Lethbridge Community College Library

FOURTH EDITION

Probation, Parole, and Community Corrections

DEAN J. CHAMPION
Texas A&M International University

Prentice Hall

Upper Saddle River, New Jersey 07458

Library of Congress Cataloging-in-Publication Data

Champion, Dean J.
  Probation, parole, and community corrections / Dean J. Champion.—4th ed.
    p.   cm.
  Includes bibliographical references and index.
  ISBN 0-13-040852-2
  1. Probation—United States.   2. Parole—United States.   I. Title.

HV9304.C463 2002
364.6'3—dc21   2001036984

Publisher: Jeff Johnston
Executive Assistant: Brenda Rock
Executive Acquisitions Editor: Kim Davies
Assistant Editor: Sarah Holle
Editorial Assistant: Korinne Dorsey
Managing Editor: Mary Carnis
Production Editor: Linda B. Pawelchak
Production Liaison: Adele M. Kupchik
Director of Manufacturing and Production: Bruce Johnson
Manufacturing Buyer: Cathleen Petersen
Art Director: Cheryl Asherman
Senior Design Coordinator: Miguel Ortiz
Cover Designer: Scott Garrison
Typesetting: Stratford Publishing Services, Inc.
Marketing Manager: Jessica Pfaff
Printing and Binding: Courier Companies, Inc.
Cover Illustration: PhotoLink/PhotoDisc
Cover Printer: Phoenix Color Corp.

Pearson Education LTD.
Pearson Education Australia PTY. Limited
Pearson Education Singapore, Pte. Ltd.
Pearson Education North Asia Ltd.
Pearson Education Canada, Ltd.
Pearson Educación de Mexico, S.A. de C.V.
Pearson Education—Japan
Pearson Education Malaysia, Pte. Ltd.

Copyright © 2002, 1999, 1996, 1990 by Pearson Education, Inc., Upper Saddle River, New Jersey 07458.
All rights reserved. Printed in the United States of America. This publication is protected by Copyright and permission should be obtained from the publisher prior to any prohibited reproduction, storage in a retrieval system, or transmission in any form or by any means, electronic, mechanical, photocopying, recording, or likewise. For information regarding permission(s), write to: Rights and Permissions Department.

10 9 8 7 6 5 4 3 2

ISBN 0-13-040852-2

Contents

Preface   **xiii**

PART I
Probation, Community Corrections,
and the Sentencing Process

CHAPTER 1
Criminal Justice System Components: **1**
Locating Probation and Parole

Introduction   3

An Overview of the Criminal Justice System   3

Types of Offenses   6
Felonies and Misdemeanors 6   Violent and Property Crimes 7   The
Uniform Crime Reports *and the* National Crime Victimization Survey *8*

Classifying Offenders   9
Traditional Offender Categorizations 9

Criminal Justice System Components   13
*Law Enforcement 13   Prosecutorial Decision Making 16   Courts and
Judges 22   Corrections 23*

Probation and Parole Distinguished   25

SUMMARY 26   KEY TERMS 27   QUESTIONS FOR REVIEW 28   SUGGESTED READINGS 28

CHAPTER 2

An Overview of Community Corrections: **29**
Types, Goals, and Functions

Introduction   31

Community Corrections and Intermediate Punishments   31

The Community Corrections Act   34

The Philosophy and History of Community Corrections   35

Characteristics, Goals, and Functions of Community
  Corrections Programs   37
  *The Goals of Community-Based Corrections 39   The Functions of
  Community-Based Corrections 39*

Selected Issues in Community Corrections   45
  *Public Resistance to Locating Community Programs in Communities
  (The NIMBY Syndrome: "Not In My Back Yard") 45   Punishment and
  Public Safety versus Offender Rehabilitation and Reintegration 46
  Net-Widening 47   Privatization of Community-Based Correctional
  Agencies 48   Services Delivery 50*

Home Confinement Programs   51
  *Home Confinement Defined 51   The Early Uses of Home
  Confinement 51   The Goals of Home Confinement Programs 57
  A Profile of Home Confinement Clients 57   Selected Issues in Home
  Confinement 58*

Electronic Monitoring Programs   60
  *Electronic Monitoring Defined 60   Early Uses of Electronic
  Monitoring 61   Types of Electronic Monitoring Systems 62   Electronic
  Monitoring with Home Confinement 63   Arguments for and against
  Electronic Monitoring 65   A Profile of Electronic Monitoring Clients 65
  Selected Issues in Electronic Monitoring 66*

Day Reporting Centers   68
  An Example of a Day Reporting Center in Action 70

SUMMARY 71   KEY TERMS 73   QUESTIONS FOR REVIEW 73   SUGGESTED READINGS 74

CHAPTER 3

Sentencing and the Presentence Investigation Report: **75**
Background, Preparation, and Functions

Introduction   77

The Sentencing Process: Types of Sentencing Systems and
  Sentencing Issues   78
  *Functions of Sentencing 78   Types of Sentencing 80   Sentencing
  Issues 84*

The Role of Probation Officers in Sentencing   86

Presentence Investigation (PSI) Reports: Interstate
  Variations   87

The Confidentiality of PSI Reports 89   The Preparation of PSI Reports 92   Functions and Uses of PSI Reports 93   The Defendant's Sentencing Memorandum 96   The Inclusion of Victim Impact Statements 97   Privatizing PSI Report Preparation 97

The Sentencing Hearing   98

Aggravating and Mitigating Circumstances   99
Aggravating Circumstances 99   Mitigating Circumstances 99

A Sample PSI Report from North Dakota   100

A PSI Report from Wisconsin   106

Changing Responsibilities of Probation Officers Resulting from Sentencing Reforms and Trends   115

SUMMARY 116   KEY TERMS 117   QUESTIONS FOR REVIEW 118   SUGGESTED READINGS 118   APPENDIX: SAMPLE PSI REPORT 119

CHAPTER 4
Probation and Probationers: History, Philosophy, Goals, and Functions

131

Introduction   133

Probation Defined   134

The History of Probation in the United States   135
Judicial Reprieves and Releases on an Offender's Recognizance 135   John Augustus, the Father of Probation in the United States 136   The Ideal-Real Dilemma: Philosophies in Conflict 137   Public Reaction to Probation 137

The Philosophy of Probation   140

Models for Dealing with Criminal Offenders   142
The Treatment or Medical Model 143   The Rehabilitation Model 143   The Justice/Due Process Model 144   The Just-Deserts Model 144   The Community Model 145

Functions of Probation   146
Crime Control 146   Community Reintegration 146   Rehabilitation 147   Punishment 149   Deterrence 149

A Profile of Probationers   150

First-Offenders and Recidivists   153

Civil Mechanisms in Lieu of Probation   154
Alternative Dispute Resolution 157   Pretrial Diversion 160   Functions of Diversion 161

Judicial Discretion and the Probation Decision 163

SUMMARY 166   KEY TERMS 168   QUESTIONS FOR REVIEW 168   SUGGESTED READINGS 168

CHAPTER 5
Programs for Probationers   **169**

Introduction   171

Standard Probation   172
Federal and State Probation Orders 173

Intensive Supervised Probation (ISP)   177
*Three Conceptual Models of ISP 178   The Georgia ISP Program 180
The Idaho ISP Program 181   The South Carolina ISP Program 181
Criticisms of the Georgia, Idaho, and South Carolina ISP Programs 184*

Shock Probation and Split Sentencing   185
*Shock Probation 185   Split Sentencing 185   The Philosophy and
Objectives of Shock Probation 186   The Effectiveness of Shock
Probation 188*

Boot Camps   188
*Boot Camps Defined 188   Goals of Boot Camps 189   A Profile of Boot
Camp Clientele 190   Boot Camp Programs 190   Jail Boot Camps 190
The Effectiveness of Boot Camps 192*

Female Probationers and Parolees: A Profile   195
Special Programs and Services for Female Offenders 195

The Probation Revocation Process   200
Special Circumstances: Federal Mandatory Probation Revocation   202

Landmark Cases and Special Issues 203

SUMMARY 210   KEY TERMS 211   QUESTIONS FOR REVIEW 211   SUGGESTED
READINGS 212

PART II
Jails, Prisons, and Parole

CHAPTER 6
Jails and Prisons   **213**

Introduction   215

Jails and Jail Characteristics   216
*Workhouses 217   The Walnut Street Jail 217   Subsequent Jail
Developments 218   The Number of Jails in the United States 219*

Functions of Jails   220

A Profile of Jail Inmates   223

Prisons, Prison History, and Prison Characteristics   224
Prisons Defined   224

Functions of Prisons   227

Inmate Classification Systems   228

A Profile of Prisoners in U.S. Prisons   235

Some Jail and Prison Contrasts   240

Selected Jail and Prison Issues   240
*Jail and Prison Overcrowding 240   Violence and Inmate Discipline 242
Jail and Prison Design and Control 244   Vocational/Technical and
Educational Programs in Jails and Prisons 245   Jail and Prison
Privatization 248   Gang Formation and Perpetuation 248*

The Role of Jails and Prisons in Probation and Parole
    Decision Making   251

SUMMARY 253   KEY TERMS 254   QUESTIONS FOR REVIEW 255   SUGGESTED
READINGS 256

CHAPTER 7
Parole and Parolees   257

Introduction   259

Parole Defined   259

The Historical Context of Parole   260

Parole and Alternative Sentencing Systems   264
*Indeterminate Sentencing and Parole 265   The Shift to Determinate
Sentencing 267*

The Philosophy of Parole   270

Functions of Parole   270
*Offender Reintegration 270   Crime Deterrence and Control 271
Decreasing Prison and Jail Overcrowding 271   Compensating for
Sentencing Disparities 272   Public Safety and Protection 273*

A Profile of Parolees in the United States   275
The Growing Gang Presence 279

SUMMARY 282   KEY TERMS 283   QUESTIONS FOR REVIEW 283   SUGGESTED
READINGS 284

CHAPTER 8
Early Release, Parole Programs, and Parole Revocation   285

Introduction   287

Prerelease Programs   289
*Definition and Examples 289   Work Release Programs 290   Study Release
Programs 293   Furlough Programs 295   Standard Parole with
Conditions 297   Intensive Supervised Parole 299   Shock Parole 307
Halfway Houses and Community Residential Centers 308*

Other Parole Conditions   312
*Day Reporting Centers 312   Fines 312   Day Fines 313   Community
Service Orders 315   Restitution 316*

Parole Boards and Early-Release Decision Making   317
  *Parole Boards, Sentencing Alternatives, and the Get-Tough Movement 317
  Parole Board Composition and Diversity 318   Functions of Parole
  Boards 319   Parole Board Decision Making and Inmate Control 322
  Parole Board Orientations 324   Developing and Implementing Objective
  Parole Criteria 325*

Salient Factor Scores and Predicting Parolee Success on
  Parole   329

The Process of Parole Revocation   333

Landmark Cases and Selected Issues   333
  Pardons 336   Parolee Program Conditions 338

SUMMARY 341   KEY TERMS 342   QUESTIONS FOR REVIEW 343   SUGGESTED
READINGS 343

PART III
The Administration of Probation and Parole
Organizational Operations: Supervising Special
Populations of Offenders

CHAPTER 9
Probation/Parole Organization and Operations: 345
Recruitment, Training, and Officer-Client Relations

Introduction   345
  *The Organization and Operation of Probation and Parole Agencies 346
  Functions and Goals of Probation and Parole Services 347   Organization
  and Administration of Probation and Parole Departments 347   Selected
  Criticisms of Probation and Parole Programs 351*

Probation and Parole Officers: A Profile   355
  *Characteristics of Probation and Parole Officers 355   What Do
  POs Do? 357   Recruitment of POs 359*

PO Training and Specialization   361
  *Assessment Centers and Staff Effectiveness 361   The Florida Assessment
  Center 362   The Use of Firearms in Probation and Parole Work 363
  Establishing Negligence in Training, Job Performance, and Retention 365
  Liability Issues Associated with PO Work 366   Probation and Parole
  Officer Labor Turnover 368*

Probation and Parole Officer Caseloads   369
  *Ideal Caseloads 369   Changing Caseloads and Officer Effectiveness 370
  Caseload Assignment and Management Models 371*

Officer/Client Interactions   372
  A Code of Ethics 376   PO Unionization and Collective Bargaining 379

SUMMARY 381   KEY TERMS 383   QUESTIONS FOR REVIEW 383   SUGGESTED
READINGS 384

CHAPTER 10
Probation and Parole Officer Roles and Responsibilities   385

Introduction   385

Probation and Parole: Risk/Needs Assessments   386
   *Assessing Offender Risk: A Brief History 386   Classification and Its
   Functions 388   Types of Risk Assessment Instruments 393   The
   Effectiveness of Risk Assessment Devices 396   Some Applications of
   Risk/Needs Measures 397   Selective Incapacitation 398*

The Changing Probation/Parole Officer Role   399

Apprehension Units   400

Gang Units   402

Research Units   405

Stress and Burnout in Probation/Parole Officer Role
   Performance   405
   *Stress 406   Burnout 407   Sources of Stress 408   Mitigating Factors to
   Alleviate Stress and Burnout 410*

Volunteers in Probation/Parole Work   411
   Criticisms of Volunteers in Correctional Work 412

Paraprofessionals in Probation/Parole Work   414
   *Roles of Paraprofessionals 414   Legal Liabilities of Volunteers and
   Paraprofessionals 416*

SUMMARY 418   KEY TERMS 420   QUESTIONS FOR REVIEW 420   SUGGESTED
READINGS 420

CHAPTER 11
Theories of Offender Treatment   421

Introduction   422

Theories of Criminal Behavior   423

Biological Theories   425
   *Abnormal Physical Structure 425   Hereditary Criminal Behaviors 427
   Biochemical Disturbances 427*

Psychological Theories   427
   *Psychoanalytic Theory 429   Cognitive Development Theory 430   Social
   Learning Theory 431*

Sociological and Sociocultural Theories   432
   *Differential Association Theory 433   Anomie Theory or Innovative
   Adaptation 434   The Subculture Theory of Delinquency 436   Labeling
   Theory 438   Social Control Theory 440   Conflict/Marxist Theory 441*

Reality Therapy   441

Social Casework   442

Which Theory Is Best? An Evaluation   443
   Theories about Adult Offenders 443   Theories about Delinquency 444

Treatment Programs and Theories   445

SUMMARY 448   KEY TERMS   449   QUESTIONS FOR REVIEW 449   SUGGESTED
READINGS 450

CHAPTER 12
Offender Supervision: Types of Offenders
and Special Supervisory Considerations   451

Introduction   451

Types of Offenders: An Overview   453
   *Coping wtih Special Needs Offenders 454   Mentally Ill Offenders 456
   Sex Offenders and Child Sexual Abusers 457   Drug- and Alcohol-
   Dependent Offenders 459   AIDS/HIV Offenders 460   Gang
   Members 461   Developmentally Disabled Offenders 462*

Mentally Ill Offenders   462

Sex Offenders   465

Offenders with HIV/AIDS   466

Substance-Abusing Offenders   467
   *Drug Screening and Methadone Treatment 470   Drug Courts and the
   Drug Court Movement 471*

Community Programs for Special Needs Offenders   476
   *Therapeutic Communities 476   Alcoholics Anonymous, Narcotics
   Anonymous, and Gamblers Anonymous Programs 477*

Gang Members   478
   Tattoo Removal Programs 481

SUMMARY 482   KEY TERMS 484   QUESTIOS FOR REVIEW 484   SUGGESTED
READINGS 484

PART IV
Juvenile Probation and Parole and Program
Evaluation

CHAPTER 13
Juvenile Probation and Parole   485

Introduction   487

Juveniles and Juvenile delinquency   488
   Delinquency and Juvenile Delinquents 489   Status Offenders 489

An Overview of the Juvenile Justice System 489
   *The Origins and Purposes of Juvenile Courts 490   Major Differences
   between Criminal and Juvenile Courts 492   Parens Patriae 494*

Arrest and Other Options 495   Intake Screenings and Detention Hearings 496   Petitions and Adjudicatory Proceedings 496 Transfers, Waivers, or Certifications 497

Types of Waivers   500
Judicial Waivers 500   Direct File 501   Statutory Exclusion 501 Demand Waivers 502   Other Types of Waivers 502   Waiver Hearings 503   Reverse Waiver Hearings 503   Time Standards Governing Waiver Decisions 504

Implications of Waiver Hearings for Juveniles   504
Positive Benefits Resulting from Juvenile Court Adjudications 504 Adverse Implications of Juvenile Court Adjudications 505

Juvenile Rights   505
Landmark Cases in Juvenile Justice 505

Offense Seriousness and Dispositions: Aggravating and Mitigating Circumstances   508
Aggravating and Mitigating Circumstances 508   Judicial Dispositional Options 509   Nominal and Conditional Sanctions 509   Custodial Sanctions 512   Nonsecure Facilities 512   Secure Confinement 515

Juvenile Probation Officers and Predispositional Reports   515
Juvenile Probation Officers 515   The Predispositional Report and Its Preparation 518

Juvenile Probation and Parole Programs 523
Unconditional and Conditional Probation 523   Intensive Supervised Probation (ISP) Programs 526   The Ohio Experience 528   The Allegheny Academy 529   Boston Offender Project 530   Other Juvenile Probation and Parole Programs 531

Revoking Juvenile Probation and Parole   533
Recidivism and Probation/Parole Revocation 535   Juvenile Case Law on Probation Revocations 536   Juvenile Case Law on Parole Revocations 538

SUMMARY 539   KEY TERMS 540   QUESTIONS FOR REVIEW 540   SUGGESTED READINGS 541

CHAPTER 14
Evaluating Programs: Balancing Service Delivery and Recidivism Considerations

543

Introduction   543

Program Evaluation: How Do We Know Programs Are Effective?   544
Some Recommended Outcome Measures 547

Balancing Program Objectives and Offender Needs   550

Recidivism Defined   552
Rearrests 555   Reconvictions 556   Revocations of Parole or Probation 556   Reincarcerations 557   Technical Program Violations 557

Recidivist Offenders and Their Characteristics   558
*Avertable and Nonavertable Recidivists 558   Public Policy and
Recidivism 560*

Probationers, Parolees, and Recidivism   560
*Probationers and Parolees Compared 561   Prison versus Probation 562
Curbing Recidivism 562*

SUMMARY 563   KEY TERMS 564   QUESTIONS FOR REVIEW 564   SUGGESTED
READINGS 565

**Internet Addresses for Professional Organizations
and Probation/Parole Agencies**   **567**

Glossary   **569**

References   **591**

Name Index   **615**

Subject Index   **622**

Case Cited   **633**

Preface

Probation, Parole, and Community Corrections, 4th edition, is about adults and juveniles who have been convicted of criminal offenses or adjudicated as delinquent and are then punished. Judges may sentence offenders to incarceration in prison or jail for a definite period or they may suspend the sentence, subject to the offender's compliance with certain conditions. Judges may also sentence offenders to incarceration for a fixed period of years, and offenders may serve only a portion of that time. Parole boards, the court, or others may authorize the early release of offenders, again subject to certain conditions.

Some adult and juvenile offenders are permitted by the courts to remain free in their communities, provided that they comply with certain stipulations. Other offenders are granted early release from incarceration under similar provisions. These offenders will be supervised by officers and agencies as provided by law. This book is also about the personnel and agencies who monitor these offenders.

The distinction between probation and parole is not clear-cut. Probation applies to a class of programs for those offenders sentenced to incarceration but who have had their incarcerative sentences conditionally suspended. Parole applies to those programs for offenders who have been incarcerated but have been released prior to serving the full term of their sentence. Therefore, parolees are convicted or adjudicated offenders who have been incarcerated but have been released before their sentences have been fully served. Probationers are convicted or adjudicated offenders who are ordered to serve nonincarcerative conditional sentences in the community in lieu of incarceration.

In both instances, parolees and probationers are supervised by parole and probation officers, but there are also other classes of offenders whose activities are monitored by these officers. Sometimes, offenders are granted diversion by the court. Diversion is a pretrial alternative whereby offenders may avoid prosecution altogether. If offenders successfully comply with the conditions of their diversion, then criminal charges against them are either dropped or reduced in seriousness when they complete their diversionary period.

Distinguishing clearly between probation and parole is difficult for at least two reasons. First, there are many probation and parole programs, and several of them overlap. Thus, the clients of a specific program may include both probationers and parolees. Second, many different kinds of probationers and parolees need to be supervised. Professionals disagree about which programs are most effective. Furthermore, there are disagreements about the philosophical objectives of probation and parole programs. This book describes the objectives of probation and parole and examines whether these objectives are achieved. Understanding these philosophies is enhanced through an examination of the history of parole and probation in the United States. Besides describing probation and parole programs, various classes of offenders are portrayed. In addition, several problems associated with the selection and training of probation and parole officers are highlighted, including their relationships with offender-clients.

Juvenile offenders pose special problems for those assigned to supervise them. A profile of juvenile offenders is also presented, together with a discussion of several controversial issues associated with processing juveniles. The juvenile justice system is gradually acquiring several characteristics that are making its distinctiveness less apparent compared with the adult criminal justice system. Larger numbers of juveniles are being processed as adult offenders, either through statutes or recommendations from prosecutors and juvenile judges. Since 1966, juveniles have been granted certain constitutional rights equivalent to those of adult offenders. Some of these rights are described, and the influence of these rights on juvenile probation and parole programs is examined.

One premise of this book is that all components of the criminal and juvenile justice sytems are interrelated to varying degrees. Although experts contend that these systems are better described as loosely related processes, each component has an effect on each of the other components. Police discretion influences the disposition of adult and juvenile offenders. In turn, the courts influence police discretion and affect prisons and jails through particular sentencing practices. Prison and jail problems such as overcrowding often burden probation and parole officers with excessive offender caseloads. Varying offender caseloads influence the quality of officer/offender interaction and the ultimate effectiveness of probation and parole programs. Ineffective probation and parole programs may increase the number of repeat offenders who come to the attention of police when they commit new crimes. Thus, probation and parole programs do not exist in a vacuum, unaffected by other agencies and organizations.

Probation and parole policy decisions are sometimes politically motivated. Economic considerations and limited human resources, however, also play important parts in shaping correctional priorities. The influence of political and economic considerations on probation and parole programs as well as on officer effectiveness is described.

The book has the following features that add to its value as a teaching tool. First, there are questions for review at the end of each chapter to facilitate group discussion and class assignments. Second, a comprehensive glossary is provided so that students can look up unfamiliar words. In addition, a comprehensive, up-to-date bibliography is included for students who wish to do additional reading and learn more about the different subjects presented. All key words that are mentioned in each chapter are in bold in the text and are listed in a key words section at the end of each chapter. Each chapter also includes suggested readings. All chapters are summarized, highlighting the major points. Each chapter includes boxes or interesting vignettes about the text material, often using the terminology or focusing on the subject matter of the sections covered. The personality highlights feature profiles of persons who work in probation and parole services. Students should find these personality highlights of interest, because they have been written by practitioners in the field in different capacities. For instructors, an Instructor's Manual is provided, together with a computerized test bank. The Instructor's Manual includes synopses of chapters; key objectives of each chapter; and true-false, multiple-choice, and short-answer essay questions to use for examination preparation.

The author wishes to acknowledge the following persons who have reviewed the manuscript for this edition and have made suggestions for improvement: George Knox, Chicago State University; Sam Torres, California State University–Long Beach; and Ed White, Florida Metropolitan University. I am grateful for their suggestions and note that any mistakes are my own. I encourage anyone using this book to contact me for additional examination information; in addition, I will be happy to provide, upon request, other ancillary materials in different software formats on diskette. I would like to thank my editor at Prentice Hall, Kim Davies, as well as my production editor, Linda Pawelchak, for the hard work that has gone into developing this project from beginning to end.

Dean J. Champion

PART I

Probation, Community Corrections, and the Sentencing Process

CHAPTER 1

Criminal Justice System Components: Locating Probation and Parole

Introduction
An Overview of the Criminal Justice System
Types of Offenses
    Felonies and Misdemeanors
    Violent and Property Crimes
    The *Uniform Crime Reports* and the *National Crime Victimization Survey*
Classifying Offenders
    Traditional Offender Categorizations
Criminal Justice System Components
    Law Enforcement

Prosecutorial Decision Making
Courts and Judges
Corrections
Probation and Parole Distinguished
Summary
Key Terms
Questions for Review
Suggested Readings

• Korn is a New York parolee. Korn is also a Muslim. Among other requirements, his parole conditions include a curfew provision that orders him confined to his home during the evening hours, specifically between 9:00 P.M. and 7:00 A.M. daily. He is obligated to remain employed, appear at his workplace regularly, and meet his familial financial responsibilities. One afternoon while meeting with his parole officer in a face-to-face office visit, Korn requests that he be allowed to attend special early-morning religious worship services at his mosque. The services begin at 4:10 A.M. The parole officer advises Korn that he may leave his home before 7:00 A.M. to attend these services. The mosque is 20 minutes from Korn's apartment. After several weeks, the parole officer visits Korn's apartment at 2:30 A.M. to see if he is observing the curfew requirement of his parole program. Korn is not at home and no one knows where he is. The parole officer files a report with the parole board. Korn is ordered to appear before the parole board and explain why he wasn't at home at 2:30 A.M. when the parole officer visited. Korn claims that he was on his way to the worship service at his mosque. The parole board rejects Korn's statement and revokes his parole. Korn is returned to prison. He appeals, but the New York high court rejects his appeal. The court concluded that there were reasonable grounds to support Korn's parole revocation. (*People ex rel. Korn v. N.Y. State Division of Parole,* 710 N.Y.S.2d 124 [N.Y. Sup. App. Div. July 2000])

• Fleming was convicted of misdemeanor assault in a Colorado court. In exchange for his plea of guilty to misdemeanor assault, the prosecutor dismissed felony sexual battery charges against him. Fleming had physically assaulted his wife. Because Fleming was a first-time offender, the judge placed him on probation and ordered him to undergo several tests and attend counseling sessions. One of the conditions of Fleming's probation was that he undergo a psychosexual evaluation in an attempt to determine the best type of treatment for Fleming. Furthermore, during his counseling sessions, Fleming was required to discuss the altercation with his wife and to take a polygraph (lie detector) test. Subsequently, psychological counselors filed papers with the court indicating that Fleming had failed to take the required polygraph test. Further, Fleming had continually refused to discuss the altercation he had had with his wife with the counselors. Because of these refusals, the required psychosexual evaluation could not be performed adequately. The judge revoked Fleming's probation and sentenced him to serve several months in the county jail. Fleming appealed, contending that the condition that he discuss the altercation with his wife violated his right against self-incrimination. The appeals court rejected his claim, noting that he was not required either to admit or deny the dismissed sexual battery charge, nor was he required to discuss other incidents that may have occurred between himself and his wife. The Colorado appeals court observed that the judges' conditions for Fleming's probation were reasonable and thus upheld the judge's order to revoke Fleming's probation program. (*People v. Fleming,* 3 P.3d 449 [Colo. App. June 2000])

• In 1996, Chatagnier was convicted in Kansas of various drug-related charges. Although he was sentenced to three to ten years in prison, the judge granted Chatagnier probation, ordered him to pay $300 restitution as a probation condition, and placed him under the supervision of community corrections for 24 months. Under an interstate compact, Chatagnier was permitted to move to Texas in 1997. As a part of his probation agreement, he agreed to be supervised by Texas probation officers for the remainder of his Kansas probationary term. He was to report to Texas probation officers regularly and refrain from using drugs or alcohol. In 1997, however, Chatagnier was convicted of a new drug-related crime in Texas and was placed on probation there until 2004. Furthermore, a random drug/alcohol check by Texas probation officers revealed that Chatagnier was using cocaine, a prohibited substance. This report was filed with Kansas probation authorities. Chatagnier was returned to Kansas, and after a probation revocation hearing, the original Kansas sentencing judge revoked Chatagnier's probation. Chatagnier was placed in a Kansas prison to commence serving his three- to ten-year sentence. Chatagnier appealed, contending that Kansas officials had no authority to revoke his probation while he was residing in Texas. A Kansas appellate court disagreed with Chatagnier and upheld his probation revocation, saying that it was reasonable for the Kansas judge to revoke his probation program for violating one or more of his probation conditions. (*State v. Chatagnier,* 3 P.3d 586 [Kan. App. June 2000])

• Haynes was convicted of a violent crime in Washington. He was sentenced to a period of years, with a specific date indicating his eligibility for parole. When his parole date occurred, Haynes met with the Washington Parole Board. The board rejected his early-release request, basing its findings on factual information from prison officials that his potential for rehabilitation was poor. Furthermore, Haynes refused to admit his guilt of the conviction offense to the parole board or accept responsibility for his actions. In addition, a report from a prison psychiatrist indicated that Haynes presented a high risk of reoffending if released on parole. Haynes appealed his parole denial, arguing that the parole board should not have had access to these psychiatric reports or prison official information. Further, Haynes contended that he should not be made to recite his guilt before the parole board again, because he had already been subjected to a trial at which he was convicted. He believed that further admissions to the parole board would constitute **double jeopardy**. The Washington court of appeals upheld the Washington Parole Board's decision to deny Haynes his parole, and it concluded that the grounds cited by the board were reasonable and that the board did not abuse its discretion in the parole denial. (*In re Haynes*, 996 P.2d 637 [Wash. App. April 2000])

INTRODUCTION

The preceding cases indicate that probation and parole are both conditional sentences and releases from incarceration, either immediately following conviction for a crime or after a period of incarceration in a prison or jail. The conditions imposed relate to behavioral requirements and involve agreements between the state and probationers/parolees based on mutual trust. The reward for probationers/parolees is freedom, which is either limited or completely unrestricted. The penalties for violating this trust involve loss of freedom through incarceration or more restrictive forms of probation/parole supervision. This book is about the diverse programs of supervised release for convicted offenders. These programs—broadly labeled probation, parole, or community corrections—are almost always operated in communities and are designed to supervise offender behaviors more or less intensively.

This chapter is an overview of the **criminal justice system**. Probation and parole are identified in relation to various criminal justice system components. The first part of this chapter defines crime and distinguishes between several types of crime. Different offense categories are listed by which offenders are classified. Two popular crime information sources, *Uniform Crime Reports (UCR)* and the *National Crime Victimization Survey (NCVS),* are described. Several criticisms of these information sources are listed. Additional descriptions are provided for both traditional offenders and special-needs offenders. These classifications include first-time offenders and recidivists, drug/alcohol-dependent offenders, offenders who are mentally and/or physically challenged, and offenders with HIV/AIDS or other communicable diseases. Major components of the criminal justice system are identified and described, including law enforcement, prosecutorial decision making, courts and court processing, and corrections. When a crime is committed and someone is charged with committing it, the criminal justice system processes the offender through a series of established stages. The final part of the chapter looks at probation and parole. Probation and parole are defined as essentially different programs, although there are many similarities among these programs for convicted offenders.

AN OVERVIEW OF THE CRIMINAL JUSTICE SYSTEM

The criminal justice system consists of law enforcement, the courts, and corrections. **Law enforcement** officers attempt to control crime and apprehend criminals. The **courts** determine a defendant's guilt or innocence and sentence convicted offenders.

Corrections punishes, manages, and rehabilitates those who have been sentenced. Ideally, this scenario is how things are supposed to work. In actual practice, however, the criminal justice system is seriously flawed. Many criminals are never caught. Many of those criminals who are apprehended never go to trial. Many of those whose cases go to trial are acquitted even though they are guilty of the offenses charged. Many convicted offenders are never incarcerated. Many incarcerated offenders are never rehabilitated; they leave prisons and jails only to resume their criminal activity. Considerable responsibility is given to corrections personnel. Much is expected of those working directly with offenders. Not only are they expected to provide inmates with food, shelter, and basic living requirements, but they are also supposed to rehabilitate them and make them suitable for return to society as law-abiding citizens. As seen in later chapters, corrections falls far short of this goal. It will also be seen, however, that it is not necessarily the fault of corrections for the low incidence of **offender rehabilitation**. Besides institutional corrections, such as prisons and jails, personnel who work in **probation**, **parole**, and **community-based corrections** are heavily involved with offender supervision and operate programs designed to rehabilitate or reintegrate offender-clients. These personnel are also expected to accomplish the difficult task of supervising and offering different forms of assistance to their clients with the express purpose of making them law-abiding citizens. Again, it will be disclosed that **probation officers (POs)** and **parole officers (POs)** often fail to achieve their personal and departmental objectives. The reasons for their client failures, however, are often beyond their direct control.

Entry into the criminal justice system begins with the commission of a crime, followed by the **arrest** of one or more suspected perpetrators of that crime. Assuming that **offenders** have been identified and apprehended, their movement through the criminal justice system is similar for both the state and federal processing. Persons suspected of committing crimes are arrested, booked, and charged with one or more offenses. If there are successful **prosecutions** of **defendants** by **prosecutors**, they are found guilty and sentenced by judges. Probation is one sentencing option imposed by judges in lieu of incarceration. **Probationers** are allowed to remain free in their communities, although they must abide by certain probation conditions for a period of time. Another option is parole. Parole is an **early release** from prison or jail, permitting convicted offenders the opportunity of living in their communities, again with parole program restrictions and conditions. Convicted offenders who have served some time in jail or prison before earning early release are called **parolees**.

This book describes what happens to offenders who are either sentenced to probation or granted parole after serving a portion of their sentence in prison. In both situations, these offenders must obey several program conditions; otherwise, their probation or parole may be revoked or canceled. A **parole revocation** means that parolees may be returned to prison for all or some of the remainder of their original sentences. For probationers, a **probation revocation** may mean incarceration or a more intensive form of supervision by probation by program officials. Enforcing the conditions of probation and parole are probation and parole officers (POs). The designation PO is used throughout this text to refer to either probation officers or parole officers. Offenders are required to report to their POs regularly and to comply with other rules and regulations. Thus, a second major goal of this book is to describe the personnel and programs that manage probationers and parolees.

Figure 1.1 is a diagram of the criminal justice system, showing the commission of a crime that leads to an arrest. Other phases of offender processing are also depicted. The figure also shows that juvenile offenders are sent to the juvenile justice system.

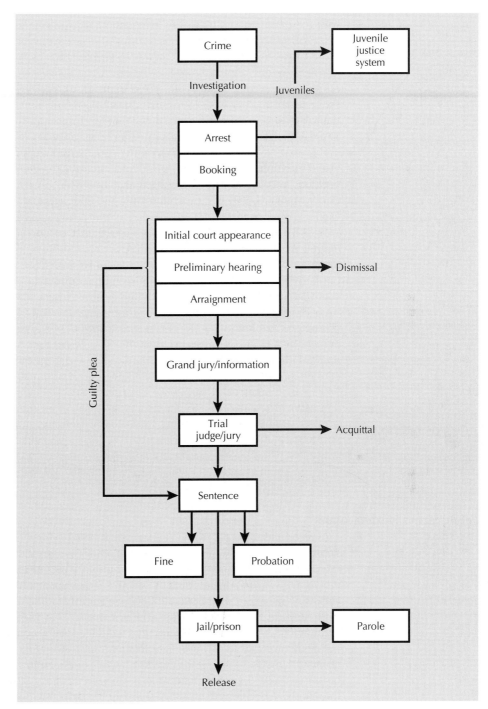

FIGURE 1.1 An overview of the criminal justice process.

POs often collaborate with community agencies that provide special services for offenders. For example, in Seattle, Washington, a program called the Special Sex Offender Sentencing Alternative (SSOSA) has been established to treat **sex offenders** (Berliner et al., 1995). Probation officers assist community **corrections officers** with their supervisory chores in overseeing large numbers of sex offenders. Some of these offenders are **recidivists**, meaning that they have been convicted of one or more previous crimes. Some amount of **recidivism** is a part of each probation and parole program, regardless of how carefully it is established and how closely offenders are supervised. Under the SSOSA program, **recidivism rates** were lower for those sex offenders who participated in the community treatment and were under the close supervision of both probation and community agency personnel. The SSOSA program has had similar results in other cities throughout the state (Song and Lieb, 1995). Thus, depending on the **jurisdiction**, POs may be assigned to supervise (1) adult probationers and/or parolees, (2) juvenile probationers and/or parolees, and/or (3) offenders with special needs. Although POs perform many other duties, their primary responsibilities are the management and supervision of nonincarcerated offenders.

All probationers and parolees are a part of corrections. **Corrections** is the aggregate of programs, services, facilities, and organizations responsible for the management of people who have been accused or convicted of criminal offenses. This book focuses largely on the nonincarcerative dimension of corrections, although some attention will be given to jails and prisons, where offenders may receive treatment or assistance for their needs or problems. More often than not, inmates of prisons or jails are influenced by those with whom they associate while confined. These associations may not be positive or therapeutic. In fact, the **criminogenic environment** of prisons and jails and social interactions with other inmates often lead to, and explain, probation or parole program failures.

TYPES OF OFFENSES

Crimes are violations of the law by people held accountable by the law. Two general categories of crime are *felonies* and *misdemeanors*.

Felonies and Misdemeanors

Felonies.   A **felony** is a major crime that carries potentially severe penalties of one or more years in prison or jail and **fines**. Fines are monetary assessments that accompany a conviction for one or more crimes. Fines are prescribed by statute. Usually, statutory penalties are associated with all felonies and include both fines and/or incarceration in a state or federal prison for one or more years. Felonies include arson, murder, rape, burglary, robbery, vehicular theft, and aggravated assault. Both misdemeanor and felony convictions mean that offenders acquire criminal records. Some jurisdictions have a third class of crimes. A certain type of minor offense may be known as a **summary offense**. These petty crimes ordinarily carry penalties of fines only. Also, convictions for these petty offenses do not result in a criminal record. Two examples of summary offenses are speeding and dumping litter from an automobile on a public highway.

Misdemeanors.   A **misdemeanor** is a minor or petty offense. Misdemeanor offenses carry less severe penalties than major crimes or felonies. Misdemeanor offenses may result in fines and/or incarceration for less than one year. A **misdemeanant** is someone who commits a misdemeanor and may be incarcerated in a local jail. Examples of misdemeanors include making a false financial statement to obtain credit, prostitution, shoplifting, and criminal trespass.

Violent and Property Crimes

Violent crimes are characterized by extreme physical force, including murder or homicide, forcible rape, child sexual abuse, assault and battery by means of a dangerous weapon, robbery, and arson (Black, 1990:371). Sometimes these offenses are referred to as **crimes of violence** or **crimes against the person**, because persons are directly involved as victims and are affected emotionally and physically as a result of the crime's commission. Nonviolent offenses include burglary, vehicular theft, embezzlement, fraud, forgery, and larceny. These crimes are often referred to as **crimes against property**, and although persons are indirectly victimized or affected by such offenses, their lives and physical well-being are not directly jeopardized by such acts. Two sources that report crime in the United States are the *Uniform Crime Reports* and the *National Crime Victimization Survey*.

The *Uniform Crime Reports* and the *National Crime Victimization Survey*

The *Uniform Crime Reports (UCR)*.   The ***Uniform Crime Reports (UCR)*** is compiled by the **Federal Bureau of Investigation (FBI)**. This publication includes statistics about the number and kinds of crimes reported in the United States annually by more than 15,000 law enforcement agencies. The *UCR* is the official compendium of crime statistics for the United States. The *UCR* is compiled by gathering information about 29 types of crime from reporting law-enforcement agencies. Crime information is requested from all rural and urban law-enforcement agencies and is subsequently reported to the FBI. The FBI has established a **crime classification index**. **Index offenses** include eight serious types of crime used by the FBI to measure crime trends: arson, murder and nonnegligent manslaughter, aggravated assault, robbery, motor vehicle theft, forcible rape, larceny-theft, and burglary. Information is also compiled about 21 less serious offenses ranging from forgery and counterfeiting to curfew violations and runaways (Gilbert, 2000). Index offense information is presented in the *UCR* for each state, city, county, and township that has submitted crime information during the most recent year. The *UCR* is published annually by the U.S. Government Printing Office.

Criticisms of the *UCR*.   Although the *UCR* publishes the most current crime figures available from reporting law enforcement agencies, this information is inaccurate in several respects. First, when criminals are questioned about other crimes they have committed, there are discrepancies between *UCR* figures and **self-reported information**. Many criminals are not caught for many of the crimes they have committed. Therefore, considerably more crime is committed annually than is disclosed by official estimates published in the *UCR*. Second, not all law enforcement agencies report crimes in uniform ways. For instance, North Dakota has no forcible rape category. That does not mean that rape does not occur in that state; rather, North Dakota classifies forcible rape as "gross sexual imposition." Third, more aggressive enforcement of certain laws in different jurisdictions may lead to more arrests, although there are few convictions. Further, not all law enforcement agencies report their crime figures consistently. Also, many crimes are never reported to the police. Finally, when a crime report is submitted to the *UCR*, often only the most serious offense is reported. Thus, if someone robs a convenience store, shoots and kills the clerk, injures customers, and steals a car before being captured by police, the police department will report only the most serious offense, "murder or nonnegligent manslaughter," rather than all the other offenses committed. Thus, there is good reason for experts to believe that the *UCR* greatly underestimates the amount of crime committed in the United States.

The *National Crime Victimization Survey (NCVS).*   The limitations of the *UCR* and other official documents measuring the amount of crime in the United States have led to comparisons between the *UCR* and the ***National Crime Victimization Survey (NCVS)***, which is conducted annually by the U.S. Bureau of the Census (Pallone and Hennessy, 1999). The *NCVS* is a random survey of approximately 60,000 dwellings, about 127,000 persons age 12 and over, and approximately 50,000 businesses. Smaller samples of persons from these original figures form the database from which annual crime estimates are compiled. Carefully worded questions lead people to report incidents that can be classified as crimes. This material, usually referred to as **victimization data**, is statistically manipulated in such a way so as to make it comparable with *UCR* statistics.

The *NCVS* distinguishes between **victimizations** and **incidents**. A victimization is the basic measure of the occurrence of a crime and is a specific criminal act that affects a single victim. An incident is a specific criminal act involving one or more victims. The *NCVS*, however, has certain persistent problems similar to those of the *UCR*. Some crime victims cannot remember when or where the offense against them occurred. Other victims are reluctant to report a rape, particularly if the rapist is known to them, such as a family member or close friend. Often, crimes are committed in the workplace, where employees steal goods from their employers. Much **white-collar crime**, or crime conducted in the course of one's occupation, is handled internally and is not reported, sometimes because those involved do not believe that the crimes are serious enough to warrant police intrusion (DeLisi and Regoli, 1999). Nonreporting is also related to victim fear, feelings of helplessness or apathy, the perceived powerlessness of police, and fear of the authorities themselves. The poor are especially reluctant to report crime because they fear reprisals from the criminals, who are often known to them. Also, police may detect evidence of other crimes or statutory violations such as health code infractions, illegal aliens, and overcrowded apartment dwellings. Regardless of these shortcomings, the *UCR* and the *NCVS* are better than no information. Researchers find many uses for the information from both sources (Osgood and Chambers, 2000; Savolainen, 2000).

In recent years, summary statistical information in the *Uniform Crime Reports* and other official sources has gradually been replaced by the **National Incident-Based Reporting System (NIBRS)**. This system involves the collection of incident-level data for a broad range of offenses. Thus, a more accurate picture of the amount of crime committed in the United States can be gleaned from an examination of NIBRS figures (Maxfield and Maltz, 1999).

CLASSIFYING OFFENDERS

Distinguishing between different types of offenders is fairly easy, particularly if they are classified strictly on the basis of the crimes they have committed. Some burglars, however, are more violent or dangerous than others. Some rapists are more aggressive than other rapists. Some murderers are more dangerous than other murderers. Prisons and jails must place their inmates according to the most appropriate form of supervision. Various classification schemes have been devised and are used by prison and jail officials to determine which **level of custody** is most appropriate for each inmate. Corrections officials want to know which inmates should be isolated from other inmates and which ones should be permitted to associate with other inmates under more general supervision. Some inmates may pose physical threats either to themselves or to other inmates. Aggressive and violent prisoners can exploit, injure, or kill weaker inmates. Some inmates are suicide risks, and yet other inmates have mental illnesses or suffer from poor social adjustment (U.S. Center for Mental Health Services, 1995).

Probation and parole agencies also have a vested interest in classifying offenders accurately. Different probation programs target particular types of offenders, although the effectiveness of classification is sometimes questionable (Dhaliwal, Porporino, and Ross, 1994). Some offenders may be impaired mentally or physically. Some may have personality disorders or poor self-concepts. Other offenders may have serious alcohol or drug dependencies. Thus, various treatment programs are designed to meet specific offender needs, such as narcotics addiction (Cooper and Bartlett, 1996). Several additional offender classifications have been developed for probation and parole programs. These traditional offender classifications include first-offenders and recidivists or career criminals.

Traditional Offender Categorizations

Besides violent and property offenders, two additional classifications are first-offenders and recidivists and career criminals.

First-Offenders. **First-offenders** or **first-time offenders** are those who commit one or more crimes but who have no previous history of criminal behavior. There is nothing especially unique about first-offenders. They may commit violent crimes or **property crimes**. First-offenders may be male or female. They may be old or young. They may or may not have records as juvenile **delinquents**. No useful blanket generalizations can be made about first-offenders other than that they have no previous criminal history. First-offenders who commit only the offense for which they were apprehended and prosecuted and who are unlikely to commit future crimes are called **situational offenders** (Wooldredge and Gordon, 1997). Situational offenders may commit serious crimes or petty offenses. The situation itself creates the unique conditions leading to the criminal act. For example, an argument between husband and wife over something trivial may lead to the death of one of the spouses. An argument between a convenience store clerk and a customer may lead to a serious altercation, even death. Serious financial pressures or setbacks may prompt situational offenders to commit embezzlement.

BOX 1.1   *First-Offenders and Repeat Offenders: Probation or Incarceration?*

Should the Following Persons Receive Prison or Probation for Their Crimes?

• *The Case of Mr. Cobb.* It happened in Dover, New Hampshire. David Cobb, 59, was an English teacher at the exclusive Phillips Academy. He was arrested August 22, 1995, for allegedly trying to molest a 12-year-old boy. A search of Cobb's dwelling yielded 300 photographs of children engaged in various sex acts. Cobb was charged with possession of child pornography in addition to child molestation. He was convicted of these offenses in May 1996. Cobb's activities were discovered when a 13-year-old boy reported Cobb to his parents. Cobb had taken photographs from pornographic magazines and superimposed photos of the heads of young boys and girls taken from department store catalogs. Subsequently, Cobb would show these photographs to various teenagers, attempting to entice them into various sex acts. He was arrested while walking with a 12-year-old. He had offered the boy $20 to assist retarded children change out of their sandy bathing suits at a camp he ran. Officers say that there was no such camp. Rather, Cobb had a list of sex acts with various dollar amounts and would offer to pay children various amounts for performing different sex acts. Cobb's knapsack contained a pay list for his sexual favors, children's underwear, a Polaroid camera, and hundreds of "fantasy photos of his naked camp." Cobb was a considered a first-offender with no prior criminal record. He was eventually convicted of possessing child pornography and solicitation to engage in child pornography. Should he receive probation or incarceration? (*Source:* Adapted from Associated Press, "Prep Teacher Convicted of Child Porn," May 7, 1996.)

• *Copperhill, Tennessee, Mayor Janelle Kimsey and Her Experiment.* Janelle Kimsey is the mayor of Copperhill, Tennessee. There had been a drug bust in the community, with arrests for trafficking in marijuana. Kimsey said that some of her constituency wanted to know what marijuana looked like, so she

accommodated them. She surreptitiously took a marijuana cigarette from those confiscated in a drug bust, extracted the marijuana seeds, and grew ten marijuana seedlings. When they were "old enough," she planted the seedlings in ten clay pots. After the plants had grown a few feet, passersby took notice and so did the police. The mayor's illegal pot plants were confiscated, but she was not immediately arrested. She explained to police that her plant-growing experiment was purely for the benefit of showing community residents what marijuana looked like. After all, she said, you need to know what something looks like if it is illegal, right? "Dumb me," Kimsey said. "We made a drug bust a couple of months ago and the citizens said they wanted to know what it [marijuana] looked like. I know that ignorance is no excuse, but in my case, it was ignorance." A Polk County grand jury was convening to consider whether to indict the mayor on pot-growing charges and marijuana possession. Is the mayor above the law? Should she be prosecuted for growing marijuana? If convicted, should she receive probation or incarceration? (*Source:* Adapted from Associated Press, "Police Confiscate Marijuana Plants Off Mayor's Porch in Tennessee Town," June 1, 1996.)

• *The Case of the Headhunters.* It happened in Buena Park, California. Two women, Alicia Howard, 25, and Alice "Brandy" Jobe, 21, were in a local hotel lobby bar. They met a German Christmas tree ornament salesman, Herbert Seidenkrantz, 36. Seidenkrantz invited the two women to his room for sex, and they complied. Unfortunately for Seidenkrantz, the women had something else on their minds. They armed themselves with knives, black lingerie, and makeup. When they got to Seidenkrantz's room, they succeeded in getting Seidenkrantz to put on a blindfold, promising exotic sexual favors in return. Once Seidenkrantz was blindfolded, however, the women pulled out knives and stabbed him repeatedly in the spleen, liver, and lungs. Miraculously, Seidenkrantz was able to escape and get medical assistance. Later in an emergency room, he underwent life-saving surgery. Meanwhile, the women were arrested and charged with premeditated attempted murder. They were subsequently convicted of assault. Jobe told police that she and Howard wanted Seidenkrantz's skull for an occult religious ritual. Howard told the same story. In the eyes of the court, the women had no prior criminal records and were first-offenders. Should they receive probation or incarceration? (*Source:* Adapted from Associated Press, "California Police Say Women Tried to Kill Man Just for His Skull," June 4, 1996.)

• *The Case of John Horace, Nurse's Aide.* It happened in Rochester, New York. John Horace, 53, was a nurse's aide in a large community hospital. A woman known only as "Kathy" was admitted to the hospital in 1985 following a serious automobile accident. Kathy remained in a coma until she died on March 18, 1997. Horace was Kathy's nurse's aide, changing Kathy's clothes and performing other duties. In 1995, it was determined that Kathy, still in a coma, was pregnant. Hospital authorities were dumbfounded and could not explain how such a thing could happen. An investigation led to police questioning John Horace, who eventually admitted that he had had sex with Kathy in her comatose state. Still comatose, Kathy gave birth to a baby boy in 1996. Her Roman Catholic family had rejected an abortion. Doctors say that Kathy's pregnancy is the first case of a woman in a comatose state becoming pregnant and giving birth. Horace's prior record of working in hospitals disclosed that he had been discharged by at least three previous health care jobs since 1982 because of his sexual abuse of comatose patients. No hospital had ever filed criminal charges against him, and so his history of raping comatose patients was never known to police and never became part of his prior employment record. Horace was charged with raping and impregnating a patient while she was comatose. He was convicted in February 1997. Should he receive probation or incarceration? (*Source:* Adapted from the Associated Press, "Nurse's Aide Sentenced for Rape," March 28, 1997.)

• *The Case of Carlos Diaz.* It happened in New York City. A man entered a downtown bank, approached a teller, and threatened to produce a gun and harm her if she did not fill a bag with money. In fear of her life, the teller complied. The man, however, was apprehended soon thereafter. Police approached him cautiously; after all, he had claimed to have a gun in his coat. After being frisked, the man was found to be carrying only a long zucchini. Nevertheless, he was charged with armed robbery. After four mistrials, Carlos Diaz, 29, was convicted of robbery. How much time can you get for holding up a bank with a zucchini? In this case, Diaz got 18 years to life in prison. Why? The reason is that Diaz had a lengthy criminal record, including six previous felony convictions for robbery, attempted robbery with a gun, assault, and selling drugs. The district attorney prosecuted Diaz as a persistent offender, and under this statute, the penalty is an automatic 15 years in prison. The defense attorney, Steven Silberblatt, unconvincingly argued that Diaz was only guilty of innocently shopping for vegetables. Should Diaz receive probation, 15 years in prison, or some other incarcerative punishment? (*Source:* Adapted from the Associated Press, "Zucchini Bandit Goes to Jail for Robbery with a Concealed Vegetable," May 29, 1997.)

• *Spec. Raymond Humphries.* Spec. Raymond Humphries, 25, was stationed at Fort Benning, Georgia. Humphries was diagnosed with AIDS and had tested positive for HIV in 1995. In 1996, Humphries began having affairs with different women, failing to notify them that he had AIDS. As a result, at least four women became pregnant, and two of them tested positive for the AIDS virus. Humphries immediately became a suspect. In the meantime, the army had assigned Humphries as a cook to a military police unit at Fort Benning, but because of his illness, he was unable to work around food or prepare it. Instead, he worked as a mechanic for the unit. Subsequently, Humphries was identified by several of the women with whom he had had unprotected sex. He was charged with knowingly infecting them with the AIDS virus. A court-martial was held for Humphries in March 1998. If found guilty on all offenses Humphries could receive up to

64 years in prison. Should he receive probation or incarceration? (*Source:* Adapted from the Associated Press, "Soldier with AIDS Gets 15 Years," March 11, 1998.)

- David Cobb was sentenced to probation and was ordered to undergo psychiatric counseling.
- Janelle Kimsey was never charged with growing marijuana.

- Alicia Howard and Alice "Brandy" Jobe each received three-year prison terms.
- John Horace was sentenced to 15 years in prison.
- Carlos Dias was sentenced to 18 years to life in prison.
- Raymond Humphries was sentenced to 15 years in prison, was given a dishonorable discharge, was reduced to the lowest military rank, and was ordered to forfeit all military pay and benefits.

Often, first-offenders are given special treatment by different components of the criminal justice system. Prosecutors are inclined to give first-offenders another chance by either diverting them from the criminal justice system entirely or downgrading the seriousness of their instant offense. These persons are frequently good candidates for community treatment programs. If they have not become deeply entrenched in criminal activity, there is a good chance that one or more programs can reach them and help them to become more law-abiding. Probation departments also target first-offenders as most eligible for their programs. Knowing one's criminal history can indicate much about whether their participation in these community programs will be worthwhile and/or successful (California Assembly, 1996).

Recidivists.   Besides first-offenders and situational criminals, some offenders are recidivists who continue to commit new offenses. Even after they have been apprehended, prosecuted, and incarcerated, many offenders continue their criminal activity when released. Sometimes these persons are called **persistent offenders**, **persistent felony offenders**, **habitual offenders**, **repeat offenders**, or **chronic offenders**. These appellations underscore the frequency and persistence of one's offending. Many programs devised by probation and parole departments are not particularly effective for helping hard-core recidivists. Some offenders will continue to reoffend no matter how carefully certain community programs are designed (Shane-Dubow et al., 1998).

Career Criminals.   **Career criminals** are offenders who earn their living from the crimes they commit (Reckless, 1961). Their criminal activity is a craft, involving expertise and special training. Career criminals are those who have reached a stage of criminality in which they view crime as an occupation or profession (Pratt and Dickson, 1997). Many of these offenders are more bothersome than dangerous. They frequently commit petty offenses involving theft, burglary, and vandalism. When they are punished, they are often overpenalized. This situation is the result of legislation in which repeat offenders are subject to harsher penalties, even life imprisonment without the possibility of parole, if they are convicted of numerous petty crimes and are nonviolent toward others (Pratt, 1996). Understandably, it is difficult for probation and parole officials to tailor programs that will rehabilitate or cure career criminals from their patterns of criminal activity.

CRIMINAL JUSTICE SYSTEM COMPONENTS

The primary components of the criminal justice system are law enforcement, prosecutorial decision making, courts and judges, and corrections.

Law Enforcement

All law enforcement agencies vest their officers with arrest powers. Police officers have the authority to make arrests whenever law violations occur within their jurisdictions. These arrest powers include apprehending anyone suspected of committing crimes. Offenses justifying arrests may range from traffic violations to first-degree murder, forcible rape, or kidnapping. Law enforcement officers are empowered to enforce the laws and statutes of their jurisdictions. The FBI, which is primarily an investigative body, has arrest powers involving violations of more than 200 federal laws. FBI agents observe all appropriate jurisdictional boundaries associated with their position. These agents do not issue traffic citations or monitor speeders on interstate highways. Accordingly, state troopers seldom investigate and arrest counterfeiters or conspirators in interstate gambling or drug trafficking.

Arrest and Booking.   An arrest means taking a crime suspect into custody. Ordinarily, police officers make arrests of those suspected of committing crimes. Once defendants have been taken into custody, they are booked. **Booking** is an administrative procedure that furnishes personal background information of offenders for law enforcement officials. It consists of compiling a file for defendants, including the defendant's name, address, telephone number, age, place of employment, relatives, and other personal data. The extensiveness of the booking procedure varies among jurisdictions. In some jurisdictions, the suspect may be photographed and fingerprinted, whereas in others, defendants may answer a few personal, descriptive questions.

Bail.   When defendants are arrested, a decision is made by prosecutors whether these persons will be brought to trial at some future date. If there is a trial, most defendants can obtain temporary release from detention. Criminal defendants may be **released on their own recognizance (ROR)**. **Bail** is only available to those entitled to bail. Those not entitled to bail include suspects likely to flee the jurisdiction if released temporarily as well as those who pose a danger to others or themselves. Bail is a surety to procure the release of those under arrest and to ensure that they will appear later to face criminal charges in court. It is ordinarily specified at the time criminal suspects are brought before a judge or magistrate in an **initial appearance**. An initial appearance involves a preliminary specification of criminal charges against the defendant. Presiding judges may specify bail or may require defendants to be held until a **preliminary hearing** or **preliminary examination** can be convened for the purpose of establishing **probable cause**. At the conclusion of preliminary hearings, bail may be ordered or suspects may be released on their own recognizance.

In the federal system, U.S. probation officers perform various **pretrial services**. These services include conducting investigations of certain persons who have been charged with federal crimes. Recommendations are often made by these federal

BOX 1.2

BOX 1.2   ***Personality Highlight***

Victor M. Villarreal
Senior Special Agent (Retired), U.S. Border Patrol, Laredo, Texas

Statistics. B.A. (political science), Laredo State University; M.A. (interdisciplinary studies), Laredo State University; Border Patrol Academy; Army Officers Candidate School;
Army Career Course and Army Command and General Staff College; M.A. in progress
(criminal justice), Texas A&M International University

Interests. I am currently a criminal justice instructor at Laredo Community
College, Laredo, Texas. I am also a real estate broker in the Laredo area. Two
years ago, I retired after serving 23 years with the U.S. Border Patrol. I served
my entire career in Laredo, Texas, as a patrol agent, intelligence officer, special
agent, and border organized crime enforcer.

I grew up traveling around the United States. My parents were farm labor
migrants, and we followed the crops as they came into season. I lived in Big
Wells, Texas; Fort Wayne, Indiana; and Fremont, California. When I was a
teenager, my father was injured working on a farm in California, and he
returned to work a small farm he owned in Mexico. I remained with my mother
and small sister to attend school in Laredo, Texas. I graduated from Martin High
School and was quickly inducted into the U.S. Army. I served three years in the
army, including one year in Vietnam, where I was an infantry platoon leader.
Upon my return to Laredo, I enrolled at Laredo Community College and joined
the Army Reserve. I was to spend a total of 30 years of active and reserve duty in
the army.

After serving in Vietnam as an infantry platoon leader, I thought I would
never want to wear or use a gun as long as I lived. My wife's grandfather, Tomas
Garcia, encouraged me to join the U.S. Border Patrol. He had been one of only
two Hispanic Border Patrol inspectors hired in 1924. I made up excuses about
why I would not join, but after his death, I joined the agency. At that time, agents
were not stationed at their home of record, but another agent (Horacio Vela)
and I were. I was to spend my entire career of 23 years working for the Border
Patrol in Laredo, Texas.

I found the U.S. Border Patrol a complete adventure. Having the army experience behind me, I had no problem with the discipline and I completely fell for
the duties. I found the outdoor duties of line watch on the riverbanks or fence
line intersections very exciting. The tracking of human beings through the chap-
arral countryside was a real challenge because it matched your wits and
endurance against that of others.

The part I found most challenging was traffic check, which consisted of manning the Border Patrol immigration checkpoints on the major highways leading
out of the border area. At the checkpoints, you were tested on your ability to
uncover counterfeit and bogus immigration documents being presented by
aliens trying to continue on their journey into the United States. Detecting and
arresting smugglers of aliens and drugs were two of our main duties at these
checkpoints.

One evening I reported to work and was assigned to work back up to the checkpoint on H-59 leading from Laredo and northeast to Freer and on to Houston. My duties included backing up the agents assigned to the temporary checkpoint and transporting any aliens detained at the checkpoint. I was the senior agent on the shift. Usually, I worked alone on this type of assignment. That evening, my supervisor, Jimmy Trevino, decided to ride with me to assist me in any chore that came with the assignment and to get a look at the field agents. That day I had purchased a new Mag-Lite metallic four-cell flashlight and was anxious to see if it would perform well.

It was beginning to get dark as I drove the patrol car east from Laredo and toward the checkpoint located about 45 miles east of Laredo. A few miles shy of the checkpoint, we spotted an old Oldsmobile parked on the side of the road. The car was typical of the ones used by alien smugglers in the area. We spotted a couple of large Hispanic men sitting inside the car. Looking toward the fence line on the side of the highway, we could see some aliens running toward the brush. We quickly concluded that the two men in the car had dropped a load of illegal aliens to walk around the checkpoint, and it was customary that they would pick them up past the Border Patrol checkpoint.

I had driven a few hundred yards past the parked car when the driver executed a turn back toward Laredo. It was obvious to us that the two men had seen us go by and were about to abandon the aliens and return to Laredo. I turned the patrol car around, got behind the Oldsmobile, and turned the overhead red lights on. The Oldsmobile came to a stop on the side of the highway, and we approached the car. I could clearly see that the driver was a big Hispanic male and that the passenger looked like his twin brother. From the corner of my eye, I could see Jimmy Trevino covering the passenger.

I was curious if there were any aliens that the smugglers had been unable to unload still in the trunk of the car, and so I asked the driver to step out of the vehicle and open the trunk. As he opened the door, he quickly began to aggressively punch and shove me. Even though I felt that I was in prime condition (after all, I had done a year in the jungles of Vietnam) and had attended jungle school and numerous other physical training, I now felt somewhat at a disadvantage. My punches seemed very ineffective against this oversized foe, while his were leaving their mark on me.

I quickly drew my prized possession, my metallic flashlight, and went to work on the guy, repelling his aggression and at the same time trying to subdue him. After a few minutes, I gained the upper hand and was able to cuff him with his hands in front, since I could not get his fat arms around his back. All the time the fight was on, I kept thinking, *Where is my partner?*

After ensuring that my prisoner was secure, I heard some yelling and grunts from the passenger's side of the car. I went around the car and found Jimmy Trevino, rolling on the ground and fighting with the other guy. After a few attention getters with the Mag-Lite, we subdued him and also cuffed him in front. We placed both men in the back seat of the patrol car, which was not easy to do because of their enormous size. Trevino and I took a few minutes to catch our breath and reflect on the encounter. We could not help but wonder why these guys had gone on the offensive and had attacked two federal officers. After all, we were in complete uniform, in a marked Border Patrol car, and had stopped them using our overhead lights.

Our question was answered rather quickly when we radioed in their identification. Both subjects were on parole and were looking at nearly ten years left on their sentences. Trevino and I both knew where these two guys were going back to. I guess these men had found it hard to go straight and had to return to criminal activity, and by doing so, they returned to prison.

Advice to Students. To any student considering a career in law enforcement, enjoy every day of your career one day at a time, because you will have very worthwhile experiences to remember. Every day you put on your uniform, take a few minutes to think of your day ahead. Don't go to work thinking of any other problems; think only of what's ahead in your upcoming shift, and be ready for anything that might come your way. Good luck!

officers to U.S. magistrates regarding an offender's bail eligibility. U.S. magistrates want to know whether a defendant poses a flight risk or poses a danger to others if freed on bail. Federal probation officers furnish the court with important information about the nature of the charges against defendants. These officers work closely with the U.S. attorney's office and determine whether to recommend bail (Wolf, 1997:19).

Prosecutorial Decision Making

Prosecutions.   After suspects have been arrested and booked for alleged violations of the law, a prosecutor examines their cases and the evidence against them and determines whether these suspects should be prosecuted. Not all arrests for serious crimes result in prosecutions. Furthermore, not all prosecutions result in convictions. A prosecution is the carrying forth of criminal proceedings against a person culminating in a trial or other final disposition, such as a guilty plea in lieu of trial. Prosecutors make these decisions and are influenced by a consideration of factors such as the adequacy of evidence, whether there are eyewitnesses, and the seriousness of the crime.

Screening and Prioritizing Cases.   The prosecuting attorney screens cases and determines which ones have the highest probability for conviction. **Screening cases** involves determining the priority to be given particular kinds of cases such as murder or vehicular theft. Some cases lack merit or have insufficient evidence to sustain a criminal conviction. In other instances, there may be so many criminal cases to prosecute that they all cannot be prosecuted. Thus, prosecutors must prioritize their cases and prosecute only the most serious ones. Prosecutors also decide whether certain cases should be dropped.

Prosecutors act as negotiators between defendants, their attorneys, and judges. They attempt to work out mutually advantageous arrangements between the state and defendants. The role of a **defense counsel** is to secure for clients the best possible outcome, preferably an acquittal. The stage is set for negotiations. Prosecutors want

BOX 1.3   *Personality Highlight*

Miguel Angel Rodriguez Jr.
Police Officer I, Laredo Police Department, Texas

Statistics. B.A. (sociology and criminal justice); M.S. (criminal justice, forthcoming), Texas A&M International University

Work History and Experience. I graduated from Laredo Community College in 1997 with an associate of applied science degree in criminal justice. At the same time, I completed 16 weeks of training from the Laredo Police Academy, making me a Texas Peace Officer at age 21. Not knowing which agency to start working with, I began working for the Webb County, Texas, constable's office as a reserve deputy constable. My goal was to earn a Ph.D. in the criminal justice field, but with experience out in the field as a peace officer. Three months later, I was sworn in as a Texas A&M International University police officer and continued my education. As I learned more about society and different subcultures that I had no idea could be seen as subcultures, like that of police officers, I decided to major in sociology. Two years later I completed a bachelor of arts degree with a major in sociology and a minor in criminal justice. One month later, I was employed by the Laredo Police Department as a police officer. Getting my degree first helped me tremendously to make better decisions in the field and to understand the police role in society much better.

While employed with Texas A&M International University, I had many opportunities to get involved in different assignments. Being a police officer for a university is not easy. Knowing that almost everybody had some kind of education kept me on my toes. I never wanted to do or say anything that might be offensive to any student because of the possibility that the student would know what a police officer should and should not do. Every day I learned something new by exchanging different information of interest with various students. When I left the university, I had some knowledge of almost every major.

I am currently employed with the Laredo Police Department in Texas as a police officer. I am assigned to the Patrol Division, District 3, which is the southeast side of Laredo. I have responded to different types of calls, from reported dogs barking to murders, while working this division. My experiences with the Laredo Police Department have been fun. Although many people don't know how hard it is to make it through the Laredo Police Department hiring process, it always comes as a surprise to them when I tell them I have a bachelor's degree. They always tell me, "You went to college to become a cop?" My answer to that is that having a degree has made being a cop much easier for me. When I got to patrol the streets of Laredo, I had some trouble adjusting to the different type of environment of the city compared with the university. I learned that it is very different dealing with people who live a criminal life than dealing with a college student. In the beginning, I started thinking that maybe the experience is what makes good officers. Then I started noticing that I would write my offense reports without any difficulties. It was easy to explain what the law is and the different avenues that could be taken in a manner a victim, witness, and suspect could understand. That's when I realized how rewarding a college education is.

One day while on patrol, I observed a vehicle doing all sorts of traffic violations. I proceeded to stop the vehicle and as I pulled him over, the driver stepped out of his car and started yelling, "Why don't you get a real job?" As polite as I could be, I immediately got out of my patrol car and told him to get back into his car. He looked at me and stated, "I am a university student majoring in business, and right now I am late for a final, but of course you wouldn't know because education is not a requirement for your job!" Then I asked him again to get inside his vehicle, and he complied. As I approached the vehicle, he said to me, "I am not giving you anything." Then I told him, "Sir, at least show me your driver's license or something that can identify you; if not, I will place you under arrest for failing to identify yourself to a police officer." He looked at me and told me that's all that he would show me. I then told him to wait inside his vehicle while I checked his driver's license. I took about five minutes to check the driver's license and another five minutes to write up all of the violations he had committed. I approached his vehicle and could tell that he was really upset. He started yelling, "Are you happy, huh? Are you?" I immediately said, "No, sir." Then I stated, "Sir, I am citing you for disregarding three stop signs, following too closely, failing to drive on a single lane, failing to signal left twice, failing to maintain financial responsibility, operating an unregistered motor vehicle, having an expired motor vehicle inspection, having a defective headlamp, and having a defective license plate light. This signature is not a plea of guilty, but just a promise to appear in court." As I gave him the citation book and showed him where he was supposed to put his signature, he saw my college graduation ring. In a different tone of voice he asked, "You went to college to become a cop?" Then I stated, "Yes, as a matter of fact, I did, and it's what has helped me make persons like you so frustrated and helpless without losing my professionalism; you see, if I didn't have an education, I would be feeling the way you are feeling right now." At the end, I told him, "Finish your education; it really does help."

Advice to Students. My advice to anyone interested in law enforcement is to earn a degree. Earning a degree will help you develop better skills. You will be more assertive in your decisions. When it comes to justify your decisions in writing, it will be as easy as writing a paragraph on half a chapter from your introduction to criminal justice class. I am still continuing my education by pursuing a master's degree in public administration with a track in criminal justice. Do not leave your education until the end. Get it as soon as possible, and remember that education will help you to succeed no matter what field you go into.

guilty pleas from defendants. Defendants, who may or may not be guilty of the offenses alleged, weigh the alternatives. Considering the strength of the evidence and other factors, defendants, after consulting with their attorneys, may decide to plead guilty, provided the government makes adequate concessions. Sentences resulting from trial convictions are often more severe than those imposed as the result of plea-bargained convictions for the same offenses.

BOX 1.4   *Personality Highlight*

Oscar Jesus Hale Jr.
Chief Prosecutor, 49th Judicial District, Webb and Zapata Counties

Statistics. B.A. (political science, history), Texas A&M International University; Juris Doctor, Texas Southern University

Work History and Experience. I graduated from Texas A&M International University (formerly Laredo State University) in May 1991 with a degree in political science and a minor in history. My intentions were to sign up with the Drug Enforcement Administration (DEA) as an agent immediately after graduation. Instead, however, I decided instead to wait until after I returned from an internship at the U.S. Congress. While in Washington, D.C., I worked for the Honorable Solomon P. Ortiz of Corpus Christi from September to December 1991 and was a Lyndon Baines Johnson Legislative Intern.

As a legislative intern, I was assigned to work on various research projects, including a project to gather statistics on controlled substance issues. Some of my other assignments included responding to written requests from constituents. While working with the congressman in Washington, I became fascinated and intrigued with our very unique legal system. In fact, when I returned to Laredo, I immediately registered to take the Law School Admissions Test (LSAT). After obtaining my LSAT results, I began to apply to law school. I only applied to two different schools, Texas Southern University (TSU) and the University of Houston (U of H). Although I received a letter of regret from U of H, I was excited and relieved when I received my law school acceptance letter from TSU (my first choice anyway).

After three years of law school, I was ready to begin the practice of law. Fortunately, I had taken the Texas bar exam early and passed, which gave me an edge in landing a job. I began working for the law firm of Person, Whitworth, Ramos, Borchers & Morales in May 1995. As an associate for this firm, I learned more about the law and about being a lawyer than I had learned in three years of law school. Law school taught me how to think like a lawyer and how to write like a lawyer, but the actual experience of being a lawyer is completely different. I gained experience in civil litigation, family law, oil and gas law, contract law, and criminal defense. My mentor, the late Charles R. Borchers, was a great person and a brilliant lawyer with whom I had the privilege of working side by side.

After about two years with the firm, March 7, 1997, to be exact, I started my first day as an assistant district attorney for the 49th Judicial District. This job was why I went to law school. My father, O. J. Hale Sr., had worked as the chief criminal investigator for this office since I was five years old (I am 32 now). In fact, the district attorney at that time was none other than the brilliant Charles R. Borchers. He was considered a hands-on D.A. Also, my three uncles have a combined 60-plus years experience in law enforcement. Law enforcement was all that I had been exposed to since I was five years old. As an assistant D.A., I have had an opportunity to handle various prosecutions including assault, driving while intoxicated, embezzlement, homicide, intoxicated manslaughter, kidnapping, theft, robbery, and many other types of offenses. On one occasion, I was asked to work on proposing a new state law that was sponsored by our state representative. I even went to the state capitol in Austin to testify in support of the proposed legislation. The proposed legislation, House Bill 2526, became law on September 1, 1999. During my four years as an assistant D.A., I have also gained extensive trial and appellate experience.

In fact, one appeal I handled involved a defendant who was challenging the legality of the revocation of his probation. In this case, the defendant's probation had terminated two weeks before the revocation hearing. The law states that the only way a court can maintain jurisdiction on a case, after the probationary period has terminated, is if two requirements are met. First, a motion to revoke must be filed in a timely manner (before termination of the probationary period). Second, a capias (arrest warrant) must be ordered prior to the termination of the probationary period. In this case, the first requirement had been met, but not the second. Instead of ordering a capias, the court issued a summons (request to appear). The defendant, however, appeared in court during the probationary period and in response to the summons. In my appeal, I argued that because the defendant had appeared voluntarily, as per the court's summons, the court maintained jurisdiction regardless of whether his revocation occurred after his probationary period had expired. The Fourth Court of Appeals agreed with me and published their ruling because this case appeared to be a case of first impression.

Advice to Students. One of the questions most frequently asked by students interested in pursuing a legal career has been, "Which major should I study to help prepare me for law school?" Students may get different responses, depending on whom they ask. If you ask me what I have learned, however, I will tell you that no single major can completely prepare you for law school. Although being an English major may help, it really does not matter what your major is as long as you have good reading and writing skills. You will find that as a lawyer, you never stop learning about the law; I guess that is why they call it the practice of law. The best advice I can pass on to you is to be well learned in areas such as art, history, music, and politics; leave the legal issues for when you get to law school and for when you begin your practice of law.

Plea Bargaining.   More than 90 percent of all felony convictions in the United States are obtained prior to trial through **plea bargaining**. A plea bargain is a preconviction agreement between the defendant and the state whereby the defendant pleads guilty with the expectation of a reduction in the charges, a promise of sentencing leniency, or some other governmental concession short of the maximum penalties that could be imposed under the law. Plea bargaining is not exclusively an American phenomenon. It is found in many other countries, such as Canada (Nasheri, 1998).

Plea bargaining is largely discretionary. Prosecutors use this tool as a means of regulating caseflow, managing case backlogs, and facilitating case completion (Pizzi, 1999). Without plea bargaining, the criminal justice system would probably be seriously impaired and grind to a halt in most jurisdictions. Almost every case would be subject to more lengthy trials, and the costs and workload involved would be prohibitive (Turpin-Petrosino, 1999).

There are four types of plea bargaining. The first type is **implicit plea bargaining**, in which defendants plead guilty with the expectation that they will receive more lenient sentences than if they were to go to trial and be found guilty by a jury. Generally, plea bargaining results in greater leniency in sentencing compared with a sentence derived from a jury finding of guilty at the conclusion of a **criminal trial** (Mitchell and Dodenhoff, 1998; Nasheri, 1998). A second type is **sentence recommendation plea bargaining**, in which the prosecutor proposes a sentence in exchange for a guilty plea. A third type is **charge reduction bargaining**, in which the prosecutor downgrades charges in exchange for a guilty plea. This type of plea bargaining is sometimes called **overcharging**. A fourth type is **judicial plea bargaining**, in which the judge makes a plea offer to a defendant such that if the defendant pleads guilty, the judge will impose a specific lenient sentence. Sentence recommendation bargaining and charge reduction bargaining are probably the most frequently used types of plea negotiating.

Prosecutors do not have the authority to grant probation to any criminal defendant in exchange for a guilty plea. They can only recommend probation to judges. Judges are the ultimate arbiters, and they decide whether to approve or disapprove any plea agreement. The plea-bargaining process is important to any criminal defendant entering into negotiations with government prosecutors. Several constitutional rights are waived by defendants, and they acquire a criminal record. In the present context, plea bargaining is any offer or recommendation of sentencing leniency in exchange for a guilty plea from a defendant (Vogel, 1999).

Informations, Indictments, and Presentments. If prosecutors persist in a prosecution against certain defendants, they have several options for commencing criminal proceedings. Prosecutors may file an **information**, or a formal criminal charge, against a defendant. In about half of all states, a **grand jury** convenes and may issue an **indictment** or **presentment** against criminal suspects. Indictments and presentments are also charges stemming from grand jury consideration of evidence against the accused. Indictments are charges against criminal suspects brought by the grand jury at the request of prosecutors. Presentments are criminal charges against the accused when the grand jury has acted on its own authority. These actions simply specify that sufficient evidence exists to establish probable cause that a crime has been committed and the accused committed it. A **true bill** indicates that the grand jury has found sufficient evidence to establish probable cause that the accused committed a crime. **No true bills** issue from grand jury action and indicate that insufficient evidence exists to establish probable cause. If a no true bill or **no bill** is issued, suspects are most often freed from further criminal prosecutions.

Arraignments. Trials are preceded by an **arraignment**, a formal proceeding in which the finalized list of charges is furnished criminal defendants. Arraignments also are held for the purposes of entering a plea (e.g., guilty, not guilty, guilty but mentally ill) and determining a trial date. In a worst-case scenario, suppose that a criminal defendant pleads not guilty to a criminal charge. A trial date is then established, and a trial is scheduled at which one's guilt or innocence can be determined by a judge or jury.

Courts and Judges

Court Dockets and Judicial Workloads.   In many federal district courts as well as state criminal courts, court calendars are glutted with cases. About 85 percent of these cases are civil, and they consume considerable court time. The remainder of the cases are criminal. The courtroom is where a defendant's guilt is ultimately determined. It functions as a public forum for the airing of all relevant information and evidence in the case. The government presents its evidence against the accused, and the defense counters with its own evidence. Witnesses are called to testify both for and against the accused, and defendants have the right to cross-examine their accusers and to offer testimony and evidence in their own behalf. The courtroom is also where the sufficiency of evidence against the accused is tested. The prosecution carries the burden of proof against the accused and must establish one's guilt **beyond a reasonable doubt**.

Speedy Trials and Case Processing.   If the charges are serious and could result in incarceration for a period of six months or more, defendants are entitled to a **jury trial** in any criminal proceeding as a matter of right. This right applies to either misdemeanors or felonies. A jury is an objective, impartial body of persons who convene to hear the case against the accused and make a determination of guilt or innocence on the basis of the factual evidence presented. Despite speedy trial measures, streamlined case processing, and other court reforms, most state and federal judges are overworked and their dockets are full of case backlogs (Jones, Wiliszowski, and Lacey, 1999; Schneider and Davis, 1995). Therefore, judges encourage prosecutors to work out arrangements with defendants, if possible, so that the number of trials can be at least minimized.

Sentencing and Implications for Convicted Offenders.   Defendants who are found not guilty are acquitted and freed from the criminal justice system. When defendants are found guilty, an appeals process exists at both the state and local levels whereby these defendants may appeal the verdict and request a new trial. In the meantime, convicted offenders are sentenced.

Several options are available to judges in **sentencing** criminal defendants. For example, first-offenders may receive light sentences and not be incarcerated. Convicted offenders with prior records, however, will probably receive harsher sentences. Judges may sentence offenders to incarceration in a local jail or regional prison for a specified period of time. If the judge sentences convicted offenders to some nonincarcerative punishment, defendants may be placed on probation for a prescribed period.

Probation is a sentence involving a conditional suspension of incarceration, usually with several behavioral provisions or conditions often prescribed by law. Although this list is not exhaustive, these conditions include (1) not associating with other known criminals, (2) refraining from committing future criminal acts, (3) obtaining and maintaining employment, and/or (4) participating in appropriate medical or counseling programs and therapy. Also, in many cases, judges must sentence convicted offenders to prison according to prescribed statutes, mandatory statutory provisions that bind judges and restrict their discretionary powers. Generally, however, convicted offenders collectively fall under the supervision of corrections.

BOX 1.5

Personality Highlight

Linda Ramirez
Graduate Student, Criminal Justice, Texas A&M International University

Statistics. B.A. (political science), St. Mary's University; M.A. (criminal justice, forthcoming), Texas A&M International University

Work History and Experience. I graduated from St. Mary's University in 2000. When first in college, I was going to major in biology. I later changed my major to political science and minored in history. I had no future plans until graduation, when I decided to pursue my education by enrolling in the criminal justice graduate program at Texas A&M International University.

During my senior year at St. Mary's, I took an introduction to criminal justice course. My professor had previously worked at a correctional institution as a correctional officer and supervisor. Throughout the course, he described in detail situations or events that occurred when he worked there. After the course, I was filled with curiosity about the criminal justice field. I began to read the book *Journey into Darkness,* which is about a profiler who helped capture some of the most wanted serial killers. Still interested in learning more about corrections, I interviewed my brother and his coworkers, who work as probation officers for Webb County, Texas. I was given the opportunity to visit my brother at his work and got a better understanding and feeling about his everyday duties.

My future plans are to continue my education until I have a doctoral degree in criminal justice. Then I plan to do research in different areas of criminal justice. For example, I would like to answer the question about how effective probation is as a rehabilitative medium for offenders. At the same time, I plan to teach at a university.

Advice to Students. Even though I have no work experience in the criminal justice field, the research and graduate courses I am currently taking have increased my knowledge of criminal justice greatly. My advice to students who plan to pursue a career in criminal justice is to take the introduction to criminal justice class and conduct a personal research project to find out if that is the path you really want to take. If, indeed, that is the field of interest for you, then go ahead and follow it. If you decide later to change your major, then that is what you want to do. Go for it!

Corrections

The last component of the criminal justice system is corrections. Corrections includes all the agencies, organizations, and personnel who deal with convicted offenders after court processing and convictions. Typically, corrections are associated with **jails** and **prisons**. Jails are usually short-term confinement facilities operated by cities and county governments. They are usually used for persons enduring short-term confinement for misdemeanor offenses or for persons charged with more serious offenses who are awaiting trial. Prisons are long-term facilities that are more

BOX 1.6   *Was the Judge Too Lenient?*

Peter Dudley Albertsen II

Matthew and Justin Wilke were 11 and 9, respectively, when they met Peter Dudley Albertsen II. Albertsen was a 23-year-old lifeguard at a summer camp in suburban Baltimore, Maryland, that the boys attended. Albertsen struck up a friendship with the two boys, and after a few years, the boys' parents would allow Matthew and Justin to spend weekends at the home of Albertsen. Soon Albertsen began sexually molesting the boys. Matthew and Justin kept the sexual abuse secret for nearly two years. Then Matthew told his mother about it. Albertsen was arrested by police in 1990. He pleaded guilty to abuse and received a three-year suspended sentence, together with an order to undergo psychological treatment and to stay away from the Wilke brothers and other children. Instead, Albertsen began to stalk the boys. He wrote letters to Justin, left notes on his car, and appeared at his high school graduation. When Albertsen was in Germany in 1995 on a student visa, he mailed a video containing child pornography to Justin on his 19th birthday, together with a birthday card and two 25-page letters.

Later in 1995, the boys' father, Don Wilke, 56, committed suicide by running a tube from his exhaust pipe into his car. On February 8, 1996, Justin committed suicide in the same way. Matthew ended his own life by suicide on August 15, 1996, by the same method. He left a note behind that said, "I hate you, Pete." It is unknown whether the suicides were directly connected to the child pornography mailed to Justin by Albertsen. Albertsen was subsequently arrested and charged with trafficking in child pornography resulting from the pornographic material he had sent to Justin. A U.S. district court found him guilty of the charge, and the judge imposed the maximum sentence of ten years in prison. The judge commented that the sentence was "unfortunately inadequate under the facts of this case." Albertsen also received three years' probation and was required to register as a pedophile, get counseling, and have no direct contact with children under 18. Prosecutor Andrew White pushed for the maximum sentence. He said, "Albertsen showed no remorse and remains unconvinced he did anything wrong." Referring to Andersen's relationship with Justin, White said, "He thinks it is beautiful." While pointing at Albertsen in the courtroom, White said, "This man right here is nothing more than a sexual predator."

Was the ten-year sentence imposed on Albertsen sufficient, considering his indirect role in the suicides of the two young men? If you had been the prosecutor, what additional charges might you have filed against Albertsen? How would you sentence Albertsen? What do you think?

Source: Adapted from the Associated Press, "Molester Gets 10-Year Sentence in Case Tied to Three Suicides," July 12, 1997.

self-contained than jails and that house inmates serving sentences of one or more years. Although prisons and jails are important features of the corrections system, they are hardly the dominant components of it. By 1997, nearly 7 million adults were under some form of correctional supervision in the United States. There were over 1 million prison inmates and about 750,000 jail inmates.

Jail and Prison Overcrowding.   Frequently, there is little room in many prisons and jails to house new convicted offenders. This condition is called **overcrowding**. By 1998, approximately 30 states were under court order to decrease their prison inmate populations to comply with health and safety standards as well as other factors (Pastore and Maguire, 2001). Along with other states, Texas, Tennessee, and Louisiana have been targeted for rehabilitative reforms by the courts. **Prison over-**

crowding and **jail overcrowding** are primarily responsible for the large increase in the number of nonincarcerated offenders currently under some form of correctional supervision. Overcrowding in jails or prisons occurs whenever the operating capacity of a facility is exceeded by the number of inmates it is intended to accommodate (Illinois Sentencing Commission, 1998). Many judges have reported that prison overcrowding is a significant factor in their sentencing decisions whether to incarcerate convicted offenders. One increasingly important factor affecting prison populations in both state and federal facilities is the growing population of noncitizen felony offenders (Florida Department of Corrections, 1999).

Judicial Discretion in Sentencing Offenders.   Judges frequently have considerable latitude in sentencing criminal offenders. Besides sentencing offenders to incarceration, judges may impose other sentences, including **community service**, restitution, and even probation. In 1997, the probation and parolee population exceeded six million. Among the factors considered by trial judge when sentencing offenders are (1) the nature and circumstances of the offense and the history and characteristics of the defendant; (2) the need for the sentence imposed to reflect the seriousness of the offense, to promote respect for the law, to afford adequate **deterrence** to criminal conduct, and to protect the public from further crimes of the defendant; (3) the kinds of educational or training services, medical care, or other correctional treatment that might be appropriate for any particular defendant; (4) the kinds of sentences available; and (5) the need to avoid unwarranted sentence disparities among defendants with similar records who have been found guilty of similar conduct. Some critics of judicial discretion say that judges have too much unregulated power that often results in questionable decision making, such as excessive leniency for violent offenders and sending nonserious juveniles to criminal courts for processing (Smith and Dickey, 1999). Numerous sentencing reforms have been dedicated to controlling judicial discretion at all levels, although no sentencing scheme seems to work perfectly (Edwards, 1999).

The Availability of Community Services and Facilities.   Many citizens equate corrections with punishment involving incarceration. In reality, a majority of convicted offenders are never incarcerated. Rather, they are permitted the freedom of living in their communities under some form of **alternative sentencing** or **creative sentencing**. Alternative sentencing involves some form of community service, some degree of restitution to victims of crimes, becoming actively involved in educational or vocational training programs, or becoming affiliated with some other productive activity. Two goals of alternative sentencing are enabling offenders to avoid the criminal label of imprisonment and allowing convicts to participate in rehabilitative and reintegrative community programs. Community programs are designed to provide convicted offenders with needed services and therapy while they remain free in their communities. Alternative sentencing is also intended to reduce jail and prison overcrowding and reduce correctional operating costs.

PROBATION AND PAROLE DISTINGUISHED

Probation is considered a front-end sentence, whereby judges impose conditional sentences in lieu of incarceration. In most cases, probationers do not serve time in either jail or prison. Rather, they must comply with an extensive list of probation program conditions as specified by the court. Probationers remain free within the jurisdiction of sentencing judges while on probation. If probationers violate one or more conditions of their probation orders while on probation, judges decide whether to revoke or terminate their probation programs.

In contrast, parole is early release from prison or jail by a **parole board**. Most states have parole boards that convene to determine whether inmates should be released short of serving their full sentences. Because almost all jails and prisons in the United States are overcrowded, any mechanism that might reduce such overcrowding is viewed favorably, particularly by state legislatures. Parole is one such mechanism. Parole differs from probation in that parolees have spent a period of time in a jail or prison. All parolees have previously been inmates of some state or federal facility. Parole boards have jurisdiction over parolees and decide whether they should be released short of serving their full incarcerative terms.

SUMMARY

The major components of the criminal justice system are law enforcement, prosecution and the courts, and corrections. Probation and parole are integral features of corrections, which includes all organizations and personnel who manage offenders convicted of crimes. Probation is a conditional sentence imposed by a judge in lieu of incarceration, whereas parole is conditional early release from prison granted by a parole board.

The entire criminal justice process starts whenever a crime is committed. Crimes are violations of the law by persons held accountable under the law. Crimes may be distinguished as either misdemeanors or felonies, and they may involve property or violence. Official sources of crime in the United States are the *Uniform Crime Reports (UCS)* and the *National Crime Victimization Survey (NCVS),* both of which are flawed in various respects. Both official sources are considered underestimates of the actual amount of crime committed in the United States annually. When persons are arrested for a crime, they are booked. Prosecutors decide whether to prosecute defendants. Prosecutors prioritize cases if their caseloads are particularly large. Over 90 percent of all criminal defendants enter guilty pleas to criminal charges in exchange for sentencing leniency in a process known as plea bargaining. For other defendants, trials are held at which juries or judges determine their guilt or innocence. If defendants are convicted through trial, judges must sentence offenders to some type of punishment. All sentences are a type of punishment, although the punishment does not always involve incarceration. Probation is a punishment, although it is a nonincarcerative alternative. Probationers must comply with numerous probation program conditions and behavioral restrictions.

Judges decide whether to place offenders on probation or send them to jails or prisons. Sentencing offenders depends on the seriousness of their offenses and their prior records. Jails are short-term facilities intended to house minor offenders and pretrial detainees. Prisons are long-term and self-contained facilities designed to accommodate more serious offenders for longer periods. Depending on the type of crime committed, offenders are classified in different ways to determine their level of custody and/or the nature of their treatment or assistance. Some offenders are first-offenders, whereas others may be recidivists or career criminals. Offenders with prior criminal records usually receive harsher treatment from judges when sentenced. Some offenders are designated as special needs criminals. They may have

AIDS or some other communicable illness, be handicapped in some respect, or be psychologically or mentally impaired. Some offenders may have drug or alcohol dependencies and require special treatment or counseling. Other offenders may be sex offenders and child sexual abusers requiring extraordinary therapy.

Corrections is expected to accommodate all types of offenders. Depending on how offenders are sentenced, different corrections agencies or institutions will be responsible for offender supervision. Those sentenced by judges to probation are supervised by probation agencies and probation officers, whereas parole officers and agencies supervise those who have been paroled from either state or federal penitentiaries by parole boards. Community-based corrections are intended to assist both probationers and parolees in various ways to enhance the likelihood that they will complete their respective probation or parole programs successfully. The long-term goal of these agencies and organizations is to cause their clients to become law-abiding so that they will refrain from future criminal activity.

KEY TERMS

Alternative sentencing
Arraignment
Arrest
Bail
Beyond a reasonable doubt
Booking
Career criminals
Charge reduction bargaining
Chronic offenders
Community-based corrections
Community service
Corrections
Corrections officers
Courts
Creative sentencing
Crime classification index
Crimes against property
Crimes against the person
Crimes of violence
Criminal justice system
Criminal trial
Criminogenic environment
Defendants
Defense counsel
Delinquents
Deterrence
Double jeopardy
Early release
Federal Bureau of Investigation (FBI)
Felony

Fines
First-offenders
First-time offenders
Grand jury
Habitual offenders
Implicit plea bargaining
Incidents
Index offenses
Indictment
Information
Initial appearance
Jail overcrowding
Jails
Judicial plea bargaining
Jurisdiction
Jury trial
Law enforcement
Level of custody
Misdemeanants
Misdemeanor
National Crime Victimization Survey (NCVS)
National Incident-Based Reporting System (NIBRS)
No bill, no true bill
Offender rehabilitation
Offenders
Overcharging
Overcrowding
Parole
Parole board

Parolees
Parole officers (POs)
Parole revocation
Persistent felony offenders
Persistent offenders
Plea bargaining
Preliminary hearing, preliminary examination
Presentment
Pretrial services
Prison overcrowding
Prisons
Probable cause
Probation
Probationer
Probation officers (POs)
Probation revocation
Property crimes
Prosecutions
Prosecutors
Recidivism
Recidivism rates
Recidivists
Released on own recognizance (ROR)
Repeat offenders
Screening cases
Self-reported information
Sentence recommendation plea bargaining
Sentencing
Sex offenders

Situational offenders

Summary offense

True bill

Uniform Crime Reports (UCR)

Victimization data

Victimizations

Violence

Violent crimes

White-collar crime

QUESTIONS FOR REVIEW

1. What is the *Uniform Crime Reports (UCR)*? What kinds of information does it report? What can you say about its accuracy relative to general crime and crime trends in the United States?

2. What is the *National Crime Victimization Survey (NCVS)*? How does it differ from the *UCR*? Explain. Do you believe that it is a more accurate reflection of the amount of crime in the United States than the *UCR*? Why or why not?

3. What are the major components of the criminal justice system? Which part of the system deals with convicted offenders? Explain briefly the functions of this component relative to convicted offenders.

4. What is a crime? Distinguish between two general categories of crime. Explain how each is treated in terms of punishment. Your answer can include both the location where offenders might be housed as well as the sentence lengths judges might commonly impose.

5. What are index offenses? What is their usefulness regarding crime in the United States and crime trends?

6. Differentiate between a victimization and an incident.

7. Who are situational offenders? What can you speculate about their amount of expected recidivism in the future? Explain.

8. What is recidivism? What are some of the ways it is measured? Why is recidivism used as a measure of a program's success or failure?

9. What are four different types of plea bargaining? Give an example of each from any hypothetical information you may have.

10. What is meant by alternative or creative sentencing? Give some examples of it.

SUGGESTED READINGS

Fox, Richard G. (1999). "Competition and Sentencing: The Rehabilitative Model versus the Punitive Model." *Psychiatry and the Law* **6:**152–162.

Roskes, Erik (ed.) (1999). "Mentally Ill Offenders: Needs and Services." *Psychiatric Services* **50:**1596–1630.

Webb, David, and Robert Harris (eds.) (1999). *Mentally Disordered Offenders: Managing People Nobody Owns.* London: Routledge.

Wilson, Martha K., et al. (1998). "Reducing Recidivism for Women Inmates: The Search for Alternatives." *Journal of Offender Rehabilitation* **27:**61–76.

Wooten, Harold B., and Herbert J. Hoover (1998). "'Operation Spotlight': The Community Probation/Community Police Team Process." *Federal Probation* **62:**30–35.

CHAPTER 2

An Overview of Community Corrections: Types, Goals, and Functions

Introduction
Community Corrections and Intermediate
  Punishments
The Community Corrections Act
The Philosophy and History of Community
  Corrections
Characteristics, Goals, and Functions of Commu-
  nity Corrections Programs
  The Goals of Community-Based Corrections
  The Functions of Community-Based Corrections
Selected Issues in Community Corrections
Public Resistance to Locating Community
  Programs in Communities (The NIMBY
  Syndrome: "Not In My Back Yard")
  Punishment and Public Safety versus Offender
  Rehabilitation and Reintegration
  Net-Widening
  Privatization of Community-Based
  Correctional Agencies
  Services Delivery
Home Confinement Programs
  Home Confinement Defined

The Early Uses of Home Confinement
The Goals of Home Confinement Programs
A Profile of Home Confinement Clients
Selected Issues in Home Confinement
Electronic Monitoring Programs
  Electronic Monitoring Defined
  Early Uses of Electronic Monitoring
  Types of Electronic Monitoring Systems
  Electronic Monitoring with Home
  Confinement
  Arguments for and against Electronic
  Monitoring
  A Profile of Electronic Monitoring Clients
  Selected Issues in Electronic Monitoring
Day Reporting Centers
  An Example of a Day Reporting Center
  in Action
Summary
Key Terms
Questions for Review
Suggested Readings

• Cobham was a Florida probationer who was sentenced to house arrest following his conviction of a felony. Cobham was ordered to remain confined to his apartment at particular times. On at least two occasions, unannounced visits from Cobham's probation officer determined that Cobham was not at home when he was supposed to be there. Accordingly, the probation officer filed a report with the court requesting that the court should revoke Cobham's probation program. The court agreed and he appealed, contending that the house arrest requirement was especially harsh and that revocation of his probation program was not warranted. The Florida appellate court upheld Cobham's probation revocation and held that the proof of Cobham's absence from his apartment on at least two occasions, as noted by the probation officer, were valid reasons for the revocation decision. (*Cobham v. State,* 736 So.2d 67 [Fla. Dist. App. June 1999])

• Johnson was convicted in a Washington state court on bad check charges. He was placed on probation, with the provisions that he must submit to random urinalysis and breathalysis and participate in a prescribed rehabilitative program, although his record revealed no misuse of alcohol or drugs. Johnson remained under community supervision by the probation department. Once, a random urinalysis determined that Johnson had consumed alcohol, and the probation department moved to have his probation program revoked. The court revoked his probation program and Johnson appealed, contending that whether or not he drank alcohol was irrelevant to the bad check charge of which he was convicted. The Washington appellate court upheld his probation revocation, holding that the court could order conditions of probation unrelated to the conviction offense. (*State v. Johnson,* 988 P.2d 460 [Wash. App. Nov. 1999])

• Ray was convicted in Georgia of a sex offense. He was incarcerated for a period of time, then placed on parole under community corrections supervision. His parole program included both house arrest and electronic monitoring. Further, he was ordered to pay victim compensation fees and electronic monitoring fees to the state as a partial reimbursement for program operation. Ray objected to having to pay such fees and appealed. The Georgia appellate court upheld these conditions as reasonable and ordered Ray to either pay them or be returned to prison. (*Hamm v. Ray,* 531 S.E.2d 91 [Ga. Sup. July 2000])

• Kelly was convicted of a felony and placed on probation in Florida. She was ordered to be placed under home confinement with electronic monitoring. One of the conditions was that she must not attempt to remove her plastic electronic bracelet. One afternoon, however, she appeared at the probation office and displayed a broken electronic bracelet. She claimed she had broken it while gardening in her yard. She was badly bruised about the eyes and arms. Subsequently, it was disclosed that her boyfriend had beaten her and had cut off the electronic bracelet. Although the probation department revoked her probation program, the Florida appellate court reversed the revocation, holding that Kelly had attempted to comply with her program rules and was essentially truthful with officials. Also, her boyfriend was prosecuted and convicted of battery, and it was determined that he had removed her electronic bracelet in a fit of rage. (*Kelly v. State,* 729 So.2d 1007 [Fla. Dist. App. April 1999])

• Sheree M. was an Arizona juvenile who was adjudicated by the juvenile court as incorrigible. She was placed under home detention under the supervision of her parents. She objected, contending that the juvenile court had no authority to incarcerate her in her home, because the juvenile court lacked the authority to place incorrigible juveniles in a juvenile detention center. The Arizona appellate court disagreed with Sheree M., holding that home confinement is not "detention" within the meaning of the statute and that one's home is not a locked and physically secure barrier with restricted ingress and egress for the protection of the juvenile or the community. Thus, the juvenile court has the authority to impose home detention as a condition of probation for incorrigible juveniles. (*In re Sheree M.*, 4 P.3d 1067 [Ariz. App. April 2000])

INTRODUCTION

The scenarios presented involve different types of offenders under supervision within their own communities. As jail and prison overcrowding have reached critical levels, it is not economically possible to lock up all convicted offenders, even though many of them deserve to be confined. It would require at least a 500 percent increase in existing jail and prison space to accommodate the present population of convicted offenders in the United States, not including the space to house new criminal offenders. One result of extreme prison and jail overcrowding is that both the states and federal government have turned to alternative supervisory methods for convicted offenders. Since the mid-1970s, increasing numbers of jurisdictions have relied on community corrections as an alternative to incarceration, believing that many offenders can be effectively monitored and supervised within their own communities. The success of community corrections has been firmly established. Most jurisdictions have discovered that community corrections not only eases prison and jail overcrowding but that the cost of supervising offenders in their own communities is but a fraction of the cost of imprisonment. Early in this chapter, the concepts of community corrections and intermediate punishments are examined to ascertain their similarities and differences, if any.

This chapter is organized as follows. First, community corrections is defined and contrasted with intermediate punishments. A historical context of the development and philosophy of community corrections is provided. Several characteristics of community-based corrections programs are described, and various goals and functions of community corrections programs are presented. Community corrections clients are also profiled. Next is an overview of different types of community corrections programs. Three kinds of community-based correctional programs—home confinement, electronic monitoring, and day reporting—and their functions and goals, advantages and disadvantages, and primary features are described.

The chapter concludes with a discussion of selected community-based correctional issues. These issues relates to public opposition toward community-based corrections programs, the privatization of such programs, and whether community-based corrections are true punishments. Some persons have been critical of community-based corrections because they have involved net-widening, or drawing in certain clients who would not be subject to any type of supervision if these programs did not exist. Other issues pertain to the management and operations of these programs, the quality of services delivery, and staff training and education.

COMMUNITY CORRECTIONS AND INTERMEDIATE PUNISHMENTS

Community-based corrections is the broad array of correctional programs established at the community level that provide alternatives to incarceration (Harris, 1999). These community-based programs are intended to continue one's punishment, but in the context of the community rather than in a prison or jail. Another term that is often used synonymously with community corrections is **intermediate punishments**. Intermediate punishments include any community-based programs that are somewhere between standard probation and incarceration. The conceptual confusion between community corrections and intermediate punishments is easily explained. This author conducted a content analysis of over 600 articles and books extracted from the *Criminal Justice Abstracts* in 2001. These articles and books were selected according to the key words *community corrections* and *intermediate punishments*. An inspection of the abstracts of these articles and books disclosed a remarkably high number of similarities.

Let's examine a few articles that focused on *intermediate punishments* or *intermediate sanctions*. For instance, Karol Lucken (1997a) examined intermediate punishments as including home confinement and day reporting programs. Henry Sontheimer and Traci Duncan (1996) investigated intermediate sanctions in Pennsylvania, including community service, restitution, house arrest/electronic monitoring, residential work release, and intensive supervision programs. David Rasmussen and Bruce Benson (1994) examined various intermediate punishment programs in Florida, including day fines, shock incarceration, intensive probation supervision, electronic monitoring, house arrest, and day reporting. A fourth source, an article by Kevin Courtright, Bruce Berg, and Robert Mutchnick (1997:19), indicated among other things that "if offenders who would have been sentenced to standard probation are now being sentenced to an intermediate punishment program, e.g., house arrest, intensive supervision, or electronic monitoring . . . then net widening would have occurred."

Next, let's examine several articles that focused on *community corrections, community-based corrections,* or *community-based sanctions*. Research reported by Jody Sundt and her associates (1998:25) investigated public opinions about different types of sanctions to be imposed on fictitious criminals with specific types of criminal histories. They reported that "given the community-based options, respondents preferred sentencing offenders to halfway houses or house arrest . . . rather than strict probation." In an essay describing Michigan's Community Corrections Act (CCA), Patricia Clark (1995:68) has noted that "since the implementation of Michigan's CCA, community service work, electronic monitoring, day reporting, employment, and drug testing and treatment programs have been initiated and expanded in most communities in the state." And in a definitive study of community corrections conducted by Robert Sigler and David Lamb (1995:7), types of community corrections included regular probation, intensive probation, shock probation, work release, electronic monitoring, house arrest, halfway house, victim restitution and fines, and community service.

What is clear is that the differences between community-based corrections and intermediate punishments are unclear. The primary reason for this lack of clarity is that virtually all intermediate punishments are community-based sanctions. All intermediate punishment programs are located in communities, where offenders are permitted various freedoms to work at jobs, attend school, and/or participate in different forms of individual or group therapy. All intermediate punishment programs have behavioral conditions. Virtually every intermediate punishment program is administered by a probation or parole agency or by a private organization. All intermediate punishment clients are under some form of supervision by these agencies or organizations. The intensity of such supervision varies according to the agency and program requirements.

Some states, such as Florida, have a program known as **community control**. According to Florida officials, community control is not intensive supervised probation or parole. Rather, it is home confinement, often coupled with *electronic monitoring*. Florida clouds the picture, however, by describing how community control involves frequent face-to-face contacts between probationers and parolees and their supervisors, that curfews are strictly enforced, and that probation and parole officers have deliberately low caseloads of 20 or fewer clients so as to allow officers to supervise offenders closely or intensively. This description of community control sounds a lot like intensive supervised probation/parole, and it has all the identifying characteristics of community corrections.

A fine line is sometimes drawn between programs that offer offenders community freedoms but require them to be monitored frequently and intensively (e.g., repeated drug and alcohol testing through urinanalysis, curfew checks, unannounced but frequent inspections of one's residence) and programs that place offenders in designated locations, such as their homes or halfway houses. The simple fact is, though, that **professionals** themselves obscure the differences between community-based programs by lumping together any and all programs that involve client freedom but some form of community supervision, regardless of its nature or intensity.

In this book, community corrections is defined as any community-based program designed to supervise convicted offenders in lieu of incarceration, either at the city, county, state or federal level; that provides various services to client/offenders; that monitors and furthers client/offender behaviors related to sentencing conditions; that heightens client/offender responsibility and accountability regarding the payment of fines, victim compensation, community service, and restitution orders; and that provides for a continuation of punishment through more controlled supervision and greater accountability (Lin-Ruey, 1997).

Various community-based correctional alternatives include programs, such as intensive probation or parole supervision, home confinement, electronic surveillance or monitoring, narcotics and drug deterrence, work furlough programs or work release, study release, day reporting centers, and probationer violation and restitution residential centers (Torres et al., 1999). Also included under the community corrections umbrella are programs such as diversion, **pretrial release** and preparole (Harris, 1999; Petersilia, 1999a). Community corrections programs can also be distinguished according to the controlling authority. The programs may be community-run (locally operated but lacking state funding and other external support); community-placed (located in communities but not networking with any community agency); and community-based (locally operated but are also financially supplemented from outside sources or networked with other community agencies and the criminal justice system). There is considerable interstate variation in community-based correctional programs (Latessa and Allen, 1999). In recent years, however, there have been efforts among different jurisdictions to network with one another as a means of information dissemination and sharing regarding particular community corrections programs (Faulkner, 1994:23).

The term may also refer to any of several different programs designed to closely control or monitor offender behaviors. Because there are several possible meanings of intermediate punishments, the term is widely applied, correctly or incorrectly, to a variety of community-based offender programs involving nonincarcerative sanctions. Major distinguishing features of intermediate punishments are the high degree of offender monitoring and control of offender behaviors by program staff. Other characteristics of intermediate punishments are curfews, whereby offenders must observe time guidelines and be at particular places at particular times, and frequent monitoring and contact with program officials (Dunlap, 1998). The amount and type of frequent monitoring or contact varies with each program, although daily visits by probation officers at an offender's workplace or home are not unusual.

One semantic problem is that the intensive supervision refers to different levels of monitoring or officer-offender contact, depending on the jurisdiction. Intermediate punishments are intended for prison- or jail-bound offenders. Therefore, offenders who are probably going to receive probation anyway are considered the least likely candidates for these more intensively supervised programs. Nonetheless, judges often assign these low-risk probation-bound offenders to intermediate punishment programs. This practice tends to defeat the goals of such programs, because the programs target offenders who would otherwise occupy valuable prison or jail space unnecessarily. Cluttering these intensive supervision programs with offenders who do not need close supervision is a waste of money, time, and personnel. This practice is referred to as **net-widening** (Palumbo and Petersen, 1994). Offenders are given considerable freedom of movement within their communities, although it is believed that such intensive monitoring and control fosters a high degree of compliance with program requirements. It is also suspected that this intensive supervision deters offenders from committing new crimes (Mitchell, 1999).

THE COMMUNITY CORRECTIONS ACT

A **community corrections act** is the enabling medium by which jurisdictions establish local community corrections agencies, facilities, and programs. A generic definition of a community corrections act is a statewide mechanism through which funds are granted to local units of government to plan, develop, and deliver correctional sanctions and services at the local level. The overall purpose of this mechanism is to provide local sentencing options in lieu of imprisonment in state institutions (Dillingham et al., 1999).

The aim of community corrections acts is to make it possible to divert certain prison-bound offenders into local-, city- or county-level programs in which they can receive treatment and assistance rather than imprisonment (U.S. Office of National Drug Control Policy, 1998). Usually, those who are eligible or otherwise qualify for community corrections programs are low-risk nonviolent, nondangerous offenders (Gitau et al., 1997). Community corrections acts also target those incarcerated offenders who pose little or no risk to the public if released into the community under close parole supervision. Thus, community corrections acts function to alleviate prison and jail overcrowding by diverting certain jail- or prison-bound offenders to community programs (U.S. Office of Justice Programs, 1998).

For instance, Wisconsin implemented a community corrections act in the early 1990s. This act was designed to provide alternatives to both incarceration and new prison construction by encouraging local communities to provide appropriate community sanctions for adult and juvenile offenders. At the time Wisconsin implemented its community-based programs, there were 196,000 crimes committed in the state annually, largely by recidivists (Mitchell, 1999). Wisconsin community corrections currently uses a variety of programs as a part of its community corrections, including home confinement, day reporting centers, halfway houses, electronic monitoring, and intensive supervised probation and parole to supervise its 68,000 offenders. Under current fiscal allocations, the annual cost of these community-based programs to the state averages $1,500 per offender (Mitchell, 1999).

In 1999, nearly 195,000 offenders were on probation in Ohio, with about 50,000 of these offenders involved in community corrections programs (Pastore and Maguire, 2001:485). Targeted offenders include nonviolent clients who participate in both residential and nonresidential placement options. These placement options include work release and halfway house programs, intensive supervised probation, day reporting centers, home confinement, community service, and standard probation. Personnel conduct urinalyses of clients as well as other forms of behavioral monitoring. Ohio programming staff look for the following resident/client traits:

1. A demonstrated willingness to comply with program rules and regulations
2. A motivation to work on individual treatment plans as described by program staff
3. A target population pool that consists primarily of nonviolent offenders, including but not limited to misdemeanants, probation-eligible felony offenders, and parolees who are amenable to community sanctions (Latessa, Travis, and Holsinger, 1997:2–10)

THE PHILOSOPHY AND HISTORY OF COMMUNITY CORRECTIONS

The philosophy of community corrections is to provide certain types of offenders with a rehabilitative and reintegrative milieu, in which their personal abilities and skills are improved and their chances for recidivism are minimized (Bayens, Manske, and Smykla, 1998). The primary purpose of community-based correctional programs is to assist probationers in becoming reintegrated into their communities, although parolees are assisted by such programs as well (Lucken, 1997b). It is not so much the case that probationers (in contrast with parolees) have lost touch with their communities through incarceration, but rather that they have the opportunity of avoiding confinement and remaining within their communities to perform productive work to support themselves and others and to repay victims for losses suffered.

A secondary purpose of community-based programs is to help alleviate prison and jail overcrowding by accepting those offenders who are not dangerous and who pose the least risk to society. Of course, the difficulty here is attempting to sort the most dangerous offenders from those least dangerous. Assessments of offender risk are not infallible, and often, persons predicted to be dangerous may never commit future violent offenses or harm others. At the same time, some risk instruments may suggest that certain offenders will be nonviolent and not dangerous, although the offender will turn out to be dangerous. These two types of offenders are called **false positives** and **false negatives**. False positives are offenders considered dangerous based on independent criteria such as their prior institutional conduct or prior record of offending, although they do not pose a danger to others. False negatives are offenders believed to be nonviolent on the basis of independent criteria, such as **risk assessment instruments** and psychological evaluations, although they turn out to be dangerous by subsequently harming others and committing violent offenses. To reduce the risks posed by false negatives and improve the likelihood of releasing false positives, Bobbie Huskey (1984:45) says that community corrections acts recognize that

1. States should continue to house violent offenders in secure facilities.
2. Judges and prosecutors need a variety of punishments.

3. Local communities cannot develop these programs without additional funding from such legislatures.

Huskey suggests eight common elements that are believed essential to the success of community-based corrections:

1. Prison- and jail-bound offenders are targeted, rather than adding additional punishments to those who would have otherwise remained in the community.
2. Financial subsidies are provided to local government and community agencies.
3. A performance factor is implemented to ensure that funds are used for the act's specific goals.
4. Local advisory boards in each local community assess local needs, propose improvements in the local criminal justice system, and educate the general public about the benefits of alternative punishments.
5. Advisory boards submit annual criminal justice plans to the local government.
6. There is a formula for allocating funds.
7. Local communities participate voluntarily and may withdraw at any time.
8. There are restrictions on funding high-cost capital projects as well as straight probation services.

Huskey believes that community-based corrections appears to be working, because these programs offer mechanisms for ensuring and maintaining public safety and security. Such programs have been demonstrated to be safer and less costly than incarceration, especially when the right, eligible nonviolent clients are targeted for inclusion in them (American Correctional Association, 1996b; Lauen, 1997; Texas Criminal Justice Policy Council, 1996).

California was one of the first states to implement a community corrections program. California's **Probation Subsidy Program**, which provided local communities with supplemental resources to manage larger numbers of probationers more closely, was implemented in 1965. A part of this subsidization provided for **community residential centers** where probationers could check in and receive counseling, employment assistance, and other forms of guidance or supervision. Soon, other states, such as Colorado and Oregon, established their own community-based programs to assist probationers and others (Lauen, 1997). Yet it took at least another decade for large-scale philosophical shifts to occur among different U.S. jurisdictions so that community corrections could be implemented more widely.

Community-based programs are geared to assist offenders by providing nonsecure lodging, vocational/educational training, job assistance, and a limited amount of psychological counseling. Such programs perform rehabilitative and reintegrative functions. One of the first official acknowledgments of the need for community-based programs as a possible front-end solution to prison and jail overcrowding was the 1967 **President's Commission on Law Enforcement and Administration of Justice**. Subsequently, the National Advisory Commission on Criminal Justice Standards and Goals as well as the Law Enforcement Assistance Administration encouraged the establishment of community-based programs as alternatives to incarceration in 1973 and provided extensive financial sponsorship for such programs (Clear and Dammer, 2000; Flanagan, 1997).

The growing use of community-based programs has occurred for at least three reasons. First, the 1967 President's Commission on Law Enforcement and Administration of Justice indicated that community-based monitoring of offenders is much cheaper than incarceration. The **Law Enforcement Assistance Administration (LEAA)** provided considerable funding for experiments in community-based programming. Second, because incarceration has been unable to offer the public any convincing evidence that large numbers of inmates emerge rehabilitated, community corrections programs will not be any worse. Community-based correctional programs are perhaps the major form of offender management today. Offender management, control, and punishment are key functions of community corrections (Clear and Dammer, 2000).

Another important reason for community-based correctional programs is that prisons are increasingly considered destructive for both offenders and society. (Flanagan, 1997). Many inmates who are confined in prisons for several years become accustomed to an alien lifestyle unlike anything occurring within their communities. There is physical separation from an offender's family unit and friends, and inmates are subject to demeaning experiences and treatment not designed to equip offenders with the necessary skills to cope with life on the outside when they are eventually released.

CHARACTERISTICS, GOALS, AND FUNCTIONS OF COMMUNITY CORRECTIONS PROGRAMS

Community-based programs vary in size and scope among communities, although they share certain characteristics such as the following:

1. Community-based program administrators have the authority to oversee offender behaviors and enforce compliance with their probation conditions.
2. These programs have job referral and placement services whereby paraprofessionals or others act as liaisons with various community agencies and organizations to facilitate offender job placement.
3. Administrators of these programs are available on the premises 24 hours a day for emergencies and spontaneous assistance for offenders who may need help.
4. One or more large homes or buildings located within the residential section of the community with space to accommodate between 20 and 30 residents are provided within walking distance of work settings and social services.
5. A professional and paraprofessional staff is on call for medical, social, or psychological emergencies.
6. A system is in place for heightening staff accountability to the court concerning offender progress. (Lauen, 1997)

Community-based corrections is not intended to free thousands of violent felons into communities. Rather, these programs advocate the continued use of incarceration for violent offenders (Flanagan, 1997). A portion of prison-bound offenders, however, might benefit by becoming involved in community-based correctional programming. Community-based corrections seeks to preserve offender attachments with their communities by diverting them from incarceration and housing them in local neighborhoods. Thus, there is a strong reintegrative objective that drives such community programming. A major obstacle for implementing community-based corrections on a large scale is community opposition because of fear and a lack of understanding about how such programming is operated.

Citizens are entitled to believe that freeing dangerous felons into their communities certainly poses some degree of risk to public safety. There is also the view that offenders who remain free also remain unpunished (Sigler and Lamb, 1996). Yet community-based corrections are replete with the characteristics associated with punishment. All community-based correctional programs are considered to be continuations of punishments for offenders. For instance, offender/clients must pay restitution to victims, perform public service, pay fines and maintenance fees, adhere to stringent rules and curfews, put up with unannounced searches of their premises by POs, and comply with other seemingly unreasonable behavioral restrictions and limitations. Indeed, some offenders have opted for imprisonment instead of probation or parole, because they regard probation or parole as a substantial intrusion on their privacy. They would rather serve out their time or "max out" their sentences and be free of the criminal justice system entirely rather than be subjected to all the rules and regulations associated with community-based corrections programs (Clear and Dammer, 2000).

The Goals of Community-Based Corrections

Goals of community corrections programs include facilitating offender reintegration, fostering offender rehabilitation, providing an alternative range of offender punishments, and heightening offender accountability.

Facilitating Offender Reintegration.   It is considered advantageous for both offenders and correctional personnel to supervise as many offenders in their communities as possible. One reason is that continued community involvement means continuous and, ideally, positive contact with one's family and close friends. Also, there is a broader range of social and psychological services available to offenders compared with their opportunities for personal growth and development while in prison or jail. Convicted offenders who remain free in their communities can help with community-based correctional programming operating costs, work at jobs to support themselves and their families, and take advantage of vocational/technical and educational programs available through local colleges and universities. Some offenders require closer monitoring than others. Therefore, it is imperative that community-based correctional programs devise effective screening mechanisms for their clients so as to diagnose their needs accurately (Auerbach and Castellano, 1998). Offender reintegration is therefore an important objective of community-based correctional programs in most states (Johnson et al., 1994). Also, community-based corrections is becoming increasingly popular in other countries, such as Canada (Linden and Clairmont, 1998).

Fostering Offender Rehabilitation.   A major goal of any community-based correctional program is rehabilitation. Rehabilitation occurs when community correctional clients, offenders, participate in vocational, educational, and/or counseling programs that are intended to improve their coping skills (Grier, 1999). These programs are particularly beneficial for first-time nonviolent offenders. Several jurisdictions disclose that they have much lower rates of recidivism among community-based correctional clientele compared with offenders who have been incarcerated. In Texas, for instance, community corrections clients have exhibited recidivism rates of 31 percent compared with a 50 percent recidivism rate among former inmates of Texas penitentiaries (Texas Criminal Justice Policy Council, 1996). In another program in a large urban probation department in another state, officials operate a program known as SAFE-T. SAFE-T adopts cognitive-behavioral approaches that target contemporary youth culture. Although SAFE-T is oriented toward more youthful offenders, it has promise also for young adults. Clients are exposed to a four-month series of 32 group sessions led by probation officers who have been intensively trained in group work methods and exposed to urban youth culture. Clients are guided in establishing personal responsibility and learning how to cope with others who may be involved in drugs, alcohol, or illicit activities (Goodman, Getzel, and Ford, 1996).

Providing an Alternative Range of Offender Punishments.   The range of punishments is vast within community-based corrections. Programs are tailored to fit clients from all age groups, including those with diverse needs and special problems, such as addictions to drugs or alcohol, learning disabilities, or vocational/educational deficiencies. Community centers are created under community corrections acts to assist clients in filling out job applications or overcoming illiteracy. Individual and group counseling are offered to different clients in need of such assistance. The private sector has become increasingly involved in the treatment of community-based correctional clients, and program expansion and diversification has occurred in many cities and communities (Bayens, Manske, and Smykla, 1998; Lucken, 1997a).

Heightening Offender Accountability.   One of the primary reasons that traditional unsupervised probation has been unsuccessful in rehabilitating offenders is that all too often, probationers are completely unsupervised. They may be permitted simply to fill out a one-page report of their work activities and submit these forms to probation offices by mail. Hence, absolutely no direct supervision of these offenders occurs. This condition exists whenever there are large numbers of offenders on probation and relatively few probation officers available to supervise them. One aim of community-based corrections is therefore to provide substantial supervision and services to those in need. Substance abusers comprise a class of clients requiring special assistance and intervention. Often these offenders have committed crimes in the past to acquire the drugs they need to satisfy their addictions. With appropriate intervention and accountability mechanisms established, many of these offenders can overcome their addictions and accept responsibility for their actions. Over time, they learn to cope and overcome their substance dependencies to the extent that they can perform full-time jobs and support their dependents (Torres et al., 1999). Heightening offender accountability is a key goal of community-based correctional programs, both in the United States and elsewhere, such as Australia and Canada (Peach, 1999; Petersilia, 1999a).

The Functions of Community-Based Corrections

Community-based corrections performs the following functions: client monitoring and supervision to ensure program compliance, ensuring public safety, employment assistance, individual and group counseling, educational training and literacy services, networking with other community agencies and businesses, and alleviating jail and prison overcrowding.

Client Monitoring and Supervision to Ensure Program Compliance.   When offenders are sentenced to a community corrections program, it is expected that they will comply with all program conditions. To ensure program compliance, the nature of their supervision is more or less intense. Victim compensation, restitution, and/or community service are often crucial program components. Public safety is enhanced to the extent that program requirements are enforced by community-based correctional personnel. Measures must be established to ensure that offenders comply with court orders and participate in designated programs (U.S. Office of Justice Programs, 1998). This step is especially important for those clients designated as having substance abuse problems and dependencies and who are in need of receiving special drugs to aid them in their withdrawal process (U.S. Office of National Drug Control Policy, 1998).

Between 1994 and 1995, for example, a sample of 109 Washington State offenders participated in a program known as moral recognition therapy (MRT). The MRT program was a community-based correctional program designed to increase moral reasoning and decrease hedonistic and sensation-seeking tendencies among offender/clients. These offenders were compared with 101 offenders in a control group who did not attend the program. Considerably more program violations occurred among offenders in the control group not exposed to the MRT program. When compared with the control group of offenders, MRT clients exhibited significantly less recidivism, much lower drug usage, a higher employment rate, more stable living conditions with their families, lower numbers of program violations, and significantly fewer rearrests (Grandberry, 1998). Greater program compliance under **community-based supervision** has been observed elsewhere, such as Idaho, California, Wyoming, Pennsylvania, and other states when national data sets have been analyzed and compared (Garcia, 1996; Gostas and Harris, 1997; Lurigio, 1996).

Ensuring Public Safety.   Community-based corrections is greatly concerned with the matter of public safety (Dillingham et al., 1999). Clients selected for inclusion in community-based programs are carefully screened so that those likely to pose the most risk or danger to others are excluded (U.S. Office of Justice Programs, 1998). The supervisory safeguards, such as curfew and drug/alcohol abuse checks, are intensive (Flanagan, 1997). Offender-clients are selected primarily on the basis of their low-risk profile and the prospect that they will complete their programs successfully. For example, several community-based programs established under Ohio's Community Corrections Act were evaluated for the years 1991–1993 by Ed Latessa, Larry Travis, and Alex Holsinger (1997). These researchers studied 1,855 offenders involved in community programs; 822 clients participating in highly supervised and regulated community homes; 1,121 offenders released from prison but without intensive supervision; and 1,515 regular probationers. Recidivism rates were lowest for those offenders involved in community-based correctional programming. The evidence clearly indicated that those prison-bound offenders who were diverted to community-based programs for the most part did not pose serious risk or danger to public safety. Further, the study demonstrated that community-based corrections is a very cost-effective way of monitoring convicted offenders compared with the considerably higher costs of incarceration.

Employment Assistance.   An important objective of community corrections is to provide offender-clients with job assistance (Auerbach and Castellano, 1998). Many of these clients do not know how to fill out job application forms; other clients

BOX 2.1   *Personality Highlight*

Whitney E. Fraley
Graduate student and former district parole officer, Texas Department of Criminal Justice

Statistics. B.A. (criminology), Arkansas State University; M.S. in progress (criminal justice), Texas A&M International University

Interests. My interest in the field of criminal justice began when I was an undergraduate at Arkansas State University in Jonesboro, Arkansas. I originally wanted to attend law school and decided that criminology would be a good major. Upon graduation in 1993, however, I was burned out on school and decided to get a job in the criminal justice field. My husband and I relocated to San Antonio, Texas, and I got a job as a case worker in a private community correctional facility, where I earned less money than men employed in the same position and endured terrible abuse from my supervisors.

One year later, I ecstatically accepted a job offer from the Texas Department of Criminal Justice (TDCJ) to be a district parole officer in Corpus Christi. A Texas State Parole Officer's duties consist mainly of home visits, office visits, documentation, and reports to the Texas State Parole Board. I loved my job. The supervision was minimal, and it was fun to get out of the office and do home visits. A fringe benefit was the flex schedule. I could work late or come in early a couple of days a week and be on the beach by 12:30 on Friday! After about six months, I was proud to be assigned a specialized substance abuse caseload.

I thoroughly enjoyed my two years as a parole officer in Corpus Christi, but when my husband got a job as Border Patrol agent, I left the agency to follow him to Uvalde, Texas where I worked as a case worker for Child Protective Services for six months before quitting and going back to the Texas Department of Criminal Justice. My new assignment was as a parole officer at the Joe Ney Substance Abuse Felony Punishment Facility (SAFPF) in Hondo, Texas, a 45-mile commute. A SAFPF resembles a typical TDJC prison unit. It is a minimum-security unit in which parole violators receive substance abuse treatment.

Unfortunately, Joe Ney was not a pleasant experience for me. There were two parole officers assigned to the unit, a man and a woman. I took the place of the woman, who had taken a position in the field. On my first day, I was told by my supervisor that the previous female parole officer had done all the clerical work, whereas the male parole officer handled all the parole officer duties. I informed my supervisors that I would handle all the professional duties for my own caseload as required by my directives.

The male parole officer was quite popular, and he resented that he would now be responsible for his own paperwork. Furthermore, the security and treatment staff had thought that the previous female parole officer was a clerk and they assumed that that was my position, too. They resented what they perceived as interference on my part. I felt as if I didn't have a friend in the world, and I wasn't getting much work done. After a year and a half, I gave up and went back to the field. I requested, and received, another substance abuse caseload, this time in San Antonio.

My new position in San Antonio came through at about the same time I found out I was pregnant. The office was 90 miles from my home in Uvalde. The commute was tough, but I loved my work, my coworkers, and just being back in the field.

I went on maternity leave in May 1999. While I was at home with my new baby, trying to figure out how I was going to manage the commute, work, and the new baby, a job my husband had put in for with the Immigration and Naturalization Service finally came through. We had been hoping that his duty station would be in San Antonio, but it turned out to be in Laredo, Texas, on the Texas-Mexico border.

I terminated my TDCJ position when we relocated to Laredo. I probably could have gotten a transfer, but I decided to take the opportunity to stay home with my daughter and attend graduate school at Texas A&M International University. I plan to complete my master of science degree in criminal justice in the fall semester of 2001. I hope to get a job as a college instructor or U.S. Probation Officer soon thereafter. For now, I am enjoying being a full-time student and stay-at-home mom.

Advice to Students. I would advise anyone who wants to work in the field of corrections to be fearless and not be dissuaded by anyone who tells them that they are too small, out-of-shape, effeminate, soft-spoken, sensitive, or "nice" to do the job. Everyone in my family laughed at me when I told them that I wanted to work in corrections, but I have had, and expect to continue to have, a rewarding career. I would further advise students to pursue an advanced degree soon after getting their bachelor's degree, and try to get a job with the federal government. In my experience, state agencies typically do not pay as well as the federal government. Entry-level state correctional jobs are best for people who are single without children or who have partners who earn more money. I "topped out" at $28,000 a year, but my health and retirement benefits were excellent.

I would like to further advise students that, if after being employed in the field of corrections for a time, they find themselves without compassion for victims, if they find themselves being cruel to offenders, or if they are unable to maintain healthy relationships with their families because of their jobs, then they should take a long leave of absence or find other work. This job is not for everyone.

I would like to direct my last bits of advice to women who want to go into the field. First, don't tolerate any type of harassment, sexual, verbal, or physical, from bosses, coworkers, or offenders. Second, demand to be paid as much as your male counterparts, even if it costs you the job. Third, don't let anyone tell you that you can't do the job because you are a woman. Fourth, do not let anyone relegate to you clerical duties instead of your professional duties. Do not take more responsibility for the clerical duties than your male counterparts, even if it results in the job not being done as effectively. And fifth, if you think that you might have a propensity for becoming romantically or sexually involved with offenders, please do not take the job. This type of behavior hurts all women in the field.

do not know how to interview properly with prospective employers. Minimal assistance from staff of community-based corrections agencies can do much to aid offenders in securing employment and avoiding further trouble with the law (Reed, 1996).

Individual and Group Counseling.   Many offender-clients who become involved in community corrections programs have drug or alcohol dependencies. Often, these offenders have difficulty getting along with others and coping with societal expectations. They may have certain social, psychological, and physical needs that must be treated, either through individual or group counseling (Lucken, 1997a). Many community corrections agencies have established such counseling programs for these offenders. In Colorado, for instance, a community-based correctional program was established to furnish offender-clients with various services, including employment assistance, counseling, and networking opportunities with various support groups, such as Alcoholics Anonymous (English, Chadwick, and Pullen, 1994). The average daily program cost per offender was only $6.07, compared with the cost of imprisonment of $52.68 per day per inmate. Furthermore, the community correctional clientele had a recidivism rate of only 23 percent, compared with a 65 percent rate of recidivism for probationers and parolees not involved in community programs. In fact, most of the recidivism among community corrections clients related to technical program violations rather than new criminal offenses. This much lower recidivism rate was attributable to the greater variety of services made available to clients through these community-based programs.

Educational Training and Literacy Services.   It is surprising for some citizens to learn that many offenders cannot read or write. Thus, whenever such offenders are released, either on probation or parole, they find it difficult to find and retain good jobs in the workplace. Most jobs require minimal reading and writing skills, but a significant proportion of offenders lack these basic skills. In Arizona, for instance, a task force investigated the literacy level of Arizonans and found that over 400,000 of them were functionally illiterate. Another 500,000 did not have a high school diploma. About 60 percent of Arizona's prison inmates had a reading level at about the sixth grade. Seeking to remedy this situation, Arizona implemented L.E.A.R.N., or Literacy, Education, and Reading Network labs, to remedy learning and educational deficiencies among its probationers and inmates. One purpose of this program is to raise the educational and reading level of offender-clients so that they will be more competitive in the workplace. Recent evidence suggests that the L.E.A.R.N. program is successful (O'Connell and Power, 1992:7).

Community-based correctional programming is increasingly offering educational experiences to offenders who are illiterate or do not have reading levels commensurate with the jobs they are seeking to provide for themselves and their families. Greater use is being made of needs instrumentation for the purpose of screening program-eligible offenders and determining which needs they have and how best those needs can be met (American Correctional Association, 1996a).

Besides working with offenders with educational deficiencies, community-based corrections also targets offenders with particular disabilities under the Americans with Disabilities Act (American Correctional Association, 1995c). Community-based correctional personnel are learning to cater to diverse offender needs, including sex offender counseling; gang affiliation and separation; cultural diversity issues; anger

---

BOX 2.2 **Community Corrections for Low-Risk Offenders?**

Should We Use Community Corrections More in Texas?

At a time when prison space is limited, some states are incarcerating offenders at record rates. For instance, in 2000, Texas, with its total prison population of 163,190, surpassed California's 163,067 prisoners, even though California's population of 32 million is over twice that of Texas. Proving that incarceration doesn't slow down the crime rate, Texas has one of the highest crime rates compared with other states with similar populations. During the 1990s, for example, Texas's prison population had an annual growth rate of nearly 12 percent. Thus, Texas incarcerated about one-fifth of the nation's inmates during the 1990s.

A research organization with an anti-incarceration agenda, the Justice Policy Institute, released these alarming figures in mid-2000. The Justice Policy Institute is a think tank of the Center on Juvenile and Criminal Justice, and the study was funded with a grant from the Center on Crime, Communities, and Culture. The groups provide programs for families of inmates and explore other solutions to punish criminal behavior beyond imprisonment, such as community correc-

tions and substance abuse treatment. Some Texas officials are also alarmed by the growing rate of incarceration. Tony Fabelo, executive director of the state Criminal Justice Policy Council, told elected officials that without a change in parole rates and policies for returning parole violators to prison, Texas will likely need prisons to hold 14,600 additional inmates by August 2005. Actually, according to Fabelo, the state's imprisonment growth occurred during a period when the state went on a prison-construction binge. Before that, Fabelo said, the state intermittently released inmates to alleviate overcrowding and comply with court-ordered lower capacity levels. In 2000, Texas was operating its prison system at about 97 percent of its rated capacity. One obvious solution is the use of more community corrections in which offenders may remain free in their communities but be under the close supervision of probation or parole officers. Certainly locking up more offenders hasn't slowed the crime rate, at least in Texas.

Should community corrections be mandated as a preferred option to incarceration, especially for lower-risk offenders? What do you think?

Source: Adapted from Associated Press, "Texas Incarceration Rate Leads Nation; Crime Rate Lags Behind," August 28, 2000.

---

management training; and health care (American Correctional Association, 1995a, 1995b).

Networking with Other Community Agencies and Businesses. An important function of community corrections is to network with various community agencies and businesses to match offender-clients with needed treatments and services. Community corrections agencies may not have a full range of offender services (Taxman, 1994). Cooperative endeavors are necessary if certain offenders are to receive the type of treatment they need most. Sometimes, the networking performed by community corrections enables offender-clients to obtain vocational and educational training, or perhaps group or individual counseling. Networking with businesses helps community corrections personnel determine job availability. Thus, community corrections offers a valuable job placement service for offenders who have difficulty finding work (Jones, 1990).

Alleviating Jail and Prison Overcrowding.   Community-based corrections alleviates some amount of jail and prison overcrowding (Mays and Gray, 1996). In New
York, for instance, it costs about $40,000 per prisoner per year for prison housing. In
contrast, community-based offender monitoring, which offers more intensive
offender supervision but less than full incarceration, costs the state about $4,500 per
prisoner (Archambeault and Deis, 1996; Pastore and Maguire, 2001).

SELECTED ISSUES IN COMMUNITY CORRECTIONS

Some important issues relating to community-based correctional programs are public resistance to locating community programs in communities, punishment and public safety versus offender rehabilitation and reintegration, net-widening, the
privatization of community-based corrections agencies, and services delivery.

Public Resistance to Locating Community Programs in Communities (The NIMBY Syndrome: "Not In My Back Yard")

Some amount of community resistance is encountered whenever any community
plans to establish a community corrections facility in a neighborhood. Community
corrections personnel desire locations for their facilities that are near city centers or
within walking distance of schools, hospitals, counseling centers, and workplaces.
Corrections personnel believe that neighborhood milieus are an integral feature of
the therapy required for more complete offender rehabilitation and reintegration.
Locating community-based services within communities is therefore critical because
offenders can experience the freedoms and responsibilities associated with their
probation and parole programs.

The view from citizens is quite different. Some citizens, especially those whose
homes are located near these community-based centers and services, believe that
they are endangered by the presence of convicted felons roaming about freely near
them and their children. Some citizens believe that their property values are
adversely affected and that they will have difficulty selling their property if they
decide to move. After all, who wants to live near a home that houses numerous convicted felons? This fairly typical community reaction stems largely from most persons not understanding what community-based corrections is all about and how it is
intended to operate (Wilkinson, 1998). It is such a typical reaction that it has been
given a name by corrections personnel: the **NIMBY syndrome**. NIMBY is an
acronym for "Not In My Back Yard." The NIMBY syndrome means that although
many citizens believe in correctional rehabilitation and believe that community corrections is an essential part of one's rehabilitation and reintegration into neighborhood life, these same citizens would prefer that such corrections agencies or
operations not be located in their own neighborhoods (Schiff, 1990). The NIMBY
syndrome has been investigated in various locations, including Canada (Gitau et al.,
1997; U.S. Office of Justice Programs, 1998).

Shereen Benzvy-Miller (1990) says that communities tend to manifest the
NIMBY Syndrome for at least three reasons: (1) they fear crime and expect that

close proximity to offenders will expose them to greater risk, (2) they have attitudes and perceptions about offenders that have little to do with reality, and (3) they are afraid that a group home will somehow taint the neighborhood and cause property values to decline. These attitudes and the problems they generate can be overcome by educating the public and increasing their awareness of what these programs are all about and how offenders are supervised or monitored. Educating the public about community-based corrections, however, is a long and sometimes difficult process (Harris, 1995).

Punishment and Public Safety versus Offender Rehabilitation and Reintegration

Public safety is a perennial issue raised whenever community corrections seeks to establish agencies within neighborhoods. There is substantial evidence that the general public has an intense fear of crime and that this fear of crime has led them to oppose the idea of community corrections programming for dangerous felons (Ambrosio and Schiraldi, 1997; Flanagan, 1996). Residents are repelled by the idea that they will have convicted felons roaming freely among them. At the same time, corrections officials cite the need to place certain offenders into communities where they can learn to function normally in law-abiding ways. Offenders need community experience, and community residents need to feel safe. Thus, public safety is often at odds with the **rehabilitative ideal** of community corrections programs (Heiner, 1996). That the cost of treating and supervising offenders in their communities is considerably less than incarcerating offenders in jails or prisons is largely undisputed (Petersilia, 1998). There is considerable disagreement, however, over whether permitting some offenders to remain in their communities either unsupervised or supervised is the functional equivalent of punishment. The dilemma is deciding whether it is therapeutic for offenders to remain within their communities where their reintegration and rehabilitation may be maximized or whether their freedom places law-abiding citizens at risk (Hahn, 1998). Both views are valid.

Interestingly, if offender-clients currently or formerly under some type of community-based supervision were to be asked whether they view their programs as punishments, they would probably agree because of the extensive behavioral restrictions and program requirements with which they obligated to comply as clients. These offenders are constantly being tested for various illegal substances. They are subject to unannounced visits from community-based correctional personnel, including probation and parole officers, at any hour of the day or night. They are monitored in diverse ways, through telephonic or face-to-face checks with employers and work associates. They must submit weekly or monthly reports and proof of employment. They must refrain from any criminal activity. They must not associate with certain types of persons. They cannot possess or use firearms for any reason, even hunting. In short, they are subject to many intrusions that ordinary citizens routinely avoid. Yet because citizens see these criminals free within their communities, this freedom is perceived as some form of leniency and certainly not punishment (Dolinko et al., 1999).

Lamont Flanagan reduces the dilemma over whether community corrections is a punishment to an issue of dollars and cents. Regarding public safety, Flanagan says that community corrections programs seek to preserve public safety by screening prospective clients and including only those most likely to succeed. He believes that imprisonment should be reserved only for the most violent offenders who pose the greatest danger to public safety (Flanagan, 1997). Furthermore, Flanagan says that the bulk of current jail and prison inmates are largely nonviolent offenders who are capable of becoming safely reintegrated into their communities under some form of monitoring or close supervision. He believes that their remediation should be a key correctional priority.

Many offenders derive numerous rehabilitative benefits from community-based programs (Stojkovic and Lovell, 1997). Proof of community-based programming effectiveness is manifested by lower recidivism rates among community corrections clientele, which is also a gauge of supervisory effectiveness of correctional staff (Goethals and Mills, 1996; Texas Criminal Justice Policy Council, 1996). It is also manifested by the increasing number of countries throughout the world that are developing community-based correctional programs for a portion of their criminal populations (Griffiths, 1996). Researchers in the United States and elsewhere declare that how offenders are supervised makes a significant difference in their potential for recidivism (Trotter, 1996). For instance, community-based correctional personnel may supervise their clients as enforcers, treating their clients in ways similar to police officer–offender encounters. Such a supervisory style emphasizes rules and punitiveness. Another supervisory style is prosocial, in which problem solving and empathy are key supervisory tactics in relation to offender-clients. Studies of this prosocial approach to offender supervision suggest that offender-clients respond more positively and perceive their supervisors as supportive rather than punitive. The result is that recidivism rates among those supervised in prosocial ways are up to 50 percent less than offenders who are supervised punitively (Trotter, 1996).

Net-Widening

Net-widening occurs whenever offender-clients are included in community programs simply because those programs exist. If the programs did not exist, then these offender-clients would probably be placed on probation (Brandau, 1992). Thus, the mere existence of a community-based correctional program raises questions about who should be included in the program. The clear intent of most community-based correctional programs is to encompass jail- or prison-bound offenders who might benefit more from community treatment rather than incarceration. Decisions about which offenders should be placed in community-based programs and which incarcerated are most often made by judges, who are influenced by the sentencing recommendations of probation officers.

Community-based correctional programs often screen prospective clients and determine their eligibility. Some of the criteria used in the screening process include whether the community agency can provide the right type of assistance for particular offenders; whether certain offenders have undesirable behaviors, habits, or prior records; and whether certain offenders are considered amenable to various treatment strategies. If community corrections officers determine that certain offenders are ineligible for their programs, then they can refuse to admit them.

Most community-based corrections agencies have a strong vested interest in including offenders in their programs who are the most likely to comply with program requirements and program completion. Often, the most nonviolent offenders are selected as clients. They have behavioral histories of compliance with authority and are considered the best risks. When these offenders are included in community programs and more serious offenders are excluded, a self-serving selection process is set in motion in which the programming outcomes for certain clients are highly predictable. Some corrections professionals refer to this process as **creaming**, as in skimming the cream from fresh milk. Applied to those considered eligible for community-based programs, creaming means that only those who show the greatest promise of being successful in their programs will be included in those programs. Program supervisors are not especially surprised when these offender-clients eventually succeed and complete their program requirements successfully. Success usually means that these same successful offender-clients will leave their programs and be the least likely to reoffend compared with more serious offenders who were barred from community corrections programs initially in the screening process. Thus, low recidivism rates among such offender-clients is quite predictable. Because most community corrections agencies depend on state or federal resources to defray their operating costs, a showing of low recidivism rates is the most direct indication of the program's success as a rehabilitative medium. The program will most likely continue to be funded by one or more government sources (Jones, 1990). This somewhat cynical view is based largely on political reality (McMahon, 1990).

Avoiding net-widening is difficult. As long as community-based corrections agencies serve gatekeeping functions and screen prospective jail- or prison-bound clients for inclusion or exclusion, only the least violent and most compliant offenders will be drawn into these programs. Judicial discretion is also important. Judges have the power to order particular jail- or prison-bound offenders to community programs, when such programs exist. All these decisions require a consideration of the value of particular types of community-based correctional programming and prospective offender-client needs and characteristics.

Privatization of Community-Based Correctional Agencies

Some proportion of the chronic overcrowding problems of jails and prisons has been alleviated through community-based correctional programs. Through community corrections acts, many communities have established programs to accommodate jail- or prison-bound offenders. Thus, some scarce prison and jail space has been made available for more serious offenders through various types of community programming. The public sector, however, has been unable to provide necessary rehabilitative services for large numbers of offenders. Increasingly, the private sector has made a concerted effort to establish itself as a legitimate alternative to public community corrections (Mays and Gray, 1996).

The **privatization** of corrections, or the intrusion of private industry into community programs and the administration of jail and prison systems, is succeeding in furthering the public relations image of corrections generally in the community by suggesting greater control of prisons and offender programs by the private sector (Mitchell, 1999). In 1999, for example, private corporations supervised at least 30,000 inmates in more than one hundred prisons, whereas over two hundred privately operated jails and detention facilities accommodated more than 50,000 prisoners (Camp and Camp, 1999). During the next decade, the proportion of offenders supervised either institutionally or in the community will multiply greatly as the demand for privately operated correctional services increases (Archambeault and Deis, 1996).

At least five reasons have been given for privately run community-based treatment programs being regarded as a progressive solution to present-day jail and prison overcrowding:

1. Privatization would break the traditional treatment-custody link and the resulting corruption from overconcern with custody and control. A greater incentive would exist to make rehabilitation work if the profit motive were present, because profits are ordinarily related to program effectiveness.

2. Privatization would result in more, not less, accountability if program rehabilitation objectives fail. Systems linking payment or contract renewal to the quality and effectiveness of services provided would make private vendors more accountable and responsive.

3. The infusion of private interests into corrections would promote experimentation with new ideas and strategies for offender treatment and rehabilitation. Under existing management schemes, the routinization of policy is common, with little or no innovativeness.

4. The introduction of business into offender rehabilitation may enhance the political acceptability of correctional treatment. In short, the public relations dimension of corrections would be enhanced and greater community acceptance would ensue.

5. Privatization is consistent with capitalist philosophy, and this basic compatibility would make sense because it offers businesses the chance to make money from corrections. (Cullen, 1986:13–15)

Major criticisms of privatization of both institutional and community corrections are that (1) private enterprise removes control of offenders from professional corrections personnel, (2) it creates accountability issues for the courts, (3) it would encourage more prisons and community-based facilities to warehouse larger numbers of offenders because of the profit motive, (4) it would lead to a downgrading of supervisory quality by reducing the standards by which personnel are trained to monitor dangerous offenders, and (5) it is unconstitutional for private enterprise to sanction state and federal offenders.

Proprivatization arguments are that (1) private agencies can respond more quickly to problems of financing than legislatures and other political organizations; (2) private enterprise can make initial capital investments in facility construction, thus saving the states billions of dollars; (3) private enterprise can decrease the amount of government liability arising from lawsuits brought by clients against program administrators and staff; (4) private enterprises can operate more efficiently and at less cost than public agencies; and (5) private enterprise staff are usually drawn from public sector correctional positions for which they have already been professionally trained.

There is no constitutional prohibition against using private enterprise as an option to publicly operated correctional facilities, either institutionally or within the community. Under the theory of **agency**, the government may direct private corporations to establish different types of correctional facilities, as long as these facilities are in compliance with state and federal guidelines. Thus, the government vests private corporations with the authority to supervise offenders, both juvenile and adult, under different conditions and for varying periods. All privately operated correctional programs are subject to the same mechanisms of accountability, control, and regulation as publicly operated facilities (Lucken, 1997b).

A major difference between private and public correctional facilities is their relative cost effectiveness. Private enterprise is able to compete more vigorously with public facilities in providing a broad range of services to offender-clients. A comparative study of privately and publicly operated correctional organizations in Louisiana, for instance, disclosed that compared with state-operated facilities, private correctional agencies were able to operate more cost-effectively; reported fewer critical incidents; provided safer work environments for employees and safer living environments for offenders; judiciously and effectively used inmate disciplinary actions to maintain order; deployed fewer security personnel while achieving higher safety levels; had proportionately more offenders complete their basic education, literacy, and vocational training courses; and equaled or surpassed the number of offender screenings for community corrections placements (Archambeault and Deis, 1996). Similar findings about privatization have been disclosed for other states, such as Florida, Washington, and Wisconsin (Lucken, 1997b; Mitchell, 1999; U.S. Office of Justice Programs, 1998). The use of privately operated correctional programs in other countries has also resulted in positive outcomes compared with publicly operated agencies and organizations (Ellem, 1995; Peach, 1999).

Services Delivery

Delivering the appropriate services for offenders is often difficult for community corrections agencies. Assessments of offender-clients are frequently superficial, largely because of understaffing or underfunding. Sometimes, offenders have several types of problems that are difficult to diagnose and treat. Historically, services delivery has been deficient in many community corrections programs in which supervisory chores and offender accountability have been regarded as primary goals (Dillingham et al., 1999).

One way to ensure that services delivery is offender-relevant and appropriate is to individualize the needs of specific offenders. For instance, many persons placed in probation and parole programs have undiagnosed mental illnesses or suffer from other mental or physical impairments (Lurigio, 1996). Appropriate diagnostic procedures must be in place for community corrections personnel to determine each offender's needs. If any particular agency is not equipped to deal with certain offender needs, then the agency should be in a position to network with other community agencies to ensure that the necessary services are provided in a timely manner. For instance, Texas has a special needs parole program that provides for an early parole review for special health needs offenders who require 24-hour skilled nursing care and supervision. Although inmates considered for special needs parole are at a higher risk of recidivating and have committed more severe offenses than regular parole cases, the parole board approves them at a higher rate for early release to particular community-based programs through which they can obtain necessary mental health services. Improved screening, referral, and review processes increase the program's use without increasing public safety risks (Texas Criminal Justice Policy Council, 2000). An additional feature of this program is that those offenders with significant medical problems and who represent little or no threat to public safety are detected and diverted from prison to more cost-effective community programs for appropriate treatment (Eisenberg, Arrigona, and Kofowit, 1999).

Many offender-clients released to community-based correctional programs have substance abuse problems and dependencies (Motiuk et al., 1994). Often, substance abuse led to their convictions, and when they are released into the community under some form of supervision, they are unable to refrain from substance abuse without strong intervention and assistance from appropriate community agencies (U.S. Office of National Drug Control Policy, 1998). Many of these offenders pose substantial supervision problems for POs and other supervisors who must monitor their progress. Any effective community-based treatment and rehabilitation program must be prepared to cope directly or indirectly with substance abusers, because they pose more significant problems for supervisory agencies than any other class of offenders (Auerbach and Castellano, 1998).

HOME CONFINEMENT PROGRAMS

There are many types of community-based correctional programs. One of the most frequently used programs is home confinement, also known as house arrest or **home incarceration**.

Home Confinement Defined

Home confinement or **house arrest** is a community-based program consisting of confining offenders to their residences for mandatory incarceration during evening hours, curfews, and/or on weekends (Enos, Holman, and Carroll, 1999). Home confinement is a sentence imposed by the court. Offenders may leave their residences for medical reasons or employment. In addition, they may be required to perform community service or pay victim restitution and/or supervisory fees. Figure 2.1 contains a typical home confinement participant agreement.

Home confinement is not new. St. Paul the Apostle was detained under house arrest in biblical times. In the 1600s, Galileo, the astronomer, was forced to live out the last eight years of his life under house arrest. In 1917, Czar Nicholas II of Russia was detained under house arrest until his death. During Czar Nicholas II's reign, Lenin was placed under house arrest for a limited period (Meachum, 1986:102). In 1971, St. Louis became the first U.S. city to use home confinement. St. Louis officials originally limited its use to juvenile offenders, although home confinement became more widespread over the next several decades in many other jurisdictions (Courtright, Berg, and Mutchnick, 1997).

The Early Uses of Home Confinement

Florida was the first state to officially use home confinement on a statewide basis (Ansay and Benveneste, 1999). As originally conceived by this act, Florida's community control house arrest is not an intensive supervision program. Offenders are confined to their own homes, instead of prison, where they are allowed to serve their sentences. The cost of home confinement is only about $10 per day, compared with about $50 per day in operating costs for imprisonment (Camp and Camp, 1999). Florida statutes regard community control as a form of intensive supervised custody in the community, including surveillance on weekends and holidays, administered by

HOME CONFINEMENT PROGRAM
PARTICIPANT AGREEMENT

1. I _____ have been placed in the Home Confinement Program. I agree to comply with all program rules set forth in this agreement and the instructions of my probation officer. Failure to comply with this Agreement or any instructions of my officer will be considered a violation of my supervision and may result in an adverse action. I agree to call my officer immediately if I have any questions about these rules or if I experience any problems with the monitoring equipment.

2. I will remain at my approved residence at all times, except for employment and other activities approved in advance by my probation or pretrial services officer. Regularly occurring activities are provided for in my written weekly schedule, which remains in effect until modified by my officer. I must obtain my officer's advance permission for any special activities (such as doctor's appointments) that are not included in my written schedule.

3. I shall not deviate from my approved schedule except in an emergency. I shall first try to get the permission of my officer. If this is not possible, I must call my officer as soon as I am able to do so. If I call during nonbusiness hours, I will leave a message on my officer's answering machine, including my name, the date, the time, a brief description of the emergency, and my location or destination. I agree to provide proof of the emergency as requested by my officer.

4. While under home confinement supervision, I agree to wear a nonremovable ankle bracelet that will be attached by my officer.

5. I agree to provide and maintain a telephone, with modular telephone connectors, at my residence and maintain telephone and electrical service there at my own expense.

6. On the line to which the monitoring equipment is connected, I agree to not have party lines, telephone answering machines, cordless telephones, "call forwarding," "Caller ID," "call waiting," and other devices and services that may interfere with the proper functioning of the electronic monitoring equipment.

7. I agree to allow a monitoring device (receiver/dialer) to be connected to the telephone and the telephone outlet at my residence.

8. I acknowledge receipt of receiver/dialer number _____ and transmitter number _____. I understand that I will be held responsible for damage, other than normal wear, to the equipment. I also understand that if I do not return the equipment, or do not return it in good condition, I may be charged for replacement or the repair of the equipment and I agree to pay these costs. I understand that I may be subject to felony prosecution if I fail to return my monitoring equipment.

9. I agree to not move, disconnect, or tamper with the monitoring device (receiver/dialer).

10. I agree to not remove or tamper with the ankle bracelet (transmitter) except in a life-threatening emergency or with the prior permission of my officer.

11. I agree to allow authorized personnel to inspect and maintain the ankle transmitter and receiver/dialer.

12. I agree to return the receiver/dialer and transmitter to my officer upon demand.

13. I agree that I will not make any changes in the telephone equipment or services at any residence without prior approval of my officer.

14. I agree to provide copies of my monthly telephone bill when requested by my officer.

15. I agree to notify my officer immediately if I lose electrical power at my residence, if I have to remove the ankle bracelet because of an emergency, or if I experience any problems with the monitoring equipment. During nonbusiness hours, I agree to call my officer and leave a message on his/her answering machine including my name, the date, the time, and the nature of my problem. If there is a power problem, I agree that I will call and leave another message when the power is restored. I also agree to notify my officer of any problems with my telephone service as soon as I am able to do so.

FIGURE 2.1   Home confinement program participation agreement.

16. I agree that I will not attempt to use my telephone when the receiver/dialer's "Phone Busy" or "Phone Indicator" light is on.

17. I understand that my officer will use telephone calls and personal visits to monitor my compliance with my approved schedule. If I fail to answer the telephone or door when I am supposed to be at home, my officer will conclude that I am absent and in violation of my curfew restrictions.

18. I understand that my officer must be able to contact me at work at any time. If I do not have a job with a fixed location (as in construction work), my officer must be able to locate me by calling my employer and promptly obtaining my work location. I also understand that jobs that do not meet these requirements are not permitted while am under home confinement supervision. I understand that all job changes must be approved in advance by my officer.

19. I agree to refrain from the excessive use of alcohol or any use of controlled substances unless the controlled substance is prescribed by a licensed medical practitioner.

20. I understand that I will be required to undergo periodic, unscheduled urine collection and testing.

21. I agree to comply with all other conditions of my release and supervision as imposed by the court or parole board.

22. I understand and agree that all telephone calls from the monitoring connector to my residence will be tape-recorded by the monitoring contractor.

23. I understand that I may be ordered to pay all or part of the daily cost of my electronic monitoring. If so ordered, I agree, as directed by my officer, to pay ____ per day directly to the monitoring service.

24. Additional Rules (As needed)

I acknowledge that I have received a copy of these rules and that they have been explained to me. I understand that I must comply with these rules until _____ or until otherwise notified by my probation/parole officer. I further understand that any violations of these rules will also constitute a violation of supervision and may cause immediate adverse action.

_____   _____

FIGURE 2.1 *(continued)*

officers with restricted caseloads. It is an individualized program in which the freedom of an offender is restricted within the community, home, or noninstitutional residential placement and specific sanctions are imposed and enforced. Community control officers work irregular hours and at nights to help ensure that offenders stay in their homes except while working at paid employment to support themselves and dependents.

In Florida, community controllees or offenders eligible for the house arrest program include low-risk, prison-bound criminals. They are expected to comply with the following program requirements:

1. Contribute from 150 to 200 hours of free labor to various public service projects during periods ranging from six months to one year.
2. Pay a monthly maintenance fee of $30 to $50 to help defray program operating costs and officer salaries.
3. Compile and maintain daily logs accounting for their activities; these logs are reviewed regularly by officers for accuracy and honesty.
4. Pay restitution to crime victims from a portion of salaries earned through employment.
5. Remain gainfully employed to support themselves and their dependents.

6. Participate in vocational/technical or other educational courses or seminars that are individualized according to each offender's needs.

7. Observe a nightly curfew and remain confined to their premises during late evening hours and on weekends, with the exception of court-approved absences for health-related reasons or other purposes.

8. Submit to monitoring by officials 28 times per month either at home or at work.

9. Maintain court-required contacts with neighbors, friends, landlords, spouses, teachers, police, and/or creditors (Ansay and Benveneste, 1999).

The record of successes through home incarceration in Florida has been impressive. By 1999, 11,500 offenders were under house arrest and intensive supervision by probation officers (Camp and Camp, 1999). There have been relatively few program failures. Most of these failures are persons who have committed technical program violations, such violating curfew.

Under Florida's home confinement program, **community control house arrest**, offenders eligible for home confinement fall into three categories: those found guilty of nonforcible felonies, probationers charged with technical or misdemeanor violations, and parolees charged with technical or misdemeanor violations. The basic conditions for home confinement cases include the following:

1. Report to the home confinement officer at least four times a week, or if employed part-time, report daily.

2. Perform at least 140 hours of public service work, without pay, as directed by the home confinement officer.

3. Remain confined to the residence except for approved employment, public service work, or other special activities approved by the home confinement officer.

4. Make monthly restitution payments for a specified total amount.

5. Submit to and pay for urinanalysis, breathalyzer, or blood specimen tests at any time as requested by the home confinement officer or other professional staff to determine possible use of alcohol, drugs, or other controlled substances.

6. Maintain an hourly account of all activities in a daily log to be submitted to the home confinement officer upon request.

7. Participate in self-improvement programs as determined by the court or home confinement officer.

8. Promptly and truthfully answer all inquiries of the court or home confinement officer, and allow the officer to visit the home, employer, or elsewhere.

9. For sex offenders, the court requires, as a special condition of home confinement, the release of treatment information to the home confinement officer or the court. (Florida Advisory Council, 1994)

House arrest programs such as Florida's are increasingly common, especially in those states with prison overcrowding problems. Home confinement programs for both juveniles and adults have been established and are proliferating in both federal and state jurisdictions (Buddress, 1997; Landreville, 1997; U.S. General Accounting Office, 1997). Additional conditions are usually imposed, including substance abuse counseling and treatment, victim compensation, and community service.

Some Examples of Home Confinement in Action.   Conventional home confinement systems usually require offenders to wear bracelets or anklets that emit elec-

---

BOX 2.3   *Two Years' House Arrest for Strawberry*

Darryl Strawberry Gets House Arrest for Probation Violations

It happened in Tampa, Florida. Darryl Strawberry, a star player for the New York Yankees baseball team, violated the terms of his probation by driving under the influence of medication and leaving the scene of an automobile accident in September 2000. The 38-year-old eight-time All-Star major league player has battled drug and alcohol abuse for several years, according to spokespersons who know him. During 1999, Strawberry was diagnosed with colon cancer. He underwent surgery and subsequently had a kidney removed. Strawberry's driving offenses occurred, according to Strawberry, as he was driving to visit his probation officer because of other criminal convictions. On Monday morning, September 11, 2000, Strawberry had taken some prescription medication before leaving his home for his appointment. An off-duty Tampa, Florida, sheriff's deputy saw Strawberry hit a road sign and turn onto another street, where he rear-ended a sports utility vehicle stopped at a red light. Strawberry drove away from the accident scene, but he was subsequently apprehended by the pursuing officer. He spent the night in the Hillsborough County Jail.

During the 1999–2000 baseball season, Strawberry was placed on suspension, not drawing any salary from the New York Yankees team. Strawberry's wife, Charisse, told reporters that her husband was sorry for what had happened and was relieved to learn that the woman whose car he struck from behind had suffered no serious injuries. Charisse Strawberry said that her husband, who had surgery in August 2000, was in a lot of pain and has had some mental difficulties. Justice was dispensed swiftly in Strawberry's case. He appeared before the original sentencing judge the following day and was sentenced to two years' house arrest. House arrest for Strawberry means that he cannot leave home except to go to the doctor's office or to work. He would need special permission from the court to attempt to rejoin his major league baseball team. Furthermore, he is prohibited from consuming any illegal drugs or alcohol and must submit to daily surprise checks from the Florida Department of Corrections. The house arrest means that Florida probation officers will check to see that Strawberry is where he is supposed to be at random times. When these officers pay Strawberry visits at his home, they are permitted to administer random drug/alcohol checks to see if Strawberry is adhering to his house arrest and probation requirements. The judge told Strawberry, "I suggest you might want to get a driver [in order to visit the probation office weekly]." The judge did not impose any community service on Strawberry, saying that he "had enough on his plate to deal with." Strawberry was ordered to pay a $265 fine, and his case was to be reviewed again in four months. Furthermore, under house arrest, Strawberry is not permitted to leave home even for an activity as mundane as going to the movies or to his children's school. Strawberry told reporters later, "I used the wrong judgment . . . taking medication because I didn't feel well. I just blacked out. I didn't know if I hurt anybody. I feel really bad about that."

Is house arrest the proper punishment for Strawberry? If a probationer convicted of various drug offenses were to commit a hit-and-run crime under the influence of drugs, what type of punishment do you think the judge would impose? Should Strawberry be subjected to imprisonment instead of house arrest? What do you think?

Source: Adapted from Vickie Chachere, Associated Press, "Strawberry Hit with 2 Years' House Arrest," September 13, 2000.

---

tronic signals. Such electronic monitoring is discussed in greater detail in the following section. Offenders must remain in their homes during evening hours, and they are permitted leave from their dwellings only for medical or work-related purposes. The electronic bracelets or anklets worn by home confinement clients are capable of detecting whether clients move out of range of their home monitoring stations, which are semipermanent fixtures in their dwellings. POs may conduct random visits to one's dwelling at times when the offender must be at home. Voice verification may be effected by telephone. Also, POs may conduct drive-bys with electronic receptors to make an unobtrusive check to see if the offender is on his or her premises at particular times. In some instances, video cameras are installed in one's home and are activated from some central location as another means of verifying the offender's whereabouts. In 2000, there were 11 companies manufacturing and distributing wrist/ankle electronic surveillance products. Targeted for inclusion in home confinement programs are carefully selected nonviolent offenders who have either been removed or diverted from high-cost incarcerative facilities (Bowers, 2000:106).

In another instance, the Dane County Sheriff's Office in Wisconsin uses SpeakerID. SpeakerID permits the sheriff's department to confine certain nonviolent offenders to their homes. The SpeakerID program started by supervising 8 to 12 offenders, and in 1998 it was supervising 30 to 35 offenders. Two staff members at the jail run the program and monitor offenders. SpeakerID uses voice verification for persons sentenced to home confinement. These persons are telephoned at random times, and their voices are compared with digitalized recordings previously made of offender's vocal patterns. Such voice verification is about 97 percent accurate. If SpeakerID does not get a successful match or an answer on the first call, then the number is automatically redialed for authentication. After a maximum of four unsuccessful attempts, the sheriff's office is notified of a possible violation, and a deputy goes to the offender's residence for a face-to-face visit. An offender's absence is grounds for terminating the program and returning the offender to jail (Listug, 1996:85). Eligibility requirements for the home confinement program include being nonviolent, being employed, and having a relatively stable family environment. If the offender has formerly been in prison or jail, then prior institutional good conduct is considered together with these other qualifying characteristics.

A third type of home confinement program used in tandem with electronic monitoring occurred from October 1992 through October 1993. It was referred to as Western County, because it was located in western Pennsylvania (Courtright, Berg, and Mutchnick, 1997:19). The Western County program primarily targeted driving under the influence (DUI) or driving while intoxicated (DWI) offenders, although other low-risk offenders were subsequently included. First-offenders are mandated to spend 48 hours in jail, second offenders 30 days in jail, and third-time offenders 90 days in jail. In Western County, however, these DWI or DUI offenders were permitted to serve their varying times under a home confinement program overseen by a probation officer. Those typically sentenced to home confinement were convicted of DUI or DWI, writing bad checks, retail theft (shoplifting), simple assault, and second-degree burglary. Excluded offenders included those previously convicted of violent crimes and sex offenses. Additional selection criteria included mandatory drug/alcohol treatment or counseling; payment of monitoring fees; and compliance with all other program rules an regulations, including curfew and periodic substance abuse checks. Home confinement participants paid a monthly maintenance fee of $25. All participants were required to be employed or be actively seeking employment if unemployed. The program compliance rate was 84 percent, meaning that only 16 percent of all clients recidivated. Most of those were technical program violations, however. Program revocation occurred in less than 2 percent of all cases. Thus, the program was considered successful and did not place the community at risk (Courtright, Berg, and Mutchnick, 1997:21–22).

The Goals of Home Confinement Programs

The goals of home confinement programs include the following:

1. To continue the offender's punishment while permitting the offender to live in his or her dwelling under general or close supervision
2. To enable offenders to perform jobs in their communities to support themselves and their families
3. To reduce jail and prison overcrowding
4. To maximize public safety by ensuring that only the most qualified clients enter home confinement programs and are properly supervised
5. To reduce the costs of offender supervision
6. To promote rehabilitation and reintegration by permitting offenders to live under appropriate supervision within their communities

Joan Petersilia (1999a) has described several advantages and disadvantages of home confinement or house arrest. Among the advantages she notes are that (1) it is cost effective, (2) it has social benefits, (3) it is responsive to local citizen and offender needs, and (4) it is easily implemented and is timely in view of jail and prison overcrowding. Some of the more important disadvantages of home confinement are that (1) house arrest may actually widen the net of social control, (2) it may narrow the net of social control by not being a sufficiently severe sentence, (3) it focuses primarily on offender surveillance, (4) it is intrusive and possibly illegal, (5) race and class bias may enter into participant selection, and (6) it may compromise public safety. Some of these advantages and disadvantages are addressed at length below as issues concerning home confinement in which electronic monitoring is also used.

A Profile of Home Confinement Clients

No precise figures exist for describing home confinement clientele. Unofficial estimates for 1999 show that approximately 50,000 offenders were in home confinement programs and were supervised generally by probation departments (Camp and Camp, 1999). An examination of the screening procedures and eligibility requirements of different home confinement programs currently operating among the states suggests that most home confinement clients are first-offenders and nonviolent offenders. They tend to have close family ties, are married and live with their spouses, and are employed full time. They do not have drug or alcohol dependencies. Compared with clients in other types of probation and parole programs, home confinement clients tend to have higher amounts of education and vocational skills. They also tend to be older, age 30 or over (*Corrections Compendium*, 1992e, 1992f).

Selected Issues in Home Confinement

Because home confinement means permitting some misdemeanants and felons the opportunity of living in personal dwellings within their communities, this type of programming is not seen by the public as particularly punitive. As a result, several issues have been raised about whether home confinement is a viable punishment option. These issues include but are not limited to the following:

1. Home confinement may not be much of a punishment.
2. Is home confinement constitutional?
3. Public safety versus offender needs for community reintegration must be considered.
4. Home confinement may not be much of a crime deterrent.

Home Confinement May Not Be Much of a Punishment.   The public tends to view offenders confined to their homes as more of a luxury than a punishment. It may even lead some persons to contemplate committing crimes, because they may reason that being confined to one's home is not that bad a punishment. The experiences of home confinement clients who have been confined to their homes for a period of weeks or months, however, suggest that home confinement is very much a punishment.

One reason home confinement is perceived as less than true punishment compared with incarceration in a jail or prison is that the courts do not equate time served at home with time served in prison. In 1990, an Illinois defendant, Ramos, was confined to his parent's home for several weeks under house arrest while awaiting trial for a crime. He was not permitted to leave the premises except to work or receive medical treatment. Later he was convicted of the crime and asked the court to apply the time he spent at home toward the time he would have to serve in prison. The court denied his request, holding that his home confinement did not amount to custody (*People v. Ramos,* 1990). Subsequent court decisions have been consistent with the Ramos ruling. Several federal cases have held that the amount of time offenders spend in house arrest cannot be counted against jail or prison time to be served (*United States v. Arch John Drummond,* 1992; *United States v. Edwards,* 1992; *United States v. Insley,* 1991; *United States v. Wickman,* 1992; and *United States v. Zackular,* 1991).

Also, when offenders leave their residences without permission while under home confinement, they are not charged with escaping from prison; rather, they are guilty of a technical program violation. Lubus, a convicted Connecticut offender, was sentenced to house arrest. At some point, he failed to report to his supervising probation officer. The officer claimed that this failure was the equivalent of an "escape" and sought to have him prosecuted as an escapee. The Connecticut Supreme Court disagreed, indicating that unauthorized departures from community residences are not the same as unauthorized departures from halfway houses, mental health facilities and hospitals, and failures to return from furloughs or work release (*State v. Lubus,* 1990). Thus, if the courts are unwilling to consider home confinement to be the equivalent of incarceration in a prison or jail, then why should the public feel differently?

Is Home Confinement Constitutional?   Some scholars have argued that home confinement is unconstitutional because it involves various warrantless intrusions into one's premises by POs at any time for supervisory purposes. This argument, however, has no legal merit. State legislatures, the U.S. Congress, and the U.S. Supreme

Court determine what is or is not unconstitutional. Thus far, home confinement has not been declared unconstitutional by the U.S. Supreme Court (Nieto, 1998). Home confinement is simply one of several approved community corrections alternatives specified under every state community corrections act. The intent of such an act is to provide alternative community punishments in lieu of incarceration in jails or prisons. A reduction in jail and prison inmate populations is sought, and more than a few offenders, particularly the least serious ones, have been diverted to some type of community corrections punishment. Offenders diverted to these programs should be those who are determined to be in need of more restrictive monitoring or supervision compared with standard probationers or standard parolees.

Perhaps the most compelling argument that overcomes the constitutionality issue is that any sentence of home confinement is strictly voluntary (Jones and Ross, 1997). Judges give offenders a choice: they can accept home confinement and its accompanying conditions and restrictions, or they can go to jail or prison. Any criminal court judge contemplating using home confinement as a punishment for any particular offender must determine whether that offender agrees in writing with the program conditions. The Fourth Amendment issue of illegal search and seizure has also been raised. Some offenders believe that one's residence is a sacred place and that random curfew checks and travel restrictions are unreasonable. If offenders do not wish to enter home confinement programs with those restrictions, then they can choose jail or prison. It is up to them, not the courts. Because those offenders who accept the program conditions waive certain constitutional rights, the Fourth Amendment issue becomes irrelevant.

In virtually every jurisdiction, the appellate courts have held that there is no fundamental right to receive probation or any other community-based sentence (*Speth v. State*, 1999). Granting probation of any kind is within the discretion of the trial court, and offenders who are sentenced to probation must declare their objections to any probation condition when they are sentenced. If any defendant finds any probation condition objectionable, then the court has the discretion to withdraw the probationary sentence and impose an incarcerative one (Tonry, 1997). Convicted offenders who receive sentences of probation are considered to have waived any issues and rights regarding any conditions imposed on appeal later. In the Alabama case of *Ford v. State* (1999), for instance, Ford was a convicted offender sentenced to a prison term, but who was subsequently ordered by the court to serve a term of probation, with conditions, in lieu of incarceration. Ford, however, objected to the stringent probationary terms and declared that he would rather serve his time in jail. An Alabama appellate court held that because Ford did not accept the judge's offer of probation, the judge cannot order probation unless Ford indicates that he is willing to accept it. In this case, Ford was sentenced to prison for the duration of his original sentence.

Public Safety versus Offender Needs for Community Reintegration Must Be Considered. In any community corrections program, corrections staff must consider public safety to be a primary consideration. Thus, eligibility requirements are strict and careful screening of potential home confinement candidates occurs. If offenders are first-timers without prior records and if their conviction offenses are nonviolent, then they are considered for inclusion. The absence of a prior record, however, is no guarantee that an offender will automatically qualify. Predictions are made, usually on the basis of sound criteria, about one's chances for success.

There are obvious problems with placing convicted felons in home confinement programs. They have the freedom to leave their dwellings and roam about their communities freely; only detection by a PO can result in terminating one's program. Home confinement does not control offender behaviors. Rather, it is a less expensive alternative to incarceration, and only the most eligible offenders are given an opportunity to participate in such programs (Marciniak, 2000). The therapeutic value of home confinement and avoiding the criminal taint of incarceration are believed essential to an offender's rehabilitation and reintegration. Public safety is enhanced through the sound application of strenuous selection criteria. No selection criteria are foolproof, however. Many criminal justice scholars and community corrections practitioners believe that house arrest is worth it, despite the occasional home confinement failures (Tolman, 1996).

Home Confinement May Not Be Much of a Crime Deterrent.   Does home confinement function as a crime deterrent? No. It isn't supposed to. The primary function of home confinement is to enable POs to maintain a high degree of supervisory control over an offender's whereabouts. No home confinement program can claim that house arrest deters crime from occurring (Anderson, 1998), but several controls, such as drug or alcohol abuse and curfew, deter those on home confinement programs from violating their program requirements.

ELECTRONIC MONITORING PROGRAMS

Frequently accompanying home confinement is **electronic monitoring** (Jones and Ross, 1997). Primarily designed for low-risk, petty offenders, particularly misdemeanants and first-offender felons, electronic monitoring is a growing alternative to incarceration in prison or jail. Several manufacturers, such as GOSSlink, BI Incorporated, and Controlec, Inc., produce tamper-resistant wrist and ankle bracelets that emit electronic signals. These signals are usually connected to telephone devices and are relayed to central computers in police stations or probation departments.

Electronic Monitoring Defined

Electronic monitoring (EM) is the use of telemetry devices to verify that offenders are at specified locations during particular times (Marciniak, 2000). Electronic devices such as wristlets or anklets are fastened to offenders and must not be removed by them during the course of their sentence. The sanction for tampering with an offender's telemetry device is strong, consisting of a revocation of privileges and return to prison or jail (Payne and Gainey, 1999). In 1999, it was reported in a survey of over 90 percent of all U.S. jurisdictions that 24,617 clients were under some form of EM supervision (Camp and Camp, 1999:126). Independent government sources, however, report that in 1998 there were over 1,500 EM programs operating in the United States, with 95,000 EM units being used (National Law Enforcement and Corrections Technology Center, 1999:1). The average cost of EM per offender per day nationally in 1997 was $8.86, with a cost variation of $5 to $25, depending on the jurisdiction (Schmidt, 1998:11). This cost is a fraction of the expense of maintaining inmates under jail or prison supervision. As a comparison, incarceration costs averaged $40 to $50 in 1998 (National Law Enforcement and Corrections Technology Center, 1999:1).

Early Uses of Electronic Monitoring

EM devices were first used commercially in 1964 as an alternative to incarcerating mental patients and certain parolees (American Correctional Association, 1996a). In subsequent years, EM was used for monitoring office work, testing employees for security clearances, and many other applications (Enos, Holman, and Carroll, 1999). The feasibility of using electronic devices to monitor probationers was investigated by various researchers during the 1960s and 1970s. New Mexico was the first state to officially sanction its use for criminal offenders in 1983 (Houk, 1984).

New Mexico Second Judicial District Judge Jack Love implemented a pilot project in 1983 to electronically monitor persons convicted of drunk driving and various white-collar offenses. The New Mexico Supreme Court examined and approved the program, subject to the voluntary consent and participation of offenders as a condition of their probation and as long as their privacy, dignity, and families were protected (Houk, 1984). Offenders were required to wear anklets or wristlets that emitted electronic signals that could be intercepted by probation officers conducting surveillance operations.

Following the New Mexico experiment, other jurisdictions began to use a variety of EM systems for supervising parolees, probationers, inmates of jails and prisons, and pretrial releasees (American Correctional Association, 1996a). Experiments with EM devices were tried in Florida, California, and Kentucky (Schmidt, 1998). Both praised and condemned by criminal justice practitioners, EM seems to be the most promising cost-effective solution to the problems of prison overcrowding and the management of **probation officer caseloads** (Bonta, Capretta-Wallace, and Rooney, 1999). Until the advent of EM devices, the idea of confining convicted offenders to their homes as a punishment was simply unworkable unless a jurisdiction was willing to pay for the continuous monitoring services of a probation officer.

The use of EM is currently global. Successful EM programs have been reported in England, Canada, and the Netherlands (Bonta, Capretta-Wallace, and Rooney, 2000a; Richardson, 1999; Spaans and Verwers, 1997; Whitfield, 1997). For instance, a study of EM was conducted in Greater Manchester, Norfolk, and Berkshire in the United Kingdom. Approximately 375 offenders were placed on EM with curfew orders in 1996 and investigated for nearly two years. These offenders were compared with 2,400 others who were given community service orders and with 2,900 offenders who were placed on probation without any type of EM. Recidivism rates were lowest, only 18 percent, among those who were electronically monitored (Mortimer and May, 1997). Those most likely to receive EM were convicted of nonviolent offenses, including theft, burglary, and driving without a license.

Similarly successful results have been reported in Canada, where numerous offenders have been placed on EM accompanied by various community-based treatments. Offender recidivism was far lower in electronically monitored programs compared with those programs where EM was not used (Bonta, Capretta-Wallace, and Rooney, 2000b). In the Canadian study, a control sample of inmates receiving treatment without the EM condition was compared with a matched sample of electronically

---

BOX 2.4   ***Does Electronic Monitoring Control Behavior? No, It's Not Supposed To***

The Cases of Scott Holmberg and Slobodan Lunic

Two swindlers bilked several thousand investors out of $38 million during a one-year fraudulent telephone marketing scheme. Scott Holmberg, 35, and his partner, Slobodan Lunic, 45, swindled 2,100 investors who thought they were getting profits from pay phones across the country but instead were really victims of a Ponzi scheme in which swindlers use money pumped in by new investors to pay "profits" to other investors. Holmberg and Lunic allegedly used their money from victims to buy yachts, fancy cars, motorcycles, and other luxuries. Federal prosecutors and the FBI eventually caught up with Holmberg and Lunic, and they were arrested. Holmberg agreed to testify against Lunic in exchange for leniency. In the meantime, over government objections, Lunic was released on $500,000 bond and placed on electronic monitoring. An electronic anklet was strapped to his ankle to make it easy for federal probation officers to track his movements. Lunic, however, cut off the plastic anklet and vanished in June 1999, two days before he was to stand trial for the fraud scheme. He has never been apprehended. Prosecutors

warned the judge who ordered the electronic monitoring that Lunic might flee to his native Serbia, which has no extradition treaty with the United States. In the meantime, Holmberg was sentenced to five years in federal prison and was ordered to repay the money he took from his victims. He could have to keep paying the rest of his life. "He will if I have anything to say about it," said Assistant U.S. Attorney Marsha McClennan, who spoke with reporters after Holmberg was sentenced in February 2000. Holmberg was also advised to stop honeymooning with the woman he plans to marry before he reports to prison in 45 days. Holmberg told the court at his sentencing hearing, "I continue to feel terrible about what I've done and the many victims that I've hurt."

If you were the judge, is a five-year sentence sufficient punishment for stealing $38 million? What steps should be taken to capture Slobodan Lunic? What punishment would you have imposed on Holmberg if you had been the judge? Does electronic monitoring control one's behavior? Should it be used in such high-profile cases involving millions of dollars? What do you think?

Source: Adapted from Associated Press, "Man Gets 5 Years for Phone Fraud," February 25, 2000.

---

monitored offenders. Rehabilitative services were more effectively delivered under EM conditions.

Types of Electronic Monitoring Systems

There are four general categories of EM equipment. Two of these categories are devices that use telephones at the monitoring location, whereas the other two are radio signal-emitting systems in which radio signals are received by either portable or stationary units.

Continuous Signaling Devices.   **Continuous signaling devices** use a miniature transmitter strapped to the offender. The transmitter broadcasts an encoded signal that is picked up by a receiver-dialer in the offender's home. The signal is relayed to a central receiver over telephone lines.

Programmed Contact Devices.   **Programmed contact devices** are similar to continuous signal units except that a central computer calls at random hours to verify that offenders are where they are supposed to be. Offenders answer the telephone, and their voices are verified by computer.

Cellular Telephone Devices. **Cellular telephone devices** are also transmitters worn by offenders. A cell phone emits a radio signal that is received by a local area monitor. Such systems can monitor as many as 25 offenders simultaneously.

Continuous Signaling Transmitters. **Continuous signaling transmitters** are also worn by the offender and emit a continuous electronic signal. Portable receiver units are used by probation officers so that they can drive by an offender's home and verify the offender's presence. Drive-by checks by POs are not only useful for detecting an offender's presence at his or her dwelling, but also verifying if the offender is attending prescribed counseling sessions or meetings, such as Alcoholics Anonymous, or is at one's workplace (Schmidt, 1998:11).

EM systems may be either passive or active. In passive systems, offenders have to answer a telephone and speak to a PO or insert the transmitter into the home monitoring device to verify one's presence. Some passive systems emit signals so that if offenders move out of range (150 to 500 yards away from the home monitoring device), an alarm sounds and the central monitoring center is alerted. Active systems emit electronic signals on a continuous basis, and such signals have their personalized signature and can be tracked by POs or by global positioning system technology. Victims may be protected from offenders as well, because these devices can be programmed to alert POs if offenders enter a specified range around the victim.

Home monitoring systems have the capability of reporting tampering or the loss of electrical power. They have memory retention capability so that all saved messages can be restored after power outages. Sufficient battery backup power is provided for up to 48 hours. Mechanisms are waterproofed to protect against pests and infestation, and internal antennae are installed to prevent offender tampering. Electronic transmitters worn on the wrist or ankle are light and manageable, no larger than a deck of cards. They are shockproof and waterproof, thus allowing offenders to bathe or swim without damaging the system's internal components. They are also tamperproof and cannot be removed except by special devices in the possession of POs. EM devices are often composed of shiny black plastic, so tampering is easily detected. POs often carry field monitoring devices and can track an offender's whereabouts anywhere in public (National Law Enforcement and Corrections Technology Center, 1999:3).

Electronic Monitoring with Home Confinement

In many jurisdictions, EM is used together with home confinement (American Correctional Association, 1996a). One of the greatest benefits of using both methods is that client reintegration and rehabilitation are facilitated. In one study of 261 probationers and parolees conducted over several years, data were compiled from a Family Environment Scale and the Beck Depression Inventory. These personality assessment devices measure a client's responsiveness to community-based treatment programming. According to this study, the most significant factor contributing to an offender's positive reintegration with his or her community was electronically monitored house arrest, which tended to facilitate one's integration and personal improvement (Enos, Holman, and Carroll, 1999). Similar outcomes have been observed in other studies (Gostas and Harris, 1997; Vitiello, 1997; Whitfield, 1997).

Some Examples of Electronic Monitoring in Action.   One particularly good example of the use of electronic monitoring with home confinement occurred in Virginia. In 1989, Chesterfield County, Virginia, received a $34,470 state grant to investigate the feasibility of home confinement as an alternative to imprisonment. The Chesterfield County Jail was suffering from chronic overcrowding with 156 inmates, nearly twice its rated capacity (*Richmond Times-Dispatch,* 1990). The county acquired 30 watch-size monitoring transmitters, activator devices, and computer equipment for a one-year trial period of an EM home incarceration program. In this case, selected inmates were fitted with a black monitoring transmitter attached to their wrists with a black plastic wristband.

With this EM system, the wristband is waterproof, and the only way it can be removed is by cutting it off. The transmitter fits into a second piece of equipment called the verifier that also goes home with the inmate. The verifier plugs into a telephonic device. The verifier is then called at random during the day by a computer located in the county jail offices. The inmate has ten seconds to answer the telephone and state his or her name and time on the receiver. Then he or she inserts the wrist transmitter into a slot on the verifier. The transmitter sends an electronic tone back to the computer, verifying that the correct monitor has responded to the telephone call. The entire system is fully automated, with the offender's voice recorded and the results of the electronic signal printed out at the jail.

If the wrist monitor fails to activate the verifier or if the inmate does not answer the telephone, then the computer redials the home in two minutes. If there is no answer, then a third call is made. If there is still no answer, then a sheriff's deputy visits the offender's home directly to verify his or her whereabouts. Violating home confinement and removing the electronic device are program violations that can result in probation or parole revocation. Further, offenders pay $5.50 daily to offset the EM costs. Because Chesterfield County uses the devices for jail-bound offenders, there is some relief from jail overcrowding (*Richmond Times-Dispatch,* 1990:100).

In another application of EM, the U.S. Probation Office for the Southern District of Mississippi experimented with EM beginning in 1994 (Gowen, 1995). The selection criteria for federal offenders included the following: no history of violence, no mental illness, and no severe substance abuse history. Subsequently, the federal EM program began to include more serious types of offenders, including substance abusers who tested positive for alcohol or drugs and irresponsible offenders, who often failed to report, failed to complete community service, or made false statements to their POs. Candidates for EM placement, however, did exhibit good work histories and relatively stable home environments. Increasing numbers of pretrial defendants and postsentence nonviolent offenders were added to the list of program-eligible clientele. For all clients, an approved daily activity schedule that permitted offenders to be "out of range" for certain periods during the day for work purposes or hospital or counseling visits was established (Gowen, 1995:11). Arrangements were made with the EM manufacturer and supplier for daily facsimile reports of offender departures from, and arrivals to, the residence. This high-precision information made it possible to detect minor violations, such as missing one's curfew.

Interestingly, program personnel found that when offender-clients began wearing electronic wristlets or anklets, an "incredible deterrent effect" was observed

(Gowen, 1995:11). The bracelet, which transmitted an electronic signal for reception by a home monitoring unit, served as a constant reminder to offenders to comply with specified program requirements. Face-to-face visits on an irregular basis and at random times further increased offender compliance with program specifications. Some EM clients were also placed in home confinement. The federal EM program exhibited a 92 percent success rate, with only 8 percent of the offenders recidivating.

Arguments for and against Electronic Monitoring

Arguments favoring the use of EM are that it (1) assists offenders in avoiding the criminogenic atmosphere of prisons or jails and helps reintegrate them into their communities; (2) permits offenders to retain jobs and support families; (3) assists probation officers in their monitoring activities and has potential for easing their caseload responsibilities; (4) gives judges and other officials considerable flexibility in sentencing offenders; (5) has the potential of reducing recidivism rate more than existing probationary alternatives; (6) is potentially useful for decreasing jail and prison populations; (7) is more cost-effective in relation to incarceration; and (8) allows for pretrial release monitoring as well as for special treatment cases such as substance abusers, the mentally retarded, women who are pregnant, and juveniles (Faulkner and Gibbs, 1998; Lucker et al., 1997; Payne and Gainey, 1998).

Arguments against EM include the following: (1) by requiring offenders to have telephones or pay for expensive monitoring equipment and/or fees, some potential exists for race, ethnic, or socioeconomic bias (ironically, some jurisdictions report that many offenders enjoy better living conditions in jail or prison custody compared with their residences outside of prison); (2) public safety may be compromised through the failure of these programs to guarantee that offenders will go straight and not endanger citizens by committing new offenses while free in the community; (3) EM may be too coercive, and it may be unrealistic for officials to expect full offender compliance with such a stringent system; (4) little consistent information exists about the impact of electronic monitoring on recidivism rates compared with other probationary alternatives; (5) persons frequently selected for participation are persons who probably do not need to be monitored anyway; (6) technological problems can make electronic monitoring somewhat unreliable; (7) EM may result in widening the net by being prescribed for offenders who otherwise would receive less costly standard probation; (8) EM raises right to privacy, civil liberty, and other constitutional issues such as Fourth Amendment search and seizure concerns; (9) much of the public interprets this option as going easy on offenders and perceives electronic monitoring as a nonpunitive alternative; and (10) the costs of electronic monitoring may be more than published estimates (Jones, 2000; Mann, 1998; Richardson, 1999; Toombs, 1995).

A Profile of Electronic Monitoring Clients

It is difficult to articulate criteria applicable to all electronically monitored clients. Some clients are juveniles, and others are awaiting trial. Many are probationers with electronic monitoring specified as a condition of probation. Others are parolees who are placed under an electronic monitoring program for short periods following their early release (Schmidt, 1998).

Electronic monitoring is not for all offenders. Ordinarily, those considered for electronic monitoring have been charged with or convicted of minor, nonviolent offenses. Prospective clients include property offenders (e.g., burglars, larcenists and thieves, automobile thieves, shoplifters, embezzlers) and those who have no prior records. Some offenders might be nonviolent, but they may be chronic offenders with lengthy criminal histories. Thus, if there is a great likelihood that certain prospective clients might reoffend, then they would be barred from participating in an electronic monitoring program (Roy, 1997).

Selected Issues in Electronic Monitoring

Invariably, electronic monitoring has generated considerable controversy since its inception in the 1960s. Any attempt to employ electronic means in offender supervision is going to raise one or more issues about the suitability and/or legality of these devices, and EM is no exception. Some of the more important issues are described here. The following discussion is fairly thorough although not comprehensive and covers: the ethics of electronic monitoring, the constitutionality of electronic monitoring and client rights, punishment versus rehabilitation and reintegration, the public safety issue, deterrence, and privatization and net-widening.

The Ethics of Electronic Monitoring.   One criticism of EM is the potential for the ultimate political control of the public. Is EM ethical? One response is to consider the fundamental purpose or intent of EM. Is EM intentionally designed to snoop on private citizens? No. Is EM intentionally designed to invade one's privacy? No. Is EM intentionally designed to assist POs in verifying an offender's whereabouts? Yes. Is EM capable of detecting program violations in lieu of direct PO supervision? Yes.

Perhaps the ethics of EM becomes more relevant or focused if we theoretically project what the limits of electronic monitoring might be in some future context. Some critics may therefore be justified in wondering that if we use EM for a limited purpose today (e.g., to verify an offender's whereabouts), what other uses might be made of electronic monitoring in future years (e.g., intruding into bedrooms to detect criminal sexual acts or other possible criminal behaviors)? At present, EM equipment is placed in convenient areas, such as kitchens or living rooms. Video-capable EM equipment is also presently limited to verifying one's identity and whether drug or alcohol program violations have occurred. No one has suggested that cameras be placed in one's bedroom or bathroom to be activated at the whim of an equipment operator. If any issue is to be raised here, then it is the reasonableness issue.

One extreme extrapolation of the use of EM has been suggested by Thomas Toombs (1995). Given present-day technology and the existence of numerous satellite surveillance systems, it may be possible to surgically implant electronic transponders in offenders in ways that would make their removal difficult. Furthermore, any attempt to remove an implanted transponder would trigger an alarm and immediately immobilize the offender. A satellite surveillance system could be significantly less costly than present prison operations. Such a system would permit community-based programs to use EM in the design of individualized treatment programs to maximize various types of assistance for offenders so that they can live acceptably in society (Toombs, 1995). There are, however, strong ethical objections to monitoring methods that involve physically intrusive procedures such as surgical implants. Less intrusive methods, such as the use of electronic pulse emission by wristlets and anklets worn by offenders and tracked by global positioning satellites or transmissions of an offender's whereabouts over either telephone lines or wireless networks, even the Internet, are being devised (Schmidt, 1998:11). Preferred EM methods aim toward supervising low-risk offenders who are least likely to reoffend (Church Council on Justice and Corrections, 1996; Virginia Department of Criminal Justice Services, 1998).

The Constitutionality of Electronic Monitoring and Client Rights. Certain legal issues about EM are currently unresolved, although the constitutionality of EM has never been successfully challenged (American Correctional Association, 1996a). Many of the same legal arguments raised regarding the constitutionality of home confinement are also raised about EM. Like home confinement, though, offenders placed in EM programs must agree to abide by all EM program conditions. If any particular offender does not want to be placed in an EM program, then the judge can impose incarceration in a jail or prison. The consensual nature of offender participation in such programs undermines virtually all constitutional challenges that might be raised. Perhaps the most compelling constitutional issue relates to whether EM discriminates against particular offenders who do not have permanent dwellings or telephones. The range of EM options, however, is such that discrimination is not a factor. Anyone can be outfitted with some type of EM device to suit the circumstance. POs can conduct drive-bys or checks with handheld EM equipment to verify an offender's whereabouts without actually using telephonic equipment.

Punishment versus Rehabilitation and Reintegration. Another criticism is that home confinement and electronic monitoring are not really punishments at all, because offenders are not assigned to hard time behind jail or prison walls. The average length of time offenders are placed on electronic monitoring is about 80 days, according to *NIJ Reports* (*Corrections Compendium,* 1991a:14). Thus, critics might claim that less than three months is insufficient time to accomplish any significant reintegration or rehabilitation. The overwhelming evidence, however, supports EM as a rehabilitative and reintegrative tool (Gostas and Harris, 1997; Mortimer and May, 1997).

The Public Safety Issue. Whenever offenders are placed on EM and/or home confinement, they are free to commit new crimes if they wish to do so. They are not incapacitated; therefore, they pose possible risks to public safety. The criteria used for selecting offenders as EM clients, however, are very strenuous. For example, the Nevada County Probation Department uses electronic monitoring with home confinement as a means of providing an alternative incarceration site besides jail. Participants are eligible for electronic monitoring if they meet the following criteria:

1. Participants must be assessed as low-risk offenders.
2. Participants must exhibit good conduct while in jail.
3. Participants must be physically and mentally capable of caring for themselves or must be in circumstances in which another person can provide their needed care.
4. Participants must have a verifiable local address as well as a telephone and electricity at their home location.
5. Participants must have no fewer than 10 days and no more than 90 days to serve in jail.

6. Participants must pay an administrative fee of $10 per day while being monitored.
7. Participants cannot have any holds or warrants from other jurisdictions while on the program.
8. Participants must wear an electronic anklet and have a field monitoring device placed in their home.
9. Participants must have the support and cooperation of family members.
10. Participants must seek and maintain employment while on the program.
11. Participants must participate in any specified rehabilitative programs while in the program.
12. Participants must volunteer to participate in the program. (Latimer, Curran, and Tepper, 1992)

Deterrence.   Despite the sophistication of technology, it can be beaten. POs have found that some offenders have installed call forwarding systems so that when the computers dial their telephone numbers automatically, the calls are forwarded electronically to cell telephones elsewhere. Also, some offenders have devised tape-recorded messages so that electronic voice verifications are deceived about the offender's actual whereabouts. Some offenders may convert their homes into a criminal base of operations, conducting fencing operations, fraud, illegal drug exchanges, and other criminal activity without attracting suspicion from the POs who supervise them. Thus, there is some question as to whether EM deters persons from committing crimes. The primary objective of EM must be remembered, however. It is not a behavior control mechanism; it is a means of determining an offender's whereabouts at particular times. Thus, although deterrence from criminal activity is desirable, it is not the primary objective of EM.

Privatization and Net-Widening.   EM is susceptible to privatization by outside interests. Companies that manufacture EM equipment and the wristlets and anklets worn by offenders are already involved to a great degree in the implementation and operation of home confinement programs in various jurisdictions. They train probation officers and others in the use of EM equipment, and they offer instruction to police departments and probation agencies on related matters of **offender control**. Thus, it is conceivably a short step to complete involvement by private interests in this growing nonincarcerative alternative.

Another concern is the potential EM has for net-widening (Mainprize, 1992). Some officials have said that judges and others may use these options increasingly for larger numbers of offenders who would otherwise be diverted to standard probation involving minimal contact with probation officers. For home confinement and EM to be maximally effective at reducing jail and prison overcrowding and not result in the feared net-widening, only jail- or prison-bound offenders should be considered for participation in these programs (Payne and Gainey, 1999).

DAY REPORTING CENTERS

For many furloughees and work-study releasees, community residences or centers are established to facilitate their work or educational placement and assist them in other needs they might have. Known as **day reporting centers** (Marciniak, 2000) or invisible jails, they are a hybrid of intensive probation supervision, house arrest, and early release. Day reporting is a highly structured nonresidential program using supervision, sanctions, and services coordinated from a central focus (Diggs and Pieper, 1994:9). In 1998, there were approximately 114 day reporting centers in the United States (Bahn and Davis, 1998). Unofficial estimates from 90 percent of the reporting state and federal jurisdictions surveyed for 1999 indicate that 10,226 offenders were under some form of day reporting center supervision (Camp and Camp, 1999:126). It is more likely that perhaps as many as 20,000 or more offenders are actually participating in day reporting center programs in the United States today.

Day reporting centers are usually located in the midst of various preparole releasees living within the community (Jones and Lacey, 1999). These centers handle daily activities and provide minimum supervision for participating work-study releasees and furloughees. Many of these offender-clients have special conditions associated with their work-study release or furlough programs, such as restitution to victims, payment of program costs, and supervisory fees. Also, clients must be checked to determine if they are involved in drug or alcohol abuse. Day reporting centers assist authorities in providing these services and offender monitoring. Another function of day reporting centers is to assist clients in job placement and completing job applications. In some instances, these programs may provide educational and vocational opportunities to prepare them for better-paying jobs.

Several guidelines for operating day reporting centers have been established, including the following:

1. Sign a contract with participants spelling out expectations about home, work, schooling, financial matters, drug tests, counseling, community service, and restitution.
2. Notify the police department in the offender's hometown.
3. Set a curfew; 9:00 P.M. is common.
4. Require an advance copy of the participant's daily itinerary points.
5. Perform spot-checks of the participant's home, job, and other itinerary points.
6. Institute proper urinalysis procedures; twice a week testing is typical.
7. Schedule telephone checks more heavily on Thursday, Friday and Saturday nights.
8. Establish services; addiction education, parenting, and transition skills are popular topics (Marciniak, 1999; Schmitz, Wassenberg, and Patterson, 2000).

Day reporting center clients should have the following characteristics:

1. Good candidates for day reporting centers include those convicted of drug offenses, larceny, DWI, breaking and entering of commercial buildings, and similar charges; Massachusetts excludes sex offenders and, for the most part, violent offenders.
2. Offenders without an identified victim are candidates for such programs.
3. Those with a home to go to may also be good candidates.
4. Typically, inmates within six months of release may also be eligible. (*Corrections Compendium*, 1990b:14)

A study of day reporting centers and their effectiveness was conducted in North Carolina for the years 1992 through 1998. A sample of 204 offenders was studied. Data were acquired from court records and follow-up investigations. The majority of offenders in the day reporting program fit the eligibility requirements. About

13 percent of the participants probably should have been assigned to standard probation instead of day reporting. Interestingly, in this particular research, about 66 percent of all participants had their programs terminated for one program violation or another. Those who successfully completed the day reporting program, however, tended to exhibit the following characteristics: (1) they were employed, (2) they had higher educational levels than other offenders, and (3) they lived alone (Marciniak, 1999). In this study, it was determined that judicial discretion led to the inclusion of many ineligible offenders into the day reporting program. Thus, the high failure rate of the clients is partially explained.

In another study of juveniles assigned to day reporting programs in several Illinois counties, day reporting was supplemented with drug treatment, individual and group counseling, education, life skills courses, and moral recognition therapy. The programs were highly successful in modifying criminal and substance-abusing behaviors of participating juveniles (Schmitz, Wassenberg, and Patterson, 2000). Reasons given for the positive results were that day reporting maximized family involvement, school enrollment, and employment.

An evaluation of several day reporting programs was made by the U.S. National Institute of Justice for the period 1990 to 1994. Three Wisconsin day reporting centers were evaluated. The study involved 277 clients who were compared with 573 probationers and 267 substance-abusing probationers ineligible for day reporting (Craddock and Graham, 1996). The study results indicated that those clients in day reporting programs had lower rates of recidivism compared with the other two groups. One major factor accounting for greater success rates among the day reporting center clientele was the availability of affordable, safe, and drug-free transitional housing, which ameliorates the stress of living in the community.

In another ambitious investigation, 496 day reporting clients were observed who were involved in the Metropolitan Day Reporting Center (MDRC) in Boston. The MDRC was established in 1987 as a residential, transitional facility to the community for inmates released early from local jails. Clients were tracked for the years 1992 through 1994. Nearly 80 percent of the clients were either employed or actively seeking employment. The typical program participant was age 25 or older, and most had serious drug or alcohol problems. Over half had no prior record, although 12 percent had been incarcerated for various reasons on three or more previous occasions. Those with prior records were primarily nonviolent property offenders. About 60 percent of all participants completed the program successfully and did not recidivate (McDevitt, Domino, and Baum, 1997). Day reporting generally appears to be a successful intervention, particularly when prospective clients are carefully screened, supervised, and given appropriate treatments or therapies (Tolman, 1996; Tonry, 1997).

An Example of a Day Reporting Center in Action

Liz Marie Marciniak (2000) has provided a detailed description of a day reporting center established in southeastern North Carolina as the result of monies supplied through the 1994 North Carolina Structured Sentencing Act. In North Carolina, day reporting center programs are a special condition of probation. That is, judges may sentence offenders to probation with the special condition that they attend day reporting centers and participate in prescribed programming. Marciniak obtained a sample of 1,026 cases where day reporting had been included in probationary sentences as a special condition. The North Carolina Day Reporting Center program was set up as follows:

1. It is a four-phase program that lasts 12 months.
2. Offenders must check in between one to six times per week, depending on the special conditions of their probation programs.
3. Clients must be employed or engaged in a concentrated job search while in the program.
4. Day reporting center clientele assess offenders for substance abuse problems, educational and vocational needs, and mental health needs, and appropriate referrals are made to other community agencies or organizations.
5. The day reporting center offers general equivalency diploma (GED) classes, literacy training, adult basic skills, parenting, Alcoholics Anonymous, Narcotics Anonymous, drug education, and individual counseling.
6. All offenders must develop and submit daily itineraries to their case managers.
7. All offenders must submit to random drug tests at the center.
8. The center operates on a three-strikes system, so that once a client accrues three strikes, he or she is terminated from the program. (Strikes include missed or late appointments, swearing, assaulting a case manager, positive drug screens, and technical or legal violations of one's probation conditions.)
9. All clients are under intensive supervised probation.
10. All clients must observe a curfew from 7:00 P.M. to 7:00 A.M.
11. All clients must have contact with their probation officer five times per week.
12. All clients must submit to warrantless searches of their residences.
13. All clients must submit to random drug tests at their residences.
14. All clients must perform community service as specified in their probation orders.
15. All clients must work or attend school.

About half of all offenders supervised by the day reporting program were sentenced to the program by a judge. The other half were sent to the program as a way of intensifying their regular probation programs, usually for committing technical program violations. Marciniak concluded as the result of her study that those who participated in the day reporting program had many rehabilitative advantages compared with probationers not involved in the program. One interesting result of Marciniak's research about day reporting centers was that the clients did not differ in their recidivism rates compared with other probationers not involved in day reporting. She observed, however, that individual clients who did participate in day reporting were able to earn their GED degrees, have substance abuse counseling, take literacy courses, and take anger management classes. Thus, recidivism rate comparisons, at least in Marciniak's view, do not give us a full and accurate portrayal of the benefits of day reporting programs for involved clients.

SUMMARY

Community corrections refers to any community-based correctional program designed to supervise convicted offenders in lieu of incarceration, including payment of fines, victim compensation and restitution, and community service. Community corrections involves any type of intermediate punishment, ranging somewhere between standard probation and incarceration. Such programs involve halfway houses, day reporting centers, work release, study release, furloughs, home confinement, electronic monitoring, and intensive supervised probation. These community-based programs are located in neighborhoods and provide a rehabilitative and reintegrative milieu for offender-clients. These facilities also function as a continuation of punishment.

Community corrections are established largely through community corrections acts. These acts fund service agencies at the local level and are intended to divert jail- or prison-bound offenders. These community-based corrections programs attempt to facilitate offender reintegration into society, aid offender rehabilitation, heighten offender accountability, and provide a range of nonincarcerative punishments. Functions of community corrections are to monitor and supervise offender-clients to ensure program compliance (e.g., victim compensation, restitution, and community service orders); ensure public safety; offer job placement and employment assistance; provide individual and group counseling; provide educational training and literacy services; network with other agencies to maximize services to offender-clients; and alleviate jail and prison overcrowding.

Major issues of community corrections concern the controversy of locating community corrections programs within communities, thereby posing a potential risk to citizens. Some persons believe that community corrections is not punishment at all. There is a struggle between meeting offender needs with reintegrative programs and ensuring public safety. Possible net-widening may occur, simply because community programs have been established. Growing privatization of community corrections suggests that large-scale use of incarceration as a punishment may occur as privatization of these programs expands. Many community corrections programs are underequipped and understaffed. Many staff members of these agencies have not been adequately trained to deal with diverse populations of offenders. Special needs offenders pose unique and sometimes difficult to resolve problems. The growth of community corrections as well as the rise of professionalization of staff suggests that these programs are becoming more effective at meeting the needs of growing numbers of offender-clients.

Home confinement is an intermediate punishment consisting of confining offenders to their residences for mandatory incarceration during evening hours, curfews, and/or on weekends. Home confinement as a punishment was first used in St. Louis, Missouri, in 1971 and was adopted statewide in Florida in 1983. Offenders on home confinement may be assigned to community service, may be required to pay maintenance fees of the program, and may be required to pay restitution to victims. Other requirements may include participation in vocational and educational courses, observance of curfews, submission to random drug and alcohol checks, and maintenance of other court-required contacts. The goals of home confinement programs are to reduce jail and prison overcrowding, reduce offender costs, foster rehabilitation and reintegration among offender-clients, ensure public safety, and continue one's punishment under nonincarcerative conditions.

Often used in conjunction with home confinement is electronic monitoring. EM is the use of telemetry devices to verify that offenders are at specified locations during particular times. It was first used in New Mexico to monitor the behaviors of those convicted of DWI. Forms of electronic monitoring include continuous signaling devices, programmed contact devices, cellular telephone devices, and continuous signally transmitters. Most persons on electronic monitoring pose little or no risk to public safety; they are often first-offenders and are nonviolent. Many issues associated with home confinement also apply to electronic monitoring. These issues pertain to the ethics of electronic monitoring, certain possible constitutional rights violations, the punishment versus rehabilitation or reintegration issue, the concern for public safety, crime deterrence, and privatization and possible net-widening.

Day reporting centers are also used as mechanisms for supervising low-risk and nonviolent offenders. Support services are made available through such programs, and most research about the successfulness of day reporting clientele has been favorable. When clients are properly screened and supervised and when they receive appropriate therapies and treatments, day reporting is regarded as an important rehabilitative and reintegrative tool.

KEY TERMS

Agency
Cellular telephone devices
Community-based supervision
Community control
Community control house arrest
Community corrections act
Community residential centers
Continuous signaling devices
Continuous signaling transmitters
Creaming
Day reporting centers
Electronic monitoring

False negatives
False positives
Home confinement
Home incarceration
House arrest
Intermediate punishments
Juvenile
Law Enforcement Assistance Administration (LEAA)
Net-widening
NIMBY syndrome
Offender control

President's Commission on Law Enforcement and Administration of Justice
Pretrial release
Privatization
Probation officer caseloads
Probation Subsidy Program
Professionals
Programmed contact devices
Rehabilitative ideal
Risk assessment instruments

QUESTIONS FOR REVIEW

1. What is meant by community-based corrections?
2. What are the major functions of community corrections programs?
3. In what sense is there a conflict between ensuring public safety and providing a community environment to promote offender therapy and reintegration? Discuss.
4. What is the general philosophy of community corrections? Based on what you have read up to now, is this philosophy consistent with the "get tough" movement? Why or why not? Explain.
5. What are some of the constitutional challenges that have been leveled against home confinement as an intermediate punishment?
6. What are some of the critical elements of Florida's community control house arrest program? What are some of the behavioral requirements of offender-clients who are sentenced to the Florida program?
7. What are the goals of home confinement? In what respects are these goals realized?
8. What are some of general characteristics of home confinement offender-clients?
9. What are some of the pros and cons associated with electronic monitoring?
10. What are the goals of day reporting centers? What are the findings regarding the recidivism among day reporting clients?

SUGGESTED READINGS

Arthur, Lindsay G. (2000). "Punishment Doesn't Work!" *Juvenile and Family Court Journal* **51:**37–42.

Harris, Patricia M. (ed.) (1999). *Research to Results: Effective Community Corrections.* Lanham, MD: American Correctional Association.

Palmer, Carleton A., and Mark Hazelrigg (2000). "The Guilty but Mentally Ill Verdict: A Review and Conceptual Analysis of Intent and Impact." *Journal of the American Academy of Psychiatry and the Law* **28:**47–54.

Payne, Brian K., and Randy R. Gainey (1998). "A Qualitative Assessment of the Pains Experienced on Electronic Monitoring." *International Journal of Offender Therapy and Comparative Criminology* **42:**149–163.

Schmidt, Annesley K. (1998). "Electronic Monitoring: What Does the Literature Tell Us?" *Federal Probation* **62:**10–19.

Sentencing and the Presentence Investigation Report: Background, Preparation, and Functions

CHAPTER 3

Introduction

The Sentencing Process: Types of Sentencing Systems and Sentencing Issues
  Functions of Sentencing
  Types of Sentencing
  Sentencing Issues

The Role of Probation Officers in Sentencing

Presentence Investigation (PSI) Reports:
  Interstate Variations
  The Confidentiality of PSI Reports
  The Preparation of PSI Reports
  Functions and Uses of PSI Reports
  The Defendant's Sentencing Memorandum
  The Inclusion of Victim Impact Statements
  Privatizing PSI Report Preparation

The Sentencing Hearing

Aggravating and Mitigating Circumstances
  Aggravating Circumstances
  Mitigating Circumstances

A Sample PSI Report from North Dakota

A PSI Report from Wisconsin

Changing Responsibilities of Probation Officers Resulting from Sentencing Reforms and Trends

Summary

Key Terms

Questions for Review

Suggested Readings

Appendix: Sample Federal PSI Report

• *The Case of the Incriminating Rap Video.* It happened in Buffalo, New York. After a three-week string of burglaries in an upscale neighborhood of Buffalo, two men were arrested after they smashed a window with a brick and stole more than $5,000 worth of clothing from a store in the Niagara Factory Outlet Mall. The two men, 21-year-old Michael Mungro and 23-year-old Eric Redfield, were apprehended and taken into custody. They gave as their address an old abandoned city-owned apartment building. Police went to the building and found over $30,000 worth of stolen merchandise, much of it from the places that had been burglarized earlier. Included in the merchandise were several videotapes. When police played the videotapes, they saw their arrestees, Mungro and Redfield, rapping and boasting of their string of burglaries before the camera. They boasted that "crime pays in many ways" and urged would-be viewers to "sit back and enjoy the show. Eat some popcorn and drink some beverages." Police said that the tape also included admissions from Mungro and Redfield that they had used drugs and committed other crimes. What type of sentence should the judge impose on these two defendants if they are convicted of the crimes? (*Source:* Adapted from Associated Press, "Pair Accused of Burglary Made Videos Boasting that 'Crime Pays,'" January 11, 1996.)

• *The Case of Governor Fife Symington.* Whenever someone is indicted, there is *always* the question of whether they are guilty of the crimes alleged in the indictment. An indictment is a charge, and like any other charge, a presumption of innocence exists until one's guilt is proved later in court beyond a reasonable doubt. Arizona Governor Fife Symington was indicted in June 1996 for allegedly cheating mortgage lenders through fraud and extortion. The government alleged that Symington made false statements to a federally insured institution, committed wire fraud, attempted extortion, and made false statements in a bankruptcy proceeding. Symington, 50, was in his second term as governor. In an earlier time, the former Arizona governor, Evan Meacham, was indicted on charges that he hid campaign loans. Subsequently, he was acquitted of all charges against him in a U.S. district court. He was later impeached on grounds unrelated to his office as governor. Had Symington been convicted, should he have been granted leniency by the sentencing judge because he had been a governor? (*Source:* Adapted from Associated Press, "Arizona Governor Indicted," June 14, 1996.)

• *The Case of Highway Mayhem.* It is happening all across the United States. One driver cuts off another, and the other driver pulls out a gun and shoots at the first driver. A driver is driving too slowly for those behind him, so others pull out their weapons and fire away at the slow driver. A driver bumps another driver. The result is the deaths of both drivers in a heated shooting exchange. Sounds like the Old West, doesn't it? Yet such occurrences on state and local highways are common. In September 1997, a man went on trial in Hastings, Minnesota, for participating in killing a Two Harbors teenager. On August 26, 1996, 17-year-old Paul Antonich was driving down a Duluth highway when he accidentally bumped a car ahead of him at a stop light. The car contained five intoxicated persons who had been drinking all day at a local bar. They got out of their car and proceeded to beat up Antonich. Next, they forced Antonich into their car, and one or two of the others drove Antonich's car about 30 miles away to a remote location. There, they shot Antonich four times, stuffed his body into the trunk of his own car, and drove the car into a water-filled ditch. Eyewitnesses led police to arrest five persons and eventually to the discovery of Antonich's car and body. All five were charged with first-degree murder, kidnapping, and aiding and abetting first-degree murder in the incident. The first two persons to go on trial for Antonich's murder were 22-year-old Andy DeVerney and 27-year-old Lester Greenleaf, both from Duluth. Others charged in the incident—John Steven Martin, John Alexander "Mike" Martin, and Jamie Lee Aubid, the alleged triggerman—were to be tried later. What type of sentence should be imposed if you were the judge in this case? (*Source:* Adapted from Associated Press, "Jury Hears Opening Arguments in Fender Bender Killings," September 3, 1997.)

• *Jose Luis Vargas.* Jose Luis Vargas, 26, and his wife, Francine Red Bear, were drinking. They got into an argument and fight, and Vargas bit off a portion of Red Bear's nose. He grabbed her face and bit off her nose because he was angry that she had left their child home alone while she went out drinking. Doctors were able to reattach the tip of Red Bear's nose, although it did not heal properly. Plastic surgeons then grafted skin from her forehead and attempt to reconstruct her nose. Later in court, the judge sentenced Vargas to six years in prison for an aggravated assault conviction stemming from the incident. Red Bear asked the judge for leniency for her husband, despite the damage to her nose. Her pleas were ignored. The judge noted that this biting incident was not the first one involving Vargas. Some years before, he had bit Red Bear on the cheek, causing permanent disfigurement. Is six years an adequate sentence for someone who bites off someone else's nose? What sort of punishment would you impose? (*Source:* Adapted from Associated Press, "South Dakota Man Gets 6 Years for Biting Off Tip of Wife's Nose," February 3, 1994.)

• *Barbara Briggs, 42-Year-Old Grandmother and Convicted Murderer.* It happened in Rochester, New York. Keith Sims, 3, and weighing only 28 pounds, was climbing up to a cupboard looking for a sandwich. Suddenly, his grandmother assaulted him with a cutting board, beating him about the head numerous times and killing him. It wasn't the first time she had unleashed violence against the toddler. Previously, she had burned him with cigarettes, beat him with belts and electrical cords, and administered other whippings for trivial misbehaviors. Often the beatings were administered because Keith had taken food without permission. The lethal beating of her grandson earned Barbara Briggs a 25-year sentence. Judge John Connell, said, "If grandmas mean something, they mean cuddles and fairy tales. And for Keith, it was a tale of terror." Briggs claimed to have loved her grandson. "I tried my best," she said, "but I was a failure. I'm sorry, I can ask for mercy but I know that I must answer to God." The boy had moved in with his grandmother because his own mother was ill. Is the 25-year sentence sufficiently severe, given the heinous murder of the toddler? What would you impose if you were the judge? (*Source:* Adapted from Associated Press, "Woman Beats Grandson to Death," May 2, 1998.)

INTRODUCTION

Each of the scenarios just presented involves a different type of crime and great variations in punishment. In each case, one or more crimes have been committed, and offenders have been convicted or are likely to be convicted. Decisions by judges about the types of sentences to be imposed are not always clear-cut. Every trial is different from the next. Sentencing offenders is not as easy as it appears at first glance. This chapter is about the sentencing process. Sentencing is a major concern of those who advocate justice reforms. The federal government and most states have passed new sentencing legislation in response to criticisms that current sentencing practices are discriminatory according to gender, race or ethnic background, and/or socioeconomic status. Four different types of sentencing schemes are described, including indeterminate, determinate, presumptive or guidelines-based, and mandatory sentencing. Several important sentencing issues are examined.

In most major felony cases and in some minor misdemeanor cases, judges ask probation officers to prepare reports about convicted offenders who are about to be sentenced. These reports, called presentence investigation, or PSI, reports and their functions, contents, and preparation are described. Probation officers have many duties and responsibilities, including a duty to the court to conduct investigations into the backgrounds of convicted offenders and determine relevant information about them. This information is eventually delivered to judges in a report that becomes useful in determining the most appropriate sentence. Besides the probation officer's observations, factual information is acquired about an offender's family, educational background, and family relations. If there are persons who have been victimized by the offender, then PSIs will sometimes contain victim impact statements to set forth the nature of injuries or damage sustained. These statements are helpful to judges as they consider if there are any circumstances that might warrant harsher penalties. Sometimes PSI reports are privately prepared. In addition, they may contain statements from offenders about their version of events. All this material is described and explained.

The next section of the chapter describes the sentencing hearing. An important part of the sentencing hearing is the opportunity for judges to weigh any aggravating or mitigating circumstances that might heighten or lessen the severity of one's sentence. Both sides speak out on behalf of or against the convicted offender in an effort to persuade the judge to be lenient or severe in the sentence imposed. Both state and federal jurisdictions have identified specific factors that are considered either aggravating or mitigating. These factors are statutory and must be considered by the sentencing authority. Several of these factors are listed and described. Whenever PSI reports are prepared for the court, it is the probation officer's responsibility to identify both aggravating and mitigating circumstances for judges and include them in their PSI reports. The chapter concludes with a discussion of the changing responsibilities of probation officers resulting from various sentencing reforms.

THE SENTENCING PROCESS: TYPES OF SENTENCING SYSTEMS AND SENTENCING ISSUES

Functions of Sentencing

The **Sentencing Reform Act of 1984** restated a number of sentencing objectives that have guided sentencing judges in their leniency or harshness toward convicted defendants. Some of these objectives have been made explicit by various states and local jurisdictions in past years, whereas others have been implicitly incorporated into prevailing sentencing guidelines (Kane, 1995). Some of the more important functions of sentencing are (1) to promote respect for the law, (2) to reflect the seriousness of the offense, (3) to provide just punishment for the offense, (4) to deter the defendant from future criminal conduct, (5) to protect the public from convicted offenders, and (6) to provide the convicted defendant with education and vocational training or other rehabilitative relief. The purposes of sentencing include punishment or retribution, deterrence, custodial monitoring or incapacitation, and rehabilitation.

To Promote Respect for the Law.   When offenders are sentenced, judges send a message to the criminal community. If the sentence is too lenient, then the message is that offenses will not be punished harshly. Therefore, many offenders may engage in further criminal conduct believing that even if they are subsequently apprehended, they will not be punished severely. Most judges attempt to impose sentences that are fair or equitable. They may use legislated standards of punishment, such as fines and prescribed terms of incarceration, or they may impose less stringent sentences than the maximums prescribed by law. Their ultimate aim is to promote respect for the law. Their intended message is that if the law is violated, violators will be sanctioned. Ideally, this view promotes respect for the law and functions as a deterrent to would-be criminals (Maxwell, 2000).

To Reflect the Seriousness of the Offense.   One objective of sentencing is to match the sentence with the seriousness of the offense. More serious crimes deserve harsher punishments. Violent criminals are usually punished more severely than property offenders, because violent crimes often result in serious bodily injury or death. Property can be replaced, but life cannot. Thus, punishments should be proportional to the seriousness of the crime. Some observers believe, however, that regardless of the punishment, no sanction is a definite deterrent to future offending (Arthur, 2000). Nevertheless, most judges tend to impose sentences that reflect a crime's seriousness. Thus, the more serious the offense, the harsher the penalty (Johnson, 2000).

To Provide Just Punishment for the Offense.   In recent years, sentencing policies in most jurisdictions in the United States have shifted to the reflect the **justice model**, which is a legitimatization of the power of the state to administer sanctions (Curry, 1996). This model emphasizes punishment as a primary objective of sentencing, an abolition of parole, an abandonment of the rehabilitative ideal, and determinate sentencing (Erez and Laster, 2000).

To Deter the Defendant from Future Criminal Conduct.   Sentencing is not only designed as a punishment to fit the crime, but also to function as a deterrent to future criminal offending. At least two major actions have been designed to equate offense seriousness with harsher penalties. The most significant legislation has been the establishment of habitual offender or repeat offender laws, whereby those convicted of three or more felonies are sentenced to life imprisonment. California has a "three strikes and you're out" law whereby repeat offenders are sentenced to life-without-parole terms (Burt et al., 2000). This get-tough action was designed to deter violent recidivists, such as robbers and murderers. The reasoning is that if repeat violent offenders have not learned their lesson by the time they are convicted of their third violent offense, then they should be locked up permanently (Harris and Jesilow, 2000).

To Protect the Public from Convicted Offenders.   Incarcerating convicted offenders is the most direct way of protecting the public from them. If they are locked up, they cannot perpetrate crimes against citizens. Longer sentences generally mean longer periods that criminals cannot victimize others. Some persons believe that to insulate a vulnerable public from their criminal activities, all criminals should be locked up for some period of time (Aguirre and Baker, 2000; Benzvy-Miller and Roach, 2000).

To Provide the Convicted Defendant with Education and Vocational Training or Other Rehabilitative Relief.   Rehabilitation has always been a fundamental goal of sentencing. A prevailing belief is that some attempt should be made to reform criminals while they are incarcerated. Offenders should not merely be warehoused. Rather,

---

BOX 3.1   *Life Imprisonment with the Possibility of Parole*

Shawn Helmenstein, 23

You are from Montana. You come to Bismarck, North Dakota, and hold up a liquor store, shoot the clerk to death, and rob the store. Later you are apprehended by police and are prosecuted for murder and robbery. You are found guilty. In North Dakota in 2000, there was no death penalty, and so you are sentenced to life with the possibility of parole. This situation happened to Shawn Helmenstein, 23. Helmenstein was convicted in December 1999 in the killing of Robbie Rahrich, 25, at the House of Bottles liquor store in north Bismarck and robbing the store of $1,600. Helmenstein, from Missoula, Montana, was living in Bismarck at the time of the murder and robbery. He had worked for a time at another House of Bottles shop and knew Rahrich. The prosecutor said, "From all of the evidence I have listened to, I believe that this was an execution. You could have taken the money if that was your motive, absent of taking a life. You chose not to do that." The main issue during the five-day trial in December 1999 was whether Helmenstein was suffering from emotional distress because his mother was ill. "We believe that his will was overborne," according to Robert Martin, Helmenstein's attorney. Others felt otherwise. Alicia Kuntz, a friend of Rahrich's

who spoke during the sentencing hearing, called Helmenstein "cold-hearted." "You stole a son, a lover, a brother, a father, an uncle, a cousin, a nephew and a best friend, and nothing you do or say will ever fill the hole in our hearts." Helmenstein said in his own behalf, "There isn't a day that goes by that I don't think about what I did, and have remorse for what I've done. Every night when I go to sleep I think about what I've caused—the pain and agony—it's unbearable." Helmenstein sobbed as South Central District Judge Donald Jorgensen handed down the sentence on February 29, 2000. According to North Dakota law, Helmenstein must spend at least 50 years in prison. Under a formula that considers his life expectancy, age, and any time already served, he will be eligible for parole after serving 85 percent of his life sentence. Burleigh County State's Attorney Richard Riha estimated that according the sentence, Helmenstein will be eligible for release when he is in his seventies.

Should Helmenstein eventually be paroled for deliberately killing and robbing another person? Under the circumstances, is life with the possibility of parole reasonable? If you had been the judge, what type of sentence would you have imposed? What do you think?

Source: Adapted from Associated Press, "Helmenstein Gets Life Imprisonment with Possibility of Parole," March 2, 2000.

---

educational and vocational programs should be offered to help those who are interested in helping themselves. It is better to provide some services for those who will use these services productively than to withhold all rehabilitative services because of those who will never be rehabilitated (Glaeser and Sacerdote, 2000; Tonry, 1999a).

Types of Sentencing

During the last several decades, sentencing practices in most states have undergone transformation. Experts disagree about the number and types of sentencing systems currently used by the states (Tonry, 1999a). Furthermore, new sentencing schemes continue to be proposed in contrast to existing ones. Four types of sentencing schemes used in most jurisdictions are indeterminate sentencing, determinate sentencing, presumptive sentencing, and mandatory sentencing.

Indeterminate Sentencing.   The most frequently used sentencing for many years was **indeterminate sentencing**. Indeterminate sentencing occurs when the court sets either explicit (according to statute) or implicit upper and lower limits on the amount of time to be served by the offender and the actual release date from prison is determined by a parole board. The judge may sentence an offender to "one to ten years," or "not more than five years," and a parole board determines when the offender may be released within the limits of those time intervals (Tonry, 1999b). In the "one- to ten-year" scenario, an inmate may be released early by a parole board after serving at least one year of the sentence. The parole board may release the inmate after two or three years. Early release is often based on an inmate's institutional behavior. Good behavior is rewarded by early release, whereas bad conduct may result in an inmate having to serve the entire ten-year sentence. At the end of the ten-year sentence, however, the jurisdiction must release the inmate, because all the sentence will have been served.

Determinate Sentencing.   **Determinate sentencing** is a fixed term of incarceration that must be served in full, less any good time earned while in prison. **Good time** is the reduction in the amount of time incarcerated amounting to a certain number of days per month for each month served. If inmates obey the rules and stay out of trouble, they accumulate good time credit, which accelerates their release from incarceration. In states using determinate sentencing, parole boards have no discretion in determining an inmate's early release (Florida Department of Corrections, 1999). In 1999, 17 states used determinate sentencing, and 24 states used both indeterminate and determinate sentencing (Camp and Camp, 1999:61).

Three types of good time credit can be accumulated by inmates to influence their early release chances: (1) **statutory good time**, in which inmates acquire good time by serving time without problems or incidents; (2) **earned good time**, in which inmates acquire good time by good behavior, participation in education or self-improvement programs, and work programs; and (3) **meritorious good time**, in which good time credit is earned by exceptional act or service. Inmates may earn all three types of good time during their imprisonment. For example, Nebraska authorizes statutory good time of 7.5 days per month, up to one-half the maximum term reduction, and earned good time of 7.5 days per month served, for a total of 15 days per month per 30 days served. In North Dakota, five days of statutory good time are allowed per month, up to two additional days per month may be granted for extraordinary acts by inmates, and five days per month of earned good time (given for performance at work, at school, or in treatment programs) may be earned. All must comply to earn good time; all inmates are given the highest possible amount of good time to be earned upon entrance; and if they become noncompliant with programming, they receive an "incident report" (write-up), and the Adjustment Committee sanctions loss of good time.

Several variations on good time accumulation are as follows. New Hampshire adds 150 days to one's minimum sentence; these days are reduced by earning 12½ days per month for exemplary conduct, and failure to earn this good time means the inmate must serve additional time beyond the minimum sentence. In Ohio, one day of statutory good time per month up to a total sentence reduction of 3 percent may be accumulated, and one day per month of earned good time can be accumulated (Ching, 1997). The Federal Bureau of Prisons permits up to 54 days per year of statutory good time. Actually, 54 days a year is approximately 15 percent of one's sentence.

This figure fits the federal sentencing model in which offenders are expected to serve at least 85 percent of their sentences before becoming eligible for parole. The federal government has encouraged individual states to adopt **truth-in-sentencing provisions** whereby incarcerated offenders must serve most of their original sentences before being considered eligible for parole. Various states have adopted these truth-in-sentencing provisions in their sentencing schemes in exchange for federal grant monies for correctional improvements (Grimes and Rogers, 1999).

Presumptive Sentencing.   **Presumptive sentencing** or **guidelines-based sentencing** is a specific sentence, usually expressed as a range of months, for each and every offense or offense class. The sentence must be imposed in all unexceptional cases, but when there are mitigating or aggravating circumstances, judges are permitted some latitude in shortening or lengthening sentences within specific boundaries (Austin et al., 1995). An example of the sentencing grids used by states with guidelines-based or presumptive sentencing schemes is the **Minnesota sentencing grid** shown in Figure 3.1.

Presumptive sentencing has the following aims: (1) to establish penalties commensurate with harm caused by the criminal activity, (2) to produce a fairer system of justice, (3) to reduce the typical severity of penalties, (4) to incarcerate only the most serious offenders, (5) to reduce discretionary power of judges and parole authorities, (6) to allow special sentences for offenders when the circumstances are clearly exceptional, (7) to eliminate early-release procedures for inmates, and (8) to make participation in treatment or rehabilitative programs completely voluntary by inmates with no effect on their terms of incarceration (Marvell, 1995).

By 1999, 90 percent of the states had reformed their sentencing laws so that an offender's parole eligibility was either eliminated or made more difficult (Leadership Conference on Civil Rights, 2000). Accompanying these reforms were changes relating to modifying the amount of good time inmates can earn and how good time should be calculated. Therefore, although the certainty of incarceration has increased under determinate sentencing, the sentences served are often shorter than they might have been under indeterminate sentencing.

Mandatory Sentencing.   **Mandatory sentencing** is the imposition of an incarcerative sentence of a specified length, for certain crimes or certain categories of offenders, and when no option of probation, suspended sentence, or immediate parole eligibility exists (Tonry, 1999a). California, Hawaii, Illinois, Kentucky, and Michigan are a few of the many states that have enacted mandatory sentencing provisions for certain offenses. As previously stated, Michigan imposes a two-year additional sentence of **flat time** (in which offenders must serve the full two years without relief from parole) if they use a dangerous weapon during the commission of a felony. In Kentucky, those convicted of being habitual offenders are sentenced to life without parole in prison for violating Kentucky's habitual offender statute. Usually, mandatory sentences are prescribed for those who use dangerous weapons during the commission of a crime, for habitual offenders with three or more prior felony convictions, and for major drug dealers (Roche, 1999). Some critics, however, question whether any significant deterrent value obtains from such mandatory sentencing laws, because attorneys and judges find numerous ways to circumvent them to suit their own purposes (U.S. Bureau of Justice Assistance, 1998).

Presumptive Sentence Lengths in Months

Italicized numbers within the grid denote the range within which a judge may sentence without the sentence being deemed a departure.

Offenders with nonimprisonment felony sentences are subject to jail time according to law.

Severity Levels of Conviction Offense		Criminal History Score						
		0	1	2	3	4	5	6 or more
Sale of a Simulated Controlled Substance	I	12*	12*	12*	13	15	17	19 *18–20*
Theft-Related Crimes ($2500 or less) *Check Forgery ($200– $2500)*	II	12*	12*	13	15	17	19	21 *20–22*
Theft Crimes ($2500 or less)	III	12*	13	15	17	19 *18–20*	22 *21–23*	25 *24–26*
Nonresidential Burglary Theft Crimes (over $2500)	IV	12*	15	18	21	25 *24–26*	32 *30–34*	41 *37–45*
Residential Burglary Simple Robbery	V	18	23	27	30 *29–31*	38 *36–40*	46 *43–49*	54 *50–58*
Criminal Sexual Conduct 2nd Degree (a) & (b)	VI	21	26	30	34 *33–35*	44 *42–46*	54 *50–58*	65 *60–70*
Aggravated Robbery	VII	48 *44–52*	58 *54–62*	68 *64–72*	78 *74–82*	88 *84–92*	98 *94–102*	108 *104–112*
Criminal Sexual Conduct, 1st Degree *Assault, 1st Degree*	VIII	86 *81–91*	98 *93–103*	110 *105–115*	122 *117–127*	134 *129–139*	146 *141–151*	158 *153–163*
Murder, 3rd Degree *Murder, 2nd Degree (felony murder)*	IX	150 *144–156*	165 *159–171*	180 *174–186*	195 *189–201*	210 *204–216*	225 *219–231*	240 *234–246*
Murder, 2nd Degree (with intent)	X	306 *299–313*	326 *319–333*	346 *339–353*	366 *359–373*	386 *379–393*	406 *399–413*	426 *419–433*

First-degree murder is excluded from the guidelines by law and continues to have a mandatory life sentence. At the discretion of the judge, up to a year in jail and/or other nonjail sanctions can be imposed as conditions of probation.

FIGURE 3.1 Minnesota sentencing grid.

Sentencing Issues

This section briefly examines some major sentencing issues that continue to plague most jurisdictions. Issues are usually questions that need to be addressed and are not, as yet, resolved. Issues also involve factors that must be considered when sentencing offenders. Although a discussion of all sentencing issues that might be included is beyond the scope of this book, several important issues have been selected here: whether convicted offenders should be placed on probation or incarcerated, jail and prison overcrowding, the ineffectiveness of rehabilitation, and offender needs and public safety.

Probation or Incarceration?   An often difficult judicial decision is, Should offenders be placed on probation or in jail or prison? Probation officers might recommend probation to judges when filing a PSI report for some convicted offender, although the court may disregard this recommendation. The just-deserts philosophy is a dominant theme in U.S. corrections today, and judges appear to be influenced by this philosophy as reflected in the sentences they impose. Generally, their interest is imposing sentences on offenders that are equated with the seriousness of the conviction offense (Shane-Dubow et al., 1998).

Jail and Prison Overcrowding.   Jail and prison overcrowding conditions influence judicial discretion in sentencing offenders (Shapiro, 1997). Judges have many sentencing options, including incarceration or a nonjail or nonprison penalty such as fines, probation, community service, restitution to victims, halfway houses, treatment, or some combination of these options. Precisely because of this broad range of discretionary options associated with the judicial role as well as the independence of other actors in the criminal justice system has jail and prison overcrowding become the most pressing problem facing the criminal justice system today.

There have been drastic changes in the sentencing policies of most states and the federal government (Grimes and Rogers, 1999). As increasing numbers of jurisdictions adopt tougher sentencing policies and implement sentencing schemes that will keep offenders behind bars for longer periods, current jail and prison overcrowding conditions are only exacerbated by these policies. In many instances, judges have no choice but to impose incarceration for specified durations on convicted offenders; they are obligated to impose mandatory terms for offenders convicted of particular offenses. Often, they have little latitude to depart from whatever sentences are required under the law. When the U.S. sentencing guidelines were implemented in 1987, for instance, the discretion of federal court judges to impose probation as an alternative to incarceration was drastically curtailed (Conaboy, 1997). Before the guidelines, the use of probation applied to over 60 percent of all convicted federal offenders. After the guidelines, less than 15 percent of all convicted federal offenders are granted probation at the discretion of federal judges. This change automatically means greater use of existing federal prison space by larger numbers of convicted offenders sentenced to incarcerative terms. An emerging dilemma is that proportionately larger numbers of nonviolent offenders are being incarcerated when it is quite likely that they would do well in community programs instead (Irwin, Schiraldi, and Ziedenberg, 1999).

The Ineffectiveness of Rehabilitation.   The failure of incarceration or various nonincarcerative alternatives to rehabilitate large numbers of offenders for long periods may not necessarily be the fault of those particular programs but rather the nature of clients served by those programs. It is generally acknowledged that jail and prison do not rehabilitate (Irwin, Schiraldi, and Ziedenberg, 1999). Although most prisons and some jails have one or more programs designed to assist inmates to develop new vocational skills and to counsel them, the effectiveness of these programs is questionable. Understaffing is a chronic problem often attributable to the lack of funding for such programs. Also, the equipment used in prison technical education programs is often outdated. If inmates earn an educational certificate, then it often bears the name of the prison facility where the degree or accomplishment was acknowledged. Thus, employers are deterred from hiring such persons with prison records. Further, many of these institutions are principally concerned with the custody and control of their inmate populations, and rehabilitation is a remote consideration for them.

One important reason that rehabilitation is less effective in prisons and jails is that they are chronically overcrowded. In some instances, the overcrowding level in certain prisons approaches the cruel and unusual punishment level, and court intervention is required (Welsh, 1995). Thus, there may be an extensive array of vocational and educational programs within different prison settings, but overcrowding means that not all inmates can take advantage of these services. Further, the effectiveness of services delivery is adversely affected because too many inmates in classes interfere with learning potential and teacher performance (Call and Cole, 1996; Virginia Joint Legislative Audit and Review Commission, 1996).

Offender Needs and Public Safety. As the courts move voluntarily or involuntarily toward the greater use of **felony probation**, judicial concern is increasingly focused on determining which offenders should be incarcerated and which should not be imprisoned. Therefore, in recent years several investigators have attempted to devise prediction schemes that would permit judges and other officials to predict a convicted defendant's dangerousness. Obviously, this concern is directed toward the preservation of public safety and minimizing public risks possibly arising from placing violent and dangerous offenders on probation rather than imprisoning them (Irwin, Schiraldi, and Ziedenberg, 1999).

Most states have laws permitting officials to detain criminal defendants on the basis of the defendant's perceived dangerousness. The legal test used is called the dangerous-tendency test, which is the propensity of a person to inflict injury (Black, 1990:394; *Frazier v. Stone*, 1974). Dangerousness is interpreted differently depending on the particular jurisdiction. In 21 states, for example, dangerousness is defined as a history of prior criminal involvement (Champion, 1994). This history may include a prior conviction, probation or parole status at the time of arrest, or a pending charge when the defendant is arrested. In 7 states, the type of crime with which the offender is charged defines dangerousness (e.g., a violent crime such as aggravated assault, robbery, homicide). And in 22 states, judicial discretion determines dangerousness. Many offenders, however, even those convicted of numerous offenses, are nonviolent and not dangerous. Some persons believe that these types of offenders are overincarcerated when they can function normally within their own communities under close supervision as an alternative in confinement in a jail or prison (Vitiello, 1997).

THE ROLE OF PROBATION OFFICERS IN SENTENCING

Probation officers are closely connected with the sentencing process, regardless of the type of sentencing scheme used by any particular jurisdiction. Different aspects of their roles relative to sentencing are listed and described below.

1. POs prepare presentence investigation reports at the request of judges. Probation officers play a fundamental role in sentencing. At the request of judges, probation officers prepare PSI reports for various convicted offenders. Although a more comprehensive definition is provided in the following section, it is sufficient for now to know that PSI reports are extensive compilations of situational and personal details about offenders, their crimes, crime victims, and any other relevant information yielded during the investigative process (Kingsnorth et al., 1999).

2. POs classify and categorize offenders. Before sentences are imposed or sentence lengths are contemplated, probation officers do some preliminary categorizing of their offender-clients. Different classification schemes are used depending on the jurisdiction (Bridges and Steen, 1998).

3. POs recommend sentences for convicted offenders. Besides preparing PSI reports, POs also make recommendations to judges about the sentences that they believe are warranted under the circumstances associated with given offenses. In several states, POs are guided by presumptive sentencing guidelines or guidelines-based sentencing schemes. Using a numerical system, they can weigh various factors and generate a score. Usually associated with this score are various incarcerative lengths, expressed in either years or months. The power of PO sentence recommendations should not be underestimated. Many POs look either for information in their investigations of offenders that confirms or justifies their sentence recommendations or for information that might lead to a modification or rejection of their recommendations. Their own work dispositions determine which investigative mode they tend to follow (Kingsnorth et al., 1999).

4. Probation officers work closely with courts to determine the best supervisory arrangement for probationer-clients. When offenders are sentenced to probation, POs may or may not supervise them closely. Usually, the greater the likelihood that an offender will recidivate, the more supervision will be directed toward that offender (Mears, 1998).

5. Probation officers are a resource for information about any extralegal factors that might either positively or adversely affect the sentencing decision. Thus, judges may rely heavily on probation officer reports about whether certain offenders are socially situated so that they can comply with different probation conditions. If judges want to impose restitution in particular cases, will offenders be able to repay the victims for damages inflicted? The PO has a fairly good sense of whether certain offenders will be able to comply with this and other probation conditions (Bowker, 1998).

PRESENTENCE INVESTIGATION (PSI) REPORTS: INTERSTATE VARIATIONS

Whether a conviction is obtained through plea bargaining or a trial, a **presentence investigation (PSI)** is often conducted on instructions from the court. The result is a **presentence investigation report**. This investigation is sometimes waived in the case of negotiated guilty pleas, because an agreement has been reached between all parties concerning the case disposition and nature of sentence to be imposed (Buddress, 1997).

When requested by federal district judges, PSI reports are usually prepared within a 60-day period from the time judges make their requests. Although there is no standard PSI format among states, most PSI reports contain similar information. A PSI report is a document usually prepared by a probation agency or officer that provides background information on the convicted offender, including name, age, present address, occupation (if any), potential for employment, the crime(s) involved, relevant circumstances associated with the crime, family data, evidence of prior record (if any), and marital status. It has been estimated that there are over one million PSI reports prepared by probation officers annually in the United States (Pastore and Maguire, 2001).

PSI reports are written summaries of information obtained by the probation officer through interviews with the defendant and an investigation of the defendant's background. An alternative definition is that PSI reports are narrative summaries of an offender's criminal and noncriminal history used to aid a judge in determining the most appropriate decision as to the offender's sentence for a crime. These documents are often partially structured in that they require probation officers to fill in standard information about defendants. PSIs also contain summaries or accounts in narrative form highlighting certain information about defendants and containing sentencing recommendations from probation officers. In some instances, space is available for the defendant's personal account of the crime and why it was committed (Albonetti, 1999; Norman and Wadman, 2000).

In most felony convictions in local, state, and federal trial courts, a presentence investigation whose purpose is to assist the judge in determining the most appropriate punishment or sentence for the convicted defendant is conducted. This investigation is usually made by a probation officer attached to the court and consists of a check of all relevant background information about a convicted defendant. Similar investigations are conducted for all juvenile offenders as well (Administrative Office of U.S. Courts, 1997; Bridges and Steen, 1998).

A presentence report is prepared from the facts revealed from the investigation. This report varies considerably in focus and scope from jurisdiction to jurisdiction, but it should contain at least the following items:

1. Complete description of the situation surrounding the criminal activity
2. Offender's educational background
3. Offender's employment history
4. Offender's social history
5. Offender's residence history
6. Offender's medical history
7. Information about the environment to which the offender will return
8. Information about any resources available to assist the offender

9. Probation officer's view of the offenders' motivations and ambitions
10. Full description of the defendant's criminal record
11. Recommendation from the probation officer as to the sentence disposition (Black, 1990:1184)

An informal component of many PSI reports is the **narrative** prepared by the probation officer. In many instances, judges are persuaded to deal more leniently or harshly with offenders, depending on how these narratives have been prepared. Probation officers exercise considerable discretion to influence the favorableness or unfavorableness of these reports for offenders. One important factor is the probation officer's judgment of the degree of public risk posed by the offender if placed on probation. Thus, probation officers must attempt to predict an offender's future behavior. This task is one of the most difficult ones associated with probation work. Assessments of offender risk to the public are given later in this chapter. A sample PSI report is illustrated in this chapter's appendix.

The PSI report is an informational document prepared by a probation officer that contains the personal data about convicted offenders, data about the conviction offense(s), and other relevant data:

1. Name
2. Address
3. Prior record including offenses and dates
4. Date and place of birth
5. Crime(s) or conviction offense and date of offense
6. Offender's version of conviction offense
7. Offender's employment history
8. Offender's known addiction to or dependency on drugs or alcohol or controlled substances of any kind
9. Statutory penalties for the conviction offense
10. Marital status
11. Personal and family data
12. Name of spouse and children, if any
13. Educational history
14. Any special vocational training or specialized work experience
15. Mental and/or emotional stability
16. Military service, if any, and disposition
17. Financial condition including assets and liabilities
18. Probation officer's personal evaluation of offender
19. Sentencing data
20. Alternative plans made by defendant if placed on probation
21. Physical description
22. Prosecution version of conviction offense
23. Victim impact statement prepared by victim, if any
24. Codefendant information, if codefendant is involved
25. Recommendation from probation officer about sentencing
26. Name of prosecutor
27. Name of defense attorney

28. Presiding judge
29. Jurisdiction where offense occurred
30. Case docket number and other identifying numbers (e.g., Social Security, driver's license)
31. Plea
32. Disposition or sentence
33. Location of probation or custody

The Administrative Office of the U.S. Courts uses standardized PSI reports that include five core categories to be addressed in the body of the report: (1) the offense, including the prosecution version, the defendant's version, statements of witnesses, codefendant information, and a victim impact statement; (2) prior record, including juvenile adjudications and adult offenses; (3) personal and family data, including parents and siblings, marital status, education, health, physical and mental condition, and financial assets and liabilities; (4) evaluation, including the probation officer's assessment, parole guideline data, sentencing data, and any special sentencing provisions; and (5) recommendation, including the rationale for the recommendation and voluntary surrender or whether the offender should be transported to the correctional institution on his own or should be transported by U.S. marshals. Under existing federal sentencing guidelines implemented in November 1987, PSIs have not been eliminated. Rather, they now include material besides that listed above regarding an offender's **acceptance of responsibility** for the crime. Judges select sentences for offenders from a sentencing table and may lessen or enhance the severity of their sentences based on probation officer recommendations, offender acknowledgment of wrongdoing or acceptance of responsibility, or other criteria.

Judges frequently treat the PSI in a way similar to how they treat plea-bargain agreements. They may concur with probation officer sentencing recommendations, or they may ignore the recommendations made in these reports. Because most convictions occur through plea bargaining, however, the only connection a judge usually has with the defendant before sentencing is through the PSI report. In federal district courts, judges may decide not to order PSI reports if they think that there is sufficient information about the convicted offender to "enable the meaningful exercise of sentencing discretion, and the court explains this finding on the record" (18 U.S.C., Rule 32[c][1], 2001). If the defendant wishes, the PSI and report may be waived, with court permission.

The Confidentiality of PSI Reports

The general public is usually excluded from seeing the contents of PSI reports. It is imperative that confidentiality be maintained. Often these reports contain the results of tests or examinations, psychiatric or otherwise. Probation officers contact one's former employers and work associates and include a summary of interview information as a part of the narrative. Ordinarily, only those court officials and others working closely on a particular case have a right to examine the contents of a PSI report. All types of information are included in these documents. Convicted offenders are entitled to some degree of privacy relative to a PSI report's contents.

The federal government requires the disclosure of the contents of PSI reports to convicted offenders, their attorneys, and attorneys for the government at least ten

BOX 3.2   *Personality Highlight*

Belinda A. Ballesteros
Federal Probation Officer, U.S. Southern District of Texas, Laredo Division, Presentence Investigation Unit

Statistics. A.A. (applied science in law enforcement), Laredo Community College; B.A. (behavioral sciences and criminal justice), Texas A&M International University

Work History and Experience. I was born and raised in Laredo, Texas, a border town in the southwest region of Texas. My interest in the legal field stemmed from my father, who was employed as a detention officer at the county jail. Although my father was opposed to my field of study due to the dangers he encountered on a daily basis, he still encouraged me to obtain an education. I attended a local community college and graduated in 1990 with an A.A. in law enforcement, and in 1992, I completed my B.A. in criminal justice. I am presently pursuing my M.A. in sociology with a minor in criminal justice and plan to complete my studies by the summer of 2001.

While attending college, I looked for a job in the legal field because I was interested in this area. Unsure as to what I actually wanted to do, I thought that the best way to find out was to come into contact with people already in this line of work. In 1989, I worked for the Laredo Police Department as a records clerk. This job allowed me to interact with law enforcement personnel such as police officers, probation officers, and parole officers on a daily basis, and it helped me to familiarize myself with legal terminology. I also did criminal records checks and read many offense reports. In 1990, I worked as an intake clerk for the Laredo Legal Aid Society, Inc. (LLASI). This agency helped the indigent population obtain free legal advice and representation. Ultimately, I was promoted to pro bono coordinator for the Webb County Volunteer Lawyers Project, which was a part of LLASI. Both jobs allowed me to interact with attorneys who assisted people in civil matters, such as housing, divorce with domestic violence issues, disability benefits, wills and testaments, bankruptcy, landlord/tenant issues, and juvenile expulsions. Through this employment, I learned a lot about poverty law and the problems people encounter. I truly enjoyed helping people and finding attorneys who would help others in need.

In my last year of college, I participated in an internship program with the local adult probation office. This internship was very instrumental in making my career choice. I learned about the job responsibilities that revolved around probation work and got firsthand knowledge about how the criminal justice system works. I met with probationers and attended court proceedings. Because I enjoyed helping people and enforcing the law, and knowing I wanted to work in the legal field, becoming a probation officer seemed like the career that would allow me to incorporate all these things. I believed in rehabilitation and that people should get a second chance. I knew, however, that apart from my education, I had to work towards getting the experience necessary to even be considered for such a job.

In 1993, I started on this journey by becoming a programs coordinator for the Webb County, Texas, Juvenile Department. In this capacity, I coordinated various programs for the detention and probation populations. Some programs involved the development of community service worksites, volunteer programs, summer recreational programs, and all other educational programs that focused on crime and drug prevention. I continued working with at-risk youth and their families while I waited for an opening as a probation officer. In 1995, due to additional funding from the Texas Juvenile Commission and the implementation of the Progressive Sanctions Guidelines, there were several openings for juvenile probation officers and I was hired. I had the opportunity to work every unit in the department—intake, deferred adjudication, court, probation, and the intensive supervision program unit—in a span of five years.

Being a juvenile probation officer is very demanding and stressful. It takes special people to work with troubled juveniles. Juvenile probationers are not just youth who violate the law. Some juveniles are mentally ill, emotionally disturbed, drug abusers, sexual offenders, victims of sexual abuse, runaways, or truants or have a combination of these characteristics. As an officer, you deal with very difficult problems and must make crucial decisions that affect a child's life and that of their families. Whether to detain, release, refer, or place a child in a secure facility is just one decision an officer must make, thereby creating an insurmountable amount of pressure on the officer to examine each case closely and with care. You have the power to make a difference and set a child on the right path.

Regardless of all the work and stress endured as a probation officer, it is a very rewarding job. There is nothing like helping a child and turning his or her life around. It is rewarding to receive a telephone call years later from a former probationer telling you that he or she has graduated from high school, is gainfully employed, or has stopped using drugs. In one instance, I encountered a parent who informed me that her son had graduated from high school and was serving as a U.S. Marine. She recalled the endless telephone calls, home visits, school visits, meetings, and detention hearings, and believe me, I did, too. It reminded me of the reasons I pursued a career in this field.

I had reached a point in my career at which I wanted new challenges and experiences and therefore decided to pursue other interests. I am now a federal probation officer in the Southern District of Texas in the Presentence Investigation Unit. My job entails interviewing defendants and preparing reports for the court. These reports consist of gathering data in reference to the defendant's personal, criminal, and financial history as well as the details of the offense and a sentencing recommendation based on the findings of the investigation that was conducted. I am very happy that I decided to make a change. My job poses different challenges and involves a great deal of investigation work, which I enjoy. It has been everything that I had expected and much more. No matter how insignificant you think your job may be, be the best at it. All my job experiences and my education have served me well in this capacity and I was thus able to reach the highest level in my professional career.

Advice to Students. Know what your interests are before making a career decision, never stop learning, always work hard, make a difference, and if you can dream it, you can do it!

days prior to actual sentencing (18 U.S.C., Sec. 3552(d), 2001). At state and local levels, this practice varies, and the PSI report may or may not be disclosed to the offender. Under 18 U.S.C., Fed. R. Cr. Proc. 32(c)(3)(B) (2001), some information in the PSI report may be withheld from the defendant. The report may contain confidential information such as a psychiatric evaluation or a sentencing recommendation. The presiding judge determines those portions of the PSI report to be disclosed to offenders and their counsels. Anything disclosed to defendants must also be made available to the prosecutors. Some federal courts have interpreted these provisions to mean that convicted offenders should have greatly restricted access to these PSI reports. Indeed, many federal prisoners have filed petitions under the **Freedom of Information Act (FOIA)** to read their own PSI reports in some judicial districts (Shockley, 1988). Among other things, this act makes it possible for private citizens to examine certain public documents containing information about them, including IRS information or information compiled by any other government agency, criminal or otherwise. This procedure is a drastic way of gaining access to a document that may or may not contain erroneous information about the offender, the circumstances of the offense, and other relevant information. Some persons believe that the postsentence disclosure of PSI reports to prisoners ought to be routine rather than a right to be enjoyed only after exhausting the provisions of the FOIA.

At least one state, California, permits an examination by the public of any PSI report filed by any state probation office for up to ten days following its filing with the court. Under exceptional circumstances, however, even California courts may bar certain information from public scrutiny if a proper argument can be made for its exclusion. Usually, a good argument is potential danger to one or more persons who have made statements or declarations in the report. Further, some witnesses or information-givers do so only under the condition that they will remain anonymous, and this anonymity guarantee must be protected by the court. As previously indicated, however, most jurisdictions maintain a high level of confidentiality regarding PSI documents and their contents.

The Preparation of PSI Reports

Most PSI reports are prepared by probation officers at the direction of criminal court judges. Todd Clear, Val Clear, and William Burrell (1989:173–175) note that there are three legal approaches to PSI report preparation. In at least 23 states, PSI report preparation is mandatory for all felony offense convictions (Clear, Clear, and Burrell, 1989:175). They note that other factors—such as when incarceration of a year or longer is a possible sentence, when the offender is under 21 or 18 years of age, and when the defendant is a first-offender—may initiate PSI report preparation in these jurisdictions. In 9 states, statutes provide for mandatory PSI report preparation in any felony case where probation is a possible consideration. When probation is not a consideration, the PSI report preparation is optional or discretionary with particular judges (North Carolina Administrative Office of the Courts, 1988). Finally, in 17 states, a PSI report is totally discretionary with the presiding judge. Clear, Clear, and Burrell give an example of various state policies about the preparation of PSI reports:

New Jersey
PSI report = required in all felony cases; suggested in misdemeanor cases involving one or more years incarceration

Connecticut
PSI report = mandatory for any case in which incarceration is one or more years

Pennsylvania
PSI report = mandatory for any case in which incarceration is one or more years

District of Columbia
PSI report = required unless offenders waive their right to one with court permission

California
PSI report = mandatory for all felony convictions; discretionary for misdemeanor cases

Arizona
PSI report = mandatory for case in which incarceration is a year or more; may be ordered in other cases

Texas
PSI report = totally discretionary with the judge (Administrative Office of U.S. Courts, 1997)

How Long Does It Take to Prepare a PSI Report?   There is no standard length of time that can be given for PSI report completion. Interstate variations are such that some PSI reports are quite short and can be completed in a few hours, whereas others are very long and take several days to complete. A large proportion of a PO's time is consumed with PSI report preparation (Norman and Wadman, 2000). The investigative time it takes for POs to verify an offender's prior employment, compile educational records, conduct interviews with family members, obtain victim and witness information, analyze court records, review police reports of the arrest and crime details, and gather other types of necessary and relevant information is only the preliminary step in the process of PSI report preparation. Officers must still sit down and prepare these reports. Most probation agencies do not have adequate secretarial staff to whom such information can be dictated and subsequently transcribed and converted into a written report, and today POs must often write their own reports. Thus, knowing how to type and to use a word processor and computer are essential PO skills. Without such training, persons wanting to become POs will be at a considerable disadvantage and will be unable to perform their jobs properly (U.S. General Accounting Office, 1998).

Functions and Uses of PSI Reports

Although no standard format exists among the states for PSI reports, many PSI reports are patterned after those used by the Administrative Office of the U.S. Courts shown in the appendix of this chapter. The PSI report was adopted formally by the Administrative Office of the U.S. Courts in 1943. Since then, the format has been revised several times. The 1984 version reflects changes in correctional law that have occurred in recent decades. Prior to 1943, informal reports about offenders were often prepared for judges by court personnel. Probably the earliest informal PSI report was prepared in 1841 by **John Augustus**, the founder of probation in the

United States (Administrative Office of U.S. Courts, 1997; American Correctional Association, 1996a; Conrad, 1987).

Although the U.S. Probation Office represents federal interests and not necessarily those of individual states, their PSI report functions have much in common with the general functions of PSI reports among the states. The PSI report for the U.S. District Courts and the U.S. Probation Office serves at least five important functions:

1. To aid the court in determining the appropriate sentence for offenders
2. To aid probation officers in their supervisory efforts during probation or parole
3. To assist the Federal Bureau of Prisons and any state prison facility in the classification, institutional programming, and release planning for inmates
4. To furnish the U.S. Parole Commission and other parole agencies with information about the offender pertinent to a parole decision
5. To serve as a source of information for research (Administrative Office of U.S. Courts, 1997)

Providing information for offender sentencing is the primary function of a PSI report because judges want to be fair and impose sentences fitting the crime. If mitigating or aggravating circumstances should be considered, then these factors appear in the report submitted to the judge. Aiding POs in their supervisory efforts is an important report objective because proper rehabilitative programs can be individualized for different offenders. The report suggests if vocational training or medical help is needed. If the offender has a history of mental illness, psychological counseling or medical treatment may be appropriate and recommended. Such information is also helpful to ancillary personnel who work in community-based probation programs and supervise offenders with special problems such as drug or alcohol dependencies. PSI reports assist prisons and other detention facilities in their efforts to classify inmates appropriately. Inmates with special problems or who are handicapped physically or mentally may be diverted to special prison facilities or housing where their needs can be addressed by professionals. Inmates with diseases or viruses such as AIDS can be isolated from others for health purposes.

The fourth function of federal PSI reports is crucial in influencing an inmate's parole chances. In jurisdictions in which parole boards determine an inmate's early-release potential, PSI reports are often consulted as background data. Decisions about early release are often contingent on the recommendation of the probation officer contained in the report. Finally, criminologists and others are interested in studying those sentenced to various terms of incarceration or probation. Background characteristics, socioeconomic information, and other relevant data assist researchers in developing explanations for criminal conduct. Also, research efforts of criminologists and those interested in criminal justice may be helpful in affecting the future design of prisons or jails. Special needs areas can be identified and programs to assist offenders with their various problems can be devised. Because most inmates will eventually be paroled, research through an examination of PSI reports may help corrections professionals devise more effective adaptation and reintegration mechanisms, permitting inmates to make a smoother transition back into their respective communities.

A General Summary of PSI Report Functions among the States. One function of the PSI report is to provide the sentencing judge with an adequate analysis of the offender's background and prospects for rehabilitation. Ideally, this review enables judges to be fairer in the sentencing process. A reasonably complete PSI report assists judges in dispensing more equitable sentences consistent with the justice model. Logically, with more factual and background information about offenses and offenders, judges can make more informed sentencing decisions, and sentencing disparities can be minimized among offenders convicted of similar offenses (Norman and Wadman, 2000; Walsh, 1997).

If offenders are placed on probation, then the PSI report permits probation officers to determine offender needs more clearly and to be more helpful in assisting offenders in locating jobs or completing applications for vocational/educational training. Thus, a second function of PSI reports is to assist probation officers in their officer/client planning. Such planning may involve community service, restitution to crime victims, assignment to community-based corrections agencies, house arrest or electronic monitoring, or some other nonincarcerative alternative.

Probation officers are expected to assess the offender's dangerousness and public risk. This assessment is a vital part of the narrative and the recommendation prepared by these officers. Probation officers have considerable influence in the sentencing disposition of offenders (Norman and Wadman, 2000). Thus, a third function of PSI reports is to classify and categorize offenders into various risk categories. These risk assessments frequently determine the level of custody or supervision imposed by judges in sentencing. Offenders considered extremely dangerous to the public are seldom granted probation. Rather, they are committed to medium- and maximum-security prisons or other facilities and for longer periods of incarceration than other offenders. Their offenses and prior records are also primary determinants of length and severity of the sentence imposed.

For incarcerated offenders, a PSI report is of value to parole boards in determining one's early release and the conditions accompanying the granting of parole, which underscores both the short- and long-term relevance and importance of PSI reports for influencing an offender's chances at securing freedom from the criminal justice system. Offenders may be prison inmates for many years. When they appear before parole boards 15, 20, or even 30 years after they have been incarcerated for their crimes, the parole boards refer to the PSI reports originally prepared at the time of their sentencing. These "ancient" documents contain important information about the offender's earlier circumstances. Even though much of this material is badly dated, parole boards consider it in their early-release decision making.

A fourth function of PSI reports is to permit probation officers or other supervisory authorities greater monitoring capability over offenders sentenced to some form of probation. The report contains background information, personal habits, and names of acquaintances of the offender. Should it become necessary to apprehend probationers for any probation violation or new crime alleged, the report also functions as a locating device.

A fifth function of PSI reports is to provide research material for scholars to conduct investigations of crime patterns, parole board decision making, judicial sentencing trends, and other related phenomenon. This function is unrelated to offender sentencing decisions and is closely tied to academic interests in the criminal justice process.

Criticisms of PSI Report Preparation.   PSI reports have been criticized in recent years because of the subjectivity inherent in their preparation. Probation officers consider both factual background information as well as their personal impressions of offenders (U.S. General Accounting Office, 1998). Some probation officers rely heavily on statistical data about offenders when making recommendations about possible public risks offenders may pose. Probation officers have overpredicted anti-social behavior and misinterpreted technical terminology. In some jurisdictions, PO supervisors encourage them not to oversimplify the background of offenders when preparing PSI reports, which is especially difficult when officers have heavy case-loads and severe time limitations.

Investigations of probation officer behaviors in PSI report preparation have disclosed diverse perspectives, ranging from rehabilitative to legalistic. A dilemma exists for many probation officers when preparing PSI reports. They must balance quantitative data (e.g., arrest reports, probation records, juvenile adjudications) with qualitative data (e.g., alcohol adjustment, social history, substance abuse). A basic requirement for probation officers is that they reflect a reasonable understanding of human nature in their report preparations. Many officers lack sufficient understanding about different types of offenders and are inclined to rely on group norms for making decisions about individual offenders (Bridges and Steen, 1998; Raynor and Honess, 1998). Thus, it is difficult to avoid subjective decision making that may have adverse consequences for convicted offenders, both at the time of sentencing and later when parole boards consider them for early release.

Not all PSI reports contain officer assessments of an offender's risk. The ones that do are founded on criteria peculiar to each probation officer. In federal district courts as well as in those states (e.g., Minnesota, Florida, Arizona, California, Washington) that have adopted sentencing guidelines, PSI reports are declining in their importance and relevance, because sentencing decisions by judges are increasingly perfunctory as sentencing tables are consulted. Their value continues, however, with evidence of mitigating or aggravating circumstances about the offense and offender that may decrease or increase the harshness of sentences imposed, provided sentencing ranges exist (Bowker, 1998).

The Defendant's Sentencing Memorandum

The Administrative Office of the U.S. Courts (Probation Division) has recommended the inclusion of the offender's version of the offense (Administrative Office of U.S. Courts, 1997). These statements are often called the **defendant's sentencing memorandum**. Although not specifically required under the 1987 federal sentencing guidelines, it is important that if such a statement is prepared, it should be prepared with assistance of defense counsel and attached to the PSI report filed by the probation officer. Often, these memorandums contain material judges regard as mitigating, and the sentence imposed may be reduced in severity accordingly. Again, these memorandums are not required by law, although the offender's acceptance of responsibility weighs heavily in affecting the sentence federal judges impose.

Whether a PSI report contains the defendant's version of the offense should be determined on the basis of the best interests of the offender. Hence, the assistance of counsel is important. If offenders decide to appeal the conviction later, then a written statement prepared by them about their version of the offense could be used by the court to impeach them and cause the appeal to fail.

The Inclusion of Victim Impact Statements

In some jurisdictions, victims of crimes are required to submit their own versions of the offense as a **victim impact statement (VIS)** (Phillips, 1997). The VIS is a statement made by the victim and addressed to the judge for consideration in sentencing. It includes a description of the harm inflicted on the victim in terms of financial, social, psychological, and physical consequences of the crime. It also includes a statement concerning the victim's feelings about the crime, the offender, and a proposed sentence (Luginbuhl and Burkhead, 1995). Although the federal government and states have no statutes currently requiring victims to file such statements with the court prior to sentencing, proponents of victim compensation regard victim impact statements as an increasingly important part of the sentencing process. This step is seen as a form of victim participation in sentencing, and a victim impact statement is given similar weight compared with the offender's version of events. Usually, these statements are not required. They pertain exclusively to the direct effects of the crime and are regarded as aggravating circumstances, just as the offender's sentencing memorandum serves as a basis for mitigating circumstances. Although victim participation in sentencing raises certain ethical, moral, and legal questions, indications are that victim impact statements are used with increasing frequency and are appended to PSI reports in various jurisdictions (Erez and Tontodonato, 1992).

Victim impact statements usually take two forms. One is as a written attachment to a PSI report in which the victim or victims describe how the crime and offender influenced them, usually adversely. The second is in the form of a speech or verbal declaration. This statement is usually a prepared document read by one or more victims at the time offenders are sentenced (Erez and Tontodonato, 1992). The admission of victim impact statements in either written or verbal form at the time of sentencing or in PSI reports is controversial. Some experts think that these statements are inflammatory and detract from objective sentencing considerations. Obviously prejudicial, these statements may intensify sentencing disparities in certain jurisdictions with sentencing schemes that rely more heavily on subjective judicial impressions compared with those jurisdictions where more objective sentencing criteria are used, such as mandatory sentencing procedures or guidelines-based sentencing schemes (*Booth v. Maryland,* 1987). Proponents of victim impact statements believe that they personalize the sentencing process by showing that actual persons were harmed by certain offender conduct. Also, victim's rights advocates contend that victims have a moral right to influence one's punishment (Davis and Smith, 1994). While this controversy continues, victims are increasingly exerting greater influence and have growing input in sentencing decisions in most jurisdictions.

Privatizing PSI Report Preparation

The Private Preparation of PSI Reports.   Sometimes PSI reports are prepared by private corporations or individuals. For example, Criminological Diagnostic Consultants, Inc. of Riverside, California, founded by brothers William and Robert Bosic, is a corporation that prepares privately commissioned PSI reports for defense attorneys and others (Kulis, 1983:11). William Bosic is a former prison counselor and probation officer, and Robert Bosic is a retired police officer. Their claim is, "We don't do anything different from the probation department; we just do it better." The average cost of a government-prepared PSI report averages about $250, but privately prepared ones cost from $200 to $2,000 or more, depending on the contents and whether psychiatric evaluations of offenders are made. The amount of investigative detail required in particular cases also influences preparation costs. Increasing numbers of PSI reports are being prepared privately, often by ex-probation officers or others closely related to corrections. The quality of private PSI report preparation varies greatly. Some private agencies prepare quite elaborate and sophisticated reports for clients able to afford them.

Many jurisdictions now accept privately prepared sentencing memorandums to accompany the official PSI report. These private-sector PSI reports are often prepared by former probation officers or criminal justice consultants. Defendant's **sentencing memorandums** contain similar PSI report information, especially the defendant's version of what happened and any mitigating factors that would lessen sentencing severity. This independently prepared report serves to make the official PSI report more objective and to clarify or resolve facts that may be in dispute (Fruchtman and Sigler, 1999).

THE SENTENCING HEARING

Under Rule 32 of the Federal **Rules of Criminal Procedure** (18 U.S.C., 2001), the contents of a PSI report must be disclosed to defendants and their counsels, although some information is exempt from disclosure. Mental or psychological reports, interviews with family members or a personalized account of the defendant's marital problems, and certain personal observations by the probation officer and court are potentially excludable.

In most jurisdictions, a **sentencing hearing** is held at which time defendants and their attorneys can respond to the contents of the PSI report. Also, an increasing number of jurisdictions are permitting crime victims to attend sentencing hearings and provide victim impact statements either orally, in writing, or both. Evidence suggests a general increase in citizen involvement at other stages of the criminal justice process as well (Atkins, 1996). Of course, many jurisdictions do not allow victims to participate in the sentencing process. The nature of victim participation varies among jurisdictions, although their participation often consists of an objective delineation of the personal and psychological effects of the crime and the financial costs incurred.

Sentencing hearings also permit offenders and their attorneys to comment on the PSI report and append to it additional informational material that may mitigate the circumstances of the conviction offense. The role of defense attorneys is important particularly at this stage because they can work with the probation officer who prepared the report as well as the victims and can make timely legal attacks on erroneous information presented to the judge. In addition to considering the contents of a PSI report, the oral and written reports furnished by victims and the offenders themselves, and attorney arguments from both the prosecution and defense, judges use their best judgment in arriving at the most equitable sentence for offenders. In arriving at a decision, they consider mitigating and aggravating circumstances surrounding the offense; the age, psychological and physical condition, and social/educational background of the offender; and the minimum and maximum statutory penalties of incarceration and/or fines accompanying the crime. Judges also take into account both aggravating circumstances and mitigating circumstances.

AGGRAVATING AND MITIGATING CIRCUMSTANCES

Aggravating Circumstances

Aggravating circumstances are those factors that increase the severity of punishment. Some of the factors considered by judges to be aggravating include the following:

1. Whether the crime involved death or serious bodily injury to one or more victims
2. Whether the crime was committed while the offender was out on bail facing other criminal charges
3. Whether the offender was on probation, parole, or work release at the time the crime was committed
4. Whether the offender was a recidivist and had committed several previous offenses for which he or she had been punished
5. Whether the offender was the leader in the commission of the offense involving two or more offenders
6. Whether the offense involved more than one victim and/or was a violent or nonviolent crime
7. Whether the offender treated the victim(s) with extreme cruelty during the commission of the offense
8. Whether the offender used a dangerous weapon in the commission of the crime and the risk to human life was high (Blankenship et al., 1997)

If the convicted defendant has one or more aggravating circumstances accompanying the crime committed, the judge is likely to intensify the punishment prescribed, which, in simple terms, means a longer sentence, incarceration in lieu of probation, or a sentence to be served in a maximum-security rather than a minimum- or medium-security prison. Mitigating circumstances may cause the judge to be lenient with the defendant and prescribe probation rather than confinement in a jail or prison. A sentence of a year or less rather than a five-year term may be imposed.

Mitigating Circumstances

Mitigating circumstances are those circumstances considered by the sentencing judge to lessen the crime's severity. Some of the more frequently cited mitigating factors in the commission of crimes are the following:

1. The offender did not cause serious bodily injury by his or her conduct during the commission of the crime.
2. The convicted defendant did not contemplate that his or her criminal conduct would inflict serious bodily injury on anyone.
3. The offender acted under duress or extreme provocation.
4. The offender's conduct was possibly justified under the circumstances.
5. The offender was suffering from mental incapacitation or a physical condition that significantly reduced his or her culpability in the offense.
6. The offender cooperated with authorities in apprehending other participants in the crime or in making restitution to the victims for losses suffered.

7. The offender committed the crime through motivation to provide necessities for himself or herself or his or her family.

8. The offender did not have a previous criminal record. (Baroff, 1990; Wilson, 1997)

If a convicted defendant has one or more mitigating circumstances associated with the crime committed, then the sentencing judge may lessen the severity of the sentence imposed. In view of the current trend toward greater use of felony probation, first-offenders and nonviolent criminals are likely to be considered prime candidates for alternative sentencing that does not involve incarceration. Recidivists, however, especially those who have committed a number of violent acts and show every likelihood of continuing their criminal behavior, are likely candidates for punishment enhancement (e.g., longer, more severe sentences and/or fines). These circumstances are usually outlined in PSI reports.

A SAMPLE PSI REPORT FROM NORTH DAKOTA

In this section, some background information has been provided for a hypothetical criminal, Jared Monroe Davis, who has been convicted of armed robbery and attempted murder in North Dakota. A North Dakota criminal court judge has ordered a probation officer, James Pangborn, to complete a presentence investigation report for Davis. Assume that the probation officer began to collect relevant information about Davis and, after extensive research and investigation, compiled the following.

Background Information

On September 8, 1999, Judge Frank Riordan of the 2nd County Court, Ward County, North Dakota, ordered a PSI report for an offender, Jared Monroe Davis, convicted by a jury trial for the armed robbery and attempted murder of a Bismarck store clerk. The judge ordered the PSI report due no later than September 30, 1999. The prosecutor is Mark Richards, State's Attorney, Minot, North Dakota. The defense attorney of record, a public defender who was court appointed, is John Jacobs, with the firm of Jacobs, Jacobs, and Bryant.

Jared Monroe Davis, 39, Social Security number 425-79-1506, NDSID No. 625-CR-21, is a white male, 6'3" tall, 220 pounds, with a prominent scar on his left forearm. Davis's telephone number is 701-555-1212. Davis has prepared a statement for the PSI report that is outlined below. Davis was born in Max, North Dakota, on January 21, 1960. He graduated from Manual Arts High School (Bismarck, North Dakota) in 1978. He attended one year at Minot State University, where he majored in history. After a year, he dropped out of school and joined the U.S. Air Force in September 1979, but he was discharged in December 1980 because of various drug infractions. Davis tested positive for cocaine and marijuana on several occasions during random drug testing. The Air Force security personnel searched Davis's locker and found drugs.

Davis held various jobs for the next ten years. He worked as a day laborer for a construction company, ABC Construction, in Bismarck for six years, but he drank heavily and frequently missed work. He was fired from ABC Construction in 1987. He was hired by U-Asked-For-It Rentals, a private rental car company in Mandan, and worked there for a year. While working for the rental car company, Davis sold one of the rental cars to one of his friends, but he later reported the car stolen. His friend painted the car a different color and put fake license plates on it. The car was never recovered. Davis's

---

BOX 3.3

Is Drunkenness a Mitigating Circumstance in Condom Theft Case?

**The Case of Keith Bradford
and the Stolen Condom Machine**

It happened in Waterford, Michigan. Keith Bradford, 34, walked into a downtown bar and began drinking. After consuming a lot of beer, Bradford disappeared toward the bathroom area. The bartender, Jodi Malone, didn't see him return. "I kind of got worried. I went to the back and looked out the window. There he was, walking away from the bar with a condom machine in his arms." Mal-

one called police, who subsequently arrested Bradford for larceny. They recovered the machine, 48 condoms, and $31.75 in quarters. "All we can figure is that he must have been planning some weekend," said Officer John Grimm, a police spokesperson.

What mitigating factors can you think of in Bradford's case? What penalty would you impose for someone who rips a condom machine off of a restroom wall? What do you think?

Source: Adapted from Associated Press, "Michigan Man Charged with Stealing Condom Machine from Restroom at Bar," November 18, 1994.

---

sneaky behavior around the car rental company aroused the suspicions of the administration, and they let Davis go. Davis did part-time work, washing dishes in a restaurant, and held other menial jobs over the next four years. In 1992, Davis connected with a friend, Oswald Clark, a burglar. Clark enlisted Davis in his burglaries, and the two stole many items from homes for about six months in the Mandan-Bismarck area. Subsequently, Davis and Clark were caught leaving a home they had just burglarized. Davis was sentenced to ten years in the North Dakota State Penitentiary. While there, Davis enrolled in some counseling and self-help sessions to overcome his alcoholism. He joined the Alcoholics Anonymous group in prison and participated in that for a few years. After four years, he was paroled.

While on parole, Davis was employed by the Danville Rug Company at a hourly rate of $7. He cut carpet and helped install it, remaining employed for almost three years. In December 1998, while still employed there, Davis met up with his old friend Oswald Clark, who had recently been paroled from prison. Davis and Clark got drunk together and then decided to hold up a convenience store. On December 29, 1998, they went to the Drive-Thru Market on Main Avenue in Bismarck. Clark remained on watch outside the store, while Davis entered and pointed a .45-caliber pistol at Maggie Smith, the store manager. Smith's address is 1818 Pine Drive, Bismarck. Smith was petrified and agreed to give Davis money from the cash register. While getting the money from the drawer, Smith began to cry. A new customer entered the store at that point and Smith yelled, "We're being robbed." Davis panicked and fired his weapon at Smith, striking her in the chest. She fell to the floor, bleeding. The customer fled from the store and called police on her cellular telephone. In the meantime, Davis ran around behind the counter and pulled money from the cash drawer.

A Bismarck city police unit was within two blocks of the Drive-Thru Market when the robbery was reported by the customer. The police unit approached the store and noted that a car was parked near the door with the motor running, and someone behind the wheel. The officers quietly exited their vehicle and approached the parked car. Clark, sitting in the car looking in the store, did not see the officers until they were nearly by his car door. He pulled out a .357-magnum revolver and emptied it at the officers. One officer took a bullet in the arm but emptied his gun into Clark. The other officer caught Davis as he was coming out of the store. Davis threw his gun down and was arrested. Clark died on the way to the hospital after an ambulance arrived an hour later. Davis was charged with armed robbery and attempted murder. Because of the charges, Davis was denied bail. He was convicted on September 8, 1999, of armed robbery and attempted murder, because Maggie Smith, the store clerk, eventually recovered. The convictions were class A felony, armed robbery, and attempted murder.

During the time Davis was in police custody awaiting trial for the armed robbery and attempted murder charges, he underwent a psychological evaluation. Doctors determined that although he was not mentally ill, he definitely had some personality problems that made him somewhat unstable. He told doctors that he regarded himself as a failure in life and thought that he never would succeed at anything. Doctors noted these statements in their analysis of Davis, but they did not say he was incapable of differentiating between right and wrong. Therefore, Davis was sane enough to stand trial.

At the time Davis was arrested, he was living at 2121 3rd Street, Bismarck and had lived there for six months. Prior to that, he lived at 15 Willow Street, Mandan, for one year. In both cases, he was renting an apartment. He was living with a girlfriend, Ima Trouble, whom he had met in a bar in Mandan in 1995. Trouble, 28, was a part-time waitress at the Watering Hole, a Bismarck bar. She liked to call Davis "Big J" for Jared, and he used that name as an alias. Police have documented the following version of events in their records.

Investigating Officer's Version of Crime. Officers Jamie Petrella and Lloyd Halvorson were patrolling the north end of Bismarck on December 29, 1998, when they received a call of an armed robbery in progress at the Drive-Thru Market. They proceeded to the Drive-Thru Market where they observed a subject, later identified as one Oswald Clark, sitting in a car with the motor running. They approached the car and drew fire from Clark. Officer Halvorson was wounded in the shooting but managed to return fire and eventually subdue and kill Clark. Officer Petrella confronted one Jared Davis leaving the Drive-Thru Market with a pistol. She immediately ordered Davis to drop his weapon and hit the pavement. Davis did so and was taken into custody. Petrella found a wounded store clerk in the store, later identified as one Maggie Smith. Ambulances were called for Smith and Clark, although Clark was D.O.A. (dead on arrival) at the Bismarck Community Hospital. Smith was treated for her wounds and released. Officer Halvorson recovered from his wounds later.

An investigation by detectives disclosed that a robbery had indeed been perpetrated and that the perpetrators were Oswald Clark and Jared Monroe Davis. Davis's gun was the weapon used to wound the store manager, Smith. The store's videotape clearly showed Davis and the robbery in progress, including Davis's demand for money. This evidence was later used at Davis's trial and helped to secure his conviction. It was also revealed that at the time of Davis's arrest, his blood alcohol level was .25, more than twice the legal limit of .10 in North Dakota for drunkenness. Oswald Clark's blood alcohol level was .19 in a postmortem examination.

Defendant's Version of Events. Jared Monroe Davis described the robbery as being Oswald Clark's idea and said that because they had been drinking heavily, he (Davis) did not recall much about the incident. Davis blamed life for his misery and failure. He does not get along well with superiors or any authority figures. He says that he loves his girl, Ima, and was probably doing it to get some money to buy an engagement ring for her. Davis says he did not mean to shoot the store clerk. He claims that he panicked and the gun just "went off." Davis says that he was walking the "straight and narrow" for several years after his earlier legal troubles, until he ran into Oswald Clark, who had recently been paroled from prison. It was Clark's idea to go out and celebrate and get drunk, and then to rob the store. Davis offered no explanation about how he came into possession of the firearm used in the robbery. He thinks that it was Clark's gun and that Clark had given it to him before going into the store. He claims that the robbery was unplanned, although Clark was carrying a complete store layout for the Drive-Thru Market on a piece of paper in his pocket when investigators catalogued his personal effects. On the paper, it said, "For Big J and me."

Davis says that he has always been misunderstood. He took drugs in the military because he hated authority. He says he was set up on the car deal at the car rental company and that he had nothing to do with stealing cars. He blames the deceased Oswald Clark for his major conviction for burglary and larceny several years earlier. He says that he was drinking heavily on those occasions as well, although investigating police reported that all these burglaries were "well-planned."

Davis says that he hangs out with four other ex-convicts. They have never engaged in any criminal activity, according to Davis, and their sole purpose in getting together is for emotional support. They meet frequently at the Horse's Mouth Tavern in Mandan. Davis likes to fish for bass in surrounding lakes and rivers, and he manages to fish with one of his ex-con buddies at least once a month when there is good weather. Davis is also a stamp collector, and he has bought thousands of stamps from mail-order catalogs and the back pages of popular magazines. He has never organized the stamps, but just throws them into a drawer. Other than these activities, Davis is somewhat inactive. He watches television. He is unaware that anyone thinks that he is a "bad guy" and that he has a bad reputation.

Comments and Sentencing Alternatives. I have met briefly with Jared Monroe Davis and have found him to have considerable resentment toward authority figures. He was reluctant to see me and disclose anything about his crimes or associates. He seems to have a severe drinking problem, which may be a major factor in explaining his criminal conduct. He is easily influenced by others, such as the now deceased Oswald Clark. Davis is definitely not a leader; rather, he is a follower. My assessment is that Davis should receive maximum sentences on both counts and that because of his prior record, he should receive consecutive sentences rather than concurrent sentences.

I recommend maximum sentences on both counts. Community control or community corrections is definitely not recommended as a punishment for Davis at this time. Perhaps after ten years or so in prison, Davis may be able to confront his inner thoughts and feelings, and he may be able to handle authority better. Right now, he poses a considerable danger to others if he were to be placed on probation.

Prepared by James Pangborn, North Dakota Parole and Probation Department.

The background information compiled for Davis has been transmitted to a standard North Dakota presentence investigation form shown in Figure 3.2.

North Dakota is not that dissimilar from other states in terms of the elements included in its PSI reports. North Dakota has three different types of forms for report preparation. The state uses a short form, a medium form, and a long form. Figure 3.2 is the short form for sentenced offenders. Other forms used by North Dakota are more detailed, complicated, and time-consuming in their preparation. For comparison, a detailed version of a federal presentence investigation report is included in this chapter's appendix.

PRE-SENTENCE INVESTIGATION REPORT I
NORTH DAKOTA PAROLE AND PROBATION DEPARTMENT
SFN 16394 (7-88)

County WARD	File No. (s)	Date PSI Ordered SEPT. 8, 1999
Judge FRANK RIORDAN	States Attorney MARK RICHARDS	Date PSI Due SEPT. 30, 1999
Defense Attorney JOHN JACOBS	☒ Appointed ☐ Retained	Date PSI Completed SEPT. 23, 1999

Name (Court Records) JARED MONROE DAVIS	Date of Birth JAN. 21, 1960	Race WHITE	Sex M

Name (Alias) BIG J	Place of Birth MAX, NORTH DAKOTA

Offense ARMED ROBBERY AND ATTEMPTED MURDER

Address 2121 3RD STREET, BISMARCK, NORTH DAKOTA	Telephone No. 701-555-1212

Lives With (Name) IMA TROUBLE	Relationship GIRLFRIEND

☐ OWNS ☒ RENTS ☐ House ☐ Apartment ☐ Room | How Long At This Address? 6 MONTHS

Marital Status SINGLE	Gross Monthy Income -All Sources $7.00 HOUR	Number of Dependents 0

Occupation CARPET INSTALLER/CUTTER	Social Security No. 425-79-1506	NDSID No. 625-CR-21

Employer DANVILLE RUG COMPANY	How Long Employed APPROX. 3YRS

Previous Employer WORKING MENIAL JOBS PART-TIME	How Long Employed 4 YRS

Reason For Leaving CONVICTED OF BURGLARIES-SENTENCED NORTH DAKOTA PENETENTIARY 10 YRS

Education COMPLETED HIGH SCHOOL/1 YR COLLEGE

Military Service (Branch & Dates) U.S. AIR FORCE SEP 79-DEC 80	Type of Discharge DISHONORABLE

Current Physical Condition GOOD

☒ Drug Use   ☐ Mental / Emotional Problems   ☒ Alcohol Use   (Give details under comments)

PRIOR RECORD (USE REVERSE SIDE IF NEEDED FOR ADDITIONAL SPACE)

Date	Offense	Arresting Agency	Disposition
1980	VARIOUS DRUG INFRACTIONS	U.S. AIR FORCE	DISHONORABLE DISCHARGE
1992	BURGLARY	BISMARCK-MANDAN POL	10YRS ND PENETENTIARY

COMMENTS AND RECOMMENDATIONS (Community Service and/or Treatment Proposals, etc.):

-Dishonorably discharged from U.S. Air Force various drug infractions 1980
-Fired ABC Construction heavy drinking, absence from work 1987
-1992-1996 while incarcerated ND Penetentiary enrolled in alcohol counseling
-Mr. Davis was drinking heavily on the night of the current incident.
-Mr. Davis is in need of extensive counseling for his drinking

MANDATORY ATTACHMENTS:
Criminal Information
Law Enforcement Investigation Report
Victim Impact Statement (If applicable)

Probation / Parole Officer _____   Date _____

FIGURE 3.2 North Dakota presentence investigation report. (Prepared with assistance from Sandra Cole.)

SFN 16395 Page 2

PRIOR RECORD (USE REVERSE SIDE IF NEEDED FOR ADDITIONAL SPACE)			
Date	Offense	Arresting Agency	Disposition

Offense and Penalty Classification	Days In Custody
CLASS A FELONY—ATTEMPTED MURDER & ARMED ROBBERY	254

Date of Offense	Arresting Agency
DEC 29, 1998	BISMARCK CITY POLICE

Co-defendants and disposition
OSWALD CLARK--DECEASED

Victim	Address
MAGGIE SMITH	1818 PINE DRIVE, BISMARCK, NORTH DAKOTA

DEFENDANT'S VERSION OF CRIME
Davis claims he had been on the "straight and narrow" for several years until Mr Clark came back into his life. He claims the robbery was unplanned and Clark's idea. Davis also claims he doesn't remember much about the incident due to his high consumption of alcohol. Davis claims he had no intention of shooting anyone the gun went off when he panicked. Another reasoning behind the incident was that he loves his girl Ima and was probably doing it so he could have enough money to buy her an engagement ring.

INVESTIGATING OFFICER'S VERSION OF CRIME
Officers Petrella and Halverson received a call of an armed robbery in progress at the drive-thru marker. As the officers approached the market they observed a subject sitting in a car (Clark). As they approached the vehicle the subject opened fire on them wounding Halvorson who returned fire killing Clark. Davis was caught leaving the market with a pistol.

OTHER INFORMATION (Reputation, Attitude, Leisure time activities, Associates, etc.)
Davis doesn't get along well with superiors or authority figures, he "hangs out" with ex-convicts at a tavern in Mandan and meets monthly with one ex-convict to go fishing. He is an unorganized stamp collector and watches TV. Davis seems to find blame for his behavior in everyone else, he is never responsible for his actions.

COMMENTS AND SENTENCING ALTERNATIVES (Community Service and/or Treatment Proposals, etc.):
Davis is not a good candidate for community service at this time, he needs a more controlled environment that he couldn't so easily pass blame for his actions and start accepting responsibility. I feel Davis would benefit in treatment programs for his obvious alcohol problem also in learning responsibility for his actions, something like the Victim-Offender reconciliation program, and to strengthen his self-esteem.

MANDATORY ATTACHMENTS:
Criminal Information / Complaint
Law Enforcement Investigation Report
Victim's Impact Statement (If applicable)

Probation / Parole Officer	Date

A PSI REPORT FROM WISCONSIN

The following material presents a more complex PSI report from the state of Wisconsin. Wisconsin authorizes general PSI preparations without adhering to a fixed PSI format. Thus, there are some components of Wisconsin PSI reports that may not be applicable for particular offenders. The intent of Wisconsin officials is to individualize these reports to fit offender characteristics, needs, and sentence recommendations. The Wisconsin Department of Corrections states that the purpose of any PSI report is a careful study of how the individual's personal characteristics, environmental factors, and behavioral patterns have interacted to produce the present situation. The agent must comply with confidentiality laws when securing and disclosing medical, psychiatric, psychological, and educational information. Courts may order PSI reports following conviction and prior to imposition of sentence for felony cases. Investigation due dates are usually set by the court.

STATE OF WISCONSIN*
DEPARTMENT OF CORRECTIONS

PRESENTENCE INVESTIGATION

Date

     August 10, 1996

Name and DOB

     John Ming
     November 20, 1962

PRESENT OFFENSE

Description of Offense

     Attempted sexual assault. Offense date is November 3, 1995. This offense involves an incident in which a 29-year-old nude woman's body was discovered on a rural road. The body had been decapitated, and the woman's head and articles of bloody clothing were discovered on another road three miles away. It was discovered that the woman, in an intoxicated condition, had accompanied some men from a tavern who reportedly took the woman to their apartment and forced her to

*This report is a real PSI report and psychiatric evaluation of an offender currently incarcerated in another state. The names of the offender, accomplices, probation officers, and physicians were changed for reasons of confidentiality.

engage in sexual intercourse. Then at least one of the men attacked the woman with a kitchen knife, cut her throat, and decapitated her. Four men were eventually charged in the offense, including the defendant, Mu Chou (life sentence), Bok Suk Kim (life sentence), and Raymond Phu (ten years). Ming admits that he resides at the apartment in which the offense occurred, but denies any involvement in or knowledge of the offense until his arrest two weeks later. He was not released on bond. Rationale: "I never see girl, I don't know about it."

Offender's Version

The subject is a 34-year-old Chinese National male, first-offender, who is currently confined in the Briggs Unit facing a ten-year sentence in Madison County for one count of attempted sexual assault. The subject states that on or about November 3, 1995, during an unknown time he allegedly committed the offense of attempted sexual assault on a 29-year-old female, but he denies the attempted sexual assault and any knowledge of the woman's murder or decapitation. He admits to occasional marijuana use at age 27 and admits to three prior arrests resulting in a two-year probationary term for DWI. He states that he left the apartment for an unknown period of time, and when he returned, his friends and the woman were gone. He admits that there was blood on the floor and in the bedroom where the woman was allegedly raped by the other men.

Victim's Statement

Not applicable.

PRIOR RECORD

Juvenile Record

No record of juvenile arrests.

Adult Record

Three prior arrests for DWI; sentenced to two years probation; claims completed.

Pending Charges

One detainer warrant from U.S. Immigration: "Hold."

Correctional Experience

Good jail report from Madison County Jail authorities.

<u>Offender's Explanation of Record</u>

Claims no contact with father, mother, or two siblings; claims single; residence unstable; education claims high school completed; employment claims "laborer"; home stability poor due to lack of contact with family; admits to experimental use of marijuana at age 27; current offense of attempted sexual assaulting a 29-year-old female and allegedly cutting her head off, subject denies; speaks little English.

PERSONAL HISTORY

<u>Academic/Vocational Skills</u>

Subject states that he completed 12 years of school in China. Subject worked as "laborer" but did not elaborate on what "laborer" did.

<u>Employment</u>

Worked as "laborer" at various jobs in different states; would not disclose which establishments employed him. No information is forthcoming about subject's past educational level or occupations in his native country of China. He had been in English classes in Indiana for about a year prior to coming to Wisconsin. While in Wisconsin, the subject worked in a few different jobs. He bused tables in a restaurant, worked in a furniture factory, and did some janitorial work. He then moved to Madison, where he worked for the ABC Packing Company as a meat cutter.

<u>Financial Management</u>

Has given no indication of ability to manage financial affairs.

<u>Marital/Alternate Family Relationships</u>

Has not seen family for many years.

<u>Companions</u>

Has no close associates presently. Admits to knowing other men who were convicted of the woman's murder only because they were also Asian and in the tavern when he was. He admits to being drunk when he left tavern but denies any involvement in the woman's murder.

<u>Emotional Health</u>

See attached psychiatric evaluation.

Physical Health

Transferred to mental health unit at Briggs for psychiatric and psychological evaluation. Subject was referred because he was mute, refused to eat, and exhibited unusual behavior. Subject appeared detached, withdrawn, in distress, and depressed. His blood pressure was low, he had lost much weight, and he appeared to be dehydrated. He would give no information to medical staff. He would sit in one place on his bunk for seven or eight hours at a time. At that time, he stated that he was very nervous and scared. He had been making statements that he needed to stay in prison because he would not have anything on the outside now. He flooded his cell on one occasion and became quite unresponsive. His physical and mental condition deteriorated further. He lost 26 pounds because he was not eating. He was transferred to the medical unit for acute care. When received, the subject was on Haldol C, 15 mg, TID, and Cogentin, 2 mg, BID. The subject may have been a suicide risk and was placed on suicide precaution status. The subject began to eat on the second day of his admission. The subject is being treated for a positive TB test with INH. The file reflects no other medical problems at this time.

Mental Ability

The subject is now a 34-year-old frail-looking Chinese male who was dressed in a disheveled Department of Corrections white uniform. He looked undernourished. He was mute and had poor eye contact. He was able to answer one question by head movement at one time. His mood seemed depressed to euthymic. He had an inappropriate smile at some part of his evaluation. There was no indication that the subject had delusions or hallucinations, although he reportedly has history of having fairly loose delusions and grandiose delusions in the past. The rest of his mental status examination was not tested because of his uncooperativeness and because he remained mute.

Chemical Usage

Subject admitted to using marijuana and drinking beer. Presently on prescribed medications as indicated.

Sexual Behavior

Convicted of attempted sexual assault; subject denies. Has no close friends or acquaintances.

Military

None.

Religion

Born into Buddhist faith; now is nondenominational.

Leisure Activities

None determined.

Residential History

Taipei, Taiwan	1962–1985
Lafayette, Indiana	1985–1986
Madison, Wisconsin	1986–present

SUMMARY AND CONCLUSIONS

Agent's Impressions

Ming is a Line Class I inmate, unassigned due to his mental health status. He needs recreational therapy. He does not attend any educational, vocational, or character development programs due to his mental status. He is not a gang member. Ming is receiving INH for TB prevention. Ming denies any mental health treatment in society and denies suicide attempts. Ming has been diagnosed with schizoeffective disorder, bipolar type rule out bipolar disorder, mixed with psychotic features, rule out schizophrenia, chronic, catatonic type with acute exacerbation. Alcohol use in remission. Addicted to cannabis; in remission due to incarceration. Interviews with Ming indicate that he is unwilling or unable to relate any new information to this officer about his present offense. Ming maintains that he is not guilty and claimed that he did not know any details about the present offense until he was arrested. Ming claims that he does not know if he was ever physically or sexually assaulted and has never been married and has no children. Ming claims that he cannot remember if he engaged in sex with prostitutes. Due to the subject's past probation for DWI, it appears that he may need monitoring in the area of alcohol usage. He may also benefit from psychological counseling.

Restitution Information

Not applicable.

Recommendation

Recommend that Ming be confined in mental unit at Briggs until such time as his eating behavior is stabilized. Recom-

mend Ming for psychological counseling. Statutory punishment
of ten years should be imposed. Ming must accept responsibility for his actions, because this officer interviewed two
other persons convicted of the murder and they give consistent accounts of Ming's involvement in the female victim's
murder and decapitation. Both subjects accused Ming of committing the decapitation and joking about it later. Other
than mental problems contained in psychiatric evaluation,
there are no outstanding mitigating circumstances that would
cause this officer to recommend sentencing leniency or a
shorter incarcerative term at this time.

1. Confinement is necessary to protect the public from
   further criminal activity.
2. The subject is in need of correctional treatment that
   can most effectively be provided through confinement.
3. Nonconfinement would unduly depreciate the seriousness
   of the instant offense.

Probation is not recommended.

John J. Beecher, Probation Officer, Madison County

PSYCHIATRIC EVALUATION
WISCONSIN DEPARTMENT OF CORRECTIONS

NAME: John Ming

WDOJ#: 47324568

DATE: July 15, 1996

EXAMINER: Dominique Daws, M.D.

Source of Information

Patient and WDOC records.

Pertinent Medical History

The patient's chart indicates that he has tuberculosis
class II and is currently taking medication for this condition. He has no allergies to medications.

Pertinent Psychiatric and Legal History

Reports in patient's brown chart indicated that he has a
history of psychiatric hospitalizations and was given the
diagnoses of psychotic disorder, NOS, alcohol abuse, and
cannabis abuse. During that hospitalization, he was given

Ativan 1 mg po hs prn for his complaint of having difficulty with his sleeping. He was also treated with other psychotropic medications prior to his discharge. His final diagnosis was schizophrenia, chronic, undifferentiated type, alcohol abuse, and cannabis abuse. His previous records also indicated that he had experienced delusional thinking such as thinking that he has special powers and special knowledge of prediction of the future and that he was involved in worldwide powerful activities. His mental status on his psychiatric hospitalization indicated that he made a statement that he went with too many gods in the war, saw them and talked to them, and went with them anywhere and that they told him things about the CIA and the life of Americans and that the American religions were always at odds with his religion. Social history done at Briggs indicated that patient reported being arrested one time in Indianapolis, Indiana, for not having any money for a bus ticket. He reportedly spent a week in jail, and a friend paid the fine and got him out. He was also arrested once in Lafayette, Indiana, for driving while intoxicated. He was released and was told to appear in court, which he did not do and which led to his later arrest for failure to appear. He reportedly paid a fine and as a result was discharged. The patient is reportedly serving a ten-year sentence for murder.

Family History

There is no available information about the patient's family or history of medical or psychiatric illness at this time.

Social History

This information is obtained from the social history compiled during the patient's hospitalization at Briggs. The patient was reportedly born in Taipei, Taiwan, and his family all reside in Taipei. He reportedly went to school there. He was not married. He came to the United States in 1985 as a refugee, stayed in Indiana for one year, and worked in a factory in Madison, Wisconsin, for three years prior to his present incarceration. For additional social history, please read social history in the brown chart.

Mental Status Examination

The patient is a 34-year-old frail-looking Chinese male who was dressed in a disheveled white WDOC uniform. He looked undernourished. He was mute and had poor eye contact. He was able to answer one question by head movement at one time. There were no indications that patient had delusions or hallucinations. The rest of his mental status examination was not tested because of his uncooperativeness and his remaining mute.

Summary of Positive Findings and Target Symptoms

This 34-year-old male reportedly came to the United States as a refugee in 1985 and has been living with friends in Madison prior to his incarceration. He reportedly is serving a ten-year sentence for murder. His records indicated that he has a history of delusions and hallucinations and was hospitalized at a mental hospital with a diagnosis of undifferentiated schizophrenia, alcohol abuse, and cannabis abuse. He reportedly was observed to have unusual behavior at Briggs, remaining mute and not making eye contact with anyone, and was observed looking at his wall while in his cell. He also started refusing to eat, causing him to lose weight. The patient was transferred to the medical unit at Briggs electively mute and not eating, although he started eating the next day. The patient at this time remains mute, although he started to answer by moving his head. It is possible that this patient has a schizoaffective disorder and a possible bipolar disorder in addition to his history of alcohol and cannabis abuse.

Diagnosis

    Axis I: 295.70 schizoaffective disorder, bipolar type

              Rule out bipolar disorder, mixed with psychotic features 296.64

              Rule out schizophrenia, chronic, catatonic type with acute exacerbation 295.24

              305.00 alcohol abuse, in remission due to incarceration

              305.20 cannabis abuse, in remission due to incarceration

    Axis II: 799.90 deferred

    Axis III: Tuberculosis class II

    Axis IV: Severe (incarceration and no family support)

    Axis V: Current GAF: 20 Highest GAF Past Year: 0

Prognosis

    Poor.

_____

Dominique Daws, M.D.

Recommendations

It is recommended that Inmate Ming be kept in acute care until he is stabilized. He should do well on a dorm unit once he has achieved some remission.

Prognosis

Guarded.

_____   _____

Raul Hastings, ACP III   William G. Fraley, Ph.D.

Staff Psychologist   Supervising Psychologist

Reason for Referral

Inmate Ming was informed that the contents of this report would be shared with the appropriate treating personnel, and the evaluation was completed following inmate's tacit consent.

This inmate is a thin, frail, 34-year-old Chinese male who understands English better than he can speak it. Records indicate that he has been hospitalized before. His travel card indicates that he is serving time for rape. He allegedly cut off the victim's head. There is some question as to whether he might have been charged with the crime and did not actually participate in the decapitation. This was a gang-rape situation. Inmate Ming has been electively mute since his admission to Briggs. He will look at this examiner, but he makes no verbal response. Records indicate that he has experienced delusional thinking in the past. He has verbalized special powers and special knowledge and has been able to predict the future. He has been diagnosed as psychotic disorder, NOS, schizoaffective disorder, depressed, and schizoaffective disorder, bipolar type. There has also been some question as to whether or not he may be a catatonic schizophrenic.

Mental Status

Inmate Ming cannot be interviewed or tested at this time because of his refusal to talk. He does not appear to be attending to hallucinations. He appears flat, withdrawn, depressed, detached, and medicated.

Psychometrics

Not applicable.

CHANGING RESPONSIBILITIES OF PROBATION OFFICERS RESULTING FROM SENTENCING REFORMS AND TRENDS

How the probation officer's role has changed as the result of changing from one type of sentencing scheme to another has already been seen. Under the previous indeterminate sentencing scheme used by the federal district courts, for example, the U.S. Probation Office used to have its probation officers collect diverse information about prospective probationers and present this information in a subsequent sentencing hearing. Probation officers frequently embellished their reports with personal observations and judgments. They also recommended sentences to federal district court judges based on their own impressions of each case. The U.S. sentencing guidelines, however, caused considerable changes in a PO's role. Now, for instance, probation officers must learn to add and subtract points from one's **offense seriousness score** according to whether a drug transaction occurred within a specified distance of a school, whether the offender used a dangerous weapon during the commission of the crime, and whether offenders accepted responsibility for their actions. In drug cases, amounts of drugs must be factored into an increasingly complex formula to determine how an offender's case might be categorized. Fortunately, much of this calculating has been computerized, making it easier for POs to determine one's offense level and crime seriousness.

Ellen Steury (1989:95–96) illustrates the complexity of score determination under the new federal sentencing guidelines with an hypothetical example. She suggests the following:

A hypothetical offense situation might be helpful in portraying the mechanics of the guidelines. Consider the case of a defendant convicted of armed robbery, where the facts are as follows: (1) the robbery offense; (2) was carefully planned; (3) $23,000 was stolen; (4) the robber pointed a gun at the teller; (5) no injuries occurred; (6) the offender had three previous felony convictions, of which two carried terms of imprisonment longer than 13 months and one carried a term of probation; (7) the offender had been out of prison six months at the time of committing the instant offense, but was not under legal sentence at the time of the offense; (8) had no other currently pending charges; (9) confessed to the crime, wholly cooperated with law enforcement authorities, and offered restitution. In the ordinary case, this fact situation would require the court to sentence the offender to a term of imprisonment between 57 months (4 years, 9 months) and 71 months (5 years, 11 months). In the hypothetical situation detailed above, each of the items would carry the following values:

1. The robbery itself carries a base level score of 18.
2. The "more than minimal planning" does not affect the sentence in the case of robbery, but it does (inexplicably) in other offenses such as burglary, property damage or destruction, embezzlement, and aggravated assault.
3. The amount of money taken increases the base level by two points.
4. Brandishing a firearm increases the base level by another three points.
5. The fact that no victim injuries occurred avoids other possible level increases, which would otherwise be calculated on the basis of the degree of the injury.
6. The criminal history score totals nine points, comprised of three points for each sentence of imprisonment longer than thirteen months, and one point for the sentence of probation; while the recency of the latest imprisonment incurs two additional points.

7. The absence of other pending charges avoids a possible score increase.
8. The confession, coupled with the cooperation and the volunteered restitution, might persuade the court to conclude that the offender had "accepted responsibility" for the crime, which could result in decreasing the offense level score by two points.

In this example, the offense points sum to 21 and the criminal history points sum to 9. The sentencing range associated with offense level 21 and the criminal history score of 9 (category IV) is 57 to 71 months. Defendants so sentenced, or the government, could appeal by claiming that the guidelines had been incorrectly applied (18 U.S.C., Sec. 3742[a][2] and Sec. 3742[b][2], 2001). An appellate court would review the case.

If the sentencing court in its wisdom believed that the offender deserved fewer than 57 months or more than 71 months, a departure from the guidelines would be allowable, provided a written justification from the judge accompanied the departure. In such cases, defendants (if the sentence were longer than the maximum specified by the guidelines) or the government (if the sentence were shorter than the minimum specified by the guidelines) could appeal for a review of the stated reasons given by the judge for the departure (18 U.S.C., Sec. 3742[a][3][A] and Sec. 3742[b][3][A], 2001) (Steury, 1989:95–96).

Frank Marshall, a federal PO with the U.S. Probation Office in Philadelphia in 1989, has observed several significant changes in PO work as the result of the federal sentencing guidelines that went into effect in November 1987. He notes that the U.S. Parole Commission was to be abolished in 1992, that all parolees were to be placed under the supervision of the U.S. Probation Office, and that a new term, *supervised release*, would replace terms such as *parole* and *special parole* in future years. Marshall also indicates that POs will acquire more sentencing responsibilities with the sentencing change as federal district court judges increasingly rely on PO work to determine appropriate sentences. At the same time, fewer convicted offenders will be eligible for probation or diversion (Marshall, 1989:153-164). In the few years following the sentencing guidelines, for example, federal sentencing patterns shifted so that probation as a sentence was imposed about 10 to 12 percent of the time in the postguidelines period compared with 60 to 65 percent probation sentences in the preguidelines period (Champion, 1994). In short, the federal sentencing guidelines have drastically reduced the number of persons eligible for and receiving probation. The work of federal POs is not substantially reduced, however, because they now supervise parolees under supervised release and their PSI report preparation has become more complex.

SUMMARY

Sentencing is a crucial stage in offender processing. Many factors are considered in determining the appropriateness of the sentences convicted criminals receive. Much depends on the type of sentencing scheme used by any particular jurisdiction. Four major sentencing schemes are indeterminate sentencing, determinate sentencing, presumptive or guidelines-based sentencing, and mandatory sentencing. Indeterminate sentencing involves a judge imposing a term of years and parole boards determining one's early release from jail or prison. Determinate sentencing also involves a sentence imposed by the judge, but offenders are released according to the amount of good time they accumulate while confined. Good time credit may be statutory, earned, or meritorious. Parole boards are not involved in the early release of inmates sentenced under determinate sentencing. Guidelines-based or presumptive sentencing involves using established sentencing ranges, usually expressed in numbers of months, that fit particular crimes and are associated with offenders with particular criminal histories. Judges are obligated to stay within preapproved guidelines in the sentences they impose, although they may depart from these guidelines provided they furnish a written rationale for doing so. Mandatory sentences must be served despite the judge's beliefs or feelings. One intent of sentencing reform and generating different sentencing schemes is to yield an equitable punishment proportional to the offense committed, removing from the sentencing equation all extralegal factors, including one's age, socioeconomic status, gender, race, or ethnicity.

Offenders who are about to be sentenced usually have a sentencing hearing. These hearings are important because they provide an opportunity for both victims and offenders to make statements favoring their respective positions. Victim impact statements reflect how the conduct of the offender influenced the lives of victims. Offenders themselves can furnish the court with positive information in an attempt to persuade sentencing judges to be lenient. Defendants' sentencing memorandums are used to detail the offender's version of the crime and why it was committed. Also considered are reports submitted by probation officers.

The role of probation officers has become increasingly varied and complex. Probation officers must classify and categorize offenders and prepare presentence investigation reports about them at the direction of criminal court judges. These reports contain recommended sentences for offenders. Judges may either consider or disregard such recommendations, but most judges seem to take such recommendations seriously. Probation officers also work closely with the courts to ensure that the best supervisory arrangement for offenders is provided if probation is used as a sentencing option.

The presentence investigation, or PSI report, is an important document. It contains many bits of information, including a summary of the offense and circumstances about it, the offender's background, and the impact of the offense on victims, if any. PSI reports are confidential court documents, although in different jurisdictions designated persons are permitted to see them at various times. Whether reports are prepared is contingent on prevailing statutes in given jurisdictions as well as the discretion of sentencing judges. PSI reports perform functions, including assisting judges in imposing the best sentences for offenders, aiding POs during their supervisory efforts with probationer-clients, assisting prison officials in their inmate classification decision making, assisting parole boards in their early-release decision making, and serving as a source for research. Offenders may attach a memorandum of their version of events as well as any exculpatory information that might mitigate their sentences.

KEY TERMS

Acceptance of responsibility	Earned good time	Guidelines-based sentencing
Aggravating circumstances	Felony probation	Indeterminate sentencing
Augustus, John	Flat time	Justice model
Defendant's sentencing memorandum	Freedom of Information Act (FOIA)	Mandatory sentencing
Determinate sentencing	Good time	Meritorious good time

Minnesota sentencing grid
Mitigating circumstances
Narrative
Offense seriousness score
Presentence investigation (PSI)

Presentence investigation report
Presumptive sentencing
Rules of Criminal Procedure
Sentencing hearing

Sentencing Reform Act of 1984
Statutory good time
Truth-in-sentencing provisions
Victim impact statement (VIS)

QUESTIONS FOR REVIEW

1. Distinguish between indeterminate and determinate sentencing. Under each sentencing scheme, how do offenders gain early release from jail or prison?
2. What is mandatory sentencing? What are some examples of mandatory sentences?
3. What are guidelines-based or presumptive sentences?
4. What are some general purposes of sentencing reform?
5. What are some general functions performed by probation officers? How do their functions relate to offender sentencing? Explain.
6. Distinguish between aggravating and mitigating circumstances. Give some examples of each. At what point in offender processing are such circumstances considered important?
7. What is a presentence investigation report? Who prepares this report? Are such reports always prepared for all offenders? Under what circumstances would PSI reports be prepared?
8. What is a victim impact statement? Is it required by law?
9. What are risk assessment measures? How are they used?
10. What information is usually provided in a PSI report? What functions do they serve?

SUGGESTED READINGS

Burt, Grant N., et al. (2000). "Three Strikes and You're Out: An Investigation of False Positive Rates Using a Canadian Sample." *Federal Probation* **64:**3–6.

Horn, Rebecca, and Martin Evans (2000). "The Effect of Gender on Pre-Sentence Investigation Reports." *Howard Journal of Criminal Justice* **39:**184–197.

Johnson, Cindy (2000). "For Better or Worse: Alternatives to Jail Time for Environmental Crimes." *New England Journal on Criminal and Civil Confinement* **26:**265–297.

Norman, Michael D., and Robert C. Wadman (2000). "Utah Presentence Investigation Reports User Group Perceptions of Quality and Effectiveness." *Federal Probation* **64:**7–12.

Steffensmeier, Darrell, and Mark Motivans (2000). "Older Men and Older Women in the Arms of American Law: Offending Patterns and Sentencing Outcomes." *Journal of Gerontology* **55:**141–151.

APPENDIX

SAMPLE PSI REPORT

IN THE UNITED STATES DISTRICT COURT
FOR THE NORTHERN DISTRICT OF OHIO

UNITED STATES OF AMERICA)

)
)
v.   )   Docket No. 00-00014-01
)
Molly McDougall   )

PRESENTENCE REPORT

<u>Prepared for:</u>	The Honorable Robert L. Taylor
	United States District Judge
<u>Prepared by:</u>	John W. Phillips
	United States Probation Officer
	(216) 633-6226
<u>Sentencing Date:</u>	September 26, 2000 at 9:00 a.m.
<u>Offense:</u>	18 U.S.C. 656, Misapplication
	of Funds
	by Bank Employee, a class D

Felony

<u>Release Status:</u>	$1,000 Personal Surety Bond (no
	presentence custodial credit)
<u>Identifying Data:</u>	
Date of Birth:	February 2, 1978
Social Security Number:	881-22-4444
Address:	24 Apple Street
	Cleveland, Ohio 44114
<u>Detainers:</u>	None.
<u>Codefendants:</u>	None.

<u>Assistant U.S. Attorney</u>	<u>Defense Counsel</u>
Michael Haynes	Jimmie Baxter
U.S. Courthouse	113 Main Street
Cleveland, Ohio 44114	Cleveland, Ohio 44114
(216) 333-3333	(216) 444-4444

Date report prepared: September 2, 2000
Revised September 12, 2000

PART A. THE OFFENSE

<u>Charge(s) and Conviction(s)</u>

   1. Molly McDougall, the defendant, was indicted by a Northern District of Ohio grand jury on June 15, 2000. The indictment alleged that on May 2, 2000 while she was employed by the Bank of Ohio in Cleveland, Ohio, the defendant misapplied bank funds, in violation of 18 U.S.C. 656. On July 25, McDougall pled guilty to the charge.

   2. Since the offense took place after November 1, 1987, the Sentencing Reform Act of 1984 is applicable.

<u>The Offense Conduct</u>

   4. The defendant McDougall began working at Bank of Ohio, 2100 Main Street, Cleveland, Ohio, in mid-January, 2000. On April 30, 2000, she went to a local furniture store to purchase some bedroom furniture. The furniture she wanted to buy cost $5,000, and McDougall asked the salesman whether she could finance the purchase. The salesman advised McDougall that because she had not established a credit rating, she could finance only one-half of the purchase price and could pay the remainder of the purchase price, $2,500, by check. McDougall did not have sufficient funds in her checking account to cover a check in that amount, but thought she would have it as soon as she could contact her boyfriend, who was going to lend her the necessary funds. Believing that her boyfriend would give her the funds before her check to the furniture company could clear, McDougall wrote the company a check for $2,500. The check was presented for payment before she could make a deposit to cover it, and the bank, as a courtesy to an employee, paid it. When her boyfriend failed to advance her any funds to cover the overdraft, McDougall became desperate.

   5. On May 2, 2000, McDougall devised a solution to her problem. On that day, Victor Garcia came to her teller's window and asked McDougall to deposit an $11,000 check to his savings account. McDougall deposited the money to her checking account, instead.

   6. On May 17, 2000, Garcia advised the bank that his account did not contain the $11,000 he had deposited on May 2. The bank immediately began an audit and soon discovered what McDougall had done. When the Audit Manager confronted McDougall with his discovery, McDougall admitted that she had placed Garcia's deposit in her account. She stated that when she diverted the check she was desperate, being fearful that she would lose her job for having overdrawn her checking account. McDougall asserts that she intended to return the money to Garcia's account but had not been able to obtain the $2,500 that she had spent when the auditor discovered the mis-

application of the money. She had planned to replace the full $11,000 in one deposit entry to Mr. Garcia's account.

7. According to bank records, on June 3, 2000, McDougall paid the bank $8,550 of the funds she diverted. She still owes the bank the remaining $2,450. The bank has not filed a claim with its bonding company, which insured McDougall's fidelity, because McDougall has agreed to pay the $2,450 balance of the embezzlement.

Adjustment for Obstruction of Justice

8. The probation officer has no information suggesting that the defendant impeded or obstructed justice.

Adjustment for Acceptance of Responsibility

9. During the interview with the probation officer, McDougall was distraught and tearful regarding the offense, stating repeatedly that she is ashamed and embarrassed. When confronted by bank officials, McDougall readily admitted that she committed the offense. Four days later, she made an $8,550 payment toward restitution. She is clearly remorseful.

Offense Level Computation

10. Base Offense Level: The guideline for an 18 U.S.S. 656 offense is found in Section 2B1.1(a) of the Guidelines. The base offense level is 4.   4
11. Specific Offense Characteristics: Section 2B1.1(b) provides that if the value of the property taken is between $10,001 and $20,000, 5 levels are added. The instant offense entailed a loss of $11,000.   5
12. Adjustment for Role in the Offense: None   0
13. Victim-Related Adjustment: None   0
14. Adjustment for Obstruction of Justice: None   0
15. Adjustment for Acceptance of Responsibility: Based on the defendant's admission of guilt, her payment of restitution, and her remorse, pursuant to Section 3E1.1(a), two levels are subtracted.   -2
16. Total Offense Level: 7

PART B. THE DEFENDANT'S CRIMINAL HISTORY

Juvenile Adjudications

17. None

Criminal Convictions

18. None

<u>Criminal History Computation</u>

19. The defendant has no criminal convictions. Therefore, she has zero criminal history points and a criminal history category of I.

<u>Other Criminal Conduct</u>

20. None

PART C. SENTENCING OPTIONS

<u>Custody</u>

21. Statutory Provisions: The maximum term of imprisonment is 5 years. 18 U.S.C. 656.

22. Guideline Provisions: Based upon a total offense level of 7 and a criminal history category of I, the guideline imprisonment range is 1 to 7 months.

<u>Supervised Release</u>

23. Statutory Provisions: If a term of imprisonment is imposed, the court may impose a term of supervised release of not more than 2 years pursuant to 18 U.S.C. 3583(b)(2).

24. Guideline Provisions: If a sentence of imprisonment is imposed within the guideline range, a term of supervised release is not required but is optional. If more than one year imprisonment is imposed on the basis of a departure, supervised release is required. According to Section 5D3.2, the term of supervised release for a class D felony is 2 years.

<u>Probation</u>

25. Statutory Provisions: The defendant is eligible for probation by statute. Because the offense is a felony, 18 U.S.C. 3563(a)(2) requires that one of the following be imposed as a condition of probation: a fine, restitution or community service. For a felony, the authorized term of probation is not less than one year nor more than five years. 18 U.S.C. 3561(b)(1).

26. Guideline Provisions: The defendant is eligible for probation provided that the court impose a condition requiring intermittent confinement or community confinement for at least one month. Section 5B1.1(a)(2). Currently there are no facilities in the Cleveland area for intermittent confinement.

However, there is currently bedspace available at the New Hope Halfway House at 500 Broadway Avenue in Cleveland. This facility appears to be a suitable facility if the defendant were ordered to serve a sentence of community confinement.

27. If the court were to impose probation, the term must be at least one year but no more than five years. Section 5B1.2(a)(1).

PART D. OFFENDER CHARACTERISTICS

Family Ties, Family Responsibilities, and Community Ties

28. Molly McDougall was born on February 2, 1978, the fourth of seven children born to John and Ann McDougall. McDougall grew up in Fargo, North Dakota and moved to Cleveland with her family at the age of 15, when her father obtained employment as a cook at a Cleveland hotel.

29. McDougall is single. She resides with her parents and younger siblings at 24 Apple Street, Cleveland. The defendant states that she has not told her parents about the criminal charges against her, as she is exceedingly embarrassed and feels that she cannot discuss the matter with them. Marcus McDougall, the defendant's older brother, verified background information about the defendant. He reported that prior to this offense, McDougall never posed any serious problems for the family.

Mental and Emotional Health

30. According to the defendant, she has never suffered from any mental or emotional problems that would require professional intervention. It was obvious to the probation officer during the interview with Ms. McDougall that she is extremely remorseful about the outcome of this case. Her brother confirmed that McDougall has no history of mental or emotional problems but recently has been very anxious about the instant case.

Physical Condition, Including Drug Dependence and Alcohol Abuse

31. Molly McDougall reports that she is in good health and has never suffered from any serious illnesses or injuries. She states that she has never used illicit drugs and does not consume alcohol.

Education and Vocational Skills

32. A transcript from Monroe High School of Cleveland indicates that Molly McDougall was graduated in June, 1996 with a grade point average of 2.5.

She attended the Bank Training Institute in Cleveland in 1999, completing a five-week training course. The probation officer verified this by examining Institute records. It was the training from this vocational school that qualified McDougall to be hired by Bank of Ohio.

Employment Record

33. At the present time, McDougall is employed as a receptionist at Video Reproductions Incorporated on Third Street in Cleveland. Her duties include answering telephones and processing invoices. Her supervisor, Howard Allen, verified that McDougall does not handle money. She has been employed at this company since July 5, 2000, and according to Allen, she has been a responsible employee. Allen is aware of the charges pending against Ms. McDougall.

34. On May 30, 2000, when McDougall was discharged from Bank of Ohio for the misapplication of the check, she had been working as a teller since January 29, 2000. From December 1997 until March 1999, McDougall was employed by Macy's department store in Cleveland as a salesclerk. She quit this job to attend the Bank Training Institute.

PART E. FINES AND RESTITUTION

Statutory Provisions

35. The maximum fine is $250,000. 18 U.S.C. 3571(b).

36. A special assessment of $50 is mandatory. 18 U.S.C. 3013.

37. Restitution is owed to Bank of Ohio in the amount of $2,450 and is payable to the following address:

Bank of Ohio Collections
Security Division
113 Grape Avenue
Cleveland, Ohio 44114
Attention: Mr. Young

Guideline Provisions About Fines

38. The fine range for this offense is from $2,450 less any restitution ordered with a minimum of $500 (Section 5E4.2(c)(1)(B) to $33,000 (Section 5E4.2(c)(2)(C).

39. Subject to the defendant's ability to pay, the court shall impose an additional fine amount that is at least sufficient to pay the costs to the government of any imprisonment, probation, or supervised release. Section 5e4.2(i).

The most recent advisory from the Administrative Office of the United States Courts, dated March 15, 2000, suggests that a monthly cost of $_____ be used for imprisonment and a monthly cost of $_____ for supervision.

Defendant's Ability to Pay

40. Based upon a financial statement submitted by McDougall, a review of her bank records and a credit bureau check, the defendant's financial condition is as follows:

Assets

    Cash

Cash on hand	$ 47
Checking account	130
U.S. Savings Bond	75

    Unencumbered Assets

Stereo system	$ 500

    Equity in Other Assets

1997 Toyota Corolla	$2,000	(equity based on Blue Book value)
TOTAL ASSETS	$2,752	

    Unsecured Debts

Loan from brother	$ 300
Attorney fees balance	1,500
TOTAL UNSECURED DEBTS	$1,800

Net Worth	$ 952

Monthly Cash Flow

    Income

Net salary	$ 752
TOTAL INCOME	$ 752

Necessary Living Expenses

Room and board	$ 150
Installment payment (car loan)	242
Gas and auto costs	50
Attorney fees	100

```
Clothing                              50

TOTAL EXPENSES                   $ 592

Net Monthly Cash Flow            $ 160
```

41. Based upon McDougall's financial profile, it appears that she has the ability to remit restitution if she makes monthly installments. However, her income is rather modest, and it does not appear that she could also pay a fine.

PART F. FACTORS THAT MAY WARRANT DEPARTURE

42. The probation officer has not identified any information that would warrant a departure from the guidelines.

Respectfully submitted,

FRANK D. GILBERT
CHIEF PROBATION OFFICER

By

_____

John W. Phillips
U.S. Probation Officer

Reviewed and Approved:

_____

WILLIAM HACKETT
SUPERVISOR

ADDENDUM TO THE PRESENCE REPORT

The probation officer certifies that the presence report, including any revision thereof, has been disclosed to the defendant, her attorney, and counsel for the Government, and that the content of the Addendum has been communicated to counsel. The Addendum fairly states any objections they have made.

OBJECTIONS

By the Government
The Government has no objections.
By the Defendant
The defense attorney maintains that the defendant's youth, lack of a prior record, and her remorse are characteristics

that should be considered for a departure from the guidelines. He will present argument at the sentencing hearing that community confinement is not necessary in this case and that the court should depart by a sentence of probation with restitution.

The probation officer does not believe that a departure is warranted. Remorse and lack of a prior record are factored into the guidelines. The Sentencing Commission policy statement on age (Section 5H1.1) suggests that youth is not a valid reason for departure.

CERTIFIED BY

FRANK D. GILBERT
CHIEF PROBATION OFFICER

By

_____

John W. Phillips
U.S. Probation Officer

Reviewed and Approved

_____

WILLIAM HACKETT
SUPERVISOR

SENTENCING RECOMMENDATION

United States v. Molly McDougall, Dkt No. 00-00014-01, U.S. District Court, District of Northern Ohio

CUSTODY

Statutory maximum:	5 years
Guideline range:	1 to 7 months
Recommendation:	1 month community confinement

Justification:

According to the Guidelines, the defendant is eligible for probation provided that she serve at least one month of intermittent or community confinement. McDougall is a good candidate for probation because she has no prior record, is willing to make restitution to the victim, and is gainfully employed. A prison sentence does not appear to be necessary in this case since the defendant does not need to be incapacitated to deter

her from further crime and other sanctions will provide sufficient punishment.

FINE

Statutory maximum:	$250,000
Guideline range:	$2,450 (or $500 if restitution is ordered) to $33,000 plus the cost of incarceration and/or supervision
Recommendation:	$0

Justification:

Restitution to the victim bank is recommended as a condition of probation. The defendant's modest income will neces-
sitate that the restitution be paid in monthly installments.
At this point, McDougall does not have the ability to pay both
restitution and a fine.

PROBATION

Statutory term:	Minimum of 1 year and a maximum of 5 years
Guideline term:	Minimum of 1 year and a maximum of 5 years
Recommended term:	4 years

Recommended conditions:

1. That the defendant not commit any crimes, federal,
   state, or local.
2. That the defendant abide by the standard conditions of
   probation recommended by the Sentencing Commission.
3. That the defendant by confined in a community
   treatment center or halfway house for 30 days, during
   which time she will be allowed to maintain employment.
4. That the defendant pay restitution to Bank of Ohio in
   the amount of $2,450 in monthly installments of $55
   per month.
5. That the defendant be prohibited from incurring new
   credit charges or opening additional lines of credit
   without the approval of the probation officer unless the
   defendant is in compliance with the payment schedule.
6. That the defendant provide the probation officer with
   access to any requested financial information.

7. That if the defendant should hold a fiduciary position in her employment, she be required to inform her employer of the instant conviction.

Justification:

A sentence of probation contingent upon 30 days' confinement in a halfway house and the payment of restitution will provide sufficient punishment for McDougall as well as a general deterrence to others. The guidelines require intermittent or community confinement as a condition of probation. Placement in a halfway house for the minimum sentence of 30 days is recommended so that McDougall can continue to work and pay restitution to the victim bank. Since she has a modest income and a substantial amount of restitution to pay, a four-year term of probation is recommended with the requirement that she pay no less than $55 per month toward restitution. Conditions of supervision requiring financial disclosure to the probation officer and a provision against incurring new credit debts are suggested in order to monitor the defendant's payments. Because the instant offense is a form of embezzlement, McDougall will be considered a third-party risk to an employer if she were to handle money. It is therefore suggested that while under supervision, she be required to inform any employer of the instant conviction if she holds a fiduciary position.

SPECIAL ASSESSMENT $50

VOLUNTARY SURRENDER
If the court imposes a custodial sentence, McDougall appears to be a good candidate for a voluntary surrender.

Respectfully submitted,

FRANK D. GILBERT
CHIEF PROBATION OFFICER

By

_____
John W. Phillips
U.S. Probation Officer

Reviewed and Approved:

_____
WILLIAM HACKETT
SUPERVISOR

Date: September 12, 2000

CHAPTER 4

Probation and Probationers: History, Philosophy, Goals, and Functions

Introduction
Probation Defined
The History of Probation in the United
  States
  Judicial Reprieves and Releases
   on an Offender's Recognizance
  John Augustus, the Father of Probation
   in the United States
  The Ideal-Real Dilemma: Philosophies in
   Conflict
  Public Reaction to Probation
The Philosophy of Probation
Models for Dealing with Criminal Offenders
  The Treatment or Medical Model
  The Rehabilitation Model
  The Justice/Due Process Model
  The Just-Deserts Model

Functions of Probation
  Crime Control
  Community Reintegration
  Rehabilitation
  Punishment
  Deterrence
A Profile of Probationers
First-Offenders and Recidivists
Civil Mechanisms in Lieu of Probation
  Alternative Dispute Resolution
  Pretrial Diversion
  Functions of Diversion
Judicial Discretion and the Probation Decision
Summary
Key Terms
Questions for Review
Suggested Readings

Are These Cases That Deserve Probation?

• *Edward Bohanon, 42.* When police investigated a cafe robbery, they didn't have to look hard to find the escaping suspect. Police report that on Thursday, January 27, 2000, a man in a wheelchair entered the Kreme Kup Dairy Bar in West Memphis, Arkansas, and ordered a Double Jumbo Cheeseburger. He then handed the waitress a threatening note written on the back of one of his personal checks. "Don't push. No pulling. You won't get hurt," the note said. The man gestured as if he were hiding a gun under his jacket. The waitress gave him $120 from the cash drawer, and the man immediately wheeled himself out of the restaurant. Police responded to the robbery call and observed a man moving down the street in a wheelchair. When they arrived at a nearby motel and confronted the man, he jumped up and immediately took off running. A police lieutenant, Mike Allen, of the West Memphis Police Department, said, "He must have rolled into a faith healer after he left the Kreme Kup." Police captured the suspect, 42-year-old Edward Bohanon, who was charged later with aggravated robbery. Interestingly, the police already had a good idea who he was anyway. He had written the robbery note on the back of a personalized check with his name, address, and telephone number. Should Bohanon be placed on probation? (*Source:* Adapted from Associated Press, "Suspect Escapes in Wheelchair," January 28, 2000.)

• *Paul Harrington, 53.* In 1975, Paul Harrington was a Detroit police officer. He was married to 28-year-old Becky Harrington, and they had two children, Pamela, 9, and Cassandra, 4. On December 19, 1975, Paul Harrington said that he received a telephone call and suddenly had a flashback to Vietnam, where he had been a soldier. He believed that he was under attack. He grabbed his service revolver and shot and killed his wife and his two daughters. He then called 911 and reported the murders. Officers arrested him for triple murder. In 1977, a court found him not guilty by reason of insanity and confined him to a mental hospital. Two months later, doctors released him. Because of the triple murders, the Detroit Police Department fired Harrington.

Later, Harrington was employed at different jobs, and in 1999, he was employed at Hercules Drawn Steel in Livonia, a Detroit suburb. He had remarried. His second wife, Wanda, had two sons, Brian, 3, and Paul Jr., 15. Doctors had prescribed medication for Harrington to calm his nerves, and he had been taking this medication for many years. One day, though, Harrington quit taking his medication. On October 15, 1999, Harrington got another gun and killed his second wife and three-year-old son, Brian. He shot Wanda in the temple while she slept; Brian was shot three times in the head. Harrington called 911 again and waited on the front porch for police. He told investigators, "The same thing happened in 1975. They should have put me away then." An investigation disclosed that Harrington was having financial trouble and had been fired from his job. According to Harrington, he had used up all his medication and couldn't afford to buy more. The medication was prescribed to control his urges and prevent him from "hearing voices." Harrington said that he had had four sleepless nights before deciding to kill his wife and son. He borrowed a gun from a neighbor to carry out the murders but said that he waited until the next morning, when everything seemed all right. Then, though, he said that his head couldn't take it any more. He waited until his 15-year-old son had gone to school, and then he shot and killed his sleeping wife and young son. His defense counsel, Donald Cutler, said that "had he been on his medication, and had he a mental health facility to utilize, probably it never would have happened again." In the meantime, Michigan revised its laws governing pleas of being mentally ill. A new law provides for a guilty but mentally ill jury decision. Under this new type of verdict, Harrington could be sent to a mental health facility until such time as he would be suited for a transfer to the state penitentiary, where he would serve a life sentence without the possibility of parole. Is Harrington a suitable candidate for probation, provided he continues his medication? (*Source:* Adapted from Associated Press, "One Ex-Cop, Two Similar Murders, 24 Years Apart," January 26, 2000.)

• *James Hornacek, Hazlet, New Jersey: Horse Batterer.* It happened in Hazlet, New Jersey. During a rowdy protest rally in 1998, James Hornacek, 35, was among nearly 40,000 construction workers marching on a government building to signify their opposition to pending legislation. Hornacek, an electrician, was confronted by several mounted police officers, including Officer John Reilly. Hornacek walked up to Reilly, looked him right in the eye, and then punched Reilly's horse "dead in the nose." According to Hornacek, he merely was raising his hands to avoid being trampled. He claimed that he didn't deliberately hit the horse. In September 1999, Hornacek was convicted for attempting to injure a police animal. He faced up to 90 days in jail for the conviction. Was Hornacek a good candidate for probation? (*Source:* Adapted from Associated Press, "Man Found Guilty of Hitting Horse," January 20, 2000.)

• *Sean Robert Francis, 21.* The terrifying telephone calls made to numerous women in the West and Midwest were placed from Middletown, New York. The caller threatened the women who answered with rape and murder. At least 75 calls were made to women in Nebraska, Kansas, Montana, North Dakota, and Oregon. In one case, a woman at Oregon State University was so terrified and believed that the caller was inside her residence that she jumped from her second-story window, seriously injuring her ankles. Tiffany Arrington, a dorm director at the University of Kansas in Lawrence, said that the telephone calls were extraordinarily upsetting. "It was not the typical heavy breathing, 'What are you wearing?' type call," said Arrington. It was, "Here's what I'm going to do to you. There was definitely the threat of violence and sexual violence." Police traced the calls to a telephone in Middletown, New York, and to Sean Robert Francis, 21. Francis lived with his father, stepmother, and stepbrother. He had recently worked as a waiter at a Cracker Barrel restaurant in Fishkill, New York. When police arrested Francis, he admitted to making the calls. In court later, Francis admitted to threatening to rape two women at the University of Nebraska in Lincoln, to rape and kill two women at Montana State University in Bozeman, to rape a woman at North Dakota State University, and to rape a woman at Oregon State. Earlier in 1999, Francis had been sentenced to three years' probation for aggravated harassment in connection with calls he made to women in Goshen, New York. According to the complaint in the federal case, Francis admitted that when he made such calls, "If I got a woman, I would threaten to rape her." The statutory maximum for these offenses is five years on each count. In the meantime, Francis was held without bail. Should Francis be placed in a probation program under intensive supervision? (*Source:* Adapted from Associated Press, "Rape Caller Pleads Guilty," December 22, 1999.)

What Happened?

• Bohanan was sentenced to five years in prison for robbery.

• Harrington was found guilty but mentally ill and confined to a mental hospital. When he is well enough, he will be transferred to the state prison, where he will serve a sentence of 25 years to life.

• Hornacek was placed on probation and ordered to perform four days' worth of community service.

• Francis was sentenced to two years in prison.

INTRODUCTION

This chapter is about probation in the United States. Probation is unique to the United States and its origins date to the 1830s. The first section defines probation and places it in an historical context. Besides describing the historical antecedents of probation and its emergence throughout the nation, the philosophy of probation is presented. Next, various models that practitioners use for dealing with probationers are described. These models are orientations that influence the types of treatments or programs designed for probationers. They also reflect the nature of political sentiment at particular points in history, ranging from primarily treatment-centered and rehabilitation-oriented to more justice-oriented, due-process frames of reference for guiding PO and probation agency thinking and practice. Several important functions of probation are also presented. The chapter continues with a profile of probationers, including first-offenders and recidivists.

The final part of the chapter examines several pretrial options available to prosecutors whenever low-level, nonserious types of offenders have committed crimes. It is not always feasible to pursue criminal charges against certain defendants, especially when such cases can resolved through less stigmatized civil proceedings. Thus, two options are presented: pretrial diversion and alternative dispute resolution. Both options require court approval, although they often result in satisfactory resolutions of disputes between complainants and offenders. In recent years, restorative justice has been used to describe a slightly different civil dispute resolution option available to prosecutors and the courts, and this process is also described. The chapter concludes with a brief discussion of judicial discretion in probation decision making.

PROBATION DEFINED

Probation is releasing convicted offenders into the community under a conditional suspended sentence, avoiding imprisonment for those offenders showing good behavior under the supervision of a probation officer (Black, 1990:1202). The word *probation* derives from the Latin ***probatio***, meaning a period of proving or trial and forgiveness. Thus, offenders who prove themselves during the trial period by complying with the conditions of their probation are forgiven and released from further involvement with the criminal justice system. Their criminal records may not be expunged or forgotten, but they avoid incarceration. Some states such as California authorize expungement of criminal records under certain conditions after a probation program has been successfully completed.

Probation is applied among the states in many different ways. In some states, probation is granted for particular crimes, whereas in others, the same type of offense might draw prison or jail time. To understand the nature and reasons for variations in probation, interstate variation of criminal statutes as well as federal criminal laws must be examined. Every state or federal criminal statute carries statutory sanctions that always provide for the *possibility* of incarceration and/or a fine, depending on the seriousness of the offense. In Tennessee, for instance, a convicted shoplifter is punished by a fine of *not more than* $300 or imprisonment for *not more than* six months, or both (T.C.A., 39-3-1124, 2001). A conviction for violating a federal criminal law, such as the willful destruction of U.S. government property not exceeding $100, is punishable by a fine of *not more than* $1,000 or by imprisonment for *not more than* one year, or both (18 U.S.C. Sec. 1361, 2001). If U.S. government property damage exceeds $100, the punishment escalates to a fine of *not more than* $10,000 or imprisonment for *not more than* ten years, or both (18 U.S.C., Sec. 1361, 2001).

The important phrase in these statutes is *not more than*. Judges have discretionary power to sentence offenders to the maximum penalties provided by law (e.g., whatever maximum penalties are provided in each criminal statute), or judges may decide to impose no penalties. A third option is that they may impose a portion of the maximum sentence prescribed by the particular criminal statute. Sometimes, a judge may declare, "You are hereby sentenced to six months in the county jail and ordered to pay a $500 fine. The six-month sentence is suspended upon the payment of a $500 fine and court costs." The judge may also say, "You are sentenced to four years in prison, but I suspend the four-year sentence and order you placed on probation for four years." All judges have diverse sentencing options.

In the federal system, until November 1987, federal judges were encouraged to refrain from incarcerating convicted offenders. In fact, 18 U.S.C., Sec. 3582 (2001), says that "recognizing that imprisonment is not an appropriate means of promoting correction and rehabilitation," the court (judge) should consider any relevant policy statements by the Sentencing Commission and recommend an appropriate sentence for the defendant. Furthermore, 18 U.S.C., Sec. 3651 (2001), provides that judges may grant probation for any offense not punishable by death or life imprisonment when they are satisfied that the ends of justice and the best interest of the public as well as the defendant will be served. Within this same section, the period of probation is limited to five years, regardless of more excessive penalties associated with the original sentence and fine. Several states have followed these federal guidelines in writing their own sentencing provisions and guidelines.

In November 1987, however, new federal sentencing guidelines were established. These presumptive guidelines were intended to establish greater uniformity and consistency among federal judges and the sentences they impose. Furthermore, these guidelines severely restrict a federal judge's sentencing options. Because of these new sentencing guidelines, every federal criminal statute has been modified (DiIulio, 1995).

The public is ambivalent about probation and who should receive it. Popular opinion views probation as a nonsentence, no punishment, or excessive leniency (Arthur, 2000). Even experts disagree about how and when probation should be used (Latessa and Allen, 1999). The word *probation* is sometimes used to indicate a legal disposition, a measure of leniency, a punitive measure, an administrative process, or a treatment method (Black, 1990:1202). Probation is the supervised release of offenders into the community in lieu of incarceration subject to conditions (Black, 1990:1202).

THE HISTORY OF PROBATION IN THE UNITED STATES

Many U.S. laws and judicial procedures have been influenced by early English common law and judicial customs. Evidence also shows a distinct British influence on U.S. prison architecture and design as well as other corrections-related phenomena (American Correctional Association, 1983).

Judicial Reprieves and Releases on an Offender's Recognizance

During the late 1700s and early 1800s, English judges increasingly exercised their discretion in numerous criminal cases by granting convicted offenders **judicial reprieves**. Under English common law, judicial reprieves suspended the incarcerative sentences of convicted offenders. They were demonstrations of judicial leniency, especially in those cases in which offenders had no prior records, had committed minor offenses, and the punishments were deemed excessive by the courts. Judges believed that in certain cases, incarceration would serve no useful purpose. Although no accurate records are available about how many convicted offenders actually received judicial reprieves in English courts during this period, the practice of granting judicial reprieves was adopted by some judges in the United States (Stastny and Tyrnauer, 1982).

Judges in Massachusetts courts during the early 1800s typically used their discretionary powers to suspend incarcerative sentences of particular offenders. Jail and prison overcrowding no doubt influenced their interest in devising options to incarceration. One of the more innovative judges of that period was Boston Municipal Judge Peter Oxenbridge Thatcher. Judge Thatcher used judicial leniency when sentencing offenders. He also sentenced some offenders to be released on their own recognizance (ROR), either before or after their criminal charges had been adjudicated. Judge Thatcher's decision to release convicted offenders on their own recognizance amounted to an indefinite suspension of their incarcerative sentences. He believed that such sentences would encourage convicted offenders to practice good behavior and refrain from committing new crimes.

While judicial reprieves and suspensions of incarcerative sentences for indefinite periods continued throughout the nineteenth century, the U.S. Supreme Court declared this practice unconstitutional in 1916. The Supreme Court believed that such discretion among judges infringed the "separation of powers" principle by contravening the powers of the legislative and executive branches to write laws and insure their enforcement. During the 1830s, however, when releases on an offender's own recognizance and judicial reprieves flourished, the stage was set for the work of another Boston correctional pioneer.

John Augustus, the Father of Probation in the United States

Many court practices in the United States have been inherited from England, but there are many exceptions. In corrections, probation is one of those exceptions. Probation in the United States was conceived in 1841 by a successful cobbler and philanthropist, John Augustus, although historical references to this phenomenon may be found in writings as early as 422–437 B.C. Of course, the actions of Judge Thatcher have been regarded by some scholars as probation, because he sentenced convicted offenders to be released on their own recognizance instead of jail. John Augustus, however, is most often credited with pioneering probation in the United States, although statutes existed at the time to label it or describe how it should be conducted (Conrad, 1987).

The temperance movement against alcohol provided the right climate for using probation (Behr, 1996). Augustus attempted to rehabilitate alcoholics and assist those arrested for alcohol-related offenses. Appearing in a Boston municipal court one morning to observe offenders charged and sentenced for various crimes, Augustus intervened on behalf of a man charged with being a "common drunkard" (Augustus, 1852). Instead of placing the convicted offender in the **Boston House of Corrections**, Augustus volunteered to supervise the man for three weeks and personally guaranteed his reappearance later. Knowing Augustus's reputation for philanthropy and trusting his motives, the judge agreed with this proposal. When Augustus returned three weeks later with the drunkard, the judge was so impressed with the man's improved behavior that he fined him only one cent and court costs, which were less than $4.00. The judge also suspended the six-month jail term. Between 1841 and 1859, the year Augustus died, nearly 2,000 men and women were spared incarceration because of Augustus's intervention and supervision.

Augustus attracted several other philanthropic volunteers to perform similar probation services with juvenile offenders as well as with adults. Few records were kept about the dispositions of juveniles, however, so the precise number of those who benefited from the work of Augustus and his volunteers is unknown. In all likelihood, several thousand youths probably were supervised effectively as informal probationers.

The Ideal-Real Dilemma: Philosophies in Conflict

Probation was a true correctional innovation in 1841. Before Augustus's work, offenders convicted of criminal offenses were fined, imprisoned, or both. Between 1790 and 1817, sentences in U.S. courts had to be served in their entirety (Bottomley, 1984). Federal prisoners increased beyond the government's capacity to confine them, and overcrowding became a critical correctional issue. Today, jail and prison overcrowding is the greatest problem confronting corrections. After 1817, prison systems began releasing some prisoners early before serving their full terms. These early-release decisions were often made informally by prison administrators, with court approval. Thus, the informal use of parole in the United States technically preceded the informal use of probation by several decades.

Currently, the **get-tough movement** is pressing for a return to sentencing policies that were practiced in the early 1800s, when convicted offenders had to serve their full incarcerative terms. The get-tough movement is not a specific association of persons with a defined membership list who band together for the purpose of creating harsher punishments for criminal offenders. Rather, the term is used to characterize a general philosophy meaning tougher criminal laws, longer imprisonment lengths for convicted offenders, greater fines, and closer supervision of those who are placed on either probation or parole.

Prison and jail overcrowding continues to frustrate efforts by judges and others to incarcerate larger numbers of convicted offenders for their full sentences. Court-ordered prison and jail inmate population reductions shorten the actual amount of time served by inmates. Logistical considerations involving where convicted offenders may be housed often conflict with the philosophy of just deserts and punishment. Furthermore, the constitutional rights of inmates, including the right to prison and jail environments that ensure inmate health and safety—must be preserved. Although no constitutional provisions exist that require prison and jail administrators to provide comfortable quarters for inmates, penal authorities are obligated to ensure that their incarcerative environments are not "cruel and unusual" and in violation of the Eighth Amendment.

Public Reaction to Probation

Many citizens believe that probation actually means coddling offenders and that it causes them not to take their punishment seriously (Arthur, 2000). In the 1840s, Augustus himself was criticized by the press, politicians, and especially jailers. The livelihood of jailers was based on the cost of care and inmate accommodations, including provisions for food and clothing. Jailer income was based on the numbers of prisoners housed in jails. The greater the occupancy, the greater the jailer's income. Under such a system of jailer rewards, some jailers embezzled funds intended for inmate food and clothing for their own use. It is unknown how much embezzlement occurred among jailers while this arrangement thrived, but it is known that more than a few jailers profited from large inmate populations.

Augustus's philanthropy directly decreased profiteering among those jailers embezzling funds allocated for inmate care. The lack of an effective system of accountability for these funds explains why the Boston House of Corrections, as well as other Massachusetts jails of that period, was described as a rat-infested hellhole to be avoided if at all possible (Lindner and Savarese, 1984). Augustus, however, could not save everyone from incarceration. In fact, that was not his intention. He only wanted to rescue those offenders he felt worthy of rehabilitation. Therefore, he screened offenders by asking them questions and engaging in informal background checks of their acquaintances and personal habits. He specifically limited his generosity to first-offenders or those never before convicted of a criminal offense. By his own account, only one offender out of nearly 2,000 ever violated his trust (Probation Association, 1939). Presentence investigation reports are now routinely conducted in all U.S. courts when defendants have been convicted of felonies or less serious crimes.

When Augustus died in 1859, probation did not die with him. Various prisoner's and children's aid societies, many religiously based, continued to volunteer their services to courts in the supervision of convicted offenders on a probationary basis. Another philanthropist, **Rufus R. Cook**, continued Augustus's work as well, particularly assisting juvenile offenders through the Boston Children's Aid Society in 1860 (Timasheff, 1941:10). **Benjamin C. Clark**, a philanthropist and volunteer probation officer, assisted in probation work with court permission throughout the 1860s.

In 1878, Massachusetts became the first state to pass a probation statute, which authorized the mayor of Boston to hire the first probation officer, Captain Savage, a former police officer. He was supervised by the superintendent of police. Thus, probation was given official recognition, although it was based on political patronage. Several other states passed similar statutes before 1900. In 1901, New York enacted a statutory probation provision similar to that of Massachusetts. Between 1886 and 1900, a number of "settlements" were established, primarily in impoverished parts of cities, for the purposes of assisting the poor and improving the lot of the disadvantaged. These settlements were "experimental efforts to aid in the solution of the social and industrial problems . . . engendered by the modern conditions of life in a great city," and they were to figure prominently in the development and use of probation during that period (Lindner, 1992a, 1992c).

In 1893, **James Bronson Reynolds**, an early prison reformer, was appointed headworker of the **University Settlement**, a private facility in New York operated to provide assistance and job referrals to community residents. When New York passed the probation statute in 1901, Reynolds seized this opportunity to involve the University Settlement in probation work. Interestingly, the statute itself prohibited compensation for persons performing "probation officer" chores. Probation work was to be simply another facet of the full-time work they did.

For example, many early probation officers worked as police officers, deputies, or clerks in district attorney's offices. The statute also provided that "private citizens would serve as probation officers without cost to the city or county" (Lindner, 1992a, 1992c). Thus, the voluntary and privately operated University Settlement project was ideally suited to experiments with future probationers. Besides, Reynolds was a member of several political committees, including the Executive Committee of the Prison Association of New York, and his connections directly benefited the University Settlement as a new probation facility. Despite political opposition to Reynolds and the program he attempted, volunteers are widely used today in various capacities by both publicly and privately operated agencies and programs that serve the needs of probationers. Volunteers work in halfway houses, provide foster care for dependent youths, and perform a large number of services that assist POs in the performance of their jobs. Without volunteers, the work of POs would be considerably more burdensome.

By 1922, 22 states had provided for probation in their corrections systems. During the late 1800s and early 1900s, federal district judges were also releasing certain offenders on their own recognizance following the pattern of Massachusetts and other states, often using the services of various state probation officers to supervise offenders. The federal government formally implemented probation through a bill sponsored by the Judicial Committee of the House of Representatives on March 4, 1925. The U.S. attorney general was given control of probation officers through another bill in 1930. The Federal Juvenile Delinquency Act was passed on June 16, 1938, so that probation could apply to juveniles as well as to adults, although "general probation" for both juveniles and adults had technically already been created through the 1925 and 1930 acts (Timasheff, 1941:64–66). Thus, all states had juvenile probation programs by 1927, and by 1957, all states had statutes authorizing the use probation as a sanction for adults where appropriate. Figure 4.1 summarizes the major developments influencing the evolution of probation in the United States.

Year	Event
1791	Passage of the Bill of Rights
1817	New York passes first good time statute
1824	New York House of Refuge is founded
1830	Judge Peter Oxenbridge Thatcher in Boston introduces release on one's own recognizance
1836	Massachusetts passes first recognizance with monetary sureties law
1841	John Augustus introduces probation in the United States in Boston
1863	Gaylord Hubbell, warden of the State of Correctional Facility at Ossining, New York (Sing Sing), visits Ireland and is influenced by Walter Crofton's ticket of leave or mark system; later led to good time credits earned by prisoners for early release
1869	Elmira Reformatory established in New York, with early release dates set by the board of managers
1870	Establishment of the National Prison Association (later the American Correctional Association), emphasizing indeterminate sentencing and early release
1876	Zebulon Brockway releases inmates on parole from Elmira Reformatory
1878	First probation law passed by Massachusetts
1899	Illinois passes first juvenile court act, creating special juvenile courts
1906	Work release originates in Vermont through informal sheriff action
1913	Huber Law or first work release statute originates in Wisconsin
1916	U.S. Supreme Court declares that sentences cannot be indefinitely suspended by courts; rather, this right was a legislative right
1918	Furlough program begun in Mississippi
1932	44 states have parole mechanisms
1954	All states and the federal government have probation and parole systems
1965	Prisoner Rehabilitation Act passed by Congress applicable to federal prisoners
1976	Maine abolishes parole

FIGURE 4.1 Major events in the development of probation and parole in the United States.

Today, probation operates very differently from the way it was originally conducted in 1841. Also, dramatic changes have occurred in the forms of probation used and approved by the court. Among other things, technological developments have spawned several different kinds of offender management systems compared with the traditional probation officer/client face-to-face relation.

THE PHILOSOPHY OF PROBATION

Probation in the 1990s has undergone significant changes in its general conception and implementation. Today, there are diverse opinions among experts about how probation should be reconceptualized and reorganized (Arthur, 2000; Johnson, 2000). One observer suggests that the reason for these disagreements and confusion is a general lack of understanding about what probation does and for whom. Even though probation supervises two-thirds of all convicted felons in the United States, it receives little publicity or financial support (Burt et al., 2000).

The idea of proving, or trial, forgiveness implied by probation says much about its underlying philosophy. The primary aim of probation is to give offenders an opportunity to prove themselves by remaining law-abiding individuals. Avoiding jail or prison is a powerful incentive to refrain from committing new crimes. Helping to promote probation as a viable alternative to imprisonment are various societal views about the rehabilitative value of prisons and jails. One belief is that incarceration does not deter crime. In fact, locking up offenders only makes matters worse, according to some observers (Brumbaugh and Birkbeck, 1999; Hofer et al., 1999). Newly confined offenders learn more about crime from more experienced hard-core prisoners. Also, new prison and jail construction is costly, and higher taxes are required to pay for this construction. Probation is far less expensive. Some forms of probation, such as electronic monitoring and home confinement, are both effective and inexpensive client management tools. This thinking minimizes the importance of rehabilitation as an important aim of incarceration. Offender punishment, containment, and control should be the priorities of incarceration. Although it may be true that some rehabilitation may occur among some offenders, that is an unintended fringe benefit (Bauer, 1999).

More than a few observers, however, question whether incarceration should be applied to all criminals. The process of differentiating those who deserve incarceration from those who do not is imperfect. Many offenders are imprisoned for minor crimes, and a significant proportion of these persons will never reoffend. Many convicted offenders are placed on probation as well, but a substantial number of these clients continue to commit new crimes. Inmates themselves have appraised incarceration and probation accordingly. Some inmates have reported that they would rather do more time in prison than adhere to a probation program with strings attached (Wood and Grasmick, 1995). At the same time, some inmates believe that probation should not be granted to certain offenders, whereas incarceration should be rejected as a sanction for other criminals.

For guidance about the general philosophy of probation, the original intent of its pioneer, John Augustus, should be examined. Augustus wanted to reform offenders. He wanted to rehabilitate common drunks and petty thieves. Thus, **rehabilitation** was and continues to be a strong philosophical aim of probation. Over time, however, probation has changed from the way Augustus originally viewed it. For example, consider how Augustus supervised his probationers. First, he stood their bail in the Boston Municipal Court. Second, he took them to his home or other place of shelter, fed them, and generally looked after them. He may have even provided them with job leads and other services through his many friendships as well as his political and philanthropic connections. In short, he provided his probationers with fairly intensive supervision and personalized assistance, financial and otherwise. He supervised approximately a hundred probationers a year between 1841 and 1859 and kept detailed records of their progress. In this respect, he compiled what are now called presentence investigation reports, although he usually made extensive notes about offenders and their progress after they had been convicted. He showed great interest in their progress, and no doubt many of these probationers were emotionally affected by his kindness and generosity. According to his own assessment of his performance, rehabilitation and reformation were occurring at a significant rate among his clients.

This example, however, oversimplifies the philosophy of probation. It has many overtones. For example, John Augustus's goal was behavioral reform, and much of his philanthropy was directed toward those offenders with drinking problems. He believed that some offenders would change from drunkenness and intemperance to sobriety and honesty if they could avoid the stigma of imprisonment. Several religious principles, as well as the views of the temperance society to which he belonged, guided his belief.

The major difficulty with pinning down a specific philosophy of probation is that among the public and professionals, there are diverse impressions of what probation is or should be. The word that recurs most often, however, is rehabilitation. Regardless of the form of rehabilitation prescribed by the court when offenders are sentenced, probation appears beneficial by diverting offenders from incarceration (Levin, Langan, and Brown, 2000).

Present-day probation has become streamlined and bureaucratic. Although there are exceptions among probation officers, relatively few take interest in their clients to the extent that they feed and clothe them and look after their other personal needs. Probation officers do not sit in municipal courtrooms waiting for the kinds of offenders who will be responsive to personalized attention and care. Probation officers do not eagerly approach judges with bail bonds and assume personal responsibility for a probationer's conduct, even if for brief periods.

Today, probation officers define their work in terms of client caseloads and officer/client ratios. Required paperwork consumes over half of a probation officer's time on the job. If society has strayed far from Augustus's original meaning of what probation supervision is and how it should be conducted, it is probably because of bureaucratic expediency. There are too many probationers and too few probation officers. It is hardly unexpected that the public has gradually become disenchanted with the rehabilitative ideal probation originally promised (Duncan, Speir, and Meredith, 1999).

The rehabilitative aim of probation has not been abandoned; rather, it has been rearranged in a rapidly growing list of correctional priorities. One dominant, contemporary philosophical aim of probation is offender control. If offenders cannot be rehabilitated, at least more effective ways of managing them while they are on probation can be devised. As a result, several alternative punishments, each connected directly with increased offender supervision and control, have been developed (American Correctional Association, 1994). The community is most frequently used for managing growing offender populations, and many community corrections programs have been established to accommodate different types of offenders. Observers generally agree that the future of probation is closely connected with the effectiveness of community corrections, and the key to effective community corrections is effective client management through more intensive supervised release (Bork, 1995). Investigators have found that in some jurisdictions, however, those placed under intensive supervision in their communities do not pose any greater risk to the public than those who have served prison terms and are subsequently paroled (Deschenes, Turner, and Petersilia, 1995).

According to some authorities, probation serves several purposes:

1. Probation keeps those convicted of petty crimes from the criminogenic environment of jails and prisons. Prisons are viewed as colleges of crime where inmates are not rehabilitated but rather learn more effective criminal techniques.

2. Probation helps offenders avoid the stigma of the criminal label. Some authorities believe that once offenders have been labeled as delinquent or criminal, they will act out these roles by committing subsequent offenses.

3. Probation allows offenders to integrate more easily with noncriminals. Offenders may hold jobs, earn a living for their families and themselves, and develop more positive self-concepts and conforming behaviors not likely acquired if incarcerated.

4. Probation is a practical means by which to ease the problems of prison and jail overcrowding. Greater use of probation is a major **front-end solution** to jail and prison overcrowding. Thus, probation serves the purely logistical function of enabling correctional institutions to more effectively manage smaller inmate populations (Johnson, 2000; Munson and Ygnacio, 2000).

MODELS FOR DEALING WITH CRIMINAL OFFENDERS

Those who supervise offenders either on probation or parole operate from a variety of different offender management assumptions. Depending on the assumptions made about offenders and the programs used to manage them, different supervisory styles and approaches may have different client outcomes. For instance, some probation officers are oriented toward law enforcement more than others. Some officers believe that their roles should be as educators or enablers. Assisting clients in finding jobs or locating housing may be more important to some officers than whether a client commits a technical program infraction, such as violating a curfew or failing a drug test. Therefore, an understanding of probation officer work ideologies can help determine which ideologies seem most effective at reducing client recidivism rates (Bazemore, 1998). Several models that represent different ways of approaching the officer/client relation—the treatment or medical model, the rehabilitation model, the justice/due process model, the just-deserts model, and the community model—are presented next.

The Treatment or Medical Model

Despite the religious, moral, and philanthropic interests that influenced the early practice of probation, its current rehabilitative nature derives from the **treatment model** of treating criminals. Also known as the **medical model**, this model considers criminal behavior as an illness to be remedied. The custodial approach of incarcerating criminals does not treat the illness; rather, it separates the ill from the well. When released from incarceration, the ill continue to be ill and are likely to commit further crimes. The nonincarcerative alternative, probation, permits rehabilitation to occur through treatment programs and therapeutic services not otherwise available to offenders under conditions of confinement. In addition, rehabilitative measures within prison and jail settings have been taken through the creation and use of vocational/technical, educational, and counseling programs as parallels to the treatment received by nonincarcerated probationers (Mason and Mercer, 1999).

Some observers claim that the fundamental flaw of the treatment model is that offenders are treated as objects (Craissati, 1998). Selectively applying probation to some offenders and not to others, however, leads to more fundamental criticisms justifiably associated with inequitable treatment on the basis of gender, race/ethnic status, socioeconomic differences, and other factors (Miller, 1996).

The Rehabilitation Model

Closely related to the treatment or medical model is the **rehabilitation model**, which stresses rehabilitation and reform. Although rehabilitation may be traced to William Penn's work in correctional reform, the most significant support for the rehabilitation orientation came from Zebulon Brockway's Elmira Reformatory in 1876. Eventually, federal recognition of rehabilitation as a major correctional objective occurred when the Federal Bureau of Prisons was established on May 14, 1930. Although the first federal penitentiary was built in 1895 in Leavenworth, Kansas, it took 35 more years for an official federal prison policy to be devised. The original mandate of the Bureau of Prisons called for rehabilitating federal prisoners through vocational and educational training as well as the traditional individualized psychological counseling that was associated with the treatment model. In later years, encounter groups, group therapy, and other strategies were incorporated into federal prison operations and policy as alternative rehabilitative methods (Roberts, 1997).

Between 1950 and 1966, more than a hundred prison riots occurred in federal facilities. These incidents were sufficient for officials to reconsider the rehabilitation model and define it as ineffective for reforming prisoners. There were other weaknesses of this model as well. Similar to the treatment model that preceded it, the rehabilitation model stresses "individual" treatment or reform, and as a result, inmate sanctions have often been individualized. Thus, those who have committed similar offenses of equal severity might receive radically different rehabilitation or punishment. The inequity of this individualized system is apparent, and in many jurisdictions, such inequities in the application of sanctions have been associated with race, ethnicity, gender, or socioeconomic status.

The 1960s and 1970s are regarded as the **progressive era** in which rehabilitation was stressed by liberals for both incarcerated and nonincarcerated offenders. Rising crime rates and the recidivism of probationers and parolees, however, stimulated a public backlash against social reform programs. Studies conducted in the 1970s disclosed the apparent lack of success of rehabilitation programs, including probation. Although some critics contend that these studies are inconclusive and misleading, one result was the general condemnation of rehabilitation and specific probation alternatives. Despite these criticisms, rehabilitation continues to be a strong correctional goal (U.S. General Accounting Office, 1994).

The Justice/Due Process Model

Although the rehabilitation ideal has not been abandoned, it has been supplemented by an alternative known as the justice or **due process model**, which is not intended to replace the rehabilitative model, but rather to enhance it (Schwartz, 1999). In recent years, probation practices in the United States have been influenced by the justice model through the imposition of more equitable sentences and fairness. Sentencing reforms have been undertaken to eliminate sentencing disparities attributable to race/ethnic background, gender, or socioeconomic status (Petersilia, 1999a). The justice model applied to probation stresses fair and equitable treatment. Probably the most important reason citizens oppose the use of probation is that they do not define probation as punishment. In response to this criticism, several justice-oriented writers (von Hirsch, 1992) have proposed the following:

1. Probation is a penal sanction whose main characteristic is punitive.
2. Probation should be a sentence, not a substitute for a real sentence threatened after future offenses.
3. Probation should be a part of a single graduated range of penal sanctions available for all levels of crime except for the most serious felonies.
4. The severity of the probation sentence should be determined by the quality and quantity of conditions (e.g., restitution or community service).
5. Neither the length of term nor any condition should be subject to change during the sentence, unless the conditions are violated.
6. Conditions should be justified in terms of seriousness of offense.
7. When conditions are violated, courts should assess additive penalties through show-cause hearings.

The Just-Deserts Model

The **just-deserts model** or **deserts model** emphasizes equating punishment with the severity of the crime. Offenders should get what they deserve; therefore, retribution is an important component. Just deserts dismisses rehabilitation as a major correctional aim. It alleges that offenders ought to receive punishments equivalent to the seriousness of their crimes. If rehabilitation occurs during the punishment process, then that is not undesirable, but it is also not essential (Miller, 1996). Applying the just-deserts philosophy, offenders sentenced to prison would be placed in custody levels fitting the seriousness of their crimes. Petty offenders who commit theft or burglary might be sentenced to minimum-security facilities with few guards and fences. Accordingly, robbers, rapists, and murderers would be placed in maximum-security prisons under close supervision. If offenders are sentenced to probation, then their level of supervision would be adjusted to fit the seriousness of their offenses. The more serious the offense, the more intensive the supervision.

The just-deserts model has emerged in recent years as a popular alternative to the rehabilitation model, which influenced correctional programs for many decades. Penal and sentencing reforms among jurisdictions are currently consistent with the just-deserts approach. Public pressure for applying the just-deserts orientation in judicial sentencing, including greater severity of penalties imposed, has stimulated the get-tough movement (Blomberg and Cohen, 1995).

The Community Model

The **community model** is a relatively new concept based on the correctional goal of offender reintegration into the community (DeLeon, 1999). Sometimes called the reintegration model, this model stresses offender adaptation to the community by participating in one or more programs that are a part of community-based corrections (Cosgrove, 1994). More judges are using community-based corrections because they are in place within the community and because they offer a front-end solution to prison and jail overcrowding (Mays and Gray, 1996). Often, offenders are accommodated in large homes where curfews and other rules are imposed. Food, clothing, and employment assistance are provided. Sometimes, counselors and psychiatrists are on call to assist with any serious adjustment or coping problems. Some community interventions are geared to helping battered women understand the abusive behaviors of others and the implications of spousal abuse for their original offending behaviors (Tolman, 1996).

The primary strengths of the community model are that offenders are able to reestablish associations with their families and that they have the opportunity to work at jobs where a portion of their wages earned can be used for victim restitution, payment of fines, and defrayment of program maintenance costs. Furthermore, offenders may participate in psychological therapy or educational and vocational programs designed to improve their work and social skills. POs often function as brokers, locating important and necessary community services for their offender-clients. POs also provide a means through which offenders can obtain employment (American Correctional Association, 1996a).

The community model uses citizen involvement in offender reintegration. Often, paraprofessionals assist probation officers in their paperwork. Community volunteers also assist offenders by performing cleaning and kitchen work. Occasionally, important community officials may be members of boards of directors of these community-based services, further integrating the community with the correctional program. The presence of community celebrities is sometimes purely symbolic, however, if they are figureheads exclusively and seldom become actively involved in these programs. Nevertheless, these healthy liaisons with community residents generally increase community acceptance of offenders and offender programs. With such community support, offenders have a better chance of adapting to community life. In recent years, operators of community-based offender programs have been keenly aware of the importance of cultivating links with the community, especially with community leaders (American Correctional Association, 1996a; Petersilia, 1999a).

FUNCTIONS OF PROBATION

The functions of probation are closely connected with its underlying philosophy. Within the rehabilitation context, the primary functions of probation are crime control, community reintegration, rehabilitation, punishment, and deterrence.

Crime Control

Crime control as a probation function stems directly from probationers often being supervised more or less closely by their POs. Jurisdictions with large numbers of probationers have difficulty supervising these offenders closely because there simply are not enough POs to do the job properly. In many cases, probationers mail in a form to the probation office either weekly or monthly. This form is usually a checklist on which the offenders report any law infractions, their most recent employment record, and other factual information. They may also pay preestablished fees to defray a portion of their probation costs and maintenance (U.S. National Institute of Corrections, 1996). Of course, much of this information is self-reported and subjective and is therefore difficult if not impossible to verify. Most of the time, probation agencies simply do not have the resources to conduct checks of this self-reported information. Offenders often come to the attention of probation offices again if they are rearrested within the jurisdiction supervising them. (Ross, 2000).

Precisely how much crime control occurs as the result of probation is unknown. When offenders are outside the immediate presence of probation officers, they may or may not engage in undetected criminal activity. Standard probation offers little by way of true crime control, because there is minimal contact between offenders and their probation officers. It is believed, however, that even standard probation offers some measure of crime control by extending to probationers a degree of trust as well as minimal behavioral restrictions. It would be misleading to believe that no monitoring occurs under standard probation supervision. Probation officers are obligated to make periodic checks of workplaces, and conversations with an offender's employer disclose much about how offenders are managing their time. Again, though, limited probation department resources confine these checks to much cursory and superficial activity. Placing offenders on probation and requiring them to comply with certain conditions succeeds to some extent as a method of crime control (Petersilia, 1999a).

Community Reintegration

One obvious benefit for offenders receiving probation is that they avoid the criminogenic environment of incarceration because they remain in their communities and benefit from **community reintegration** (Glaser, 1995). Offenders on probation usually maintain jobs, live with and support their families, engage in vocational/technical training or other educational programs, receive counseling, and lead otherwise normal lives. Although minimum-security prisons and some jails do afford prisoners opportunities to learn skills and participate in programs designed to rehabilitate them, nothing about prisons and jails comes close to the therapeutic value of remaining free within the community.

BOX 4.1   *Automated Drive-in Windows for Probationers?*

The Case of the New York City Probation Department

The electronic age has finally arrived. New York City has more than its fair share of probationers. The New York City Probation Department also has a problem typical of most other probation agencies: not enough money to run its department properly. There aren't enough probation officers to go around, and there are lots of probationers. Some of these probationers are dangerous; others aren't. What, if anything, can be done to assist the probation department and free up its limited probation officer staff to work primarily with the more dangerous probationers? In 1994, New York City implemented a new automated program through which terminals similar to automated bank machines are placed in key locations like kiosks throughout the city. These machines enable low-risk probationers, about 60,000 of them annually, to check in on regular bases and answer a series of questions relative to their current behavior and possible criminal conduct. The machines are equipped to conduct thumbprint analyses and verifications, palm print and voice print analyses and identifications, or retina scans. Those offenders requiring special help or referrals to various agen-

cies or human resources will receive such referral information from these machines, based on their answers to questions asked. Commissioner Michael Jacobson, head of the New York City Probation Department, says that this system is not a passing fancy or fad. In fact, it is his expectation that the automated check-in devices will only get better and more sophisticated in future years.

Especially for low-risk probationers, this tactic seems workable as a supervisory tool. In Los Angeles, for example, caseloads of probation officers can be as high as 2,000 clients per officer. There is no way officers can meet face-to-face with all their probationer-clients on monthly or even semimonthly. Many officers in Los Angeles tell their probationer-clients to call in once in a while, and that is the extent of the supervision they will receive. Is it any wonder why recidivism among these probationers is as high as 65 or 70 percent?

Should probationers be required to have face-to-face visits with their probation officers regularly? Is enough money being spent on probation services? Are such check-in devices violative of any of our constitutional rights? Should machines be vested with referral authority?

Source: Adapted from "Automation Reporting for New York City's Low-Risk Offenders," *Corrections Compendium,* **18**, October 1993, p. 21.

Rehabilitation

 One benefit of probation is that it permits offenders to remain in their communities, work at jobs, support their families, make restitution to victims, and perform other useful services. In addition, offenders avoid the criminogenic influence of jail or prison environments. It is most difficult to make the transformation from prison life to community living, especially if an inmate has been incarcerated for several years. Prison life is highly regulated, and the nature of confinement bears no relation to life on the outside. The community reintegration function of probation is most closely associated with its rehabilitative aim (Watterson, 1996).

BOX 4.2   ***Unusual Conditions of Probation***

- Lose weight or go to jail! That's what Arthur Younkin was told by a Wichita, Kansas, judge in November 1994. Younkin, who weighed 490 pounds, was convicted of forging $11,000 in checks in 1991. He was sentenced to probation and ordered to pay restitution. Younkin made several payments toward restitution, but then the payments ceased. Younkin was called back into court. The judge wanted to know why Younkin wasn't repaying the money as originally directed. Younkin said that it was because he was too heavy and nobody would hire him. The judge, Clark Owens, ordered Younkins to a halfway house where he could go on a diet. The judge ordered him to lose weight so that he could become more employable. Younkins lost 60 pounds after rigidly adhering to a 1,200-calorie-per-day diet. He was allowed to leave the halfway house following the weight loss, but Younkin's probation officer noted that Younkins had gained 4 pounds during court-ordered weekly weigh-ins. His probation officer threatened to contact the judge again if Younkins continued to gain weight. Younkins found a telemarketing job that enabled him to make periodic payments as restitution. (*Source:* Adapted from Associated Press, "Judge Orders 490-pound Probationer to Lose Weight or Go to Jail," November 18, 1994.)

- Thornton was convicted of cruelty to animals and ordered by the judge to pay restitution to a dog he had harmed. The nature of the dog's injuries was unclear, although the dog's medical bills were substantial. The Illinois judge ruled, however, that Thornton must make restitution to cover the dog's medical bills as a part of his sentence of probation. Subsequently, Thornton protested, arguing that he couldn't be required to pay restitution to a dog. The Illinois Court of Appeals heard Thornton's case and ruled that under Illinois's restitution statute, the definition of "victim" specifies that the victim must be a "person." Because the dog did not qualify as a person, the restitution law did not apply to it. Thus, Thornton was relieved of having to pay the dog's medical bills. He was not, however, relieved of having to pay his lawyer's fees. (*Source: People v. Thornton,* 676 N.E.2d 1024 [Ill. App. February 1997].)

- Seventy-nine-year-old Mildred Kaitz of Monticello, New York, didn't think anything about the ten-foot high plant growing in her yard beside her front porch. Curious neighbors wondered what it was. Pointing at the large plant, they asked Mildred, "What is that?" "Marijuana," said Mildred. For many months, Mildred escaped police scrutiny until a neighborhood teenager who knew what the plant really was reported it to authorities. Mildred was promptly arrested and her plant was confiscated. In court later, Mildred told the judge that she was growing the marijuana to give to her son who was suffering from multiple sclerosis. It seems that the marijuana was alleviating the racking pain and nausea associated with the disease. Regardless of Mildred's altruistic motives and love for her son, the judge placed Mildred on probation for six months, with no fine and no time. Mildred said, "I don't feel guilty. I didn't grow it to sell it. I did it for my son." (*Source: People,* January 10, 1994:94.)

- A convicted sex offender, Inman, was sentenced to probation by a judge in a Florida court in 1993. Among other conditions, Inman was forbidden to have any contact with children under the age of 18. One afternoon in July 1993, Mrs. Inman, Inman's ex-wife, brought her two sons to see their father. The sons, ages 7 and 8, were ushered into Inman's presence inside his new apartment. At the time, Inman was residing with his fiancée and advised his ex-wife that it was not a good time to visit. Furthermore, Inman advised, he was not permitted to be around children under the age of 18. Despite this advice, Inman's ex-wife left the two boys with their father and left abruptly. Shortly thereafter, a probation officer showed up at Inman's apartment and demanded entry. Seeing the two boys in the presence of Inman, the probation officer removed them from the premises. Subsequently, a judge revoked Inman's probation and ordered him to jail. Inman protested, and his appeal was heard by a higher court. The court reversed Inman's probation revocation, saying that there was no evidence that Inman had initiated any contact with his two boys. Further, there was evidence that he attempted to avoid the unauthorized visitation. There was no evidence of a willful or substantial probation violation. (*Source: Inman v. State,* 684 So. 2d 899 [Fla. Dist. App. December 1996].)

- Rodriguez was convicted of leaving the scene of an accident that resulted in death. Rodriguez was a first-offender, and thus the Florida judge was inclined to grant him probation instead of incarceration. The judge, however, ordered that as a part of Rodriguez's probation, he must clean the victim's grave site monthly. Further, Rodriguez was required to work at the grave site at the direction of the victim's family. Rodriguez appealed, and a higher court modified the probation conditions. Although the appellate court held that the condition requiring Rodriguez to clean the victim's grave site was valid, it was neither proper nor within the scope of judicial authority to require that the victim's family should direct Rodriguez's work at the grave site. (*Source: Rodriguez v. State,* 684 So. 2d 864 [Fla. Dist. App. December 1996].)

These scenarios show that probation is a sentence, a punishment. Many diverse conditions may be imposed with a probation order. Judges have considerable discretion about the nature of probation imposed and any accompanying conditions. In some instances, judges have ordered pregnant women convicted of cocaine possession to be sterilized as a probation condition or go to prison. Other judges have ordered convicted rapists to be castrated as a condition of their probation or face lengthy prison terms. Yet other judges have ordered mothers handcuffed to their daughters as a probationary condition as a way of ensuring the child's continuous adult supervision. Many other bizarre probation conditions have been imposed by judges. Some of these conditions have subsequently been set aside because they violate the civil rights of probationers, but many seemingly peculiar probation conditions have been validated by appellate courts.

Punishment

Is probation a punishment? Those on probation think that it is. There are many behavioral conditions accompanying probation orders. Any violation can lead to having one's probation program revoked, and the offender may be incarcerated in a jail or prison as a result. Filing a late monthly report is a technical violation. Being absent from work without a legitimate excuse might also be a violation of an offender's probation terms. Other sanctions may be imposed as a part of standard probation, although they do not involve direct or frequent contact with the probation officer. For example, the judge may order the convicted offender to make restitution to victims, to pay for damages and medical bills sustained through whatever crime was committed. Public service of a particular type may be required, and others may be asked to report on the offender's work quality. And, of course, the offender may be fined. A portion of an offender's wages may be garnished by the court regularly during the term of probation as payment toward the fine assessed. Obviously, the offender must sustain regular employment to meet these court-imposed fine obligations and community service (Majer, 1994). These punishments place virtually all probationers at risk of losing their freedom for violating one or more conditions of their probation programs.

Deterrence

Does probation deter criminals from committing new crimes? The answer is not much. Because of the low degree of offender control associated with standard probation supervision, which often means no supervision at all, recidivism rates are higher than those of offenders in more intensively supervised intermediate punishment programs. Observers disagree about the deterrent effect probation serves (Petersilia, 1999a). Although no national standard exists about what is a respectable or successful recidivism level, 30 percent has been defined by various researchers as a cutting point, with more successful probation programs having recidivism rates below 30 percent. Thus, the deterrent value of probation may vary according to the standard by which deterrence is measured (Shearer, 2000). Traditional probation programs have recidivism rates of about 65 percent, meaning that only 35 percent of the probationers do not commit new crimes (Maxwell and Gray, 2000; Tonry, 1999a, 1999b).

A PROFILE OF PROBATIONERS

The profile of probationers in the United States changes annually. Each year, the probation population includes increasing numbers of felony offenders (U.S. Department of Justice, 2000). At the beginning of 2000, there were 3,773,624 adults on probation in the United States, an increase of 2.7 percent since 1998 and 44.6 percent since 1990. The average annual increase in probationers was 4.2 percent. Several states with the largest numbers of probationers were Texas (447,100), California (332,414), Georgia (307,653), and Florida (292,399). Table 4.1 shows a distribution of the number of adults on probation at the end of 1999.

TABLE 4.1 Adults on Probation, 1999

Region and Jurisdiction	Probation Population				Percent Change during 1999	Number on Probation on 12/31/99 per 100,000 Adult Residents
	1/1/99	1999		12/31/99		
		Entries	Exits			
U.S. total	3,670,591	1,819,403	1,714,630	3,773,624	2.8%	1,864
Federal	33,390	14,571	14,793	32,816	-1.7%	16
State	3,637,201	1,804,832	1,699,837	3,740,808	2.8	1,848
Northeast	572,832	195,038	187,977	575,270	0.4%	1,465
Connecticut	55,000	30,000	29,930	55,070	0.1	2,244
Maine	6,953	5,379	4,808	7,524	8.2	782
Massachusetts[a]	46,567	40,676	40,976	46,267	-0.6	983
New Hampshire	5,175	:	:	3,160	. . .	. . .
New Jersey[a]	129,377	58,500	59,543	128,634	-0.6	2,095
New York[a]	178,612	45,618	40,544	183,686	2.8	1,335
Pennsylvania[a,b]	121,094	1,072	623	118,635	-2.0	1,298
Rhode Island	21,049	7,972	7,268	21,753	3.3	2,902
Vermont	9,005	5,821	4,285	10,541	17.1	2,320
Midwest	849,703	458,923	436,681	871,319	2.5%	1,858
Illinois	131,850	58,695	56,275	134,270	1.8	1,501
Indiana[a]	104,624	87,517	86,270	105,871	1.2	2,399
Iowa[a]	18,447	18,863	17,635	19,675	6.7	915
Kansas	17,219	21,090	20,542	17,767	3.2	909
Michigan[a]	170,997	69,124	69,210	170,978	**	2,341
Minnesota	100,818	60,872	58,164	104,615	3.8	2,986
Missouri	49,992	26,037	23,536	52,493	5.0	1,290
Nebraska	16,527	19,095	15,160	20,462	. . .	1,674
North Dakota	2,726	1,620	1,617	2,729	0.1	576

| Region and Jurisdiction | Probation Population | | | | Percent Change during 1999 | Number on Probation on 12/31/99 per 100,000 Adult Residents |
	1/1/99	1999 Entries	Exits	12/31/99		
Ohio[a,c]	178,830	68,480	60,661	184,867	5.2	2,198
South Dakota	3,441	3,064	3,044	3,461	0.6	647
Wisconsin	54,232	24,466	24,567	54,131	-0.2	1,387
South	1,503,679	837,091	783,397	1,556,507	3.5%	2,170
Alabama	40,379	15,835	14,457	41,757	3.4	1,264
Arkansas	28,698	8,537	6,755	30,480	6.2	1,612
Delaware	20,030	11,015	10,069	20,976	4.7	3,673
District of Columbia	11,234	10,877	9,265	12,129	8.0	2,863
Florida[a]	283,965	194,529	189,140	292,399	3.0	2,533
Georgia[a]	278,669	183,322	154,944	307,653	...	5,368
Kentucky[a]	17,594	16,848	12,311	18,988	7.9	634
Louisiana	33,028	14,425	12,335	35,118	6.3	1,104
Maryland	78,051	41,117	37,882	81,286	4.1	2,105
Mississippi[a]	11,530	5,748	4,830	12,448	8.0	618
North Carolina	105,227	59,195	59,327	105,095	-0.1	1,841
Oklahoma	29,093	12,257	13,213	27,997	-3.8	1,131
South Carolina	46,482	15,244	16,797	44,929	-3.3	1,534
Tennessee[a,d]	38,924	23,289	22,153	40,060	2.9	967
Texas	443,688	198,573	195,161	447,100	0.8	3,121
Virginia	30,576	26,280	24,758	32,098	5.0	616
West Virginia	6,511	:	:	5,994	-7.9	427
West	710,987	313,780	291,782	737,712	3.8%	1,653
Alaska[a]	4,274	1,795	1,552	4,517	5.7	1,069
Arizona	51,329	32,611	26,864	57,076	11.2	1,657
California	324,427	162,543	152,604	332,414	2.5	1,372
Colorado[a]	45,502	26,601	26,613	45,339	-0.4	1,516
Hawaii	15,711	7,228	7,232	15,707	**	1,753
Idaho	31,172	2,970	3,033	36,705	17.7	4,073
Montana[a]	5,358	1,102	634	5,906	10.2	896
Nevada	12,561	:	:	11,787	-6.2	894
New Mexico[a]	10,397	8,850	7,956	11,291	8.6	907
Oregon	44,809	17,140	16,459	45,490	1.5	1,828
Utah	9,482	3,843	3,899	9,426	-0.6	663
Washington[a]	152,140	47,213	43,088	158,213	4.0	3,705
Wyoming	3,825	1,884	1,848	3,841	0.4	1,089

Note: Because of nonresponse or incomplete data, the probation population for some jurisdictions on December 31, 1999, does not equal the population on January 1, 1999, plus entries, minus exits. During 1999 an estimated 2,042,500 persons entered probation supervision, and 1,927,700 exited, based on imputations for agencies which did not provide data.

: Not known.

... Comparable percentage or rate could not be calculated.

**Between -0.05% and 0.05%.

[a]Data do not include cases in one or more of the following categories: absconder, out of state, inactive, intensive supervision, or electronic monitoring.
[b]Entries and exits do not include county data.
[c]Percent change in probation population during 1999 excludes 134 local probation agencies for which a single population estimate was obtained for 12/31/99.
[d]Data are for the period beginning May 1, 1999, and ending April 30, 2000.

Source: U.S. Department of Justice, *Probation and Parole, 1999.* (Washington, DC: U.S. Department of Justice, 2000), 4.

Some of the characteristics of persons on probation in the United States are illustrated in Table 4.2, which compares probationers for the years 1990 and 1999. Approximately 78 percent of all probationers were male in 1999. Between 1990 and 1999, the proportion of female probationers increased from 18 percent to 22 percent. The racial distribution of probationers has not changed much in this ten-year period. White probationers declined to 63 percent in 1999 from 68 percent in 1990, whereas black probationers increased from 31 percent in 1990 to 35 percent in 1999. The proportion of Hispanic probationers declined slightly from 18 percent to 16 percent from 1990 to 1999.

TABLE 4.2 Characteristics of Adults on Probation, 1990 and 1999

Characteristic	1990	1999
Total	100%	100%
Gender	100%	100%
Male	82	78
Female	18	22
Race	100%	100%
White	68	63
Black	31	35
Other	1	2
Hispanic origin	100%	100%
Hispanic	18	16
Non-Hispanic	82	84
Status of supervision	100%	100%
Active	83	77
Inactive	9	10
Absconded	6	9
Supervised out of State	2	2
Other	—	2
Adults entering probation	100%	100%
Without incarceration	87	79
With incarceration	8	16
Other	5	5
Adults leaving probation	100%	100%
Successful completion	69	61
Returned to incarceration	14	14
With new sentence	3	4
With the same sentence	11	7
Type of return unknown	0	3
Absconder	7	3
Other unsuccessful	2	11
Death	**	1
Other	7	9
Severity of offense		100%
Felony	—	51

Misdemeanor	—	48
Other infractions	—	1
Status of probation	100%	100%
Direct imposition	38	58
Split sentence	6	10
Sentence suspended	41	22
Imposition suspended	14	8
Other	1	3

Note: For every characteristic there were persons of unknown status or type. Detail may not sum to total because of rounding.

—Not available.

**Less than 0.5%.

Source: U.S. Department of Justice, *Probation and Parole, 1999* (Washington, DC: U.S. Department of Justice, 2000), 6.

Table 4.2 also shows that proportionately fewer probationers are entering probation programs without serving any jail time first. In 1999, 79 percent of the probationers entered probation without incarceration, down from 87 percent in 1990. There were proportionately fewer successful completions of probation programs in 1999 (61 percent) compared with a successful completion of 69 percent in 1990. About 14 percent of all probationers were returned to incarceration for both 1990 and 1999 for various program violations. About half (51 percent) of all probationers in 1999 were on probation for felony convictions. One of the largest differences between 1990 and 1999 was a direct imposition of probation. In 1990, 38 percent of all probationers were sentenced directly to probation, whereas 58 percent were sentenced directly to probation in 1999. Greater use was made of split sentencing, in which offenders sentenced to probation were also obligated to do some jail time, in 1999. About 10 percent of all probationers received split sentences in 1999 compared with 6 percent in 1990. There were fewer suspended sentences (22 percent) in 1999 compared with 41 percent suspended sentences in 1990.

FIRST-OFFENDERS AND RECIDIVISTS

Probation decision making is solely at the discretion of criminal court judges. Judges receive sentencing assistance from probation officers, who are frequently directed to prepare the background investigations for the PSI reports of convicted offenders. To the extent that judges must impose specific sentences in particular cases under mandatory sentencing laws, their hands are tied. For instance, if an offender uses a firearm during the commission of an offense in Michigan, criminal court judges there must impose a two-year additional sentence. This mandatory punishment, which must be served after one's original sentence for the conviction offense is imposed, is intended to deter the use of dangerous weapons by criminals. It does not always work.

Because of the diversity of offenders and their crimes, prior records or criminal histories, ages, family stability, work record, and a host of other factors, judges attempt to develop and apply a consistent set of sentencing standards to cover each convicted offender. Thus, some individuality in sentencing occurs. When such individualization occurs, extralegal factors such as race or ethnicity, gender, age, socioeconomic status, and demeanor and attitude often function to influence judicial decision making. Many offenders are habitual offenders and chronic recidivists. Judges tend to impose harsher sentences on such persons. Those with extensive prior records of offending, especially those previously convicted of violent offenses, are less likely to be considered for probation (Olson and Lurigio, 2000).

Other factors are considered as well, and judges are virtually powerless to do anything about them. For example, if a state has jail or prison overcrowding, then this overcrowding might obligate judges to impose nonincarcerative sentences, such as probation, more often than incarcerative sentences. In many jurisdictions, however, judges are ignorant of the overcrowding conditions of their jails and prisons, and they may impose jail or prison terms for convicted offenders only to find out later that the convicted offenders were released because there were no accommodations for them.

Most probationers share the following characteristics:

1. Probationers tend to be first-offenders or low-risk offenders.
2. More property offenders than violent offenders are considered for probation.
3. More convicted females are considered for probation than convicted males.
4. Not having a history of drug or alcohol use or abuse is considered as a positive factor in granting probation.
5. If there are no physical injuries resulting from the convicted offender's actions or if no weapons were used to commit the crime, then the chances for probation are greater.

CIVIL MECHANISMS IN LIEU OF PROBATION

Because of the large volume of offenders being arrested for various crimes, prosecutors are increasingly faced with burgeoning numbers of criminal cases. Many of these cases involve petty offenses, although even the least serious crimes consume valuable court time. Thus, not every criminal case can be prosecuted, even if prosecutors had the time and people to initiate such prosecutions. There simply are not enough courts and judges to handle the great volume of criminal cases. Two alternative solutions chosen by prosecutors in a growing number of jurisdictions are to target certain low-level criminal cases for alternative dispute resolution, whereby a civil court or other authorized body meets with victims and offenders to work out a civil remedy, and diversion, whereby a criminal case is temporarily suspended from the criminal justice system while offenders must engage in constructive, remedial work or programs and resolve their disputes with victims. Consider the following scenarios:

- A man gets drunk in a bar and insults the girlfriend of another man. The two men get into a brief fight, and one man knocks out two teeth of the other man. Police arrive quickly, break up the fight, and arrest the two men for aggravated assault.

- A man is driving his car down a street well known for its streetwalkers, hookers, and prostitutes. He is looking for a prostitute for a brief sexual interlude. He pulls up to a woman in a short skirt, and they converse through his open car window. Suddenly, the woman pulls out a badge and arrests the man for soliciting prostitution. She is an undercover police officer. The man is a respected physician who is married with four children.

- A 19-year-old breaks into the garage of a neighbor and steals some power tools. A few days later, the neighbor sees the young man using some of the stolen power tools and calls the police. The police arrest the 19-year-old for theft and burglary. The young man has no record of prior offenses and is enrolled at a local community college, where he is receiving good grades.

- A man and a woman leave a Las Vegas casino late at night. The man is shoving the woman and cursing at her. Suddenly the woman turns on the man and scratches his face with her fingernails. The man and woman are married to each other, and the man just lost a lot of money gambling. Police break up the fight and arrest the man for spousal abuse.

- An 18-year-old drives her new car out of the driveway of her home and accidentally drives over her neighbor's flower garden, which is growing near the driveway. The neighbor sees this incident and accuses her later of damaging his flowers. She gets angry and drives her car at the man, trying to run him down. Instead, she drives through the man's garage door, smashing it and damaging her own car. The police arrest her for assault with a deadly weapon. She has no record of prior arrests and is an excellent student at a local college.

- A 23-year-old man is working at a car dealership as a car salesman. One day, he walks past the office of a coworker and sees the woman's purse on her desk. The woman has stepped away from her desk and is waiting on a customer in another part of the large automobile showroom. The man enters her office and rifles through her wallet, stealing $200. Later, he spends the money at a local bar, buying drinks and meals for his friends. The woman reports the theft, and police determine that the man's fingerprints are on her purse. Also, another coworker who happened to be passing by unnoticed saw the man going through the woman's purse and gave this information to investigating police. It turns out that the man had been drinking before coming to work that morning. He was drunk at the time, or so he claims, and thus didn't know what he was doing.

None of these cases excites prosecutors. Bar fights, driving over a neighbor's geraniums, stealing money from a coworker's purse, soliciting a prostitute, getting into a spat over gambling, or stealing a neighbor's power tools are bothersome cases for most prosecutors. Yes, they are crimes, and justice says that people should pay for the crimes they commit. Yet should each and every one of these cases be prosecuted to the fullest extent of the law? Should trials be held for all these cases? For many prosecutors, the idea of a civil resolution for some of or all these cases seems like a reasonable alternative, especially under the different circumstances of the individual scenarios above. Thus, prosecutors may opt for diversion or alternative dispute resolution. Both procedures effectively remove a case from the criminal justice system, at least temporarily, while one or more civil remedies are sought.

Civil procedure and criminal procedure involve two separate systems. The most common portrayal of civil procedure is *Judge Judy* on television. This popular program resolves disputes between parties within certain monetary limits, with Judge Judy in action as the impartial arbiter. Civil wrongs or **torts** are commonly settled in civil actions. In all civil actions, damages are sought, not criminal convictions. The man in the bar fight would like to have his missing teeth replaced. The man soliciting for prostitution might be obligated to receive some type of counseling. The man whose tools were stolen would like them replaced or returned. The man whose garage door was smashed would like it, as well as his dead flowers, replaced. The couple who fought outside the Las Vegas casino could profit from some marital counseling. The woman whose money was stolen would like to have her money back.

Many of these solutions are restorative in nature, with stolen or damaged property restored. In the process, however, the perpetrators should be held accountable for their actions with some type of punishment. They must do something besides pay for damages to show their contrition, and they must accept responsibility for whatever they did. In recent years, this process has become known as **restorative justice**, which is every action that is primarily oriented toward doing justice by repairing the harm that has been caused by a crime (Bazemore and Walgrave, 1999:48). Restorative justice usually means a face-to-face confrontation between the victim and perpetrator at which time a mutually agreeable restorative solution is proposed and agreed on. A key feature of restorative justice is equity, whereby all parties not only agree on the proposed solution, but offender accountability is also heightened. The offender needs to know that whatever was done has serious consequences: a victim suffered either through injuries or property loss. The offender must realize the consequences of whatever was done and accept responsibility for those consequences. Two types of programs similar to restorative justice—alternative dispute resolution and diversion—are presented in the next section.

Any victim can seek damages in a civil court as a remedy for being victimized. In an increasing number of cases, however, those who allegedly offend against victims may be prosecuted as criminals in the criminal justice system. In numerous instances, though, the offenses alleged are petty or minor. Even though the criminal justice system might define certain conduct as criminal, that conduct might be redefined as a civil wrong. If conduct that could be defined as criminal is actually reinterpreted as a civil wrong or a tort, then civil mechanisms can be brought into action to resolve or mediate disputes between victims and offenders. Besides pursuing cases against offenders in civil actions, victims can seek compensation through other means, such as alternative dispute resolution.

Alternative Dispute Resolution

In cases involving minor criminal offenses, one option increasingly used by the prosecution is **alternative dispute resolution (ADR)**, a community-based, informal dispute settlement between offenders and their victims (Cimini, 1997). Most often targeted for participation in these programs are misdemeanants. A growing number of ADR programs are being implemented throughout the nation. With its early roots in the Midwest, **victim-offender reconciliation** or ADR programs now exist in more than a hundred U.S. jurisdictions. There are 54 such programs in Norway, 40 in France, 25 in Canada, 25 in Germany, 18 in England, 20 in Finland, and 8 in Belgium (Griffiths and Bazemore, 1999).

In growing circles, ADR is also known as restorative justice (Bazemore and Walgrave, 1999). ADR involves the direct participation of the victim and offender, with the aim of mutual accommodation for both parties. The emphasis of ADR is on restitution rather than punishment. Compared with trials, the costs associated with it are small, and criminal **stigmatization** is avoided. It is sometimes difficult to decide, however, which cases are best arbitrated through ADR and which should be formally resolved through trial. In addition, specific programs in various jurisdictions are especially tailored for juvenile offenders (Miclityinen, 1999; Parton and Wattam, 1999). In a growing number of jurisdictions, many criminal cases are being diverted from the criminal justice system through ADR. It is a relatively new phenomenon, but it is recognized increasingly as a means whereby differences between criminals and their victims can be resolved through conciliation, mediation, or arbitration. **Restitution** or **victim compensation** also makes such programs easier for victims to accept.

The Dispute Settlement Center, Durham, North Carolina. A good example of ADR is the Dispute Settlement Center of Durham (DSCD), which was established in North Carolina in 1983 (McGillis, 1998:2). Originally, the DSCD received financial assistance from the Orange County Dispute Settlement Center, the Human Relations Commission of the City of Durham, and Hassle House, a local drop-in center for youths. Michael Wendt was hired as the first DSCD director in March 1983. By 1988, the DSCD was a full-time operation with a board of directors.

Early activities of the DSCD included training staff members in the art of **mediation**, the process of working out amicable and mutually satisfactory agreements between offenders and victims in disputes. Training was conducted by attorneys affiliated with the North Carolina division of the American Bar Association. A balanced pool of mediators was selected to represent a cross-section of the gender, racial, and ethnic composition of the community. A total of 38 volunteers were trained in the first mediator pool for the DSCD. In 1990, an office building was constructed to accommodate all DSCD activities.

The DSCD considers numerous minor criminal cases that have been referred by the Durham County District Court. Referrals come from a daily review of new arrest warrants issued at the court clerk's office. Some of the cases heard by the DSCD include writing bad checks, divorce and family mediation, drive-by shooting injuries, landlord-tenant disputes, traffic and parking complaints, workplace mediation, school mediation, shoplifting cases, petty theft, burglary, and criminal trespass. Some of the cases excluded from DSCD action include domestic violence, child abuse, alcohol and drug abuse, and incidents involving serious and untreated mental illness.

Criminal matters are usually referred to the DSCD with a letter from the court, which says, "A warrant has been sworn out against you by _____

_____ alleging that you committed the criminal offense of _____
____. You can avoid having to appear in criminal court by submitting this matter to mediation." Respondents are provided with a specific hearing time and informed that they may reschedule if necessary, as long as the revised time occurs prior to the court date set for the case. The letter closes by saying, "If you choose not to appear at the Dispute Settlement Center or mediation is not successful, you must be in Criminal Court at [specific time and place]" (McGillis, 1998:8–9).

The process of mediation involves two mediators, the victim, and the perpetrator. Ground rules are established whereby neither party may interrupt the other while speaking. Complainants are then asked to describe the problem from their perspective. Respondents are asked to respond to complainants' comments and to indicate their views regarding the dispute. Mediators focus on having the parties clearly state their positions and on exploring common perspectives and areas of disagreement.

If the mediation session does not appear to be working out, the mediators may meet with each party individually to discuss their particular perceptions and possible solutions. Such private meetings with individual participants may disclose evidence or information that one of the parties feels uncomfortable about sharing among all present. Mediators may also ask each party to consider further steps. If and when disputants reach an agreement, the terms are written down and signed by both parties. The agreement has the legal status of a written contract and is enforceable. About 90 percent of all mediations result in such agreements. If the case was originally referred by the district attorney's office, the parties also sign a letter stating, "As a result of mediation, an agreement has been reached. We, the undersigned, request that all pending criminal charges in the above case be dismissed." The letter is signed by the complainant, the respondent, and the two mediators who handled the case.

In 1998, there were 24 community dispute settlement centers throughout North Carolina. Over 16,000 disputes have been satisfactorily resolved without further criminal prosecution. About 50 percent of these disputes were originally referred by the criminal court. The DSCD receives its funding from state appropriations and the Administrative Office of the U.S. Courts. The impact of volunteer mediators should not be underestimated. In 1995, for example, the average mediator spent 460 hours performing board service, 450 hours mediating disputes, 132 hours performing clerical and other support functions, 83 hours facilitating groups, 65 hours conducting training sessions, 40 hours of fund-raising, and 10 hours engaging in community outreach (McGillis, 1998:10).

Not all DSCD cases are successfully resolved. In fact, in some isolated instances, there have been lethal consequences. For instance, a name-calling incident involving two students at a local high school escalated to a beating of one of the students by friends of the other student. Subsequently, some of the students in one of the groups engaged in a drive-by shooting of an innocent pedestrian while attempting to kill another student. Warrants were sworn out for attempted murder against several students believed to be involved in the drive-by shooting, but police were unable to positively identify the shooter. The prosecutor feared that the case might be dropped for lack of evidence and therefore referred the case to the DSCD for mediation between the two student groups. Fifteen students and 30 parents agreed to participate in mediation. Student peer mediators ensured that all involved in the shooting participated in the mediation hearing. After one hour, the two groups apologized to each other. Parents of 11 of the 13 students who had sworn out warrants against other students agreed to have their cases dismissed. The parties signed forms requesting dismissals, and the cases were dismissed by the criminal court judge. The parents of two other students persisted in their complaints, however, and took their cases to court, but when the parties reached court, the judge dismissed the two cases because the two larger groups of students had reconciled.

The DSCD conducted a survey of all disputants who had been served by the center several years after it had been operating. About 88 percent of all disputes had resulted in agreements. Between 85 to 95 percent of all disputants indicated that they were satisfied with the results from DSCD mediation. The primary result of the DSCD program was that it showed how an energetic and creative mediation program can provide a wide range of rehabilitative services to the community. Although the DSCD was not 100 percent successful, it is clear that numerous cases that otherwise would have consumed valuable criminal court time were resolved through civil means, and to most everyone's satisfaction.

Victim-Offender Reconciliation Projects.   Another version of alternative dispute resolution is victim-offender reconciliation. Victim-offender reconciliation is a specific form of conflict resolution between the victim and the offender. Face-to-face encounter is the essence of this process (Shichor and Sechrest, 1998). Elkhart County, Indiana, has been the site of the **victim-offender reconciliation project (VORP)** since 1987. The primary aims of VORPs are (1) to make offenders accountable for their wrongs against victims, (2) to reduce recidivism among participating offenders, and (3) to heighten responsibility of offenders through victim compensation and repayment for damages inflicted (Roy and Brown, 1992).

Officially, VORP was established in Kitchener, Ontario, in 1974 and was subsequently replicated as PACT, or Prisoner and Community Together, in northern Indiana near Elkhart. Subsequent replications in various jurisdictions have created different varieties of ADR, each variety spawning embellishments, additions, or program deletions deemed more or less important by the particular jurisdiction. The Genessee County (Batavia), New York, Sheriff's Department established a VORP in 1983, followed in 1985 by programs in Valparaiso, Indiana; Quincy, Massachusetts; and Minneapolis, Minnesota. In Quincy, for instance, the program, named EARN-IT, was operated through the probation department. More than 25 different states have one version or another of VORP (Umbreit, 1994; Umbreit and Coates, 1993). One of these sites involved a study of offender recidivism and ADR. During the 1987–1991 period, an investigation of ADR and its effectiveness was undertaken and the results evaluated (Roy and Brown, 1992). A VORP significantly reduced recidivism among offenders. Both juvenile and adult offenders have been involved in this project over the years, and results suggest that it will be continued.

Cross-site analyses of ADR programs in other jurisdictions suggest results comparable to those in Indiana. VORPs have been evaluated in several other jurisdictions, including Orange County, California. Over a thousand interviews were conducted in both premediation and postmediation periods as well as with persons in several groups not participating in ADR. Most victims and offenders reported greater satisfaction and perceptions of fairness for victims as well as a much higher rate of restitution completion by offenders (Niemeyer and Shichor, 1996). VORPs have been increasingly established outside of the United States with similar success (Sawyer, 2000).

Pretrial Diversion

Pretrial diversion is a procedure whereby criminal defendants are diverted to either a community-based agency for treatment or assigned to a counselor for social and/or psychiatric assistance (Shichor and Sechrest, 1998). Pretrial diversion may involve education, job training, counseling, or some type of psychological or physical therapy. **Diversion** is the official halting or suspension of legal proceedings against a criminal defendant or juvenile after a recorded justice system entry and possible referral of that person to a treatment or care program administered by a nonjustice agency or private agency. Technically, diversion is not true probation in that the alleged offender has not been convicted of a crime. The thrust of diversion is toward an informal administrative effort to determine (1) whether nonjudicial processing is warranted; (2) whether treatment is warranted; (3) if treatment is warranted, which one to use; and (4) whether charges against the defendant should be dropped or reinstated (National Association of Pretrial Services Agencies, 1995).

Diversion is intended for first-offenders who have not committed serious crimes. It is similar to probation because offenders must comply with specific conditions established by the court. Successful completion of those conditions usually leads to a dismissal of charges against the defendant. A **totality of circumstances** assessment of each offender's crime is made by the prosecutor and the court, and a decision about diversion is made. Each case is considered on its own merits. Those charged with DWI may be diverted to attend Alcoholics Anonymous meetings or special classes for drunk drivers as a part of their diversion. Often, diverted defendants must pay monthly fees or **user fees** during the diversion period to help defray expenses incurred by the public or private agencies who monitor them.

Unconditional and Conditional Diversion. Most **diversion programs** in the United States include one or more behavioral conditions and prescribe involvement in treatment programs such as Alcoholics Anonymous, driver's training schools, and/or individual or group psychological counseling. A diversion program, however, may simply specify that offenders, known as **divertees**, should be law-abiding and should submit monthly reports and user fees for the duration of their diversion terms. Such a program is called an **unconditional diversion program**. Unconditional diversion programs place no restrictions on a divertee's behavior, and there are no formal controls operating through which divertee behaviors can be monitored.

A **conditional diversion program** involves some behavioral monitoring by probation officers or personnel affiliated with local probation departments in cities or counties. The degree of monitoring depends on the conditions of the diversion program and the special needs of divertees. For the least monitored divertees, monthly contact with the probation department by letter or telephone, together with the payment of a monthly maintenance fee that may range from $10 to $100 or more, may be all that is required. Divertees are often required to submit a regular statement (usually monthly or weekly) indicating their current successful employment, family support, and other pertinent data.

The History and Philosophy of Diversion. Diversion originated in the United States through the early juvenile courts in Chicago and New York in the late 1800s. There were concerted efforts by religious groups and reformers to keep children from imprisonment of any kind, because children over eight years of age were considered eligible for adult court processing. Cook County, Illinois, implemented a diversion program for youthful offenders in 1899 (Doeren and Hageman, 1982:23). The underlying philosophy of diversion is community reintegration and rehabilitation, whereby offenders avoid the stigma of incarceration and the public notoriety accompanying appearances and trials. In most state courts where diversion is condoned, diversion does not entirely remove offenders from court processing, because the court usually must approve prosecutorial recommendations for diversion in each case. Because these approvals are often conducted in less publicized hearings, a divertee's crimes are less likely to be scrutinized publicly. When an offender completes his or her diversion program successfully, one of two things happens. The first result is that the offender's arrest record pertaining to that offense is erased through an **expungement** and the prosecution is terminated. If this event does not occur, then the second optional result is a downgrading of the original criminal charge to a lesser offense and a resulting conviction. For instance, a first-offender charged with felony theft may have his or her offense downgraded to misdemeanor theft following the successful completion of the diversion program. Either way for offenders who are permitted diversion, their diversion programs are win-win situations.

Functions of Diversion

Some of the more important functions of diversion are the following:

1. To permit divertees the opportunity of remaining in their communities where they can receive needed assistance or treatment, depending on the nature of the crimes charged
2. To permit divertees the opportunity to make restitution to their victims when monetary damages were suffered and property destroyed
3. To permit divertees the opportunity of remaining free in their communities to support themselves and their families, and to avoid the stigma of incarceration
4. To help divertees avoid the stigma of a criminal conviction
5. To assist corrections officials in reducing prison and jail overcrowding by diverting less serious cases to nonincarcerative alternatives
6. To save the courts the time, trouble, and expense of formally processing less serious cases and streamlining case dispositions through informal case handling
7. To make it possible for divertees to participate in self-help, educational, or vocational programs
8. To preserve the dignity and integrity of divertees by helping them avoid further contact with the criminal justice system and assisting them to be more responsible adults capable of managing their own lives
9. To preserve the family unit and enhance family solidarity and continuity

This list highlights the rehabilitative nature of diversion. It is unknown about how much diversion affects the court system and court caseloads. Accurate estimates of those placed on diversion are difficult to determine, primarily because of the potential for record expungements. Once these criminal records or arrest warrants for various charges have been expunged, the media and official agencies usually cannot access them. Literally, they cease to exist.

Criteria Influencing Pretrial Diversion.   Who qualifies for pretrial diversion? First, it helps to be a first-offender. First-offenders who are charged with petty crimes are the most likely candidates for diversion programs. Those barred from such programs might include the following:

1. Those with prior drug offense convictions, former drug offense divertees, and/or who traffic in drugs
2. Those convicted of a felony within the previous five-year period
3. Those whose current offense involves violence
4. Those who are past or present probation or parole violators (National Association of Pretrial Services Agencies, 1995)

Other relevant criteria used by different jurisdictions for deciding which offenders deserve to be included in diversion programs are the following:

1. The age of the offender
2. The residency, employment, and familial status of the offender
3. The prior record of the offender
4. The seriousness of the offense
5. Aggravating or mitigating circumstances associated with the commission of the offense

Criticisms of Diversion.   Not everyone favors using diversion as a means of removing those charged with crimes from the criminal justice system, even on a temporary basis. Some believe that diversion is too lenient on criminals. Critics of diversion generally focus on the nonpunitive nature of diversion conditions, which are often no conditions.

Other criticisms are that diversion is an inappropriate punishment for criminals and that it does not deal effectively with offenders. Furthermore, some critics allege that diversion leads to net-widening. Another criticism is that diversion excludes female offenders. Some observers think that diversion resolves an offender's case without the benefit of due process. For instance, whenever a prosecutor examines a case, the evidence against the defendant, and other pertinent circumstances, an offer of diversion may be made. If the offer is accepted, then this acceptance is a tacit admission by the defendant that he or she is guilty of the offense(s) alleged. If the offer of diversion is rejected, then prosecutors can always exercise their option to pursue criminal charges against the defendant later in court. Thus, diversion assumes guilt without a trial.

Supporters of diversion, however, say that diversion greatly reduces offender recidivism when applied appropriately. For instance, a sample of first-time offenders was placed on diversion in Vanderburgh County, Indiana, during the mid-1990s. A sample of 243 divertees was studied. The recidivism rate for those who successfully completed their diversion programs was only 9 percent, whereas those who did not successfully complete their programs had 39 percent recidivism (Walsh et al., 1997). Those favoring diversion also counter by arguing that diversion enables divertees to avoid the stigma and criminogenic atmosphere of prisons and jails. Furthermore, there does not appear to be any gender discrimination that applies to diversion programs in any jurisdiction. Men appear equally likely to receive diversion compared with women. The idea that guilt is assumed without the benefit of a criminal trial is difficult to overcome because prosecutors assume precisely that. The benefit of freedom to live within the community without restriction and the fact that participation in diversion is strictly voluntary, however, outweigh the argument that one's right to due process is somehow jeopardized. If those charged with crimes really want to fight in court, then they can exercise their constitutional rights and have trials in the matters (National Association of Pretrial Services Agencies, 1995).

JUDICIAL DISCRETION AND THE PROBATION DECISION

Criminal court judges play a pivotal role in the sentencing process. They decide which sentences to impose, and they determine the severity or leniency of those sentences. Most judges have a variety of sentencing options, ranging from probation to incarceration. They can even impose some incarceration interspersed with some probation.

Judges are guided in their sentencing decisions by the different standards of the jurisdictions of their criminal courts. Probation officers assist them by preparing PSI reports. Probation officers frequently append their own sentencing recommendations to these PSI reports, although judges are only obligated to consider them. No judge is bound by the contents of PSIs. If, however, judges are in jurisdictions with sentencing guidelines or presumptive sentencing schemes, then these schemes provide for particular sentencing ranges, usually expressed in months, that function as guides for judges to follow. Again, there is no hard-and-fast rule obligating judges to follow these guidelines, no matter how binding they may appear. The only constraints on judges are mandatory sentencing provisions. If cases come before them where particular sentences are mandated, then they must impose these sentences. For instance, if a repeat offender is convicted of being an habitual offender, many state statutes provide for mandatory terms of life without parole. Therefore, judges have no discretion in these cases and must impose a term of life without parole.

Under most sentencing scenarios, though, judges have considerable latitude in the sentences they impose. They may impose probation, or they may also impose probation with special conditions appended to probation orders. These special conditions are not uncommonly applied (Hemmens, 1999:16). Probationers must comply with all these conditions or they are subject to having their probation programs revoked. They may be placed in a jail or prison for the duration of their sentences. Although most states by law suggest conditions to be imposed on new probationers, judges generally have complete discretion to accept, modify, or reject these conditions (Hemmens, 1999:16). In Texas, for instance, judges may impose some of the following special conditions of probation on offenders:

1. Probationer shall not open a checking account.
2. Probationer must attend basic education or vocational training as directed by the supervising probation officer.
3. Probationer must notify any prospective employer regarding criminal history, if a position of financial responsibility is involved.
4. Probationer shall be assigned to the highest level of supervision or supervision caseload until appropriate level of supervision is further established by objective assessment instrument and supervision case classification.
5. Probationer shall comply with any other condition specified herein (e.g., no controlled substances).

6. Probationer shall participate in a mental health/mental retardation treatment or counseling program as directed by the supervising probation officer.

7. Probationer shall make restitution payments as required by supervising probation officer in an amount to be set by the court. By the tenth of each month, payments (cashier's check or money order) shall be paid to the Texas Department of Criminal Justice Probation Division, Capital Station, Texas, 78711.

8. Probationer shall submit to substance (alcohol/narcotics) treatment program, which may include urinalysis monitoring, attendance at scheduled counseling sessions, driving restrictions, or related requirements as directed by supervising probation officer.

9. Probationer shall not contact victim(s).

10. Probationer shall not enter the specified county without prior written judicial approval.

Judges circle the appropriate special conditions and attach the sheet to the probation order. The probationer must agree with these conditions and other program requirements and must sign the form. If the prospective probationer refuses to sign the form, then probation will be denied. Judges cannot force offenders into probation programs against their wishes.

Probation conditions are usually classified as general or specific. General conditions are imposed on all probationers, whereas specific conditions are only applied to certain probationers. Judges usually use a previously adopted set of standard probation conditions that include the following: (1) make periodic reports to their probation officer, (2) notify the officer about changes in employment or residence, (3) obtain permission for out-of-state travel, (4) refrain from possessing firearms, (5) not associate with known criminals, and (6) obey the law (Hemmens, 1999:16).

Original sentencing judges or their courts maintain jurisdiction over all probationers for the duration of their probationary terms. If any probationer violates one or more program conditions and these violations are detected, then the information is transmitted to the court. The judge considers the evidence in a special hearing before the court and decides what to do. The judge may intensify a probationer's supervision or place the offender under home confinement with electronic monitoring. The judge may require probation officers to make frequent checks of the offender's premises and test the offender for drugs, alcohol, or other substances that may be prohibited.

Judges are responsive to what the public wants and attempt to impose sentences that fit the particular offense, but those most directly involved in the enforcement of conditions of a probationer's program are probation officers. These officers are the primary link between the court and their probationer-clients. As far as the court is concerned, probation officers should stress the following in their supervisory responsibilities:

1. The public wants probation to deliver public safety.
2. Probation can both raise public safety and help probationers become law-abiding citizens.
3. Probation needs to enforce probation orders and help offenders.
4. The "get tough on probationers" idea does not need to lead to more imprisonment; in fact, it could lead to an increase in general deterrence. (Evans, 1999:30)

Recommendations from judges to probation officers include the following admonitions:

1. Public safety comes first.
2. Probation officers should spend more time supervising offenders who pose the greatest risk to public safety.
3. Probation officers should be assigned to supervise specific geographical areas rather than being randomly assigned to offenders.
4. Permissive practices should be abandoned and replaced with a response that is certain and incorporates graduated sanctions to deal with technical violations.
5. Probation should encourage involvement of other agencies, organizations, and interest groups in offender treatment.
6. Program performance should be used as the measure for the allocation of resources. (Evans, 1999:31)

Although probation officers are given a great deal of supervisory responsibility over sentenced offenders on probation, their initial input through PSI report preparation in certain jurisdictions is mixed. For example, a study was conducted of PSI report preparation for 468 persons convicted of sexual assault in Sacramento County, California during the 1992–1994 period (Kingsnorth et al., 1999). Probation officers were excluded entirely from sentencing decisions in 23 percent of the cases that were plea-bargained. Furthermore, probation officers made more severe sentencing recommendations than those contemplated by plea agreements in 29 percent of these cases, and the judges ignored their PSI reports and recommendations in all cases. Even though probation officers relied on the same sentencing criteria as prosecutors and judges in all their recommendations, they were nevertheless viewed negatively by defense attorneys who perceived them as agents of the state. Thus, judicial discretion may operate to the probation officer's disadvantage in some cases. Part of the problem is the growing bureaucratization of probation services and a general breakdown in communication between judges and probation agencies (MacDonald and Baroody-Hart, 1999).

Judges therefore have broad discretion in promoting offender accountability. They may impose restitution orders or community service as a means of heightening offender responsibilities. In some jurisdictions, restitution to victims by offenders is mandated by legislative statute. In Pennsylvania, for instance, judges must impose restitution on probationers whenever damages are easy to quantify. Some experiments have shown that whenever restitution orders are imposed, they operate in ways to minimize one's likelihood of being rearrested. Also influential in heightening offender accountability are if many offenders are married, employed, and older.

Judicial discretion and the special conditions of probation they impose are valid as long as they (1) do not violate the Constitution, (2) are reasonable, (3) are unambiguous, and (4) are intended to promote the rehabilitation of the offender and/or the protection of society (Hemmens, 1999:17). In recent years, the job of sentencing offenders has become less perfunctory. Judges are increasingly exercising what some persons call **therapeutic jurisprudence**, which attempts to combine a "rights" perspective (focusing on justice, rights, and equality issues) with an "ethic of care" perspective (focusing on care, interdependence, and response to need) (Rottman and Casey, 1999:13). Thus, sentencing offenders is increasingly becoming a collaborative enterprise between the court and community. Sentencing judges attempt to create appropriate dispositional outcomes, including securing treatment and social services for offenders who are sentenced, which is where the special conditions of probation can come into play and influence the offender's life chances significantly. The public seems to desire a more involved and responsive judiciary. Thus, the judiciary is gradually being transformed into a process removed somewhat from the traditional one followed for so many decades. A comparison of the traditional process with the transformed court process is as shown:

Traditional Process	Transformed Process
• Dispute resolution	• Problem-solving dispute avoidance
• Legal outcome	• Therapeutic outcome
• Adversarial process	• Collaborative process
• Claim- or case-oriented	• People oriented
• Rights-based	• Interest- or needs-based
• Emphasis placed on adjudication	• Emphasis placed on postadjudication and alternative dispute resolution
• Interpretation and application of law	• Interpretation and application of social science
• Judge as arbiter	• Judge as coach
• Backward looking	• Forward looking
• Precedent-based	• Planning-based
• Few participants and stakeholders	• Wide range of participants and stakeholders
• Individualistic	• Interdependent
• Legalistic	• Commonsensical
• Formal	• Informal
• Efficient	• Effective

Thus, the orientation underlying therapeutic jurisprudence directs the judge's attention beyond the specific dispute before the court and toward the needs and circumstances of the individuals involved in the dispute (Rottman and Casey, 1999:14; Warren, 1998). All participants in the process of creating safer communities, including judges and probation officers, must stay focused on their areas of influence, ensure ongoing interagency training needs to become the norm, and continue to focus on policy development built on reliable research. Many criminal justice organizations, including the courts and probation departments, are increasingly coordinating with other criminal justice organizations in a greater effort to create safer communities and more law-abiding probationer-clients (Cochran and McDevitt, 1998).

SUMMARY

Probation derives from the word *probatio,* which means a period of proving or trial and forgiveness. It was formally recognized by statute in Massachusetts in 1878, although a Massachusetts reformer, John Augustus, is credited with introducing it in the United States in 1841 as part of his philanthropy and temperance beliefs. Those most likely placed on probation include first-time offenders, particularly those convicted of nonviolent crimes. Currently, probation refers to any conditional nonincarcerative sentence imposed by judges for a criminal conviction. Probation differs from parole in that probationers do not ordinarily serve time in either a prison or jail, whereas parolees are former inmates of such institutions who have been released early by parole boards. Judges control probationers, whereas parolees are dependent on parole board discretion for their early release from incarceration.

Not everyone agrees that probation is a suitable punishment for criminal offenders. Those most likely to receive sentences of probation are nondangerous first-offenders, whereas recidivists and dangerous offenders are least likely to receive it. Proponents of probation argue that it prevents persons from succumbing to the criminogenic influence of prisons and jails. The stigma of being labeled as a criminal may compel some persons to commit new crimes as one result of being incarcerated. Probation means avoiding to some extent this criminal label. Probation also alleviates prison and jail overcrowding. In addition, probation permits offenders to remain in their communities and become reintegrated to do lawful and useful activities. Opponents of probation say that it coddles offenders and creates attitudes among criminals that they will not really be punished if they commit crimes.

Those most likely to receive probation are property offenders or those who have been convicted of less serious offenses. Virtually *every* crime category, however, has at least some persons who have been granted probation. The average length of probation for most offenders is between 24 and 36 months, although those convicted of the most serious crimes have the longest probation lengths. The use of probation is also contingent on the nature of the sentencing scheme in any jurisdiction. Guidelines-based sentencing schemes and mandatory sentencing procedures restrict judicial options in sentencing considerably. Nevertheless, most jurisdictions throughout the United States report greater use of probation annually.

Before criminal cases are prosecuted, prosecutors, judges, and offenders sometimes enter into agreements to have their cases disposed of through civil mechanisms. An umbrella term, restorative justice, has been used to depict any action that is primarily oriented toward doing justice by repairing the harm that has been caused by a crime. One civil mechanism involving offender mediation with one or more victims is alternative dispute resolution (ADR), a community-based, informal dispute settlement process. Usually targeted for involvement in such programs are misdemeanants, although low-level nonviolent felons may become involved in the ADR process, depending on the circumstances. Another option available to prosecutors is pretrial diversion. Diversion means to suspend a case from the criminal justice process temporarily and divert offenders to community-based agencies for treatment and/or supervision for a period of time. Once this process is completed, one's criminal record may be either downgraded to a lesser offense or completely expunged. Victim-offender reconciliation projects (VORPs) are becoming increasingly common as methods for reducing clogged criminal court dockets and case backlogs in prosecutors' offices.

At the hub of any preconviction action is the criminal court judge. Criminal court judges have broad discretionary powers and can impose any one of several different punishments. Judges may impose probation for offenders who are considered good candidates for such programs. These offenders are usually low-risk, nonviolent offenders with no prior criminal records. Increasing numbers of offenders have substance abuse problems or mental illnesses, and judges can proscribe special conditions of probation for these persons to receive appropriate treatment from community-based agencies. Increasingly, the judiciary is moving toward greater collaboration with community agencies and organizations to deliver sentences that not only preserve public safety, but tend to hold offenders accountable to their victims in restorative ways.

KEY TERMS

Alternative dispute resolution (ADR)
Boston House of Corrections
Clark, Benjamin C.
Community model
Community reintegration
Conditional diversion program
Cook, Rufus R.
Crime control
Deserts model
Diversion
Diversion programs
Divertees
Due process model
Expungement

Front-end solution
Get-tough movement
Judicial reprieves
Just-deserts model
Mediation
Medical model
Pretrial diversion
Probatio
Progressive era
Reynolds, James Bronson
Rehabilitation
Rehabilitation model
Restitution
Restorative justice

Stigmatization
Therapeutic jurisprudence
Tort
Totality of circumstances
Treatment model
Unconditional diversion program
University Settlement
User fees
Victim compensation
Victim-offender reconciliation
Victim-Offender Reconciliation Project (VORP)

QUESTIONS FOR REVIEW

1. What does probation mean? Where and when did it originate in the United States?
2. Describe the early use of probation in the United States.
3. Compare and contrast the rehabilitative, treatment-oriented correctional philosophy with the justice model. Give some arguments favoring either perspective.
4. What do you see as the relative merits of probation as an alternative to incarceration? Do you think everyone is in favor of probation? Why or why not? Explain.
5. What do you think would happen to our crime rate if probation were done away with completely? Explain.
6. Who was John Augustus, and why was he critical to the subsequent adoption of probation as an alternative to incarceration?
7. Describe four different functions of probation.
8. What is meant by alternative dispute resolution? What are some of its functions?
9. What is restorative justice, and why is it important?
10. What is the nature of judicial discretion in probation decision making?

SUGGESTED READINGS

Anderson, David C. (1998). *Sensible Justice: Alternatives to Prison.* New York: New Press.
Bayens, Gerald J., Michael W. Manske, and John Ortiz Smykla (1998). "The Impact of the 'New Penology' on ISP." *Criminal Justice Review* **23:**51–62.
Latessa, Edward J., et al. (1998). *Evaluating the Prototypical ISP: Final Report.* Washington, DC: U.S. National Institute of Justice.
Marciniak, Liz Marie (2000). "The Addition of Day Reporting to Intensive Supervision Probation: A Comparison of Recidivism Rates." *Federal Probation* **64:**34–39.
Maxwell, Sheila Royo, and M. Kevin Gray (2000). "Deterrence: Testing the Effects of Perceived Sanction Certainty on Probation Violations." *Sociological Inquiry* **70:**117–136.

Programs
for Probationers

CHAPTER 5

Introduction
Standard Probation
   Federal and State Probation Orders
Intensive Supervised Probation (ISP)
   Three Conceptual Models of ISP
   The Georgia ISP Program
   The Idaho ISP Program
   The South Carolina ISP Program
   Criticisms of the Georgia, Idaho, and South
   Carolina ISP Programs
Shock Probation and Split Sentencing
   Shock Probation
   Split Sentencing
   The Philosophy and Objectives of Shock
   Probation
   The Effectiveness of Shock Probation
Boot Camps

Boot Camps Defined
Goals of Boot Camps
A Profile of Boot Camp Clientele
Boot Camp Programs
Jail Boot Camps
The Effectiveness of Boot Camps
Female Probationers and Parolees: A Profile
   Special Programs and Services for Female
   Offenders
The Probation Revocation Process
   Special Circumstances: Mandatory Federal
   Probation Revocation
Landmark Cases and Special Issues
Summary
Key Terms
Questions for Review
Suggested Readings

Do Any of These Persons Qualify for Probation?

• *Timothy Boomer, 25, the Cussing Canoeist.* What does it take to get arrested and convicted in Michigan? Cussing in your canoe, that's what. At least that's what happened to Timothy Boomer, 25, in June 1999 in Standish, Michigan. In the summer of 1998, Timothy Boomer was canoeing on the Rifle River when his canoe hit a rock, throwing him into the water. Boomer allegedly used the "f-word" anywhere from 25 to perhaps 70 times with children present. Witnesses described Boomer's neck with veins popping out; he was enraged. Boomer claims in his own defense that he didn't know children were present when he uttered the string of profanity. Boomer is a factory worker from nearby Detroit. He did not deny letting off steam when his canoe hit a rock in the river. William Street, Boomer's attorney, who defended him on behalf of the American Civil Liberties Union, said, "Boomer at worst said an 'f-word' or two when he fell into the Rifle River. It was the sort of event that has now been exaggerated and blown all out of proportion. The people are trying to make a mountain out of a molehill." Street also said, "As much as they would like to have been able to ticket Timothy Boomer for being drunk, they didn't bring the charge because they didn't have the facts. So they scraped 102 years deep into the bottom of the Michigan Criminal Code to bring this offense to the top." Boomer faced up to 90 days in jail. Should he be placed on probation or put in jail? (*Source:* Adapted from Associated Press, "Canoeist Convicted of Cussing in Michigan," June 12, 1999.)

• *Paul Wilson, Pierre, South Dakota.* A 15-minute ride down Main Street on a horse may not seem like much, but if you are intoxicated while riding the horse, you can be charged with DWI. That's what happened to Paul Wilson, 42, of Pierre, South Dakota. Police say that Wilson rode his horse to a local cafe in the downtown business district, tethered the animal outside, and went inside to eat. He was later arrested as he rode away from the restaurant. According to Hughes County State's Attorney Mark Smith, "It is illegal to ride a horse while intoxicated. Driving under the influence is operating a vehicle under the influence of alcohol, and by definition of the word, vehicle, it includes a ridden animal. Laugh as you will, it's true." Drunken driving, or drunken horse riding, is punishable by up to one year in jail and a $1,000 fine. Wilson was released on bond and was scheduled to appear in court later. There is some question as to whether the DWI statute applies only to motorized vehicles, in which case horses would be excluded. Is Wilson a good candidate for probation? (*Source:* Adapted from Associated Press, "Horseman Charged with Drunken Driving," June 4, 1999.)

• *Rodney Hosler, 27, Child Molester and Victim.* In Delaware, Ohio, a strange event occurred. Rodney Hosler, 27, had been convicted of molesting a five-year-old child. He served a two-year prison sentence and returned to his home. Within a short time following his release from prison, Hosler was found wrapped only in a blanket behind a pizza parlor in Delaware. Someone had brutalized him sexually and had scribbled "I am a child molester" on his body. When police sorted out what happened to Hosler, they arrested three women and charged them with kidnapping and rape. Arrested were Hosler's wife, Jewell, 28; Hosler's mother, Mary Franks, 44; and Mrs. Hosler's aunt, Vickie Coulter, 39. According to Rodney Hosler, he was at home watching television when the women burst in, wrestled him to the floor, and cut off his sweatpants and underwear. They then shaved his head and pubic hair, assaulted him anally with a cucumber, put a heat-producing ointment on his genitals, and threatened him with a hammer. Hosler resisted, screaming in pain. Next, the women scribbled "child molester" all over his body and drove him 70 miles away to his hometown of McComb, leaving him behind a pizza parlor wrapped only in a pink-and-green Minnie Mouse blanket. Keith Ruhl, 19, of Delaware, Ohio, regarded the incident as a form of rough justice. "It was kind of funny and I think he deserved it," Ruhl said. Police investigating the incident took a different view. "I don't know what their motive was but it's apparent that they were trying to send the victim a message. I don't know if it was a warning or revenge. What was written on the body, you can draw your own conclusions," said Captain Pat Yankie of the Delaware Police

Department. Are these women good candidates for probation? (*Source:* Adapted from Associated Press, "Women Charged with Attack on Child Molester," August 8, 1999.)

• *Charles Bauld.* It happened in San Francisco. A 90-year-old man, Charles Bauld, and his wife had entered into a suicide pact to die earlier that day. Bauld later told police that he and his wife discussed the idea of a murder-suicide frequently, but that his wife was reluctant to go through with it. Later that day, Bauld elected to make the decision for them. He picked up a dumbbell and bludgeoned her over the head with it. Then, he leaped from a second-story window in an attempt to kill himself. He succeeded only in fracturing his arm and leg. Police found Bauld lying in the backyard of the couple's home. Entering the home, they discovered Mrs. Bauld with a plastic bag over her bloody head. Subsequent investigation revealed that Bauld had become increasingly agitated over his wife's diabetes condition. He said that his wife had gotten out of the hospital, was incontinent, and couldn't move anymore. There were indications at the crime scene that Mrs. Bauld had struggled with her husband before he had killed her. Is Bauld a good candidate for probation? (*Source:* Adapted from Associated Press, "90-Year-Old Man Bludgeons Wife," April 25, 1998.)

What Happened?

• Boomer was convicted of violating an obscenity ordinance and was placed on probation for six months and ordered to pay a fine and court costs.

• Wilson was placed on probation.

• The three women were convicted of assault and placed on probation for two years, each having to perform 200 hours of community service.

• Bauld was convicted of manslaughter but a psychiatric examination was ordered. After being treated in a mental hospital, he was placed on intensive supervised probation.

INTRODUCTION

This chapter begins with an examination of standard probation and intensive supervised probation as alternatives to incarceration. After a determination of guilt in criminal court, some convicted offenders are sentenced to probation for a period of years. The history, philosophy, and functions of probation have already been described. In this chapter, several popular probation options, including specific programs of intensive supervised probation, are explored.

The final part of this chapter examines shock probation, split sentencing, and boot camps as increasingly used probation variations and options. The goals and effectiveness of shock probation are presented. Boot camps, including some of the more popular models developed in various states, are described, and boot camp participants are profiled. The effectiveness of boot camps is also discussed, as well as several criticisms of it. The costs of these nonincarcerative options are compared with the costs of incarceration, and several trends in diversion and probation are described.

STANDARD PROBATION

Standard probation supervision in many jurisdictions is essentially no supervision at all. When offenders are convicted of one or more crimes, judges sentence a portion of these convicted offenders to a probation program in lieu of incarceration. These programs may or may not have conditions. Prospective probationers are required to sign a form outlining the conditions of their probation. Compliance with the probation program conditions is monitored closely by POs. These officers, however, are often so overworked and understaffed that they cannot possibly oversee all the activities of their probationer-clients. The caseloads or numbers of offenders POs are assigned to supervise vary among jurisdictions. They may be as high as 2,000 in some cities or counties, whereas in others, the caseloads may be 30 or fewer. Caseloads vary according to the type of program, the number of offenders, and the number of probation officers who are available.

Standard probation is considered by many critics to be the most ineffective probationary form. Often, probationers may contact their probation officers by telephone and avoid face-to-face visits. In addition, the requirements of their probationary programs are often less stringent compared with more intensive probation programs. The caseloads of POs in some jurisdictions are so high that officers cannot devote special attention to those offenders in the greatest need of special attention. That is the great failing of standard probation. There are no easy solutions to this problem. The probation department can only do so much in view of its staffing problems and varying clientele, and there is no relief in sight. The chances are that this probation form is growing rather than declining, despite high recidivism rates among standard probationers (Petersilia, 1999a).

Another problem with probation is that often, those in administrative positions in probation departments attach greater importance to those things that enhance paper processing, office efficiency, and career development rather than to those things that directly affect probationers. For instance, a study of the Massachusetts probation system involved a mail survey that yielded 500 responses. These responses were supplemented with interviews and field efforts involving 60 different criminal courts and more than 400 individuals. The resulting report addressed at least 60 different improvements in Massachusetts probation programs. A more selective list of those improvements receiving the greatest priority and attention is significant, though, not because of what is included, but rather what is excluded. The 11 priority concerns are as follows:

1. The review and redefinition of the overall mission of probation
2. Career advancement opportunities for all personnel
3. Greater emphasis on affirmative action
4. Adjustments in the staffing level in some courts
5. Increased training opportunities
6. Substantially improved physical facilities
7. Immediate attention to computerizing the central file

8. Formation of citizen advisory groups
9. Substantially improved social services for offenders
10. Specific attention to the unique needs of the various trial court departments
11. An immediate and forceful public education campaign to enlist support for improved social services from all branches of government and the general public (Spangenberg et al. 1987)

All but one of these improvement recommendations has to do with office policy, office efficiency, office work, office environment, public relations with the community, and office relations with courts. It is unclear about what is meant by "improved social services for offenders." Ideally, probation offices exist to supervise offenders. Many probation departments act as brokers between the agency and various community businesses, to identify potential workplaces where probationer-clients might find and maintain employment. Probationer assistance has always been a mission of probation departments, but most of these key priorities are unrelated directly to assisting probationers, except for improving their social activities, whatever they may be. This reason may help explain why some observers have declared that probation is in trouble (Orchowsky, Merritt, and Browning, 1994).

Federal and State Probation Orders

Standard probation among the states is quite diverse, although the conditions of probation share many of the same characteristics. The U.S. Probation Department oversees adult probationers as well as certain juveniles who have been sentenced by U.S. magistrates or federal district court judges for federal crimes. As the result of the U.S. sentencing guidelines, the use of probation in the federal system since 1987 has been drastically reduced. In the preguideline period prior to 1987, probation was granted by federal district court judges about 65 percent of the time. Today, the proportion of federal offenders who are granted probation is about 10 to 15 percent (U.S. Department of Justice, 2000). Below are some examples of standard probation orders. Figure 5.1 shows a U.S. district court probation form indicating specific standard conditions of probation. A reading of these conditions shows that federal standard probation and supervised release is geared toward crime control and heightening offender accountability. Besides paying fines and restitution, federal offenders must periodically report to the probation office. Probationers cannot possess firearms. They cannot leave their jurisdictions without permission from the federal court. Probationers must work at jobs unless otherwise involved in educational or vocational programs or if they are undergoing psychological counseling for mental health or substance abuse problems. They must refrain from excessive use of alcohol, and they are forbidden from taking illegal drugs. Even their associations with others and the places they may visit are restricted. Probationers must make their dwellings available at any time for a PO's inspection and search for contraband. Also note in Figure 5.1 that space has been provided for judges to add special conditions of probation, which may include various community-based sanctions, including home confinement, electronic monitoring, day reporting, and other activities deemed necessary for an offender's rehabilitation and reintegration.

The conditions of standard probation for prospective Florida probationers are fairly standard for state standard probation programs. Under Florida probation

PROB 7A
(Rev. 10/89)

Conditions of Probation and Supervised Release

UNITED STATES DISTRICT COURT

FOR THE

_____

Name _____   Docket No. _____

Address _____

Under the terms of your sentence, you have been placed on probation/supervised release (strike one) by the Honorable _____ , United States District Judge for the District of _____ . Your term of supervision is for a period of _____ , commencing _____ .

While on probation/supervised release (strike one) you shall not commit another Federal, state, or local crime and shall not illegally possess a controlled substance. Revocation of probation and supervised release is mandatory for possession of a controlled substance.

CHECK IF APPROPRIATE:

☐ As a condition of supervision, you are instructed to pay a fine in the amount of _____ ; it shall be paid in the following manner _____ .

☐ As a condition of supervision, you are instructed to pay restitution in the amount of _____ to _____ ; it shall be paid in the following manner _____ .

☐ The defendant shall not possess a firearm or destructive device. Probation must be revoked for possession of a firearm.

☐ The defendant shall report in person to the probation office in the district to which the defendant is released within 72 hours of release from the custody of the Bureau of Prisons.

☐ The defendant shall report in person to the probation office in the district of release within 72 hours of release from the custody of the Bureau of Prisons.

It is the order of the Court that you shall comply with the following standard conditions:

(1) You shall not leave the judicial district without permission of the Court or probation officer;

(2) You shall report to the probation officer as directed by the Court or probation officer, and shall submit a truthful and complete written report within the first five days of each month;

(3) You shall answer truthfully all inquiries by the probation officer and follow the instructions of the probation officer;

FIGURE 5.1 U.S. District Court conditions of probation and supervised release. (*Source:* Administrative Office of the U.S. Courts, 1997:21.)

(4)   You shall support your dependents and meet other family responsibilities;

(5)   You shall work regularly at a lawful occupation unless excused by the probation officer for schooling, training, or other acceptable reasons;

(6)   You shall notify the probation officer within 72 hours of any change in residence or employment;

(7)   You shall refrain from excessive use of alcohol and shall not purchase, possess, use, distribute, or administer any narcotic or other controlled substance, or any paraphernalia related to such substances, except as prescribed by a physician;

(8)   You shall not frequent places where controlled substances are illegally sold, used, distributed, or administered;

(9)   You shall not associate with any persons engaged in criminal activity, and shall not associate with any person convicted of a felony unless granted permission to do so by the probation officer;

(10)   You shall permit a probation officer to visit you at any time at home or elsewhere, and shall permit confiscation of any contraband observed in plain view by the probation officer;

(11)   You shall notify the probation officer within 72 hours of being arrested or questioned by a law enforcement officer;

(12)   You shall not enter into any agreement to act as an informer or a special agent of a law enforcement agency without the permission of the Court;

(13)   As directed by the probation officer, you shall notify third parties of risks that may be occasioned by your criminal record or personal history or characteristics, and shall permit the probation officer to make such notifications and to confirm your compliance with such notification requirement.

The special conditions ordered by the Court are as follows:

Upon a finding of violation of probation or supervised release, I understand that the Court may (1) revoke supervision or (2) extend the term of supervision and/or modify the conditions of supervision.

These conditions have been read to me. I fully understand the conditions, and have been provided a copy of them.

(Signed) _____   _____
                  Defendant   Date

_____   _____
U.S. Probation Officer/Designated Witness   Date

guidelines supplied to judges, the following conditions do not require oral pronouncement in court by a judge. Rather, they are prepared in written form and a copy is submitted to the offender for his or her consent and signature. These conditions are as follows:

1. Probationer must report to the probation supervisor as directed.
2. Probationer must permit supervisors to visit him or her at his or her home or elsewhere.
3. Probationer must work faithfully at suitable employment insofar as may be possible.
4. Probationer must remain within a specified place.
5. Probationer must make reparation or restitution to the aggrieved party for the damage or loss caused by his or her offense in an amount to be determined by the court.
6. Probationer must make payment of the debt due and owing to a county or municipal detention facility for medical care, treatment, hospitalization, or transportation received by the probationer while in that detention facility.
7. Probationer must support his or her legal dependents to the best of his or her ability.
8. Probationer must make payment of debt due and owing to the state subject to modification based on change in circumstances.
9. Probationer must pay any application fee assessed and attorney's fees and costs assessed subject to modification based on change of circumstances.
10. Probationer must not associate with persons engaged in criminal activities.
11. Probationer must submit to random testing as directed by the correctional probation officer or the professional staff of the treatment center where he or she is receiving treatment to determine the presence of alcohol or use of alcohol or controlled substances.
12. Probationer is prohibited from possessing, carrying, or owning any firearm unless authorized by the court and consented to by the probation officer.
13. Probationer is prohibited from using any intoxicants to excess or possessing any drugs or narcotics unless prescribed by a physician. The probationer shall not knowingly visit places where intoxicants, drugs, or other dangerous substances are unlawfully sold, dispensed, or used.
14. Probationer will attend an HIV/AIDS awareness program consisting of a class of not less than 2 hours or more than 4 hours in length, the cost of which shall be paid by the offender, if such a program is available in the county of the offender's residence.
15. Probationer shall pay not more than $1 per month during the term of probation to a nonprofit organization established for the sole purpose of supplementing the rehabilitative efforts of the Department of Corrections. (Florida Department of Corrections, 2001)

Florida also imposes certain special conditions of probation similar to the federal standard probation conditions, as follows:

1. Probationer is required to be intensively supervised and under probation officer surveillance.
2. Probationer is required to maintain specified contact with the probation officer.
3. Probationer shall be confined to an agreed-upon residence during hours away from employment and public service activities.
4. Probationer shall perform mandatory public service.

5. Probationer shall be supervised by means of an electronic monitoring device.
6. Probationer placed on electronic monitoring shall be monitored 24 hours a day.
7. Probationers placed on electronic monitoring will be subject to investigation and supervision by a probation officer 24 hours a day.
8. The court shall receive a diagnosis and evaluation of any probationer for appropriate community treatment. (Florida Department of Corrections, 2001)

In the Florida Department of Corrections, for instance, several different types of public service or **community service** are prescribed, such as (1) maintenance work on any property or building owned or leased by any state, county, or municipality or any nonprofit organization or agency; (2) maintenance work on any state-owned, county-owned, or municipally owned road or highway; (3) landscaping or maintenance work in any state, county, or municipal park or recreational area; and (4) work in any state, county, or municipal hospital or any developmental services institution or other nonprofit organization or agency. Florida offenders convicted of drug crimes may be required to pay a fine ranging from $500 to $10,000; to perform at least 100 hours of public service; to submit to routine and random drug testing; and to participate, at their own expense, in some appropriate self-help group, such as Narcotics Anonymous, Alcoholics Anonymous, or Cocaine Anonymous, if available. In 2001, the Florida Department of Corrections reported that 145,098 offenders were on probation, with 107,078 or 81 percent on standard probation. The remainder of nonincarcerated clients were under other forms of supervision, such as community control, pretrial intervention, or postprison release (Florida Department of Corrections, 2001:1).

A major problem with standard probation is high offender recidivism. Most jurisdictions throughout the United States report recidivism rates of 60 percent or higher for offenders who are placed on standard probation. Some attempt has been made to reduce these high recidivism rates by establishing programs that involve much more intensive offender monitoring and supervision. These programs are categorically called intensive supervised probation (ISP) programs.

INTENSIVE SUPERVISED PROBATION (ISP)

An **intensive supervised probation (ISP) program** or an **intensive probation supervision (IPS) program** is an increasingly common method of supervising offenders who require closer monitoring (Bayens, Manske, and Smykla, 1998). Also known as traditional probation, ISP is a type of intermediate punishment somewhere between standard probation and incarceration (Petersilia, 1999a). One short-range goal of intermediate punishments is to reduce prison and jail overcrowding. There is government endorsement of this ISP program goal as well as support within the professional community. Other types of intermediate punishments are electronic monitoring, home incarceration, community-based supervision, and community-based corrections. These programs will be examined at length in subsequent chapters. Offenders are assigned probation officers who arrange frequent face-to-face contacts with their clients. These contacts may be weekly, a few times a week, or daily. ISP is a special form of traditional probation in which the intensity of offender monitoring is greatly increased and the conditions of probation are considerably more stringent. The logic is that the greater amount of contact between the probationer and PO will function as an incentive for greater offender compliance with program requirements. Known in some circles as smart sentencing, ISP often involves greater client/officer contact, which may mean that POs are more frequently accessible to clients if they are experiencing personal or financial difficulties, social stresses, or other problems (Fulton et al., 1997; Jones and Lacey, 1999).

There is considerable variation in ISP programs among jurisdictions, mostly because probation officer caseloads vary. These caseloads depend on the financial resources of the jurisdiction and local definitions of the maximum number of clients probation officers must supervise. ISP in many jurisdictions limits the number of offender-clients to 30 per probation officer. In some jurisdictions, the maximum number of offenders supervised may be limited to 15 or 20 (Administrative Office of the U.S. Courts, 1997; Kushner et al., 1995).

Intensive supervised probation programs have received mixed reactions among the public. One problem is that many of these programs, their objectives, and the ways they are being implemented are misunderstood by community residents and interpreted in the most unfavorable light. Even though these programs monitor probationers more closely than standard probation supervision and are tougher on offenders by comparison, many citizens believe that offender freedom in the community is not an acceptable punishment.

There is no standard definition for ISP, although all ISP programs feature small offender caseload sizes (Sundt et al., 1998). *Intensive* is a relative term, but the basic idea is to increase the intensity of supervision for designated probationers to satisfy public demand for applying a just punishment (Erwin, 1986:17). Some persons distinguish between standard probation and intensive surveillance coupled with substantial community service and/or restitution. Probably the best way of conceptualizing what ISP means is to identify ISP program components that have been operationalized in several states (Petersilia, 1998).

Three Conceptual Models of ISP

Before examining several state ISP programs, three conceptual models of ISP—the justice model; the limited risk control model; and the traditional, treatment-oriented model—are described. These models help explain not only interstate variations in ISP programs but also their individual rationales. Table 5.1 contrasts these three models and highlights several of their important features.

The Justice Model.   The justice model makes no pretense of being anything other than punishment-centered, but not to the point of being unfair to offenders. The penalty should fit the crime committed, and the offender should receive his or her just deserts. This model emphasizes daily contact between offenders and probation officers, community service orders, and/or restitution. No counseling is required, nor is any participation in any specific rehabilitative program (Maxwell and Gray, 2000).

The Limited Risk Control Model.   The **limited risk control model** is based on anticipated future criminal conduct and uses risk assessment devices to place offenders within an effective control range. This model fits a presumptive sentencing format

TABLE 5.1 The Justice, Limited Risk Control, and Traditional Treatment-Oriented Models Compared by Intensive Supervised Probation Factors

Program Elements	Justice Model	Limited Risk Control Model	Traditional Treatment-Oriented Model
1. Recommended caseload	"Low"	10	"Low"
2. Daily contact with probation officer	Yes	No	No
3. Weekly contact with probation officer	No	Yes	20 times per month, variable
4. Community service	Yes	Optional	Yes
5. Restitution	Yes	Optional	Yes
6. Field visits	Yes	Yes	Optional
7. Probation fees	Yes	Yes	Optional
8. Curfew	Yes	Optional	Yes
9. Shock probation	Optional	No	Yes
10. Offender volunteers for program	No	No	Yes
11. Periodic committee review of offender progress	No	Yes	Yes
12. Use of risk assessment devices	No	Yes	Optional
13. Minimum time in ISP	6 months	Individual, but 90 days minimum	12 months
14. Normal program length	6–36 months	Variable	18 months
15. House arrest	Optional	No	Optional
16. Fines	Optional	Optional	Yes
17. Counseling	No	Probably	Probably
18. Vocational/rehabilitation training	No	Probably	Probably

Source: James M. Byrne, "The Control Controversy: A Preliminary Examination of Intensive Supervision Programs in the United States," *Federal Probation* **50:**4–12, 1986.

specifying ranges of penalties or varying control levels depending on risk assessment scores (Byrne, 1986:7). Thus, judges rely on predictions of probable future criminal conduct and sentence offenders to one of three degrees of community supervision (e.g., minimum, regular, and intensive). Compared with the justice model, the limited risk control model appears more flexible and provides for periodic reassessments of predicted offender behaviors and corresponding adjustments of degrees of community supervision.

The Traditional, Treatment-Oriented Model. The **traditional treatment-oriented model** stresses traditional rehabilitative measures that seek to reintegrate the offender into the community through extensive assistance. Although this model may include elements of the justice and limited risk control models, its primary aim is "long-term change in offender behavior" (Byrne, 1986:8). Therefore, it includes strategies such as developing individual offender plans for life in the community such as work, study, or community service; full-time employment and/or vocational training; and/or using community sponsors or other support personnel to provide assistance and direction for offenders (Byrne, 1986:8).

No states currently use the justice model exclusively. States using the limited risk control model include Oregon and Massachusetts. Several other states have initiated ISP programs as well. Georgia created an ISP program in 1982 (Erwin, 1986:17), and programs in Idaho and South Carolina began in 1984. The Georgia, New Jersey, Idaho, and South Carolina plans are featured here because they represent four different approaches to the problem of managing probationers and because other states have incorporated many of the elements of these programs into their own ISP programs.

The Georgia ISP Program

In the 1970s, Georgia had the highest per capita incarceration rate in the United States (Erwin, 1986:17). Because of prison overcrowding and the spillover effect into Georgia's jails to house their prison overflow, the state was desperate to devise a workable probation program. After spending much money on feasibility studies and considering alternatives to incarceration, Georgia's ISP was put into effect in 1982.

Georgia Program Elements.   The **Georgia Intensive Supervision Probation Program (GISPP)** has established several punitive intensive probation conditions that parallel the justice model. Three phases of the program were outlined according to the level of control, phase I being the most intensive supervision and phase III being the least intensive. These standards include the following:

1. Five face-to-face contacts per week in phase I (decreasing to two face-to-face contacts per week in phase III)
2. 132 hours of mandatory community service
3. Mandatory curfew
4. Mandatory employment
5. Weekly check of local arrest records
6. Automatic notification of arrest elsewhere via State Crime Information Network listings
7. Routine alcohol and drug screens
8. Assignment of one probation officer and one surveillance officer to 25 probationers or one probation officer and two surveillance officers to 40 probationers (surveillance officers have corrections backgrounds or law enforcement training and make home visits, check arrest records, and perform drug/alcohol tests among other duties)
9. Determination by probation officer of individualized treatment (e.g., counseling, vocational/educational training) for offender
10. Probation officer as liaison between court and offender to report to court regularly on offender's progress from personal and surveillance observations and records

The Success of the Georgia ISP Program.   The success of the GISPP thus far has been demonstrated by low recidivism rates among offenders under ISP (recidivism rates are almost always used as measures of probation program effectiveness). Compared with paroled offenders and others supervised by standard probation practices, the GISPP participants had systematically lower recidivism rates depending on their risk classification, which were low, medium, high, and maximum. Reconvictions for these groups were 25 percent, 16 percent, 28 percent, and 26 percent, respectively, compared with parolees who had considerably higher reconviction rates for all risk groupings. By comparison, Figure 5.2 shows the New Jersey conditions of placement of individuals on intensive supervised probation.

The Idaho ISP Program

The **Idaho Intensive Supervised Probation Program** was launched as a pilot project in 1982 (Brown, 1992:7). Initially, a team consisting of one PO and two surveillance officers closely supervised a small group of low-risk offenders who normally would have been sent to prison. The program was quite successful. In October 1984, Idaho established a statewide ISP program with legislative approval, a step seen as a major element in the get-tough-on-crime posture taken by the state.

Elements of the Idaho ISP Program. When implemented in 1984, the ISP program operated in teams, consisting of two POs and a section supervisor responsible for supervising a maximum of 25 high-risk clients. This team was required to work evenings and in shifts. POs carried firearms while performing their duties. The court-referred clientele for these POs and supervisors consisted of felony probationers or parolees who were classified at a maximum level of supervision. All clients had lengthy criminal records of violent crimes and were in need of intensive supervision. Clients were obligated to stay in their programs for four to six months and had to complete two major phases of supervision.

The first phase consisted of seven face-to-face visits per week, four of which occurred in the clients' homes. Phase II reduced the number of face-to-face contacts with clients per week to four. Both phases included random day or night checks for possible curfew violations, drug and/or alcohol abuse, and any other possible program violation. Probationers who violated one or more program conditions received either verbal warnings or informal staff hearings, at which several additional program conditions might be imposed, including community service. Another possibility is that those probationers in phase II would be returned to phase I.

Idaho ISP Program Effectiveness. Between 1984 and 1992, the Idaho Department of Corrections has processed 2,487 clients, and about 63 percent of these probationers have completed the ISP program successfully. During 1992, 179 clients were under ISP of one form or another. The overall rate of technical violations, such as curfew violations, drinking, and unauthorized travel, was only about 28 percent, and the rate of new felonies charged was only 1.3 percent (Brown, 1992:7-8). The major result of this ISP program has been a drastic reduction in new convictions for felonies among successful program participants.

The South Carolina ISP Program

To ease prison overcrowding in South Carolina, a legislative mandate was given in 1984 to establish an ISP program for statewide use. The South Carolina Department of Probation, Parole, and Pardon Services (DPPPS) was responsible for the **South**

NEW JERSEY CONDITIONS OF PLACEMENT OF
ADULTS ON INTENSIVE SUPERVISION

I have applied for, and been granted, an opportunity to be placed on intensive supervision by the Resentencing Panel for a period of_____. Based on the plan I submitted, the Resentencing Panel believes that I am capable of living a useful and law-abiding life in the community and has suspended my sentence with the condition that I comply with the provisions of the intensive supervision program. My being granted the opportunity of intensive supervision is subject to my compliance with the plan I submitted as part of my application along with the conditions listed below. If there is probable cause to believe that I have committed another offense or if I have been held to answer thereto, the Resentencing Panel will commit me to the institution to which I have been sentenced, without bail, to await trial on the new charges. I am required to notify promptly my ISP officer if I am arrested at any time during my sentence to the intensive supervision program.

1. I will obey the laws of the United States and the laws and ordinances of any jurisdiction to which I may be assigned.
2. I will report as directed by the court or my ISP officer.
3. I will permit the ISP officer to visit my home.
4. I will answer promptly, truthfully, and completely all inquiries made by my ISP officer and report any address or residence change to that officer. If the change of address or residence is outside the region in which I am under supervision, I will request approval of my ISP officer at least thirty days in advance of such change.
5. I will cooperate in any medical and/or psychological examination, tests and/or counseling my ISP officer recommends.
6. I will support my dependents, meet my family responsibilities, continue gainful employment, and/or pursue such alternatives as may be part of the program and promptly notify my ISP officer prior to any change in my place of employment or if I find myself out of work.
7. I will participate in a counseling program as scheduled by my ISP officer.
8. I will not leave the State of New Jersey without permission from my ISP officer.
9. I will not have in my possession any firearm or other dangerous weapon.
10. I will perform community service in accordance with the ISP officer.
11. I will participate in group activities scheduled by my ISP officer.
12. I will maintain a diary of my activities while under supervision.
13. I will maintain weekly contact with my community sponsor and network team.

I will comply with the following conditions of intensive supervision imposed in accordance with N.J.S.A. 2C:45-1 et. seq., as communicated to me by my ISP officer.

_____I will pay a fine of $_____in strict accord with the terms described.
_____I will make restitution of $_____in strict accord with the terms described.
_____I will pursue the course of study or vocational training described.
_____I will attend/reside in the facility described for the required period of time.
_____I will refrain from frequenting the unlawful or disreputable places or consorting with the disreputable persons described.

_____

Signature of ISP Client

_____

Date

FIGURE 5.2 New Jersey Conditions of Placement of Adults on Intensive Supervision.

Carolina Intensive Supervised Probation Program implementation. The primary aims of the ISP program were to heighten surveillance of participants, increase PO/client contact, and increase offender accountability. Like Idaho, South Carolina started its ISP program as a pilot or experimental project. Their program goal was to involve 336 probationers during the first year of operation. By 1991, 13,356 offenders had been processed through the ISP program. During that year, South Carolina was supervising 1,589 probationers and 480 parolees (Cavanaugh, 1992:1,5).

South Carolina ISP Program Elements. Offenders placed in South Carolina ISP programs must pay a $10 per week supervision fee. Supervision fees are not particularly unusual in many ISP programs. Clients are supervised by specialized POs known as intensive agents with caseloads of no more than 35 offenders at any given time. Weekly face-to-face contacts with offenders are mandatory, together with visits to neighbors, friends, employers, and service providers of probationers. POs in the South Carolina program act as liaisons between the private sector and their clients, lining up job possibilities. Thus, POs do some employment counseling when necessary.

Offender Classification for Participation. Each offender is classified according to risk and needs, and POs then tailor individual program requirements to fit these offender needs. The level of supervision over particular offenders is influenced by their particular risk level determined through risk assessment. The goal of DPPPS POs is to provide offenders with the proper balance of control and assistance. Thus, the ISP program is also supplemented with curfews, electronic monitoring, and house arrest or home incarceration elements for certain high-risk offenders. Offenders sentenced to home incarceration are in a program known as ISP Home Detention and are confined to their homes from 10:00 P.M. to 6:00 A.M. excepting authorized leaves from home by their supervising POs. Offenders are subject to random visits from POs, day or night. Clients must work or seek employment; undergo medical, psychiatric, or mental health counseling or other rehabilitative treatment; attend religious services; or perform community service work (Cavanaugh, 1992:5–6).

The length of their stay in this ISP program varies from three to six months. Electronic monitoring is used to supplement this program whereby offenders are placed on EM and must wear an electronic wristlet or anklet for the first 30 days. After successfully completing the first 30-day period of ISP, they are taken off EM and subject to a 60-day period of simple voice verification. Such verification occurs by telephone, with POs calling offenders at particular times to verify their whereabouts. Offenders give requested information over the telephone, and electronic devices verify whether the voice pattern transmitted matches that of the offender being called.

Like POs in the Idaho program, POs in the DPPPS work in shifts so that offenders can be checked both day and night. The DPPPS also uses paraprofessionals in operation specialist capacities who assist POs in performing surveillance work, particularly in the state's larger counties (Cavanaugh, 1992:6).

Effectiveness of the South Carolina ISP Program. The ISP program in South Carolina appears successful. Less than 10 percent of the probationers who have participated in the South Carolina ISP program have had their programs revoked due to new offenses rather than for technical program violations. Using the arbitrary 30 percent recidivism standard for determining whether a program is or is not successful, the South Carolina ISP program is successful for both its probationers and its parolees.

Criticisms of the Georgia, Idaho, and South Carolina ISP Programs

A general criticism leveled at any ISP program is that it does not achieve its stated goals (Fulton and Stone, 1993:43). Some observers say that victims are ignored in probation decision making (Heisel, 1992:38). Yet others say that by bringing certain offenders under the ISP program umbrella who really do not need to be intensively supervised, ISP programs contribute to net-widening (Palumbo and Snyder-Joy, 1990). Simultaneously, an equally vocal aggregate of critics praises ISP for alleviating prison inmate overcrowding and providing a meaningful option to incarceration (Lemov, 1992:134). Among the ISP program components in certain jurisdictions that have drawn criticism have been supervision fees (Mills, 1992:10), which are normally incurred by probationer-clients. Even this particular issue is hotly debated, however. The controversy over ISP programs will likely remain unresolved for many years.

Regardless of their disputed effectiveness, different ISP programs have been developed and used in other states. For example, several elements of the Georgia model have been adopted by Colorado, Nevada, Oregon, and Washington. These states have not copied Georgia precisely in their probation guidelines, but their newly developed programs resemble the Georgia program to a high degree.

The Georgia program has been both praised and criticized. First, it has demonstrated low rates of recidivism. Convicted criminals who participate in the program do not commit new offenses with great frequency. The ISP program has alleviated some prison overcrowding by diverting a large number of offenders to probationary status rather than incarceration. The most important criticism of Georgia's program credibility pertains to those selected for inclusion in it. Fewer than 30 percent of the offenders placed on ISP in Georgia consist of maximum-risk cases. Thus, most Georgia ISP probationers are those least likely to recidivate anyway (Petersilia, 1999a). Also, the division of labor between probation officers and surveillance officers has not been as clear as originally intended. Surveillance officers perform many of the same functions as standard probation officers. Therefore, it is difficult to formulate a clear caseload picture for regular Georgia probation officer functions.

Another criticism is that Georgia handpicks its clients for ISP involvement. The selection process deliberately includes low- to medium-risk offenders with the greatest potential to succeed. Deliberately excluded are the most serious offenders with the least success likelihood. In fact, some researchers have said the current composition of ISP clients consists of persons who would have been diverted from prison anyway (Petersilia, 1999a). For ISP programs to be effective, more high-risk offenders ought to be targeted for inclusion rather than those most likely to succeed (Dickey and Wagner, 1990).

New Jersey's ISP program has received several criticisms. First, offenders must volunteer, and only 25 percent of all applicants are accepted. The most serious felons are excluded, thus creating a "bias" toward lower recidivism among those served by the program. Furthermore, that participants must be incarcerated for a short time is tantamount to shock probation or shock parole. Therefore, space in prison is consumed at least temporarily by persons eventually selected for ISP.

The Idaho and South Carolina ISP programs exhibit relatively low rates of recidivism for their participating offenders. Compared with the Georgia and New Jersey programs, these programs rely fairly heavily on the use of risk assessment instruments for recruiting clients and determining their level of intensive supervision. The

South Carolina program element involving the payment of a $10 per week supervision fee is only a token amount, but it is nevertheless regarded by staff as heightening offender accountability and serves as a reminder that they are paying for their crimes, even if the payment is hardly excessive. POs in both Idaho and South Carolina act as liaisons and unite clients with receptive employers. Further, the integrated use of home confinement and electronic monitoring, together with frequent face-to-face visits and checks by supervising POs, means that offender control is heightened.

SHOCK PROBATION AND SPLIT SENTENCING

Shock Probation

Shock probation, also referred to as **split sentencing**, first appeared as a federal split sentencing provision in 1958, although the California legislature had authorized a bill permitting judges to impose a combination of incarceration and probation for the same offender in the early 1920s (New York State Division of Parole, 1998). The term *shock probation,* was later coined by Ohio, the first state to use shock probation, in 1964. It has been characterized as a brief application of the rigors of imprisonment (in Ohio, 90 to 130 days served) that will deter criminal behavior and not impede the readjustment of the individual upon release. Shock probation has been used increasingly in other states in recent years. In more than a few jurisdictions, problem drinkers, DWI cases, and drug abusers have been targeted for **shock probation programs** (Vaughn, 1993).

Because offenders sentenced to shock probation are actually incarcerated in a jail or prison for a short period, primarily for shock value, some persons have wondered whether shock probation is an appropriate term. Shock probation stems from judges initially sentencing offenders to lengthy terms of incarceration, usually in a jail. After offenders have been in jail for a short interval (e.g., 30, 60, 90, or 120 days), they are brought before the judge and are sentenced to probation. This type of sentence shocks and surprises these offenders, because they didn't expect to receive probation. Offenders who have been resentenced under these circumstances are **shock probationers**. The shock of incarceration is supposed to be a deterrent against further offending. It is anticipated that recidivism rates among shock probationers will be low.

Split Sentencing Distinguished from Shock Probation. There is a difference between split sentencing and shock probation (Burns and Vito, 1995). Split sentencing means that the judge imposes a **combination sentence**, a portion of which includes incarceration and a portion of which includes probation. Thus, the judge may sentence the offender up to one year, with a maximum incarceration of six months. The remainder of the sentence is to be served on probation. Violating one or more conditions of probation may result in reincarceration, however.

Split Sentencing

Most states have authorized the use of one of three general types of either split sentencing or shock probation by judges in the sentencing of low-risk offenders (Byrne, 1990a). These types include the California scheme, in which jail is attached as a condition of probation; the federal scheme under the 1987 sentencing guidelines, in which supervised release of up to five years may follow sentences of imprisonment of more than one year (the length of supervised release varies according to the crime classification and ranges from one year for misdemeanors to five years); and the Ohio scheme, in which a judge resentences offenders within a 130-day incarcerative period to a probationary sentence. Other states, including Texas, have similar systems, although incarcerative periods are often longer than 130 days before resentencing to probation is considered (U.S. General Accounting Office, 1994).

Other terms used to describe these schemes are **mixed sentence**, **intermittent confinement**, and **jail as a condition of probation**. A mixed sentence is imposed by a judge whenever an offender has committed two or more offenses. The judge imposes a separate sentence for each offense. One sentence may involve probation, whereas the other may involve incarceration. The judge decides whether the two sentences are to be served concurrently or consecutively. The **intermittent sentence** is imposed whenever the offender is sentenced to a term requiring partial confinement. Perhaps the offender must serve weekends in jail, or a curfew may be imposed. In all other respects, the nature of intermittent sentencing is much like probation. Finally, jail as a condition of probation is an option whereby the judge imposes a fixed jail term to be served prior to the offender's completion of a sentence of probation.

The Philosophy and Objectives of Shock Probation

Shock Probation and Deterrence.   Deterrence is one of shock probation's primary themes. Another prominent philosophical objective is reintegration. Confining offenders to jail for brief periods and obligating them to serve their remaining months on probationary status enables them to be employed, support themselves and their families, and otherwise be productive citizens in their communities. The freedom shock probation allows permits offenders to receive specialized attention and to participate in programs designed to deal with their problems. Ideally, exposure to jail should be sufficiently traumatic to cause offenders to want to refrain from further criminal activity.

Shock Probation and Rehabilitation.   Consistent with the philosophy of shock probation and split sentencing generally are community reintegration and rehabilitation. A brief exposure to incarceration followed by release into the community permits offenders to hold jobs, support themselves and their families, pay restitution to victims, perform various public services, and/or participate in therapeutic or educational programs designed to help them with their special problems.

Shock Probation and Creative Sentencing.   Judges are permitted greater flexibility in the punishments they impose for low-risk offenders. Short-term incarceration is one form of creative sentencing.

Shock Probation as a Punishment.   The confinement phase of shock probation is considered a punishment. Low-risk offenders who have never been incarcerated are able to understand what it is like to be locked up without the freedoms to which they have become accustomed while living in their communities.

BOX 5.1   *Shock Probation Isn't Shock Probation When It Isn't Shocking!*

Atascosa County, Texas, and Shock Probation

It is called shock probation. Under ordinary circumstances, convicted offenders receive it when they don't know they are getting it. Suppose that you are a first-offender and are convicted of a crime, and the punishment for that crime is up to two years in prison. Suppose that the judge sentences you to two years in jail. You are placed in jail, and after three months, the judge orders your release from jail and resentences you to probation, which you will serve for the remaining one and a half years. You are genuinely surprised; you didn't expect to be released after serving only three months in jail. You fully expected to serve a large portion of the two-year sentence you originally received. Indeed, you are shocked by this experience, particularly since you are a first-offender and jail is very unpleasant for you. The intent of shock probation is therefore to deter you from reoffending by showing you how unpleasant jail confinement can be, even for 90 days. What if, however, you knew that you could be sentenced to ten years in prison and that the judge was going to sentence you to shock probation instead of the full ten years? You would know that after serving 90 or 120 days in jail, you would be released and placed on probation. You would feign surprise over this expectation and would avoid the ten-year prison term. Would shock probation really be "shocking" under this scenario? No. Would it have the deterrent value it was intended to have? No.

In a strange turn of events in Atascosa County, Texas, a former county clerk was convicted of stealing $283,662 in tax payments over a ten-year period. Royetta Hon, 56, was arrested in April 1999 and pleaded no contest to first-degree felony theft by a public servant. The district attorney sought two 15-year sentences and one 10-year sentence for the crimes as well as a restitution of $317,204. The judge, however, sentenced Hon to ten years in prison. Hon, however, was under the impression that if she begins immediate repayment of the stolen funds, she will receive shock probation, serving no more than 180 days in jail. Hon immediately made a payment of $100,000 toward her restitution order. According to Hon, State District Judge Pat Priest told her that he would consider an application for shock probation under which she would serve no more than 180 days behind bars if pledges made by her husband to make a $100,000 down-payment were quickly fulfilled. The judge gave no guarantee that he would grant Hon shock probation, though, even if the county receives the $100,000. District Attorney Lynn Ellison said, "I've never seen a judge mention shock probation where [the defendant] didn't get it. My interpretation of the sentence is if she pays $100,000 up front, she gets shock probation." Hon's coworkers, however, say that she did much to tarnish their own reputations, especially when the Atascosa County Tax Assessor–Collector's Office was under investigation by federal and state authorities. They favored hard time for Hon, because they became targets of ridicule and suspicion. One tax office clerk said, "She did the damage and left us to face it."

Should Hon get shock probation? Is it really shock probation if she knows that it is going to be imposed? Is a judge's imposition of a ten-year sentence on someone for stealing a large amount of money and violating the public trust an especially wise use of shock probation, if it is imposed? What do you think?

Source: Adapted from Associated Press, "Former Atascosa County Clerk Sentenced for Stealing Payments," October 22, 2000.

Shock Probation and Offender Needs.   Short-term confinement in a jail enables judges to determine appropriate services and therapies needed by offenders. Jail reports often disclose certain offender needs that must be addressed through community agencies. Judges can configure a suitable probationary punishment that includes programs that directly address particular offender needs.

Shock Probation and Offender Accountability.   Shock probation heightens offender awareness of the seriousness of their crimes. For many low-risk offenders, spending three or four months in jail is a sufficiently punishing experience to cause them to reflect on the seriousness of the crimes they committed and to accept responsibility for their actions.

Shock Probation and Community Safety.   There is some question as to whether short-term incarceration ensures community safety. Eventually, shock probationers will be placed on probation within their communities. Some authorities, however, have acknowledged that short-term incarceration does satisfy the public's demand for punitiveness when the law has been violated (Talarico and Myers, 1987).

The Effectiveness of Shock Probation

Is shock probation effective? The answer to this question depends on what is expected from shock probation. If shock probation is expected to deter offenders from future offending, then it appears to be modestly successful (New York State Division of Parole, 1998; U.S. General Accounting Office, 1998). Recidivism rates among shock probationers tend to be fairly low, averaging under 30 percent, perhaps due primarily to low-risk, nonviolent offenders being most often selected as targets of shock probation sentences (Vaughn, 1993). Thus, those least likely to reoffend are included in the broad class of shock probationers and receive this special sanction.

If shock probation is expected to alleviate prison and jail overcrowding, then the results are mixed. Some professionals have observed that shock probation is one viable alternative to alleviating prison overcrowding (Vito, Holmes, and Wilson, 1985), because most offenders sentenced to shock probation will serve brief terms of confinement, usually in county jails. Thus, they will not occupy valuable long-term prison space that should be reserved for more serious or dangerous offenders (Massachusetts Legislative Research Council, 1987; South Carolina State Reorganization Commission, 1991, 1992). Nevertheless, shock probationers do occupy some jail space, even if their periods of confinement are relatively short. The high turnover among jail inmates suggests that shock probation has only an imperceptible effect on jail overcrowding.

BOOT CAMPS

Closely related to shock probation is **shock incarceration** or **boot camps**, where convicted offenders are jailed or otherwise confined, but their confinement resembles military boot camp training. Shock probation involved sentencing offenders to a plain jail term, with no participation in any military-like programs. In contrast, shock incarceration or boot camp programs do provide military-like regimentation and regulation of inmate behavior.

Boot Camps Defined

Boot camps are highly regimented, military-like, short-term correctional programs (90 to 180 days) where offenders are provided with strict discipline, physical training, and hard labor resembling some aspects of military basic training; when successfully completed, boot camps provide for transfers of participants to community-based facilities for nonsecure supervision. By 1998, boot camps had been formally established in most of the states (Gover, MacKenzie, and Styve, 2000; Stinchcomb, 1999).

Boot camps were officially established in 1983 by the Georgia Department of Corrections Special Alternative Incarceration, but the general idea for boot camps originated in the late 1970s, also in Georgia (Parent, 1989b). The usual length of incarceration in boot camps varies from three to six months. During this period, boot camp participants engage in marching, work, and classes that are believed useful in one's rehabilitation. Usually, youthful offenders are targeted by these programs (Dieterich, Boyles, and Colling, 1999).

The Rationale for Boot Camps.   Boot camps were established as an alternative to long-term, traditional incarceration. A brief rationale for boot camps is as follows:

1. A substantial number of youthful first-time offenders now incarcerated will respond to a short but intensive period of confinement followed by a longer period of intensive community supervision.
2. These youthful offenders will benefit from a military-type atmosphere that instills a sense of self-discipline and physical conditioning that was lacking in their lives.
3. These same youths need exposure to relevant educational, vocational training, drug treatment, and general counseling services to develop more positive and law-abiding values and become better prepared to secure legitimate future employment.
4. The costs involved will be less than a traditional criminal justice sanction that imprisons the offender for a substantially longer period of time (Austin, Jones, and Bolyard, 1993:1).

Goals of Boot Camps

Boot camps have several general goals, including rehabilitation/reintegration; discipline; deterrence; easing of prison and jail overcrowding; and vocational, educational, and rehabilitative services.

To Provide Rehabilitation and Reintegration.   Boot camp programs are designed to improve one's sense of purpose, self-discipline, self-control, and self-confidence through physical conditioning, educational programs, and social skills training, all within the framework of strict military discipline (Lutze and Murphy, 1999). The time youthful offenders spend in boot camps is not especially lengthy. The emphasis on discipline and educational skills is calculated to provide structure lacking in a participant's previous family and social environment. Thus, both rehabilitative and reintegrative objectives are sought by most boot camp programs.

To Provide Discipline.   Boot camps are intended to improve one's discipline (Gover, MacKenzie, and Styve, 2000). Many youthful offenders find it difficult to accept authority and often refuse to learn in traditional classroom or treatment environments. Within the context of a boot camp program, however, are incentives to become involved in program activities. Most boot camp programs also include educational elements pertaining to literacy, academic and vocational education, intensive value clarification, and resocialization (Taylor, 1992:124).

To Promote Deterrence.   Being thrust into a military-like atmosphere is a frightening experience for many boot camp clients. It is believed that a highly regimented boot camp experience will cause most participants to lead more law-abiding lives when they successfully complete their programs (Mitchell et al., 1999). There have, however, been numerous boot camp failures that have caused some observers to regard these programs with some amount of skepticism. It has been recommended, for instance, that more selective criteria should be used to include those clients most amenable to change under military-like boot camp conditions. Furthermore, post-release follow-ups should be conducted of boot camp clientele to gauge program effectiveness (Stinchcomb, 1999). In some instances, boot camp staff have appeared to be overzealous in exercising their authority over youthful offenders. Thus, several ethical questions have been generated about how much control these authorities should have and how that control should be applied, especially when youthful offenders are involved (Hemmens and Stohr, 2000; Mitchell et al., 1999).

To Ease Prison and Jail Overcrowding.   Boot camps are believed to have a long-term effect on jail and prison overcrowding (Wood and Grasmick, 1999). One primary purpose of boot camps is to divert prison-bound youthful offenders to a structured environment in which they can learn discipline and become rehabilitated. Compared with the population of jail and prison inmates, the total number of boot camp clientele accounts for only a small fraction of these populations, however, so it is doubtful whether boot camps seriously ease prison or jail overcrowding to a significant degree (Anderson and Dyson, 1999; Maryland Commission on Criminal Sentencing Policy, 1998).

To Provide Vocational and Rehabilitative Services.   Most boot camp programs offer educational and/or vocational training to clients (Anderson and Dyson, 1999). Rehabilitative services can include drug abuse intervention counseling, mental health services, and sex offender therapy (Mitchell et al., 1999; Toombs, Benda, and Tilmon, 1999).

A Profile of Boot Camp Clientele

Who can participate in boot camps or shock incarceration programs? Participants may or may not be able to enter or withdraw from boot camps voluntarily; it depends on the particular program. Most boot camp participants are prison-bound youthful offenders convicted of less serious, nonviolent crimes and who have never been previously incarcerated (Bilchik, 1996a:1). Depending on the program, there are some exceptions (Albright et al., 1996). Participants may either be referred to these programs by judges or corrections departments or they may volunteer. They may or may not be accepted, and if they complete their programs successfully, they may or may not be released under supervision into their communities.

Boot Camp Programs

Although all boot camp programs share certain features, different program components make them fairly distinctive from one another. It is interesting to note which features are included or excluded from one program to the next.

Jail Boot Camps

Jail boot camps are short-term programs for jail inmates serving short sentences of less than one year (Radli, 1997:87–88). In 1999, there were 18 jail boot camp programs operating in U.S. jails involving 3,004 inmates (Camp and Camp, 1999:43). In Washoe County, Nevada, for instance, a jail boot camp was established in May 1995.

BOX 5.2 *Four Boot Camps Compared*

Michigan Department of Corrections Special Alternative Incarceration. The Michigan Department of Corrections has implemented a 90-day boot camp program called Special Alternatives Incarceration. Program elements include the following:

1. Physical training
2. Work at a trade
3. Life skills course
4. Stress management training
5. Group counseling
6. Job seeking
7. Substance abuse awareness
8. Adult basic education

Education sessions are conducted over ten weeks, with each weekly session lasting 70 minutes. Clients are assessed for substance abuse problems. Michigan's intensive postrelease program may include a 120-day residential placement and electronic monitoring. All graduates are required to undergo a minimum of 18 months of community supervision, with the first four months including intensive daily supervision.

The Harris County (Texas) Regimented Intensive Probation Program. The Harris County, Texas, program has the following features:

1. It uses a military model, militaristic chain of command.
2. Staff consists of volunteers from deputies of Harris County Sheriff's Department.
3. It handles convicted criminal offenders under probation supervision.
4. Probationers are supervised for a 90-day period by drill instructors.
5. The program accommodates 48 probationers as a "group" who begin and end as a group.
6. Regimen: breakfast at 4:00 A.M.; physical training; lunch at 11:00 A.M.; more physical training; barracks clean-up; general orders; dinner at 3:00 P.M.; more physical training; day ends with lights out at 10:00 P.M.; participants wear uniforms and combat boots, and different types of uniforms distinguish between different levels of probationers.
7. Services provided include medical, vocational, physical, social (drug and alcohol counseling), coping, and life skills programs.
8. Participants are required to practice good grooming and personal hygiene habits; structured activities are designed to prepare them for successful reintegration into society.
9. Program activities are mandatory.

The Mississippi Regimented Inmate Discipline Program. The program established in Mississippi has the following program features:

1. There are 140 inmates in a minimum-security camp.
2. Judges control the inmate selection process, according to broad statutory criteria.
3. The program features physical training, drill and ceremony, hard labor, and treatment.
4. No vocational or educational program.
5. Released inmates live in halfway houses and perform community service; they are subsequently released to regular probation supervision.

The Alabama Disciplinary Rehabilitation Unit. The Alabama program includes the following characteristics:

1. It is a 12-step program used by Alcoholics Anonymous.
2. Drug and alcohol services are provided.
3. Camp psychologist counseling sessions are provided.
4. Judges control the selection process, with this program as a condition of probation.
5. The program includes physical training, drill, and hard work, with two exercise and drill periods daily and eight hours of hard labor periods in between.
6. Participants perform limited community services.
7. Drug abuse education and information about sexually transmitted diseases are provided. (Cowles, Castellano, and Gransky, 1995:14–22)

A wide range of ages was represented, with no explicit minimum or maximum age restrictions. The main goals of the Washoe program were to instill in inmates a positive attitude by stressing academic achievement, coping skills, anger and money management, and good work habits. The intent was to inspire the inmate to succeed in society after he or she leaves jail (Radli, 1997:87). Six basic objectives were sought: (1) inmates will develop good work habits and skills, (2) inmates will no longer sit idle while they are held in jail, (3) members will partially repay the community for the cost of their incarceration, (4) members will become more self-sufficient, (5) members will adjust more smoothly back into society, and (6) the recidivism rate will be reduced.

Known as the Highly Intensive Supervision, Training, and Education Program (HISTEP), the Washoe County program was implemented through the Washoe County Sheriff's Office and involved 452 inmates. Five levels were incorporated in the program. Levels I and II ran for six weeks during which inmates were introduced to the military way of life. Physical training, inspections, and educational classes were conducted in somewhat of a shock environment, breaking inmates out of the traditional general inmate population mold. Various tests were administered to determine their educational and personality maturity levels. Skills classes were taught, emphasizing anger management, communication, building self-esteem, decision making, parenting techniques, and financial management. Core values—a sense of responsibility, pride, and acceptable behavior in various real-life situations—were also taught. Level III, lasting eight weeks, initiated members to the fundamentals of seeking employment, writing resumes, exploring employment resources, and learning interviewing techniques. Levels IV and V included work at the jail at a jail industry job. The inmate received a small hourly wage, part of which was used to support the program. Work furloughs were made available to certain inmates who would reside within the jail during evening hours but would work at a job outside the jail during the day. Again, jail inmate wages were divided into offsetting program costs, establishing a small inmate savings account, and commissary items. Levels IV and V lasted eight weeks. Thus, the program was designed for inmates to leave the jail with a job skill, a job, and money in the bank (Radli, 1997:87–88).

Washoe County Jail officials have conducted a follow-up of the number of inmates who went through the program during May 1995 through August 1996. Of the 452 entering the HISTEP program, 30 percent or 138 completed it. Of the successful jail boot camp inmates who completed the program, the recidivism rate was only 11 percent. Considering substantially higher rates of recidivism associated with standard probation and parole programs and other community-based or intermediate punishments, the 11 percent recidivism figure was interpreted by Washoe officials as a very positive indicator of their HISTEP program success (Radli, 1997:90). It is not possible to generalize Washoe County's HISTEP success rate to other jurisdictions with substantial accuracy, although this program does seem to be typical of other jail boot camp programs operating in other jurisdictions (Wood and Grasmick, 1999).

The Effectiveness of Boot Camps

Are boot camps or shock incarceration programs successful? Programs with recidivism rates of 30 percent or less are considered successful by many criminal justice professionals. If this standard is used as a measure of boot camp effectiveness, there

---

BOX 5.3   *Are Boot Camps Getting the Boot?*

Throwing the Baby Out with the Bath Water?

Are boot camps good for juveniles? During the 1990s, boot camps were touted as the "magic bullet" to cure delinquency, instill discipline and self-pride, and ensure accountability. Skeptics had their doubts. Do we have enough information about boot camps today to determine whether they are accomplishing their objectives and decreasing and/or preventing delinquency? During the period of 1998 to 1999, several boot camps in various states were scenes of camp guards brutalizing juvenile inmates. During 1999, five juvenile justice officials lost their jobs in Maryland after Governor Parris Glendening found a pattern of abuse by guards that had begun shortly after the first three boot camps were opened in 1996. The guards have also become targets of criminal child abuse and federal civil rights investigations. In the early years when boot camps were being established, some critics warned that the rigorous discipline demanded of juveniles might be too rigorous and perhaps punitive. One critic, Jann Jackson, executive director of Advocates for Children and Youth, who served on the task force that investigated abuses in Maryland boot camps, said, "For three years, this administration was touting its 'get tough' boot camps when from the first week the camps opened there was clear evidence that the tactical officers were manhandling youths."

More than 60 juvenile boot camps have been established in various states since Louisiana opened the first boot camp in 1985. Usually, the juveniles are subjected to a demanding schedule, with 16-hour days filled with discipline, physical training, and military-style drills. The public has been fed up with violent youth, and the boot camp idea seemed a good one at the time. Other states have been implicated in boot camp abuses besides Maryland. Five Arizona Boys Ranch employees were charged in early 1999 with first-degree murder in the death of a 16-year-old who was punished for discipline violations. Although those charges were dismissed, one worker remains accused of manslaughter and child abuse. The paramilitary boot camp was closed amid criminal and state regulatory investigations. Also, two former South Dakota boot camp women were charged with manslaughter and child abuse in the death of a 14-year-old girl who collapsed and died from heat stroke after being compelled to drill in the sun for hours. She had begged for water and attention, but authorities believed that she was faking it and ignored her cries for help. In Georgia, officials overhauled their boot camp program in December 1999 after it was found to be overcrowded and dangerous to the point of being unconstitutional. Those in favor of boot camps claim that the boot camp concept is valid. It is poor guard training that has created the problems of Maryland, Arizona, South Dakota, and Georgia boot camps. Citing research that shows lower recidivism rates among boot camp participants compared with juvenile delinquents who do not go to boot camps, some authorities believe that they should be continued. Guards, however, should be training better in dealing with anger management. Other researchers dispute the idea that boot camps do anything to deter offenders from committing more delinquency in future years. In fact, one research agency, the Koch Crime Institute in Topeka, Kansas, reported that recidivism rates for boot camps across the country ranged between 64 percent and 75 percent, slightly higher than for those subjected to traditional correctional facilities. Attesting to the authenticity of this finding, Professor Doris MacKenzie of the University of Maryland says that "boot camps don't have any impact on recidivism." Nevertheless, Maryland officials believe that a revamped boot camp program that does not tolerate violence should be created and perpetuated for youths.

Maryland Governor Glendening appointed a task force in late December 1999 to study ways of providing boot camp graduates with a strong follow-up program. David Altschuler, a researcher at Johns Hopkins University Institute for Policy Studies, says, "Where the rubber meets the road is what happens when these kids are in the community where there are temptations, where there may be very little left for them to do and where programs or services that they received when they were in these facilities are no longer in place."

Should boot camps throughout the United States be discontinued because of their failure to reduce juvenile delinquency and reduce recidivism? Is there any redeeming value from the discipline received by these boot camp clients in those states without abusive procedures? Should a few bad examples cause the entire boot camp concept to be scrapped? What do you think?

Source: Adapted from Associated Press, "States Reassessing Boot Camps Due to Abuses," December 27, 1999.

seems to be considerable support in the literature for their effectiveness. For instance, a Louisiana Intensive Motivational Program of Alternative Correctional Treatment program reported that during the first six months of community supervision following boot camp participation, between 7 to 14 percent of the boot camp clients recidivated compared with from 12 to 23 percent of the boot camp dropouts or those who failed to complete the program (MacKenzie 1993:7). A New York Rikers Boot Camp has reported recidivism rates of 23 percent among its graduates (Mack, 1992:65). On the other hand, a 38 percent recidivism rate was reported by a Georgia Special Alternative Incarceration program (MacKenzie, 1993:9).

The simple fact is that because most of these boot camp programs were established in the late 1980s and 1990s, there has not been much research on their effectiveness. One study was conducted by Kathleen Albright and her colleagues, who from 1990 to 1995 investigated boot camps in Cleveland, Ohio; Denver, Colorado; and Mobile, Alabama (Albright et al., 1996). The findings were disappointing. Recidivism figures were about the same for boot camp participants compared with youthful offenders who participated in traditional probation programs, averaging between 65 and 70 percent. The cost-effectiveness of the boot camp programs, however, was considerably lower than housing youths in secure confinement. For instance, residential services for boot camp youths averaged $54 per day compared with $139 per day for those in secure confinement and who did not participate in boot camp programming. Thus, boot camp programming and aftercare were substantially cheaper than institutional confinement. The cost of supervising youths on standard probation, however, averaged about $2 per day. Their rates of recidivism were only about 10 percent higher, on the average, than boot camp participants. Therefore, boot camp youths had somewhat lower rates of recidivism compared with standard probationers, although the boot camp costs were 27 times as high ($54 compared with $2).

It is difficult to draw clear conclusions from these preliminary investigations of boot camp costs. At first glance, it may appear that boot camps do not affect recidivism rates of participants significantly compared with standard probationers. Yet only three jurisdictions were investigated by Albright and colleagues (1996). In 2001, there were between 50 and 100 different boot camps operating in the United States, and little research has been made available about them and whether they are effective. There are also major differences among these boot camps in the clientele selected for inclusion. Some boot camps are designated for those with substance abuse problems, whereas other programs are intended for those with disciplinary problems and who are relatively drug-free. Different selection criteria exist, and each program is different. The general impression that might be drawn from existing literature about boot camps is that they appear to be reasonably successful for those who complete programming requirements (American Correctional Association, 1996c). This impression suggests that more rigorous criteria ought to be used when targeting participants for boot camp involvement.

FEMALE PROBATIONERS AND PAROLEES: A PROFILE

In 1999, women accounted for 18 percent of all probationers and 10 percent of all parolees (Pastore and Maguire, 2001). Women were most represented proportionately in various property offense categories, such as fraud (40 percent) and larceny (24 percent). Overall, women made up 22 percent of all probationers convicted of property offenses. On the average, women are sentenced to probation more often than men, which is likely attributable to male and female offenders having different offending patterns. Men are involved to a greater degree in violent offending, whereas women are involved to a greater degree in property offending. Another explanation for these sentencing differences is that judges have tended to be more paternalistic toward female offenders in the past. In recent years, however, presumptive or guidelines-based sentencing schemes used by different states and the federal government have caused male-female sentencing differentials to narrow. Generally, the rate of female offending and incarceration has increased both dramatically and systematically since the early 1980s (Nesbitt, 1992:6). This increase does not necessarily mean that there is a new breed or a more dangerous female offender in society; rather, more women are being subject to less lenient treatment by a more equitable criminal justice system (Erez, 1992). Some observers have labeled this phenomenon gender parity (Steffensmeier, Kramer, and Streifel, 1993).

Regarding parole, women tended to be distributed in ways similar to their conviction patterns, which are similar to the proportionate distribution of women incarcerated in federal and state prisons. With a few exceptions, female parolee distributions by conviction offense were similar to their original conviction offense patterns. The female failure rate while on probation or parole is about 65 percent, approximately the same as it is for male probationers and parolees (Pastore and Maguire, 2001).

Special Programs and Services for Female Offenders

In 1992, the American Correctional Association formulated a National Correctional Policy on Female Offender Services (Nesbitt, 1992:7). This policy is as follows.

Introduction. Correctional systems must develop service delivery systems for accused and adjudicated female offenders that are comparable to those provided to male offenders. Additional services must also be provided to meet the unique needs of the female offender population.

Statement. Correctional systems must be guided by the principle of parity. Female offenders must receive the equivalent range of services available to other offenders, including opportunities for individualized programming and services that recognize the unique needs of this population. The services should:

1. Assure access to a range of alternatives to incarceration, including pretrial and posttrial diversion, probation, restitution, treatment for substance abuse, halfway houses, and parole services

2. Provide acceptable conditions of confinement, including appropriately trained staff and sound operating procedures that address this population's needs in such areas as clothing, personal property, hygiene, exercise, recreation, and visitation with children and family

3. Provide access to a full range of work and programs designed to expand economic and social roles of women, with emphasis on education; career counseling and exploration of nontraditional as well as traditional vocational training; relevant life skills, including parenting and social and economic assertiveness; and prerelease and work/education release programs

4. Facilitate the maintenance and strengthening of family ties, particularly those between parent and child

5. Deliver appropriate programs and services, including medical, dental, and mental health programs, services to pregnant women, substance abuse programs, child and family services, and provide access to legal services

6. Provide access to release programs that include aid in establishing homes, economic stability, and sound family relationships (Nesbitt, 1992:7)

Criticisms of Women's Prison and Community Programming. A Minnesota study highlights some of the continuing problems associated with women's prisons and community-based treatment services. Shirley Hokanson (1986) gathered information about female inmates from 87 county correctional facilities and 31 jails. She found that the typical female offender was young, either single, divorced, or separated; educated at a level approximating the general population; lacking in work skills and dependent on public assistance; overrepresentative of minority groups; and having a high probability of physical and/or sexual abuse victimization and a history of substance abuse. Similar observations have been made about female offenders by others (Carp and Schade, 1992:152).

It is generally acknowledged that women's prisons and programming for women in community-based correctional programs have not compared favorably with programs and facilities for men. For instance, programs for female offenders have been poorer in quality, quantity, variability, and availability in both the United States and Canada. Despite these inequities, courts generally declare that men and women in prisons do not have to be treated equally and that separate can be equal when men's and women's prisons are compared (Knight, 1992). There are exceptions, however. In 1979, the case of *Glover v. Johnson* (1979) involved the Michigan Department of Corrections and the issue of equal programming for female inmates. A class action suit was filed on behalf of all Michigan female prison inmates to the effect that their constitutional rights were violated because they were being denied educational and vocational rehabilitation opportunities that were then being provided to male inmates only. Among other things, the Michigan Department of Corrections was ordered to provide the following to its incarcerated women: (1) two-year college programming, (2) paralegal training and access to attorneys to remedy past inadequacies in law library facilities, (3) a revised inmate wage policy to ensure that female inmates were provided equal wages, (4) access to programming at camps previously available only to male inmates, (5) enhanced vocational offerings, (6) apprenticeship opportunities, and (7) prison industries that previously existed only at men's facilities (American Correctional Association, 1993c:32). Several similar cases in other jurisdictions (Connecticut, California, Wisconsin, and Idaho) have been settled without court action.

The *Glover* case is like the tip of an iceberg when it comes to disclosing various problems associated with women's prisons and other corrections institutions for women. The following are criticisms leveled against women's correctional facilities in the last few decades. Some of these criticisms have been remedied in selected jurisdictions.

1. No adequate classification system exists for female prisoners. Women from widely different backgrounds with diverse criminal histories are celled with one another in most women's prisons, a practice that is conducive to greater criminalization during the incarceration period. Further, most women's prisons have only medium-security custody rather than a wider variety of custody levels to accommodate female offenders of differing seriousness and dangerousness. Better classification methods should be devised (Culliver, 1993).
2. Most women's prisons are remotely located; thus, many female prisoners are deprived of immediate contact with out-of-prison educational or vocational services that might be available through study or work release.
3. Women who give birth to babies while incarcerated are deprived of valuable parent-child contact. Some observers contend that this practice is a serious deprivation for newborn infants.
4. Women have less extensive vocational and educational programming in the prison setting than men.
5. Women have less access to legal services than men; in the past, law libraries in women's facilities were lacking or nonexistent, but recent remedies have included provisions for either legal services or more adequate libraries in women's institutions.
6. Women have special medical needs, and women's prisons do not adequately provide for meeting these needs.
7. Mental health treatment services and programs for women are inferior to those provided for men in men's facilities.
8. Training programs that are provided women do not permit them to live independently and earn decent livings when released on parole (Culliver, 1993:407).

Because of the rather unique role of women as caregivers for their children, many corrections professionals regard the imprisonment of women differently from the imprisonment of men. For various reasons, female imprisonment is opposed on moral, ethical, and religious grounds. Legally, these arguments are often unconvincing. In an attempt to at least address some of the unique problems confronting female offenders when they are incarcerated or when they participate in community-based programs, some observers have advocated the following recommendations:

1. Institute training programs that would enable imprisoned women to become literate
2. Provide female offenders with programs that do not center on traditional gender roles, programs that will lead to more economic independence and self-sufficiency
3. Establish programs that would engender more positive self-esteem for imprisoned women and enhance their assertiveness and communication and interpersonal skills
4. Establish more programs that would allow imprisoned mothers to interact more with their children and assist them in overcoming feelings of guilt and shame for having deserted their children; in addition, visitation areas for mothers and children should be altered to minimize the effect of a prison-type environment

5. Allow imprisoned mothers to spend more time with their children outside the prison

6. Provide imprisoned mothers with training to improve parenting skills

7. Establish more programs to treat drug-addicted female offenders

8. Establish a community partnership program to provide imprisoned women with employment opportunities

9. Establish a better classification system for incarcerated women, one that would not permit the less hardened offender to be juxtaposed with the hardened female offender

10. Provide in-service training (sensitivity awareness) to assist staff members (wardens, correctional officers) in understanding the nature and needs of incarcerated women (Culliver, 1993:409–410)

Other observers have recommended the establishment and provision for an environment that would allow all pregnant inmates the opportunity to rear their newborn infants for a period of one year and provide counseling regarding available parental services, foster care, guardianship, and other relevant activities pending their eventual release. Some women's facilities have cottages on prison grounds where inmates with infants can accomplish some of these objectives. One such program is the **Program for Female Offenders, Inc. (PFO)**, established in 1974 as the result of jail overcrowding in Allegheny County, Pennsylvania (Arnold, 1992:37). PFO is a work-release facility operated as a nonprofit agency by the county, designed to accommodate up to 36 women with space for six preschool children. Although originally created to reduce jail overcrowding, because of escalating rates of female offending and jail incarceration the overcrowding problem persists.

When PFO was established, the Allegheny County Jail was small, and only 12 women were housed there. Nevertheless, agency founders worked out an agreement with jail authorities so that female jail prisoners could be transferred to PFO by court order. Inmate-clients would be guilty of prison breach if they left PFO without permission. While at PFO, the women would participate in training, volunteering in the community, and learning how to spend their leisure time with the help of a role modeling and parent education program for mothers and children. The program is based on freedom reached by attaining levels of responsibility. In the mid-1980s, a much larger work-release facility was constructed in Allegheny County. Currently, over 300 women per year are served by PFO. PFO authorities reserve the right to screen potential candidates for work release. During 1992, the following companion projects were implemented in Allegheny County:

1. Good-time project at the county jail

2. Male work-release center accommodating 60 beds

3. Development of criminal justice division in county government

4. Drug treatment/work-release facility at St. Francis Health Center's Chemical Dependency Department

5. Development of a male job placement program

6. Expansion of the existing THE PROGRAM Women's Center

7. Expansion of the retail theft project (Arnold, 1992:38).

The success of PFO is demonstrated by its low 3.5 percent recidivism rate in the community program and only a 17 percent recidivism rate at the residential facility. Over $88,000 has been collected in rent, $27,000 in fines, and $8,000 in restitution to victims of the female offenders. For the male offenders, $106,500 has been collected in rent and $107,400 in fines and restitution. Long-range plans for PFO call for a crime prevention program, including a day care center, intervention therapy for drug-abusing families, intensive work with preschool children who are already giving evidence of impending **delinquency**, and a scholarship program (Arnold, 1992:40). Plans also include expanding services to more areas throughout Pennsylvania.

In the early 1990s, the Kansas Department of Corrections established a program for women with children that has been patterned after PATCH (Parents and Their Children), which was created by the Missouri Department of Corrections, and MATCH (Mothers and Their Children) operated by the California Department of Corrections. The Kansas program is known as the **Women's Activities and Learning Center (WALC)**, started with a grant from the U.S. Department of Education under the Women's Educational Opportunity Act and based in Topeka (Logan, 1992:160). WALC has a primary goal of developing and coordinating a broad range of programs, services, and classes and workshops that will increase women offender's chances for a positive reintegration with their families and society upon release (Logan, 1992:160). A visiting area at the Topeka center accommodates visitations with female inmates and their children, thus giving mothers a chance to take an active part in caring for their children. Mothers acquire some measure of a mother-child relationship during incarceration. They are able to fix meals for their children and recreate with them in designated areas. Various civic and religious groups contribute their volunteer resources to assist these women. Both time and money are expended by outside agencies and personnel, such as the Kiwanis, the Kansas East Conference of the United Methodist Church, and the Fraternal Order of Police (Logan, 1992:161).

One advantage of WALC is that it provides various programs and courses in useful areas such as parenting, child development, prenatal care, self-esteem, anger management, nutrition, support groups, study groups, cardiopulmonary resuscitation, personal development, and crafts. The parenting program, for instance, is a ten-week course in which inmate-mothers meet weekly to discuss their various problems. To qualify for inclusion in this program, female inmates must be designated as low risk and minimum security and have no disciplinary reports filed against them during the 90 days prior to program involvement. When the ten-week course is completed, the women are entitled to participate in a three-week retreat sponsored by the Methodist Church. The retreat includes transportation for inmates, with fishing, horseback riding, hay rides, and games for mothers and their children. Volunteers and a correctional officer are present during the retreat experience. Since September 1991, more than 300 women and 500 children have participated in the WALC program, with a low rate of recidivism (Logan, 1992:161).

New York's Prison Nursery/Children's Center.   At the Bedford Hills, New York, Correctional Facility, a 750-woman maximum-security prison constructed in 1933, a Children's Center was completed in 1990. Since 1930, New York legislation provided for women in prison to keep their babies. Authorities at Bedford Hills believe that it is important for women to maintain strong ties with their families during incarceration. Further, they believe that women will have a greater chance at reintegration and lower recidivism as the opportunity for familial interaction increases. Further, there is a positive effect on babies, because they can remain with and be nurtured by their mothers. Not all mothers incarcerated at Bedford Hills are eligible to participate in the prison nursery program. A woman's criminal background, past parenting performance, disciplinary record, and educational needs are examined and assessed before they are accepted. Women who are selected are expected to make the best use of their time by developing their mothering skills and caring for their infants. They are also expected to participate in various self-help programs of a vocational and educational nature. The center's main program goals are to help women preserve and strengthen family ties and receive visits from their children as often as possible in a warm, nurturing atmosphere. Through the various classes and programs offered at Bedford Hills, women acquire a better understanding of their roles as parents and are able to reinforce their feelings of self-worth (Roulet, 1993:5).

Sister Elaine Roulet (1993:6) says that women whose babies are born while incarcerated may keep them at Bedford for up to one year. Babies are delivered in a hospital outside of prison, and the mother and infant live in the nursery for as long as the child remains. If it is likely that the mother will be paroled by the time the infant is 18 months old, then the infant may remain with the mother with special permission until that date. It is important to keep mothers and children together as much as possible while at Bedford Hills. The child's welfare is of utmost concern to authorities (Roulet, 1993:6). Such bonding is considered significant at reducing rates of recidivism among paroled Bedford Hills women.

More women are being convicted of drug offenses annually. Three-fourths of all women inmates are in need of substance abuse treatment, although only 30 percent of all incarcerated women have conviction offenses involving drugs. Most offenders had dropped out of high school or had not received a GED. Most had been unable to hold a job for longer than six months. Most of the surveyed institutions now offer vocational and educational courses for these women. Two-thirds offer college courses, and 70 have prerelease programs. Most facilities have institutional work assignments, and about half have parenting programs (Davis, 1992b:8). These policy changes involve increased opportunities for women to work and/or participate in vocational and educational programming originally available only to male inmates. Major changes have occurred in classification, visitation, housing, and clothing policies. Some changes have been occasioned by the parity issue, whereby women's facilities are brought more in line with men's facilities, which in most instances has meant improved services delivery to women's prisons. Most prison and community correctional policy changes have benefited women generally. Each year, the conditions in women's facilities are being improved and services delivery to these institutions and community agencies is being expanded.

THE PROBATION REVOCATION PROCESS

What if probationers violate one or more conditions of their probation? First, the program violation must be detected. Second, if it is detected, then the detector, usually the PO, must decide whether to report it. Third, if it is reported, then it may or may not be serious enough to warrant a hearing by a judge. Fourth, if it is serious enough to warrant a hearing by a judge, then it may or may not result in the termination of the probationer's program. Fifth, if the probationer's probation program is terminated, then it may or may not result in prison or jail confinement. Hence, a judge could resentence the probationer to a different type of probation program involving more intensive supervised probation, perhaps a program involving home confinement or electronic monitoring. The probationer may even be directed to participate in some form of mediation if the violation involved property loss or physical injury to others (Cook, 1995). Therefore, the probation revocation process, whenever it is initiated, may lead anywhere (Crew et al., 1998; Kaden, 1998).

Technically, any probation program violation is regarded seriously whenever it is detected. A PO could determine, for instance, that the probationer violated curfew by one or more minutes, which is a curfew violation, and could report the incident. A program violation such as a probationer testing positive for drugs or alcohol is regarded as serious and could be reported. Much discretionary power rests with the PO and his or her relationship with the particular probationer-client. Usually an attempt is made to determine why the program violation occurred. Notes maintained by the PO indicate whether or not the offense has occurred before, and if so, how often. In reality, POs prioritize probation program requirements and treat their seriousness on a graduated scale known only to them. Reporting a probationer for a technical program violation involves a certain amount of paperwork and a subsequent court appearance; thus POs often seek to avoid this time-consuming process. Therefore, only the most serious program violations, such as committing new crimes or being visibly impaired from chronic substance or alcohol abuse, are often considered for formal action (Hepburn and Albonetti, 1994; Morgan, 1994).

Interestingly, POs know much about their probationer-clients and whether they will complete their probation programs successfully. For instance, probationers with minimal education (i.e., not completing high school) and a record of numerous prior arrests are more likely to fail in their probation programs. Offenders with a history of substance abuse and who were under- or unemployed preceding their instant conviction offenses are also more likely to fail during the period of their probation. Those POs who take greater interest in their clients might likely refer them to certain community services where some or all of their needs can be addressed, but high caseloads in many jurisdictions often mean that POs can spend very little or no time face to face with their clients.

Whether formal probation revocation proceedings will occur involves a great deal of PO discretion. Certain factors or events, however, are beyond a PO's direct control. For instance, a probationer may be arrested and charged with a crime. The probationer may be carrying a concealed weapon and the weapon is discovered by police officers or detectives interviewing witnesses at a crime scene. The probationer may get in an automobile accident while driving a car he or she is not supposed to be driving. Official reports filed by different law enforcement agencies cannot be ignored. That a person is on probation is a matter of public record. When a probationer gets into any type of trouble with a law enforcement agency of any kind, there is bound to be a report made of that trouble to the court that has jurisdiction over that probationer.

Under current law in every U.S. jurisdiction, probationers are entitled to a hearing before the judge if their probation is in jeopardy. Thus, if a probationer is charged with committing either a technical probation program violation (e.g., curfew violation or frequenting a place where alcoholic beverages are served) or a crime, then the matter of revoking one's probation is referred to the original sentencing court for further action.

The court must conduct a two-stage proceeding. In the first stage, allegations against the probationer must be heard by the judge, and supporting evidentiary information must be presented to show the probationer's guilt relating to the charges filed. Then the probationer is permitted to introduce exculpatory information on his or her own behalf and to offer supporting testimony. Therefore, the first stage of a probation revocation hearing is to determine the guilt or innocence of the accused relating to the probation program violation, whatever it may be. If the judge determines that there is no basis for the allegations, then the matter is concluded and the probationer remains on his or her probation program. If the judge determines that the probationer is guilty of the allegations, however, then a second stage is conducted during which the judge determines the penalty for violating the particular program requirement(s). This second stage may be conducted in court after a recess.

Judges are encouraged to avoid incarcerating probationers if it is reasonable to do so under particular circumstances. Many options are available to judges. They may determine that even though the probationer has violated one or more program conditions based on the evidence presented, the probationer should be permitted to continue in his or her probation program for its duration. Judges may decide to impose additional conditions to one's program as sanctions or penalties. The offender may be required to make restitution to victims, pay a fine, or enter into mediation with one or more other parties. The offender may be placed in home confinement and/or electronic monitoring or may be required to have more frequent face-to-face visits with the PO in an intensive supervision scenario. If the program violation is serious enough, the judge has the authority to terminate one's probation program and order the probationer incarcerated. Below are some leading cases relating to probation revocation. The next section also contains several common scenarios involving probationers and how different state jurisdictions have concluded these revocation actions.

Special Circumstances: Mandatory Federal Probation Revocation

Federal district court judges were exposed to numerous changes in sentencing laws during the 1980s and 1990s. The Sentencing Reform Act of 1984 led to the promulgation of **U.S. sentencing guidelines** that went into effect in October 1987. Federal district court judges are obligated to follow these guidelines as closely as possible, although they have been allowed to engage in upward or downward departures from these guidelines in sentencing certain offenders provided that they furnish a written rationale for doing so.

In 1994, Congress passed the Violent Crime and Law Enforcement Act (VCCA), which further affected federal judges and the sentences they imposed. Of particular interest are changes in sentencing regulations that pertained to revoking the probation programs of federal offenders. In the pre-VCCA period (pre-September 1994), federal district court judges could revoke a federal probationer's probation program, but the revocation sentence must fall within the guideline range available for the original sentence. In the post-VCCA period, however, a revocation sentence could be any sentence that the court could have imposed at the time of the original sentence. For example, if a probationer had originally been sentenced to 12 months of probation resulting from a recommendation from the federal prosecutor for a downward guideline departure, then a subsequent revocation sentence from the court could be for a 24-month probationary sentence or even imprisonment, absent a renewal motion from the federal prosecutor. Under the post-VCCA sentencing scheme, a federal judge could impose any sentence that could have been imposed at the original sentencing date, regardless of prosecutorial recommendations.

Under a new post-VCCA provision, a revocation sentence resulting from drug possession must result in a term of imprisonment, which is a new mandatory sentence. Although it is mandatory, the court may determine that the revoked probationer may benefit from drug treatment as an alternative to incarceration. This very narrow option is contained in the new post-VCCA provisions. If the mandatory incarcerative term is imposed, however, then it must be at least one-third of the maximum guideline provision for the original offense. Thus, if the original sentence had an upper guideline of 30 months, then the term of incarceration that the court must impose would be 10 months, absent any consideration given to one's amenability to drug treatment (Adair, 2000:67–68).

LANDMARK CASES AND SPECIAL ISSUES

In this section, several U.S. Supreme Court cases that have affected probationers and the conditions under which judges may revoke their probation programs are examined. Several cases that have had national significance and application are highlighted. Other cases are described at the state level, where individual state supreme or appellate courts have ruled in particular probation revocation matters. The issues described in each of the following scenarios are generally applicable among the states, with very few and limited exceptions.

Mempa v. Rhay (1967). Jerry Mempa was convicted of "joyriding" in a stolen vehicle on June 17, 1959. He was placed on probation for two years by a Spokane, Washington, judge. Several months later, on September 15, 1959, Mempa was involved in a burglary. The county prosecutor in Spokane moved to have Mempa's probation revoked. Mempa admitted participating in the burglary. At his probation revocation hearing, the sole testimony about his involvement in the burglary came from his probation officer. Mempa was not represented by counsel, was not asked if he wanted counsel, and was not given an opportunity to offer statements in his own behalf. Furthermore, there was no cross-examination of the probation officer about his statements. The court revoked Mempa's probation and sentenced him to ten years in the Washington State Penitentiary.

Six years later in 1965, Mempa filed a writ of **habeas corpus**, alleging that he had been denied a right to counsel at the revocation hearing. The Washington Supreme Court denied his petition, but the U.S. Supreme Court elected to hear it on appeal. The U.S. Supreme Court overturned the Washington decision and ruled in Mempa's favor. Specifically, the Court said that Mempa was entitled to an attorney but was denied one. Although the Court did not question Washington authority to defer sentencing in the probation matter, it said that any indigent (including Mempa) is entitled at every stage of a criminal proceeding to be represented by court-appointed counsel, where "substantial rights of a criminal accused may be affected." Thus, the U.S. Supreme Court considered a probation revocation hearing to be a "critical stage" that falls within the due process provisions of the Fourteenth

Amendment. In subsequent years, several courts also applied this decision to parole revocation hearings.

Gagnon v. Scarpelli (1973). Gerald Scarpelli pleaded guilty to a charge of robbery in July 1965 in a Wisconsin court and was sentenced to 15 years in prison. The judge suspended this sentence on August 5, 1965, and placed Scarpelli on probation for seven years. The next day, August 6, Scarpelli was arrested and charged with burglary. His probation was revoked without a hearing and he was placed in the Wisconsin State Reformatory to serve his 15-year term. About three years later, Scarpelli was paroled. Shortly before his parole, he filed a habeas corpus petition, alleging that his probation revocation was invoked without a hearing and without benefit of counsel, constituting a denial of due process. Following his parole, the U.S. Supreme Court acted on his original habeas corpus petition and ruled in his favor. Specifically, the Court said that Scarpelli was denied his right to due process because no revocation hearing was held and because he was not represented by court-appointed counsel within the indigent claim. In effect, the Court, referring to *Morrissey v. Brewer* (1972), said that "a probation revocation, like parole revocation, is not a stage of a criminal prosecution, but does result in loss of liberty. . . . We hold that a probationer, like a parolee, is entitled to a preliminary hearing and a final revocation hearing in the conditions specified in *Morrissey v. Brewer*."

The significance of this case is that it equated probation with parole as well as with the respective revocation proceedings. Although the Court did not say that all parolees and probationers have a right to representation by counsel in all probation and parole revocation proceedings, it did say that counsel should be provided in cases in which the probationer or parolee makes a timely claim contesting the allegations. Although no constitutional basis exists for providing counsel in all probation or parole revocation proceedings, subsequent probation and parole revocation hearings usually involve defense counsel if legitimately requested. The U.S. Supreme Court declaration has been liberally interpreted in subsequent cases.

Bearden v. Georgia (1983). Bearden's probation was revoked by Georgia authorities because he failed to pay a fine and make restitution to his victim as required by the court. He claimed that he was indigent, but the court rejected his claim as a valid explanation for his conduct. The U.S. Supreme Court disagreed. It ruled that probation may not be revoked in the case of indigent probationers who have failed to pay their fines or make restitution. They further suggested alternatives for restitution and punishments that were more compatible with the abilities and economic resources of indigent probationers such as community service. In short, the probationer should not be penalized when a reasonable effort has been made to pay court-ordered fines and restitution.

Offender indigence does not automatically entitle offenders to immunity from restitution orders. In a 1993 case, *United States v. Bachsian* (1993), Bachsian was convicted of theft. He was required to pay restitution for the merchandise still in his possession under the Victim Witness Protection Act. Bachsian claimed, however, that he was indigent and was unable to make restitution. The Ninth Circuit Court of Appeals declared in Bachsian's case that it was not improper to impose restitution orders on an offender at the time of sentencing, even if the offender was unable to pay restitution then. In this instance, records indicated that based on a presentence investigation report Bachsian was considered by the court as having a future ability to pay. Eventually, Bachsian would become financially able and in a position to make restitution to his victim. His restitution orders were upheld. Also, bankruptcy does not discharge an offender's obligation to make restitution, although the amount and rate of restitution payments may be affected (*Baker v. State,* 1993; *State v. Hayes,* 1993).

Black v. Romano (1985).   A probationer had his probation revoked by the sentencing judge because of alleged program violations. The defendant had left the scene of an automobile accident, a felony in the jurisdiction in which the alleged offense occurred. The judge gave reasons for the revocation decision, but did not indicate that he had considered any option other than incarceration. The U.S. Supreme Court ruled that judges are not generally obligated to consider alternatives to incarceration before they revoke an offender's probation and place him in jail or prison. Clearly, probationers and parolees have obtained substantial rights in recent years. U.S. Supreme Court decisions have provided them with several important constitutional rights that invalidate the arbitrary and capricious revocation of their probation or parole programs by judges or parole boards. The two-stage hearing is extremely important to probationers and parolees in that it permits ample airing of the allegations against offenders, cross-examinations by counsel, and testimony from individual offenders.

Probationers who are acquitted of other crimes while on probation must be represented by counsel at subsequent probation revocation proceedings. Furthermore, judges may not use evidence from their trial acquittals against them to enhance the punishment in a probation revocation proceeding. Gibbs was a Delaware probationer (*Gibbs v. State,* 2000). During his probationary term, he was arrested and charged with a crime and was subsequently acquitted. In a unilateral action, the original sentencing judge ordered Gibbs's probation program revoked. The judge did not allow Gibbs to be represented by counsel, nor did he permit Gibbs to offer testimony in his own behalf. The judge summarily revoked Gibbs's probation, citing as evidence some of the information from the trial at which Gibbs was acquitted. Furthermore, the judge declared that on the basis of the **preponderance of evidence**, he found that Gibbs had indeed violated one or more of his probation program conditions. Gibbs appealed, arguing that he was entitled to counsel and that he should be permitted to give testimony in his own behalf. A Delaware appellate court agreed and overturned the judge's revocation order. Probationers are entitled to counsel in their probation revocation proceedings.

Statements made to a PO while being interrogated, not in custody, are admissible in court for the purpose of supporting new criminal charges. In *Minnesota v. Murphy* (1984), Murphy, a probationer, was serving a three-year probation term for criminal sexual conduct. Murphy's probation conditions included that he report regularly to his PO and answer all questions truthfully. Another condition was that he seek sexual therapy and counseling. During one of these counseling sessions, Murphy confessed to one of his counselors that he had committed a rape and murder in 1974. The counselor told Murphy's probation officer, who in turn interrogated Murphy at his residence. Murphy admitted the crime (responding truthfully) after extensive interviewing and interrogation by the PO. The PO gave this incriminating information to police who arrested Murphy later and charged him with the 1974 rape and murder. Murphy later claimed that the PO had not advised him of his Miranda rights (e.g., right to an attorney, right to terminate questioning at any point, right against making self-incriminating statements) and thus his confession should not be admitted later in court against him. As a general rule, criminal suspects who are the targets of a police investigation must be advised of their Miranda rights if undergoing an interrogation, whether or not they are in custody. A similar rule pertains to probationers. It might be argued, for instance, that their probation itself is a form of "custody." Thus, all probationers (and parolees) might be considered "in custody" during their program terms. "Custody," however, implies being unable to leave the presence of the interrogator. When suspects conclude their interrogation, they may or may not be permitted to leave. If they leave, then they are not considered to be in custody; otherwise, they are. In Murphy's case, he was not in custody and was not compelled to answer the PO's questions. Obviously, this case is a complex one involving seemingly conflicting obligations and constitutional rights.

Search and seizure grounds are less stringent for POs who intend to search their client's homes for illegal contraband. In *Griffin v. Wisconsin* (1987), Griffin was placed on probation after being convicted of resisting arrest, disorderly conduct, and obstructing a Wisconsin police officer in 1980. One condition of Griffin's probation was that he not possess a firearm. An informant advised Griffin's PO that Griffin had a weapon on his premises. Based on previous reliable information provided by the informant, the PO believed that reasonable grounds existed to conduct a warrantless search. The PO went to Griffin's home, searched it without a warrant, and discovered a gun. Griffin was subsequently arrested, prosecuted, and convicted for being a convicted felon in possession of a firearm and was sentenced to two years. He appealed on the grounds that the PO's search of his premises should have been conducted with a properly issued warrant and based on probable cause. The U.S. Supreme Court declared that in Griffin's case, POs are entitled to special consideration because of their demanding jobs. They should not be held to the more stringent standard of "probable cause" because they must often take immediate action to detect crimes or seize illegal contraband relating to their probationer-parolee clients. The "reasonable grounds" standard, a lesser standard than probable cause, is upheld to the extent that probation or parole agency policies make provisions for such warrantless searches of offender premises in their jurisdictions. The ruling is not intended as a blanket right to violate one's Fourth Amendment rights on a whim. An even broader search and seizure case was upheld in the case of *Crooker v. Metallo* (1993). In that case, POs conducted a sweep of a parolee's premises on the basis of a search incident to an arrest for alleged parole violations. The sweep included a quick search between the parolee's box springs and mattress of his bed, where illegal contraband were found. The First Circuit Court of Appeals held for the POs and indicated that they possessed qualified immunity while conducting the search and that their search was objectively reasonable.

An interesting case of *Davis v. State* (1992), however, provides an exception for POs and police relative to warrantless searches of probationer's premises. Davis, a probationer convicted of a controlled substance charge, was away from his home one evening when his 10-year-old son dialed 911 and summoned police to the home. The boy had found drugs in the house and had called police. These drugs were later used as evidence against Davis to revoke his probation. A Georgia Court of Appeals, however, threw out this evidence, concluding that a 10-year-old, regardless of his motives, has no authority to give police permission to enter his father's home and search his bedroom for illegal contraband. Police would have to find some other means to use the illegally seized evidence. In this instance, the police intrusion into Davis's home constituted unlawful entry, and no basis could be shown upon which to issue a warrant on probable cause, using a telephone call from a 10-year-old to support such an action. The case against Davis was thrown out, and his probation was reinstated.

Conditions of probation/parole, including victim restitution payments, are legitimate; there are, however, situations in which offenders may or may not be able to pay restitution ordered by the court. In the case of *Bearden v. Georgia* (1983), it was seen that an inability to pay restitution cannot entitle judges to automatically revoke one's probation program. In Bearden's case, the judge had not examined other options in lieu of the restitution order. More recent cases have upheld *Bearden,* and some interesting spins have been added. For instance, a Florida man, Moore, was convicted of purchasing a stolen truck (*Moore v. State,* 1993). The original truck's owner, the victim, claimed that there were tools worth $500 in the truck when it was stolen initially by the person who later sold the truck to Moore. Nevertheless, the judge imposed a sentence of probation, with a restitution condition that Moore repay the victim $500 for the loss of the tools. A Florida Court of Appeals set aside this condition, because it did not show that the loss was caused by Moore's action and that there was a significant relation between the loss and the crime of purchasing a stolen vehicle.

In a federal case, Lombardi was convicted of mail fraud involving over $190,000 of unaccounted-for funds (*United States v. Lombardi,* 1993). He was fined $60,000 as a part of his sentence and was obligated to make restitution in the sum of $190,000. Lombardi protested, claiming that he was unable to pay these amounts. The First Circuit Court of Appeals disagreed, however, indicating that Lombardi had never accounted for the whereabouts of these illegally obtained funds. His restitution order remained effective. Failure to make restitution, in Lombardi's case, would result in incarceration.

Judges who impose probation in lieu of mandatory sentences for particular offenses may have their probation judgments declared invalid. In a New York case, a plea bargain was worked out between the state and a defendant, Hipp (*People v. Hipp,* 1993). Hipp was determined by the court to be addicted to gambling. The nature of the conviction offense and the gambling addiction compel the court under mandatory sentencing to prescribe a jail term as well as accompanying therapy for the addiction. In this instance, the judge simply accepted a plea agreement, accepting the defendant's guilty plea in exchange for a term of probation. The New York Court of Appeals overruled the judge in this case, indicating that New York statutes do not authorize a trial court to ignore clearly expressed and unequivocal mandatory sentencing provisions of the New York Penal Law. In Florida, however, a judge imposed probation on an offender convicted under a habitual offender statute (*McKnight v. State,* 1993). McKnight, a habitual offender, was convicted of being a habitual felony offender. Ordinarily, this conviction carries a mandatory life-without-parole penalty, but the judge imposed probation. Although the members of the Florida Court of Appeals did not like the judge's decision, they upheld it anyway, supporting the general principle of judicial discretion.

Probationers can be barred from using computers if computers were involved in their conviction offenses. In the case of *State v. Combs* (2000), Combs was a Washington probationer who had been convicted of second-degree child molestation. He was placed on probation with the provision that he was forbidden to use a computer. Furthermore, he was required to submit to a polygraph (lie detector) test as a means of monitoring his compliance with program requirements. Combs objected to these conditions and appealed, but an appellate court upheld the terms of his probation. The court reasoned that the polygraph test was a reasonable condition as long as it did not amount to a fishing expedition to discover additional criminal activity. Regarding the prohibition of computer use, it was known that Combs had used the computer to transmit pornographic images to his female victims, who were five and six years old at the time. He then required the young girls to pose with him in the same positions they had just viewed on the computer. Because the computer was a major device used in his crimes, the court upheld the judge's order forbidding him to use one.

Probation officers are forbidden from creating their own rules for their probationer-clients in addition to those imposed by the sentencing judge. In the Massachusetts case of *Commonwealth v. MacDonald* (2000), MacDonald was placed on probation in relation to a felony conviction. Among other requirements, MacDonald was ordered by the sentencing judge to "stay away" from Cynthia Evans. He was also ordered to submit to counseling for drug and alcohol abuse. When MacDonald arrived at the probation office, however, the PO advised him that he was to have "no contact" with Evans. Subsequently, MacDonald sent a letter to Evans regarding an upcoming care and protection hearing concerning their two minor children. The PO considered this letter to be a violation of the "no contact" order he had issued and moved to revoke MacDonald's probation. The judge revoked MacDonald's probation program and he appealed. An appellate court overturned the revocation, saying that the PO illegally added the "no contact" provision and that this differed significantly from the "stay away" provision contemplated by the judge. POs cannot write new rules for their clients.

Defendants can refuse probation if the court imposes probation as a sentence. In a rather unique case, the defendant, Cannon, was convicted of criminally negligent homicide after entering a guilty plea (*Cannon v. State*, 1993). In open court, however, after probation was imposed, Cannon refused the probation and demanded to be incarcerated instead. The judge insisted that the probation sentence be accepted, and Cannon appealed. In an Alabama Court of Appeals decision, the court upheld Cannon's right to refuse probation, and he was remanded to prison instead. This situation is not as bad as it sounds, however. Cannon had been incarcerated for some time prior to his criminally negligent homicide conviction. By accepting probation, Cannon would have been obligated to adhere to certain restrictive conditions for a period of time far in excess of the time remaining to be served. In effect, he had only a few more months to serve of his original sentence, counting the many months he had been behind bars before his trial and conviction. Thus, a probation sentence in Cannon's case would have involved a longer term of conditional freedom rather than the number of months remaining before his **unconditional release** from prison. The court said, "Our holding merely recognizes a convict's right to reject the trial court's offer of probation if he or she deems it to be more onerous than a prison sentence."

Judges may revoke one's probation program or supervised release and impose a new sentence of which the offender must serve the remainder in confinement. A federal probationer, Levi, was under supervised release (*United States v. Levi*, 1993). During his first 11 months of supervised release, Levi committed one or more probation violations. The judge revoked Levi's probation and declared that he must spend the remaining 13 months incarcerated. The Eighth Circuit Court of Appeals upheld the judge's action, because the 13-month imprisonment was within the two-year sentence of probation originally imposed by the same judge.

Sometimes POs obligate their probationer-clients to conform to rules outside of those specified in probation orders. Such extra orders are considered unconstitutional in some jurisdictions. In the case of *Lemon v. State* (1993), Lemon, a probationer convicted of misappropriate of property, was required by a judge to perform community service at the orders or discretion of his probation officer. The Texas Court of Appeals reversed this condition of the probation, because the nature of community service had not been articulated by the judge. It is improper for POs to determine the nature of one's community service to be performed under a sentence of probation with conditions.

Ordinarily, sentences of probation cannot be served simultaneously with sentences of incarceration. If a judge imposes incarceration for an offender for offense A and if that same judge imposes probation for the same offender for offense B, then both the incarcerative sentence and the probationary sentence cannot be served concurrently, at least in Florida courts. In the case of *Hill v. State* (1993), Hill, a convicted Florida offender, was sentenced to probation and to incarceration for different offenses. He wanted to serve both sentences concurrently. The Florida Court of Appeals denied his request, particularly in view of a prior case which was decided on the same issue (*Nobles v. State*, 1992).

Probationers admitting to probation violations and waiving direct appeal actions does not prevent them from being entitled to a transcript of the proceedings so as to attack the revocation proceeding itself. In an Arizona case, *Wilson v. Ellis* (1993), an indigent defendant had his probation revoked after admitting to a probation violation. His request for a transcript of his revocation proceedings was denied. The Arizona Court of Appeals rejected this lower court denial and declared that the offender did have a right to pursue a challenge of the revocation proceeding itself, despite his waiver of appeal rights, in the context of a postconviction remedy.

Probationers are obligated to pay certain supervision fees to defray some of their program expenses, if they are financially able to do so. Failure to pay one's supervisory costs may be grounds for a probation revocation. In the Florida case of *Anderson v. State* (1993), Anderson, the probationer, failed to pay his supervisory fees imposed by the court, which were due and payable on the fifth day of each month. Anderson was employed and was able to pay these fees; he simply elected not to. In this case, based on his ability to pay, his probation was revoked by the judge. A higher court declared that the judge was justified in this probation revocation.

SUMMARY

When offenders are convicted of crimes, they may receive probation in lieu of incarceration. The most common form of probation is standard probation. Offenders are expected to comply with a list of behavioral requirements. Ordinarily, some form of reporting to probation agencies is specified so that probationers can have contact with their POs at regular intervals. Some offenders require closer supervision. Increasing the amount of contact between probationers and their supervising officers is called intensive supervised probation. Intensive supervised probation, which refers to a wide range of nonincarcerative programs exerting variable control over probationers, means different things depending on the jurisdiction. Most corrections professionals consider intensive supervision to mean frequent face-to-face contact with probationers. Thus, intensive supervision means to supervise probationers more closely than standard probationers. Often, intensive supervision is accompanied by home confinement and electronic monitoring as well as other program conditions.

Unpopular with the general public, probation of any kind is designed to reintegrate offenders into their respective communities and to assist jail and prison officials with their overcrowding problems. Intensive supervised probation programs in current use among the states are based on one or more correctional philosophies stressing contrasting orientations toward how offenders on probation ought to be controlled. The justice model is most punitive and emphasizes penalties for offenders that fit the crimes they committed. The limited risk control model is founded on the ideas that an offender's degree of risk to the public can be measured and that the intensity of supervision imposed should vary with the severity of the offense. The treatment-oriented model is most closely aligned with the rehabilitative ideal of corrections and emphasizes community reintegration, community service, restitution, curfew, and home confinement alternatives.

Most intensive supervised probation programs are characterized with low probation officer caseloads and frequent face-to-face contact with probationers either at home or at work. Many programs include counseling or some form of vocational/educational training, restitution, and/or public service. The Georgia ISP program, the Idaho ISP program, and the South Carolina ISP program have similar elements and characteristics and are designed for low-risk nonviolent offenders. Georgia handpicks its probationers; therefore, only the most eligible offenders are included. This practice biases the program in such a way so as to maximize its success for clients. The Idaho ISP program uses teams of two POs and a supervisor who work in shifts to monitor offender conduct. South Carolina's ISP program uses specialized POs who have training specific to different offender needs. Offenders must also pay a regular, nominal program maintenance fee.

Another incarcerative alternative is shock probation, also known as split sentencing. It involves a short period of incarceration followed by participation in a probation program. Shock probation was pioneered in Ohio, although it is currently used in many other states as a sanction. The philosophy of shock probation is that offenders will be shocked into the realization that their crimes are serious and that incarceration is undesirable. Shock incarceration is sometimes known as a boot camp experience. Boot camp goals are multifaceted, emphasizing self-discipline, self-awareness, and various educational and vocational skills. They are aimed primarily at more youthful offenders, although older offenders are not excluded by most programs. Most states have either developed or are in the process of developing these programs. Boot camp graduates tend to have low recidivism rates compared with standard probationers. Some boot camps, known as jail boot camps, are operated by county jails. Boot camps have been instrumental in upgrading one's social and vocational skills as well as preparing participants for entering the workforce and supporting their families.

When one or more probation program requirements are violated, POs initiate action against probationers. Some program requirements are more important than others; thus, in certain instances, no action is taken. When new crimes are alleged or drug or alcohol dependencies are detected, however, some probationers are in jeopardy of having their probation programs revoked by their original sentencing judges. The probation revocation process is a formal, two-stage proceeding. The first stage determines one's guilt or innocence relating to the allegations of program violations. If judges find that probationers have indeed violated one or more probationary terms, then they must decide the punishment to impose. This decision process is in the second phase of the proceeding. Punishment may be a simple return to one's probation program, but in other instances, it may be a resentence to more intensive supervised probation. In yet other instances, some probationers may be placed in jails or prisons for a period of time. Several landmark cases have been decided by the U.S. Supreme Court to govern the probation revocation process.

KEY TERMS

Boot camps

Combination sentence

Delinquency

Georgia Intensive Supervision Probation Program (GISPP)

Habeas corpus

Idaho Intensive Supervised Probation Program

Intensive probation supervision (IPS) programs

Intensive supervised probation (ISP) programs

Intermittent confinement

Intermittent sentence

Jail as a condition of probation

Jail boot camps

Limited risk control model

Mixed sentence

Preponderance of evidence

Program for Female Offenders, Inc. (PFO)

Runaways

Shock incarceration

Shock probation

Shock probationers

Shock probation program

South Carolina Intensive Supervised Probation Program

Split sentencing

Traditional treatment-oriented model

Unconditional release

U.S. sentencing guidelines

Women's Activities and Learning Center (WALC)

QUESTIONS FOR REVIEW

1. What is meant by intensive supervised probation?
2. How does intensive supervised probation differ from standard probation?
3. Differentiate between the Georgia and South Carolina intensive supervised probation models. How are participants selected for each program?
4. What are three correctional models that have influenced intensive supervised probation programs in recent years? How does each model modify or shape existing probation programs?
5. What are some principal program components of the South Carolina and Idaho ISP programs?
6. What is a boot camp? What are its goals?
7. What is the philosophy of shock probation? Has shock probation achieved its general objectives? Why or why not?
8. What are two important landmark cases in the probation revocation process?

9. Would probationers not being able to afford to pay their probation fees necessarily bar them from participating in probation programs? Why or why not?
10. What is meant by mandatory probation revocation?

SUGGESTED READINGS

Ardovini-Brooker, Joanne, and Lewis Walker (2000). "Juvenile Boot Camps and the Reclamation of Our Youth: Some Food for Thought." *Juvenile and Family Court Journal* **51:**21–29.

Crew, B. Keith, et al. (1998). *An Analysis of Probation Revocation in the First Judicial District of Iowa.* Cedar Falls: College of Social and Behavioral Sciences, University of Northern Iowa.

Gover, Angela R., Doris Layton MacKenzie, and Gaylene J. Styve (2000). "Boot Camps and Traditional Correctional Facilities for Juveniles: A Comparison of the Participants, Daily Activities, and Environments." *Journal of Criminal Justice* **28:**53–68.

Stinchcombe, Jeanne B. (1999). "Recovering from the Shocking Reality of Shock Incarceration: What Correctional Administrators Can Learn from Boot Camp Failures." *Corrections Management Quarterly* **3:**43–52.

Wood, Peter B., and Harold G. Grasmick (1999). "Toward the Development of Punishment Equivalencies: Male and Female Inmates Rate the Severity of Alternative Sanctions Compared to Prison." *Justice Quarterly* **16:**19–50.

CHAPTER 6   # Jails and Prisons

Introduction
Jails and Jail Characteristics
  Workhouses
  The Walnut Street Jail
  Subsequent Jail Developments
  The Number of Jails in the United States
Functions of Jails
A Profile of Jail Inmates
Prisons, Prison History, and Prison
  Characteristics
  Prisons Defined
Functions of Prisons
Inmate Classification Systems
A Profile of Prisoners in U.S. Prisons
Some Jail and Prison Contrasts

Selected Jail and Prison Issues
  Jail and Prison Overcrowding
  Violence and Inmate Discipline
  Jail and Prison Design and Control
  Vocational/Technical and Educational
  Programs in Jails and Prisons
  Jail and Prison Privatization
  Gang Formation and Perpetuation
The Role of Jails and Prisons in Probation and
  Parole Decision Making
Summary
Key Terms
Questions for Review
Suggested Readings

• *Daniel Altstadt, 43.* It happened in San Diego, California, in February 1975. Daniel Altstadt, then 18, took a hatchet and slaughtered his father, mother, and sister. He also attempted to kill his brother, Gary, but Gary survived. Gary's spinal cord was severed, however, and he was paralyzed for life. Daniel Altstadt was an Eagle Scout and honors student at school. He had never exhibited any personal problems and was well liked by others. Daniel was convicted of multiple murders and given several life sentences. On May 11, 2000, he was transferred from the minimum-security California Men's Colony in San Luis Obispo to another California prison in Coalinga. Prison officials processed Altstadt and placed him in a cell. On Sunday, May 28, 2000, authorities found Daniel Altstadt dead in his cell. He had hanged himself with a shoelace around his neck. How can prison or jail officials prevent inmate suicides? Is it possible to design a suicide-proof cell? What preventive measures would you employ? Is the placement of closed-circuit cameras in all prison cells the answer? What do you think? (*Source:* Adapted from Associated Press, "Prisoner Hangs Himself," May 29, 2000.)

   • *The Federal Prison at Harrisburg, Pennsylvania.* There are many stories about what prison correctional officers do, both good and bad. Some correctional officers have been indicted and convicted of smuggling contraband into or out of prisons in exchange for money from prisoners. Some prisoners are members of gangs or organized crime with incredible assets, and the rewards to correctional officers willing to violate the law are enormous. In October 2000, though, a new twist was made of correctional officer misconduct, this time involving smuggling inmate sperm outside of prison to be used to impregnate girlfriends of inmates. Interestingly, the alleged smuggling operation was carried out at the federal penitentiary at Allenwood, Pennsylvania, a medium- to maximum-security federal prison with strict rules governing visitation and inmate-visitor contact. Conjugal visits are not permitted. In fact, no direct contact between visitors and inmates is permitted. Nevertheless, as many as five New York mobsters housed at Allenwood for lengthy incarcerative terms have boasted that they are proud fathers of newly born children to their women outside of prison. Suspicious behaviors among inmates had been observed by watchful correctional officers at Allenwood over the last several years. One convicted Colombo family hitman, Kevin Granato, was seen in the Allenwood visitation room in 1997 showing off a toddler he called "my son." The incident raised eyebrows because he had been at the prison since 1988. No one knows the source for their information, but government investigators began to closely monitor correctional officers at Allenwood. In fact, a sting operation of sorts was established in which an undercover FBI female agent posing as an inmate's girlfriend gave an Allenwood correctional officer, Troy Kemmerer, 33, $5,000 in exchange for smuggling some of her boyfriend's sperm from the prison in a cryogenic sperm kit she provided. Kemmerer was arrested following that incident, and several other correctional officers were implicated, including Todd Swineford. Both men were arrested and charged with bribery and released pending trial. Both declined comment when the news media attempted to contact them. One inmate involved in the alleged scheme was a New York mob associate, Antoninio Parlevecchio. Thousands of dollars were exchanged so that inmates could smuggle their sperm in cryogenic sperm kits to their girlfriends outside of prison, and the scheme had gone on for some time. It was unknown how much the correctional officers had profited from the illegal sperm smuggling. According to investigators, the sperm kits and sperm-filled vials were taken from the prison and delivered on several occasions to the Park Avenue Fertility Laboratory in New York City. A prison spokesperson at Allenwood said that the two correctional officers charged in the incident have quit. "We have a zero tolerance policy for staff misconduct," said Edward Berry, prison spokesperson. Should inmates have the right to father children while in prison? Should there be a law prohibiting the sending of sperm outside of prisons to the families of inmates so that they can have children? What do you think? (*Source:* Adapted from Hope Yen and Associated Press, "Prison Guards Accused of Taking Bribes to Smuggle Inmate Sperm," October 11, 2000.)

   • *Who Says 78 Is Too Old to Rob Banks?* Forrest Silva Tucker, 78, has a criminal record dating back to the 1930s. He was convicted of several crimes, including bank robbery, in California during the 1950s and was incarcerated in San Quentin, one of California's toughest prisons. In 1979, Tucker and two other inmates built a crude boat and set out from the beach. The flimsy vessel, assembled from plastic sheets, wood, duct tape, and Formica, held together long enough for them to paddle several hundred yards to their freedom. Police couldn't find Tucker for more than 20 years, but his luck finally ran out in Florida. He was arrested in a Pompano Beach school parking lot following a local bank robbery. Authorities determined that he was a California fugitive, and the judge ordered him held without bail. He had been arrested a few years earlier in Boston, although authorities there didn't realize that he was wanted in California. According to Massachusetts police, Tucker joined the Over-the-Hill Gang, a group of elderly thieves who robbed supermarkets in the Boston area. When Tucker was apprehended in Florida, he had been visiting a girl-friend. He tried to elude police but crashed his vehicle into a palm tree. Should Tucker be placed in jail? Is Forrest Tucker an exception, or is he indicative of a growing trend among elderly criminals to commit new crimes? How is crime among the elderly contributing to jail problems? What do you think? (*Source:* Adapted from Associated Press, "Elderly Robber Escaped San Quentin," April 29, 1999.)

• *Robert Washington, Fort Worth, Texas.* You've been acquitted of murder charges, but you wind up in jail for six months. What's the story? In Fort Worth, Texas, Robert Washington was charged with murder and a trial was set. After hearing the evidence, the jury returned their verdict: not guilty. Washington and his mother were so overjoyed by the verdict that they hooted and hollered and engaged in a celebration dance. The judge wasn't impressed. He found both Washington and his mother in contempt of court and sentenced Washington to six months in jail. The mother got 30 days in jail. Before reading the verdict, Judge George Gallagher gave a common warning to both the defense and prosecution against any outbursts. He said later, "It was as if he had caught the winning touchdown and spiked the ball in front of the defensive back. I didn't hear a word. All I saw was the physical response, and it was totally inappropriate. The celebration was so blatant that a message had to be sent." A subsequent meeting was scheduled with Washington's attorney to review the charges. Should acquitted defendants be penalized for celebrating in court over being acquitted? Is a six-month jail term deserved for spontaneously reacting to being acquitted of murder charges? What proper punishment should have been imposed? Would a fine have been more appropriate? Is this sentence an appropriate use of scarce jail space? What do you think? (*Source:* Adapted from Associated Press, "Innocent Verdict: Jail Time Anyway," April 14, 2000.)

INTRODUCTION

This chapter is about jails and prisons. Jails in the United States are one of the most maligned and forgotten components of the criminal justice system. In the first section, a brief history of jails in the United States is presented, and jail inmates are profiled. Typically, jails are facilities designed to confine offenders serving short sentences as well as those awaiting trial and are funded and operated by cities or counties. Jails are an integral feature of U.S. corrections. In contrast, prisons are intended as long-term custodial facilities for more serious offenders. The second section of this chapter presents a brief history of prisons in the United States and discusses their characteristics and functions. In past years, prisons and jails could be clearly distinguished by whether convicted offenders had committed felonies or misdemeanors. Misdemeanants were usually sent to jails, whereas convicted felons were sent to prisons. This situation is no longer the case, because prison overcrowding has caused prison officials to negotiate with smaller jails to accommodate some of their inmate overflow. These inmates housed in local jails are **contract prisoners**. Both state and federal governments have contracted with many local jails as a means of housing a certain proportion of their offender populations. This contracting has directly aggravated existing jail overcrowding. Later in the chapter, prison inmates are profiled and compared with jail inmates.

The last section of the chapter discusses several important issues relevant for both jails and prisons, including the overcrowding problem, the problem of inmate violence and discipline, the design and control of jails and prisons, vocational and educational programs for inmates, and privatization. It is important to understand some of the functions and culture of jails and prisons, because inmate conduct is one determinant of early release decisions by parole boards. Also, inmate conduct is important for those offenders experiencing shock probation. Shock probation prescribes one to four months of incarceration, whereupon judges remove offenders from jails and resentence them to probation. Inmates who behave poorly while confined for these short terms, however, may not be resentenced to probation. Judges exercise discretion and are influenced by inmate conduct. They must decide whether to continue incarcerating offenders or resentence them to probation after one or more months of confinement. Thus, jails and prisons play an important role in probation and parole programs.

JAILS AND JAIL CHARACTERISTICS

In 1999, there were 14 million admissions to and 13.9 million releases from U.S. jails, with an average daily jail population of 687,973 (Beck, 2000a:5), an increase of over 23,000 inmates since midyear 1998, when the average was 664,847. This jail population increase has created serious overcrowding problems in city and county jails in most jurisdictions. In turn, jail overcrowding has been directly or indirectly responsible for numerous inmate deaths and extensive violence, much offender litigation challenging among other things the constitutionality of the nature of their confinement and treatment, and administrative and/or supervisory problems of immense proportions (Welch, 1999). How did jails reach this stage and acquire these problems? A brief history of jails in the United States explains several contemporary jail problems.

The term *jail* is derived from old English term, ***gaol*** (also pronounced "jail"), which originated in A.D. 1166 through a declaration by Henry II of England. Henry II established gaols as a part of the Assize or Constitution of Clarendon (American Correctional Association, 1983:3). Gaols were locally administered and operated, and they housed many of society's misfits. Paupers or vagrants, drunkards, thieves, murderers, debtors, highwaymen, trespassers, orphan children, prostitutes, and others made up early gaol populations. Because the Church of England was powerful and influential, many religious dissidents were housed in these gaols as a punishment for their dissent, a practice that continued for several centuries.

Local control over the administration and operation of jails by **shire-reeves** in England was a practice continued by the American colonists in later years. Most jails in the United States today are locally controlled and operated; thus, political influence upon jails and jail conditions is strong. In fact, changing jail conditions from one year to the next are often linked to local political shifts through elections and new administrative appointments. Also, local officials controlling jails and jail operations meant that no single administrative style typified these facilities. Each county (shire) was responsible for establishing jails and managing them according to their individual discretion. Current U.S. jail operations in most jurisdictions are characterized by this same individuality of style.

Originally, jails were designed as holding facilities for persons accused of crimes. Alleged law violators were held until court convened, when their guilt or innocence could be determined. Today, pretrial detainees make up a significant proportion of the U.S. jail population. Shire-reeves made their living through reimbursements from taxes collected in the form of fees for each inmate housed on a daily basis. For instance, the reeve would receive a fixed fee, perhaps 50 or 75 cents per day, for each inmate held in the jail. Therefore, more prisoners meant more money for reeves and their assistants. Such a reimbursement scheme was easily susceptible to corruption, and much money intended for inmate food and shelter was pocketed by selfish reeves. Quite logically, the quality of inmate food and shelter was very substandard, and jails became notorious because of widespread malnutrition, disease, and death among prisoners.

Workhouses

Deplorable jail conditions continued into the sixteenth century, when workhouses were established largely in response to mercantile demands for cheap labor. A typical **workhouse** in the mid-sixteenth century was the **Bridewell Workhouse**, established in 1557. This London facility housed many of the city's vagrants and general riffraff (American Correctional Association, 1983). Jail and workhouse sheriffs and administrators quickly capitalized on the cheap labor these facilities generated, and additional profits were envisioned. Thus, it became common for sheriffs and other officials to "hire out" their inmates to perform skilled and semiskilled tasks for various merchants. Although the manifest functions of workhouses and prisoner labor were supposed to improve the moral and social fiber of prisoners and train them to perform useful skills when they were eventually released, profits from inmate labor were often pocketed by corrupt jail and workhouse officials. Workhouses were also established in other countries such as Italy and the Netherlands during the same period (Spruit et al., 1998). In the United States, workhouses were prevalent well into the 1800s and existed to house disreputable persons, such as prostitutes and drunkards (Adler, 1992).

Jails were common throughout the colonies. Sheriffs were appointed to supervise jail inmates, and the fee system continued to be used to finance these facilities. All types of people were confined together in jails, regardless of their gender or age. Orphans, prostitutes, drunkards, thieves, and robbers were often contained in large, dormitory-style rooms with hay and blankets for beds. Jails were great melting pots of humanity, with little or no regard for inmate treatment, health, or rehabilitation. Even today, jails are characterized similarly (Kerle, 1998).

The Walnut Street Jail

In 1790, the Pennsylvania legislature authorized the renovation of a facility originally constructed on Walnut Street in 1776, a two-acre structure initially designed to house the overflow resulting from overcrowding of the High Street Jail. The **Walnut Street**

Jail was both a workhouse and a place of incarceration for all types of offenders. The 1790 renovation, however, was the first of several innovations in U.S. corrections. Specifically, the Walnut Street Jail was innovative because (1) it separated the most serious prisoners from others in 16 large solitary cells, (2) it separated other prisoners according to their offense seriousness, and (3) it separated prisoners according to gender. Besides these innovations, the Walnut Street Jail assigned inmates to different types of productive labor according to their gender and conviction offense. Women made clothing and performed washing and mending chores. Skilled inmates worked in carpentry, shoemaking, and other crafts. Unskilled prisoners beat hemp or jute for ship caulking. With the exception of women, prisoners received a daily wage for their labor that was applied to defray the cost of their maintenance. The Society of Quakers and other religious groups provided regular instruction for most offenders. The Walnut Street Jail concept was widely imitated by officials from other states during the next several decades. Many prisons were modeled after the Walnut Street Jail for housing and managing long-term prisoners (Okun, 1997).

The Quakers in Pennsylvania were a strong influence in jail reforms. In 1787, they established the **Philadelphia Society for Alleviating the Miseries of Public Prisons**, made up of many prominent Philadelphia citizens, philanthropists, and religious reformers who believed that prison and jail conditions ought to be changed and replaced with a more humane environment. Members of this society visited each jail and prison daily, bringing food, clothing, and religious instruction to inmates. Some were educators who sought to assist prisoners in acquiring basic skills such as reading and writing. Although their intrusion into prison and jail life was frequently resented and opposed by local authorities and sheriffs, their presence was significant and brought the deplorable conditions of confinement to the attention of politicians.

Subsequent Jail Developments

Information about the early growth of jails in the United States is sketchy. For one reason, many inmate facilities were established during the 1800s and early 1900s, serving many functions and operating under different labels. Sheriffs' homes were used as jails in some jurisdictions, and workhouses, farms, barns, small houses, and other types of facilities served similar purposes in others. Thus, depending on who did the counting, some facilities would be labeled as jails and some would not. Limiting jail definitions only to locally operated short-term facilities for inmates also excluded state-operated jails in some states, such as Alaska, Delaware, and Rhode Island. Another reason for inadequate jail statistics and information was that there was little interest in jail populations. Yet another problem was the difficulty in transmitting information from jails and jail inmates to any central location during that period. Often, local records were not maintained, and many sheriff's departments were not inclined to share information about their prisoners with others. Streamlined communications systems did not exist, and information was compiled very slowly, if at all. State governments expressed little or no interest in the affairs of jails within their borders, because they were largely local enterprises funded with local funds. Even if there had been a strong interest in jail information among corrections professionals and others, it would have been quite difficult to acquire.

The U.S. Census Bureau began to compile information about jails in 1880 (Cahalan and Parsons, 1986:73). At ten-year intervals following 1880, general jail information was systematically obtained about race, ethnicity, gender, and age. Originally, the U.S. Census Bureau presented data separately for county jails, city prisons, workhouses, houses of correction, and leased county prisoners (Cahalan and Parsons, 1986:73), but in 1923, these figures were combined to reflect more accurately what is now described as jail statistics. A special report was prepared by the U.S. Census Bureau entitled *Prisoners 1923*. In that same year, Joseph Fishman, a federal prison inspector, published a book, *Crucible of Crime,* describing living conditions of many U.S. jails (Cahalan and Parsons, 1986:73). Comparisons with 1880 base figures show the jail population of the United States to be 18,686 in 1880 and almost doubling to 33,093 by 1890.

Most reports about jail conditions in the United States have been largely unfavorable. The 1923 report by Fishman was based on his visits to and observations of 1,500 jails, and he described the conditions he saw as horrible. More recent reports suggest that conditions have not changed dramatically since Fishman made his early observations. Not until 1972 did national survey data about jails become available. Exceptions include the years 1910, 1923, and 1933, when jail inmate characteristics were listed according to several offense categories. A majority of jail inmates each of those years had committed petty offenses such as vagrancy, public drunkenness, and minor property crimes (Cahalan and Parsons, 1986:86). Even since 1972, jail data have not been regularly and consistently compiled (Kerle, 1998).

There are several reasons for many of the continuing jail problems in the United States. Although some of these persistent problems are examined in depth later in this chapter, it is sufficient for now to understand that (1) most of the U.S. jails today were built before 1970, and many were built five decades or more before that; (2) local control of jails often results in erratic policies that shift with each political election, thus forcing jail guards and other personnel to adapt to constantly changing conditions and jail operations; and (3) jail funding is a low-priority budget item in most jurisdictions, and with limited operating funds, the quality of services and personnel jails provide and attract is considerably lower compared with state and federal prison standards and personnel (Wooldredge, 1991).

The Number of Jails in the United States

No one knows the exact number of jails in the United States at any given time. One reason is that observers disagree about how jails ought to be defined. Some people count only locally operated and funded, short-term incarceration facilities as jails, whereas others include state-operated jails in their figures. In remote territories such as Alaska, World War II Quonset huts may be used to house offenders on a short-term basis. Work release centers, farms for low-risk inmates, and other facilities may be included or excluded from the jail definition. Sometimes, a **lockup** (drunk tank, holding tank) might be counted as a jail, although such a facility exists primarily to hold those charged with public drunkenness or other minor offenses for up to 48 hours. They are not jails in the formal sense; rather, they are simple holding tanks or facilities. The American Jail Association suggests that to qualify as a bona fide jail, the facility must hold inmates for 72 hours or longer, not 48 hours (Kerle, 1998). One of the more accurate estimates of the number of jails in the United States is 3,328, reported by the U.S. **Department of Justice** jail census in 1997 (Harlow, 1998:1).

FUNCTIONS OF JAILS

John Irwin (1985) says that jails are more likely to receive, process, and confine mostly detached and disreputable persons rather than true criminals. He says that many noncriminals are arrested simply because they are offensive and not because they have committed crimes. Irwin worked as a caseworker in several county jails in San Francisco, California, during the early 1980s, and he based his conclusions on personal observations as well as conversations and interviews with county pretrial release and **public defender** personnel.

Jails were originally conceived as short-term holding facilities for inmates serving short sentences as well as for those awaiting trial. The general and most basic function of jails is security. Since 1980, however, jails have changed considerably in response to public policy and practicality. Today, jails perform myriad functions, some unrelated to their original historical purpose (Kerle, 1998). The following functions characterize a majority of jails in the United States.

Jails Hold Indigents, Vagrants, and the Mentally Ill.   Jails are generally ill-equipped to handle those with mental or physical disorders. Often, physicians are available only on an on-call basis from local clinics in communities, and no rehabilitative programs or activities exist (Ditton, 1999).

Jails Hold Pretrial Detainees.   Offenders arrested for various crimes who cannot afford or are denied bail are housed in jails until their trial. For most defendants awaiting trial, their period of **pretrial detention** is fairly short. **Pretrial detainees** may be held in jail without bail if they pose an escape risk or are considered dangerous. Such action is sometimes known as **preventive detention**.

Jails House Witnesses in Protective Custody.   Material witnesses to crimes in key cases may be housed in jails until trials can be held if it appears that their lives are in danger or their safety is threatened. Some witnesses may be reluctant to testify; thus, prosecutors may wish to guarantee their subsequent appearance by placing them in protective custody. Often, jails are designed so that special accommodations are provided these witnesses, and they do not ordinarily associate with offenders.

Jails House Convicted Offenders Awaiting Sentencing.   Convicted offenders awaiting sentencing are usually held in local jail facilities. These offenders may be federal, state, or local prisoners. When these offenders are housed in local jails, the jurisdiction is ordinarily reimbursed for offender expenses from state or federal funds.

Jails House Persons Serving Short-Term Sentences.   Jails were never designed to accommodate offenders for lengthy incarcerative periods beyond one year. Prisons were constructed and intended for that type of long-term inmate confinement. Many offenders still serve relatively short terms in jails, but increasing numbers of inmates are incarcerated for periods exceeding the one-year standard.

Jails House Some Juvenile Offenders.   Because of the **jail removal initiative**, most juveniles have been diverted from jails for processing, but some juveniles are still incarcerated in jails for short periods until their identity can be verified. Many juveniles have fake IDs and lie to police about who they are and where they live, and some juveniles appear to be much older than they really are. Thus, jail authorities may not know that they are incarcerating juveniles if IDs say otherwise and the juveniles appear to be adults. When juveniles are held in jails for brief periods, they are usually segregated from adult offenders, unless jail conditions do not permit such segregation. Despite the jail removal initiative and efforts from various vested interest groups to remove juveniles from adult jails, their numbers have increased over the years. For instance, there were 5,900 juveniles held in adult jails in 1995, a figure that rose to 8,598 in 1999 (Beck, 2000a:6). One reason for this increase is that more jurisdictions are getting tough with youthful offenders and changing laws so that incarceration of younger youths in adult facilities is approved.

Jails Hold Prisoners Wanted by Other States on Detainer Warrants.   Jails must often accommodate prisoners wanted by other jurisdictions in other states. **Detainer warrants** are notices of criminal charges or unserved sentences pending against prisoners. Even though these types of prisoners will eventually be moved to other jurisdictions when authorities from those jurisdictions take them into custody, detainees take up space and time when initially booked and processed.

Jails Hold Probation and Parole Violators.   If probationers or parolees violate one or more of their program conditions, then they are subject to arrest and incarceration until authorities can determine what to do about their program violations. Often, sentencing judges will return probation program violators to the streets after finding that their program violations were not especially serious. Parole boards may release a certain proportion of parolees for similar reasons. Nevertheless, these persons take up valuable jail space while they are confined, even if the periods of confinement are brief.

Jails Hold Contract Prisoners from Other Jurisdictions.   More than a few jails in Texas, Virginia, Oregon, Washington, and other states work out agreements with state and federal prison systems to house a certain portion of their inmate population overflows. Many jurisdictions have serious inmate overcrowding problems; thus, the existence of available jail space to accommodate some of this overflow is appealing to these state and federal jurisdictions. In effect, the state or federal government pays the county jail, wherever it is located, to house a certain number of prisoners, known as contract prisoners, for a specified period. For instance, Hawaii has exported a large number of its state prisoners to Texas jails to be held for periods of one or more years. This transportation of inmates from Hawaii to the mainland has caused the families of many inmates to complain, because they cannot afford to visit incarcerated relatives on a regular basis. Prisoners, however, have no right to determine where they are housed, as long as their accommodations are not cruel and unusual. Furthermore, family members of inmates have no legal rights in this decision making.

Jails Operate Community-Based Programs and Jail Boot Camps.   Increasingly, some of the larger jails are offering some inmates an opportunity to improve their employability by taking vocational and educational training at nearby schools. Some jails operate jail boot camps that give inmates an opportunity to participate in counseling and self-help programs. For example, if certain inmates are alcohol or

---

BOX 6.1

County Jail Cannot Accommodate Federal Prisoners from Penitentiary Overflow

The Webb County, Texas Jail

They call them contract prisoners. They are from other jurisdictions, such as the federal or state prisons, but they are housed in county jails. The state and federal governments pay the county government a fee per prisoner per day to accommodate them. Webb County Jail in Laredo, Texas, is one jail that houses contract prisoners. The federal government pays Webb County about $50 per day for each federal inmate housed there, but jail officials say that the inmate influx is running far ahead of available bed space. "We simply don't have enough beds to accommodate more federal prisoners. We can't even take the state prisoners they're sending us," says Webb County Executive Administrator Carlos Villarreal. Villarreal also adds, "If somebody needs to be incarcerated, then we are not going to let anybody out. There are a lot of things that we can do to deal with the over-inmate housing situation." He says that it would help if police officers file their reports more rapidly with the district attorney's office, which must,

in turn, make a decision as to what they're going to do with the prisoner in custody. Justices of the peace need to assign attorneys or public defenders to inmates more quickly. As a result, some inmates can get out of jail temporarily shortly after they're arrested and while they're awaiting a trial.

During October 2000, the Commission on Jail Standards approved the addition of 170 new beds at the Webb County Jail, but these beds would not become available until December 2000. Villarreal says that one option is to send state prisoners to a private company, Corrections Corporation of America, that operates prisons and jails throughout the United States. Villarreal says, however, "If we have state prisoners, we can't house federal inmates and we can't send the state prisoners to Corrections Corporation of America because it will cost us."

Does the contract prisoner system make sense? Should local jails accommodate state and federal prisoners to ease their own overcrowding problems, or should the state and federal governments simply build more prisons? What do you think?

Source: Adapted from Robert Garcia, "Sheriff's Office Waits on Bed Space Ahead of Prisoners," *Laredo Morning Times,* October 19, 2000:7A.

---

substance abusers, then they are permitted to join local Alcoholics Anonymous or Narcotics Anonymous groups for brief periods.

Jails Hold Mentally Ill Inmates Pending Their Removal to Mental Health Facilities. No one knows for sure how many mentally ill inmates pass through jails annually. The mentally ill pose supervisory and medical problems for jail staff, because often specific illness are undiagnosed and there is inadequate medical assistance available on the jail premises (Gallemore, 2000:67). Furthermore, some of the more serious mentally ill inmates may injure themselves or other inmates by committing acts of violence. No official estimates are available, although some observers have indicated that jails hold as many as 600,000 mentally ill persons annually (Cornelius, 1996). One major reason for larger numbers of mentally ill persons winding up in jails is massive deinstitutionalization of the mentally ill. In 1955, for example, there were 559,000 patients in state mental hospitals. In 1999, there were fewer than 60,000 patients in these same hospitals (Torrey, 1999:12). Theoretically, at least, patients who were discharged were supposed to receive outpatient follow-up care and services in their communities, but such care and services occurred in only a fraction of these cases. In recent years, this problem has received significant media attention as well as government recognition, and growing numbers of mentally ill offenders currently housed in jails and prisons are being discharged to appropriate medical and mental health centers for treatment rather than punishment (Torrey, 1999:13).

A PROFILE OF JAIL INMATES

In 1999, approximately 89 percent of all jail inmates were male, and 41 percent were white and non-Hispanic (Beck, 2000a:6). The number of female arrestees has climbed slowly, from 9.2 percent in 1990 to 11.2 percent in 1999. Figures for different ethnicities and races remained fairly constant during the 1990s. Some observers believe that selective law enforcement and racial profiling have contributed to the disproportionately large number of black jail inmates, about 42 percent of all jail inmates, over the years (Beck, 2000a:6). More than half of all jail inmates were not convicted of any crime. At midyear 1999, about 93 percent of all available jail space in the United States was occupied. Some of the types of occupants in U.S. jails are described below.

Drunks, Vagrants, and Juveniles.   Many sorts of persons are processed through jails daily. In recent years, virtually every large U.S. city has experienced an escalation in the number of homeless persons, or those without any means of support and nowhere to stay except on city streets, in doorways, or in public parks. Police officers may bring loiterers and vagrants to jail and hold them temporarily until they can establish their identities and account for their conduct. These arrests and detentions most often result in releases several hours later. Drunk drivers are taken to jails by police officers every evening, and they are released in the morning after they have sobered up. Some juveniles whose identities are unknown may be held in separate areas of jails for brief periods until they can be reunited with their families or guardians.

Pretrial Detainees and Petty Offenders.   Many jail inmates are held for the purpose of awaiting trial on assorted criminal charges. Other inmates are held for periods of less than a year for petty offense convictions.

Shock Probationers and Prison Inmate Overflow.   Scarce jail space must be found for a certain number of jail inmates known as shock probationers, persons sentenced by judges to long prison terms. The judge's intention, however, is to hold these persons in jails for periods ranging from 30 to 120 days. Then, these persons will be brought back before the judge and resentenced to probation. The judge merely wishes to scare these persons by incarcerating them for brief periods. The belief is that the shock value of short-term incarceration will act as a deterrent to further offending. Despite this noble crime prevention objective, shock probationers take up valuable jail space and are not considered particularly serious. Another contingent of jail inmates, however, consists of more serious offenders from various state and federal jurisdictions. State and federal prisons with overcrowding problems contract with jail authorities to house a certain number of prisoners, thus reducing a certain amount of prison overcrowding. These contract prisoners are usually held for periods of one year or longer in designated jails with sufficient space to accommodate them. They take up scarce jail space on a long-term basis.

Contract prisoners are usually held in special cell blocks or on designated floors of jails. Further, they are supervised more closely than other jail inmates, because they constitute a general inmate class that is considered more dangerous. Contract prisoners cost jails more to supervise, but this cost is offset by state and federal government funds that are allocated to particular counties where jail space is used. In 1999, there were 43,270 contract prisoners being housed in U.S. jails (Camp and Camp, 1999:9).

Work Releasees and the Mentally Ill.   Jail services also include managing a certain portion of offenders on work release programs in those jurisdictions that have them. Jail inmates sentenced to work release programs are low-risk and nonviolent offenders. Some observers question whether these persons should be incarcerated at all compared with those who have been sentenced to standard probation (Dubler, 1998).

Psychologically disturbed inmates may prove bothersome or disruptive to other inmates. These people pose additional problems to jail staff, because in especially small jail facilities, there are no separate facilities for segregating them from serious offenders (Midkiff, 2000:49). Often, local jail facilities are ill-equipped to meet the special needs of mentally ill offenders or those who may be retarded (Cornelius, 1996). In 1999, about a fourth of all U.S. jails had no psychological or health staff (Camp and Camp, 1999:91).

Probationers and Parolees.   A small proportion of jail inmates consists of probationers and parolees who have violated one or more conditions of their programs and are awaiting hearings to determine their dispositions and whether their programs should be revoked. About 3,500 jail inmates were probation or parole violators in 1998 (Pastore and Maguire, 2001:493). About a fourth of these offenders (865) were being held in jails for allegedly committing new crimes.

PRISONS, PRISON HISTORY, AND PRISON CHARACTERISTICS

Prisons Defined

Prisons are state or federally funded and operated institutions that house convicted offenders under continuous custody on a long-term basis. Compared with jails, prisons are completely self-contained and self-sufficient. In 1999, there were 1,366,721 inmates in both federal and state penitentiaries (Beck, 2000b:1). Overall, prisons were operating at 101 percent of their operating capacity. The Federal Bureau of Prisons was operating at 132 percent of its operating capacity, whereas New Jersey and Wisconsin were operating at 143 percent and 139 percent, respectively, of their operating capacities (Beck, 2000b:8). Erving Goffman (1961) has described a prison as a **total institution**, because it is an environmental reality of absolute dominance over prisoners' lives. These self-contained facilities have recreational yards, workout rooms, auditoriums for viewing feature films, and small stores for purchases of toiletries and other goods.

The Development and Growth of U.S. Prisons.   Early English and Scottish penal methods were very influential on the subsequent growth and development of U.S.

prisons (American Correctional Association, 1983; Hughes, 1987). Most English and Scottish prisons that existed to house criminals and others often had operational policies that were influenced by economic or mercantile interests as well as those of the church. **John Howard** (1726–1790), an influential English prison reformer, criticized the manner and circumstances under which prisoners were administered and housed. Howard had been a county squire and later, in 1773, the sheriff of Bedfordshire. He conducted regular inspections of gaol facilities and found that prisoners were routinely exploited by gaolers, because gaolers had no regular income other than that extracted from prisoners through their labor. Howard visited other countries to inspect their prison systems. He was impressed with the Maison de Force (House of Enforcement) of Ghent, where prisoners were treated humanely. They were clothed, lodged separately from others during evening hours, and well fed. He thought that these ideas could be used as models for British prisons and gaols, and succeeded in convincing British authorities that certain reforms should be undertaken. In 1779, the Penitentiary Act was passed.

The Penitentiary Act provided that new facilities, in which prisoners could work productively at hard labor rather than suffer the usual punishment of **banishment**, be created. Prisoners were to be well fed, clothed, and housed in isolated, sanitary cells. They were to be given opportunities to learn useful skills and trades. Fees for their maintenance were abolished, rigorous inspections were conducted regularly, and balanced diets and improved hygiene were to be strictly observed. Howard believed that prisoners should be given a hearty work regimen. Through hard work, prisoners would realize the seriousness and consequences of their crimes; thus, work was a type of penance. A new word, *penitentiary,* was originated and was synonymous with reform and punishment. Currently, penitentiaries in the United States are regarded as punishment-centered rather than reform-oriented, because significant philosophical shifts have occurred in American corrections (American Correctional Association, 1983:15).

State Prisons.   The first state prison was established in Simsbury, Connecticut, in 1773. This prison was actually an underground copper mine that was converted into a confinement facility for convicted felons. It was eventually made into a permanent prison in 1790. Prisoners were shackled about the ankles, worked long hours, and received particularly harsh sentences for minor offenses. Burglary and counterfeiting were punishable in Simsbury by imprisonment not exceeding ten years, whereas a second offense meant life imprisonment (American Correctional Association, 1983:26–27).

Actually, the Walnut Street Jail was the first true U.S. prison that attempted to correct offenders. Compared with the Simsbury, Connecticut, underground prison, a strictly punishment-centered facility, the Walnut Street Jail operated according to rehabilitation model. A signer of the Declaration of Independence, Dr. Benjamin Rush (1745–1813) was both a physician and a humanitarian. He believed that punishment should reform offenders and prevent them from committing future crimes. He also believed that they should be removed temporarily from society until they became remorseful. Rush believed that prisoners should exercise regularly and eat wholesome foods; thus, he encouraged prisoners to grow gardens where they could produce their own goods. Prisoner-produced goods were so successful at one point that produce and other materials manufactured or grown by inmates were marketed to the general public. Therefore, Rush pioneered the first prison industry, whereby prisoners could market goods for profit and use some of this income to defray prison operating expenses. Some of Rush's ideas were incorporated into the operation of the Walnut Street Jail, and eventually, the pattern of discipline and offender treatment practiced there became known popularly as the **Pennsylvania System**. The Walnut Street Jail Pennsylvania System became a model used by many other jurisdictions (American Correctional Association, 1983:31).

Auburn State Penitentiary.   New York correctional authorities developed a new type of prison in 1816, the **Auburn State Penitentiary**, designed according to **tiers**, with inmates housed on several different levels. The **tier system** became a common feature of subsequent U.S. prison construction, and today, most prisons are architecturally structured according to tiers. The term *penitentiary* is used to designate an institution that not only segregates offenders from society but also from each other. The original connotation of penitentiary was a place where prisoners could think, reflect, and repent of their misdeeds and possibly undergo reformation (Spiegel and Spiegel, 1998). Today, the words *prison* and *penitentiary* are used interchangeably, because virtually every prison has facilities for isolating prisoners from one another according to various levels of custody and control. Thus, each state has devised different names for facilities designed to house its most dangerous offenders. Examples are Kentucky State Penitentiary, California State Prison at San Quentin, New Jersey State Prison, North Dakota Penitentiary, and Maine State Prison.

At the Auburn State Penitentiary, prisoners were housed in solitary cells during evening hours. This practice was the beginning of what is now known as **solitary confinement**. Another innovation at Auburn was that inmates were allowed to work together and eat their meals with one another during daylight hours, a practice known as the **congregate system** (American Correctional Association, 1983). The Auburn State Penitentiary also provided for divisions among prisoners according to the nature of their offenses. The different tiers conveniently housed inmates in different offense categories, with more serious offenders housed on one tier and less serious offenders on another. Certain tiers were reserved for the most unruly offenders who could not conform their conduct to prison policies. The most dangerous inmates were kept in solitary confinement as punishment for periods ranging from a few days to a few months, depending on the prison rule violated. Therefore, the Auburn State Penitentiary is significant historically because it provided for the minimum-, medium-, and maximum-security designations by which modern penitentiaries are known.

Prisoners were also provided with different uniforms to set them apart from one another. The stereotypical striped uniform of prison inmates, a novelty at Auburn, was widely copied as well. Over half of all state prisons patterned their structures after the Auburn system during the next half century, including the style of prison dress and manner of separating offenders according to their crime seriousness (American Correctional Association, 1983:49–54). Striped prison uniforms for prisoners continued until the 1950s.

Other Prison Developments.   Between 1816 and 1900, many other state prisons were established. One of the first successful prisons was constructed in Cherry Hill, Pennsylvania, in the early 1830s. This prison was considered successful because it was the first to offer a continuing internal program of treatment and other forms of assistance to inmates (Johnston, 1973). The first state penitentiary in Ohio was opened in Columbus in 1834. The largest state prison of that time was established in

Jackson, Michigan, in 1839. By 1999, this State Prison of Southern Michigan had been torn down and rebuilt; it now houses 615 male inmates. Another large state prison was built in Parchman, Mississippi, in 1900. In 1999, it housed 4,836 inmates. Louisiana claims one of the largest and oldest state prisons. Built in 1866 with a capacity of 4,747 inmates, by 1999 the Louisiana State Penitentiary in Angola housed 5,108 males (American Correctional Association, 2000).

The American Correctional Association and Elmira Reformatory. In 1870, the **American Correctional Association (ACA)** was established, and Rutherford B. Hayes, a future U.S. president, was selected to head that organization. The goals of the ACA were to formulate a national correctional philosophy, to develop sound correctional policies and standards, to offer expertise to all interested jurisdictions in the design and operation of correctional facilities, and to assist in the training of correctional officers. The ACA was originally called the National Prison Association, then the American Prison Association, and finally and more generally, the American Correctional Association.

The United States was entering a new era of correctional reform with the establishment of the ACA. Six years later, in 1876, the Elmira State Reformatory in Elmira, New York, was constructed. The **Elmira Reformatory** experimented with certain new rehabilitative philosophies espoused by various penologists, including its first superintendent, Zebulon Brockway (1827–1920). Brockway was critical of the harsh methods employed by the establishments he headed, and he envisioned better and more effective treatments for prisoners. Elmira was considered an example of the new penology and used the latest scientific information in its correctional methods. **Captain Alexander Maconochie** and **Sir Walter Crofton**, penologists from Scotland and Ireland, respectively, were instrumental in bringing about changes in European correctional methods in the early 1870s. These men influenced U.S. corrections by introducing the **mark system**, in which prisoners could accumulate **tickets-of-leave** that would enable them to be released early from their lengthy incarcerative sentences. Through hard work and industry, prisoners could shorten their original sentences, which earlier had to be served in their entirety (American Correctional Association, 1983:67).

Elmira was truly a reformatory and used a military model comparable to contemporary boot camps. Prisoners performed useful labor and participated in educational or vocational activities, and their productivity and good conduct could earn them shorter sentences. Elmira inmates were trained in close-order drill, wore military uniforms, and paraded about with wooden rifles. Authorities regarded these practices as a way of instilling discipline in inmates and reforming them. Historians credit Elmira Reformatory with individualizing prisoner treatment and with the use of indeterminate sentencing directly suited for parole actions. The reformatory was subsequently widely imitated by other state prison systems (Rafter, 1997).

FUNCTIONS OF PRISONS

The functions served by prisons are closely connected with the overall goals of corrections. Broadly stated, correctional goals include deterrence, rehabilitation, societal protection, offender reintegration, just-deserts, justice and due process, and retribution or punishment. Some goals of prisons are listed and described next.

Prisons Provide Societal Protection.   Locking up dangerous offenders or those who are persistent nonviolent offenders means that society will be protected from them for variable time periods. It is not possible at present to lock up all offenders who deserve to be incarcerated. Space limitations are such that at least four or five times the number of existing prisons would be required to incarcerate all convicted felons and misdemeanants. Thus, the criminal justice system attempts to incarcerate those most in need of incarceration.

Prisons Punish Offenders.   Restricting one's freedoms, confining inmates in cells, and obligating inmates to follow rigid behavioral codes while confined is regarded as punishment for criminal conduct. Incarceration is a punishment compared with the greater freedoms enjoyed by probationers and parolees.

Prisons Rehabilitate Offenders.   Few criminal justice scholars accept the idea that prisons rehabilitate inmates. Little support exists for the view that imprisonment does much of a rehabilitative nature for anyone confined. Nevertheless, many prisons have vocational and educational programs, psychological counselors, and an array of services available to inmates so that they might improve their skills, education, and self-concept (American Correctional Association, 2000). Prisons also have libraries for inmate self-improvement. More often than not, prisons also socialize inmates in adverse ways, so that they might emerge from prisons as better criminals who have learned ways of avoiding detection when committing future crimes.

Prisons Reintegrate Offenders.   It might be argued that moving offenders from higher security levels, where they are more closely supervised, to lower security levels, where they are less closely supervised, helps them understand that conformity with institutional rules is rewarded. As prisoners near their release dates, they may be permitted unescorted leaves, known as furloughs, or work/study release, whereby they may participate in work or educational programs and visit with their families during the week or on weekends. These experiences are considered reintegrative. Most prisons have such programs, but they are presumably aimed at certain offenders who are believed to no longer pose a threat to society. Occasionally, officials wrongly estimate the nondangerousness of certain furloughees and work releasees. In any case, the intent of reintegrative prison programs is to provide those wanting such programs the opportunity of having them. At least some inmates derive value from such programs, although some observers believe that the costs of operating them are far outweighed by the lack of rehabilitation and reintegration that actually occurs.

INMATE CLASSIFICATION SYSTEMS

Religious movements are credited with establishing early prisoner classification systems in the eighteenth century (American Correctional Association, 1983:194). The Walnut Street Jail in 1790 in Philadelphia attempted to segregate prisoners according to age, gender, and offense seriousness. Subsequent efforts were made by penal authorities to classify and separate inmates according to various criteria in many state and federal prison facilities, but adequate classification schemes for prisoners have yet to be devised (California Department of Corrections, 1998). **Inmate classification** schemes are based largely on psychological, behavioral, and sociodemo-

BOX 6.2   *Personality Highlight*

Efran R. Rangel Jr.
Formerly with Webb County Sheriff's Office; U.S. Border Patrol; United South Middle School teacher

Statistics. A.A. (law enforcement), Laredo Junior College; B.A. (criminal justice, political science), Laredo State University; M.A. (criminal justice), Texas A&M International University

Background and Work Experience. I grew up in a very humble, yet loving and caring, environment. Both my parents encouraged me and my two sisters to excel in our education. My father taught me to work hard at anything I do, including ranch work, carpentry, welding, auto mechanics, and any other job having to do with manual labor. My mother, however, inspired me to pursue my college education. She managed to get her education degree while working as a beautician and raising a family of three. As a young boy, I was taken to Laredo State University while my mother took courses. Ironically, I graduated from that same university 20 years later with my criminal justice degree.

My reasons for entering law enforcement were attributed to my first goal of becoming an attorney. I was unaware of how rewarding and challenging it is to be a police officer, deputy, or border patrol agent. One can encounter exciting situations that involve dealing with people daily. That, I think, is the most rewarding aspect of law enforcement: the close interaction with the people within your community. Having the power to help others is just as rewarding.

I am currently employed as an eighth-grade teacher at United South Middle School in Laredo, Texas. Prior to this position, I was employed as a Border Patrol agent with the U.S. government for a brief time. As a part of my internship during my undergraduate studies, I worked on a volunteer basis with the Webb County Sheriff's Office. One of our most memorable days on the job was the day we went to serve a warrant on a man who had been previously arrested for drug trafficking. He lived in an area of Laredo near the Rio Grande River known for its drug smuggling. Because I was not able to carry a weapon yet, the officer with whom I was riding gave me his bulletproof vest and a flashlight. He simply said, "Back me up and cover the rear entrance of the shabby dwelling." I asked, "What do I do?" He answered, "If he comes your way, just shine the light on him, and if he shoots at you, just hit the ground." Needless to say, I was scared out of my mind. It was dark and cold. When the officer knocked on the door, the offender answered and was taken into custody without any incident. The officer later confessed that he knew that the offender would not be any trouble and simply wanted to see if I had the courage to stand there in the dark, alone, and be willing to back him up if necessary. After proving myself in that manner, we later handled many calls with an ongoing trust between us.

Advice to Students. My advice to students is to get informed about the field you are contemplating. Questions about job duties, pay, and training requirements should be answered before you decide to enter any area in law enforcement. You can find out so much by just taking time to talk to a police officer, probation officer, or any law enforcement officer. I encourage anyone to simply begin their classes and by just listening to your instructors, a huge curiosity will be created in this great field. Go for it and good luck!

graphic criteria. The use of psychological characteristics as predictors of risk or dangerousness and subsequent custody assignments for prisoners was stimulated by research during the 1910 to 1920 period (American Correctional Association, 1983:196).

No single scheme for classifying offenders is foolproof, although several instruments have been used more frequently than others for inmate classification and placement. The Megargee Inmate Typology presumes to measure inmate adjustment to prison life (Megargee and Carbonell, 1985). Several items were selected from the Minnesota Multiphasic Personality Inventory, a psychological assessment device, to define ten prisoner types and to predict an inmate's inclination to violate prison rules or act aggressively against others. The Megargee Inmate Typology, a psychological tool, has been adopted by various state prison systems for purposes of classifying prisoners into different custody levels. The predictive use of this instrument is questionable, however. One problem Megargee himself detected was that prisoner classification types based on his index scores change drastically during a one-year period. For some observers, this finding has caused serious questions about the reliability of Megargee's scale. For other observers, however, inmate score changes on Megargee's scale indicate behavioral change, possibly improvement. Thus, reclassifications are conducted of most prison inmates at regular intervals to chart their behavioral progress.

Besides Megargee, other professionals have devised useful inmate classification criteria but have not been particularly fruitful. For example, Norman Holt (1996) found that inmate misconduct is correlated with being affiliated with street gangs. Other criteria have been used in different research throughout each of the state and federal systems with varying results (Austin and Alexander, 1996; Owens, Will, and Camp, 1997; U.S. Sentencing Commission, 1994). One's prior record of offending, age, unemployment history, and race have functioned as both legal and extralegal criteria and have been associated with program failures or successes under different research conditions. The present generation of objective prison classification systems must be capable of more than simple risk assessment. Systems must be able to identify the needs of an increasingly diverse population with changing characteristics to provide appropriate programs, services, and treatment opportunities, and prepare offenders for reentry into their communities. The focus of risk assessment development is currently about identifying high-risk, disruptive offenders so as to foster more effective correctional planning and monitoring, as well as promoting safer environments for staff and inmates (Brown, 2000:138).

One thing is certain about risk instruments and inmate classifications resulting from applications of these instruments: how prison inmates are initially classified and housed will directly influence their parole chances (Gottfredson and Gottfredson, 1988, 1990; Hoffman, 1983). Inmates classified as maximum security may not deserve this classification, because it means that the inmate is considered dangerous. Inmate opportunities for personal development and rehabilitation are limited by these classifications. Inmates who are classified as minimum security, however, have a wide variety of prison benefits and programs. They are neither supervised as closely nor considered dangerous. When minimum-security inmates face parole boards, their custody levels are assets. When maximum-security inmates face parole boards, their classification is a liability. An example of a prison risk assessment instrument to determine an inmate's placement or security level, the one used by the Alaska Department of Corrections, is illustrated in Figure 6.1.

All prisons in the United States have classifications that differentiate between prisoners and cause them to be placed under various levels of custody or security. A main purpose for the initial inmate classification is to identify those likely to engage in assaultive or aggressive disciplinary infractions. Prisoners are eventually channeled into one of several fixed custody levels known as minimum-security, medium-security, and maximum-security.

Minimum-Security Classification. **Minimum-security prisons** are facilities designed to house low-risk, nonviolent first-offenders. These institutions are also established to accommodate those serving short-term sentences. Sometimes, minimum-security institutions function as intermediate housing for those prisoners leaving more heavily monitored facilities on their way toward parole or eventual freedom. Minimum-security housing often has a dormitory-like quality, with grounds and physical plants resembling a university campus rather than a prison. Those assigned to minimum-security facilities are trusted to comply with whatever rules are in force.

Administrators place greater trust in inmates in minimum-security institutions, and these sites are believed to be most likely to promote greater self-confidence and self-esteem among prisoners. The rehabilitative value of minimum-security inmates is high. Also, family visits are less restricted. The emphasis of minimum-security classification is definitely on prisoner reintegration into society.

Medium-Security Classification. Sixty percent of all state and federal prisons in the United States are minimum- and **medium-security prisons**. The American Correctional Association (2000) says that a majority of state and federal prison facilities are designed to accommodate minimum- and medium-security inmates. As of 1999, of all U.S. penitentiaries, all but the one in Atlanta, Georgia, were classified as medium security (American Correctional Association, 2000). Medium-security facilities at both state and federal levels offer inmates opportunities for work release, furloughs, and other types of programs.

Maximum-Security Classification. Forty percent of all U.S. prisons are **maximum-security prisons**. Ordinarily, those sentenced to serve time in maximum-security facilities are considered among the most dangerous, high-risk offenders. Maximum-security prisons are characterized by many stringent rules and restrictions, and inmates are isolated from one another for long periods in single-cell accommodations. Closed-circuit television monitors often permit correctional officers to observe prisoners in their cells or in work areas which are limited. Visitation privileges are minimal. Most often, no efforts are made by officials to rehabilitate inmates.

An example of one of the most memorable maximum-security penitentiaries ever constructed was the federal prison at Alcatraz in San Francisco Bay. Alcatraz was constructed in 1934 but closed in 1963 because of poor sanitation and the great expense of prisoner maintenance. During the period Alcatraz was operated, Alcatraz

STATE OF ALASKA
DEPARTMENT OF CORRECTIONS

SECURITY DESIGNATION FORM FOR LONG-TERM SENTENCED PRISONERS

(1) _____   (3) _____
     Institution   Designation Staff Member

(2) _____   (4) _____
     Date   Supt. Signature (exception case only)

SECTION A   IDENTIFYING DATA

(1) _____
     Prisoner's Name   Last   First   Middle Initial

(2) _____
     Date of Birth

(3) Type of Case: Regular _____ Exception _____ (4) OBSCIS _____

(5) Separatees: _____
_____
_____

SECTION B   SECURITY SCORING

1. Type of Detainer:

   0 = None   3 = Class C Felony   7 = Unclassified or
   1 = Misdemeanor   5 = Class B Felony   Class A Felony   [ ] 1

2. Severity of Current Offense:

   1 = Misdemeanor   3 = Class C Felony   7 = Unclassified or
                       5 = Class B Felony   Class A Felony   [ ] 2

3. Time to Firm Release Date:

   0 = 0–12 months   3 = 60–83 months
   1 = 13–59 months   5 = 84+ months   _____   [ ] 3
                                             Firm Release Date

FIGURE 6.1 Alaska long-term prisoner classification form. (Courtesy of the Alaska Department of Corrections, 2000.)

4. Type of Prior Convictions:

   0 = None   1 = Misdemeanor   3 = Felony   [ ] 4

5. History of Escapes or Attempted Escapes:

	None	+15 Years	10-15 Years	5-10 Years	-5 Years	
Minor	0	1	1	2	3	
Serious	0	4	5	6	7	[ ] 5

6. History of Violent Behavior:

	None	+15 Years	10-15 Years	5-10 Years	-5 Years	
Minor	0	1	1	2	3	
Serious	0	4	5	6	7	[ ] 6

7. SECURITY TOTAL   [ ] 7

8. Security Level:

   Minimum = 0-6 points   Medium = 7-13 points   Maximum = 14-36 points

9. Designated Custody Level:

Community/Minimum	Medium	Close	Maximum
0-6	7-13	14-25	26-36

10. Designation Staff Comments:

_____

_____

_____

_____

SECTION C   MANAGEMENT CONSIDERATION

1. Release Plans	5. Special Treatment	9. Residence
2. Medical	6. Ethnic/Cultural	10. Restitution Center
3. Psychiatric	Consideration	11. Contract Misdemeanant
4. Education	7. Overcrowding	Housing
	8. Judicial Recommendation	

held over 1,500 prisoners, including Al Capone and Robert "Birdman" Stroud. In maximum-security prisons, inmate isolation and control are stressed, and close monitoring by guards either directly or through closed-circuit television reduces prisoner misconduct significantly.

Maxi-Maxi, Admin Max, and Supermax Prisons. Prisons such as the federal penitentiary at Marion, Illinois, are considered maxi-maxi prisons. The Marion facility accommodated only 568 inmates in 1999, and those incarcerated there are considered the very worst prisoners (American Correctional Association, 2000). Marion inmates are the most violence-prone prisoners, are inclined to escape whenever the opportunity arises, and are extremely dangerous. In one instance, two correctional officers were killed by prisoners in the Control Unit. When the riot was contained, Marion officials ordered a **lockdown**, whereby all prisoners were placed in solitary confinement and severe restrictions were imposed. For Marion inmates, lockdown meant confinement in isolation for 23½ hours per day, with a half hour for exercise. Privileges were extremely limited. Prisons with the highest levels of security and inmate supervision are designated as **maxi-maxi prisons**. In Colorado, the U.S. Bureau of Prisons operates the United States Penitentiary at Florence. This facility, designated as an **admin max**, houses only inmates with extensive criminal histories (American Correctional Association, 2000:648). Sometimes these prisons are known as **supermax** facilities. It is believed that maxi-maxi, admin max, and supermax all refer to essentially the same types of facilities with equivalent levels of the highest supervision and custody for the most dangerous offenders (Shepperd, Geiger, and Welborn, 1996).

An example of a supermax facility is Illinois's new Closed Maximum Security Correctional Center in Tamms, designed to house 520 of the state's most violent offenders. The closed maximum-security unit is the most secure. It is podular, with each pod containing 60 cells, ten in each of six cellblocks. The cellblocks are arranged around a control station strategically positioned with visual access to all cells. Correctional officers assigned to each pod carry weapons and have access to tear gas. The facility supports the use of deadly force against inmates should it become necessary. Cell furniture includes a concrete sleeping platform with a pad, a wall-mounted writing surface and shelf, a stainless steel "combi unit" (water closet, lavatory, and drinking fountain), and a small, stainless steel mirror. Strategically placed security vestibules provide additional circulation control and allow portions of the facility to be sealed off at will. Each bank of pods has an exterior evacuation area surrounded by a chain-link fence and capped with razor wire (Shepperd, Geiger, and Welborn, 1996).

It is apparent that there are many types of prisons, ranging from minimum-security, honor farm–type facilities to maxi-maxi penitentiaries. A low degree of violence is associated with minimum-security facilities because inmates there tend to be less dangerous and pose the least risk to the safety of correctional officers and others. Each prison setting, with its peculiar inmate profile, means that wardens or superintendents are presented with different kinds of problems to resolve.

The Importance of Classification for Prisoners.   Whether prisoners realize it or not, their classification when they enter prison has substantial influence on their early-release eligibility. Other factors—such as institutional conduct, not getting into fights with other inmates, avoiding disruptive behavior, controlling anger, participating in self-help programs, and enrolling in counseling and other available prison services—combine to influence the parole board when it comes time to decide whether a particular inmate should be released.

Paroling authorities consider it significant, for instance, if an inmate enters prison and is placed in maximum-security or medium-security custody and if that same inmate eventually works his or her way down to minimum-security custody; the inmate has earned a level-of-custody reduction through good behavior. Parole boards are not going to grant parole easily to an inmate who has been placed in maximum-security custody and has remained there for several years. Furthermore, an inmate's advance to a higher custody level, such as moving from minimum security to medium security, is evidence of poor conduct. The inmate may have a bad attitude, reject authority or any type of helpful intervention, or engage in disruptive behavior. Thus, it is definitely to an inmate's advantage to do the right types of things that will earn level-of-custody reductions.

In Nevada, for instance, a parole-eligible inmate faced the parole board. He was a young man in his mid-twenties. His record indicated that he lacked a high school education. He had been unemployed and on drugs at the time of his arrest for a property offense. He had served two years of a six-year term. The parole board asked him, "Why should we release you now? Have you worked on your GED? Have you done anything to correct your drug problem?" The inmate, condemning himself to further confinement, said, "No, I haven't done any of that. I don't like education. I hate teachers. I don't think I've got a drug problem. I've been in this place for a few years and I don't do drugs. I'm just not interested in those different things they say we can get involved in. I just hate authority." The Nevada Parole Board rejected his parole application. In this case, his own attitude about self-improvement was sufficient to cause the parole board to turn down his early-release request. Perhaps the parole board may have granted him early release on that occasion had he obtained a GED or participated in drug therapy and counseling.

Many self-help options are available to most prisoners in both the state and federal systems. They have to assist in their own defense, however; they cannot wait for a parole board to grant them early release. They can do things to speed up the early-release process, such as earning a lower level of custody by following institutional rules and not causing trouble (Gido, 1998).

A PROFILE OF PRISONERS IN U.S. PRISONS

Considerable diversity exists among prisoners in state and federal institutions, including the nature and seriousness of their conviction offenses, age, and psychological or medical problems. To cope more effectively with meeting the needs of such diverse offenders, prisons have established different confinement facilities and levels of custody, depending on how each prisoner is classified. Between 1980 and 1999, a majority of states more than quadrupled their number of sentenced prisoners (Beck, 2000b:2). Overall, state and federal prisoner populations increased by 473 percent between 1980 and 1999. Generally, the average increase in the federal and state prison inmate population was about 6 percent per year. This information is shown in Table 6.1.

A survey of state prison inmates was conducted in 1999 by the **Bureau of Justice Statistics** and compared with 1990 figures. The percentage of white prison inmates declined from 35.6 percent in 1990 to 33 percent in 1999. The percentage of black inmates increased from 44.5 percent in 1990 to 45.7 percent in 1999. Asian, Native American, and Pacific Islander inmates increased from 2.5 percent in 1990 to 3.4 percent in 1999. There was little change in the percentage of Hispanic inmates from 1990 to 1999, with about 17.9 percent represented in 1999.

TABLE 6.1 Change in the State and Federal Prison Populations, 1980–1999

Year	No. of Inmates	Annual Percent Change	Total Percent Change Since 1980
1980	329,821	—	—
1981	369,930	12.2%	12.2%
1982	413,606	11.9	25.5
1983	436,855	5.6	32.5
1984	482,002	5.8	40.1
1985	502,752	8.8	52.4
1986	546,378	8.5	65.4
1987	585,292	7.3	77.5
1988	631,990	8.0	91.6
1989	712,967	12.8	116.2
1990	773,124	8.4	134.4
1991	824,133	6.6	149.9
1992	883,593	7.2	167.9
1993	932,074	5.4	182.6
1994	1,016,691	9.0	208.2
1995	1,585,586	5.6	380.7
1996	1,646,020	3.8	399.0
1997	1,743,643	5.9	428.6
1998	1,816,931	4.2	450.8
1999	1,890,837	4.1	473.2

Source: Allen J. Beck, *Prisoners in 1999* (Washington, DC: U.S. Department of Justice, Bureau of Justice Statistics, 2000), 1.

In 1999, about 7.5 percent of all state and federal prisoners were women (Beck, 2000b:5). Women were incarcerated at increasing rates during the 1990s. For instance, during 1999 the percentage of female inmates increased by 4.4 percent, outpacing male incarcerations, which rose by 3.3 percent. Between 1990 and 1999, the female inmate population doubled. During the 1990s, the average growth of state and federal female inmates was 8.3 percent, considerably larger than the 6.4 percent increase in male state and federal inmates (Beck, 2000b:5). The more rapid rise in female incarceration is attributable to more drug-related arrests and convictions among women than among men. For instance, there was an 18 percent rise in the state and federal inmate population between 1990 and 1999 for drug convictions, whereas there was a 36 percent rise in the number of female commitments in state and federal facilities for the same types of offenses. The largest gains for male commitments were for violent crimes (56 percent increase between 1990 and 1999). Female commitments for violent crimes increased by 27 percent during the same period (Beck, 2000b:10).

Table 6.2 shows the distribution of state and federal prisoners according to their respective jurisdictions for 1999, with contrasting information provided from 1998. Table 6.3 shows a distribution of sentenced prisoners by offense according to their gender, race, and ethnicity. Table 6.4 shows the number of sentenced prisoners under state or federal jurisdiction, by gender, race, and age, for 1999.

TABLE 6.2 Prisoners under the Jurisdiction of State and Federal Correctional Authorities, by Region and Jurisdiction, Year End 1998 and 1999

Region and Jurisdiction	Total			Sentenced to More Than 1 Year			Incarceration Rate, 1999[a]
	Advance 1999	1998	Percent change, 1998–99	Advance 1999	1998	Percent change, 1998–99	
U.S. total	1,366,721	1,300,573	3.4%	1,305,393	1,245,402	3.2%	476
Federal	135,246	123,041	9.9	114,275	103,682	10.2	42
State	1,231,475	1,177,532	2.7	1,191,118	1,141,720	2.5	434
Northeast	179,758	175,681	1.5%	171,234	167,376	1.5%	330
Connecticut[b]	18,639	17,605	5.9	13,032	12,193	6.9	397
Maine	1,716	1,691	1.5	1,663	1,641	1.3	133
Massachusetts[c]	11,356	11,799	–3.8	10,282	10,744	–4.3	266
New Hampshire	2,257	2,169	4.1	2,257	2,169	4.1	187
New Jersey[d]	31,493	31,121	1.2	31,493	31,121	1.2	384
New York[e]	73,233	70,001	2.6	72,896	70,001	2.1	400
Pennsylvania	36,525	36,377	0.4	36,525	36,373	0.4	305
Rhode Island[b]	3,003	3,445	–12.8	1,908	2,175	–12.3	193
Vermont[b]	1,536	1,473	4.3	1,178	959	22.8	198
Midwest	232,905	228,116	2.1%	231,961	227,270	2.1%	367
Illinois[d,f]	44,660	43,051	3.7	44,660	43,051	3.7	368
Indiana	19,309	19,197	0.6	19,260	19,016	1.3	324
Iowa[d,f]	3,232	7,394	–2.2	7,232	7,394	–2.2	252
Kansas[d]	8,567	8,183	4.7	8,567	8,183	4.7	321
Michigan[f]	46,617	45,879	1.6	46,617	45,879	1.6	472
Minnesota	5,969	5,572	7.1	5,955	5,557	7.2	125
Missouri	26,155	24,974	4.7	26,133	24,950	4.7	477
Nebraska	3,688	3,676	0.3	3,632	3,588	1.2	217
North Dakota	943	915	3.1	866	834	3.8	137
Ohio[d]	46,842	48,450	–3.3	46,842	48,450	–3.3	417
South Dakota	2,506	2,422	3.5	2,498	2,417	3.4	339
Wisconsin	20,417	18,403	10.9	19,699	17,951	9.7	375
South	551,284	512,271	3.7%	528,377	493,488	3.4%	543
Alabama	24,658	22,676	8.7	24,109	22,214	8.5	549
Arkansas	11,415	10,638	7.3	11,336	10,561	7.3	443
Delaware[b]	6,983	5,558	—	3,730	3,211	—	493
Dist. of Columbia[b]	8,652	9,829	–12.0	6,730	8,144	–17.4	1,314
Florida[f]	69,596	67,224	3.5	69,594	67,193	3.6	456
Georgia[f]	42,091	39,262	7.2	42,008	38,758	8.4	532
Kentucky	15,317	14,987	2.2	15,317	14,987	2.2	385
Louisiana	34,066	32,228	5.7	34,066	32,228	5.7	776
Maryland	23,095	22,572	2.3	22,184	21,540	3.0	427
Mississippi	18,247	16,678	9.4	17,410	15,855	9.8	626
North Carolina	31,086	31,961	–2.7	26,635	27,244	–2.2	345
Oklahoma[d]	22,393	20,892	7.2	22,393	20,892	7.2	662

(continued)

TABLE 6.2 *(continued)*

Region and Jurisdiction	Total			Sentenced to More Than 1 Year			Incarceration Rate, 1999[a]
	Advance 1999	1998	Percent change, 1998–99	Advance 1999	1998	Percent change, 1998–99	
South Carolina	22,008	21,764	1.1	21,228	20,910	1.5	543
Tennessee[d,e]	22,502	17,738	4.5	22,502	17,738	4.5	408
Texas[e]	163,190	144,510	1.9	154,865	139,863	0.7	762
Virginia	32,453	30,276	7.2	30,738	28,672	7.2	447
West Virginia	3,532	3,478	1.6	3,532	3,478	1.6	196
West	267,528	261,464	1.9%	259,546	253,586	2.0%	421
Alaska[b]	3,949	4,097	–3.6	2,325	2,541	–8.5	374
Arizona[f]	25,986	25,515	1.8	23,944	23,500	1.9	495
California	163,067	161,904	0.7	160,517	159,201	0.8	481
Colorado	15,670	14,312	9.5	15,670	14,312	9.5	383
Hawaii[b]	4,903	4,924	–0.4	3,817	3,670	4.0	320
Idaho[e]	4,842	4,083	12.9	4,842	4,083	12.9	385
Montana	2,954	2,734	8.0	2,954	2,734	8.0	335
Nevada	9,494	9,651	–1.6	9,413	9,651	–2.5	509
New Mexico	5,124	5,078	0.9	4,730	4,825	–2.0	270
Oregon	9,810	8,981	9.2	9,792	8,935	9.6	293
Utah[e]	5,426	4,453	4.2	5,271	4,402	4.8	245
Washington	14,590	14,161	3.0	14,558	14,161	2.8	251
Wyoming	1,713	1,571	9.0	1,713	1,571	9.0	355

—Not calculated.

[a]The number of prisoners with sentences of more than 1 year per 100,000 U.S. residents.

[b]Prisons and jails form one integrated system. Data include total jail and prison population.

[c]The incarceration rate includes an estimated 6,200 inmates sentenced to more than 1 year but held in local jails or houses of corrections.

[d]"Sentenced to more than 1 year" includes some inmates "sentenced to 1 year or less."

[e]Reporting changed in 1999; percents calculated on counts adjusted for comparable reporting.

[f]Population figures are based on custody counts.

Source: Allen J. Beck, *Prisoners in 1999* (Washington, DC: U.S. Department of Justice, 2000), 3.

TABLE 6.3 **Estimated Number of Sentenced Prisoners under State Jurisdiction, by Offense, Gender, Race, and Hispanic Origin, 1998**

Offenses	All	Male	Female	White	Black	Hispanic
Total	1,141,700	1,071,400	70,300	380,400	531,100	194,000
Violent offenses	545,200	525,100	20,100	180,300	357,700	87,600
Murder[a]	134,600	128,500	6,100	42,400	67,100	21,500
Manslaughter	17,600	15,800	1,800	6,200	7,100	3,400
Rape	29,600	29,300	300	13,500	12,100	2,400
Other sexual assault	71,200	70,500	700	41,400	17,500	9,300

Offenses	All	Male	Female	White	Black	Hispanic
Robbery	159,600	154,600	5,000	33,000	96,700	25,400
Assault	109,500	104,500	5,000	33,800	48,800	22,000
Other violent	23,100	21,800	1,300	10,000	8,400	3,800
Property offenses	242,900	224,500	18,500	104,200	97,700	34,000
Burglary	118,000	114,400	3,600	49,900	48,100	16,600
Larceny	45,500	39,600	5,900	17,200	20,500	6,100
Motor vehicle theft	20,100	19,400	800	8,000	7,300	4,400
Fraud	30,200	23,300	6,900	15,700	11,100	2,800
Other property	29,100	27,800	1,300	13,300	10,700	4,100
Drug offenses	236,800	212,900	23,900	46,300	134,800	51,700
Public-order offenses[b]	113,900	106,500	7,500	49,200	39,400	20,100
Other/unspecified[c]	2,800	2,500	200	400	1,500	700

Note: Data are for inmates with a sentence of more than 1 year under the jurisdiction of state correctional authorities. The number of inmates by offense were estimated using 1997 Survey of Inmates in State Correctional Facilities and rounded to the nearest 100.

[a]Includes nonnegligent manslaughter.

[b]Includes weapons, drunk driving, court offenses, commercialized vice, morals and decency charges, liquor law violations, and other public-order offenses.

[c]Includes juvenile offenses and unspecified felonies.

Source: Allen J. Beck, *Prisoners in 1999* (Washington, DC: U.S. Department of Justice, 2000), 3.

TABLE 6.4 Number of Sentenced Prisoners under State or Federal Jurisdiction, by Gender, Race, Hispanic Origin, and Age, 1999

	Number of Sentenced Prisoners							
	Males				Females			
Age	Total[a]	White[b]	Black[b]	Hispanic	Total[a]	White[b]	Black[b]	Hispanic
Total	1,222,799	403,700	558,700	219,500	82,594	27,100	38,300	14,100
18–19	33,200	7,700	16,000	7,600	1,100	500	500	200
20–24	197,900	52,100	95,900	42,300	7,700	2,600	3,100	1,700
25–29	229,500	61,800	115,900	44,100	14,500	4,100	6,800	2,800
30–34	231,300	75,600	106,600	42,400	20,700	6,500	10,200	3,300
35–39	210,300	73,200	99,300	32,000	18,000	5,900	8,800	2,700
40–44	147,300	54,000	63,000	25,700	10,000	3,200	5,000	1,400
45–54	126,700	56,100	47,900	18,500	8,200	3,000	3,200	1,500
55 or older	41,400	22,100	11,000	6,400	1,900	1,000	600	200

Note: Based on custody counts from National Prisoners Statistics (NPS1-A) and updated from jurisdiction counts by gender at year end. Estimates by age derived from the Surveys of Inmates in State and Federal Correctional facilities, 1997. Estimates were rounded to the nearest 100.

[a]Includes American Indians, Alaska Natives, Asians, Native Hawaiians, and other Pacific islanders.

[b]Excludes Hispanics.

Source: Allen J. Beck, *Prisoners in 1999* (Washington, DC: U.S. Department of Justice, 2000), 9.

SOME JAIL AND PRISON CONTRASTS

Prisons are constructed to house long-term offenders who are convicted of serious offenses compared with those housed in jails. Below are some of the contrasts between prisons and jails. Compared with prisons:

1. The physical plant of jails is poorer, with many jails under court order to improve their physical facilities to comply with minimum health and safety standards.

2. Jails usually do not have programs or facilities associated with long-term incarceration such as vocational, technical, or educational courses to be taken by inmates, jail industries, recreation yards, or psychological or social counseling or therapy.

3. Jails have a greater diversity of inmates, including witnesses for trials; suspects or detainees, defendants awaiting trial unable to post bail or whose bail was denied; juveniles awaiting transfer to juvenile facilities or detention; those serving short-term sentences for public drunkenness, driving while intoxicated, or city ordinance violations; mentally ill or disturbed persons awaiting hospitalization; and overflow from state and federal prison populations (Virginia Joint Legislative Audit and Review Commission, 1996).

4. Jail inmate culture is less pronounced and persistent. There is a high inmate turnover in jails, with the exception of the state and federal convict population.

5. The quality of jail personnel is lower, with many jail personnel untrained, undertrained, or otherwise less qualified to guard prisoners compared with their counterparts, prison correctional officers.

6. Jails are not usually partitioned into minimum-, medium-, or maximum-security areas. Control towers do not exist, where armed correctional officers patrol regularly. Jails are not surrounded by several perimeters, with barbed wire areas, sound-detection equipment, and other exotic electronic devices (Gido, 1998).

SELECTED JAIL AND PRISON ISSUES

This section examines briefly six major issues representing problems for both jails and prisons: (1) jail and prison overcrowding, (2) violence and inmate discipline, (3) jail and prison design and control, (4) vocational/technical and educational programs in jails and prisons, (5) jail and prison privatization, and (6) gang formation and perpetuation.

Jail and Prison Overcrowding

Jails are expected to accommodate almost everyone brought to them for booking or processing. Murder suspects as well as public intoxication cases may be housed temporarily in the same tank or detention area to await further processing. The millions of admissions to and releases from jails annually only aggravate persistent jail overcrowding problems, despite the fact that most of those admitted to jails are not confined for lengthy periods. The volume of admissions and releases is severe enough and persistent enough to cause continuing jail overcrowding problems. Law enforcement arrest policies in many jurisdictions seriously aggravate jail overcrowding as well, as millions of arrestees occupy valuable jail space during booking and other perfunctory jail processing (Welch, 1999). The fact that numerous state and federal prisons contract with local jail authorities to house some of the prison inmate over-flow suggests serious prison overcrowding as well (Call and Cole, 1996).

Violent deaths, suicides, psychiatric commitments, and disciplinary infractions have been linked to jail and prison overcrowding (Cornelius, 1996). Some observers have argued that these results are very predictable. For instance, Reginald Wilkinson and Tessa Unwin (1999:98) have indicated, "Take a prison with inmates of many cultures, ethnic backgrounds and a basic tendency toward xenophobia; add a pinch of politically driven tightening of privileges; fold in a large dollop of life long lessons in mistrust and hatred; cook at 170 percent of design capacity and top off with hot and humid summer months . . . even the most bucolic of communities would be hard-pressed to exist, much less thrive, in such an environment. . . . Yet we ask this of prison inmates every day." These researchers also note that many inmates come from backgrounds that allow little exposure to people of different races, religions, behaviors, and attitudes and that this ignorance becomes the root of many street and prison gangs. The overcrowding problem and the many conditions it generates that are adverse for inmates, however, have often been handled piecemeal. For instance, Ohio conducts a Corrections Training Academy at which cultural diversity is taught to prospective correctional officer recruits. Thus, staff are sensitized to overcrowding and the multicultural blend of inmates, but the inmates themselves are not offered similar experiences.

An endless string of solutions has been suggested to ease jail and prison over-crowding. Some are labeled as front-door solutions, because they pertain to policies and practices by criminal justice officials who deal with offenders before and during sentencing. Others are back-door solutions in which strategies are suggested to reduce existing prison populations through early release or parole, furlough, administrative release, and several other options (Welsh, 1995).

Typically, front-door solutions to prison overcrowding are frequently directed at prosecutors and judges and at the way they handle offenders. Some observers suggest greater use of diversion and/or assignment to community service agencies, where offenders bypass the criminal justice system altogether and remain free within their communities. Greater use of probation by judges and recommendations of leniency from prosecutors have also been suggested, with an emphasis on some form of restitution, community service, victim compensation, and/or fine as the primary punishment (Waits, 1993). Other solutions include greater plea bargaining when probation is included; selective incapacitation, where those offenders deemed most dangerous are considered for incarceration; assigning judges a fixed number of prison spaces so that they might rearrange their sentencing priorities and incarcerate only the most serious offenders; and decriminalization of offenses to narrow the range of crimes for which offenders can be incarcerated (Bazemore and Maloney, 1994; Yuslum, 1990).

Some of the back-door proposals by observers include easing the eligibility criteria for early release or parole, the administrative reduction of prison terms through the governor or others shortening originally imposed sentences for certain offenders, modifying parole revocation criteria so as to encourage fewer parole violations, expanding the number of community programs such as mediation, and including the use of intensive supervised parole for more serious offender groups (Adair, 2000; Albonetti and Hepburn, 1997; Burke, 1994; Cook, 1995).

Probably the most serious effect of prison overcrowding for inmates is on their early-release chances. Parole-eligible inmates often find that their parole chances are lessened because of prison overcrowding and the violence it generates. There are far more inmates than self-help programs and prison labor can accommodate. Prisoners benefit if they can become involved in prison labor programs, but only about 20 percent of all prisoners in the United States are included in such programs. Many services, such as group or individual counseling and vocational/technical and educational programs, are chronically understaffed and cannot be offered to all inmates who need or desire them. Even when inmates want to become involved in these programs, the mere fact that so many inmates must be accommodated means that some inmates will be excluded from them. As a result, some inmates will not receive the needed services or programs. Even if they do receive some of these services, then the quality of services or programming will be adversely affected because of larger numbers of inmates who must be accommodated. Many parole-eligible inmates therefore will not have adequate opportunities to show parole boards what they have accomplished, one of the adverse consequences of warehousing offenders under conditions of limited services and self-help programs.

Violence and Inmate Discipline

Prisons and jails are breeding grounds for inmate violence. Contributing to this potential for violence is the great mixture of races, ethnicities, and ages of inmates, together with chronic overcrowding. The increasingly visible presence of gangs has also increased prison and jail violence as inmates become affiliated with one gang or another, often for the purpose of self-protection (Knox, 2000). Every prison has screening mechanisms for new inmates according to standard criteria, but misclassifications frequently occur. Dangerous offenders and the mentally retarded or ill often commit aggressive acts against other inmates. Yet it is difficult to detect and distinguish between all offenders in terms of who poses the greatest risk to themselves or others (Kennedy, 1986). Placing inmates in solitary confinement for their own protection is most often not an option for the average prison; there is simply insufficient maximum-security space to accommodate all those inmates who seek escape from other inmates who might wish to injure or exploit them. Also, there are limited policy provisions for ensuring inmate safety from other violent inmates, although these provisions are not applied because of the exigencies of the situation (Memory et al., 1999).

Much prison violence goes undetected. Inmate-on-inmate assault, in which one or more inmates physically or sexually assault another inmate, is the most frequent type of violence. The assaulted inmate often does not report the incident for fear of retaliation, which is highly foreseeable. Not all assaults are sex-oriented or initiated. Many assaults by inmates on other inmates are started over something as trivial as disagreements over telephone use (LaVigne, 1994). Many prisoners suffer physical injuries, which are frequently unreported or unrecorded. Even when correctional officers suspect or observe rule-breaking and certain forms of inmate violence, this behavior is frequently ignored. Some researchers indicate that correctional officers often ignore this misconduct to obtain inmate cooperation and compliance with prison rules (American Correctional Association, 1993d). This fact gives prisoners some degree of psychological control or power over those correctional officers who look the other way when they observe rule infractions.

Increasingly common are sexual assaults and psychological harassment in jails and prisons (Braswell and Miller, 1989). Prison violence has been mitigated successfully in at least some state prisons. In the Washington State Penitentiary at Walla Walla, for example, administrators have trained staff to cope with inmate violence through an approach known as prevention and reaction (Buentello et al., 1992). With appropriate staff training, Washington correctional officers are learning to prevent new prisoners from joining prison gangs through various intervention activities.

Probably the most visible forms of prison violence are riots, which are on the rise in U.S. prisons (Taylor, 1996:9). Rioting among jail and prison inmates is not unique to the United States; it occurs in virtually every prison in every country at one time or another (Eskridge and Newbold, 1996; Lewis, 1997; Walmsley, 1996). Whenever prisoners riot, they cause considerable damage to prison property and inflict physical injuries on inmates and prison and/or jail staff. Between 1990 and 1995, for instance, there were 1,334 incidents of inmate rioting in U.S. prisons and jails (Montgomery and Crews, 1998). Causes of these riots have been attributable to racial tension, changes in rules and regulations, mass escape attempts, gang conflicts, rumors, disputes among inmates and between inmates and staff members, drug and alcohol use, complaints about food, and security procedures (Adams and Campling, 1994). Usually, riots are instigated as the result of multiple factors rather than a single issue (Goldstone and Useem, 1999).

It is difficult for jail and prison administrators to prepare effectively for riots. Sometimes informants from among the prisoners will give correctional officers some advance warning that a riot is about to occur (Taylor, 1996:6), but most often, riots are spontaneous and unplanned, at least from an administrator's perspective. Therefore, administrators have devised various strategies for coping with, containing, and eliminating riot behavior when it erupts (Useem, Camp, and Camp, 1996). One strategy includes control of the news media, which often plays into the hands of inmates who are seeking external recognition of their grievance or plight (Mahan and Lawrence, 1996). Force, negotiations, and administrative concessions are other strategies that help end rioting. Whenever rioting ends, command and control structures are reexamined. Some reorganization occurs, with prison and jail administrators attempting to implement new policies and procedures that will minimize or even eliminate further rioting (Boin and Van Duin, 1995). A typical response by prison administrators is to impose greater restrictions and rule enforcement on inmates following rioting. This action, however, often causes more disciplinary problems than it resolves (Stevens, 1997:1). It has been recommended that an official nonviolent attitude should be adopted by prison administrators in high-custody facilities while using whatever force is necessary to confine and control high-risk inmates. Such a nonviolent stance from administrators helps to ease inmate tensions and reduce the level of prison violence (Stevens, 1997:3).

Some observers note that far more is known about the causes of aggression and violence among inmates than about their treatment (Van Voorhis, Cullen, and Applegate, 1995:19). Aggressive behavior is typically the result of an interaction between personal characteristics and situational factors. Technology supplies the capability of reasonably identifying the perceptual and cognitive patterns, coping skills, contingencies, and values of those most deserving of special attention from prison programs. Those most likely to engage in violence and aggressive behavior or are at the greatest risk levels, however, are often the same persons who are least amenable to treatment. Thus, some intervention programs offered in prisons fail because they target inmates who cannot benefit from the program. Or, intervention programs work for some offenders but not for others. Or, the program was a true failure because it did not provide a specific service that targeted a factor unrelated to violent conduct (Van Voorhis, Cullen, and Applegate, 1995:19).

One administrative change that has had somewhat positive results is the establishment of inmate councils. These councils, sometimes called inmate disciplinary councils, exist apart from administrative sanctioning mechanisms. They hear and decide many low-level, nonserious inmate complaints against other inmates and even correctional officers or administrative policies. Usually, these councils can reach problem resolutions that satisfy most parties. All state- and federal-level prisons currently have formal grievance procedures. Some councils consist of inmates and a few prison correctional officers. Prisoners regard the addition of corrections officers as a way of provide these councils with some objectivity when hearing and deciding inmate grievances.

Hans Toch (1995:35) says that prisons gain from prison democracy when prisoners become committed to the improvement of prisons and from participating in decisions that affect their lives. From the perspective of prisoners, there are several positive benefits from greater participation in prison governance and self-regulation. Prisoners say, for instance, that they (1) have a chance to get rid of the them-and-us attitude, (2) have a more relaxed community atmosphere, (3) have more integration with staff, (4) have less boredom, (5) have less paranoia about release, (6) have more emphasis on the rehabilitation factor, and (7) have less bitterness against the system when released (Toch, 1995:36). For prospective parolees, these positive benefits can ultimately drive down the amount of recidivism that typifies their conduct upon release.

Jail and Prison Design and Control

Some observers see a direct connection between new jail and prison design and a reduction in inmate violence (Cronin, 1992). Two proposals for resolving jail and prison problems are to create new jails and prisons constructed in ways that will conserve scarce space and require fewer correctional officers and to reconstruct existing facilities to minimize prison violence and house more inmates. Prison construction in recent years has included increasingly popular modular designs. These designs also permit layouts and arrangements of cell blocks to enhance officer monitoring of inmates. New prison construction is expensive, however, and many jurisdictions are either unwilling or unable to undertake new prison construction projects. One idea is to expand existing facilities to accommodate larger numbers of prisoners (Erickson et al., 1992).

New jail and prison construction, the renovation or expansion of existing facilities, or the conversion of existing buildings previously used for other purposes takes into account the matter of security and safety for both staff and inmates (Chapman, 1998). Stairwells and areas otherwise hidden from the view of correctional officers encourage inmate sexual or otherwise physical assaults. These areas can either be reduced or eliminated entirely with new architectural designs. It is generally conceded that reducing blind spots or areas not directly visible to officers and other corrections officials helps to reduce the incidence of inmate assaults (Bogard et al., 1993; Collins, 1994; Erickson et al., 1992). The construction of safer jail and prison facilities can do much to minimize the incidence of inmate violence. Further, institutional programming is enhanced, because better organization and planning result from being able to anticipate the characteristics of future jail and prison clientele (Spens, 1994). If jail and prison officials have a better idea about the characteristics of those entering their facilities in future years, then they can develop more effective programming to meet their needs. In the long run, inmates benefit from such planning (Burns, 1998:56).

Vocational/Technical and Educational Programs in Jails and Prisons

Most jails are not equipped to provide inmates with any vocational/technical and educational programs, because most jails are not equipped with the space to offer such educational programming, jail inmates do not have parole and good time credit incentives compared with prison inmates, and jail inmates are usually serving short-term sentences that would interrupt any meaningful educational programming. Even when jail educational programs have been devised and offered on a short-term basis to inmates, recidivism rates of graduates have not differed significantly from those who have not participated in educational programs offered at the jails (Vito and Tewksbury, 1999).

Many prisons lack a broad variety of programs geared to enhance inmate skills and education (Schlossman and Spillane, 1992). This state of affairs seems consistent with the view that the rehabilitation orientation in U.S. prisons is on the decline (Shichor, 1992). There have, however, been several successes among state and federal prison systems. For instance, drug offenders in the U.S. Bureau of Prison's Choice program, a drug treatment and intervention program, have for the most part been successfully treated. Inmates with drug dependencies are subjected to a ten-month program, including intake/evaluation/follow-up, drug education, skills development, lifestyle modification, wellness, responsibility, and individualized counseling/case supervision. The emphases in the Choice program are on education and the development of cognitive skills rather than on treatment and insight-oriented therapy (Walters et al., 1992).

In Washington, McNeil Island houses 1,300 medium-security inmates. In 1996, the prison facility implemented an educational program known as the Work Ethic Camp (WEC) (Gianas, 1996). The camp recruits volunteers from among interested inmates who want to improve themselves. Designated correctional officers behave in ways that model demanding employers, although they develop a personally supportive relationship between themselves and participating inmates. Inmates, known as WECies, are expected to put in eight-hour workdays at different tasks. There is demanding work at the island's power station, motor pool, recycling plant, water-filtration plant, meat-packaging plant, and other facilities. Inmates learn boat repair and maintenance, road repair, building construction, facility maintenance, clerical work, farm work, and forest maintenance. WEC inmates are also taught basic work habits, including cleanliness, following instructions, planning tasks, teamwork, interpersonal skills, tool care, and supervisor-employee relationships. They take courses in reading, writing, and math; adult basic education preparation; anger/stress management; victim awareness; community responsibility; dependable strengths articulation process; family dynamics; unlocking your potential; chemical dependency; health and wellness; job readiness; and transition planning. The WEC's objective is to produce productive, employable inmates who will leave McNeil Island ready to

---

BOX 6.3   *Cons Behind Bars Run 4-H Program for Children*

The Long-Distance Dads Program

It is happening in many states around the country. Although many prison wardens remain wary, fatherhood programs are springing up in different prisons in states such as North Carolina, Florida, and Missouri. These programs are teaching inmate-fathers, some of whom are barely literate, how to read and become better parents. Parenting skills, together with other family values, are taught. More than 700,000 inmate-fathers were incarcerated in federal and state prisons in 2000. One fairly popular program is called Long-Distance Dads. In Pennsylvania, for example, the Long-Distance Dads program works with fatherhood groups in a 12-week program. The curriculum is created in part by inmates, and inmates are used as group leaders. The program encourages fathers to assume responsibility for their children while in prison and after they get out. Pennsylvania State University was in the process of evaluating the program in September 2000. Early reports suggest that better behavior from participating inmates has been observed and that more father-child interaction has occurred in prison visiting rooms. Another program that has achieved some visibility is a 4-H Club started at Missouri's maximum-security Potosi Correctional Center. Inmates there plan monthly meetings, organize family dinners and guide their children in community service activities. Lynna Lawson, a 4-H Club specialist who assists the club, said that the inmates show a keen interest even though most are serving lengthy sentences. She said, "It's an attitude like, 'This is my life. I have to make the best of it.'" Lawson added that inmates can be crushed if a child unexpectedly fails to show up for a monthly meeting, which means that the father cannot participate in the program. She said, "All the fathers in prison have expressed frustration about having no control over their kids."

In Florida, a program called Reading Family Ties has been implemented for inmates. In this program, initially offered to imprisoned mothers and recently extended to two men's prisons, participants attend an 80-hour parenting course and can insert personal greetings on the recordings they send home. The idea of speaking into a tape recorder is significant for many inmates. It makes it possible for them to communicate with their children indirectly. Many inmates have trouble expressing their intimate feelings to others. The program seems to be making a difference. Another program undertaken in New York State is Conscious Parenting. This program, started in 1996 by suburbanite volunteers from neighboring Connecticut, has reached more than 250 inmates thus far. It features a children's day every few months, when children of inmates are bused to prison for daylong festivities, including games and a meal organized by the inmates themselves. According to one of the volunteers, some of the children have never met their fathers. One reason the program is only slowly expanding is that many inmates feel that there is no hope; there seems to be an attitude of dismissal of their ability to care. Some persons are also reluctant to do volunteer work in men's prisons. According to national figures, there are 1.5 million children who have a parent in prison. Although many programs for women are currently operating in various prisons around the country, 93 percent of the imprisoned parents are men. Typically, their role as fathers has been neglected by corrections officials. One unidentified source said the prevailing attitude of many wardens is, "Nobody gets out, nobody gets hurt. If they can do that, they've had a good day."

Should more parenting programs be created for male inmates? Are such programs rehabilitative? What do you think?

Source: Adapted from David Crary, Associated Press, "Men Behind Bars Strive to Become Better Dads," September 15, 2000.

---

go to work for an employer on the outside. Evaluation of the program thus far has been favorable. Inmates are developing better self-images and self-respect and are acquiring the skills necessary to make it more effectively on the outside when released. Yet much depends on whether inmates are motivated to become involved in programs such as the WEC.

Some vocational/technical and educational programs are tailored to meet the needs of female inmates. In an Oregon prison, for example, a program was established in 1992 called the Women in Community Service program (WICS). This program was assessed from 1992 to 1995 and was determined to be effective for female offenders in different ways. The WICS was established to improve one's life skills, self-esteem, and motivation to change behavior. Vocational skills as well as drug- and alcohol-awareness courses and programs were emphasized. The program's success has been determined by low recidivism rates among WICS participants in follow-up investigations (Day, Friedman, and Christophersen, 1998).

By the early 1990s, participation in jail or prison educational programs was mandatory in at least 13 states (DiVito, 1991). Of those states making education mandatory, the primary inmate targets were those with obvious educational deficiencies who did not meet minimum educational criteria. Reduced sentence lengths were offered as incentives to participate in educational programs. The measure of success of these programs was whether inmates continue their education in jail or prison beyond the mandatory minimum. One of the more innovative inmate literacy programs is operated by the Virginia Department of Corrections. Commencing in 1986, the "no read, no release" program has emphasized literacy achievement at no lower than the sixth-grade level and has made such an achievement part of the parole decision-making process. Results have been favorably viewed by various states. Compulsory educational programs in jails and prisons, however, have been subjected to several constitutional challenges (DiVito, 1991).

In recent years, more than a few prison systems have gravitated toward offering life skills programs as a part of their educational services. The Delaware Department of Correction, for instance, established a life skills program in 1997. This program was offered in each of its four state prisons, where 5,000 inmates were housed. Participation in the program was voluntary, but each year approximately 300 inmates have enrolled. Nearly 85 percent have graduated from the program. The Delaware Life Skills Program, as it is called, runs three hours a day for four months. Each of five teachers conducts a morning and an afternoon course with 12 to 15 inmates in each course. The curriculum stresses three areas: academics, violence reduction, and applied life skills. Academics includes reading comprehension, mathematics, and language expression. The violence reduction component includes moral recognition therapy, anger management, and conflict resolution training. The applied life skills component includes credit and banking, job search, motor vehicle regulations, legal responsibilities and restitution, family responsibilities and child support, health issues, social services, educational services, cultural differences, and government and law (Finn, 1998:4-5). An evaluation of the life skills program offered by Delaware shows that the recidivism rate among program graduates was only 19 percent, which compares quite favorably with a control group with a recidivism rate of 27 percent. Thus, the objective of reducing recidivism among life skills participants was realized at all four Delaware institutions.

Parolees often benefit from the array of services extended to them in prison settings. Participation in educational programs, Alcoholics Anonymous, or some other educational or counseling is viewed as a desire to better oneself and indicative that rehabilitation may have occurred. Rehabilitation may or may not occur for particular inmates, depending on whether they manipulate the system or use it for true self-improvement (Whitesell and Anderson, 1990). In any case, parole boards seem impressed with whatever progress inmates manifest, regardless of an inmate's motives. Indeed, some research indicates that at least some parolees benefit in their postrelease after participating in correctional higher education programs (Brandon and Chard-Wierschem, 1997).

Jail and Prison Privatization

A proposal that has received mixed reactions in recent years is the privatization of jail and prison management by private interests (Moser, 1994). Legally, there is nothing to prevent private enterprises from operating prisons and jails as extensions of state and local governments and law enforcement agencies (Bowman, Hakim, and Seidenstat, 1993). Privatization has been most noticeable in the juvenile justice system (McDonald, 1993). In fact, in 1989, over 40 percent of all incarcerated juveniles were being held in facilities owned and operated by private interests (McDonald, 1993). Private interests argue that they can manage and operate jails and prisons more effectively and economically than many government agencies. This issue remains unresolved today. There is no debating, however, that private sector proposals for the management of jails and other facilities have been increasing in recent years and result in considerable savings for the contracting local and state governments (Thompson and Mays, 1991). In fact, the privatization phenomenon in corrections is not unique to the United States. Many other countries are currently experimenting with it (Mays and Gray, 1996).

A significant hurdle is the political control issue. Who has control over offenders housed in and managed by persons in the private sector? Another issue is an administrative one. Should private enterprises be allowed to sanction convicted offenders? Will the current level of quality of inmate care be maintained when operated by private interests? Many government facilities are currently under court order to improve their living conditions for inmates. Although it is unlikely that the private sector would do a poorer managerial task relating to inmate management, the accountability issue persists (Harding, 1999; Ogle, 1999).

Privatization has spread to probation and parole program operations (McDonald and Fournier, 1998). Private corporations can prepare presentence investigation reports, or PSIs. They can also assist probation and parole departments in supervising probationer- or parolee-clients. In fact, guidelines are currently available to local and state governments about how private interests can interface with their own program operations and organization.

A positive view of privatization in corrections is to view this phenomenon as an extension and a complement to existing public correctional programs (Harding, 1997). Private interests have been instrumental in devising many correctional innovations, including electronic monitoring and new technology for surveillance, control, and drug testing (Feeley, 1991). Private innovators in corrections have made it possible for many convicted offenders to become enrolled in intermediate punishment programs and endure many sanctions imposed in lieu of traditional incarceration in a jail or prison.

Gang Formation and Perpetuation

One of the most serious problems in jails and prisons today is the prevalence and influence of gangs (Knox, 2000). A 1999 survey of all major U.S. prisons disclosed that although two-thirds had specific policies that prohibited gang recruitment, there was a gang presence in almost all facilities surveyed. About one-sixth of all institutions reported that gang members had assaulted correctional staff. Two-thirds of all institutions were providing some form of gang training for their correctional officers. Such training included recognition signs such as tattoos, clothing colors and trinkets, and hand gestures.

No one knows precisely how many gang members there are in U.S. prisons and jails today (Fong, Vogel, and Buentello, 1996). Gangs are found in virtually all prisons throughout the world (Houston and Prinsloo, 1998; Miller and Rush, 1996). Estimates of 100,000 or more prison inmates involved in formal gang activity have been made, although the figure is probably much higher (Miller and Rush, 1996). Because many prison gang members were former street gang members, some idea of the prevalence of gangs in prisons can be gleaned by examining the prevalence and numbers of street gangs and their memberships. In 1998, for example, there were 28,700 gangs and 780,000 gang members in the United States (Moore and Cook, 1999:1). Self-reports from a sample of gang members surveyed by researchers indicated that most of these gang members were involved in one or more illegal activities and were committing crimes. A sizable portion of these gang members had served time in juvenile secure facilities, jails, or prisons.

Generally for prisons but also for jails, gang members are believed responsible for 50 percent or more of all institutional disturbances and problems. For this reason, several correctional systems have aggressively established programs designed to defeat gang influence and discourage gang recruitment and membership practices in a variety of ways. One effort is the Gang-Free Environment Program established in Illinois in 1996. Through this program, the Taylorville Correctional Center (TCC) was created as a gang-free institution. Inmates were selected on the basis of their nongang status. Programs were created to emphasize self-improvement, education, and employability and to deemphasize any need for gang affiliation. Thus, the institution had to create a safe environment for all inmates. Correctional officers received various types of training calculated to help them relate more effectively with inmates and to recognize any attempt at gang formation among the prisoners. One goal of the TCC is to encourage inmates to make general changes in their lifestyles. The Lifestyle Redirection Program's various courses are offered to all inmates. Inmates are virtually free from any pressure to join gangs. The inmate selection process has been mostly successful (Gransky and Cowles, 1999). Unfortunately, not all prisons are capable of offering such a luxury to their inmates.

Prison gangs are not only pervasive, but they are also powerful (Hassine, 1996; Knox, 2000; Miller and Rush, 1996). Prospective recruits for existing prison gangs enter prison with feelings of fear of the new setting. They sense danger, feel isolated, and are lonely. There are virtually no rules for acceptance, no commitment to any group, no rules of conduct that are immediately apparent, and no formal leadership. Subsequently, many inmates gravitate toward one gang or another, often along racial or ethnic lines. The prison gang itself is characterized as having (1) formal rules and constitution, (2) well-defined goals and philosophy, (3) hierarchy of formal leadership with clearly defined authority and responsibility, (4) membership for life, (5) members who wear gang tattoos, (6) wholesale involvement in gang activities both inside and outside of the penal institution, and (7) ongoing criminal enterprise (Fong, Vogel, and Buentello, 1996:107).

Figure 6.2 shows four different gang tattoos from inmates in the Texas Department of Criminal Justice prison system. Featured are tattoos of the Ayran Nations,

AYRAN NATIONS   MEXICAN MAFIA

TEXAS SYNDICATE   TEXAS MAFIA

FIGURE 6.2 Prison gang tattoos.

Mexican Mafia, the Texas Syndicate, and Texas Mafia. In the tattoo of the Texas Syndicate, for instance, there is a visible "T" and "S" in the background. Tattoos vary in complexity and design, but members of the Texas Syndicate will always have a "T" and an "S" somewhere visible within their particular tattoos. Membership in these prison gangs is for life and is continued once prisoners are paroled or max out their sentences.

In many instances, gangs have controlled prison culture and what transpires behind prison walls. They have intimidated prison staff. Furthermore, there is evidence that the same gangs have affiliate gangs in prisons in other states besides the ones from which they originate (Miller and Rush, 1996; Valdez, 1997). Beyond the disruptive effects of gangs on prison order and their influence over others within institutions, far-reaching effects extend to those released from prison. Once someone has joined a prison gang, he or she is a part of that gang for life. Usually the only way to leave a gang is to die. The thought of betraying another gang member either within or without prison walls is reprehensible for most gang members (Rees, 1996). Therefore, when a gang member leaves prison either by serving his or her time or through parole, a continuing allegiance to the gang is expected. If the gang member outside of prison can do one or more favors or perform services for other gang members inside prison, then he or she will perform these favors or services. In most instances, these favors involve criminal activity of one type or another (Valentine, 1995).

POs have a strong interest in determining whether their clients are affiliated with gangs. They learn gang recognition signals and familiarize themselves with gang territories in areas where their clients live. Gangs are considered community threat groups. Different states and the U.S. Probation Office have established specialized threat group programs through which they attempt to coordinate their resources to combat those gang members on probation or parole who pose a serious threat to their communities (Casilias, 1994). Certain POs have special gang expertise and work with offenders who are gang members. It is their responsibility to identify telltale signs of gang activity and whether their clients are continuing their gang affiliations and traditions despite probation or parole program requirements to the contrary.

For probationers and parolees, gangs have a pervasive influence on whether these persons can remain law abiding and conform with their different programs (Harland, Buentello, and Knox, 1993). There is ample evidence that prison and street gangs are closely intertwined (Hunt et al., 1993). If gang membership requires probationers or parolees to commit new offenses, such as requisitioning drugs or money for currently incarcerated inmate-gang members, then POs must confront and resolve this serious situation (Ralph, 1992; Rolf and Greeson, 1992).

Several methods are currently being employed to minimize the influence of gangs in both prisons and on the streets. Sophisticated tracking programs are being devised so that computer tracking of gang members can occur. Understanding the communication patterns of gang members both inside and outside of prison is crucial to effective PO work, especially for those POs who work closely with known gang members (California Department of Justice, 1990; New Mexico Governor's Organized Crime Prevention Commission, 1990).

THE ROLE OF JAILS AND PRISONS IN PROBATION AND PAROLE DECISION MAKING

Whether in jails or prisons, inmates are obligated to comply with specific behavioral guidelines that will permit jail and prison officials to maintain order and discipline. Besides these requirements, many prisons and some jails have programs designed to assist inmates in different ways. Educational or vocational training is more readily available in prison settings, although some of the larger jails offer similar programs for long-term offenders. Remember that many jails have contracts with state and federal prison systems to house some of their inmate overflow; thus, not every jail inmate is incarcerated for shorter intervals of a year or less. Counseling and other forms of assistance are available to inmates if they want such services (Munson and Ygnacio, 2000).

Jail and prison officers and administrators are in positions of submitting written reports about inmate conduct while confined. These reports may contain favorable or unfavorable information. Ultimately, this information is made available to paroling authorities so that a more informed parole decision can be made. If inmates cannot conduct themselves in a setting with explicit rules and regulations, then it is presumed that they cannot function well in their communities if released short of serving their full prison terms (Hemmens and Stohr, 2000).

The federal government has experimented with various predictive classification systems used for pretrial detainees (Garner, 1991). Therefore, even in instances in which one's guilt or innocence has not yet been established through trial, some preliminary screening mechanisms have already been implemented that may impact either favorably or unfavorably on a judge's sentencing decision later. In the Federal Bureau of Prisons, for instance, pretrial detainees have been screened by various instruments and according to different predictive criteria to determine which alleged offenders would be good candidates for pretrial release. The results of such experimentation have been thus far inconclusive.

Attempts have also been made to forecast the successfulness of probationers based, in part, on their incarcerative experiences (Nieto, 1998). In Eastern Pasco County, Florida, for example, a sample of 427 probationers sentenced to community supervision was examined between 1980 and 1982, with a follow-up investigation in 1987 (Liberton, Silverman, and Blount, 1992). Some of the probationers had been held in jails in pretrial detention until their trials. Others had been released on their own recognizance (ROR). Interestingly, researchers found that those offenders who had been incarcerated for periods exceeding two days had a much higher rate of recidivism compared with those offenders who were ROR. Specifically, the researchers found an inverse relationship between the length of pretrial commitment and the successful completion of probation. Factors relating to one's successful probation completion included being older, employed, married, and having some previous military service. Perhaps those offenders who were held in pretrial detention may have been more serious offenders compared with the ROR sample. Obviously, there were reasons for not allowing them to remain free in their communities pending their trial.

Some jails and most prisons attempt to screen incoming inmates according to their risk or dangerousness as well as their special needs (Krauth, 1991). Screening is also conducted to evaluate offenders and determine their most suitable level of custody (Alexander and Austin, 1992). Because it becomes increasingly expensive to monitor offenders as the level of custody increases (e.g., from minimum security to medium security, from medium security to maximum security), it is in an institution's best economic interest to maintain prisoners at the least intense custody level while they are confined. Hence, most prisons have reassessments of inmates periodically (e.g., every six months or a year) to determine whether their present level of custody should be increased or decreased.

For inmates in various state and federal prison systems, inmate classifications are very important in several respects. Imposing more stringent monitoring and closer custody on those prisoners considered most aggressive and violent serves to protect less serious and nonviolent inmates. The lower one's classification level, the more the trust accorded that inmate. Parole boards consider one's present level of custody and whether one has behaved well while at that particular custody level. Again, it is in a prisoner's best interests to be confined at the lowest security level possible. Therefore, periodic reclassifications of offenders that tend to downgrade their present levels of custody are positive moves that influence one's parole chances accordingly. The prison system itself plays a crucial role in determining whether parole will be granted. Other relevant factors are the seriousness of the conviction offense, length of the original sentence, and the amount of time served in relation to that sentence length.

In sum, jails and prisons are playing increasingly important roles in probation and parole decision making. Jails are devising more sophisticated classification procedures commensurate with those used in most prison systems. These classification systems are helpful in separating offenders according to several criteria that optimize their safety and needs (Tonry, 1998). As jails become more like prisons by establishing a broader array of inmate programs of an educational and vocational nature, inmates themselves will be able to do more to influence their chances of more favorable treatment (California San Diego Association of Governments, 1998). They can take affirmative steps to ensure their involvement in community correctional programs in which fewer restrictions exist.

SUMMARY

Jails were originally conceived as short-term facilities to house offenders charged with minor offenses, pretrial detainees, and those serving relatively short sentences. The American Jail Association considers a facility a jail if it houses inmates for periods of 72 hours or longer. Those facilities holding persons overnight are either lock-ups or holding tanks. In 2001, there were between 3,300 and 3,400 jails in the United States. In recent decades, jails have inadvertently assumed additional functions and responsibilities, including housing juvenile offenders for short periods, holding federal and state prisoner overflows on a contractual basis with various government agencies, housing witnesses, and providing a temporary haven for those suffering from psychological or mental problems. Jails also house probation and parole violators. Jails have little or no control over the types of inmates housed. About half of all jail inmates are unconvicted offenders, including drunks and vagrants. Shock probationers are also accommodated for short periods as a part of their split sentences. Most jails in the United States are old, many having been constructed prior to 1950.

Prisons are long-term facilities designed to hold more serious offenders. Early U.S. prisons were constructed in the late 1700s in Connecticut and Pennsylvania. Auburn (New York) State Penitentiary introduced several important innovations in U.S. corrections in the early 1800s, including the tier system, solitary confinement, and the congregate system. Striped uniforms also were pioneered by Auburn State Penitentiary. Prisons are designed to provide societal protection, punish offenders, rehabilitate offenders, and assist in their eventual reintegration into society. Inmate classification is an important feature of prison systems. Prisons classify inmates into different security levels, such as minimum, medium, and maximum. Inmate housing costs rise as their custody level increases.

Jails are acquiring many of the characteristics of prisons as officials acknowledge a growing jail population consisting of federal and state prisoners in need of rehabilitative services and other amenities. Jails and prisons share several problems, including chronic overcrowding, inmate violence, and various types of inmate programs. Prison and jail overcrowding is chronic and is a problem for most institutional administrators. Many other problems faced by prison and jail staffs are directly or indirectly influenced by overcrowding. Efforts to alleviate overcrowding have included innovations in building design and architectural rearrangements that permit more effective use of space and promote greater officer efficiency. Podular direct supervision jails and prisons are rapidly becoming popular as the most effective inmate management strategy. The private sector is gradually moving into jail and prison management and operations, effectively reducing inmate maintenance costs. Much privatization has thus far been restricted to juvenile facilities and aftercare, although more privately operated adult facilities are being established in different localities.

Prisons and jails also influence probationers and parolees by providing the courts and parole boards with feedback about inmate conduct while confined. Especially in prisons, an inmate's level of custody can be changed, either upwardly or downwardly, depending on his or her bad or good conduct. Favorable behavioral reports encourage judges and parole boards to grant probationers and parolees greater benefits and freedoms.

Several issues affect jails and prisons. They are chronically overcrowded, which occurs because there is insufficient space to accommodate all persons who should be incarcerated and there are inadequate resources for new jail and prison construction. Overcrowding contributes to and causes various problems for administrators and other inmates, such as increasing prison violence and inmate rioting for various reasons. Efforts have been made to reduce the amount of inmate violence. Changes in the architectural design and structuring of jails and prisons have lessened the incidence of violence in certain jurisdictions. Furthermore, the addition of helpful programs and services for inmates has helped many inmates improve their personal skills and self-images. Thus, both jails and prisons today have made a concerted effort to provide inmates with ample opportunities for self-improvement through vocational/technical and educational classes, group or individual counseling programs, and courses relating to anger management and improvement in social skills and interpersonal relations. Increasingly, the privatization of jails and prisons is occurring, although only a small fraction of the U.S. jail and prison inmate population today is under the control of private interests. Finally, gang presence in jails and prisons has increased over the past several decades. The formation and perpetuation of gangs as well as the continuing effects of gang membership on parolees when they reenter their communities affect all in corrections.

KEY TERMS

Admin max
American Correctional Association (ACA)
Auburn State Penitentiary
Banishment
Bridewell Workhouse
Bureau of Justice Statistics
Congregate system

Contract prisoners
Crofton, Sir Walter
Department of Justice
Detainer warrants
Direct supervision jails
Elmira Reformatory
Gaol
Howard, John

Inmate classification
Jail removal initiative
Lockdown
Lockup
Mark system
Maxi-maxi prisons
Maximum-security prisons
Medium-security prisons

Minimum-security prisons
Penitentiary
Pennsylvania System
Philadelphia Society for Alleviating the Miseries of Public Prisons
Pretrial detainees

Pretrial detention
Preventive detention
Public defender
Shire-reeves
Solitary confinement
Supermax

Tickets-of-leave
Tiers
Tier system
Total institution
Walnut Street Jail
Workhouse

QUESTIONS FOR REVIEW

1. What are some important events in the evolution of jails in the United States?
2. What are some general functions of jails? How do they contrast with the functions of prisons?
3. What were some of the innovations introduced by the Auburn State Penitentiary? Are any of these innovations still in evidence in modern-day prisons?
4. How do jails differ from lockups and drunk tanks?
5. What innovations did the Walnut Street Jail introduce? What was the influence of religion in correctional reforms during the 1700s and 1800s in the United States?
6. What is a detainer warrant? Who is likely to be served with a detainer warrant?
7. How do prisons and jails influence probation and parole violators?
8. What are some general factors considered important when classifying offenders for placement in prisons? What are risk elements?
9. Identify three major issues of relevance to both prisons and jails. Indicate in a brief paragraph how these issues are important to prison and jail operations and management.
10. What is a direct supervision jail? What are some of its characteristics for offender management?

SUGGESTED READINGS

Birmingham, Luke, et al. (2000). "Mental Illness at Reception into Prison." *Criminal Behaviour and Mental Health* **10:**77–87.

Knox, George W. (2000). "A National Assessment of Gangs and Security Threat Groups (STGs) in Adult Correctional Institutions: Results of the 1999 Adult Corrections Survey." *Journal of Gang Research* **7:**1–45.

Lindquist, Christine H., and Charles A. Lindquist (1999). "Health Behind Bars: Utilization of Medical Care among Jail Inmates." *Journal of Community Health* **24:**285–303.

Memory, John M., et al. (1999). "Comparing Disciplinary Infraction Rates of North Carolina Fair Sentencing and Structured Sentencing Inmates: A Natural Experiment." *Prison Journal* **79:**45–71.

U.S. General Accounting Office (1999). *Women in Prison: Issues and Challenges Confronting U.S. Correctional Systems.* Washington, DC: U.S. General Accounting Office.

CHAPTER 7 # Parole and Parolees

Introduction
Parole Defined
The Historical Context of Parole
Parole and Alternative Sentencing Systems
   Indeterminate Sentencing and Parole
   The Shift to Determinate Sentencing
The Philosophy of Parole
Functions of Parole
   Offender Reintegration
   Crime Deterrence and Control

Decreasing Prison and Jail Overcrowding
Compensating for Sentencing Disparities
Public Safety and Protection
A Profile of Parolees in the United States
The Growing Gang Presence
Summary
Key Terms
Questions for Review
Suggested Readings

• Moore was a convicted sex offender who was sentenced to life imprisonment in New York in 1963. In 1982, a change in the law provided that Moore was eligible for parole. Accordingly, he applied, and the parole board rejected his request on several subsequent occasions. In the most recent rejection of Moore's parole request, the parole board cited the especially violent and heinous nature of his crime, strangling a teenage girl to death and committing an act of necrophilia with her corpse later. Furthermore, he had molested two young girls shortly after being released from probation for another crime. In his own defense, Moore showed that he had exhibited exemplary conduct while imprisoned, that he completed several educational achievements, and that he had solid and acceptable postrelease plans, including potential employment and a suitable residence. The parole board ignored these factors and denied his parole. Moore appealed, contending that the parole board should have considered only his mental health status and whether he can remain law-abiding in contemporary society. An appellate court disagreed with Moore and upheld the parole board's decision to deny him early release. (*Moore v. New York State Bd. of Parole,* 712 N.Y.S.2d 179 [N.Y. Sup. App. Div. July 2000])

• Wilson was charged with a federal offense. While in custody awaiting trial for that offense, he assaulted a jail inmate in the cell in which he was being confined. As a result, he was charged with assault. In the meantime, Wilson went to trial on the federal charges and was convicted. Following his conviction and sentencing, Wilson was advised by the U.S. Parole Commission that his parole eligibility date was rescinded because of his unlawful conduct while awaiting trial in jail. The result was that Wilson would not become eligible for parole until much later into his federal sentence. Wilson appealed. The Third Circuit Court of Appeals heard his case and overturned the U.S. Parole Commission's decision to rescind Wilson's early-release date. The court was particularly influenced by the commission's own statement to the effect that "the following guidelines shall apply to the sanctioning or disciplinary infractions or new criminal behavior committed by a prisoner subsequent to the commencement of his sentence and prior to his release on parole." Because Wilson had not been tried or convicted at the time he committed the jail assault, the particular guideline followed by the U.S. Parole Commission did not apply to him. Thus, the commission was barred from preventing Wilson from being released on parole in accordance with his original presumptive or effective date. (*Wilson v. United States Parole Commission,* 193 F.3d 195 [U.S.3d Cir. September 1999])

• Bollinger was an Oregon inmate serving time for a crime. When he became eligible for parole, the Oregon Board of Parole and Post-Prison Supervision held a parole hearing and granted him parole. Bollinger, however, shocked the Board of Parole and refused their parole offer. The board claimed that Bollinger had to accept parole under their conditions. Bollinger disagreed and appealed. An appellate court heard the case and determined the following facts. When Bollinger was originally sentenced, the sentence was a determinate one, which meant that Bollinger could be released by statute upon completing an amount of hard time minus credit accumulated for good time. His release as the result of accumulating good time credit meant that he would not be subject to traditional parolee restrictions and conditions. Rather, he would be free of the criminal justice system entirely. His release date through calculating good time credit was only a few months beyond the parole date specified by the Board of Parole. Thus, Bollinger reasoned that if he stayed in prison a few months longer, the prison would have to release him unconditionally anyway. He preferred this method of release rather than the conditional one imposed by the board and thus refused their parole offer. The appellate court reversed the Board of Parole and said that Bollinger had a right to refuse their parole offer and its conditions. The court cited the statement that "the board shall determine and may at any time modify the conditions of parole, which may include among other conditions, that the parolee shall accept the parole granted subject to all terms and conditions specified by the board." (*Bollinger v. Bd. of Parole & Post-Prison Supervision,* 992 P.2d 445 [Or. Sup. December 1999])

• Trantino was convicted of first-degree murder and was sentenced to death in New Jersey in 1964. Subsequently, his death sentence was commuted to life imprisonment, with Trantino becoming eligible for parole after serving 25 years of his life sentence. In 1996, he applied for parole, and the New Jersey Parole Board rejected his parole request. Trantino appealed and an appellate court remanded the case back to the New Jersey Parole Board, which again rejected Trantino's early-release request and cited the following reasons: (1) the defendant became upset when confronted about the results of a personality test, (2) the inadequacy of the defendant's parole plan, (3) the defendant's plan to write a book regarding his commission of the crime, (4) the defendant's alleged memory loss regarding the circumstances surrounding the offense, and (5) the defendant's violation of a previous parole program in the state of New York. The appellate court heard Trantino's appeal and overruled the New Jersey Parole Board, ordering them to grant Trantino parole. The court said that the defendant's conduct in New York 39 years earlier had no relevance for their current early-release decision, that his book-writing was irrelevant, that his memory loss was reasonable, and that there was ample evidence of his good behavior and rehabilitation while imprisoned. (*Trantino v. N.J. State Parole Bd.*, 752 A.2d 761 [N.J. Sup. June 2000])

INTRODUCTION

The previous scenarios suggest that parole is a complex decision often involving criteria that are not clear-cut. In Moore's case, for instance, his institutional conduct seemed to have little or no weight in whether Moore received early release. The parole board was persuaded more by the seriousness of Moore's offense than by any other criteria. It is clear that a great deal of subjectivity entered into the decision to reject his parole request. In Wilson's case, he was being punished by the parole board for an offense committed before he was convicted of a federal crime. The parole board simply exceeded its authority in punishing him for something he did while not under their jurisdiction. In Bollinger's case, he simply refused the offer of a parole board to parole him. He calculated that he would fare better if stayed in prison a few more months and would be released unconditionally anyway. And in Trantino's case, a parole board seemed to be inventing reasons to keep him behind bars, despite his good works in prison during a 35-year period.

This chapter looks at parole or early release from prison. A brief history of parole in the United States is provided. Included is a discussion of the philosophy of parole as well as several of its important functions. Parole has been criticized in recent years for various reasons. In some instances, dangerous persons have been paroled and have committed serious crimes while under parole supervision. Some states have abolished parole outright. Thus, some consideration is given to the positive and negative aspects of parole decision making. Alternatives to parole are also examined. One consideration when contemplating parole for any particular offender is that offender's prior record. Thus, an examination of the types of persons who are paroled is provided. Because many parolees have joined gangs while imprisoned, some attention is given to the growing presence in communities and how parolees are affected by such gangs.

PAROLE DEFINED

Parole is the conditional release of a prisoner from incarceration (either from prison or jail) under supervision after a portion of the sentence has been served (West-Smith, Pogrebin, and Poole, 2000). The major distinguishing feature between probation and parole is that parolees have served some time incarcerated in either jail or prison, whereas most probationers are not incarcerated. Some common characteristics shared by both parolees and probationers are that: (1) they have committed crimes, (2) they have been convicted of crimes, (3) they are under the supervision or control of probation or parole officers, and (4) they are subject to one or more similar conditions accompanying their probation or parole programs. Some general differences are that, in general, parolees have committed more serious offenses than probationers. Also, parolees have been incarcerated for a portion of their sentences, whereas probationers are not generally incarcerated following their convictions for crimes. Furthermore, parolees may have more stringent conditions (e.g., curfew, participation in drug or alcohol rehabilitation, counseling, halfway house participation, more face-to-face contacts with their POs) accompanying their parole programs compared with probationers.

THE HISTORICAL CONTEXT OF PAROLE

Parole existed in eighteenth-century Spain, France, England, and Wales (Bottomley, 1984). British convicts under sentence of death or convicted of other serious offenses created for England a problem currently confronting the United States: prison overcrowding. In the eighteenth century, Britain had no penitentiaries, but one option available was to export excess prisoners to the American colonies. After the Revolutionary War, this option no longer existed.

Seeking new locations for isolating its criminals from the rest of society, England selected Australia, one of several remote English colonies that had accommodated small numbers of offenders during the American colonial period when prisoner exportation was popular. The first large-scale **transportation** of convicts from England came to Australia in 1788. Although many of these transportees were convicted of minor theft, it was intended by the English government that they should become builders and farmers. These trades, however, were ones at which they were highly unsuccessful. It became apparent that officials needed to establish prisons to house some of their prisoner-transportees. One such outpost 1,000 miles off the coast of Australia was **Norfolk Island**, where a penal colony was established. Another was **Van Dieman's Land** (Hughes, 1987).

The private secretary to the lieutenant governor of Van Diemen's Land in 1836 was a former Royal Navy officer and social reformer, **Alexander Maconochie** (1787–1860). In 1840, Maconochie was appointed superintendent of the penal colony at Norfolk Island. When he arrived to assume his new duties, he was appalled by what he found. Prisoners were lashed repeatedly and tortured frequently by other means. Maconochie had personal views and a penchant for humanitarianism, and his lenient administrative style toward prisoners was unpopular with his superiors as well as other penal officials. For instance, Maconochie believed that confinement ought to be rehabilitative, not punitive. Also, he felt that prisoners ought to be granted early release from custody if they behaved well and did good work while confined. Thus, Maconochie established the *mark system* whereby he gave prisoners **marks of commendation** and authorized the early release of certain inmates who demonstrated a willingness and ability to behave well in society on the outside. This action was the early manifestation of indeterminate sentencing that was subsequently established in the United States. Maconochie's termination as superintendent at Norfolk Island occurred largely because he filed a report that condemned the English penal system and the disciplinary measures used by the island penal colony. He was sent back to England in 1844.

| BOX 7.1 | **Rehabilitation through Breaking in Wild Horses?** |

The Four Mile Correctional Center, Colorado Springs, Colorado

How should prison inmates be rehabilitated? In Colorado Springs, Colorado, state officials think that they have found at least one way that seems to work. At the Four Mile Correctional Center near Colorado Springs, some of the inmates are involved in a new program to work with wild horses, training them to be tame for horse ranches. In the program, wild horses are collected on federal lands in Nevada, Wyoming, and Colorado and are brought to the state prison under an agreement with the Colorado Department of Corrections and the U.S. Bureau of Land Management. According to Sheri Bell, a Bureau of Land Management spokesperson, "We formed a partnership with the prison in which they could give inmates the opportunity to learn new skills and a meaningful job and also serve a need we had in terms of marketing. It was really a success from the very instant it started."

The horses are rounded up and offered for adoption because they reproduce so quickly and would starve if left unattended in the desert wilderness. Summer droughts have killed most of the grass horses would ordinarily eat. More than 2,000 horses, or 200 per year, have been trained at the 8,500-acre prison ranch since the program began in 1986.

For inmates to become eligible to participate in the horse program, they must apply. They are paid for their work in the program by the Corrections Department. All the inmates are minimum-security prisoners who aren't considered dangerous, according to George Uhland, the prison's agribusiness production manager. One inmate, Jaime Chapa, works with a six-year-old black mustang to accept a saddle. The horse is taught to walk, trot, and canter around a ring after about two months of training. The program has assisted numerous inmates in various ways. One spokesperson said, "It takes a lot of patience to train a horse, and to train others how to train a horse." The program also teaches the inmates communication skills and responsibility and gives them goals.

Inmates indicate that the program also gives them a sense of pride. One inmate, 26-year-old Manuel Torres, said, "We're doing this for people on the streets. It makes you feel good to send home a good horse." People can adopt tamed animals for a $125 fee. For an additional $650, owners can get horses already walking on a lead and ready to ride, thanks to the work of dedicated inmates.

Is this type of program workable in all states? Should all inmates have access to such a program? What eligibility criteria would you adopt for such a program if you had to handpick inmates to become involved in it? What do you think?

Source: Adapted from Tiffany Meredith and the Associated Press, "Inmates Train Wild Horses for Adoption," November 26, 2000.

Maconochie's prison reform work did not end with this dismissal. During the next five years, he was transferred from one desk job to another, although he continued to press for penal reforms. Eventually he was reassigned, probably as a probationary move by his superiors, to the governorship of the new Birmingham Borough Prison. His position there lasted less than two years. His superiors dismissed him for being too lenient with prisoners. In 1853, he successfully lobbied for the passage of the English Penal Servitude Act that established several rehabilitation programs for inmates and abolished transporting prisoners to Australia. Because of these significant improvements in British penal policy and the institutionalization of early-release provisions throughout England's prison system, Maconochie is credited as being the father of parole.

Sir Walter Crofton, a prison reformer and director of Ireland's prison system during the 1850s, was impressed by Maconochie's work and copied his three-stage intermediate system whereby Irish prisoners could earn their early conditional release. Crofton, also known as another father of parole in various European countries, modified Maconochie's plan whereby prisoners would be

1. subject to strict imprisonment for a time
2. transferred to an intermediate prison for a short period where they could participate in educational programs and perform useful and responsible tasks to earn **good marks**
3. given tickets-of-leave whereby they would be released from prison on license under the limited supervision of local police

Under this third ticket-of-leave stage, released prisoners were required to submit monthly reports of their progress to police who assisted them in finding work. A study of 557 prisoners during that period showed only 17 had their tickets-of-leave revoked for various infractions. Thus, Crofton pioneered what later came to be known as several major functions of parole officers: employment assistance to released prisoners, regular visits by officers to parolees, and the general supervision of their activities (Bottomley, 1984).

The U.S. connection with the European use of parole allegedly occurred in 1863 when Gaylord Hubbell, the warden at Sing Sing Prison, New York, visited Ireland and conferred with Crofton about his penal innovations and parole system. Subsequently, the National Prison Association convened in Cincinnati, Ohio, in 1870 and considered the Irish parole system as a primary portion of its agenda. Attending that meeting were Crofton, Hubbell, and other reformers and penologists. The meeting resulted in the establishment of a Declaration of Principles that promoted an indeterminate sentence and a classification system based largely on Crofton's work (Bottomley, 1984). Table 7.1 shows Crofton's mark system, which functioned as a pattern for various states to follow after formally adopting versions of Crofton's scheme.

Zebulon Brockway became the new superintendent of the New York State Reformatory at Elmira in 1876 and was instrumental in the passage of the first indeterminate sentencing law in the U.S. (American Correctional Association, 1983). He is also credited with introducing the first **good time system** in which an inmate's sentence to be served is reduced by the number of good marks earned. **Good time** or credit applied to one's maximum sentence, was given. If an inmate accumulated sufficient good time credit, then he or she could be released short of serving the full sentence originally imposed by the judge. Once this system was in operation and shown to be moderately effective, several other states patterned their own early-release standards after it. Elmira Reformatory was important in part because it used the good time release system for prisoners in 1876. Actually, the practice of using early release for inmates occurred in the United States much earlier. Parole was officially established in Boston by Samuel G. Howe in 1847. From 1790 to 1817, convicts were obligated to serve their entire sentences in prison (American Correctional Association, 1983).

In 1817, New York adopted a form of commutation or lessening of sentence which became known as good time. Through the accumulation of sufficient good time, an inmate could be granted early release through his good behavior. This good

TABLE 7.1 Mark System Developed by Sir Walter Crofton

| Class and Number of Marks to be Gained for Admission to the Intermediate Prisons for Different Sentences[a] | Sentences of Penal Servitude (Years) | Shortest Periods of Imprisonment | | | | Periods of Remission on License |
| | | In ordinary prisons | | Shortest period of detention in intermediate prisons | | |
		Years	Months	Years	Months	
Class 1st 100‰	3	2	2	0	4	
			2– –6			
Class 6 A, or 6 months in A class	4	2	10	0	5	
			3– –3			
Class 14 A, or 14 months in A class	5	3	6	0	6	The periods remitted on License will be proportionate to the length of sentences and will depend upon the fitness of each Convict for release after a careful consideration has been given to his case by the government.
			4– –0			
Class 17 A, or 17 months in A class	6	3	9	0	9	
			4– –6			
Class 20 A, or 20 months in A class	7	4	0	1	3	
			5– –3			
Class 28 A, or 28 months in A class	8	4	8	1	4	
			6– –0			
Class 44 A, or 44 months in A class	10	6	0	1	6	
			7– –6			
Class 59 A, or 59 months in A class	12	7	3	1	9	
			9– –0			
Class 68 A, or 68 months in A class	15	8	0	2	0	
			10– –0			

Source: Mary Carpenter, *Reformatory Prison Discipline as Developed by the Rt. Hon. Sir Walter Crofton in the Irish Convict Prison* (Montclair, NJ: Patterson-Smith, 1967, reprint of 1872 ed.).

[a]The earliest possible periods of removal to Intermediate Prisons apply only to those of the most unexceptionable character, and no remission of the full sentence will take place unless the prisoner has qualified himself by carefully measured good conduct for passing the periods in the Intermediate Prisons prescribed by the Rules; and any delay in this qualification will have the effect of postponing his admission into the Intermediate Prisons, and thereby deferring to the same extent the remission of a portion of his sentence.

time early release was essentially a **pardon**, an executive device designed to absolve offenders of their crimes committed and release them, thus alleviating the prison overcrowding situation. The unofficial practice of parole therefore preceded the unofficial practice of probation by several decades. Officially, however, true parole resulted from the ticket-of-leave practice and was first adopted in 1884 by Massachusetts, also the first state to officially implement the practice of probation in 1878 (Bottomley, 1984).

PAROLE AND ALTERNATIVE SENTENCING SYSTEMS

A general relation exists between indeterminate sentencing and parole. Jurisdictions' adoption of indeterminate sentencing schemes does not mean, however, that either parole or parole boards are automatically established. Indeterminate sentencing indicates a minimum and a maximum term of years or months inmates may serve. Ordinarily, inmates must serve the minimum amount of time specified, but they may be released in different ways short of serving their full terms. Parole boards determine early-release dates for inmates under this type of sentencing system, but there are other early-release options besides parole board actions. For example, by 1911, nine states were using indeterminate sentencing. Eleven years earlier, in 1900, however, 20 states had established parole plans to effect the early release of prison inmates. Some of these jurisdictions had mandatory sentencing provisions, whereas others had determinate sentencing schemes. Early release short of serving one's full term could be administratively granted from prison officials or the governor or through the accumulation of good time credits applied against the maximum time to be served. In short, it is not the case that indeterminate sentencing and parole boards must coexist in any jurisdiction simultaneously (Shane-DuBow, Brown, and Olsen, 1985:6).

Usually, a parole system in any state prison consisted of the warden and other local authorities, including the prison physician, the superintendent of prisons, and certain community officials. The federal prison system had no formal parole board until 1910, and then it was similarly composed of officials making up state parole boards. Prior to the establishment of these boards and within the context of indeterminate sentencing, the discretion to release a prisoner short of serving his or her full term rested with the prison warden, superintendent, or state governor.

By 1944, all states had parole systems. The U.S. Congress formally established a U.S. Board of Parole in 1930. By the 1960s, all states had some form of indeterminate sentencing. Apart from the obvious benefits of alleviating prison overcrowding, parole and indeterminate sentencing were perceived for nearly a century as a panacea for reforming criminals. The rehabilitative ideal dominated the structure and process of all phases of corrections as well as most corrections programs (American Correctional Association, 1983).

Not all states used parole for rehabilitative purposes, however. In 1893, California adopted parole as (1) a way of minimizing the use of clemency by governors and (2) to correct and/or modify excessive prison sentences in relation to certain crimes committed. In fact, officials who favored parole in California were skeptical about its rehabilitative value. Parole was seen primarily as a period during which the end of a determinate sentence would occur that was originally imposed by the court (Messinger et al., 1985). A majority of the states, though, stressed the rehabilitative value of indeterminate sentencing and parole generally. Although the principle of deterrence dominated corrections philosophy for most of the 1820 to 1900 period, from 1900 to 1960 the principle of rehabilitation was of primary importance. Indeterminate sentencing was largely in the hands of corrections "observers" such as social workers, wardens, and probation and parole officers (Rothman, 1983).

One early criticism of parole was contained in a series of reports issued in 1931 by the **Wickersham Commission**, a National Commission on Law Observance and Enforcement (National Commission on Law Observance and Enforcement, 1931). The Wickersham Commission derived its name from its chairman, George W. Wickersham, a former U.S. Attorney General. Prepared shortly after Prohibition and the Depression, the Wickersham reports were very critical of most criminal justice agencies and how they dealt with crime and criminals. Although parole was not the sole target of criticism by the Wickersham Commission, it did receive many criticisms, among which were that parole released many dangerous criminals into society and that those offenders were not rehabilitated and unsupervised. Also, the Wickersham Commission did not believe that a suitable system for determining which prisoners should be eligible for parole existed. Although these reports caused considerable debate among corrections professionals for several years, nothing was done to alter the existing operations of state or federal parole systems. The rehabilitation or medical model, together with social work and psychiatry, became increasingly popular as members of these helping professions attempted to treat prisoner adjustment problems through therapy, medicine, and counseling.

Indeterminate Sentencing and Parole

Indeterminate sentencing is the only sentencing scheme that involves the intervention of parole boards. Because parole boards are vested with virtually absolute discretion concerning who does and does not get paroled, they are considered powerful entities, but because they have been responsible for the release of more than a few inmates who have subsequently committed violent crimes, they have attracted considerable adverse criticism. The major positive and negative aspects of indeterminate sentencing have already been described. Some of the positive features of indeterminate sentencing are that it

1. Allows for full implementation of rehabilitative ideal
2. Offers the best means of motivating involuntarily committed inmates to work for rehabilitation
3. Offers maximum protection to society from hardcore recidivists and mentally defective offenders
4. Helps maintain an orderly environment within the institution
5. Prevents unnecessary incarceration of an offender and thus helps prevent the correctional system from becoming a factory from which offenders emerge as hardened criminals
6. Offers a feasible alternative to capital punishment
7. Removes judgment as to length of incarceration from the trial court and puts it in the hands of a qualified panel of behavioral observers that makes its final decision based on considerably more evidence than is available at the postconviction stage of the trial

8. Reflects the needs of the offender and not the gravity of the crime, in the best interests of both society and offender
9. Prevents correctional authorities from being forced to release from custody an offender who is clearly not ready to rejoin society
10. Prevents a problem offender from retreating into a "sick" role during rehabilitation
11. Acts as a deterrent to crime

Some of the negative features of indeterminate sentences are the following:

1. Treatment is a myth and vocational training is a fraud; inmates are neither treated, trained, nor rehabilitated.
2. Even if treatment were honestly attempted by staffs, psychotherapy with involuntarily committed patients is generally considered difficult; indeterminate sentencing supplies only negative motivation, which will be insufficient for long-range results.
3. Even if effective therapy were plausible for some offenders, it is neither justified nor proper for all offenders, and there should be a right not to receive unwanted therapy.
4. Treatment is tokenism and rehabilitation is almost nonexistent; therefore, the indeterminate sentence is a device to hide society's dehumanizing treatment of criminals, particularly those who are poor or are members of minority groups.
5. Taking criminals off the street makes it easy for society to ignore the underlying causes of crime.
6. The indeterminate sentence is most often used as an instrument of inmate control.
7. Psychiatrists become more jailers than healers; they know that they will have to testify later in court about the patient and recommend or not recommend a prisoner's release.
8. Designations of some offenders as mentally ill are extremely arbitrary; therefore, single treatment approaches are impossible to devise.
9. There is great danger that indeterminate sentencing will be used to punish persons for unpopular political beliefs and views; religious and political nonconformists are most likely to rebel against a therapeutic system.
10. Indeterminate sentence encourages the smart or cunning offender and is more favorable to him or her than to the less intelligent offender.
11. Even though courts are supposed to retain some measure of control, there is no adequate protection from life imprisonment under the guise of indeterminate sentencing. (Fogel and Hudson, 1981:72–75)

Because of rising crime rates, unacceptable levels of recidivism among parolees, and general dissension among the ranks of corrections professionals about the most effective ways of dealing with offenders, the 1970s reflected a gradual decline in the significance and influence of the rehabilitation model. Selected jurisdictions, however, have reported success with parole programs in which effective community supervision and offender management have been provided or in which POs have performed their supervisory roles properly (Byrne and Brewster, 1993). Whether parole rehabilitates is arguable. In any case, the rehabilitation model has been largely replaced by the justice model (Dickey, 1989). The mission of the justice model or perspective is fairness, with prison regarded as the instrument whereby sentences are implemented without being held accountable for rehabilitating offenders (Fogel, 1979:202). The justice model has assisted greatly in prompting most states as well as the federal government to undertake extensive revisions of their sentencing guidelines. The general thrust of these revisions is toward a get-tough-on-crime crusade that is replacing reform with retribution (Petersilia, 1999a).

Another goal of the justice model is to minimize if not eliminate entirely any sentencing disparities often associated with indeterminate sentencing schemes and the arbitrariness of parole board decisions. It is questionable, however, whether any sentencing scheme will achieve such desirable results. Some authorities suggest that there is every reason to believe that judges will continue to impose sentences according to previous discriminatory patterns where extralegal factors are influential. Such extralegal factors include race, ethnicity, gender, age, and socioeconomic status (Steffensmeier, Kramer, and Streifel, 1993).

The Shift to Determinate Sentencing

Nearly half the states had shifted from indeterminate to determinate sentencing by 1995 (Marvell and Moody, 1996), resulting in the abolition of paroling authority in a few states for making early prisoner release decisions. An additional consequence has been to limit the discretionary sentencing power of judges. The remaining states and the District of Columbia have also instituted numerous sentencing reforms calculated to deal more harshly with offenders; to reduce or eliminate sentencing disparities attributable to race, ethnicity, or socioeconomic status; to increase prisoner release predictability as well as the certainty of incarceration; and/or to deter or control crime. In many of these states, the authority of parole boards to grant early release as well as the calculation of good time credits have been restricted to varying degrees (Tonry, 1999b).

On November 1, 1987, the U.S. Sentencing Commission entirely revamped existing sentencing guidelines for federal district judges (Champion, 1989). The long-range implications of these changes are unknown, but some preliminary estimates have been projected. For instance, the average time served prior to November 1, 1987, for kidnapping was from 7.2 to 9 years. The new guidelines provide an incarcerative term for offenders of from 4.2 to 5.2 years. For first-degree murder convictions, however, the new guidelines prescribe 30 years to life for all offenders, compared with 10 to 12.5 years time served, on the average, under old sentencing practices by federal judges. Therefore, more convicted felons will go to prison, but many of these offenses will carry shorter incarceration terms (Tonry, 1999b).

Although these sentencing guidelines are only applicable to U.S. district courts and federal judges and magistrates, some states have similar guidelines-based or presumptive sentencing schemes (Mitchell and Dodenhoff, 1998). Other states such as California, Minnesota, Pennsylvania, and Washington already have existing penalties for certain offenses that are similar in severity to those prescribed for the same offenses by the U.S. sentencing guidelines. By 1998, 26 states had established sentencing guidelines for their prison inmates (Albonetti, 1999; Tonry, 1999b).

In Pennsylvania, sentencing guidelines were introduced in the early 1980s (*Corrections Compendium,* 1992d:18). Compared with an indeterminate sentencing scheme used prior to these guidelines, actual sentences imposed have become more severe for violent offenders. Yet sentencing severity has also increased for many nonviolent property offenders. It is unclear whether this outcome was contemplated by the Pennsylvania State Legislature when the guidelines were determined. At least one objective of Pennsylvania's guidelines was to remedy sentencing disparities. Some evidence suggests that this outcome has been realized in part. Pennsylvania state prison growth, however, was 171 percent during the 1980s, so that by 1990, the prison system housing accommodated more than 24,000 inmates in space actually designed for 16,000 inmates. At the time of this writing, Pennsylvania authorities were constructing new prison space to house 10,000 additional offenders at a cost of $1.3 billion (*Corrections Compendium,* 1992d:18).

Critics contend that although determinate sentencing may provide prisoners with release certainty and possibly result in more fairness in the sentencing process, several discretionary decisions at various stages in the adjudication and postadjudication period are uncontrolled by this sentencing form. Six decision-making stages or factors have been identified as critical to sentencing equity and predictability:

1. The decision to incarcerate
2. The characteristics of the penalty scaling system, including the numbers of penalty ranges and offense categories
3. The presence or absence of aggravating or mitigating circumstances
4. The parole review process
5. The use of good time in calculating early release
6. Revocation from supervised release (Goodstein, Kramer, and Nuss, 1984)

In addition, prosecutorial discretion concerning which cases should be prosecuted, reports of arresting officers and circumstances surrounding arrests, evidentiary factors, and judicial idiosyncrasies figure prominently in many sentencing decisions at state and federal levels. Thus, regardless of the nature and scope of existing sentencing provisions, the prospects for the effective control over all the relevant discretionary decisions that influence sentencing are not overwhelmingly favorable. Although parole boards in 36 states have continued to exercise discretion over the early release of prisoners, parole continues to draw criticism from both the public and corrections professionals (Metchik, 1992a, 1992b).

The American Correctional Association established a Task Force on Parole to examine how states have established and implemented their present parole policies and guidelines (American Correctional Association, 1995c). This task force has found that parole is undergoing alteration in various jurisdictions because of both political and public pressures. States such as Pennsylvania have established guidelines for their parole boards to follow for making their early release decisions about offenders. These guidelines are similar to the ones created in these same states for judicial sentencing decisions.

Good Time Credits and Early Release.   Good time credits may be called gain time, earned time, statutory time, meritorious time, commutation time, provisional credits, good conduct credits, or disciplinary credits (Davis, 1990a:1). Whatever the term, good time is a reward for good behavior and a prevalent management tool in most U.S. prisons. For instance, Arkansas uses the good time standard of 30 days of good time for every 30 days served. Thus, when offenders are sentenced to ten years in Arkansas, offenders know that for every month they serve, 30 days will be deducted from their ten-year maximum term. In Iowa, the standard of 15 days of good time for every 30 days served is used. Therefore, serving six years in an Iowa prison means that three years is deducted from one's original ten-year sentence. Accumulating good time and being released is not the same thing as being paroled. In the case of an Arkansas inmate who has served one-half of his or her original sentence, he or she is free from prison without conditions. This practice is not absolute in all jurisdictions, however. In some states, inmates released as the result of good time credit accumulation must serve some of or all their remaining time on supervised **mandatory release** (Jankowski, 1991:5). Table 7.2 shows various states with different good time provisions.

A majority of states permit the accumulation of good time credit at the rate of 15 days or more per month served. The Federal Bureau of Prisons permits 54 days per year as good time credit to be earned by federal prisoners. Some states permit additional credits to be accumulated for participation in vocational or educational programs. Some states, such as New Hampshire, have an interesting variation on this theme. Instead of rewarding prisoners with good time credits, New Hampshire authorities add 150 days to the minimum sentences imposed. These 150 days can be reduced at the rate of 12½ days per month of good behavior or exemplary conduct, according to the New Hampshire prison system (Griset, 1996).

There are various motives behind different state provisions for good time, with prison overcrowding being perhaps the most frequently cited reason. Good time credit allowances, however, can also encourage inmates to participate in useful vocational and educational programs. More than a few inmates abuse the good time system by enrolling in these programs in a token fashion, but many inmates derive good benefits from them as well. Also, good time credits influence one's security placement while institutionalized. Those inmates who behave well may be moved from

TABLE 7.2 Good Time Credits for Different State Jurisdictions

More than 30 days per month

Alabama, Oklahoma, South Carolina, Texas

30 days per month

Arkansas, Florida, Illinois, Indiana, Kansas, Louisiana, Nevada, New Mexico, Virginia, West Virginia

20 days per month

Maryland, Massachusetts

15 days per month

Arizona, California, Connecticut, Kentucky, Maine, Nebraska, New Jersey, Rhode Island, South Dakota, Vermont, Washington, Wyoming

Fewer than 15 days per month

Alaska, Colorado, Delaware, District of Columbia, Federal Bureau of Prisons, Iowa, Michigan, Mississippi, Missouri, New Hampshire, New York, North Carolina, North Dakota, Oregon, Tennessee

No good time given

Georgia, Hawaii, Idaho, Minnesota, Ohio, Pennsylvania, Utah, Wisconsin

Source: Adapted from James Ching, "Credits as Personal Property: Beware of the New *Ex Post Facto Clause*," *Corrections Compendium*, **22:**1–16, 1997.

maximum- to medium- or from medium- to minimum-security custody levels over time. In addition, one's immediate classification level preceding a parole board hearing is taken into account as a factor influencing one's parole chances. Another reason for good time allowances or credits is to maintain and improve inmate management by prison administrative staff. Well-behaved inmates make it easier for officials to administer prison affairs. Those who do not obey prison rules are subject to good time credit deductions and are "written-up" by correctional officers for their misconduct. If inmates accumulate enough of these paper infractions, they may lose good time credits or, as in New Hampshire, they may fail to reduce the extra time imposed above their minimum sentences.

THE PHILOSOPHY OF PAROLE

Like probation, parole has been established for the purpose of *rehabilitating* offenders and *reintegrating* them into society. Parole is a continuation of a parolee's punishment, under varying degrees of supervision by parole officers, ending when the originally imposed sentence has been served. Officials have noted that parole is *earned* rather than automatically granted after serving a fixed amount of one's sentence. The punitive nature of parole is inherent in the conditions and restrictions accompanying it that other community residents are not obligated to follow (Rhine, Smith, and Jackson, 1991).

Parole's eighteenth-century origins suggest no philosophical foundation. In the 1700s, penological pragmatism permitted correctional officials to use parole to alleviate prison overcrowding. Between roughly 1850 and 1970, the influence of social reformers, religious leaders, and humanitarians on parole as a rehabilitative medium was quite apparent (Bottomley, 1984). Yet as has been seen, the pendulum has shifted away from rehabilitation (not entirely) and toward societal retribution. The early California experience with parole was anything but rehabilitative; rather, it was a bureaucratic tool to assist gubernatorial decision making in clemency cases involving excessively long sentences (Messinger et al., 1985).

FUNCTIONS OF PAROLE

The functions of parole are probably best understood when couched in terms of manifest and latent functions. **Manifest functions** are intended or recognized, apparent to all. **Latent functions** are also important, but they are hidden and less transparent (Castellano et al., 1993). Two important manifest functions of parole are to reintegrate parolees into society and to control and/or deter crime. Three latent functions of parole are to ease prison and jail overcrowding, to remedy sentencing disparities, and to protect the public.

Offender Reintegration

Incarcerated offenders, especially those who have been incarcerated for long periods, often find it difficult to readjust to life in the community. Inmate idleness and a unique prison subculture, regimentation and strict conformity to numerous rules, and continuous exposure to a population of criminals who have committed every offense imaginable simply fail to prepare prisoners adequately for noncustodial living (Yeboah, 2000). Parole provides a means through which an offender may make a smooth transition from prison life to living in a community with some degree of freedom under supervision (West-Smith, Pogrebin, and Poole, 2000). Parole functions as a reintegrative mechanism for both juveniles and adults (Altschuler, Armstrong, and MacKenzie, 1999).

Crime Deterrence and Control

It is believed by some correctional authorities that rewarding an inmate for good behavior while in prison through an early conditional release under supervision will promote respect for the law. Some persons believe that keeping an offender imprisoned for prolonged periods will increase the offender's bitterness toward society and result in the commission of new and more serious offenses. Yet there is some evidence to the contrary. For instance, a study of parole board decision making in Nebraska showed that parole-eligible inmates who were denied parole were more likely to comply with institutional rules and behave well following their parole denials. Institutional misconduct also decreased for offenders not granted parole hearings. This information suggests that once these inmates have been rejected for early release or denied a parole hearing, they may seek to conform with institutional rules to a greater degree than before (Proctor and Pease, 2000). Therefore, the prospect of parole provides a strong incentive for inmates to comply with institutional rules. Although that does not mean that they will obey societal rules if released into their communities later, it is a good indication that they have the capacity to follow rules when they choose to do so and if it is in their best interests. Parole boards are persuaded to grant early release to offenders with good conduct records while incarcerated. They are deemed better risks than those who engage in institutional misconduct.

Early release from prison, under appropriate supervision, implies an agreement of trust between the state and offender (Josi and Sechrest, 1999). In many instances, this trust instills a degree of self-confidence in the offender, which yields the desired law-abiding results. Then again, some claim that parole is a failure, although they cannot say for certain whether the problem rests with parole itself or with the abuse of discretion on the part of parole-granting bodies (Petersilia, 1999a). Deterrence and crime control actually extend beyond parole board decision making. PO supervisory practices within the community play an important part in controlling offender behaviors. Furthermore, POs can be of assistance in linking their clients with necessary community services, such as psychological counseling and programming, vocational/technical and educational programs, and other services (Burns et al., 1999).

Decreasing Prison and Jail Overcrowding

Another function of parole is to alleviate jail and prison overcrowding. Parole is a back-end solution inasmuch as parole boards exercise considerable discretion about which offenders will be released short of serving their full terms, although more than a few parole board members in various jurisdictions do not perceive their decision making to be affected by prison overcrowding conditions (Burns et al., 1999). Every state has a paroling authority, although several states have eliminated parole as an early-release option. That some states and the federal government have abolished parole and substituted other means whereby inmates may be freed short of serving their full sentences does not mean that those previously sentenced under an indeterminate sentencing scheme are no longer within the jurisdiction of parole boards (U.S. Sentencing Commission, 1996). For instance, Maine was the first state to abolish parole in 1976, yet its parole board continues to meet from time to time to hear early-release petitions from inmates who were convicted prior to 1976. The old rules for early release still apply to these offenders, but their numbers are diminishing. In 1999, for instance, Maine had only 31 parolees, with two released from parole supervision. The Maine Parole Board will continue to exist as long as there are parolees in the state. If one or more parolees violate their parole conditions, then the Maine Parole Board must determine whether such violations are sufficient to revoke their parole programs. If so, then some Maine parolees may be returned to prison.

Most states have significant numbers of parolees and are quite different from Maine. In fact, there were 696,385 persons on parole in the United States in 1999, a sizable number given that the total number of those incarcerated in jails and prisons in 1999 was about 1.8 million. Parole is definitely making a difference to jail and prison populations, because parolee numbers are about a third of the number of all incarcerated offenders. Also, there is a fairly brisk turnover among parolees annually, with slightly more parolees entering parole programs than are released from them. For instance, in 1999, there were 429,172 new parolees entering parole programs and 412,167 exits or persons leaving parole supervision, an increase of 2.3 percent from 1998 (U.S. Department of Justice, 2000:5).

Interestingly, the influence of parole boards on prison population sizes may be overstated. Some jurisdictions, such as Florida, report that following the abolition of parole in 1983 and a transformation from indeterminate to determinate sentencing, average prison sentences of convicted offenders were reduced to a greater degree through statutorily mandated earned good time credits. Thus, larger numbers of offenders were being released from Florida prisons earlier under determinate sentencing than under indeterminate sentencing in which parole board discretion was exercised (Florida Department of Corrections, 1999).

Compensating for Sentencing Disparities

One criticism of sentencing practices in both the states and federal system is that judges impose disparate sentences on the basis of race/ethnicity, age, gender, and/or socioeconomic status. In an effort to remedy sentencing disparities, parole boards can exercise their discretion and adjust the sentences of those who appear to be unfairly penalized because of extralegal factors. Evidence exists to suggest that some disparities in sentencing have been minimized through determinate sentencing in selected jurisdictions (Hofer et al., 1999).

Among the states to implement wholesale changes in their sentencing practices is Minnesota. This state established sentencing guidelines in 1980, and officials noted substantial decreases in prior sentencing disparities attributable to race, ethnicity, age, gender, and socioeconomic status (Albonetti, 1999; D'Alessio and Stolzenberg, 1995). Sentences were more uniform as to who goes to prison and how long they serve. Similar results have been found as the result of sentencing reforms in North Carolina and Georgia (Duncan, Speir, and Meredith, 1999; Lillis, 1994).

An informed parole board is capable of making decisions about early releases of inmates that are fairer than those calculated through determinate sentencing provisions. In Ohio, parole boards permit victims of crimes, the sentencing judge, prosecutor, and the media to be notified of and attend parole hearings, and they actively solicit essential documentation to support their subsequent parole decision (Ohio Parole Board, 1992). Inmates have an opportunity to present evidence of their progress in prison as well as their constructive parole plans. If granted early release, then they must sign an agreement to abide by the conditions required for successful parole supervision, and they are ultimately responsible for their own conduct while completing the term of their parole (Stolzenberg, 1993).

Public Safety and Protection

A primary area of concern for citizens relating to parole is offender **risk** (Champion, 1994). There are no foolproof ways of forecasting an offender's future dangerousness, yet dangerous offenders are freed by parole boards daily throughout the United States. Many of these offenders have demonstrated by their work in prison that they are potentially capable of leading law-abiding lives (Gillis, Motiuk, and Belcourt, 1998). Parole boards use different methods for determining which offenders should be released. Such forecasts of offender risk have been used since the 1920s (Bruce et al., 1928). Predicting offender success on parole is a major policy issue in most jurisdictions. This issue has led to numerous reforms relating to sentencing and parole board decision making and to the criteria used for risk forecasting (Pratt, Maahs, and Stehr, 1998). There is currently no universal policy in effect throughout all U.S. jurisdictions. Each state and the federal government have independent criteria that are used for early-release decision making.

One critical issue is determining whose interests are more important, the public's or the inmate's. Parole offers inmates a chance to live reasonably normal lives in society, but some risk is assumed by parole boards when parole is granted. No one knows for sure how each parolee will respond to his or her parole program. Parolee failures cause people to view the whole idea of parole with skepticism (Grant and Gal, 1998; Shearer, 2000). Many other parolees, however, have successful experiences while on parole. They are able to readjust to community living and refrain from committing new offenses. For all practical purposes, they have become rehabilitated. In 1999, 412,167 parolees were discharged from their parole programs, meaning that they endured their parole programs without incident and refrained from violating the law or their parole program conditions (U.S. Department of Justice, 2000:5). Proportionately, about a third of all parolees remain violation-free within their jurisdictions. This fact does not mean that the other two-thirds commit new crimes, but they may violate one or more of their parole program conditions, such as curfew, or failing an alcohol or drug test (New York State Division of Parole, 1998).

Parole departments throughout the United States supervise their clients more or less intensively. Most departments have specialized units of parole officers to deal with parolees with particular problems, such as alcohol or substance abuse issues. Different types of community services are available to parolees with various problems to enable them to improve themselves in different ways (Wright, 1997). Evidence suggests,

---

BOX 7.2   ***More Prisoners and Parolees on the Internet***

Databases of Prisoners and Parolees on the Internet?

Do you want to know if your neighbor is a parolee or a probationer? Do you want to know if your cousin is in prison somewhere? If you get on the Internet and enter certain Web sites, you might find out. A growing number of states are offering online databases of inmates and parolees, permitting citizens to check out convicted neighbors and employers to screen prospective employees. Civil liberty groups say that the Internet sites are making it harder for ex-convicts to return to society and become reintegrated and rehabilitated.

Ari Schwartz, policy analyst for the Center for Democracy and Technology headquartered in Washington, D.C., says that there has always been a desire among the public to get criminal information online. Yet it really raises the issue of just because it's possible, is it desirable? In 2000, at least 18 states operated Web sites through which citizens can find the names, pictures, criminal records, and sentences for current inmates and those on parole. Some states include both federal and state records.

In 2001, Indiana was planning on establishing such a Web site, and several other states have indicated their intention to offer limited databases for narrower prison populations such as sex offenders, death row inmates, and fugitives. One of the first states to put the names of prisoners on the Internet was Florida, which opened its Web site in 1997. Kentucky followed in December 2000. The Kentucky Offender Online Lookup site will soon carry the records of 22,500 inmates and parolees going back to 1978. State officials contend that such information is a matter of public record and can contribute to public safety. Once a person finishes parole, his or her name is purged from the site. C. J. Drake, a spokesperson for the Florida Department of Corrections, says, "It gives the public, the press, law enforcement agencies and inmate relatives as well as victims immediate access to inmate information."

There is growing popularity among U.S. citizens for having such information available on the Internet. More than 2.2 million hits were recorded by Florida's inmate and parolee sites in December 2000 alone. Persons supporting such sites say that citizens are permitted to check whether any parolees live in their neighborhood or when a convicted neighbor is leaving prison, and employers can check to see if a prospective hire is on parole. The National Center for the Victims of Crime (NCVC) is very much in favor of such databases. Susan Howley, director of public policy for the NCVC, says, "Whenever you're talking about managing offenders, you're having to balance public safety concerns with individual rights. But we think where there is a victim, a witness, or even a neighbor, that balance weighs in favor of public safety."

Critics contend, however, that although the information may be useful for some, it can detract from another worthy goal: reintegrating and rehabilitating inmates. Larry Spalding, legislative counsel for the American Civil Liberties Union, says, "You probably catch some dangerous offenders, but you also do a lot of damage to people who are legitimately trying to make a new start to improve themselves. When you've got the information on the Web, it's very difficult to get or keep a job." One ex-offender, William Stillwell, a federal criminal from Oshkosh, Wisconsin, said that he felt blackballed in society because of his prison record. He said that it's difficult to find a job or housing because of public access to this information. Despite these objections, there is little hope of preventing Web sites from posting information about offenders, because their offending behavior is a matter of public record.

Should prisoner information be available for public scrutiny on the Internet? Should the names of prisoners and parolees be posted for citizens to access at their will? What are the benefits and liabilities for posting such information? Are prisoners really harmed by such information? Whose rights are more important, the victim's or the perpetrator's? What do you think?

Source: Adapted from D. Ian Hopper and Associated Press, "More Prisoners, Parolees on Web," December 28, 2000.

however, that some parole departments and POs have negative views toward their clients and are predisposed to view them unfavorably. Thus, the assistance parolees receive from their POs may not be entirely supportive (Lynch, 2000; Petersilia, 1999b).

Society must cope with eventual offender releases, because many offenders serve their time and are released unconditionally anyway. The early release of a portion of these offenders is based on prior department practices and parole board dispositions. No offender who is seriously believed to pose a public risk is deliberately released short of serving his or her full term of confinement (Nieves, Draine, and Solomon, 2000). Paroling authorities believe that they can predict with a reasonable degree of certainty that most of those who receive early release will be properly supervised and will live law-abiding lives. From the perspective of inmates, they deserve a chance within their communities to prove themselves capable of earning societal trust through their good works (Altschuler, Armstrong, and MacKenzie, 1999; Wheeler-Cox, Arrigona, and Reichers, 1998).

A PROFILE OF PAROLEES IN THE UNITED STATES

Numbers of Parolees under Supervision.   In 1999, 6.3 million persons were under some form of correctional supervision in the United States. Of these, 712,713, or about 11.3 percent, were on parole. About 9 percent of these were federal parolees, whereas the remainder were from state prisons. The parole population grew in the United States by 2.3 percent between 1998 and 1999. Seven states reported parolee increases greater than 10 percent: Ohio (39.6 percent), South Dakota (20.9 percent), West Virginia (18.8 percent), Louisiana (16.8 percent), Iowa (14.6 percent), Hawaii (12.1 percent), and Minnesota (10.4 percent) (U.S. Department of Justice, 2000:5). Substantial parolee decreases were reported by Washington (–46.7 percent) and North Carolina (–24.4 percent). Table 7.3 shows the number of state and federal offenders on parole, according to both state and U.S. region.

Methods of Release from Prison.   Releases of large numbers of inmates on parole are the result of many factors, such as prison overcrowding and good behavior of prisoners while confined. Also, prisons are attempting to manage their scarce space to accommodate the most dangerous offenders. Court-ordered prison population reductions, because of health and safety regulations and cruel and unusual punishment conditions associated with some prison facilities that have been unable to comply with federally mandated guidelines under which inmates may be confined, are another major contributing factor. Some of the older prisons in the United States are rat-infested, roach-ridden structures without proper heat or ventilation in winter or summer months. Coupled with chronic overcrowding, some of these institutions are simply inhumane. Courts draw the line and require minimal conditions under which human beings can be held in confinement.

A primary method of releasing inmates from prison is through parole board discretion. Parole board decision making accounts for approximately 42 percent of all inmate releases. For those states and the federal government that have abolished parole, usually the method of release has been designated as supervised mandatory release in which a parole board has not intervened. Approximately 50 percent of all inmate releases occur through this method. These types of releases are consistent with determinate sentencing, whereby inmates accrue sufficient good time credits to

TABLE 7.3 Adults on Parole, 1999

Region and Jurisdiction	Parole Population				Percent change during 1999	Number on Parole on 12/31/99 per 100,000 Adult Residents
	1/1/99	1999				
		Entries	Exits	12/31/99		
U.S. total	696,385	429,172	412,167	712,713	2.3%	352
Federal	67,169	26,653	22,575	71,020	5.7%	35
State	629,216	402,519	389,592	641,693	2.0	317
Northeast	162,006	49,962	51,023	162,840	0.5%	415
Connecticut	1,396	1,338	1,208	1,526	9.3	62
Maine	33	0	2	31	–6.1	3
Massachusetts*	4,489	4,033	3,689	4,304	–4.1	91
New Hampshire	1,141	:	:	1,146	0.4	128
New Jersey	13,218	10,394	10,644	12,968	–1.9	211
New York	59,548	25,200	26,792	57,956	–2.7	421
Pennsylvania	81,001	8,199	7,917	83,702	3.3	916
Rhode Island	432	515	534	413	–4.4	55
Vermont*	748	283	237	794	6.1	175
Midwest	94,110	77,648	71,737	100,021	6.3%	213
Illinois	30,432	25,422	25,370	30,484	0.2	341
Indiana*	4,258	4,898	4,617	4,539	6.6	103
Iowa*	2,194	2,805	2,485	2,514	14.6	117
Kansas	6,025	5,352	5,468	5,909	–1.9	302
Michigan	15,331	9,681	9,471	15,541	1.4	213
Minnesota	2,995	3,464	3,308	3,151	5.2	90
Missouri	10,366	8,501	7,419	11,448	10.4	281
Nebraska*	624	687	699	612	–1.9	50
North Dakota	174	370	387	157	–9.8	33
Ohio	11,304	11,237	6,765	15,776	39.6	188
South Dakota*	1,125	964	729	1,360	20.9	254
Wisconsin	9,282	4,267	5,019	8,530	–8.1	219
South	223,922	96,430	94,250	223,469	–0.2%	312
Alabama*	5,221	1,861	2,170	5,005	–4.1	151
Arkansas	6,979	5,519	4,853	7,645	9.5	404
Delaware*	572	268	206	634	10.8	111
District of Columbia	7,055	:	:	5,103	. . .	1,204
Florida*	6,487	4,780	4,413	6,418	–1.1	56
Georgia	20,482	12,149	10,290	22,003	7.4	384
Kentucky*	4,508	3,117	2,757	4,868	8.0	163
Louisiana	18,759	14,185	11,040	21,904	16.8	688
Maryland*	15,528	8,059	8,580	15,007	–3.4	389
Mississippi	1,489	688	821	1,356	–8.9	67
North Carolina	5,806	5,603	7,020	4,389	–24.4	77
Oklahoma	1,532	610	615	1,527	–0.3	62
South Carolina	4,404	786	1,246	3,944	–10.4	135

Region and Jurisdiction	Parole Population					Number on Parole on 12/31/99 per 100,000 Adult Residents
	1/1/99	1999 Entries	Exits	12/31/99	Percent change during 1999	
Tennessee	7,605	3,288	3,555	7,338	–3.5	177
Texas	109,820	30,316	30,826	109,310	–0.5	763
Virginia	6,700	4,357	5,197	5,860	–12.5	113
West Virginia	975	844	661	1,158	18.8	83
West	149,178	178,479	172,582	155,363	4.1%	348
Alaska*	478	321	306	493	3.1	117
Arizona*	3,742	6,490	6,517	3,715	–0.7	108
California*	108,424	153,571	148,303	114,046	5.2	471
Colorado*	5,204	3,979	3,920	5,263	1.1	176
Hawaii*	2,009	1,058	911	2,252	12.1	251
Idaho*	1,309	873	872	1,310	0.1	145
Montana*	667	500	618	549	–17.7	83
Nevada	4,055	:	:	3,893	–4.0	295
New Mexico	1,773	1,710	1,561	1,922	8.4	154
Oregon	17,270	7,485	6,881	17,874	3.5	718
Utah	3,424	2,249	2,285	3,388	–1.1	238
Washington	375	15	190	200	–46.7	5
Wyoming	448	228	218	458	2.2	130

Source: U.S. Department of Justice, *Probation and Parole, 1999* (Washington, DC: U.S. Department of Justice, 2000), 5.

Note: Because of nonresponse or incomplete data, the probation population for some jurisdictions on December 31, 1999, does not equal the population on January 1, 1999, plus entries, minus exits. During 1999, an estimated 451,600 persons entered parole supervision, and 434,300 exited, biased on imputations for agencies that did not provide data.

. . . Comparable percentage could not be calculated.

:Not known.

*Data do not include parolees in one or more of the following categories: absconder, out of state, inactive, intensive supervision, or electronic monitoring.

apply against their maximum sentences to be released automatically. Thus, inmates serving determinate sentences of 10 years but who are accruing good-time at the rate of 30 days per month for every 30 days served will be released after serving five years. In many jurisdictions, these inmates are free from further supervision by corrections authorities. In other jurisdictions, these inmates must serve some time on parole under the supervision of POs. The remaining 8 percent of releases are parolees who have had their parole programs reinstated or have been paroled for other reasons. Some inmates max out their sentences by serving them in their entirety or through administrative actions. In some instances, court-ordered reductions in inmate populations will cause administrators to release some inmates deemed to pose the least risk to society, regardless of the proportion of their sentences actually served (U.S. Department of Justice, 2000:2).

Profiling Parolees. Table 7.4 shows some primary characteristics of parolees in the United States for 1999 compared with the parolee population from 1990. One of the

TABLE 7.4 Characteristics of Adults on Parole, 1990 and 1999

Characteristic	1990	1999
Total	100%	100%
Gender	100%	100%
Male	92	88
Female	8	12
Race	100%	100%
White	52	55
Black	47	44
Other	1	1
Hispanic origin	100%	100%
Hispanic	18	21
Non-Hispanic	82	79
Status of supervision	100%	100%
Active	82	83
Inactive	6	5
Absconded	6	7
Supervised out of State	6	5
Other	—	**
Adults entering parole	100%	100%
Discretionary parole	59	42
Mandatory parole	41	50
Reinstatement	—	6
Other	—	2
Adults leaving parole	100%	100%
Successful completion	50	43
Returned to incarceration	46	42
With new sentence	17	11
Other	29	31
Absconder	1	10
Other unsuccessful	1	2
Transferred	1	1
Death	1	1
Other	—	2
Length of sentence	100%	100%
Less than 1 year	5	3
One year or more	95	97

Source: U.S. Department of Justice, *Probation and Parole, 1999* (Washington, DC: U.S. Department of Justice, 2000), 6.

Note: For every characteristic, there were persons of unknown status or type. Detail may not sum to total because of rounding.

—Not available.

**Less than 0.5%.

most significant changes from 1990 to 1999 is that female parolees increased from 8 percent to 12 percent of the parolee population. Racially, white parolees increased proportionately from 52 to 55 percent, and black parolees declined from 47 percent to 44 percent. That a somewhat larger proportion of parolees is white and that there are fewer black parolees might mean that blacks are serving longer sentences compared with whites before being paroled. The proportion of Hispanic parolees increased from 18 percent to 21 percent during the 1990 to 1999 period. Overall, however, the proportion of non-Hispanics declined from 82 percent to 79 percent (U.S. Department of Justice, 2000:6).

Not much changed between 1990 and 1999 regarding the status of supervision. Approximately 83 percent of all parolees are actively supervised. About 7 percent of all parolees have absconded and are being hunted as fugitives. Another 5 percent have had their parole programs transferred to other states. It is not uncommon for some parolees to request that they be transferred to their home states for parole supervision if they have been convicted for a crime and are serving time in another state. This action is usually accomplished through interstate pacts or agreements among parole departments. Consent of both departments in the different jurisdictions is required.

Successful completion of parole declined between 1990 and 1999. In 1990, 50 percent of all parolees had completed their parole programs successfully. By 1999, only 43 percent of all parolees had done so. In 1999, about 42 percent of all parolees had been returned to incarceration, with 25 percent of these being returned to serve a new sentence; the remaining 75 percent were returned for one or more parole program violations. About 3 percent of all parolees had been serving sentences of less than one year, and 97 percent were serving sentences of one or more years. There are some preliminary observations about why parolees fail to complete their programs successfully. Parole revocations are highly correlated with excessive alcohol use and substance abuse (Kassebaum, Davidson-Coronado, and Silverio, 1999). Furthermore, it would appear that at least for some samples of parolees studied, the greater the length of time spent in prison, the more they are likely to recidivate (Brumbaugh and Rouse, 1998; Kronick, Lambert, and Lambert, 1998). Of course, longer prison terms usually mean that more serious types of offenders are involved. Thus, it might be anticipated that more serious and/or violent offenders serving longer prison terms would be more likely to recidivate when paroled compared with less dangerous and nonviolent offenders serving shorter incarcerative terms.

Another factor relating to one's success while on parole is whether offenders have been employed full- or part-time. Those employed on a full-time basis are less likely to reoffend or violate their parole program conditions compared with those who are underemployed or unemployed while on parole (California Department of Corrections, 1997; Hanlon et al., 1998).

THE GROWING GANG PRESENCE

Increasing numbers of parolees are affiliated with gangs (Tonry, 1998). If convicted offenders are not gang members when they enter prison, the likelihood is that they will be affiliated with a gang when they leave prison on parole (American Correctional Association, 1993d). Gang membership increases one's propensity to reoffend, because most gangs are involved in illicit criminal activities and induce their membership to engage in such criminal enterprises as drug trafficking.

Also, increasing numbers of offenders who enter jails and prisons are already affiliated with gangs. Most of these new inmates joined gangs as juveniles (Buentello et al., 1992; Spergel et al., 1994). It is generally acknowledged that gangs exist in all states, that they are involved with drug sales and distribution, and that they are highly structured (Joo, 1993; Joo, Ekland-Olson, and Kelly, 1995). The variety and nature of gangs is explained by personal factors such as class, culture, race, and ethnicity along with community factors such as poverty, social instability, and social isolation (Spergel, 1993). Intergang violence is fairly common. Gang members are becoming older and remaining in gangs longer. Many of those entering prisons perpetuate their gang affiliations by joining existing gangs or by forming their own groups for self-protection and other interests.

Parole officers have reported that one of their major problems in dealing with parolees is gang affiliation, which is not always apparent. Many parolees attempt to disguise their gang affiliation by removing recognizable gang tattoos or by denying that they are gang members when visited by their POs (Texas Office of the Comptroller, 1992). It is often difficult for POs to prescribe treatments or needed community services for those affiliated with gangs, because there is strong resistance from parolee-clients who are gang-affiliated to becoming meaningfully involved in helpful interventions (California Assembly, 1996). Early research by Mark Wiederanders (1983) is indicative of more recent findings that parolee failure is strongly associated with prior records of delinquency and belonging to gangs prior to being arrested and convicted for present offenses (Fong, Vogel, and Buentello, 1996; Tonry, 1998).

Overcoming gang influence is difficult. POs may attempt to initiate contacts between parolees and their victims when personal injuries or property losses were sustained as the result of crimes committed. Sometimes restorative justice methods are effective in increasing the likelihood that parolees will remain law-abiding while on parole (Seiter, 2000). Yet despite the best intentions of POs and their agencies, there will always be a hardcore contingent of parolees who will prove to be unstable and will not abide by their parole program conditions. Some may even abscond from their jurisdictions (Williams, McShane, and Dolny, 2000). Greater police presence in gang-dominated neighborhoods assists POs in their attempts to keep parolees from engaging in further criminal activities as the result of gang influence (Grimes and Rogers, 1999).

The pervasiveness of gangs in areas where parolees are likely to reside together with ready access to addictive substances and alcohol, however, mean that POs are fighting an uphill battle in their efforts to reform, rehabilitate, and reintegrate their parolee-clients. In many jurisdictions, parolee failures are drug-related (Young and Porter, 1999). Parolee failures attributable to substance abuse can sometimes be converted into positive experiences, however. In Kentucky, for example, a program known as the Halfway Back Program provides an alternative to incarceration for parolees with nonviolent technical violations that might otherwise trigger revocation proceedings. In this program, parolees caught violating technical program conditions sign an agreement to complete their programs and refrain from committing future technical violations. These agreements between parolees and their POs seem to offer strong incentives to remain law-abiding, despite the adverse influence gangs in the area may have (Munden, Tewksbury, and Grossi, 1999). Other strategies, such as home confinement and electronic monitoring, may be necessary, however (Enos, Holman, and Carroll, 1999).

The Idea of Parole in Retrospect.   It is evident that parole in the United States is increasing annually, but that does not mean that the successfulness of parole is increasing to an equivalent degree. On the contrary, it seems that much depends on the nature of particular parole programs and the intensity of supervised release relating to how parolees are managed. The federal government has replaced parole with supervised release. Parole has already been abolished in Maine, and several other states have given serious consideration to proposals for its elimination. At one extreme, the just-deserts philosophy is that offenders should be punished for their crimes in accordance with whatever the law prescribes. The laws, however, are not formulated with the right degree of precision. For example, most offenses prescribe a term of incarceration up to x years or months and/or a fine of not more than x dollars. Thus, important decisions must be made by prosecutors, judges, and other officials in an attempt to match the severity of the punishment imposed with the seriousness of the crime committed. This decision process is far from an exact science, although social scientists and others have wrestled for centuries with the problems of defining appropriate punishments that fit each crime. Scientific investigations have attempted to evolve ideal models or schemes that might fit neatly into a sentencing scheme that states or the federal government might adopt. In fact, there is little or nothing scientific about state and federal statutes and their accompanying sentencing patterns in any jurisdiction.

At the other extreme are those labeled as rehabilitation-oriented and/or those who promote or endorse nonincarcerative, reintegrative programs or the early release of offenders so as to minimize the criminogenic effects of prisons and jails. It is unlikely that parole will be abolished on a national scale, at least for the next several decades. Methods for controlling or monitoring offenders while on probation or parole are constantly being improved, and new and better devices are being developed to ensure greater supervisory effectiveness. Thus, better control of persons currently under PO supervision appears to be the most logical solution to current problems.

Prison overcrowding enters the picture as an extremely important intervening variable. Many state prison systems have contracts with local city or county jails to house some of their inmate overflow. Several state prison systems are currently under zero population growth court orders, whereby maximum prison capacities cannot be exceeded. A general shift in sentencing from indeterminate to determinate has eroded or eliminated parole board authority to grant prisoners early release. Under determinate sentencing, however, considerable latitude in sentencing decisions and charging decisions exists for judges and prosecutors. One result of these sentencing reforms has been to increase the likelihood of being incarcerated for various offenses, although the length of incarceration has been significantly shortened.

The just-deserts and rehabilitative philosophies present corrections officials with an unresolvable dilemma. Standing on the sidelines of the great debate are observers who claim that nothing works (Martinson, 1974). No offender rehabilitation program is 100 percent recidivism-free, but that does not mean that a program ought to be scrapped. When particular parole programs have recidivism rates of 30 percent or less, they also have success rates of 70 percent or higher. Some offenders appear to benefit from program participation. One costly solution is to construct and staff more prisons to house more prisoners, but can the states and the federal government afford to do so? Consider California's dilemma. Currently, California places approximately 70 percent of its convicted felons on probation (Pastore and Maguire, 2001). What if these felons had been sentenced to incarceration, even for short terms? Where would California prison officials put them? Furthermore, it is difficult and costly to attract and hire educated and competent persons to work in correctional officer and PO positions to supervise and manage offenders, in or out of prison.

Communities are, however, playing an increasingly important role in offender management. In fact, many organizations are being established in the private sector to assume roles and offender management functions originally performed by under-staffed and underpaid government bureaucracies. Parolees are becoming involved in new and innovative community programs featuring useful activities, such as employment assistance, individual and group counseling, educational training, liter-acy services, and valuable networking with other community agencies and busi-nesses. More dangerous offenders who are released on parole are often placed in electronic monitoring programs and/or are subject to house arrest or home confine-ment.

In addition, inmates who are within a few months of their prospective parole dates are being released, with or without supervision, for short periods through work or study release programs. Other inmates are permitted short leaves from prison through furloughs. Yet other inmates are housed temporarily in halfway houses in communities, where they can ease back into community life gradually. Halfway houses are facilities with some rules and regulations, including curfew and drug and alcohol checks. Some inmates have a particularly difficult time coping with the rela-tively new freedoms of community life after the strict discipline and regimentation they experienced while incarcerated. These halfway houses and community residen-tial centers provide diverse functions for many recently paroled offenders.

Almost all the programs available to probationers are also made available to parolees. Although differences between probationers and parolees were more pro-nounced in past decades, it is becoming increasingly the case that they bear more similarities to one another than differences. One reason is that there is so little room available in prisons and jails that many felons cannot be accommodated. Some states, such as California, place as many as 70 percent of their convicted felons on probation annually, simply because there is no room for them in existing prison and jail facilities. Even the vast construction programs in California and other states are falling behind in their attempt to keep pace with increasing numbers of offenders falling within some form of probation or parole supervision annually.

One prediction is that government will rely more heavily in future years on private interests for offender management responsibilities. Numerous experiments are under way to see which programs have the best results and minimize parolee failures. Failures most often occur because many parolees are either unsupervised or undersupervised during their parole activity. Many of them lack the ability to fill out application forms for jobs. Also, many have drug- or alcohol-related problems that got them into trouble initially. Rapidly expanding community services are doing more to fill important parolee needs. Volunteers and paraprofessionals are becom-ing more valuable components of these growing community programs as well.

SUMMARY

Parole is early release from prison short of serving one's full sentence originally imposed by the court. Parole originated in the eighteenth century in Spain, France, and England and became popular in the United States in the mid-1800s as a means of alleviating prison overcrowding. The father of parole, Alexander Maconochie, was an early prison reformer who sought to assist prisoners earn early release through marks of commendation or good marks. These types of rewards have been continued in United States prisons as good time credits against time served.

U.S. sentencing reforms have resulted in the abolishment of parole boards in several states, although a majority of states continue to use indeterminate sentencing and parole boards as decision-making bodies to grant or refuse to grant prisoners early release. Parole boards have been criticized for their failure to recognize recidivists and/or dangerous prisoners who should be confined. No foolproof prediction tools, however, currently exist to permit accurate predictions of dangerousness of prisoners or the risk to the public if offenders are released short of serving their full terms.

The philosophy of parole is prisoner rehabilitation through reintegrating offenders into society. The manifest and latent functions of parole include reintegrating offenders into society; controlling or deterring crime; alleviating prison overcrowding; remedying sentencing disparities attributable to race, ethnicity, or socioeconomic status; and public protection. No current profile of parolees exists other than selected characteristics of persons currently incarcerated in prisons. Few prisoners serve their full terms, and most are released either through parole board discretion or mandatorily after serving approximately one-third of their sentences.

Shifts in the nature of sentencing have done much to influence how parole is treated. Many states continue to use parole boards with discretionary powers to release inmates short of serving their full terms. Other states use mandatory supervised release as a way of rewarding those who have accumulated sufficient good time credits and show promise for successful adaptations to community life if released. Many states are currently reevaluating their sentencing provisions and standards. There is considerable controversy today concerning the contrasting philosophies of rehabilitation and just deserts, in which some corrections professionals seriously question the rehabilitative value of parole programs.

KEY TERMS

Brockway, Zebulon	Maconochie, Alexander	Pardon
Good marks	Mandatory release	Risk
Good time	Manifest functions	Transportation
Good time system	Marks of commendation	Van Dieman's Land
Latent functions	Norfolk Island	Wickersham Commission

QUESTIONS FOR REVIEW

1. What is parole? What are some manifest and latent functions of parole?
2. What are some of the goals of parole? Do corrections professionals agree on these goals and the extent to which they are being achieved?
3. What contributions have the following persons made to the use of parole in the United States?
   a. Alexander Maconochie
   b. Sir Walter Crofton
   c. Gaylord Hubbell
4. What is the relation between indeterminate sentencing and parole?

5. How does determinate sentencing modify parole?
6. What was the Wickersham Commission, and what were some of its functions?
7. What are some of the pros and cons of indeterminate sentencing in relation to parole?
8. Contrast the rehabilitative and justice models relative to parole.
9. What are some of the characteristics of parolees in the United States?
10. Do you think that parole deters crime? Why or why not?

SUGGESTED READINGS

Butzin, Clifford et al. (1999). "Measuring the Impact of Drug Treatment: Beyond Relapse and Recidivism." *Corrections Management Quarterly* **3:**1–7.

Mitchell, George (1999). *Privatizing Parole and Probation in Wisconsin: The Path to Fewer Prisons.* Thiensville: Wisconsin Policy Research Institute.

Munson, Michelle, and Tom Reed (2000). *Goal Met: Violent Offenders in Texas are Serving a Higher Percentage of Their Prison Sentences.* Austin: Texas Criminal Justice Policy Council.

Proctor, Jon L., and Michael Pease (2000). "Parole as Institutional Control: A Test of Specific Deterrence and Offender Misconduct." *Prison Journal* **80:**39–55.

Tonry, Michael (ed.) (1998). *The Handbook of Punishment.* New York: Oxford University Press.

Early Release, Parole Programs, and Parole Revocation

CHAPTER 8

Introduction
Prerelease Programs
  Prerelease Programs
  Work Release Programs
  Study Release Programs
  Furlough Programs
  Standard Parole with Conditions
  Intensive Supervised Parole
  Shock Parole
  Halfway Houses and Community
  Residential Centers
Other Parole Conditions
  Day Reporting Centers
  Fines
  Day Fines
  Community Service Orders
  Restitution
Parole Boards and Early-Release
  Decision Making
  Parole Boards, Sentencing Alternatives,
  and the Get-Tough Movement

Parole Board Composition and Diversity
Functions of Parole Boards
Parole Board Decision Making
  and Inmate Control
Parole Board Orientations
Developing and Implementing Objective
  Parole Criteria
Salient Factor Scores and Predicting Parolee
  Success on Parole
The Process of Parole Revocation
Landmark Cases and Selected Issues
  Pardons
  Parolee Program
  Conditions
Summary
Key Terms
Questions for Review
Suggested Readings

• *Matthew Curtis Marshall, 21.* In June 2000, Matthew Curtis Marshall, 21, set fire to a cross in the front yard of a black family, the Rosses, in Houston, Texas. He was one of five persons eventually caught and convicted of violating the civil rights of Dwayne and Maria Ross and their two children. Marshall pleaded guilty to the crime and stood before the federal district court judge awaiting sentencing. Speaking out on his own behalf, he said, "It was a foolish act of vandalism, your honor. It was not personal because I didn't even know their names [the Rosses]. Can't I have probation, or boot camp, or some other alternative besides prison? It was not about hate, because I am not a racist." Marshall's family and friends wrote numerous letters on his behalf, attesting to his good nature and behavior in past years. His attorney, Ken Mingledorff, said that drugs and alcohol were to blame and that Marshall just sort of got "caught up." U.S. District Court Judge David Hittner saw things differently. He noted that in a presentence investigation report filed by the U.S. Probation Office, Marshall had organized the crime and had provided the gasoline to ignite the cross. Marshall had also brought a post-hole digger to place the cross in the front yard, but the post-hole digger hit a tree root. Instead, the men leaned the burning cross against a tree near the house. The judge said, "The house could have gone up." The judge also cited documented instances of Marshall dragging a dog to death with his car and forcing a high school classmate of American Indian descent to eat a feces-laden sandwich in lieu of paying a debt. He also used numerous racial and ethnic slurs against Hispanics, blacks, and Chinese Americans. It was also observed that Marshall's father was similarly inclined. The judge observed, "It appears that the seeds of your racism were sown at home." Marshall was sentenced to ten years in prison. Under the U.S. Sentencing Guidelines, he will not be eligible for parole until he serves at least 8½ years of that sentence. (*Source:* Adapted from Associated Press, "Fifth Hate Defendant Sentenced," February 6, 2001.)

• Noble was a parolee under the supervision of the District of Columbia Department of Corrections. He had been on parole for several months until a parole officer determined that Noble had violated one or more of his parole conditions. Noble appeared later before a parole board to determine whether his parole should be revoked. After a two-stage hearing, the parole board revoked his parole and returned him to prison to continue serving his original sentence. Noble appealed, alleging a Fourteenth Amendment equal rights violation, contending that he should be given time off of his maximum sentence for the months he had spent under parole supervision. The Department of Corrections denied his request, and a U.S. district court heard his appeal. One of the arguments Noble raised was that other District of Columbia prisoners under similar circumstances had been given time off of their maximum sentences for their time served while on parole. The court determined that these allegations were false and that these named prisoners had not been given such credit. The court determined that his equal protection rights under the Fourteenth Amendment had not been violated and that he must serve out the rest of his prison term. (*Noble v. United States Parole Commission,* 194 F.3d 152 [U.S.D.C. Cir. November 1999])

• Christianson was eligible for parole after serving several years for the murder of his three-year-old daughter. He had struck her with a vicious blow after she ran between him and his video player and accidentally spilled his beer. Christianson became angry and struck her in the stomach with a backhanded blow severe enough to cause a rupture of his daughter's bowels. Although the girl continued to complain of being sick throughout the day, Christianson ignored her and did not seek medical assistance. Eventually, she began to cough up blood, and he finally took her to a hospital emergency room. By the time he arrived, however, she had lost consciousness, and she died a few minutes later. Christianson claimed that he ought to be paroled, because other murderers he knew were being paroled. The parole board, however, cited the especially heinous nature of his daughter's murder as a primary reason for declining parole. An appellate court upheld the parole board's decision and agreed that Christianson's crime and its circumstances justified the imposition of a term of parole ineligibility. (*State v. Christianson,* 983 P.2d 909 [Mont. Sup. July 1999])

• Heckman was convicted of child sexual abuse and was incarcerated for several years. Eventually he was paroled. The Pennsylvania Parole Board ordered, among other things, that he participate in a mandatory sex offender treatment program. During the treatment program, it was learned that Heckman was frequently around or in the company of children to the extent that several of them became suspicious of him and reported him to police. A police investigation disclosed that although Heckman had not sexually abused any of the children or engaged in any lewd conduct, he nevertheless was a convicted child sex offender, and this information was relayed to his parole officer. It was also learned that Heckman had acquired some pornographic material and had been deceptive during therapy sessions regarding his thoughts or behavior in relation to sexually inappropriate targets. The same information became known to the psychotherapist who was conducting the sex offender treatment program in which Heckman was a participant. The psychotherapist discharged Heckman from her program, stating that he was unsuitable for treatment because of his continued association with children under questionable circumstances and his possession of pornographic materials. Because Heckman did not complete the mandatory sex offender treatment program, the Pennsylvania Parole Board revoked his parole and he was returned to prison. He appealed, arguing that he had done nothing wrong to merit revocation. The appellate court disagreed and upheld his revocation. The court determined that Heckman admitted to contacting someone via the Internet who was under the age of 19, when he was supposed to refrain from having any contact with any person 18 or under. All things considered, there was sufficient evidence to support the revocation. (*Heckman v. Pa. Bd. of Probation and Parole,* 744 A.2d 371 [Pa. Commw. January 2000])

• Foshee, a Louisiana parolee, had previously been convicted of a sex offense. At the time of his sentencing, the judge ordered that whenever Foshee was paroled in the future, he must participate in an anger management program, obtain his GED, and not have unsupervised contact with anyone under the age of 18. Foshee was subsequently paroled and placed under the supervision of a parole officer. Later, it was determined that Foshee had been seen in the company of persons under the age of 18. This information was transmitted to the original sentencing judge, who ordered the parole revoked because Foshee had violated the court's orders. Foshee appealed, contending that the sentencing judge had no discretionary authority over him once he was imprisoned and that the parole board is the sole determinant of his parole program conditions. Because contact with persons under the age of 18 was not prohibited by the parole board, Foshee claimed that he had done nothing to warrant parole revocation. The appellate court agreed with him. Sentencing judges have no authority to set conditions for one's parole; that is the exclusive province of parole boards. Foshee's parole revocation was therefore set aside. (*State v. Foshee,* 756 So.2d 693 (La. App. April 2000])

INTRODUCTION

This chapter is about parole board early-release decision making. It examines the options and alternatives available to parolees when parole is granted. With the exception of life imprisonment and death penalty cases, most offenders sentenced to incarceration are eventually released back into their communities, either through the natural conclusion of their original sentences or through some alternative early release scheme such as parole. Parole is most frequently conditional, and parole programs involve filing reports with parole agencies, observing curfew, making restitution, performing community service, participating in individual or group counseling, or participating in educational or vocational/technical programs. There is considerable diversity among programs for parolees. In this chapter, some of these programs are described. Furthermore, some parolees may need to be supervised intensively, whereas other clients may simply be required to report in a manner similar to standard probation. Many parolees may only be required to make contact by letter or telephone with their POs, whereas others must make themselves accessible to random face-to-face visits at home or in the workplace.

Compared with programs designed for probationers such as pretrial diversion, shock probation, split sentencing, and various forms of intensive probation supervision, programs for parolees are rather unique in that they are, for the most part, transitional programs. These programs are designed to assist recently imprisoned offenders make any necessary psychological and social adjustments to become reintegrated into their communities. Parolees with special problems (e.g., mental illness, mental retardation, alcohol or drug dependencies, and sex offenders) may be required to participate in community activities and programs that deal directly with these problems. Sometimes parolees will be expected to make restitution to their victims or perform a limited amount of community service for the duration of their original sentences. Parole boards may see fit to make these additional conditions a part of an offender's parole program.

The first section of this chapter describes several prerelease programs that involve releases of inmates for limited purposes, such as short-term work assignments, and for the purpose of taking academic courses at nearby schools. Some inmates take courses to complete their GEDs. Other clients take courses or participate in group or individual therapy not ordinarily offered in prison settings. Work and study release are defined, and their advantages and disadvantages for participating offenders are described. Furlough programs are also examined. Furloughs, or short leaves from prison, are usually limited to weekends and involve visits with family members. Some furloughs may serve other purposes, such as performing work or community service or making restitution to victims. The functions, goals, and advantages and disadvantages of furlough programs are discussed. Most parole program options are community-driven, which means that community-based corrections often manages or supervises parolees.

The parole-granting process is also described. This section includes a discussion of parole board conduct as it relates to early-release decision making for eligible jail or prison inmates. Parole boards exist in most states, and their composition and their diversity are also discussed. Numerous modifications in sentencing strategies among the states and federal government, however, have greatly modified parole-granting practices in more than a few jurisdictions. In some instances, parole has been eliminated entirely as an early-release option for inmates. Parole boards orient themselves in various ways toward inmates, and some of these orientations are described. Because parole boards also attempt to employ objective criteria when making parole decisions, some of these criteria are also examined.

Risk assessment instruments, which provide parole boards with important data about the future conduct of inmates, are also used. Parole boards are fallible entities, and their decision making is imperfect, but that does not deter them from attempting to make accurate forecasts of future parolee conduct. The final part of this chapter describes several landmark cases pertaining to parole revocation. Parolees are entitled to two-stage hearings before their parole boards and have minimum due process rights. The chapter catalogues several important legal rights of parolees and presents various scenarios involving legal challenges to the different conditions of their parole programs.

PRERELEASE PROGRAMS

Most programs available to parolees are similar to those for probationers. In some states and in the federal system, parolees and probationers report to the same persons or agencies. One distinction previously made between probationers and parolees is that parolees have served time in prison. For this reason alone, parolees are considered more dangerous as an offender class compared with probationers. Parolees are granted early release from incarceration by parole boards or some other paroling authority, but that does not mean that they will be removed entirely from supervision. Several different kinds of programs exist for particular types of parolees and require varying levels of parolee supervision and monitoring. This section examines eight such programs: prelease, work release, study release, furloughs, standard parole with conditions, intensive supervised parole, shock parole, and halfway houses.

Definitions and Examples

Prerelease is any action that results in a jail or prison inmate being granted a temporary leave from his or her institution for various purposes. Usually these purposes include meeting with prospective employers and working at part-time jobs until one's parole or early release is granted, studying or taking courses at nearby schools for the purpose of completing degrees, and visiting with families for the purpose of reuniting with them and establishing harmonious familial relations (Bouffard, MacKenzie, and Hickman, 2000). A **prerelease program** is any activity that enables inmates to leave their institutions on a temporary basis for purposes of employment, work, study, or familial contact. Prerelease programs are available to both male and female inmates (Ammar and Erez, 2000). For example, the Program for Female Offenders, Inc., is operated by the Pennsylvania Department of Corrections to assist female inmates in learning word processing, data entry, and telecommunications skill training (Arnold, 1992). Sometimes prerelease programs are calculated to assist particular inmates with various addictions or dependencies. For instance, prerelease might enable some inmates with drug, alcohol, or gambling problems to receive needed assistance from community services through their temporary releases from custody (Anderson, 1999).

Prerelease programs, sometimes programs called **preparole programs**, are transitional in that they enable inmates to make a smoother transition into their communities through gradual reentry and temporary leaves from jail or prison. Oklahoma operates a Pre-Parole Conditional Supervision Program, or PPCSP (*Corrections Compendium*, 1991a). PPCSP is a traditional exit from the prison system for many inmates (*Corrections Compendium*, 1991a:1). In Oklahoma, many prisoners about to be paroled are released under close supervision for limited periods. Commenced in 1988, the PPCSP requires inmates to submit a weekly parole plan to their POs, submit to drug and/or alcohol checks, observe curfew, maintain employment, and pay court costs. They must return to their prisons on weekends. If an inmate does not have a job, then he or she must obtain one within 30 days following preparole release. Over 80 percent of all PPCSP releasees have some sort of job lined up before being released. To qualify for inclusion in this program, inmates must have served at least 15 percent of their time and be within one year of their scheduled parole eligibility date. Any institutional infraction will delay an inmate's acceptance into the program. PPCSP clients must pay a $20 monthly supervision fee, restitution, court costs, and child support. Since the PPCSP was established in 1988, a 26 percent failure rate has been reported, meaning that 26 percent of inmate-clients violated one or more of the preparole program conditions (*Corrections Compendium,* 1991c:7).

Work Release Programs

Work release, also called **work furlough**, **day parole**, **day pass**, and **community work**, refers to any program that provides for the labor of jail or prison inmates in the community under limited supervision. Sometimes work release and work furlough are used interchangeably, referring to similar activities such as an inmate's participation in a job not ordinarily available to other prison inmates. Work release programs are also available to older youthful offenders (Altschuler and Armstrong, 1991, 1993, 1994). These programs are designed to ease inmates gradually back into their communities by permitting them short leaves from prison to perform jobs and assist in supporting their dependents. For instance, Illinois established a PreStart Program in 1991 intended to assist inmates about to be paroled in making easier transitions back into their communities. The program was implemented largely because the public was increasingly disenchanted with standard parole and because of the abrupt changes for inmates into society; more than a few parolees have failed in their parole programs because of this difficult transition. PreStart was designed to reintroduce inmates gradually back into their communities by providing temporarily leaves for the purpose of locating employment and performing part-time jobs (Castellano et al., 1993).

Work release was actually an integral feature of Alexander Maconochie's plan for prison improvement in the 1840s and 1850s (Miller, 1984). The first informal use of work release in the United States occurred in Vermont in 1906 when sheriffs, acting on their own authority, assigned inmates to work outside jail walls in the community (Busher, 1973). At that time, county sheriffs issued passes to certain low-risk inmates to work in the community during daytime hours, but they were obligated to return to jail at particular curfew periods. The first formal acknowledgment of work release occurred in Wisconsin when the **Huber Law** was passed in 1913. Senator Huber of Wisconsin successfully secured the passage of a bill that permitted Wisconsin correctional institutions to grant temporary releases to low-risk misdemeanants (Johnson and Kotch, 1973). Most states have work release programs today, with 37,950 inmates involved in such programs in 1998 (Camp and Camp, 1999:126). Work release was not popular and was only sluggishly adopted on a large scale as an alternative to incarceration during the 1960s and 1970s. By the early 1980s, almost all states had work release programs.

BOX 8.1   *Are Work Releasees Dangerous?*

Charles Rodman Campbell

It happened in 1974. Charles Rodman Campbell, 19, was a drifter who came through Clearview in Snohomish County near Seattle, Washington. He encountered and savagely raped Renae Wicklund, 23, a resident of Clearview. Subsequently, he was identified by Wicklund and her family friend, Barbara Hendrickson, 43. Eyewitness testimony from Wicklund and Hendrickson at Campbell's trial resulted in his conviction for rape. He was sentenced to 15 years in Washington State Penitentiary. During his incarceration, he conformed to prison rules and policies. In 1982, he became eligible for work release. While on work release, Campbell sought out Wicklund and Hendrickson for revenge. He had murder on his mind. He found Wicklund with her eight-year-old daughter, and in the company of Barbara Hendrickson. He bludgeoned each of the women to death and slit their throats. He almost beheaded Wicklund's daughter, Shannah. Another trial for these crimes resulted in a death sentence for Campbell.

On May 27, 1994, Campbell was scheduled for execution. Mrs. Iverson, Wicklund's sister, wants to

watch. "It will be an emotion of foreclosure. The fear of him getting out hangs on us very heavily. As victims of a vicious murder, we comfort each other in full awareness that along with those who were murdered, we too have become victims who have had to endure endless pain and suffering." Campbell was belligerent to the very end. When given a choice between hanging or lethal injection as his preferred execution method, Campbell said some censored things to prison officials, essentially stating that he was not going to be a party to helping Washington administer a death penalty that he, Campbell, finds objectionable and unconstitutional. Washington officials hanged Campbell, on schedule, May 27, 1994. Because of this case and others like it, Washington has enacted laws to protect victims of violent crimes, especially victims who eventually give incriminating testimony. Victims now have the right to be notified when their attackers are released and be told the outcome of cases.

Is Campbell the sort of inmate who should have been granted work release? Do you think he would have eventually killed these women if he had served his full incarcerative term?

Source: Adapted from Associated Press, "Triple Murderer Faces Hanging: N.D. Relatives of Victims Say They'll Be Glad When Case Is Over," May 26, 1994.

The Goals and Functions of Work Release Programs.   The goals of work release programs are to

1. Reintegrate the offender into the community
2. Give the offender an opportunity to learn and/or practice new skills
3. Provide offenders with the means to make restitution to victims of crimes
4. Give offenders a chance to assist in supporting themselves and their families
5. Help authorities to predict the likelihood of offender success if paroled more effectively
6. Foster improvements in self-images or self-concepts through working in a nonincarcerative environment and assuming full responsibility for one's conduct

Specific benefits accruing to offenders and the community are that at least some inmates are not idle and exposed to continuous moral decay associated with incarceration, that prisoners pay confinement costs and can support their families, and that prisoners can receive rehabilitative treatment and possibly make restitution to their victims (Fitzharris, 1971).

The primary functions of work release for parolees are community reintegration, promotion of inmate self-respect, repayment of debts to victims and society, and provision of support for self and dependents.

Community reintegration. Work release enables the parolee to become reintegrated into the community (Ely, 1996). Even though parolees must return to their prisons or other places of confinement during nonworking hours, they enjoy temporary freedoms while performing useful work. Thus, when it comes time for them to be officially released through a parole board decision, through administrative action, or from the normal completion of their sentences, the adjustment to community life will not be abrupt and potentially upsetting psychologically or socially.

A study of postrelease employment, known as the Post-Release Employment Project, investigated the pre- and postrelease behaviors of a large sample of federal inmates who were placed in work release programs before their paroles were granted (Saylor and Gaes, 1992). Researchers report that inmates who receive training and work experience during their incarceration tend to have more favorable conduct reports in prison, are likely to be employed during their halfway house stay and after release, and are less likely to recidivate than similar inmates who are not trained or who are unemployed during their imprisonment. Thus, the work release experience of these federal releasees proved valuable to their subsequent community reintegration.

Work release has been particularly effective for female inmates involved in a Delaware-sponsored program known as CREST (Farrell, 2000). In this program, female inmates with drug dependencies and other problems seek and receive treatment from community agencies. Furthermore, these women have been able to work at jobs and form networks of social support among themselves. About 39 percent of the women who have been involved in CREST have relapsed, although this relapse figure is not particularly high. Usually, the relapse occurs through a resumption of alcohol consumption and drug use. The social support groups women have formed, however, have helped most to avoid these relapses and successfully reintegrate within their communities later.

Promotion of inmate self-respect. Plans for inmate labor in some jurisdictions are designed with rehabilitation in mind. Most work study programs attempt to instill self-esteem within those inmates originally untrained and incapable of performing even menial labor in the private sector. These work experiences are designed to equip inmates with skills useful to employers on the outside. Furthermore, inmates can earn sufficient income to offset some of their own housing expenses while in prison and provide supplementary amounts to their families (Castellano and Soderstrom, 1997).

In Philadelphia, Pennsylvania, a prison prerelease program that includes a prerelease center was established in 1990 (Philadelphia Prison System, 1990). The program encourages inmates to work, study, or obtain medical assistance outside the prisons while they are still serving their sentences. It aims to ease the transition from institutional to community life. Offender-clients receive room and board at a modest cost as well as assistance and counseling in the management of their financial affairs. Social awareness groups provide new participants with instruction in communication and problem-solving skills, financial management, legal procedures, and other topics necessary for successful social integration (Philadelphia Prison System, 1990).

Repayment of debts to victims and society. On October 12, 1984, President Ronald Reagan signed Public Law 98-473, the **Victims of Crime Act of 1984** (Peak, 1986:39–40). Currently, all states and the federal government have victim compensation programs. As a part of offender work release requirements, a certain amount of an offender's earned wages may be allocated to restitution and to a general victim compensation fund. Thus, fines, restitution, and some form of community service have become common features of federal sentencing (18 U.S.C. Sec. 3563[a][2], 2001). Almost every state has adopted some form of victim restitution program for offenders.

Provision of support for self and dependents. Those prisoners with wives and/or children ordinarily do not earn enough on work release to support their dependents totally, but their income does help provide a portion of their dependents' necessities. It is also apparent that the potential for becoming involved in a work release program can function as an incentive for prisoners to comply with prison rules. Thus, prison officials sometimes reveal that one means of eliciting prisoner compliance with prison rules is to hold out to them the prospect of work release or a denial of such participation, depending on inmate behavior while in custody (Nieto, 1998). Increasing numbers of states are obligating work releasees to contribute some of their earnings toward program costs as well as pay for some of their dependent support (Hill, 1998).

Determining Inmate Eligibility for Work Release Programs.   Not all inmates in prisons and jails are eligible for work release programs. Before an inmate may become eligible for such programs in some jurisdictions, they must serve a minimum portion of their originally prescribed sentences. Long-term inmates who have committed serious crimes are often automatically excluded from participation in work release because of their projected public risk if free in their communities. Statutory provisions in several states specify the minimum amount of time that must be served before inmates may make application to participate in work release. Of course, an advantage of being able to participate in these programs is that it weighs heavily and favorably when one is eventually considered for parole. Inmates who have completed work release programs successfully stand a much better chance of being paroled than those who have not been selected for participation. In short, they have proven themselves capable of living and working with others on the outside and are not considered potentially troublesome (Grant and Beal, 1998).

Study Release Programs

Study release programs are essentially the same as work release programs, but for the express purpose of securing educational goals. Types of **study release** are adult basic education, high school or high school equivalency (GED), technical or vocational education, and college (Siegel, 1994). In 1999, there were 103 inmates in study release programs (Camp and Camp, 1999:126). One reason for such low numbers of study releasees is that many educational programs are offered on-line by computer or are available through correspondence. Also, most prison systems have educational programs that enable inmates to receive degrees at various educational levels (Goodman, 1992; Leonardson, 1997).

Determining Inmate Eligibility for Study Release.   An inmate's eligibility for study release involves several factors. First, study release may be granted to those within a year or less of being paroled. A second criterion is whether inmates have behaved well while institutionalized. Good behavior on the inside does not necessarily mean that inmates will behave well when on study release, but compliance with institutional rules is generally a good indicator of compliance with program rules for study release. Few offenders wish to jeopardize their parole chances by violating program rules while on study release. Absconding or escaping while on work or study release results in additional time to be served when these inmates are apprehended. Usually, if an inmate has previously absconded, the time to be served becomes flat time that must be served. Study release involves an element of trust on the part of the releasing institution. Violations of this trust by inmates are not favorably viewed by paroling authorities (Washington Department of Corrections, 1993).

Inmates must also file a plan indicating the reasons for acquiring additional education and where their educational goals will lead them when they are released into the community. Educational training enhances an inmate's eligibility for particular kinds of work when parole is granted or whenever the offender is released from the system. More educated inmates are more employable. If restitution is a part of one's parole program, then acquiring greater amounts of education can assist in making restitution payments later (Waits, 1993).

Advantages and Disadvantages of Study Release Programs.   Study release programs prompt concern among community residents that some study releasees or other types of releasees will harm them or pose various threats to community safety. The failure rate of study releasees, however, is so low that program advantages far outweigh these disadvantages (Stiles, 1994; U.S. Department of Justice, 1991). Study release helps to prepare inmates for different types of occupations or professions. The Tennessee Department of Corrections, for instance, has a study release program through which selected inmates can learn data entry, building construction, welding, food services, industrial maintenance, surveying, and drafting. Upon completing their study release programs, they become certified. Many of their educational credits are transferable to colleges and universities, if they are interested (Tennessee Department of Corrections, 1994). Some jurisdictions, however, have reported inmate discontent with the types of jobs their education has qualified them to perform (MacGrady, Bemister, and Fontaine, 1991).

Some inmates do not actually use these study release programs for anything other than their cosmetic value for parole board appearances. For instance, a study of work and study release programs in two states, Oregon and California, has shown that many prisoners believe that they are "under pressure" to participate in these types of prison programs. Many prisoners believe that such participation would look good to their parole boards (U.S. Department of Justice, 1996). Tennessee and other jurisdictions, however, report that inmates have demonstrated remarkable progress related to greater knowledge about the harmful effects of drug abuse, greater discipline, and improved development in self-awareness and self-concept (Tennessee Department of Corrections, 1994).

Furlough Programs

A **furlough** is an authorized, unescorted leave from confinement granted for specific purposes and for designated time periods, usually from 24 to 72 hours, although it may be as long as several weeks or as short as a few hours (Grant and Johnson, 1998). The overall aim of **furlough programs** as a form of temporary release is to assist the offender in becoming reintegrated into society. In 1918, Mississippi became the first state to use furloughs on a limited basis for low-risk, minimum-security prison inmates who had served at least two or more years of their sentences and who were regarded as good security risks (Marley, 1973). These furloughs usually involved conjugal visits with families or Christmas holiday activities for brief, ten-day periods and were believed valuable for preparing offenders for permanent reentry into their respective communities once parole had been granted. In 1998, 8,681 inmates participated in 95,079 furloughs (Camp and Camp, 1999:128). Thirty states and the federal government used furloughs for eligible offenders. Florida granted the largest number of furloughs (67,790), followed by Rhode Island (4,621), Vermont (3,848), the federal system (3,365), and Nebraska (2,728). Arkansas, Tennessee, and Wisconsin, with two each, had the fewest. During 1998, only 65 inmates absconded from their furlough programs.

The prime beneficiaries of furlough programs are the prisoners themselves. It is likely that the trust placed in them by the prison system is psychologically beneficial, at least for some. There is always the possibility that offenders on furlough from prison unescorted or unsupervised may commit new crimes. Furloughs are an outgrowth of work release programs in which select inmates are chosen, usually through application, for participation. Typically, inmates have served a significant portion of their originally prescribed sentences and are eligible for parole consideration. The success of an inmate's furlough experience figures prominently in early release decisions by parole boards. Thus, offenders granted furloughs who successfully comply with their requirements have an advantage over others.

Furloughs have many of the same characteristics as work release programs. There are about three times as many furloughs granted than work releases. The length of a furlough varies by jurisdiction. Most furlough programs throughout the United States range from 24 to 72 hours, although some programs may offer inmates up to two weeks or more of freedom for special activities (Smith and Sabatino, 1990).

The Goals of Furlough Programs.   Furloughs have several purposes. Offenders are given a high degree of trust by prison officials and are permitted leaves to visit their homes and families. Interestingly, such furloughs are beneficial to both prisoners and their families, because they permit family members to get used to the presence of the offender after a long incarcerative absence. Sometimes prisoners participate in educational programs (like study release) outside of prison. They can arrange for employment once paroled, or they can participate in vocational training for short periods. In Canada, for instance, furloughs may be granted to eligible inmates to make contacts for employment, to visit close relatives, to obtain medical or psychiatric services, to visit seriously ill relatives or attend the funerals of close relatives, to appear before study groups, to make contacts for discharge, and to secure a residence upon release on parole or discharge (Grant and Millson, 1998). Such programs in Canada are called temporary absence programs (Motiuk and Belcourt, 1996).

Furloughs also provide officials with an opportunity to evaluate offenders and determine how they adapt to living with others in their community. Thus, the furlough is a type of test to determine, with some predictability, the likelihood that inmates will conform to society's rules if they are eventually released through parole (Glaser, 1995). For some prisoners, furloughs function as incentives to conform to prison rules and regulations, because only prisoners who have demonstrated that they can control their behaviors in prison will be considered for temporary releases. Usually, although not always, prisoners selected for participation in furlough programs are nearing the end of their sentences and will eventually be paroled or released anyway. They are good risks because the likelihood they will abscond while on a furlough is quite remote (Birkbeck, Wilson, and Hussong, 1996).

The Functions of Furlough Programs.   Furloughs provide offender rehabilitation and reintegration, the development of self-esteem and self-worth, opportunities to pursue vocational/educational programs, and aid parole boards in determining when inmates are ready to be released.

Offender rehabilitation and reintegration. The manifest intent of furloughs is to provide offenders with outside experiences that enable them to become accustomed to living with others in the community apart from the highly regulated life in prison or jail settings. Indications are that furloughs fulfill this objective in most instances (Chard-Wierschem, 1995). Furloughs assist inmates in making successful transitions from prison life to community living.

The development of self-esteem and self-worth. Furloughs instill within inmates feelings of self-esteem and self-worth. Again, the element of trust plays an important role in enabling those granted furloughs to acquire trust for those who place trust in them. The development of self-esteem and self-worth are unmeasurable, yet many of those granted furloughs report that they have benefited from their temporary release experiences (Ryan, 1997).

Opportunities to pursue vocational/educational programs. Another benefit of furlough programs for those in jurisdictions where furloughs are permitted and granted is the opportunities for inmates to participate in programs not available in prisons or jails. Thus, inmates can take courses in typing, art, automobile repair, or social science and related areas. Sometimes, these furloughs are labeled as study release, because they involve a program of study designed for the offender's specific needs (Glaser, 1995).

Aiding parole boards in determining when inmates ought to be released. A key function of furloughs as tests of inmate behavior is to alert parole boards about which inmates are most eligible to be released and about who will likely be successful on parole (Glaser, 1995; Motiuk and Belcourt, 1996). Indiana, for instance, has an 80 percent success rate with its furlough program as used for parole board decision making. In that jurisdiction, inmates are granted furloughs if they are within 60 days of being paroled. They are limited to three-day furloughs, during which time they can make home visits, obtain required medical treatment or psychological counseling, participate in special training courses, and perform work or other duties (Indiana Department of Corrections, 2001).

Determining Inmate Eligibility for Furloughs.   In most jurisdictions, furloughs are granted only to inmates who meet special eligibility requirements. Usually, program participation is restricted as follows: inmates must be at minimum-custody status, they must have served a fixed amount of their sentences and be within some fixed time of release, approval must be obtained from a committee that reviews all furlough applications, a clean institutional record is required, they must have a stable home environment, and they must not have prior records of violent offending (e.g., murder, aggravated assault, armed robbery, rape) (Birkbecj, Wilson, and Hussong, 1996).

Weaknesses and Strengths of Furlough Programs.   Not all states have furlough programs. One reason is that under certain types of sentencing systems, any **temporary release program** is not permitted. Those offenders sentenced to mandatory prison terms cannot be released prior to serving their entire sentences, less the good time credits they may have acquired during the initial incarceration period. Under indeterminate sentencing, there is considerable latitude for paroling authorities to grant furloughs or work releases to those inmates who have shown that they can conform their conduct to the institutional rules (Harer and Eichenlaub, 1992).

One possible consequence in the reduction of furlough programs nationwide is that inmates in prisons and jails have less incentive to abide by institutional rules. In some jurisdictions that have abolished parole, furloughs and work release were considered incentives to comply with prison and jail regulations, because parole boards viewed favorably any offender who successfully completed such a program. Even though these programs have been terminated in some jurisdictions, however, there are still incentives such as the accumulation of good time credits that may be applied against an offender's original sentence. The success of furlough programs is demonstrated by the relatively low recidivism rates in certain jurisdictions using such programs on a limited basis (Glaser, 1995; Ryan, 1997).

Standard Parole with Conditions

In 1999, every state had parolees, and many of these offenders were granted early release by a parole board. There are some exceptions, however. In California, for example, most prison inmates receive a determinate sentence and are released on parole once they have served their prison terms, less any good time credit they have accumulated. Following their release from prison, they have a three-year parole that involves supervision by POs wherever these offenders choose to locate within the state. They must abide by the same types of conditions required of probationers. Once they have successfully completed their three-year parole terms, they are officially released from the criminal justice system. More serious California offenders who have been convicted of first- or second-degree murder have usually been sentenced to life terms with the possibility of parole. The California Board of Prison Terms meets and considers whether any of these offenders should be paroled. If they are eventually paroled, then the length of their parole is for the rest of their lives; that is, they will be under PO supervision until they die. Both life and nonlife parolees are periodically reviewed during their parole periods to determine their suitability for discharge from parole prior to their maximum discharge dates (Stephens, 2001:1).

Parolees in virtually every jurisdiction must comply with certain program conditions. All parole programs are conditional in that they indicate what parolees must and must not do during their parole periods. For offenders with particular needs, such as alcohol or drug dependencies or gambling addictions, the conditions of their parole programs may include special provisions for community treatment on a regular basis, such as a requirement to attend Alcoholics Anonymous, Narcotics Anonymous, or Gamblers Anonymous meetings. Parole boards usually determine whatever additional conditions should be included.

Most parole agreements include standard conditions and a space for special conditions of parole, at the parole board's discretion. For instance, to be admitted to the Ohio parole program, parole-eligible inmates must sign the following document containing these provisions:

In consideration of having been granted supervision on December 1, 2001, I agree to report to my probation/parole officer within 48 hours or according to the written instructions I have received and to the following conditions:

1. I will obey federal, state, and local laws and ordinances, and all rules and regulations of the Fifth Common Pleas Court or the Department of Rehabilitation and Correction.

2. I will always keep my probation/parole officer informed of my residence and place of employment. I will obtain permission from my probation/parole officer before changing my residence or my employment.

3. I will not leave the state without written permission of the Adult Parole Authority.

4. I will not enter upon the grounds of any correctional facility nor attempt to visit any prisoner without the written permission of my probation/parole officer nor will I communicate with any prisoner without first informing my probation/parole officer of the reason for such communication.

5. I will comply with all orders given to me by my probation/parole officer or other authorized representative of the court, the Department of Rehabilitation and Correction, or the Adult Parole Authority, including any written instructions issued at any time during the period of supervision.

6. I will not purchase, possess, own, use, or have under my control any firearms, deadly weapons, ammunition, or dangerous ordnance.

7. I will not possess, use, purchase, or have under my control any narcotic drug or other controlled substance, including any instrument, device, or other object used to administer drugs or to prepare them for administration, unless it is lawfully prescribed for me by a licensed physician. I agree to inform my probation/parole officer promptly of any such prescription and I agree to submit to drug testing if required by the Adult Parole Authority.

8. I will report any arrest, citation of a violation of the law, conviction, or any other contact with a law enforcement officer to my probation/parole officer no later than the next business day, and I will not enter into any agreement or other arrangement with any law enforcement agency that might place me in the position of violating any law or condition of my supervision unless I have obtained permission in writing from the Adult Parole Authority, or from the court if I am a probationer.

9. I agree to a search without warrant of my person, my motor vehicle, or my place of residence by a probation/parole officer at any time.

10. I agree to sign a release of confidential information from any public or private agency if requested to do so by a probation/parole officer.

11. I agree and understand that if I am arrested in any other state or territory of the United States or in any foreign country, my signature as witnessed at the end of the page will be deemed to be a waiver of extradition and that no other formali-

ties will be required for authorized agents of the State of Ohio to bring about my return to this state for revocation proceedings.

12. I also agree to the following Special Conditions as imposed by the court or the Adult Parole Authority:

I have read or had read to me, the foregoing conditions of my parole. I fully understand these conditions, I agree to comply with them, and I understand that violation of any of these conditions may result in the revocation of my parole.

In addition, I understand that I will be subject to the foregoing conditions until I have received a certificate from the Adult Parole Authority or a Journal Entry from the Court if I am a probationer, stating that I have been discharged from supervision.

The parolee signs this form and a witness also signs.

This agreement contains several important stipulations contained in virtually every parole agreement. First, the prospective parolee must agree to stay in continuous contact with his or her parole officer during the parole period, however long it may be. The offender may not possess firearms or dangerous weapons. The offender must remain in the state unless permission to leave it is obtained from the PO in advance. Drugs and alcohol are to be avoided, and drug and alcohol checks are to be permitted whenever the PO sees fit to administer them. In this particular form, the offender agrees to be extradited from external jurisdictions, even foreign countries, in the event that he or she absconds. In addition, the prospective parolee agrees to warrantless searches at any time by his or her PO. Any special conditions of parole must be complied with to the letter. If counseling or sex offender treatment is required, then the parolee must satisfy that condition. If attending Alcoholics Anonymous or some other group is required, then this condition is mandatory. All conditions are mandatory.

The prospective parolee *must* agree to all these conditions. Failure to sign the document will mean that parole will not be granted. Although it may seem unusual for a prospective parolee not to sign this document and obtain early release, some inmates believe that the conditions are too stringent. They may exercise their right to remain in prison and serve out their sentences, particularly if they are within a few months or years of mandatory release anyway. If the offender accepts these conditions and violates any one or more of them, he or she is liable of having his or her parole program revoked. A majority of parolees in the United States are currently under standard parole with conditions (Pastore and Maguire, 2001).

Intensive Supervised Parole

Parolees are often subject to precisely the same kinds of behavioral requirements as probationers who are involved in intensive supervision programs. The **New Jersey Intensive Probation Supervision Program** is made up of inmates who have served at least three or four months of their prison terms (Ciancia and Talty, 1999). In fact, the term *shock parole* has been applied to this and similar programs, because an inmate is shocked with what it is like to be incarcerated. The use of house arrest, electronic monitoring, and several other programs may be a part of one's conditional early release from prison. The level of monitoring will vary according to the risk posed by the offender, but it is quite difficult to predict accurately one's risk to the public or general dangerousness.

Most parolees are **standard parolees** in the sense that they are obligated to adhere to certain standard early release agreements formulated by paroling authorities. In 1987, the U.S. Sentencing Commission implemented new guidelines that included the following policy statement of recommended conditions of probation and **supervised release**:

1. The defendant shall not leave the judicial district or other specified geographical area without the permission of the court or PO.
2. The defendant shall report to the PO as directed by the court and shall submit a truthful and complete written report within the first five days of each month.
3. The defendant shall answer truthfully all inquiries by the PO and follow the instructions of the PO.
4. The defendant shall support his dependents and meet other family responsibilities.
5. The defendant shall work regularly at a lawful occupation unless excused by the PO for schooling, training, or other acceptable reasons.
6. The defendant shall notify the PO within seventy-two hours of any change in residence or employment.
7. The defendant shall refrain from excessive use of alcohol and shall not purchase, possess, use, distribute, or administer any narcotic or other controlled substance, or any paraphernalia related to such substances, except as prescribed by a physician.
8. The defendant shall not frequent places where controlled substances are illegally sold, used, distributed, or administered, or other places specified by the court.
9. The defendant shall not associate with any persons engaged in criminal activity, and shall not associate with any person convicted of a felony, unless granted permission to do so by the PO.
10. The defendant shall permit a PO to visit him at any time at home or elsewhere and shall permit confiscation of any contraband observed in plain view by the PO.
11. The defendant shall notify the PO within seventy-two hours of being arrested or questioned by a law enforcement officer.
12. The defendant shall not enter into any agreement to act as an informer or a special agent of a law enforcement agency without the permission of the court.
13. As directed by the PO, the defendant shall notify third parties of risks that may be occasioned by the defendant's criminal record or personal history or characteristics, and shall permit the probation officer to make such notifications and to confirm the defendant's compliance with such notification requirement (U.S. Sentencing Commission, 1987).

Additional special provisions pertain to possession of weapons, restitution, fines, debt obligations, access to financial information, community confinement, home detention, community service, occupational restrictions, substance abuse program participation, and mental health program participation (U.S. Sentencing Commission, 1987:5.7–5.10).

The New Jersey Intensive Supervision Parole Program.   One of the better **intensive supervised parole (ISP)** programs in the United States has been devised by New Jersey. The New Jersey Intensive Supervision Program (NJISP) was established in June 1983. Originally, the program was influenced by the traditional, treatment-oriented rehabilitation model and was designed to target the least serious incarcerated offenders (Ciancia and Talty, 1999). Since 1983, the NJISP has become a model program emulated by other states. Its program components are discussed at length in this section because of its success.

Program goals. The goals of the NJISP are to reduce the number of offenders serving state prison sentences by permitting them to be resentenced to an intermediate form of punishment, to improve the use of correctional resources by making additional bed space available for violent criminals, and to test whether supervising selected offenders in the community is less costly and more effective than incarceration.

Program eligibility. Who qualifies for the NJISP? First, anyone incarcerated in a New Jersey prison may apply for admission to the program. In fact, once an offender has been convicted of a crime and incarcerated in a New Jersey prison or county jail, he or she may apply for admission into the NJISP. There are, however, mandatory exclusions:

1. Persons convicted of homicide, a sex offense, a crime of the first degree, and robbery.
2. Persons serving sentences of life without the possibility of parole.
3. Persons convicted of organized crime activity.

For all other offenders, applications are received and reviewed by an ISP Screening Board composed of three members drawn from 25 judges and citizen members. The board screens applications received from eligible inmates, and screening standards are rigorous. Between 1983 and 1999, for instance, 38,000 applications from inmates were received, but only 19 percent (7,220) were approved.

The application process is more than merely rubber-stamping someone's application for inclusion. Applicants deemed eligible for the NJISP are interviewed by program staff. They must develop detailed case plans that set forth their goals and objectives for achieving program success. Participant goals include remaining free from illegal substances, strengthening relationships, maintaining steady employment, resolving legal problems, and paying required financial obligations. Applicants must also state that they will attend self-help sessions of Alcoholics Anonymous, take adult education courses, or receive family counseling, depending on individual offender circumstances. Applicants must indicate their willingness to abide by the NJISP conditions by signing their case plans.

Applicants must also obtain a sponsor within the community, and they are encouraged to develop network teams. Community sponsors help participants comply with the program's conditions. They may provide transportation to and from required meetings or to obtain employment. Community sponsors also sign an applicant's case plan and can offer suggestions about how to strengthen it. During the applicant investigation process, recommendations are solicited from the original sentencing judge, the prosecutor, previous probation and parole officers, victims, and the local police. This information, referred to as an assessment report, is forwarded to the ISP Screening Board for review. The Board deliberates in groups of three and decides whether to accept or reject a particular applicant.

The provisional process. An ISP Resentencing Panel receives recommendations from the ISP Screening Board and admits or denies program admission for each applicant. Accepted applicants are immediately released from prison or jail and placed into the NJISP. Those denied admission are returned to the New Jersey Department of Corrections.

All applicants must endure a 90-day trial period. The progress of each participant is tracked and reviewed by the panel in 90-day intervals. Participants reappear before the panel for formal resentencing into the program after they have been under supervision for 180 days. Prior to resentencing, participants are considered to be on conditional release from their prisons or jails.

The ISP Resentencing Panel stresses that it does not overturn the original sentencing judge's decision; rather, it merely changes the place of confinement. Further, the panel does not declare that the original sentence was inappropriate; it stands by the original sentence imposed and deems it proper and justified. The NJISP is not a slap on the wrist. It is a demanding program requiring the participant to adhere to many stringent program requirements. Some applicants have been known to withdraw their applications once they learn that they will be under ISP supervision for 16 to 22 months. Finally, the NJISP is not a widening of the net of social control over offenders. Only those sentenced to serve incarcerative terms are considered eligible for program admission. Judges are prohibited from sentencing offenders directly into the NJISP.

Participants are advised that if admitted into the program, then they can expect to be on the program for at least 16 months, and for a longer period if their original sentence was five or more years. If any program condition is violated while they are in the NJISP, then they may be expected to remain in the program longer.

Program requirements. The NJISP requirements that follow are among the most rigorous found in any state or federal ISP program.

Conditions of the Intensive Supervision Program (ISP)

You have been placed on the Intensive Supervision Program (ISP) by the ISP Resentencing Panel for a trial period of 90 days subject to your compliance with your case plan and the conditions listed below. If you are arrested for a new offense, the ISP Resentencing Panel may issue a warrant to detain you in custody, without bail, to await disposition on the new charges.

1. I will obey the laws of the United States, and the laws and ordinances of any jurisdiction in which I may be residing.
2. I am required to promptly notify my ISP Officer if I am arrested, questioned, or contacted by any law enforcement official whether summoned, indicted, or charged with any offense or violation.
3. I will report as directed to the Court or to my ISP Officer.
4. I will permit the ISP Officer to visit my home.
5. I will answer promptly, truthfully, and completely all inquiries made by my ISP Officer and must obtain approval prior to any residence change. If the change of address or residence is outside the region in which I am under supervision, I will request approval at least 30 days in advance.
6. I will participate in any medical and/or psychological examinations, tests, and/or counseling as directed.
7. I will support my dependents, meet my family responsibilities, and continue full time (35 hours or more per week), gainful employment. I will notify my ISP Officer prior to any change in my employment or if I become unemployed.
8. I will not leave the State of New Jersey without permission of my ISP Officer.
9. If I abscond from supervision (keep my whereabouts unknown to my ISP Officer), I may be charged with a new crime of Escape under 2C: 29-5, which may subject me to an additional sentence of up to five years consecutive to any ISP violation time.
10. I will not have in my possession any firearm or other dangerous weapon.

11. I will perform community service of at least 16 hours per month, unless modified by the ISP Resentencing Panel.

12. I will participate in ISP group activities as directed.

13. I will maintain a daily diary of my activities and a weekly budget while under supervision.

14. I will not borrow any money, loan any money, or make credit purchases without permission of my ISP Officer. I may be required to surrender any credit cards in my possession to my officer.

15. I will maintain weekly contact with my community sponsor and network team.

16. I will comply with the required curfew of 6 P.M. to 6 A.M. unless modified by my ISP Officer. If unemployed, I will abide by a 6 P.M. curfew unless modified by my ISP Officer.

17. I will submit at any time to a search of my person, places, or things under my immediate control by my ISP Officer.

18. I will abstain from all illegal drug use and consumption of alcohol (including nonalcoholic beer) and submit to drug and/or alcohol testing as directed. I also will not ingest any product containing poppy seeds. I will not use any medications, including over-the-counter medications, that contain alcohol.

19. I will notify my employer of my participation in ISP within 30 days after commencing employment.

20. I will not ingest any medication prescribed to someone else and will inform my ISP Officer of any medication prescribed to me by a physician or dentist.

21. I will file my Federal and State tax returns by the lawfully prescribed date and provide copies of the returns to my ISP Officer.

22. In accordance with State law, I cannot vote in any public election while under ISP supervision.

23. I will maintain telephone service at my approved residence. If the telephone service is discontinued, I will notify my ISP Officer immediately. I am not permitted to have caller ID or call forwarding services on my telephone.

24. I cannot collect unemployment benefits, disability assistance, or welfare benefits without permission.

25. I cannot possess a pager (beeper) and/or cellular telephone unless approved by my ISP Officer.

26. I cannot visit inmates in county or state correctional facilities until I have completed six months of satisfactory ISP supervision and with the permission of the ISP Regional Supervisor.

27. I may not serve in the capacity of an informant for a law enforcement agency. If requested to do so, I must decline and inform my ISP Officer of the request.

28. I will not engage in any gambling including the purchase of lottery tickets. I will not enter a gambling establishment (casino) unless employed at such an establishment or given permission to visit such establishment by my ISP Officer.

29. I will turn in to my ISP Officer my driver's license (if driving privileges have been revoked), firearms ID card, and hunting license if any of them are in my possession.

30. I will comply with any and all directives from the ISP Resentencing Panel or my officer.

These conditions are very rigorous. All participants must agree to them in writing. A violation of one or more conditions means that the ISP Resentencing Panel will hear the charges and decide on the punishment. Program violations are cause for terminating one's involvement in the program and returning the offender to prison. The panel usually sits in parties of three and conducts hearings at least two times per month. Hearings are held in various locations throughout New Jersey's 21 counties in an effort to acquaint judges and other judicial employees with the functions of the ISP Resentencing Panel.

PO responsibilities. ISP officers spend about 80 percent of their time in direct field supervision. In 1998, for instance, officers conducted 556,202 participant contacts. Since 1984, POs have conducted almost four million contacts. Caseloads of POs are a maximum of 20 clients. Participants do not visit regional officers; rather, POs visit participants at their workplaces, homes, and other places as deemed appropriate by the PO. Participants can reach their POs 24 hours a day. All POs are equipped with a message paging device accessed through a toll-free telephone number. If a participant absconds from the program, then the ISP arranges for and assists in the execution of arrest warrants. Violators will be tracked down by any and all means available to the state.

POs are unarmed, which is a concern for many involved in the NJISP. Strategies for working in unsafe areas, including arranging meetings with community sponsors as escorts and using prearranged sites, have been devised. All ISP officers and community development specialists are equipped with portable cellular telephones to assist in their monitoring and surveillance duties. ISP officers may search a participant's home, person, or vehicle without a warrant. Searches are conducted at random to determine whether participants are in possession of firearms or illegal contraband or if they have any other prohibited items such as credit cards or cellular telephones or pagers.

Client responsibilities. All ISP participants must maintain employment and must be economically self-sufficient. During 1998, for instance, ISP participants had an average full-time income of $15,000. Participants are obligated to observe a curfew ranging from 6 P.M. to 6 A.M. These curfews may be changed with PO approval. Curfews are monitored through random visits, telephone calls, and electronic surveillance and by community sponsors and network team and family members. Participants can modify their curfews as they progress successfully through their programs. Participants must pay all court-ordered financial obligations which may include restitution, child support, court-mandated fines, drug penalties, Victim Crime Compensation Board fees, and other payments. Participants must perform at least 16 hours of community service each month. Projects may include maintenance work at hospitals, nursing homes, and geriatric institutes; cleaning municipal vehicles; picking up litter at parks and roadways; stuffing envelopes for nonprofit agencies; painting; carpentry; plumbing; tutoring; and clerical work for charitable organizations.

Clients must submit to urine monitoring to detect drug use. Alcohol ingestion is detected by using a Breathalyzer. The majority of participants have substance abuse problems. Participants are screened as often as three times a week. Positive tests are often confirmed by gas chromatography, and participants with positive tests are immediately confronted. Admission of drug use is considered a crucial element in the recovery process, and most participants admit to using drugs when confronted. ISP uses more than a hundred outpatient and inpatient substance abuse, alcohol abuse, and psychological treatment providers. Educational seminars are held regularly for participants, and their attendance at these seminars is mandatory.

Sanctions are imposed for any program violation. The seriousness of the sanction depends on the seriousness of the violation. The most commonly applied sanctions are increased curfew restrictions, additional community service hours, increased treatment requirements, home detention, and short-term incarceration.

The successfulness of the NJISP. The NJISP measures the success of its program through client recidivism rates. By March 1999, there were 7,154 participants, with about 44 percent (3,164) graduating. There were 2,774 (39 percent) participants returned to custody for violating program conditions. Of the program graduates, the recidivism figures have been most impressive. Using a 60-month follow-up of the NJISP graduates, only 7.5 percent had recidivated, for a success rate of 92.5 percent.

The cost of the NJISP is low compared with incarceration. In New Jersey, it cost $31,000 to house one offender in prison or jail for a year. The NJISP program costs for each participant per year were only $7,158.

A profile of NJISP clientele. In 1999, the active caseload of all NJISP clients was 1,133. Of these, 86 percent were male. The average sentence length for males was 51 months, compared with 49 months for female offenders participating in the program. A majority of offenders were convicted for drug use and sales (63.7 percent for men and 73.1 percent for women). A majority of participants were never married; about 12 percent of all participants, both men and women, were married. The median educational level of all participants was 11 years, and about 60 percent of all participants were high school graduates. A majority were employed (62 percent for men and 53 percent for women). About 38 percent of all male participants were first-offenders, whereas 49 percent of all female participants were first-offenders.

In New Jersey, at least, the public likes the NJISP, and the media have given the NJISP very favorable coverage. There have been relatively few incidents involving victimizations through violent offending, perhaps because applicants are so rigorously screened before they are accepted into the program. Through educational seminars, courses in parenting skills, GED preparation, job searches and job application form assistance, and literacy courses, the NJISP has had a very positive effect on most participants.

This program is by no means the only one of its type in the United States. One common thread running through almost all these ISP programs is the continuous monitoring and random checking of offenders (Marciniak, 2000; Maxwell and Gray, 2000). ISP means closer offender monitoring, which means that fewer clients will have a chance to use drugs or alcohol and avoid being detected through random checks. This constant monitoring seems to work in most ISP programs (Latessa et al., 1998; Petersilia, 1999a). Face-to-face contacts improve client compliance with program conditions (Bayens, Manske, and Smykla, 1998). There is some variation among programs relating to client recidivism. Not all offenders are monitored as closely as they are in the NJISP. The two most important factors relating to program failure, however, were drug/alcohol abuse and unemployment (English, Pullen, and Colling-Chadwick, 1996; Garcia, 1996).

The Nevada Intensive Supervision Program.   Nevada has established an intensive supervision program for both its probationers and parolees. The Nevada ISP program is one component of case management and is a tool to assist the Nevada Division of Parole and Probation achieve its overall mission. It is also the ultimate level of supervision that the Nevada agency can provide for community safety and offender rehabilitation. The common elements of Nevada's ISP are as follows:

1. Frequent contacts with offenders
2. Smaller caseloads
3. A system of phases or levels
4. Curfews or electronic monitoring
5. Drug and alcohol testing
6. Graduated internal sanctions
7. Treatment and other interventions
8. Required employment
9. Employment-seeking activities or schooling

All specialized caseloads are fielded to District IV (Las Vegas), the largest ISP unit within Nevada. These caseloads encompass residential confinement, mandatory parole release, offenders in need of true ISP monitoring, and the sex offender unit. In 2001, these caseloads totaled 1,044 offenders. The Nevada legislature authorized a 30–1 ratio for residential confinement and ISP offenders and a 40–1 ratio for all others. The Division of Parole and Probation screens offenders for inclusion in its ISP program according to (1) crimes of violence, (2) crimes involving drug trafficking or sales of controlled substances, (3) criminal activity of a sophisticated nature, (4) active gang affiliation, (5) sustained or chronic substance abuse history, (6) history of mental illness, and (7) court/board ordered. One or all of these criteria might function to deny admission to the ISP program for any particular offender.

The ISP encompasses two phases of specific periods of time. The first phase is 90 days during which the offender is placed either on court/board house arrest or curfew. The house arrest monitoring is provided by a contracted private company that sets the fee for such service, and the offender is required to meet that financial obligation. Curfew can either be monitored by the appropriate officer or the offender may be referred to the private company offering that service (the offender is responsible for fee assessments when referred to the private company). During this initial 90-day period, the offender is aggressively encouraged to enroll in and complete short-term goals such as outpatient substance abuse or alcohol counseling, employment counseling, and anger management.

The second phase of this program consists of either a 30- or 60-day period during which the offender is made ready to enter the general supervision population. In this phase, the offender is taken off residential confinement or curfew and supervision requirements are greatly relaxed. If the offender relapses during this phase of supervision, then he or she is allowed one more opportunity to reenter the first phase and again attempt to change his or her behavior, indicating that he or she can be managed in a general supervision population. Thus, the ISP was structured with intent of providing an ultimate level of ISP and rehabilitation to promote long-term behavioral change that would eventually lead to enhanced public safety. If those efforts fail and result in a violation process, then the Nevada Division of Parole and Probation could positively assure that there would be no other supervision strategies available to the offender.

The following are contract requirements for each phase or level of supervision:

Phase/Level I
1 home contact
1 monthly report

2 field contacts or 2 surveillance contacts or 1 each
1 employment program/program verification
Special conditions as applicable

Phase/Level II
1 home contact
1 monthly report
1 field contact or 1 surveillance
1 employment/program verification
Special conditions as applicable

Offenders on Residential Confinement
2 home contacts
1 monthly report
1 residence verification
1 face-to-face contact
2 employment/program verifications
Special conditions as applicable

Surveillance of an offender may be considered to be a field contact with supervisory approval. All surveillance time shall be recorded in a surveillance log that is turned into and maintained by the officer's immediate supervisor at the end of each month. At the beginning of 2001, the ISP unit worked a seven-day schedule, with a day shift and a swing shift. Caseloads were assigned according to geographic location. The team concept is used within this unit, and the officers usually work with assigned partners when working the field. Most caseloads are integrated with both the residential confinement and ISP offenders because of two factors: the geographic location and because every officer cross-trains in all phases, therefore making it easier to have the same level of expertise throughout the seven-day period. The sex offender sub-unit currently has ten officers, and their contact requirements are constantly changing. These officers generally work alone with the exception of a planned search and arrest. The program was implemented during the spring and summer of 2000. As of March 2001, 10 percent of all offenders were returned to either the court or the parole board, resulting in a 3 percent revocation rate (Konopka, 2001:1–4).

Shock Parole

Shock parole, sometimes called shock probation, refers to a planned sentence whereby judges order offenders imprisoned for periods ranging from 30, 60, 90, or even 120 days. The terms of imprisonment are actually longer, such as one or more years, but offenders are removed from their jails or prisons after these short periods and resentenced to probation or parole provided that they behaved well while incarcerated. The shock factor relates to the shock of being imprisoned. Theoretically, this trauma will be so dramatic that offenders will not want to reoffend and return to prison; thus, there is a strong deterrent factor associated with these shock parole sentences. Ohio introduced the first shock probation law in 1965. Several other states have adopted similar laws in recent years (New York State Department of Correctional Services, 1994). Offenders who are sentenced to shock parole do not know that this sentence is actually being imposed. In their own minds, they are being sentenced to terms of one or more years in prison. Thus, when they are suddenly removed from prison and resentenced to parole, this shock of resentencing sends them an important message to refrain from lawless conduct and remain law-abiding.

The success of shock parole is measured by the recidivism rates of shock parolees. New York State Department of Corrections estimates savings per inmate of up to $10,000 per year, and other jurisdictions using shock incarceration report similar savings (New York State Department of Correctional Services, 1994). Recidivism figures for shock probationers in Ohio and other jurisdictions have been unusually low compared with the recidivism rates of offenders involved in other types of programs such as intensive supervised probation, furloughs, or work release (Vito, Holmes, and Wilson, 1985). It is perhaps too early to tell whether shock incarceration will make an important difference in the long run as a crime control strategy, although preliminary reports are favorable.

Halfway Houses and Community Residential Centers

Halfway Houses Defined.   One of the most important components of transitional corrections is the **halfway house**, either publicly or privately operated facilities staffed by professionals, paraprofessionals, and volunteers. Designed to assist parolees make the transition from prison to the community, halfway houses provide food, clothing, temporary living quarters, employment assistance, and limited counseling. Again, if the parolee has been confined for a long period, the transition can be difficult, possibly even traumatic (Bouffard, MacKenzie, and Hickman, 2000). Sometimes these facilities are known as **community residential centers**.

In 1999, 29 states and the federal government operated halfway houses for parolees. There were 19,490 halfway house clients (Camp and Camp, 1999:124). Although the precise origin of halfway houses is unknown, some observers say evidence of halfway houses existed during the Middle Ages as a part of Christian charity (Pratt and Winston, 1999). The Salvation Army was associated with halfway house operations in the United States in the early 1900s, although shelters such as the Philadelphia House of Industry were in existence to serve the various needs of parolees as early as 1889. Much earlier, in 1817, some reformist groups lobbied for halfway houses as a means of solving prison overcrowding problems. At that time, these proposals were rejected because of the belief that prisoners would contaminate one another if they lived together in common quarters, spreading their criminality like a disease. Temporary facilities for released prisoners were established also in New York City as early as 1845. In that year, the Society of Quakers opened the **Isaac T. Hopper Home** in New York City, followed by the Temporary Asylum for Disadvantaged Female Prisoners established in Boston in 1864 by a reformist group (G. Wilson, 1985:153). In 1889, the House of Industry was opened in Philadelphia, and in 1896, Hope House was established in New York City by Maud and Ballington Booth. Receiving considerable financial support from a missionary religious society called the Volunteers of America, the Boothes were able to open what became known as **Hope Houses** in future years in Chicago, San Francisco, and New Orleans (G. Wilson, 1985:153).

In many jurisdictions, halfway houses offer services to offenders on a voluntary basis. They assist greatly in helping former inmates make the transition from rigid prison life to community living. There was resistance to halfway houses when they were first proposed, because the public feared **criminal contamination**. The public subsequently warmed to the idea of halfway houses once it was learned that they exerted a high degree of supervision and control over their clientele.

State and federal governments during the 1800s and early 1900s continued to work toward the creation of halfway houses apart from those established in the private sector, however. In 1917, the Massachusetts Prison Commission recommended the establishment of houses to accommodate recently released offenders who were indigent, but this plan was rejected. Eventually, in the 1960s, Attorney General Robert F. Kennedy recommended government sponsorship and funding for halfway house programs. In 1965, the Prisoner Rehabilitation Act, which authorized the establishment of community-based residential centers for both juvenile and adult prerelease offenders, was passed (G. Wilson, 1985:154).

One of the most significant events to spark the growth of state-operated halfway houses was the creation of the **International Halfway House Association (IHHA)** in Chicago in 1964. Although many of the halfway house programs continued to be privately operated after the formation of the IHHA, the growth in the numbers of halfway houses was phenomenal during the next decade. For instance, from 1966 to 1982, the number of halfway houses operating in the United States and Canada rose from 40 to 1,800 (G. Wilson, 1985:154). These figures are probably lower than the actual number of halfway houses in existence during those periods, because these numbers were based on affiliation with the IHHA and the American Correctional Association, through which a directory was devised. Other researchers have reported as many as 2,300 halfway house facilities with over 100,000 beds existing in 1981 (Gatz and Murray, 1981).

Halfway House Variations. Because so many different government-sponsored and private agencies claim to be halfway houses, it is impossible to devise a consistent definition of one that fits all jurisdictions. There is extensive variation in the level of custody for clients, ranging from providing simple shelter on a voluntary basis to mandatory confinement with curfew. Halfway houses also provide many different services such as alcohol or drug-related rehabilitation facilities with some hospitalization on premises, minimal or extensive counseling services, and/or employment assistance. Halfway house programs are designed for offenders ranging from probationers and prereleasees to parolees and others assigned to community service with special conditions (Bouffard, MacKenzie, and Hickman, 2000).

Halfway-In and Halfway-Out Houses. The concept of a halfway house is closely connected with the reintegrative aim of corrections. In recent years, at least two hyphenated versions of the term have emerged. **Halfway-out houses** are facilities designed to serve the immediate needs of parolees from those established to accommodate probationers in the community. **Halfway-in houses** provide services catering to probationers in need of limited or somewhat restricted confinement apart from complete freedom of movement in the community (Travis, 1985).

Halfway-in houses are deliberately intended to create uncomfortable atmospheres. These houses structure the lives of probationers in various ways, mostly by making them comply with various program requirements (e.g., curfew and random drug and alcohol checks). In contrast, halfway-out houses, for parolees, are designed to provide homelike and supportive environments aimed at aiding the offender's readjustment to society. Like halfway-in houses, these homes also continue punishment through the high degree of supervision or offender control exerted by halfway-out house staff (Ely, 1996). Yet because their clientele are parolees and have served substantial time behind bars, their functions are more therapeutic, rehabilitative, and reintegrative rather than punishment-centered (Twill et al., 1998).

The Philosophy and Functions of Halfway Houses.   More than any other parole program, the halfway house typifies the transition prisoners must make from the unique custodial world of prisons and jails to the outside community. Today, halfway houses furnish not only living accommodations and food, but also job placement services for parolees, group and/or individual counseling, medical assistance, placement assistance in vocational/technical training programs, and numerous other opportunities for self-development (Munden, Tewksbury, and Grossi, 1999).

The major functions of halfway houses overlap some of those associated with other programs for parolees. They include parolee rehabilitation and reintegration into the community; provisions for food and shelter; job placement, vocational guidance, and employment assistance; client-specific treatments; alleviating jail and prison overcrowding; supplementing supervisory functions of probation and parole agencies; and monitoring probationers, work/study releasees, and others with special program conditions.

Parole rehabilitation and reintegration into the community.   The major function of halfway houses is to facilitate offender reintegration into the community. This function is accomplished, in part, by providing necessities and making various services accessible to offenders. The administrative personnel of halfway houses as well as professional and paraprofessional staff members assist in helping offenders with specific problems they might have, such as alcohol or drug dependencies. Often, parolees have worked out a plan for themselves in advance of their parole date. This plan is subjected to scrutiny by parole board members, and the parolee often has the assistance of a PO in its preparation.

Provisions for food and shelter.   Some parolees have acquired savings from their work in prison industries, whereas other parolees have no operating capital. Thus, halfway houses furnish offenders with a place to stay and regular meals while they hunt for new occupations and participate in self-help programs. Furthermore, halfway house personnel help offenders locate apartments or more permanent private housing for themselves and their families.

Job placement, vocational guidance, and employment assistance.   Almost every halfway house assists offenders by furnishing them job leads and negotiating contacts between them and prospective employers. Some halfway houses provide offenders with financial subsidies that must be repaid when the offender has successfully acquired employment and is relatively stable (Twill et al., 1998).

Client-specific treatments.   Offenders with special needs or problems, such as sex offenders, drug addicts or alcoholics, or mentally retarded clients, benefit from halfway houses by being permitted the freedom to take advantage of special treatment programs. They may receive counseling, medical treatment, or other services custom designed for their particular needs. If these offenders were to be placed on the street on parole directly from a prison or jail, then the transition for some would be very traumatic, and it is likely that they would revert to old habits or dependencies.

Alleviating jail and prison overcrowding. Any program that provides a safety valve for prison or jail populations contributes to alleviating overcrowding problems. Probably the major function of halfway houses is to assist offenders in becoming reintegrated into society after long periods in secure confinement, but the functions of such houses have become diversified over the years. In any case, the existence of halfway houses has contributed to some reduction in jail and prison overcrowding as both a front-end and a back-end solution (Ely, 1996; Munden, Tewksbury, and Grossi, 1999).

Supplementing supervisory functions of probation and parole agencies. A latent function of halfway houses is to exercise some degree of supervision and control over both probationers and parolees. These supervisory functions are ordinarily performed by probation or parole officers. When some inmates are released to halfway houses, however, halfway house staff assume considerable responsibility for client conduct (Bouffard, MacKenzie, and Hickman, 2000; Pratt and Winston, 1999).

Monitoring parolees, work/study releasees, and others with special program conditions. Many parolees have conditional parole programs that require their attendance at meetings and regular counseling. Thus, halfway houses cannot only provide the basic necessities such as food, clothing, and shelter, but they can also offer assistance in transporting clients to and from their required meetings and counseling sessions (Pratt and Winston, 1999).

Strengths and Weaknesses of Halfway Houses. Blanket generalizations about halfway house effectiveness are difficult because there is so much diversity among the programs (Bouffard, MacKenzie, and Hickman, 2000). Furthermore, these programs have been established on widely different philosophical bases or rehabilitative models. Several attempts to measure halfway house effectiveness, however, primarily one of three ways, have been made. First, are halfway houses more cost-effective compared with incarceration? Second, do halfway houses actually assist in reintegrating offenders into society? Third, do halfway houses reduce recidivism to a greater degree among parolees compared with other programs such as standard parole? The cost-effectiveness of halfway houses is undisputed when contrasted with the cost of maintaining inmates in prisons or jails. For instance, it costs about $43 per day to maintain a client in a halfway house (Camp and Camp, 1999:124), less than half the cost of incarcerating offenders in most prisons.

Some of the major strengths and weaknesses of halfway house programs are as follows:

1. Halfway houses are effective in preventing criminal behavior in the community as alternatives that involve community release.
2. The placement of halfway houses in communities neither increases nor decreases property values.
3. Halfway houses assist their clients in locating employment but not necessarily in maintaining it.

4. Halfway houses are able to provide for the basic needs of their clients as well as other forms of release.

5. At full capacity, halfway houses cost no more, and probably less, than incarceration, although they do cost more than straight parole or outright release from correctional systems (Jones, 1997).

OTHER PAROLE CONDITIONS

Parolees are subject to several different conditions while serving their parole terms, such as attending Alcoholics Anonymous meetings, Narcotics Anonymous meetings, or Gamblers Anonymous meetings; participating in individual or group counseling; taking vocational/educational training, and seeking and obtaining continuous employment to support their dependents. Other conditions include day reporting centers, fines, day fines, community service orders, and restitution.

Day Reporting Centers

For parolees, day treatment centers are operated primarily during daytime hours for the purpose of providing diverse services to offenders and their families. Day reporting centers are highly structured nonresidential programs that use supervision, sanctions, and services coordinated from a central focus (Jones and Lacey, 1999). Offenders live at home and report to these centers daily. As a part of community residential treatment centers, day treatment programs provide services according to offender needs, such as employment assistance, family counseling, and educational/vocational training (Chard-Wierschem, 1995). Day treatment centers can also be used for supervision or monitoring. Client behavior modification is a key goal of such centers. Limited supervisory functions such as employment verification and evidence of law-abiding conduct for probationers and parolees can be performed by day treatment centers as well. These centers are also operated for the purpose of providing family counseling in **juvenile delinquency** cases through parent education and support groups (Bahn and Davis, 1998).

Fines

Fines and Criminal Statutes.   An integral part of sentencing in an increasing number of cases is the use of fines (U.S. General Accounting Office, 1998). The use of fines as sanctions can be traced to preindustrialized and non-Western societies (Winterfield and Hillsman, 1993:1). Estimates suggest that over 14 million persons are arrested each year in the United States and that a significant portion of these people receive fines upon conviction. Ordinarily, state and federal criminal statutes provide for various incarcerative lengths upon conviction. In addition, various fines are imposed as and/or conditions exercised at the discretion of sentencing judges. For instance, if law enforcement officers were to violate one's civil rights by the unlawful use of physical force or excessive force in making an arrest, they might be subject to penalties, including confinement in a state penitentiary up to five years and a fine of "not more than" $10,000. Thus, if these law enforcement officers are convicted of violating one's civil rights, the judge can sentence them to prison for up to five years and impose a fine of $10,000. This sentence would be within the judge's discretionary powers (McDonald, Greene and Worzella, 1992:1).

Types of Fines and Fine Collection Problems.   There are different types of scenarios involving fines: fines plus jail or prison terms; fines plus probation; fines plus suspended jail or prison terms; fines or jail alternatives ($30 or 30 days); fines alone, partially suspended; and fines alone (Winterfield and Hillsman, 1993). The arguments for and against the use of fines as sanctions have also been clearly delineated. For instance, Douglas McDonald, Judith Greene, and Charles Worzella (1992:1) say that (1) fines are logically suited for punishment because they are unambiguously punitive; (2) many offenders are poor and cannot afford fines; (3) because the poor cannot afford fines as easily as the rich, there is obvious discrimination in fine imposition; (4) someone else may pay the fine other than the offender; (5) often, fine payments are unenforceable because of offender absconding; (6) courts lack sufficient enforcement capability; and (7) fines may actually increase crime so that the poor can get enough money to pay previously imposed fines. The problems of fine collection are such that fewer than half the fines imposed are ever collected in most U.S. courts. Billions of dollars are involved in fine nonpayment. In more than a few jurisdictions, fine payment rates at the time of conviction have only been 14 percent (McDonald, Greene, and Worzella, 1992:33).

Suspending Fines.   In many criminal cases, however, fines are suspended. Often, indigent or poor offenders cannot pay these fines or would have great difficulty paying them and supporting their families or fulfilling any of their other financial obligations. From an examination of probation and parole revocation, it is known that one's probation or parole program cannot be revoked simply because of one's inability to pay program fees or fines. Thus, many judges do not impose fines because they will be uncollectible (Wheeler and Rudolph, 1990). Also, fines are not imposed in many cases because of certain jurisdictional precedents. In other instances, fines may be imposed but those obligated to pay fines will abscond. Even if those assessed fines do not abscond, the collection procedures in some jurisdictions are lax or unenforced.

Day Fines

Historically, the fine was not a prominent intermediate penalty in the United States because of deep skepticism among U.S. criminal justice professionals (Winterfield and Hillsman, 1993:1). During the late 1970s and early 1980s, considerable effort was expended investigating alternative sentencing for offenders different from traditional indeterminate sentencing. Besides attempting to devise more equitable sentencing schemes through guidelines-based sentencing, determinate sentencing, and mandatory sentencing, offender accountability was heightened in various ways. A key issue, however, was how much should fines be in relation to an offender's ability to pay.

One solution is the use of **day fines**, an early European invention. Day fines are a two-step process whereby courts use a unit scale or benchmark to sentence offenders to certain numbers of day-fine units (e.g., 15, 30, 120) according to offense severity and without regard to income and determine the value of each unit according to a percentage of the offender's daily income; total fine amounts are determined by multiplying this unit value by the number of units accompanying the offense (Winterfield and Hillsman, 1993:2). For instance, Offender X's conviction of simple assault might have a unit value of 30. The offender may have a net daily income of $50. Suppose that the percentage of one's net daily income to be assessed as a fine is 10 percent. Therefore, Offender X's total fine would be $50 × 10% × 30 units (for simple assault), or $5 × 30 = $150. This $150 fine would be assessed an offender at the time of sentencing, and the method of fine payment would also be determined. Fine payments may be in installments, usually over no longer than a three-month period (McDonald, Greene and Worzella, 1992:35-37).

The Staten Island Day-Fine Experiment.   In August 1988, judges in the New York City borough of Staten Island established a day-fine system similar to that developed earlier in Europe. This experiment was conducted because this jurisdiction and others like it in New York had considerable trouble collecting fines imposed when offenders were convicted of crimes. It was believed by Staten Island officials that day fines would actually increase the rate of fine payments, because day fines were determined in accordance with one's ability to pay. The project's planners had several goals in mind:

1. A system of sentencing benchmarks proposing a specific number of day-fine units for each criminal offense
2. A system for collecting necessary information about offenders concerning their ability to pay
3. Policy guidelines and easy-to-use methods for establishing the value of each day-fine unit imposed for each offender
4. Strategic improvements in the court's collection and enforcement mechanisms
5. A microcomputer-based information system that automates and records collection and enforcement activities (McDonald, Green and Worzella, 1992:19–22)

Establishing the amount of a day-fine unit involved determining one's net daily income expected as well as the number of one's dependents. Day-fine unit amounts were scaled down according to increased numbers of dependants, for instance. Thus, every effort was made to distribute day fines equitably, according to one's ability to pay, in stark contrast with the idea of a fixed-fine system imposed on offenders, regardless of their earnings or numbers of dependents. The Staten Island experiment wanted to determine several things. First, were day fines higher or lower than fines previously assessed for similar offenses? Second, would the burden of calculating one's day-fine amount deter fine collection? Third, would the new collection techniques used with day fines have any favorable impact on collection outcomes? The results were favorable. For instance, between April 1987 and March 1988, the total fine amounts imposed by the courts increased by 14 percent, and fines for average penal law offenses increased by 25 percent. Most important, collection rates under the new day-fine system rose to 85 percent. Capped collection amounts were those governed by statute. Thus, day-fine payments could not exceed statutory maximum fines for specific offenses, even though a day-fine amount may be generated in excess of this statutory maximum. An average of $440.83 was collected using uncapped day fines compared with $205.66 collected under traditional fine methods (Winterfield and Hillsman, 1993:3–5).

Laura Winterfield and Sally Hillsman (1993:5–6) say that the new collection techniques established by the Staten Island project has had the following advantages over traditional or more routine court procedures related to fine assessments and payment:

1. More extended terms for payment of the larger day fines
2. Fewer costly court appearances
3. Fewer warrants for nonappearance at postsentence hearings

Considered significant in the Staten Island experiments was the individualized nature of fine assessments and collection. Clearly, determining one's fine according to ability to pay and arranging for installment payments of these fines is a more profitable way of court operation as well as a means of enhancing offender accountability. Similar experiments with consonant results have been conducted in Milwaukee.

Community Service Orders

Increasingly, conditions are imposed on parolees that provide for fines, some amount of restitution, and community service (Bazemore and Maloney, 1994). Community service sentencing is one of the best examples of the use of parole as a means of achieving offender accountability (Allen and Treger, 1990). Under the **Victim and Witness Protection Act of 1982** (18 U.S.C. Sec. 3579-3580, 2001), community service orders were incorporated as an option in addition to incarceration at the federal level. One flaw of the act was that it left unspecified when community service orders were to be imposed. Thus, judges could impose community service orders at the time of sentencing, or parole boards could make community service a provisional requirement for an inmate's early release. Victim advocates strongly urge that community service orders be an integral feature of the sentencing process. For instance, California has adopted community service orders as part of their parole process (Stephens, 2001).

Community service means that parolees perform services for the state or community. The nature of community service to be performed is discretionary with the sentencing judge or paroling authority. In some jurisdictions, prisoners must perform a specified number of hours of community service such as lawn maintenance, plumbing and other similar repairs, or services that fit their particular skills. The philosophy underlying community service is more aligned with retribution than rehabilitation (Florida House of Representatives, 1994).

Forms of Community Service.   Community service is considered a punishment and is imposed by the court. Many types of projects are undertaken by offenders as community service. Usually, these projects are supervised by POs or other officials, although reports are sometimes solicited from private individuals such as company managers or supervisors. A portion of the offender's earnings is allocated to victims as well as to the state or local public or private agencies overseeing the community services provided. In New Jersey, for example, community service orders include the following: assisting Community Food Banks throughout New Jersey with food drives, working on Adopt-a-Highway programs, participating in the March of Dimes Walk-A-Thon, and assisting various Goodwill sites with sorting and cleaning donated items. Other community service projects include scraping, sanding, and digging; building renovations; maintenance of recreational areas; and assistance in the operation of governmental facilities and nonprofit charitable events (Ciancia and Talty, 1999:7).

The Effectiveness of Community Service.   Serious questions are raised by authorities about the effectiveness of community service and restitution as sentencing options or parole program requirements. That offenders are released into their communities for the purpose of performing community service raises a **public risk** issue for some people, although those offenders ordinarily selected for community service are low risk and nonviolent (Majer, 1994). Other questions relate to the personal philosophies of judicial and correctional authorities, the offender eligibility and selection criteria used among jurisdictions, organizational arrangements, the nature of supervision over offenders performing community services, and how such services are evaluated (Meeker, Jesilow, and Aranda, 1992). Community service is a just and fitting accompaniment to whatever sentence is imposed by judges or whatever conditions are established by paroling authorities when considering inmates for early release. The element of retribution is strong, and it is believed by some observers that through community service, offenders are better able to understand the significance of the harm they inflicted on others by their criminal acts (Yuslum, 1990).

Restitution

An increasingly important feature of probation programs is restitution (Crew, 1994). Restitution is the practice of requiring offenders to compensate crime victims for damages offenders may have inflicted. Several models of restitution have been described.

The Financial/Community Service Model.   The financial/community service model stresses the offender's financial accountability and community service to pay for damages inflicted on victims and to defray a portion of the expenses of court prosecutions. It is becoming more common for probationers and divertees to be ordered to pay some restitution to victims and to perform some type of community service. Community service may involve clean-up activities in municipal parks, painting projects involving graffiti removal, cutting courthouse lawns, or any other constructive project that can benefit the community. These community service sentences are imposed by judges. Probation officers are largely responsible for overseeing the efforts of convicted offenders in fulfilling their community service obligations. These sentencing provisions are commonly called **community-service orders**.

Community service orders are symbolic restitution, involving redress for victims, less severe sanctions for offenders, offender rehabilitation, reduction of demands on the criminal justice system, a reduction of the need for vengeance in a society, or a combination of these factors. Community service orders are found in many different countries and benefit the community directly (Roy, 1993). Further, when convicted offenders are indigent or unemployed, community service is a way of paying their fines and court costs. S. M. Donnelly (1980) summarizes some of the chief benefits of community service: (1) the community benefits because some form of restitution is paid, (2) offenders benefit because they are given an opportunity to rejoin their communities in law-abiding responsible roles, and (3) the courts benefit because sentencing alternatives are provided. Usually, between 50 and 200 hours of community service might be required for any particular convicted offender (Byrne, Lurigio, and Petersilia, 1992).

The Victim/Offender Mediation Model. The victim/offender mediation model focuses on victim-offender reconciliation. Alternative dispute resolution is used as a mediating ground for resolving differences or disputes between victims and perpetrators (Patel and Soderlund, 1994). Usually, third-party arbiters, such as judges, lawyers, or public appointees, can meet with offenders and their victims to work out mutually satisfactory arrangements whereby victims can be compensated for their losses or injuries.

The Victim/Reparations Model. The victim/reparations model stresses that offenders should compensate their victims directly for their offenses. Many states have provisions that provide **reparations** or financial payments to victims under a Crime Victims Reparations Act, which establishes a state-financed program of reparations to persons who suffer personal injury and to dependents of persons killed as the result of certain criminal conduct. In many jurisdictions, a specially constituted board determines, independently of court adjudication, the existence of a crime, the damages caused, and other elements necessary for reparation. Reparations cover such economic losses as medical expenses, rehabilitative and occupational retraining expenses, loss of earnings, and the cost of actual substitute services. Restitution can heighten accountability and result in a reduction in recidivism among offenders. If, however, restitution is not properly implemented by the court or carefully supervised, then it serves little deterrent purpose.

PAROLE BOARDS AND EARLY-RELEASE DECISION MAKING

Parole Boards, Sentencing Alternatives, and the Get-Tough Movement

By 1988, most states had changed their sentencing provisions (Champion, 1994). In many instances, these changes in sentencing provisions significantly limited the discretionary authority of parole boards to grant prisoners early release. By 1999, 12 states and the federal government had abolished parole in favor of determinate sentencing. Nevertheless, all states continue to use parole boards for those offenders sentenced under indeterminate sentencing and prior to parole's abolishment in specified jurisdictions.

Maine became the first state to abolish parole in 1976. The following states abolished parole in subsequent years: Minnesota (1982), Florida (1983), Washington and the Federal Bureau of Prisons (1984), Oregon (1989), Delaware (1990), Kansas (1993), Arizona and North Carolina (1994), Virginia (1995), Ohio (1996), and Wisconsin (1999) (Camp and Camp, 1999:60–61). By 1983, the Maine legislature enacted certain good time provisions for the prison population. The primary reason given for abolishing parole in these jurisdictions was to remove early-release authority from parole boards, which tended to exhibit discrimination and often used extralegal factors in the parole-granting process. Furthermore, concerned critics of the parole system believed that many offenders were being released too soon; that is, they were not serving sufficient portions of their sentences. Thus, whenever parole boards released inmates short of serving their full sentences, criticism from those opposing parole inevitably resulted. Ironically, since parole has been abolished in the states noted above, the amount of time actually served by state and federal inmates has decreased through the accumulation of good time credits under substituted determinate and guidelines-based sentencing schemes. Thus, if critics worried about offenders being released too soon under their parole board systems, then how must they feel now, considering offenders are being released much earlier, unconditionally in fact, from their prison systems? Unfortunately, no sentencing scheme or reform has satisfied all critics. Both violent and nonviolent offenders are being released daily from U.S. prisons, and many of those released are subject to little or no supervision or PO control (Colorado Legislative Council, 1998; Edwards, 1999).

The question of abolishing parole boards in any jurisdiction is hotly contested and one not likely resolvable in the near future. Whenever persons currently on parole commit new offenses, angry community residents want to know why they were released short of serving their full terms in the first place. It is acknowledged that community corrections programs can greatly enhance a parolee's success chances by providing valuable employment assistance, food, clothing, counseling, and a host of other services (Bosoni, 1992). If parolees are released to some type of intensive parole supervision (ISP) program within their communities, then it is not always the case that the ISP program will be beneficial to certain clients. Joan Petersilia (1999b) suggests that if jurisdictions are primarily interested in providing flexibility in sentencing decisions by imposing ISP that more closely fits the crimes of offenders, then ISP will likely be fruitful. If jurisdictions are mainly concerned with reducing recidivism and system costs, however, then ISP programs, as they are currently structured, will focus more on surveillance as opposed to treatment and thus will have a greater failure rate, where failure is defined as greater parolee-client recidivism.

Parole Board Composition and Diversity

There is considerable diversity among parole boards in the United States. Most parole board members, whether full- or part-time, are appointed by the governor of their state, and there are no special qualifications for parole board membership in most jurisdictions. Some parole board members may be former correctional officers or prison superintendents, whereas others may be retired judges, school teachers, or university professors.

Compared with other jurisdictions, Massachusetts probably has the most stringent criteria for parole board membership compared with other jurisdictions. Members of the Massachusetts Parole Board must possess a bachelor's degree and have at least five or more years of experience in corrections, law enforcement, social work, or other related field. One parole board member must be an attorney, and another must be a physician. States such as Texas, Oregon, and North Dakota do not require their parole board members to possess special qualifications. Because governors make parole board appointments in most jurisdictions, membership on these boards is largely political.

Subtleties in Parole Name-Changing: Politically Correct and Client-Friendly Labels. In many jurisdictions, parole is a bad word. Simply using the word *parole* draws much criticism. Parole, however, is indispensable. Without it, at least four, perhaps five times as many prisons and jails than presently exist would have to be constructed to accommodate all of those not granted this bad word. One way of living with this bad word without using it is to use a good word instead, similar to changing the name of insane asylum to mental hospital to the institute for the psychologically impaired.

How does this discussion apply to parole? Maine and several other states have abolished it. In subsequent years, however, Maine and Florida have been reconsidering reestablishing it. Maine also continues to have a parole board that convenes to hear parole-eligible cases of those convicted prior to 1976, when parole was formally abandoned. Several other states have abolished parole as well, believing that more equitable early-release mechanisms should be used rather than the discretionary power of parole boards. The federal government has established an alternative program for its prior parolees. Although there is still a U.S. Parole Commission, the U.S. Probation Office of each U.S. district court is responsible for supervising federal releasees. The diversity of labels applied to parole boards is evident in Table 8.1, which shows various state parole board labels for 2001.

Arkansas uses the name Post-Prison Transfer Board, Illinois uses Prisoner Review Board, Maryland uses Parole Commission, North Carolina uses Post-Release Supervision and Parole Commission, and Ohio uses Adult Parole Authority. These creative names do not disguise that they are all parole boards. When these various bodies convene and hear inmate requests for early release, the requests are either granted or denied. Regardless of the labels these jurisdictions choose to apply, these boards performed parole functions (Jayjohn, 1995).

Functions of Parole Boards

Each parole board in the United States has different functions; no two parole boards are identical. A synthesis of functions, however, is possible by comparing the goals and philosophical statements of various boards. A result of this synthesis includes the following major functions of parole boards:

1. To evaluate prison inmates who are eligible for parole and act on their application to approve or deny parole
2. To convene to determine whether a parolee's parole should be revoked on the basis of alleged parole violations
3. To evaluate juveniles to determine their eligibility for release from detention
4. To grant pardons or a **commutation** of sentences to prisoners, when mitigating circumstances or new information is presented that was not considered at trial
5. To make provisions for the supervision of adult offenders placed on parole; to establish supervisory agencies and select parole officers to monitor offender behavior
6. To provide investigative and supervisory services to smaller jurisdictions within the state
7. To grant reprieves in death sentence cases and to commute death penalties
8. To restore full civil and political rights to parolees and others on **conditional release**, including probationers
9. To review disparate sentences and make recommendations to the governor for clemency
10. To review the pardons and executive clemency decisions made by the governor (American Correctional Association, 2001)

TABLE 8.1 Parole Boards for Federal and State Jurisdictions, 2001

State	2001 Parole Board Name
Alabama	Board of Pardons and Paroles (3 full-time members; governor-appointed)
Alaska	Board of Parole (5 part-time members; governor-appointed)
Arizona	Board of Executive Clemency (5 full-time members; governor-appointed)
Arkansas	Post-Prison Transfer Board (7 members, 3 full-time, 4 part-time; independent)
California	Board of Prison Terms (7 full-time members; governor-appointed)
Colorado	Board of Parole (7 full-time members; governor-appointed)
Connecticut	Board of Parole (12 part-time members, chairperson full-time; governor-appointed)
Delaware	Board of Parole (1 full-time, 4 part-time members; governor-appointed)
District of Columbia	U.S. Parole Commission (7 full-time members; appointed by U.S. attorney general)
Florida	Parole Commission (3 full-time members; governor-appointed)
Georgia	Board of Pardons and Paroles (5 full-time members; autonomous)
Hawaii	Paroling Authority (3 full-time, 2 part-time, 1 full-time chairman; governor-appointed)
Idaho	Commission of Pardons and Parole (5 part-time members; appointed by Board of Corrections)
Illinois	Prisoner Review Board (12 full-time members; governor-appointed)
Indiana	Parole Board (5 full-time members; governor-appointed)
Iowa	Board of Parole (5 full-time members; governor-appointed)
Kansas	Parole Board (4 full-time members; governor-appointed)
Kentucky	Parole Board (8 full-time members; governor-appointed)
Louisiana	Board of Parole (7 full-time members; governor-appointed)
Maine	Parole Board (5 part-time members; governor-appointed; hears only cases pre–April 1976)
Maryland	Parole Commission (8 full-time members; appointed by the secretary of Public Safety and Correctional Services)
Massachusetts	Parole Board (6 full-time members; governor-appointed)
Michigan	Parole Board (10 full-time unclassified employees; appointed by the director of the Department of Corrections)
Minnesota	Board of Pardons (3 full-time members: governor, chief justice, attorney general); Hearings and Release Unit (8 full-time officers set terms of supervised release for adults and parole for juveniles)
Mississippi	Parole Board (5 full-time members; governor-appointed)
Missouri	Board of Probation and Parole (6 full-time members; governor-appointed)
Montana	Board of Pardons (3 part-time and 2 auxiliary members; governor-appointed)
Nebraska	Board of Parole (5 full-time members; governor-appointed)
Nevada	Board of Parole Commissioners (7 full-time members; governor-appointed)
New Hampshire	Board of Parole (7 part-time members; governor-appointed)
New Jersey	Parole Board (9 full-time members; governor-appointed)
New Mexico	Adult Parole Board (4 full-time members; governor-appointed)

State	2001 Parole Board Name
New York	Board of Parole (19 full-time members; governor-appointed)
North Carolina	Post-Release Supervision and Parole Commission (5 full-time commissioners; governor-appointed)
North Dakota	Parole Board (3 part-time members; governor-appointed)
Ohio	Adult Parole Authority (12 full-time members; 3 chief hearing officers; 19 hearing officers; 24 parole board parole officers appointed by the director of the department)
Oklahoma	Pardon and Parole Board (5 part-time, 3 appointed by governor, 1 by Court of Criminal Appeals, and 1 by the Oklahoma Supreme Court)
Oregon	Board of Parole and Post-Prison Supervision (3 full-time members; governor-appointed)
Pennsylvania	Board of Probation and Parole (5 full-time members; governor-appointed)
Rhode Island	Parole Board (6 part-time members; governor-appointed)
South Carolina	Board of Paroles and Pardons (7 part-time members; governor-appointed)
South Dakota	Board of Pardons and Paroles (7 part-time members; independent and responsible to Department of Corrections)
Tennessee	Board of Paroles (7 full-time members; governor-appointed)
Texas	Board of Pardons and Paroles (18 full-time members; convene in 3-member panels; independent)
Utah	Board of Pardons and Parole (5 full-time members; governor-appointed)
Vermont	Board of Parole (5 part-time members; governor-appointed)
Virginia	Parole Board (5 full-time members; governor-appointed)
Washington	Indeterminate Sentence Review Board (3 part-time members, governor-appointed; determines parole for offenders sentenced prior to July, 1984)
West Virginia	Parole Board (5 full-time members; governor-appointed)
Wisconsin	Parole Commission (5 full-time members; governor-appointed)
Wyoming	Board of Parole (7 full-time members; governor-appointed)
Federal	U.S. Parole Commission (7 full-time members; appointed by U.S. Attorney General)

Source: Compiled by author from the American Correctional Association, *Probation and Parole Directory 2001–2003* (Lanham, MD: American Correctional Association, 2001).

Most parole boards make parole decisions exclusively. In a limited number of jurisdictions, additional functions are performed, either according to statute or at the pleasure of the governor. In a limited number of jurisdictions, the paroling authority is vested in agencies independent of the governor.

Parole Board Standards. Parole boards may evolve their own standards, subject to legislative approval. For instance, the Connecticut Parole Board has several standards that govern each early-release decision:

1. The nature and circumstances of inmate offenses and their current attitudes toward them
2. The inmate's prior record and parole adjustment if paroled previously
3. Inmate's attitude toward family members, the victim, and authority in general

4. The institutional adjustment of inmates, including their participation in vocational/educational programs while incarcerated
5. Inmate's employment history and work skills
6. Inmate's physical, mental, and emotional condition as determined from interviews and other diagnostic information available
7. Inmate's insight into the causes of his or her own criminal behavior in the past
8. Inmate's personal efforts to find solutions to personal problems such as alcoholism, drug dependency, and need for educational training or developing special skills
9. The adequacy of the inmate's parole plan, including planned place of residence, social acquaintances, and employment program (Connecticut Board of Parole, 2001)

Parole Board Decision Making and Inmate Control

A major factor influencing parole board decision making is prison overcrowding, which has a tremendous effect on how corrections professionals do their jobs. Dramatic increases in parole supervision have been observed, and the number of parole release and revocation hearings has grown markedly over the years (Runda, Rhine, and Wetter, 1994). The aims of parole boards are similar to those of sentencing: treatment, incapacitation, deterrence, and deserts (Kansas Legislative Division of Post Audit, 1994). Parole boards, however, appear to receive more criticism from the public about the decisions they make compared with earlier similar judicial decisions. The significant question for parole boards is *when* to release inmates rather than *whether* to release them. Some states have attempted to adopt parole guidelines as a means of objectifying early-release decision making, but parole boards in these jurisdictions have been hesitant, if not resistant, to adopt objective parole guidelines. One reason is that parole boards fear losing a certain amount of control over inmate releases. Also, parole boards do not know for sure which variables are most crucial in making these early-release decisions for particular parole-eligible inmates. The use of risk-screening instruments for determining which offenders should be paroled has exhibited results that are unimpressive (Champion, 1994).

Cases Parole Boards Must Review.   A majority of parole board decisions, however, involve property offenders, although persons convicted of murder, robbery, assault, rape, and other violent crimes also face parole boards regularly. Facing parole boards at one time or another have been Sirhan Sirhan, convicted killer of Robert Kennedy; Charles Manson, Patricia Krenwinkle, and Leslie Van Houten, convicted murderers of several persons, including heiress Abigail Folger and actress Sharon Tate; convicted murderer James Richardson, who murdered his seven children by using a poison insecticide in Arcadia, Florida, on October 25, 1967; and confessed serial killer Joel Rifkin, who murdered at least 13 prostitutes on Long Island and in upstate New York between 1990 and 1993.

Cases Parole Boards Do Not Have to Review.   Sometimes, parole boards do not have to make difficult early-release decisions. They narrowly missed having to make a decision in the case of Dalton Prejean, who was only 17 when he murdered a Louisiana state trooper in 1977. He was convicted for shooting Louisiana trooper Donald Cleveland, who had stopped Prejean and his brother for a routine traffic violation. Prejean fired two shots through Cleveland's head, killing him outright. Three years earlier when Prejean was only 14, he had shot and killed a cab driver during an aborted robbery attempt. Subsequently, he was sentenced to the death penalty for the state trooper murder. After exhausting almost every appeal, his execution in the electric chair was scheduled for May 1990.

Amnesty International and other capital punishment opponents appealed to the Louisiana Governor Buddy Roemer to commute his sentence to life through executive clemency. Prejean was black, convicted by an all-white jury, suffered from partial brain damage, claimed he was remorseful, and had a history of abuse as a child. Candy Cleveland, the widow of the murdered state trooper, though, made a judgment of her own: "There is always the possibility of good time, good behavior . . . who knows, in 20 or 30 years, Prejean could be back on the street [to kill again]" (Shapiro, 1990:23). Roemer denied Prejean's request for clemency, and Prejean was electrocuted on schedule at Angola Prison. If Prejean's death sentence had been commuted to life without parole, then it is possible that Candy Cleveland's prediction would have come true.

Another case parole boards will not review is Danny Harold Rolling, a drifter who, in 1994, was convicted of murdering five University of Florida students in Gainesville in 1990. There were numerous aggravating circumstances and only a few questionable mitigating ones. Rolling had stabbed his victims repeatedly, bound them with duct tape, raped and mutilated them, and decapitated one victim. Persuasive evidence indicates that he tortured his victims prior to killing them in a brutal manner. In March 1994, a second-phase jury decision recommended the death penalty for Rolling. Barring any compelling appeals, which are unlikely, Rolling will eventually be executed by Florida authorities.

Just because an offender becomes eligible for parole does not mean that it will automatically be granted by the parole board. These boards have considerable discretionary power, and in many jurisdictions, they have absolute discretion over an inmate's early release potential. In fact, when federal courts have been petitioned to intervene and challenge parole board actions, the decisions of parole boards have prevailed (*Tarlton v. Clark,* 1971). In deciding whether to grant parole for given inmates or not grant parole, the following factors are considered:

1. The commission of serious disciplinary infractions while confined
2. The nature and pattern of previous convictions
3. The adjustment to previous probation, parole, and/or incarceration
4. The facts and circumstances of the offense
5. The aggravating and mitigating factors surrounding the offense
6. Participation in institutional programs that might have led to the improvement of problems diagnosed at admission or during incarceration
7. Documented changes in attitude toward self or others
8. Documentation of personal goals and strengths or motivation for law-abiding behavior
9. Parole plans
10. Inmate statements suggesting the likelihood that the inmate will not commit future offenses
11. Court statements about the reasons for the sentence.

If the parole board reacts favorably and grants an inmate parole, then it is usually conditional and subject to compliance with various rules and regulations (Seiter,

2000). If the parole board reacts unfavorably and denies the inmate parole, then usually one or more reasons are provided by the board for their action taken. Most jurisdictions obligate their parole boards to outline the reasons for their actions or at least make their reasons for denial of early release known to the inmate, giving the inmate an opportunity to improve in those areas cited by the board as unsatisfactory or unfavorable. Rehearings in some jurisdictions are conducted at regular intervals, usually annually (American Correctional Association, 2001).

Parole boards often rely on the idea that an inmate's good behavior while confined indicates that they might behave well if paroled, but parole-release policies that use this idea as a crucial factor in determining early release are in for a rude awakening. Evidence suggests that good behavior while incarcerated does not necessarily mean that an inmate will successfully adapt to the community and be law-abiding following a favorable early-release decision (Kassebaum, Davidson-Coronado, and Silverio, 1999). In fact, many criminal justice professionals believe that a prisoner's behavior, either before or during prison confinement, does not correlate highly with recidivism.

It is often the case that factors outside of prison are better predictors of parolee success. For instance, do parolees have favorable job prospects? Can they obtain jobs and retain them? Are they married? Are they participating in academic or vocational training programs while on parole? Do certain parolees have prior problems with drug or alcohol abuse? Are they taking steps to see that these particular addiction or dependency problems will not reoccur? In one study reporting largely favorable results about parolee success that examined 760 adult prison releasees from a Midwestern prison, it was found that only 177 of them became parole violators. Factors such as those listed above appeared crucial in determining success. Most parole violators had no job contacts following their release. Drug-dependent or alcohol-dependent releasees who did not seek treatment for their dependencies were more likely to recidivate while on parole. Those who had good job contacts, manifested marital stability, and participated in constructive educational, vocational, or counseling programs, however, were more apt to be successful while on parole (Anderson, Schumacker, and Anderson, 1991).

At the same time, some community pressures are exerted on known releasees. Sometimes these pressures create obstacles to effective parolee reintegration, particularly if community residents actively reject parolees socially (Enos, Holman, and Carroll, 1999). Ex-offenders sometimes have great difficulty finding jobs and housing if it is known to employers and rental agencies that these persons have prior records. Thus, through no particular fault of their own (short of having a prior record), parolees who make an honest effort to become reintegrated into their communities are frustrated by community residents unwilling to accept them (Schwaner, 1998).

Parole Board Orientations

Decisions made by parole boards can be classified into six general categories, each manifesting a particular value system: the jurist value system, the sanctioner value system, the treater value system, the controller value system, the citizen value system, and the regulator value system (Gottfredson and Gottfredson, 1988:231–233). The **jurist value system** regards parole decisions as a natural part of criminal justice in which fairness and equity predominate. Emphasized are an inmate's rights, and parole board members strive to be sensitive to due process. The **sanctioner value system** equates the seriousness of the offense with the amount of time served. In some respects, this system is closely connected with the just-deserts philosophy. The **treater value system** is rehabilitative in orientation, with decisions made in the context of what might most benefit the offender if parole is granted. Thus, participation in various educational or vocational programs, therapy or encounter groups, restitution, and other types of conditions might accompanying one's early release. The **controller value system** emphasizes the functions of parole supervision and monitoring. The conditions are established that increase the degree of control over the offender. Perhaps electronic monitoring or house arrest might be a part of one's parole program. In any case, the controller value system sees offender incapacitation or severe restrictions of freedom while on parole as desirable. The controller value system is most concerned with the risk posed to the public by an offender's early release.

The **citizen value system** is concerned with appealing to public interests and seeing that community expectations are met by making appropriate early-release decisions. How will the public react to releasing certain offenders short of serving their full terms? Will public good be served by such decisions? Community harmony and social order should be preserved, and parole board decisions that promote community harmony and order should be made. In view of mixed public sentiment and current dissatisfaction with parole board decision making in general, this task seems impossible. Finally, the **regulator value system** is directed toward inmate reactions to parole board decisions. How will current inmates react to those decisions in view of their own circumstances? Will the parole supervision system be undermined or enhanced as the result of parole board decision making? Therefore, inmate reaction is of paramount concern to parole board authorities who seek to maintain their credibility among the very persons their decisions directly affect (Hill, Thoma, and Birkbeck, 1996; Pearl, 1998).

When parole board decision making is considered in these diverse and sometimes conflicting contexts, it is easier to understand why extensive variability exists among boards in different jurisdictions. Each parole board member possesses one or another of these value systems. It is not likely that an entire parole board is associated with a single viewpoint or value system; rather, these different value systems help to account for inconsistent decision making about early releases of inmates with similar criminal histories and instant conviction offenses, even by the same parole boards, at different points in time.

Developing and Implementing Objective Parole Criteria

With such diversity among parole board members and the values they reflect, is it possible to establish objective parole criteria to govern all parole board decision making? Ideally, objective parole criteria would insulate parole board members from criticisms of racism when releasing disproportionately large numbers of offenders of particular races or ethnic backgrounds. Parole board member liability would be limited in instances in which offenders are granted early release and are especially dangerous and pose the greatest risk to their communities.

Objective parole criteria have been compared with determinate sentencing policies, whereas traditional parole criteria have been equated with indeterminate sentencing systems (Lombardi and Lombardi, 1986:86). Among the advantages of objective parole criteria are the following:

1. Inmates know their presumptive release dates within several months of their incarceration.
2. The paroling authority is bound or obligated to meet the presumptive release date.
3. The paroling authority uses scores consisting of an inmate's criminal history and offense severity to determine time ranges for parole release.
4. The paroling authority uses a composite group score representing criminal histories of similar offenders to predict parole success. (Lombardi and Lombardi, 1986)

Ironically, these objective parole criteria function to restrict the discretionary power and flexibility of parole boards. Therefore, although fairness to offenders and parole board accountability are increased by making the parole release decision-making process more explicit and consistent, there are some undesirable, unanticipated consequences. For example, the Florida Parole Commission implemented new objective parole criteria in 1980 (Lombardi, 1981). Prior to 1980, adult inmates of Florida's prisons had filed an average of 400 civil lawsuits annually. After the objective criteria went into effect, the number of lawsuits increased to more than 1,800 per year. The Florida Parole Commission's legal department had to increase its staff of attorneys from two to seven. Florida inmate lawsuits involved primarily four issues directly related to the new objective parole criteria. First, inmates alleged that objective scoring system errors led to unfavorable classifications and unjustifiably longer incarceration terms. Second, inmates claimed that they had originally been placed in the wrong level of offense severity, often stemming from an erroneous interpretation of their plea agreements. Third, inmates claimed that parole board members inconsistently extended or shortened their incarceration length by either considering or failing to consider certain aggravating circumstances such as using a weapon during the commission of the crime or causing serious injury to victims. The fourth issue alleged parole board failure to consider mitigating circumstances that would lessen the length of incarceration. All these issues could seemingly be remedied by close monitoring of all parole board decision making and a demand for fairness and consistency in the application of objective parole criteria (Lombardi, 1981).

Interest in devising consistent and objective early release criteria is probably as old as parole itself. Most of the popular and more scientific methods for devising predictive criteria, however, have been developed since the late 1960s. In 1972, the U.S. Parole Commission started to use an actuarial device in predicting parole success of federal prisoners (Hoffman, 1983). By the early 1980s, every state had either devised a system or was using one originated by another jurisdiction whereby parole decision making could be objectified (Gottfredson and Tonry, 1987).

Corrections observers currently contend that technology that can classify offenders accurately on the basis of their potential risk to public safety, social service, educational and vocational needs, and individual behavioral profiles exists. These observers also charge, however, that many paroling bodies have not as yet fully exploited this technology in a cooperative and systematic manner (Olbrich, 1997). At the same time, other observers caution that the current state-of-the-art in statistical risk prediction is such that many developed models are unstable when applied to various prisoner populations from one state to the next. Furthermore, insufficient validation of prediction instruments has occurred. When a parole risk assessment device was developed by Wisconsin officials for parole board decision making, for example, the device became popular in several other states, especially after being recognized as a useful instrument by the National Institute of Corrections. The Wisconsin instrument, however, appeared to lack validity when applied to a sample of New York parolees (Wright, Clear, and Dickson, 1984). This shortcoming strongly suggests the need to devise measures that are applicable for selected inmate populations on a state-by-state basis. For example, the Ohio Parole Board uses the following criteria as guidelines:

1. Current offense and details of the crime
2. Prior record: felonies, misdemeanors, juvenile offenses
3. Supervision experiences: parole, furlough, probation
4. Institution adjustment: job assignment, work evaluation, rule infractions
5. Substance abuse program participation
6. Vocational or academic training
7. Personality evaluation: I.Q., highest grade completed
8. Psychological reports
9. Psychiatric reports
10. Personal history factors: marital status, employment history, work skills, special problems
11. Parole plan: living arrangements, employment plans
12. Community attitude: prosecutor's recommendation, judge's recommendation, police or sheriff's recommendation, victim's statement
13. Detainers
14. Type and number of prior hearings
15. Results of prehearing conference with case manager or unit manager (Ohio Department of Correction and Rehabilitation, 2001)

These criteria are only guidelines, as noted by the Ohio Adult Parole Authority. Therefore, there may be departures based on the degree of aggravation or mitigation accompanying any eligible inmate's early-release request. It is Ohio's experience that using these criteria in conjunction with several other measures increases their adult parole authority effectiveness to about 75 percent. In short, Ohio authorities believe that 75 percent of their early-release decision making with these guidelines will result in successful decision making. Viewed another way, Ohio authorities expect no more than a 25 percent degree of recidivism among those paroled. Ohio bases their guidelines system on five major components:

1. *Risk instrument:* The risk instrument is critical to the guidelines system. It looks at several factors dealing with an inmate's prior criminal history, including the number of probations, paroles, and revocations. Age at first felony conviction and substance abuse history are also related to risk assessed points. The risk level totals equal 1, 2, or 3. The higher the number, the higher the risk.

2. *Offense score:* Included in the guideline system are several offenses designated as "endangering offenses." If an inmate has ever been convicted of an endangering offense, either as a juvenile or adult, one point is assessed toward the total score.

3. *Institutional score:* The parole board will make a determination of the inmate's institutional adjustment at the time of the hearing. If the inmate is now serving or has recently served time in disciplinary control, local control, or administrative control, one point will be assessed towards the total score.

4. *Aggregate score:* The sum total of the risk score, the offense score, and the institution score equals the aggregate score.

5. *Matrix:* The matrix is a grid containing 24 cell divisions. Each cell contains the guidelines procedure into which an inmate is placed and a continuance range if the decision is not to release. The horizontal axis of the grid is the "aggregate score" of 1 to 5. The vertical axis is the felony level reflecting the inmate's sentence. Sentences range from fourth degree to life (Ohio Department of Correction and Rehabilitation, 2001).

Each state has devised independent criteria governing early-release decision making for its parole board. All these criteria are related to a degree, although there are significant variations. For example, the Massachusetts Parole Board uses a release risk classification instrument consisting of (1) the number of returns to higher custody since the controlling effective date of commitment; (2) custody standing prior to the controlling effective date of commitment; (3) total number of parole revocations; (4) number of adult convictions for property offenses; (5) number of charges for a person offense as a juvenile; (6) age at release hearing; and (7) evidence of heroin, opiate, or crack cocaine use. Both the number of returns to higher custody and age have maximum scores of 6 for four or more returns to higher custody and being 23 years of age or younger. One's custody standing and evidence of drug use each contribute 2 points, whereas the other factors are weighted by 1 point each. A high score of 19 points is possible. Such a person might be a 22-year-old cocaine addict who has prior offenses of burglary as an adult and robbery as a juvenile, has been returned to a higher custody level on four previous occasions, has one previous parole revocation, and was incarcerated prior to the controlling effective date. A three-part scale is used: 0–4 = low risk, 5–10 = moderate risk, and 11+ = high risk.

Utah uses the following factors to determine one's parole eligibility: (1) age at first arrest, (2) prior juvenile record, (3) prior adult arrests, (4) correctional supervision history, (5) supervision risk, (6) percentage of time employed in last 12 months, prior to incarceration, (7) alcohol usage problems, (8) drug usage problems, (9) attitude (motivation to change, willing to accept responsibility), (10) address changes during last 12 months (prior to incarceration), (11) family support, and (12) conviction or juvenile adjudication for assaultive offense in last five years.

Age, prior record, and drug/alcohol dependencies are obviously considered significant risk factors, at least for these instruments developed in these particular jurisdictions. In fact, they are critical components of most scales examined. Many jurisdictions believe that one's employment history and attitude (measured in different ways) are also crucial to good parole decision making. The rationale for including these different components is grounded in considerable empirical research. As already seen, many studies have focused on recidivism and the characteristics of recidivists. Most of these studies have provided the bases for making actuarial predictions for various offender aggregates. Thus, younger offenders have higher recidivism rates than older offenders (English et al., 1996). The age of onset of criminal behavior is an important predictor. The earlier the onset of criminal conduct, the more likely recidivism will occur.

Similar to initial classifications conducted by prison officials and subsequent reassessments of inmates, parole boards also use reassessments of client risk after parolees have functioned for several months in their respective parole programs. Some jurisdictions have established rather specific prediction schemes based on some or all of these criteria. For example, Michigan has created five risk groupings based primarily on one's age, marital status, and previous institutional conduct, as shown next.

Risk Group
Very high risk: Instant offense of rape, robbery, or homicide and serious misconduct or security segregation and first arrest before 15th birthday

High risk: Instant offense of rape, robbery, or homicide and serious misconduct and age of first arrest was 15 or over

Middle risk: Instant offense of rape, robbery, or homicide and no serious misconduct; or instant offense not rape, robbery, or homicide (may be other assaultive crime) and no reported felony while juvenile and never been married at time of instant offense

Very low risk: Instant offense not rape, robbery, or homicide and no reported felony while juvenile and not serving on other assaultive crime and has been married (Michigan Department of Corrections, 1999)

The National Council on Crime and Delinquency has examined risk prediction extensively and has constructed risk assessment devices for various states, including California, South Carolina, Oregon, Alaska, Illinois, Louisiana, and Tennessee (National Council on Crime and Delinquency, 1990a, 1990b). The council's survey of existing or currently used instruments indicates the following factors that most often appear as risk predictors:

1. Number of prior convictions
2. Number of prior incarcerations
3. Age at first commitment, conviction, or arrest
4. Drug abuse history
5. Convictions for burglary, forgery, theft
6. Alcohol abuse history
7. Employment history
8. School adjustment
9. Probation/parole history
10. Peer involvement

Regardless of the predictive utility of these items, the council has exhibited a failure rate for various sample predictions of about 30 percent. According to the council, the primary problem is that accurate data concerning prospective parolees are often difficult to obtain. Therefore, predictions of success for different offender aggregates are always tainted by the unknown influence of extraneous variables (National Council on Crime and Delinquency, 1990b:6–7).

SALIENT FACTOR SCORES AND PREDICTING PAROLEE SUCCESS ON PAROLE

Although a weighting system for parole prognosis was developed by **Ernest W. Burgess** of the University of Chicago in 1928, the development of currently applicable objective parole decision-making guidelines can be traced to the pioneering work of Don Gottfredson and Leslie Wilkins, leaders of the Parole Decision-Making Project in the early 1970s. At that time, the National Council on Crime and Delinquency and the

U.S. Parole Commission (originally the U.S. Board of Parole) were interested in parole decision making and solicited the assistance of social scientists to examine various criteria involved in early-release decisions (Glaser, 1987:256). The Parole Decision-Making Project led to the adoption of a preliminary set of guidelines that provided parole board members with specific criteria to assess the successfulness of granting parole to various offenders. Categories of offenders were established by these guidelines and based, in part, on a ranking of **offense severity** as well as a salient factor score (Gottfredson, Wilkins, and Hoffman, 1978). A salient factor score (SFS) is a numerical classification that supposedly predicts the probability of a parolee's success if parole is granted.

The SFS was designed to help parole board members make fair, objective, and just parole decisions. Unusual departures from these guidelines by parole boards were to be accompanied by written rationales outlining the reasons for such departures. In 1973, the U.S. Parole Commission formally adopted these parole decision guidelines, and SFSs were used in all federal parole hearings. This step was largely the result of a federal court order for the U.S. Board of Parole to articulate specifically its policies for granting parole (*Childs v. United States Board of Parole,* 1973). Subsequently, the Federal Bureau of Prisons devised several prediction devices to determine early release for parole-eligible federal inmates. One of these devices is the salient factor score or SFS 81. An earlier version was the SFS 76 (Hoffman, 1994).

The Federal Bureau of Prisons devised the **salient factor score 81 (SFS 81)** for determining parole eligibility or, more recently, supervised release, for its eligible inmates. The salient factor score index consists of six criteria: (1) prior convictions/delinquency adjudications, (2) prior commitments of more than 30 days (either as an adult or as a juvenile), (3) age at current offense/prior commitments, (4) recent commitment-free period (three years), (5) probation/parole/confinement/escape status violator this time, and (6) heroin/opiate dependence. Eligible federal inmates receive up to 3 points for no prior convictions or delinquency adjudications; up to 2 points for no prior commitments of more than 30 days (as either an adult or a juvenile); up to 2 points for being 26 or older at the time of the current offense; and 1 point each for no prior commitment (in last three years), no probation/parole/confinement/escape status at time of current offense, and no history of opiate addiction. Thus, federal inmates can score a possible 10 points and minimize their parole risk status. Scores of zero or close to zero mean higher or highest parole risk.

At the federal level, the salient factor score was made up of seven criteria and was refined in 1976 to SFS 76. In August 1981, the salient factor scoring instrument underwent further revision and the new, six-factor predictive device was constructed (Hoffman, 1983). A comparison of the revised SFS 81 with SFS 76 was made according to validity, stability, simplicity, scoring reliability, and certain ethical concerns. Both instruments appeared to have similar predictive characteristics, although the revised device possesses greater scoring reliability. Of even greater significance is that SFS 81 places considerable weight on the extent and recency of an offender's criminal history. Up to seven points can be earned by having no prior convictions or adjudications (adult or juvenile), no prior commitments of more than 30 days, and being 26 years of age or older at the time of the current offense (with certain exceptions). Figure 8.1 shows the six-item SFS 81 (Hoffman, 1983). Classification systems such as the SFS 81 instrument are simply models, assigned such names as the National Institute of Corrections Prison Classification Model or the Iowa Risk Assessment Model (Rans, 1984:50).

Salient Factor Score Index

1. Prior convictions/adjudications (adult or juvenile):
   None (3 pts)
   One (2 points)
   Two or three (1 point)
   Four or more (0 points) _____

2. Prior commitments of more than 30 days (adult or juvenile):
   None (2 points)
   One or two (1 point)
   Three or more (0 points) _____

3. Age at current offense/prior commitments:
   25 years of age or older (2 points)
   20–25 years of age (1 point)
   19 years of age or younger (0 points) _____

4. Recent commitment free period (three years):
   No prior commitment of more than 30 days (adult or juvenile)
   or released to the community from last such commitment
   at least three years prior to the commencement of the current
   offense (1 point)
   Otherwise (0 points) _____

5. Probation/parole/confinement/escape status violator this time:
   Neither on probation, parole, confinement, or escape status
   at the time of the current offense, nor committed as a probation,
   parole, confinement, or escape status violator this time (1 point)
   Otherwise (0 points) _____

6. Heroin/opiate dependence:
   No history of heroin/opiate dependence (1 point)
   Otherwise (0 points) _____

   Total score = _____

Source: U.S. Parole Commission, *Rules and Procedures Manual* (Washington, DC: U.S. Parole Commission, 1985).

FIGURE 8.1 Salient factor score index, SFS 81.

Several dimensions of the SFS 81 are worth noting. First, great emphasis is placed on one's prior juvenile record. Items 1, 2, and 4 refer to prior behaviors of parolees that may have involved their juvenile pasts. A total of six points on this ten-point scale may be accumulated, depending on whether one has a juvenile record. Further, age is considered significant. The younger one enters a life of crime, the more seriously it is regarded. There are sound sociological and psychological reasons for this assumption. Thus, further adverse emphasis is placed on one's prior record as a juvenile. Finally, the SFS 81 contains information about drug use, specifically heroin or opiate dependence. Therefore, one's youthfulness when committing offenses, prior juvenile adjudications, and involvement with heroin or opiates serve to undermine one's parole chances.

The SFS 81 is scored in the following manner:

Raw Score	Parole Prognosis
0–3	Poor
4–5	Fair
6–7	Good
8–10	Very good

Thus, the lower the score, the better the prognosis for parole. Federal paroling authorities are not bound by the results of this instrument. They have at their disposal the contents of an offender's PSI report, together with information from victims or victims' relatives, and judicial recommendations and commentary are also available to them. Ultimately, the parole decision involves numerous factors, some legal, others extralegal. It is difficult to determine when extralegal factors are operative, because they are used in subtle ways (Hess et al., 1990). Their use *is* illegal, however. Parole board members should not consider one's race, ethnicity, gender, social class, or any other extralegal factor when attempting to make an objective parole decision (Burns et al., 1999).

The parole agreement is a contract between the offender and the state. The parole officer is usually responsible for ensuring offender compliance with the conditions set forth in the contract. In the event that one or more conditions of the agreement are not complied with by the parolee, the discretionary power of the parole officer is invoked. The parole officer may choose to overlook the violation, depending on its seriousness, or the officer may decide to recommend parole revocation. In some jurisdictions, the discretionary power of these officers is severely limited by judges, parole boards, or statute.

One continuing issue often contingent on parole officer action is recidivism. If the officer reports parole violators for violating curfew (e.g., not being on their premises by 9:00 P.M. each evening), then the violators stand a good chance of being returned to prison. Some persons consider this action an indication that the parole program has somehow failed. This technical violation, however, is not evidence of new criminal activity. Circumstances beyond a parolee's control may prevent the parolee from complying with parole requirements. On the other hand, a technical violation may be deliberate. Also, some technical violations are common occurrences for anyone else other than parolees. The use of alcohol and firearms possession are taken for granted by most citizens, but for parolees, these technical violations may result in parole revocation. Random drug/alcohol tests may disclose that parolees have done something prohibited by the rules governing their parole. Complying with the rules of parole is an indication that parolees can comply with societal rules when they are completely free from the correctional system. Thus, minor infractions are indicators of future deviant behavior and criminality for some authorities. Some parole board members may regard rule infractions as sufficient to deny a parolee continuation of parole.

Others say that the program fails only when parolees commit and are convicted of new crimes. In any case, an important discretionary function is performed by the parole officer whenever parole violations are apparent. The decision made affects the life of the parolee as well as the life or lives of others dependent on the parolee (e.g., supported children, spouse, and victim, in the case of restitution forthcoming from monies earned through offender employment).

THE PROCESS OF PAROLE REVOCATION

Parole revocation is a two-stage process. Parolees in jeopardy of having their parole programs revoked through **revocation actions** are entitled to **minimum due process** rights (Roberts et al., 1999). The governing case in all parole revocation proceedings is *Morrissey v. Brewer* (1972), discussed in the following section. The primary reason for extending minimum due process rights to parolees is that they are in jeopardy of losing their liberty. They can be reincarcerated if the parole board determines that the nature of their parole program violation is sufficiently serious (Burke, 1997).

A majority of parolees, however, are not returned to prison; rather, they are placed under more restrictive supervision from their POs. Some parolees are electronically monitored and are subjected to home confinement with strictly enforced curfews. Those who failed in their programs because of alcohol or substance abuse may be obligated to participate in counseling or group therapy. Self-help groups, such as Alcoholics Anonymous or Narcotics Anonymous, may be recommended as a part of their continuing parole program (DiIulio and Mitchell, 1996; U.S. Parole Commission, 1994).

The first stage of the parole revocation process is when the offender appears before the parole board to answer the allegations relating to the parole program violation(s). If the parole board determines that the offender is guilty of one or more program rule infractions, then it must decide the punishment in the second stage. If a parolee's program is revoked, then the parole board is obligated to furnish the parolee with its reasons in writing. Further, the parole board recommends what the parolee must do if reincarcerated to earn another chance at parole (Irwin and Austin, 1994). Below are several cases involving parole revocation.

LANDMARK CASES AND SELECTED ISSUES

***Morrissey v. Brewer* (1972).** The first landmark case involving the constitutional rights of parolees was *Morrissey v. Brewer* (1972). In 1967, John Morrissey was convicted by an Iowa court for "falsely drawing checks" and was sentenced to not more than seven years in the Iowa State Prison. He was paroled from prison in June 1968. Seven months later, however, his parole officer learned that while on parole, Morrissey had bought a car under an assumed name and had operated it without permission, had obtained credit cards under a false name, and had given false information to an insurance company when he was involved in a minor automobile accident. Also, Morrissey had given his parole officer a false address for his residence.

The parole officer interviewed Morrissey and filed a report recommending that parole be revoked. The reasons given by the officer were that Morrissey

---

BOX 8.2

A Parole Officer Lists Excuses Given by Parolees for Parole Program Violations

Montie Guthrie, Dallas, Texas Parole Officer

During the 1990s, Montie Guthrie was employed with the Texas Department of Criminal Justice Parole Division supervising hundreds of parolees and preparing thousands of reports. He visited his parolee-clients in dangerous gang-infested Dallas, Texas, neighborhoods. On more than one occasion, his life was threatened by neighborhood toughs. Luckily for Guthrie, his parolee-clients always bailed him out. Once, for example, Guthrie was visiting a parolee who had been convicted of aggravated assault and murder. The parolee was gigantic, with massive arms and chest and was known to pummel his victims into submission or death. When Guthrie visited, another man, a gang member, was at the parolee's residence. The visitor didn't like Guthrie's inquiries of his parolee-client and that Guthrie was looking around the apartment for possible illegal contraband. The visitor insulted Guthrie and invited him outside to fight. Instead, the parolee rose from his chair and advised his visiting friend that he, the parolee, would be stepping outside with his friend, not the parole officer. He advised his friend to "keep quiet" or suffer the consequences. He pointed his finger at his parole officer and said, "That's the man keeping me out of prison. Nobody lays a finger on him. Now sit down and keep quiet."

As Guthrie reflects on his years as a parole officer, he is amused at some incidents involving some of his parolee-clients. For example, Guthrie described a parolee who went hunting and shot an award-winning 18-point buck with a high-powered rifle. The shooting merited a visit from photographers and a reporter from a Dallas newspaper, resulting in the parolee's picture, holding the buck for everyone to see, being printed in the paper. The caption read, "Mr._____ shot his trophy 18-point buck in northeast Coleman County just before Christmas. Mr. _____ said the buck would field dress about 150 pounds. The rack measured 18 inches. Mr. _____ was headed for the taxidermist and will probably soon have a fine trophy on the wall of his home." Ironically, Mr. _____ was a parolee, with a parole program condition that he not possess or use firearms. This hunting antic came to Guthrie's attention when he read the morning newspaper. Mr._____ had his parole revoked for the firearms violation and was returned to prison.

Early in his career as a parole officer, Guthrie visited numerous clients, some of whom tested positive for drugs or alcohol. Others weren't home when they were supposed to be. Some clients didn't report to his office when scheduled to do so at regular intervals, and still others absconded from the jurisdiction, only to be apprehended later. Each parolee had one or more excuses for violating his or her parole conditions. Guthrie catalogued these excuses:

- I didn't report because I was shot.
- I forgot.
- I don't know.
- My Corry [family member] died.
- I thought you said I didn't have to.
- I thought I was an annual [meaning once-a-year visit].
- I thought I would be arrested.
- I went to jail.
- I was sick.
- I came up here but you weren't here.
- My car broke down.
- I couldn't report because of my sister's drinking problem and I had to stay and watch her kids.
- I got married.
- My family said he [the parole officer] had homosexual tendencies, and I was afraid he would come on to me.
- The reason I was positive [for cocaine] was my girlfriend put it on my ———— and then sucked it.
- You see, I'm always positive [for cocaine] because I go out to these clubs and these girls, man, they always want to get with me, right? So, when I'm not looking, they put coke in my drink to get me high so I'll get with them.
- Well, I didn't do no crack, man, I was just cookin' the stuff.
- I was just around a bunch of people smokin'.

- I didn't do no drugs! My girl, man, she smoked the stuff, and it must have got on me when I went down on her.
- My neighbors sneaked into my house and put cocaine in my sugar.
- It was on the counter, and when I brushed it off, it must have got in me.
- They do coke at this bar a lot on the table, and when I put the pretzels on the bar, some must a got on them and me when I ate them.
- I smoke weed because I'm trying to gain weight and I know I'll get the munchies if I do.
- I was having sex with a guy who was high and he ejaculated in me.
- I was at a club, and my friend saw a guy put something in my drink and didn't tell me.
- It's just weed!
- I'm taking vitamins and antibiotics.
- I smoke because I want to get with women.

- My girl was going back to school, and I wanted to be sure to give it to her good before she went back so she'll think about me.
- I cut so much cocaine it must have absorbed into my skin.
- They're not as bad as they seem.
- My friends stole the car, and then they picked me up at the house in it.
- It wasn't crack. It was just a ball of soap.
- I don't remember.
- It was self-defense. He started calling my grandmother bad names, and so I stabbed him.
- I left because they were selling drugs where I lived. I didn't have time to tell you where I moved to.
- I didn't go to GED classes because someone is trying to kill me. They'll kill me if I go to that class.

As Guthrie says, once you think you've heard it all, you hear something new. There's never a dull moment in parole work!

Source: Courtesy of Montie Guthrie. Compiled by author, February 2001.

admitted to buying the car and obtaining false identification, to obtaining credit under false pretenses, and to being involved in the auto accident. Morrissey claimed that he "was sick" and that this condition prevented him from maintaining continuous contact with his parole officer. The parole officer claimed that Morrissey's parole should be revoked because Morrissey had a habit of "continually violating the rules." The parole board revoked Morrissey's parole, and he was returned to the Iowa State Prison to serve the remainder of his sentence. Morrissey was not represented by counsel at the revocation proceeding. Furthermore, he was not given the opportunity to cross-examine witnesses against him, he was not advised in writing of the charges against him, no disclosure of the evidence against him was provided, and reasons for the revocation were not given. Morrissey was also not permitted to offer evidence in his own behalf or give personal testimony.

Morrissey's appeal to the Iowa Supreme Court was rejected, but not his appeal to the U.S. Supreme Court. Although the Court did not directly address the question of whether Morrissey should have had court-appointed counsel, it did make a landmark decision in his case, overturning the Iowa Parole Board action and establishing a two-stage proceeding for determining whether parole ought to be revoked. The first or preliminary hearing is held at the time of arrest and detention, when it is determined whether probable cause exists that the parolee actually committed the alleged parole violation. The second hearing is more involved and establishes the guilt of the parolee relating to the violations. This proceeding must extend to the parolee certain minimum due process rights:

1. The right to have written notice of the alleged violations of parole conditions
2. The right to have any evidence of the alleged violation disclosed to the parolee

3. The right of the parolee to be heard in person and to present **exculpatory evidence** as well as witnesses on his behalf
4. The right to confront and cross-examine adverse witnesses, unless cause exists why they should not be cross-examined
5. The right to a judgment by a neutral and detached body, such as the parole board itself
6. The right to a written statement of the reasons for the parole revocation

Thus, the significance of *Morrissey* is that it set forth minimum due process rights for all parolees, creating a two-stage proceeding whereby the alleged infractions of parole conditions could be examined and a full hearing conducted to determine the most appropriate disposition of the offender.

For several decades, interest in the rights of probationers and parolees has increased considerably (South Carolina Department of Probation, Parole, and Pardon Services, 1993). Not only has more attention been devoted to this subject in the professional literature, but various courts in different jurisdictions, including the U.S. Supreme Court, have set forth landmark decisions that influence either positively or negatively the lives of those in probation or parole programs (Vigdal and Stadler, 1994:44).

***Pennsylvania Board of Probation and Parole v. Scott* (1998).**   Scott, a parolee, was suspected of possessing firearms in violation of his parole conditions. Parole officers conducted a warrantless search of his premises and discovered firearms. Scott's parole was revoked on the basis of the discovered evidence, and he was recommitted to prison. He appealed, alleging that his Fourth Amendment right against unreasonable searches and seizures had been violated and that evidence thus seized was not admissible in a **parole revocation hearing**. The U.S. Supreme Court held that a parolee's Fourth Amendment rights do not apply in parole revocation hearings and that incriminating evidence discovered and seized in violation of a parolees' Fourth Amendment rights may be introduced at parole revocation proceedings.

***Pennsylvania Department of Corrections v. Yeskey* (1998).**   Yeskey was a Pennsylvania prison inmate who was sentenced to 18 to 36 months in a correctional facility, but was recommended for placement in a motivational boot camp program that, if successfully completed, would have led to his parole in just six months. Yeskey was rejected by the boot camp officials because of a medical history of hypertension. He sued the Pennsylvania Department of Corrections, alleging that the exclusion violated the Americans with Disabilities Act (ADA). The federal court rejected his claim, contending that the ADA was inapplicable to state prison inmates. The Third Circuit Court of Appeals reversed and remanded, and the government appealed to the U.S. Supreme Court, which heard the case. The U.S. Supreme Court affirmed the appellate court, declaring that the ADA provision prohibiting a public entity from discriminating against qualified individuals with disabilities on account of that person's disability applied to inmates in state prisons.

Pardons

When the U.S. president or a state governor pardons someone who may or may not be on probation or parole, the effect of these pardons varies, depending on the jurisdiction (Cavender and Knepper, 1992). Generally, a pardon is tantamount to absolution for a crime previously committed. Someone has been convicted of the crime, and the intent of a pardon is to terminate whatever punishment has been imposed. In *United States v. Noonan* (1990), for instance, Gregory Noonan was convicted and sentenced in 1969 for "failing to submit to induction into the armed forces." President Jimmy Carter granted a pardon to Noonan on January 21, 1977, wherein Carter declared a "full, complete and unconditional pardon" to persons convicted during the Vietnam War of refusing induction. Noonan sought to have his record of the original conviction expunged. An **expungement order** has the effect of wiping one's slate clean, as though the crime and the conviction had never occurred. Noonan believed that his conviction, which remained on his record, adversely affected his employment chances. Thus, he sought to expunge his record because of the pardon. The Third Circuit Court of Appeals, a federal appellate court, refused to grant him this request. The court declared that "a pardon does not blot out guilt nor does it restore the offender to a state of innocence in the eye of the law." In short, at least in Noonan's case, the presidential pardon was effective in removing the punishment but not the criminal record.

Not all courts agree with the Third Circuit Court of Appeals. In some state appellate courts, a different position has been taken regarding the influence of a pardon on one's criminal record. Following the lead of a Pennsylvania court of appeals, the Indiana Court of Appeals declared in the case of *State v. Bergman* (1990) that a pardon does expunge one's criminal record. The governor of Indiana had pardoned a convict, Bergman, for a crime that he had previously committed. Bergman sought to have his record expunged, in much the same way as Noonan. The Indiana Court of Appeals declared that pardons "block out the very existence of the offender's guilt, so that, in the eye(s) of the law, he is thereafter as innocent as if he had never committed the offense." Subsequent state court decisions have concurred with both Pennsylvania and Indiana.

In Florida, for instance, an appellant was convicted of being an accessory to robbery in 1976. In 1986, after completing his full sentence, he was granted a full and unconditional pardon for his offense. He sought to expunge his record, and at first, Florida authorities acceded to his request for expungement. The state, however, subsequently objected to this expungement order and sought to have it set aside. Eventually, the case reached the Florida Court of Appeals, which held that "when the pardon is full, it remits the punishment and blots out the existence of guilt, so that in the eyes of the law the offender is as innocent as if he had never committed the crime. After a full pardon, the person who has been granted the pardon is no longer considered 'convicted' or 'adjudicated guilty' of that crime." (*Doe v. State,* 1992).

These cases are exceptions. In Rhode Island, for instance, in the case of *State v. Gervais* (1992), Gervais had been convicted of a crime after entering a plea of nolo contendere, the equivalent of a guilty plea. The conviction was suspended pending the satisfactory completion of a term of probation. When the probation was completed, Gervais's conviction was dismissed. Gervais subsequently sought to expunge his record of the original charges. The holding in Gervais's case turned on a technicality. The Rhode Island Court of Appeals declared that "expungements of records can occur within forty-five days only when a person is acquitted or exonerated from the offense with which he or she is charged. A plea of nolo contendere and a successfully served term of probation, while not constituting a conviction, remains as a record and does not constitute exoneration of that charge." In effect, if Gervais had served a probationary term of fewer than 45 days, then he could have had his criminal record expunged. His term of probation, however, went well beyond 45 days; thus, a denial of his request for expungement was based on this technicality. Another technicality interfered with an Oregon resident's claim for a certification of rehabilitation and pardon in a California Court. In the case of *People v. Matthews* (1993), Matthews completed a term of probation relative to a crime committed in California. His application for a pardon and certification of rehabilitation from California was denied because to qualify for the pardon and certification of rehabilitation, one must be a California resident for at least three years. Matthews did not qualify.

Parolee Program Conditions

When probationers or parolees are subject to having their programs revoked by respective authorities, what is the nature of evidence that can be used against them to support their program revocation (Harer, 1994)? What are their rights concerning PO searches of their premises? What about the program conditions they have been obligated to follow? What about parole board recognition of and obligation to follow minimum-sentence provisions from sentencing judges (Blumstein and Beck, 1999)? These issues and several others are discussed briefly below.

Parole Board Actions and Rights.   Parole boards have considerable discretionary powers. They may deny parole or grant it. They may revoke one's parole and return the offender to prison, or they may continue the offender's parole program, with additional supervision and other conditions (Archwamety and Katsiyannis, 2000). Below are a variety of cases dealing with numerous issues. Although some of these issues may appear trivial, their significance to affected probationers or parolees is profound.

Inmates who become eligible for parole are not automatically entitled to parole. Parole boards have considerable discretion whether to grant or deny parole to any inmate. Short of serving their full sentences or completing a portion of their term less any applicable good time credit, inmates are not automatically entitled to be paroled. In the case of *Williams v. Puckett* (1993), a Mississippi man convicted of armed robbery and forgery was sentenced to a mandatory sentence of ten years plus a five-year term for the forgery conviction. In Mississippi, inmates become eligible for parole after serving ten years of terms imposed in excess of ten years, by statute. Because this armed robbery conviction involved a mandatory prison term of ten years, however, the entire sentence of ten years must be served. Thus, according to Mississippi law, the inmate must serve at least one-fourth of the five-year term for the forgery conviction before actual parole eligibility occurred. Even then, the Mississippi Parole Board is not obligated to automatically grant his early release.

Parole boards do not have to recognize minimum-sentence provisions from sentencing judges when considering an inmate's parole eligibility. In another case, this time in Oregon, an inmate became eligible for parole after serving his minimum sentence, under a determinate minimum-maximum sentence originally imposed by a judge (*Carroll v. Board of Parole*, 1993). The Oregon Parole Board is vested with the power to override any minimum-sentence provision that might otherwise provide a means whereby an offender might be paroled automatically. In this case, the inmate had been convicted of murder and had served the minimum sentence prescribed by law. The parole board, however, voted to override the minimum sentence and to continue the inmate's incarceration, considering the seriousness of the crime and other factors. The inmate contested this parole board action, but the Oregon Court of Appeals upheld the action as legitimate, because a unanimous vote was required to override the minimum sentence and the parole board had voted unanimously.

Inmates who serve some of their parole program time in a halfway house are entitled to credit equal to the time served in the halfway house applied against their maximum sentences. In Ohio a parolee, Fair, was placed in a halfway house. During the time Fair spent there, he was closely supervised by halfway house staff. After several months of living there, he violated one or more halfway house rules, and his parole program was revoked. The parole board denied him credit against his maximum sentence for the time he spent in the halfway house. Fair appealed, and an Ohio court of appeals ordered the parole board to credit him with the time he had served at the halfway house. The court reasoned that the halfway house was a "confinement facility" and thus Fair's time spent there should be credited toward his maximum prison sentence (*State v. Fair,* 2000).

Inmates who have been sentenced under an indeterminate sentencing scheme and are subsequently paroled cannot change their sentence to a determinate sentence if their parole is revoked. Perez was a Kansas parolee who had originally been sentenced under an indeterminate sentencing scheme (*State v. Perez,* 2000). Subsequently, his parole was revoked because of one or more program violations. Perez sought to have his sentence changed to a determinate one, because under a determinate sentencing scheme, he would be eligible for release in a shorter time and without the restrictive conditions of a parole program. The parole board denied his request to change his sentence to a determinate one. Perez appealed, contending that the parole program violation amounted to a new crime and that he should be sentenced under the new determinate sentencing scheme Kansas had adopted since he was originally incarcerated. The Kansas Supreme Court upheld the parole board action, saying that Perez's parole violation was not a crime in the same sense that an offender would be convicted of a crime. Thus, the appellate court distinguished between crimes and parole violations and held that Perez would continue to serve his indeterminate sentence subject to its original conditions.

Inmates who have been paroled and who subsequently commit a new violent act while on parole may have their parole programs revoked and be returned to prison to serve the remainder of their sentences in their entirety. In New York, a parolee, Richardson, committed a new violent felony while on parole. The parole board revoked his parole and returned him to prison without further parole consideration, even though he had not, as yet, been tried and convicted on the new violent offense charge (*Richardson v. New York State Executive Department,* 1993).

If a paroling authority does not hold a revocation hearing for a parolee in a timely manner, it may not revoke his parole. Shivers was a Pennsylvania parolee who committed a new offense during his parole program. He was subsequently convicted of the new offense through a plea bargain. The Pennsylvania Parole Board was obligated to hold a revocation hearing regarding Shivers's parole program within 120 days of notice to the board of the new conviction. It delayed the revocation hearing, however, so as to obtain "further information" about Shivers's new offense to determine how much more time Shivers should serve in prison. The 120-day time limit expired, and eventually the parole board met and revoked Shivers's parole. Shivers appealed, citing the timeliness of the board's revocation proceeding and that it violated his due process rights. An appellate court agreed with Shivers and said that the simple fact that the board wanted to accumulate "further information" about Shivers's case was inadequate and not "good cause" to delay his revocation proceeding. Thus, the revocation decision was set aside (*Shivers v. Pa. Bd. of Probation and Parole*, 2000).

A paroling authority imposition of a special condition of parole, such as submitting to penile plethysmography, is not considered an unusual and unconstitutional parole condition. Penile plethysmography is a test administered to convicted sex offenders. It involves attaching devices to a prospective parolee's penis to determine the parolee's subsequent reaction to various forms of sexual stimuli. An erection response to various stimuli is incriminating in this instance, and the offender may be denied parole. The test is also used to determine whether a sex offender continues to pose a threat to society. In an Illinois federal action, a convicted sex offender, Walrath, was required to submit to a penile plethysmograph test as one condition preceding his parole by the Illinois Parole Board (*Walrath v. United States*, 1993). Walrath claimed that such a test would violate his Fifth Amendment right against self-incrimination. The U.S. District Court in Illinois upheld the U.S. Parole Commission's administration of the test to Walrath, holding that "there is no indication that any results from Walrath's plethysmograph could be used to criminally prosecute him for other acts. Instead, the results, like the treatment, might legitimately be used to assess the threat Walrath poses to society."

If a parole board's action in revoking one's parole is shown to be vindictive, then the parole revocation decision can be rescinded. Hammond was a parolee in the District of Columbia. During his term on parole, he allegedly violated four different program conditions. His PO moved to have his parole program revoked, but during the parole revocation hearing, Hammond was able to show that he was innocent of three of the charges. Thus, the parole board was faced with a single, minor charge involving a technical program violation. The board decided to revoke Hammond's parole and, furthermore, extended Hammond's original sentence. Hammond appealed. An appellate court ruled that Hammond was being punished by the District of Columbia Board of Parole for failing to prove the other charges against him. The board's vindictiveness was supported by its extending Hammond's prison time as a punishment. The court ordered Hammond's parole revocation overturned (*Hammond v. District of Columbia Board of Parole*, 2000).

Other interesting decisions are legitimizing life sentences of probation (*People v. Shafer*, 1992); consecutive probation sentences for two or more offenses (*Menifee v. State*, 1992); that prisoners who complete their sentences less "gain" time have served their "full" sentences (*State v. Green*, 1989); that admissions about probation violations must be entered by probationers themselves, not their attorneys (*State v. Lavoy*, 1992); that urinalyses are improper if not made conditions of a probation program, especially when drugs and/or alcohol were *not* involved (*Patterson v. State*, 1992); that new programs for offenders cannot be imposed as parole-eligibility criteria after offenders have been convicted and sentenced under earlier laws (*Pareton v. Armontrout,* 1993); that ex post facto laws for parolees and probationers are unconstitutional (*Roller v. Cavanaugh,* 1993); that credit for the amount of time served on probation or parole may not be credited against incarcerative sentences if revocation of one's program occurs for one or more program violations (*State v. Oquendo,* 1993); that probationers cannot have their probation revoked for violating a probation condition that is not in their probation orders or if they have not received a copy of such probation orders (*State v. Alves,* 1992); and that judges have no authority to set parole conditions (*State v. Beauchamp,* 1993).

SUMMARY

Several prerelease programs are available to parole-eligible inmates who are within a short time of being released. Some of these programs include work release, through which inmates may be granted temporary leaves from their prisons to work at jobs in their communities. Other temporary leaves may be used for earning academic degrees through programs known as study release. Variations from standard parole include halfway houses and furloughs, community-based programs that provide offenders with opportunities for reintegration into the community. Halfway houses or community residential centers may be either publicly or privately operated. They exist to provide offenders with housing, food, counseling, and other services while on parole. These programs are considered transitional because they permit offenders to gradually reenter society and make an adjustment from highly structured and regulated prison life. Furloughs are temporary leaves designed to permit offenders to become reunited with families or to engage in employment. Most of the time, these programs are granted to low-risk minimum-security offenders.

Other programs include standard parole with conditions. All parole programs are conditional in that certain expectations are made of all parolees. These conditions prohibit the use of alcohol or illegal drugs, ownership of firearms, and possession of cellular telephones and beepers. Further, parolees must permit their supervising POs to visit their premises and conduct searches without warrant at any time. Some parole programs involve intensive parolee supervision. The New Jersey Intensive Supervision Program selects participants from numerous applicants annually. Any interested New Jersey jail or prison inmate may apply for entry into the NJISP, but authorities only accept about 19 percent of all applicants. Several types of inmates are automatically excluded, including those with violent criminal records, sex offenders, and those affiliated with organized crime. The New Jersey program boasts a recidivism rate of less than 10 percent and has operated successfully since 1983.

Other conditions, including community service and victim restitution, may be imposed by a paroling authority. Together with fines and day fines, community service partially defrays the costs associated with the offender's crime, such as medical bills and property damage. There are many forms of community service and restitution. Not everyone agrees how or when these types of sanctions ought to be applied, however. Also, it is difficult to evaluate the effectiveness of these sanctions as deterrents to further criminal activity.

By 1988, all states had modified their existing sentencing provisions. Maine abolished parole in 1976, and the federal government technically abolished parole in

1992, although supervised early-release procedures have been continued. Many states are moving toward some form of determinate sentencing or presumptive or guidelines-based sentencing schemes. A majority of states continue to use parole boards for granting early release to prisoners. Parole board composition varies among jurisdictions, and the criteria for granting parole vary considerably as well. In many jurisdictions, prisoners may acquire good time credits that serve to reduce their sentences a certain number of days for each month served.

Parole boards attempt to predict which inmates should receive early release. They also determine dates for first parole consideration, fix the minimum time to be served, and award good time credits to inmates who have earned them. Studies of parole board decision making reveal that predictions of risk are complex and far from error-free. Parole board members further complicate the early-release decision-making process by reflecting different correctional orientations, including jurist, treater, sanctioner, controller, citizen, and regulator philosophies. The primary criticisms of parole boards focus on a lack of consistent parole criteria. Many parole boards use salient factor scores made up of an inmate's prior record, age, and prospects for adjusting to community life.

Parole revocation is the process of returning an inmate to prison for one or more technical violations or for committing new crimes. The revocation process has been examined by the U.S. Supreme Court, and several landmark cases have presented parolees with specific rights. Parole revocation now consists of two hearings, one to determine if probable cause exists that a violation occurred and the other to determine whether parole ought to be revoked.

Parolees and probationers have been vested with several important constitutional rights in the last few decades, as the U.S. Supreme Court has extended due process and equal protection to encompass them as well as other citizens. It is likely that other significant rights will obtain for parolees in future years as the U.S. Supreme Court faces new and different appeals from parolees and probationers.

KEY TERMS

Burgess, Ernest W.
Community residential centers
Community-service orders
Community work
Commutation
Conditional release
Criminal contamination
Day fines
Day parole
Day pass
Exculpatory evidence
Expungement order
Furlough programs
Furloughs
Halfway house
Halfway-in houses
Halfway-out houses
Hope Houses

Huber law
International Halfway House Association (IHHA)
Isaac T. Hopper Home
Citizen value system
Controller value system
Intensive supervised parole (ISP)
Jurist value system
Juvenile delinquency
Minimum due process
New Jersey Intensive Supervision Program
Objective parole criteria
Offense severity
Parole revocation hearing
Preparole programs
Prerelease
Prerelease program

Public risk
Regulator value system
Reparations
Revocation actions
Salient factor score (SFS), SFS 81
Sanctioner value system
Shock parole
Standard parolees
Study release
Study release programs
Supervised release
Temporary release programs
Treater value system
Victim and Witness Protection Act of 1982
Victims of Crime Act of 1984
Work furlough
Work release

QUESTIONS FOR REVIEW

1. What is meant by prerelease? What are several types of prerelease programs? Describe each.
2. What is work release? What are some potential benefits for inmates who participate in work release?
3. What are furloughs? Are furloughs the same as work release? What are some advantages of furloughs for prisoners?
4. What are some important functions performed by parole boards? What criteria do they usually employ when reaching decisions about individual inmates?
5. What is the salient factor score index? Is there any apparent bias associated with this index?
6. What rights do offenders have before officials can revoke their parole? Cite several cases that are important in the matter of parole revocation.
7. Who makes up a parole board? Are these persons corrections observers? Why or why not?
8. Identify five different orientations of parole board members besides the sanctioner orientation. Define each.
9. What are some objective parole criteria? Why are they considered objective?
10. What is a salient factor score? How is it used by parole boards to determine one's early-release eligibility?

SUGGESTED READINGS

Farrell, Amy (2000). "Women, Crime, and Drugs: Testing the Effect of Therapeutic Communities." *Women and Criminal Justice* **11:**21–48.

Hanlon, Thomas E., Richard W. Bateman, and Kevin E. O'Grady (1999). "The Relative Effects of Three Approaches to the Parole Supervision of Narcotic Addicts and Cocaine Abusers." *Prison Journal* **79:**163–181.

Kassebaum, Gene, Janet Coronado, and Mel Silverio (1999). *Survival on Parole: A Study of Post-Prison Adjustment and the Risk of Returning to Prison.* Honolulu: Hawaii Department of the Attorney General.

Twill, Sarah E., et al. (1998). "Changes in Measured Loneliness, Control, and Social Support among Parolees in a Halfway House." *Journal of Offender Rehabilitation* **27:**77–92.

Walters, Glenn D. (1999). "Short-Term Outcome of Inmates Participating in the Lifestyle Change Program." *Criminal Justice and Behavior* **26:**322–337.

PART III

**The Administration of Probation
and Parole Organizational Operations:
Supervising Special Populations of Offenders**

Probation/Parole Organization
and Operations:
Recruitment, Training,
CHAPTER 9 # and Officer-Client Relations

Introduction
The Organization and Operation of Probation
   and Parole Agencies
   Functions and Goals of Probation and Parole
   Services
   Organization and Administration of Probation
   and Parole Departments
   Selected Criticisms of Probation and Parole
   Programs
Probation and Parole Officers: A Profile
   Characteristics of Probation and Parole
   Officers
   What Do POs Do?
   Recruitment of POs
PO Training and Specialization
   Assessment Centers and Staff Effectiveness
   The Florida Assessment Center

The Use of Firearms in Probation and Parole
Work
   Establishing Negligence in Training, Job
   Performance, and Retention
   Liability Issues Associated with PO Work
   Probation and Parole Officer Labor Turnover
Probation and Parole Officer Caseloads
   Ideal Caseloads
   Changing Caseloads and Officer Effectiveness
   Caseload Assignment and Management Models
Officer/Client Interactions
A Code of Ethics
PO Unionization and Collective Bargaining
Summary
Key Terms
Questions for Review
Suggested Readings

INTRODUCTION

This chapter is about the recruitment, selection, and training of probation and parole officers. When a mandate was issued by the President's Commission of 1967, significant developments occurred in corrections and probation/parole that led to improvements in programs, personnel, and policies in almost every local, state, and federal jurisdiction. In this chapter, the contemporary condition of probation and parole services as well as the state of these services in previous years are examined. Although considerable improvements have been made in efforts to recruit and retain quality personnel and upgrade the quality of services provided to offenders, much more needs to be done. This chapter assesses the progress made as well as highlights areas in need of improvement.

Correctional officers are prison or jail staff and their supervisors who manage inmates, whereas probation and parole officers supervise and manage probationers and parolees in a variety of offender aftercare programs (American Correctional Association, 2001). Because the departments of correction in many states select POs as well as prison staff and conduct training programs for all their correctional personnel, similar criteria are often used for selecting correctional officers as well as for POs. Thus, useful information can be gleaned from the general correctional literature, which is applicable to POs as well as prison and jail personnel. Prison and jail correctional officers, however, do not necessarily share the same characteristics of POs. One major difference is that correctional officers manage and interact with incarcerated offenders, whereas POs manage and interact with nonincarcerated criminals. There are also differing pay scales, work requirements, and other important characteristics that serve to distinguish between these two officer populations.

There has been a substantial and continuing increase in the number of personnel working in the area of adult and juvenile corrections. In 2001, there were over 630,000 personnel in corrections for both adults and juveniles, an increase of nearly 300 percent compared with the 214,000 personnel reported in 1986 (American Correctional Association, 2001:44–46). There were 250,000 correctional officers in U.S. jails and prisons in 2001. Also, there were 380,000 personnel working in adult and juvenile probation and parole services for the same period (American Correctional Association, 2001:44–46). Thus, probation and parole personnel made up about 60 percent of all persons working with convicted offenders.

Probation officers are hired to manage probationers exclusively in many jurisdictions, whereas parole officers deal only with parolees. Some observers believe that probation officers deal with lower-risk and less dangerous offenders than do parole officers. Parole officers are assigned ex-convicts who have already served a portion of their sentences in prisons or jails, usually because of felony convictions. Confinement implies a greater level of dangerousness compared with those who are selected to participate in probation programs. Evidence, however, suggests that probation officers are receiving more dangerous offenders into their charge annually through felony probation, as prison and jail overcrowding make it impossible to incarcerate all criminals who should be incarcerated (Johnson and Jones, 1994).

In many jurisdictions, probation and parole officers supervise both types of offenders interchangeably (American Correctional Association, 2001). In many states, probation and parole officers are combined in official reports of statistical information to organizations such as the American Correctional Association. Within the adult category, states such as Alabama, Florida, Virginia, Washington, and Wyoming report total numbers of probation and parole aftercare personnel rather than distinguish them.

THE ORGANIZATION AND OPERATION OF PROBATION AND PAROLE AGENCIES

Different departments and agencies in each state administer probation and parole departments. Most states have departments of corrections that supervise both incarcerated and nonincarcerated offenders, but these tasks are sometimes overseen in other jurisdictions by departments of human services, departments of youth services, or some other umbrella agency.

Functions and Goals of Probation and Parole Services

The functions and goals of probation and parole services are to

- Supervise offenders
- Ensure offender-client compliance with program conditions by conducting random searches of offender premises, maintaining contact with offender-client employers, and otherwise maintaining occasional face-to-face spot checks
- Conduct routine and random drug/alcohol checks
- Provide networking services for employment assistance
- Direct offender-clients to proper treatment, counseling, and other forms of requested assistance
- Protect the community and its residents by detecting program infractions and reporting infractions to judges and parole boards
- Assist offenders in becoming reintegrated into their communities
- Engage in any rehabilitative action that will improve offender-client skills and law-abiding behavior

Organization and Administration of Probation and Parole Departments

Each state and large city has its own organization for administering and supervising probationers and parolees. The volume of offenders makes a significant difference in how departments are managed and the sizes of POs' caseloads. In some areas of the country, such as New York, PO caseloads for supervising probationers are as high as 400. In other parts of the country, PO caseloads may be as low as 10. Obviously, in those areas where PO caseloads are sizable, the nature of supervision exercised over these offenders is different from the supervision received by clients when client caseloads are under 25 (Baird, 1992a).

Some jurisdictions have drive-in windows established in shopping centers. Clients drive up to a window like they are going to withdraw cash from an automated teller machine, but instead, they place their hands on a surface that reads their palm prints and verifies their whereabouts. In other locations, such as Long Beach, California, large numbers of probationers and some parolees report to a central office monthly to verify that they are employed and are remaining law-abiding. These check-ins mean that numerous offenders can be supervised, but the nature of the supervision is questionable. Without frequent, random, and direct face-to-face contact with offender-clients, POs have no way of knowing whether these clients are law-abiding or whether they are engaging in some illicit behavior. Only those brought to the attention of police come to the attention of POs. Also, POs may detect probation or parole program violations during random visits to offender-clients' premises at odd hours (Kushner et al., 1995).

Most states and the federal government attempt to divide clients according to the seriousness of their prior offending. Some offenders are deemed at greater risk of reoffending than others and are therefore targeted for more intensive supervision. Lower-risk offenders are less likely to reoffend; therefore, their supervision does not need to be that intense.

One example of a probation and parole agency is the Field Services Division Central Office in North Dakota, which has a director, a program manager, a business officer, a release program manager, three community offender services program managers, and an institutional offender services manager. Figure 9.1 shows a diagram of this office. One good feature of this figure is that it is relatively simple, because there simply are not many persons on probation or parole in North Dakota. For example, in 1999, there were 2,991 probationers and 212 parolees in North Dakota to be supervised (Camp and Camp, 1999:166–167). Despite these low numbers, even the North Dakota Probation and Parole Field Services division can be fairly complex. Figure 9.2 shows a diagram of the division of labor for Parole and Probation Field Services.

Figure 9.2 shows a general manager over four major regions of North Dakota together with a manager who supervises an intensive program for offenders who need to be more closely monitored. North Dakota is a large state geographically; thus, it is imperative to divide it according to quadrants, with a West Region Supervisor, a Central Region Supervisor, a South Region Supervisor, and a North Region Supervisor. Notice that there are 14 major cities and surrounding areas served by these four regions. Under the intensive supervision program, there are four supervisors and support staff to supervise offenders. These programs operate primarily out of Bismarck or Fargo.

The general mission of the Field Services Division overseeing probationers, parolees, and other community-based clients is to protect society by ensuring that the

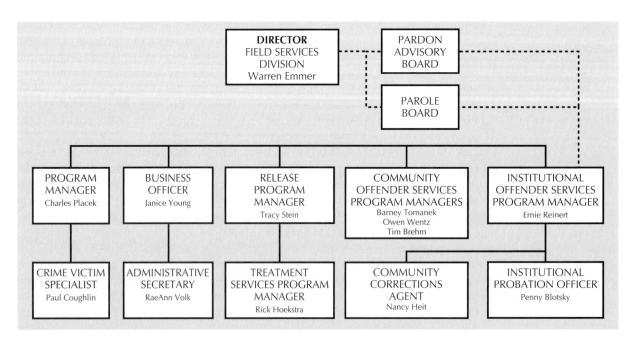

FIGURE 9.1 North Dakota Field Division Central Office. (*Source:* Courtesy of Elaine Little, Director, North Dakota Department of Corrections and Rehabilitation.)

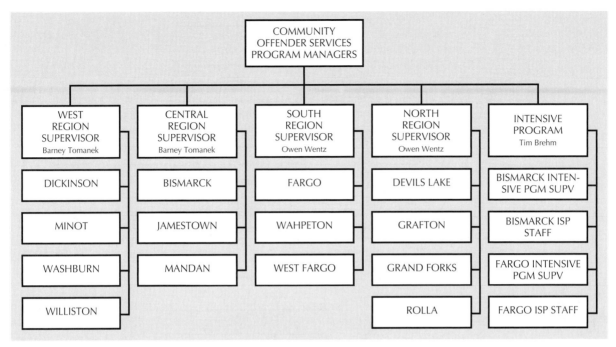

FIGURE 9.2 North Dakota Parole and Probation Field Services. (*Source:* Courtesy of Elaine Little, Director, North Dakota Department of Corrections and Rehabilitation.)

community-placed offenders are provided responsible supervision that requires them to be active participants in their rehabilitation. Supervising offenders requires proactive intervention and case management strategies. The Field Services Division continuously reviews and modifies programs it provides to address community safety issues, prison overcrowding, and offender needs. The intensive supervision program and comprehensive day reporting program typify programming designed to facilitate the supervision of those offenders posing the greatest risks and needs. Halfway houses, home confinement programs, and curfews are some of the intermediate sanctions used to verify compliance with supervision sanctions. Electronic monitoring and on-site drug testing are also tools used regularly by POs to supervise offenders.

A prototype of an intensive supervision program for community-based correctional services has been established by the American Probation and Parole Association. Figure 9.3 shows this prototypical intensive supervision program, beginning with the offender-client population to be served by different community agencies. These agencies devise mission statements that articulate clearly their goals and policies. Relations with local law enforcement agencies, parole boards, judges, and courts are lumped under "Other CJS Components." The community in which the agency is based is considered another significant piece of input that influences agency policy and protocol. A primary goal of these community-based agencies is to reduce offender recidivism. This goal is achieved in part through shifting from a custodial, incapacitative, and punitive mode to a more integrated approach of interventions and risk-control strategies. A balanced approach to offender supervision is stressed, whereby individual offender needs are prioritized and met. Prior agency goals were short-term ones; under future agency planning, goals are projected as long-range

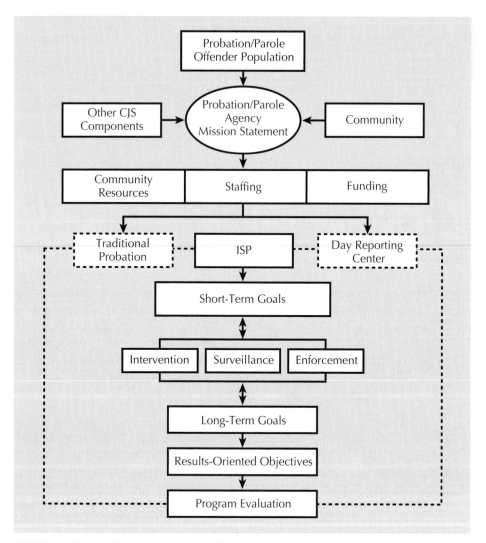

FIGURE 9.3 Program development process. (*Source:* From Fulton, Gendreau, and Paparozzi, 1995:26; reprinted with the permission of the American Probation and Parole Association.)

ones. Better risk control is both a short-term and long-term goal sought by all community-based agencies. Such risk control is achieved to a greater degree when agencies provide a greater range of assistance and offender services that meet offender needs, particularly in the areas of employment and substance abuse. The prototype also encourages focusing on results of programs rather than program activities. It is accepted that the two primary missions of probation and parole are to protect society and to rehabilitate offenders.

Critical factors in effective program development include (1) needs assessment, (2) adequate staffing, (3) proper and ample funding, (4) engaging stakeholders, including establishing working task forces and creating more effective public relations, (5) networking with community service providers, (6) close program monitoring and evaluation, (7) targeting greater numbers of high-risk/high-need offenders for program involvement and treatment, and (8) developing better selection instruments for the inclusion of program participants (Fulton, Gendreau, and Paparozzi, 1995:27–30). Several ambitious goals are outlined for the ideal community-based ISP agency: (1) increased public safety, (2) rehabilitation of offenders, (3) provision of intermediate punishments, (4) reduction in prison and jail overcrowding, and (5) reduction in operating costs. ISP objectives should be specific, measurable, achieved within a limited time, and identified with an actual result (Fulton, Gendreau, and Paparozzi, 1995:31). Critical elements for successful program implementation include smaller PO caseloads, a greater range of correctional interventions, a more objectives-based management system, systematic case review, a system of positive reinforcement for clients, a system of control and accountability, victim restitution, community involvement, and aftercare. Several successful community-based ISP programs include New Jersey's ISP program devised in 1983, the Massachusetts Intensive Probation Supervision Program implemented in 1985, and the Colorado Judicial Department's Specialized Drug Offender Program created in the early 1990s.

Probation and parole departments in various states are administered by different agencies and organizations. Although most states have departments of corrections that supervise both incarcerated and nonincarcerated offenders, in other jurisdictions these tasks are sometimes overseen by departments of human services, departments of youth services, or some other umbrella agency that may or may not have the expertise to service these clients adequately.

During the 1990s, a growing concern has been the professionalization of all correctional personnel (Read et al., 1997; Sieh, 1990). When the President's Commission on Law Enforcement and Administration of Justice made its recommendations in 1967, few standards were in place in most jurisdictions to guide administrators in their selection of new recruits. Thus, it was not unusual for critics of corrections to frequently make unfavorable remarks about and unflattering characterizations of those who manage criminals and oversee their behaviors. Because of the complexity of contemporary correctional roles, new pools from which to recruit, and greater social science training, different types of officers with a broader range of skills may be required in future years (Storm, 1997).

Selected Criticisms of Probation and Parole Programs

Probation and parole programs have been viewed unfavorably over the years, both in the United States and in other countries such as England (Middleton, 1995). There have been claims that probation and parole do not work as rehabilitative strategies and that POs are not doing their jobs properly because of the actions of their probationers and parolees (Hill, 1994). Consequently, both state and federal policy makers have targeted probation, parole, and the field of corrections in general for massive institutional changes and reforms. In the early years of correctional reforms, officials believed that the treatment or medical model was sound and that rehabilitation on a large scale was possible for both incarcerated and nonincarcerated offenders. Of course, rehabilitation was projected as the direct result of proper therapeutic programs and treatments. Educational and vocational-technical programs were coupled with group and individual counseling in prisons and jails. Offenders sentenced to probation were slotted for involvement in various training courses and assigned to programs designed to improve their self-concept, skills, and marketability as job holders and breadwinners.

The rehabilitative aim of corrections was not entirely abandoned, but over the years, an increasingly skeptical public became disenchanted with what corrections officials espoused and how they sought to rehabilitate offenders. Too many ex-convicts were committing new crimes and were subject to rearrests. Former clients of probation or parole programs were also apprehended for new law violations. Furthermore, rearrests of offenders frequently occurred while they were on probation or parole.

Robert Martinson (1974), a criminologist, asked a crucial question concerning the criminal justice system: What works? His response to his own question was, "Nothing works." This answer has became a widely used cliché, but at the time, it had an immediate influence on both popular and professional thinking about rehabilitation as a correctional aim in all criminal justice system components. Martinson's proclamation was seriously received by the criminal justice community. In effect, he had issued a challenge to probation and parole and to the general field of criminal justice to show precisely what had been accomplished as the result of a massive infusion of funds by the federal government and private resources since the original President's Commission recommendations in 1967 and the establishment of the Law Enforcement Assistance Administration.

Martinson's own research critically evaluated studies of probation and parole programs between 1945 and 1967. He found only 231 studies during that period worthy of scientific merit, and even those studies were beset with methodological and theoretical faults that seriously questioned the findings. Martinson concluded that both probation and parole officials and the academic community at large were grossly negligent by failing to provide a means whereby self-assessments and effectiveness evaluations of programs could be conducted. Thus, it was impossible to determine any particular program's effectiveness and whether Law Enforcement Assistance Administration monies had been wisely invested. Martinson believed the case to be largely one of massive professional irresponsibility. In fairness to him as well as to probation and parole organizations, Martinson did not reject all programs outright. Elements of success were associated with many of the programs studied, although frequently the level of success was not as high as he and others desired.

Following Martinson's criticisms, the New York Governor's Special Committee on Criminal Offenders, the committee that originally sponsored Martinson's research, sought to suppress his report from public disclosure. It was well known that fairly large sums of money were being extended to this and other committees from the Law Enforcement Assistance Administration and other government sources during that period, and the release of such unfavorable information about probation and parole might cause the curtailment of these monies. Martinson's work was eventually published despite committee objections and legal problems, and a special National Academy of Sciences Panel on Research on Rehabilitative Techniques later supported him by affirming that his findings were essentially correct (Walker, 1989).

Efforts have been made to link the failure of rehabilitation in probation and parole with specific programs and personnel. The most common criticisms of rehabilitation programs are that they are disorganized and are inadequately funded and staffed (Orchowsky, Merritt, and Browning, 1994). Few programs dependent on public funds for their operation and continuation will acknowledge adequate staffing and funding. Thus, most programs are perpetually in a state of need, with requests made annually for larger portions of public resources and budgets stretched to justify greater allocations for agency funding (Lindner and Bonn, 1996; Sluder, Garner, and Cannon, 1995).

What evidence suggests that enlarging correctional staffs and spending more money on correctional programs will necessarily result in lower recidivism rates? Interestingly, the enlargement of correctional staffs, especially in probation and parole, has made it possible in some jurisdictions for officers to supervise their clients more closely through lower offender caseloads. Greater supervision of offenders, however, has occasionally resulted in an increase in the number of reported technical violations of an offender's probation or parole program (Walker, 1989). Technical violations do not mean that crime among probationers and parolees has increased, but only that they are now more frequently observed and recorded. These offenders stand a good chance of having their probation or parole revoked because of such violations, thus giving the public the impression that their criminal activity is increasing.

Criticisms of POs generally have centered on the inadequacy of their training, lack of experience, and poor educational background. For example, studies of POs have shown that they are typically white, come from rural areas, are politically conservative, have mixed job histories, have entered corrections work at a turning point or after failure in another career, or are merely holding their present job while anticipating a career move to a more promising alternative (DelGrosso, 1997; Sieh, 1992).

To the extent that probation and parole officers are similar in their backgrounds and training compared with corrections officers who perform inmate management chores, these characteristics have implications for the quality of services delivered by probation and parole agencies. If it is true that a majority of probation and parole officers enter this work with little or no training, that they lack the enthusiasm and energy to perform their jobs efficiently and effectively, and that they lack basic educational skills for dealing with offender clients, then it may be that these factors significantly influence the quality of services delivered to offenders (Bishop, 1993). If probation and parole officers cannot cope effectively with the demands of their jobs because of their own limited resources and experiences, then suggested reforms involving their professionalization would be justified.

Professionalization is often equated with acquiring more formal education rather than practical skills involving one-to-one human relationships with different types of offender-clients. Educational programs for officers often overemphasize the laws and rules of institutions and the mechanics of enforcement. Often underemphasized are people skills and the ability to cope with human problems (e.g., physically or mentally impaired clients), abilities required if the quality of officers is to be raised (Campbell, 1998). Although the following list is not exhaustive, it contains some of the more prevalent reasons for criticisms of probation and parole programs and personnel:

1. Probation and parole programs have historically been fragmented and independent of other criminal justice organizations and agencies. Without any centralized planning and coordinating, probation and parole programs have developed haphazardly in response to varying jurisdictional needs (Sluder, Garner, and Cannon, 1995).

2. The general field of corrections has lacked the professionalism associated with established fields with specialized bodies of knowledge (Whitehead and Lindquist, 1992:13–15). Often, corrections officers have secured their training through affiliation with an academic program in sociology, criminal justice, or political science. Although these programs offer much relating to the correctional field, they are not designed to give corrections career–oriented students the practical exposure to real problems faced by officers on duty and dealing with real offenders.

3. Most jurisdictions have lacked licensing mechanisms whereby officers can become certified through proper in-service training and education. However, this situation has greatly improved during the last few decades. In 1999, probation and parole officers averaged 246 hours of training, including 38 hours of in-service training. In 1999, there were formal training programs in all U.S. jurisdictions (Camp and Camp, 1999:204–205).

4. Until the early 1980s, only one state required a college education of probation or parole officer applicants, and some states had as their only prerequisite the ability to read and write, presumably for the purpose of completing PSI reports (Read et al., 1997; Storm, 1997). Even though the relation between a college education and probation or parole officer effectiveness has not been demonstrated conclusively, some evidence suggests that college training is particularly helpful in preparing presentence investigations and in understanding criminal law and potential legal issues and liabilities that might arise in the officer-client relationship (Cosgrove, 1994).

5. Past selection procedures for probation and parole officers have focused on physical attributes and security considerations (Brown, 1993). An emphasis in recruitment on physical attributes has historically operated to exclude women from probation and parole work, although there is evidence showing a greater infusion of women into correctional roles in recent years (Read et al., 1997; Storm, 1997). For example, in 1986, only 12 percent of all POs in the United States were women (American Correctional Association, 1993b), but by 1999, the proportion of female POs had risen to about 50 percent (Camp and Camp, 1999:200–201). In recent years, screening mechanisms have changed to include psychological interviews and personality assessment inventories for the purpose of identifying those most able to handle the **stress** and psychological challenges of probation and parole work, with less emphasis on physical abilities (Lindner and Bonn, 1996). Several studies have found that PO work in general is more enriching and complicated in the sense that one's personal problem-solving skills are becoming more important compared with past years, when learned standard solutions were applied consistently to situations with general similarities (Leonardi and Frew, 1991; Whitehead and Lindquist, 1992). Thus, PO work is become more of an art rather than the application of a limited range of standard strategies for diverse client problems, regardless of whether those strategies are applicable or inappropriate (Crosland, 1995).

6. Probation and parole officer training has often been based on the military model used for police training (Tarr, 1997). In those states with centralized corrections officer training and in-service programs for those preparing for careers in probation and parole work, a fundamental program flaw has been overreliance on police training models, whose relevance is frequently questioned by new recruits. Highly structured training programs frequently fail to provide prospective probation and parole officers with the sorts of practical experiences they will encounter face to face with offender-clients.

PROBATION AND PAROLE OFFICERS: A PROFILE

Interacting with ex-offenders, visiting their homes or workplaces, and generally overseeing their behavior while on probation or parole is stressful (Maggio and Terenzi, 1993). The danger associated with PO work is well-documented, and most POs are exposed to risks similar to those encountered by police officers daily. Of course, offenders are obliged to comply with probation or parole program requirements, whatever they might be, and to be responsive and accessible whenever POs wish to contact them (Cornelius, 1994).

The primary control mechanism that POs exercise over offenders is the probation or parole revocation power possessed by POs. Although their recommendations for a parole or probation revocation are not binding on any parole board convened to hear allegations of violations against an offender, reports filed by POs commence revocation proceedings. An unfavorable report about an offender may involve a technical violation or a serious criminal allegation. POs often overlook minor supervision violations, in part because they judge such violations not to be serious and also because they do not wish to prepare the extensive paperwork that is a preliminary requirement for a formal probation or parole revocation hearing. Despite the leverage POs have over their offender-clients, the possibility of violent confrontation with injury or death and hostility from the public-at-large make PO work increasingly stressful and demanding.

Characteristics of Probation and Parole Officers

Who are probation and parole officers? What are their characteristics? Although little comprehensive information about POs exists, surveys that depict the characteristics of those performing various correctional roles have been conducted in recent years. These surveys indicate a gradual move toward greater corrections officer professionalization. Historically, evidence of professionalizing probation work has been found in various cities, such as Chicago, during the 1900–1935 period (Knupfer, 1999). One indication of greater professionalization of the corrections profession has been the movement toward accreditation and the establishment of accreditation programs through the American Correctional Association (ACA) and the American Probation and Parole Association (APPA) (American Correctional Association, 2001). A majority of PO staff are women (57.5 percent), white (77 percent), possess bachelor's degrees (75 percent), and have 9 to 12 years of experience. Entry-level salaries for POs ranged in 1999 from a low of $17,900 in Kentucky to a high of $43,600 in California, with the average entry-level salary being about $26,000 (Camp and Camp, 1999:206). Maximum salaries among jurisdictions for POs ranged from a low of $30,000 in West Virginia to a high of $85,000 in Alaska (Camp and Camp, 1999:206), with the average highest salary at $52,000. The federal probation system

BOX 9.1   *Personality Highlight*

Sonia Martinez
U.S. Probation Officer, Laredo, Texas

Statistics. B.S. (criminal justice), Laredo State University; Texas Teacher's Certificate (elementary education), Laredo State University; M.A. (criminal justice), Texas A&M International University

Work History and Experience. I obtained my bachelor's degree from Laredo State University in 1992, where I majored in criminal justice, and in 1995, I returned to the university and obtained my Texas Teacher's Certificate in elementary education.

I first became interested in the criminal justice/corrections field in 1989, when I enrolled in a corrections internship course at our local community college. That same year, I completed an internship program with the adult state probation office. Following that experience, I knew that I had chosen the right field of study. Immediately following graduation, I accepted employment with the Laredo State Center as a social worker/rape crisis counselor. In 1993, I became an adult state probation officer with Webb County, Texas. I thoroughly enjoyed my experience there and acquired a wide range of knowledge dealing with corrections. I used this knowledge to develop a better understanding of the population with which I was dealing. In 1995, I took a teaching position at the Webb County Juvenile Justice Alternative School, with the challenging task of teaching juvenile delinquents who were thought to be on the road to self-destruction. I must say that my time spent with these students through their difficult times proved to be the most rewarding experience I have encountered. I wholeheartedly believe that the school and the staff had a positive effect on at least a couple of these young lives.

In 1997, I left school to pursue a career in law enforcement. Early that year I attended the U.S. Customs Academy in Glynco, Georgia. Upon graduating from the academy, I returned to Laredo as a U.S. customs inspector. I remained in this capacity for over three years, and my experience proved to be exciting, interesting, and at times, monotonous. I enjoyed the camaraderie that came with working with a close group of individuals. I had to learn to trust and be trusted by my colleagues because of the possibility of encountering life-threatening situations. During my tenure, I made a few lifelong friends whom I knew I could count on in a moment's notice.

In April 2000, however, I made the decision to return to my roots in the corrections field. I accepted my current position as a U.S. probation officer. I was saddened to leave my good friends and coworkers, but I am confident that I made the right choice. I am also confident that my experiences in other fields have enhanced my ability to meet the organizational goals and to assist offenders in becoming productive citizens in their respective communities.

As noted earlier, I have explored various fields in social work, law enforcement, and corrections. I firmly believe that my past experiences have made me the officer I am today: a well-rounded individual, highly equipped to handle a multitude of tasks and challenges effectively.

Advice to Students. Follow your dreams wherever they may lead you, because you are essentially paving the road to your future. Don't be afraid to explore different areas of interest in different fields; that is the only way to be sure you have chosen the right career. During my career changes, I was often told that I "did not know what I wanted to do with my life," and my response was that it was not that I did not know what I wanted; it was simply that I wanted it all and did not plan to sell myself short.

had an entry-level salary of $25,000 and a high salary of $93,400, with an average of $47,900. Most state systems currently require a bachelor's degree as the minimum education for an entry-level parole officer position. In a few states, the general entry-level requirements for PO positions are less stringent. In 1990, for instance, a few jurisdictions required either a bachelor's degree or equivalent experience. By 1999, a majority of jurisdictions required a bachelor's degree for an entry-level position (Camp and Camp, 1999).

Considering the relatively low salaries of POs compared with those in other correctional positions and in the private sector, their higher median ages, and their comparatively lower educational levels, it is understandable that probation and parole have drawn criticism in the last few decades concerning the lack of professionalism POs seem to exhibit (Crank, 1996). This problem is explained, in part, by the lack of professional identity characterizing PO work, a lack of any recognized professional schools to prepare leaders for probation, and a lack of nationally recognized scholars or administrators who can be called eminent leaders in this field (Hill, 1997).

What Do POs Do?

Studies of correctional personnel have focused on prison and jail correctional officers, their behaviors and backgrounds, and work orientations (Storm, 1997). It has been reported that POs have negative self-images and impressions (Crank, 1996; Read et al., 1997). Although there have been gains in the selection, recruitment, and professionalization of POs, attitudes about their work roles and relationships with offender-clients have been slow to change (Read et al., 1997). The highest labor turnover among POs usually occurs during the early years of their employment (Wiggins, 1996).

At least 23 different PO functions have been identified, reflecting considerable diversity associated with PO roles. These functions are supervision, surveillance, investigation of cases, assist in rehabilitation, develop and discuss probation conditions, counsel, visit homes and work with clients, make arrests, make referrals, write PSI reports, keep records, perform court duties, collect fines, supervise restitution, serve warrants, maintain contracts with courts, recommend sentences, develop community service programs, assist law enforcement officers and agencies, assist courts in transferring cases, enforce criminal laws, locate employment for clients, and initiate program revocations (Read et al., 1997; Storm, 1997).

A direct relation exists between professionalism and the nature and quality of work performed in the organization (Fulton et al., 1997). Because POs lack self-esteem and are often scorned by others because of their apparent leniency with the offenders they manage, they have sometimes acquired counterproductive definitions of their work roles and functions (Courtright, 1995). An element of cynicism has been detected by Jeffrey Rush (1992), who investigated POs and their work attitudes. Some of the major orientations manifested by POs are summarized as follows:

1. Probation officers are mere instruments to be used for larger organizational ends. Their body of professional skills cannot be autonomously employed but must be exercised within the framework of precise organizational limits and objectives.
2. Probation officers' lack of genuine professional status in the court is a constant source of personal anxiety, work alienation, and general dissatisfaction.
3. The presentence investigation document is often cynically employed to validate judicial behavior or is otherwise used to reinforce administrative action already taken. The circumstances under which probation reports are prepared cast serious doubts as to their objectivity, validity, and integrity.
4. Frustrated as professionals, stripped of real decision-making power, lacking a genuine career motif, and assigned relatively low status by the community, it is not surprising that probation workers often develop a high degree of cynicism.
5. Probation officers "come to view their administrators as frightened, insecure, petty officials who will respond to any organization need at the expense of workers and clients. There is a constant undercurrent of antagonism between probation workers and their supervisors" (Lawrence, 1984:15).

Although POs themselves may be at fault directly or indirectly by being ill-prepared or undereducated for the roles they perform, probation and parole agencies must absorb some of the blame (Read et al., 1997). It has been suggested by more than one critic that probation and parole organizations and agencies often fail to clarify their own goals and objectives for the staff to achieve (Crank, 1996). If the goals of the organization itself are diffuse, then it is difficult for agency members to adhere to particular policies or move in constructive directions when helping their offender-clients.

Some fragmentation of effort exists among many POs who have their own ideas about how their jobs ought to be performed and what correctional philosophies should guide their own thinking about themselves and what they do (Spica, 1993:24–25). Increasing PO accountability through more effective leadership from administrators is one possible solution. Agency management must be willing to establish reasonable standards of performance for both staff and clients and must then follow through by monitoring and assessing performance objectively.

Frequently, organizational constraints inhibit the development of professional orientations toward probation and parole work. Although more educated POs are sought by probation/parole agencies, when they begin their job, these duties remain perfunctory or routine and custodial. Thus, more educated POs are not permitted the latitude to adapt their skills and education to their supervisory tasks and dealings with offender-clients (Texas Office of the State Auditor, 1996). Many PO training programs, when they exist, simply fail to train new POs to deal effectively with the practical problems they will encounter on the job. It also seems that they are neither allowed nor encouraged to use the skills they have developed (Wiggins, 1996).

Tenured POs feel threatened by what they perceive as greater emphasis on education, which operates to the exclusion of prior experience. These feelings foster interpersonal strains between senior/experienced POs and newer POs with vastly different educational backgrounds and experiences. The importance of dealing effectively with the offender-client is shifted to a lower priority, as POs spend more time dealing with conflicting role and training expectations and less time helping offenders. Accordingly, more highly educated POs reflect greater disappointment with their work, where they were promised more challenging tasks but must often perform routine and menial ones (Fulton et al., 1997).

Observers have concluded that POs experience much frustration in the performance of their work roles and associations with colleagues and clients and that much of this frustration is organizationally induced (Markley, 1994; May and Vass, 1996). Greater professionalism is called for, and it has been suggested that such professionalism can be engendered through greater participation in decision making by the POs themselves (Wiggins, 1996).

POs must prepare reports or PSI reports for convicted offenders at the request of judges. They must maintain contact with all offenders assigned to their supervision. They must be aware of community agencies and employment opportunities so that their function as resource staff may be maximized. They must perform informal psychological counseling. They must enforce the laws and ensure offender compliance with the requirements of the particular probation or parole program. When faced with dangerous or life-threatening situations in their contacts with offenders, they must be able to make decisions about how best to handle these situations. They must be familiar with their legal rights, the rights of offenders, and their own legal liabilities in relation to clients. POs must be flexible enough to supervise a wide variety of offender-clients. Increasing numbers of PO clients are from different ethnicities and cultures. Thus, greater cultural awareness is required of today's POs (Murphy, 1994; Stewart, 1994).

Recruitment of POs

When POs are recruited, what type of training should they receive? How much education should be required, and what educational subjects have the greatest relevance for correctional careers? No immediate answers are available for these questions. Although most people would agree that a Ph.D. is not essential for the effective performance of PO work, some educational training is desirable. Currently, observers disagree about how much education should be officially required as a part of the recruitment process.

The selection requirements and recruitment procedures included in this section are not exhaustive, but they serve as a set of standards against which PO recruitment, selection, and training programs may be evaluated. Traditional PO selection procedures have tended to focus on weeding out those unfit for PO work rather than on selecting those possessing the skills needed for successful job performance (Storm, 1997). PO training in most states includes several weeks of class time (e.g., social sciences, humanities, and/or police sciences) and two or more weeks of in-service training (American Correctional Association, 2001; Camp and Camp, 1999).

Some states, however, have no in-service or course requirements in place for those aspiring to PO roles. By 1999, most states had minimum numbers of introductory hours that ranged from 40 to 1,460, whereas in-service hours ranged from 20 to 140 (Camp and Camp, 1999:204–205).

Minimum Educational Requirements for POs. In 1999, minimum educational requirements of those entering the correctional field were a high school diploma or the GED for an entry-level PO position, community college (two years) diploma, or some college work. Because of the recent emphasis on professionalization, increasing numbers of jurisdictions are requiring a bachelor's degree for entry-level PO jobs (American Correctional Association, 2001:10-11).

The Use of Written Examinations for Screening Applicants. Although over 80 percent of the programs required a written examination, only about 20 percent subjected recruits to psychological screening. The Minnesota Multiphasic Personality Inventory and Inwald Personality Inventory appear to be those most popularly applied tools when any are used. Very few programs included physical examinations, medical checks, or FBI inquiries. Several programs had no formal testing or examination procedures as a means of screening PO candidates (American Correctional Association, 2001). By 2000, most jurisdictions had considerably more rigorous physical and psychological qualifications for starting positions (American Correctional Association, 2001).

In 1981, the National Institute of Corrections (NIC) responded to the need for greater **professionalization** and training among POs by sponsoring a series of training programs in various jurisdictions. The ACA was selected to administer some of these programs and eventually came out with the Development of Correctional Staff Trainers program, which provided comprehensive, experience-based training for more than 1,000 trainers and other professionals between 1981 and 1985. In 1985, over 6,000 individuals had enrolled in ACA correspondence courses and had participated in related programs, seminars, and workshops on a variety of correctional topics. These training programs continue, and enrollments have escalated considerably (American Correctional Association, 2001).

Stressed in these programs and workshops have been legal liabilities of POs and other types of corrections officers as well as the cultivation of skills in the management and supervision of offender-clients. In addition, programs and courses are offered for managing stress, crisis intervention and hostage negotiations, proposal and report writing, legal issues training, managing community corrections facilities, dealing with the mentally ill offender, and suicide prevention (Bernat, 1994).

One way of gauging the nature and quantity of education that should logically be expected of potential POs is to examine the situations they would ordinarily encounter. That POs interact with violent and nonviolent offenders requires more than one approach or solution to any situation. Certain types of offenders on probation or parole are dangerous, and incarceration has not necessarily made them less dangerous than they were when they originally committed serious crimes (Wilkinson, 1993). For example, female POs risk sexual assault if they are assigned especially violent sex offenders with one or more previous rape convictions. Both male and female POs risk injury through assault if they make decisions that affect offender freedoms, such as recommendations for parole or probation revocations because of program violations they detect. Furthermore, drug- or alcohol-dependent offenders are less predictable than other offenders and may become violent even if they were convicted of nonviolent offenses (DelGrosso, 1997).

Offenders on probation or parole as well as those incarcerated are frequently adept at manipulating those supervising them. Thus, in some jurisdictions, POs receive training for resisting group pressure, acquiring self-control, and making less risky decisions (American Correctional Association, 2001). In addition, they receive offensive and defensive training for self-protection as well as their own manipulative skills for eliciting and altering offenders' values and beliefs about themselves in both formal and informal counseling (Brown, 1994).

Increasing the amount of training considered relevant by prospective POs through simulated situations of officer-offender interactions is one means of increasing the professionalism of officers in general. Many POs believe that they need more practical training as a part of their training programs, rather than mere attendance in awareness or other related educational courses. One reason for a more practical training emphasis is that the kinds of persons traditionally attracted to corrections positions have not been particularly excited about or motivated to participate in academic programs. Thus, topics such as when to use deadly force and spotting those situations likely to create legal liability are directly relevant to the future tasks performed by POs. Those officers most likely to leave the correctional field often lack motivation, education, and commitment, but a more relevant curriculum could function to reduce labor turnover significantly in various training programs (Cornelius, 1994; Crank, 1996).

PO TRAINING AND SPECIALIZATION

The amount of PO training is mandated by the different states and the federal government (American Correctional Association, 2001).

Assessment Centers and Staff Effectiveness

The focus on behaviorally based methods for selecting and evaluating POs not only results in the hiring of better line personnel, but it also functions to identify those most able to perform managerial tasks. It is clear that a key element in the success of any probation program is the quality of line staff (Crank, 1996; Smith, 1993a), and a key element in maintaining the quality of line staff is managerial adequacy (Virginia State Crime Commission, 1998).

Assessment centers are useful for identifying potential chief probation officers and administrators for probation/parole programs (Page, 1995). These assessment centers are often patterned after those used in the selection of law enforcement officers. Personality tests are often used to identify those prospective officers who would have the right temperament for PO work (Sluder and Shearer, 1992).

If the right kinds of managers can be selected and promoted, then line staff can be molded into productive work units to serve offender-clients better. Managers can assist their probation and parole organizations to devise more clearly defined mission statements of goals and objectives and to establish greater uniformity of quality of performance among staff members (Wiggins, 1996). Although assessment centers are not foolproof and should not be considered as cookbook methods for selecting "good managers," they help by providing specific tests and assessments of those desirable qualities of leadership and managerial effectiveness that should be seriously considered by administrators. Criminal justice generally has had a continuing need for better managers, and thus criminal justice professionals, including corrections personnel, should explore every management evaluation tool available, such as assessment centers (Siegel, 1996).

The Florida Assessment Center

The Dade County, Florida, Department of Corrections and Rehabilitation was one of the first state corrections agencies to establish an **assessment center** for the selection of entry-level officers (Page, 1995). Although using assessment centers to screen personnel for organizational positions is not a new concept, especially in private industry, the use of such centers in corrections recruitment and training is innovative. Currently, a large number of law enforcement agencies employ assessment centers or other pivotal screening facilities to separate the fit from the unfit among applicants for law enforcement positions.

The **Florida Assessment Center** moves beyond traditional selection mechanisms such as the use of paper-and-pencil measures and standard personality, interests, and aptitude and IQ tests or inventories by examining a candidate's potential on the basis of the full scope of the job. This examination is accomplished by a previously established job task analysis made of the different correctional chores to be performed by prospective applicants. The Dade County Assessment Center has identified the following skills associated with corrections work of any kind:

1. The ability to understand and implement policies and procedures
2. The ability to be aware of all elements in a given situation and to use sensitivity to others and good judgment in dealing with the situation
3. The ability to communicate effectively (Page, 1995)

On the basis of various measures designed to tap into each of these personal and social skills, the most qualified candidates are targeted for further testing and interviews. These tests include preparations of written reports, role playing and acting out problem situations, and videotaped situational exercises. The center strives to provide candidates with as much realism as possible concerning the kinds of situations they will encounter when dealing with criminals either inside or outside of prison. Also emphasized is an awareness of race, gender, and ethnicity in the social dimension of relating with offenders. Three-person teams of evaluators screen applicants on the basis of their objectivity and manner in responding to various job-related simulated challenges. A key objective is to assist prospective corrections personnel in avoiding legal challenges and suits by clients or prisoners. Thus, when subsequent decisions are made by corrections officers and others and are challenged in court, the basis for the challenges will be unlikely attributable to faults associated with the selection process (Page, 1995).

The evaluators in the Florida Assessment Center are themselves trained by other assessors or correctional officers so that they may more readily determine the most appropriate candidates for correctional posts. Observing, categorizing, and evaluating candidate skills are procedures requiring extensive training, and the assessment center continually subjects its own selection process to both internal and external scrutiny and evaluation. Assessment center officials in both Florida and other jurisdictions where such centers are used believe that the training their officers receive also helps reduce their potential for lawsuits from clients (Morgan, Belbot, and Clark, 1997).

The Use of Firearms in Probation and Parole Work

Because the idea of POs carrying firearms is fairly new, little information exists about it. Also, it is too early to evaluate the long-range implications of PO firearm use in the field. In 2000, 24 states authorized the use of firearms for parole officers; 26 states authorized firearms use for their probation officers (American Correctional Association, 2001:14–15). More probation and parole officer training programs are featuring topics related to PO safety, especially in view of the shift from the medical model toward more proactive, client-control officer orientations (Arola and Lawrence, 1999). Few professionals in criminology and criminal justice question that each generation of probationers and parolees includes more dangerous offenders. Largely because it is impossible at present to incarcerate everyone convicted of crimes, the use of probation and parole as front-end and back-end solutions to jail and prison overcrowding is increasing. Also increasing are reports of victimization from POs working with probationers and parolees in dangerous neighborhoods (DelGrosso, 1997). It is not necessarily the case that probationer-clients or parolee-clients are becoming more aggressive or violent toward their PO supervisors, although there have been reports of escalating client violence against their supervising POs. Yet POs are obligated to conduct face-to-face visits with their clients, and in many instances, these visits involve potentially dangerous situations or scenarios. Some evidence, however, suggests a decline in the future of home visits as a standard PO function (Arola and Lawrence, 1999).

Life-Threatening Situations and Assaults against POs by Their Clients. Anonymous interviews with POs supervising both adults and juveniles give some insight as to the potential hazards of PO work. One PO supervising juvenile offenders in Cincinnati, Ohio, for instance, reported that she was assaulted and physically beaten by youthful gang members associated with one of her juvenile clients. The juvenile client himself was apologetic and promised to advise his gang members to leave her alone the next time she appeared in his neighborhood. In another situation, a male PO visited a parolee in a run-down section of Los Angeles. The parolee had been drinking excessively. When the PO entered the client's apartment, the parolee held a rifle to his own chin, threatening suicide. At one point, as the parolee continued to drink, he pointed the rifle at the PO and said, "You're the reason it's come to this. I might as well blow your head off too." After three hours of talking, the parolee was coaxed into surrendering his weapon with a promise from the PO "not to do anything." The PO left and never said a word about the incident but within a month had resigned. Increasingly, PO training involves understanding about how to deal with drug- or alcohol-dependent clients in productive ways (Read, 1992:4–6).

The hazards of PO work are clearly portrayed in the results of a nationwide survey conducted by the Federal Probation and Pretrial Officers Association in 1993 that disclosed the following assaults or attempted assaults against officers nation-wide since 1980 (Bigger, 1993:14–15):

Murders or attempted murders	16
Rapes or attempted rapes	7
Other sexual assaults or attempted sexual assaults	100
Shot and wounded or attempted shot and wounded	32
Use or attempted use of blunt instrument or projectile	60
Slashed or stabbed or attempted slashed or stabbed	28
Car used as weapon or attempted use of car as weapon	12
Punched, kicked, choked, or other use of body/attempted	1,396
Use or attempted use of caustic substance	3
Use or attempted use of incendiary device	9
Abducted or attempted abduction and held hostage	3
Attempted or actual unspecified assaults	944
Total	2,610

A more recent survey of 1,120 state and county probation and parole officers in Minnesota raises several concerns about officer safety. Of the sample surveyed, 19 percent reported one or more physical assaults during their career, and 74 percent reported being verbally or physically threatened one or more times. About 4 percent were actually physically assaulted one or more times in the past year, and 37 percent reported being physically or verbally threatened one or more times during the past year (Arola and Lawrence, 1999:32).

Self-Protection of Provocation?   Whether POs should arm themselves during their visits to clients is often a moot question, because they arm themselves anyway, regardless of probation/parole office policy. When POs are put to a vote, however, the results are often divided 50–50. For instance, a study of 159 POs attending an in-service training session during 1990 at a state probation training academy investigated these POs' opinions about their right to carry firearms while on the job. A carefully worded question, "Should POs be given the legal option to carry a firearm while working?" was asked of these 159 POs. Responses indicated that 59 percent of the officers believed that they should have the legal option to carry a firearm. This figure does not mean that 59 percent of these officers would carry firearms on the job; rather, they supported the idea of one's choice to carry a firearm while working if such a choice were made available (*Corrections Compendium,* 1992b; Sluder, Shearer, and Potts, 1991). In the same study, POs were asked whether they would endorse a requirement to carry a firearm as a part of one's PO work. Over 80 percent of the female POs interviewed opposed such a requirement, whereas about 69 percent of the male POs responded similarly. Yet, 80 percent of all officers interviewed said that they would carry a firearm if required to do so.

Opposition to POs carrying firearms is largely that it moves POs into a law enforcement function (Brown, 1993). Furthermore, if it becomes generally known that POs carry firearms, a situation between a PO and an armed client may escalate to the point where injuries or deaths could occur. In contrast, other professionals argue that changing offender populations have transformed into successive generations of more dangerous, violent clientele (Brown, 1994). A fundamental issue at the center of this controversy is the amount and type of training POs receive who will carry these firearms (Arola and Lawrence, 1999). States such as Florida have authorized their POs to use firearms as of July 1992. Their POs, however, have received extensive firearms training as well as psychological training so that the necessity of using a firearm will be for self-protection and as a last resort (*Corrections Compendium,* 1992b, 1992c).

Establishing Negligence in Training, Job Performance, and Retention

Not only is PO work increasingly hazardous, but POs are become increasingly liable for their actions taken in relation to the clients they supervise. Lawsuits against POs are becoming more common. Many are frivolous, but they consume much time and cause many job prospects to turn away from PO work (Jones and del Carmen, 1992). There are three basic forms of immunity: (1) absolute immunity, meaning that those acting on behalf of the state can suffer no liability from their actions taken while performing their state tasks (e.g., judges, prosecutors, and legislators); (2) qualified immunity, such as that enjoyed by probation officers if they are performing their tasks in good faith; and (3) quasi-judicial immunity, which generally refers to PO preparation of PSI reports at judicial request (Jones and del Carmen, 1992:36–37). In the general case, POs enjoy only qualified immunity, meaning that they are immune only when their actions were taken in good faith. There is, however, some evidence that the rules are changing related to the types of defenses available to POs, although the limits of immunity continue to be vague and undefined. Mark Jones and Rolando del Carmen (1992) have clarified at least two different conditions that seem to favor POs in the performance of their tasks and the immunity they derive from such conditions:

1. Probation officers are considered officers of the court and perform a valuable court function, namely the preparation of PSI reports.
2. Probation officers perform work intimately associated with court process, such as sentencing offenders.

Despite these conditions, Jones and del Carmen (1992) believe that it is unlikely that POs will ever be extended absolute immunity to all of their work functions. In some later and related research, Rolando del Carmen and James Pilant (1994:14–15) described judicial immunity and qualified immunity as two types of immunity that are generally available to public officials including POs. Judicial liability is like absolute immunity described earlier. Judges must perform their functions and make decisions that may be favorable or unfavorable to defendants. Lawsuits filed against judges are almost always routinely dismissed without trial on the merits. Parole boards also possess such judicial immunity in most cases. In contrast, qualified immunity ensues only if officials, including POs, did not violate some client's constitutional rights according to what a reasonable person would have known (del Carmen and Pilant, 1994:14).

One of the ambiguities of PO work is that the letter of the law is often replaced by the spirit of the law. POs may simply create their own informal rules for dealing with their clients (Morgan, Belbot, and Clark, 1997). Annual regional and national conferences of probation and parole officers—such as those sponsored by the American Correctional Association, the American Jail Association, and the American

Probation and Parole Association—optimize conditions in which officers from different jurisdictions can exchange information with one another about how their work is performed. Much of this informal dialogue is casual conversation, but in many instances, POs glean from their counterparts in other jurisdictions certain ideas about bending the rules. Not all this dialogue is nefarious, however. Often, a PO in South Carolina will tell another PO from California that South Carolina POs have a right to do one or more different things that affect client programs. The California PO may be surprised, because in California, PO interference with or modification of client programs may be prohibited.

For example, Tim Matthews (1993) reports that in South Carolina, POs may place clients in halfway houses for up to 75 days, they may place offenders in residential or nonresidential treatment, they may restructure the supervision of a client's plan of action, they may increase the numbers of supervisory contacts, and they may order up to 40 hours of community service. In Florida, though, some or all of these actions by POs are strictly prohibited. For instance, in *Reynard v. State* (1993), a PO had ordered a client to perform a number of hours of community service, but a Florida Appellate Court struck down the community service orders because the sentencing judge had not included them as probation conditions.

Liability Issues Associated with PO Work

A summary of some of the key liability issues related to PO work is as follows:

1. Some information about a PO's clients is subject to public disclosure, whereas some information is not. Del Carmen (1990:34) says that POs must constantly reassess their working materials about specific clients and decide which information is relevant under certain circumstances. It would be advisable, for instance, to inform prospective employers of certain probationers or parolees if the work involves custodial services in a large apartment complex and the particular probationers/parolees are convicted voyeurs, rapists, exhibitionists, or burglars. POs might also inform banks that particular probationers/parolees have been convicted of embezzlement if these clients are seeking work in a bank setting or any other business where they will be working around and handling money. It may not be appropriate to advise an employer that the probationer/parolee is a convicted drug dealer if the client is seeking to become a car salesperson or factory worker. Also, in most states, if POs know that a client has AIDS, it is improper for them to report this fact to a client's employer because of statutory prohibitions against such disclosures except under certain circumstances. These circumstances vary considerably among state jurisdictions, and some states have no policy on this issue. Thus, it is up to individual agencies to adopt their own policies (Barrineau, 1994). A general rule within most PO agencies is that "if a probationer or parolee obtains a job on his or her own, there is no officer or agency liability because reliance is absent. However, an agency's rules may require disclosure by the officer when he or she learns of the probationer or parolee's job, even if the job was obtained by the offender" (del Carmen, 1990:36).

2. POs have a duty to protect the public. Their work in this regard may subject them to lawsuits. This issue relates closely to the first. If particular probationers or parolees have made threats to seek revenge against particular persons or organizations, then it would be advisable for POs to report that these clients are in the community and may pose a risk to one or more former victims. There are some notable distinctions in degrees of liability, however. Del Carmen (1990:36) indicates that if a probationer says that he is going to kill his wife and the PO does nothing about it, liability may attach and the PO may be liable for not warning the wife or notifying authorities. If a parolee tells his PO that he feels like going out to commit armed robbery and actually carries it out, however, the liability of the PO is questionable, because it is unreasonable to assume that the PO knew where and when the client would commit the robbery. Furthermore, saying that one may go out and commit armed robbery and actually committing the robbery are two different matters. The PO may conclude that her client is simply "blowing off steam," "getting emotions out in the open where they can be dealt with productively," or some other such similar interpretation.

3. PO use of firearms may create hazards for both POs and their clients. POs are increasingly carrying firearms for their personal protection when entering dangerous neighborhoods or housing projects where their clients reside. If they use their firearms, then there is some likelihood that someone—possibly the probationer/parolee, the PO, or an innocent bystander or relative—may be seriously or fatally injured. Liability of this sort is always possible. One way of minimizing such liability is to provide POs with proper firearms training prior to authorizing them to carry dangerous weapons (Morgan, Belbot, and Clark, 1997). Although this precaution does not guarantee that lawsuits and liability will be avoided, it does minimize the risk of such legal actions by others. Often, when POs are sued by their clients or others, the **Civil Rights Act** (U.S. Code, Title 42, Sec. 1983) applies. Civil rights actions are usually tort actions and are settled in civil courts rather than criminal courts.

4. POs may supervise their clients in a negligent manner. Watkins (1989:30–31) describes an Arizona case in which several POs were sued because of injuries sustained by a victim as the result of failing to properly supervise a dangerous client. In the Arizona case (*Acevedo v. Pima County Adult Probation Department,* 1984), a convicted felon and child sexual abuser was placed on probation and subsequently sexually molested several of the plaintiff's children. The POs supervising this offender knew of his sexual deviance and propensities, yet they allowed him to rent a room on premises where the plaintiff and her five children resided. The Arizona Supreme Court observed that although POs do many diverse tasks and have demanding responsibilities, they must not knowingly place clients in situations in which their former conduct might create a hazard to the public. In this case, the lawsuit against the POs was successfully pursued. It may also be argued that these POs failed to warn the plaintiff of their client's sexual propensities, which also could have warranted a lawsuit against these POs.

5. PO PSI report preparation may result in liability. One of the more important PO functions is the preparation of PSI reports at the request of judges prior to offender sentencing. Some of the information contained in these PSI reports may not be directly relevant to sentencing; thus, it may not be necessary to disclose the entire contents of PSI reports at any particular time. At the federal level, at least, judges may disclose the contents of PSI reports except when (a) disclosure might disrupt rehabilitation of the defendant, (b) the information was obtained on a promise of confidentiality, and (c) harm may result to the defendant or to any other person. Subsequently, when inmates are about to be paroled, the PSI report may again be consulted. Obviously, the long-term impact of a PSI report is substantial. Errors of fact, unintentional or otherwise, may cause grievous harm to inmates and may seriously jeopardize their chances for early release. If the information barring them from early release is contained in the PSI report, if the parole board relies heavily on this information in denying parole to particular offenders, and if the information contained therein is inaccurate or false, then a cause of action or lawsuit may be lodged against the PO who prepared the original PSI report (U.S. Department of Justice, 1997).

6. Liabilities against POs and/or their agencies may ensue for negligent training, negligent retention, and deliberate indifference to client needs. POs may not have particular counseling skills when dealing with certain offenders who have psychological problems and may give poor advice. Such advice may cause offenders to behave in ways that harm others. Also, POs may not be adequately prepared or trained to carry firearms. They may discharge their firearms under certain circumstances that can cause serious injury or death. These situations are examples of negligent training. Negligent retention might result when certain POs are maintained by a probation agency after they have exhibited certain conduct or training deficiencies that they have failed to remedy. Failing to rid an organization of incompetent employees is negligent retention. Finally, when POs meet with their probationer/parolee/clients, they may believe that particular offenders need certain community services or assistance but these POs may deliberately refrain from providing such assistance or making it possible for their clients to receive such aid. If certain clients are drug dependent and obviously in need of medical services, deliberate indifference on the part of the PO would be exhibited if the PO did nothing to assist the client in receiving the needed medical treatment. This situation is an example of deliberate indifference. Deliberate indifference may be a vengeful act on the part of the PO, an omission, or simple failure to act promptly.

Although the above list of PO legal liabilities is not exhaustive, it represents the major types of situations in which POs incur potential problems from lawsuits. Jones and del Carmen (1992:36) and Richard Sluder and del Carmen (1990:3–4) suggest at least three different types of defenses used by POs when performing their work. These defenses are not perfect, but they do make it difficult for plaintiffs to prevail under a variety of scenarios.

1. POs were acting in good faith while performing the PO role.
2. POs have official immunity, because they are working for and on behalf of the state, which enjoys sovereign immunity.
3. POs may not have a special relationship with their clients, thus absolving them of possible liability if their clients commit future offenses that result in injuries or deaths to themselves or others.

Probation and Parole Officer Labor Turnover

In 1999, turnover among probation and parole officers was 15.4 percent. Among probation/parole officer recruits in training, turnover was higher at 22 percent (Camp and Camp, 1999:152). In view of a number of continuing problems confronting those entering probation and parole service as a career, the high degree of **labor turnover** among POs is understandable (Brown, 1993; Maggio and Terenzi, 1993). There are several explanations for this turnover. First, the rapid increase in the offender population managed by POs has created significant logistical problems. Some observers have indicated that POs must continue to maintain their current level of activity in an environment in which the public demands greater punishment, incarceration, and a decrease in public expenditures (Camp and Camp, 1999). Furthermore, there is a lack of consensus among POs about their goals and professional objectives as well as how these goals ought to be realized. Some POs see themselves as **brokers** who provide referral services to their offender-clients or arrange offender contacts with community agencies that provide special services, including counseling and training. Other POs see themselves as **caseworkers** who attempt to change offender behavior through educating, enabling, or mediating whenever offender problems occur. Many POs have asked whether the public has come to expect too much from them, particularly in view of financial cutbacks and greatly increased offender caseloads (Crosland, 1995; Storm, 1997).

PROBATION AND PAROLE OFFICER CASELOADS

The **caseload** of a probation or parole officer is considered by many authorities to be significant in affecting the quality of supervision POs can provide their clients. Caseloads are the numbers of offender-clients supervised by POs. Caseloads vary among jurisdictions (American Correctional Association, 2001:16–17). Theoretically, the larger the caseload, the poorer the quality of supervision and other services. Intensive probation supervision (IPS) programs are based on the premise that low offender caseloads maximize the attention POs can give their clients, including counseling, employment, social, and psychological assistance. The success of such programs suggests that lower caseloads contribute to lower recidivism rates among parolees and probationers. Other program components such as fines, curfews, and community service may also have some influence on the overall reduction of these rates.

Ideal Caseloads

The earliest work outlining optimum caseloads for professionals was done by C. L. Chute (1922), who advocated caseloads for POs no larger than 50. Similar endorsements of a 50-caseload limit were made by Edwin Sutherland in 1934, the American Prison Association in 1946, the Manual of Correctional Standards in 1954, and the National Council of Crime and Delinquency in 1962 (Gottfredson and Gottfredson, 1988:182). The 1967 President's Commission on Law Enforcement and Administration of Justice lowered the optimum caseload figure to 35.

In 1999, actual caseloads of POs varied greatly, ranging from a low of 40 clients in Nebraska to a high of 81 clients in California (Camp and Camp, 1999:176). IPS programs had caseloads ranging from 9 per officer in Wyoming to a high of 51 in Rhode Island (Camp and Camp, 1999:176). Considerable jurisdictional variation exists regarding both regular and intensive supervision caseloads for POs.

There is at present no agreement among professionals regarding an ideal PO caseload. On the basis of evaluating caseloads of POs in a variety of jurisdictions,

Michael Gottfredson and Don Gottfredson (1988:182) have concluded that "it may be said with assurance . . . that (1) no optimal caseload size has been demonstrated, and (2) no clear evidence of reduced recidivism, simply by reduced caseload size, has been found." This declaration applies mainly to standard probation/parole supervision, and it is not intended to reflect on the quality of recent IPS programs established in many jurisdictions. Because the composition of parolees and probationers varies considerably among jurisdictions, it is difficult to develop clear-cut conclusions about the influence of supervision on recidivism and the delivery of other program services (Texas Office of the State Auditor, 1996). An arbitrary caseload figure based on current caseload sizes among state jurisdictions would be about 30 clients per PO, which is perhaps the closest number to an ideal caseload size. The average caseload for POs in 1999 was 124, whereas the average intensive supervision caseload was 25. This small difference suggests that different jurisdictions have variable ideas about what is or is not standard or intensive supervision (Camp and Camp, 1999:176).

Changing Caseloads and Officer Effectiveness

Do smaller PO caseloads mean greater effectiveness and quality of services provided clients by their supervising POs? It is assumed that if POs have fewer clients to supervise, then they will be able to supervise their clients more effectively. There is great variation among jurisdictions about how optimum caseloads, large or small, should be defined (Baird, 1992a). If asked, then POs will almost always say that the lower their caseload, the more effective they are at helping their probationers and parolees (Kushner et al., 1995). If probationers and parolees are asked the same question, then they will tell a similar story. Close supervision of their behaviors while on probation or parole is more often viewed as assistance rather than punishment (Parker-Jimenez, 1997). This fact is especially true for those clients with drug or alcohol dependencies (Read, 1995).

The nature of PO client supervision is changing. POs are increasingly relying on technology in their relations with probationers and parolees (Sluder, Garner, and Cannon, 1995). Electronic monitoring and home confinement, drive-by check-ins at probation department offices, and distance contacts between offenders and their supervisors by mail or other means suggest less face-to-face encounters. It is clear that officer safety is becoming increasingly crucial and is a dominant issue in discussions of how best to supervise offenders (Courtright, Berg, and Mutchnik, 1997).

PO jobs are becoming increasingly complex, and POs are learning to be more effective as service brokers. They are networking their clients with more community services annually to provide improved treatments and other offender needs (Arthur, 2000). At the same time, some jurisdictions are experimenting with group reporting. In Anoka County, Minnesota, group reporting involves offender/clients reporting to their probation departments at particular times and meeting as a group with their assigned POs (Soma, 1994). Thus, POs have a chance to meet face to face with a large number of clients at any given time, rather than to hazard visits to dangerous neighborhoods for one-on-one face-to-face visits (Arola and Lawrence, 1999).

Technology is being incorporated into the PO-client relation in other ways as well. More probationers are having to undergo polygraph or lie detector testing as a condition of their probation or parole programs (Basta, 1995; Falkin, Strauss, and Bohen, 1999). In a criminal investigation, some clients on probation or parole may become suspects; therefore, their submission to a polygraph test will either include or exclude them as suspects. Also, these clients can be asked about program infractions that are not easily detected, such as drug use or associating with known criminals. If the answers to these questions are incriminating, then the preliminary grounds to seek a revocation of one's program may exist.

Caseload Assignment and Management Models

The court sentences offenders to probation, whereas parole boards release many prisoners short of serving their full terms. POs must reckon with fluctuating numbers of offenders monthly, as new assignments are given and some offenders complete their programs successfully (Baird, 1992a). No particular caseload assignment method has been universally adopted by all jurisdictions (Baird, Wagner, and DeComo, 1995). Rather, depending on the numbers of offenders assigned to probation and parole agencies, PO caseload assignment practices vary. Eric Carlson and Evalyn Parks (1979) have studied various caseload assignment schemes. Their investigation has led to the identification of four popular varieties of assignment methods: the conventional model, the numbers game model, the conventional model with geographic considerations, and the specialized caseload model.

The Conventional Model.   The **conventional model** involves the random assignment of probationers or parolees to POs. Thus, any PO must be prepared to cope with extremely dangerous offenders released early from prison on parole, those with drug or alcohol dependencies or in need of special treatment programs, and those requiring little if any supervision. Those convicted of violent offenses, however, may no longer be violent. For example, spouses may kill in the heat of passion, but it is highly unlikely that they will kill again. By the same token, it is possible that low-risk, less dangerous property offenders may become violent through offense escalation, although this rarely occurs.

The conventional model is probably used most frequently in probation and parole agencies throughout the United States. There are no specific logistical problems to handle, and POs can be assigned offender-clients on an as-needed basis. The major drawback is that POs must be extremely flexible in their management options, because of the diverse clientele they must supervise.

The Numbers Game Model.   The **numbers game model** is similar to the conventional model. To apply this model, the total number of clients is divided by the number of POs, and POs are given randomly the designated number. For instance, if there are 500 offenders and 10 POs, then there would be 500/10, or 50, offenders per PO. Another version of the numbers game model is to define an optimum caseload such as 40 and determine how many POs are required to supervise 40 offenders each. Thus, PO hiring is directly influenced by the numbers of offenders assigned to the jurisdiction and whatever is considered the optimum caseload.

The Conventional Model with Geographic Considerations.   The **conventional model with geographic considerations** is applied on the basis of the travel time required for POs to meet with their offender-clients regularly. Those POs who supervise offenders in predominantly rural regions are given lighter caseloads so that they may have the time to make reasonable numbers of contacts with offenders monthly or weekly. Those POs who supervise largely urban offenders are given heavier caseloads because less travel time between clients is required.

The Specialized Caseloads Model.   Sometimes caseload assignments are made on the basis of PO specialties. The **specialized caseloads model** pertains to PO assignments to clients who share particular problems, such as drug or alcohol dependencies. The POs assigned to these clients have special skills relating to these dependencies. Often, these POs have developed liaisons with Alcoholics Anonymous or other organizations so that their service to clients can be enhanced (Falkin, Strauss, and Bohen, 1999). Perhaps certain POs have had extensive training and education in particular problem areas to better serve certain offender-clients who may be retarded or mentally ill. Some POs, by virtue of their training, may be assigned more dangerous offenders. Those POs with greater work experience and legal training can manage dangerous offenders more effectively than new PO recruits. In some respects, this model is close to client-specific planning, in which individualization of cases is stressed (English et al., 1996; Torres, 1997a).

Some observers such as Ray Ferns (1994) believe that caseloads ought to be refocused to heighten offender accountability through cognitive restructuring and restorative case management. Traditional caseloads are oriented largely toward offender monitoring and control. Ferns suggests that offenders need to experience some actual change in their behavior while on probation or parole and need to learn about the adverse impact they had on possible victims of their crimes. Their accountability should be heightened and their self-awareness in this regard sharpened. Ferns says that the intent of restorative case management is to provide an ethical foundation and specific direction for the function of offender case management. Attention of supervising POs is shifted toward the offender's level of cognitive distortion and skill defects, the level of antisocial behaviors, and the ability of offenders to provide restoration to communities and victims. The emphasis of restorative case management is on the victims of offenders, although offenders themselves should acquire a greater degree of empathy with their victims. This program, as Ferns notes, is similar to the balanced approach. The **balanced approach**, devised originally for juvenile offenders, stresses heightening offender accountability, individualizing sanctions or punishments, and promoting community safety as critical program components (Bazemore and Walgrave, 1999). Ferns's restorative case management synthesizes these elements and blends them with heightened offender awareness through cognitive restructuring.

OFFICER/CLIENT INTERACTIONS

Although recruitment for POs is designed to identify and select those most capable of performing increasingly demanding PO tasks, little uniformity exists among jurisdictions regarding the types of POs ultimately recruited. Each PO brings to the job a philosophy of supervision based, in part, on agency expectations. Furthermore, each PO has individual differences and attitudes toward work that influence his or her supervisory style. Some POs are more punitive than others, whereas some see themselves as rehabilitators or therapists.

In the course of interacting with different kinds of offenders, it is not unusual for POs to acquire a certain amount of cynicism about their jobs and those they

BOX 9.3   ***Personality Highlight***

Montie Guthrie
Senior Patrol Agent, U.S. Border Patrol, Department of Justice, Immigration and Naturalization Service

Statistics. B.S. (criminal justice), Tarlton State University; M.S. (criminal justice), Texas A&M International University

Work History and Experience. Currently I am a senior patrol agent with the U.S. Border Patrol, having entered the Immigration and Naturalization Service in 1995. Prior to my tenure as a federal agent, I was a district parole officer with the State of Texas in Dallas for over three years, with the last two of those years concentrating mostly on street and prison gang members.

As a federal agent with the U.S. Border Patrol in Laredo, Texas, I have literally arrested thousands of individuals, ranging from honest workers trying to make a better life for themselves and their families to serious, hardened criminals convicted of crimes ranging from murder and rape to drug delivery charges. In addition, I have seized tens of thousands of pounds of illegal drugs, with my largest single seizure being 1,800 pounds of marijuana. That is quite a sight to see. Many people do not realize that over half of the drugs reported as seized by the DEA every year in the United States come from the seizures made by the U.S. Border Patrol. I have traveled all over the country and have even been detailed to the South Pacific to interdict illegal Chinese freighters bringing more than 600 Chinese people into Guam. I've worked with practically every federal (FBI, DEA) and state (local police, Department of Public Safety, Texas Rangers) agency that exists in Texas. I have interdicted drugs along the banks of the Rio Grande with U.S. Special Forces members, including Army Rangers and Navy Seals, and I have executed warrants with U.S. Customs and U.S. Marshals agents. All in all, it's been quite a ride.

In my time as district parole officer, I concentrated and focused on gang members and served as one of the gang liaisons with the Dallas Police Department, Sheriff's Office, and various state, local, and federal agencies under my immediate supervisor, who was the primary liaison. I supervised prison as well as street gang members. Some of the more interesting prison gangs were the Mexican Mafia, Texas Mafia, Texas Syndicate, and the Aryan Brotherhood. The street gangs were the various Crip and Blood sets as well as several independent Mexican-American gangs. I observed firsthand two gang drive-by shootings, one of which was directed at my parole office. The area of Dallas to which I was assigned was Fair Park, which is generally considered to be one of the roughest ghetto areas in the entire state. The area was an excellent testing ground to study street gangs, with approximately 20 major street gang sets within a five-square-mile area. I also spoke at several conferences about my insights and experiences with street gangs. That was a learning experience, working with so many highly trained and experienced veterans of the war against street gangs.

My work has given me a wide range of experience from which to draw. I have seen horrible sights, such as bodies I have personally discovered in the Rio

Grande that were dumped after prolonged torture and execution by having their throats cut or being shot in the head. I've also experienced incredibly humorous situations. One was the illegal alien who was trying to get to San Antonio, Texas, who locked himself in a railroad boxcar full of Corona beer and started drinking. It took two hours and over 20 police officers, border patrol agents, and firefighters to secure this one extremely drunk, beer-bottle throwing Mexican who weighed about 110 pounds soaking wet. I have more amusing anecdotes than I can honestly remember, and many terrible experiences that I cannot forget.

Working in the field of criminal justice, you find yourself in an almost continual state of change and flux, because the job is almost never the same. Although there are, of course, routine aspects of the job, something new always comes up. For those looking for a career free from the confines of the desk and office, it is unparalleled.

Advice to Students. If you truly feel that this career is for you, then fully commit yourself and begin the process. Look into the agency of your choice and see what it requires. A college degree, although not always a must, is very important for pay and advancement potential. Keep your nose clean and avoid situations and people who will get you into legal trouble, which will certainly derail your career plans. Get yourself into sufficient physical shape to do the job. Bone up on your writing skills; they are extremely important regardless of which branch of criminal justice you wish to enter. Finally, you must have a serious mindset in this line of work. It is not for the slacker or the faint of heart. That is not to say that you must have zero sense of humor. It is, however, a difficult and demanding career that will test you every day and will take its toll, if you let it.

This type of work requires a person to be able to go from controlled destructiveness to sympathy and caring, sometimes in a matter of minutes. You must be willing to take a life as well as risk your own to save one. If you cannot use violence or if you have little compassion for others, then this career is not for you. Those are the two spectra of the job. Usually the job falls somewhere in between, but those two ends are always possibilities. It is neither a job for the meek nor the bully. It is for those who sincerely want to try to make their little piece of the world a better place and are willing to get dirty to do so. If, after investigating and thinking about this, you feel that you still want a career in this line of work, then go for it. Best of luck to you in whatever endeavor you choose.

supervise. If an offender recidivates by committing a new offense, then some POs may take this new offense personally and consider it an indication of their failure at helping certain offender-clients. Edward Read et al. (1997), John Storm (1997), and others have examined the multifaceted nature of PO work and have identified a variety of roles performed by POs. Sometimes, these work roles come into conflict with one another.

Work roles include but are not limited to the following: (1) the **detector**, whereby the PO attempts to identify troublesome clients or those who have one or more problems that could present the community with some risk; (2) the **broker**, whereby the PO functions as a referral service and supplies the offender-client with contacts with agencies who provided needed services; (3) the **educator**, **enabler**, and **mediator**, whereby the PO seeks to instruct and assist offenders to deal with problems as they arise in the community; and (4) the **enforcer**, whereby POs perceive themselves as enforcement officers charged with regulating client behaviors (Strong, 1981).

Because POs are obligated to check up on their clients, they are viewed with suspicion and apprehension by probationers and parolees. One important concern for parolees is the confidentiality of the relationship between themselves and their supervisors (Whitehead and Lindquist, 1992). According to the rules and terms of one's probation or parole, infractions of any kind are to be reported to agency authorities and dealt with accordingly. If every single infraction observed by POs were reported and acted on officially, however, then there would be an endless series of hearings about whether probation or parole should be revoked in each reported case. The required attendance and participation of POs at such hearings would consume virtually every minute of their time, and little or no time would be left to supervise and help other offenders. Therefore, the PO/offender-client relationship often becomes one of negotiation, with the PO conveniently overlooking certain rule infractions, particularly minor ones, and the offender-client conscientiously attempting to adhere to the more important probation or parole provisions. Often, an unwritten relationship is established whereby the PO and offender can help each other in complementary ways.

Role conflict is inherent in the PO/offender relationship; it cannot be eliminated. The PO desires a successful outcome for the client, with the terms of the probation or parole fulfilled and the client emerging from the program to lead a productive life. Often, however, the circumstances leading to an offender's original arrest and conviction continue to exist and influence offender behaviors. Old acquaintances, family circumstances, and the added pressures of maintaining a job and complying with stringent probation or parole program conditions cause problems for more than a few offenders. Many revert to their old ways by committing new crimes or violating one or more program requirements.

If a PO reports a parolee or probationer for violating a program rule, then a possibility exists that the offender will eventually retaliate by either threatening the PO or by carrying out aggressive acts. At the same time, the PO has considerable power and can significantly influence the life chances of those supervised. An unfavorable report may mean prison for probationers or a longer term in prison for parolees. Objectivity is required of all POs, although achieving objectivity and detachment in performing the PO role is difficult. Many POs take it personally whenever one of their offenders fails or is returned to prison. They regard offender failure as their own failure. After all, some of these POs entered their profession originally to help others. When their strategies for helping others are apparently ineffective, this failure reflects adversely on their own job performance. Seasoned POs recommend to those entering the field initially not get too friendly with their offender-clients. They must constantly divorce their emotions from their work roles. There is some evidence, however, that POs find this detachment difficult. POs attempt to perform helping functions while simultaneously being enforcers of legal conditions (Jones and Lurigio, 1997).

Women on probation or parole are considered troublesome by many POs (Stephen, 1993). Some POs believe that women take up too much of their time with a variety of what agents consider minor problems. In addition, female clients evidence problems of adjustment related to family, children, and employment. For these and related reasons, women are less likely than men to be reported for anything but the most serious rule infractions. Researchers suggest that POs treat female probationers and parolees differently than males because of their paternalistic beliefs that womens' family-based obligations are more important than mens' (American Correctional Association, 1993c).

Many POs are frustrated because they lack the time and resources to do the kind of job that they believe is maximally helpful to their clients. Because of their increasing caseload responsibilities, POs cannot possibly devote the proper amount of time to any given offender without interfering with their time allocations to other clients. The immense paperwork associated with the PO's role has caused more than few POs to opt for alternative professions. The progress of offenders must be reported regularly to the courts, parole boards, and various agencies, and these reports are tedious to complete. Increased caseloads and work pressures are not only stressful, but they also lead to a reduction in the quality of general services and supervision extended to offender-clients (Read et al., 1997).

One important implication for POs of the reduced quality of client supervision is the increased potential for lawsuits arising from their negligent supervision of clients (Morgan, Belbot, and Clark, 1997). Although POs cannot guarantee public safety completely by their supervision of offenders, it is generally believed that the more intense the supervision, the less likely offenders will commit dangerous offenses. When supervision by POs is less intense, the risk to the public posed by the offender theoretically increases. In a 1986 case, the Alaska Supreme Court ruled that state agencies and their officers may be held liable for **negligence** when probationers and parolees under their supervision commit violent offenses (*Division of Corrections v. Neakok,* 1986). Thus, POs are increasingly at risk through tort actions filed by victims harmed by the crimes committed by their offender-clients (del Carmen, 1990; Wicklund, 1996). The American Correction Association currently conducts seminars and other types of training to make POs more knowledgeable about their personal liabilities, especially if one or more of their clients harm victims while under PO supervision.

A CODE OF ETHICS

Ethical codes have been developed for most professional organizations, and POs abide by a general code of ethics. A **code of ethics** refers to regulations formulated by major professional societies that outline the specific problems and issues frequently encountered by persons who practice the profession. POs are in continuous contact with criminals who are either on probation or parole. Often, POs must make ethical choices that involve moral dilemmas. POs exercise considerable discretion over their clients, and they are expected to exercise their discretion wisely. Thus, they have a responsibility to act properly in controlling individual clients. At the same time, they must balance societal interests against the interests of their clients.

For example, POs are expected to monitor their clients closely and report any infractions of probation or parole programs. Yet, POs have been known to give second and third chances to their clients to help them avoid imprisonment (Jones and Lurigio, 1997:26). Furthermore, depending on how probation officers prepare PSI reports for judges, they can sway the judge toward or against the offender. POs choose what should be entered into PSI reports and on occasion may omit a fact that could seriously affect a convicted offender's freedom. For instance, if the offender used a firearm during the commission of a felony, which would lead to a mandatory period of incarceration, then the PO could omit this fact from the PSI report. Mitigating circumstances, however, may change how the PO views the use of the firearm by the particular offender. POs also work closely with prosecutors and are intimately familiar with the nuances of plea bargaining. Often, prosecutors will reduce charges against criminal suspects in exchange for a guilty plea to a less serious offense. More often than not, the prosecutor will encourage the PO to prepare a PSI report that omits certain factual information that the judge might otherwise consider. With the information included, the judge may not accept the plea agreement and the case might have to be tried before a jury. This outcome is not always desirable for prosecutors. Thus, there is an element of collusion between prosecutors and POs, which for some POs presents an ethical dilemma.

POs who are considered educators and enablers may wish to maintain clients under their supervision in the belief that they can make a difference in their lives. If their clients violate minor program rules, such as curfew, then POs may overlook the violation so as to continue the offender's treatment in counseling or participation in an educational or vocational program.

POs are not supposed to have malicious motives when referring their clients to judges or parole boards for revocation actions. One situation is if a PO reports a program violation to teach the client the importance of obeying program rules. If the PO reports a program violation to the parole board because the offender is black or Hispanic, however, then this action is discriminatory and clearly wrong (Jones and Lurigio, 1997:28). In another situation, if a PO does not violate a probationer or parolee for failing a drug test, then the PO may be facilitating their program success by encouraging them to be law-abiding and refrain from further drug use. The PO may also, however, be enabling the offender's addictive behavior.

The American Probation and Parole Association has evolved a code of ethics for its membership:

1. I will render professional service to the justice system and the community at large in effecting the social adjustment of the offender.
2. I will uphold the law with dignity, displaying an awareness of my responsibility to offenders while recognizing the right of the public to be safe-guarded from criminal activity.
3. I will strive to be objective in the performance of my duties, recognizing the inalienable rights of all persons, appreciating the inherent worth of the individual, and respecting those confidences which can be reposed with me.
4. I will conduct my personal life with decorum, neither accepting nor granting favors in connection with my office.
5. I will cooperate with my co-workers and related agencies and will continually strive to improve my professional competence through the seeking and sharing of knowledge and understanding.
6. I will distinguish clearly, in public, between my statements and actions as an individual and as a representative of my profession.
7. I will encourage policy, procedures, and personnel practices which will enable others to conduct themselves in accordance with the values, goals, and objectives of the American Probation and Parole Association.

8. I recognize my office as a symbol of public faith and I accept it as a public trust to be held as long as I am true to the ethics of the American Probation and Parole Association.

9. I will constantly strive to achieve these objectives and ideals, dedicating myself to my chosen profession (American Probation and Parole Association, 1997).

Federal probation officers have also established an ethical code to abide by when supervising offenders:

1. As a Federal Probation Officer, I am dedicated to rendering professional service to the courts, the parole authorities, and the community at large in effecting the social adjustment of the offender.

2. I will conduct my personal life with decorum, will neither accept nor grant favors in connection with my office, and will put loyalty to moral principles above personal consideration.

3. I will uphold the law with dignity and with complete awareness of the prestige and stature of the judicial system of which I am a part. I will be ever cognizant of my responsibility to the community which I serve.

4. I will strive to be objective in the performance of my duties; respect the inalienable rights of all persons; appreciate the inherent worth of the individual; and hold inviolate those confidences which can be reposed with me.

5. I will cooperate with my fellow workers and related agencies and will continually attempt to improve my professional standards through seeking of knowledge and understanding.

6. I recognize my office as a symbol of public faith and I accept it as a public trust to be held as long as I am true to the ethics of the Federal Probation Service. I will constantly strive to achieve these objectives and ideals, dedicating myself to my chosen profession (Administrative Office of U.S. Courts, 2001).

Marylouise Jones and Arthur Lurigio (1997:29–32) have typified several different kinds of probation/parole officers. They have classified them into punitive officers, welfare officers, passive officers, and synthetic officers.

Punitive Officers. Punitive officers are very dogmatic and orient themselves toward their clients as law enforcement officers. They put societal interests above the interests of their clients. They file petitions to violate their clients' programs with great frequency. The punitive officer seeks to control offender behavior through threats and intimidation.

Welfare Officers. Welfare officers are like social workers in that they focus on treatment and rehabilitation. Such officers focus their attention on advocating, brokering, education, enabling, and mediating. They assist their clients in finding employment and even help them fill out job applications. They consider their roles as largely therapeutic.

Passive Officers. Passive officers care little about the needs of society or their clients. They merely go through the day in a perfunctory way, performing their jobs in minimal ways. Their primary interest is getting through the day, the week, the month, and the year and eventually retiring with full pension and benefits. They seek to advance their own positions within their agencies. They simply follow the rules set forth for them to follow, nothing more, nothing less.

Synthetic Officers.   Synthetic officers are actually a blend of enforcers and social workers. They want very much to supervise their offenders so that they will remain law-abiding. They work closely with police departments. Yet at the same time, they understand the complexities of probationers' and parolees' problems and the limitations of working through those problems. These officers are both humanitarian and justice oriented (Jones and Lurigio, 1997:30–31).

It is unknown how many officers of particular types there are throughout the different state and federal agencies and organizations. All officers share a common bond, however, in that they should be guided by the ethic of care, the central goal of which is to reintegrate offenders into their communities (Jones and Lurigio, 1997:31). Thus, they must continually reevaluate their positions and how they relate with their clients. The PO/client relation is dynamic and ever changing.

PO UNIONIZATION AND COLLECTIVE BARGAINING

Historically, U.S. probation and parole officers have been among the last professional aggregates to organize for the purpose of forming unions and engaging in collective bargaining. A survey of the professional literature found in the source files of *Criminal Justice Abstracts* during the period 1968 to 1999 reveals that 90 percent of all references to unions and collective bargaining relate primarily to police organizations (Champion, 2001). Most of the remaining articles and books on the subject of unions and collective bargaining pertain to correctional officers who are affiliated with prisons and jails. One reason for these early developments and the emphasis on unionization for police officers and correctional staff is that criminal suspects and inmates have been the most volatile aggregates to file lawsuits against specific officers. Often these lawsuits have proved groundless, yet individual officers have had to hire their own defense counsels for the purpose of self-protection against frivolous suits (More, 1998). Through unionization, police officer and correctional officer unions now provide ample funds for defense work when individual officers are sued by citizens or inmates. Another objective of these unions is to secure additional benefits pertaining to working conditions, officer safety, and retirement (Burpo, DeLord, and Shannon, 1997; Philadelphia Police Department, 1998; Zhao and Lovrich, 1997).

During the 1990s, POs organized at local, state, and federal levels to establish collective bargaining mechanisms and unions for common purposes. Virtually every major city and all states today have probation and parole officer unions that represent PO interests. One of the oldest unions is the L.A. (Los Angeles) County Probation Officers Union, an outgrowth of the American Federation of State, County, and Municipal Employees (AFSCME), one of the country's largest public employees' unions. AFSCME, which is affiliated with the AFL-CIO, began as a series of smaller unions during the 1930s. In 1955, the membership of AFSCME numbered 100,000 employees. In 1945, a group of World War II veterans who became employed as probation officers in Los Angeles County in California founded AFSCME Local 685. In 1969, Local 685, under the strong leadership of Henry Fiering, began to fight aggressively for the rights of its employees with the L.A. County Probation Department in all matters concerning wages, hours, benefits, and working conditions, including case-load assignments.

The L.A. County Probation Officers Union is only one of hundreds of local unions across the country today that lobby for the rights and entitlements of POs. In New York, for example, the New York State Probation Officers Association (NYSPOA) was formed during the late 1960s to represent the interests of line officers working in the field of probation. The preamble to the NYSPOA's constitution says that the association, recognizing the need to preserve human dignity through acceptance, empathy, and understanding, advocates the use of those corrective facilities, professions, skills, and rehabilitative procedures that will best protect society through the reduction of crime and delinquency. Over the years, the NYSPOA has strived to write, influence, and support legislative endeavors that would permit probation officers to perform their functions effectively, efficiently, and safely. The NYSPOA works with other professional organizations, such as the American Probation and Parole Association, to further its interests and objectives. The NYSPOA is continually striving to upgrade the quality of professional services rendered by its affiliate officers. In 1991, for instance, an annual conference was proposed to provide low-cost training for interested POs and address their diverse needs.

Probation and parole officer unions also arbitrate and settle grievances, whether they are generated by probationers or parolees or by POs themselves. In some instances, grievances pertain to the pay POs should receive for overtime they engage in while supervising their clients. For instance, a New Jersey county settled a grievance originating from New Jersey PO supervisors who had been given additional supervisory responsibilities to supervise other POs. The pay differential was 94 cents per hour, and the county balked at paying the additional hourly wage. The union representing the POs arbitrated a settlement, however, with the county paying over $5,800 owed to PO supervisors.

Salary increases at fixed rates are also negotiated by unions through collective bargaining. In one county, for example, a cost-of-living pay raise was negotiated at 4 percent for January 1998, 3 percent for January 1999, 3 percent for January 2000, and 2 percent for January 2001. If POs in this particular county should be promoted, demoted, or transferred, contract provisions call for salary adjustments to levels consistent with the salary range held prior to the promotion, transfer, or demotion.

At the city level, probation and parole unions are having a more significant voice and power over the lives of affiliate POs. In Portland, Oregon, for instance, the city council has recognized the Parole and Probation Employees' Association (PPEA) to represent its membership as a collective bargaining unit. Some issues negotiated include caseloads, working hours, compensation for overtime, confidentiality issues, PSI report preparation time, fringe benefits relating to vacations, and retirement. Regarding caseloads, the Department of Corrections has alleged that POs have caseloads of 8 per PO under ISP programs and 50 per PO under standard supervision. The PPEA has alleged, however, that standard caseloads are closer to 100 clients per PO. A PPEA representative said that because of the sheer volume of cases, "we've become a bunch of desk-bound pencil pushers" (Probation and Parole Employees' Association, 2001:2). One issue of importance to POs in the PPEA is whether POs should be permitted to possess and carry firearms during the performance of their work tasks. A bill was before the Oregon legislature in early 2001 to authorize firearms use by POs, including an appropriate amount of firearms safety training. These issues illustrate the types of problems unions attempt to resolve for their memberships.

Probation and parole officer unions are not unique to the United States. For instance, there are probation and parole officer unions in Canada and other countries. In Ontario, Canada, the Probation Officers Association of Ontario, Inc. (POAO), is committed to the following objectives:

1. To speak with credibility on issues in criminal justice
2. To facilitate increased understanding of the specialized role of the probation officer
3. To provide representative perspectives on legislative issues to policy makers
4. To provide a forum for an exchange of professional experience and opinion
5. To promote good fellowship and esprit de corps among members
6. To foster good will, understanding, and cooperation with others working in the criminal justice system
7. To educate and involve the community in corrections

The POAO expects its membership to subscribe to the following values:

1. That Probation Officers achieve professional status and continue to receive on ongoing education
2. That its members are fully committed to a code of ethics
3. That community corrections programs retain their validity as an effective means of rehabilitation for offenders
4. That autonomy be maintained, while at the same time the responsibilities of the ministries, OPSEU, and other components of the criminal justice system be acknowledged
5. That involvement in the decision-making process be democratic and participatory at all levels

More than 600 probation and parole officers who supervise more than 60,000 offenders in the community belong to the POAO. POs supervise probation orders, parole, conditional sentences, and conditional supervision orders. They monitor and enforce compliance with these court orders and others such as restitution to victims and community service orders. These professionals prepare detailed and comprehensive presentence investigation reports and predispositional reports for juveniles. Preparole reports are also prepared for the Ontario Board of Parole.

SUMMARY

Both adult and juvenile corrections has escalated during the last few decades. POs have assumed increased responsibilities and supervisory tasks in dealing with an increasingly diverse and dangerous clientele. In 2001, there were over 630,000 personnel working in corrections, with about 60 percent of these working in probation and parole services. The functions of probation and parole services are to supervise offenders; ensure offender compliance with program goals and provisions; conduct routine alcohol and drug checks; provide networking services for employment assistance; direct offender-clients to proper treatment, counseling, and other forms of assistance; protect the community by detecting a client's program infractions and reporting them to judges or parole boards; assisting offenders in becoming integrated into their communities; and engaging in any useful rehabilitative enterprise that will improve offender-client skills.

The organization and administration of probation and parole services is most often within the scope of a state's department of corrections. Services vary among the states, although some elements to all probation and parole services and programs are common. The complexity of organizational structure is highly dependent on the nature of clientele supervised and their special needs. The rehabilitative aim of corrections has not been particularly successful. For this and other reasons, probation and parole departments have drawn extensive criticism from an increasingly discontent public, focusing on the lack of skills and training of POs and the ineffectiveness of their performance. Professionalization through organizations such as the American Correctional Association and the American Probation and Parole Association has attempted to raise standards relating to the selection, recruitment, and training of POs throughout the nation.

In 2001, POs averaged $23,000 as an entry-level salary, whereas top PO positions reached $93,400. Few jurisdictions required a bachelor's degree for PO work, yet a majority of POs had some college education or had completed college. Increased education is the primary means for improving one's professionalization. Observers suggest that there is a high correlation between higher education achieved and work effectiveness among POs. Because of an increasingly ethnically and racially diverse clientele, POs have received additional training in cultural diversity. Some POs are recruited for dealing with special offender populations in which English is a second language.

One important issue being raised in greater numbers of jurisdictions is whether POs should carry firearms. About half the states authorized the use of firearms for POs in 1999. Other states without such provisions were considering legislation in 2001. There is a controversy over whether POs should be armed. Some persons feel that armed POs tend to provoke their clients, whereas others see being armed as a reasonable means of self-protection, particularly if POs must enter dangerous, gang-controlled neighborhoods to visit their clients. A hazard of PO work is the lawsuit syndrome, whereby clients sue POs for various reasons. Thus, a part of PO training is designed to acquaint POs with the conditions and situations most likely to result in lawsuits, thus avoiding or minimizing the potential for lawsuits. POs are continually subjected to periodic evaluations to determine their competence in job performance. Labor turnover among POs averages about 15 percent per year. Most POs who leave the profession tend to seek better jobs in the private sector or graduate to federal employment, with pay and benefits substantially greater than state compensation.

Another important issue is the matter of caseloads, or the number of clients managed by POs in any state or federal agency. POs supervise offenders either intensively or generally, depending on the programs imposed by judges and parole boards. No precise figures have been agreed upon as to what constitutes an optimum caseload size for POs. There are different caseload assignment models, such as the conventional model, the numbers game model, the conventional model with geographic considerations, and the specialized caseloads model. Officer/client interactions are affected by different factors, including the orientations of POs toward offenders. Some of these orientations are detectors, brokers, enablers, educators, mediators, and enforcers. Depending on a PO's orientation, interactions with clients are positively or negatively influenced. Some amount of role conflict therefore exists, as POs attempt to perform their jobs under different sets of circumstances established by each jurisdiction. Most POs belong to one or more organizations in which codes of ethics have been promulgated. These codes obligate POs to adhere to stringent behavioral guidelines in the performance of their jobs. It is expected that PO adherence to these codes of ethics will eventually improve their effectiveness and job performance and that, ultimately, client recidivism will decline.

Probation and parole officers have formed unions and engage in collective bargaining in all states. Many of these unions are at local, county, and state levels, and all unionization is designed to achieve better conditions for POs. Issues involve pay, retirement benefits, caseloads and assignments, promotional opportunities, and various types of grievances about the job and its benefits. Each union has articulated objectives. Union representatives are authorized to negotiate contracts with city, county, state, and federal governments to determine pay scales, working hours and conditions, and other matters of relevance to their memberships. Unions also attempt to improve the quality of professionalism among their memberships by sponsoring annual conferences at which workshops are conducted to learn various skills. All union members are encouraged to improve their skills on a regular basis to promote their own interests within their respective probation or parole agencies.

KEY TERMS

Assessment center
Balanced approach
Broker
Caseload
Caseworker
Civil Rights Act
Code of ethics
Conventional model

Conventional model with geographic considerations
Detector
Educator
Enabler
Enforcer
Florida Assessment Center
Florida community control program (FCCP)

Labor turnover
Mediator
Negligence
Numbers game model
Professionalization
Role conflict
Specialized caseloads model
Stress

QUESTIONS FOR REVIEW

1. What are some functions and goals of probation and parole services?
2. Are all probation and parole agencies organized in the same way? What are some reasons for different organizational arrangements?
3. What are several criticisms of probation and parole programs?
4. What are some of the major duties and responsibilities of POs?
5. Identify and describe four types of caseload assignment methods.
6. What is meant by the professionalization of probation and parole?
7. What are some arguments for and against the use of firearms by POs during the performance of their tasks? What proportion of the states authorized firearms for their POs in 1999?
8. How is negligence established in PO training? What are some of the bases for lawsuits filed against POs?
9. What are some of the key orientations of POs toward their clients? How do each of these orientations influence officer/client interactions?
10. What are codes of ethics? Why are they important? How do codes of ethics influence how POs perform their work?

SUGGESTED READINGS

Finn, Peter (1999). "Correctional Officer Stress: A Cause for Concern and Additional Help." *Federal Probation* **62:**65–74.

Hemmens, Craig, and Mary K. Stohr (eds.) (2000). "Ethics in Corrections." *Prison Journal* **80:**123–222.

Simmons, Calvin, John K. Cochran, and William R. Blount (1997). "The Effects of Job-Related Stress and Job Satisfaction on Probation Officers' Inclinations to Quit." *American Journal of Criminal Justice* **21:**213–229.

Torres, Sam, and Robert M. Latta (2000). "Selecting the Substance Abuse Specialist." *Federal Probation* **64:**46–50.

Probation and Parole Officer
Roles and Responsibilities

CHAPTER 10

Introduction
Probation and Parole: Risk/Needs Assessments
  Assessing Offender Risk: A Brief History
  Classification and Its Functions
  Types of Risk Assessment Instruments
  The Effectiveness of Risk Assessment Devices
  Some Applications of Risk/Needs Measures
  Selective Incapacitation
The Changing Probation/Parole Officer Role
Apprehension Units
Gang Units
Research Units
Stress and Burnout in Probation/Parole Officer
  Role Performance
  Stress

Burnout
  Sources of Stress
  Mitigating Factors to Alleviate Stress and
  Burnout
Volunteers in Probation/Parole Work
  Criticisms of Volunteers in Correctional
  Work
Paraprofessionals in Probation/Parole Work
  Roles of Paraprofessionals
  Legal Liabilities of Volunteers
  and Paraprofessionals
Summary
Key Terms
Questions for Review
Suggested Readings

INTRODUCTION

This chapter examines the changing role of probation and parole officers. There are serious concerns throughout the correctional community about whether POs are peace officers or police officers. PO responsibilities include supervising dangerous clients and ensuring that they comply with their probation or parole program requirements. One of the first things POs attempt is to ascertain the degree of risk posed by the offenders they supervise. The first part of this chapter examines the assessment of offender risk, and several risk measures are presented. Because POs are expected to assist their clients as well as monitor their behaviors, some of these instruments attempt to determine offender needs as well. For POs to network and coordinate the most appropriate community services as interventions on a client's behalf, it is very important that an offender's needs be defined.

PO work is increasingly specialized. Some offenders who are freed on probation or parole abscond or leave their jurisdictions without PO permission and cannot be immediately be located. As a result, many probation and parole agencies have established apprehension units to track down absconders and return them to their jurisdictions. If absconders are located and returned, then they face possible probation or parole program revocation. Therefore, it is dangerous to be a part of apprehension units and hunt fugitives who want to avoid capture.

Gangs, thousands of which exist throughout the United States, are a pervasive part of society. Gangs are common in prisons and jails as well as on city streets. Therefore, it is essential that POs familiarize themselves with gang recognition signs and symbols. Often, particular neighborhoods in which their clients reside are gang-dominated. Thus, an element of danger exists merely during the act of checking up on a PO's clients. The gang phenomenon is examined to the extent that it influences PO work and how POs do their jobs, especially when a portion of one's probationer- or parolee-clients are gang members. Probation and parole agencies also have research units whose task it is to study client profiles and devise new and improved supervision procedures, and some of the activities of these research units are described.

PO work is stressful. There are numerous demands on these officers, including their work for criminal courts and their supervision of dangerous clientele. The stresses of PO work are examined, including a discussion of possible sources of stress. Stress often leads to burnout, which in turn causes POs to become less effective in their work performance. Burnout is also examined, including a discussion of how it is assessed. Several solutions to alleviate stress and burnout are proposed.

The final part of this chapter examines the roles of volunteers and paraprofessionals who often assist with offender management in a variety of ways. **Volunteers** are unsalaried workers. They are often found working with offenders in halfway houses, helping them to fill out job applications and teaching. Usually, volunteers have no legal training or qualifications that authorize them to direct probationers or parolees in their required programming by the court or parole board. Nevertheless, they perform several valuable services for probation and parole departments and officers. Paraprofessionals have some amount of formal training working with offenders. Many paraprofessionals have college degrees in disciplines that complement probation and parole work, such as criminal justice, sociology, political science, psychology, or social work. Their roles are also described in this chapter. Finally, because volunteers and paraprofessionals are not as well trained as regular POs, they are unusually vulnerable to legal liabilities of different kinds. They may give offenders the wrong type of advice, or they may give illegal assistance to offenders without the knowledge that what they are doing is wrong. Thus, the legal liabilities of these volunteers and paraprofessionals are examined and discussed.

PROBATION AND PAROLE: RISK/NEEDS ASSESSMENTS

Assessing Offender Risk: A Brief History

Many **risk assessment** measures have been devised, and they are used largely for the purpose of determining probabilities that offender-clients will engage in dangerous or maladjusted behaviors (Bjorkly, Havik, and Loberg, 1996). These probabilities are subsequently used for placement, program, and security decision making (Wicharaya, 1995). Needs measures and instruments enable corrections personnel and administrative staffs to highlight client weaknesses or problems that may have led to their convictions or difficulties initially. Once problem areas have been targeted, specific services or treatments may be scheduled and provided. Various Christian Reform movements have been credited with establishing an early prisoner **classification system** in the eighteenth century (American Correctional Association, 1983:194). Behavioral scientists, especially psychiatrists and psychologists, who conducted research during the period of 1910 to 1920 found that custody-level placements of inmates as well as other program assignments could be made by using certain psychological characteristics as predictors (American Correctional Association, 1983:196).

Criminologists and criminal justice scholars have become increasingly involved in devising risk assessment inventories and needs indices, using combinations of psychological, social, socioeconomic, and demographic factors and related criteria to make dangerousness forecasts and behavioral predictions. Formal, paper-and-pencil risk and needs instruments began to proliferate during the 1960s (Champion, 1994). Some of this instrumentation was used with juvenile offenders. Later, numerous behavioral and psychological instruments were devised and used for the purpose of assessing client risk or inmate dangerousness. The Minnesota Multiphasic Personality Inventory (MMPI), consisting of 550 true-false items, was originally used in departments of corrections for personality assessments. Although this instrument is still applied in many correctional settings, some researchers, such as Edwin Megargee, have extracted certain items from the MMPI for use as predictors of inmate violence and adjustment. The use of **classification** devices such as Megargee's are often designated as MMPI-based assessments or classifications. Applications of scales such as Megargee's have received mixed results and evaluations. In at least some studies, such scales have demonstrably low reliability (Bohn, Carbonell, and Megargee, 1995).

Herbert Quay's work preceded the work of Megargee (Quay and Parsons, 1971). Quay devised a relatively simple typology of delinquent behavior, classifying delinquents into four categories: undersocialized aggression, socialized aggression, attention deficit, and anxiety-withdrawal-dysphoria. Juveniles would complete a self-administered questionnaire, and their personality scores would be quickly tabulated. Different treatments would be administered to help particular juveniles, depending on how they were depicted and classified. Later, Quay devised a scale that he called AIMS, or the Adult Internal Management System (Quay, 1984). Again, Quay used a self-administered inventory, the Correctional Adjustment Checklist and the Correctional Adjustment Life History. His adult typology consisted of five types of inmates: aggressive psychopathic, manipulative, situational, inadequate-dependent, and neurotic-anxious. Another system is the I-Level Classification, referring to the Interpersonal Maturity Level Classification System. This system, originally devised by C. Sullivan, M. Q. Grant, and J. D. Grant (1957), is based on a mixture of developmental and psychoanalytic theories and is administered by psychologists or psychiatrists in lengthy clinical interviews. Clients are classified as being at particular "I-levels," such as I-1, I-2, and so on, up to I-7. Each I-level is a developmental stage reflecting one's ability to cope with complex personal and interpersonal problems. The higher the I-level, the better adjusted the client.

Not until the 1980s, however, did state corrections departments begin to create and apply risk assessment schemes with some regularity and in correctional areas beyond the institutional setting (Virginia Commission on Sentencing and Parole Reform, 1995). For example, Arizona created its first Offender Classification System manual in 1986 (Arizona Department of Corrections, 1991). Instrumentation for risk assessment was established in Illinois in the mid-1980s. Tennessee sought requests for proposals in 1987 to devise risk measures for its inmate population. Missouri introduced a variation of AIMS for use in its Department of Corrections in 1988. Many jurisdictions are currently revising or have recently revised their risk and needs instruments (Campbell, 1995). Iowa's Risk/Needs Classification System was implemented in December, 1983 and revised extensively in 1992 (Iowa Department of Correctional Services, 1992). The Iowa Department of Corrections Reassessment of Client Risk is shown in Figure 10.1.

Classification and Its Functions

1. Classification systems enable authorities to make decisions about appropriate offender program placements.
2. Classification systems help identify one's needs and the provision of effective services in specialized treatment programs.
3. Classification assists in determining one's custody level if confined in either prisons or jails.
4. Classification helps adjust one's custody level during confinement, considering behavioral improvement and evidence of rehabilitation.
5. While confined, inmates may be targeted for particular services and/or programs to meet their needs.
6. Classification may be used for offender management and deterrence relative to program or prison rules and requirements.
7. Classification schemes are useful for policy decision making and administrative planning relevant for jail and prison construction, the nature and number of facilities required, and the types of services to be made available within such facilities.
8. Classification systems enable parole boards to make better early-release decisions about eligible offenders.
9. Community corrections agencies can use classification schemes to determine those parolees who qualify for participation and those who do not.
10. Classification systems enable assessments of risk and dangerousness to be made generally in anticipation of the type of supervision best suited for particular offenders.
11. Classification schemes assist in decision making relevant for community crime control, the nature of penalties to be imposed, and the determination of punishment.
12. Classification may enable authorities to determine whether selective incapacitation is desirable for particular offenders or offender groupings.

The terms *dangerousness* and *risk* are often used interchangeably; they both convey propensities to cause harm to others or oneself. What is the likelihood that any particular offender will be violent toward others? Does an offender pose any risk to public safety? What is the likelihood that any particular offender will commit suicide or attempt it? Risk (or dangerousness) instruments are screening devices intended to distinguish between different types of offenders for purposes of determining initial institutional classification, security placement and inmate management, early release eligibility, and the level of supervision required under conditions of probation or parole (Krauss et al., 2000). Most state jurisdictions and the federal government refer to these measures as risk instruments rather than dangerousness instruments. There is considerable variance among states regarding the format and content of such measures. An example of one of the less elaborate versions of a risk assessment instrument is one used by the Massachusetts Parole Board illustrated in Figure 10.2.

IOWA DEPARTMENT OF CORRECTIONS REASSESSMENT OF CLIENT RISK

Client Name_____ICBC#_____
        Last   First   Middle

Date of Reassessment_____ Officer's Name_____

Offense_____

INSTRUCTIONS: SCORE ITEMS AND ADD TOTAL SCORE.   **SCORE**

1. Age at first Adult Conviction/Juvenile Adjudication (include deferreds)
   - 24 or older = -2 [ ]
   - 20 to 23 = 0 [ ]
   - 19 or younger = 1 [ ]

2. Prior Juvenile Commitments
   - None = 0 [ ]
   - One or more = 2 [ ]

3. Prior Probations/Parole Supervisions (Adult/Juvenile Adjudications)
   - None = 0 [ ]
   - One or more = 2 [ ]

4. Number of Prior Probation/Parole Revocations (Adult/Juvenile Adjudications)
   - None = 0 [ ]
   - One or more = 2 [ ]

5. Felony/Misdemeanor Convictions (include present offense, deferreds, juvenile adjudications); Circle applicable and add for score. Do not exceed a total of 3.
   - Burglary or Robbery = 1 [ ]
   - Theft, Forgery, FUFI, Fraudulent Practices = 1
   - Assault, Weapons Public Order Offenses = 1

6. Misdemeanor Conviction History (Simple & Serious Misdemeanors Only); Include present offense, deferreds & Juvenile Adjudications.
   - None = 0 [ ]
   - None or one = 0
   - Two or more = 1 [ ]

7. Sex
   - Female = 0
   - Male = 1 [ ]

8. Alcohol Usage Problems
   - No interference = 0
   - Occasional abuse = 1
   - Frequent abuse = 2 [ ]

9. Drug Usage Problems
   - No interference = 0
   - Occasional abuse = 1
   - Frequent abuse = 2 [ ]

*10. **Employment** Satisfactory
    one year or longer = -2
    Secure or not applicable = 0
    Unsatisfactory or
    Unemployed, unemployable = 2 [ ]

(continued)

FIGURE 10.1 Iowa reassessment instrument.

```
*11. Companions No adverse
     relationships                =    0
     Associations occasionally
     negative                     =    1
     Associations almost
     completely
     negative                     =    2  [     ]
*12. Problems with Current
     Living Situation Relatively
     stable relationships
     and/or address               =    0
     Moderate disorganization
     or stress                    =    1
     Major disorganization/
     stress                       =    2  [     ]
*13. Response to Supervision
     Conditions No problems of
     consequence                  =    0
     Moderate compliance problem  =    1
     Frequently unwilling to
     comply                       =    3  [     ]
*14. New Arrests None            =    0
     One or more arrests          =    3  [     ]
*15. Use of Community Resources
     Not needed                   =    0
     Productively utilized        =    0
     Needed, but not available    =    1
     Utilized, but not beneficial =    2
     Client rejected referral     =    3  [     ]
```

```
     TOTAL SCORE                          [     ]
```

Clients are assigned to the highest level of supervision indicated on the following scale:

Risk

```
31 to 15   Intensive
14 to  8   Normal
 7 to  2   Minimum
 1 to -5   Administrative
```

Levels of Supervision

```
1 Intensive
2 Normal
3 Minimum
4 Administrative
```

FIGURE 10.1 *(continued)*

<u>Reason for Override</u>

0 Assaultive offense
1 Severity of offense
2 Special conditions set by parole board, court, or district
3 Client not available for active supervision
4 Force field indicates high needs

5 Other _____

_____

_____

_____

_____

_____

_____

Comments_____

_____

_____

_____

_____

Level   [   ]

Revised Level   [   ]

Override reason code [   ]

_____

Override approval/date

      In addition, needs assessment devices are instruments that measure an offender's personal and social skills, health well-being and emotional stability, educational level and vocational strengths and weaknesses, alcohol and drug dependencies, mental ability, and other relevant life factors and that highlight those areas for which services are available and could or should be provided (Wilson et al., 2000). Needs assessment devices, measures, scales, or inventories identify the types of services offenders might require if incarcerated (Hoffman, 1994). Illiterate offenders may be placed, either voluntarily or involuntarily, into an educational program at

MASSACHUSETTS PAROLE BOARD
Release Risk Classification Instrument

Name: _____ MCI-Number: _____

SID: _____ Actual Release Date: _____

Hearing Location: _____ Hearing Date: _____

Completed By: _____ Completion Date: _____

Controlling Effective Date of Commitment: _____

1. Number of returns to higher custody since the Controlling Effective Date of Commitment (Count all revocations, returns from escape and probation surrenders):	0 = 0 points 1 = 2 points 2, 3 = 4 points 4 or more = 6 points	[ ]
2. Custody standing prior to the Controlling Effective Date of Commitment:	Not under custody = 0 points On street supervision = 1 point Incarceration = 2 points	[ ]
3. Total number of parole revocations on prior state sentences:	None = 0 points 1 or more = 1 point	[ ]
4. Number of adult convictions for property offenses prior to the Controlling Effective Date of Commitment:	None = 0 points 1 or more = 1 point	[ ]
5. Number of charges for a person offense as a juvenile:	None = 0 points 1 or more = 1 point	[ ]
6. Age at release hearing:	34 or older = 0 points 28–33 = 2 points 24–27 = 4 points 23 or younger = 6 points	[ ]
7. Evidence of heroin, cocaine, or crack cocaine use: Notes (verbal admission): _____	No = 0 points Yes = 2 points	[ ]

_____

8. SCORE: Add the numerical scores of questions 1 through 7 and enter the total score in this box.   [ ]

SCORING: A score between 0–4 = Low Risk; 5–10 = Moderate Risk; 11 or more = High Risk

FIGURE 10.2 Massachusetts Parole Board release risk classification instrument.

some level, depending on the amount of remedial work deemed necessary (Bjorkly, Havik, and Loberg, 1996). Psychologically disturbed or mentally ill offenders may require some type of counseling or therapy (Silver, 2000). Some offenders may require particular medications for illnesses or other maladies. Sometimes instruments are designed in such a way so as to assess both needs and risk. Figure 10.3 shows the Kansas Department of Corrections risk and needs assessment coding form for assessing the future conduct and needs of parolees.

Risk and need assessments may also be referred to jointly and contained in a longer inventory or measure, labeled a risk/needs assessment. An inspection of these devices and the individual items included within them will indicate which factors seem to have the greatest priority and predictive utility. The offender needs assessment inventory shown in Figure 10.3 also assigns greater or lesser weight to different items that focus on various dimensions of one's life. Those areas having the largest number of potential points assigned include employment, emotional stability, and alcohol usage, with possible large scores of 5, 6, and 5, respectively. All other items, including academic/vocational skills, financial status, other substance abuse, mental ability, health, living arrangements, sexual behavior, and the officer's impression of a client's needs, have a largest weight of 4 or less. Interpretive tables are consulted to determine, based on one's cumulative score, the level of needs and types of needs that should be addressed with one or more services. These services might include alcohol or drug abuse treatment programs, vocational/educational training, employment counseling, or individual/group therapy (Motiuk, Belcourt, and Bonta, 1995). Those areas most indicative of one's greatest weaknesses or needs are typically those with the largest score.

Types of Risk Assessment Instruments

Three basic categories of risk classifications have been identified (Morris and Miller, 1985:13–14): anamnestic prediction, actuarial prediction, and clinical prediction.

1. Anamnestic prediction is a prediction of offender behavior according to past circumstances. The circumstances are similar now; therefore, it is likely that the offender will behave the same way now. For example, a presentence investigation report may show that an offender was alcohol- and drug-dependent, unemployed, inclined toward violence because of previous assault incidents, and poorly educated. Recidivists convicted of new crimes may experience present circumstances similar to those that prevailed when they were convicted of their earlier offense. Thus, judges and others might rely heavily on the situational similarity of past and present circumstances to measure offender risk. If some offenders have made a significant effort between convictions to obtain additional education or training for better job performance or if they are no longer alcohol- or drug-dependent, however, other types of behavioral forecasts will have to be made because different circumstances exist.

2. Actuarial prediction is based on the characteristics of a class of offenders similar to offenders being considered for probation, parole, or inmate classification. Considering others like them, situated as they are, shows how they behaved in the past; therefore, it is likely that those persons who exhibit similar characteristics to the general class of offenders considered for these different sanctioning and classification options will behave in ways similar to that particular class. In effect, this method is an aggregate predictive tool. For instance, given a large sample of persons placed on probation and tracked over a two-year period, it is determined that 65 percent of these

Kansas Department of Corrections

Parolee Risk and Needs Assessment Coding Form

Name _____

Number _____

Assessment Date

| MO | DA | YR |

Type of Assessment _____

Action Code: [ ]

District [ ]

PO NO. _____

Risk Assessment

Pts	Item	Code
[ ]	1. Severity Level I Offense	[ ]
[ ]	2. # Prior Periods Prob/Par Sup	[ ]
[ ]	3. Attitude	[ ]
[ ]	4. Age 1st Felony Conviction	[ ]
[ ]	5. # Prior Felony Convictions	[ ]
[ ]	6. Convictions/Certain Offenses	[ ]
[ ]	7. # Prior Prob/Par Revocations	[ ]
[ ]	8. Alcohol Usage Problems	[ ]
[ ]	9. Other Drug Usage	[ ]
[ ]	10. # Address Changes	[ ]
[ ]	11. % Time Employed	[ ]
[ ]	12. Social Identification	[ ]
[ ]	13. Problem Interpersonal Rel.	[ ]
[ ]	14. Use of Community Resources	[ ]
[ ]	15. Response to Supervision	[ ]
[ ]	16. Risk Total	[ ]

Needs Assessment

Pts	Item	Code
[ ]	17. Academic/Vocational	[ ]
[ ]	18. Employment	[ ]
[ ]	19. Financial Management	[ ]
[ ]	20. Marital/Family	[ ]
[ ]	21. Companions	[ ]
[ ]	22. Emotional Stability	[ ]
[ ]	23. Alcohol Usage	[ ]
[ ]	24. Other Drug Usage	[ ]
[ ]	25. Mental Ability	[ ]
[ ]	26. Health	[ ]
[ ]	27. Sexual Behavior	[ ]
[ ]	28. Officer Impression	[ ]
[ ]	29. Needs Total	[ ]

Decision

		Code
	30. Supervision Determination	[ ]
	31. Override	[ ]
	32. Supervision Level Assigned	[ ]
	33. Next Assessment Date _____ MO _____ YR	

ASSESSMENT COMPLETED BY: Signature

Distribution
Original—Data Entry
Copy—PO File
Copy—Deputy Secretary If Override Required

May 20, 1988 (Amended)

FIGURE 10.3 Kansas Department of Corrections parolee risk and needs assessment coding form.

probationers did not complete their probationary periods satisfactorily. These failures are described as predominantly young, black, unemployed or underemployed, lacking a high school education, victims of child abuse, and drug-dependent. Now, whenever young, black, unemployed, less educated, drug-dependent, former child-abuse victims are considered for probation, parole, inmate classification, or some intermediate sanctioning option, their chances of being placed in one program or another, or of being classified one way or another, may be influenced greatly by the general characteristics of previous program failures. Interestingly, it seems that program failures are more often described and used to structure risk instruments than are program successes (Grann, Belfrage, and Tengstrom, 2000).

3. Clinical prediction is based on the predictor's professional training and experience working directly with the offender. Based on extensive diagnostic examinations, the belief is that the offender will behave in a certain way. The subjectivity inherent in clinical prediction is apparent. The skills of the assessor are prominent. Such prediction, however, is more expensive, because each clinical prediction is individualized. Both anamnestic and actuarial prediction use, respectively, situational factors and general characteristics of offenders in forecasting their future risk. Interestingly, the highest degrees of validity are associated with actuarial and anamnestic predictions (for instance, those currently used by parole boards), and they are considered very reliable. Predictors in clinical predictions are usually psychiatrists or psychologists with extensive clinical training and experience with deviant conduct and criminal behavior (Prins, 1999). Some research has found that actuarial prediction is superior in its predictive utility compared with clinical prediction (Gardner et al., 1996).

Any prediction tools used and any claims about their validity, reliability, and/or the recommendations concerning their applicability to specific offender situations are subject to certain limitations (Dillingham et al., 1999). For instance, Norval Morris and Marc Miller (1985:35–37) have suggested three guiding principles for parole boards to consider when making early-release decisions:

1. Punishment should not be imposed, nor the term of punishment extended, by virtue of a prediction of dangerousness, beyond that which would be justified as a deserved punishment independently of that prediction.
2. Provided this limitation is respected, predictions of dangerousness may properly influence sentencing decisions and other decisions under criminal law.
3. The base expectancy rate of violence for the criminal predicted as dangerous must be shown by reliable evidence to be substantially higher than the base expectancy rate of another criminal with a closely similar criminal record and convicted of a closely similar crime but not predicted as unusually dangerous, before the greater dangerousness of the former may be relied on to intensify or extend his or her punishment.

Judges and especially probation officers are also interested in behavioral prediction. The PSI report prepared for any offender sometimes contains a recommendation for some form of probation or incarceration (American Correctional Association, 1994), based on the probation officer's belief that the offender will either be a good risk or a poor risk for probation. Such a recommendation is behavioral prediction. **Prediction** means an assessment of some expected future behavior of a person, including criminal acts, arrests, or convictions. Predictions of future criminal behavior date back to ancient times, although our concern here is with contemporary developments and the current state-of-the-art prediction and assessment devices. Assessments of offender risk have been devised by most departments of corrections throughout the United States. Iowa, Kansas, and Massachusetts are only a few of the states that have devised such instruments. Several important and desirable characteristics of these instruments have been outlined:

1. The model should be predictively valid.
2. The model should reflect reality.
3. The model should be designed for a dynamic system and not remain fixed over time.
4. The model should serve practical purposes.
5. The model should not be a substitute for good thinking and responsible judgment.
6. The model should be both qualitative and quantitative. (Rans, 1984:50)

The paroling authority next consults a table of offense characteristics consisting of categories varying in offense severity. Adult ranges in numbers of months served are provided for each category and are cross-tabulated with the four-category parole prognosis above. Thus, a parole board can theoretically apply a consistent set of standards to prisoners committing similar offenses. When the board departs from these standards, especially when parole is possible for an offender but is denied, a written rationale is provided for both the prisoner and appellate authorities. An inmate also has the right to appeal the decision of the parole board to a higher authority such as the National Appeals Board (18 U.S.C., Sec. 4215, 2001). Consistency is highly desirable in the application of any parole criteria. Many inmate lawsuits involve allegations of inconsistent application of parole eligibility guidelines.

The Effectiveness of Risk Assessment Devices

Current efforts to develop classification schemes to predict offender future behavior remain at best an unstable business. This criticism applies to both adult and juvenile risk assessment measures that are currently applied (Fagan and Guggenheim, 1996). Risk assessment devices developed and used in one state are often not applicable to offenders in other states. In some states such as Massachusetts, risk assessment instruments are used by probation officers to decide which probationers should be supervised with varying frequency. Results were favorable (i.e., lower recidivism rates were observed) when certain high-risk offenders received greater supervision by probation officers compared with high-risk offenders not receiving greater supervision.

Two important questions in designing any instrument to predict future criminal conduct are Which factors are most relevant in such predictions? and What weight should be given each of these factors? The answers are not known for sure. One recurring criticism of prediction studies and the development of risk assessment instruments is that much work is needed on the definition and measurement of criteria (Gottfredson and Gottfredson, 1990). All the instruments now developed are not worthless as predictors of success on probation or parole, but perhaps these measures are imperfect. Therefore, it may be premature to rely exclusively on instrument scores to decide who goes to prison and who receives probation. In many jurisdictions, however, risk assessment scores are used precisely for this purpose (Cuvelier and Potts, 1993).

Some Applications of Risk/Needs Measures

Several of the many potential applications of **risk/needs instruments** and measures have already been discussed. One convenient way of highlighting the most common applications of these instruments by the different states is to examine their own utilization criteria and objectives. The following state utilization criteria are not intended to represent *all* other states or to typify them; rather, they have been highlighted because of their diversity of objectives. For example, Iowa's Classification Risk Assessment Scale is used for the following purposes:

1. Program planning
2. Budgeting and deployment of resources
3. Evaluating services, programs, procedures, and performances
4. Measuring the potential impact of legislative and policy changes
5. Enhancing accountability through standardization
6. Equitably distributing the workload
7. Improving service delivery to clients (Iowa Department of Correctional Services, 1992:6)

These goals for Iowa are couched in the context of initial placement decisions and are closely related to management objectives, including allocating scarce resources most profitably in view of system constraints. Theoretically, if the system's processual features are optimized, then offender management is also. Presumably, the quality of services available to offender-clients would also be improved. Yet, as seen, risk assessments serve some purposes. For instance, the Ohio Parole Board uses a guideline system for determining early releases of certain offenders through parole or furlough. This system incorporates a risk assessment instrument and has the following objectives:

1. To provide for public protection by not releasing those inmates who represent a high risk of repeating violent or other serious crimes
2. To provide an appropriate continuum of sanctions for crime
3. To cooperate with correctional management in providing safe, secure, and humane conditions in state correctional institutions
4. To recognize the achievement of those inmates with special identifiable problems relating to their criminal behavior who have participated in institutional programs designed to alleviate their problems
5. To make the decision-making process of the Adult Parole Authority more open, equitable, and understandable both to the public and to the inmate. (Ohio Parole Board, 1992:2)

The parole board guideline system objectives of Ohio differ substantially from those of Iowa. The Ohio risk assessment objectives are more offender-oriented, with emphases on the appropriateness of sanctions and identifying offender-client needs that may be met by particular services (Escoto et al., 1995). There are also greater concerns for public safety and greater community comprehension of the parole decision-making process. Most states distinguish between offender evaluations for the purpose of determining their *institutional risk* and their public risk. Again, the device contents are often identical or very similar. An examination of the utilization criteria for other state risk assessment devices yields similar diversity of instrument goals. These diverse objectives can be grouped according to several general applications. Thus, for most states, the following general applications are made of risk assessment instruments at different client-processing stages:

1. To promote better program planning through optimum budgeting and deployment of resources
2. To target high-risk and high-need offenders for particular custody levels, programs, and services without endangering the safety of others
3. To apply the fair and appropriate sanctions to particular classes of offenders and raise their level of accountability
4. To provide mechanisms for evaluating services and programs as well as service and program improvements over time
5. To maximize public safety as well as public understanding of the diverse functions of corrections by making decision making more open and comprehensible to both citizens and offender-clients (Champion, 1994)

Selective Incapacitation

Selective incapacitation is incarcerating certain offenders deemed high risks to public safety and not incarcerating other offenders determined to be low risks, given similar offenses. Selective incapacitation applies to certain high-risk offenders and is designed to reduce the crime rate by incapacitating only those most likely to recidivate. Obviously, selective incapacitation is discriminatory in its application, and the ethics and fairness of predictive sentencing are frequently called into question (Marvell and Moody, 1996). Professionals who deal with violent persons on a regular basis, such as mental health professionals and psychiatrists, also question the accuracy of dangerousness indices, especially when such devices are used for justifying preventive detention (Cleary and Powell, 1994). Too many variables can interfere with proper prediction of individual behaviors. If one's drug abuse, substance abuse, or some other chemical dependency is factored in, prediction attempts become increasingly unreliable (Makkai, 1999).

In Washington, for instance, specific types of offenders have been targeted for special punishment following their conventional sentences. Washington State's legislature passed the Sexual Predator Act in 1990, which allows for the civil commitment of sex offenders in a mental health facility if they are deemed to pose a future danger to others. Identifying a specific offender aggregate for more extensive punishment when they have served their full terms raises questions about the fairness of their extended terms, even though these extended terms are in mental hospitals and not prisons. Some critics label Washington's Sexual Predator Act as premature and unscientific (Brody and Green, 1994), because the scientific skills to make precise predictions about one's future conduct are currently lacking. Similarities have been drawn between the treatment of habitual sex offenders and habitual drunk drivers, for example. One conclusion is that a special category of offenders for whom there is no escape has been created. The only real predictor to be inferred based on current knowledge is that patients with a history of sexually violent behavior are in a high-risk group for committing future acts of this nature. Therefore, anyone treated for sexual deviance is at high risk for repeating such acts (Hanson and Thornton, 1999). In many of these situations, the law selects poor candidates for more extensive treatment in mental hospitals. The use of preventive detention for such purposes raises both moral and legal questions for analysis (Corrado, 1996).

THE CHANGING PROBATION/PAROLE OFFICER ROLE

The quality of PO personnel is increasing compared with past years (Davis, 1990b:7). The American Correctional Association and several other agencies are expanding their training options and arrangements to permit larger numbers of prospective corrections recruits to acquire skills and training. Raising the minimum standards and qualifications associated with corrections positions generally and with PO work specifically will eventually spawn new generations of better-trained officers to manage growing offender populations. Those new POs also need to familiarize themselves with computers and computer software programs designed for offender control and surveillance (Read et al., 1997; Storm, 1997).

One belief is that better-educated POs may be able to manage the stress associated with PO work better. At the same time, however, there are indications that more educated POs and other corrections officers have higher levels of dissatisfaction with their work compared with less educated officers. Personality factors appear crucial for making successful adaptations to PO work. In addition, the high labor turnover among corrections personnel means that comparatively few officers remain in PO work long enough to acquire useful skills and abilities to assist their clients effectively (Cosgrove, 1994). Although the composition of the PO workforce is changing gradually each year, technological developments and changes in the laws governing PO/offender-client interactions and the rights of offenders are also occurring. For instance, the use of electronic monitoring of offenders is making it possible to increase officer caseloads dramatically without seriously affecting the amount of time officers spend monitoring offender's whereabouts. These changes are especially applicable in the case of low-risk offenders sentenced to probation or paroled property offenders.

Electronic monitoring, together with home incarceration, is inadvertently changing the qualifications of those who supervise offenders with these electronic devices. Private enterprises are entering the correctional field in increasing numbers, and their involvement in probation or parole programs in which electronic monitoring and house arrest are used as sanctions is apparent. What kinds of POs will be needed in the future to read computer printouts, drive by offender homes with electronic receiving devices, and conduct telephonic checks of offenders? Not all clients on probation or parole are nonviolent, low-risk offenders. Increasing numbers are dangerous felons who have committed violent crimes (Johnson and Jones, 1994). Therefore, POs who possess more than minimal qualifications are required to supervise uncharacteristic probationers or parolees adequately. Although in-service training is desirable, not all states include it in their recruitment process. Unless there are drastic changes in both the image and rewards associated with PO work in the near future, more offenders will receive increasingly inadequate services from probation and parole professionals as caseloads are enlarged. This circumstance will only serve to increase recidivism rates associated with various probation and parole programs (Camp and Camp, 1999).

Global Positioning Satellite Systems: Tracking Offenders from Outer Space. Technological advancements in offender monitoring also modify PO roles and how they do their jobs. One of the more recent developments is the **global positioning satellite (GPS) system**, a network of satellites used to locate an offender. In 1997, the Florida Department of Corrections began a pilot project using this technology in Tampa and Clearwater to track the location and movements of offenders in real time, 24 hours a day, and notify probation officers of any violations as they occurred. The U.S. Department of Defense uses GPS to pinpoint targets and guide bombs. It has been used for everything from helping hikers find their way through the woods to guiding law enforcement to locate stolen vehicles. With GPS, POs can track an offender on a computer screen and can tell on which street the offender is, anywhere in the state (Mercer, Brooks, and Bryant, 2000:77).

GPS systems can actually customize equipment for particular offenders and create zones of inclusion or exclusion. Thus, POs can be warned if offenders approach their former victims in any way or enter their neighborhoods. Some areas can simply be declared off-limits, and such rules can be enforced easily through GPS. Offenders strap pager-size units to their ankles and carry lunchbox-size personal tracking devices (PTDs). POs can send instant messages to their clients through these PTDs and can warn offenders to leave particular locations immediately. One immediate benefit of such a system is to protect victims from various clients.

A survey of Florida POs who have used GPS and PTD reveals mixed feelings. Some Florida POs say that the primary usefulness of GPS is to enforce curfews and determine if offenders are present or absent in their homes or other places. The GPS system is not designed to show where offenders are during approved absence. Furthermore, the GPS system does not show what an offender is doing at any particular location. Most POs agreed that those offenders who could use GPS and PTDs the most were violent sex offenders and predators with prior criminal histories. According to some Florida POs, the technology is so new that some Florida judges do not know what they are dealing with. They sometimes assign traffic violators, bad check writers, and drug users to GPS and PTDs, offenses for which these systems were not designed to deter. Another problem is technical failure, such as battery failure or system malfunctions. One skeptic, Judge John Kuder of Pensacola, decided to test the GPS system before sentencing convicted offenders to it. He wore GPS and PTD devices for five days, doing everything he could to try to outsmart the system. He went to a movie theater that had been designated as "off-limits" for the test and left a note at the box office saying, "The mouse was here." Four minutes later, a Florida Department of Corrections PO signed the same note at the box office, saying "So was the smart cat. Busted!" Judge Kuder said, "This is one challenge I'm very glad I lost" (Mercer, Brooks, and Bryant, 2000:80).

Is technology going to replace PO surveillance functions? The answer is, probably not; it will operate similar to electronic monitoring and home confinement programs that are a part of Florida's community control program. GPS and PTDs are simply alternative systems for tracking offenders' whereabouts. POs are still needed to conduct face-to-face visits with their clients, administer substance abuse kits and determine program violations related to illegal substances or alcohol, and determine other types of program violations. The system does seem to suggest, however, that surveillance techniques in the future will become increasingly sophisticated and that perhaps POs can use the extra time for more important ways of assisting clients in becoming reintegrated and rehabilitated.

APPREHENSION UNITS

One fact of life faced by all probation and parole agencies is that some proportion of their clients will abscond or flee the jurisdiction. After all, probationers and parolees have the freedom and mobility to move about within their communities. If they choose to, they can flee the jurisdiction and attempt to elude their supervisors by living in other jurisdictions. Absconders also include a portion of jail and prison inmates who have been placed on work release, study release, or furloughs. These inmates, however, are almost always within a few months of being released anyway. Thus, prisons and jails do not regard them as serious escape risks if they are entrusted not to abscond when given temporary leaves for various purposes. Fortunately, the proportion of absconders in probation and parole is quite low, less than 5 percent (Camp and Camp, 1999). The same is true for inmates of prisons and jails who abscond while on work and study release or in furlough programs. The rate of apprehension of these fugitives is over 90 percent.

All departments of correction throughout the United States have **apprehension units** to track **absconders**. Absconders are persons who are on work release, study release, furlough programs, probation, or parole who flee their jurisdictions without permission. Apprehension units are dedicated departments consisting of specialists engaged in offender tracking and apprehension. Their business is to find absconders and bring them back to their jurisdictions for punishment. Absconders are subject to penalties such as five years' imprisonment for escape in addition to the sentences they are serving for other crimes. For instance, when offenders sign intensive supervised probation documents, they often agree not to oppose extradition from another jurisdiction if they flee and are eventually apprehended. Probation and parole departments attempt to cover all contingencies relating to the retrieval of escapees from their various programs. Responses to absconders have included greater line officer responsibility, new information sources to locate absconders, expanded agency fugitive units, and tying sanctions for absconding to offender risk (Parent et al., 1994).

For example, New York State has an apprehension unit dedicated to tracking down offenders who escape from work release and other temporary leave programs (New York State Department of Correctional Services, 1993). The Maricopa County, Arizona, Adult Probation Department also has an apprehension unit for locating absconders (Taxman and Byrne, 1994); its goal is to locate absconders before they have an opportunity to commit new offenses. They rely primarily on case files and telephone contact for potential leads about absconders. In the early 1990s, for instance, absconders were often detected when they committed crimes in other jurisdictions. Cursory records checks by other jurisdictions revealed detainer warrants that had been issued by the originating jurisdictions. These jurisdictions were therefore notified of the offender's whereabouts, and POs could travel to these other jurisdictions and bring back the absconders. About 50 percent of all absconders were tracked according to their new offense records. Using case files and telephone contacts also resulted in a drastic improvement in apprehension rates. Nearly 65 percent of all absconders were located shortly after their escapes from supervision. In these instances, family members and friends were called and told authorities where these persons could be located. Thus, many absconders were caught before they could commit new crimes.

Tracking absconders through case files is not new. The U.S. Probation Office and the U.S. Marshals Service have tracked offenders in this fashion for decades. When offenders are processed during booking, they are fingerprinted, photographed, and interviewed by authorities. They are required to provide all relevant contact information, including names, addresses, and telephone numbers of family members and details on where they have lived during the most recent ten-year period. This information is cross-checked to determine its validity and reliability. If some of these offenders escape later, then this case file information is consulted and greatly assists U.S. Marshals in finding federal fugitives.

There have been numerous attempts to forecast potential absconders in advance. Using actuarial methods, potential Texas absconders seem to exhibit the following characteristics. They are often older; minorities; have fewer skills, outstanding debts, credit problems or bad credit, prior extensive unemployment, or greater drug or alcohol abuse; had more unsavory friends with prior criminal records; and were serving longer sentences (McReynolds, 1987). Interestingly, many of these characteristics typified absconders from New York (New York State Department of Correctional Services, 1993). Even absconders from halfway houses shared many of these same traits (Eisenberg, 1990). More recent evidence about absconders from parole programs has shown that they tend to be less dangerous and pose less societal risk, although they do have extensive prior criminal records, are emotionally unstable, and have more parole supervisions and revocations (Schwaner, 1997; Williams, McShane, and Dolny, 2000). Some prior evidence of mental illness seems associated with absconding in selected jurisdictions (Anderson, 1998).

One major issue that has arisen to confront probation and parole agencies is how to punish absconders. Before extensive prison and jail overcrowding, the simple solution was simply to reconfine these offenders for prolonged periods. With chronic prison and jail overcrowding, however, this option is rapidly diminishing. Also, more than a few probation and parole departments have oversized caseloads and cannot allocate sufficient resources to locate absconders. The reduced availability of prison sanctions whenever absconders are located underscores the need to highlight and target high-risk offenders as potential absconders and streamline the procedures for apprehending and returning them to custody (Parent et al., 1994). Those considered to be high risk are clients who are serving longer prison terms and who have previously been in prison or jail (Chard-Wierschem, 1995). Yet no current method is foolproof in identifying those most likely to abscond (Fields, 1994; New York State Department of Correctional Services, 1993; Williams, McShane, and Dolny, 2000).

GANG UNITS

In 1998, there were 28,707 known gangs in the United States (Wilson, 2000:12), with a total membership of 780,233. About 21,000 of them were in large and small cities compared with suburban or rural counties. Because gangs are a pervasive phenomenon in American society, they have become a major problem for POs, who have found that increasing numbers of their clients are current or former gang members (Miethe and McCorkle, 1997). One response has been the formation of **gang units**, which were originally created to identify gang presence in neighborhoods as well as gang influence. Gang units were formed by police departments to combat gang-related crime in larger cities in which gangs were most visible (Katz, 1997; Klein, Maxson, and Gordon, 1987). Because most gangs are involved in illicit activities, particularly drugs and drug trafficking, gang membership was also indicative of likely criminality. Gangs have increasingly been linked with violent crimes, including homicides (Kennedy and Braga, 1998).

During the last few decades, both juvenile and adult probation and parole departments have established specialized gang units to learn more about their gang-

BOX 10.1

Personality Highlight

Rick V. Lopez
Senior Prosecutions Agent, U.S. Border Patrol–Prosecutions Unit, Laredo, Texas

Statistics. B.A. (sociology), Texas A&I University–Kingsville; Del Mar Police Academy; U.S. Border Patrol Academy; M.S. (criminal justice, forthcoming), Texas A&M International University

Background and Work Experience. I am a senior prosecutions/warrants agent for the U.S. Border Patrol. This position is located at the U.S. Border Patrol Sector Headquarters in Laredo, Texas. My experiences include working as a deputy sheriff, drug counselor, and Border Patrol agent.

The position of senior prosecutions/warrants agent is an extremely difficult position to define. I conduct investigations of considerable difficulty and complexity to apprehend and prosecute individuals who have violated the Immigration and Nationality Act or the related criminal provisions of the U.S. Code. Investigations of this type usually include the use of surveillance, undercover operations, audio/video consensual monitoring, record searches, interrogations, and information development. The skills necessary to perform this position are the preparation of reports and other written technical material that deal with the collection, protection, and recording of evidence and the presentation of testimony. This position also requires me to be able to communicate with different audience levels. This communication is necessary to present facts and evidence to the U.S. District Court, the federal grand jury, and the U.S. Attorney, immigration courts as well as to explain rights and complicated legal proceedings to persons apprehended or held as material witnesses.

The direct training I received to perform these tasks came from working as a Border Patrol agent. At the Border Patrol Academy, I was trained in immigration and nationality law, criminal law, and statutory law. I also received extensive training in Titles 8, 18, 19, and 21 of the U.S. Code, Rules of Federal Criminal Procedure, Rules of Evidence, and of appellate decisions. This position also requires the proficiency in the use of Spanish and knowledge of the socioeconomic cultures of various Spanish-speaking countries. Skills in detecting differences in such areas as patterns of speech, accents, and manner of dress that may be useful during in-depth interviews of defendants and material witnesses in identifying the suspects' countries of origin and truthfulness are also needed.

Advice to Students. Most of my experiences as a Border Patrol agent and as a prosecutions agent have been positive. One aspect of being a federal agent that I cannot explain is the identity that you acquire after your training. I am and will always consider myself a federal agent, no matter where my career path takes me from here. At times, as in any career, I would rather be doing something else. I have to add that some of the cases that come through our office are so frustrating that I'd wish they would just go away. Unfortunately, they would just get more complicated. The U.S. Border Patrol has been in existence for over 75 years. During that time, the agency has seen many changes, most of them for the best. The mission in the Border Patrol is clear: "To uphold the Constitution and the Laws of this Country." I highly recommend anyone interested in law enforcement to look into the U.S. Border Patrol as a possible career. You'll be glad you did.

affiliated clientele (Finn, 1999; Jenson and Howard, 1998). The result is that POs have learned a lot more in recent years about gang activities in neighborhoods in which clients are supervised, about gang member personal alcohol and drug use, and about antisocial peer networks distinguishing between gang and nongang members. Even more compelling about the work of probation and parole agency gang units is the discovery of a closer connection between prison and street gangs and their relation with organized crime on several levels (Decker, Bynum, and Weisel, 1998). Examples of the interplay between prison and street gangs are Chicago's Gangster Disciples and Latin Kings. These gangs have moved from disorganized collectivities to smooth-running organized crime groups with corporate divisions of labor and contemporary conceptual frameworks for conducting illegal businesses.

Not all gang activity occurs in major cities in states with large populations, however. In Virginia, for instance, there are approximately 320 gangs. According to probation department personnel, many of these gang members are probationers or have previously been on probation. Assault, vandalism, and intimidation are most often linked with gang activities, although about half appear to be involved in drug trafficking and gun distribution (Johnson, Wilson, and Wright, 1999). Gangs are not strictly a U.S. phenomena. Often, gangs in other countries are loosely linked with their U.S. counterparts (Gordon, 2000).

Of particular concern to POs is the link between street gangs and prison gangs. Many inmates of prisons and jails are gang members. When they are eventually released on parole, they link up with their gang counterparts in the cities in which they become involved in their parole programs. POs are concerned because when ex-convicts return to the streets and reinvolve themselves in gang activities, they have a proclivity toward greater violence that spills over into street gang activities. Thus, the involvement of ex-convicts in youth gangs increases the life of the gangs and their level of violent crime (Wilson, 2000:35). Nearly half of all gangs report such increased violence as the result of ex-convicts returning to their gangs.

POs strive to enhance their knowledge of both street and prison gangs so as to more effectively supervise them through learning gang jargon and prison argot or the use of special phrases and hand gestures that are relevant only to gang members. Such signals are ways of communicating among gang members, even with prison staff or POs present, and without their awareness or knowledge. As POs become more aware of this new language, however, they can interdict at appropriate times and take the necessary steps to control their clients. Thus, an important training component for both POs and correctional officers in institutions is gang interpersonal communications skills to help prepare them to interact with offender populations whose speech is intended to manipulate or misdirect (Wittenberg, 1996). Sometimes, POs work with tactical police officers, community youth workers, and neighborhood representatives to work toward reducing violent criminal activity. In the Little Village Gang Violence

Reduction Project in Chicago, Illinois, POs learn much about general gang phenomena and become better at performing their supervisory responsibilities, particularly when gang members were involved (Spergel and Grossman, 1997). Some results of such experiments are more effective social intervention by POs of specific gang members as clients, greater crime prevention, and general gang suppression.

The U.S. Probation Office currently has special teams to handle community threat groups in designated areas of the country, such as San Antonio, Texas. In that city, there are street and youth gangs, former inmate gang members, organized crime groups, and prison gangs. The presence of these gangs in the San Antonio area grew during the 1980s and shows no signs of abating. A specialized community threat group program has been established, the two primary activities of which are to assign probation office personnel to specialized work with community threat group offenders and to develop an intensive training curriculum for the general staff. The ultimate objective is a massive interdiction effort to reduce or eliminate gang activity in San Antonio, especially pertaining to federal offenders (Tonry, 1998).

RESEARCH UNITS

Research units, essential components of any probation or parole department, compile extensive information about probationer and parolee characteristics as well as information about inmate populations of jails and prisons. POs need accurate profiles of their clients. Research units are essential to effective probation and parole program planning. Networking with established community services can be achieved more effectively if offender needs can be anticipated.

Research units are also in the business of devising risk/needs instrumentation for use by judges and paroling authorities. Again, it is imperative for these persons and agencies to have at their disposal indicators concerning offender needs and the risks they might pose if granted probation or parole. Research units are also involved in departmental and organizational programming, both within their own agencies and throughout the community. They devise new and improved strategies for offender supervision and management as well as better ways of administering agency resources. For example, Kentucky's Criminal Justice Statistical Analysis Center compiles much valuable information about offenders and their risks and needs (Johnson, Burgess, and Hutcherson, 1985).

Research units are also important in effective court management, which can eventually ease the problems of POs in their supervisory duties. Research units for the courts, probation and parole departments, and police agencies have existed for several decades and have proved instrumental at providing essential information for task coordination and crime reduction (Abt Associates, Inc., 1976; Adams, 1975; Zurawski and Brooks, 1975).

STRESS AND BURNOUT IN PROBATION/PAROLE OFFICER
ROLE PERFORMANCE

The selection and recruitment of the right kinds of personnel to perform PO work roles are designed to identify those most able to handle the stresses and strains accompanying the job. The concern about occupational stress has been rising steadily in recent years (Cornelius, 1994). Virtually all occupations and professions have varying degrees of stress associated with them. Probation and parole work is not immune from stress and **burnout**. John Whitehead and Charles Lindquist (1992) studied 400 probation and parole officers in various states and found that they tended to offer more negative than positive comments about their work. In fact, these researchers reported that the POs studied had stress levels comparable to police officers as well as significant job burnout, stress levels, and **job dissatisfaction** (Whitehead, 1989). Similar findings have been reported by Peter Finn (1999) relating to correctional officer stress levels and the reasons given for stress through self-reports.

Possible Gender and Age Differences in Stress and Burnout Associated with PO Work.   Do female POs have more or less stress and burnout compared with their male PO counterparts? The answer is, not according to a review of research on the subject (Cornelius, 1994). Apparently, the problems of female officers are the problems of male officers, so that neither gender requires special attention. Both men and women who pursue PO careers may have similar personality backgrounds. The premise of personality as a determinant has not been systematically studied thus far (Pelletier, Coutu, and Lamonde, 1996). This lack of study applies similarly to studies of male and female police officer stress levels (Hendricks and McKean, 1995).

Age as a factor in burnout also seems to be a contributing factor. Some studies show that as POs get older, they experience more burnout. This postulation, however, has little consistent empirical support. For instance, one study has reported that older POs (age 51 or older) tend to experience more emotional exhaustion and low feelings of personal accomplishment. In turn, this sensed lack of accomplishment has led to decreased client contact, which, in turn, has decreased PO work effectiveness (Holgate and Clegg, 1991). In the same study, however, younger POs often exhibited greater role conflict and emotional exhaustion accompanied by greater client contact. Apparently, in this study at least, younger officers are driven toward greater client contact to resolve role conflict situations and reduce emotional exhaustion, whereas older officers are driven away from clients because of feelings of depersonalization and a lack of accomplishment.

Stress

Stress is a nonspecific response to a perceived threat to an individual's well-being or self-esteem (Cornelius, 1994). It is important to recognize that these stress responses are not specific and that each person reacts differently to the same situation triggering stress. Some people react to stress with somatic complaints of aches and pains, whereas others may exhibit irritability, loss of attention span, or fatigue. Furthermore, what is stressful for one person may not be stressful to another. Therefore, several factors, including one's previous experiences with the event, constitutional factors, and personality, may function to mediate the stress and one's reaction to the event (Pelletier, Coutu, and Lamonde, 1996). In-service training is regarded by many departments of correction as important, because it exposes new recruits to different officer/offender relationships that generate stress. Becoming familiar with a variety of officer-offender interactions and recognizing potentially problematic interpersonal situations is one means of effectively combating, or at least minimizing, stress.

Although it is not known precisely how education relates to
educated POs are probably more aware of several beha·
options whenever problems arise between themselves and p₁
(Simmons, Cochran, and Blount, 1997). Although this fir
among all jurisdictions, greater stress has been reported in
caseload assignments are received (Soma, 1994).

Some stress is good. A moderate amount enhances the learning and creative
processes, and too little stress may induce boredom or apathy. It is not known, however, how much stress is too much. It is known that correctional officers have twice
the national average divorce rate and the highest heart attack rates among all types of
state employees, including police officers. These statistics appear to result directly
from the stressful aspects of corrections work. A study by Bernie Patterson (1992) of
4,500 police, correctional, and probation/parole officers, however, showed a curvilin-
ear relation between perceived stress and time on the job. This result might be interpreted as follows: There is considerable stress among many of these officers in their
early years on the job, followed by a stress decline. In turn, this stress increases as on-
the-job experience increases. Obviously, blanket generalizations about stress and the
amount of one's job experience are difficult to formulate (Maggio and Terenzi, 1993).

Burnout

Burnout is one result of stress. Burnout emerged as a popular term in the mid-1970s
to describe work alienation, apathy, depersonalization, depression, and a host of
other job-related complaints (Cornelius, 1994). Not everyone agrees about how
burnout ought to be defined. Christina Maslach (1982a:30-31) has identified at least
fifteen different connotations of the term:

1. A syndrome of emotional exhaustion, depersonalization, and reduced personal accomplishment that can occur among individuals who do people work of some kind
2. A progressive loss of idealism, energy, and purpose experienced by people in the helping professions as a result of the conditions of their work
3. A state of physical, emotional, and mental exhaustion marked by physical depletion
   and chronic fatigue, feelings of helplessness and hopelessness, and the development of a
   negative self-concept and negative attitudes toward work, life, and other people
4. A syndrome of inappropriate attitudes toward clients and self, often associated with
   uncomfortable physical and emotional symptoms
5. A state of exhaustion, irritability, and fatigue that markedly decreases the worker's
   effectiveness and capability
6. Depleting oneself; exhausting one's physical and mental resources; wearing oneself out
   by excessively striving to reach some unrealistic expectations imposed by oneself or by
   the values of society
7. Wearing oneself out doing what one has to do; an inability to cope adequately with the
   stresses of work or personal life
8. A malaise of the spirit; a loss of will; an inability to mobilize interests and capabilities
9. Becoming debilitated, weakened, because of extreme demands on one's physical and/or
   mental energy
10. An accumulation of intense negative feelings that is so debilitating that a person with-
    draws from the situation in which those feelings are generated

11. A pervasive mood of anxiety giving way to depression and despair
12. A process in which a professional's attitudes and behavior change in negative ways in response to job strain
13. An inadequate coping mechanism used consistently by an individual to reduce stress
14. A condition produced by working too hard for too long in a high-pressure environment
15. A debilitating psychological condition resulting from work-related frustrations, which results in lower employee productivity and morale

The common elements of these definitions are emotional, mental, and physical exhaustion that debilitates and weakens one's ability to cope with situations. Definitions 2, 3, and 4 are particularly crucial for PO work, because POs must maintain effective relations with their clients continuously and evaluate their progress regularly (Patterson, 1992). When stress rises to the level of burnout, offender-clients experience corresponding decreases in the quality of delivery services from probation/parole personnel (Cornelius, 1994). The importance of burnout is that it signifies a reduction in the quality or effectiveness of an officer's job performance (Maggio and Terenzi, 1993). Such debilitating reductions in effectiveness are often accompanied by higher recidivism rates among probationers and parolees, more legal problems and case filings from officer/client interactions, and greater turnover among POs (Holgate and Clegg, 1991).

Sources of Stress

Stress among POs and other professionals emanates from several sources. Stress researchers have targeted the following as the chief sources of stress among POs: job dissatisfaction, role conflict, role ambiguity, officer/client interactions, excessive paperwork and performance pressures, low self-esteem and public image, and job risks and liabilities.

Job Dissatisfaction.   Job dissatisfaction is somewhat unwieldy, because it occurs as the result of a variety of factors, some of which overlap those that generate work-related stress. Low pay, burgeoning caseloads, and unchallenging work figure prominently in an officer's decision to leave PO work for better employment opportunities (Patterson, 1992).

Role Conflict.   Role conflict occurs as the result of having to adhere to conflicting expectations. For example, a PO's collection of supervision fees from his or her indigent clients often creates a type of conflict about the role of rehabilitator and enforcer. The expectations of the probation officer role are unusual and sometimes conflicting. They may be those of supervisors, and they are sometimes in conflict with a PO's concept of how the job ought to be performed (Finn and Parent, 1992b). Sometimes role conflict occurs when the probation supervisor and administrator each expects the PO to complete different tasks at the same time. The logistical complications are apparent, and role conflict ensues (Clear and Latessa, 1993). Darrell Mills (1990:3–6) summarizes many feelings of POs who sense the frustrations of role conflict: Nobody said it would be like this; Why do you think they call them [probationer/clients] cons?; If there is a problem, see the probation officer; How am I doing so far?; I never took this job to get rich; and Will this ever end? Mills (1990:7) says that "for the probation officer, it is important to maintain a freshness and enthusiasm toward the career. In part this calls on the officer to establish and maintain a well-balanced life." Unfortunately, nobody ever explains to the average PO how all that can be accomplished.

Role Ambiguity. Closely related to role conflict is **role ambiguity**, which occurs whenever POs have inadequate or even conflicting information about their work roles, the scope and responsibilities of the job, and the ethics of certain unwritten practices that are common among many POs (Read et al., 1997). Observers have long been critical of probation and parole agencies and organizations for failing to make explicit program goals and mission statements (Crank, 1996). That probation and parole program goals are often diffuse or unspecified makes it difficult for POs working with those programs to focus their energies in productive directions consistent with program objectives (Johnson and Grant, 1999).

Officer/Client Interactions. Work overload, inadequate agency resources, and problems related to client contact often contribute to job stress. In some instances, officers felt that their efforts in relating to offender-clients were frequently misunderstood and that they were perceived as antagonistic toward those they were supposed to help. Mismatching of officers and their clients also accounts for a certain proportion of interpersonal problems that arise in various agencies. Workload deployment systems based on a successful match between officer skills and clients to be supervised can make a significant difference in the day-to-day operation of probation/parole agencies (Burke, 1990:37–39).

Excessive Paperwork and Performance Measures. The larger a PO's caseload, the more paperwork associated with the clients supervised (Goldsmith and Libonate, 1990). A growing problem in many jurisdictions is increased caseloads without an accompanying increase in the numbers of POs to perform the work. Officers working under increased pressure must produce more work in the same amount of time. The preparation of PSI reports takes time. During any given period, the amount of time devoted to report preparation accounts for almost three-fourths of the PO's 40-hour work week (Smith, 1992:136–138). Closely related to excessive paperwork and performance pressures is bureaucratization, which stresses adherence to abstract rules, a hierarchy of authority, task specialization, explicit spheres of competence, emotional neutrality, and promotion on the basis of merit and expertise (Champion, 1998). Probation departments have been depicted by various investigators as more or less bureaucratic. As a result of these variable bureaucratic features either present or absent in probation/parole agencies, POs acquire different orientations toward their work (Horn, 1992).

Low Self-Esteem and Public Image. The low self-esteem and public image of POs are well known, and they invariably influence the quality of work they perform. There is little POs can do in the short term to significantly modify their low public image, but as recruitment efforts are more successful in attracting better qualified applicants for PO positions, it is likely that the quality of services delivered will improve. One result of improved delivery of services may be a better public image associated with PO work (Matthewson, 1991).

Job Risks and Liabilities.   Persons working with criminals incur several risks. Some risk may be associated with the type of offender clientele served (Johnson and Jones, 1994). Parolees who have been formerly convicted of aggravated assault, murder, rape, or some other type of violent crime may pose a degree of risk to the personal safety of POs. An element of risk is also incurred from a client's associates who may be violent criminals. These hazards are unknown and incalculable. In addition to these personal risks are legal liabilities incurred by POs who must interact with their offender-clients. In the course of furnishing them with counseling, job assistance, and other services, POs risk giving them poor advice, violating their privacy, maligning them to others, and preventing them from participating in various programs. POs must be aware of their legal responsibilities (Patterson, 1992). They must also be aware of actions that may lead to lawsuits from dissatisfied offender clientele. Many POs say that their training may not be sufficient to equip them with the legal and practical expertise needed to do good jobs (Vohryzek-Bolden, Croisdale, and Barnes, 1999).

Mitigating Factors to Alleviate Stress and Burnout

Many authorities believe that probation and parole organizations and agencies are at fault in creating dangerously high stress and burnout levels among POs and other correctional officers (Cornelius, 1994). One theory is that organizational factors directly contribute to employee stress (Maslach, 1982b). When a calling becomes the job, one no longer lives to work but works to live. Thus, POs may lose enthusiasm, excitement, and a sense of mission about the work. Although some observers say that it is virtually impossible to prevent burnout among POs, regardless of their coping strategies and mechanisms, it is possible for the organization to implement changes to minimize it. If organizational heads will recognize what causes stress and burnout, then they have a better than even chance of dealing with it effectively (Crank, 1996). One way of alleviating stress and burnout is to incorporate features into PO training programs to make POs more streetwise and therefore safer when face to face with their clients (Morrisson, 1992). Such programs may encompass hand-to-hand combat training and other self-defense skills.

Participative Management.   Participative management is the philosophy of organizational administration whereby substantial input is solicited from the work staff and used for decision making when one's work might be affected. Thus, as lower-level participants are given a greater voice in how the organization is operated or administered, subordinates' opinions become crucial to organizational decision making. Organizational solutions stress greater employee involvement in decision making relating to offender treatment and supervision (Cushman and Sechrest, 1992). Generally, a lack of participation in decision making is a key source of stress and burnout. Employee commitment to do better work can be enhanced through bringing a PO's goals into harmony with those of the organization (Rath, 1991). Management by objectives, or MBO, has been suggested as one means of accomplishing participatory goal setting between organizational heads and agency personnel, although it has lost momentum as a goal-setting and motivating strategy in recent years.

The Kalamazoo, Michigan, Probation Enhancement Program developed in 1981 used employment skills classes, a job club, peer support groups, basic life skills classes, and general equivalency diploma preparation to assist probationers and parolees. POs involved in this project derived considerable satisfaction from it. The evaluation of the program by Kalamazoo probation office officials focused primarily on the success rates of program participants rather than on the POs who worked closely with them to achieve those success rates. Such a limited focus is one indication of the failure of agency leaders to reward their staffs properly for work they are "expected" to do anyway (Minor and Hartmann, 1992).

VOLUNTEERS IN PROBATION/PAROLE WORK

Who Are Volunteers?　A **corrections volunteer** is any unpaid person who performs auxiliary, supplemental, augmentative, or any other work or services for any law enforcement, court, or corrections agency. Corrections volunteers vary greatly in their characteristics and abilities, in their ages, and in their functions. For instance, Girl Scouts, aged 12 to 16, work closely with female inmates and their children at the Maryland Correctional Institution for Women in Jessup, Maryland (Moses, 1993:132). Girl Scouts play with the daughters of female inmates during twice-monthly troop meetings. Troop projects as well as future activities, with female inmates and their daughters becoming involved and experiencing more intimate bonding not ordinarily possible under penal conditions, are planned (American Probation and Parole Association, 1996).

What Do Corrections Volunteers Do?　Some volunteers are retired schoolteachers who work with jail and prison inmates in various literacy programs (Tracy, 1993:102). The Gray Panthers, an organization of elderly volunteers, provide various services and programs specifically targeting older inmates (Lehman, 1993:84). Some volunteers, such as septuagenarian Brigitte Cooke in Huntington, Pennsylvania, work with death row inmates or those serving life sentences. Her services include spiritual guidance, support, and compassion (Love, 1993). Some volunteers are crime victims who confront criminals who have committed crimes suffered by victims (Costa and Seymour, 1993:110). Yet other volunteers provide religious training and conduct services for inmates and others (Pace, 1993:114). Other types of volunteers work as day care service personnel caring for young children of female parolees and probationers who work full time in connection with their probation or parole programs (Arnold, 1993:118).

Some Examples of Correctional Volunteer Work.　One volunteer program designed for working with female offenders both in prison and community-based programs is the Program for Female Offenders. This program provides for volunteers who visit the Allegheny County, Pennsylvania, Jail three times a week and the State Correctional Institution at Muncy on a less frequent but regular basis (Arnold, 1993:120). Incarcerated women are assisted by volunteers who help them adjust to prison life. Certain family and legal problems may be handled, using the volunteers as intermediaries. The agency operates a training center, two residential facilities and a day treatment program for women who have been recently released. All these facilities are located in Pittsburgh (Arnold, 1993:120). One facility, the Program Center, is a work release facility that serves 34 female prisoners. Volunteers provide job assistance, GED preparation, and life skills. Parenting programs and day care services are also provided, largely through the use of volunteer services. Charlotte Arnold (1993:120–122) says that volunteers deserve special recognition for the unpaid services. This Pennsylvania program has outlined some valuable types of functions performed by these volunteers:

1. Serving as tutors at the skill training center and handling most GED preparation
2. Providing transportation to parenting sessions at their residential centers
3. Teaching women hobby skills such as knitting, sewing, and dressmaking
4. Teaching computer and job search skills at the skill training center
5. Providing gifts for women and their children every Christmas

Arnold says that these tasks often lead to friendships between volunteers and inmate-clients. Arnold also advises that it is important to place volunteers in positions in which they will feel safe and comfortable. She suggests the following guidelines:

1. Do not take offenders home or lend them money.
2. Do not share your troubles with offenders.
3. Learn to listen effectively.
4. Do not try to solve offenders' problems.
5. Do not make judgments.
6. Report irregular behavior to the agency staff. You are not being disloyal.
7. Do not provide drugs or alcohol to offenders.
8. Do not always expect to be appreciated.
9. Do have empathy and patience.
10. Do care. (Arnold, 1993:122)

Criticisms of Volunteers in Correctional Work

There Is Pervasive Volunteer Naivete.   Not everyone is enthusiastic about volunteer involvement in law enforcement, the courts, or corrections. From time to time, unusual situations in which inmates and other types of offenders might harm volunteers or be harmed by the very volunteers trying to help them arise. One problem frequently cited by critics of correctional volunteerism is volunteer naivete.

Volunteers Do Not Make Long-Term Commitments with Clients.   Because of the voluntary, unpaid nature of volunteer work, many volunteers may be in correctional settings for brief periods, tire of their activities, and leave. Although POs generally hold positive attitudes about the influence of volunteers in assisting them in their regular duties, the most frequent criticism is that a significant proportion of volunteers do not stay with their clients for an adequate time. Clients are often shuffled between volunteers and regular POs. As a result, clients feel manipulated or let down by the particular volunteer absence.

Volunteers Often Do Not Want to Work Independently.   Some volunteers do not wish to work independently from POs in assisting their clients. This situation has necessitated a considerable and unnecessary expenditure of valuable time on the part of the supervising PO, often already overworked with heavy caseloads and numerous other required duties.

Volunteers Often Lack Expertise and Experience. One chief concern of POs is that volunteers lack general knowledge about the specific rules and policies of their probation/parole offices (Florida Department of Corrections, 1993). Thus, if some offenders violate program rules, volunteers may experience difficulty reporting them for these infractions. Volunteers seem to be more easily manipulated than regular POs.

Law Enforcement Agencies and the Courts Are Reluctant to Share Information about Offenders with Volunteers Serving PO Functions. It is probably natural for law enforcement organizations and the courts to take a dim view of disclosing confidential information about offender-clients to volunteers operating in unofficial capacities. Thus, the confidentiality issue continues to be pervasive among probation departments (American Correctional Association, 1993e).

Volunteers Threaten Job Security. It follows that if a department or agency uses volunteers to supplement the work performed by full-time staff, then some of those full-time staff may not be needed in the future. Some employees of corrections agencies have expressed this particular fear, regardless of its foundation in truth (Winter, 1993:20).

Because Volunteers Are Unpaid, They Do Not Respond to Orders Like Regular Staff Do. Unpaid personnel who work with corrections agencies on a voluntary basis are under no special obligation to adhere to specific working hours or schedules. Most volunteers wish to comply with the requirements of the tasks they are assigned, but they may have a totally different commitment to work compared with paid staff members. If volunteers do not like certain tasks they are assigned, they do not have to reappear at work in the future.

Some Volunteers May Be Aiders and Abetters. D. J. Bayse (1993:16) describes a situation at a prison in which a local pastor regularly brought church members to the prison for worship services with inmates. He allowed a woman from a nearby church to join the group one Sunday at the last moment. The pastor did not know that the woman was wearing two dresses and a wig. When she excused herself to go to the bathroom, an inmate discretely followed her and outfitted himself in her extra dress and wig. Dressed as a woman, he returned with her to the church group and left with them when they exited the prison. He was apprehended a few days later. This story illustrates the potential harm volunteers can cause to corrections officials if they develop close relationships with prisoners or if their backgrounds are not carefully screened.

Because of the nonprofessional nature of volunteer work in general, questions often arise concerning the quality of work volunteers can perform (Connelly, 1995). If volunteers are assigned case-sensitive work, such as working with probationers or parolees, then they must necessarily become exposed to confidential materials or information about their clients. In fact, some volunteers in certain probation/parole agencies often act on instructions from these agencies to obtain such information from law enforcement sources or the courts (Onek, 1994). Should these volunteers be granted access to this information? Kevin Ogburn (1993:66) has provided the following admonitions to persons or organizations interested in establishing volunteer programs:

1. Evaluate the need.
2. Develop goals and job descriptions.
3. Involve staff.
4. Actively recruit volunteers.
5. Educate volunteers about inmates.
6. Explain security needs to volunteers.
7. Give volunteers the big picture.
8. Evaluate program effectiveness.
9. Recognize your volunteers' contributions.

Further, Bayse (1993:43–47) admonishes volunteers to be ethical, good listeners, empathetic but not gullible, respectful, genuine, patient, trustworthy, confrontive, objective, nonhostile, nonexpectant of thanks.

PARAPROFESSIONALS IN PROBATION/PAROLE WORK

Paraprofessionals in virtually every field are salaried assistants who work with professionals. A corrections paraprofessional is a someone who possesses some formal training in a given correctional area, is salaried, works specified hours, has formal duties and responsibilities, is accountable to higher-level supervisors for work quality, and has limited immunity under the theory of agency. **Agency** is the special relation between an employer and an employee through which the employee acts as an agent of the employer, and is able to make decisions and take actions on the employer's behalf (Black, 1990:62).

Roles of Paraprofessionals

The quality of paraprofessional work reflects the amount of training these personnel receive (Enos and Southern, 1996). For instance, in various prisons, paraprofessionals are used to assist mental health professionals and psychiatrists. Some correctional staff may have demonstrable abilities as mental health caregivers. Others are especially good when working with children (Godwin, Steinhart, and Fulton, 1996). In some jurisdictions, corrections personnel are given specialized mental health training and experience with mental health counseling. Although the primary professional goals of clinical and correctional staff may conflict from time to time, it is apparent that the two professions share common functions. Actually, properly trained correctional staff as mental health paraprofessionals can supply quality mental health care compared with the work quality of many professionals who work with inmates (Ellsworth, 1996).

Virginia's Department of Corrections has invested considerable time and effort to establish literacy programs for its prison inmates and community corrections clients, and paraprofessionals have been used extensively in several of their projects. The Wechsler Adult Intelligence Scale was used by Virginia officials to

BOX 10.2   *On the Ethics of Using Volunteers*

D. J. Bayse (1993:48–50) also provides prospective volunteers with some suggestions and rules:

1. Use appropriate language. Don't pick up inmate slang or vulgarity. Using language that isn't a part of your style can label you a phoney.

2. Do not volunteer if you are a relative or visitor of an inmate in that institution.

3. Do not engage in political activities during the time voluntary services are being performed.

4. Do not bring contraband into prison. If you are not sure what is contraband, ask the staff. People who bring in contraband are subject to permanent expulsion and/or arrest.

5. Do not bring anything into or out of a facility for an inmate at any time, no matter how innocent or trivial it may seem, unless with the written permission of the superintendent. Volunteers should adopt a policy of saying no to any request by an inmate to bring in cigarettes, money, magazines, or letters. If in doubt, ask a staff member.

6. Keep everything in the open. Do not say or do anything with an inmate you would be embarrassed to share with your peers or supervisors.

7. Do not give up if you failed at your first try. Try again.

8. Don't overidentify. Be a friend, but let inmates carry their own problems. Be supportive without becoming like the inmates in viewpoint or attitude.

9. Do not take anything, including letters, in or out of a correctional facility without permission. Respect the confidentiality of records and other privileged information.

10. Do not bring unauthorized visitors or guests with you to the institution. They will be refused admission.

11. Do not give out your address or telephone number. If asked, you might say, "I'm sorry, but I was told that it was against the rules to do that."

12. Do not correspond with inmates in the facility in which you volunteer or accept collect telephone calls from them at your place of residence.

13. Be aware that the use of, or being under the influence of, alcohol or drugs while on institution grounds is prohibited.

14. Don't impose your values and beliefs on inmates. Do not let others impose a lower set of values on you.

15. Don't discuss the criminal justice system, the courts, inconsistency in sentencing, or related topics. Although everyone is entitled to his or her own opinion, what volunteers say can have serious repercussions in the dorms or with staff.

16. Ask for help. If you are uncertain about what to do or say, be honest. It is always best to tell the inmate that you will have to seek assistance from your supervisor. Inmates don't expect you to have all the answers.

17. Know your personal and professional goals. Be firm, fair and consistent.

18. If you have done something inappropriate, tell your coordinator regardless of what happened. It is far better to be reprimanded than to become a criminal.

Source: Adapted from D.J. Bayse, *Helping Hands: A Handbook for Volunteers in Prisons and Jails* (Laurel, MD: American Correctional Association, 1993), 48–50.

define offenders with IQs ranging from 72 to 90. Also chosen were males age 16 to 19 who had reading levels from 50 to 83 percent below normal grade level. Paraprofessionals were hired to read in unison with these offenders. Reading material was chosen and read several times to establish a fluent, normal reading pattern. Through the use of paraprofessionals in these educational endeavors, Virginia officials estimate that they were able to raise the reading level of most offenders by more than four years (Traynelis-Yurek and Yurek, 1990).

Paraprofessionals who work with family therapists learn about family and juvenile laws and how youths should be counseled and treated. In Seattle, Washington, for instance, paraprofessionals are used to counsel repeat runaway offenders through the Community Services Section of the Seattle Police Department (Gaudin, 1993). Paraprofessionals have also been used in mediation projects, such as alternative dispute resolution, when impartial arbiters reconcile differences between offenders and their victims and attempt to mediate these conflicts in an equitable manner.

Legal Liabilities of Volunteers and Paraprofessionals

The Case of *Hyland v. Wonder* (1992).   One of the few high-profile legal cases involving volunteers was the case of *Hyland v. Wonder* (1992). This case involved a volunteer who had worked at a juvenile probation department for several years. After serving as a volunteer and working with juveniles during this period, the volunteer became critical of how the probation office was being managed and wrote a letter to those overseeing the probation department, outlining various complaints and asserting how certain improvements would benefit the office. His services as a volunteer were subsequently terminated. He sued, claiming that his criticisms of the probation department were protected by the free speech provision of the First Amendment. Furthermore, he contended that he had a protected liberty interest in his continued status as a volunteer and that this liberty interest was protected by the due process clause of the Fourteenth Amendment. The Ninth Circuit Court of Appeals heard his appeal after his complaint had been dismissed by a U.S. District Court. The appellate court determined that the agency could not deprive the defendant of a valuable government benefit as punishment for speaking out on a matter of public concern. The nature of his public concern was government inefficiency, incompetence, and waste. The court did declare, however, that the man was not vested with a property or liberty interest in his volunteer position. Thus, he was not in the position of being able to state or create a claim of entitlement for the purposes of the due process clause of the Fourteenth Amendment.

In *Hyland,* a volunteer had spent so much time in his volunteer work with the probation department that he came to regard his position and opinions as equivalent to those of regular full-time employees, or so it would appear. His lawsuit is evidence of his enthusiasm for the work and the seriousness he attached to it. The court, however, was unsympathetic to the extent that his volunteer time accrued did not vest him with any real standing regarding office policies. *Hyland* is a good example of how some volunteers can lose their perspective of who they are and why they are there. It is also a good example of one pitfall of volunteer work.

As employees of various helping agencies associated with law enforcement, the courts, and corrections, paraprofessionals enjoy immunity from prosecution similar to that of regular law enforcement officers, corrections officers, and POs. This immunity is not absolute, but rather is limited to acts within the scope of one's duties and responsibilities. Thus, paraprofessionals act on behalf of the agencies employing them. Under certain conditions, staff who injure or cause harm to others may be liable under the theory of ***respondeat superior,*** a doctrine based on the principle of master and servant. If the servant does something to harm others while performing work for the master, then the master might be liable. For example, if a Los Angeles County probation officer shot and wounded a probationer during a confrontation, then the Los Angeles County Probation Department might be liable under certain conditions. Public agencies such as the Los Angeles County Probation Department, however, enjoy some qualified immunity from lawsuits, many of which are often frivolous.

The liability coverage of paraprofessionals is very similar to that of volunteers. Organizations are subject to lawsuits if an action by one of their paraprofessionals or volunteers results in damages to inmates or offender-clients. Organizations are especially liable if paraprofessionals are used in counseling and other programs involving sex offenders, when their potentially insufficient training may generate various issues (Lee, Auburn, and Kibblewhite, 1999). These damages may be monetary, physical, or intangible, such as psychological harm. Title 42, Section 1983, of the **U.S. Code Annotated** (U.S. Code Annotated, 2001) outlines various types of civil rights violations that can be used as bases for lawsuits. Among the bases for different lawsuits by offender-clients are allegations of negligence. **Negligence** may be

1. Negligent hiring (e.g., organization failed to "weed out" unqualified employees who inflicted harm subsequently on an inmate or probationer/parolee)
2. Negligent assignment (e.g., employee without firearms training is assigned to guard prisoners with a firearm; firearm discharges, wounding or killing an inmate)
3. Negligent retention (e.g., an employee with a known history of poor work and inefficiency is retained; subsequently, work of poor quality performed by that employee causes harm to an inmate or offender-client)
4. Negligent entrustment (e.g., employee may be given confidential records and may inadvertently furnish information to others that may be harmful to inmates or offender-clients)
5. Negligent direction (e.g., directions may be given to employees that are not consistent with their job description or work assignment that may result in harm to inmates or offender-clients)
6. Negligent supervision (e.g., employee may supervise prisoners such that inmate problems are overlooked, causing serious harm and further injury or death to inmate or offender-client) (Barrineau, 1994:55–58)

One way of minimizing lawsuits against paraprofessionals and other employees of correctional agencies is to train them so that they can perform their jobs appropriately. H. E. Barrineau (1994:84) lists several criteria that are important to establish as a part of a training program for paraprofessionals and others in the event subsequent lawsuits are filed:

1. The training was necessary as validated by a task analysis.
2. The persons conducting the training were, in fact, qualified to conduct such training.
3. The training did, in fact, take place and was properly conducted and documented.
4. The training was state of the art and up to date.
5. Adequate measures of mastery of the subject matter can be documented.
6. Those who did not satisfactorily "learn" in the training session have received additional training and now have mastery of the subject matter.
7. Close supervision exists to monitor and continually evaluate the trainee's progress.

Barrineau notes that these criteria alone are insufficient to insulate fully one's organization against lawsuits from offender-clients. Nevertheless, they provide some suitable guidelines to cite in the event that an organization or its employees are ever sued. The rule recommended by Barrineau is to document that such training is provided and has occurred (*Whitley v. Warden,* 1971). The theory is that if an event is not documented, it did not happen, as in training (Shearer, 2000).

SUMMARY

POs are supervising an increasingly dangerous clientele. The number of probationers and parolees is escalating annually. Many new entries to probation and parole programs are gang members with prior histories of violence; therefore, it is imperative for POs to have some detailed information about the clientele they will be supervising. One method of determining the risk posed by such clients is to apply risk assessment measures. Probationers as well as parolees are administered risk assessment instruments, either by probation departments or by parole boards. The intent is to determine which offenders are most likely to reoffend and pose safety risks to the public and their supervising POs.

Assessing offender risk has been done for many decades. All states and the federal government have devised risk inventories with differing degrees of sophistication to anticipate one's future dangerousness. Classification is an attempt to place offenders in those programs that will enable them to maximize the program benefits. Some offenders have needs resulting from low levels of education and a lack of work skills. Such offenders will need more assistance than others when it comes to networking with community agencies. Thus, one function of classification is to identify not only the level of risk posed by offenders but also some indication of the types of needs that must be addressed. PO supervisory responsibilities can be enhanced to the extent that they can anticipate offender needs and match them with appropriate community agencies for counseling or treatment.

Risk assessments can be classified according to whether they are actuarial, anamnestic, or clinical. Actuarial devices, which are the most popular, attempt to identify the characteristics of program failures. Thus, the focus is on which characteristics tend to be associated with probationers and parolees who do not succeed in their programs. Probation- or parole-eligible offenders may either be granted or denied probation or parole on the basis of the extent to which they match the characteristics of program failures. Actuarial prediction is popular largely because anyone can administer a paper-and-pencil questionnaire delving into superficial details of one's background and prior criminal record. Anamnestic prediction is using one's past experiences and comparing them with one's anticipated future experiences. Parole boards are especially adept at ascertaining whether one's parole plan is sufficiently unique to show them that the conditions under which a parolee will be living will be substantially different from the conditions that originally led to trouble with the law. Thus, anamnestic prediction compares past circumstances with future circumstances, and predictions are made about how these changed circumstances will modify the future behaviors of prospective parolees. Clinical prediction is the least used of the three types of prediction, mainly because it is too costly to administer on a large-scale basis. Clinicians, psychologists, and psychiatrists must become involved with probationers or parolees, a time-consuming and expensive process. Few jurisdictions have the resources to apply clinical prediction. Ultimately, no single prediction method is foolproof, and virtually every method by which future behaviors are predicted is flawed. Thus, one method is about as good as the others for predicting one's future risk or dangerousness, despite how much one prediction form is marketed or promoted over the others as the best method.

Risk assessment instruments are used for diverse purposes. Not only are they useful for making offender forecasts of future conduct while on probation or parole, but they are also used for classifying offenders for institutional custody levels, such as minimum-, medium-, or maximum-security confinement. Some parole-eligible inmates may not be granted parole because they are deemed to pose too great a risk to society and because their recidivism potential is high. Therefore, selective incapacitation is used to confine those least likely to complete their parole programs successfully.

The roles of POs are gradually changing. One reason for such change is technological advancements relating to client supervision. Global positioning satellite systems are currently being used in growing numbers of jurisdictions to determine an offender's whereabouts. Further, like electronic monitoring, although such tracking systems cannot control behavior, they can warn probation agencies and POs whether their clients are entering restricted areas in which former victims of their crimes reside. Thus, there is a safety element introduced through such tracking systems, although there is currently some controversy among POs about the usefulness and applications of such technology.

In every probation and parole department are apprehension units, or special departments whose personnel have the responsibility of tracking down program absconders. Every year, a proportion of absconders leave their jurisdictions without permission and attempt to elude capture. In 1999, about 4 percent of all clients under different forms of supervision in the community were absconders, including some inmates who were granted temporary releases, such as work release, study release, or furloughs. Even some halfway house residents have absconded from their parole programs. Several factors were identified with absconders. Most probation and parole departments in the larger cities have gang units, or special task forces who study gang formation and operations. More POs are interacting with gang members who not only are affiliated with street gangs but are associated with other gang members while incarcerated in prisons and jails. Finally, most larger probation and parole departments have research units that compile valuable statistical information about those supervised and their characteristics.

PO work is stressful. Stress is a nonspecific response to a perceived threat to an individual's well-being or self-esteem. Stress may lead to burnout, which directly interferes with a PO's work performance. Some of the sources of stress are job dissatisfaction, role conflict, role ambiguity, excessive paperwork obligations, high caseloads, and high risks and liabilities that accompany supervising dangerous offenders. Assisting POs in their supervisory work are volunteers and paraprofessionals. Volunteers are unpaid, yet they perform valuable services such as teaching parolees and probationers how to read and fill out job applications. They perform other tasks as well, depending on the particular jurisdiction and PO needs. Paraprofessionals have had some training related to the work they perform, although they do not have the requisite skills to be full-fledged POs. Their work is more advanced compared with volunteers, and they are paid for what services they render. Both volunteers and paraprofessionals are at risk regarding their legal liabilities. No one working with probationers or parolees is immune from lawsuits that might be filed. Usually, the least-experienced workers are most vulnerable to lawsuits from clients, because they may offer adverse advice unintentionally.

KEY TERMS

Absconders

Actuarial prediction

Agency

Anamnestic prediction

Apprehension units

Burnout

Classification

Classification system

Clinical prediction

Corrections volunteer

Gang units

Global positioning satellite (GPS) system

Job dissatisfaction

Negligence

Paraprofessional

Prediction

Professional

Respondeat superior

Risk assessment

Risk/needs instruments

Role ambiguity

Selective incapacitation

U.S. Code Annotated

Volunteers

QUESTIONS FOR REVIEW

1. What is risk assessment? What are risk assessment instruments?
2. What is meant by classification? What are some of its functions?
3. Identify three types of prediction. Which type of prediction is best? Discuss.
4. What is meant by selective incapacitation? Is it constitutional? Why or why not?
5. How is technology changing the PO role?
6. What is a global positioning satellite system? How is it used to monitor an offender's whereabouts?
7. What can POs do to alleviate stress and burnout?
8. How do volunteers differ from paraprofessionals?
9. What is the doctrine of *respondeat superior*? Do organizations have absolute immunity against lawsuits filed against them because of poor work done by their employees?
10. What was significant about the case of *Hyland v. Wonder*?

SUGGESTED READINGS

Celinska, Katarzyna (2000). "Volunteer Involvement in Ex-Offenders' Readjustment: Reducing the Stigma of Imprisonment." *Journal of Offender Rehabilitation* **30:**99–116.

Dillingham, David D., et al. (1999). *Annual Issue 1999: Classification and Risk Assessment.* Longmont, CO: U.S. National Institute of Corrections.

Lea, Susan, Tim Auburn, and Karen Kibblewhite (1999). "Working with Sex Offenders: The Perceptions and Experiences of Professionals and Paraprofessionals." *International Journal of Offender Therapy and Comparative Criminology* **43:**103–119.

Shearer, Robert A. (2000). "Coerced Substance Abuse Counseling Revisited." *Journal of Offender Rehabilitation* **30:**153–171.

Wilson, Robin J. et al. (2000). "Community-Based Sexual Offender Management: Combining Parole Supervision and Treatment to Reduce Recidivism." *Canadian Journal of Criminology* **42:**177–188.

Theories of Offender Treatment

CHAPTER 11

Introduction
Theories of Criminal Behavior
Biological Theories
   Abnormal Physical Structure
   Hereditary Criminal Behaviors
   Biochemical Disturbances
Psychological Theories
   Psychoanalytic Theory
   Cognitive Development Theory
   Social Learning Theory
Sociological and Sociocultural Theories
   Differential Association Theory
   Anomie Theory or Innovative Adaptation
   The Subculture Theory of Delinquency

Labeling Theory
Social Control Theory
Conflict/Marxist Theory
Reality Therapy
Social Casework
Which Theory Is Best? An Evaluation
   Theories about Adult Offenders
   Theories about Delinquency
Treatment Programs and Theories
Summary
Key Terms
Questions for Review
Suggested Readings

- "About 11:30 P.M. Mrs. Lloyd was awakened by Leonore's crying, 'Oh, God, John. You're going to kill me. Help, mother. Help. John is killing me.' [Mrs. Lloyd] jumped out of bed, opened the door, and saw Leonore in bed and [John] standing over her, his right hand raised and his left hand on her throat. When Mrs. Lloyd got her daughter, Leonore, to the hospital, she was dead. The doctor counted 43 stab wounds on her body, 19 in the chest, 5 on the face, 5 on the right hand, 13 on the left hand, and one on the left thigh. There was a laceration of [a large vein] and two lacerations on the trachea, any one of which could have caused her death." (*Government of Virgin Islands v. Lake*, 362 F.2d 770 1966)

John Lake, husband of Leonore Lake, pleaded not guilty to a charge of first-degree murder because he claimed that his state of mind ruled out the criminal element of premeditation. He was subsequently convicted of first-degree murder, and his appeal was affirmed, or upheld, by the U.S. Court of Appeals.

INTRODUCTION

For several centuries, scientists have attempted to explain crime, what causes it to occur, and how it most effectively can be treated. This chapter describes several theories or explanations for committing crimes. Theories are explanatory schemes that attempt to link events with presumed causes of those events. Subsequent research attempts to show the predictive utility of theories and the events they are designed to explain.

There are important contrasts between how the criminal justice system handles a case like Lake's when determining guilt or innocence and how criminologists might explain or account for the same behavior. The criminal justice system processed Lake for his crime. The criminologist would attempt to account for Lake's actions by asking questions about Lake's sanity or mental capacity or condition. What was his mental state when the crime was committed? Although not all criminologists agree on which explanations are best under these circumstances, criminology does focus on the forms of criminal behavior, the causes of crime, the definition of criminality, and societal reaction to crime. This chapter looks at several explanations for criminal behavior. Several of these explanations have influenced the criminal justice system in different ways.

Because probationers and parolees have been convicted of crimes, they have often been studied by researchers who delve into their motives and intent. This inquiry has led to the formulation of various treatments, known as interventions, designed to rehabilitate offenders or cause them to change their criminal ways. Interventions are experiences interjected into the lives of persons at different ages to cause changes in their future circumstances. For instance, some students in elementary school have been identified as being at risk of becoming delinquent. They may be socially isolated or may exhibit psychological problems. They may be indifferent to authority or may simply refuse to obey a teacher's instructions. Psychologists and others have devised terms to account for some of this behavior. Attention deficit hyperactivity disorder, or ADHD, is used to explain why some students have difficulty staying on task in classroom situations. Some students are hyperactive, and they have medications prescribed for them to control their hyperactivity.

In short, interventions with at-risk youths or with adult probationers and parolees are intended to correct their current behaviors and cause them to become law-abiding. A hard look at any particular intervention will usually find some criminological theory lurking in the background. Some, for example, believe that youthful offenders should not be exposed to the trappings of juvenile courts, which are increasingly like criminal courts in their appearance. Thus, it has been advocated that many of these youths should be sheltered from these formal proceedings and diverted from the juvenile justice system if possible. In the interest of protecting or insulating certain youths from criminal courtlike proceedings, it is therefore believed that they will not define themselves as criminals or delinquents. And as a result, they may be saved from a life of crime by being treated in some way rather than punished through incarceration or probation. Labeling theory is the explanatory scheme behind this type of diversionary action. Youths can avoid the criminal taint or label of being criminal or delinquent. Thus, if they do not define themselves that way, they will have a better chance of becoming rehabilitated.

Interventions in preschool or in one's early school years that target at-risk youths are designed to provide opportunities they might not otherwise have because of their socioeconomic circumstances. Being at-risk does not always mean being socioeconomically deprived, however. Risk factors such as family violence or insta-bility, drug use, alcohol consumption, social isolation, bullying, and other circum-stances cause some youths to be identified by authorities as being at risk. What should be done to rescue these youths from the circumstances that are believed to contribute to their future potential criminal conduct? Various types of counseling and therapeutic interventions that target some of these at-risk youths are attempted. The idea is to help them understand themselves and acquire better self-concepts and self-esteem. Social isolates are drawn out and into school groups and activities. They are provided with social opportunities and learning experiences they otherwise might not have. Behind these types of interventions are theories known as differen-tial or limited opportunity.

For other youthful offenders in their teens, boot camps are used to instill disci-pline. Boot camps and their military-like interventions where self-esteem, self-respect, acceptance of responsibility, and respect for authority are heightened were already examined. Many juveniles are attracted to gangs and engage in delinquent or criminal conduct because they lack the resistance to avoid delinquent groups or criminal organizations. Boot camps are designed, in part, to assist participants in act-ing independently without having to rely on delinquent gangs for esteem and recog-nition. A theory of delinquent subcultures underlies many boot camp programs operating in the United States today.

This chapter describes different theories of criminal and delinquent behavior. Explored are biological theories, psychological theories, and sociological theories that have been used to explain deviant and criminal conduct. These theories are important because they are linked closely with the interventions used by POs in relation with their clients. Further, these theories are the basis for many of the expe-riences and programs to which probationer/parolee/clients are exposed. The chapter concludes by evaluating these theories in terms of their predictive utility. Which the-ory is best? No single theory is universally accepted by all criminologists. No single theory dominates PO policy and practice. Nevertheless, PO work is often couched in one type of theory or another. Thus, why POs orient themselves to clients in particu-lar ways can be more effectively understood through a knowledge of the theories that drive their behaviors and the interventions they utilize.

THEORIES OF CRIMINAL BEHAVIOR

A **theory** is a set of assumptions that attempts to explain and predict relationships between phenomena. The primary functions of theories are to explain and predict. Regarding probationer recidivism, explaining why certain probationers commit new offenses while on probation and predicting the occurrence of these crimes are topics of interest. Criminologists conduct statistical studies to identify circumstances of probationers who cannot remain law-abiding. They might suggest that such proba-tioners were unemployed or underemployed, were on drugs or under the influence of alcohol, or had associated with other known criminals prior to committing these new offenses. If adolescents join a delinquent gang and commit burglaries or engage in gang fights, the criminologist might say that these adolescents had unstable home environments, were not doing well in school, or needed peer companionship and esteem. Thus, several theories may be needed to account for one's criminal conduct.

Observers disagree about the objectives of probation and parole. Some see probation and parole as rehabilitative, whereas others see it as a deterrent to crime.

Yet others see the objective of probation and parole as purely punitive. And some believe that probation and parole embrace all these objectives. Understanding the causes of crime and criminal behavior is useful in designing effective treatment strategies that might be useful in the rehabilitative and reintegrative process. The criminal justice system, including the statutes applicable to sanctioning criminal offenders, has evolved over several centuries. The influence of various theories of criminal behavior on probationer and parolee conduct and the development of subsequent interventions used in their treatment are apparent. Many theories of criminal behavior can be grouped into three general categories that stress different causal factors: biological theories, psychological theories, and sociological or sociocultural theories.

Between 1890 and 2000 there was a major theoretical shift in the thinking of criminologists about why people commit crimes. Early theories of crime emphasized factors inside persons or internal to them. Bad blood, malfunctioning glands, physical deformities, having a criminal personality, having criminal drives or tendencies, possession by evil spirits, heredity, and mental illness are some of the many internal concepts advanced to explain deviant behavior generally and criminal behavior specifically. (Hooton, 1939; Mednick and Volavka, 1980; Montagu, 1968; Yochelson and Samenow, 1976).

During the 1940s and 1950s, some criminologists changed their thinking about criminal behavior to those phenomena occurring external to the individual such as the person's social status or sociocultural position, group pressures and gang conformity, antisocial criminal patterns, associating with criminals, labeling one's self as a criminal, or learning to be a criminal (Cohen, 1955; Nettler, 1974; Thornton, James, and Doerner, 1982). Although this shift has not been overtly acknowledged, it is apparent that the emergence of violent delinquent gangs and social circumstances of adult offenders have undermined existing internal explanations of criminal behavior. Another indication of this shift is the subtle change in research literature that explains crime and describes criminality. Although interpretations of trends in the criminological research literature are largely impressionistic, explanations of crime today emphasize causal factors that differ from those emphasized in the 1920s and 1930s.

This shift does not mean that professionals have abandoned internal explanations for external ones. Rather, external theories are currently more popular than internal theories. This popularity may be seen in the treatment and rehabilitation of criminal offenders. Manipulating the external environment of criminals, their home life, or associates seems easier to accomplish than modifying their genetic structure, driving out evil spirits, or erasing criminal propensities, whatever they might be. Of course, there are other explanations for this shift. Recent theoretical developments in sociology and psychology have emphasized the importance of social or external factors in predicting criminal behavior. Also, criminologists have learned more about genetic makeup, the role of diet in altering personality characteristics, and the medical control of various psychological disorders. Interestingly, these and similar developments have recently renewed interest in some of the more popular internal explanations for criminal behavior.

For example, sociobiologists believe that body chemistry and genetic makeup are crucial in determining all human behavior, including deviance and criminal conduct (Jeffery, 1978; Wilson, 1975; Wilson and Herrnstein, 1985). **Sociobiology** is the scientific study of the causal relation between genetic structure and social behavior.

Some of the treatment programs currently used for offenders are based, in part, on this biological explanation for criminal behavior.

One important issue shared by all these theories, regardless of their intuitive value, innovativeness, or general interest, is whether they can be used to explain and predict criminal behavior. How can each theory be applied? Can effective rehabilitative programs be developed for probationers and parolees? Can any of these theories be used to control criminal behavior or prevent crime? These practical questions are often used to assess the adequacy of any of the theories described here.

Some of these theories of criminal behavior may seem archaic in view of the current state of scientific knowledge, but their effect may be measured or evaluated according to their influence on correctional policies and other criminal justice issues. Thus, although a theory of criminal behavior may be refuted and found to be false, it nevertheless may have important implications for the policies of various agencies within the criminal justice system. For instance, one theory of criminal behavior shown to be false was that heredity transmitted criminal characteristics genetically from one generation to the next. During the 1930s and 1940s, thousands of state and federal prisoners were sterilized, because it was believed that their sterilization would prevent the birth of new generations of criminal offspring.

Evaluations of these theories are not limited to strictly pragmatic criteria. Sometimes, explanations of criminal behavior are abstract and provide contextual backgrounds for other, more practical, theories. For instance, sociologists say that the social class structure of the United States explains certain kinds of crimes. Crime fluctuates among neighborhoods as well as among social classes. Evidently, there is a some connection between the social class structure and crime, but it is unlikely that major changes will soon occur in the social class structure of the United States that affect crime or crime rates. Yet that does not preclude criminologists from using social class as an explanation for crime and crime trends. In addition, it probably encourages POs to orient themselves in particular ways toward probationers or parolees according to the nature of the neighborhoods in which they live as well as their ethnic or racial backgrounds and general socioeconomic information.

BIOLOGICAL THEORIES

Biological theories of criminal behavior include abnormal physical structure, hereditary criminal behaviors, and biochemical disturbances.

Abnormal Physical Structure

One biologically based set of theories has attempted to link **abnormal physical structures** with criminal behaviors. A pioneer of the school of thought that criminals may be identified by their abnormal or unusual physical characteristics was Italian physician Cesare Lombroso (1835–1909), who coined the expression "born criminals." In fairness to Lombroso, his beliefs about the relation between physique and criminal propensities were developed during the period when Charles Darwin's theory of evolution was deemed quite credible in science. Darwin argued that humans evolved from lower life forms and that some humans were more advanced in their biological development than others. Less advanced humans had visible physical characteristics closely associated with the physical features of criminals. Thus, Lombroso's explanation of crime made much more sense then than it does today.

Lombroso said that (1) criminals are, by birth, a distinct type; (2) this type can be recognized by asymmetrical craniums, long lower jaws, flattened noses, scanty beards, and low sensitivity to pain; (3) these characteristics do not themselves cause crime but assist in our identification of personalities disposed toward criminal behavior; (4) such persons cannot refrain from criminal behavior except under unusual social circumstances; and (5) different physical features are associated with different kinds of crime (Vorenberg, 1981:33–34).

Originally, Lombroso argued that 100 percent of the prison population was composed of born criminals, but in subsequent years, he modified this figure to about 40 percent. His treatise on the subject was published in 1876 and was expanded into three volumes (Lombroso, 1918). His views later were known as the Italian school or the positive school, because direct empirical indicators of criminal tendencies could be identified (i.e., cranium shape, jaw angles, body hair) compared with other speculation about criminal conduct.

Lombroso's studies of Italian prison inmates led him to observe that many had long, sloping foreheads, pointed ears, narrow or shifty eyes, receding chins, and overly long arms. Subsequent comparisons of other prisoners with the nonincarcerated population at large have revealed no significant differences in physical characteristics between criminals and noncriminals, however. One explanation for Lombroso's views about physique and criminal behavior is that persons with odd appearances are often rejected by others. This rejection might lead them to follow deviant or criminal paths. The labeling theory of deviant behavior described later in this chapter examines this phenomenon more fully.

Lombroso's views still enjoy popularity in the media whenever particularly bizarre events occur. For instance, the late Truman Capote wrote a nonfictional work entitled *In Cold Blood* that detailed the murder of an entire Kansas family by two drifters. These men were apprehended, tried and convicted of murder, and executed. At or about the time of their execution, their photographs appeared in the *Saturday Evening Post*. The writer of the article suggested that readers observe that one of the murderers had a face made up from two parts and the two parts did not quite match up with one another. Attention was drawn to portions of the murderer's photograph showing that one eye was not level or even with the other, that the mouth curved down on one side and up on the other side, and that the ears were unevenly matched. This physical description was provided in a popular national magazine in the late 1960s.

A popular outgrowth of Lombroso's positivist thinking was the concept of various body types by Sheldon (1949), who classified persons into three distinct categories: **endomorphs** (fat, soft, plump, jolly); **ectomorphs** (thin, sensitive, delicate); and **mesomorphs** (strong, muscular, aggressive, tough). Sheldon wrote extensively about the behavioral characteristics of each body type. He devised a complex numerical system in which persons possessed features of one body type to a greater degree than the other two types. He eventually developed crude indices from which generalizations about criminal behavior could be made. He said that ectomorphs tend to commit forgery, fraud, or burglary (passive, nonviolent crimes), whereas mesomorphs tend to commit robbery, rape, murder, assault, and other physically demanding crimes. Sheldon believed that body type was a cause of particular types of criminal conduct. Subsequent studies and extensive research by criminologists and others have failed to support Sheldon's theory.

Hereditary Criminal Behaviors

Heredity as a cause of criminal conduct suggested the inheritance of certain physical and behavioral characteristics from parents or ancestors. Whether people became criminals depended on their lineage or hereditary background. If one's ancestors were cattle rustlers, thieves, or rapists, then their offspring would also tend to be cattle rustlers, thieves, or rapists. Little scientific evidence exists supporting this theory.

A more recent heredity-based theory of criminal behavior is the XYY syndrome, where X and Y are labels assigned to the human sex chromosomes. Males are XY, and females are XX. These sex chromosomes X and Y are inherited from the mother and father. The father transmits the Y or aggressive chromosome, and the X or passive chromosome comes from the mother. Occasionally, infants are born with an XYY (doubly aggressive?) chromosomatic pattern.

In the 1960s, researchers were intrigued by the discovery that Richard Speck had an XYY chromosomatic pattern. At the time, Speck was in prison for the brutal murder of eight student nurses in Chicago. Could this extra Y chromosome have caused his violent behavior? Geneticists have investigated the XYY syndrome in selected, captive-audience situations: prisons (McClearn, 1969; Mednick and Volavka, 1980; Shah and Roth, 1974). Their studies show that (1) there appear to be more XYY people in the criminal population compared with the general population and (2) fewer than 5 percent of the prison population has the XYY syndrome (Shah and Roth, 1974). Thus, the XYY syndrome is not a consistent cause of criminal behavior (Sarbin and Miller, 1970).

Biochemical Disturbances

A third group of biologically based theories of criminal behavior focuses on biochemical disturbances and glandular malfunctions as inducing criminal acts. The thyroid, adrenal, pituitary, and hypothalamus glands have been linked with different kinds of aggressive and antisocial behavior. Glands have been shown to control metabolism, growth, and activity levels. Hyperactivity, or abnormally active behavior, is often associated with oversecretions or undersecretions of various hormones (Hippchen, 1981; Yaryura-Tobias and Neziroglu, 1975). Recent medical developments have led to a greater understanding of biochemical functions and to the development of drugs and synthetic chemicals that can control abnormal behavior. For example, Thorazine is administered to mental patients to control various psychotic disorders. Diazepam, an antidepressant, is used to treat severe alcohol withdrawal or to help patients manage severe anxiety or stress. These products alter hormonal states and permit some regulation of deviant and criminal behavior.

Various drugs have been used to contain the sexual urges of more than a few probationers and parolees who are sex offenders. Together with counseling and medicine, many sex offenders are leading normal lives today as probationers and parolees, because their problems are believed to be hormone related to a degree. Chemical imbalances can also be regulated with proper drug therapies.

PSYCHOLOGICAL THEORIES

Another set of theories about criminal conduct is based in psychology, the study of individual behavior. By studying individual behavior, psychologists try to explain the inner workings of the mind. Because various components of the criminal justice system must determine criminal intent and the defendant's mental competence to stand

BOX 11.1   *Will Castration Prevent Sex Crimes?*

The Case of Jeffrey Morse. Jeffrey Morse, 30, of Schaumburg, a Chicago suburb, wants to be castrated. Why? He is a sex offender who cannot control his sexual impulses. He attacked a 12-year-old girl in 1996 and molested her sexually. He tried to attack an 11-year-old girl in 1997, but was unsuccessful. He tried to lure her to his car, where he planned to rape her. Morse was convicted of the 1996 sexual molestation charge, and he faced 6 to 100 years in prison for the crime. His sentencing was scheduled for February 1998. Morse's attorney, Paul B. Wharton, advised news sources that Morse planned to have himself castrated, because, as Wharton put it, "someone said that if the flagpole isn't flying, the compulsion to sing the *Star-Spangled Banner* is not the primary thought in the man's mind." Wharton said that a group of anonymous donors has contributed over $5,000 to cover the cost of the castration for Morse. Morse was permitted a one-day furlough from jail to have the castration. An anonymous group of doctors would perform the operation, Wharton said. Why would a sex offender such as Morse undergo castration? One explanation is that Morse believes that besides minimizing his sex drive, it will also have some weight in mitigating his potentially lengthy sentence. Morse hoped that his decision to have the castration surgery would persuade the judge to be lenient with him. This procedure is not a compulsory order from the court. Rather, Morse himself initiated the idea and believes that it is the best alternative in his case. In other jurisdictions, judges have attempted to impose castration of sex offenders in lieu of lengthy prison terms, but the U.S. Supreme Court has ruled that they cannot offer convicted offenders this alternative, because it would violate their constitutional rights. Should the judge be lenient in sentencing Morse because he underwent voluntary castration? What do you think? (*Source:* Adapted from Associated Press, "Sex Offender Wants Castration," January 17, 1998.)

The Case of Larry Don McQuay. Larry Don McQuay, 32-year-old convicted child molester, was serving a lengthy prison term in Texas. In March 1996, he became eligible for parole, and early release was granted. Everyone seemed satisfied with the early-release decision, everyone except Larry Don McQuay. Prior to appearing before the Texas Board of Pardons and Paroles, McQuay had requested that he be castrated. His reason: to curb his desire to attack and sexually molest children, especially young boys. He carried on a relentless letter-writing campaign with state officials, demanding that the State of Texas castrate him for their own good and his own good. McQuay even referred to himself as a "child molesting demon" who would do even more harm to children if released. Texas authorities rejected his request. The reason given was that castration is *elective surgery,* and thus it cannot be performed at state expense.

Victor Rodriguez, chairman of the Texas Board of Pardons and Paroles, said that McQuay was to be released to a halfway house. Halfway houses are usually located in neighborhoods, and halfway house clients may come and go as they please. Halfway house personnel are in positions to monitor client behaviors when those clients are on site, but such monitoring is impossible when clients are out during daytime hours. McQuay sent at least six letters to a victim's rights group known as Justice for All, a Houston-based organization concerned with the rights of victims of violent crimes. The organization notifies victims whenever convicted felons become eligible for parole so that victims might appear and speak against such early-release decision making by paroling authorities. Dianne Clements, president of Justice for All, said that the letters she has received from McQuay are perverse and "sick stuff," a "dissertation of his fantasies." McQuay has said a few things himself. "I have been busting my butt to do everything possible to keep me from reoffending, but everyone seems to be dead set against it," said McQuay to reporters. "I got away with molesting over 240 children before getting caught for molesting just one little boy. With all that I have cold-heartedly learned while in prison, there is no way that I will ever get caught again. Will *your* children be my next victims?" McQuay posed.

McQuay further stated that "I am doomed to eventually rape then murder my poor little victims to keep them from telling on me. Sometimes I wish I was born a hundred years ago when you could marry a 12-year-old girl and nobody would think twice about it; or back in the Greek culture when they had sex with boys; but in today's society, that's not acceptable and I'm not a time traveler, so I can't go back into another society or another culture." Texas officials are required under a 1995 state law to notify local law enforcement authorities if a convicted child molester is moving into their community. Interestingly, McQuay is exempt from this law, because he was convicted before the law was enacted. Betty Frank, a neighbor living near the halfway house where McQuay will be housed, said, "It terrifies me!" When released, McQuay was given a $50 check, a bus ticket out of town, and the promise of another $50 for reporting, on his own, to the Texas House in Houston, the halfway house where he is to serve the remainder of his sentence. The halfway house serves at least 210 offenders at any given time.

What if McQuay strikes again and molests children once he is placed in the halfway house? Who would be to blame? McQuay himself? The Texas Board of Pardons and Paroles? After all, McQuay has warned that he is coming out and will be dangerous. Will this warning absolve him of future criminal conduct if authorities don't intervene? (*Source:* Adapted from Associated Press, "Texas Delays Release of Convicted Pedophile," April 3, 1996.)

trial, prosecutors and defense attorneys often turn to psychologists for help. Psychologists and psychiatrists, physicians who specialize in treating mental disorders, are often asked to examine defendants and give their expert testimony in court. Psychological theories of criminal behavior have also influenced correctional and rehabilitative programs. Psychological counselors and psychiatrists play key roles in contemporary criminal rehabilitative therapy. Three psychological theories are presented here: psychoanalytic theory, cognitive development theory, and social learning theory.

Psychoanalytic Theory

Psychoanalytic theory was created by the Austrian neurologist Sigmund Freud (1856–1939). Frustrated by the primitive technology of his day, Freud tried to explain the human personality and mental disorders through the interaction of the concepts of the **id**, the **ego**, the **superego**, and the **libido**. The id is the "I want" associated with the behavior of infants. Getting a two-year-old to share his or her jelly-beans or ice cream is near impossible. As children grow, they learn that the id cannot always be satisfied. The child cannot have everything he or she wants. Therefore, the id is eventually controlled by the ego, which embodies society's standards and conventional rules. As the child matures into adolescence, moral values are incorporated into the personality. Moral values are the domain of the superego. The libido is the sex urge or drive that Freud believed was inborn. He explained criminal behavior as a function of an inadequately developed ego, the controlling mechanism for the id. When persons fail to control their impulses and disregard the rights and feelings of others, their aggressive behaviors often follow deviant paths and criminal acts occur. According to Freud, rape may be the result of an uncontrollable libido, and theft may be the result of a poorly developed ego.

Some counseling centers and rehabilitative agencies work with offenders to assist them in improving their self-concept as well as their ability to function normally around others. Encouraging people to talk out their problems and exchange personal information with others through group therapy and encounter sessions are ways for offenders to gain greater control over their behaviors. The halfway house concept is one intervention designed to gradually assist offenders back into society once they have left prison or jail, because the transition experience may be abrupt. Halfway house personnel, together with other offenders, provide a social support system for newly released inmates learning to cope with societal demands for law-abiding behavior. Furthermore, these houses provide some amount of counseling assistance. If they cannot, then a community network of services is available to halfway house clients. All probationers and parolees have access to necessary community services if needed, and many of these services are oriented toward improving one's self-concept and feelings of self-worth.

More than a few POs have bought into the idea that some of their clients have underdeveloped egos and psychological problems that must be resolved through some form of counseling or therapy. This type of approach is used by enablers, brokers, and educators, and it reflects a social work orientation toward the PO role. POs using this approach in dealing with their clients are more inclined to recommend some form of counseling, individually or in a group, for offenders who violate one or more program conditions. Compared with enforcers, they are less likely to report program infractions.

Cognitive Development Theory

Cognitive development theory stresses **cognitive development** through a learning process involving various stages. Jean Piaget (1896–1980) was one of the first to stress the importance of cognitive stages of development and the idea that all normal individuals pass through the same sequential periods in the growth or maturing of their ability to think or to gain knowledge and awareness of themselves and their environment (VanderZanden, 1984:116-117). As a child moves through various stages of development, he or she acquires an awareness of people, objects, and, especially, standards of behavior or judgments of right and wrong (Boehm, 1962; Piaget, 1948).

Piaget's notions about cognitive development have been modified and expanded by L. Kohlberg (1963), who has described six stages in the development of a person's moral judgment. These levels or stages, according to Kohlberg, reflect a different type of relationship between the individual and his or her society (VanderZanden, 1984:123). Kohlberg divides the six stages into three categories: the preconventional level, the conventional level, and the postconventional level. Kohlberg says that very young children, some adolescents, and many criminals are in the preconventional stage of development. Thus, psychologists supporting this theory associate criminal behavior with inadequate moral development during childhood. Some gender bias is inherent in Kohlberg's scheme, because conventional role conformity traditionally encourages men in our culture to acquire protective/aggressive behaviors, whereas women are socialized to be more submissive and nurturing.

A contrary perspective has been devised by Samuel Yochelson and Stanton Samenow (1976). These researchers reject the notion that criminal behavior is the direct result of one's environment. Rather, they believe that those who become criminals do so because they want to. At a very early age, youths seek associations with others who may be delinquent. The excitement of committing delinquent acts becomes a self-perpetuating influence in their lives. As these youths graduate to more serious offenses as adults, the same excitement urges them to carry out criminal acts. Yochelson and Samenow believe that free will rather than one's environment determines whether a criminal career pattern will be pursued. Thus, if criminal behavior is to be decreased or eliminated by any conventional treatment program, then it is imperative that psychologists and others try to dissuade these people from thinking about committing crimes. Changing their thoughts about crime will lead to a cessation of their criminal behaviors. Yochelson and Samenow, however, do not answer the question of why these people "think" about engaging in criminal acts. In short, little support exists for their position. Their theorizing is, though, an interesting contrast with the work of Kohlberg and others who stress environmental experiences as primary ingredients for stimulating criminal behavior.

Social Learning Theory

Applied to criminology, **social learning theory** is that criminal behavior is learned by modeling the behaviors of others who are criminal. It does not propose that criminal conduct is copied or imitated. Rather, those who use others as models for their criminal behavior do so as the result of strong incentives to do so (Bandura, 1977). Deviant and criminal conduct as well as conventional conduct stems from the process of reinforcement, through which people perceive others who are rewarded (by goods, money, or social status) for conforming to conventional rules or are punished for deviating from those same rules. This type of reinforcement, called external reinforcement, is seen as a crucial social reinforcement mechanism that propels people toward conventional behavior. People also derive reinforcement from internal sources. Some people may engage in self-punishment when they perceive themselves behaving badly, or they may reward themselves for self-perceptions of conformity and appropriate behavior. Most important, reinforcement arises from observing others being rewarded for their conduct. Depending on the environment in which people are socialized, reinforcement may stem from conventional sources or from unconventional ones. Those who observe a criminal being rewarded with goods, money, social status, or acclaim may be motivated to model or emulate this deviant or criminal behavior.

When people do not fit in with certain social groups, or when they are unsuccessful in adapting to social situations and perceive little or no reward for their conventional behavior, they may learn other behaviors for which rewards of various kinds are forthcoming. Such conduct may be criminal conduct, and it can yield rewards from others who are criminal. This situation reinforces deviant conduct and dissuades people from adopting conventional modes of behavior.

Social learning theory fails to explain the roles played by close friends, family, and other agencies of socialization in modifying one's conventional or unconventional conduct. It stresses psychological factors and alludes to certain stimulus-response behavior patterns reflected by behaviorism. Its main value is that it focuses attention on the social contexts in which conventional or unconventional conduct is acquired. It does not, however, adequately explain the process of acquiring these behaviors.

BOX 11.2   *Tougher Gun Laws or Tougher Enforcement for Medication*

Sergei Babarin

Sergei Barbarin, 71, is dead. On April 16, 1999, he walked into the Mormon Family History Library in Salt Lake City and sprayed the first floor with .22-caliber handgun fire, killing two people and wounding four others before being shot to death by police. The library shooting was shocking, but also shocking was when just months earlier, on January 14, in the same city, 24-year-old Di-Kieu Duy walked into a downtown office building with a grocery sack full of bullets and opened fire on office workers. One person died and another suffered minor gunshot wounds. Immediately following the shootings in both cases, Salt Lake City Police Chief Ruben Ortega issued a call for stricter state law to keep guns from those with mental illnesses. Ortega says, "It's happening too much all over the country."

Are stiffer gun laws needed? Both Babarin and Duy were diagnosed as paranoid schizophrenics and placed on medication to control their emotional outbursts and mental instability. Utah is one of many states with laws prohibiting the sale of firearms to those who have been declared mentally incompetent. In the case of Utah's 100,000 mentally ill persons on record, this legal threshold is difficult to meet. Technically, Babarin and Duy were not "mentally incompetent." Both Babarin

and Duy had previous brushes with the law. Police had taken a .22-caliber semiautomatic handgun from Babarin after he was arrested and charged with assault and carrying a concealed weapon in a 1995 fight at a downtown department store. It was similar to the handgun he used at the Mormon Family History Library.

Police Chief Ortega believes that psychiatrists should be ordered to report to state authorities the names of persons they diagnose with certain mental illnesses. Gun dealers would then be forbidden from selling guns to them. Babarin's son, Alex, however, said he didn't think a stiffer gun law would have deterred his father from committing these acts of violence. "He could just take his car and run people down," said Alex Babarin. Alex said that he had fought to get his father committed for nearly a year. Just two days before the shooting, his father had accused him of spying and being out to get him, the same charges he had leveled against his neighbors and even against people passing on the street.

How is it known whether someone is mentally ill? If someone is mentally ill, then how can he or she be compelled to take appropriate medication? Should psychiatrists be more accountable? What do you think?

Source: Adapted from Associated Press, "Police Chief Calls for Tougher Gun Laws in Wake of Shooting." April 17, 1999.

SOCIOLOGICAL AND SOCIOCULTURAL THEORIES

Sociological and sociocultural theories are as equally diverse as psychological theories. There is considerable interplay between psychological and sociological perspectives, but sociologists focus more closely on the social processes involved in criminal conduct as well as the importance of social structure. They believe that forces or processes in the external social environment lead people to commit criminal acts. **Social process theories** stress external forces as causes of criminal conduct, in contrast to the internal forces, emphasized by biological and psychological theories. Several popular sociological theories of criminal behavior are differential association theory, anomie theory, subculture theory, labeling theory, social control theory, and conflict/Marxist theory.

Differential Association Theory

Sociologist Edwin Sutherland (1893–1950) is credited with formulating perhaps the best-known sociological theory of crime. His theory, known as **differential association theory**, was formally presented in the 1920s, and a few researchers still use to it to explain some forms of adult crime (Fannin, 1984). Sutherland used the differential association concept to explain the process by which persons became criminals. As the name implies, association with criminals is an important part of this process. Yet it is an oversimplification of Sutherland's theory to state that simple association with criminals causes a person become a criminal; the theory is more complex than that. In some respects, Sutherland's theory is an outgrowth of **cultural transmission theory** developed by Clifford Shaw and Henry McKay (1929). These sociologists believed that criminal behavior patterns are transmitted in much the same manner as culture is transmitted through **socialization**. Socialization is learning through contact with others or social learning.

Expanding on the work of Shaw and McKay, Sutherland outlined a fairly elaborate multidimensional social interaction process that would induce a person to adopt criminal behaviors. The dimensions of differential association theory are frequency, duration, priority, and intensity. The transmission of deviant (and criminal) cultural values and behaviors occurs in a social learning context in which the potential criminal has frequent contact of some lasting duration with criminals. Priority and intensity are more elusive concepts in Sutherland's scheme. Priority refers to either the lawful or criminal behavior learned in early childhood. This learning persists throughout a person's life to reinforce criminal behaviors whenever associations with criminals occur. Intensity is the degree of emotional attachment to either conventional or criminal groups and the prestige allocated each. Thus, criminal behaviors acquired at an early age and reinforced through frequent and lengthy emotional attachments with one or more criminals are seen as primary contributing factors to explain why people become criminals.

Professionals involved in corrections programs have shown some respect for Sutherland's differential association ideas over the years. In some jurisdictions, first-offenders are not placed in the same cells with more seasoned offenders. This policy is a luxury, though, relinquished when incarceration rates are high and prison funding is low. Thus, because of overcrowding, penal authorities sometimes mix all inmates, regardless of the nature or seriousness of the crimes they have committed. This overcrowding situation has caused some observers to label prisons and jails as institutions of higher criminal learning, with more seasoned criminals teaching first-offenders how to avoid being apprehended the next time.

Critics of differential association theory have said that Sutherland's terms are difficult to define and understand. What is meant by an intense relation? How frequent is frequent? Also, Sutherland's theory does not explain all types of criminal conduct. Although Sutherland intended his theory to account for most criminal behavior, numerous exceptions to his scheme over the years caused him to believe that additional factors such as opportunity and individual needs were equally important and ought to be considered. Therefore, he eventually adopted multiple-factor theoretical explanations for criminal conduct and gave less attention to differential association.

Closely related to differential association theory and applied to juveniles is **neutralization theory**. POs who work with juveniles frequently encounter youths who deny responsibility for what they have done. They deny that they caused any-one injury, or they claim that the victim deserved whatever injuries were received. These youths are living examples of what Gresham Sykes and David Matza (1957) called neutralization theory. This theory holds that delinquents experience guilt whenever they commit crimes, because simultaneously, they respect the legitimacy of the social order of their community. Their delinquency is episodic rather than chronic. They are said to drift into delinquent conduct, first neutralizing their legal and moral values with rationalizations of various kinds.

Most juveniles spend their early years on a behavioral continuum ranging between unlimited freedom and total control or restraint. These persons drift toward one end of the continuum or the other, depending on their social and psychological cir-cumstances. If youths have strong attachments with those who are delinquent, then they drift toward the unlimited freedom end of the continuum and perhaps engage accordingly in delinquent activities. The behavioral issue is not clear-cut, however. Juve-niles are most likely to have associations with normative culture as well as the delin-quent subculture. Therefore, at least some delinquency results from rationalizations created by youths that render delinquent acts acceptable under the circumstances. Appropriate preventative therapy for such delinquents might be to undermine their rationales for delinquent behaviors through empathic means.

Rationalizations used by juveniles to account for their misconduct include that there is no real victim, that they believe their victim deserved to be injured, that they committed their crimes for family members or friends, that the police and others are out to get them, that no one actually was hurt by whatever they did, and that the delinquency was not really their fault. PO dealings with juveniles frequently disclose such rationalizations. Thus, they are able to understand why some delinquents do not accept any responsibility or exhibit remorse when they have done something wrong. Neutralization theory, however, posits that delinquents do indeed feel guilt at some level, and POs can use this guilt to their advantage when prescribing appropriate community therapies for juvenile offenders.

Anomie Theory or Innovative Adaptation

The use of anomie in **anomie theory** is a misnomer. **Anomie** literally means norm-lessness, or a condition when the norms or behavioral expectations are unknown, undefined, or in conflict. People seldom experience true normlessness. Robert King Merton (1938, 1957) is credited with developing anomie theory, which was originally proposed by the French sociologist, Emile Durkheim (1858–1917). Anomie theory states that all people in society are taught to pursue certain culturally approved goals. People are also taught socially acceptable or approved institutionalized means by which these goals may be achieved. Merton's theory of anomie emphasized the ways that persons adapt to goal attainment and the means they use to achieve these goals, which he referred to as the **modes of adaptation**. Merton said that persons either accept or reject the goals of their society. Also, they either accept or reject the approved means to achieve those goals (Merton, 1938).

According to Merton, conformity is the most common adaptation. People accept the culturally approved goals and the socially approved means to achieve them. People might want a new car or a new home, and they will work patiently at socially acceptable jobs so that they may eventually acquire these possessions. Some people, however, accept the culturally approved goals, but they reject the means to achieve those goals. For instance, an inmate at a state prison once confided that he had been an A student at a large California university, majoring in business administration and planned a business career. At the end of his third year, however, he decided that the educational process was too slow, and that his calculations of future earnings were too low for his particular desires. He said, "I decided that to get what I want fast, I've got to have a lot of money. The best place to get a lot of money fast is a bank. So I started robbing banks." His adaptation to the goals/means relation was innovation. His criminal behaviors were the innovative means he substituted to achieve certain desired, culturally approved goals.

Much criminal behavior, according to Merton, is innovative behavior, and this mode of adaptation was the focus of his theory of anomie. Merton's theory also tried to explain drug abusers and alcohol users. These people have been labeled as retreatists because they withdraw from others and reject the culturally approved goals as well as the means to achieve them. Such people may be unemployed, vagrant, or otherwise indifferent about achieving the culturally approved goals sought by others. Other adaptation forms included in Merton's scheme are ritualism (rejecting the goals, accepting the means) and rebellion (accepting and rejecting some of the goals and means and substituting new goals and means). Ritualists might be people who conclude that they will never have the nice home and new car, but they will nevertheless work at their socially approved jobs until retirement. In contrast, rebels reject the goals and the means and are interested in creating new societal goals through revolution or rebellion.

Merton's theory of anomie is particularly relevant for explaining property crimes such as burglary and larceny. The people who commit these crimes may want material wealth or expensive possessions, but they are unwilling or unable to earn money through socially acceptable occupations. Thus, they will likely seek goal attainment through innovative means. Merton's theory is economically based and concerned with gaining access to certain success goals. Some critics say that Merton made an erroneous assumption that poor persons are more prone to criminal behavior than rich persons (Thio, 1975). Furthermore, Merton has not explained the embezzlement or tax fraud of successful business executives (Thio, 1975). It might be, however, that such criminals are simply seeking a culturally approved goal through innovative means. Another criticism is that the theory does not explain noneconomic crimes such as aggravated assault or rape. Anomie, however, is not intended to explain these kinds of offenses. Finally, some critics have said that Merton's scheme does not deal with criminal behavior as a process (Gibbons, 1968).

Merton's scheme presents several adaptations people can make in attaining goals and choosing the means to achieve those goals. It is a static rather than dynamic theory. Merton's innovative mode is more or less an automatic response that is almost always regarded as deviant and/or criminal. By comparison, differential association theory analyzes such dynamic processes as the duration and intensity of social associations that encourage and condone criminal acts. Sutherland's differential association theory about white collar criminals and Merton's innovative modes of adaptation may be linked theoretically to the **theory of opportunity**. According to this theory, middle- and upper-class persons have more opportunities to gain access to and achieve success goals, whereas lower-class persons lack these opportunities. Therefore, lower-class persons tend to achieve success by achieving certain deviant and/or criminal objectives that are respected by other criminals.

The Subculture Theory of Delinquency

During the 1950s, sociologist Albert Cohen (1955) focused on and described **delinquent subcultures**, which exist, according to Cohen, within the greater societal culture. These **subcultures**, though, contain value systems, modes of achievement, and gaining status and recognition apart from the mainstream culture. Thus, to understand why many juveniles behave as they do, attention must be paid to the patterns of their particular subculture.

The notion of a delinquent subculture is fairly easy to understand, especially in view of the earlier work of Shaw and McKay (1929). Although middle- and upper-class children learn and aspire to achieve lofty ambitions and educational goals and receive support for these aspirations from their parents as well as predominantly middle-class teachers, lower-class youths are at a distinct disadvantage at the outset. They are born into families in which these aspirations and attainments may be alien and rejected. Their primary familial role models have not attained these high aims themselves. At school, these youths are often isolated socially from upper- and middle-class juveniles; therefore, social attachments are formed with others similar to themselves. Perhaps these youths dress differently from other students, wear their hair in a certain style, or use coded language when talking to peers in front of other students. They acquire a culture unto themselves that is largely unknown to other students. In a sense, much of this cultural isolation is self-imposed, but it functions to give them a sense of fulfillment, reward, self-esteem, and recognition apart from other reward systems. If these students cannot achieve one or more of the various standards set by middle-class society, then they create their own standards and prescribe the means to achieve those standards.

Cohen is quick to point out that delinquency is not a product of lower socioeconomic status per se. Rather, children from lower socioeconomic statuses are at greater risk than others of being susceptible to the rewards and opportunities a subculture of delinquency might offer in contrast with the system's middle-class reward structure. Several experiments in which these subcultures have been targeted and described and in which the norms of these subcultures have been used as intervening mechanisms to modify delinquent behaviors toward nondelinquent modes of action have subsequently been implemented with delinquents. The Provo Experiment was influenced, to a degree, by the work of Cohen (Empey and Rabow, 1961). In the late 1950s, samples of delinquent youths in Provo, Utah, were identified and were given an opportunity to participate in group therapy sessions at Pine Hills, a large home in Provo that had been converted to an experimental laboratory. In cooperation with juvenile court judges and other authorities, Pine Hills investigators began their intervention strategies assuming that juvenile participants had limited access to success goals, performed many of their delinquent activities in groups rather than alone, and committed their delinquent acts for nonutilitarian objectives rather than for money (Empey and Rabow, 1961). These investigators believed that because the delinquents had acquired their delinquent values and conduct through their subculture of delinquency, they could "unlearn" these values and learn new values by the same means. Thus, groups of delinquents participated extensively in therapy directed at changing their behaviors through group processes. The investigators believed that their intervention efforts were largely successful and that the subcultural approach to delinquency prevention and behavioral change was fruitful.

An interesting variation on the subcultural theme is the work of Marvin Wolfgang and Franco Ferracuti (1967). Wolfgang and other associates investigated large numbers of Philadelphia, Pennsylvania, boys in a study of birth cohorts. In that study, they found that approximately 6 percent of all boys accounted for more than 50 percent of all delinquent conduct from the entire cohort of more than 9,000 boys (Wolfgang, Figlio, and Sellin, 1972). These boys were chronic recidivists who were also violent offenders. Wolfgang has theorized that there are subcultural norms of violence in many communities that attract male youths. They regard violence as a normal part of their environment; they use violence and respect the use of violence by others. On the basis of evidence amassed by Wolfgang and Ferracuti, it appeared that predominantly lower-class and less-educated young men formed a disproportionately large part of this **subculture of violence**. When violence is accepted and respected, its use is considered normal and normative for the users. Remorse is an alien emotion to those using violence and who live with it constantly. Thus, it is socially ingrained as a subcultural value.

The subcultural perspective toward delinquent conduct is indicative of a strain between the values of society and the values of a subgroup of delinquent youths. Therefore, some researchers have labeled the subcultural perspective a **strain theory**. The strain component is apparent because although many youths in the lower socioeconomic strata have adopted middle-class goals and aspirations, they may be unable to attain these goals because of their individual economic and cultural circumstances. This experience is frustrating for many of these youths, and such frustration is manifested by the strain to achieve difficult goals or objectives. Although middle-class youths also experience strain in their attempts to achieve middle-class goals, it is particularly aggravating for many lower-class youths, because they sometimes do not receive the necessary support from their families. Merton's anomie theory greatly influenced the development of strain theory.

Obviously, myriad other explanations for delinquent conduct have been advanced by various theorists. Those selected for more in-depth coverage above are by no means the best theories to account for delinquency. Their inclusion here is merely to describe some of the thinking about why juveniles might be attracted toward delinquent conduct. Two other approaches that have been advocated are **containment theory** and **differential reinforcement theory**.

Containment theory is closely associated with the work of sociologist Walter Reckless (1967), who outlined a theoretical model consisting of "pushes" and "pulls" in relation to delinquency. By pushes he referred to internal personal factors, including hostility, anxiety, and discontent. By pulls he meant external social forces, including delinquent subcultures and significant others. The containment dimension of his theoretical scheme consisted of both outer and inner containments. Outer containments, according to Reckless, are social norms, folkways, mores, laws, and institutional arrangements that induce societal conformity. By inner containments, Reckless referred to individual or personal coping strategies to deal with stressful situations and conflict. These strategies might be a high tolerance for conflict or frustration and considerable ego strength. Thus, Reckless combined both psychological and social elements in referring to weak attachments of some youths to cultural norms, high anxiety levels, and low tolerance for personal stress. These persons are most inclined to delinquent conduct. A key factor in whether juveniles adopt delinquent behaviors is their level of self-esteem. Those with high levels of self-esteem seem most resistant to delinquent behaviors if they are exposed to such conduct while around their friends.

In 1966, Robert Burgess and Ronald Akers attempted to revise Sutherland's differential association theory and derived what they called differential reinforcement theory. This theory actually combines elements from labeling theory and a psychological phenomenon known as conditioning. Conditioning functions in the social learning process as persons are rewarded for engaging in certain desirable behaviors and refraining from certain undesirable behaviors. Juveniles perceive how others respond to their behaviors (negative reactions) and may be disposed to behave in ways that will maximize their rewards from others. Also, in some respects, Burgess and Akers have incorporated certain aspects of the "looking-glass self" concept originally devised by the theorist Charles Horton Cooley, who theorized that people learned ways of conforming by paying attention to the reactions of others in response to their own behavior. Therefore, Cooley would argue that we imagine how others see us. We look for other's reactions to our behavior and make interpretations of these reactions as either good or bad reactions. If we define others' reactions as good, then we will feel a degree of pride and likely persist in the behaviors. As Cooley indicated, however, if we interpret their reactions to our behaviors as bad, we might experience mortification. Given this latter reaction or at least our interpretation of it, we might change our behaviors to conform to what others might want and thereby elicit approval from them. Although these ideas continue to be of interest, they are difficult to conceptualize and investigate empirically. Akers and others have acknowledged such difficulties, yet their work is insightful and underscores the reality of a multidimensional view of delinquent conduct.

Labeling Theory

A third popular sociological theory of criminal behavior is **labeling theory**. This theory is associated with the work of Edwin Lemert (1951), although Howard S. Becker (1963) and John Kitsuse (1962) have also been credited with being among its early advocates. Labeling theory is concerned with the social definitions of criminal acts rather than the criminal acts themselves. It attempts to answer at least two questions: What is the process through which persons become labeled as criminals or deviants? and How does such labeling influence the persons labeled as deviant?

The basic assumptions of labeling theory are as follows: (1) no act is inherently criminal, (2) persons become criminals by social labeling or definition, (3) all persons at one time or another conform to and deviate from laws, (4) getting caught begins the labeling process, (5) the person defined as criminal will develop a criminal self-definition, and (6) the person will seek others similarly defined and develop a criminal subculture (Bernstein, Kelly, and Doyle, 1977; Schrag, 1971; VanderZanden, 1984:206; Wellford, 1975).

According to Edwin Lemert (1951), there are two types of deviation: primary and secondary. **Primary deviations** involve violations of law that often can be and frequently are overlooked. College students who pull pranks such as disassembling the university president's car and reassembling it on the roof of a dormitory are mildly chided by police rather than arrested for criminal vehicular theft. **Secondary deviations** occur when violations of the law have become incorporated into a person's lifestyle or behavior pattern. Usually, by the time secondary deviations have occurred, the offender has accepted the label of deviant or criminal and is on the road toward joining a criminal subculture.

Many labeling theorists say they are not interested in explaining criminal acts. Instead, they want to explain the social process of labeling and one's personal reaction to being labeled. Nevertheless, a strong explanatory element is prevalent. In effect, the labeling theorist is saying that persons who react to social labeling by defining themselves as deviant or criminal will not only engage in further criminal activity but will also seek out others like themselves and form criminal subcultures. This subcultural development is the equivalent of rejecting the rejectors (Schrag, 1971).

Some evidence of the influence of labeling may be found by examining arrest rates by race and social class. Labeling theorists argue that the most likely targets of labeling are persons who are young, nonwhite, and of lower socioeconomic statuses. These persons are most likely to be labeled by police and others as deviant or inclined to be criminal.

More arrests tend to be made in high-crime areas. Coincidentally, high-crime areas tend to be low-rent districts that attract a disproportionately large number of the poor and ethnic and racial minorities. These same areas tend to attract larger numbers of police such that arrest rates will be increased. Also, law enforcement officers may be more inclined to take advantage of persons of lower socioeconomic statuses. When compared with middle- or upper-class citizens, lower-class persons have fewer resources and lack the legal sophistication to resist or retaliate within the legal system. Again, deviance or criminal conduct is like a social status that, once assigned, changes the relationship the person has with others (VanderZanden, 1984:206).

Labeling theory is an external explanation for criminal behavior. Criminal behavior is whatever lawmakers—an external source—say it is. A criminal is whoever a society labels as criminal. The offender's acceptance of the label criminal merely completes the process and leads the offender to seek the companionship of others labeled as deviants. In some respects, labeling theory involves some interplay between the social and psychological realms. The offender reacts to social definitions, interprets or defines himself or herself as deviant or criminal, and forms subcultures with others in an effort to win acceptance and preserve self-worth.

Labeling theory, however, fails to account for the people who either reject deviant labels or successfully unlabel themselves as criminals or deviants. It also inadequately explains occasional offenders or weekend deviants, persons leading two morally different lives by associating with diverse community elements. Finally, persons who engage in victimless crimes or crimes in which the victim is a willing participant (e.g., gambling and prostitution) seem to escape the psychological effects of being labeled deviants. The theory does not explain the mental compartmentalization these people seem to use in refusing to define themselves as deviants.

Most probation and parole program agreements reflect critical elements of labeling theory. Among most provisions are that probationers and parolees are not to associate or have contact with any known criminals. Furthermore, visits to prisons or jails to visit incarcerated friends or relatives are strictly prohibited. PO approval is required for any contact to be made among offenders. What other reason would there be to deny one a chance to visit his or her friends acquired while incarcerated or to associate with friends in the community who also happen to have criminal records?

Social Control Theory

Sometimes referred to as **bonding theory**, **social control theory** focuses on the processual aspects of becoming bonded or attached to the norms and values of society (Hirschi, 1969). As the bonds between society and people become stronger, the possibility that people will engage in deviant or criminal behaviors becomes weaker. Bonding consists of several dimensions (Hirschi, 1969), including attachment, the emotional or affective dimension linking us with significant others whose opinions we respect and whose admonitions we follow; commitment, the energy expended by an individual in particular activities, either conventional or unconventional; belief, a person's moral definition of the propriety of particular conduct, that the laws and rules should be obeyed; and involvement, the degree of intensity with which one is involved in conventional conduct or with which one espouses conventional values.

Persons who have strong attachments with conventional groups and their opinions, who manifest beliefs in the values of the group, who are intensely involved in these groups' activities, and who expend considerable energy in these activities will probably not become deviant or exhibit criminal conduct. If one or more of these bonding dimensions are weakened, however, then people stand a better chance of deviating from the expectations of conventional society. For instance, when people cease to believe that the group with which they associate is important and/or exhibits the right values or standards, a weakening of the bond occurs. It may be that a delinquent gang can lure youths away from conventional groups by permitting them to develop close attachments and involvements in delinquent gang activity. A type of rivalry occurs between one's conventional bonds and the developing bonds of less conventional social groups.

Hirschi's social control theory builds on the differential association theory developed by Sutherland, whose dimensions of intensity and priority appear closely related to Hirschi's notions of attachment, commitment, and involvement. Although Sutherland attempted to account for white-collar crime, Hirschi has used his bonding theory to explain juvenile delinquency. In Hirschi's investigation of a sample of junior and senior high school youth in California, he found that those students who exhibited strong attitudes and attachments to teachers and school officials were less inclined to engage in delinquent activity than others. These students were also those earning higher grades and making a more successful adjustment to the rigors of school than students with weaker bonds. As for youths engaged in delinquent activity, Hirschi found that they were frequently the poor performers academically, disliked school, and had few positive experiences with school faculty and officials (Hirschi, 1969).

Hirschi's theory has been criticized for several reasons. First, it fails to specify the precise relation between these bonding dimensions and conventional and nonconventional conduct. Many youths have attachments to both conventional and nonconventional groups, yet no clear pattern of delinquency or nondelinquency emerges as a result. Which dimensions have the greatest weight in predicting deviant conduct? What are the roles of parents and church officials in the lives of these youths? How does social class function as an explanatory variable (Nettler, 1974)?

Social control theory is strongly psychological, because it holds that one's mental attachments and beliefs are critical in linking the individual to society's conventional norms. This theory may explain why certain individuals reject conventional behavior for deviant conduct, but it cannot be used to predict which youths among large groups will turn to crime (Nettler, 1974). Hirschi's emphasis on school experiences is an inherent weakness, because it does not account for bonding processes that take place outside of school settings. Its application is restricted to explaining deviance among adolescents who are in school.

Conflict/Marxist Theory

Sometimes called **Marxist criminology**, **conflict criminology**, **critical criminology**, or **radical criminology**, **conflict/Marxist theory** explains criminal conduct by focusing attention on the people who have the political power to define crime for the rest of society. According to this theory, the masses can be divided into the haves, the rich and powerful people who have vested interests in capital, industry, and business, and the have-nots, the poor people who are manipulated and controlled by the haves.

Statistically, persons in the lower socioeconomic strata are arrested more frequently than those in the upper socioeconomic strata. These statistics do not mean that those in the lower socioeconomic categories commit more crime; instead, they show that the ruling elite has targeted these poor people for harassment. This harassment is a strategy for maintaining the status quo and preserving existing societal arrangements that perpetuate and legitimize the power of the haves (Manning, 1977; Sykes, 1974). This theory also asserts that one reason for the formal creation of the police in 1829 was to protect the interests of those in power. These interests exert considerable influence on how crime is defined. Vagrancy and loitering laws were created, in part, as a means for keeping people from wandering about, looking for better jobs and work (Manning, 1977).

Conflict/Marxist theory is a general scheme to account for societal characteristics. It does not explain individual behaviors or the behavior of small groups. It is not linked with any particular social process of acquiring criminal behaviors, and it defines criminal behavior as the result of legislative definitions created by the rich and powerful. To use this theory for creating a specific plan to deal with crime and influence the lives of probationers and parolees, the basic social and economic structure would have to change.

REALITY THERAPY

Reality therapy was created by William Glasser (1976), a psychiatrist by training who accepted developmental theory as an explanation of deviant conduct up to a point. Glasser rejected the developmental theoretical explanation that once a cause is known for a particular criminal behavior, the problem can be dealt with by having the probationer/parolee/client understand the problem's origins. Reality therapy is a confrontational method of behavior modification in which one's criminality is simply unacceptable to a PO. Glasser contends that all persons are born with two primary psychological needs: a need for love and a need for acceptance, self-worth, or recognition. Those POs who practice reality therapy must acquire the trust of their clients and get close to them emotionally. POs must therefore cultivate a tentative friendship between themselves and their clients so that their clients can feel free to disclose things about themselves.

POs using reality therapy must get emotionally involved with their clients. The PO is not interested in trying to understand one's prior circumstances and what led to present circumstances; instead, the focus is on the present, and the intent of the PO is to assist clients in evaluating their behavior and why it is unacceptable. Thus, it is unimportant to know the etiology of one's criminality, which the client all too often uses as a crutch. Many clients love to rationalize their conduct as being the product of a miserable childhood, poor upbringing, or bad social circumstances in their school years.

Reality therapy works best if the PO is able to establish a support group of several clients. Sympathy and excuses are rejected. The PO does not label the client as sick or disturbed. Rather, there are problems that are unacceptable that need to be handled and resolved. The PO is an enabler in this regard. Glasser says the POs can assist their clients by helping them devise better plans for the future. When appropriate, the PO should lavish the client with praise for acceptable, law-abiding conduct as a reinforcement.

Reality therapy has been criticized because some clients feel uncomfortable disclosing things about themselves on an intimate level. Some clients prefer rejecting a PO's help rather than risk accepting it, because they expect to be disappointed if the therapy does not work. POs who work hard to cultivate close relationships with clients may actually drive them away emotionally. Therefore, reality therapy is an intervention that should be used only by selected POs who are qualified and disposed to working with hard-to-manage offenders.

SOCIAL CASEWORK

Social casework is a service-oriented intervention technique. It is the development of a relation between the PO and his or her clients within a problem-solving context and coordinated with the appropriate use of community resources. Social casework rests on three basic tenets: assessment, or gathering and analyzing relevant information on which to base a plan for one's client; planning, or thinking about and organizing facts into a meaningful, goal-oriented explanation; and intervention, or implementation of the plan.

Social casework is a product of social work, which emerged as an intervention strategy during the 1920s. Important to social workers are human relations skills and the capacity to mobilize community resources to assist clients. POs who use the social casework method for assisting their clients attempt to find solutions for their problems that interfere with or minimize their effectiveness as persons. If parolees or probationers have difficulty seeking and maintaining continuous employment, social caseworker–POs can assist them in resolving problems that may be inhibiting them from being successful in this regard.

Good social caseworkers acquire understandings of their clients and attempt to assist them in developing constructive solutions to their problems. They are concerned with client self-esteem and feelings of self-worth. They want clients to be able to function apart from the caseworker. Thus, they provide clients with encouragement and moral support, together with necessary training from community resources.

They are reassuring and believe strongly in counseling and guidance as strategies for coping and behavioral changes.

WHICH THEORY IS BEST? AN EVALUATION

Theories about Adult Offenders

No single theory is universally accepted by all researchers as the best one to explain crime or criminal conduct. Each theory has strengths and weaknesses and has exerted varying degrees of influence on the criminal justice system in processing offenders. An important criterion for evaluating theories of criminal behavior is the extent to which they enable us to explain and predict that behavior. An evaluation of these theories suggests that creating a satisfactory theory stringently meeting this criterion is quite difficult.

Most of the theories presented, regardless of whether they were biological, psychological, or sociological, emphasized single-factor causation. One factor (e.g., glands, genes, improper or inadequate ego development, or anomie) was usually featured as the chief cause of criminal behavior, and all other factors were either subordinated or ignored.

One problem with evaluating these theories is that the historical context in which they were generated is often overlooked. As already seen, Cesare Lombroso's work on the relation between physique and criminal behavior was devised during the time when Charles Darwin's *Origin of the Species* was popular. Biological evolution was considered an important explanation for certain kinds of social behaviors in the 1870s as well as for the next several decades. Assessing Lombroso's work in view of our current knowledge makes his theorizing seem comical. In contrast, psychologists investigated the influence of an air pollutant, ozone, on criminal behavior in 1987. James Rotton, a psychologist at Florida International University, has estimated that every year, ozone provokes hundreds of cases of family violence in large cities with bad air (Londer, 1987). How will this theory be viewed by criminologists and others a hundred years from now?

In all likelihood, criminal behavior is the result of a combination of these factors. It is insufficient to rely entirely on a single cause for such a complex phenomenon. There are criminals of every size and shape and variety. The same crimes such as murder or robbery are committed by many different kinds of people for a variety of reasons. It may be that in time of war, murdering the enemy will cause someone to be a hero, whereas murder in other contexts and at other times would be punished severely. There is a problem with developing conglomerate or "holistic" theories, however, because they may not be theories at all in the formal sense.

Obviously, explanations advanced by Lombroso and Sheldon attaching significance to one's body structure have little or no predictive value. It cannot be determined by looking at someone's physical features whether they are criminals or will become criminals. Also, genetic structure fails to explain and predict criminal behavior. Theories emphasizing the id, ego, and superego as crucial determinants of social conduct are very difficult to test empirically. Such phenomena cannot be extracted from persons and dissected and examined microscopically. If the standards of science and empiricism are applied to all explorations, and if the most scrupulous

Jails, Prisons, and Parole

experiments and tests are rigorously applied, then all theories of criminal behavior presented in this chapter fail such tests.

Theories about Delinquency

Assessing the importance or significance of theories of delinquency is difficult. First, almost all causes of delinquent conduct that have been advocated by experts during the past century continue to interest contemporary investigators. The most frequently discounted and consistently criticized views are the biological ones, although as seen, sociobiology and genetic concomitants of delinquent conduct persist to raise unanswered questions about the role of heredity in the delinquency equation. Psychological explanations seem more plausible than biological ones, although the precise relation between the psyche and biological factors remains unknown. If the focus is on psychological explanations of delinquency as important in fostering delinquent conduct, almost invariably certain elements of one's social world in such explanations are involved. Thus, one's mental processes are influenced in various ways by one's social experiences. Self-definitions, important to psychologists and learning theorists, are conceived largely in social contexts, in the presence of and through contact with others. It is therefore not surprising that the most fruitful explanations for delinquency are those that seek to blend the best parts of different theories that assess different dimensions of youths, their physique and intellectual abilities, their personalities, and their social experiences. Intellectual isolationism or complete reliance on biological factors, psychological factors, or sociological factors exclusively may simplify theory construction, but in the final analysis, such isolationism is unproductive. Certainly, each field has importance and contributes to explaining why some youths exhibit delinquent conduct and others do not. By applying a purely pragmatic approach in assessing the predictive and/or explanatory utility of each of these theories, contemporary interventionist efforts that seek to curb delinquency or prevent its resurgence can be examined.

Program successes are often used as gauges of the success of their underlying theoretical schemes. Because no program is 100 percent effective at preventing delinquency, it follows that no theoretical scheme devised thus far is fully effective. Yet the wide variety of programs applied to deal with different kinds of juvenile offenders today indicates that most psychological and sociological approaches have some merit and contribute differentially to delinquency reduction. As will be seen in subsequent chapters, policy decisions are made throughout the juvenile justice system and are often contingent on the theoretical views adopted by politicians, law enforcement personnel, prosecutors and judges, and correctional officials at every stage of the justice process. For now, most views can be appreciated because of their varying intuitive value and particular approaches to accommodate different types of juvenile offenders can be applied.

A bottom line concerning theories of delinquency generally is that their effect has been felt most strongly in the area of policy making rather than in behavioral change or modification. Virtually every theory is connected in some respect to various types of experimental programs in different jurisdictions. The intent of most programs has been to change behaviors of participants. Yet high rates of recidivism characterize all delinquency prevention innovations, regardless of their intensity or ingenuity. Policy decisions implemented at earlier points have long-range implications for current policies in correctional work. Probationers and parolees as well as inmates and divertees, adults and juveniles alike, are recipients or inheritors of previous policies laid in place by theorists who have attempted to convert their theories into practical experiences and action.

Current policy in juvenile justice favors the get-tough orientation, and increasingly, programs that heavily incorporate accountability and individual responsibility elements are sponsored. Earlier in time, projects emphasizing rehabilitation and reintegration were rewarded more heavily through private grants and various types of government funding. No particular prevention or intervention or supervision program works best. Numerous contrasting perspectives about how policy should be shaped continue to vie for recognition among professionals and politicians. The theories described here are indicative of the many factors that have shaped present policies and practices.

TREATMENT PROGRAMS AND THEORIES

One way of evaluating these theories is to examine the successes that have resulted when these theories have been applied at various stages of the criminal justice process. Which theories seem to be most influential in formulating policies in various correctional institutions? Which theories receive the most consistent emphasis and support from foundations that underwrite research projects examining the causes of criminal behavior? To identify which theories seem most popular, it helps to study parole board hearings. Parole boards determine whether incarcerated prisoners should be released before serving their full sentences and consider many factors before deciding (Hoffman and Adelberg, 1980). Did the inmate behave properly in prison? Did the inmate exhibit any unusual behavioral disorders? What is the likelihood that these offenders will be able to cope effectively with life on the "outside"? Halfway houses, where parolees can stay temporarily in the community until they can find appropriate employment and housing, were created to help offenders adjust to life outside prison.

Have inmates had vocational training or group therapy or rehabilitative counseling? What are the reports of the counselors who interacted with these inmates and listened to their problems? All answers to these questions combine to form a release quotient or salient factor score, a numerical value that predicts an inmates' chances of living on the outside in the community with others and not committing new crimes.

Differential association theory seems influential in parole decisions and the conditions prescribed for parolees. For instance, persons who are paroled are required not to associate with other known criminals as one of several parole conditions, but many parolees violate this condition because the community has labeled them as ex-convicts. This community rejection makes it difficult for these former criminals to obtain employment. Thus, in a sense, society compels these persons to seek social attachments with other criminals, which frustrates efforts to refrain from further criminal activity.

One way to determine which delinquency theories are most popular or influence policy and administrative decision making relative to juveniles is to catalogue the ways offenders are treated by the juvenile justice system after their apprehension by police or others. A preliminary screening of juvenile offenders may result in some being diverted from the juvenile justice system. One manifest purpose of such diversionary action is to reduce the potentially adverse influence of labeling on these youths. A long-term objective of diversion is to minimize recidivism among divertees. Although some experts contend that the intended effects of diversion, such as a reduction in the degree of social stigmatization toward status offenders, are currently unclear, inconsistent, and insufficiently documented, other professionals endorse diversion programs and regard them as effective in preventing further delinquent conduct among first-offenders. In fact, the preponderance of evidence from a survey of available literature is that diversion, although not fully effective at preventing delinquent recidivism, nevertheless tends to reduce it substantially.

During the period 1983 to 1984, for example, the probation departments of Los Angeles and Contra Costa Counties, together with several community service agencies in southern California, conducted a Youth at Risk Program, consisting of ten-day rural training courses for large samples of youths aged 13 to 19 (MetaMetrics, Inc., 1984). These Youth at Risk programs included classes, outdoor recreational activities, and an emphasis on self-reliance and individual responsibility. Youths participating in the program were the subject of a 15-month follow-up that sought to identify their recidivism rates. Compared with samples of delinquent youths not involved in this diversion program, the amount of recidivism among program participants was quite low. Program officials concluded that their program was a significant improvement over traditional processing methods by the juvenile justice systems in these same jurisdictions. Diversionary programs in Denver, Colorado, and in various Midwestern cities have yielded similar results (Davidson et al., 1987).

These and other similar diversionary studies have reported lower rates of recidivism among participating youths. Implicit in most of these studies has been the idea that minimizing formal involvement with the juvenile justice system has been favorable for reducing participants' self-definitions as delinquent and avoiding the delinquent label. Thus, labeling theory seems to have been prominent in the promotion of diversionary programs. Furthermore, many divertees have been exposed to experiences that enhance or improve their self-reliance and independence. Many youths have learned to think out their problems rather than act them out unproductively or antisocially. When the contents of these programs are examined closely, it is fairly easy to detect aspects of bonding theory, containment theory, and differential reinforcement theory at work in the delinquency prevention process.

Besides using diversion per se with or without various programs, elements or overtones of other theoretical schemes may be present in the particular treatments or experiences juveniles receive as they continue to be processed throughout the juvenile justice system. At the time of adjudication, for example, judges may or may not impose special conditions to accompany a sentence of probation. Special conditions may refer to obligating juveniles to make restitution to victims, to perform public services, to participate in group or individual therapy, or to undergo medical treatment in cases of drug addiction or alcohol abuse. Some investigators have suggested that those youths who receive probation accompanied by special conditions are less likely to recidivate compared with those youths who receive probation unconditionally (Nagoshi, 1986).

Learning to accept responsibility for one's actions, acquiring new coping skills to face crises and personal tragedy, improving one's educational attainment, and improving one's ego strength to resist the influence of one's delinquent peers are individually or collectively integral parts of various delinquency treatment programs, particularly when the psychological approach is strong. For example, a juvenile education program was implemented at the East Lansing (Kansas) Penitentiary in the late 1970s. Delinquent youths then on probation and residing in three Kansas counties near the penitentiary were obligated from June to October 1980 to participate in the program, which stressed introducing them to the realities of prison life (Locke et al., 1986). In a follow-up investigation of their recidivism rates compared with a sample of other delinquents not exposed to the program, self-reported delinquency was considerably lower among previous program participants than among those who did not participate in the program. Researchers concluded that the experience of life in prison was to a degree therapeutic, and it appeared to change the perceived status of most participants.

Peter Greenwood (1986) has described programs in various jurisdictions that function as alternatives to state training schools, including outdoor educational activities and wilderness challenges that encourage youths to learn useful skills and confront their fears. For children designated "at risk," preschool programs such as Headstart, parent training programs such as the Oregon Learning Center, selected school programs intended to increase the achievement of lower income children, and voluntary youth service programs such as California's Conservation Corps provide many participating youths with opportunities to avoid delinquent behavioral patterns (Greenwood, 1986). Together with psychodrama, behavioral-cognitive techniques were used by the Clinic of the Wayne County, Michigan, Juvenile Court and were intended to reduce participants' acting out, aggressive tendencies and build their ego strength (Carpenter and Sandberg, 1985). A High School Personality Questionnaire was administered to all adolescents participating in the program to chart before-and-after program changes. Researchers reported positive results, with juveniles tending to exhibit higher ego strength, less introversive tendencies, and less antisocial behavior after program participation. Intervention techniques included behavioral contracting, monetary reinforcement, and alternative behavior rehearsals, together with psychodrama, as methods for reducing these delinquents' acting-out tendencies (Jesness, 1987).

Several psychologists have conducted an extensive review of group therapy literature as applied to the treatment of juvenile delinquents (Lavin et al., 1984). They conclude that group therapy is particularly effective for more aggressive adolescents. They also report that much of the research surveyed is conducted in residential settings, such as group homes. In these less traditional, nonthreatening circumstances, juveniles seem to be more amenable to behavioral change and improved conduct.

During the late 1970s, a program known as Getting It Together was established in a large city juvenile court jurisdiction (Carpenter and Sugrue, 1984). The program emphasized a combination of affective (emotional) and social skills training designed to assist those with immature personalities who exhibited neurotic behaviors. Over the next several years, many delinquent youths participated in this program. A majority reported improved self-esteem and socially mature behavior, better communication skills with authorities and parents, greater self-control, more positive values, and more adequate job skills. Ego strength levels for most participating youths improved, as did the quality of peer relationships, and a reduction of various sexual problems was seen. This program, in addition to other similar enterprises, has been guided to a great degree by social learning theory.

SUMMARY

Theories explain and predict relationships between various phenomena. Criminologists theorize about criminal behavior and describe the characteristics of persons convicted of crimes as well as their motives. Efforts are made to determine whether or not criminals have a predisposition to commit crimes. Nineteenth-century biological theories of criminal behavior stressed the importance of physical characteristics as indicators of criminal propensities. One biological theory determined that criminal behavior was hereditary. Other biological explanations focused on body type as a predictor. These theories have been discounted. Biochemical imbalance or glandular problems were also believed linked with criminal conduct, although no consistent evidence exists to support such beliefs.

Psychoanalytic theory developed by Sigmund Freud emphasizes early selfish behaviors of infants that sometimes remain uncontrolled as children grow older. The id, or "I want" part of the personality, remains unchecked by the ego, or that part of the personality that includes the standards and conventional rules of society. Again, criminal behavior is one predictable result. The psychological theory of moral development emphasizes developmental stages in the lives of children. As they grow and mature, they incorporate into their personality systems certain socially acceptable behavior patterns. Sometimes, disruptions occur in these stages, and criminal conduct results.

Sociological or sociocultural theories of criminal behavior stress social and environmental factors as influential in promoting criminal conduct. One sociological theory, anomie, is that people experience a conflict between aspiring to achieve socially acceptable goals and the culturally approved means to achieve those goals. People adapt to this conflict in different ways. Some persons engage in innovative or unconventional behavior to achieve desired objectives. According to a third sociological theory, labeling, deviance is whatever a group says it is. Labeling theory involves no moral judgments of criminal actions. Rather, attention is directed at social definitions of criminal behavior and a person's responses to being labeled as criminal.

An evaluation of these theories may be made according to several criteria. Can they be used to predict criminal behavior? Which theories are most useful for understanding why people commit crimes? In addition to evaluating their usefulness in predicting crime, these theories can be evaluated by considering the importance each is given in various sectors of the criminal justice system. Counseling programs and group therapy and rehabilitative practices in prison settings are strongly influenced by psychological theories. Correctional institutional policies and guidelines are strongly influenced by differential association theory and the labeling perspective. Finally, single-factor explanations of criminal behavior have inherent weaknesses, because they highlight one variable or circumstance and ignore others. The best explanations are those that combine the best elements of several theoretical schemes.

Similar to theories about adult criminality, theories of delinquency may be grouped into biological, psychological, and sociological explanations. Biological theories strongly imply a causal relation between physique and other genetic phenomena and delinquent behaviors. Psychological theories include psychoanalytic theory devised by Freud and promoted by others. Social learning theory is similar to psychoanalytic theory, although it stresses imitation of significant others.

A popular sociological view of delinquency is labeling theory. Those who engage in wrongdoing may come to adopt self-definitions as delinquents, particularly if significant others and the police define them as delinquents. Having frequent contact with the juvenile justice system enhances such labeling for many youths. Labeling theorists often argue that delinquents are acting out the behaviors others expect from them. Closely related to labeling theory is bonding theory, in which juveniles develop either close or distant attachments to schools, teachers, and peers. Delinquency is regarded as a function of inadequate bonding or a weakening of social attachments. Other theories are containment theory, neutralization or drift theory, and differential association, each of which suggests the power or attraction of group processes in the onset of delinquent conduct.

Theories of delinquency are often evaluated according to how they influence public policy relating to juvenile conduct and its prevention or treatment. Diversionary programs that prevent further juvenile contact with the juvenile justice system are influenced largely by labeling theory, because it is believed that youths will become more deeply entrenched in juvenile conduct to the extent that they are exposed to the formal system and juvenile courts. Individual and group therapy, often components of treatment programs for errant juveniles, seek to use ego-development strategies coupled with various learning methods to improve self-definitions, reduce antisocial behaviors, and promote more healthy attitudes toward others. Programs that emphasize personal responsibility for one's actions or encourage youths to become more active in decision making seem to make a difference in reducing recidivism among program participants. No theory is universally accepted, however.

KEY TERMS

Abnormal physical structure	Ectomorph	Secondary deviation
Anomie	Ego	Social casework
Anomie theory	Endomorph	Social control theory
Biological theories	Heredity	Socialization
Bonding theory	Id	Social learning theory
Cognitive development	Labeling theory	Social process theories
Cognitive development theory	Libido	Sociobiology
Conflict/Marxist theory	Marxist criminology	Strain theory
Conflict criminology	Mesomorph	Subculture of violence
Containment theory	Modes of adaptation	Subcultures
Critical criminology	Neutralization theory	Superego
Cultural transmission theory	Primary deviation	Theory
Delinquent subcultures	Psychoanalytic theory	Theory of opportunity
Differential association theory	Radical criminology	XYY syndrome
Differential reinforcement theory	Reality therapy	

QUESTIONS FOR REVIEW

1. Which theory of criminal behavior discussed in this chapter do you think most appropriately applies to the case discussed at the beginning of the chapter, *Government of Virgin Islands v. Lake*? Explain your reasons by citing theory characteristics and the nature of the crime committed by Lake.

2. Compare and contrast labeling theory with differential association theory. Which theory directs attention to the nature of the crime committed? Which theory directs attention to the societal reaction toward the offender? Which theory do you think is the more "sociological" of the two?

3. What is a theory of criminal behavior? What are some important objectives of such theories? Can these objectives be used to evaluate whether certain criminal theories are good or bad? Why or why not? Give an example.

4. Of the three different categories of criminal behavior theories, which one do you prefer and why? Name your favorite theory discussed in the category you have chosen, and explain why it is your favorite.

5. Some people read about differential association theory and decide that Edwin Sutherland meant that associating with criminals would make someone turn out to be a criminal. Is that what Sutherland was really saying? What are the characteristics of differential association theory? Why are they important in explaining criminal conduct?

6. Discuss the labeling process of becoming a deviant. What factors seem to be most important in this theoretical explanation of criminal behavior? What are the assumptions or principles of labeling theory?

7. Differentiate between primary and secondary deviation. Give two examples of situations in which two different persons would commit the same criminal acts, but one person gets arrested and convicted and the other is only scolded. Why do you think situations like that occur?

8. In determining prisoner living arrangements and policies in various correctional institutions, which theory or theories of criminal behavior appear to be most influential and why?

9. What is meant by reality therapy? Are there special qualities POs must have in order to apply reality therapy properly?

10. What is the relation between social work and social casework? To what extent is social casework effective in working with probationers and parolees?

SUGGESTED READINGS

Greenberg, David F. (1999). "The Weak Strength of Social Control Theory." *Crime and Delinquency* **45:**66–81.

Harrower, Julie (1998). *Applying Psychology to Crime.* Abingdon, UK: Hodder and Stoughton.

Jones, Marshall B., and Donald R. Jones (2000). "The Contagious Nature of Antisocial Behavior." *Criminology* **38:**25–46.

Pratt, Travis C., and Francis T. Cullen (2000). "The Empirical Status of Gottfredson and Hirschi's General Theory of Crime: A Meta-Analysis." *Criminology* **38:**931–964.

Offender Supervision: Types of Offenders and Special Supervisory Considerations

CHAPTER 12

Introduction
Types of Offenders: An Overview
  Coping with Special Needs Offenders
  Mentally Ill Offenders
  Sex Offenders and Child Sexual Abusers
  Drug- and Alcohol-Dependent Offenders
  AIDS/HIV Offenders
  Gang Members
  Developmentally Disabled Offenders
Mentally Ill Offenders
Sex Offenders
Offenders with HIV/AIDS
Substance-Abusing Offenders

Drug Screening and Methadone Treatment
Drug Courts and the Drug Court Movement
Community Programs for Special Needs
  Offenders
  Therapeutic Communities
  Alcoholics Anonymous, Narcotics Anonymous,
    and Gamblers Anonymous Programs
Gang Members
  Tattoo Removal Programs
Summary
Key Terms
Questions for Review
Suggested Readings

INTRODUCTION

Probation and parole officers supervise an increasingly diverse clientele. In the 1950s and 1960s, POs enjoyed far greater predictability in their work than they do today. Conventional distinctions were made between property offenders (e.g., burglars, thieves, those convicted of vehicular theft) and violent offenders, or those who committed crimes against the person (e.g., homicide, aggravated assault, forcible rape, and robbery). Although there always have been offenders with problems, substance abuse, mental illness, and communicable diseases have become pervasive in American society, especially since the 1970s. Contemporary probationers and parolees as clients have special problems and are in need of unconventional services and resources.

In 1998, for instance, an estimated 283,800 mentally ill offenders were incarcerated in U.S. prisons and jails. Among probationers that same year, 547,800 were identified as mentally ill, 473,000 reported a mental or emotional condition, and 281,200 had been admitted overnight to a mental hospital for treatment (Ditton, 1999:3). Over half of all mentally ill clients have prior histories in jails and prisons of institutional violence. Therefore, it is not unexpected that such violence will carry over into their probation and parole programs as a part of a continuing pattern. Relatively little has been done to intervene and assist mentally ill inmates and subsequent PO clients. They continue to pose supervisory hazards for their POs, largely because of their unpredictability. Thus, the first part of this chapter examines mentally ill offenders who are under PO supervision.

A second type of offender POs supervise is the sex offender, some of whom are child sexual abusers. They may be required to avoid frequenting places where small children are located, such as schools and parks. Although sex offenders are not especially abundant, there are sufficient numbers such that POs assigned to supervise them must pay particular attention to their whereabouts and activities. Many sex offenders are obligated to attend individual and group counseling and participate in sex offender programs as a part of their special parole and probation program conditions. These activities require continuous monitoring by attentive POs. Also, because offenders cannot be monitored around the clock, their freedom to roam in their communities means that they may be able to reoffend without their PO's knowledge. Problems of monitoring sex offenders are also examined.

A third type of offender is also described: those with AIDS or HIV. Increased numbers of AIDS/HIV cases have occurred largely because of indiscriminate drug use, needle-sharing, and unprotected sex. Prisons and jails are optimum breeding grounds for the transmission of AIDS/HIV, because offenders are in close proximity with one another and stronger offenders can sexually exploit the weaker ones. Some same-sex relations are consensual. Furthermore, AIDS/HIV is not restricted to the male inmate population. Female inmates are exhibiting increased rates of AIDS/HIV in recent years. Therefore, POs are supervising increased numbers of clients with such communicable diseases as AIDS/HIV. Tuberculosis among offenders has also increased in the United States in recent years. This highly contagious disease presents greater risk and dangers for POs because it can be transmitted more easily than AIDS/HIV. AIDS/HIV offender-clients are described as well as the special supervisory provisions for POs who must monitor them.

By far the largest category of offenders in need of close supervision are substance abusers. Substance abuse is considered the single most important problem among probation and parole offenders. It has been estimated that between 55 and 80 percent of all probationers and parolees have been involved with drugs or alcohol and that illicit substances were involved in their original offenses. The incidence of relapse is especially high for substance-abusing offenders, and POs must devise innovative strategies for their supervision. Because substance-abusing offenders are so prevalent within the probationer and parolee community and because of the unique problems they pose for their supervising POs, improved screening mechanisms have been devised to detect offenders' illegal drug use. POs have had to work harder to link these offenders with necessary community services so that they can receive appropriate therapy and treatment. Furthermore, because substance abusers are inclined to relapse at high rates, POs must be more vigilant at detecting relapses and rapidly moving to control such behavior when it occurs.

One response to greater drug use among offenders has been the development of specialized courts to deal only with drug abusers. These drug courts provide therapies and recommended programs to involve those most in need of treatment and community services. They also make provisions for follow-up monitoring by POs as well as appropriate sanctions if their relapses are chronic or repetitive over time. Drug courts, including their operations and services, are described. POs increasingly rely on therapeutic communities, or treatment models that emphasize integrated community services at several different levels to meet the complex needs of substance-abusing offenders and others, and these communities and their functions are described. A part of the therapeutic community are interventions such as Alcoholics Anonymous for those with alcohol addictions, Narcotics Anonymous for those with drug dependencies, and Gamblers Anonymous for those addicted to gambling. Therapeutic communities also exist for developmentally disabled, handicapped, and/or mentally retarded offenders.

The chapter concludes with a discussion of gang members on probation and parole. A growing segment of the offender population both within and without the prison setting are gang members. One reason gang members present supervision problems for POs is that gangs tend to form subcultures with strong group norms that, in turn, create a substantial resistance to change. Thus, when POs attempt to intervene in the lives of gang members and help them become more law-abiding, they often encounter subcultural barriers that are gang-generated. Thus, the process of coping with gang-affiliated clients is discussed. Some of the strategies for overcoming resistance to change are also highlighted, including recently developed tattoo removal programs.

TYPES OF OFFENDERS: AN OVERVIEW

In this section, an overview of **special needs offenders** is presented. This overview is intended to describe the various types of offender populations that POs supervise. Special services from POs and an extraordinary amount of care and supervision are required when certain probationers and parolees have serious needs and dependencies. In some probation and parole agencies, special assignments, referred to as specialized caseloads, are made to certain POs with skills relevant for those clients with particular disabilities or problems. Many probation and parole departments do not have the resources or labor to allocate POs for specialized services. Thus, POs must supervise all offenders, regardless of whether or not they have special problems requiring unconventional community intervention, assistance, or programming.

The first part of this section describes problems of coping with special needs offenders. What must POs do to manage or supervise offenders with serious dependencies and other problems? What are the pressures on POs to monitor these offenders closely? What should POs do when they detect program violations among those most likely to relapse and commit program violations? There are no easy answers to these questions. As each offender aggregate is described, some idea of the magnitude of the problem is also presented. Thus, the significance these offenders pose for their supervising POs is seen. In subsequent sections of this chapter, these different types of special needs offenders are examined in closer detail. In these latter sections, several interventions and community programs that are used in conjunction with their supervision are also presented.

Coping with Special Needs Offenders

Any correctional program, whether institutional corrections or community-based corrections, will inevitably have to deal with and make provisions for special needs offenders. Special needs offenders include physically, mentally, psychologically, or socially impaired or handicapped offenders who require extraordinary care and supervision. Sometimes, elderly offenders are classified as special needs offenders to the extent that they might require special diets, medicines, or environments. Mental retardation, illiteracy, and physical disabilities are some of the many kinds of problems associated with special needs offenders. Some definitions of special needs offenders include women, although female offenders and their problems and programs are treated elsewhere (Gowdy et al., 1998). Operators of community-based correctional facilities face continual dilemmas over the need to accommodate these offenders in special facilities and the need to move offender-clients generally into mainstream society and help them live independently.

Major problems in the provisions for special needs offenders in many community corrections programs have been identified, including lack of access to adequate mental health services, inadequate information and training among court and corrections personnel, and insufficient interagency coordination and cooperation. In more than a few instances, some of these inmates have attempted suicide or have assaulted other inmates. Some suicide attempts have been successful, and some inmate assaults have been fatal (Canada Solicitor General, 1998; Victoria Department of Justice, 1998). Some community corrections facilities are linked closely with other close-custody prisons, such as the Massachusetts Correctional Institution for women at Framingham. That institution, which houses 530 female convicts, offers assistance in mental health counseling; substance abuse treatment; parenting and family services; employment planning, education, and vocational counseling; and health screenings, treatment, and referrals (American Correctional Association, 1994). These services are offender-relevant, because a lack of education and drug abuse are two of the major obstacles to finding employment.

In Texas, for example, a Special Needs Parole Program has been established to provide for an early parole review for special health needs offenders who require 24-hour skilled nursing care. Between 1995 and 1999, for instance, the number of cases screened for the program declined markedly by 54 percent, as did those referred to the parole board for early release. Those released on Special Needs Parole declined by 67 percent. These declines were attributable to ineffective and inadequate screening procedures as well as tougher parole criteria. It was found that over 50 percent of all referred cases in 1999 were simply ineligible for parole because of Texas statutes, yet 38 percent were referred for parole anyway, and of these, 22 percent were granted early release (Texas Criminal Justice Policy Council, 2000).

Almost contemporaneously with the Texas Special Needs Program was an independent survey of U.S. state prisons during the period 1991 to 1997. It was found that the number of inmates age 50 and above increased by 115 percent during this period, whereas the overall prison population grew by almost 84 percent. It was also found that increasing numbers of prisons were housing special needs offenders, older offenders with health problems, and disabled inmates in special prison areas or were including them in programs specifically designed for their conditions (Edwards, 1998). Thus, Texas and perhaps other jurisdictions are retaining more special needs offenders for longer prison terms, although corrections officials are having to make special (and more expensive) arrangements for their care and treatment. Eventually, a portion of these offenders will be released on parole, and the problems of the institution will be passed along to paroling authorities.

Community corrections may not provide the degree of protection that might need to be extended to persons with one or more disabilities or handicaps. Those who are mentally ill may not be able to function normally in their communities. Some offenders who are mentally impaired may require constant monitoring and supervision, primarily for their own protection (Silver, 2000). Some observers believe that it will be necessary for entire departments of corrections in each state to address the problems of special needs offenders from a total systems approach. A comprehensive corrections plan can be effective at maximizing the cost-efficiency of correctional construction. The growing number of special needs populations will require new thinking by architects and administrators to meet inmates' and clients' special health, program, and management needs (Anderson, Sestoft, and Lilleback, 2000).

Sex offenders often pose special problems for community corrections staff. Sex offenders may have committed rape, incest, voyeurism, or any of several other sexual behaviors or perversions. Treatments of sex offenders sometimes involve the hormonal drug Depo-Provera, and some patients may be monitored by a penile plethysmograph, a device that measures the significance of various sexual stimuli relating to one's arousal (Dutton, 2000; Johnson and Knight, 2000).

Many offenders involved in community-based corrections programs have learning disabilities. Special education courses and services are needed to meet their needs more effectively (Eisenberg, Arrigona, and Kofowit, 1999). Several components of successful correctional special educational programs have been identified, including functional assessments of the skills and learning needs of handicapped offenders, a curriculum that teaches functional academic and living skills, vocational special education, and transitional programs that facilitate moving from correctional systems to community living. In more than a few instances, inmate mothers about to be released may have previously been addicted to crack cocaine or other drugs. It is imperative that they be put in contact with appropriate agencies or community centers upon their release so that they can continue to receive information and education about the dangers of drug use and how it might imperil their children (Humphries, 1999).

Correctional agencies must manage a wide range of offenders, including those with special problems. These offenders or clients present unusual challenges for POs as well as program administrators who must adjust their supervisory methods and program components accordingly. Special types of offenders may have deep-seated psychological problems that are not immediately diagnosed. They may react in unpredictable ways to various types of treatments or therapy. Because their behaviors may be unexpected or unanticipated, they may become violent and harm themselves or others. Persons who are abnormal in some respects behave in abnormal ways. Probation and parole personnel are not always prepared for each and every contingency that may arise; therefore, it is beneficial to know about these special types of offenders, their needs, their behavior patterns, and what, if anything, of an unusual nature might be expected from them.

Unfortunately, there is often inadequate communication between institutional staff and community services or institutional care officials who can intercede and recommend appropriate treatment for inmates who misbehave or exhibit unconventional behaviors. For example, frontline correctional staff of prisons may not deem it necessary to report to mental health officials that certain inmates are cutting themselves, masturbating publicly, or smearing feces on their cell walls. One reason for not reporting such incidents is that some correctional staff have acquired cynical attitudes about inmates and their attempts to seek recognition from others. Attracting officer and medical attention by engaging in unconventional behaviors is sometimes used to manipulate staff. Thus, correctional officers may dismiss such behaviors as unimportant when they may, indeed, be indicative of deep-seated personality disturbances in need of attention or treatment (Lovell and Rhodes, 1997:40).

This overview encompasses the following offender aggregates: mentally ill offenders; sex offenders and child sexual abusers; drug- and alcohol-dependent offenders; AIDS/HIV offenders; gang members; and developmentally disabled offenders.

Mentally Ill Offenders

No one knows how many mentally ill inmates are in prisons and jails throughout the United States (Cornelius, 1996). Estimates suggest that as many as 600,000 mentally ill offenders are currently incarcerated (Pastore and Maguire, 2001). These inmates present correctional officials with problems similar to those who have drug or alcohol dependencies. Frequently, inadequate staffing makes diagnoses of inmates and their problems difficult. Because of the short-term confinement purpose of jails, these facilities are not prepared to adequately treat those inmates with serious mental disturbances or deficiencies. Suicides in jails and prisons are frequently linked with the mental condition of inmates unable to cope with confinement. Mentally ill inmates also exhibit a high degree of socially disruptive behavior, which occurs not only during confinement but also later, when these inmates are discharged. In many jurisdictions, treatment services for mentally retarded offenders receive a low budgetary and program priority (Paradis et al., 2000).

Offenders who are mentally ill are incarcerated disproportionately in relation to other offenders (Mastrofski et al., 2000). Mentally ill inmates tend to mask their limitations and are highly susceptible to prison culture and inmate manipulation. Also, these offenders are often unresponsive to traditional rehabilitation programs available to other inmates. They present correctional officers with discipline problems unlike those of other inmates. Corrections officers often have little, if any, training in dealing with mentally ill individuals. Obviously, proper classification systems should be devised to identify different types of disabled inmates. Evidence indicates that such classification systems are currently being devised in many jail settings and that corrections generally is becoming more responsive to the needs of these types of offenders (California Board of Corrections, 2000).

A deinstitutionalization movement commenced in 1968 in the United States, when mentally ill offenders were increasingly shifted from institutional to community care. This movement has not been uniform throughout all jurisdictions, however. One aim of deinstitutionalization has been to reduce jail and prison populations by diverting the mentally ill or retarded to nonincarcerative surroundings such as hospitals, but it has not been entirely successful in this respect. One unintended consequence of deinstitutionalization has been to discharge large numbers of mentally disturbed offenders back into the community prematurely, after a short hospitalization. Police once again encounter these offenders because of their inability to cope with the rigors of the street. In fact, the police bring these same individuals back into jails and prisons through "mercy bookings," mistakenly believing that correctional personnel can take care of them more effectively. Thus, the cycle is repeated, and the stresses of jail or prison exacerbate latent psychotic, convulsive, and behavioral factors (California Board of Corrections, 2000).

Of course, deinstitutionalization of mentally ill offenders does not significantly alleviate the burden on probation and parole departments that must supervise these clients. POs and their agencies have had to make significant adjustments and programmatic changes to accommodate mentally ill offenders. One of the greatest areas of concern, from the standpoint of agency personnel, relates to supervising those who are learning disabled or mentally retarded. Because these offenders cannot express themselves or indicate their needs, it is often difficult to identify the most appropriate services or legal assistance they might require. Many POs lack skills in dealing with these clients, although many agencies throughout the United States are improving their services delivery (Corrado et al., 2000).

Sex Offenders and Child Sexual Abusers

Another category of offenders receiving special emphasis from corrections are sex offenders, including child sexual abusers. Sometimes these offenders are grouped with criminals who are mentally ill and deserve special services, whereas other officials think that they should receive no unique consideration. Because many sex offenses are committed against victims known by the offender as a friend or family member, a large number of these incidents are not reported to the police. Thus, no one really knows how many sex offenders there are in the United States at any given time.

It has been estimated that convicted rapists made up about 2 percent of the prison population in the United States in 1998 (Beck, 2000b:10). About 234,000 sex offenders were under some form of correctional supervision during the same period (Robinson, 1998). Sex offenders are persons who commit a sexual act prohibited by law. Fairly common types of sex offenders are rapists and prostitutes, although sex offenses may include voyeurism (Peeping Toms), exhibitionism, child sexual molestation, incest, date rape, and marital rape, but this list is not exhaustive. Child sexual abusers are adults who involve minors in virtually any kind of sexual activity, ranging from intercourse with children to photographing them in lewd poses. Although the exact figure is unknown, it is believed that approximately two million children are sexually victimized annually. It is also estimated that 90 percent of all child sexual abuse cases are never prosecuted, although this situation appears to be changing (Kruttschnitt, Uggen, and Shelton, 2000).

Public interest in and awareness of sex offenders is based on the belief that most convicted sex offenders will commit new sex offenses when released. Regardless of the diverse motives of sex offenders, there is general agreement among professionals that these offenders usually need some form of counseling or therapy. Many jurisdictions currently operate sex therapy programs designed to rehabilitate sex offenders, depending on the nature of their sex crime (Marshall and Serran, 2000).

Sex offenders offer POs a unique challenge. First, sex offenders expect some amount of assistance from community programs designed to counsel and treat them.

BOX 12.1   *Child Molesters on CD-ROM*

Dial-a-Molester

In Los Angeles and other cities around the United States, the government is establishing databases of sex offenders. As growing numbers of sex offenders are loosed into communities through probation and parole, there is increased concern among a wary public about the safety and security of their children. One controversial strategy is the creation of Internet databases, including listings of known convicted sex offenders. California is one of several states that have generated databases on CD-ROM of known sex offenders. The California CD-ROM directory of sex offenders shows their names, photographs, and zip codes. A convicted child molester, Chuck, is worried about the new directory. He is middle-aged, employed, church-going, and articulate. He says that it will be only a matter of time before someone knocks on his neighbors' doors and notifies them about his past and conviction as a sex offender. Chuck feels that he has served his time in prison some years ago for this crime, and he has no intention of committing new offenses. Chuck says, "I'm not afraid of the notification and the reaction so much as that there doesn't seem to be an end to it." He says that the usual reaction from residents is pressure for him to move. He envisions another knock on another door, another move to another city, a repetitive process. "It's a fresh experience each time you move," he says. "It is very

debilitating." Some convicted sex offenders oppose the notification law. Some say that part of the law is self-defeating. Former offenders are less likely to seek treatment or build healthy relationships. Chuck says, "I myself personally have many, many people who are in support of me. I have disclosed everything about my past to them. I don't have to hide what I've done. If I feel uncomfortable about my life, I can speak to almost anyone about it. Long before I get to the point of even considering to re-offend, I have an outlet to deal with it. The more you feel isolated and hunted, the less you want to be helped and the less you're going to ask for help and reach out to support groups. Once you kick someone out, then they start looking at everyone else in the neighborhood wondering if there's somebody else they should kick out. It never stays with one person. Whether or not this group is dangerous or should be locked up is a moot point. The whole society needs to realize that the more government can confine and control without due process, the less freedom is available to the average human being."

What is your reaction to a CD-ROM directory of known sex offenders distributed in your state? Would you favor or oppose such a directory? How could such a directory be used to help known sex offenders? In what ways might such a directory hurt the chances of these persons leading normal lives? What do you think?

Source: Adapted from Associated Press, "Convicted Molester: CD-ROM List Won't Solve the Problem," July 8, 1997.

Thus, they believe that they are in a therapeutic milieu whenever they are freed on probation or parole with conditions. In accordance with their program expectations, they obtain honest employment and attempt to lead law-abiding lives. Most sex offenders do not have lengthy criminal records, nor do they have moderate or severe substance-abuse problems or dependencies or unstable lifestyles, but the media and public have quite a different view of sex offenders. They are viewed as unstable predators who seek to repeat their victimizations whenever possible (Firestone et al., 2000). Reports of escapes of violent sexual predators from treatment centers and mental hospitals do little to dispel public sentiment against sex offenders (Dolan, Harkness, and McGuire, 2000). In support of this belief, 48 states had passed community notification legislation by 1998 requiring sex offenders to register whenever they relocate to a different community. Obviously the public regards sex offending as a most egregious activity and desires to punish it most severely. Thus, the dilemma arises about how POs can effectively supervise these offenders without posing a risk to public safety and at the same time avoid undercutting the offender's ability to get back on to a crime-free path (Robinson, 1998). There are no easy answers to this dilemma.

Drug- and Alcohol-Dependent Offenders

Drug and alcohol abuse are highly correlated with criminal conduct (Deschenes, Turner, and Clear, 1992). Large numbers of pretrial detainees are characterized as having drug and/or alcohol dependencies. Furthermore, there is evidence that many offenders suffer from polysubstance abuse (Capodanno and Chavaria, 1991). Offenders with drug or alcohol dependencies present several problems for correctional personnel (Kraus and Lazear, 1991). Often, jails are not equipped to handle their withdrawal symptoms, especially if they are confined for long periods. Also, the symptoms themselves are frequently dealt with rather than the social and psychological causes for these dependencies. Thus, after offenders go through alcohol detoxification programs or are treated for drug addiction, they are placed back into the same circumstances that caused the dependencies originally.

A fairly common offender category under PO supervision is the DWI or DUI offender, persons who have been convicted of driving while intoxicated or driving under the influence of alcohol or drugs (U.S. Department of Justice, 1999:1). It has been estimated that 513,200 persons convicted of DWI were under correctional supervision during 1999. Of these, about 454,500 were on probation, 41,100 were in local jails, and another 17,600 were in prisons. For POs, it is important to note that during the 1990s, the correctional supervision rate for DWI offenders rose from 151 for every 1,000 DWI arrests to 347 for every DWI arrests (U.S. Department of Justice, 1999:1). DWI or DUI offenders must complete special conditions of probation relating to attending Alcoholics Anonymous meetings, Mothers Against Drunk Drivers meetings, and driving schools in various jurisdictions. All information must be documented and filed with the probation office. POs must keep track of all these offenders to ensure program compliance.

Prisons and jails do not always insulate inmates from continued drug or alcohol abuses. Illegal substance abuse is prevalent among inmates in state and federal prisons (Straub, 1997). Corrections employees are often about as likely as prisoners to abuse drugs, because the employees themselves are frequently the major conduits for smuggling drugs into prison settings. Currently, many state, local, and federal agencies conduct routine urinalyses of their employees to detect and deter drug abuse among them (Ellsworth, 1996).

Pretrial detainees have often been involved in additional criminality while awaiting trial. Even samples of pretrial detainees who were subjected to periodic drug tests as a specific deterrent were found to have high failure-to-appear rates and rearrests (Britt, Gottfredson, and Goldkamp, 1992). Drug dependencies also account for greater numbers of dropouts and failures among those involved in both juvenile and adult intervention programs. For those on either probation or parole, drug and/or alcohol dependencies present various problems and account for program infractions, rearrests, and general adjustment and reintegration problems.

Those reentering the community on parole after years of incarceration are especially vulnerable to drug dependencies during the first six months following their release (Nurco, Hanlon, and Bateman, 1992). Individual or group counseling and other forms of therapy are recommended for drug- or alcohol-dependent clients, although many clients are considered treatment-resistant (Dawson, 1992). Since 1972, various community-based treatment programs have been implemented to treat and counsel drug-dependent clients. These community-based programs have been collectively labeled **treatment alternatives to street crime (TASC)** and are currently operating in numerous jurisdictions throughout the United States to improve client abstinence from drugs, increase clients' employment potential, and improve clients' social/personal functioning.

AIDS/HIV Offenders

A growing problem in corrections is AIDS/HIV, or acquired immune deficiency syndrome/human immunodeficiency virus. Estimates are that by 1997, there were over 3 million AIDS/HIV cases in the United States and that the number of AIDS cases was doubling about every eight to ten months (Office of Justice Programs, 2001). AIDS is particularly prevalent among jail and prison inmates (Correctional Association of New York, 2000; Shewan and Davies, 2000). Prisoners living in close quarters are highly susceptible to the AIDS virus because of the likelihood of anal-genital or oral-genital contact. Although there has been much improvement in creating greater AIDS awareness among inmates through educational programs, AIDS education in incarcerative settings has not slowed the spread of this disease appreciably (Marcus, Amen, and Bibace, 1992). By the beginning of 1998, for instance, there were 22,548 AIDS-infected inmates in state prisons and 1,030 AIDS-infected inmates in federal penitentiaries (Office of Justice Programs, 2001:1). Interestingly, female inmates in state and federal prisons had a higher AIDS infection rate compared with men. For male prisoners, about 2.2 percent were AIDS-infected, compared with 3.5 percent of all female inmates.

It follows that if AIDS is prevalent and increasing among jail and prison inmates, then it is prevalent and increasing among probationers and parolees as well. Thus, AIDS has become a primary topic of concern among POs and their agencies (Lurigio, Bensinger, and Laszlo, 1990). In view of the various circumstances under which AIDS has been transmitted in recent years, including from saliva or blood residue from dentists and others working in different health professions, POs have perceived that their risk of being infected with the AIDS virus has increased greatly. Many probationers and parolees are former drug offenders. Drug-dependent clients represent a special danger, because AIDS is known to be easily transmitted when drug addicts share their needles used to inject heroin and other substances. It is widely known from media reports that some crimes have been perpetrated by some offenders wielding needles and other objects that they say have been infected with AIDS. Thus, these actions pose additional risks for supervising POs.

Indirectly related to the rise in AIDS/HIV in prisons, jails, and probation and parole programs is the rise in tuberculosis. Between 1976 and 1996, for instance, there was a 50 percent increase in the number of New York State prison inmates infected with tuberculosis. Much of this tuberculosis is untreatable and fatal. It is more easily transmitted than AIDS/HIV, although AIDS/HIV inmates and clients seem at greater risk of contracting tuberculosis than AIDS/HIV-free inmates. Today, virtually every prison conducts a routine tuberculosis skin test to determine whether particular inmates are infected. If so, then they are almost always isolated from the general inmate population in an effort to control the spread of this disease. Some of the nation's larger jails, such as the Los Angeles County Jail, conduct routine mini chest films, which are single-view, low-dose, screening radiographs to detect active pulmonary disease. Thus, early detection of this disease can be immediately isolated and treated (Andrus, Fleming, and Knox, 1999).

Gang Members

In 1998, there were 780,200 active gang members in 28,700 youth gangs throughout the United States, both on the streets and in U.S. prisons and jails (Wilson, 2000). Virtually every city with a population of 250,000 or greater reported the presence of gangs. Furthermore, there were significant gang increases in suburban and rural areas of the United States, with the number of gang members in these areas increasing by 43 percent from 1996 to 1998.

It is difficult to understand why youth gangs form and perpetuate themselves over long periods of time. Gangs emerge, grow, dissolve, and disappear for reasons that are poorly understood (Wilson, 2000:1). Gangs are defined as self-formed associations of peers, united by mutual interests, with identifiable leadership and internal organization, who act collectively or as individuals to achieve specific purposes, including the conduct of illegal activity and control of a particular territory, facility, or enterprise. They may include either adults or juveniles (Wilson, 2000:1).

Several problems confront POs who must supervise gang members. When gang members have been incarcerated for a period of time, they emerge from prisons or jails and seem to increase the level of violence among their street gang affiliate memberships (Wilson, 2000:35-36). POs must interact with these gang members, often on their own turfs, where gang members use hand signs and special language to deceive and mislead POs. There are also dangers whenever POs enter known gang-controlled neighborhoods for the purpose of visiting other gang-member clients (Knox, 2000). It has been reported that over 50 percent of all gang members in the United States have used firearms at one time or another during the commission of a violent crime (Wilson, 2000:28–29). This reason is why many POs have sought to carry firearms when they make house visits to their clients. About half of all states have approved firearms use for their POs, in part because of these potential dangers to PO lives and security.

Gangs are prevalent in schools throughout the United States (Howell and Lynch, 2000). In fact, the number of students reporting the presence of gangs in schools doubled between 1989 and 1995. A high percentage of students reported that gang members brought firearms to their schools at different times. Many students also reported a high degree of illicit drug use among gang members on school property. Eighty percent of students interviewed in a 1998 survey about gang presence in their schools replied that they knew of the presence of specific gangs by their names. About 80 percent also said that they recognized gang associations through particular student groupings during the school day. About 56 percent reported tagging, or the presence of gang graffiti, on their school property, and 71 percent said that gang members usually wore identifying clothing to set themselves apart from other students (Howell and Lynch, 2000).

Gangs also create a pattern of resistance to change. Thus, when POs attempt to intervene and intercede with any particular offender, there is an overpowering sense of betrayal on the part of the gang member-client if he or she accepts the PO's suggested intervention. Betrayal does not always occur, but POs encounter resistance from more than a few gang member-clients nevertheless (Kelly, 2000).

Many gangs are involved in illicit activities, such as dealing drugs or transporting firearms (Decker, 2000). There is always the possibility that gang-member offenders are continuing their involvement in these illicit activities. Actual drug use by probationers or parolees, however, can easily be checked with various devices at random times. Thus, many gang members are smart enough not to get caught doing drugs while serving time in probation or parole programs. Despite these checks, POs often regard their interventions with gang members as unproductive, because it is difficult to overcome the influence of gang membership.

Developmentally Disabled Offenders

A growing but neglected population of offenders are those with physical handicaps. Some offenders are confined to wheelchairs, and therefore special facilities must be constructed to accommodate their access to probation or parole offices or community-based sites. Other offenders have hearing or speech impairments that limit them in various ways. Counselor Kay McGill of the Rehabilitation Services Division of the Georgia Department of Human Resources has described her role in dealing with certain handicapped parolees (*Georgia Parole Review*, 1990). One of her parolee-clients was described as suffering from tinnitus, an inherited condition involving a constant roaring in one's head and amplified and unfiltered sound. The client had difficulty holding a job and suffered from depression and insecurity stemming from his condition. McGill arranged for him to acquire a job involving working with an electronics program with low noise levels and some isolation. In the general case, the Georgia Rehabilitation Services Division is an agency whose mission is to get their clients functioning at an optimal level so that they may adjust more normally within their communities (*Georgia Parole Review*, 1990:176).

Physically challenged offenders often require greater attention from their POs. Acquiring and maintaining employment is sometimes difficult for persons with different types of physical handicaps, such as the parolee-client managed by McGill. Many POs become brokers between their own agencies and community businesses that are encouraged to employ certain clients with special problems. Community volunteers are increasingly helpful in assisting probation and parole agencies with physically handicapped clients.

MENTALLY ILL OFFENDERS

Thousands of mentally ill individuals pass through local correctional facilities annually. One quarter of all inmates in prisons and jails in 1996 reported that they had been diagnosed or treated for one type of mental illness or another (Conly, 1999:3). Nearly 89,000 of these inmates said that they were on some form of prescription medication for a mental illness, and another 51,000 reported that they had been admitted to a mental health program at one time or another during their commission of crimes.

For institutional corrections, the problems of mentally ill are manifold. Many mentally ill offenders are violent, and they are recidivists (Grisso et al., 2000). A 1998 study of mentally ill patients known as the MacArthur Violence Risk Assessment Study investigated 1,136 persons who had been hospitalized for mental disorders. Many of these persons had criminal records, and self-disclosures by these patients revealed that about a third had violent thoughts. Many patients were self-proclaimed substance abusers, and they predicted that they would leave their institutions and commit violent acts if given the opportunity. A correlation among their psychopathy, anger, and impulsiveness was demonstrated (Grisso et al., 2000). The disturbing fact is that many of these patients, when released, will actually carry out their violent thoughts and act accordingly. Therefore, many new commitments to jails and prisons are former mental patients with histories of violence. A sample of New York inmates revealed that a high percentage of older detainees, age 62 or older, were charged with violent felonies and had previously been hospitalized in New York or elsewhere (Paradis et al., 2000). Many of those committed to jails reported that they previously had been diagnosed with mental problems and reportedly had paranoid delusions that were known to psychiatric staff. Little or no attempt was made to detain them beyond short-term observation periods in the facilities in which they were confined, however.

Many mentally ill inmates of prisons and jails slip through the cracks and are not diagnosed as mentally ill. Rather, they are simply regarded by correctional officers as violent inmates and thus avoid treatment for their mental problems altogether. Some prisoners develop psychoses of one type or another as the result of confinement. For instance, prisoners placed in solitary confinement seem to have a higher incidence of onset of psychiatric disorders compared with those not placed in solitary confinement (Anderson, Sestoft, and Lilleback, 2000).

Most prisons in the United States and in other English-speaking countries such as England and Canada attempt to screen incoming inmates for mental disorders. For instance, at the Durham Prison in England, new inmates undergo health assessments designed to determine their mental conditions. Many of these inmates were improperly diagnosed, however, and almost all were placed in the general population with other inmates. Researchers who investigated this situation concluded that these misclassifications and misdiagnoses were attributable to inappropriate staff training and experience. Furthermore, when screened, incoming prisoners were discouraged by staff from carrying on conversations in which their mental illnesses might become more apparent (Birmingham et al., 2000). Even when mentally ill offenders are processed or screened properly, they may not receive the appropriate therapy. In some instances, they may receive no therapy at all (Hodgins and Muller-Isberner, 2000; Timonen et al., 2000).

Court intervention has not always been helpful. During the 1980s and 1990s, the verdict of guilty but mentally ill was increasingly used. This verdict enabled juries to convict mentally ill offenders of crimes that resulted in their hospitalization rather than incarceration. Supposedly, these offenders would receive appropriate treatment and then be released into the general inmate population of the nearest prison. Many of these offenders, however, have escaped incarceration when civil authorities have authorized their release from hospital custody (Palmer and Hazelrigg, 2000; Sreenivasan et al., 2000).

When these offenders are eventually transferred to parole services, their mental problems accompany them. In more than a few instances, POs do not know that these persons are mentally disturbed. Increasing numbers of states, however, are devising risk/needs assessment devices that permit POs the opportunity of detecting some of the more mentally disordered clients (Simourd and Hoge, 2000). Despite these advancements in technology and test improvements, it is still difficult for many authorities to detect antisocial personalities and those most likely to become violent and re-offend (Rogers et al., 2000). The most direct indicators of problem parolees is through contacts with prison officials who have supposedly had an opportunity to examine these parole-eligible inmates and determine their psychopathy. All too often, however, inmates with serious psychological problems are improperly diagnosed or are not diagnosed at all. Therefore, it is unexpected whenever POs discover mentally unstable clients among their caseloads when no prior warning had been given from institutional officials. Again, the problem is often attributable to a lack of properly trained jail or prison staff who either did not take the time to diagnose certain inmates properly or failed to recognize the signs of mental illness when they were prevalent (Borum, 1999).

One attempt to deal aggressively with the mentally ill population was implemented in Maryland in 1994 following a pilot study of assessing mental illness among inmates in jails and prisons and how communities and institutions were coping with it. In the early 1990s, it was estimated that approximately 700 inmates were being confined in local facilities in Maryland, yet the state, not unlike other jurisdictions, lacked sufficient and adequately trained staff to screen and treat the mentally ill properly as they were processed by local jails. Often, mentally ill individuals were simply ignored unless they proved disruptive or attempted suicide. Early in the development of the program, some Maryland officials asked whether "we could shoot them up with something to calm them down and just let them sleep while they are here?" (Conly, 1999:5). After several pilot projects, Maryland officials created the Community Criminal Justice Treatment Program, or MCCJTP. This program is founded on two principles: the target population requires a continuum of care provided by a variety of service professionals in jail and in the community that is coordinated at both the state and local levels, and local communities are in the best position to plan and implement responses to meet the needs of the mentally ill offenders in their jurisdictions.

The goals of the MCCJTP are to improve the identification and treatment of mentally ill offenders and increase their chances of successful independent living, thereby preventing their swift return to jail, mental hospitals, homelessness, or hospital emergency rooms. In some locations, MCCJTP also aims to reduce to period of incarceration, through postbooking diversion and even reduce the likelihood of incarceration altogether.

The MCCJTP works as follows:

1. Preliminary identification of candidates for program services is made following arrest, after self-referral by the defendant, or as the result of referrals by the arresting officer, the classification officer, jail medical staff, the substance abuse counselor, or other jail personnel.
2. The MCCJTP case manager meets with candidates to conduct an in-jail diagnostic interview and an individual needs assessment.
3. While in jail, the inmate meets with the case manager for counseling and the development of an aftercare plan. A typical plan will include substance abuse counseling, edu-

cational services, recreational services, employment training, and eventually, suitable housing.

4. MCCJTP case mangers help link clients to specified services, such as psychiatric day treatment, substance abuse treatment, vocational rehabilitation, and educational services.

5. Case managers are responsible for monitoring offenders for program compliance and to ensure their compliance with housing agreements and participation in daily activities and treatment plans.

6. The length of stay in the MCCJTP depends on client progress, which is monitored daily. Judicial approval is required. The case is left open for one year. At the end of the year, the judge either closes or reopens the case.

The probation department actively assists the MCCJTP in a variety of ways, usually through networking with community agencies to provide clients with needed services and programs. Between 1994 and 1998 the program was highly successful. Although persons with mental illnesses have not been cured outright, most have been brought to a level where they can function fairly normally with assistance from caregivers provided through the MCCJTP.

State and federal probation and parole services have gradually increased their roles in assessing the prevalence of mental illness among their clientele. In 1995, 41 states indicated that mental health agencies, private practitioners, or the courts were the primary determinants of one's mental condition. Only nine states had provisions for and kept records of the prevalence of mental illness among their probation and parole populations (Boone, 1995:34). Although these figures have improved somewhat since 1995, there are still inadequate assessments of mentally ill clients among a majority of state probation and parole agencies (Camp and Camp, 1999; Pastore and Maguire, 2001).

SEX OFFENDERS

The **Missouri Sexual Offender Program (MOSOP)** targets the needs of incarcerated, nonpsychotic sexual offenders. The program can effectively supervise over 700 offenders who are required to complete the program before becoming eligible for parole. MOSOP approaches sex offenders on the assumption that their offenses resulted from learned patterns of behavior associated with anxious, angry, and impulsive individuals. The three-phase program obligates offenders to attend ten weeks of courses in abnormal psychology and the psychology of sexual offending. In other phases, inmates attend group therapy sessions with counselors and other inmates. MOSOP officials believe that if the program can reduce sex offender recidivism by only 3 percent, it will pay for itself from the savings of court costs and inmate processing and confinement (Kuznestov, Pierson, and Harry, 1992).

The Minnesota Department of Corrections operates a project known as **180 Degrees, Inc.** This program, similar to a halfway house for parolees, is designed for those who have received no previous treatment for their sex offenses (Driggs and Zoet, 1987). Participation in 180 Degrees, Inc. is limited only to those offenders willing to admit that they have committed one or more sex offenses and who can function as group members. Offenders form men's sexuality groups that meet for 90-minute meetings over thirteen weeks. All participants contract with officials to write an autobiography of their offense, a description of the victim, a listing of sexual abuse cues, the development of a control plan, and personal affirmations (Driggs and Zoet, 1987:126). Although this program is not fully effective, it does seem to help some offenders understand their behavior.

Sex offenders, especially child sexual abusers, pose significant problems for jail and prison authorities as well as for community-based corrections personnel. Child sexual abusers are often abused themselves by other inmates when their crimes become known to others. Other sex offenders become the prey of stronger inmates, who use these offenders for their own sexual gratification. Many sex offenders request that they be segregated from other prisoners because of danger to themselves, yet because of limited resources and space, jail and prison officials often cannot segregate these offenders effectively from other inmates.

Within communities, many sex offenders and child sexual abusers are placed in community-based facilities for treatment and counseling (Wilson et al., 2000). A survey of 2,961 juvenile and adult sex offender treatment programs has indicated an increase of 133 percent in the number of these providers between 1986 and 1990 (Knopp, Freeman-Longo, and Stevenson, 1992). The most frequently used treatment method in sex offender treatment agencies is peer group counseling. For example, the state of Washington operates the Special Sex Offender Sentencing Alternative that permits community treatment in lieu of determinate sentences for adult, felony sex offenders (Washington State Department of Social and Mental Health Services, 1991). The Washington program has found that intensive counseling and therapy for many of these clients has substantially reduced their recidivism within the community.

Various models of PO training and caseload assignments that include sex offender specialization have been described. Some officers are specialists in that they have received unique training in counseling sex offenders. Some POs have acquired master of social work degrees and are certified counselors for those with sex or alcohol problems. One PO training model is the specialized caseloads model, in which clients are assigned according to their particular offenses and/or psychological problems (Firestone et al., 2000). Sex offenders and child sexual abusers are among those clients receiving particular supervision from PO specialists, just as chemically dependent persons might be supervised by POs who have acquired additional chemical dependency training (Fisher, Beech, and Browne, 2000; Marshall and Serran, 2000).

OFFENDERS WITH HIV/AIDS

Inmates, probationers, and parolees with AIDS/HIV are at risk of transmitting their disease to others. While institutionalized, inmates with AIDS/HIV are often isolated physically from the general inmate population to prevent the spread of their disease to other inmates (Shewan and Davies, 2000). Their isolation cannot be continued indefinitely, however. Some authorities believe that institutionalization is the last chance many of these persons will have to receive appropriate treatment under any type of meaningful supervision (Marquart et al., 1999). Although some prisoners with AIDS/HIV are confined, particularly in local jails, sometimes they are also ill-treated or denied treatment by insensitive jail personnel as a punishment for their condition (Vaughn and Smith, 1999). At some point, most of these offenders will be paroled. When they come under the supervision of paroling authorities, they are often assigned to a PO who is trained in sexually transmitted diseases. POs with special knowledge can be more effective in the management and supervision of AIDS/HIV-infected clients and this specialized caseload.

AIDS/HIV-infected inmates are often known to POs before their arrival. With this advance knowledge, POs can arrange appropriate community services and treatment so that when their clients arrive, their therapy can continue without interruption (Anno, 1998). Often, new clients with AIDS/HIV have other problems such as drug dependencies, and POs must also plan to address these types of problems. Increasing numbers of AIDS/HIV-infected clients are women. If some of these women are pregnant or have borne children prior to their earlier confinement, then POs must arrange to educate them about how to prevent the spread of AIDS/HIV. Some investigations have revealed that the knowledge among women with AIDS/HIV, how it was acquired and how it can be transmitted, is extremely low. Thus, it is critical that these persons receive special education courses or a general exposure to knowledge about AIDS/HIV and its transmission (Brewer, Marquart, and Mullings, 1998). Usually, a community agency can assist in this regard (Maxwell and Wallisch, 1998).

Some inmates with AIDS/HIV who are within a short time of early release may be granted work or study release from their confinement. There are obvious risk factors associated with permitting these persons to work for limited periods outside of prison walls. Yet, it has been found that if these persons are properly supervised within a supportive community environment, then their transition back into their communities later goes more smoothly (Harrison et al., 1998).

SUBSTANCE-ABUSING OFFENDERS

Offenders who are arrested and convicted for substance abuse are increasing compared with other offender groups. It is estimated that when alcohol abusers are combined with drug abusers within the offender population, between 80 and 90 percent of them have some type of addiction or problem (Shearer and Carter, 1999:30). Between 1980 and 1994, for instance, the number of state and local arrests for drug offenses rose from 581,000 to 1,350,000 (Corbett and Harris, 1999:67). The population of chronic illicit drug users consists largely of poor, undereducated, unemployed, and uninsured persons. These persons commit crimes at disproportionately higher rates than other criminals, and they pose substantial health risks to their associates (Lurigio and Swartz, 1999:67). Furthermore, they comprise the population of probationers and parolees most likely to relapse while free within their communities under PO supervision. Thus, they present fairly serious monitoring problems for POs in all jurisdictions, and this problem is increasing rather than diminishing.

For POs, an effective supervision strategy requires a reliable drug-testing program as well as a consistent and well-formulated policy that holds offenders accountable for their decision to use drugs or otherwise violate the special drug aftercare consideration. The range of consequences for drug aftercare violations must be clearly spelled out in the office policy manual and overseen by unit supervisors; the expectations of abstinence and possible sanctions must be carefully reviewed with the offender during the initial interview; and, most essential, the threatened sanctions must be imposed when and if violations occur if controlling and treating drug offenders is to be effective (Torres, 1998:36).

In the early 1990s, the typical response whenever drug or alcohol abusers were encountered in courts was to place them under intensive probation or parole supervision, with considerable monitoring and randomized drug and alcohol checks. Although these types of checks are still conducted in most if not all state and federal jurisdictions, they do not appear to be working to decrease the extent of substance abuse (Martin and Lurigio, 1994:25). What is acknowledged as the most effective strategy for reducing drug demand is combining prevention and education programs for non-drug users with treatment programs for users. Treatment for incarcerated and nonincarcerated offenders not only reduces drug use but also suppresses the criminal activity associated with it. Moreover, offenders who are forced into drug treatment by legal mandates are just as successful in recovery as those who voluntarily enter treatment programs, and they often remain in their programs for longer periods (Martin and Lurigio, 1994:25).

In Cook County, Illinois, during 1989, an Evening Narcotics Court was established due to the high volume of felony drug cases. Between 1989 and 1993, the Evening Narcotics Court had handled 19,485 probation cases and conducted 3,900 presentence and pretrial investigations. Contemporaneous with the Evening Narcotics Court, an Illinois Drug Offender Specialized Supervision Program as well as a Home Confinement Unit were established. These additional programs enabled Cook County authorities the opportunity of providing larger numbers of drug offenders with nonincarcerative options. The Cook County Jail inmate population was greatly alleviated as a result. What, though, did the program accomplish since its inception?

The first major hurdle was to screen prospective applicants for inclusion. Probation officers conducted interviews with likely candidates and selected approximately 600 offenders who were considered eligible. Subsequently, as resources and personnel expanded, more offenders became involved in the program. Courts ordered these offenders to maintain employment, complete their education, participate in outpatient treatment, and remain at home with their families under mild supervision from the probation department. During 1992, for instance, home confinement officers made approximately 122,000 face-to-face visits and 77,700 telephone contacts with program participants. Drug tests and urinalyses were conducted thousands of times for these offenders. Initially, about 46 percent of all participants tested positive for at least one illegal drug, but, they were permitted to remain in their programs, with intensified supervision. After a while, only 33 percent tested positive for one or more illegal drugs, mostly cocaine. Offenders who continued to test positive for illegal drugs were referred to drug treatment programs for additional assistance. Although the program was not 100 percent effective in eliminating illicit drug use, it did divert a substantial number of drug abusers to a therapeutic environment in which they could withdraw from drugs over time and remain connected with their families (Martin and Lurigio, 1994:26-27).

In other jurisdictions, more aggressive offender monitoring and supervision has been proposed. For instance, some observers contend that the traditional medical model, which considers drug and alcohol dependence a disease that can be cured with some type of long-term therapy and treatment, is not suitable for criminal offenders who have serious addictions (Torres, 1998:36). The medical model is closely associated with the social work approach and places POs in positions to be manipulated by their addicted clients. Few offenders are willing to oblige their supervising POs or anyone else to give up their drugs or alcohol voluntarily. The usual scenario is that there are frequent relapses and POs merely suggest starting over or trying again with a particular therapy. Also, many addicted clients are master manipulators and design various methods to beat the drug tests. It is not unusual for

POs to give offenders chance after chance following drug tests that are "dirty" or disclose the use of one or more drugs within the past 24 or 48 hours (Torres, 1997b:17). For many POs, this part of establishing rapport with their clients and earning their trust is necessary. Some clients, for instance, object to being ordered to refrain from using alcohol if their addiction happens to be cocaine. Why should they be expected to refrain from alcohol use if they have another type of addiction? One answer is that alcohol consumption is associated with a higher rate of relapse involving their drug of choice, whether it is cocaine, heroin, or some other addictive substance (Torres, 1997a). The most common positives for drugs include cocaine, amphetamines, morphine, and marijuana. Other drugs include anabolic steroids, barbiturates, phencyclidine (PCP), and prescription medications such as diazepam (Valium), codeine, and methadone (Torres, 1998:38).

Many offenders attempt to beat the tests administered by POs or private contractors by doing different things to contaminate their urine or blood specimens. Some of the techniques offenders use include using a rubber penis filled with clean urine; attaching to the unobserved side of the penis a tube leading to a container under the armpit; inserting a small bottle of clean urine into the vagina; pouring clean urine into a specimen bottle; dipping the bottle into the urinal or toilet and filling it with water; and contaminating the urine sample with various foreign substances, such as Drano, chlorine, or bleach. Other clients flush their systems and consume large quantities of water, coffee, or other liquids to dilute the concentration of drugs in the body and accelerate the excretion. The greater the liquid intake, the lower the concentration of the drug and the quicker the excretion rate. Some offenders simply fail to show up for their counseling sessions or treatment. Skipping meetings means no test and no detection (Torres, 1996). For many POs, a "no show" at a counseling session is less serious than testing positive for drugs.

Sam Torres, a former federal probation officer, believes that a continuum of sanctions should be imposed instead of the usual course of treatment prescribed by the medical model. The sanctions are as follows:

1. Admonishment, which is a verbal warning that the test was positive or that the offender failed to report for testing
2. Verbal admonishment by a probation officer, which is a verbal warning issued to the offender that further drug use will have consequences, such as mandatory participation in a 12-step program or other activities
3. Written admonishment by the probation officer, which is a formal letter to the offender advising him or her of consequences for continuing to test positive for drug use
4. Verbal admonishment by the probation officer and supervisor, which adds weight to the admonishment
5. Written admonishment by the U.S. Parole Commission, if the client is a federal probationer or parolee
6. Verbal admonishment by the court
7. Lengthen the time in the current phase, or simply extend the period of their current phase level
8. Increase the client's phase level to closer supervision and testing
9. Increase the level of supervision, including more frequent offender monitoring
10. Community service as a punishment
11. Alcoholics Anonymous or Narcotics Anonymous mandatory meetings; offenders must sign cards at these meetings to signify that they attended

12. Outpatient counseling
13. Electronic monitoring
14. Community correctional center participation
15. Reside and participate in a sober-living program
16. Arrest, short-term custody, and reinstatement to supervision
17. Intermittent incarceration
18. Therapeutic community (residential drug treatment)
19. Arrest, custody, and recommendation for program revocation (Torres, 1998:38–44)

The importance of these different stages of increasing sanctions is to make clear to offenders that their relapses will have specific consequences. It is insufficient to merely threaten to do something; the PO actually has to follow through and do it. Torres recommends a zero tolerance policy, and he believes that offenders should be held accountable for their decision to use drugs because they are engaging in a rational choice to violate program requirements. Clients are given numerous opportunities to overcome their addictions. Complete abstinence is the recommended therapy according to this model (Torres, 1997b).

Unfortunately, it is a fact that if drug-abusing offenders are eventually incarcerated, they can easily acquire drugs from other inmates. There is about as much drug use, if not more, in prisons and jails than there is on city streets. Inmates use a multitude of methods to smuggle drugs into their institutions. And, there are many creative ways of paying for these drugs to continue their addictions (Lurigio and Swartz, 1999:67–70).

Drug Screening and Methadone Treatment

Detecting drug abuse is most often accomplished through clinical screenings performed by addiction counselors or others. A clinical screening is an initial gathering and compiling of information to determine if an offender has a problem with alcohol or drug (AOD) abuse and if so, whether a comprehensive clinical assessment is warranted. Screening is accomplished through a structured interview or instruments designed to get offenders to self-report information. Screening also filters out individuals who have medical, legal, or psychological problems that must be addressed before they can fully participate in treatment (Shearer and Carter, 1999:30).

Some agencies use the Psychopathic Personality Inventory, a 56-item self-report inventory that provides a total score on psychopathy and factor scores on eight dimensions of psychopathy: Machiavellian egocentricity, social potency, coldheartedness, carefree nonplanfulness, fearlessness, blame externalization, impulsive nonconformity, and stress nonimmunity. The major screening and assessment is a standardized set of procedures designed to:

1. Establish baseline information about AOD dependence
2. Assess client readiness for counseling
3. Serve as treatment planning tools for counseling by identifying (a) the client's high-risk situations for AOD use and (b) the client's coping strengths and weaknesses (Shearer and Carter, 1999:31)

Clients are considered ready for treatment when they perceive and accept that they have a problem or "own" the problem. In many instances, however, clients do not appear ready for treatment. They tend to minimize, deny, or reject and resist any attempt to help them from counselors. Certainly a part of this resistance or denial is related to their present addictive state, because they are not rational enough to appreciate the logical curative consequences of withdrawal (Shearer and Carter, 1999:32).

Perhaps the most serious problem associated with deterring substance abusers from persisting in their addictions is the physical reactions offenders experience during the withdrawal period. In instances of heroin addiction, for instance, complete and immediate abstinence from heroin causes intense pain throughout the body, complete with nausea, vomiting, and cramping, that continues for several days. In addition, there is always the possibility that because of one's bodily condition and weakness, the physical stress of withdrawal can be debilitating, causing permanent nerve damage, even death. Therefore, in cases in which serious addictions to drugs exist, the withdrawal treatment is gradual. Several drugs are used in the withdrawal process. These drugs, such as methadone, are also narcotics, but they cause fewer violent withdrawal symptoms. For instance, methadone is a synthetic narcotic used to treat morphine and heroin addiction. It is actually more powerful than morphine, but it has fewer debilitating side effects and the body can withstand adverse withdrawal reactions more easily. In short, drug withdrawal with the assistance of other drugs is more easily tolerated by the body. Many treatment programs conducted under controlled hospital conditions use methadone and other substances to treat serious addictions.

Some observers believe that the use of methadone in treating heroin and morphine addiction is merely substituting one narcotic for another and that one can become addicted to methadone. This observation, however, neglects that there are other dimensions to one's overall treatment program, such as chemical dependency education, counseling, and other nondrug therapies. Furthermore, an offender receives continuous monitoring and is medically evaluated on a regular basis to determine how his or her body is responding to treatment (Fogg, 1992). With the volume of drug-abusing offenders entering the criminal justice system, one increasingly used response is the drug court.

Drug Courts and the Drug Court Movement

Drug courts are special courts dedicated exclusively to the needs of drug-abusing offenders in which prosecutors, defense counsels, treatment professionals, probation officers, and other community agencies work to achieve case outcomes for drug abusers that will maximize their successful treatment. Drug courts were established in 1989 in Dade County, Florida (Goldkamp, 2000). Drug courts had been implemented in over 400 jurisdictions by 1998. More than 100,000 drug-using offenders have participated in drug court programs. Of these, about 71 percent have successfully completed their programs or are actively participating in them (Huddleston, 1998:98).

One unique feature of drug courts is the specialization they exhibit toward drug-abusing offenders. Most other courts are courts of general criminal jurisdiction, and drug offenders are combined with other types of criminals and are punished similarly. Drug courts, however, recognize the atypicality of drug abusers and their need for special services provided only through an integrated community program involving several helping agencies. Although these courts are currently enjoying a

472   *Jails, Prisons, and Parole*

remarkable degree of success in the treatment of drug-abusing offenders, not everyone is enthusiastic about their emergence and persistence. One criticism is that for some drug abusers, being sent to a drug court for processing is more stigmatizing than therapeutic, so the reintegrative intentions of drug courts may be defeated in part because of their specialization. Thus, diversion to drug court may be regarded as discriminatory by some drug abusers, who in turn, will reject the reintegrative efforts of those seeking to assist them (Miethe, Lu, and Reese, 2000).

Despite this criticism, drug courts show no signs of abating in the near future. If anything, they are being expanded in more diverse areas of the country annually, and at a phenomenal growth rate (Goldkamp, 2000; Taxman, 1999). Furthermore, drug courts are not exclusively focused on drugs. Some drug courts address alcohol dependency as well as hard drugs. For example, a unique DWI drug court has been established in Las Cruces, New Mexico, with specially trained court personnel assessing first- and second-time DWI offenders for symptoms of alcoholism. A subsequent treatment program that includes individual, group, and family counseling sessions is prescribed by the judge. Results from a 24-month follow-up suggest that this DWI drug court is having a substantial effect on decreasing the recidivism rates of DWI offenders who participate in the program compared with nonparticipants (Breckenridge et al., 2000).

One feature of drug courts is that they provide for more consistent and frequent monitoring of participating offenders who are ordered into particular therapies (Belenko, 1999). Not only is the supervision more comprehensive, but there are increased rates of retention in treatment and reduced drug use and criminal behavior while participants are in these programs. Drug courts are designed to handle more serious offenders, many of whom have prior criminal histories with myriad physical and mental health needs. Recidivism rates almost always decline following one's participation in such programs (Belenko, 1999; National Drug Court Institute, 1999a, 1999b).

The Drug Court Model. The model typically followed by drug courts entails the following characteristics:

1. A single drug court judge and staff who provide leadership and focus
2. Expedited adjudication through early identification of appropriate program participants and referral to treatment as soon as possible after arrest
3. Intensive long-term treatment and aftercare for appropriate drug-using offenders
4. Comprehensive and well-coordinated supervision through regular status hearings before a single drug court judge to monitor treatment progress through program compliance
5. Increased defendant accountability through a series of graduated sanctions and rewards
6. Mandatory and frequent drug testing (Huddleston, 1998:98)

A study of 24 drug courts by Columbia University's National Center on Addiction and Substance Abuse (CASA) has provided one of the first major academic reviews and analyses of drug court effectiveness. How has the model worked with offenders? Essentially, the study found that drug courts provide closer, more comprehensive supervision and much more frequent drug testing and monitoring than conventional forms of community supervision, such as probation or parole. More important, drug use and criminal behavior are substantially reduced while offenders are participating in drug court programs. The CASA study further summarizes findings from older and newer drug courts. The results are fairly consistent in that

1. Drug courts have been successful in engaging and retaining felony offenders in programmatic and treatment services who have substantial substance abuse and criminal histories but little prior treatment engagement.
2. Drug courts provide more comprehensive and closer supervision of the drug-using offender than other forms of community supervision.
3. Drug use and criminal behavior are substantially reduced while clients are participating in drug court.
4. Criminal behavior is lower after program participation, especially for graduates, although few studies have tracked recidivism for more than one year post-program
5. Drug courts generate cost savings, at least in the short term, from reduced jail/prison use, reduced criminality, and lower criminal justice system costs.
6. Drug courts have been successful in bridging the gap between the court and the treatment/public health systems and spurring greater cooperation among the various agencies and personnel within the criminal justice system as well as between the criminal justice system and the community. (Belenko, 1999; Huddleston, 1998:99–100)

The cost-effectiveness of drug courts has been assessed. In Multnomah County, Oregon, a program known as the STOP Drug Court Diversion Program was evaluated. A sample of 150 participants was compared with three other groups, including STOP noncompleters (persons who failed drug tests or did not appear at their status hearings). For every taxpayer dollar spent on programming costs of STOP, a $2.50 savings was realized. If victimization costs are factored in, then the cost savings rises to about $10 for every dollar spent on programming (Finigan, 1999). Similar savings have been reported by other jurisdictions (Peters and Murrin, 2000; Winfree and Giever, 2000).

The Jefferson County (Kentucky) Drug Court Program.   An example of one drug court in action is the Jefferson County Drug Court Program in Kentucky. Based on the Dade County, Florida, model, this program diverts first-time, drug possession offenders into a 12-month community treatment program that includes acupuncture and the development of social and educational skills (Vito and Tewksbury, 1998:46). It is monitored directly by the drug court judge, who helps supervise the offender's treatment program. The model breaks down the traditional adversarial roles of prosecutors and defense attorneys. If the judge believes that offenders are trying to break the pattern of addiction, then the offenders remain in treatment even after they test positive for drugs several times. Therefore, the treatment program may be continued indefinitely until the offender successfully completes it.

The drug court judge extends judicial oversight throughout all phases of the program. Clients are required to attend sessions of drug court on a schedule set by the judge. Before weekly sessions of drug court, the judge is provided with individualized progress reports for all participants. During these court sessions, the judge reviews the program progress of each client. Upon review, the judge may (1) continue client participation, (2) permanently remove the client from the program, or (3) remand the client to a term of jail incarceration for failure to meet program requirements.

Participation in drug court is voluntary. Referrals are made to the drug court from prosecutors or from public or private attorneys. Clients must be 18 years of age and meet the following criteria established by the prosecutor:

1. Possession versus trafficking cases: preference is given to cocaine possession cases; trafficking cases are considered after a review of possession cases.
2. Prior drug arrests: defendants with multiple trafficking arrests in their history are not considered.
3. No history of violent offenses: offenders with a history of violent crimes are not eligible for inclusion in the program.
4. Eligibility: only Jefferson County cases are eligible for inclusion.
5. Police approval: the lead officer in the case is consulted in the decision to recommend a client for diversion into the drug court program.
6. Quantity of cocaine: any offender in possession of one or more ounces of cocaine is not eligible for drug court; any offender with five or more grams of cocaine is presumed to be trafficking in drugs and is placed on the trafficking list of offenders eligible for program review (Vito and Tewksbury, 1998:46)

After all applicants are screened and meet the initial screening criteria, they must undergo a psychological assessment. The purpose of the assessment is to determine whether the client is amenable to treatment and does not pose a risk to the community. Drug court participants must abide by all program conditions and must be punctual, attend all required program sessions, be nonviolent, refrain from attending treatment sessions while under the influence of drugs, and behave lawfully. The aim is to create and maintain a receptive treatment environment, promote prosocial behavior, and establish a sense of individual accountability among clients. The various treatment programs offered through the drug court include acupuncture, meditation, individual counseling, group therapy, Alcoholics Anonymous (AA), Narcotics Anonymous (NA), and chemical dependency education (Vito and Tewksbury, 1998:46–47).

The three treatment phases. are follows:

Phase I: Detoxification (10 days)

1. Four random drug tests
2. Attendance at a minimum of five weekly meetings of AA/NA
3. Participation in all individual and group counseling sessions as determined by program staff
4. Optional acupuncture and/or meditation sessions

To move to phase II, the client must receive a maximum of four negative drug screens, attend all assigned individual and group therapy sessions, and attend all weekly AA/NA meetings.

Phase II: Stabilization (108 days)

1. Acupuncture and/or meditation sessions as needed/requested
2. Two weekly drug tests (a minimum number of positive drug screenings during each of the first four weeks and no positive drug screens by the sixth week of this phase are necessary to move to phase III)

3. Attendance at a minimum of four AA/NA meetings as prescribed by the treatment plan; clients must obtain an AA/NA sponsor
4. Attendance at all individual and group counseling sessions as prescribed by the treatment plan
5. Significant progress toward meeting treatment plan goals as determined by treatment program staff and the drug court judge

Phase III: Aftercare (6 months)

1. Acupuncture and/or meditation sessions as requested by the client
2. Random drug tests
3. Participation in educational, vocational, remedial, and other training programs as specified in the individual treatment plan
4. Individual and group counseling as needed
5. Attendance at a minimum of three AA/NA meetings per week
6. Maintenance of and regular contact with a full-time AA/NA sponsor

To graduate from the drug court program, clients must meet (1) remain drug free as shown by the results of their drug tests in the last two months of this phase and (2) secure or maintain employment, enroll or maintain enrollment in an educational program and/or engage in full-time parenting responsibilities. Only those clients who have paid all accrued fees will be permitted to graduate from drug court (Vito and Tewksbury, 1998:47–48).

Results from the Jefferson County Drug Court Program were based on an analysis of 237 clients who were screened and included in the program. They were compared with a sample of 76 persons who were screened but not included in the program. Reconviction was used as the recidivism measure and an indicator of program failure. There were significant differences in failure rates of graduates compared with nonparticipants. Graduates of drug court had a reconviction rate of 13 percent, whereas the reconviction rate of the comparison group was 55 percent. This finding suggests that the Jefferson County Drug Court treatment program has been successful. The graduates were also compared, however, according to whether they were subsequently charged with a drug/alcohol-related offense. This time, about 43 percent of the graduates had been charged during the follow-up period, but these figures are slightly lower than the nongraduates, of whom 46 percent were charged with new drug offenses. Thus, nearly half of all drug court graduates were unable to avoid relapses back to drugs. One recommendation was that drug court graduates should continue to receive regular drug testing and monitoring so as to maintain their resistance to drugs (Vito and Tewksbury, 1998:50–51).

Drug court programs in other jurisdictions have had similar success rates. The Brooklyn, New York, Treatment Court started in 1996. More than 1,000 drug abusers were placed in treatment programs by this drug court from 1996 to 1999. Two-thirds were still actively involved in the program, and about one-third had completed 180 days of treatment. Although there were relapses, relapse rates were similar to the Jefferson County, Kentucky, rates of about 50 percent (Harrell and Roman, 1999). And in Riverside, California, a drug court operated a Recovery Opportunity Center, a drug treatment day program, with 103 clients. After 20 months from program admission, 58 percent of the graduates showed no signs of substance abuse. Recidivism rates for graduates were about 15 percent, again comparable with the Jefferson County, Kentucky, program (Sechrest et al., 1998).

COMMUNITY PROGRAMS FOR SPECIAL NEEDS OFFENDERS

Therapeutic Communities

A **therapeutic community** is a treatment model in which all activities, both formal and informal, are viewed as interrelated interventions that address the multidimensional disorder of the whole person. These activities include educational and therapeutic meetings and groups as well as interpersonal and social activities of the community. Within this theoretical framework, social and psychological change evolves as a dynamic interaction between the individual and the peer community, its context of activities, and expectations for participation (Deitch et al., 2001:24). Therapeutic communities are often mandated by the courts or parole boards for persons with particular substance-abuse problems or chemical dependencies (Maxwell, 2000). For instance, 720 offenders were mandated by the court for drug treatment into three highly structured therapeutic communities in the northeastern United States from 1990 to 1993. These offenders were subjected to a battery of tests, including the Circumstances, Motivation, Readiness, and Suitability attitudinal scale. The periods of the detention of these court-placed offenders were unspecified. It remained at the discretion of program authorities to determine when they had successfully completed their programs by participating in community programming as outlined by their therapeutic community plan (Maxwell, 2000).

Many therapeutic community models are commenced in prison or jail settings and subsequently continued in an offender's city or town. Therefore, therapeutic community clientele have the benefit of continuing their treatment and programming under limited supervision following their release from incarceration. Often, these therapeutic community programs are designed for offenders with chemical dependencies rather than for mentally ill patients (Hiller, Knight, and Simpson, 1999; Messina, Wish, and Nemes, 1999). Programs have been established in Texas, Washington, D.C., and Delaware.

In Delaware, a therapeutic community known as CREST has been created. CREST is prison-based and is applied to women who are encouraged to form networks of support for one another. During an experimental period in the mid-1990s, 41 female participants were involved in CREST, including a control group of 39 female work releasees. Both groups were compared while in prison as well as in 6- and 18-month follow-ups after they were released from incarceration. Women participating in the CREST program were more successful in remaining law-abiding, with a 39 percent recidivism rate. Those who were on standard work release, however, had a recidivism rate of 50 percent. Thus, the likelihood of relapse was greater for those who were not a part of the CREST program (Farrell, 2000). A similar study of substance-abusing clients was conducted in Washington, D.C. Two therapeutic communities were studied and involved 412 randomly drawn drug-abusing clients (Nemes, Wish, and Messina, 1999). The program lasted 12 months and involved numerous community interventions and experiences. Subsequently, the clients were placed on outpatient services. Marked reductions in illicit drug use and crime were found among the clients who completed the program.

For POs, therapeutic community involvement of parolees alleviates some of their pressure to locate and integrate offender programming. It is already in place for some of these offenders. Thus, a PO's job is made much easier by simply having to supervise offenders already networked within their therapeutic community environments. A PO's work might consist primarily of performing periodic and random drug or curfew checks. The concept of therapeutic community is being considered and applied in countries outside of the United States. It appears to be gaining in popularity as an intervention for persons with serious addiction problems (Klingemann and Hunt, 1998).

Alcoholics Anonymous, Narcotics Anonymous, and Gamblers Anonymous Programs

As seen in therapeutic community and drug court interventions, Alcoholics Anonymous and Narcotics Anonymous programs have played major roles as community support mechanisms to provide social support for recovering alcohol and drug abusers (Cunningham et al., 1998). Alcoholics Anonymous and Narcotics Anonymous programs are designed to provide information and guidance for those with alcohol and drug dependencies. They are offered to inmates in prisons and jails as well as in their communities (Alcoholics Anonymous World Services, Inc., 1991). They both involve a series of steps through which participants admit that they are powerless to control their cravings for alcohol or drugs (Mumola and Bonczar, 1998). These programs are frequently linked with probation and parole programs. Judges and parole boards often require probationers and parolees to attend their meetings as one of their special conditions of probation or parole (English, Pullen, and Colling-Chadwick, 1996).

Similar to the 12-step program used by Alcoholics Anonymous, the 12-step program for Narcotics Anonymous is as follows:

1. We admitted that we were powerless over our addiction, that our lives had become unmanageable.
2. We came to believe that a Power greater than ourselves could restore us to sanity.
3. We made a decision to turn our will and our lives over to the care of God as we understood Him.
4. We made a searching and fearless moral inventory of ourselves.
5. We admitted to God, to ourselves, and to another human being the exact nature of our wrongs.
6. We were entirely ready to have God remove all these defects of character.
7. We humbly asked Him to remove our shortcomings.
8. We made a list of all persons we had harmed, and became willing to make amends to them all.
9. We made direct amends to such people whenever possible, except when to do so would injure them or others.
10. We continue to take personal inventory and when we were wrong promptly admitted it.
11. We sought through prayer and meditation to improve our conscious contact with God as we understood Him, praying only for knowledge of His will for us and the power to carry that out.
12. Having had a spiritual awakening as a result of these steps, we tried to carry this message to addicts, and practice these principles in all our affairs. (Narcotics Anonymous, 1999)

Meetings of these groups are usually announced in local newspapers daily throughout the nation, and street locations and times are given. Some meetings are "closed," meaning that they are not open to the general public. Closed meetings are occasions for the permanent membership to band together and discuss intimate details of their alcohol and narcotics addictions with one another. Other meetings are open, and the public is invited. Only those with drug or alcohol dependencies are encouraged to attend these open meetings, although it is unlikely that someone wishing to see what goes on at these meetings would be barred from participating. During the meetings, which usually last one hour, people are given an opportunity to stand, identify themselves by first name only, and indicate the nature of their addiction. Some attendees take this opportunity to apologize to the group for their addictions, and they elicit acceptance and empathy from other attendees. At the end of the meeting, a prayer is uttered, with all those willing to do so linking hands in a large circle.

The religious components in both Alcoholics Anonymous and Narcotics Anonymous have alienated certain drug abusers who are atheists and do not believe in God. Several options have been made available to them, including various secular organizations organized along lines similar to those of AA and NA. In some areas of the country, such as Tampa, Florida, groups of substance-abusing adult probationers have been encouraged to form associations and hold meetings that emphasize positive behaviors (Peters et al., 1993).

Some observers question the value of AA and NA as viable interventions. When convicted offenders are required to attend such meetings as a part of their probation programs, there is no way that they can be induced to participate actively in these meetings once there. They sign a card signifying their attendance, and there is no pressure on them to become actively involved in discussions. No one can compel them to say anything about themselves (O'Callaghan, Gagnon, and Brochu, 1990). Nevertheless, POs continue to encourage those with alcohol and drug dependencies to attend these meetings and to attend them with great frequency (Read, 1990).

Increasingly recognized as a serious addiction is gambling. Gambling is legal in many areas. It is addictive in much the same sense that alcohol and drugs are addictive. In many areas of the country, organizations have been established to treat gambling addiction, especially when it has been related to criminal activity. Persons who gamble may lose a lot of money and may resort to crime to obtain additional money to pursue their gambling addiction. Usually, Gamblers Anonymous organizations have included 12-step programs similar to AA and NA, although they also include educational programming emphasizing personal financial counseling. Individual and group therapy also accompany Gamblers Anonymous programming, depending on the jurisdiction (Gowen and Speyerer, 1995). Gamblers Anonymous organizations have been in existence for several decades (Livingston, 1974).

GANG MEMBERS

The National Youth Gang Survey is disturbing in a number of respects. First, it demonstrates the pervasiveness of gangs in American society. Second, it shows the strength gangs have in virtually every locality where they exist. Third, it demonstrates the interaction between prison/jail inmates and street gangs. Fourth, it illustrates the diverse forms of criminal activities associated with gang membership

---

BOX 12.2   ***About the GREAT Program***

GREAT = Gang Resistance Education and Training

Established in Phoenix, Arizona in 1991, the goal of the GREAT Program, for Gang Resistance Education and Training, was to reduce gang activity in the schools. The program has now spread to many communities throughout the nation, particularly as gang presence has proliferated and gang violence has escalated. The program involves visits to local and area schools by police officers who are members of special gang units in police departments. These police officers are quite familiar with gang terms and signs and can recognize gang presence whenever they see it. This skill is not easily acquired by others, particularly schoolteachers and other students. In Bismarck, North Dakota, for instance, some samples of student art were on display for a parent-student night at a high school. Displayed in a main hallway of the high school was a large mural painted by several students. The teachers and students seemed proud of it. When one of the fathers of a student entered the building and saw the mural, he was appalled; the mural was nothing more than a gigantic display of gang graffiti. He was a police officer with the Bismarck Police Department and a member of a special gang unit and task force. Once advised about its significance, teachers and the principal hurriedly removed the mural.

The GREAT Program has been quite useful in deterring many students from gang affiliation in local schools. Usually, several police officers with special training visit these schools and educate the students about the various pitfalls of joining gangs. In Webb County, Texas, for instance, Sheriff Juan Garza says, "School violence revolves around gangs and we must teach students to become better citizens. Counselors are going to work to identify where the root of the problem is." In preparation for their educational experience, various police officers are handpicked for their community involvement. At a two-week training course in Phoenix, Arizona, they receive intensive instruction on gang recruitment tactics and activities. The Laredo, Texas (Webb County), GREAT Program was implemented in September 2000. School counselors normally work together with police officers during their educational sessions with children. Because Laredo does not have a major gang problem yet, Sheriff Garza says that prevention rather than reaction is the objective. A secondary objective of the program is to point out to students other gang activities, such as involvement with drugs, alcohol, and tobacco.

Should antigang programs be created and operated in all schools throughout the United States? Should persons identified as gang members be barred from attending school? What do you think?

Source: Adapted from Erick Santos and Associated Press, "Anti-Gang Program Sends Deputies to Local Schools," September 24, 2000.

(Wilson, 2000). As seen, in 1998, there were at least 780,200 known gang members in 28,700 gangs in the United States.

Even more disturbing is that since the 1950s, there have been numerous changes in the structure, organization, and activities of gangs. Gangs are increasingly lethal in their choice of weaponry, which often includes automatic weapons. Other changes include the fact that gangs are no longer confined to large urban centers; they have branched out into smaller communities and towns. Further, more gang members are remaining in their gangs well into their adult years. More gangs are graduating into large-scale drug trafficking and gun sales both nationally and internationally (Elder, 1996). Gangs are big business, and many gangs are increasingly organized according to corporate structural models, complete with executive boards and chairmen (Triplet and Ross, 1998:29–30).

The public is more frequently aware of gang presence by the incidence of drive-by shootings that occur in large cities such as Los Angeles, New York, and Chicago. Often, these drive-by shootings involve deaths of innocent bystanders who are standing in close proximity to the intended targets, rival gang members (Levine and Parra, 2000). Relatively little is known by the public about gang involvement in large-scale drug trafficking and other criminal enterprises.

Considerable investigation has been conducted concerning why persons become affiliated with gangs initially. Psychological and social maladjustments such as low self-esteem and being an isolate in schools and other social settings are often cited (Lynskey and Winfree, 2000). Both male and female gang members appear to have joined gangs for essentially the same reasons (Miller and Brunson, 2000). Other persons join gangs for mutual protection. They feel safe where there is strength in numbers (Aguirre and Baker, 2000).

POs have an uneasy relation with clients who are affiliated with gangs. Some of these reasons were examined earlier in this chapter. Gangs exert considerable social and psychological influence over their memberships, and this influence often undermines PO attempts to change the attitudes of gang member-clients. Further, there is the possibility and likelihood that gang member-clients will continue to engage in illicit activities of their gangs without PO knowledge.

Community and PO response to gangs and gang interventions have usually broken down into the following categories:

1. Community organization or neighborhood mobilization
2. Social intervention, which involves youth outreach and street work counseling
3. Opportunities provision, which involves jobs, job training, and education
4. Suppression, which involves arrest, incarceration, and supervision
5. Organizational development, which involves adapting organizations to facilitate dealing with gangs, such as the development of gang units in police departments (Triplet and Ross, 1998:30)

Increasingly, gang intervention programs are emphasizing partnerships with different agencies, including schools. The GREAT (Gang Resistance Education and Training) program involves school resource officers and works in conjunction with gang units from police departments to educate nongang members in schools to avoid gangs. Other programs are geared toward younger youths. For instance, the Montreal Preventive Treatment Program is a multicomponent prevention program designed to prevent antisocial behavior among boys of lower socioeconomic statuses who display disruptive problem behavior in kindergarten (Howell, 2000:7). Parent training was combined with individual social skills for boys age seven to nine. Parents received an average of 17 training sessions to improve social skills and self-control. The training was implemented in small groups containing both disruptive and nondisruptive boys and used coaching, peer modeling, self-instruction, reinforcement contingencies, and role-playing to build skills (Tremblay et al., 1996). Follow-up evaluations of this research showed less delinquency, substance abuse, and gang involvement by age 15 among those studied.

For early childhood or adolescent programs to maximize their effectiveness, they must target those most susceptible to gang membership, those known as at-risk children. One way of identifying at-risk factors is to study the characteristics and background of known gang members and work backwards to nongang adolescents with those same characteristics. For example, gang members exhibit the following characteristics: they are largely male, are socially inept, are maladjusted, are sexually promiscuous, suffer from low self-esteem, are ethnic minorities, exhibit sociopathic personalities, and are closely associated with antisocial peers. Geographically, areas characterized with high unemployment, poverty, the absence of meaningful jobs, and economically distressed neighborhoods seem to be breeding grounds for prospective gang members. Clearly, the identification of at-risk youths is at best diffuse (Esbensen, 2000:9). Given this diffuseness, a comprehensive gang model that is a multifaceted approach targeting individual youths, peer groups, families, and the community has been recommended.

What can POs do to intervene where gang members form a portion of their clientele? One program initiated in Boston, Massachusetts, is Operation Night Light. Started in 1992, Operation Night Light is a specialized unit with two goals: curbing gang violence and enforcing court-ordered conditions of probation. The program involves teams of police officers and probation officers who visit the homes of probationers who are known gang members. The objective of these visits is to ensure program compliance with curfews and to conduct visual inspections of one's premises for illegal contraband, cellular telephones, illegal beepers, and other items that might be used for illicit purposes. Operation Night Light, which eventually became Operation Tracker, has been successful enough to eliminate the blind spots of communication between the police and POs (Triplet and Ross, 1998:31).

What seems to have emerged from Operation Tracker and similar programs is that to maximize their effectiveness, POs need to be in greater contact with police organizations and communicate with them. Probation officers need to equip themselves with the knowledge and techniques to recognize the presence of gang activity. One method of obtaining such knowledge is increased communication with various criminal justice agencies, primarily police departments. Whenever police officers stop a person on the street for investigation, they may not know that the person is a parolee or probationer. With more frequent communication between POs and police officers, these communication gaps can be narrowed and offender accountability can be improved (Triplet and Ross, 1998:34).

Tattoo Removal Programs

Whenever gang members wish to leave gangs, they often find it hard to do so. If they relocate to other regions of the country, then chances are that affiliate gangs in those new territories will recognize those who recently moved there. One of the tell-tale signs of gang membership is a gang **tattoo**. Gang members place tattoos on their hands, arms, feet, faces, and other places on their bodies as symbols of their gang affiliation. The conspicuous placement of tattoos attracts the attention of affiliate gang members. Tattoos are frequently given to new gang members in prisons and jails, with other inmates using crude instruments to install permanent tattoos on their new members. The tattoo is seemingly a symbol of ownership, implying that the gang owns the gang member forever. Once a gang member, always a gang member, or so some gang members would like their membership to believe. Some gangs are so deeply entrenched in one's social and personal world that they will not let anyone leave their gang under penalty of death. Gang membership is often taken that seriously. More than a few deaths have been the result of persons attempting to leave their gangs.

Increasingly, POs and police agencies are offering to remove these symbols of gang membership for those desiring to detach themselves from gangs. The Ventura County, California, Sheriff's Department has a **tattoo removal program** in which gang members can have their tattoos removed through laser surgery at no charge. According to this program, whenever a gang member wants to get out of the gang and find employment, it is almost impossible because employers fear gang members and can easily recognize them through their tattoos. Tattoos are essentially a stigma that follows them through life. They cannot get a job, nor can they have lasting relationships with anyone. Thus, they cannot become productive members of society.

The tattoo removal program operated by the Ventura County Sheriff's Department consists of the following process. First, gang members must attend a tattoo removal screening and are interviewed about why they want their tattoos removed. They are asked about where they plan to relocate to escape contact with their former gang associates. They must perform a certain number of community service hours to pay for the removal. Once they have been interviewed and have performed the necessary hours of community service, which may include graffiti removal of their own gangs' symbols, their tattoos are removed free of charge. Thus, they can detach themselves from gang membership by having the most visible signs of gangs removed from their bodies. Once these tattoos are removed, these persons can leave their communities and establish new lives elsewhere where others do not know about their prior affiliation with gangs (Ventura County Sheriff's Department, 2001). Tattoo removal programs similar to the one operated by the Ventura County Sheriff's Department are operated in other parts of the country with positive results.

SUMMARY

Special needs offenders present diverse problems for probation agencies and paroling authorities throughout the United States. Special needs offenders include those who are drug- or alcohol-dependent, the mentally ill, sex offenders and child sexual abusers, developmentally disabled offenders, and offenders with AIDS/HIV or other communicable diseases such as tuberculosis. POs have increasing responsibilities for networking among various community-based agencies that offer diverse services for offender-clients. Many communities do not have adequate services to coincide with some of the problems manifested by offenders. Attempts are being made to individualize offender treatments, to provide family counseling and parenting education as a means of preventing family violence, and to provide offenders with parenting skills so that better childhood interventions can be employed. Supervising offenders is hazardous work. POs need to acquire greater training to anticipate the types of offenders they will supervise and how different psychological and social offender problems should be resolved.

Mentally ill offenders are abundant in our prisons and jails. Many of these persons become clients of POs, and POs must learn different ways of supervising clients whose behaviors are often violent and unpredictable. Another class of special needs offender is the sex offender. Although making up only a small proportion of jail and prison inmates as well as clients of POs, sex offenders are regarded as a most heinous aggregate by citizens in general. Thus, POs have increased responsibilities to monitor sex offenders of different types very closely as a way of protecting the community from them. Most, however, have no prior criminal histories, are nonviolent, and pose little or no danger to others.

Drug- and/or alcohol-dependent offenders are associated with over 80 percent of all criminal activity and arrests. The likelihood of relapse is greatest among this offender aggregate; therefore, POs must monitor their progress closely, often by administering urinalyses and other tests to determine the presence of illegal substances. Another class of offender is the client with AIDS/HIV and/or tuberculosis. Tuberculosis cases have been rising in the United States at an alarming rate. Although POs have a low likelihood of contracting AIDS/HIV from their clients, they are at far greater risk when interacting with tuberculosis-infected clients.

Gang members are another offender category that requires special treatment and supervision. POs must be cognizant of gang signs and symbols as well as of the dangers of entering gang territories for the purpose of visiting their gang member clientele. Developmentally disabled offenders must be accommodated as well. Although there are not many of these offenders in the population, their numbers are growing. POs must increasingly network with various community agencies to see that these persons have their needs met appropriately.

Various types of interventions have been recommended for each of these offender groupings. For sex offenders, community treatment programs and sex therapy classes are often required as a part of their probation or parole programs. Offenders with AIDS/HIV or tuberculosis must be linked with appropriate agencies so that they can learn how to avoid transmitting their diseases to others, and educational courses of various kinds are recommended or required as a part of their therapeutic treatment. The largest aggregate of offenders under PO supervision have drug or alcohol dependencies. In recent years, most jurisdictions have established drug courts that hear only DWI or drug cases. Appropriate treatments are recommended or required. Drug courts work closely with a network of persons and agencies to ensure that drug-dependent offenders receive appropriate instruction and treatment as needed. Often, counseling on an individual or group basis is recommended.

Increasingly, therapeutic communities are being established in different communities as treatment models for persons with different types of addictions or dependencies. Therapeutic community refers to multiple interventions and agencies networked in such a way to achieve a positive result for participating clients. They are often started in prisons and jails, although they continue once offenders leave incarceration on probation or parole. Assisting offenders in their rehabilitation are private self-help organizations, such as Alcoholics Anonymous, Narcotics Anonymous, and Gamblers Anonymous. Often, attendance at these meetings is compulsory for probationers or parolees with drug or alcohol or gambling addictions.

Gang members are pervasive in American society. Their numbers, organizational structure, and operational sophistication are such that many POs find it difficult to relate with them. Learning programs are established to inform and advise POs about the latest advancements in gang psychology and methodology. Police agencies and parole/probation departments are working closer together in those areas where gang presence is especially strong. Greater communication between these agencies assists POs in heightening offender accountability. If gang members want to leave their gangs, tattoo removal programs assist them free of charge in ridding themselves of telltale tattoos that often are used to control and manipulate them. Without identifying tattoos, such persons can move to other areas and start new lives without the fear of being recognized by other gang members and enlisted involuntarily into illicit gang activities.

KEY TERMS

Community Services System
Drug courts
Missouri Sexual Offender Program (MOSOP)

180 Degrees, Inc.
Services to Unruly Youth Program
Special needs offenders
Tattoo

Tattoo removal program
Therapeutic community
Treatment alternatives to street crime (TASC)

QUESTIONS FOR REVIEW

1. Who are special needs offenders? What problems do they pose for supervising POs?
2. How many mentally ill offenders are under the supervision of POs throughout the United States? In what ways do mentally ill offenders pose a danger to POs during their supervision?
3. Identify some of the special programs that have been created for sex offenders and are a mandatory part of their probation or parole programs.
4. Drug- and alcohol-dependent offenders are associated with 80 percent of all crimes committed. Why is this offender aggregate troublesome for their supervising POs? What is the rate of relapse among drug- and alcohol-dependent offenders?
5. What are some of the problems posed by gang members for supervising POs? How can POs overcome the influence of gangs on their gang member-clients?
6. What are drug courts? When and where were they created?
7. What is meant by therapeutic community, and why is it important in an offender's rehabilitation?
8. Sam Torres recommends a continuum of sanctions against drug and alcohol abusers. Identify some of these sanctions.
9. What are Alcoholics Anonymous, Narcotics Anonymous, and Gamblers Anonymous? What is their relation to religion, if any? How do they operate in relation to various offender treatment programs?
10. What is a tattoo removal program, and what are its objectives?

SUGGESTED READINGS

Birmingham, Luke, et al. (2000). "Mental Illness at Reception into Prison." *Criminal Behaviour and Mental Health* **10:**77–87.

Clear, Todd R., and Harry R. Dammer (2000). *The Offender in the Community.* Belmont, CA: Wadsworth.

Hodgins, Sheilagh, and Rudiger Muller-Isberner (eds.) (2000). *Violence, Crime, and Mentally Disordered Offenders: Concepts and Methods for Effective Treatment and Prevention.* New York: Wiley.

Peterson, Rebecca D. (2000). "Definitions of a Gang and Impacts on Public Policy." *Journal of Criminal Justice* **28:**139–149.

Strang, John, et al. (2000). "Is Prison Tattooing a Risk Behaviour for HIV and Other Viruses? Results from a National Survey of Prisoners in England and Wales." *Criminal Behaviour and Mental Health* **10:**60–65.

Juvenile Probation and Parole

CHAPTER 13

Introduction
Juveniles and Juvenile Delinquency
    Delinquency and Juvenile Delinquents
    Status Offenders
An Overview of the Juvenile Justice System
    The Origins and Purposes of Juvenile Courts
    Major Differences between Criminal
    and Juvenile Courts
    Parens Patriae
    Arrest and Other Options
    Intake Screenings and Detention Hearings
    Petitions and Adjudicatory Proceedings
    Transfers, Waivers, or Certifications
Types of Waivers
    Judicial Waivers
    Direct File
    Statutory Exclusion
    Demand Waivers
    Other Types of Waivers
    Waiver Hearings
    Reverse Waiver Hearings
    Time Standards Governing Waiver Decisions
Implications of Waiver Hearings for Juveniles
    Positive Benefits Resulting from Juvenile
    Court Adjudications
    Adverse Implications of Juvenile Court
    Adjudications
Juvenile Rights
    Landmark Cases in Juvenile Justice

Offense Seriousness and Dispositions:
    Aggravating and Mitigating Circumstances
    Judicial Dispositional Options
    Nominal and Conditional Sanctions
    Custodial Sanctions
    Nonsecure Facilities
    Secure Confinement
Juvenile Probation Officers and Predispositional
    Reports
    Juvenile Probation Officers
    The Predispositional Report and Its
    Preparation
Juvenile Probation and Parole Programs
    Unconditional and Conditional Probation
    Intensive Supervised Probation (ISP)
    Programs
    The Ohio Experience
    The Allegheny Academy
    Boston Offender Project
    Other Juvenile Probation and Parole
    Programs
Revoking Juvenile Probation and Parole
    Recidivism and Probation/Parole Revocation
    Juvenile Case Law on Probation Revocations
    Juvenile Case Law on Parole Revocations
Summary
Key Terms
Questions for Review
Suggested Readings

• Allen N. was a California juvenile delinquent. The juvenile court ordered him to the adult authority, where he would be supervised by adult probation officers. Allen N. appealed, contending that the judge did not have the authority to sentence him to the adult authority, and a California appeals court agreed. The juvenile court did not have the authority to both order the commitment of the juvenile to the adult authority and impose conditions of supervision regarding the juvenile's rehabilitation. This function rests solely with the California Youth Authority, which supervises youthful offenders once the juvenile is ordered committed. (*In re Allen N.,* 100 Cal. Rptr. 2d 902 [Cal. App. October 2000])

• S.R.A. and S.S. were two juveniles in two Florida cases who were disposed by their respective juvenile courts to terms of probation. The period of supervision for both offenders extended well beyond their 19th birthday, and they appealed. The Florida Court of Appeals reversed the juvenile court judges in both instances, saying that the terms of both offenders, which were supervised under Florida's community control program, would end when they each reached their 19th birthdate. (*S.R.A. v. State,* 766 So.2d 277 [Fla. Dist. App. February 2000]; *S.S. v. State,* 765 So.2d 949 [Fla. Dist. App. August 2000])

• G.C.A. was a juvenile delinquent in Puerto Rico. He was adjudicated delinquent and placed on probation until his 21st birthday. One month before he turned 21, however, he violated several terms of his probation program. The juvenile court judge revoked his probation and resentenced G.C.A. for the original offense, which included incarceration in a juvenile facility. G.C.A. appealed, contending that the nearness of his 21st birthday to the revocation date nullified the revocation order issued by the judge. The appellate court disagreed and upheld the judge's order to revoke G.C.A.'s probation program. (*United States v. G.C.A.,* 83 F.Supp.2d 253 [U.S.D.P.R. February 2000])

• B.K. was a Georgia juvenile who was informally disposed by a juvenile court judge as a status offender. The judge advised B.K. that he should remain law-abiding and stay out of trouble. Subsequently, a juvenile probation officer visited B.K.'s home and found that he was not there. It was late at night, and the juvenile PO, believing that this absence involved a curfew violation, reported it to the juvenile court judge. The judge adjudicated B.K. delinquent on the curfew violation charge. B.K. appealed, contending that there never was a formal determination of his delinquency or status offending, but rather, only an informal hearing at which several behavioral options were implied by the judge but not committed to writing; therefore, there was no record of any probation order with a curfew condition. The appellate court reversed the juvenile court judge and threw out the delinquency adjudication, holding that no written evidence existed to show that B.K. was on probation and had violated a probation order. (*In re B.K.,* 522 S.E.2d 255 [Ga. App. September 1999])

• D.L.J. is a Florida juvenile who was adjudicated delinquent for a second-degree misdemeanor by a juvenile court judge and disposed to a period of residential commitment for 60 days and a term of community control for an additional 60 days. The maximum term of commitment to either a residential facility or community control for an adult would be 60 days maximum. Therefore, D.L.J. appealed, seeking relief from an appellate court. The court heard D.L.J.'s case and reversed the judge's order of the two 60-day terms. The court held that juveniles are subject to the same maximum limitations as adults regarding community control orders or residential commitments. (*D.L.J. v. State,* 765 So.2d 740 [Fla. Dist. App. May 2000])

• Pedro M. is a California juvenile sex offender who was adjudicated delinquent by the juvenile court. As a part of his probation orders, he was to attend a sex offender treatment program that required that he disclose the details of his sex actions; his feelings about such actions; and the acquisition of empathy, development, and relapse prevention. Pedro M. failed to cooperate in the sex offender treatment program. He did not attend some sessions, and other sessions he attended were unproductive because he failed to talk about what he had done. He was reported as a probation violator, and the judge revoked his probation. Pedro M. appealed, contending that there is a confidentiality agreement between the psychotherapist and the patient and that the psychotherapist should be barred from testifying about Pedro M.'s failure to disclose about his sex acts. The appellate court disagreed and upheld Pedro M.'s revocation order. It held that failure to cooperate in the sex offender treatment program directly violated the judge's probation condition that had been imposed. (*In re Pedro M.,* 96 Ca. Rptr. 2d 839 [Cal. App. June 2000])

INTRODUCTION

This chapter is about juvenile probation and parole. There is little consistency among jurisdictions throughout the United States about how juvenile probation and parole are handled. No national policies exist that apply to every jurisdiction. Thus, it is impossible to make blanket generalizations about the juvenile probation and parole process, except in the broadest of terms. The first section describes juveniles and juvenile delinquency. How are juvenile delinquents defined? Another class of juvenile is the status offender, who differs in several significant ways from juvenile delinquents. The deinstitutionalization of status offenders is a movement that began in the 1970s to remove status offenders from incarcerative settings normally used for more serious juveniles. Although many states have implemented the deinstitutionalization of status offenders, other states are either undecided on the issue or are moving slowly toward such a policy. This policy is described and its significance and relevance for affected juveniles are explained.

The second section presents an overview of the juvenile justice system, describing briefly the origins and functions of juvenile courts. The doctrine of *parens patriae,* inherited from England, has had a profound influence on juvenile courts in the United States. The juvenile justice system or process, as some professionals prefer to label it, is presented from the point of juvenile arrests, intake, petitions and adjudicatory proceedings, and judicial dispositions. Various dispositional options available to juvenile court judges, including nominal, conditional, and custodial dispositional options, are listed and described. The next section of the chapter examines various juvenile probation and parole programs. It is not intended to be comprehensive, because juvenile justice textbooks cover this information in far greater detail. Nevertheless, several key programs that provide a broad perspective of available juvenile probation and parole programs are described.

The final section examines the juvenile probation and parole revocation process. Almost no U.S. Supreme Court action has been taken regarding revocations of juvenile probation and parole. Often, state and local jurisdictions have followed the guidelines of probation and parole revocations set forth by various precedent-setting landmark cases for adult criminals. Such cases include *Mempa v. Rhay* (1967), *Gagnon v. Scarpelli* (1973), and *Morrissey v. Brewer* (1972). Juvenile courts and revocation proceedings are not bound by these adult cases, but the cases do serve as guidelines for juvenile courts. Several state cases involving juvenile probation and parole revocation are presented, however, to illustrate how different jurisdictions deal with juvenile probation or parole program violations.

JUVENILES AND JUVENILE DELINQUENCY

Juvenile Offenders.   **Juvenile offenders** or **juvenile delinquents** are classified and defined according to several different criteria. For instance, the 1899 Illinois **Juvenile Court Act** that created juvenile courts determined that the jurisdiction of juvenile courts extended to all juveniles under the age of 16 who were found to be in violation of any state or local laws. About a fifth of all states, including Illinois, currently place the upper age limit for juveniles at either 15 or 16. In the remaining states, the upper limit for juveniles is 17 (except for Wyoming, where it is 18). Ordinarily, the jurisdiction of juvenile courts includes all young persons who have not yet attained the age at which they should be treated as adults for purposes of criminal law (Black, 1990:867). At the federal level, juveniles are considered to be persons who have not yet attained their 18th birthday (18 U.S.C., Sec. 5031, 2001).

Upper and Lower Jurisdictional Age Limits.   Although fairly uniform upper age limits for juveniles have been established in all U.S. jurisdictions (either under 16, under 17, or under 18 years of age), there is no uniformity concerning applicable lower age limits. English common law placed juveniles under age seven beyond the reach of criminal courts, because it was believed that those under age seven were incapable of formulating criminal intent, or *mens rea.* Many juvenile courts throughout the United States, however, have no specified lower age limits for those juveniles within their purview. Few, if any, juvenile courts will process three-year-olds who kill others through the juvenile court, although these courts technically can do so in some jurisdictions.

Treatment and Punishment Functions of Juvenile Courts.   The idea that for juvenile courts to exercise jurisdiction over juveniles, the youths must be offenders and have committed criminal acts is misleading. Many youths who appear before juvenile court judges have not violated any criminal laws. Rather, their status as juveniles renders them subject to juvenile court control, provided certain circumstances exist. These circumstances may be the quality of their adult supervision, if any. Other circumstances may be that they run away from home, are truant from school, or loiter on certain city streets during evening hours. Runaways, truants, or curfew violators are considered **status offenders**, because their actions would not be criminal ones if committed by adults. In addition, children who are physically, psychologically, or sexually abused by parents or other adults in their homes are brought within the scope of juvenile court authority. Some of these children are PINS, or persons in need of supervision. These youths are often supervised and treated by community social welfare agencies.

Delinquency and Juvenile Delinquents

The majority of youthful offenders who appear before juvenile courts have violated state or local laws or ordinances. The jurisdiction of juvenile courts depends on the established legislative definitions of juveniles among the different states. The federal government has no juvenile court. Rather, federal cases involving juveniles are infrequently heard in federal district courts, but adjudicated juveniles are housed in state or local facilities if the sentences involve commitment to secure youth facilities. Ordinarily, upper and lower age limits are prescribed. In reality, the most liberal definition of juvenile delinquency is whatever the juvenile court believes should be brought within its jurisdiction. This definition vests juvenile judges and other juvenile authorities with broad discretionary powers to define almost any juvenile conduct as delinquent conduct. Today, the majority of U.S. jurisdictions restrict their definitions of juvenile delinquency to any act committed by a juvenile that, if committed by an adult, would be considered a crime (Zhang and Messner, 2000).

Status Offenders

Status offenses are any acts committed by juveniles that would (1) bring the juveniles to the attention of juvenile courts and (2) not be crimes if committed by adults. Common juvenile status offenses include running away from home, truancy, and curfew violations. Many of the youths who engage in this conduct are incorrigible, habitually disobedient, and beyond parental control. Truants and liquor law violators may be more inclined to become chronic offenders and to engage in more serious, possibly criminal, behaviors (Grisso and Schwartz, 2000). An influential factor contributing to juvenile offender chronicity and persistence is contact with juvenile courts. Contact with these courts, especially frequent contact, is believed by some researchers to stigmatize youths and cause them either to be labeled or acquire self-concepts as delinquents or deviants (Kowalski-Jones, 2000). Therefore, diversion of certain types of juvenile offenders from the juvenile justice system has been advocated and recommended to minimize these potentially adverse consequences of systemic contact.

AN OVERVIEW OF THE JUVENILE JUSTICE SYSTEM

The **juvenile justice system** consists of a more or less integrated network of agencies, institutions, organizations, and personnel that process juvenile offenders. This network is made up of law enforcement agencies, prosecutors, and courts; corrections, probation, and parole services; and public and private community-based treatment programs that provide youths with diverse services. The definition is intentionally qualified by the phrase "more or less integrated" because the concept of juvenile justice means different things to the states and to the federal government. Also, in some jurisdictions, the diverse components of the juvenile justice system are closely coordinated, whereas in other jurisdictions, these components are at best loosely coordinated, if they are coordinated at all (Torbet et al., 2000).

The Origins and Purposes of Juvenile Courts

Juvenile Courts as an American Creation.   Juvenile courts are a relatively recent American creation. Modern U.S. juvenile courts, however, have various less formal European antecedents. Although the origin of this cutting point is unknown, the age of seven was used in Roman times to separate **infants** from older children who were accountable to the law for their actions. During the Middle Ages, English **common law** established under the monarchy adhered to the same standard. In the United States, several state jurisdictions currently apply this distinction and consider all children below the age of seven not accountable for any criminal acts they may commit. This distinction is a common-law practice.

Early Juvenile Reforms.   Reforms in the American colonies relating to the treatment and punishment of juvenile offenders occurred slowly. Shortly after the Revolutionary War, religious interests in the United States moved forward with various proposals designed to improve the plight of the oppressed, particularly those who were incarcerated in prisons and jails. In 1787, the Quakers in Pennsylvania established the Philadelphia Society for Alleviating the Miseries of Public Prisons. This largely philanthropic society composed of prominent citizens, religious leaders, and philanthropists was appalled by existing prison and jail conditions. Male, female, and juvenile offenders alike were housed in common quarters and treated poorly. In 1790, the society's efforts were rewarded. The Philadelphia Walnut Street Jail described in Chapter 5 had considerable historical significance for corrections as well as for juvenile offenders. One of its major innovations was that women and children were maintained in separate rooms apart from adult male offenders during evening hours.

The **New York House of Refuge** was established in New York City in 1825 by the Society for the Prevention of Pauperism (Cahalan and Parsons, 1986:101). This institution was largely devoted to managing status offenders, such as runaways or incorrigible children. Compulsory education and other forms of training and assistance were provided to these children. The strict, prisonlike regimen of this organization, however, was not entirely therapeutic for its clientele. Many of the youthful offenders sent to such institutions, including the House of Reformation in Boston, were offspring of immigrants.

The Case of *Ex parte Crouse*.   Until the late 1830s, little consistency was apparent related to the division of labor between parental, religious, and state authority over juveniles. In 1839, a decision in a state case invested juvenile authorities with considerable parental power. The case of *Ex parte Crouse* (1839) involved a father who sought custody of his daughter from the Philadelphia House of Refuge. The girl had been committed to that facility by the court because she was declared unmanageable. She was not given a jury trial; rather, the judge arbitrarily committed her. A higher court rejected the father's claim that parental control of children is exclusive, natural, and proper. It upheld the power of the state to exercise necessary reforms and restraints to protect children from themselves and their environments. Although this decision was only applicable to Pennsylvania citizens and their children, other states took note of it and sought to invoke similar controls over errant children in their jurisdictions. In effect, children (at least in Pennsylvania) were temporarily deprived of any legal standing to challenge decisions made by the state on their behalf. This was the general state of juvenile affairs until the post–Civil War period known as Reconstruction.

Extensive family migration toward large cities occurred after the Civil War. New York, Philadelphia, Boston, and Chicago were centers where fragmented families attempted to find work. Often, both parents had to work extended working hours (e.g., 16-hour work periods). While parents worked, increasing numbers of children roamed city streets unsupervised. Religious organizations subsequently intervened as a way of protecting unsupervised youths from the perils of life in the streets. Believing that these youths would subsequently turn to lives of crime as adults, many reformers and philanthropists sought to save them from their plight. Thus, in different cities throughout the United States, various groups were formed to find and control these youths by offering them constructive work programs, healthful living conditions, and above all, adult supervision. Collectively, these efforts became widely known as the **child-saver movement**. **Child-savers** came largely from the middle and upper classes, and their assistance to youths took many forms. Food and shelter were provided to children who were in trouble with the law or who were simply idle. Private homes were converted into settlements where social, educational, and other important activities could be provided for needy youths.

Reform Schools. In a period prior to the Civil War, **reform schools** were established and proliferated. One of the first state-operated reform schools was established in Westboro, Massachusetts, in 1848. By the end of that century, all states had reform schools. All these institutions were characterized by strict discipline, absolute control over juvenile behavior, and compulsory work at various trades. Another common feature was that they were controversial.

Children's Tribunals. Although Illinois is credited with establishing the first juvenile court system in the United States, an earlier juvenile justice apparatus was created in Massachusetts in 1874. Known as **children's tribunals**, this system was used exclusively as a mechanism for dealing with children charged with crimes; it was kept separate from the system of criminal courts for adults. Some years later, in 1899, Colorado passed an education law known as the Compulsory School Act.

Dependent and Neglected Children. Few legal challenges of state authority over juveniles were lodged by parents during the 1800s. In 1870, however, an Illinois case made it possible for special courts to be established to dispose of juvenile matters and represented an early recognition of certain minimal rights they might have. Daniel O'Connell, a youth who was declared vagrant and in need of supervision, was committed to the Chicago Reform School for an unspecified period. O'Connell's parents challenged this court action, claiming that his confinement for vagrancy was unjust and untenable. Existing Illinois law vested state authorities with the power to commit any juvenile to a state reform school as long as a reasonable justification could be provided. In this instance, vagrancy was a reasonable justification. The Illinois Supreme Court distinguished between misfortune (vagrancy) and criminal acts in arriving at its decision to reverse O'Connell's commitment. In effect, the court nullified the law by declaring that reform school commitments of youths could not be made by the state if the "offense" was simple misfortune. The court reasoned that the state's interests would be better served if commitments of juveniles to reform schools were limited to those committing more serious criminal offenses rather than those who were victims of misfortune. Those considered victims of misfortune were called **dependent and neglected children**.

The First Juvenile Court.   Three decades later, the Illinois legislature established the first juvenile court on July 1, 1899, by passing the Act to Regulate the Treatment and Control of Dependent, Neglected, and Delinquent Children, or the Juvenile Court Act. This act provided for limited courts of record, in which notes might be taken by judges or their assistants, to reflect judicial actions against juveniles. The jurisdiction of these courts, subsequently designated as "juvenile courts," would include all juveniles under the age of 16 who were found in violation of any state or local law or ordinance. Also, provision was made for the care of dependent and/or neglected children who had been abandoned or who otherwise lacked proper parental care, support, or guardianship. No minimum age was specified that would limit the jurisdiction of juvenile court judges. The act provided, however, that judges could impose secure confinement on juveniles ten years of age or older by placing them in state-regulated juvenile facilities such as the state reformatory or the State Home for Juvenile Female Offenders. Judges were expressly prohibited from confining any juvenile under 12 years of age in a jail or police station. Extremely young juveniles would be assigned POs to look after their needs and placement on a temporary basis. Between 1900 and 1920, 20 states passed similar acts to establish juvenile courts. By the end of World War II, all states had created juvenile court systems. Considerable variation existed among these court systems, however, depending on the jurisdiction.

Major Differences between Criminal and Juvenile Courts

The intent of this section is not to describe either criminal or juvenile courts in depth, but rather to show several major similarities and differences between them. Also, the diversity among juvenile courts in every jurisdiction is such that it precludes blanket generalizations about them. Generally, the following statements about these different courts are accurate.

1. Juvenile courts are civil proceedings exclusively designed for juveniles, whereas criminal courts are proceedings designed for alleged violators of criminal laws. In criminal courts, alleged criminal law violators are primarily adults, although selected juveniles may be tried as adults in these same courts.
2. Juvenile proceedings are informal, whereas criminal proceedings are formal. Attempts are made in many juvenile courts to avoid the formal trappings that characterize criminal proceedings.
3. In most states, juveniles are not entitled to a trial by jury, unless the juvenile judge approves.
4. Both juvenile and criminal proceedings are adversarial. Juveniles may or may not wish to retain or be represented by counsel. Today, most states make provisions in their juvenile codes for public defenders for juveniles if they are indigent and cannot afford to hire private counsel.
5. Criminal courts are courts of record, whereas juvenile proceedings may or may not maintain a running transcript of proceedings.
6. The standard of proof used for determining one's guilt in criminal proceedings is beyond a reasonable doubt. In juvenile courts, judges use the same standard for juvenile

---

BOX 13.1   *Personality Highlight*

Yolanda G. Castillo
Student, Postgraduate Studies Texas A&M International University

Statistics. B.S. (criminal justice, cum laude), Texas A&M International University

Background and Interests. I am currently working on my master's degree in criminal justice with a minor in sociology. After being out of school for 20 years, I never dreamed it would be possible to accomplish what I have in the past four years.

Through being involved with my 13-year-old son's education, teachers, school PTA, and sports activities, I have seen how the students are becoming more and more outspoken. So much, that it makes me wonder if in the future there will be a shortage of teachers nationwide. That could be a reason why some students are falling through the cracks and becoming juvenile delinquents.

During one of my spring semesters at the university, I took a criminal justice course that required us to attend the Juvenile Alternative Education Program once a week for credit. While working with these troubled juveniles, I realized that many of these students wanted to learn, but they needed some attention and positive reinforcement to become successful in society. I would like to continue helping juveniles that want to learn and maybe even be successful with one or two that do not want to change. To be able to help those who are labeled as chronic juveniles would certainly be my greatest satisfaction.

In attempting to gain valuable experience, I recently completed a tour of three months working with the Drug Enforcement Administration, which was part of my internship. I am in the process of obtaining full-time employment with federal, state, or local law enforcement agencies. I would like to stay in my community and make a difference. I will make every attempt to stay in the law enforcement field. Many of my family members have dedicated their lives to law enforcement. My brother was with the local police department and my sister works with the federal government.

Advice to Students. Do not wait until you are over 37 years old to decide to join a law enforcement agency. If you decide at an early age, do some sort of volunteer or part-time work for some law enforcement agency. I was told that not only did I need a college degree, but that I also needed experience in the field. That is one thing I don't have, although I am quickly getting it.

---

delinquents who face possible commitment to secure juvenile facilities. In other court matters leading to noncommitment alternatives, the court uses the civil standard of preponderance of the evidence.

7. The range of penalties juvenile judges may impose is more limited than criminal courts. Both juvenile and criminal courts can impose fines, restitution, community service, probation, and other forms of conditional discharge. Juvenile courts can also impose residential secure or nonsecure placement, group homes, and camp/ranch experiences. Long terms of commitment to secure facilities are also within the purview of juvenile court

judges. In most criminal courts, however, the range of penalties may include life imprisonment or the death penalty in those jurisdictions in which the death penalty is used.

This comparison indicates that criminal court actions are more serious and have more significant long-term consequences for offenders compared with actions taken by juvenile courts. Juvenile courts do, however, have sanctioning power to place juveniles in secure confinement for lengthy periods, if circumstances warrant. This type of court power should not be discounted just because the court deals with juvenile matters and not criminal cases. Juvenile courts are guided by strong rehabilitative orientations in most jurisdictions, despite a general get-tough movement that has occurred during the 1980s and 1990s, whereas criminal courts are seemingly adopting more punitive sanctions for adult offenders. Although many critics see juvenile courts moving toward a just-deserts philosophy in the treatment and **adjudication** of juveniles, many youths are still subject to treatment-oriented nonsecure alternatives rather than custodial options. Furthermore, overcrowding is a chronic problem in many juvenile facilities. Thus, correctional agencies for juveniles mirror many of the same problems of adult corrections. It is in the best interests of the state to provide alternatives to incarceration for both adult and juvenile offenders. This "best interests" philosophy of juvenile courts is based on an early doctrine known as *parens patriae*.

Parens Patriae

Juvenile courts have always had considerable latitude in regulating the affairs of juveniles. This freedom to act on a child's behalf was rooted in the largely unchallenged doctrine of ***parens patriae***. This doctrine received formal recognition in U.S. courts in the case of *Ex parte Crouse* (1839), which involved the commitment of an unruly and incorrigible female child to a state agency. When the parents of the child attempted to regain custody over her later, their request was denied; she remained a ward of the state by virtue of the power of the state agency charged with her supervision. This case set a precedent in that the state established almost absolute control over juvenile custody matters.

The primary elements of *parens patriae* that have contributed to its persistence as a dominant philosophical perspective in the juvenile justice system are summarized as follows:

1. *Parens patriae* encourages informal handling of juvenile matters as opposed to more formal and criminalizing procedures.
2. *Parens patriae* vests juvenile courts with absolute authority to provide what is best for youthful offenders (e.g., support services and other forms of care).
3. *Parens patriae* strongly encourages benevolent and rehabilitative treatments to assist youths in overcoming their personal and social problems.
4. *Parens patriae* avoids the adverse labeling effects that formal court proceedings might create.
5. *Parens patriae* means state control over juvenile life chances.

One early example of *parens patriae* is when police officers interacted with juveniles during the 1940s, 1950s, and 1960s. Whenever juveniles were apprehended by police officers for alleged infractions of the law, they were eventually turned over to juvenile authorities or taken to juvenile halls for further processing. Juveniles were not advised of their right to an attorney, to have an attorney present during any interrogation, and to remain silent. They were subject to lengthy interrogations by police, without parental notification and consent or legal counsel. Juveniles had virtually no protection against adult constitutional rights violations by law enforcement officers and/or juvenile court judges. Due process simply did not apply to juveniles.

Because of the informality of juvenile proceedings in most jurisdictions, there were frequent and obvious abuses of judicial discretion. These abuses occurred because of the absence of consistent guidelines through which cases could be adjudicated. Juvenile POs might casually recommend to judges that particular juveniles ought to do a few months in an industrial school or other secure detention facility, and the judge might be persuaded to adjudicate these cases accordingly. Several forces simultaneously at work during the 1950s and 1960s, however, would eventually have the conjoint consequence of making juvenile courts more accountable for specific adjudications of youthful offenders. One of these forces was increased parental and general public recognition of and concern for the liberal license taken by juvenile courts in administering the affairs of juveniles. The abuse of judicial discretion was becoming increasingly apparent and widely known. In addition, there was a growing disenchantment with and apathy for the rehabilitation ideal, although this disenchantment was not directed solely at juvenile courts.

Barry Feld (1995) says that the juvenile court as originally envisioned by Progressives was procedurally informal, characterized by individualized, offender-oriented dispositional practices, but the contemporary juvenile court has departed markedly from this ideal. Today, juvenile courts are increasingly criminalized, featuring an adversarial system and greater procedural formality that effectively inhibits any individualized treatment the courts might contemplate. This change has increased the perfunctory nature of sentencing juveniles adjudicated as delinquent.

The major shift from *parens patriae,* state-based interests to a due process juvenile justice model gradually occurred during the 1970s. This shift signified a general abandonment of most of these *parens patriae* elements. Decision making relative to youthful offenders became more rationalized and the philosophy of just deserts became more dominant as a way of disposing of juvenile cases. Thus, this shift meant less discretionary authority among juvenile judges, because they began to decide each case more on the basis of offense seriousness and prescribed punishments rather than disposing of such cases on the basis of individual characteristics of youthful offenders (Kirkish et al., 2000).

Arrests and Other Options

In general, police officers need little justification to apprehend juveniles or take them into custody. Little uniformity exists among jurisdictions about how an "arrest" is defined. There is even greater ambiguity about what constitutes a juvenile arrest. Technically, an arrest is the legal detainment of a person to answer for criminal charges or (infrequently at present) civil demands. By degree, arrests of juveniles are more serious than taking them into custody. Because any juvenile may be taken into custody for suspicious behavior or on any other pretext, all types of juveniles may be detained at police headquarters or at a sheriff's station, department, or jail temporarily. Suspected runaways, truants, or curfew violators may be taken into custody for their own welfare or protection, not necessarily for the purpose of facing subsequent offenses. It is standard police policy in most jurisdictions, considering the sophistication of available social services, for officers and jailers to turn over juveniles to the appropriate agencies as soon as possible after these youths have been apprehended and taken into custody. The first screening of juveniles before further proceedings occur is intake.

Intake Screenings and Detention Hearings

Intake or an **intake screening** is the second major step in the juvenile justice process. It is a more or less informally conducted screening procedure whereby intake POs or other juvenile court functionaries decide whether detained juveniles should be (1) unconditionally released from the juvenile justice system, (2) released to parents or guardians subject to a subsequent juvenile court appearance, (3) released or referred to one or more community-based services or resources, (4) placed in secure detention subject to a subsequent juvenile court appearance, or (5) waived or transferred to the jurisdiction of criminal courts.

During intake hearings, intake POs have virtually unbridled discretion regarding a youth's chances in the system. Apart from certain state-mandated hearings that must precede formal adjudicatory proceedings by juvenile judges, no constitutional provisions require states to conduct such hearings. Intake officers seldom hear legal arguments or evaluate the sufficiency of evidence on behalf of or against youths sitting before them. These proceedings, which most often are informally conducted, usually result in adjustments, with intake officers adjusting the particular matter informally to most everyone's satisfaction. A more formal proceeding, a **detention hearing**, is held for the purpose of determining whether a juvenile ought to be held until his or her case can be heard by a juvenile court judge.

Petitions and Adjudicatory Proceedings

Jurisdictional Variations in Juvenile Processing.   There is considerable variation in different jurisdictions about how juvenile courts are conducted. Increasingly, juvenile courts are emulating criminal courts in many respects (Snyder, Sickmund, and Poe-Yamagata, 2000). Most of the physical trappings are present, including the judge's bench, tables for the prosecution and defense, and a witness stand. In some jurisdictions such as Ocean County, New Jersey, however, these facilities are being redesigned to appear less courtlike and threatening. Manuals that catalogue various pleadings defense attorneys may enter in juvenile courtrooms are currently available, and there is growing interest in the rules of juvenile court procedure. Further, there appears widespread interest in holding juveniles more accountable for their actions than in the past (Feld, 1995).

Petitions.   Prosecutors either file **petitions** or act on the petitions filed by others. Petitions are official documents filed in juvenile courts on the juvenile's behalf, specifying reasons for the youth's court appearance. These documents assert that juveniles fall within the categories of dependent or neglected, status offender, or delinquent and usually give the reasons for such assertions. Filing a petition formally places the juvenile before the juvenile judge in many jurisdictions, but juveniles may come before juvenile judges in less formal ways. Those able to file petitions against juveniles include their parents, school officials, neighbors, and any other interested party. The legitimacy and factual accuracy of petitions are evaluated by juvenile court judges (Applegate et al., 2000).

Juvenile Court Judicial Discretion.   In most jurisdictions, juvenile judges have almost absolute discretion in how their courts are conducted. Juvenile defendants alleged to have committed various crimes may or may not be granted a trial by jury, if one is requested. Few states permit jury trials for juveniles in juvenile courts, according to legislative mandates. After hearing the evidence presented by both sides in any juvenile proceeding, the judge decides or adjudicates the matter. An adjudication is a judgment or action on the petition filed with the court by others. If the petition alleges delinquency on the part of certain juveniles, then the judge determines whether the juveniles are delinquent or not delinquent. If the petition alleges that the juveniles involved are dependent, neglected, or otherwise in need of care by agencies or others, then the judge decides the matter. If the adjudicatory proceeding fails to support the facts alleged in the petition filed with the court, then the case is dismissed and the youth is freed. If the adjudicatory proceeding supports the allegations, then the judge must adjudicate the youth as either a delinquent, a status offender, or a youth in need of special treatment or supervision. Then, the juvenile court judge must dispose of the case according to several options. The judge may order a predispositional report to be prepared by a juvenile probation officer. Another option is for the judge to declare the juvenile to be an adult and transfer or waive the youth to a criminal court for processing.

Transfers, Waivers, or Certifications

Transfers refer to changing the jurisdiction over certain juvenile offenders to another jurisdiction, usually from juvenile court jurisdiction to criminal court jurisdiction (Ruddell, Mays, and Giever, 1998). Transfers are also known as waivers, referring to a **waiver** or change of jurisdiction from the authority of juvenile court judges to criminal court judges. Prosecutors or juvenile court judges decide that, in some cases, juveniles should be waived or transferred to the jurisdiction of criminal courts. Presumably, those cases that are waived or transferred are the most serious cases, involving violent or serious offenses, such as homicide, aggravated assault, forcible rape, robbery, or drug-dealing activities.

In some jurisdictions, such as Utah, juveniles are waived or transferred to criminal courts through a process known as **certification**. A certification is a formal procedure through which the state declares the juvenile to be an adult for the purpose of a criminal prosecution in a criminal court. The results of certifications are the same as for waivers, or transfers. Thus, certifications, waivers, and transfers result in juvenile offenders being subject to the jurisdiction of criminal courts where they can be prosecuted as though they were adult offenders. A 14-year-old murderer, for instance, might be transferred to criminal court for a criminal prosecution on the murder charge. In criminal court, the juvenile, now being treated as though an adult, can be convicted of the murder and sentenced to a prison term for one or more years. If the juvenile is charged with capital murder, is 16 or older, and lives in a state where the death penalty is administered to those convicted of capital murder, then he or she can potentially receive the death penalty as the maximum punishment for that offense, provided there is a capital murder conviction (Ziedenberg and Schiraldi, 1997). Or, criminal court judges might impose life-without-parole sentences on these convicted 16- or 17-year-olds. Imposing life-without-parole sentences or the death penalty are *not* within the jurisdiction of juvenile court judges; their jurisdiction ends when an offender becomes an adult. Thus, a delinquency adjudication on capital murder charges in juvenile court might result in a juvenile being placed in the state industrial school until he or she is 18 or 21, depending on whichever is the age of majority or adulthood.

The Rationale for the Use of Transfers or Waivers.   The basic rationale underlying the use of waivers is that the most serious juvenile offenders will be transferred to the jurisdiction of criminal courts where the harshest punishments, including capital punishment, may be imposed as sanctions. Because juvenile courts lack the jurisdiction and decision-making power to impose anything harsher than secure confinement dispositions of limited duration in industrial or reform schools, the waiver would seem be an ideal way to impose the most severe punishments on those juveniles who commit the most violent acts. All states have provisions that allow juveniles under certain conditions to be tried as if they were adults in criminal court by one or more transfer or waiver provisions (Torbet and Szymanski, 1998:2). Reasons for the use of transfers, waivers, or certifications include the following:

1. To make it possible for harsher punishments to be imposed
2. To provide just deserts and proportionately severe punishments on those juveniles who deserve such punishments by their more violent actions
3. To foster fairness in administering punishments according to one's serious offending
4. To hold serious or violent offenders more accountable for what they have done
5. To show other juveniles who contemplate committing serious offenses that the system works and that harsh punishments can be expected if serious offenses are committed
6. To provide a deterrent to decrease juvenile violence
7. To overcome the traditional leniency of juvenile courts and provide more realistic sanctions
8. To make youths realize the seriousness of their offending and induce remorse and acceptance of responsibility

Youths designated for transfer or waiver by various participants in the juvenile justice process should exhibit certain consistent characteristics. Age, offense seriousness, and prior record (including previous referrals to juvenile court, intake proceedings and dispositions, or juvenile court delinquency adjudications) are some of these characteristics. For example, Thomas Grisso, Alan Tomkins, and Pamela Casey (1988) indicate that several extralegal factors function to enhance the likelihood that a juvenile will be waived to criminal court. These researchers gathered data from 50 state juvenile codes and, using content analysis, searched court records and read decisions involving transferred juveniles, appeals of these transfers to appellate courts, and various law review articles pertaining to transfers. They supplemented their analysis with interviews of 85 court personnel and a survey of 1,423 representatives from 127 courts in 34 states. They concluded several things about the juveniles who were subjects of transfers.

First, those with extensive prior records or involvement with the juvenile justice system were more frequently detained and subjected to transfer. Second, many of these youths exhibited emotional disturbances of various kinds. Such disturbances seemed to promote self-destructive behavior and poor school adjustment. These youths were most unwilling to accept interventions suggested by juvenile courts and intake officers. Thus, unwillingness to accept intervention became an important extralegal factor that adversely influenced the transfer decision. Third, the researchers found that those transferred tended to lack self-discipline and failed to comply with rules or court orders and conditional sanctions imposed by juvenile court judges. Therefore, a youth's unwillingness to comply with institutional rules became another extralegal factor impinging on the waiver decision.

In 1994, 12,400 youths were transferred to criminal court. Most juveniles transferred were young men, with only 600 young women (0.5 percent) being waived (Butts and Snyder, 1997). About 6,800 (55 percent) of all transferred juveniles were black or another minority, even though white juveniles comprised about 64 percent of all cases referred to juvenile court. Furthermore, those charged with person offenses and waived to criminal court made up only 42 percent of those transferred. About 46 percent of those charged with property or public order offenses were waived to criminal courts, whereas about 10 percent of those waived were charged with drug offenses (Butts and Snyder, 1997).

Youngest Ages for Transfers to Criminal Court.   In 1997, 18 states and all federal districts indicated no specified age for transferring juveniles to criminal courts for processing. Two states, Vermont and Wisconsin, specified 10 as the minimum age at which a juvenile could be waived. Colorado, Missouri, Montana, and Oregon established 12 as the earliest age for a juvenile waiver. Eighteen states used 14 as the youngest transfer age, whereas the District of Columbia set the minimum transfer age at 15, and one state, Hawaii, used the minimum transfer age of 16. Thus, since 1987, a majority of states substantially reduced the age at which juveniles could be tried as adults in criminal courts.

Under judicial waiver modifications, four states lowered the age limit at which juveniles can be transferred to criminal court. One example of a significant age modification is Missouri, where the minimum age for juvenile transfers was lowered from 14 to 12 for any felony. In the case of Texas, the minimum transfer age was lowered from 15 to 10. Virginia lowered the transfer age from 15 to 14. Other modifications were made to get tough toward juvenile offenders. Ten states added crimes to the list of those qualifying youths for transfer to criminal courts. In six states, the age of criminal accountability was lowered, and 24 states authorized the inclusion of additional crimes that would automatically direct that the criminal court rather than the juvenile court have jurisdiction (Butts and Snyder, 1997).

Waiver Decision Making.   Organizational and political factors are at work to influence the upward trend in the use of transfers. Politicians wish to present a get-tough facade to the public by citing waiver statistics and showing their increased use is the political response to the rise in serious youth crime. Despite political rhetoric, there has been an increase in the use of waivers. Between 1989 and 1993, for instance, the use of transfers increased by 41 percent. A majority of those transferred were charged with felonies (Ruddell, Mays, and Giever, 1998).

Several types of waivers can be used to negotiate transfers of jurisdiction from juvenile to criminal courts. One is the automatic transfer or automatic waiver currently employed in several jurisdictions. If youthful offenders are within a particular age range, such as 16 or 17, and if they are charged with specific types of offenses (usually murder, robbery, rape, aggravated assault, and other violent crimes), then they will be automatically transferred to criminal courts. These types of waivers, also known as legislative waivers because they were mandated by legislative bodies in various states and carry the weight of statutory authority, involve no discretionary action among prosecutors or judges. For other types of waivers, the decision-making process is largely discretionary (Torbet and Szymanski, 1998).

Because of the discretionary nature of the waiver process, large numbers of the wrong types of juveniles are transferred to criminal courts. Such juveniles are the wrong type because they are not those originally targeted by juvenile justice professionals and reformers to be the primary candidates for transfers. The primary targets of waivers are intended to be the most serious, violent, and dangerous juveniles who also are the most likely to deserve more serious sanctions that criminal courts can impose. Yet there is a serious credibility gap between the types of juveniles who are actually transferred each year and those who should be transferred. In 1994, for instance, nearly half (46 percent) of all youths transferred to criminal court were charged with property or public order offenses. These types of offenses include theft, burglary, petty larceny, and disturbing the peace. Only 42 percent of those transferred in 1994 were charged with person offenses or violent crimes. If transfers, waivers, or certifications were applied as they should be applied, 100 percent of those transferred annually would be serious, violent offenders, and juvenile courts would handle all the other cases.

TYPES OF WAIVERS

Waiver actions include judicial waivers, direct file, statutory exclusion, and demand waivers, among others.

Judicial Waivers

The largest numbers of waivers from juvenile to criminal court annually come about as the result of direct judicial action. **Judicial waivers** give the juvenile court judge the authority to decide whether to waive jurisdiction and transfer the case to criminal court (Bilchik, 1996b:3).

There are three kinds of judicial waivers. The first type, **discretionary waivers**, empower the judge to waive jurisdiction over the juvenile and transfer the case to criminal court. Because of this type of waiver, judicial waivers are sometimes known as discretionary waivers. The second type of judicial waiver is the **mandatory waiver**. In the case of a mandatory waiver, the juvenile court judge *must* waive jurisdiction over the juvenile if probable cause exists that the juvenile committed the alleged offense. The third type of judicial waiver is a **presumptive waiver**. Under the presumptive waiver scenario, the burden of proof concerning a transfer decision is shifted from the state to the juvenile. It requires that certain juveniles be waived to criminal court unless they can prove that they are suited to juvenile rehabilitation.

Judicial waivers are often criticized because of their subjectivity. Two different youths charged with identical offenses may appear at different times before the same judge. On the basis of impressions formed about the youths, the judge may decide to transfer one youth to criminal court and adjudicate the other youth in juvenile court. Obviously, the intrusion of extralegal factors into this important action generates a degree of unfairness and inequality. A youth's appearance and attitude emerge as significant factors that will either make or break the offender in the eyes of the judge. These socioeconomic and behavioral criteria often overshadow the seriousness or pettiness of offenses alleged. In the context of this particular type of transfer, it is easy to see how some persistent, nonviolent offenders may suffer waiver to criminal court.

Although judges have this discretionary power in most jurisdictions, youths are still entitled to a hearing at which they can protest the waiver action. It is true that the criminal court poses risks to juveniles in terms of potentially harsher penalties, but it is also true that being tried as an adult entitles youths to all the adult constitutional safeguards, including the right to a trial by jury. In a later section of this chapter, this and other options that may be of benefit to certain juveniles are closely examined. Thus, some juveniles may not want to fight waiver or transfer actions, largely because they may be treated more leniently by criminal courts.

Direct File

Whenever offenders are screened at intake and referred to the juvenile court for possible prosecution, prosecutors in various jurisdictions conduct further screenings of these youths. They determine which cases merit further action and formal adjudication by judges. Not all cases sent to prosecutors by intake officers automatically result in subsequent formal juvenile court action. Prosecutors may decline to prosecute certain ones, particularly if there are problems with witnesses who are either missing or who refuse to testify, if there are evidentiary issues, or if there are overloaded juvenile court dockets. A relatively small proportion of cases may warrant waivers to criminal courts.

Under **direct file**, the prosecutor has the sole authority to decide whether any given juvenile case will be heard in criminal court or juvenile court. Essentially, the prosecutor decides which court should have jurisdiction over the juvenile. Prosecutors with direct file power are said to have **concurrent jurisdiction**, which is another name for direct file. In Florida, for example, prosecutors have concurrent jurisdiction. They may file extremely serious charges (e.g., murder, rape, aggravated assault, robbery) against youths in criminal courts and present cases to grand juries for indictment action. Or, prosecutors may decide to file the same cases in the juvenile court.

Statutory Exclusion

Statutory exclusion means that certain juvenile offenders are automatically excluded from the juvenile court's original jurisdiction. Legislatures of various states declare a particular list of offenses to be excluded from the jurisdiction of juvenile courts. Added to this list of excluded offenses is a particular age range. Thus, in Illinois, if a 16-year-old juvenile is charged with murder, rape, or aggravated assault, then he or she is automatically excluded from the jurisdiction of the juvenile court; instead, the case will be heard in criminal court. In 1997, 16 states had statutory exclusion provisions and excluded certain types of offenders from juvenile court jurisdiction. Because state legislatures created statutory exclusion provisions, this waiver action is sometimes known as a **legislative waiver**. Because these provisions mandate the automatic waiver of juveniles to criminal court, they are also known as **automatic waivers**.

Demand Waivers

Under certain conditions and in selected jurisdictions, juveniles may submit motions for **demand waivers**, which are requests or motions filed by juveniles and their attorneys to have their cases transferred from juvenile courts to criminal courts. Why would juveniles want to have their cases transferred to criminal courts? One reason is that most U.S. jurisdictions do not provide jury trials for juveniles in juvenile courts as a matter of right (*McKeiver v. Pennsylvania,* 1971). About a fifth of the states, however, have established provisions for jury trials for juveniles at their request and depending on the nature of the charges against them. In the remainder of the states, jury trials for juveniles are granted only at the discretion of the juvenile court judge. Most juvenile court judges are not inclined to grant jury trials to juveniles. Thus, if juveniles are (1) in a jurisdiction in which they are not entitled to a jury trial even if they request one from the juvenile court judge, (2) face serious charges, and (3) believe that their cases would receive greater impartiality from a jury in a criminal courtroom, then they may seek a demand waiver so as to have their cases transferred to criminal court. Florida permits demand waivers as one of several waiver options (Bilchik, 1996b:3).

Other Types of Waivers

Reverse Waivers.   **Reverse waivers** are actions by the criminal court to transfer direct file or statutory exclusion cases from criminal court back to juvenile court, usually at the recommendation of the prosecutor. Typically, juveniles involved in these reverse waiver hearings are those who were automatically sent to criminal court because of statutory exclusion. Thus, criminal court judges can send at least some of these juveniles back to the jurisdiction of the juvenile court. Reverse waiver actions may also be instigated by defense counsels on behalf of their clients. **Reverse waiver hearings** are held in these matters.

Once an Adult, Always an Adult.   The **once an adult, always an adult provision** is perhaps the most serious and long-lasting provision for affected juvenile offenders. This provision means that once juveniles have been convicted in criminal court, they are forever after considered adults for the purpose of criminal prosecutions. For instance, suppose that a 12-year-old is transferred to criminal court in Vermont and is subsequently convicted of a crime. Then, at age 15, if the same juvenile commits another crime, such as vehicular theft, he or she would be subject to prosecution in criminal court. Thus, a criminal court conviction means that the juvenile permanently loses access to the juvenile court. In 1997, 31 states had once an adult, always an adult provisions.

    The once an adult, always an adult provision is not as ominous as it appears. It requires that particular jurisdictions keep track of each juvenile offender previously convicted of a crime. This documentation is not particularly sophisticated in different jurisdictions. Some juveniles may simply move away from the jurisdiction in which they were originally convicted. A 14-year-old juvenile who is convicted of a crime in California may move to North Dakota or Vermont, where he or she may be treated as a first-offender in those juvenile courts. How are North Dakota and Vermont juvenile courts supposed to know that a particular 14-year-old has a criminal conviction in California? Information sharing among juvenile courts throughout the United States is extremely limited or nonexistent. Thus, the intent of the once an adult, always an adult provision can often be defeated simply by relocating to another jurisdiction. The most popular type of waiver action is the judicial waiver, and 46 states had judicial waiver provisions in 1997 (Torbet and Szymanski, 1998:4). Over half of all states, 28, had statutory exclusion provisions in 1997. Reverse waivers, which result from automatic or legislative waivers, were used in 23 states in 1997. Also, 31 states enacted the once waived, always waived provision.

Waiver Hearings

All juveniles who are waived to criminal court for processing are entitled to a hearing on the waiver if they request one (Bilchik, 1996b). A **waiver hearing** is a formal proceeding designed to determine whether the waiver action taken by the judge or prosecutor is the correct action and the juvenile should be transferred to criminal court. Waiver hearings are normally conducted before the juvenile court judge. They are initiated through a **waiver motion** through which the prosecutor usually requests the judge to send the case to criminal court. Because a case must be made for why criminal courts should have jurisdiction in any specific instance, these hearings are to some extent evidentiary. Usually, juveniles with lengthy prior records, several previous referrals, and/or one or more previous adjudications as delinquent are more susceptible to being transferred. Although the offenses alleged are most often crimes, it is not always the case that the crimes are the most serious ones. Depending on the jurisdiction, the seriousness of crimes associated with transferred cases varies. Disproportionately large numbers of cases involving property crimes are transferred to criminal courts for processing. In some instances, chronic, persistent, or habitual status offenders have been transferred, particularly if they have violated specific court orders to attend school, participate in therapeutic programs, perform community service work, make restitution, or engage in some other constructive enterprise. If waivers are to be fully effective, then only the most serious offenders should be targeted for transfer. Transferring less serious and petty offenders accomplishes little in the way of enhanced punishments for these offenders.

Reverse Waiver Hearings

In those jurisdictions with direct file or statutory exclusion provisions, juveniles and their attorneys may contest these waiver actions through reverse waiver hearings. These hearings are conducted before criminal court judges to determine whether to send the juvenile's case back to juvenile court. For both waiver and reverse waiver hearings, defense counsel and the prosecution attempt to make a case for their desired action. In many respects, these hearings are similar to preliminary hearings or preliminary examinations conducted within the criminal justice framework. Some evidence and testimony are permitted, and arguments for both sides are heard. Once all arguments have been presented and each side has had a chance to rebut the opponents' arguments, the judge decides the matter.

Time Standards Governing Waiver Decisions

Although only less than 1 percent of all juveniles processed by the juvenile justice system annually are transferred to criminal courts for processing as adults, only eight states—Arizona, Indiana, Iowa, Maryland, Massachusetts, Michigan, Minnesota, New Mexico, and Virginia—had time limits governing transfer provisions for juveniles as of 1993 (Butts, 1996b:559). Maryland, for example, has a 30-day maximum time limit between one's detention and the **transfer hearing**. If the transfer hearing results in a denial of the transfer, then there is a 30-day maximum between the denial of the transfer and the juvenile court adjudication. In contrast, Minnesota provides only a one-day maximum between placing youths in adult jails and filing transfer motions by juvenile court prosecutors. New Mexico's provisions are similar to Maryland's.

IMPLICATIONS OF WAIVER HEARINGS FOR JUVENILES

Those juveniles who contest or fight their transfers to criminal courts or attempt to obtain a reverse waiver wish to remain within the juvenile justice system, be treated as juveniles, and be adjudicated by juvenile court judges, but not all juveniles who are the subject of transfer are eager to contest the transfer. There are several important implications for youths, depending on the nature of their offenses, their prior records, and the potential penalties the respective courts may impose. Under the right circumstances, having one's case transferred to criminal court may offer juvenile defendants considerable advantages not normally enjoyed if their cases were to remain in the juvenile court. In the following discussion, some of the major advantages and disadvantages of being transferred are examined.

Positive Benefits Resulting from Juvenile Court Adjudications

Among the positive benefits of having one's case heard in juvenile court are that:

1. Juvenile court proceedings are civil, not criminal; thus, juveniles do not acquire criminal records.
2. Juveniles are less likely to receive sentences of incarceration.
3. Compared with criminal court judges, juvenile court judges have considerably more discretion in influencing a youth's life chances prior to or at the time of adjudication.
4. Juvenile courts are traditionally more lenient than criminal courts.
5. There is considerably more public sympathy extended to those who are processed in the juvenile justice system, despite the general public advocacy for a greater get-tough policy.
6. Compared with criminal courts, juvenile courts do not have as elaborate an information-exchange apparatus to determine whether certain juveniles have been adjudicated delinquent by juvenile courts in other jurisdictions.

7. Life imprisonment and the death penalty lie beyond the jurisdiction of juvenile judges, and they cannot impose these harsh sentences.

Adverse Implications of Juvenile Court Adjudications

Juvenile courts are not perfect, however, and may be disadvantageous to many youthful offenders. Some of their major limitations are that:

1. Juvenile court judges have the power to administer lengthy sentences of incarceration, not only for serious and dangerous offenders, but for status offenders as well.

2. In most states, juvenile courts are not required to provide juveniles with a trial by jury.

3. Because of their wide discretion in handling juveniles, judges may overpenalize a large number of those appearing before them on various charges.

4. Juveniles do not enjoy the same range of constitutional rights as adults in criminal courts.

JUVENILE RIGHTS

During the mid-1960s and for the following 20 years, significant achievements were made in the area of juvenile rights. Although the *parens patriae* philosophy continues to be somewhat influential in juvenile proceedings, the U.S. Supreme Court has vested youths with certain constitutional rights. These rights do not encompass all of the rights extended to adults who are charged with crimes, but they thus far have had far-reaching implications for how juveniles are processed from arrest through probation and parole.

Landmark Cases in Juvenile Justice

***Kent v. United States* (1966).** The first major juvenile rights case to preface further juvenile court reforms, *Kent v. United States* (1966), established the universal precedents of (1) requiring waiver hearings before juveniles can be transferred to the jurisdiction of a criminal court (excepting legislative or automatic waivers, although reverse waiver hearings must be conducted at the juvenile's request) and (2) entitling juveniles to consult with counsel prior to and during such hearings. In 1959, Morris A. Kent Jr., a 14-year-old in the District of Columbia, was apprehended and charged with several housebreakings and attempted purse snatchings. He was adjudicated delinquent and placed on probation. Subsequently, in 1961, an intruder entered the apartment of a woman, took her wallet, and raped her. Fingerprints at the crime scene were later identified as those of Kent, who had been fingerprinted in connection with his delinquency case in 1959. On September 5, 1961, Kent admitted to the offense as well as to other crimes, and the juvenile court judge voiced his intent to waive Kent to criminal court. In the meantime, Kent's mother had obtained an attorney who advised the court that he intended to oppose the waiver. The judge ignored the attorney's motion and transferred Kent to the U.S. District Court for the District of Columbia, where he was tried and convicted of six counts of housebreaking by a federal jury, although the jury found him "not guilty by reason of insanity" on the rape charge. Kent's conviction was reversed by the U.S. Supreme Court. The majority held that Kent's rights to due process and to the effective assistance of counsel were violated when he was denied a formal hearing on the waiver and his attorney's motions were ignored. The U.S. Supreme Court said that the matter of a waiver to criminal court was a "critical stage" and thus attorney representation was fundamental to due process. In adult cases, for instance, critical stages are those that relate to the defendant's potential loss of freedoms (i.e., incarceration). Because of the Kent decision, waiver hearings are now considered critical stages.

In re Gault **(1967).**   The Gault case is the most significant of all landmark juvenile rights cases. It is certainly considered the most ambitious. In a 7–2 vote, the U.S. Supreme Court articulated the following rights for all juveniles: (1) the right to a notice of charges, (2) the right to counsel, (3) the right to confront and cross-examine witnesses, and (4) the right to invoke the privilege against self-incrimination. The petitioner, Gault, requested the Court to rule favorably on two additional rights sought: the right to a transcript of proceedings and the right to an appellate review. The Court did not rule on either of these additional rights. The facts are that Gerald Francis Gault, a 15-year-old, and a friend, Ronald Lewis, were taken into custody by the sheriff of Gila County, Arizona, on the morning of June 8, 1964, for allegedly making an obscene telephone call to a female neighbor. At the time, Gault was on probation for of purse-snatching. A verbal complaint was filed by the neighbor of Gault, Mrs. Cook, alleging that Gault had called her and made lewd and indecent remarks. When Gault was taken into custody by police, his mother and father were at work; indeed, they did not learn where their son was until much later that evening. A subsequent informal adjudication hearing of Gault was held, at which a one-sided presentation was given about Gault's alleged obscene conduct. The witness against him, Mrs. Cook, did not appear or offer testimony and thus was unavailable for cross-examination by Gault or his attorney. A court probation officer gave the essentially one-sided account incriminating Gault. Subsequently, the judge ordered Gault to the Arizona State Industrial School until he became 21. (If an adult had made an obscene telephone call, he would have received a $50 fine and no more than 60 days in jail. In Gault's case, he was facing nearly six years in a juvenile prison for the same offense.) After exhausting their appeals in Arizona state courts, the Gaults appealed to the U.S. Supreme Court. The U.S. Supreme Court reversed the Arizona Supreme Court, holding that Gault did, indeed, have the right to an attorney, the right to confront his accuser (Mrs. Cook) and to cross-examine her, the right against self-incrimination, and the right to have notice of the charges filed against him. All these rights had been violated by the original juvenile court judge during the adjudicatory proceedings.

In re Winship **(1970).**   *Winship* established an important precedent in juvenile courts relating to the standard of proof used in established defendant guilt. The U.S. Supreme Court held that "beyond a reasonable doubt," a standard ordinarily used in adult criminal courts, was henceforth to be used by juvenile court judges and others in establishing a youth's delinquency. Formerly, the standard used was the civil application of "preponderance of the evidence." The facts in the Winship case are that Samuel Winship was a 12-year-old charged with larceny in New York City. He purportedly entered a locker and stole $112 from a woman's pocketbook. Under Section 712 of the New York Family Court Act, a juvenile delinquent was defined as "a person over seven and less than sixteen years of age who does any act, which, if done by an adult, would constitute a crime." Interestingly, the juvenile judge in the case acknowledged that the proof to be presented by the prosecution might be insufficient to establish the guilt of Winship beyond a reasonable doubt, although he did indicate that the New York Family Court Act provided that "any determination at the conclusion of an **adjudicatory hearing** that a juvenile did an act or acts must be based on a preponderance of the evidence" standard (397 U.S. at 360). Winship was adjudicated as a delinquent and ordered to a training school for 18 months, subject to annual extensions of his commitment until his 18th birthday. Appeals to New York courts were unsuccessful. The U.S. Supreme Court subsequently heard Winship's appeal and reversed the New York Family Court ruling because the "beyond a reasonable doubt" standard had not been used in a case in which incarceration or loss of freedom was likely.

***McKeiver v. Pennsylvania* (1971).**   The McKeiver case was important because the U.S. Supreme Court held that juveniles are not entitled to a jury trial as a matter of right. The facts are that in May 1968, Joseph McKeiver, 16, was charged with robbery, larceny, and receiving stolen goods. He was represented by counsel who asked the court for a jury trial "as a matter of right." This request was denied. McKeiver was subsequently adjudicated delinquent. On appeal to the U.S. Supreme Court later, McKeiver's adjudication was upheld. The U.S. Supreme Court said that jury trials for juveniles are not a matter of right but rather at the discretion of the juvenile court judge. In about a fifth of the states today, jury trials for juveniles in juvenile courts are held under certain conditions.

***Breed v. Jones* (1975).**   The significant constitutional issue of "double jeopardy" was raised in *Breed v. Jones.* In this case, the U.S. Supreme Court concluded that after a juvenile has been adjudicated as delinquent on specific charges, those same charges may not be subsequently alleged against those juveniles in criminal courts through transfers or waivers. The facts are that on February 8, 1971, in Los Angeles, California, Gary Steven Jones, 17, was armed with a deadly weapon and allegedly committed robbery. He was subsequently apprehended, and an adjudicatory hearing was held on March 1. Jones was adjudicated delinquent on these robbery charges, after which the juvenile court judge transferred Jones to criminal court to stand trial on these same charges. Jones was subsequently convicted of robbery. He appealed the decision, and the U.S. Supreme Court reversed the robbery conviction, concluding that the robbery adjudication was considered the equivalent of a criminal trial on the same charges, a dual court action constituting double jeopardy. The juvenile court judge should have disposed Jones to secure confinement following his adjudication on the robbery charges or simply waived jurisdiction over Jones initially to criminal court.

***Schall v. Martin* (1984).**   In *Schall v. Martin,* the U.S. Supreme Court issued juveniles a minor setback regarding the state's right to hold them in preventive detention pending a subsequent adjudication. The Court said that the preventive detention of juveniles by states is constitutional if judges perceive these youths to pose a danger to the community or an otherwise serious risk if released short of an adjudicatory hearing. This decision was significant, in part, because many observers advocated the separation of juveniles and adults in jails, those facilities most often used for preventive detention. Also, the preventive detention of adults was not ordinarily practiced at that time. (Since then, the preventive detention of adults who are deemed to pose societal risks has been upheld by the U.S. Supreme Court [*United States v. Salerno,* 1987].) The facts are that 14-year-old Gregory Martin was arrested at 11:30 P.M. on December 13, 1977, in New York City and was charged with first-degree robbery, second-degree assault, and criminal possession of a weapon. Martin lied to police at the time, giving a false name and address. Between the time of his arrest and the fact-finding hearing on December 29 (a total of 15 days), Martin was detained. His detention was based largely on the false information he had supplied to police and the seriousness of the charges pending against him. Subsequently, he was adjudicated delinquent and placed on two years' probation. His attorney later filed an appeal, contesting his preventive detention as violative of the due process clause of the Fourteenth Amendment. The U.S. Supreme Court eventually heard the case and upheld the detention as constitutional.

OFFENSE SERIOUSNESS AND DISPOSITIONS: AGGRAVATING AND MITIGATING CIRCUMSTANCES

In 1999, an estimated 1.8 million delinquency cases were disposed of in the juvenile justice system. About 12,000 cases were transferred to criminal court, and less than 10 percent of these cases resulted in incarceration. Most were either downgraded or dismissed, or sentences of probation were imposed (Pastore and Maguire, 2001). Whether juveniles are first-offenders or have prior juvenile records is crucial to many prosecutorial decisions. The overwhelming tendency among prosecutors is to divert petty first-offenders to some conditional program. Influencing prosecutorial decision making is the presence of aggravating and/or mitigating factors.

Aggravating and Mitigating Circumstances

Aggravating Circumstances.   Aggravating circumstances enhance penalties imposed by juvenile court and criminal court judges. Key aggravating factors include the following:

1. Death or serious bodily injury to one or more victims
2. An offense committed while an offender is awaiting resolution of other delinquency charges
3. An offense committed while the offender is on probation, parole, or work release
4. Previous offenses for which the offender has been punished
5. Leadership in the commission of a delinquent act involving two or more offenders
6. A violent offense involving more than one victim
7. Extreme cruelty during the commission of the offense
8. The use of a dangerous weapon in the commission of the offense, with high risk to human life

Mitigating Circumstances.   Mitigating factors lessen penalties imposed by these respective courts. Key mitigating factors include the following:

1. No serious bodily injury resulting from the offense
2. No attempt to inflict serious bodily injury on anyone
3. Duress or extreme provocation

4. Circumstances that justify the conduct
5. Mental incapacitation or physical condition that significantly reduced the offender's culpability in the offense
6. Cooperation with authorities in apprehending other participants, or making restitution to the victims for losses they suffered
7. No previous record of delinquent activity

Judicial Dispositional Options

Judges in juvenile courts may exercise several options when deciding specific cases. These judges may adjudicate youths as delinquent and do no more than record the event. If the juvenile appears again before the same judge, then harsher sentencing measures may be taken. The judge might divert juveniles to community-based services or agencies for special treatment. Those youths with psychological problems or who are emotionally disturbed, sex offenders, or those with drug and/or alcohol dependencies may be targeted for special community treatments. Various conditions as punishments such as fines, restitution, or some form of community service may also be imposed by judges. The more drastic alternatives are varying degrees of custodial sentences, ranging from the placement of juveniles in foster homes, camp ranches, reform schools, or industrial schools. These nonsecure and secure forms of placement and/or detention are usually reserved for the most serious offenders. One or more of the following eleven judicial options may be exercised in any delinquency adjudication:

Nominal Sanctions
1. A stern reprimand may be given.
2. A verbal warning may be issued.

Conditional Sanctions
3. An order may be given to make restitution to victims.
4. An order may given to pay a fine.
5. An order may be given to perform some public service.
6. An order may be given to submit to the supervisory control of some community-based corrections agency on a probationary basis.
7. A sentence may be imposed, but the sentence may be suspended for a fixed term of probation.

Custodial Sanctions (Nonsecure and Secure)
8. An order may be issued for the placement of the juvenile in a foster home.
9. An order may be issued for the placement of the juvenile in a residential center or group home.
10. An order may be given to participate under supervision at a camp ranch or special school (either nonsecure or secure detention).
11. An order may be given to be confined in a secure facility for a specified period.

Nominal and Conditional Sanctions

Nominal dispositions are verbal and/or written warnings issued to low-risk juvenile offenders, often first-offenders, for the purpose of alerting them to the seriousness of their acts and their potential for receiving severe conditional punishments if they ever should reoffend. These sanctions are the least punitive alternatives.

Conditional sanctions include probation and a variety of other community placements and interventions. These programs include those discussed next.

Youth Diversion and Community-Based Programs.   One of the earliest delinquency prevention strategies that can be implemented by juvenile court judges and other actors throughout the juvenile justice system is diversion. It is the temporary directing of youths from the juvenile justice system so that they can remain with their families or guardians, attend school, and be subject to limited supervision on a regular basis by a juvenile PO.

Youth Service Bureaus (YSBs).   Diversion programs have operated in the United States for many years. In the early 1960s, **Youth Service Bureaus (YSBs)** were established in numerous jurisdictions to accomplish diversion's several objectives. Although those youths considered delinquency-prone or youths at risk still cannot be identified precisely, YSBs were created, in part, as places within communities where such youths could be referred by parents, schools, and law enforcement agencies. Actually, YSBs were forerunners of the contemporary community-based correctional programs, because they were intended to solicit volunteers from among community residents and to mobilize a variety of resources that could assist in a youth's treatment. The nature of treatments for youths, within the YSB concept, originally included referrals to a variety of community services, educational experiences, and individual or group counseling. YSB organizers compiled lists of existing community services, agencies, organizations, and sponsors who could cooperatively coordinate these resources in the most productive ways to benefit affected juveniles (Romig, 1978).

Diversion may be either unconditional or conditional. Unconditional diversion simply means that the divertee will attend school, behave, and not reappear before the juvenile court for a specified period. Conditional diversion may require juveniles to attend lectures, individual or group psychotherapy, drug or alcohol treatment centers, police department–conducted DUI classes, and/or vocational or educational classes or programs. Successful completion of the diversion program likely means dismissal of the case. These programs are of variable lengths, but most run for periods of six months to a year.

Juvenile Diversion/Noncustody Intake Program.   In 1982, officials in Orange County, California, implemented a diversionary program called the **Juvenile Diversion/Non-Custody Intake Program**. Diversionary efforts in previous years by county officials had been ineffective. This program was designed to target more serious juvenile offenders by giving them more concentrated attention by police, probation, community agencies, schools, and families (Binder et al., 1985). The program was a type of conditional diversion, because juvenile clients were required to pay restitution to their victims. Arnold Binder and colleagues reported that the program successfully diverted a large proportion of intake cases ordinarily referred to the district attorney for formal processing. Besides easing the juvenile court caseload, program clients tended to have lower recidivism rates compared with those in more traditional programs, although these differences were not substantial.

The Juvenile Diversion Program (JDP).   Gilbert Litton and Linda Marye (1983) have described a reasonably successful diversion program. A **juvenile diversion pro-**

gram (JDP) was established in New Orleans, Louisiana, in 1981 by the district attorney's office through which youths could receive diversion before being petitioned and adjudicated delinquent. During the 1981 to 1983 period, 233 juveniles were accepted into the program, although the program capacity was estimated at 400. This JDP consisted of intensive counseling and evaluative and social services. Other elements included family and individual counseling, parent involvement, restitution to victims, and use of various community services. After a one-year follow-up, results disclosed only a 20 percent recidivism rate among program participants. Although the researchers complained that the program was ineffective because it did not serve the full complement of 400 juveniles as it was originally conceived, there is certainly nothing wrong with a 20 percent recidivism rate. This rate is even more significant when those accepted into the program were first-offender felons (excluding murder, rape, and robbery) and serious misdemeanants.

Youth-at-Risk Program.   Significant success rates (i.e., lower recidivism) have been reported by another California program known as the **Youth-at-Risk program**, which operated in Los Angeles and Contra Costa Counties during 1982 to 1984 for youths age 13 to 19. The program consisted of a ten-day rural training course composed of classes; outdoor sites for running and other physical activities; and emphasis on self-reliance, peer resistance, peer and staff support, and individual responsibility. A community follow-up program was implemented as a continuation of these experiences. Of the 155 youths participating in the program during the period 1982 to 1983, 49 were studied over a 15-month period and were compared with a matched group of probationers with similar characteristics and delinquency histories. Youth-at-risk program participants had incident recidivism rates of 34.7 percent compared with 55.1 percent for the comparison group and a serious offense recidivism rate of only 18.4 percent compared with 40.8 percent for the comparison group. These figures led program officials to conclude that their program had a profound positive effect on their juvenile clients (MetaMetrics, Inc., 1984).

See Our Side Program.   In Prince George's County, Maryland, the **See Our Side (SOS) Program** was established in 1983 (Mitchell and Williams, 1986:70). SOS is referred to by its directors as a "juvenile aversion" program and dissociates itself from "scare" programs such as Scared Straight. SOS seeks to educate juveniles about the realities of life in prison through discussions and hands-on experience and attempts to show them the types of behaviors that can lead to incarceration (Mitchell and Williams, 1986:70). Clients are referred from various sources, including juvenile court, public and private schools, churches, professional counseling agencies, and police and fire departments. Youths served by SOS range in age from 12 to 18, and they do not have be adjudicated as delinquent to be eligible for participation. SOS consists of four three-hour phases:

> Phase I: Staff orientation and group counseling session at which staff attempt to facilitate discussion and ease tension among the youthful clients; characteristics of jails are discussed, including age and gender breakdowns, race, and types of juvenile behavior that might result in jailing for short periods.
>
> Phase II: A tour of a prison facility.
>
> Phase III: Three inmates discuss with youths what life is like behind bars; inmates who assist in the program are selected on the basis of their emotional maturity, communications skills, and warden recommendations.

Phase IV. Two evaluations are made, the first an evaluation of SOS sessions by the juveniles; a recidivism evaluation is also conducted for each youth after a one-year lapse from the time they participated in SOS; relative program successfulness can therefore be gauged.

SOS officials conducted an evaluation of the program in September 1985 and found that SOS served 327 youths during the first year of operation and that a total of 38 sessions were held. Recidivism of program participants was about 22 percent. Again, this low recidivism rate is favorable. Subsequent evaluations of the SOS program showed that the average rate of client recidivism dropped to only 16 percent. The cost of the program was negligible; during the first year, the program cost was only $280, or about 86 cents per youth served.

Custodial Sanctions

The custodial options available to juvenile court judges are of two general types: nonsecure facilities and secure facilities. Nonsecure custodial facilities are those that permit youths freedom of movement within the community. Youths are generally free to leave the premises of their facilities, although they are compelled to observe various rules, such as curfew, avoidance of alcoholic beverages and drugs, and participation in specific programs that are tailored to their particular needs. These types of nonsecure facilities include foster homes, group homes and halfway houses, camps, ranches, experience programs, and wilderness projects.

Nonsecure Facilities

Foster Homes.   If the juvenile's natural parents are considered unfit, or if the juvenile is abandoned or orphaned, **foster homes** are often used for temporary placement. Youths placed in foster homes are not necessarily law violators. They may be **children in need of supervision (CHINS)** or **persons in need of supervision (PINS)** (*Matter of Zachary "I"*, 1993). Foster home placement provides youths with a substitute family. A stable family environment is believed by the courts to be beneficial in cases in which youths have no consistent adult supervision or are unmanageable or unruly in their own households.

Foster home placements are useful in many cases in which youths have been apprehended for status offenses. Most families that accept youths into their homes have been investigated by state or local authorities in advance to determine their fitness as foster parents. Socioeconomic factors and home stability are considered important for child placements. Foster parents often typify middle-aged, middle-class citizens with above-average educational backgrounds. Despite these positive features, it is unlikely that foster homes are able to provide the high intensity of adult supervision required by more hard-core juvenile offenders. Further, it is unlikely that these parents can furnish the quality of special treatments that might prove effective in the youth's possible rehabilitation or societal reintegration. Most foster parents simply are not trained as counselors, social workers, or psychologists. For many nonserious youths, however, a home environment, particularly a stable one, has certain therapeutic benefits.

BOX 13.2

Personality Highlight

Nelda De La Garza
Formerly with the Webb County, Texas Juvenile Detention Center

Statistics. A.A. (criminal justice), Laredo Community College; B.A. (criminal justice), Texas A&M International University; M.A. (criminal justice and sociology), Texas A&M International University

Background and Interests. I am a 1999 graduate of Texas A&M International University with a bachelor's degree and master's degree in criminal justice. Previously I attended Laredo Community College, where I received an associate's degree in criminal justice.

It was always my life's dream to enroll in a law school to become a prosecuting attorney, but that all changed once I interned with the Webb County Juvenile Detention Center. I felt that I would be better suited in the area of social work. While at the detention center, I worked with juvenile probation officers, which involved interaction with juveniles and their parents. Visits were routinely held to discuss their progress, or why they were having difficulties with their families and school.

Then I became employed with the Texas Department of Protective and Regulatory Services as a Child Protective Service Specialist II. This work involved taking courses in the education of conducting investigations, interviews, and learning the legalities of the job. My duties were to find a placement for children who had been removed from their homes. Then I had to appear in court to inform the judge as to what services Child Protective Services would offer to the child and family. Then I had to follow up with the family and the family's counselor to see if court-ordered services were being used. Another duty included being placed on night duty. A different worker would be placed on call each night in case an emergency removal was necessary or if a family disturbance occurred.

My experience with Child Protective Services was positive, but I felt the need to continue my education. Working with Child Protective Services involved a great deal of time with each case.

Advice to Students. My advice to any student interested in this line of work is to contact their local agency and ask for a complete list of job requirements and find out what the agency's expectations of them would be. This job is for someone who is willing to work long hours and who is able to communicate with children. One must be able to make a child feel safe and cared for.

Group Homes.   Another nonsecure option for juvenile judges is the assignment of juveniles to **group homes**. Placing youths in group homes is considered an intermediate option available to juvenile court judges. Group homes are community-based operations that may be either publicly or privately administered. Usually, they will have counselors or residents to act as parental figures for youths in groups of 10 to 20. Certain group homes, referred to as family group homes, are actually family-operated, and thus are, in a sense, an extension of foster homes for larger numbers of youths. In group homes, nonsecure supervision of juvenile clients is practiced (Haghighi and Lopez, 1993). Both privately and publicly operated group homes require juvenile clients to observe the rights of others, participate in various vocational or educational training programs, attend school, participate in therapy or receive prescribed medical treatment, and observe curfew. Urinalyses or other tests may be conducted randomly as checks to see whether juveniles are taking drugs or are consuming alcohol contrary to group home policy. If one or more program violations occur, then group home officials may report these infractions to juvenile judges, who retain dispositional control over the youths. Assignment to a group home is usually for a determinate period.

Positively, group homes provide youths with the companionship of other juveniles. Problem sharing often occurs through planned group discussions. Staff are available to assist youths secure employment, work through certain school problems, and absorb emotional burdens arising from difficult interpersonal relationships. These homes, however, are sometimes staffed by community volunteers with little training or experience with a youth's problems. Certain risks and legal liabilities may be incurred as the result of well-intentioned but bad advice or inadequate assistance. Currently, there are limited regulations among states for how group homes are established and operated. Training programs for group home staff are scarce in most jurisdictions, and few standards on staff preparation and qualifications exist. Therefore, considerable variation exists among group homes.

Camps, Ranches, Experience Programs, and Wilderness Projects. Camps and **ranches** are nonsecure facilities that are sometimes referred to as wilderness projects or experience programs. A less expensive alternative to the detention of juvenile offenders, even those considered chronic, is participation in experience programs. **Experience programs** include a wide array of outdoor programs designed to improve a juvenile's self-worth, self-concept, pride, and trust in others.

Hope Center Wilderness Camp.   An example of a fairly successful wilderness experiment is the **Hope Center Wilderness Camp** in Houston, Texas. This camp has an organized network of four interdependent, small living groups of 12 teenagers each. The camp's goals are to provide quality care and treatment in a nonpunitive environment with specific emphases on health, safety, education, and therapy. Emotionally disturbed youths whose offenses range from truancy to murder are selected for program participation. Informal techniques are used, including "aftertalk" (informal discussion during meals), "huddle up" (a group discussion technique), and "pow wow" (a nightly fire gathering). Special nondenominational religious services are conducted. Participants are involved in various special events and learn how to cook meals outdoors, how to camp, and other survival skills. Follow-ups by camp officials show that camp participants exhibit recidivism rates of only about 15 percent (Clagett, 1989).

Homeward Bound.   A program known as **Homeward Bound** was established in Massachusetts in 1970. Designed to provide juveniles with mature responsibilities through the acquisition of survival skills and wilderness experiences, this six-week training program subjected 32 boys to endurance training, physical fitness, and performance of community service. In addition, officials of the program worked with the boys to develop a release program in which they completed the project requirements successfully. During the evenings, the juveniles were given instruction in ecology, search

and rescue, and overnight treks (Haghighi and Lopez, 1993). Toward the end of th
gram, the boys were subjected to a test: surviving a three-day, three-night trip in the
wilderness to prove that each boy had acquired the necessary survival skills. Although
these programs serve limited numbers of juveniles and some authorities question their
value in deterring further delinquency, some evidence suggests that these wilderness
experiences generate less recidivism among participants compared with those youths
who are institutionalized in industrial schools under close custody and monitoring.

Secure Confinement

Short-Term and Long-Term Facilities. **Secure confinement** for juveniles in the
United States emulates adult prisons or penitentiaries in several of their characteristics. They are also either short term or long term. These terms are ambiguous as they
pertain to juvenile secure custody facilities. Short-term confinement facilities, sometimes referred to as **detention**, are designed to accommodate juveniles on a temporary basis. These juveniles are awaiting a later juvenile court adjudication,
subsequent foster home, group home placement, or transfer to criminal court. Sometimes youths will be placed in short-term confinement because their identity is
unknown and it is desirable that they not be confined in adult lockups or jails. When
juveniles are placed in these short-term facilities, they are considered held in detention. On the other side of detention, juveniles placed in long-term facilities may be
confined for several days or years, although the average duration of juvenile incarceration across all offender categories nationally is about six or seven months. The
average short-term incarceration in public facilities for juveniles is about 30 days.
Most juvenile court judges use incarceration as a last-resort disposition, if the circumstances merit incarceration. By far the most frequently used sanction against
juveniles is probation (Snyder, Sickmund, and Poe-Yamagata, 2000).

JUVENILE PROBATION OFFICERS AND PREDISPOSITIONAL REPORTS

Juvenile Probation Officers

Many probation officers who work with juveniles report that their work is satisfying.
Many see themselves as playing an important part in shaping a youth's future by the
nature of the relationships they can establish between themselves and the juveniles
with whom they work. James R. Davis, a probation officer with the Department of
Probation in New York City for 22 years, has supervised both adults and juvenile
offenders. Usually, the juveniles he supervises are those age 16 and over who have
been transferred to criminal courts because of more serious offenses they have committed. He shares his experiences:

> Generally, I supervise adults from the age of 16 and over who are placed on probation
> by the court. Sometimes, I have supervised juveniles under age 16 who are tried in adult
> courts under the New York State Juvenile Laws. Although I have had only a few cases of
> juveniles who are tried as adults, they present the worst cases to me, and, I am sure, to
> other probation officers. This is logical, since they are accused of violent crimes. Now there
> is a special worker who handles these [kinds of] cases. I remember a case of a juvenile who
> was 15 and tried as an adult. He was charged with felonious assault. He was hostile and

noncooperative when supervised by me. For example, he didn't report on time, he was verbally abusive to me, and [he was] loud and hostile. He was arrested while on probation for another felony assault charge. He was known to have beaten up his grandmother. When I initiated a violation of probation for the new arrest, he became quite hostile and wanted to know why I did this. He even followed me one night into the street and I had to get into a cab to escape him. He beat up another probationer in the waiting area of the office and was finally transferred to an intensive probation caseload.

I was supervising another juvenile who was placed on adult probation at the age of 15 for robbery. He had an arrest prior to being placed on probation for robbery and was arrested again during supervision for another robbery. He always tried to work, and at first he was cooperative. However, during supervision he became hostile, noncooperative, failing to keep appointments, and failing to wait for his turn in the office. He was black and insisted that he wanted a black probation officer, since I was white. However, the judge incarcerated him for a few weeks because of this new robbery charge. He is now awaiting the disposition of his new robbery case. Although I am still supervising him, the relationship between him and me is tense and fragile; he is still nervous and impatient, and he doesn't keep appointments on time. He minimizes his arrest record. He claims that blacks do not receive justice with white agents of the criminal justice system. His mother absconded from the home, and he is now supervised by his grandmother.

Although I [now] supervise [primarily] adults, anyone from the age of 16 to 19 is given a youthful offender status except for a few violent offenders. However, I believe that juveniles under 16 who are tried as adults present some special problems and do need supervision in a special caseload by experienced probation officers who are trained for this type of experience. (Interview with James R. Davis, January 1999)

Probation Work and Professionalism.   There is a keen sense of professionalism among most probation and parole officers. The American Correctional Association and the American Probation and Parole Association are two of the most important professional organizations today that disseminate information about corrections and probation and parole programs and provide workshops and various forms of professional training. Many probation and parole officers attend the meetings of these and other professional organizations to learn about the latest innovations and probation programs. Joseph Sweet (1985) views probation work with juveniles as a timely opportunity to intervene and make a difference in their lives. Thus, he sees probation as a type of therapy. He divides the therapy function that probation officers can perform into five simple steps:

1. Case review: probation counselors need skills to read the behaviors of the youths they supervise and their probable antecedents.
2. Self-awareness: probation counselors need to inspect their own reactions to youths; are they too impatient or overly sensitive? Traditional transference, countertransference issues must be addressed.
3. Development of a relationship: great patience is required; children are often rejected, and probation officers must learn to accept them and demonstrate a faith in their ability to achieve personal goals.
4. The critical incident: the testing phase of the relationship, when juveniles may deliberately act up to test honesty and sincerity of PO.
5. Following through: successive tests will be made by juveniles as they continue to verify the PO's honesty and sincerity; POs do much of the parenting that their clients' parents failed to do. (Sweet, 1985:90)

Sweet considers these stages integral features of action therapy that can often be more effective than insight-oriented therapy.

Because of their diverse training, POs often orient themselves toward juvenile clients in particular ways that may be more or less effective. Because many juvenile offenders are considered manipulators who might take advantage of a PO's sympathies, some POs have devised interpersonal barriers between themselves and their youthful clients. Other POs have adopted more productive interpersonal strategies. In most juvenile cases, POs seek to instruct and help offenders in dealing with their personal and social problems to fit into their community environments better. If POs continuously check up on their youthful clients or regard them with suspicion, they inhibit the growth of productive interpersonal relations that might be helpful in facilitating a youth's reentry into society. Enforcement-oriented officers and those who attempt to detect rule infractions almost always create a hostile working relationship with their clients, and communication barriers are often erected that inhibit a PO's effectiveness.

Juvenile Probation Officer Functions.   The functions of juvenile POs are diverse and include report preparation, home and school visits, and a variety of other client contacts. POs often arrange contacts between their clients and various community-based corrections agencies that provide services and specific types of psychological and social treatments. POs themselves perform counseling tasks with their clients. They must also enforce laws associated with probation or parole program conditions. Thus, if offenders have been ordered to comply with a specific curfew and/or reimburse victims for their financial losses, POs must monitor them to ensure that these program conditions have been fulfilled.

The most important PO dimensions include the following:

1. Problem solving (problem analysis: the ability to grasp the source, nature, and key elements of problems; judgment: recognition of the significant factors to arrive at sound and practical decisions)
2. Communication (dialogue skills: effectiveness of one-on-one contacts with youthful clients, small group interactions; writing skills: expression of ideas clearly and concisely)
3. Emotional and motivational (reactions to reassure: functioning in a controlled, effective manner under conditions of stress; keeping one's head; drive: the amount of directed and sustained energy to accomplish one's objectives)
4. Interpersonal (insight into others: the ability to proceed, giving due consideration to the needs and feelings of others; leadership: the direction of behavior of others toward the achievement of goals)
5. Administrative (planning: forward thinking, anticipating situations and problems, and preparation in advance to cope with these problems; commitment to excellence: determination that the task will be done well)

In 2000, it was estimated that there were 20,000 juvenile probation officers in the United States (Pastore and Maguire, 2001). These officers provided intake services for nearly 1.8 million juveniles, predispositional studies of over 800,000 cases, and received over 600,000 cases for supervision (American Correctional Association, 2001). These cases are not distributed evenly throughout the various juvenile probation departments in the United States. Thus, caseloads for some POs are considerably larger than they are for others. A high caseload is arbitrarily defined as 50 or more juvenile clients, although caseloads as high as 300 or more have been reported in some jurisdictions. When caseloads are particularly high, an even greater burden is placed on the shoulders of juvenile POs who must often prepare predispositional reports for youths at the juvenile court judge's direction.

The Predispositional Report and Its Preparation

Juvenile court judges in many jurisdictions order the preparation of **predispositional reports**, the functional equivalent of presentence investigation reports for adults. Predispositional reports are intended to furnish judges with background information about juveniles so that judges can make a more informed sentencing decision. They also function to assist probation officers and others target high-need areas for youths and specific services or agencies for individualized referrals. This information is often channeled to information agencies such as the National Center for Juvenile Justice in Pittsburgh, Pennsylvania, so that researchers may benefit in their juvenile justice investigations. They may analyze the information compiled from various jurisdictions for their own research investigations (Rogers and Williams, 1995).

Predispositional reports are completed for more serious juveniles and function like presentence investigation reports prepared by POs for adults. Juvenile court judges order these reports prepared in most cases, unless statutory provisions in certain jurisdictions govern their automatic preparation. These predispositional reports contain much of the same information as PSI reports. Sometimes, juveniles whose families can afford them have private predispositional reports prepared to influence judges to exert leniency on the juvenile offender (Rogers and Williams, 1995). In fact, that is precisely what Peter Greenwood and Susan Turner found when they compared case dispositions of youths who had private predispositional reports prepared against those cases that had standard reports compiled by juvenile POs. Greenwood and Turner described client-specific planning as the name given by the National Center on Institutions and Alternatives to its process of developing alternative sentencing plans designed to minimize the incarceration of its clients (Greenwood and Turner, 1993:232).

Harold Trester (1981:89-90) has summarized four important reasons predispositional reports should be prepared:

1. These reports provide juvenile court judges with a more complete picture of juvenile offenders and their offenses, including the existence of any aggravating or mitigating circumstances.
2. These reports can assist the court in tailoring the disposition of the case to an offender's needs.
3. These reports may lead to the identification of positive factors that would indicate the likelihood of rehabilitation.
4. These reports provide judges with the offender's treatment history, which might indicate the effectiveness or ineffectiveness of previous dispositions and suggest the need for alternative dispositions.

It is important to recognize that predispositional reports are not required by judges in all jurisdictions. By the same token, legislative mandates obligate officials in other jurisdictions to prepare them for all juveniles to be adjudicated. Also, there are no specific formats universally acceptable in these report preparations. Figure 13.1 is an example of a predispositional report.

Joseph Rogers (1990:44) indicates that predispositional reports contain insightful information about youths that can be helpful to juvenile court judges prior to sentencing. Six social aspects of a person's life are crucial for investigations, analysis, and treatment: personal health, physical and emotional; family and home situation;

THE PREDISPOSITION REPORT

**A Model Set of Field Notes to Guide Preparation of
Juvenile Court Predisposition Reports**

COURT REPORT OUTLINE

CASE NO:_____ HEARING DATE:_____

ADDRESS:_____PHONE:_____

1.	REASON FOR HEARING:	PETITION NO.:	PETITION DATE:	W&I	SUB:
	NAME: (AKA):			AGE:	
	ALLEGATION AND REFERENCE TO P.D. REPORT OR COMPLAINT:				
2.	PRESENT SITUATION	FIRST COURT WARD		REFERRAL DATE AND AGENCY:	
	PLACE AND DATE OF DETENTION OR CUSTODY:		RELEASED TO:	DATE:	
3.	CITATION / SERVED / MAILED	TO:			
	SERVED BY:	LOCATION		DATE:	
4.	LEGAL RESIDENCE	DETERMINING PARENT:	ARRIVED IN SAN DIEGO COUNTY:		
	VERIFICATION:		RESIDENCE OF CHILD:		
5.	PREVIOUS HISTORY:				
6.	STATEMENT OF CHILD (Description, attitude, and statements re: allegation and home):				
	RACE: / HAIR: / EYES: / HT: / WT: / MARKS:				

FIGURE 13.1 A predispositional report. (*Source:* Joseph W. Rogers, "The Predisposition Report: Maintaining the Promise of Individual and Juvenile Justice." *Federal Probation* **54:**51–52, 1990.)

7. STATEMENT OF PARENTS (Description, attitude, and statement re: allegation and child):

8. STATEMENT OF VICTIM, WITNESSES, RELATIVES OR OTHERS (Name, Address, Date and Relation to Case):

9. FAMILY HISTORY

MARRIAGE OF NATURAL PARENTS, DATE AND PLACE:

CHILDREN AND ORDER OF BIRTH

AGE, EDUCATIONAL LEVEL AND BACKGROUND OF NATURAL PARENTS

DATE, PLACE, REASON AND EFFECTS OF SEPARATION, DIVORCE, REMARRIAGE (CUSTODY):

PREVIOUS RESIDENCE; EMPLOYMENT; DATE ARRIVED S. D. CO.; PRESENT FAMILY UNIT:

DESCRIPTION OF HOME AND FURNISHINGS:

OWNED		$
RENTED		$

COMMUNITY RELATIONSHIP AND ENVIRONMENTAL FACTORS: POLICE RECORD OF PARENT AND/OR SIBLINGS:

DISEASES IN HISTORY OF EITHER PARENT: HANDICAPS, MENTAL DISORDERS, ALCOHOLISM, SUICIDE; HEALTH INSURANCE AND HOSPITAL ELIGIBILITY:

RELIGION AND ATTENDANCE:

PARENT - CHILD RELATIONSHIP:

recreational activities and use of leisure time; peer group relationships (types of companions); education; and work experience. According to the National Advisory Commission on Criminal Justice Standards and Goals as outlined in 1973, predispositional reports have been recommended in all cases in which the offenders are minors. In actual practice, however, predispositional reports are only prepared at the request of juvenile court judges. No systematic pattern typifies such report preparation in most U.S. jurisdictions. Table 13.1 shows the type of information reported in a sample of 162 predisposition reports.

TABLE 13.1 Percentage of Juvenile Case Records in Which Line Item Information Was Located

Variable Identification	Item Number	Percentage
Case code number	1–3	
Sex	4	100
Ethnic status	5	100
Age, 1st juv. ct. appearance	6	100
Source of 1st referral	7	100
Reason for 1st referral/ct. hearing	8–9	100
Recoding of prior item	10	100
Formal court disposition	11	100
Youth's initial placement by court	12	100
Miscellaneous court orders	13	100
Detention prior to 1st hearing	14	100
Type of counsel retained	15	100
Initial plea	16	100
Presiding, initial ct. hearing	17	99
Number of prior offenses	18	100
Age, time of initial offense	19	100
Number of off. after 1st hearing	20	100
Youth's total offense number	21	100
Number companions, 1st offense	22	100
Usual companionship portrait	23	92
Living arrangements 1st ct. hearing	24	99
Parents' marital status	25	99
Youth's age at divorce/death	26	93
Household economic status	27	95
Public assistance recipient?	28	88
Income dependence number	29	96
Type of neighborhood	30	60
Home assessment	31	85
Parental work situation	32	94
Parental education background	33	19
Father's health	34	78
Mother's health	35	85
Youth's school academic standing	36	94
Youth's school attendance	37	94

(continued)

TABLE 13.1 *(continued)*

Variable Identification	Item Number	Percentage
Youth's att./perception: sch.	38	83
Parents' att. toward youth's educ.	39	59
Child's birth	40	72
Organic/emotional dysfunctions	41	85
Other educational problems	42	80
Youth's church attendance	43	28
Youth's job record	44	73
Leisure-time interests	45	64
Youth's mental health portrait	46	86
Highest IQ recorded	47	45
Psychological intervention	48	85
Community outpatient care	49	35
Residential inpatient care	50	43
Statement of juvenile	51	92
Statement of mother	52	83
Statement of father	53	56
Youth's generalized explanation	54	95
Parent's generalized explanation	55	88
JPO's generalized explanation	56	93
Alienation	57	96
Childhood rejection	58	88
Child's concept of self	59	90
Dominant manifest personality	60	97
Personality direction	61	93
Usual peer group relationship	62	89
Achievement orientation	63	77
Siblings relationships	64	74
Mother/child relationship	65	93
Father/child relationship	66	84
Principal discipline source	67	85
Quality of discipline	68	77
Family difficulty with police	69	76
Last known offense	70–71	99
Decoding of prior item	72	99
Time under JPO supervision	73	93
Number of detentions	74	100
Number of out-of-home placements	75	100
Dominant form of JPO contact	76	83
JPO home visit frequency	77	67
Overall frequency of contact	78	78
Final status of case	79	95
Judge, last court hearing	80	99

Source: Joseph W. Rogers, "The Predisposition Report," *Federal Probation* **54:**48 (1990).

Rogers (1990:46) says that the following characteristics were included in 100 percent of the cases: (1) gender, (2) ethnic status, (3) age at first juvenile court appearance, (4) source of first referral to juvenile court, (5) reason(s) for referral, (6) formal court disposition, (7) youth's initial placement by court, (8) miscellaneous court orders and conditions, (9) type of counsel retained, (10) initial plea, (11) number of prior offenses, (12) age and time of initial offense, (13) number of offenses after first hearing, (14) youth's total offense number, (15) number of companions at first offense, (16) number of detentions, and (17) number of out-of-home placements. These predispositional reports may or may not contain victim impact statements. Presentence investigation reports or PSIs prepared for adults convicted of crimes are the equivalent of predispositional reports. It is more common to see such victim impact statements in adult PSI reports, although some predispositional reports contain them in certain jurisdictions. These statements are often prepared by victims themselves and appended to the report before the judge sees it. They are intended to provide judges with a sense of the physical harm and monetary damage victims have sustained and thus often detail aggravating factors that weigh heavily against the juvenile to be sentenced.

JUVENILE PROBATION AND PAROLE PROGRAMS

About 1.8 million juvenile cases are processed annually by juvenile courts. About 700,000 of these are assigned to POs for predispositional study, whereas 500,000 cases are assigned for supervision (Pastore and Maguire, 2001). The most common form of probation is standard probation. Standard juvenile probation is more or less elaborate, depending on the jurisdiction. Of all sentencing options available to juvenile court judges, standard probation is the most commonly used. The first probation law was enacted in Massachusetts in 1878, although probation was used much earlier; John Augustus is credited with inventing probation in Boston in 1841. **Standard probation programs** are either a conditional or unconditional nonincarcerative sentence of a specified period following an adjudication of delinquency.

Unconditional and Conditional Probation

Probation programs for juveniles are either unconditional or conditional and exhibit many similarities with adult probation programs. Unconditional standard probation involves complete freedom of movement within the juvenile's community, perhaps accompanied by periodic reports by telephone or mail with a PO or the probation department. Because a PO's caseload is often high, with several hundred juvenile clients to be managed, individualized attention cannot be given to most juveniles on standard probation. The period of unsupervised probation varies among jurisdictions depending upon offense seriousness and other circumstances.

Conditional probation programs may include optional conditions and program requirements such as performing a certain number of hours of public or community service; providing restitution to victims; payment of fines; employment; and/or participation in specific vocational, educational, or therapeutic programs. It is crucial to any probation program that an effective classification system be in place so that juvenile judges can sentence offenders accordingly. S. Christopher Baird (1985:32–34) suggests that a variation of the National Institute of Corrections' Model Classification Project scheme, in which both risk and needs are assessed, be

BOX 13.3   *Personality Highlight*

Sara L. Trujillo
Juvenile Probation Officer, Webb County, Laredo, Texas

Statistics. B.A. (sociology, criminal justice), Texas A&M International University; M.A. (criminal justice, forthcoming), Texas A&M International University

Work Experience and Background. I first became interested in the criminal justice field when I began to work at Laredo Community College as a police aide. My duties included issuing parking citations, radio dispatching, computer data entry, filing complaints, and report writing. I had applied for the part-time job just to make ends meet. With time, however, I became very interested in the daily activities that took place on campus and I observed the campus police officers' duties as well. It was at that point that I decided to minor in criminal justice because I knew that it was the career path that I wanted to take. My role as a police aide lasted for two and a half years. During that same period, I was also working as an English tutor at a local middle school. I then discovered that I had a good rapport with students. I worked as a tutor for three school years.

After that period, a friend later told me that detention officer part-time positions were available at Webb County Juvenile Detention Center. I was nearing completion of my bachelor's degree at the university when I decided to apply. I submitted my application, and the three years of working with students helped me land the job. I was thrilled! I worked as a detention officer for one year. My job enabled me to work with juvenile offenders, especially young women. My daily duties consisted of conducting female room inspections, strip searches, supervision of family visitations, manning the control room, writing daily logs, counseling, and disciplining female detainees. When needed, I also supervised male detainees. I became aware of the life of delinquent youths. Most of the juveniles were involved in hard-core drug problems, family conflicts, dysfunctional home surroundings, sexual and physical abuse, and gang affiliation, among other problems, but the work only interested me more. I enjoyed helping as many offenders as walked through the doors.

I eventually graduated and applied for a juvenile probation officer position at the same center, and I was hired. I was even more excited about my new career. I transferred to the administrative unit, and then I was able to talk to the families as a whole. I dedicated a lot of my time in working with juveniles by providing them with services, such as psychological and family counseling, drug prevention and intervention programs, drug rehabilitation placement settings, boot camps, medical treatment, and school hearings. My career as a juvenile probation officer lasted four years, and I can honestly say that it was a humbling experience. I gained a lot of work experience, and I especially enjoyed representing the department and families in court proceedings. I am now working as a criminal justice instructor at a local high school. I teach students the basics of the field of criminal justice, and I have enjoyed this career as well because I have continued to work with adolescents.

Advice to Students. My advice to others interested in the field is to continue to work hard to achieve their goals. It takes special people to work in this field!

used for juvenile classifications. General terms of standard probation usually include the following:

1. To obey one's parents or guardians
2. To obey all laws of the community, including curfew and school laws
3. To follow the school or work program approved by the PO
4. To follow instructions of the PO
5. To report in person to the PO or court at such times designated by the PO
6. To comply with any special conditions of probation
7. To consult with the PO when in need of further advice

Juveniles sentenced to standard probation experience little change in their social routines. The inclusion of special conditions of probation usually means more work for POs. Some of these conditions may include medical treatments for drug or alcohol dependencies, individual or group therapy or counseling, and participation in a driver's safety course. In some instances involving theft, burglary, or vandalism, restitution provisions, whereby youths must repay victims for their financial losses, may be included. Most standard probation programs in the United States require little, if any, direct contact with the probation office, which logistically works out well for POs, who are frequently overworked. Greater caseloads, however, mean less individualized attention devoted to youths by POs, and some of these youths require more supervision than others while on standard probation.

Standard probation exhibits relatively high rates of recidivism, ranging from 40 to 75 percent. Even certain youth camps operated in various California counties have reported recidivism rates as high as 76 percent (Levin, Langan, and Brown, 2000). Therefore, it is often difficult to forecast which juveniles will have the greatest likelihood of reoffending, regardless of the program being examined.

According to Baird (1985:36), the following elements appear to be predictive of future criminal activity and reoffending by juveniles: (1) one's age at first adjudication, (2) a prior criminal record (a combined measure of the number and severity of priors), (3) the number of prior commitments to juvenile facilities, (4) drug/chemical abuse, (5) alcohol abuse, (6) family relationships (parental control), (7) school problems, and (8) peer relationships. An additional factor not cited by Baird that may have significant predictive value is whether youths who are currently on probation violate one or more conditions of their probation programs. Needs assessments should be individualized, based on the juvenile's past record and other pertinent characteristics, including the present adjudication offense (Baird, 1985:36). The level of supervision should vary according to the degree of risk posed to the public by the juvenile. Although Baird does not provide a weighting procedure for the different risk factors listed earlier, he does describe a supervisory scheme that acts as a guide for juvenile probation and aftercare. This scheme would be applied based on the perceived risk of each juvenile offender and would include the following:

Regular or Differential Supervision
1. Four face-to-face contacts per month with youth
2. Two face-to-face contacts per month with parents
3. One face-to-face contact per month with placement staff
4. One contact with school officials

Intensive Supervision
1. Six face-to-face contacts per month with youth
2. Three face-to-face contacts per month with parents
3. One face-to-face contact per month with placement staff
4. Two contacts with school officials

Alternative Care Cases
1. One face-to-face contact per month with youth
2. Four contacts with agency staff (one must be face to face)
3. One contact every two months with parents

An assignment to any one of these supervision levels, including **alternative care cases**, should be based on both risk and needs assessments. Baird says that agencies often make categorical assignments of juveniles to one level of supervision or another, primarily by referring to the highest level of supervision suggested by two or more scales used (1985:38). Each juvenile probation agency prefers specific predictive devices, and some agencies use a combination of them. Again, no scale is foolproof, and the matter of false positives and false negatives arises because some juveniles receive more supervision than they really require, whereas others receive less than they need.

Not all probation orders involving juveniles are lenient. In the *Matter of Jessie GG* (1993), for instance, a New York high school student was placed on a two-year probationary term and ordered to pay $1,500 restitution for damages to a victim's property. The two-year probationary period coincided with his ability to pay. Further, it was the harshest disposition the juvenile court judge could impose.

Juvenile probationers do not have the same rights as adult probationers. For instance, a California juvenile probationer, Michael T., was placed on probation with the provision that supervising POs and police could conduct warrantless searches of his premises at any time (*In re Michael T.*, 1993). A similar provision for warrantless searches and seizures on a juvenile probationer's premises has been made in the case of *In re Bounmy V.* (1993) in which the offender was a known cocaine dealer and was suspected of secreting cocaine on his premises at different times.

Intensive Supervised Probation (ISP) Programs

Intensive supervised probation (ISP) programs, alternatively known as intensive probation supervision (IPS) programs, have become increasingly popular for managing nonincarcerated offender populations. Since the mid-1960s, these programs have been aimed primarily at supervising adult offenders closely, and in recent years,

ISP programs have been designed for juvenile offenders as well. ISP is a highly structured and conditional program for either adult or juvenile offenders that serves as an alternative to incarceration and provides for an acceptable level of public safety. Some researchers argue that the effectiveness of ISP is how well certain risk control factors are managed by supervising POs rather than the sheer intensity of their supervision over clients (Pullen, 1996).

Characteristics of ISP Programs.   ISP programs for juveniles have been developed and are currently operating in about one-third to one-half of all U.S. jurisdictions (Pullen, 1996). Similar to their adult ISP program counterparts, **juvenile intensive supervision programs (JISPs)** are ideally designed for secure detention-bound youths and are considered acceptable alternatives to incarceration. JISPs are differentiated from other forms of standard probation programs by the obvious differences in the amount of officer/client contact during the course of the probationary period. For example, standard probation is considered no more than two face-to-face officer/client contacts per month. JISP programs might differ from standard probation according to the following face-to-face criteria: (1) two or three times per week versus once per month, (2) once per week versus twice per month, or (3) four times per week versus once per week (the last figure being unusually high for standard probation contact) (Armstrong, 1988:346).

Different types of POs' dispositions toward work are evident in descriptions of the various services provided by the different JISP programs investigated by Troy Armstrong. For example, of the 55 programs he examined (92 percent of his total program sample), he found that the following range of services, skills, and resources were mentioned as being brokered by POs in different jurisdictions:

1. Mental health counseling
2. Drug and alcohol counseling
3. Academic achievement and aptitude testing
4. Vocational and employment training
5. Individual, group, and family counseling
6. Job search and placement programs
7. Alternative education programs
8. Foster grandparents programs
9. Big Brother/Big Sister programs

Not all ISP programs are alike, however (Wiebush, 1990:26). Nevertheless, many juvenile ISP programs share similarities, including the following:

1. Recognition of the shortcomings of traditional responses to serious and/or chronic offenders (e.g., incarceration or out-of-home placement)
2. Severe resource constraints within jurisdictions that compel many probation departments to adopt agency-wide classification and workload deployment systems for targeting a disproportionate share of resources for the most problematic juvenile offenders
3. Program hopes to reduce the incidence of incarceration in juvenile secure detention facilities and reduce overcrowding
4. Programs tend to include aggressive supervision and control elements as a part of the get-tough movement
5. A vested interest in rehabilitation of youthful offenders

From these analyses of ISP program content in general, the following basic characteristics of ISP programs can be gleaned:

1. Low officer/client caseloads (i.e., 30 or fewer probationers)
2. High levels of offender accountability (e.g., victim restitution, community service, payment of fines, partial defrayment of program expenses)
3. High levels of offender responsibility
4. High levels of offender control (home confinement, electronic monitoring, frequent face-to-face visits by POs)
5. Frequent checks for arrests, drug and/or alcohol use and employment/school attendance (drug/alcohol screening, coordination with police departments and juvenile halls, teachers, family) (Armstrong, 1988:342–343; Wiebush, 1990)

The Ohio Experience

The value of JISP programs can be appreciated by what Richard Wiebush has described as the **Ohio Experience**. Wiebush has compared three different Ohio counties—Delaware County (predominantly rural), Lucas County (Toledo), and Cuyahoga County (Cleveland)—that have used different ISP programs for their juvenile offenders as well as the Ohio Department of Youth Services (ODYS). The ODYS is state operated and manages the most serious offenders, exclusively felony offenders on parole from secure detention. In each county jurisdiction, most of the offenders are bound for detention, with the exception of the Lucas County juveniles, who are sentenced to ISP after having their original sentences of detention reversed by juvenile court judges.

Targeted by the Delaware County JISP program are those juveniles with a high propensity to recidivate as well as more serious felony offenders who are bound for detention. Youths begin the program with a five-day detention followed by two weeks of house arrest. Later, they must observe curfews, attend school and complete school work satisfactorily, report daily to the probation office, and submit to periodic urinalysis. Each youth's progress is monitored by intensive counselors and surveillance staff 16 hours a day, seven days a week. Weibush says that although the Delaware County program has a rather strict approach, it embodies rehabilitation as a primary program objective. This program has about a 40 percent recidivism rate, which is high, although it is better than the 75 percent rate of recidivism among the general juvenile court population of high-risk offenders elsewhere in Ohio jurisdictions.

In Lucas County, program officials select clients from those already serving sentences of detention and who are considered high-risk offenders. Lucas County officials wanted to use this particular selection method to avoid any appearance of net-widening that their JISP program might reflect. Drawing from those already incarcerated seemed the best strategy in this case. The Lucas County program is similar to the Delaware County program in its treatment and control approaches, but the Lucas program obligates offenders to perform up to 100 hours of community service as a program condition. House arrest, curfew, and other Delaware County program requirements are also found in the Lucas County program. The successfulness of the Lucas County program has not been evaluated fully, although it does appear to have reduced institutional commitments by about 10 percent between 1986 and 1987.

The Cuyahoga County program (Cleveland) was one of the first of several ISP programs in Ohio's metropolitan jurisdictions. It is perhaps the largest county program, with 1,500 clients at any given time as well as six juvenile court judges and 72 supervisory personnel. One innovation of the Cuyahoga County program was the development of a team approach to client surveillance and management. This program, like the other county programs, performs certain broker functions by referring its clients to an assortment of community-based services and treatments during the program duration. There are currently six teams of surveillance officers who each serve about 60 youths. These teams are composed of a team leader, two counselors, and three surveillance staff. Recidivism rates averaged about 31 percent in a longitudinal follow-up.

In addition to supervising the 3,000 youths each year who are released on parole, the ODYS program operates the state's nine training schools. The ODYS has 93 youth counselors to staff seven regional offices. The JISP program started in February 1988 and supervised those high-risk offenders with a predicted future recidivism rate of 75 percent or higher. Because these clients were all prior felony offenders with lengthy adjudication records, they were considered the most serious group to be supervised compared with the other programs. Accordingly, the ODYS supervision and surveillance structure exhibited the greatest degree of offender monitoring. The team approach is used by the ODYS, with teams consisting of three youth counselors and two surveillance staff. Since its creation, the JISP program operated by the ODYS has exhibited a drop in its recidivism rate. On the basis of a comparison of the first year of its operation with recidivism figures for its clients from the previous year, the ODYS program had a 34 percent reduction in its rate of recidivism. Further, a 39 percent reduction in parole revocations occurred, which is significant given the high-risk nature of the offender population being managed.

All these programs have required enormous investments of time and energy by high-quality staff, according to Weibush. Further, each program has illustrated how best to use existing community resources to further its objectives and best serve juvenile clients in need. Weibush says, however, that what is good for Ohio probationers and parolees may not necessarily be suitable for those offenders of other jurisdictions. Nevertheless, these programs function as potential models after which programs in other jurisdictions may be patterned.

The Allegheny Academy

In February 1982, the **Allegheny Academy** in Pennsylvania was opened and operated by the Community Specialists Corporation, a private, nonprofit corporation headquartered in Pittsburgh and specializing in the community-based treatment of young offenders (Costanzo, 1990:114). The program's general aim is to change the negative behavior of offenders. The targets of the Allegheny Academy are those juvenile offenders who have failed in other, traditional probation programs in Pennsylvania. Thus, the youthful clients are recidivists who, academy officials believe, would not particularly benefit from further institutionalization through secure detention. The Allegheny Academy was originally designed as a facility to provide meaningful aftercare to adjudicated offenders. Clients are referred to the academy by juvenile court judges in lieu of incarceration. The program may be completed by clients in about six months. Youths live at home, but they must attend the academy each day after school and also on weekends. Buses carrying 15 passengers each pick clients up daily and return them to their homes in the evenings. They receive two full-course meals a day and arrive at their homes around 8:00 or 9:00 P.M. Supervisors who monitor the program-imposed curfew of 10:30 P.M. make follow-up telephone calls to the youths' homes. The academy offers instruction and other forms of assistance enable participants to acquire greater responsibilities. After they have successfully complied with program requirements for 28 days in a row, they are gradually allowed community days at home on weekends. Student failure to attend classes or observe curfews may result in sending them to the county juvenile detention facility for 2 to 14 days (Costanzo, 1990:116).

The Allegheny Academy includes in its program various student activities, such as woodworking, carpentry, masonry, painting, electrical and structural repair, food services, vehicle maintenance, graphic arts, and computer skills. Clients also receive individual or group counseling as well as some family counseling. Clients are encouraged to learn about substance abuse and to behave well in their schools and homes. Between 1982 and 1990, the cost of operating Allegheny Academy has been only a fraction of what it would have required to impose long-term detention on all the juveniles served. Further, clients have paid out over $100,000 in restitution to various victims through earnings from summer work programs.

Boston Offender Project

Sometimes, a compromise relating to the custody imposed in various juvenile probation programs in which some degree of secure custody over youths is necessary for a short time but nonsecure supervision is also permitted and desirable is preferred. One of the most frustrating aggregates of juvenile offenders is that small minority that commits violent offenses (Murphy, 1985:26). Judges and POs are often at a loss for strategies to deal effectively with such offenders. Often, the options are secure custody in a reform school or a waiver to criminal courts, presumably for more stringent punishments and longer sentences of confinement. Some professionals in juvenile corrections continued to believe, however, that other options were available, provided that the time and resources could be allocated properly.

In 1981, an experimental program was commenced in Boston, one of five demonstration sites, to give some of these professionals their chance to put into practice what they believed could be done in theory. The Massachusetts Department of Youth Services was awarded a grant to implement what eventually became known as the **Boston Offender Project (BOP)**. Its target was violent juveniles, and its goals included reducing recidivism, enhancing public protection by increasing accountability for major violators, and improving the likelihood of successful reintegration of juveniles into society by focusing on these offenders' academic and vocational skills (Murphy, 1985:26).

BOP sought to improve the typical handling of a violent juvenile case in the following ways:

1. By developing three coordinated phases of treatment that include initial placement in a small, locked, secure-treatment program, followed by planned transition into a halfway house, and finally, a gradual return to the juvenile's home community
2. By assuring the delivery of comprehensive services by assigning particularly experienced caseworkers responsible for working intensively with a caseload of not more than eight violent offenders and their families

3. By providing services focused on increasing the educational level of offenders and tying educational programs to the marketplace, significantly increasing the prospects of meaningful employment (Murphy, 1985:26)

BOP was similar to shock probation in that violent juvenile offenders would experience some confinement in a secure facility, but after a short time, they would be released to less secure surroundings. Thus, a shock element was included, at least implicitly, in the BOP structure. The BOP has several important features compared with the treatment received by those juveniles in the control group. First, diagnostic assessments of juveniles in BOP went well beyond standard psychological assessments, and these measures charted, on an ongoing basis, developments in psychological, vocational, and medical areas. Second, caseworkers in the BOP program were three times more experienced (in numbers of years) than standard program caseworkers. Third, BOP caseworker loads were limited to seven, whereas caseloads for workers in the standard program were as high as 25. A fourth feature was that BOP caseworkers were actively involved in the treatment phase, whereas the standard program caseworker involvement was passive. Fifth, caseworker visits to juveniles were eight times as frequent per month compared with standard program visits. Sixth, juveniles were automatically assigned to nonsecure residential facilities once the first secure phase of the program was completed. For standard program participants, this step was not necessarily an option. Furthermore, in the BOP program, continued violence would subject a participant to regression, so that the offender could be placed back in secure confinement. In the standard program, there was only limited flexibility to make this program shift. Finally, the standard program was terminated for youths when they reached 18 years of age, whereas the BOP could be discontinued or continued before or after age 18, depending on caseworker judgment.

Some important differences between the two groups emerged over the next several years. For instance, 79 percent of BOP clients found unsubsidized employment compared with only 29 percent of the control group. Also, only about a third of the BOP clients had been rearrested, which was about half the rearrest rate exhibited by the control group. Thus, although the BOP may not be the most perfect solution to the problem of violent juvenile offenders, it does offer a viable, middle-ground alternative that has demonstrable success, at least with some offenders. For the chronic, hard-core, and most dangerous offenders, detention is one of the last judicial options.

Other Juvenile Probation and Parole Programs

Electronic Monitoring for Juvenile Offenders. Michael Charles (1989a) describes the implementation of one electronic monitoring program for juvenile offenders. The Allen County, Indiana, Juvenile Electronic Monitoring Program Pilot Project began as an experimental study in October 1987 and ran through May 1988. At the time the study started, the probation department had 25 POs who were appointed by the court and certified by the Indiana Judicial Conference. During 1987, 2,404 juveniles were referred to the probation department by the court, about 34 percent of whom were female offenders. During that same year, 167 youths were incarcerated in secure facilities for delinquents at a total cost of $1.5 million. Charles (1989b:152–153) indicates that because of fiscal constraints, Allen County agreed to place only six juveniles in the electronic monitoring program, but two of these youths recidivated and were quickly dropped. The remaining four youths stayed in the program. The juvenile judge in these cases sentenced each youth to a six-month probationary period with electronic monitoring. Each youth wore a conspicuous wristlet, which eventually became a symbol of court sanctions. Like the proverbial string tied around one's finger, the wristlet was a constant reminder that these juveniles were "on probation." Further, others who became aware of these electronic devices helped these youths to avoid activities that might be considered violations of probation program conditions.

Despite the small number of participants in Charles's research, his findings are of interest and suggest similar successful applications on larger offender aggregates. The juveniles were interviewed at the conclusion of the program and reported that their wristlets were continuous reminders of their involvement in the probation program. They did not, however, feel as though program officials were spying on them. In fact, one of the youths compared his experience with electronic monitoring with his previous experience of being supervised by a PO. He remarked that whenever he was under the PO's supervision, he could do whatever he wished, and there was little likelihood that his PO would ever find out about it. With the wristlet, however, he was always under the threat of being discovered by the computer or by the surveillance officer.

Another interesting phenomenon was that the wristlet enabled certain offenders to avoid peer pressure and "hanging out" with their friends. Their wristlets provided good excuses to return home and not violate their curfews. Also, the families of these juveniles took a greater interest in them and their program. In short, at least for these four youths, the program was viewed very favorably and was considered successful. Parents interviewed at the conclusion of the program agreed that the program and monitoring system had been quite beneficial for their sons. Although electronic monitoring for juveniles is still in its early stages of experimentation in various jurisdictions, Charles (1989b) believes that it is a cost-effective alternative to incarceration.

Home Confinement and Juveniles.   In many jurisdictions, home confinement is supplemented with electronic monitoring (Schlatter, 1989). Relatively little is known about the extent to which home confinement is used as a sentencing alternative for juvenile offenders. Because probation is so widely used as the sanction of choice except for the most chronic recidivists, home confinement is most often applied as an accompanying condition of electronic monitoring. This type of sentencing may be redundant, however, because curfew for juvenile offenders means home confinement anyway, especially during evening hours. As a day sentence, home confinement for juveniles would probably be counterproductive, because juveniles are often obligated to finish their schooling as a probation program condition. Again, because school hours are in the day, it would not make sense to deprive juveniles of school opportunities through some type of home detention.

Shock Probation and Boot Camps.   Shock probation has sometimes been compared erroneously with **Scared Straight**, a New Jersey program implemented in the late 1970s. Scared Straight sought to frighten samples of hard-core delinquent youths by having them confront inmates in a Rahway, New Jersey, prison. Inmates would yell at and belittle them, calling them names, cursing, and yelling. Inmates would tell them about sexual assaults and other prison unpleasantries in an attempt to get them to refrain from reoffending. The program was unsuccessful, however. Despite early favorable reports of recidivism rates of less than 20 percent, the actual rate of recidivism among these participating youths was considerably higher. Furthermore, another control group not exposed to Scared Straight had lower recidivism.

The juvenile version of shock probation or shock incarceration is perhaps best exemplified by juvenile boot camps. Also known as the Army Model, boot camp programs are patterned after basic training for new military recruits. Juvenile offenders are given a taste of hard military life, and such regimented activities and structure for up to 180 days are often sufficient to "shock" them into giving up their lives of delinquency or crime and staying out of jail (Ratliff, 1988:98). Boot camp programs in various states such as the Regimented Inmate Discipline program in Mississippi, the About Face program in Louisiana, and the shock incarceration program in Georgia have been established.

Two good examples of boot camp programs are the U.S. Army Correctional Activity in Fort Riley, Kansas, established in 1968 (Ratliff, 1988), and the Butler (New York) Shock Incarceration Correctional Facility (Waldron, 1990) In both programs, inmates wear army uniforms, learn basic army drills, salute, and participate in a rigorous correctional treatment program. Ordinarily, youthful first-offender felons are targeted for involvement in these programs. The Butler program, for instance, involves young offenders ranging in age from 16 to 29 who must stay in the camp for six months and comply with all program rules. About 88 percent of all boot camp trainees are successful and win a parole later. The Butler facility has inmates who have been heavily involved in dealing drugs with about 90 percent of all participants having been convicted of drug offenses. They have rigorous work details, must complete school work, and must adhere to a highly disciplined regimen. They are given eight minutes for meals, and they must carry their leftovers in their pockets.

Their days begin at 5:30 A.M., with reveille blaring over the intercom. Immediately, drill instructors start screaming at them. Besides military drilling, all inmates must experience drug counseling and study. At the Fort Riley facility, inmates may learn vocational skills and crafts. They also receive counseling and other therapy and treatment. At both camps, physicians and other support staff are ready to furnish any needed medical treatment. When they eventually leave the facility, most have changed their outlook on life and have acquired new lifestyles not associated with crime. Again, recidivism rates among these inmates are under 30 percent, which is considered an indication of program success.

REVOKING JUVENILE PROBATION AND PAROLE

Parole for juveniles is similar to parole for adult offenders. Those juveniles who have been detained in various institutions for long periods may be released prior to serving their full sentences.

Purposes of Juvenile Parole.   The general purposes of parole for juveniles are to

1. Reward good behavior while youths have been detained
2. Alleviate overcrowding
3. Permit youths to become reintegrated into their communities and enhance their rehabilitation potential
4. Deter youths from future offending by ensuring their continued supervision under juvenile parole officers

Numbers of Juveniles on Parole.   Estimates about how many juvenile offenders are on parole at any given time vary. The current lack of coordination among jurisdictions relating to juvenile offender record-keeping makes it difficult to determine actual numbers of juvenile parolees or probationers at any given time. Further, some jurisdictions continue to prevent public scrutiny of juvenile court adjudicatory proceedings or their results. Because one's juvenile record is expunged or sealed upon reaching adulthood, even historical research on this subject is limited by various systemic constraints. About 20,000 youths were involved in some form of juvenile parole program in 2000 (American Correctional Association, 2001).

Juvenile parolees share many of the same programs used to supervise youthful probationers. ISP programs are used for both probationers and parolees in many jurisdictions. Further, juvenile probation officers often perform dual roles as juvenile parole officers, supervising both types of offenders. Studies of juvenile parolees show that the greater the intensity of parole, the lower the recidivism (Altschuler, Armstrong, and MacKenzie, 1999; Lewis and Howard, 2000). Influencing the successfulness of juvenile parole is whether juveniles are successfully employed or actively involved in development or counseling programs. For most juveniles who spend time behind bars or reform school walls, the experience is traumatic. About 65 percent of the juveniles on parole refrain from committing new offenses (American Correctional Association, 2001).

Juvenile Parole Decision Making.   The decision to parole particular juveniles is left to different agencies and bodies, depending on the jurisdiction. Studies of imposing secure confinement on juvenile delinquents indicate that in 45 state jurisdictions, the lengths of secure confinement are indeterminate. In 32 states, early-release decisions are left to the particular juvenile correction agency, whereas six states use parole boards exclusively and five other states depend on the original juvenile court judge's decision. Only a few states had determinate schemes for youthful offenders; therefore, their early release from secure custody would be established by statute in much the same way as it is for adult offenders (American Correctional Association, 2001).

A governor-appointed seven-member parole board in New Jersey grants early release to both adult and juvenile inmates. Utah uses a Youth Parole Authority, a part-time board consisting of three citizens and four staff members from the Utah Division of Youth Corrections. This board employs objective decision-making criteria to determine which juveniles should be paroled. Sometimes, however, discrepancies exist between what the authority actually does and what it is supposed to do. One criticism is that the primary parole criteria are related to one's former institutional behavior rather than to other factors, such as one's prospects for successful adaptation to community life, employment, and participation in educational or vocational programs (Norman and Wadman, 2000).

A similar criticism has been made about youth parole boards in other states. Many of these juvenile parole boards consist of persons who make subjective judgments about youths on the basis of extralegal and subjective criteria. Predispositional reports prepared by juvenile POs, records of institutional behavior, a youth's appearance and demeanor during the parole hearing, and the presence of witnesses or victims have unknown effects on individual parole board members. Parole decision making is not an exact science; subjectivity is endemic to this process. When subjective criteria affect this process, a juvenile's parole chances are significantly subverted. Thus, parole board decision-making profiles in various jurisdictions may show evidence of early-release disparities attributable to racial, ethnic, gender, or socioeconomic factors (Norman and Wadman, 2000).

Juvenile Parole Policy.　Jose Ashford and Craig LeCroy (1993:186) undertook an investigation of the various state juvenile parole programs and provisions. They sent letters and questionnaires to all state juvenile jurisdictions, soliciting any available information on their juvenile paroling policies. Their response rate was 94 percent, with 47 of the 50 states responding. One interesting result of their survey was the development of a typology of juvenile parole. They discovered eight different kinds of juvenile parole used more or less frequently among the states:

1. Determinate parole (length of parole is linked closely with the period of commitment specified by the court; paroling authorities cannot extend confinement period of juvenile beyond original commitment length prescribed by judge; juvenile can be released short of serving the full sentence)
2. Determinate parole set by administrative agency (parole release date is set immediately following youth's arrival at secure facility)
3. Presumptive minimum with limits on the extension of the supervision period for a fixed or determinate length of time (minimum confinement period is specified, and youth must be paroled after that date unless there is a showing of bad conduct)
4. Presumptive minimum with limits on the extension of supervision for an indeterminate period (parole should terminate after fixed period of time; parole period is indeterminate, with the PO having discretion to extend parole period with justification; parole length can extend until youth reaches age of majority and leaves juvenile court jurisdiction)
5. Presumptive minimum with discretionary extension of supervision for an indeterminate period (same as item 4 except that the PO has discretion to extend parole length of juvenile with no explicit upper age limit; lacks explicit standards limiting the extension of parole)
6. Indeterminate parole with a specified maximum and a discretionary minimum length of supervision
7. Indeterminate parole with legal minimum and maximum periods of supervision
8. Indeterminate or purely discretionary parole (Ashford and LeCroy, 1993:187–191)

Recidivism and Probation/Parole Revocation

Juvenile Probation and Parole Revocation.　Probation and parole revocations are the termination of one's probation or parole program (PPP), usually for one or more program violations. When one's PPP is terminated, regardless of who does the terminating, there are several possible outcomes. The most severe result is that the offender will be returned to secure detention. A less harsh alternative is that offenders will be shifted to a different kind of PPP. For instance, if a juvenile is assigned to a halfway house as a part of a parole program, then the rules of the halfway house must be observed. If one or more rules are violated, such as failing to observe curfew, failing drug or alcohol urinalyses, or committing new offenses, then a report is filed with the court or the juvenile corrections authority for possible revocation action. If it is decided later that one's PPP should be terminated, then the result may be to place the offender under house arrest or home confinement, coupled with electronic monitoring for a specified period. Other program conditions would be applied as well. One is not automatically returned to detention following a parole revocation.

Usually, if a return to incarceration or detention is not indicated, then the options available to judges, parole boards, or others are limited only by the array of supervisory resources in the given jurisdiction. These options ordinarily involve more intensive supervision or monitoring of offender behaviors. Severe overcrowding in many juvenile detention facilities discourages revocation action that would return large numbers of offenders to industrial schools or youth centers. Intermediate punishments therefore function well to accommodate larger numbers of serious offenders, including those who have their parole revoked.

The process of PPP revocation for juveniles is not as clear-cut as it is for adult offenders. The U.S. Supreme Court has not ruled decisively thus far about how juvenile PPP revocation actions should handled. Prior to several significant U.S. Supreme Court decisions, PPP revocation could be accomplished for adult offenders on the basis of reports filed by POs that offenders were in violation of one or more conditions of their program. Criminal court judges, those ordinarily in charge of determining whether to terminate one's probationary status, could decide this issue on the basis of available evidence against offenders. For adult parolees, former decision making relative to terminating their parole could be made by parole boards without much fanfare from offenders. In short, parole officers and others might simply present evidence that one or more infractions or violations of PPP conditions had been committed. These infractions could then be the basis and the justification for revoking PPPs.

Juvenile Case Law on Probation Revocations

When youths are placed on probation, the most frequently used dispositional option by juvenile court judges, they are subject to having their program revoked for one or more violations of program conditions. Several cases presented below show how different juvenile courts handle probation revocations.

The Case of *In re Kazuo G.* (1994).   A California youth, Kazuo G., was charged with various offenses, and the court imposed a term of commitment to a secure facility for six months. This commitment was suspended and probation ordered instead. Shortly thereafter, the youth was adjudicated delinquent for misdemeanor battery. The juvenile court judge ordered Kazuo G. committed to a boy's ranch for six months, but again suspended this order and placed him on probation. Two more misdemeanor charges were filed against him within a few weeks, and he was adjudicated delinquent on one of these charges. This time, the judge ordered Kazuo G. to the boy's ranch. The youth contested this decision, arguing that he was not given a dispositional hearing. The California Court of Appeals rejected this appeal, and Kazuo G. was finally placed in the boy's ranch for six months.

The Case of *In re F.N.* (1993).   F.N., a juvenile, was adjudicated delinquent on an attempted murder charge in Illinois and was placed on probation. Subsequently, he was arrested on new charges involving criminal assault, and a petition was filed to revoke his probation. He admitted the offense. In exchange for this admission (a form of plea bargaining), his original probation was continued. The judge also ordered F.N. to a youth home for 30 days, with credit for time served while in custody earlier. Another court disagreed, noting that F.N. had participated in a gang-related shooting and was belligerent toward officers seeking to search his home with a warrant. Numerous probation program violations were noted by authorities, and F.N. was subsequently placed in the Kane County, Illinois, Youth Home for 30 days. That the trial court was justifiably concerned with F.N.'s activities that indicated an "aggressive nature" is an understatement.

The Case of *Matter of Tammy JJ* (1993).   Tammy JJ was a New York juvenile who was adjudicated as a status offender and placed on probation, but she violated several probation conditions, including running away from home, not attending school, and failing to keep her appointments with her PO. The court ordered her probation revoked after a showing of the factual accuracy of these allegations, and Tammy JJ was placed in the custody of the Department of Social Services.

The Case of *J.G. v. State* (1992).   J.G. was a Florida juvenile who was adjudicated delinquent and placed in a community control program. Subsequently, he violated several program rules and requirements. Florida authorities held him in contempt of court for these program violations and placed him in a secure facility for a period of months. He appealed, in this case successfully. The Florida District Court of Appeals held that his punishment should have been more intensive supervised probation rather than confinement in a secure facility.

The Case of *State v. H.B.* (1992).   A New Jersey juvenile was placed on probation. Two of several probation conditions were that he remain in school and get a C+ grade average or better and not go out after dark unless accompanied by a parent. Subsequently, he was apprehended by police late at night and was charged with possession of a stolen automobile. The juvenile court judge revoked the probation, and H.B. was committed to a one-year term in a New Jersey youth center. H.B. appealed, claiming that the one-year term was "not rehabilitative" consistent with the family court policies of New Jersey. The court, however, declared that although rehabilitation is desirable, a breach of probation conditions is serious and may lead to the imposition of more coercive penalties. That the judge could impose such an incarcerative penalty was viewed as a proper means to encourage compliance with probationary conditions. Otherwise, the whole process would be farcical and ineffective.

The Case of *Avery v. State* (1993).   In the peculiar case of *Avery v. State,* an Arkansas juvenile was placed on probation; subsequently, a motion filed to revoke his probation was denied. Instead, the court lengthened the term of the youth's probation. A few months later, the court found that the juvenile was not in compliance with certain probation program requirements, revoked the probation, and fined the juvenile. An appeals court held that although the original trial court had the right to deny the revocation motion and extend one's probationary term, it could wait several months, change its mind, and grant the original motion to revoke probation. This decision raised a double jeopardy issue (*Breed v. Jones,* 1975).

The Case of *Matter of J.K.A.* (1993).   It is not always necessary for the court to adjudicate juveniles for new offenses if they are currently on probation and probation revocation is a consideration. In the Texas case of *Matter of J.K.A.* (1993), J.K.A. was charged with violating his probation by possessing an illegal weapon. He was not adjudicated delinquent on the new charge, although he could have been. The court, however, revoked his probation simply because of a valid probation program condition that he not violate the law. Possessing an illegal firearm violated the law; hence, his probation was revoked.

Juvenile Case Law on Parole Revocations

There is very little current information about juvenile parole revocation. A few of the more recent cases involving parole eligibility and/or revocation involving juveniles are reported below.

The Case of *Patuxent Institution Board of Review v. Hancock* (1993).   A juvenile, Hancock, was found to be a "defective delinquent" and was ordered committed to Patuxent Institution in Jessup, Maryland. Patuxent Institution, which holds 750 young men and 50 young women, provides various services for offenders of diverse ages. Hancock served several months in Patuxent and sought parole. His parole application was denied. On appeal, the Institutional Board of Review found that Hancock had been wrongfully denied parole and ordered Patuxent authorities to release him. The institutional paroling authorities cited numerous institutional infractions committed by Hancock and "revoked" his parole again. Because of a procedural technicality, Hancock was subsequently paroled. Essentially, he was denied the basic due process right to advance notice of the conditions he allegedly violated, and no hearing was held at which he could contest these charges. The order of parole revocation in Hancock's case was reversed and Hancock was finally paroled.

The Case of *C.D.R. v. State* (1992).   A Texas juvenile was adjudicated delinquent after being charged with aggravated sexual assault. He was placed in a facility under the direction of the Texas Youth Commission. One month before his 18th birthday, he petitioned for parole, which was denied. He was subsequently transferred to the adult Texas Department of Corrections to serve more time. The Texas Court of Appeals upheld these proceedings.

Prospective juvenile parolees are entitled to certain minimum due process rights in various states similar to those articulated in the adult case of *Morrissey v. Brewer* (1972). Similar procedures are followed in several other states (Josi and Sechrest, 1999). Despite these procedural safeguards, parole revocation hearings for juveniles are often scripted in advance (Altschuler, Armstrong, and MacKenzie, 1999).

Because the literature on juvenile parole violators is scant, it is difficult to profile them. Early research has shown, however, that those parolees who have had the longest institutional commitment lengths are also the more likely to have their parole revoked (Cavender and Knepper, 1992). This observation may be somewhat self-fulfilling, however, because the most serious offenders are given the longest sentences anyway, and they are more likely to recidivate.

A study of some magnitude was conducted by Christy Visher, Pamela Lattimore, and Richard Linster (1991). This study, involving 1,949 juveniles paroled from the California Youth Authority between July 1, 1981 and June 30, 1982, reported an 88 percent failure rate. This result is somewhat misleading, however, because a failure was any rearrest or parole revocation following parole. Only 14 percent failed because of a parole revocation. Hence, there were many rearrests, but apparently they were unsubstantiated, and these parolees were released or, if charges had been filed against them, had their cases dismissed. The 14 percent failure figure is impressive. At least for this sample of juvenile offenders, parole seemed to work for 86 percent of them, despite the failures observed by these researchers. The average length of time between one's parole and rearrest was ten months. Considering what is known about juvenile offending, most juvenile delinquents eventually "grow out of" delinquent conduct anyway as they mature. This process is also known as aging out.

SUMMARY

Juvenile delinquents commit acts that would be crimes if committed by adults. Status offenders commit acts that would not be crimes if committed by adults. Considerable variation exists among juvenile court jurisdictions. Most juvenile court jurisdictions throughout the United States deal with juveniles charged with delinquent offenses. In a minority of jurisdictions, status offenders are coprocessed with delinquent offenders. The juvenile court is a civil court. Thus, the result of a juvenile's case being presented and decided is adjudication or judgment. This adjudication is not the same as a criminal conviction. Juveniles do not acquire criminal records from juvenile court adjudications of any kind. Sometimes, if the offense warrants, juveniles may be waived, certified, or transferred to criminal courts and tried as if they were adults. A greater range of severe penalties may be imposed on those convicted of crimes in criminal courts. Most cases commenced in the juvenile justice system remain within it, and juvenile court judges have various options if offenders are adjudicated delinquent. These options include nominal, conditional, and custodial sanctions. The most frequently used option by juvenile court judges is probation. Frequently, juveniles who have been adjudicated delinquent and have recidivated at a later date will be placed on probation again. In fact, secure confinement of juveniles is considered a last resort in most juvenile court jurisdictions.

Many of the probation and parole programs for adults are emulated in the juvenile justice system. Juveniles may be placed on unconditional or conditional diversion, unconditional or conditional probation, intensive supervised probation, and with or without conditions including victim compensation or restitution, fines, community service, electronic monitoring, home confinement, and/or suggested psychological treatments or counseling. No U.S. Supreme Court case law exists governing probation and parole revocation proceedings for juveniles.

Many jurisdictions are influenced by some of the major cases decided for adult probationers and parolees facing revocation of their programs. In some instances, juvenile court judges require juvenile POs to prepare predispositional reports to assist judges in the dispositions they impose for adjudicated juveniles.

The most successful probation and parole programs for juveniles involve activities that improve their coping skills, self-images, and self-respect. Accountability is an important component of these programs as well. The Ohio Experience emphasizes community protection, offender accountability, and individualizing sanctions for specific youths. This particular program underscores the continuing importance of the *parens patriae* doctrine. Boot camps and shock probation or incarceration also seem useful for instilling youths with greater individual responsibility and accountability.

KEY TERMS

Adjudication
Adjudicatory hearing
Allegheny Academy
Alternative care cases
Automatic waivers
Boston Offender Project (BOP)
Camps
Certification
Children in need of supervision (CHINS)
Children's tribunals
Child-saver movement
Child-savers
Common law
Concurrent jurisdiction
Conditional sanctions
Demand waivers
Dependent and neglected children
Detention
Detention hearing
Direct file
Discretionary waivers
Experience programs
Foster homes
Group homes

Homeward Bound
Hope Center Wilderness Camp
Infants
Intake
Intake screening
Judicial waivers
Juvenile Court Act
Juvenile delinquents
Juvenile Diversion/Non-Custody Intake Program
Juvenile diversion program (JDP)
Juvenile intensive supervision programs (JISP)
Juvenile justice system
Juvenile offenders
Legislative waiver
Mandatory waivers
New York House of Refuge
Nominal dispositions
Ohio Experience
Once an adult/always an adult provision
Parens patriae
Persons in need of supervision (PINS)

Petitions
Predispositional reports
Presumptive waiver
Project New Pride
Ranches
Reform schools
Reverse waiver hearings
Reverse waivers
Scared Straight
Secure confinement
See Our Side (SOS) Program
Standard probation programs
Status offenders
Status offenses
Statutory exclusion
Transfer hearing
Transfers
Waiver hearing
Waiver motion
Waivers
Wilderness program
Youth-at-risk program
Youth Service Bureaus (YSBs)

QUESTIONS FOR REVIEW

1. Distinguish between delinquents and status offenders. What are several "official" definitions of delinquency? What seem to be the major criteria used in these different definitions?

2. What is the extent of juvenile court jurisdiction over children who are dependent and neglected?

3. What are some general criticisms of the deinstitutionalization of status offenses?

4. What was the significance of the following cases: (a) *Schall v. Martin,* (b) *Ex parte Crouse,* (c) *In re Gault,* (d) *In re Winship.*

5. Describe some of the major differences between criminal and juvenile courts.

6. What are waivers? What are four different types of waivers? Do waiver proceedings require a hearing? Why or why not?

7. Describe nonsecure and secure custodial sanctions. Give some examples of programs or circumstances that might portray these types of sanctions.

8. What is a predispositional report? Does it bear some resemblance to a PSI report?

9. Describe three conditional probation programs for juveniles. In your own words, describe the successfulness of each of these programs.

10. What is the Ohio Experience? How does it differ from the Boston Offender Project?

SUGGESTED READINGS

Bazemore, Gordon, and Leslie Leip (2000). "Victim Participation in the New Juvenile Court: Tracking Judicial Attitudes Toward Restorative Justice Reforms." *Justice System Journal* **21:**199–226.

Fielding, Ellen Wilson (ed.) (1999). "Centenary of the Juvenile Justice System." *Federal Probation* **63:**4–77.

Justice Research and Statistics Association (1999). *Juvenile Justice Evaluation Needs in the States: Findings of the Formula Grants Program Evaluation Needs Assessment.* Washington, DC: Justice Research and Statistics Association.

Leon, Ana M., Sophia F. Dziegielewski, and Christine Tubiak (1999). "A Program Evaluation of a Juvenile Halfway House: Considerations for Strengthening Program Components." *Evaluation and Program Planning* **22:**141–153.

O'Mahony, David (2000). "Young People, Crime, and Criminal Justice: Patterns and Prospects for the Future." *Youth and Society* **32:**60–80.

Wilson, Sandra Jo, and Mark W. Lipsey (2000). "Wilderness Challenge Programs for Delinquent Youth: A Meta-Analysis of Outcome Evaluations." *Evaluation and Program Planning* **23:**1–12.

Evaluating Programs: Balancing Service Delivery and Recidivism Considerations

CHAPTER 14

Introduction
Program Evaluation: How Do We Know Programs
    Are Effective?
    Some Recommended Outcome Measures
Balancing Program Objectives and Offender
    Needs
Recidivism Defined
    Rearrests
    Reconvictions
    Revocations of Parole or Probation
    Reincarcerations
    Technical Program Violations

Recidivist Offenders and Their Characteristics
    Avertable and Nonavertable Recidivists
    Public Policy and Recidivism
Probationers, Parolees, and Recidivism
    Probationers and Parolees Compared
    Prison versus Probation
    Curbing Recidivism
Summary
Key Terms
Questions for Review
Suggested Readings

INTRODUCTION

How do we know if community-based correctional programs for probationers and parolees work? Which ones are most effective? Do these many programs achieve their objectives, and to what degree?

This chapter is about program evaluation and recidivism. Every intervention program applied to both juveniles and adults is subject to evaluation at one time or another. Investigators want to know whether a particular program is cost-effective and whether it accomplishes its stated goals. Programs are either successful or unsuccessful. Offender-clients either "fail" or "succeed." How is the successfulness or unsuccessfulness of programs and offender-clients measured? The first part of this chapter examines the criteria conventionally used to evaluate program effectiveness. Both objective and subjective criteria are considered in this discussion.

Because of the many different kinds of offenders of various ages, numerous intervention, rehabilitation, and reintegration programs are designed to assist them

in meeting their diverse needs. Program success is subject to widely different interpretations, and many professionals use diffuse and even inconsistent criteria to evaluate whether a program's goals are attained. Because the successfulness of programs
often depends on the nature of the program clientele, some attention is given to how
clients are selected for inclusion in particular programs. Some programs engage in
creaming, a practice through which only the most low-risk and eligible offenders are
included. Thus, some bias favoring program successfulness exists at the outset. If
only the most desirable clients are included, then more favorable results will be
expected, compared with those programs that include more dangerous and higher-
risk clientele.

Recidivism is an important measure of program success or failure; therefore,
considerable attention is devoted to its description and its many varieties. Recidivism is examined in the context of both juvenile and adult probationers and
parolees. Probationer recidivism is compared with parolee recidivism to determine
significant differences, if any (Schwaner, 1998). What kinds of offenders are more
likely to recidivate, and under what types of conditions? What factors are useful in
decreasing recidivism? Recidivism seems to fluctuate among probationers and
parolees according to various program conditions. Which program conditions seem
most likely to reduce recidivism? The chapter concludes with an examination of attitudes expressed by probationers and parolees themselves about their reasons for
recidivating.

PROGRAM EVALUATION: HOW DO WE KNOW PROGRAMS ARE EFFECTIVE?

Program evaluation is the process of assessing any corrections intervention or program for the purpose of determining its effectiveness in achieving manifest goals.
Program evaluation investigates the nature of organizational intervention strategies,
counseling, interpersonal interactions, staff quality, expertise, and education and the
success or failure experiences of clients served by any program. Several examples
below illustrate what is meant by program evaluation.

Example 1.   *The rapid rise in juvenile delinquency during the late 1980s and 1990s
prompted experiments with various interventions, one of which was the use of boot
camps. Boot camps are military-like experiences designed to instill discipline, self-
worth, self-esteem, and obedience to the law within their recruits. Social scientists
believe that if juvenile delinquents are exposed to or participate in boot camps, then
their delinquency recidivism will decline.* Agreement or disagreement with this statement is irrelevant. The fact is, some researchers believe it. During the period 1992 to
1993, the National Institute of Justice experimented with three boot camp projects in
Cleveland, Ohio; Denver, Colorado; and Mobile, Alabama.

In each of the three projects, program goals were articulated and shared,
including the goals that boot camps would (1) serve as a cost-effective alternative to
institutionalization; (2) promote discipline through physical conditioning and teamwork; (3) instill moral values and a work ethic; (4) promote literacy and increase academic achievement; (5) reduce drug and alcohol abuse; (6) encourage participants to
become productive, law-abiding citizens; and (7) ensure that offenders are held
accountable for their actions. During the initial phase of the experiment, 119 youths
were admitted to the Cleveland boot camp, 76 were admitted to the Denver site, and

122 participants were admitted to the Mobile boot camp. All the sites implemented 90-day residential programs that put youths through an intensive daily regimen of military drills and discipline and physical conditioning. The sites offered rehabilitative activities, including remedial education, life skills education and counseling, and substance abuse education. A platoon structure was used in which 10 to 13 youths entered the program every 4 to 6 weeks and were expected to graduate together. On-site drill instructors, teachers, and case managers were provided. Staff had military backgrounds. Military-style uniforms were worn by all youths. An exhausting daily routine, starting at 5:30 A.M. and ending with lights out at 9 P.M., was enforced. Summary punishments were administered for minor breaches of the rules, culminating in removal from the program for the more serious offenders. A public graduation ceremony was held upon successful completion of the program.

The program evaluation consisted of several criteria. First, program costs were calculated and compared with the costs of institutionalization. Second, recidivism figures were compared for boot camp graduates and institutionalized delinquents. Third, failure rates at each site were assessed, both during and following the boot camp experience in community aftercare. Boot camp costs ranged from $66 to $75 per day per youth, whereas the costs of incarceration in institutions ranged from $99 in Ohio to $138 in Denver. From a cost-effectiveness perspective, the program was successful. The boot camps, however, graduated only about 50 percent of all participating clients. Finally, recidivism rates of clients assessed during a follow-up period in aftercare averaged 71 percent. This rate was regarded as an indication of program failure compared with traditional institutionalization (Bourque et al., 1996).

Example 2.   *Local, state, and federal officials have been concerned with various interventions that have been attempted to cut down on driving while intoxicated. The most common sanction applied to drivers convicted of DWI was probation. An electronic monitoring and home confinement program was implemented for a sample of drivers convicted of DWI in "Western County" in Pennsylvania between October 1992 and October 1993 as an experimental intervention. It was believed that if these offenders were placed in home confinement and were subject to electronic monitoring and other program conditions, their DWI recidivism would be greatly reduced. Again, whatever one believes is irrelevant.*

In this study, an experiment was planned that would place a sample of drivers convicted of DWI under house arrest and electronic monitoring for a specified period. Furthermore, these clients would be subject to the following conditions. They would have to: (1) undergo drug/alcohol treatment and/or counseling; (2) be placed on electronic monitoring and the subsequent rules and restrictions of the program; and (3) pay a fee of $8 per day to cover the cost of the monitoring, although offenders would not be excluded from participating because of indigence. Once they completed their electronic monitoring phase, they would be required to pay a $25 per month supervision fee for regular supervision. Offenders were required to have a residence and a telephone compatible with electronic monitoring. Finally, all participants were required to be employed. The program evaluation would consist of the cost-effectiveness of the electronic monitoring and house arrest compared with traditional probation supervision. A second evaluation would be made by examining recidivism rates of participants following their completion of the program.

During the period of the experiment, "Western County" collected $12,805 in supervision fees and $21,650 in fines from 600 clients under active supervision. It was estimated that confining a convicted DWI offender in the county jail would cost $42 per day. During the experiment, a total of 1,742 days of incarceration were avoided at a savings of $73,164. The collection of electronic monitoring supervision fees brought in $13,512, and monthly supervision fees generated $12,805, for a total of $99,481. Deducted from this figure was the actual cost of operating the house arrest/electronic monitoring program for one year, which amounted to $24,758. Thus, a cost savings to "Western County" amounted to $74,722. Furthermore, a follow-up of all participants in the study showed a recidivism rate of less than 2 percent. This intervention program was therefore regarded as successful (Courtright, Berg, and Mutchnick, 1997).

Example 3.   *Adult offenders who are on probation often have educational deficits. Some of them cannot read or write. Therefore, they may get into trouble again because they may not qualify for employment in which reading and writing proficiency are required. A program designed to improve the literacy levels of adult offenders on probation might decrease their recidivism rate.* Again, agreement with this point of view or argument is irrelevant. In 1987, Arizona implemented 31 different reading labs in probation departments throughout the state in an effort to improve the reading ability of adult probationers. GED courses were offered, together with remedial reading education, and Literacy, Education, and Reading Network (LEARN) labs were established. In addition, an innovative, computer-assisted literacy program developed by IBM and known as PALS was used to teach reading and writing. Adult basic education classes, which included life skills courses, GED testing, math, grammar and writing, and other subjects, were offered to adult probationers. Between 1988 and 1992, a large sample of adult probationers was selected for inclusion in the LEARN program. Probationers included ranged in age from 18 to 67. Ten variables were identified and collected on each probationer: age, how and when probation was completed, gender, race, education level, risk and needs assessment scores, types of probation supervision, length of probation, sentence, and date of sentencing. The information was collected for five groups: PALS graduates, PALS dropouts, GED graduates, GED dropouts, and a control group of probationers with characteristics similar to those who were not referred to the LEARN group. The evaluation amounted to a comparison of recidivism rates between the LEARN group who successfully graduated from the program and the dropouts. The results revealed that the PALS or LEARN graduates had a low recidivism rate of 23 percent compared with a 36 percent recidivism rate of nonparticipants. The Bureau of Justice Statistics reports that on the average, adult probationers throughout the United States have a 43 percent recidivism rate. Thus, the LEARN program was considered effective at reducing recidivism by improving one's reading ability and through graduation (Siegel, 1994).

Example 4.   *Some researchers think that if juveniles were obligated to make restitution whenever they commit crimes involving property loss to victims, this act of restitution will heighten their accountability and be an important factor in deterring them from further delinquent activity.* Whether this view is believed is irrelevant. A study conducted in Indiana from January 1989 through December 1990 involved 113 juveniles who had been adjudicated delinquent for various property offenses. These 113 juveniles were placed in a program requiring that they make restitution to their victims. They were compared with a sample of 148 juvenile delinquents who were placed on standard probation without a restitution requirement. It was believed that the restitution group would exhibit greater accountability and have lower recidivism compared with the probation-only group. The evaluation variable, recidivism, was measured according to the number and types of subsequent offenses as well as reconvictions of the successful participants during a follow-up period. The types of subsequent offenses were categorized as "felony" and "nonfelony."

Both groups of juvenile offenders were tracked through 1992 to permit an adequate follow-up period. Of the 113 restitution group participants, 32 percent recidivated during the follow-up, whereas 43 percent of the probation-only group recidivated. In addition, of the probation-only group members who recidivated, 73 percent of them committed felony offenses, whereas only 26 percent of the restitution group committed new felony offenses. Thus, it was concluded that at least for this sample of subjects, the imposition of restitution as a condition of probation was significant in reducing serious recidivism and was regarded as an important intervention (Roy, 1995a).

Some Recommended Outcome Measures

The American Probation and Parole Association (APPA) has been involved in a longitudinal investigation and survey to determine various alternative outcome measures for assessing intermediate punishment program effectiveness. The APPA Board of Directors consists of probation and parole administrators, probation and parole line staff, and representatives from various affiliate organizations (American Correctional Association, American Jail Association) throughout the United States and Canada. The APPA distributed a survey to all APPA board members and prefaced their questionnaire with the following:

> Assume that your department is going to be evaluated by an outside evaluator. The results of the evaluation will determine the level of funding for the next fiscal year. What outcome measure(s) would you want the evaluator to use in "measuring" the success of your program(s)? What outcome measure(s) would you not want the evaluator to use in the evaluation?

The survey yielded a response from 30 different board members, a response rate of 31 percent. Table 14.1 shows the relative rankings and ratings of the top 23 criteria cited by these board members as alternative outcome measures they would like to see used. The table shows that the amount of restitution collected tops the list of criteria preferred by these board members. Logically, this finding would be a direct empirical, tangible indicator of agency effectiveness. As seen in previous chapters, community-based programs are increasingly incorporating elements that heighten offender accountability, and making restitution to victims or to the community is an increasingly common program element. Employment is also a key agency goal of many community-based agencies. Thus, many board members selected number of offenders employed as another preferred indicator of agency effectiveness. Other criteria in the top five included technical violations, alcohol/drug test results, and new arrests. Possibly because agencies have more effective monitoring mechanisms in place and improved supervision styles, it is less likely for program clients to engage in technical program violations, fail in drug/alcohol test results, and be rearrested for new offenses.

When asked which measures were not preferred for program evaluation, the responding board members cited 12 program components, shown in Table 14.2.

TABLE 14.1 Alternative Outcome Measures from APPA Board of Directors Survey: Top 23

Measure	No. of Board Members Selecting Measure
Amount of restitution collected	10
Number of offenders employed	10
Technical violations	9
Alcohol/drug test results	9
New arrests	8
Fines/fees collected	7
Number completed supervision	6
Hours community service	6
Number sessions of treatment	5
Number/ratio revocations	5
Percent financial obligations collected	5
Employment stability/days employed	5
New arrests: crime type/seriousness	4
Meeting needs of offenders	4
Family stability	4
Education attainment	4
Costs/benefits/services/savings	4
Days alcohol/drug free	4
Number of treatment referrals	3
Time between technical violations	3
Marital stability	3
Wages/taxes paid	3
Compliance with court orders	3

Source: Harry N. Boone Jr., "Recommended Outcome Measures for Program Evaluation: APPA's Board of Directors Survey Results," *APPA Perspectives* **18:**19 (1994). Reprinted by permission of the American Probation and Parole Association.

The table shows that board members would at least downplay recidivism rates, revocation rates, technical violations, and new arrests as outcome measures of program effectiveness. Boone (1994b:20) said that "there was considerable confusion among the 30 respondents as to exactly what outcome measures should or should not be used to evaluate their respective programs." Ideally, more effective programs have lower recidivism rates than less effective programs. All agencies want to exhibit low rates of recidivism among their clientele. Any agency disclosing a recidivism rate of 10 percent or less would most certainly be considered for federal or private funding, because the program would be demonstrably successful. Yet such low recidivism rates are hard to obtain in most agencies. Again, an informal standard of 30 percent has existed for several decades. This 30 percent standard suggests that programs with recidivism rates 30 percent or less are successful programs, whereas those with rates above 30 percent are not successful. Some observers use the word *failure* to describe such programs.

In many respects, it is unfair to label any particular program as a failure or a success on the basis of demonstrated client recidivism rates (Seiter, 2000). Every agency deals with a different breed of offender: sex offenders, property offenders, chronic delinquents, persistent property offenders, shoplifters, robbers, and thieves.

TABLE 14.2 Outcome Measures Not to Use to Measure Program Success

Measure	No. of Board Members Selecting Measure
Recidivism	8
Revocation rates	6
Technical violations	5
New arrests	4
Single measure	2
Public/media perception	2
New conviction	2
Number of positive drug tests	2
Cost of services/efficiency	2
Number of contacts	2
Number of clients	2
Client evaluation	2

Source: Harry N. Boone Jr., "Recommended Outcome Measures for Program Evaluation: APPA's Board of Directors Survey Results," *APPA Perspectives* **18**:20 (1994). Reprinted by permission of the American Probation and Parole Association.

For instance, Deborah Wilson and Gennaro Vito (1990) describe samples of persistent felony offenders they investigated in Kentucky. Designing intervention programs that will decrease the chronicity of such offenders is probably impossible, because these offenders persist in their offending, no matter what types of intervention strategies are applied. Also, different time lengths are used to gauge recidivism. Some standards are one year following one's program commencement, whereas other standards are two or three years. Some standards are even shorter, as short as three or six months. With such different time dimensions over which to determine recidivism of clientele, a meaningful discussion of recidivism in any general sense is of little or no consequence when assessing the merits and weaknesses of particular programs.

Another factor is that many program and agency personnel wish to include those offenders most likely to succeed in those programs. These clients, however, may not be the ones who need the particular program intervention. Ideally, if jail- or prison-bound offenders, and both high- and low-risk types, are program targets, then any program that reduces recidivism among these offenders will deserve more careful consideration and should be given greater funding priority. Many community-based intervention programs, however, are designed to work with low-risk offenders as a means of keeping them integrated in their communities. These persons are usually first-offenders with little likelihood of reoffending. Unfortunately, net-widening occurs with the establishment of such programs (Kassebaum, Davidson-Coronado, and Silverio, 1999). The effect is that many persons who would be placed on standard probation or whose cases might otherwise be dismissed as a matter of prosecutorial priority may find their way into community programs designed to keep them from reentering the criminal justice system. Thus, some persons are served by programs but do not need to be in these programs. Also, programs that select only those offenders most likely to succeed—offenders with jobs, stable families, good education, middle-class social standing, first-offenders, low-risk offenders—actually create a clientele milieu with a predictably low "failure rate." This practice is called creaming.

BOX 14.1   **A Self-Fulfilling Prophecy for Successfulness?**

On the Notion of Creaming

Probably every community-based corrections program has eligibility criteria used for selecting prospective clientele from among the offender population. Many programs regarded as "successful" in fulfilling their objectives and aims are guilty of selecting only the most success-prone clients, such as low-risk offenders and first-offenders. Particular types of offenders are deliberately excluded. For instance, some programs declare that if offenders have a history of violent conduct, are mentally ill or psychologically disturbed, or are sex offenders, then they will be ineligible for inclusion in those programs. If only the most problem-free offenders are selected from the jail- or prison-bound offender population for probation or placement in a community-based correctional program, then the program effectiveness will be enhanced simply because a higher quality of clientele is being included. Those who are unlikely to succeed in these programs are systematically excluded. This practice is called creaming.

The term *creaming* no doubt derives from dairying, when the cream is skimmed from fresh milk. In a sense, the "cream of the crop" of eligible offenders is herded into intervention programs. Agency heads can later say, "See, we have a successful program. Look at our low rates of recidivism among our clients." Certainly they have low recidivism rates: they have excluded those least likely to succeed, probably the very offenders that need the intervention programs they are capable of providing. The New Jersey ISP program for parolees is an example of creaming. This program had a strict client selection process consisting of several screening stages. Final decisions on which applicants were accepted were made by a resentencing panel of Superior Court judges. Reasons for rejecting applicants included first- and second-degree felonies, too many prior felony convictions, prior crimes of violence, and applicant reluctance to comply with ISP provisions. Thus, the New Jersey program was targeted for low-risk offenders with the least likelihood of recidivating. Not unexpectedly, this program reported recidivism rates of less than 20 percent. Thus, a type of self-fulfilling prophecy is created, wherein the program will succeed because everything has been done to enhance the success of the program, including a careful screening of program applicants. The true test of any intervention program is whether it can make a difference for the hard-core offender aggregate. Short of permanently incarcerating all hard-core offenders, one important goal of community-based intervention programs should be to reintegrate unreintegratable offenders into their communities with some measure of success. Not many community-based corrections organizations are willing to implement programs that cater to the least successful clientele pool.

BALANCING PROGRAM OBJECTIVES AND OFFENDER NEEDS

The major objectives of community-based probation and parole programs for juveniles and adults are summarized as follows:

1. Facilitating offender reintegration
2. Continuing offender punishment
3. Heightening offender accountability
4. Ensuring community protection or safety
5. Promoting offender rehabilitation
6. Improving offender skills and coping mechanisms

7. Resolving offender social and psychological problems
8. Alleviating jail and prison overcrowding
9. Monitoring offender behaviors
10. Reducing offender chemical dependencies
11. Collecting fines, restitution payments, and other fees
12. Enforcing the law, including community service orders
13. Employing support personnel, corrections workers, and professionals/paraprofessionals
14. Producing low rates of recidivism among agency clientele
15. Coordinating and networking agency tasks and functions with other community agencies
16. Justifying agency budget

This list is not exhaustive. Many functions or objectives overlap. Agencies are multifaceted, striving to achieve diverse goals or aims. Many of these organizational aims are mentioned by Joan Petersilia and Susan Turner (1993), who note the following agency goals with accompanying performance indicators:

1. Assessing offender's suitability for placement (performance indicators = accuracy and completeness of PSI reports, timeliness of revocation and termination hearings, validity of classification/prediction instrument, percent of offenders receiving recommended sentence or violation action, and percent of offenders recommended for community who violate)
2. Enforcing court-ordered sanctions (performance indicators = number of arrests and technical violations during supervision, percent of ordered payments collected, number of hours/days performed community service, number of favorable discharges, numbers of days employed in vocational education or school, and drug-free and/or alcohol-free days during supervision)
3. Protecting the community (performance indicators = number and type of supervision contacts, number and type of arrests during supervision; number and type of technical violations during supervision, and number of absconders during supervision)
4. Assisting offenders to change (performance indicators = number of times attending treatment/work programming, employment during supervision, number of arrests and/or technical violations during supervision, number drug-free and/or alcohol free days during supervision, and attitude change)
5. Restoring crime victims (performance indicators = payment of restitution and extent of victim satisfaction with service and department)

Thus, these programs exist for a variety of reasons. Some are totally unrelated to offender needs, such as employment of agency personnel and justifying the agency budget. It is important to coincide agency processes with offender needs as a way of demonstrating program effectiveness. Petersilia and Turner (1993) have reduced almost all these agency functions to things that can be counted: the amount of collected fine payments and restitution, numbers of days alcohol-free or drug-free, numbers of rearrests, numbers of favorable discharges, or numbers of days employed. Many intangibles, however, cannot be counted. For instance, it is not known whether offender familial relations are actually improving. The number of 911 calls, however, for reports of spousal abuse or other forms of familial conflict for various offender-clients may be counted. This finding might be a negative gauge of positive family functioning. Also, it is not known whether true psychological changes are occurring within any particular offender-client, only that these offender-clients have been provided with the means for change. Nor is it known for sure whether changes actually occur in designated or targeted program areas.

When PSI reports are prepared for any offender, POs make a point of identifying problem areas, identified as offender needs, that could or should be addressed by subsequent programming. An array of risk-needs instruments are available to assess both an offender's dangerousness and the special needs they might exhibit. When inmates are classified upon entry into jails or prisons, they are usually assessed with either self-administered or other types of paper-and-pencil tests or devices that seek to determine their most appropriate placement, whether it is a particular custody level or a rehabilitation/educational/vocational/counseling program. In Virginia, for instance, inmates with low reading levels are tracked to special educational classes designed to improve their literacy levels (Hawk et al., 1993). It is logical to assume that if the literacy levels of inmates can be improved, then their chances for employment are also improved. Completing job application forms requires a minimum amount of literacy, for example. Offenders with psychological or social adjustment problems may benefit from individual or group therapy or various forms of sensitivity training.

What about alcohol or drug usage? In prison, there is a low likelihood that alcoholism or drug dependency will continue to be problematic for inmates. Inmates have access to drugs in most prisons or jails, but what can be done now to help offenders cope with their community environment when they are subsequently released from prison? If alcohol or drug dependencies contributed to their crimes, then what coping mechanisms can be provided these offenders while they are institutionalized? Classes are provided to inmates with these kinds of problems (identifiable need areas), but do these classes prevent subsequent recurrences of alcohol and drug dependency? Every day, parole boards in most jurisdictions face offenders who are chronic recidivists with drug and alcohol dependencies. The board members ask prospective parolees, "Did you participate in Alcoholics Anonymous while in prison?" Prospective parolee: "Yes." Parole board: "Yet you have been convicted of a new crime, and when you were caught, you were drunk. What happened?" Prospective parolee: "I got in with the wrong crowd" or "I had a setback" or "I had some personal problems" or "I just couldn't pass up a drink" or "I went along with the crowd for old time's sake." Some offenders never escape the problems that contributed to their criminal activity, no matter how much training, coursework, therapy, or counseling they receive.

Any community-based corrections program attempts to provide useful interventions that will assist offender-clients in various ways. Volunteers and paraprofessionals assist offender-clients in filling out job application forms, in reading programs, or in other reintegrative or rehabilitative activities. Meeting diverse offender needs is viewed as a primary way of reducing or eliminating recidivism, and recidivism is probably the most direct way of measuring program effectiveness, despite other program components, aims, or alternative outcome measures.

RECIDIVISM DEFINED

A conceptual Tower of Babel exists regarding recidivism. Numerous investigations of this phenomenon have been conducted, although no consensus exists about the meaning of the term. Criminologists and other observers can recite lengthy lists of characteristics that describe recidivists, but doing so and using those characteristics as effective predictors of recidivism are two different matters. For example, if a parole board uses a salient factor score to predict an offender's degree of success on parole, some inmates will be refused parole because their scores suggest that they are poor risks. At the same time, other inmate scores may indicate good risks. The poor risks are denied parole, whereas the good risks are granted it. Among the poor risks, however, are inmates who will never recidivate, and among the good risks (who eventually become parolees) are serious recidivists. Parole boards are interested in minimizing the frequency of both false positives and false negatives. When a false positive is denied parole, certain moral, ethical, and legal issues are raised about continuing to confine otherwise harmless persons. When a false negative is granted parole and commits a new, serious offense, the public is outraged, the parole board is embarrassed, and the integrity of test developers and the validity of prediction instruments are called into question. Judges who impose probation instead of incarceration or incarceration instead of probation are subject to similar attacks on similar grounds. Numerical scales are often used as more objective criteria for probation or parole decision making. It is not necessarily true that these scales are superior to personal judgments by judges or parole boards, but references to numbers seem to objectify early-release or probation-granting decisions compared with visual appraisals of offenders and subjective interpretations of their backgrounds contained in PSI reports. Several problems have been identified relating to recidivism and its measurement. A brief listing of some of the more common problems is as follows:

1. The time interval between commencing a probation or parole program and recidivating is different from one study to the next. Some studies use six months, whereas others use one year, two years, or five years (Boone, 1994a:13; Langan and Cunniff, 1992; Smith and Akers, 1993).

2. There are at least 14 different meanings of recidivism (Maltz, 1984). Comparing one definition of recidivism with another is like comparing apples with oranges.

3. Recidivism is often dichotomized rather than gradated. Thus, people either recidivate or they do not recidivate. No variation exists to allow for degrees of seriousness of reoffending of any type (Boone, 1994a:13).

4. Recidivism rates are influenced by multiple factors, such as the intensity of supervised probation or parole, the numbers of face-to-face visits between POs and their clients, and even the rate of prison construction (Ekland-Olson and Kelly, 1993; Kelly and Ekland-Olson, 1991).

5. Recidivism rates may be indicative of program failures rather than client failures (Waldo and Griswold, 1979).

6. Recidivism only accounts for official rule or law violations; self-reported information indicates that higher rates of recidivism may actually exist compared with those that are subsequently reported and recorded (Waldo and Griswold, 1979).

7. Considerable client variation exists as well as numerous programmatic variations. Depending on the client population under investigation, recidivism is more or less significant.

8. Policy shifts in local and state governments may change how recidivism is used or defined as well as the amount of recidivism observed in given jurisdictions (Maltz and McCleary, 1977).

One knows, or at least one thinks he or she knows, that recidivists tend to be male, black, younger, less educated, and have lengthy prior records. In fact, having a lengthy prior record appears to be most consistently related to recidivism. There-fore, should it be official judicial or parole board policy not to grant probation or parole to younger, less educated, black males with lengthy prior records? The answer is no; these aggregate characteristics do not easily lend themselves to individ-ualized probation or parole decision making.

One continuing problem is that while these and other characteristics describe the general category of recidivists (whomever they may be), they are also found among many nonrecidivists. Thus, based on relevant information about offenders, prediction measures must be devised and tested to improve their validity. A related problem is determining whether recidivism has occurred. Therefore, some degree of agreement needs to be established concerning what does and does not mean recidivism.

Existing measures of recidivism complicate rather than simplify its definition. Because probation or parole program failures and successes are measured by recidi-vism rates, it is important to pay attention to how recidivism is conceptualized in the research literature. A general standard has emerged among professionals that a fail-ure rate above 30 percent means that a probation or parole program is ineffective, but in what sense? Reducing crime? Rehabilitating offenders? Both?

Recidivism means program failure, or does it? A wide variety of probation and parole programs is available to the courts and corrections officials for many differ-ent kinds of offenders. One common problem faced by all programs is that observers have trouble matching the right programs with the right clientele. There is much descriptive information about recidivists. Numerous evaluation studies are con-ducted annually of various offender programs, and virtually all strategies for dealing with offenders are examined and reexamined. No matter the cure proposed, the ill-ness remains. Treatments are rarely pure, however, and therefore their evaluations are necessarily complicated. Probationers or parolees who violate one or more terms of their probation or parole, regardless of the type of program examined, are considered recidivists. Yet, as we have seen, recidivism has various meanings. It may be more helpful if we distinguish recidivists according to a graduated scale of the seriousness of the recidivism observed, and whether it is a technical program viola-tion or an acutal crime.

Barry Nidorf, chief probation officer for Los Angeles County, takes issue with using recidivism as a measure of program failure (Petersilia, 1987a:89). He says that if rehabilitation is the probation or parole program goal, then recidivism rates seem appropriate measures of program success or failure. If control and community protec-tion are [program] goals, however, then a success might be viewed as the identification and quick revocation of persons who are committing crimes. After all, the police are in the business of surveillance and control, and they judge an arrest a success, whereas others deem it a failure. If community safety is the primary goal, then perhaps an arrest and revocation should be seen as a success and not a failure. Nidorf's argument is per-suasive in that persons should consider *how* they wish program success or failure to be evaluated. Recidivism seems relevant when one is interested in the rehabilitative value of programs, but many programs involving intensive supervision of parolees and probationers seem focused primarily on crime control (Kronick, Lambert, and Lam-bert (1998). Some of the different ways of operationalizing recidivism include:

1. Rearrest
2. Parole or probation revocation or unsatisfactory termination
3. Technical parole or probation rule violations

4. Conviction for a new offense while on parole or probation

5. Return to prison

6. Having a prior record and being rearrested for a new offense

7. Having a prior record and being convicted for a new offense

8. Any new commitment to a jail or prison for 60 days or more

9. Presence of a new sentence exceeding one year for any offense committed during a five-year parole follow-up

10. Return of released offenders to custody of state correctional authorities

11. Return to jail

12. Reincarceration

13. The use of drugs or alcohol by former drug or alcohol abusers

14. Failure to complete educational or vocational/technical course or courses in or out of prison/jail custody

The most commonly used conceptualizations include rearrests, reconvictions, revocations of parole or probation, reincarcerations, and technical program violations (Maltz, 1984).

Rearrests

As a measure of recidivism, **rearrest** is frequently used in evaluation studies of parole/probation program effectiveness, although rearrests are highly misleading (Marciniak, 2000). The most obvious flaw is that it is uncertain whether offenders have actually committed new offenses. Sometimes, if a crime has been committed in the neighborhood where particular clients are residing in a halfway house, *and* if the crime is similar in nature to the crime(s) for which the ex-offenders were previously convicted, then detectives and police may look up the offenders and interview them. Because offender associations with police authorities are inherently strained anyway, it is likely that police would interpret an offender's nervousness as a sign of guilt (Steiner, Cauffman, and Duxbury, 1999). Thus, the offender might be subject to rearrest based on the suspicions of officers. The crucial element is whether the officers have probable cause to justify the client's arrest. The totality of circumstances may be such that officers may in good faith believe that they have reasonable suspicion that the client has committed a crime or has guilty knowledge (Lucker et al., (1997). They have wide discretion to question ex-offenders in an effort to learn more about the crime and the potential culpability of those they interview. In New York, for instance, whenever an inmate is granted parole, the supervising PO brings the parolee's fingerprints and criminal record to the local police precinct in which the offender resides. Thus, police are notified of the parolee's return to the community. Constitutional safeguards exist, of course, to protect all citizens from unreasonable arrests by police. Yet law enforcement officers find it relatively easy to justify their actions to the court when dealing with former offenders and parolees, even where the constitutional rights of ex-offenders have been infringed (Stanz and Tewksbury, 2000).

Another flaw associated with using rearrests to measure recidivism is that ex-offenders may be released after police determine that they are not likely suspects (Orchowsky, Merritt, and Browning, 1994). A rearrest, however, is interpreted as recidivism by some researchers, which means program failure. Rearrested offenders are not necessarily taken to jail or returned to prison; they may continue in their present probation or parole programs. Of course, it is also possible that the ex-offender did, indeed, commit a new crime, but that must be proved beyond a reasonable doubt in a court of law. Some jurisdictions use the preponderance of evidence standard for probation/parole revocations. This standard is less stringent than the beyond-a-reasonable-doubt standard.

In New York, for instance, many probationers/parolees adjourn their revocation hearings pending the outcome of their court cases. Being acquitted of criminal charges obviously affects their probation/parole revocation process favorably. If the result of a trial is a conviction for the probationer/parolee, then a revocation hearing on the violation will not be conducted; a certificate of disposition would suffice as evidence of a conviction and sentence. Not all parolees or probationers who are rearrested for new crimes are prosecuted for those crimes, however: they may instead be sent to prison. Due to the *Morrissey v. Brewer* (1972) decision, though, two hearings (i.e., one to determine probable cause and the other an actual revocation proceeding) are required before the paroling authority can summarily revoke parole.

Reconvictions

Reconviction for a new offense is probably the most reliable indicator of recidivism as well as the most valid definition of it (Breckenridge et al., 2000). Reconviction represents that at least one new crime has been committed by an offender while on probation or parole, and the court has determined offender guilt beyond a reasonable doubt. Arguably, some observers counter by saying that any failure to observe probation or parole conditions or that placing oneself in a position of increasing the likelihood of arrest (e.g., violating curfew or associating with other offenders) is evidence that offender rehabilitation has not occurred. If crime control is of primary importance to those involved with probationers and parolees, however, then this argument fails to hold (Pratt, 2000).

In a well-publicized study conducted by the **Rand Corporation**, approximately 16,500 men in 17 of California's largest counties were sentenced to either prison or probation (Petersilia et al., 1985:vi). Of these 16,500 men, a subsample of 1,672 felony probationers sentenced in Los Angeles and Alameda Counties were tracked by researchers for 40 months, with recordings made of arrests, filings, convictions, and incarcerations. During the 40-month follow-up period, researchers found that 65 percent of the probationers (1,087) were rearrested and 51 percent (853) were reconvicted for one or more new offenses. Using the violent-nonviolent crime distinction, however, most (82 percent) of these new convictions involved nonviolent crimes (e.g., burglary and larceny). Rand researchers also found that 34 percent (568) were reincarcerated. Interestingly, 285 reconvictions (17 percent) resulted in a continuation of probation. Many of the reconvictions were for misdemeanor offenses, and PSI report recommendations favored probation being continued.

Revocations of Parole or Probation

A **revocation** of parole or probation means that parolees or probationers have violated one or more of the conditions associated with their supervision status (Jones and Lacey, 2000). These conditions may be as harmless as missing a 10:00 P.M. curfew by five minutes or as serious as committing and being convicted of a new felony. POs have some discretionary authority when technical program violations are involved. They may overlook or report these incidents. If the incident is a rearrest, then the discretion passes to others such as arresting officers and prosecutors or is at least "shared." If interpersonal relations between clients and POs have become strained, then the PO may exaggerate the violation, regardless of how minor it may be.

Many factors, including prison or jail overcrowding, influence a parole or probation revocation decision. The seriousness of the violation is also considered. A third factor is the recommendation of the PO. The main problem with a technical violation of parole or probation, however, is that it is often not related to crime of any kind. Therefore, a revocation based solely on technical criteria is irrelevant as a crime control strategy, unless it can be demonstrated empirically that failure to revoke would have resulted in a new crime being committed. In addition, most, if not all, observers are not prepared to make such assertions at present. A revocation of probation or parole does not necessarily mean a return to prison or jail, however. Depending on the grounds for the revocation and other factors, an offender may be placed on a probation or parole program with a higher control level. For this reason, revocations of probation and parole cannot be equated directly with reincarceration.

Reincarcerations

The use of **reincarceration** as a measure of recidivism is as misleading as counting the numbers of rearrests and revocations among probationers and parolees (Joo, 1993). Reincarceration does not specify the type of incarceration. After probation is revoked, a probationer may be placed in a state or federal prison. After a federal parolee's status has been revoked, the parolee may be placed in a city or county jail for a short period rather than be returned to the original federal prison. The most frequent usages of recidivism are rearrests, reconvictions, and reincarcerations, although many other meanings have been given it. Arguably, it seems that the most relevant connotation applied to recidivism is a new conviction for a criminal offense as opposed to a simple rearrest or parole revocation for a technical program violation, both of which might be grounds for reincarceration. Reincarceration as a measure of recidivism is unreliable as well because it fails to distinguish between the true law breaker and the technical rule violator.

Technical Program Violations

Technical program violations include curfew violation, failing a drug or alcohol urinalysis, failing to report employment or unemployment, failing to check in with the PO, failing to file a monthly status report in a timely way, or missing a group therapy meeting. Technical program violations are not crimes, but they are enforceable, legitimate conditions of probation or parole. Failure to comply with one or more of these program requirements (e.g., making restitution to victims, performing so many hours of community service) may be the basis for a possible probation or parole revocation action. Technical program violations have been used in more than a few studies as a measure of recidivism (Stanz and Tewksbury, 2000).

Although used as recidivism measures, technical program violations are not particularly the best indicators (California Department of the Youth Authority,

1997). The most frequently used measures of recidivism are reconvictions, reincarcerations, rearrests, and probation/parole revocations, probably in that order. Harry Boone (1994a) has offered some suggestions to clarify the use of recidivism in program evaluation and research:

1. Standardize the definition of recidivism.
2. Discourage the use of recidivism as the only outcome measure for community corrections programs.
3. Define alternative outcome measures for the evaluation of community corrections programs.
4. Educate interested stakeholders, including the general public, on the alternative measures.
5. Encourage researchers, evaluators, and agency personnel to use appropriate outcome measures to evaluate program success/failure. (Boone, 1994a:17)

It is unlikely that Boone's first two suggestions will ever be implemented; there is simply too much variety among community corrections programs. Too many different vested interests have a stake in seeing recidivism conceptualized in different ways to fit neatly into particular funding priorities by showing program "successes." The public as well as stakeholders definitely need to be educated concerning various ways of measuring agency success or effectiveness. It is true that recidivism is not the only way successfulness or effectiveness should be measured. Boone's last three suggestions suggest both short- and long-range planning to allow for testing alternative outcome measures of program accomplishments.

RECIDIVIST OFFENDERS AND THEIR CHARACTERISTICS

A nationwide survey of 153,465 male felony offenders admitted to state prisons in 1979 was conducted and sponsored by the Bureau of Justice Statistics (Greenfeld, 1985). Of these offenders, 94,134, or 61.3 percent, had been incarcerated previously in either a state prison (58.7 percent), jail (28.4 percent), juvenile detention (9.5 percent), or federal/military facilities (3.4 percent). First-offenders accounted for 38.7 percent or 59,331 new prison admissions.

Avertable and Nonavertable Recidivists

One of most innovative aspects of the study was the classification of recidivists with prior records of incarceration into avertable recidivists and nonavertable recidivists. **Avertable recidivists** are offenders who would have still been in prison serving their original sentences in full at the time they were confined in 1979 for committing new offenses. **Nonavertable recidivists** are offenders whose prior sentences would not have affected the commission of new crimes. Examples of avertable and nonavertable recidivists using more recent sentencing periods are as follows. Suppose that John Doe is a new 1995 prison admission. He was previously incarcerated in 1990 for armed robbery and was given a 2- to 15-year sentence in a state prison. The parole board released Doe in 1993, whereupon he committed several burglaries. He was apprehended by police and eventually convicted of burglary in 1995. Had he still been in prison serving his entire 15-year sentence, the burglaries he committed never would have occurred. Doe is called an avertable recidivist, because his crimes occurred within the maximum range of his original sentence (e.g., 1990–2005).

John Doe's sister, Jane, was convicted in 1991 of vehicular theft and was sentenced to three years. She served her time and was eventually released. Jane Doe obeyed the law for several years, but in 1999, she was arrested for and convicted of stealing another automobile. Because she had already served the maximum sentence of three years for vehicular theft from 1991 to 1994, the maximum range of her original sentence no longer applied, so she is classified as a nonavertable recidivist. Both she and her brother, John, are recidivists, because they are criminal offenders who have been convicted of previous crimes, but John's new crimes may have been averted had he been forced to serve his maximum sentence. Of course, the possibility exists that when John finally served the maximum 15-year sentence for armed robbery, he could commit new crimes and therefore be classified as a nonavertable recidivist like his sister.

Nonavertable recidivists tend to account for substantially higher percentages of crimes compared with avertable recidivists in virtually every crime category. Second, nonavertable recidivists compared with first-timers account for substantially smaller percentages of violent crimes and drug offenses but somewhat higher percentages of property crimes, with few exceptions. The percent of offenses under the avertable recidivists category theoretically represents the proportion of crimes that would not have been committed by these offenders had they been obligated to serve out their entire sentences.

The work of Alfred Miranne and Michael Geerken (1991) is significant here. These investigators tested a seven-item scale devised by Peter Greenwood at the Rand Corporation (Chaiken and Chaiken, 1982; Greenwood, 1982). This scale purportedly differentiated between high- and low-rate offenders on the basis of their responses to seven items on a self-report instrument. The Miranne-Geerken study used a similar, but more elaborate, form of the original Greenwood instrument and obtained self-reports from 200 convicted inmates at facilities operated by the Orleans (Louisiana) Parish Criminal Sheriff in New Orleans. Essentially, their findings were similar to Greenwood's. High-rate and low-rate offenders could be identified, although the findings were inconclusive to the extent that a change in public policy about selective incapacitation could not be substantiated. Miranne and Geerken do highlight an important consideration, however. They note that "if high-rate offenders could be accurately identified and distinguished from low-rate offenders, sentencing the former to a longer period of incarceration than the latter could possibly increase cost-effectiveness" and conceivably lower the crime rate by incarcerating the high-rate offenders for longer periods (Miranne and Geerken, 1991:514).

Public Policy and Recidivism

State legislators and policy makers have seized results such as these as foundations for arguments that mandatory and/or determinate sentencing and more rigorous parole criteria ought to be employed. In view of the sentencing reforms enacted by various states and current trends, these figures have apparently been persuasive or at least influential in changing sentencing policies and parole criteria.

The study conducted by the Bureau of Justice Statistics is one of the larger surveys of recidivists and their characteristics. Each year, though, new waves of offenders enter jails and prisons. The profile changes, probably daily. Yet some general patterns emerge, not only from this analysis but from other research as well. According to the survey, using reconviction as an indicator of an adult recidivist, recidivists appear to share the following characteristics:

1. Recidivists tend to be male.
2. Recidivists tend to be younger (under 30), and recidivism declines with advancing age.
3. Recidivists tend to have an educational level equivalent to high school or less.
4. Recidivists tend to have lengthy records of arrests and/or convictions.
5. Recidivists tend to be under no correctional supervision when committing new offenses.
6. Recidivists tend to have a record of juvenile offenses.
7. Recidivists tend to commit crimes similar to those for which they were convicted previously.
8. Recidivists tend to have alcohol or drug dependency problems associated with the commission of new offenses.
9. Recidivists tend not to commit progressively serious offenses compared with their prior records.
10. Recidivists tend to be unmarried, widowed, or divorced.
11. Recidivists tend to be employed, either full-time or part-time, when committing new offenses.

Again, these characteristics considered singly or in any combination make predictions of dangerousness or public risk difficult at best. Parole boards might use such supplemental information when interviewing prospective parolees. Judges might consider such information when deciding the appropriate sentence for a convicted offender. The odds favor future offender behaviors consistent with previous offender behaviors. The odds increase as the number of characteristics associated with recidivists increases. Yet the certainty of recidivism for any specific offender can never be predicted in any absolute sense. Prediction schemes seem more effective when large numbers of offenders sharing similar characteristics are aggregated, but parole boards and judges make decisions about individual offenders, not groups of them.

PROBATIONERS, PAROLEES, AND RECIDIVISM

The immense interest of states in sentencing reforms directed away from rehabilitation and toward justice with greater certainty of punishment stems, in part, from public dissatisfaction with how the courts and corrections have dealt with offenders in recent decades. Recidivism spells failure to many citizens, and judicial leniency in sentencing, real or imagined, has contributed to a backlash of sorts. This backlash is similar to the public reaction to John Hinckley's acquittal on charges that he attempted to assassinate President Ronald Reagan on the grounds that he was insane at the time. The insanity defense was quickly abolished in several states and was vastly overhauled in others, even though the insanity defense is used in fewer than 1 percent of all criminal prosecutions and is successfully used in only a small fraction of those cases.

Alarming statistics stimulate public concern about parole and probation programs. The U.S. Department of Justice says that 65 percent of released prisoners will return to prison within two years, and most of these returns will occur within one year from the time of release. Parole may hold down prison populations, but there may be a trade-off through increased street crime (Petersilia, 1987a:vi). Greater certainty of incarceration coupled with longer terms of confinement for law violators are advanced by reformers as solutions for reducing and controlling crime. Research, however, has never demonstrated conclusively that longer prison sentences make ex-offenders less likely to commit new crimes. In view of public sentiment favoring longer prison sentences for offenders, it may be concluded that the primary goal achieved by longer incarcerative sentences is incapacitation and control rather than deterrence. Getting tough on crime is best illustrated to the public by imposing harsher and longer sentences on convicted offenders. Again, the deterrent value of lengthy incarceration is questionable.

Probationers and Parolees Compared

Few studies have actually directly compared probationers with parolees regarding their recidivism. As has been seen, there is an abundance of research about recidivists and their characteristics, but few investigators have focused on probationers and parolees simultaneously to see whether two reasonably matched sets of offenders differ in their recidivism rates and other related characteristics. Rand Corporation researchers, however, used an existing database of 16,500 men convicted of felonies in several California counties in 1980 to compare probationers and parolees regarding their recidivism (Petersilia, Turner, and Peterson, 1986). The Rand offender database consisted of persons convicted of robbery, assault, burglary, larceny/theft, forgery, and drug sale/possession, crimes selected because offenders convicted of them may be sentenced to either prison or probation. Offenders were compared according to age, race, gender, employment, juvenile/adult criminal history, and several other salient factors. Eventually, 511 probationers and 511 parolees were roughly matched according to several criteria. The probationers tended to be more serious probationers than probationers in general, whereas the parolees were among the least serious offenders imprisoned. In short, Rand researchers selected the least serious offenders from the more serious offending group and the most serious offenders from less serious offending group. On this basis, Rand researchers argued that the two offender samples were generally comparable in terms of their offense seriousness (Petersilia, Turner, and Peterson, 1986:12).

This study examined more dimensions of offender behaviors than are reported here. Also, the Rand researchers found that parolees recidivated more quickly compared with probationers. These investigators used rearrests, charges filed, reconvictions, and reincarceration as various recidivism dimensions. In virtually every category, parolees had higher recidivism scores than probationers, although these differences were not that dramatic for all categories. For example, 19 percent of the probationer sample was incarcerated in prison compared with 26 percent of the parolees. Another comparison showed 72 percent of the parolees were rearrested compared with 63 percent of the probationers.

The Rand researchers concluded that at least for their sample, parolees had higher recidivism rates than probationers, although their new crimes were not more serious. These investigators also found little influence of incarceration on recidivism. Interestingly, incarceration tended to *increase* recidivism rates slightly, especially for property offenders who historically have higher recidivism rates anyway. Finally, serving longer prison terms did not significantly influence the rate of recidivism for most offense categories, although a slight decrease in recidivism occurred with longer prison terms.

These findings are consistent with a study sponsored by the U.S. Department of Justice. Although between 1979 and 1986 average lengths of regular prison sentences increased by 32 percent, the rate of parole revocations for both technical violations and major crimes doubled for parolees during the same period. Of more than 20,000 federal offenders leaving probation and parole between July 1, 1985 and June 30, 1986, more than one in five had committed a new crime or violated the technical conditions of their release. Again, incarceration seemed to make little difference. When it did make a difference, it only seemed to increase recidivism rates (Abt Associates, Inc., 1987:2).

Prison versus Probation

The question was raised in the Rand study about whether the greater cost of confinement in jail or prison was worth the small differences in recidivism rates observed between prisoners and probationers. That study demonstrated that probation/parole programs costs are about half the costs of incarceration. For example, average costs per offender on probation in California for the samples studied were $11,600 compared with $23,400 for incarcerated offenders (Petersilia, Turner, and Peterson, 1986:34).

The Rand researchers concluded that

1. Public safety would clearly benefit from somehow incapacitating a larger proportion of the felons represented in the study's matched sample of prisoners and felony probationers.
2. Building more prisons can move toward accomplishing this goal, but cannot fully realize it.
3. Relying on only one form of incapacitation necessarily limits society's ability to respond to the overall crime problem. In addition to imprisonment, other means of incapacitating felony offenders may be necessary to control the threat of serious crimes from felony offenders released to the community from prison and on probation. (Petersilia, Turner, and Peterson, 1986:37)

Curbing Recidivism

Strategies for decreasing recidivism rates include incarceration, intensive supervised probation/parole, and a wide range of intermediate punishments already discussed, including electronic monitoring, house arrest, and community-based treatment programs. The more intensive monitoring an offender receives, the less the recidivism, although some intensively supervised offenders recidivate. The treatment or rehabilitation orientation is not a bad one, although many observers think that many established treatment programs do not fulfill their stated goals. That 50 percent or more of all offenders, incarcerated or on probation, will recidivate in the future at some unspecified time is evidence of the rehabilitative failure of any program, including incarceration. One influential but conservative voice favoring incapacitation, James

Q. Wilson, argues that although imprisonment may not rehabilitate offenders, it does keep them off the streets away from the general public, which may be the most effective means of crime control (D. Wilson, 1985). Another controversial solution recommended by some observers is selective incapacitation.

A report prepared by the National Council on Crime and Delinquency (NCCD) examined parolee recidivism in California and found that parolee failures increased from 23 percent in 1975 to 53 percent in 1983 (Austin, 1987). This report yields findings similar to those presented by Rand researchers. Administrative parole revocations have jumped from 5 to 35 percent since 1975, but the proportion of parolees being returned for new felonies committed while on parole increased by only 5 percent. Parolee failures do not seem related to program failures, however; rather, external and administrative factors appear largely to blame. The following factors contribute significantly to the growing numbers of administrative parole revocations:

1. Declining levels of financial assistance and narcotic treatment resources for parolees
2. Increases in parole supervision caseloads
3. A shift in public and law enforcement attitudes regarding parolees and law violators in general
4. Jail overcrowding
5. A more efficient law enforcement/parole supervision system (Austin, 1987)

Thus, recidivism rates might be curbed by more effective implementation of probation/parole program goals, smaller caseloads for POs (probably resulting in more frequent contact with probationer or parolee clients), and increasing the capacity of delivery systems (i.e., greater funding) to meet the specialized needs of offenders such as those with drug or alcohol dependencies. The NCCD findings and corresponding recommendations are shared by other researchers as well. Paradoxically, more frequent contact between POs and their clients may make POs more aware of client technical violations of their program requirements. This awareness does not mean that PO clients are committing more program violations, but rather that POs are in the position of observing their clients more frequently and therefore the likelihood of observing program infractions is increased.

SUMMARY

Program evaluation is the process of assessing any corrections intervention or program to determine its effectiveness in achieving manifest goals. Program evaluation almost always involves recidivism as an indicator of program goal attainment. Other alternative outcome measures, including costs, benefits, and savings to communities, wages and taxes paid, and compliance with court orders, are also used. Recidivism refers to repeat offending, although it has no universally applicable definition. It applies to criminals who commit or are suspected of committing new offenses, and connotations of the term are associated with rearrests, reconvictions, reincarcerations, parole/probation revocations, and technical program violations.

Parole boards and judges are interested in minimizing recidivism in their parole-granting and sentencing capacities. Often, salient factor scores are useful in forecasting one's potential successfulness as a parolee, and judges rely on presentence investigations of offenders when deciding the correct sentence to impose. No technique or measure accurately forecasts recidivism, however. False positives and false negatives attest to the low predictive power of instruments purportedly designed to measure dangerousness or public risk. Recidivists tend to be younger men with lengthy prior records of convictions. They usually, although not always, have less education, are from lower socioeconomic statuses, and tend to commit new offenses similar to their prior offense convictions. Recidivism declines with advancing age.

Factors influencing recidivism appear to be probation or parole status, length of prison term, and type of offense. Property offenders tend to recidivate more than violent offenders, and parolees tend to recidivate more than probationers. The greater the level of probation/parole supervision, the less the recidivism while on probation/parole. The length of incarceration appears to have little influence on recidivism. This finding undermines arguments advanced by observers that longer prison terms will reduce crime and recidivism.

Probation and parole programs and their administration can be improved. Many programs are either new or in early experimental stages, so definite conclusions about their effectiveness cannot be drawn. Probationers themselves believe that increased contact with probation officers and program incentives and rewards for compliance ought to be incorporated as a means of increasing program effectiveness and reducing recidivism. Differential supervision may actually be an incentive for many probationers/parolees. The longer one remains violation-free while under supervision, the less intense the supervision will be. Some states have automatic probation/parole program discharges, with probationers/parolees automatically being released from the criminal justice system after successfully completing a three-year term of supervision without incurring revocations or program violations.

KEY TERMS

Avertable recidivists	Rand Corporation	Reincarceration
Nonavertable recidivists	Rearrest	Revocation
Program evaluation	Reconviction	Technical program violations

QUESTIONS FOR REVIEW

1. What is a needs instrument? What types of items are included on needs instruments?
2. Differentiate between avertable recidivists and nonavertable recidivists. Give some examples.
3. Identify at least six different connotations of recidivism. Which recidivism measures are most popular?
4. How well can recidivist characteristics be used to predict offender risk or dangerousness?
5. Does the length of incarceration exert any effect on the likelihood of recidivism?
6. Some researchers believe that recidivists tend to commit more serious offenses. Is that true? Why or why not?
7. Why are parole boards and judges concerned about false positives and false negatives?
8. Does a parole revocation mean that the offender has committed a new crime? Why or why not?
9. What are some factors influencing a decision to revoke parole or probation?
10. What is meant by program evaluation? What are some alternative outcome measures to assess program effectiveness?

SUGGESTED READINGS

Minnesota Department of Corrections (1999). *Community-Based Sex Offender Program Evaluation Project.* St. Paul: Minnesota Department of Corrections.

Motiuk, Larry, et al. (2000). "What Works in Corrections?" *Forum on Corrections Research* **12:**3–60.

Norton, Douglas R. (1999). *Adult Probation Programs: Program Evaluation.* Phoenix: Arizona Office of the Auditor General.

Seiter, Richard P. (ed.). (1998). "Strategic Management: Moving the Organization Forward." *Corrections Management Quarterly* **2:**1–85.

Internet Addresses for Professional Organizations and Probation/Parole Agencies

Academy of Criminal Justice Sciences   www.acjs.org
Administrative Office of U.S. Courts   www.uscourts.gov
American Academy of Forensic Sciences   aafs.org
American Bar Association   www.abanet.org
American Correctional Association   corrections.com/aca/
American Judges Association   aja.ncsc.dni.us
American Probation and Parole Association   www.appa-net.org
American Society of Criminology   asc41@infinet.com   *also*   bsos.umd.edu/asc/
American Sociological Association   asanet.org
Bureau of Justice Statistics   www.ojp.usdoj.gov/bjs/
Bureau of Prisons   www.bop.gov
Department of Justice   usdoj.gov
FBI Academy   fbi.gov/academy/academy.htm
FBI Laboratory   fbi.gov/lab/report/labhome.com
FBI Law Enforcement Bulletin   leb@fbiacademy.edu
Federal Bureau of Investigation   fbi.gov
Federal Judicial Center   www.fjc.gov
Federation of Law Societies of Canada   flsc.ca
Freedom of Information Act   citizen.org
Immigration and Naturalization Service   ins.usdoj.gov/
Law and Society Association   webmaster@lawandsociety.org
National Association for Court Management   nacm.ncsc.dni.us/
National Association of Counsel for Children   naccchildlaw.org
National Association of Drug Court Professionals   www.drugcourt.org
National Association of Pretrial Services Agencies   napsa.org

National Association of State Judicial Educators   www.nasje.org

National Center for State Courts   www.ncsc.dni.us

National Center for Youth Law   www.youthlaw.org

National Clearinghouse for Judicial Educational Information   jeritt.msu.edu

National Council of Juvenile and Family Court Judges   www.ncjfcj.unr.edu

National Criminal Justice Reference Service   www.ncjrs.org

National District Attorneys Association   www.ndaa.org

National Institute of Corrections   nicic.org/inst/

National Institute of Justice   www.ojp.usdoj.gov/nij

National Institute of Justice Data Resources Program   nacjd@icpsr.umich.edu

National Law Enforcement and Corrections Technology Center   www.nlectc.org/

Office of Justice Programs   ojp.usdoj.gov/

Office of Juvenile Justice and Delinquency Prevention (OJJDP)   www.ojjdp.ncjrs.org

OJP Drug Court Clearinghouse and Technical Assistance Project   www.american.edu/academic.depts/spa/justice/dcclear.htm

Pacific Sociological Association   psa@csus.edu

Sentencing Project   www.sentencingproject.org

Sex Offender Awareness Page   www.sharlow.com/

Sourcebook of Criminal Justice Statistics   albany.edu/sourcebook/

Southern Sociological Society   levin@soc.msstate.edu

State Judicial Institute   www.statejustice.org

Uniform Crime Reports   fbi.gov/ucr

U.S. Customs Service   customs.ustreas.gov

U.S. Federal Judiciary   www.uscourts.gov/

U.S. Government Printing Office   access.gpo.gov

U.S. Marshals Service   us.marshals@usdoj.gov

U.S. Parole Commission   usdoj.gov/parole.htm

U.S. Sentencing Commission   www.usscr.gov

U.S. Supreme Court   supct.law.cornell.edu/supct/

Vera Institute of Justice   broadway.vera.org

Victim-Offender Reconciliation Project (VORP)   vorp.com

Western and Pacific Association of Criminal Justice Educators   WPACJE@boisestate.edu

Glossary

Abnormal physical structure Explanation of criminal conduct using physical indicators such as the shape of earlobes, head shapes and contours, and body deformities that are viewed as contributory to deviance or crime.

Absconders Persons who flee their jurisdictions while on probation, parole, work release, study release, or furloughs without permission.

Acceptance of responsibility Acknowledgment by convicted offenders that they are responsible for their actions and have rendered themselves totally and absolutely accountable for the injuries or damages they may have caused; used by judges to mitigate sentences during sentencing hearings; an integral factor in U.S. sentencing guidelines offense severity calculations, influencing numbers of months of confinement offenders may receive.

Actuarial prediction Prediction of future inmate behavior based on a class of offenders similar to those considered for parole.

Adjudication Decision by juvenile court judge deciding whether juvenile is delinquent, a status offender, or dependent/neglected; finding may be "not delinquent."

Adjudicatory hearing Formal proceeding involving a prosecutor and defense attorney at which evidence is presented and the juvenile's guilt or innocence is determined by the juvenile court judge.

Admin max Level of security designation to denote a penitentiary that holds only prisoners with extensive criminal histories and who are escape-prone or especially violent. The highest security level exists at such facilities.

Aggravating circumstances Circumstances that enhance one's sentence; they include whether serious bodily injury or death occurred to a victim during crime commission and whether offender was on parole at time of crime.

Allegheny Academy A Pennsylvania facility opened in 1982 and operated by the Community Specialists Corporation, a private, nonprofit corporation headquartered in Pittsburgh and specializing in the community-based treatment of young offenders; general aim is to change the negative behavior of offenders; targeted are juvenile offenders who have failed in other, traditional probation programs.

Alternative care cases Borderline cases in which judges may sentence offenders to either incarceration or probation subject to compliance with various conditions.

Alternative dispute resolution (ADR) Procedure whereby a criminal case is redefined as a civil one and the case is decided by an impartial arbiter and both parties agree to amicable settlement; criminal court is not used for resolving such matters; usually reserved for minor offenses.

Alternative sentencing Also called creative sentencing; where judge imposes sentence other than incarceration; often involves good works such as community service, restitution to victims, and other public service activity.

American Correctional Association (ACA) Established in 1870 to disseminate information about correctional programs and correctional training; designed to foster professionalism throughout the correctional community.

Anamnestic prediction Prediction of inmate behavior according to past circumstances.

Anomie Condition of normlessness as set forth in Robert K. Merton's theory of anomie.

Anomie theory Robert Merton's theory, alleging persons acquire desires for culturally approved goals to strive to achieve, but they adopt innovative, sometimes deviant, means to achieve these goals; anomie implies normlessness; innovators accept societal goals but reject institutionalized means to achieve them.

Apprehension units Specific departments within correctional services that pursue those who leave their jurisdictions without permission or who abscond; probation and parole departments have apprehension units dedicated to hunting down absconders.

Arraignment Proceeding following an indictment by a grand jury or a finding of probable cause from a preliminary hearing; determines (1) plea, (2) specification of final charges against defendant(s), and (3) trial date.

Arrest Taking persons into custody and restraining them until they can be brought before court to answer the charges against them.

Assessment center Agency designed for selecting entry-level officers for correctional work; assessment centers hire correctional officers and probation or parole officers.

Auburn State Penitentiary Prison constructed in New York in 1816; known for its creation of tiers, or different levels of custody for different types of offenders; also known for use of "striped" clothing for prisoners to distinguish them from the general population if prisoners escape confinement; also known for congregate system, wherein offenders could dine in large eating areas; also used solitary confinement; custody levels are medium and maximum.

Augustus, John Private citizen acknowledged as formulator of probation in U.S. in Boston, Massachusetts, 1841.

Automatic waivers (Also **Legislative waivers**) Actions initiated by state legislatures whereby certain juvenile offenders are sent to criminal courts for processing rather than to juvenile courts; usually requires a certain age range (16–17) and prescribed list of offenses (e.g., rape, homicide, armed robbery, arson); a type of certification or waiver or transfer.

Avertable recidivists Offenders who would still have been in prison serving a sentence at a time when new offense was committed.

Bail A surety to procure the release of those under arrest and to ensure that they will appear later to face criminal charges in court; also known as a bailbond.

Balanced approach View of offender rehabilitation that stresses heightening offender accountability, individualizing sanctions or punishments, and promoting community safety.

Banishment (See also **Transportation**) Punishment form used for many centuries as a sanction for violations of the law or religious beliefs; those found guilty of crimes or other infractions were ordered to leave their communities and never return; in many instances, this punishment was the equivalent of the death penalty, because communities were often isolated and no food or water were available within distances of hundreds of miles from these communities.

Beyond a reasonable doubt Standard used in criminal courts to establish guilt or innocence of criminal defendant.

Biological theories Explanations of criminal conduct that emphasize the genetic transmission of traits that figure prominently in deviant behavior; any explanation that focuses on biology and heredity as sources of criminal behavior.

Bonding theory A key concept in a number of theoretical formulations. Emile Durkheim's notion that deviant behavior is controlled to the degree that group members feel morally bound to one another, are committed to common goals, and share a collective conscience. In social control theory, the elements of attachment, commitment, involvement and belief; explanation of criminal behavior implying that criminality is the result of a loosening of bonds or attachments with society; builds on differential association theory. Primarily designed to account for juvenile delinquency.

Booking An administrative procedure designed to furnish personal background information to a bonding company and law enforcement officials; includes compiling a file for defendants, including their name, address, telephone number, age, place of work, relatives, and other personal data.

Boot camps Highly regimented, military-like, short-term correctional programs (90–180 days) in which offenders are provided with strict discipline, physical training, and hard labor resembling some aspects of military basic training; when successfully completed, boot camps provide for transfers of participants to community-based facilities for nonsecure supervision.

Boston House of Corrections Jail where convicted offenders were confined for various offenses, including drunkenness and disorderly behavior; operated during 1830s and 1840s.

Boston Offender Project (BOP) Experimental juvenile treatment program commenced in 1981 through the Massachusetts Department of Youth Services; aimed at reducing recidivism, reintegrating youths, and increasing offender accountability.

Bridewell Workhouse Established in 1557 in London, England; designed to house vagrants and general riffraff; noted for exploitation of inmate labor by private mercantile interests.

Brockway, Zebulon First superintendent of New York State Reformatory at Elmira in 1876; arguably credited with introducing first "good time" system whereby inmates could have their sentences reduced or shortened by the number of good marks earned through good behavior.

Broker PO work role orientation in which PO functions as a referral service and supplies offender-client with contacts with agencies that provide needed services.

Bureau of Justice Statistics Bureau created in 1979 to distribute statistical information concerning crime, criminals, and crime trends.

Burgess, Ernest W. Collaborated with Robert Park to devise concentric zone hypothesis to explain crime in different Chicago city sectors.

Burnout Psychological equivalent of physical stress, characterized by a loss of motivation and commitment related to task performance.

Camps Nonsecure youth programs, usually located in rural settings, designed to instill self-confidence and interpersonal skills for juvenile offenders; also known as wilderness programs.

Career criminals Offenders who earn their living through crime; they go about their criminal activity in much the same way workers or professional individuals engage in their daily work activities; career criminals often consider their work as a "craft," because they acquire considerable technical skills and competence in the performance of crimes.

Caseload The number of clients or offenders probation or parole officers must supervise during any given time period, such as one week or one month.

Caseworker Any probation or parole officer who works with probationers or parolees as clients; term originates from social work, with caseworkers attempting to educate, train, or rehabilitate those without coping skills.

Cellular telephone devices Electronic monitoring equipment worn by offenders that emits radio signal received by local area monitor.

Certification (See **Transfers**)

Charge reduction bargaining Type of plea bargaining in which the inducement from the prosecutor is a reduction in the seriousness of charge or number of charges against a defendant in exchange for a guilty plea.

Children in need of supervision (CHINS) Any youth who has no responsible parent or guardian and needs one.

Children's tribunals Early form of court dealing with juvenile offending; 1850s through 1890s; informal judicial mechanisms for evaluating seriousness of juvenile offenders and prescribing punishments for them.

Child-saver movement Largely religious in origin, a loosely organized attempt to deal with unsupervised youth following the Civil War; child-savers were interested in the welfare of youths who roamed city streets unsupervised.

Child-savers Philanthropists who believed that children ought to be protected; originated following the Civil War.

Child sexual abusers Adults who involve minors in virtually any kind of sexual activity, ranging from intercourse with children to photographing them in lewd poses.

Chronic offenders Repeat offenders who continually reoffend; repeat offenses and new convictions may be for misdemeanors or felonies, but there is a continuation of offending over a period of years; persistent offenders.

Citizen value system Parole board decision-making model appealing to public interests in seeing that community expectations are met by making appropriate early release decisions.

Civil Rights Act Title 42, Section 1983, of the U. S. Code permitting inmates of prisons and jails as well as probationers and parolees the right to sue their administrators and/or supervisors under the due process and equal protection clauses of the Fourteenth Amendment.

Clark, Benjamin C. Philanthropist and "volunteer" probation officer who assisted courts with limited probation work during 1860s; carried on John Augustus's work commenced in early 1840s.

Classification Attempts to categorize offenders according to type of offense, dangerousness, public risk, special needs, and other relevant criteria; used in institutional settings (prisons) for purposes of placing inmates in more or less close custody and supervision.

Classification system Means used by prisons and probation/parole agencies to separate offenders according to offense seriousness, type of offense, and other criteria; no classification system has been demonstrably successful at effective prisoner or client placements; any means of determining the dangerousness or risk of offenders to place them in either specific community programs or appropriate custody levels while confined.

Clinical prediction Prediction of inmate behavior based on professional's expert training and working directly with offenders.

Code of ethics Regulations formulated by major professional societies that outline the specific problems and issues frequently encountered in the types of research carried out within a particular profession. Serves as a guide to ethical research practices.

Cognitive development Stages in the learning process when one acquires abilities to think and express himself or herself; thoughts about the feelings of others are acquired.

Cognitive development theory Also called developmental theory. Stresses stages of learning process in which persons acquire abilities to think and express themselves, respect the property and rights of others, and cultivate a set of moral values.

Combination sentence (See **Split sentencing**)

Common law Authority based on court decrees and judgments that recognize, affirm, and enforce certain usages and customs of the people. Laws determined by judges in accordance with their rulings.

Community-based corrections Several types of programs that manage offenders within the community instead of prison or jail; includes electronic monitoring, day-fine programs, home confinement, and intensive supervised probation/parole.

Community-based supervision Reintegrative programs operated publicly or privately to assist offenders by providing therapeutic, support, and supervision programs for criminals; may include furloughs, probation, parole, community service, and restitution.

Community control   A Florida community-based correctional program involving home confinement and electronic monitoring for offender supervision.

Community control house arrest   A Florida program in which offenders are confined to their own homes, instead of prison, where they are allowed to serve their sentences.

Community corrections   Any one of several different types of programs designed to supervise probationers and parolees; includes but is not limited to home confinement, electronic monitoring, day reporting centers, probation, parole, intensive supervised probation, intensive supervised parole, furloughs, halfway houses, work release, and study release.

Community corrections act   Statewide mechanism included in legislation whereby funds are granted to local units of government and community agencies to develop and deliver "front-end" alternative sanctions in lieu of state incarceration.

Community model   Relatively new concept based on the correctional goal of offender reintegration into the community; stresses offender adaptation to the community by participating in one or more programs that are a part of community-based corrections.

Community reintegration   Process by which offender who has been incarcerated is able to live in community under some supervision and gradually adjust to life outside of prison or jail; theory is that transition to community life from regimentation of prison life can be eased through community-based correctional program and limited community supervision.

Community residential centers   Transitional agencies located in neighborhoods where offenders may obtain employment counseling, food and shelter, and limited supervision pertaining to one or more conditions of probation or parole; example is day reporting/treatment program.

Community service   Sentence imposed by judges in lieu of incarceration whereby offenders are obligated to perform various tasks that assist the community and help to offset the losses suffered by victims or the community at large.

Community-service orders   Symbolic restitution involving redress for victims, less severe sanctions for offenders, offender rehabilitation, reduction of demands on the criminal justice system, and a reduction of the need for vengeance in a society, or a combination of these factors.

Community work (See **Work release**)

Commutation   Administratively authorized early release from custody; e.g., prisoners serving life terms may have their sentences commuted to ten years.

Concurrent jurisdiction (See **Direct file**)

Conditional diversion program   Program in which divertee is involved in some degree of local monitoring by probation officers or personnel affiliated with local probation departments.

Conditional release   Any release of inmates from custody with various conditions or program requirements; parole is a conditional release; any release to a community-based corrections program is a conditional release.

Conditional sanctions   Juvenile punishment options including probation, community service, restitution, or some other penalty after an adjudication of delinquency has been made.

Conflict criminology (See **Radical criminology**)

Conflict/Marxist theory (See **Radical criminology**)

Congregate system   A system that allowed inmates to work together and eat their meals with one another during daylight hours.

Containment theory   Explanation elaborated by Walter Reckless and others that positive self-image enables persons otherwise disposed toward criminal behavior to avoid criminal conduct and conform to societal values. Every person is a part of an external structure and has a protective internal structure providing defense, protection, and/or insulation against one's peers, such as delinquents.

Continuous signaling devices   Electronic monitoring devices that broadcast an encoded signal that is received by a receiver-dialer in the offender's home. (See **Electronic monitoring**.)

Continuous signaling transmitters   Apparatuses worn about the ankle or wrist that emit continuous electronic signals that may be received by POs with a reception device as they drive by an offender's dwelling.

Contract prisoners   Inmates from state or federal prison systems who are accommodated in local jails for designated periods such as one or more years at reduced rates so as to reduce prison overcrowding.

Controller value system   Parole board decision-making system emphasizing the functions of parole supervision and management.

Conventional model   Caseload assignment model in which probation or parole officers are assigned clients randomly.

Conventional model with geographic considerations   Similar to conventional model; caseload assignment model is based on the travel time required for POs to meet with offender-clients regularly.

Cook, Rufus R.   Philanthropist who continued John Augustus's work, particularly assisting juvenile offenders through the Boston Children's Aid Society in 1860.

Corrections   The aggregate of programs, services, facilities, and organizations responsible for the management of people who have been accused or convicted of criminal offenses.

Corrections officers   Personnel who work in any correctional institution, such as a jail, prison, or penitentiary; formerly known as guards; currently the preferred term per American Correctional Association and American Jail Association resolutions.

Corrections volunteer   Any unpaid person who performs auxiliary, supplemental, augmentative, or any other work or services for any law enforcement, court, or corrections agency.

Courts Public judiciary bodies that apply the law to controversies and oversee the administration of justice.

Creaming Term to denote taking only the most qualified offenders for succeeding in a rehabilitative program; these offenders are low risk, unlikely to reoffend.

Creative sentencing Name applied to a broad class of punishments that offer alternatives to incarceration and that are designed to fit a particular crime.

Crime classification index Selected list of offenses that are used to portray crime trends; index offenses are usually divided into type I or more serious offenses and type II offenses or less serious offenses; compiled by Federal Bureau of Investigation and Department of Justice.

Crime control A model of criminal justice that emphasizes containment of dangerous offenders and societal protection.

Crimes Violations of the law by persons held accountable under the law; must involve *mens rea* and *actus reus* as two primary components.

Crimes against property Any criminal act not directly involving a victim, such as burglary, vehicular theft (not car-jacking), larceny, or arson (of an unoccupied dwelling); more recently designated as property crime.

Crimes against the person Less frequently used term to describe a criminal act involving direct contact with another person and/or injury to that person, usually when a dangerous weapon is used; person crimes include aggravated assault; rape; homicide; robbery; more recently designated as violent crime; such crimes are currently considered violent crimes or crimes of violence.

Crimes of violence Any crime involving potential or actual injury to a victim and when a weapon is used to facilitate the offense; usually includes homicide, rape, or aggravated assault.

Criminal contamination Belief that if ex-offenders live together or associate closely with one another, they would spread their criminality like a disease; fear originally aroused from construction of halfway houses for parolees.

Criminal justice system Integrated network of law enforcement, prosecution and courts, and corrections designed to process criminal offenders from detection to trial and punishment; interrelated set of agencies and organizations designed to control criminal behavior, detect crime, and apprehend, process, prosecute, rehabilitate, and/or punish criminals.

Criminal trial An adversarial proceeding within a particular jurisdiction, at which a judicial determination of issues can be made and at which a defendant's guilt or innocence can be decided impartially.

Criminogenic environment Typically, prisons are viewed as "colleges of crime" where inmates are not rehabilitated but rather learn more effective criminal techniques; any interpersonal situation in which the likelihood of acquiring criminal behaviors is enhanced.

Critical criminology A school of criminology that holds that criminal law and the criminal justice system have been created to control the poor and have-nots of society. Crimes are defined depending on how much power is wielded in society by those defining crime.

Crofton, Sir Walter Director of Ireland's prison system during 1850s; considered father of parole in various European countries; established system of early release for prisoners; issued tickets of leave as an early version of parole.

Cultural transmission theory Explanation emphasizing transmission of criminal behavior through socialization. Views delinquency as socially learned behavior transmitted from one generation to the next in disorganized urban areas.

Dangerousness Defined differently in several jurisdictions; prior record of violent offenses; potential to commit future violent crimes if released; propensity to inflict injury.

Day fines A two-step process whereby courts (1) use a unit scale or benchmark to sentence offenders to certain numbers of day-fine units (e.g., 15, 30, 120) according to offense severity and without regard to income and (2) determine the value of each unit according to a percentage of the offender's daily income; total fine amounts are determined by multiplying this unit value by the number of units accompanying the offense.

Day parole (See **Work release**)

Day pass (See **Work release**)

Day reporting centers Operated primarily during daytime hours for the purpose of providing diverse services to offenders and their families; defined as a highly structured nonresidential program using supervision, sanctions, and services coordinated from a central focus; offenders live at home and report to these centers regularly; provides services according to offender needs; these services might include employment assistance, family counseling, and educational/vocational training; may be used for supervisory and/or monitoring purposes; client behavior modification is a key goal of such centers.

Defendants Persons who have been charged with one or more crimes.

Defendant's sentencing memorandum Version of events leading to conviction offense in the words of the convicted offender; version may be submitted together with a victim impact statement.

Defense counsel Any lawyer who represents and defends in court someone accused of a crime.

Delinquency Any act committed by an infant of not more than a specified age who has violated criminal laws or engages in disobedient, indecent, or immoral conduct and is in need of treatment, rehabilitation, or supervision; status acquired through an adjudicatory proceeding by juvenile court.

Delinquents Juveniles who commit an offense that would be a crime if committed by an adult.

Delinquent subcultures Close associations formed between youths who have committed crimes; bonds formed and patterns of behavior closely resemble societal rules such that these groupings are referred to as subcultures; characteristics include ways of gaining status and recognition or promotion.

Demand waivers Actions filed by juveniles and their attorneys to have a case in juvenile court transferred to the jurisdiction of criminal courts.

Department of Justice Organization headed by the attorney general of United States; responsible for prosecuting federal law violators; oversees the Federal Bureau of Investigation and the Drug Enforcement Administration.

Dependent and neglected children Official category used by juvenile court judges to determine whether juveniles should be placed in foster homes and taken away from parents or guardians who may be deemed unfit; children who have no or little familial support or supervision.

Deserts model Way of viewing punishment in proportion to offense seriousness; the punishment should fit the crime.

Detainer warrants Notices of criminal charges or unserved sentences pending against prisoners in the same or other jurisdictions.

Detector PO work role orientation in which the PO attempts to identify troublesome clients or those who are most likely to pose high community risk.

Detention Any holding of a juvenile for a specified period to await an adjudicatory proceeding.

Detention hearing Judicial or quasi-judicial proceeding held to determine whether or not it is appropriate to continue to hold or detain a juvenile in a shelter facility.

Determinate sentencing Sentence involving confinement for a fixed period of time and which must be served in full and without parole board intervention, less any "good time" earned in prison.

Deterrence Actions designed to prevent crime before it occurs by threatening severe criminal penalties or sanctions; may include safety measures to discourage potential lawbreakers such as elaborate security systems, electronic monitoring, and greater police officer visibility.

Differential association theory Edwin Sutherland's theory of deviance and criminality through associations with others who are deviant or criminal. Theory includes dimensions of frequency, duration, priority, and intensity; persons become criminal or delinquent because of a preponderance of learned definitions that are favorable to violating the law over learned definitions unfavorable to it.

Differential reinforcement theory In social learning theory, strengthening or increasing the likelihood of the future occurrence of some voluntary act. Positive reinforcement is produced by rewarding behavior, negative reinforcement by an unpleasant or punishing stimulus. Differential reinforcement is produced when a person comes to prefer one behavior over another as the result of more rewards and less punishment. Self-reinforcement refers to self-imposed positive or negative sanctions.

Direct file Condition in which prosecutor has sole authority to determine whether a juvenile will be prosecuted in juvenile or criminal court.

Direct supervision jails Constructed so as to provide officers with 180-degree lines of sight to monitor inmates; employ a podular design; modern facilities also combine closed-circuit cameras to observe inmates continuously while celled.

Discretionary waivers (See **Judicial waivers**)

Diversion The official halting or suspension of legal proceedings against criminal defendants after a recorded justice system entry, and possible referral of those persons to treatment or care programs administered by a nonjustice or private agency. (See also **Pretrial release**.)

Diversion programs (See also **Diversion**.) Several types of programs preceding formal court adjudication of charges against defendants; defendants participate in therapeutic, educational, or other helping programs; may result in expungement of criminal charges originally filed against defendant; may include participation in Alcoholics Anonymous or driver's training programs.

Divertees Persons who participate in a diversion program or who are otherwise granted diversion.

Double jeopardy Fifth Amendment guarantee that protects against a second prosecution for the same offense following acquittal or conviction for the offense and against multiple punishments for the same offense.

Drug courts Special courts that handle only drug cases and are designed to work with prosecutors, defense counsels, treatment professionals, and probation officers to achieve a case outcome that is in the best interests of drug-involved offenders; established in 1989.

Due process model (See also **Justice model**) Emphasizes one's constitutional right to a fair trial and consistent treatment under the law; the equal protection clause of the Fourteenth Amendment is also stressed; sentencing disparities attributable to race, ethnic origin, gender, or socioeconomic status should not be tolerated.

Earned good time Credit earned and applied against one's maximum sentence through participation in GED programs, vocational/technical programs, counseling, and self-help groups while in prison.

Early Release (See **Parole**)

Ectomorph Body type described by William Sheldon; person is thin, sensitive, and delicate.

Educator (See **Enabler**)

Ego Sigmund Freud's term describing the embodiment of society's standards, values, and conventional rules.

Electronic monitoring Use of telemetry devices to verify that an offender is at a specified location at specified times.

Elmira Reformatory Institution constructed in Elmira, New York, in 1876; experimented with certain new rehabilitative philosophies espoused by various penologists including its first superintendent, Zebulon Brockway (1827–1920); considered the new penology and used the latest scientific information in its correctional methods; used a military model comparable to contemporary boot camps; prisoners performed useful labor and participated in educational or vocational activities, in which their productivity and good conduct could earn them shorter sentences; inmates were trained in close-order drill, wore military uniforms, and paraded about with wooden rifles; authorities regarded this method as a way of instilling discipline in inmates and reforming them; Elmira Reformatory is credited with individualizing prisoner treatment and the use of indeterminate sentencing directly suited for parole actions; widely imitated by other state prison systems subsequently.

Enabler PO work role orientation in which a PO seeks to instruct and assist offenders in dealing with problems as they arise.

Endomorph Body type described by Sheldon; person is fat, soft, plump, and jolly.

Enforcer PO work role orientation in which POs see themselves as enforcement officers charged with regulating client behaviors.

Exculpatory evidence Any evidence or material that shows or supports a defendant's innocence.

Experience programs (See **Wilderness programs**)

Expungement The act of removing one or more records of an arrest or conviction from an offender's court files and other legal documents; usually ordered by the court following a successful diversion program.

Expungement order (See also **Sealing of Record**) Act of removing a juvenile's record from public view; issued by juvenile court judges; order instructs police and juvenile agencies to destroy any file material related to juvenile's conduct.

False negatives Offenders predicted not to be dangerous but who turn out to be.

False positives Offenders predicted to be dangerous but who turn out not to be.

Federal Bureau of Investigation (FBI) Investigative agency that is the enforcement arm of the Department of Justice; investigates over 200 different kinds of federal law violations; maintains extensive files on criminals; assists other law agencies.

Felony Crime punishable by imprisonment in prison for a term of one or more years; a major crime; an index crime.

Felony probation Procedure of granting convicted felons probation in lieu of incarceration, usually justified because of prison overcrowding; involves conditional sentence in lieu of incarceration.

Fines Financial penalties imposed at time of sentencing convicted offenders; most criminal statutes contain provisions for the imposition of monetary penalties as sentencing options.

First-offenders Criminals who have no prior record of criminal activity.

First-time offenders Criminals who have no previous criminal records; these persons may have committed crimes, but they have only been caught for the instant offense.

Flat time Actual amount of incarceration inmates must serve before becoming eligible for parole or early release.

Florida Assessment Center One of the first state corrections agencies to establish a center for selection of entry-level correctional officers; uses intensive screening procedures for selecting applicants for officer positions.

Florida Community Control Program (FCCP) Florida program seeking to provide a milieu of accountability for offender-clients; established in 1983, the FCCP has served more than 40,000 clients; supervision of Florida offenders placed in this program is intense; offenders must have a minimum of 28 supervisory contacts per month; supervising officers have caseloads of between 20 and 25 offenders; caseloads are very low compared with standard probation or parole supervision; uses home confinement; offenders are regularly screened for drug and alcohol use, and offenders are monitored to ensure their payment of victim compensation, restitution, and/or community service; offenders also pay supervision fees to offset some of the program costs; recidivism is less than 20 percent for FCCP clients.

Foster homes Temporary placements in a home where family setting is regarded as vital; children in need of supervision targeted for out-of-own-home placement.

Freedom of Information Act (FOIA) Act that makes it possible for private citizens to examine certain public documents containing information about them, including IRS information or information compiled by any other government agency, criminal or otherwise.

Front-end solution Any solution for jail and prison overcrowding prior to placement of convicted offenders in jail or prison settings; programs include diversion, probation, and any community-based correctional program.

Furlough programs Authorized, unescorted leaves for inmates; designed to permit incarcerated offenders the opportunity of leaving prison temporarily to visit their homes with the promise to return to facility at expiration of furlough.

Furloughs Authorized, unescorted leaves from confinement granted for specific purposes and for designated time periods.

Gaol Early English term for a contemporary jail (pronounced "jail").

Gang Self-formed associations of peers, united by mutual interests, with identifiable leadership and organization, who act collectively or as individuals to achieve specific purposes, including the conduct of illegal activity or the control of a particular territory, facility, or enterprise.

Gang units Special departments in police, probation, or parole agencies dedicated to identifying and supervising the activities of gang members.

Georgia Intensive Supervision Probation Program (GISPP) Program commenced in 1982 that established three phases of punitive probation conditions for probationers; phases moved probationers through extensive monitoring and control to less extensive monitoring, ranging from 6 to 12 months; program has demonstrated low rates of recidivism among participants.

Get-tough movement General trend among sentencing reformers and others to toughen current sentencing laws and punishments to require offenders to serve more time; philosophy of punishment advocating less use of probation and more use of incarceration.

Global positioning satellite (GPS) system Network of satellites, used by the U.S. Department of Defense, that pinpoints targets and guides bombs. Currently used by some jurisdictions for the purpose of tracking probationers and parolees and their whereabouts.

Good marks Marks obtained by prisoners in nineteenth-century England whereby prisoners were given credit for participating in educational programs and other self-improvement activities.

Good time Credit applied to a convicted offender's sentence based on the amount of time served; states vary in allowable good time; average is 15 days off of maximum sentence for every 30 days served in prison or jail; incentive for good behavior, thus called good time; the amount of time deducted from the period of incarceration of a convicted offender; calculated as so many days per month on the basis of good behavior while incarcerated.

Good time system System introduced by Elmira Reformatory in 1876 in which an inmate's sentence to be served is reduced by the number of good marks earned; once this system was in operation and shown to be moderately effective, several other states patterned their own early-release standards after it in later years.

Grand jury Special jury convened in about one-half of all states; composed of various citizens; numbers vary among states; purposes are to investigate criminal activity or determine probable cause that a crime has been committed and a designated suspect probably committed it; yields "true bill" or indictment or presentment, or "no true bill," finding insufficient probable cause to merit indictment.

Group homes Also known as group centers or foster homes, facilities for juveniles that provide limited supervision and support; juveniles live in a homelike environment with other juveniles and participate in therapeutic programs and counseling; considered nonsecure custodial.

Guidelines-based sentencing Also known as presumptive sentencing, this form of sentencing specifies ranges of months or years for different degrees of offense seriousness or severity and one's record of prior offending; the greater the severity of conduct and the more prior offending, the more incarceration time is imposed; originally used to create objectivity in sentencing and reduce sentencing disparities attributable to gender, race, ethnicity, or socioeconomic status.

Habeas corpus Writ meaning "produce the body"; used by prisoners to challenge the nature and length of their confinement.

Habitual offenders Criminals who engage in continuous criminal activity during their lives; recidivists who continually commit and are convicted of new crimes.

Halfway house Any nonconfining residential facility intended to provide alternative to incarceration as a period of readjustment of offenders to the community after confinement.

Halfway-in houses Houses that provide services catering to probationers in need of limited or somewhat restricted confinement apart from complete freedom of movement in the community.

Halfway-out houses Facilities designed to serve the immediate needs of parolees contrasted with those established to accommodate probationers in the community.

Heredity Theory that behaviors are the result of characteristics genetically transmitted; criminal behaviors are explained according to inherited genes from parents or ancestors who are criminal or who have criminal propensities.

Home confinement Also called house arrest or home incarceration; intended to house offenders in their own homes with or without electronic devices; reduces prison overcrowding and prisoner costs; intermediate punishment involving the use of offender residences for mandatory incarceration during evening hours after a curfew and on weekends.

Home incarceration (See **Home confinement**)

Homeward Bound Program established in Massachusetts in 1970 designed to provide juveniles with mature responsibilities through the acquisition of survival skills and wilderness experiences; six-week training program subjected 32 youths to endurance training, physical fitness, and performing community service.

Hope Center Wilderness Camp Organized network of four interdependent, small living groups of 12 teenagers each; goals are to provide quality care and treatment in a nonpunitive environment, with specific emphases on health, safety, education, and therapy; emotionally disturbed youths whose offenses range from truancy to murder are selected for program participation; informal techniques used, including "aftertalk" (informal discussing during meals), "huddle up" (a group discussion technique), and "pow wow" (a nightly fire gathering); special nondenominational religious services are conducted; participants involved in various special events and learn to cook meals outdoors, to camp, and other survival skills.

Hope Houses In 1896, Hope House was established in New York City by Maud and Ballington Booth; receiving considerable financial support from a missionary religious society called the Volunteers of America, the Booths were able to open additional Hope Houses in future years in Chicago, San Francisco, and New Orleans.

House arrest (See **Home confinement**)

Howard, John (1726–1790) English prison reformer who influenced upgrading prison conditions throughout England and the United States.

Huber law Legislation passed in Wisconsin in 1913 authorizing the establishment of work release programs.

Id The "I want" part of a person, formed in one's early years; Sigmund Freud's term to depict that part of personality concerned with individual gratification.

Idaho Intensive Supervised Probation Program Launched as a pilot project in 1982; a team consisting of one PO and two surveillance officers closely supervised a small group of low-risk offenders who normally would have been sent to prison; the program was quite successful; in October 1984, Idaho established a statewide ISP program with legislative approval; this step was seen as a major element in the get-tough posture taken by the state.

Implicit plea bargaining Entry of guilty plea by defendant with the expectation of receiving a more lenient sentence from authorities.

Incidents A specific criminal act involving one or more victims.

Indeterminate sentencing Sentences of imprisonment by the court for either specified or unspecified durations, with the final release date determined by a parole board.

Index offenses Includes eight serious types of crime used by the FBI to measure crime trends; information is also compiled about 21 less serious offenses ranging from forgery and counterfeiting to curfew violations and runaways; index offense information is presented in the *Uniform Crime Reports* for each state, city, county, and township that has submitted crime information during the most recent year.

Indictment A charge against a criminal defendant issued by a grand jury at the request of the prosecutor; the establishment of probable cause by a grand jury that a crime has been committed and that a specific named individual committed it.

Infants Legal term applicable to juveniles who have not attained the age of majority; in most states, age of majority is 18.

Information Prosecutor-initiated charge against criminal defendant; a charge against a criminal defendant issued by a prosecutor and based on a finding of probable cause.

Initial appearance First formal appearance of criminal suspect before a judicial magistrate, usually for the purpose of determining the nature of criminal charges and whether bail should be set.

Inmate classification Classification schemes based largely on psychological, behavioral, and sociodemographic criteria; the use of psychological characteristics as predictors of risk or dangerousness and subsequent custody assignments for prisoners was stimulated by research during the period 1910 to 1920.

Intake Process of screening juvenile offenders for further processing within the juvenile justice system.

Intake screening Critical phase at which determination is made by probation officer to release juvenile, to detain juvenile, or to release juvenile to parents pending subsequent court appearance.

Intensive probation supervision (IPS) programs Programs designed to supervise probationers closely, with increased numbers of face-to-face visits by POs and more frequent drug and alcohol checks.

Intensive supervised parole (ISP) Intensified monitoring by POs where more face-to-face visits and drug/alcohol testing are conducted; seems to result in a lower amount of recidivism than more standardized parole programs.

Intensive supervised probation (ISP) programs Also called intensive probation supervision; supervised probation under probation officer; involves close monitoring of offender activities by various means.

Intermediate punishments Sanctions involving punishments existing somewhere between incarceration and probation on a continuum of criminal penalties; may include home incarceration and electronic monitoring.

Intermittent confinement (See also **Split sentencing**) Sentence in which the offender must serve a portion of the sentence in jail, perhaps on weekends or specific evenings; considered similar to probation with limited incarceration.

Intermittent sentence Sentence that occurs when offenders are sentenced to a term requiring partial confinement; perhaps the offender must serve weekends in jail; a curfew may also be imposed; in all other respects, the nature of intermittent sentencing is much like probation.

International Halfway House Association (IHHA) State-operated halfway houses were the creation of the IHHA in Chicago, 1964; although many of the halfway house programs continued to be privately operated after the formation of the IHHA, the growth in the numbers of halfway houses was phenomenal during the next decade; for instance, from 1966 to 1982, the number of halfway houses operating in the United States and Canada rose from 40 to 1,800.

Isaac T. Hopper Home In 1845, the Quakers opened the Isaac T. Hopper Home in New York City, followed by the Temporary Asylum for Disadvantaged Female Prisoners established in Boston in 1864 by a reformist group.

Jail as a condition of probation (See also **Split sentencing**) Sentence in which judge imposes limited jail time to be served before commencement of probation.

Jail boot camps Short-term programs for offenders in a wide age range; those in New York and New Orleans have age limits of 39 years and 45 years, respectively; many of the existing jail boot camps target probation or parole violators who may face revocation and imprisonment.

Jail overcrowding Condition that exists whenever the number of inmates in a jail exceeds the number designated as the operating capacity for the jail.

Jail removal initiative Movement to remove juveniles from adult jails.

Jails Facilities designed to house short-term offenders for terms of less than one year; also a place for persons awaiting trial or on trial; funded and operated by city/county funds; American Jail Association defines jails as facilities that hold offenders for periods of 72 hours or longer.

Job dissatisfaction Lack of interest in work performed by correctional officers; apathy or discontentment with tasks or assignments.

Judicial plea bargaining Type of plea bargaining in which judge offers a specific sentence.

Judicial reprieves Temporary relief or postponement of the imposition of a sentence; commenced during the Middle Ages at the discretion of judges to permit defendants more time to gather evidence of their innocence or to allow them to demonstrate that they had reformed their behavior.

Judicial waivers (Also called **discretionary waivers**); transfer of jurisdiction over juvenile offenders to criminal court, where judges initiate such action.

Jurisdiction Power of a court to hear and determine a particular case.

Jurist value system Category of decision making by parole boards in which parole decisions are regarded as a natural part of the criminal justice process in which fairness and equity predominate.

Jury trial An entitlement of being charged with a crime carrying a penalty of incarceration of six months or more; an adversarial proceeding involving either a civil or criminal matter that is resolved by a vote of a designated number of one's peers, usually 12 members; as opposed to a "bench trial" at which a judge hears a case and decides guilt or innocence of defendants or whether plaintiffs have prevailed against defendants in civil cases.

Just-deserts model (See also **Deserts model**)

Justice model Punishment orientation emphasizing fixed sentences, abolition of parole, and an abandonment of the rehabilitative ideal; philosophy that emphasizes punishment as a primary objective of sentencing.

Juvenile Also known as an infant legally; a person who has not attained his or her 18th birthday.

Juvenile Court Act Provided for limited courts of record in 1899 in Illinois, where notes might be taken by judges or their assistants, to reflect judicial actions against juveniles; the jurisdiction of these courts, subsequently designated as "juvenile courts," would include all juveniles under the age of 16 who were found in violation of any state or local law or ordinance; also, provision was made for the care of dependent and/or neglected children who had been abandoned or who otherwise lacked proper parental care, support, or guardianship.

Juvenile delinquency Violation of the law by a person prior to his or her 18th birthday; any illegal behavior committed by someone within a given age range punishable by juvenile court jurisdiction.

Juvenile delinquents Minors who commit acts that would be crimes if committed by an adult.

Juvenile Diversion/Non-Custody Intake Program California juvenile program implemented in 1982 targeted for more serious juvenile offenders; characterized by intensive supervised probation, required school attendance, employment, and counseling.

Juvenile diversion program (JDP) (See also **Diversion**) Any program for juvenile offenders that temporarily suspends their processing by the juvenile justice system; similar to adult diversion programs; also program established in 1981 in New Orleans, Louisiana, by the district attorney's office in which youths could receive treatment before being petitioned and adjudicated delinquent.

Juvenile intensive supervision programs (JISPs) Intensive supervision programs for youthful offenders; they possess many of the same features as programs for adults, including more frequent face-to-face visits, curfews, drug and alcohol checks, electronic monitoring, and home confinement.

Juvenile justice system The process through which juveniles are processed, sentenced, and corrected after arrests for juvenile delinquency.

Juvenile offenders (See **Juvenile delinquents**)

Labeling theory Explanation of crime attributed to Edwin Lemert whereby persons acquire self-definitions that are deviant or criminal; persons perceive themselves as deviant or criminal through labels applied to them by others; the more people are involved in the criminal justice system, the more they acquire self-definitions consistent with the criminal label.

Labor turnover The degree to which new POs and correctional officers replace those who quit, die, or retire.

Latent functions Unrecognized, unintended functions; associated with probation or parole, latent functions might be to alleviate prison or jail overcrowding.

Law enforcement The activities of various public and private agencies at local, state, and federal levels that are designed to ensure compliance with formal rules of society that regulate social conduct.

Law Enforcement Assistance Administration (LEAA) Program commenced in 1968 and terminated in 1984, designed to provide financial and technical assistance to local and state police agencies to combat crime in various ways.

Legislative waiver (See **Statutory exclusion**)

Level of custody Degree of supervision and confinement for inmates, depending on their type of crime committed, whether they pose a danger to themselves or other prisoners, and their past institutional history; varies from minimum-security, medium-security, to maximum-security conditions.

Libido Sigmund Freud's term describing the sex drive believed innate in everyone.

Limited risk control model Model of supervising offenders based on anticipated future criminal conduct;

uses risk assessment devices to place offenders in an effective control range.

Lockdown   Security measure implemented in prisons that have undergone rioting; usually involves solitary confinement of prisoners for undetermined period and removal of amenities, such as televisions, store privileges.

Lockup   Short-term facilities to hold minor offenders; includes drunk tanks, holding tanks; although these facilities are counted as jails, they exist primarily to hold those charged with public drunkenness or other minor offenses for up to 48 hours; the American Jail Association suggests that to qualify as a bona fide jail, the facility must hold inmates for 72 hours or longer, not 48 hours.

Maconochie, Captain Alexander   (1797–1860)   Prison reformer and former superintendent of the British penal colony at Norfolk Island and governor of Birmingham Borough Prison; known for humanitarian treatment of prisoners and issuance of "marks of commendation" to prisoners that led to their early release; considered the forerunner of indeterminate sentencing in the United States.

Mandatory release   Type of release from jail or prison whereby inmates have served their full terms or when they have fulfilled sentences specified according to particular sentencing scheme, such as guidelines-based sentencing or determinate sentencing; mandatory releasees would be subject to automatic release upon serving some portion of their incarcerative terms less good time credits applied for so many months or days served.

Mandatory sentencing   Court is required to impose an incarcerative sentence of a specified length, without the option for probation, suspended sentence, or immediate parole eligibility.

Mandatory waivers   Transfers initiated by judges who are required to waive jurisdiction over a juvenile to criminal court.

Manifest functions   Intended or recognized functions; associated with probation and parole, manifest functions are to permit offender reintegration into society.

Marks of commendation   Points accrued by convicts for good behavior under Alexander Maconochie's (1840s) term of leadership at Norfolk Island; authorized early release of some inmates who demonstrated a willingness and ability to behave well in society on the outside; this action was forerunner of indeterminate sentencing subsequently practiced in the United States.

Mark system (See **Tickets-of-Leave**)

Marxist criminology (See **Radical criminology**)

Maxi-maxi prisons (See **Maximum-security prisons**) Level of custody that accommodates the most violence-prone inmates who are inclined to escape whenever the opportunity arises and who are considered extremely dangerous; in many cases, maxi-maxi prison inmates are placed in solitary confinement and severe restrictions are imposed; confinement in isolation for 23½ hours per day, with a half hour for exercise is not uncommon; privileges are extremely limited.

Maximum-security prisons   Level of custody in which prisoners are closely supervised and given little freedom; subject to constant surveillance, often solitary confinement; limited privileges.

Mediation   The process of working out mutually satisfactory agreements between victims and offenders; an integral part of alternative dispute resolution.

Mediator (See **Enabler**)

Medical model   Also called treatment model; this model considers criminal behavior as an illness to be treated.

Medium-security prisons   Level of custody in a prison in which inmates are given more freedoms compared with maximum-security facilities; their movements are monitored; often, these facilities are dormitory-like, and prisoners are eligible for privileges.

Meritorious good time   Credit earned and applied against one's maximum sentence to be served in prison for engaging in acts of heroism or other feats that should be recognized for their merit; used in conjunction with determinate sentencing schemes.

Mesomorph   Body type described by Sheldon; person is strong, muscular, aggressive, and tough.

Minimum due process (See also **Due process model**) Rights accorded parolees resulting from *Morrissey v. Brewer* (1972) landmark case; two hearings are required: a preliminary hearing to determine whether probable cause exists that a parolee has violated any specific parole condition and a general revocation proceeding; written notice must be given to the parolee prior to the general revocation proceeding; disclosure must be made to the parolee concerning the nature of parole violation(s) and evidence obtained; parolees must be given the right to confront and cross-examine their accusers unless adequate cause can be given for prohibiting such a cross-examination; a written statement must be provided containing the reasons for revoking the parole and the evidence used in making that decision; the parolee is entitled to have the facts judged by a detached and neutral hearing committee.

Minimum-security prisons   Level of custody in a prison that is designated for nonviolent, low-risk offenders; housed in efficiency apartments; inmates permitted family visits, considerable inmate privileges.

Minnesota sentencing grid   Sentencing guidelines established by Minnesota legislature in 1980 and used by judges to sentence offenders; grid contains criminal history score, offense seriousness, and presumptive sentences to be imposed; judges may depart from guidelines upward or downward depending on aggravating or mitigating circumstances.

Misdemeanants   Those who commit misdemeanors.

Misdemeanor   Crime punishable by confinement in city or county jail for a period of less than one year; a lesser offense.

Missouri Sexual Offender Program (MOSOP)   Program targeted to serve the needs of incarcerated, nonpsychotic sexual offenders; the program can effectively supervise over 700 offenders who are required to complete the program before becoming eligible for parole; approach is that sex offenders' behaviors resulted from learned patterns of behavior associated with anxious, angry, and impulsive individuals; the three-phase program obligates offenders to attend ten weeks of courses in abnormal psychology and the psychology of sexual offending. In other phases, inmates meet in group therapy sessions to talk out their problems with counselors and other inmates.

Mitigating circumstances   Factors that lessen the severity of the crime and/or sentence; such factors include old age, cooperation with police in apprehending other offenders, and lack of intent to inflict injury.

Mixed sentence (See also **Split sentencing**)   Two or more separate sentences imposed in which offenders have been convicted of two or more crimes in the same adjudication proceeding.

Modes of adaptation   Robert Merton's typology of how persons orient themselves to societal goals and the means used to achieve those goals.

Narrative   Portion of presentence investigation report prepared by probation officer or private agency in which a description of the offense and offender are provided; culminates in and justifies a recommendation for a specific sentence to be imposed on the offender by judges.

National Crime Victimization Survey (NCVS)   A random survey of approximately 60,000 dwellings, about 127,000 persons age 12 and over, and approximately 50,000 businesses; smaller samples of persons from these original figures form the database from which crime figures are compiled; carefully worded questions lead people to report incidents that can be classified as crimes. This material is statistically manipulated in such a way so as to make it comparable with *Uniform Crime Report* statistics; this material is usually referred to as victimization data.

National Incident-Based Reporting System (NIBRS)   A compendium of incident-level data for a broad range of offenses; all incidents involving crimes are counted, even if they arise out of an ongoing sequence of criminal events (e.g., a suspect robs a liquor store, shoots the clerk, assaults customers, steals a car, and commits vehicular homicide before being arrested by police).

Negligence   Liability accruing to prison or correctional program administrators and POs as the result of a failure to perform a duty owed clients or inmates or the improper or inadequate performance of that duty; may include negligent entrustment, negligent training, negligent assignment, negligent retention, or negligent supervision (for example, providing POs with revolvers and not providing them with firearms training).

Net-widening   Also called widening the net; pulling juveniles into the juvenile justice system who would not otherwise be involved in delinquent activity; applies to many status offenders.

Neutralization theory   Explanation that holds that delinquents experience guilt when involved in delinquent activities and that they respect leaders of the legitimate social order. Their delinquency is episodic rather than chronic, and they adhere to conventional values while drifting into periods of illegal behavior. To drift, the delinquent must first neutralize legal and moral values.

New Jersey Intensive Supervision Program   Program commenced in 1983 to serve low-risk incarcerated offenders that draws clients from inmate volunteers; program selectivity limits participants through a seven-stage selection process; participants must serve at least four months in prison or jail before being admitted to the program, which monitors their progress extensively; similar to Georgia Intensive Probation Supervision Program in successfulness and low recidivism scores among participants.

New York House of Refuge   Established in New York City in 1825 by the Society for the Prevention of Pauperism; an institution largely devoted to managing status offenders, such as runaways or incorrigible children; compulsory education and other forms of training and assistance were provided to these children; the strict, prisonlike regimen of this organization was not entirely therapeutic for its clientele; many of the youthful offenders sent to such institutions, including the House of Reformation in Boston, were offspring of immigrants.

NIMBY syndrome   Meaning "Not in my back yard"; refers to attitudes of property owners who live near to where community-based correctional facilities are planned for construction; property owners believe that they will suffer declined property values and will be at risk because of felons roaming freely near their homes; opposition opinion toward construction of community-based correctional facilities.

Nominal dispositions   Juvenile punishments resulting in lenient penalties such as warnings and/or probation.

Nonavertable recidivists   Offenders whose prior sentence would not have affected the commission of new crimes.

Norfolk Island   Penal colony established on this island in 1840s supervised by Alexander Maconochie; noted for establishment of mark system and marks of commendation leading to contemporary use of good time credits in U.S. prisons and jails.

No bill, no true bill   Finding of a grand jury that insufficient evidence exists to find probable cause against a criminal defendant that a crime was committed and that the suspect committed it.

Numbers game model   Caseload assignment model for probation or parole officers in which the total number of offender/clients is divided by number of officers.

Objective parole criteria   General qualifying conditions that permit parole boards to make nonsubjective parole decisions without regard to an inmate's race, religion, gender, age, or socioeconomic status.

Offender control   Philosophy that says if offenders cannot be rehabilitated, then their behavior while on probation cannot be controlled; priority shift in probationer management toward greater use of intermediate punishments designed for better offender monitoring.

Offender rehabilitation Condition achieved when criminals are reintegrated into their communities and refrain from further criminal activity (See Rehabilitation).

Offenders Persons convicted of a crime.

Offense seriousness score Score based on criminal offense severity; often used in guidelines-based sentencing schemes such as are used in Minnesota; U.S. sentencing guidelines use offense seriousness scores to calculate numbers of months of incarceration for convicted offenders, together with one's criminal history score.

Offense severity Seriousness of offense, according to monetary amount involved in theft or embezzlement; degree of injuries inflicted on one or more victims; amount of drugs involved in drug transactions; other alternative measures of crime seriousness.

Ohio Experience Several different types of programs established in Ohio during late 1980s for juvenile offenders; uses home confinement, electronic monitoring, intensive supervised probation; has three goals of heightening offender accountability, individualizing punishments, and promoting community safety.

Once an adult, always an adult provision When juveniles are transferred to criminal court for processing in particular jurisdictions, they will forever after be treated as adults if they commit new offenses, regardless of whether they are still juveniles.

180 Degrees, Inc. Program similar to a halfway house for parolees, but is designed for those who have received no previous treatment for their sex offenses; participation is limited only to those offenders willing to admit that they have committed one or more sex offenses and who can function as group members; offenders form men's sexuality groups that hold 90-minute meetings over 13 weeks; all participants contract with officials to write an autobiography of their offense, a description of the victim, a listing of sexual abuse cues, the development of a control plan, and personal affirmations.

Overcharging Action by prosecutors of charging a defendant with more crimes than are reasonable under the circumstances; raising the charge to a more serious level, expecting a conviction of lesser crime.

Overcrowding Condition that exists when numbers of prisoners exceed the space allocations for which the jail or prison is designed; often associated with double-bunking or putting two prisoners per cell.

Paraprofessional Someone who possesses some formal training in a given correctional area, is salaried, works specified hours, has formal duties and responsibilities, is accountable to higher-level supervisors for work quality, and has limited immunity under the theory of agency.

Pardon An executive device designed to absolve offenders of their crimes committed and release them; can be used to alleviate prison overcrowding.

Parens patriae Literally "parent of the country"; refers to doctrine in which the state oversees the welfare of youth; originally established by the king of England and administered through chancellors.

Parole Status of offenders conditionally released from a confinement facility prior to expiration of their sentences and placed under supervision of a parole agency.

Parole board Body of governor-appointed or elected persons who decide whether eligible inmates may be granted early release from incarceration.

Parolees Offenders who have served some time in jail or prison, but have been released prior to serving their entire sentences imposed upon conviction.

Parole officers (POs) Corrections officers who supervise and counsel parolees and perform numerous other duties associated with parolee management.

Parole revocation Two-stage proceeding that may result of a parolee's reincarceration in jail or prison; first stage is a preliminary hearing to determine whether parolee violated any specific parole condition; second stage is to determine whether parole should be canceled and the offender reincarcerated.

Parole revocation hearing A formal meeting of a parolee with a parole board at which the parole board determines whether a parolee is guilty or innocent of a parole program infraction or rule violation; if guilt is established, then the parole board must determine punishment to be imposed, which may include intensification of supervision in current parole program or return to prison; two-stage proceeding to determine whether parolee has committed offense or offenses requiring revocation of parole and what punishment should be imposed; a critical stage.

Penitentiary Facility generally designed to be self-contained and to house large numbers of serious offenders for periods of one year or longer; characterized by manned perimeters, walls, electronic security devices, and high custody levels.

Pennsylvania System Devised and used in the Walnut Street Jail in 1790 to place prisoners in solitary confinement; predecessor to modern prisons; used solitude to increase penitence and prevent cross-infection of prisoners; encouraged behavioral improvements.

Persistent offenders Persons who are convicted multiple times for crimes during their lives.

Persistent felony offenders Persons who continually commit new felonies and are convicted of them; repeat offenders.

Persons in need of supervision (PINS) Youths who need the supervision and management of an adult guardian or parent.

Petitions Official documents filed in juvenile courts on the juvenile's behalf specifying reasons for court appearance.

Philadelphia Society for Alleviating the Miseries of Public Prisons Established in 1787; Quaker society devoted to improving jail conditions in Philadelphia; consisted of philanthropists and religionists.

Plea bargaining A preconviction agreement between the defendant and the state in which the defendant pleads guilty with the expectation of a reduction in the charges, a promise of sentencing leniency, or some other government concession short of the maximum penalties that could be imposed under the law.

Prediction An assessment of some expected future behavior of a person including criminal acts, arrests, or convictions.

Predispositional reports Documents prepared by juvenile intake officers for juvenile judges; purpose of reports is to furnish judges with background about juveniles to make more informed sentencing decisions; similar to PSI reports.

Preliminary hearing, preliminary examination Hearing by a magistrate or other judicial officer to determine if the person charged with a crime should be held for trial; proceeding to establish probable cause; does not determine guilt or innocence.

Preponderance of evidence Standard used in civil courts to determine defendant or plaintiff liability.

Preparole programs Any transitional programs, including work release, study release, furloughs, or other temporary leaves for various purposes; inmates are usually within several months of being granted early release; the intent of such programs is to reintegrate these offenders into their communities gradually and avoid the shock of shifting from highly structured and regulated prison life into community living without prison restrictions and regulations.

Prerelease Any transitional program that assists inmates in prisons or jails in adapting or adjusting to life in their communities by offering them temporary leaves from their institutions.

Prerelease program Prior to granting parole, inmates may be placed on furloughs or work or study release to reintegrate them gradually back into their communities.

Presentence investigation (PSI) Report prepared either by a probation officer or private organization to assist judges in sentencing convicted offenders; includes description of offense, work background and social history of offender, victim impact statement, educational attainment, work record, and other important details.

Presentence investigation report Document prepared by a probation officer, usually at the request of a judge, wherein a background profile of a convicted offender is compiled; includes PO's version of crime committed, convicted offender's statement, victim impact statement, and other relevant data compiled from court records and interviews with persons who know offender and victim.

Presentment A charge issued by a grand jury upon its own authority against a specific criminal defendant; a finding of probable cause against a criminal suspect that a crime has been committed and the named suspect committed it.

President's Commission on Law Enforcement and Administration of Justice 1967 panel empowered to investigate the state of training and standards used for police officer selection; made recommendations to the president of United States to authorize funds to improve officer selection and training methods for general improvement of law enforcement effectiveness.

Presumptive sentencing Punishment prescribed by statute for each offense or class of offense; the sentence must be imposed in all unexceptional circumstances, but when there are mitigating or aggravating circumstances, the judge is permitted some latitude in shortening or lengthening the sentence within specific boundaries, usually with written justification.

Presumptive waiver Burden of proof in transfer decision making shifts from the state to the juvenile; juvenile must be waived to criminal court for processing unless he or she can prove that he or she is suitable for rehabilitation.

Pretrial detainees Persons charged with crimes and who are placed in custody, usually a jail, prior to their trial.

Pretrial detention Order by court for the defendant (juvenile or adult) to be confined prior to adjudicatory proceeding; usually reserved for defendants considered dangerous or likely to flee the jurisdiction if released temporarily.

Pretrial diversion Act of deferring prosecution of a criminal case by permitting a defendant to complete a specified period of months or years, usually with conditions; usually persons who comply with behavioral requirements of diversion may have their original charges dismissed, reduced, or expunged.

Pretrial release (See also **Released on own recognizance**) Freedom from incarceration prior to trial granted to defendants.

Pretrial services Various duties performed by probation officers for either state or federal courts; may include investigations of persons charged with crimes and bail recommendations.

Preventive detention Constitutional right of police to detain suspects prior to trial without bail, when suspects are likely to flee from the jurisdiction or pose serious risks to others.

Primary deviation Minor violations of the law that are frequently overlooked by police (including "streaking" or swimming in a public pool after hours).

Prison overcrowding Condition resulting whenever inmate population exceeds rated or design capacity.

Prisons Facilities designed to house long-term serious offenders; operated by state or federal government; houses inmates for terms longer than one year.

Privatization General movement in corrections and law enforcement to supplement existing law enforcement agencies and correctional facilities with privately owned and operated institutions, organizations, and personnel; theory is that private management of such organizations can be more cost-effective and reduce capital outlays (taxation) associated with public expenditures for similar functions.

Probable cause   Reasonable belief that a crime has been committed and that a specified person accused of the crime committed it.

Probatio   A period of proving or trial or forgiveness.

Probation   Sentence not involving confinement that imposes conditions and retains authority in sentencing court to modify conditions of sentence or resentence offender for probation violations.

Probationer   Person who does not go to jail or prison, but rather serves a term outside of prison subject to certain behavioral conditions.

Probation officer caseloads   The number of probationer-clients supervised by probation officers; caseloads are determined in different ways, depending on particular probation agency policies.

Probation officers (POs)   Corrections officials who monitor convict's progress outside of prison.

Probation revocation   The process in which a judge conducts a two-stage proceeding to determine whether a probationer's probation program should be revoked or terminated; such terminations are based on one or more program infractions, which may include curfew violation, use of illegal drugs, possession of illegal contraband, or commission of a new offense.

Probation Subsidy Program   California program implemented in 1965 and providing local communities with supplemental resources to manage larger numbers of probationers more closely; a part of this subsidy is provided for community residential centers where probationers could "check in" and receive counseling, employment assistance, and other forms of guidance or supervision.

Professionalization   Equated with acquiring more formal education rather than practical skills involving one-to-one human relationships with different types of offender-clients; more recently associated with improvements in officer selection, training, and education; accreditation measures are implemented to standardize curricula and acquisition of skills that improve one's work proficiency.

Professionals   Persons who are members of a learned profession or who have achieved a high level of proficiency, competency, and training.

Program evaluation   The process of assessing any corrections intervention or program for the purpose of determining its effectiveness in achieving manifest goals; investigates the nature of organizational intervention strategies, counseling, interpersonal interactions, staff quality, expertise, and education and the success or failure experiences of clients served by any program.

Programmed contact devices   Electronic monitoring devices; similar to continuous signal units, except that a central computer calls at random hours being monitored to verify that offenders are where they are supposed to be; offenders answer the telephone and their voices are verified by computer.

Program for Female Offenders, Inc. (PFO)   Pennsylvania program commenced in 1974, guided by two goals: reforming female offenders and creating economically dependent women; started with a job placement service; training centers were eventually created and operated by different counties on a nonprofit basis; center offerings have included remedial math instruction, English instruction, and clerical classes such as word processing, data entry, and telecommunications skill training; counseling has also been provided for those women with social and psychological problems; currently serves 300 women per year, and the community facilities have a low recidivism rate of only 3.5 percent.

Progressive era   1960s and 1970s time period where liberals stressed rehabilitation for convicted offenders rather than lengthy prison sentences.

Project New Pride   Program established in Denver, Colorado, in 1973 that blends education, counseling, employment, and cultural education for children ages 14 through 17; eligible juveniles include those with two prior adjudications for serious misdemeanors and/or felonies; goals are to reintegrate juveniles into their communities through school participation and employment and reduce recidivism rates of juveniles.

Property crimes   Crimes that do not involve direct contact with specific victims; examples include theft, burglary of unoccupied dwellings, vehicular theft (not car-jacking), embezzlement, and fraud.

Prosecutions   Carrying forth of criminal proceedings against a person culminating in a trial or other final disposition such as a plea of guilty in lieu of trial.

Prosecutors   Court officials who commence criminal proceedings against defendants, represent state interests or government interests, and prosecute defendants on behalf of state or government.

Psychoanalytic theory   Sigmund Freud's theory of personality formation through the id, ego, and superego at various stages of childhood; maintains that early life experiences influence adult behavior.

Public defender   Court-appointed attorney for indigent defendants who cannot afford private counsel.

Public risk   A subjective gauge of an offender's perceived dangerousness to the community if released, either on probation or parole; sometimes assessed through risk assessment instruments.

Radical criminology   Stresses control of the poor by the wealthy and powerful. Crime is defined by those in political and economic power in such a way so as to control lower socioeconomic classes (e.g., vagrancy statutes are manifestations of control by wealthy over the poor).

Ranches   (See also **Wilderness programs**) Nonsecure facilities for juvenile delinquents designed to promote self-confidence and self-reliance; located in rural settings;

involves camping out and other survival activities for building confidence.

Rand Corporation   Private institution that conducts investigations and surveys of criminals and examines a wide variety of social issues; located in Santa Monica, California; distributes literature to many criminal justice agencies; contracts with and conducts research for other institutions.

Reality therapy   Behavior modification method focusing on the collaborative relation between a PO and a client; client is accepted for what he or she is, but whose behavior is unacceptable; rationalization for behavior is rejected; an outgrowth of developmental theory.

Rearrest   One indicator of recidivism; consists of taking parolee or probationer into custody for investigation in relation to crimes committed; not necessarily indicative of new crimes committed by probationers or parolees; may be the result of police officer suspicion.

Recidivism   New crime committed by an offender who has served time or was placed on probation for previous offense; tendency to repeat crimes.

Recidivism rates   Proportion of offenders who, when released from probation or parole, commit further crimes; measured several different ways, including probation revocation, parole revocation, violating curfew, testing positive for drugs or alcohol, or failing to appear for weekly or monthly meetings with POs.

Recidivists   Offenders who have committed previous offenses and are convicted of new crimes.

Reconviction   Measure of recidivism in which former convicted offenders are found guilty of new crimes by a judge or jury.

Reform schools   Early establishments providing secure confinement for more serious types of juvenile offenders; juvenile equivalent to prisons; taught youths various crafts and trade skills; intended to reform youth's behavior; unsuccessful at behavior modification.

Regulator value system   Parole board orientation directed toward inmate reactions to parole board decisions; deals with issues such as how current inmates will react to those decisions in view of their own circumstances or how the parole supervision system could be undermined or enhanced as the result of parole board decision making.

Rehabilitation   Correcting criminal behavior through educational and other means, usually associated with prisons.

Rehabilitation model   Orientation toward offenders that stresses reintegration into society through counseling, education, and learning new ways of relating to others.

Rehabilitative ideal (See **Rehabilitation**)

Reincarceration   Return to prison or jail for one or more reasons including parole or probation violations and revocations, rearrests, and reconvictions.

Released on own recognizance   Also called ROR; act of releasing defendants charged with crimes into the community prior to trial, without bail or other restrictions; usually ROR defendants have strong community ties and have committed minor or nonviolent offenses.

Reparations   Damages paid an offender to victims for injuries and property loss because of a crime.

Repeat offenders   Habitual offenders who continually reoffend and are convicted of new offenses during a span of years.

Respondeat superior   Doctrine that holds master (supervisor, administrator) liable for actions of slave (employees).

Restitution   Stipulation by court that offenders must compensate victims for their financial losses resulting from crime; compensation for psychological, physical, or financial loss by victim; may be imposed as a part of an incarcerative sentence.

Restorative justice   Every action that is primarily oriented toward doing justice by repairing the harm that has been caused by a crime.

Reverse waiver hearings   Formal meetings with the juvenile court judge and criminal court to determine whether youths who have been transferred to criminal court for processing as the result of an automatic waiver or legislative waiver can have this waiver set aside so that the case may be heard in juvenile court.

Reverse waivers   Actions filed by juveniles to have their transferred cases waived from criminal court back to juvenile court.

Revocation   Action taken by a parole board or judge to revoke or rescind the parolee's or probationer's program because of one or more program violations.

Revocation actions   Any decision by a judge or parole board to consider revoking a probationer's or parolee's program based on one or more reasons related to program violations.

Reynolds, James Bronson   Early prison reformer; established the University Settlement in 1893 in New York; settlement project ultimately abandoned after Reynolds and others could not demonstrate its effectiveness at reform to politicians and the public generally.

Risk   Danger or potential harm posed by an offender, convicted or otherwise; likelihood of being successful if placed in a probation or parole program intended to reintegrate or rehabilitate through community involvement.

Risk assessment   Any attempt to characterize the future behaviors of persons charged with or convicted of crimes; involves behavioral forecasts of one's propensity to pose harm or a danger to themselves or to others; usually paper-and-pencil devices that yield scores of one's potential dangerousness; used for probation and parole decision making.

Risk assessment instruments   Predictive device intended to forecast an offender's propensity to commit new offenses or recidivate.

Risk/needs instruments   The same type of device as a risk assessment instrument, with the exception that items are included that attempt to determine or define necessary services, counseling, education, or any other helpful strategy that will deter offenders from future offending.

Role ambiguity Lack of clarity about work expectations; unfamiliarity with correctional tasks.

Role conflict Clash between personal feelings and beliefs and job duties as a probation, parole, or correctional officer.

Rules of Criminal Procedure Formal rules followed by state and federal governments in processing defendants from arrest through trial; these rules vary from state to state.

Runaways Juveniles who leave their homes for long-term periods without parental consent or supervision; unruly youths who cannot be controlled or managed by parents or guardians.

Salient factor score (SFS), SFS 81 Score used by parole boards and agencies to forecast an offender's risk to the public and future dangerousness; numerical classification that predicts the probability of a parolee's success if parole is granted; different numerical designations indicate years when scoring devices were created.

Sanctioner value system Model used by parole boards in early release decision making in which the amount of time served is equated with seriousness of conviction offense.

Scared Straight New Jersey program devised in 1980s in which juveniles visit inmates in prisons; inmates talk to youths and scare them with stories of their prison experiences; intended as a delinquency deterrent.

Screening cases Procedure used by prosecutor to define which cases have prosecutive merit and which do not; some screening bureaus are made up of police and lawyers with trial experience.

Secondary deviation Law violations that have become incorporated into person's lifestyle or behavior pattern.

Secure confinement Confinement of juvenile offender in facility that restricts movement in community; similar to an adult penal facility involving total incarceration.

See Our Side (SOS) program Prince George's County, Maryland, program established in 1983; SOS is referred to by its directors as a "juvenile aversion" program and dissociates itself from "scare" programs such as Scared Straight; seeks to educate juveniles about the realities of life in prison through discussions and hands-on experience and attempts to show them the types of behaviors that can lead to incarceration; clients coming to SOS are referrals from various sources, including juvenile court, public and private schools, churches, professional counseling agencies, and police and fire departments; youths served by SOS range in age from 12 to 18, and they do not have to be adjudicated as delinquent to be eligible for participation. SOS consists of four, three-hour phases.

Selective incapacitation Selectively incarcerating individuals who show a high likelihood of repeating their previous offenses; based on forecasts of potential for recidivism; includes but not limited to dangerousness.

Self-reported information Any data about one's personal criminal offending disclosed by the offender other than by official recordings of arrests; any disclosures of crimes committed by offenders that are otherwise unknown to police.

Sentence recommendation plea bargaining Agreement between defense counsel and prosecutor in which prosecutor recommends a specific sentence to the judge in exchange for a defendant's guilty plea.

Sentencing Phase of criminal justice process in which a judge imposes a penalty for a criminal conviction; penalty may include a fine and/or incarceration in a jail or prison for a period of months or years; may also include numerous nonincarcerative punishments, such as community-based corrections.

Sentencing hearing A formal procedure following one's criminal conviction at which a judge hears evidence from a convicted offender and others concerning crime seriousness and impact; PSI report introduced as evidence to influence judicial decision making; additional testimony heard to either mitigate or aggravate sentence imposed.

Sentencing memorandum, defendant's Core element of presentence investigation report in which offenders provide their version of the offense and the nature of their involvement in that offense; may include mitigating factors that might lessen sentencing severity.

Sentencing Reform Act of 1984 Act that provided federal judges and others with considerable discretionary powers to provide alternative sentencing and other provisions in their sentencing of various offenders.

Sex offenders Persons who commit a sexual act prohibited by law; common types of sex offenders include rapists and prostitutes, although sex offenses may include voyeurism (Peeping Toms), exhibitionism, child sexual molestation, incest, date rape, and marital rape.

Shire-reeves The early English term used to refer to the chief law enforcement officer of counties (shires) who was known as a reeve. Contemporary usage of the term has been abbreviated to sheriff, who is the chief law enforcement officer of U.S. counties.

Shock incarceration (See **Shock probation**)

Shock parole (See **Shock probation**)

Shock probation (See also **Shock probation program**) Placing an offender in prison for a brief period, primarily to give him or her a taste of prison life (for "shock value") and then releasing the person into the custody of a probation/parole officer.

Shock probationers Any convicted offenders sentenced to a shock probation program.

Shock probation program Derives from judges initially sentencing offenders to terms of incarceration, usually in a jail; after offenders have been in jail for a brief period (e.g., 30, 60, 90, or 120 days), they are brought back to reappear before their original sentencing judges; these judges reconsider the original sentences they imposed on these offenders; provided that these offenders behaved well while incarcerated, judges resentence them to probation for specified terms; first used in Ohio in 1964.

Situational offenders   First-offenders who commit only the offense for which they were apprehended and prosecuted and are unlikely to commit future crimes.

Social casework   An approach to modifying the behavior of criminals by developing a close relation between the PO and client, within a problem solving context, and coordinated with the appropriate use of community resources.

Social control theory   Explanation of criminal behavior that focuses on control mechanisms and techniques and strategies for regulating human behavior, leading to conformity or obedience to society's rules, and that posits that deviance results when social controls are weakened or break down so that individuals are not motivated to conform to them.

Socialization   Learning through contact with others.

Social learning theory   Applied to criminal behavior, the theory stressing importance of learning through modeling others who are criminal; criminal behavior is a function of copying or learning criminal conduct from others.

Social process theories   Explanations of criminal conduct that arise from one's social environment and close associations with others.

Sociobiology   Scientific study of causal relation between genetic structure and social behavior.

Solitary confinement   Technically originated with the Walnut Street Jail; used subsequently by and originally attributed to the Auburn (New York) State Penitentiary in 1820s, where prisoners were housed individually in separate cells during evening hours.

South Carolina Intensive Supervised Probation Program   Program implemented in 1984; primary aims were to heighten surveillance of participants, increase PO/client contact, and increase offender accountability; started as a pilot or experimental project.

Specialized caseloads model   PO caseload model based on POs' unique skills and knowledge relative to offender drug or alcohol problems; some POs are assigned particular clients with unique problems who require more than average PO expertise.

Special needs offenders   Inmates, probationers, and parolees with unique problems, such as drug or alcohol dependencies, communicable diseases such as tuberculosis or AIDS/HIV, mental illness, or developmental disabilities and mental retardation; may include gang members who require unconventional interventions.

Split sentencing   Procedure by which judge imposes a sentence of incarceration for a fixed period followed by a probationary period for a fixed duration; similar to shock probation.

Standard parolees   Anyone on parole who must comply with the basic parole program conditions, as opposed to someone who is intensively supervised by POs with frequent face-to-face visits and random drug and alcohol checks.

Standard probation programs   Probationers conform to all terms of their probation program, but their contact with probation officers is minimal; often, their contact is by telephone or letter once or twice a month.

Status offenders   Any juveniles who commit offenses that would not be crimes if committed by adults (e.g., runaway behavior, truancy, curfew violation).

Status offenses   Violations of statutes or ordinances by minors that, if committed by adults, would not be considered either felonies or misdemeanors.

Statutory exclusion   Certain juveniles, largely because of their age and offense committed, are automatically excluded from juvenile court jurisdiction.

Statutory good time   Credit prescribed by the U.S. Congress and state legislatures that prisoners may apply toward their maximum sentences; a method of obtaining early release under determinate sentencing schemes.

Stigmatization   Social process in which offenders acquire undesirable characteristics as the result of imprisonment or court appearances; undesirable criminal or delinquent labels are assigned those who are processed through the criminal and juvenile justice systems.

Strain theory   A criminological theory positing that a gap between culturally approved goals and legitimate means of achieving them causes frustration that leads to criminal behavior.

Stress   Negative anxiety accompanied by an alarm reaction, resistance, and exhaustion; such anxiety contributes to heart disease, headaches, high blood pressure, and ulcers.

Study release   Essentially the same as work release programs, but for the express purpose of securing educational goals; several types of study release have been identified: adult basic education, high school or high school equivalency (GED), technical or vocational education, and college.

Study release programs (See **Study release**)

Subculture of violence   Subculture with values that demand the overt use of violence in certain social situations. Marvin Wolfgang and Franco Ferracuti devised this concept to depict a set of norms apart from mainstream conventional society, in which the theme of violence is pervasive and dominant. Learned through socialization with others as an alternative lifestyle.

Subcultures   Social cliques and behavior patterns of selected groups, such as gangs.

Summary offense   Any petty crime punishable by a fine only.

Superego   Sigmund Freud's term describing that part of personality concerned with moral values.

Supermax   Level of security designed for the most dangerous inmates with extensive criminal histories.

Supervised release   Any type of offender management program in which clients must be supervised by probation/parole officers more or less intensively.

Tattoo Symbol of gang membership that is placed on the body to signify one's gang affiliation.

Tattoo removal program Any process by which gang members can have their gang tattoos removed in order to escape gang control.

Technical program violations Any infractions by probationers or parolees of the terms of their probation or parole agreements; some violations include failing drug or alcohol checks, violating curfew, associating with known felons, and possessing firearms or cellular telephones or pagers.

Temporary release programs Any type of program for jail or prison inmates designed to permit them absence from confinement, either escorted or unescorted, for a short time; work release, study release, and furloughs are most common types of temporary release.

Theory An integrated body of propositions, definitions, and assumptions that are related in such a way so as to explain and predict the relation between two or more variables.

Theory of opportunity Explanation of deviant behavior and criminality that is class-based and that suggests that persons in the lower socioeconomic classes have less opportunity to acquire scarce goods; therefore, they obtain these goods by illegal means.

Therapeutic community A treatment model in which all activities, both formal and informal, are viewed as interrelated interventions that address the multidimensional disorder of the whole person. These activities include educational and therapeutic meetings and groups, as well as interpersonal and social activities of the community; within this theoretical framework, social and psychological change evolves as a dynamic interaction between the individual and the peer community, its context of activities, and expectations for participation.

Therapeutic jurisprudence View of judges which attempts to combine a "rights" perspective—focusing on justice, rights, and equality issues—with an "ethic of care" perspective—focusing on care, interdependence, and response to need.

Tickets-of-leave Document given to a prisoner as the result of accumulating good time marks and which would obligate the prisoner to remain under limited jurisdiction and supervision of local police.

Tiers Different floors of a prison or penal institution designed to hold prisoners who have committed various types of offenses.

Tier system Auburn (New York) State Penitentiary innovation in 1820s designed to establish multiple levels of inmate housing, probably according to type of conviction offense and institutional conduct.

Tort Civil wrong, omission in which plaintiff seeks monetary damages; as distinguished from crimes, for which incarceration and fines may be imposed.

Total institution Erving Goffman's term describing self-contained nature of prisons; depicts all community functions inside prison walls, including social exchange and living.

Totality of circumstances Sometimes used as the standard by which offender guilt is determined or search and seizure warrants may be obtained; officers consider the entire set of circumstances surrounding apparently illegal event and act accordingly.

Traditional treatment-oriented model Stresses traditional rehabilitative measures that seek to reintegrate the offender into the community through extensive assistance; may include elements of the justice and limited risk control models, its primary aim is long-term change in offender behavior; includes strategies such as (1) developing individual offender plans for life in the community such as work, study, or community service; (2) full-time employment and/or vocational training; and/or (3) using community sponsors or other support personnel to provide assistance and direction for offenders.

Transfer hearing Also known as certification or waiver; a proceeding to determine whether juveniles should be certified as adults for purposes of being subjected to jurisdiction of adult criminal courts where more severe penalties may be imposed.

Transfers Also known as certification and waiver; proceedings at which juveniles are remanded to the jurisdiction of criminal courts to be processed as though they were adults.

Transportion This form of punishment was banishment to remote territories or islands where law violators would work at hard labor in penal colonies isolated from society.

Treater value system Parole board decision-making system in which emphasis is on rehabilitation and early release decisions are made on the basis of what will best suit the offender.

Treatment alternatives to street crime (TASC) Since 1972, various community-based treatment programs have been implemented to treat and counsel drug-dependent clients; collectively labeled treatment alternatives to street crime (TASC) and currently operating in numerous jurisdictions throughout the United States to improve client abstinence from drugs, increase their employment potential, and improve their social/personal functioning.

Treatment model (See **Medical model**)

True bill Finding by a grand jury that probable cause exists that a crime was committed and that a specific person or persons committed it; an indictment; a presentment.

Truth-in-sentencing provisions Legislatively mandated proportionately longer incarcerative terms that must be served by inmates before they become eligible for parole; the federal government requires that its inmates must serve at least 85 percent of their imposed sentences before they are eligible for supervised release.

Unconditional diversion program No restrictions are placed on offender's behavior; no formal controls operate to control or monitor divertee's behavior.

Unconditional release   Any authorized release from custody, either as a defendant or convicted offender, without restriction; usually applicable to inmates who have served their statutory time in jail or prison; diversion or probation may be unconditional.

Uniform Crime Reports (UCR)   Published annually by the Federal Bureau of Investigation; includes statistics about the number and kinds of crimes reported in the United States annually by over 15,000 law enforcement agencies; the major sourcebook of crime statistics in the United States; compiled by gathering information on 29 types of crime from participating law enforcement agencies; crime information is requested from all rural and urban law enforcement agencies and is reported to the FBI.

University Settlement   Privately operated facility in New York commenced in 1893 by James Bronson Reynolds to provide assistance and job referral services to community residents; settlement involved in probation work in 1901; eventually abandoned after considerable public skepticism and when political opponents withdrew their support.

User fees   Monthly fees paid by divertees or probationers during the diversion or probationary period to help defray expenses incurred by the public or private agencies that monitor them.

U.S. Code Annotated   Comprehensive compendium of federal laws and statutes, including landmark cases and discussions of law applications.

U.S. sentencing guidelines   Standards of punishment implemented by federal courts in November 1987 obligating federal judges to impose presumptive sentences on all convicted offenders; guidelines exist based on offense seriousness and offender characteristics; judges may depart from guidelines only by justifying their departures in writing.

Van Dieman's Land   1780s English island penal colony established off the coast of Australia; used to accommodate dangerous prisoners convicted of crimes in England.

Victim and Witness Protection Act of 1982   Federal act designed to require criminals to provide restitution to victims; provides a sentencing option that judges may impose.

Victim compensation   Any financial restitution payable to victims by either the state or convicted offenders.

Victim impact statement (VIS)   Statement filed voluntarily by victim of crime, appended to the presentence investigation report as a supplement for judicial consideration in sentencing offender; describes injuries to victims resulting from convicted offender's actions.

Victimization data   Carefully worded questions lead people to report incidents that can be classified as crimes; this material is statistically manipulated in such a way so as to make it comparable with *UCR* statistics.

Victimizations   The basic measure of the occurrence of a crime and a specific criminal act that affects a single victim.

Victim-offender reconciliation   Any mediated or arbitrated civil proceeding or meeting between offender and victim at which a mutually satisfactory solution is agreed upon and criminal proceedings are avoided.

Victim-Offender Reconciliation Project (VORP)   A specific form of conflict resolution between the victim and the offender; face-to-face encounter is the essence of this process; Elkhart County, Indiana, has been the site of VORP since 1987; primary aims of VORP are to make offenders accountable for their wrongs against victims, to reduce recidivism among participating offenders, and to heighten responsibility of offenders through victim compensation and repayment for damages inflicted.

Victims of Crime Act of 1984   Under Public Law 98-473, the Comprehensive Crime Control Act was established; Chapter 14 of this act is known as the Victims of Crime Act of 1984; as a part of all state and federal government victim compensation programs and work release requirements, a certain amount of earned wages of work releasees may be allocated to restitution and to a general victim compensation fund.

Violence   Behaviors of individuals that intentionally threaten, attempt, or inflict physical harm on others.

Violent crimes   Any criminal act involving direct confrontation of one or more victims; may or may not involve injury or death; examples are aggravated assault, robbery, forcible rape, homicide.

VisionQuest   A type of wilderness program; a private, for-profit enterprise operated from Tucson, Arizona; program operates in about 15 states, serves about 500 juveniles annually, and costs about half that of secure institutionalization.

Volunteers   Hardworking, unpaid, dedicated individuals who fill in the gaps for correctional agencies and provide much-needed services that victims, inmates, parolees, probationers and their families might otherwise not receive because of limited program funding.

Waiver hearing   Motion by a prosecutor to transfer a juvenile charged with various offenses to a criminal or adult court for prosecution; waiver motions make it possible to sustain adult criminal penalties.

Waiver motion   Move by defense or prosecution to transfer a juvenile to jurisdiction of criminal court.

Waivers (See **Transfers**)

Walnut Street Jail   Pennsylvania legislature authorized in 1790 the renovation of a facility originally constructed on Walnut Street in 1776 to house the overflow resulting from overcrowding of the High Street Jail; used as both a workhouse and a place of incarceration for all types of offenders; 1790 renovation was the first of several innovations in U.S. corrections, including separating the most serious prisoners from others in 16 large solitary cells, separating other prisoners according to their offense seriousness, and separating prisoners according to gender.

White-collar crime   Offenses committed by someone in the course of performing his or her job or occupation; embezzlement and fraud are examples.

Wickersham Commission   A National Commission on Law Observance and Enforcement established in 1931 and chaired by George W. Wickersham; evaluated and critiqued parole as well as the practices of various criminal justice agencies in managing the criminal population.

Wilderness program Any nonsecure outdoors program that enables juvenile delinquents to learn survival skills, self-confidence, self-reliance, and self-esteem; used for secure-confinement bound offenders.

Women's Activities and Learning Center Program (WALC) The Kansas Department of Corrections established a program for women with children that has been patterned after PATCH (Parents and Their Children) commenced by the Missouri Department of Corrections and MATCH (Mothers and Their Children) operated by the California Department of Corrections; Topeka facility's primary goal is developing and coordinating a broad range of programs, services, and classes and workshops that will increase women offender's chances for a positive reintegration with their families and society upon release.

Work furlough (See **Work release**)

Workhouse Incarcerative facilities in England in 1700s where sheriffs and other officials "hired out" their inmates to perform skilled and semiskilled tasks for various merchants; the manifest functions of workhouses and prisoner labor were supposed to improve the moral and social fiber of prisoners and train them to perform useful skills when they were eventually released; profits from inmate labor, however, were often pocketed by corrupt jail and workhouse officials.

Work release Any program in which inmates in jails or prisons are permitted to work in their communities with minimal restrictions and supervision, are compensated at the prevailing minimum wage, and must serve their nonworking hours housed in a secure facility.

XYY syndrome Theory of criminal behavior suggesting that some criminals are born with an extra "Y" chromosome, characterized as the "aggressive" chromosome compared with the "passive X" chromosome. An extra Y chromosome produces greater agitation, greater aggressiveness, and criminal propensities.

Youth-at-risk program Any juvenile program targeting youths considered at risk because of low socioeconomic status, poor family relationships, or members of families with known criminal parents or siblings; any program designed to improve a youth's skills in various educational and social areas, where such immediate limitations make conditions favorable for acquiring delinquent characteristics and behaviors.

Youth Service Bureaus (YSBs) Established in numerous jurisdictions to accomplish several objectives of diversion; places within communities where "delinquent-prone" youths could be referred by parents, schools, and law enforcement agencies; forerunners of contemporary community-based correctional programs, because they were intended to solicit volunteers from among community residents and to mobilize a variety of resources that could assist in a youth's treatment; the nature of treatments for youths, within the YSB concept, originally included referrals to a variety of community services, educational experiences, and individual or group counseling; original YSBs attempted to compile lists of existing community services, agencies, organizations, and sponsors who could cooperatively coordinate these resources in the most productive ways to benefit affected juveniles.

References

Abt Associates, Inc. (1976). *Court Planning and Research: The Los Angeles Experience.* Washington, DC: U.S. National Institute of Law Enforcement and Criminal Justice, U.S. Government Printing Office.

Abt Associates, Inc. (1987). *Sentencing and Time Served.* Washington, DC: Bureau of Justice Statistics.

Adair, David N., Jr. (2000). "Revocation Sentences: A Practical Guide." *Federal Probation* **64:**67–73.

Adams, Robert, and Jo Campling (1994). *Prison Riots in Britain and the USA.* London: Macmillan.

Adams, Stuart (1975). *Perceived Impact of Research on Corrections.* Washington, DC: U.S. National Institute of Law Enforcement and Criminal Justice.

Adler, Jeffrey S. (1992). "Streetwalkers, Degraded Outcasts, and Good-for-Nothing Huzzies: Woman and the Dangerous Class in Antebellum St. Louis." *Journal of Social History* **25:**737–755.

Administrative Office of U.S. Courts (1997). *PSI Reports: Preparation and Examples.* Washington, DC: Administrative Office of U.S. Courts.

Administrative Office of U.S. Courts (2001). *Federal Probation Officer Code of Ethics.* Washington, DC: Administrative Office of U.S. Courts.

Aguirre, Adalberto, Jr., and David Baker (eds.) (2000). "Latinos and the Criminal Justice System." *Justice Professional* **13:**3–102.

Albonetti, Celesta A. (1999). "The Avoidance of Punishment: A Legal-Bureaucratic Model of Suspended Sentences in Federal White-Collar Cases Prior to the Federal Sentencing Guidelines." *Social Forces* **78:**303–329.

Albonetti, Celesta A., and John R. Hepburn (1997). "Probation Revocation: A Proportional Hazards Model of the Conditional Effects of Social Disadvantage." *Social Problems* **44:**124–138.

Albright, Kathleen, et al. (1996). *Evaluation of the Impact of Boot Camps for Juvenile Offenders.* Washington, DC: U.S. Department of Justice.

Alcoholics Anonymous World Services, Inc. (1991). *A.A. in Prison: Inmate to Inmate.* New York: Alcoholics Anonymous World Services, Inc.

Alexander, Jack, and James Austin (1992). *Handbook for Evaluating Objective Prison Classification Systems.* Washington, DC: U.S. National Institute of Corrections.

Allen, G. Frederick, and H. Treger (1990). "Community Service Orders in Federal Probation: Perceptions of Probationers and Host Agencies." *Federal Probation* **54:**8–14.

Altschuler, David M., and Troy L. Armstrong (1991). "Intensive Aftercare for the High-Risk Juvenile Parolee: Issues and Approaches in Reintegration and Community Supervision in Juvenile Probation and Parole." In *Intensive Interventions with High-Risk Youths: Promising Approaches,* Troy L. Armstrong (ed.). Monsey, NY: Criminal Justice Press.

Altschuler, David M., and Troy L. Armstrong (1993). "Intensive Aftercare for High-Risk Juvenile Parolees: Program Development and Implementation in Eight Pilot Sites." Unpublished paper presented at the annual meeting of the American Society of Criminology, Phoenix, AZ, October.

Altschuler, David M., and Troy L. Armstrong (1994). *Intensive Aftercare with High-Risk Juveniles.* Washington, DC: U.S. Office of Juvenile Justice and Delinquency Prevention.

Altschuler, David M., Troy L. Armstrong, and Doris Layton MacKenzie (1999). *Reintegration, Supervised Release, and Intensive Aftercare.* Washington, DC: U.S. Office of Juvenile Justice an Delinquency Prevention.

Ambrosio, Tara Jen, and Vincent Schiraldi (1997). *From Classrooms to Cell Blocks: A National Perspective.* Washington, DC: Justice Policy Institute.

American Correctional Association (1983). *The American Prison: From the Beginning . . . A Pictorial History.* College Park, MD: American Correctional Association.

American Correctional Association (1993a). *Classification: A Tool for Managing Today's Offenders.* Laurel, MD: American Correctional Association.

American Correctional Association (1993b). *Community Partnerships in Action.* Laurel, MD: American Correctional Association.

American Correctional Association (1993c). *Female Offenders: Meeting Needs of a Neglected Population.* Laurel, MD: American Correctional Association.

American Correctional Association (1993d). *Gangs in Correctional Facilities: A National Assessment.* Laurel, MD: American Correctional Association.

American Correctional Association (1993e). *Juvenile and Adult Correctional Departments, Institutions, Agencies and Paroling Authorities: United States and Canada.* Laurel, MD: American Correctional Association.

American Correctional Association (1994). *Field Officer and Resource Guide.* Laurel, MD: American Correctional Association.

American Correctional Association (1995a). *Community Partnerships in Action.* Laurel, MD: American Correctional Association.

American Correctional Association (1995b). *Standards for Adult Community Residential Services,* 3d ed. Laurel, MD: American Correctional Association.

American Correctional Association (1995c). *The State of Corrections.* Laurel, MD: American Correctional Association.

American Correctional Association (1996a). *Community Corrections.* Lanham, MD: American Correctional Association.

American Correctional Association (1996b). *Creative Therapies and Programs in Corrections.* Lanham, MD: American Correctional Association.

American Correctional Association (1996c). *Juvenile and Adult Boot Camps.* Lanham, MD: American Correctional Association.

American Correctional Association (2000). *Juvenile and Adult Directory.* Lanham, MD: American Correctional Association.

American Correctional Association (2001). *Probation and Parole Directory 2001–2004.* Lanham, MD: American Correctional Association.

American Probation and Parole Association (1996). *Restoring Hope through Community Partnerships: The Real Deal in Crime Control—A Handbook for Community Corrections.* Lexington, KY: American Probation and Parole Association.

American Probation and Parole Association (1997). *The American Probation and Parole Association Code of Ethics.* Lexington, KY: American Probation and Parole Association.

Ammar, Nawal H., and Edna Erez (2000). "Health Delivery Systems in Women's Prisons: The Case of Ohio." *Federal Probation* **64:**19–26.

Anderson, David C. (1998). *Sensible Justice: Alternatives to Prison.* New York: New Press.

Anderson, Dennis B. (1999). "Problem Gambling Among Incarcerated Felons." *Journal of Offender Rehabilitation* **29:**113–127.

Anderson, Dennis B., Randall E. Schumacker, and Sara L. Anderson (1991). "Releasee Characteristics and Parole Success." *Journal of Offender Rehabilitation* **17:**133–145.

Anderson, H. S., D. Sestoft, and T. Lilleback (2000). "A Longitudinal Study of Prisoners on Remand: Psychiatric Prevalence, Incidence and Psychopathology in Solitary vs. Non-Solitary Confinement." *Acta Psychiatrica Scandinavica* **102:**19–25.

Anderson, James F., and Laronistine Dyson (1999). *Boot Camps: An Intermediate Sanction.* Lanham, MD: University Press of America.

Andrus, J. K., D. W. Fleming, and C. Knox (1999). "HIV Testing in Prisoners: Is Mandatory Testing Mandatory?" *American Journal of Public Health* **79:**40–42.

Ansay, Sylvia J., and Deena Benveneste (1999). "Equal Application of Unequal Treatment: Practical Outcomes for Women on Community Control in Florida." *Women and Criminal Justice* **10:**121–135.

Applegate, Brandon K., et al. (2000). "Individualization, Criminalization, or Problem Resolution: A Factorial Survey of Juvenile Court Judges' Decisions to Incarcerate Youthful Felony Offenders." *Justice Quarterly* **17:**310–331.

Archambeault, William G., and Donald R. Deis Jr. (1996). *Cost Effectiveness Comparisons of Private versus Public Prisons in Louisiana.* Baton Rouge: School of Social Work, Louisiana State University.

Archwamety, Teara, and Antonis Katsiyannis (2000). "Academic Remediation, Parole Violations, and Recidivism Rates." *Remedial and Special Education* **21:**161–170.

Arizona Department of Corrections (1991). *Offender Classification System (OCS): Classification Operating Manual.* Phoenix: Arizona Department of Corrections.

Armstrong, Troy L. (1988). "National Survey of Juvenile Intensive Probation Supervision, Part I." *Criminal Justice Abstracts* **20:**342–348.

Arnold, Charlotte S. (1992). "The Program for Female Offenders, Inc.—A Community Corrections Answer to Jail Overcrowding." *American Jails* **5:**36–40.

Arnold, Charlotte S. (1993). "Respect, Recognition Are Keys to Effective Volunteer Programs." *Corrections Today* **55:**118–122.

Arola, Terryl, and Richard Lawrence (1999). "Assessing Probation Officer Assaults and Responding to Officer Safety Concerns." *APPA Perspectives* **22:**32–35.

Arthur, Lindsay G. (2000). "Punishment Doesn't Work!" *Juvenile and Family Court Journal* **51:**37–42.

Ashford, Jose B., and Craig Winston LeCroy (1993). "Juvenile Parole Policy in the United States: Determinate versus Indeterminate Models." *Justice Quarterly* **10:**179–195.

Atkins, Elliot (1996). "Post-Verdict Psychological Consultation in the Federal Courts." *American Journal of Forensic Psychology* **14:**25–35.

Auerbach, Barbara J., and Thomas C. Castellano (eds.) (1998). *Successful Community Sanctions and Services for Special Offenders: Proceedings of the 1994 Conference of the International Community Corrections Association.* Lanham, MD: American Correctional Association.

Augustus, John (1852). *A Report of the Labors of John Augustus for the Last Ten Years: In Aid of the Unfortunate.* New York: Wright and Hasty.

Austin, James (1987). *Success and Failure on Parole in California: A Preliminary Evaluation.* San Francisco: National Council on Crime and Delinquency.

Austin, James, and Jack Alexander (1996). *Evaluation of the Colorado Department of Corrections Inmate Classification System.* San Francisco: National Council on Crime and Delinquency.

Austin, James, Michael Jones, and Melissa Bolyard (1993). *The Growing Use of Jail Boot Camps: The Current State of the Art.* Washington, DC: U.S. Department of Justice, Office of Justice Programs.

Austin, James, et al. (1995). *National Assessment of Structured Sentencing: Final Report.* Washington, DC: U.S. Bureau of Justice Statistics.

Bahn, Charles, and James R. Davis (1998). "Day Reporting Centers as an Alternative to Incarceration." *Journal of Offender Rehabilitation* **27:**139–150.

Baird, Christopher S. (1985). "Classifying Juveniles: Making the Most of an Important Management Tool." *Corrections Today* **47:**32–38.

Baird, Christopher (1992a). "The Management of Probation Caseloads: A National Assessment." Unpublished paper presented at the annual meeting of the American Society of Criminology, New Orleans, LA, November.

Baird, Christopher (1992b). *Validating Risk Assessment Instruments Used in Community Corrections.* Madison, WI: National Council on Crime and Delinquency.

Baird, Christopher S., Dennis Wagner, and Robert DeComo (1995). *Evaluation of the Impact of Oregon's Structured Sanctions Program.* San Francisco: National Council on Crime and Delinquency.

Bandura, Albert (1977). *Social Learning Theory.* Englewood Cliffs, NJ: Prentice Hall.

Baroff, George S. (1990). "Establishing Mental Retardation in Capital Defendants." *American Journal of Forensic Psychology* **8:**35–45.

Barrineau, H. E., III (1994). *Civil Liability in Criminal Justice,* 2d ed. Cincinnati, OH: Anderson Publishing Company.

Basta, Joanne (1995). *Evaluation of the Intensive Probation Specialized Caseload for Graduates of Shock Incarceration.* Tucson, AZ: Adult Probation Department, Pima County Superior Court.

Bauer, Jere M. (1999). *Felony Sentencing and Probation.* Madison: Wisconsin Legislative Fiscal Bureau.

Bayens, Gerald J., Michael W. Manske, and John Ortiz Smykla (1998). "The Attitudes of Criminal Justice Workgroups toward Intensive Supervised Probation." *American Journal of Criminal Justice* **22:**189–206.

Bayse, D. J. (1993). *Helping Hands: A Handbook for Volunteers in Prisons and Jails.* Laurel, MD: American Correctional Association.

Bazemore, Gordon (1998). "Restorative Justice and Earned Redemption: Communities, Victims, and Offender Reintegration." *American Behavioral Scientist* **41:**768–813.

Bazemore, Gordon, and Dennis Maloney (1994). "Rehabilitative Community Service: Toward Restorative Service Sanctions in a Balanced Justice System." *Federal Probation* **58:**24–34.

Bazemore, Gordon, and Lode Walgrave (eds.) (1999). *Restorative Juvenile Justice: Repairing the Harm of Youth Crime.* Monsey, NY: Criminal Justice Press.

Beck, Allen J. (2000a). *Prison and Jail Inmates at Midyear 1999.* Washington, DC: U.S. Department of Justice.

Beck, Allen J. (2000b). *Prisoners in 1999.* Washington, DC: U.S. Department of Justice.

Becker, Howard S. (1963). *Outsiders: Studies in the Sociology of Deviance.* New York: Free Press.

Behr, Edward (1996). *Prohibition: Thirteen Years That Changed America.* New York: Arcade Publishing.

Belenko, Steven R. (1999). "Research on Drug Courts: A Critical Review 1999 Update." *National Drug Court Institute Review* **2:**1–58.

Benzvy-Miller, Shereen (1990). "Community Corrections and the NIMBY Syndrome." *Forum on Corrections Research* **2:**18–22.

Benzvy-Miller, Shereen, and Kent Roach (2000). "Changing Punishment at the Turn of the Century: Finding the Common Ground." *Canadian Journal of Criminology* **42:**249–404.

Berliner, Lucy, et al. (1995). "A Sentencing Alternative for Sex Offenders: A Study of Decision Making and Recidivism." *Journal of Interpersonal Violence* **10:**487–502.

Bernat, Frances P. (1994). "Public Sector Worker Safety and Legal Remedies." *American Journal of Criminal Justice* **18:**307–326.

Bernstein, Ilene N., William R. Kelly, and Patricia A. Doyle (1977). "Societal Reaction to Deviants: The Case of Criminal Defendants." *American Sociological Review* **42:**743–755.

Bigger, Phillip J. (1993). "Officers in Danger: Results of the Federal Probation and Pretrial Officers Association's National Study on Serious Assaults." *APPA Perspectives* **17:**14–20.

Bilchik, Shay (1996a). *Juvenile Boot Camps: Lessons Learned.* Washington, DC: U.S. Department of Justice.

Bilchik, Shay (1996b). *State Responses to Serious and Violent Juvenile Crime.* Pittsburgh, PA: National Center for Juvenile Justice.

Binder, Arnold, et al. (1985). "A Diversionary Approach for the 1980s." *Federal Probation* **49:**4–12.

Birkbeck, Christopher, Nora Campbell Wilson, and Michelle Hussong (1996). *Furloughs Granted to Minimum-Security Inmates in New Mexico.* Albuquerque: New Mexico Criminal Justice Statistical Analysis Center.

Birmingham, Luke, et al. (2000). "Mental Illness at Reception into Prison." *Criminal Behaviour and Mental Health* **10:**77–87.

Bishop, Bill (1993). "New York's Crime War: The Empire Strikes Out!" *APPA Perspectives* **17:**13–14.

Bjorkly, Stal, Odd E. Havik, and Tor Loberg (1996). "The Interrater Reliability of the Scale for the Prediction of Aggression and Dangerousness in Psychotic Patients." *Criminal Justice and Behavior* **23:**440–454.

Black, Henry Campbell (1990). *Black's Law Dictionary,* 6th ed. St. Paul, MN: West.

Blomberg, Thomas G., and Stanley Cohen (eds.) (1995). *Punishment and Social Control: Essays in Honor of Sheldon L. Messinger.* Hawthorne, NY: Aldine de Gruyter.

Blumstein, Alfred, and Allen J. Beck (1999). "Population Growth in U.S. Prisons, 1980–1996." In *Prisons,* Michael Tonry and Joan Petersilia (eds.). Chicago: University of Chicago Press.

Boehm, L. (1962). "The Development of Conscience." *Child Development* **33:**575–590.

Bogard, David M., et al. (1993). "Architecture, Construction, and Design." *Corrections Today* **55:**74–128.

Bohn, Martin J., Joyce L. Carbonell, and Edwin I. Megargee (1995). "The Applicability and Utility of the MMPI-Based Offender Classification System in a Mental Health Unit." *Criminal Behaviour and Mental Health* **5:**14–33.

Boin, R. Arjen, and Menno J. Van Duin (1995). "Prison Riots as Organizational Failures: A Managerial Perspective." *Prison Journal* **75:**357–379.

Bonta, James, Suzanne Capretta-Wallace, and Jennifer Rooney (1999). *Electronic Monitoring in Canada.* Ottawa: Solicitor General Canada.

Bonta, James, Suzanne Capretta-Wallace, and Jennifer Rooney (2000a). "Can Electronic Monitoring Make a Difference?" *Crime and Delinquency* **46:**61–75.

Bonta, James, Suzanne Capretta-Wallace, and Jennifer Rooney (2000b). *Criminal Justice and Behavior* **27:**312–329.

Boone, Harry N., Jr. (1994a). "An Examination of Recidivism and Other Outcome Measures: A Review of the Literature." *APPA Perspectives* **18:**12–18.

Boone, Harry N., Jr. (1994b). "Recommended Outcome Measures for Program Evaluation: APPAs Board of Directors Survey Results." *APPA Perspectives* **18:**19–20.

Boone, Harry N., Jr. (1995). "Mental Illness in Probation and Parole Populations: Results from a National Survey." *APPA Perspectives* **19:**32–44.

Bork, Michael V. (1995). "Five-Year Review of United States Probation Data, 1990–1994." *Federal Probation* **59:**27–33.

Borum, Randy (1999). *Misdemeanor Offenders with Mental Illness in Florida: Examining Police Response, Court Jurisdiction, and Jail Mental Health Service.* Tallahassee: Florida Department of Children and Families.

Bosoni, Anthony J. (1992). *Post-Release Assistance Programs for Prisoners: A National Directory.* Jefferson, NC: McFarland and Company.

Bottomley, A. Keith (1984). "Dilemmas of Parole in a Penal Crisis." *Howard Journal of Criminal Justice* **23:**24–40.

Bouffard, Jeffrey A., Doris Layton MacKenzie, and Laura J. Hickman (2000). "Effectiveness of Vocational Education and Employment Programs for Adult Offenders: A Methodology-Based Analysis of the Literature." *Journal of Offender Rehabilitation* **31:**1–42.

Bourque, Blair B., et al. (1996). *Boot Camps for Juvenile Offenders: An Implementation Evaluation of Three Demonstration Programs.* Washington, DC: U.S. National Institute of Justice.

Bowers, Dan M. (2000). "Home Detention Systems." *Corrections Today* **62:**102–106.

Bowker, Arthur L. (1998). "REDUCE: The Six Aims of Financial Investigations for Probation Officers." *Federal Probation* **62:**22–25.

Bowman, Gary W., Simon Hakim, and Paul Seidenstat (eds.) (1993). *Privatizing Correctional Institutions.* New Brunswick, NJ: Transaction.

Brandau, Timothy J. (1992). *An Alternative to Incarceration for Juvenile Delinquents: The Delaware Bay Marine Institute.* Ann Arbor, MI: University Microfilms International.

Brandon, Ann, and Deborah Chard-Wierschem (1997). *Vocational Programs: Description and Exploratory Study.* Albany: New York State Department of Correctional Services.

Braswell, Michael C., and Larry S. Miller (1989). "The Seriousness of Inmate Induced Prison Violence: An Analysis of Correctional Personnel Perceptions." *Journal of Criminal Justice* **17:**47–53.

Breckenridge, James F., et al. (2000). "Drunk Drivers, DWI 'Drug Court' Treatment, and Recidivism: Who Fails?" *Justice Research and Policy* **2:**87–105.

Brewer, Victoria E., James W. Marquart, and Janet L. Mullings (1998). "Female Drug Offenders: HIV-Related Risk Behavior, Self Perceptions, and Public Health Interpretations." *Criminal Justice Policy Review* **9:**185–208.

Bridges, George S., and Sara Steen (1998). "Racial Disparities in Official Assessments of Juvenile Offenders: Attributional Stereotypes as Mediating Mechanisms." *American Sociological Review* **63:**554–570.

Britt, Chester L., III, Michael R. Gottfredson, and John S. Goldkamp (1992). "Drug Testing and Pretrial Misconduct: An Experiment on the Specific Deterrent Effects of Drug Monitoring Defendants on Pretrial Release." *Journal of Research in Crime and Delinquency* **29:**62–78.

Brody, Arthur L., and Richard Green (1994). "Washington State's Unscientific Approach to the Problem of Repeat Offenders." *Bulletin of the American Academy of Psychiatry and the Law* **22:**343–356.

Brown, Paul W. (1993). "Probation Officer Safety and Mental Conditioning." *Federal Probation* **57:**17–21.

Brown, Paul W. (1994). "Mental Preparedness: Probation Officers Need to Rely on More Than Luck to Ensure Safety." *Corrections Today* **56:**180–187.

Brown, Sammie (2000). "Into the Millennium with Comprehensive Objective Prison Classification Systems." *Corrections Today* **62:**138–139.

Brown, Valerie (1992). "Idaho's Intensive Supervision Program." *Corrections Compendium* **17:**7–8.

Bruce, A. A., et al. (1928). *Parole and the Indeterminate Sentence.* Springfield: Illinois Parole Board.

Brumbaugh, Susan, and Chris Birkbeck (1999). *Sentencing in New Mexico: 1997 Followup.* Albuquerque: New Mexico Criminal and Juvenile Justice Coordinating Council.

Brumbaugh, Susan, and Amelia A. Rouse (1998). *A Profile of Probationers and Parolees in New Mexico.* Albuquerque: Institute for Social Research, University of New Mexico.

Buddress, Loren A. N. (1997). "Federal Probation and Pretrial Services: A Cost-Effective and Successful Community Corrections Program." *Federal Probation* **61:**5–14.

Buentello, Salvador, et al. (1992). "Gangs: A Growing Menace on the Streets and in Our Prisons." *Corrections Today* **54:**58–97.

Burke, Peggy B. (1990). "Classification and Case Management for Probation and Parole: Don't Shoot the Messenger." *APPA Perspectives* **14:**37–42.

Burke, Peggy B. (1994). "Probation Violation and Revocation Policy: Opportunities for Change." *APPA Perspectives* **18:**24–31.

Burke, Peggy B. (1997). *Policy-Drive Responses to Probation and Parole Violations.* Washington, DC: U.S. National Institute of Corrections.

Burns, Jerald C., and Gennaro F. Vito (1995). "An Impact Analysis of the Alabama Boot Camp Program." *Federal Probation* **59:**63–67.

Burns, Ronald (1998). "Forecasting Bollinger: Methods for Projecting the Future of Jails." *American Jails* **12:**55–56.

Burns, Ronald, et al. (1999). "Perspectives on Parole: The Board Members' Viewpoint." *Federal Probation* **63:**16–22.

Burpo, John, Ron DeLord, and Michael Shannon (1997). *Police Association Power, Politics, and Confrontation: A Guide for the Successful Police Labor Leader.* Springfield, IL: Charles C Thomas.

Burt, Grant N., et al. (2000). "Three Strikes and You're Out: An Investigation of False Positive Rates Using a Canadian Sample." *Federal Probation* **64:**3–6.

Busher, Walter (1973). *Ordering Time to Serve Prisoners: A Manual for the Planning and Administering of Work Release.* Washington, DC: U.S. Government Printing Office.

Butts, Jeffrey A. (1996a). *Offenders in Juvenile Courts, 1994.* Washington, DC: Office of Juvenile Justice and Delinquency Prevention.

Butts, Jeffrey A. (1996b). "Speedy Trial in Juvenile Court." *American Journal of Criminal Law* **23:**515–561.

Butts, Jeffrey A., and Howard N. Snyder (1997). *The Youngest Delinquents: Offenders under Age 15.* Washington, DC: Office of Juvenile Justice and Delinquency Prevention.

Byrne, James M. (1986). "The Control Controversy: A Preliminary Examination of Intensive Probation Supervision Programs in the United States." *Federal Probation* **50:**4–16.

Byrne, James M. (1990a). "Evaluating the Effectiveness of the 'New' Intermediate Sanctions: A Nationwide Review of Intensified Community Corrections Programs." Unpublished paper presented at the annual meeting of the American Society of Criminology, Baltimore, MD, November.

Byrne, James M. (1990b). "Intensive Probation Supervision: An Alternative to Prison." *Crime and Delinquency* **36:**3–191.

Byrne, James M. (1990c). "Intermediate Sanctions and the Search for a Theory of Community Control." Unpublished paper presented at the annual meeting of the American Society of Criminology, Baltimore, MD, November.

Byrne, James M., and Mary Brewster (1993). "Choosing the Future of American Corrections: Punishment or Reform?" *Federal Probation* **57:**3–9.

Byrne, James M., Arthur J. Lurigio, and Joan M. Petersilia (eds.) (1992). *Smart Sentencing: The Emergence of Intermediate Sanctions.* Newbury Park, CA: Sage.

Cahalan, Margaret Werner, and Lee Anne Parsons (1986). *Historical Corrections in the United States, 1850–1984.* Washington, DC: Bureau of Justice Statistics.

Calathes, William (1991). "Project Green Hope, a Halfway House for Women Offenders: Where Do They Go from Here?" *Journal of Contemporary Criminal Justice* **7:**135–145.

California Assembly (1996). *Summary of Significant Juvenile Justice Assembly Bills Passed by the Public Safety Commission.* Sacramento: California Assembly Public Safety Committee, Subcommittee on Juvenile Justice.

California Board of Corrections (2000). *Improving California's Response to Mentally Ill Offenders: An Analysis of County-Level Needs.* Sacramento: California Board of Corrections.

California Department of Corrections (1997). *Historical Trends: Institution and Parole Population, 1976–1996.* Sacramento: California Department of Corrections.

California Department of Justice (1990). *Organized Crime in California, 1989: Annual Report to the California Legislature.* Sacramento: California Department of Justice Bureau of Organized Crime and Criminal Intelligence.

California Department of the Youth Authority (1997). *LEAD: A Boot Camp and Intensive Parole Program.* Sacramento: California Department of the Youth Authority.

California San Diego Association of Governments (1998). *Staying Out Successfully: An Evaluation of an In-Custody Life Skills Training Program.* San Diego: California San Diego Association of Governments.

Call, Jack E., and Richard Cole (1996). "Assessing the Possible Impact of the Violent Crime Control Act of 1994 on Prison and Jail Overcrowding Suits." *Prison Journal* **76:**92–106.

Camp, Camille Graham, and George M. Camp (1999). *The Corrections Yearbook 1999.* Middletown, CT: Criminal Justice Institute, Inc.

Campbell, Jacquelyn C. (ed.) (1995). *Assessing Dangerousness: Violence by Sexual Offenders, Batterers, and Child Abusers.* Thousand Oaks, CA: Sage.

Campbell, Ralph, Jr. (1998). *Performance Audit: Department of Correction, Division of Adult Probation and Parole.* Raleigh: North Carolina Office of the State Auditor.

Canada Solicitor General (1998). *Towards a Just, Peaceful, and Safe Society: The Corrections and Conditional Release Act Five Years Later.* Ottawa: Public Works and Government Services of Canada.

Capodanno, Daniel J., and Frederick R. Chavaria (1991). "Polysubstance Abuse: The Interaction of Alcohol and Other Drugs." *Federal Probation* **55:**24–27.

Carlson, Eric W., and Evalyn Parks (1979). *Critical Issues in Adult Probation: Issues in Probation Management.* Washington, DC: U.S. Department of Justice.

Carp, Scarlett V., and Linda S. Schade (1992). "Tailoring Facility Programming to Suit Female Offenders' Needs." *Corrections Today* **54:**152–159.

Carpenter, Patricia, and Salek Sandberg (1985). "Further Psychodrama and Delinquent Adolescents." *Adolescence* **20:**599–604.

Carpenter, Patricia, and Dennis P. Sugrue (1984). "Psychoeducation in an Outpatient Setting: Designing a Heterogeneous Population of Juvenile Delinquents." *Adolescence* **19:**113–122.

Casilias, Victor A. (1994). "Identifying and Supervising Offenders Affiliated with Community Threat Groups." *Federal Probation* **58:**11–19.

Castellano, Thomas C., and Irina R. Soderstrom (1997). "Self-Esteem, Depression, and Anxiety: Evidenced by a Prison Inmate Sample." *Prison Journal* **77:**259–280.

Castellano, Thomas C., et al. (1993). *The Implementation of Illinois' PreStart Program: An Initial Assessment.* Chicago: Illinois Criminal Justice Information Authority.

Cavanaugh, Michael J. (1992). "Intensive Supervision in South Carolina: Accountability and Assistance." *Corrections Compendium* **17:**1–6.

Cavender, Gray, and Paul Knepper (1992). "Strange Interlude: An Analysis of Juvenile Parole Revocation Decision Making." *Social Problems* **39:**387–399.

Chaiken, Jan M., and Marcia R. Chaiken (1982). *Varieties of Criminal Behavior.* Santa Monica, CA: Rand Corporation.

Champion, Dean J. (ed.) (1989). *The U.S. Sentencing Guidelines: Implications for Criminal Justice.* New York: Praeger.

Champion, Dean J. (1994). *Measuring Offender Risk: A Criminal Justice Sourcebook.* Westport, CT: Greenwood Press.

Champion, Dean J. (1998). *Corrections in the United States: A Contemporary Perspective,* 2d ed. Upper Saddle River, NJ: Prentice Hall.

Champion, Dean J. (2001). *Review of Literature Relating to Collective Bargaining and Probation and Parole Officers.* Laredo: Texas A&M International University.

Chapman, Jack (1998). "Bigger, Better, Safer, Faster, and Less Expensive." *American Jails* **12:**9–17.

Chard-Wierschem, Deborah J. (1995). *Day Reporting Program Profile, 1994.* Albany: New York Department of Correctional Services, Division of Program Planning, Research and Evaluation.

Charles, Michael T. (1989a). "The Development of a Juvenile Electronic Monitoring Program." *Federal Probation* **53:**3–12.

Charles, Michael T. (1989b). "Electronic Monitoring for Juveniles." *Journal of Crime and Justice* **12:**147–169.

Ching, James (1997). "Credits as Personal Property: Beware of the New *Ex Post Facto* Clause." *Corrections Compendium* **22:**1–16.

Church Council on Justice and Corrections (1996). *Satisfying Justice: Safe Community Options That Attempt to Repair Harm from Crime and Reduce the Use or Length of Confinement.* Ontario: Correctional Service of Canada.

Chute, C. L. (1922). "Probation and Suspended Sentence." *Journal of the American Institute of Criminal Law and Criminology* **12:**558.

Ciancia, James J., and Richard B. Talty (1999). *New Jersey Intensive Supervision Program.* Trenton, NJ: Division of Parole and Community Programs.

Cimini, Joseph F. (1997). "Alternative Dispute Resolution in the Criminal Justice System." *Justice Professional* **10:**105–125.

Clagett, Arthur P. (1989). "Effective Therapeutic Wilderness Camp Programs for Rehabilitating Emotionally-Disturbed, Problem Teenagers and Delinquents." *Journal of Offender Counseling, Services, and Rehabilitation* **14:**79–96.

Clark, Patricia M. (1995). "The Evolution of Michigan's Community Corrections Act." *Corrections Today* **57:**38–39, 68.

Clear, Todd R., Val B. Clear, and William D. Burrell (1989). *Offender Assessment and Evaluation: The Presentence Investigation Report.* Cincinnati, OH: Anderson.

Clear, Todd R., and Harry R. Dammer (2000). *The Offender in the Community.* Belmont, CA: Wadsworth.

Clear, Todd R., and Edward J. Latessa (1993). "Probation Officers' Roles in Intensive Supervision: Surveillance versus Treatment." *Justice Quarterly* **10:**441–462.

Cleary, Jim, and Michelle Powell (1994). *History, Issues, and Analysis of Pretrial Release and Detention: A Policy Analysis.* St. Paul: Minnesota House of Representatives Research Department.

Cochran, Donald, and John F. McDevitt (1998). "Probation: The Times Are Changing." *APPA Perspectives* **22:**20–25.

Cohen, Albert K. (1955). *Delinquent Boys.* Glencoe, IL: Free Press.

Collins, William C. (1994). *Jail Design and Operation and the Constitution: An Overview.* Boulder, CO: U.S. National Institute of Corrections.

Colorado Legislative Council (1998). *Legislative Council Staff Study on the State Parole System.* Denver: Colorado Legislative Council.

Conaboy, Richard P. (1997). "The United States Sentencing Commission: A New Component in the Federal Criminal Justice System." *Federal Probation* **61**:58–62.

Conly, Catherine (1999). *Coordinating Community Services for Mentally Ill Offenders: Maryland's Community Criminal Justice Treatment Program.* Washington, DC: National Institute of Justice.

Connecticut Board of Parole (2001). *Mission, Functions, and Procedures.* Hartford: Connecticut Board of Parole.

Connelly, Michael (1995). "Mentors and Tutors: An Overview of Two Volunteer Programs in Oklahoma Corrections." *Journal of the Oklahoma Criminal Justice Research Consortium* **2**:80–88.

Conrad, John P. (1987). "Return to John Augustus." *Federal Probation* **51**:22–27.

Cook, Stephen S. (1995). "Mediation as an Alternative to Probation Revocation Proceedings." *Federal Probation* **59**:48–52.

Cooper, Caroline S., and Shanie R. Bartlett (1996). *Drug Courts: A Profile of Operational Programs.* Washington, DC: American University.

Corbett, Ronald P., Jr., and M. Kay Harris (1999). "Up to Speed: A Review of Research for Practitioners." *Federal Probation* **63**:67–71.

Cornelius, Gary F. (1994). *Stressed Out: Strategies for Living and Working with Stress in Corrections.* Laurel, MD: American Correctional Association.

Cornelius, Gary F. (1996). *Jails in America: An Overview of Issues,* 2d ed. Laurel, MD: American Correctional Association.

Corrado, Michael Louis (1996). "Punishment and the Wild Beast of Prey: The Problem of Preventive Detention." *Journal of Criminal Law and Criminology* **86**:778–814.

Corrado, Raymond R., et al. (2000). "Diagnosing Mental Disorders in Offenders: Conceptual and Methodological Issues." *Criminal Behaviour and Mental Health* **10**:29–39.

Correctional Association of New York (2000). *Health Care in New York State Prisons: A Report of Findings and Recommendations by the Visiting Committee on Correctional Association of New York.* New York: Correctional Association of New York Prison Visiting Committee.

Corrections Compendium (1989). "Medal of Valor to Charles Smith." *Corrections Compendium* **14**:14.

Corrections Compendium (1990a). "Privatization Gains as Marshals Service Contracts for New Jail." *Corrections Compendium* **15**:21.

Corrections Compendium (1990b). "Use of Prison Alternatives Could Save New York Millions." *Corrections Compendium* **15**:14.

Corrections Compendium (1991a). "Electronic Monitoring Programs Grow Rapidly from 1986 to 1989." *Corrections Compendium* **16**:1–4.

Corrections Compendium (1991b). "Survey: Sentencing Guidelines Determine Penalties in 17 Systems." *Corrections Compendium* **16**:10–18.

Corrections Compendium (1991c). "Survey Shows High Public Support for Community Programs." *Corrections Compendium* **16**:1–15.

Corrections Compendium (1992a). "ACA's Medal of Valor Goes to Michigan Parole Officer." *Corrections Compendium* **17**:13–14.

Corrections Compendium (1992b). "Florida Authorizes Probation, Parole Officers to Carry Firearms." *Corrections Compendium* **17**:2.

Corrections Compendium (1992c). "Florida's P&P Officers Train for Concealed Weapons." *Corrections Compendium* **17**:16.

Corrections Compendium (1992d). "Greater Jail Terms Have Not Cut Crime Rates in Pennsylvania." *Corrections Compendium* **17**:18.

Corrections Compendium (1992e). "Home Confinement." *Corrections Compendium* **17**:16.

Corrections Compendium (1992f). "IPS Use of House Arrest and Electronic Monitoring." *Corrections Compendium* **17**:13.

Cosgrove, Edward J. (1994). "ROBO-PO: The Life and Times of a Federal Probation Officer." *Federal Probation* **58**:29–30.

Costa, Jeralita, and Anne Seymour (1993). "Experienced Volunteers: Crime Victims, Former Offenders Contribute a Unique Perspective." *Corrections Today* **55**:110–111.

Costanzo, Samuel A. (1990). "Juvenile Academy Serves as Facility without Walls." *Corrections Today* **52**:112–126.

Courtright, Kevin Edward (1995). "A Rational Examination of the Policy Issues Surrounding the Privatization of Probation and Parole Supervision." *APPA Perspectives* **19**:14–20.

Courtright, Kevin E., Bruce L. Berg, and Robert J. Mutchnick (1997). "The Cost Effectiveness of Using House Arrest with Electronic Monitoring for Drunk Drivers." *Federal Probation* **61**:19–22.

Cowles, Ernest L., Thomas C. Castellano, and Laura A. Gransky (1995). *Boot Camp Drug Treatment and Aftercare Intervention: An Evaluation Review.* Washington, DC: U.S. Government Printing Office.

Craddock, Amy, and Laura A. Graham (1996). *Day Reporting Centers as an Intermediate Sanction: Evaluation of Programs Operated by the ATTIC Correctional Services.* Chapel Hill, NC: Pacific Institute for Research and Evaluation.

Craissati, Jackie (1998). *Child Sexual Abusers: A Community Treatment Approach.* East Sussex, UK: Psychology Press.

Crank, John P. (1996). "The Construction and Meaning During Training for Probation and Parole." *Justice Quarterly* **13**:265–290.

Crew, B. Keith, et al. (1998). *An Analysis of Probation Revocation in the First Judicial District of Iowa.* Cedar Falls: College of Social and Behavioral Sciences, University of Northern Iowa.

Crew, Robert E., Jr. (1994). "Managing Victim Restitution in Florida." *Justice System Journal* **17**:241–249.

Cronin, Mary (1992). "Gilded Cages: New Designs for Jails and Prisons are Showing Positive Results: The Question Is, Can We Afford Them?" *Time,* May 25, 1992:52–54.

Crosland, Paul (1995). "Searching for Proof of Probation Officer Effectiveness." *Probation Journal* **42**:126–134.

Cullen, Francis T. (1986). "The Privatization of Treatment: Prison Reform in the 1980's." *Federal Probation* **50**:8–16.

Culliver, Concetta C. (1993). *Female Criminality: The State of the Art.* New York: Garland Press.

Cunningham, John A., et al. (1998). "Current Research and Clinical Practice." *Journal of Offender Rehabilitation* **27**:167–208.

Curry, Theodore R. (1996). "Conservative Protestantism and the Perceived Wrongfulness of Crimes: A Research Note." *Criminology* **34**:453–464.

Cushman, Robert C., and Dale Sechrest (1992). "Variations in the Administration of Probation Supervision." *Federal Probation* **56**:19–29.

Cuvelier, Steven Jay, and Dennis W. Potts (1993). *Bail Classification Profile Project Harris County, Texas: Final Report.* Alexandria, VA: State Justice Institute.

D'Alessio, Stewart J., and Lisa Stolzenberg (1995). "The Impact of Sentencing Guidelines on Jail Incarceration in Minnesota." *Criminology* **33:**283–302.

Davidson, William S., et al. (1987). "Diversion of Juvenile Offenders: An Experimental Comparison." *Journal of Consulting and Clinical Psychology* **55:**68–75.

Davis, Robert C., and Barbara E. Smith (1994). "The Effect of Victim Impact Statements on Sentencing Decisions: A Test in an Urban Setting." *Justice Quarterly* **11:**453–512.

Davis, Su Perk (1990a). "Good Time." *Corrections Compendium* **15:**1–12.

Davis, Su Perk (1990b). "Survey: Parole Officers' Roles Changing in Some States." *Corrections Compendium* **15:**7–16.

Davis, Su Perk (1992a). "Survey: Number of Offenders Under Intensive Probation Increases." *Corrections Compendium* **17:**9–17.

Davis, Su Perk (1992b). "Survey: Programs and Services for the Female Offender." *Corrections Compendium* **17:**7–20.

Dawson, Roger E. (1992). "Opponent Process Theory for Substance Abuse Treatment." *Juvenile and Family Court Journal* **43:**51–59.

Day, Michael, Sharon Friedman, and Kristin Christophersen (1998). *A Women-Centered Approach to Correctional Programming: The WICS Lifeskills Program in Portland, OR.* Portland, OR: Portland State University.

Decker, Scott H. (2000). "Legitimating Drug Use: A Note on the Impact of Gang Membership and Drug Sales on the Use of Illicit Drugs." *Justice Quarterly* **17:**393–410.

Decker, Scott H., Tim Bynum, and Deborah Weisel (1998). "A Tale of Two Cities: Gangs as Organized Crime Groups." *Justice Quarterly* **15:**395–425.

Deitch, David A., et al. (2001). "Does In-Custody Therapeutic Community Substance Abuse Treatment Impact Custody Personnel?" *Corrections Compendium* **26:**1–24.

del Carmen, Rolando V. (1990). "Probation and Parole: Facing Today's Tough Liability Issues." *Corrections Today* **52:**34–42.

del Carmen, Rolando V., and James Alan Pilant (1994). "The Scope of Judicial Immunity for Probation and Parole Officers." *APPA Perspectives* **18:**14–21.

DeLeon, William Granados (1999). *Travels through Crime and Place: Community Building as Crime Control.* Boston: Northeastern University Press.

DelGrosso, Ernest J. (1997). "Probation Officer Safety and Defensive Weapons: A Closer Look." *Federal Probation* **61:**45–50.

DeLisi, Matt, and Bob Regoli (1999). "Race, Conventional Crime, and Criminal Justice: The Declining Importance of Skin Color." *Journal of Criminal Justice* **27:**549–557.

Deschenes, Elizabeth, Susan Turner, and Todd Clear (1992). "The Effectiveness of ISP for Different Types of Drug Offenders." Unpublished paper presented at the annual meeting of the American Society of Criminology. New Orleans, LA, November.

Deschenes, Elizabeth Piper, Susan Turner, and Joan Petersilia (1995). "A Dual Experiment in Intensive Community Supervision: Minnesota's Prison Diversion and Enhanced Supervised Release Programs." *Prison Journal* **75:**330–356.

Dhaliwal, Gurmeet K., Frank Porporino, and Robert R. Ross (1994). "Assessment of Criminogenic Factors, Program Assignment, and Recidivism." *Criminal Justice and Behavior* **21:**456–467.

Dickey, Walter J., and Dennis Wagner (1990). *From the Bottom Up: The High Risk Offender Intensive Supervision Program.* Madison: Continuing Education and Outreach, University of Wisconsin Law School.

Dieterich, William, Cecilia E. Boyles, and Susan Colling (1999). *Colorado Regimented Juvenile Training Program Evaluation Report.* Denver: Colorado General Assembly.

Diggs, David W., and Stephen L. Pieper (1994). "Using Day Reporting Centers as an Alternative to Jail." *Federal Probation* **58:**9–23.

DiIulio, John J. (1995). *How to Stop Federal Judges from Releasing Violent Criminals and Gutting Truth-in-Sentencing Laws.* Washington, DC: The Heritage Foundation.

DiIulio, John J., and George A. Mitchell (1996). *Who Really Goes to Prison in Wisconsin? A Profile of Urban Inmates in Wisconsin Prisons.* Milwaukee: Wisconsin Policy Review Institute.

Dillingham, David D., et al. (1999). *Annual Issue 1999: Classification and Risk Assessment.* Longmont, CO: U.S. National Institute of Corrections.

Ditton, Paula M. (1999). *Mental Health Treatment of Inmates and Probationers.* Washington, DC: U.S. Bureau of Justice Statistics.

DiVito, Robert J. (1991). "Survey of Mandatory Education Policies in State Penal Institutions." *Journal of Correctional Education* **42:**126–132.

Doeren, Stephen E., and Mary J. Hageman (1982). *Community Corrections.* Cincinnati, OH: Anderson.

Dolan, Richard, Marti Harkness, and Kathy McGuire (2000). *Special Preview: Escape from Martin Treatment Centerfor Sexually Violent Predators.* Tallahassee: Office of Program Policy Analysis and Government Accountability, Florida Legislature.

Dolinko, David, et al. (1999). "The Future of Punishment." *UCLA Law Review* **46:**1719–1940.

Donnelly, S. M. (1980). *Community Service Orders in Federal Probation.* Washington, DC: National Institute of Justice.

Driggs, John, and Thomas H. Zoet (1987). "Breaking the Cycle: Sex Offenders on Parole." *Corrections Today* **49:**124–129.

Dubler, Nancy Neveloff (1998). "The Collision of Confinement and Care: End-of-Life Care in Prisons and Jails." *Journal of Law, Medicine, and Ethics* **26:**149–156.

Duncan, Randall W., John C. Speir, and Tammy Meredith (1999). "An Overlay of the North Carolina Structured Sentencing Guidelines on the 1996 Georgia Felony Offender Population." *Justice Research and Policy* **1:**43–59.

Dunlap, Karen L. (1998). *Community Justice Concepts and Strategies.* Lexington, KY: American Probation and Parole Association.

Dutton, Donnie W. (ed.) (2000). "Post-Conviction Sex Offender Testing." *Polygraph* **29:**1–115.

Edwards, Todd (1998). *The Aging Inmate Population.* Atlanta, GA: Southern Legislative Conference, Council of State Governments.

Edwards, Todd (1999). *Sentencing Reform in Southern States: A Review of Truth in Sentencing and Three-Strikes Measures.* Atlanta, GA: Council of State Governments Southern Office.

Eisenberg, Michael (1990). *Special Release and Supervision Programs: Two-Year Outcome Study: Halfway House/PPT Placements.* Austin: Texas Department of Criminal Justice.

Eisenberg, Michael, Nancy Arrigona, and Dee Kofowit (1999). *Overview of Special Needs Parole Policy.* Austin: Texas Criminal Justice Policy Council.

Ekland-Olson, Sheldon, and William R. Kelly (1993). *Justice under Pressure: A Comparison of Recidivism Patterns among Four Successive Parolee Cohorts.* New York: Springer-Verlag.

Elder, Alice P. Franklin (1996). "Inside Gang Society: How Gang Members Imitate Legitimate Social Forms." *Journal of Gang Research* **3:**1–12.

Ellem, Barry (ed.) (1995). *Beyond Catching and Keeping: Police, Corrections, and the Community.* Monash, Australia: Centre for Police and Justice Studies, Monash University.

Ellsworth, Thomas (ed.) (1996). *Contemporary Community Corrections.* Prospect Heights, IL: Waveland Press.

Ely, John Frederick (1996). *Inside Out: Halfway House Staff Management of Punishment and Empathy on the Ambiguous Boundary Between Prison and the Outside.* Ann Arbor, MI: University Microfilms International.

Empey, Lamar T., and Jerome Rabow (1961). "The Provo Experiment in Delinquency Rehabilitation." *American Sociological Review* **26:**679–695.

English, Kim, Susan M. Chadwick, and Suzanne K. Pullen (1994). *Colorado's Intensive Supervision Probation.* Denver: Colorado Division of Criminal Justice.

English, Kim, Suzanne Pullen, and Susan Colling-Chadwick (1996). *Comparison of Intensive Supervision Probation and Community Corrections Clientele: Report of Findings.* Denver: Colorado Division of Criminal Justice.

English, Kim, et al. (1996). *How Are Adult Felony Sex Offenders Managed on Probation and Parole? A National Survey.* Denver: Colorado Department of Safety.

Enos, Richard, John E. Holman, and Marnie E. Carroll (1999). *Alternative Sentencing: Electronically Monitored Correctional Supervision,* 2d ed. Bristol, IN: Wyndham Hall Press.

Enos, Richard, and Stephen Southern (1996). *Correctional Case Management.* Cincinnati, OH: Anderson.

Erez, Edna (1992). "Dangerous Men, Evil Women: Gender and Parole Decision-Making." *Justice Quarterly* **9:**105–126.

Erez, Edna, and Kathy Laster (eds.) (2000). "Special Issue on Domestic Violence." *International Review of Victimology* **7:**1–242.

Erez, Edna, and Pamela Tontodonato (1992). "Victim Participation in Sentencing and Satisfaction with Justice." *Justice Quarterly* **9:**393–417.

Erickson, Lori, et al. (1992). "Architecture, Construction, and Design." *Corrections Today* **54:**80–133.

Erwin, Billie S. (1986). "Turning Up the Heat on Probationers in Georgia." *Federal Probation* **50:**17–24.

Esbensen, Finn-Aage (2000). *Preventing Adolescent Gang Involvement.* Washington, DC: U.S. Department of Justice.

Eskridge, Chris W., and Greg Newbold (1996). "Global Perspectives: Crime, Justice, Corrections." *Journal of Offender Rehabilitation* **24:**1–202.

Escoto, Henry A., et al. (1995). "Juvenile Detention Symposium." *District of Columbia Law Review* **3:**193–439.

Evans, Donald G. (1999). "Broken Windows: Fixing Probation." *Corrections Today* **61:**30–31.

Fagan, Jeffrey A., and Martin Guggenheim (1996). "Preventive Detention and the Judicial Prediction of Dangerousness for Juveniles: A Natural Experiment." *Journal of Criminal Law and Criminology* **86:**415–448.

Falkin, Gregory P., Shiela Strauss, and Timothy Bohen (1999). "Matching Drug-Involved Probationers to Appropriate Drug Interventions." *Federal Probation* **63:**3–8.

Fannin, Leon F. (1984). "Indian Thugs as Professional Criminals." Paper presented at the annual meeting of the Eastern Sociological Society, April, Boston.

Farrell, Amy (2000). "Women, Crime, and Drugs: Testing the Effect of Therapeutic Communities." *Women and Criminal Justice* **11:**21–48.

Faulkner, David, and Anita Gibbs (eds.) (1998). *New Politics, New Probation? Proceedings of the Probation Studies Unit Second Colloquium.* Oxford, U.K.: Centre for Criminological Research, University of Oxford.

Faulkner, Rick (1994). "Networking in Community Corrections." *APPA Perspectives* **18:**23.

Feeley, Malcolm M. (1991). "The Privatization of Prisons in Historical Perspective." *Criminal Justice Research Bulletin* **6:**1–10.

Feld, Barry C. (1995). "Violent Youth and Public Policy: A Case Study of Juvenile Justice Law Reform." *Minnesota Law Review* **79:**965–1128.

Ferns, Ray (1994). "Restorative Case Management: The Evolution of Correctional Case Management." *APPA Perspectives* **18:**36–41.

Fields, Charles B. (ed.) (1994). *Innovative Trends and Specialized Strategies in Community-Based Corrections.* New York: Garland.

Finigan, Michael W. (1999). "Assessing Cost Off-Sets in a Drug Court Setting." *National Drug Court Institute Review* **2:**59–91.

Finn, Peter (1998). *The Delaware Department of Correction Life Skills Program.* Washington, DC: U.S. Department of Justice.

Finn, Peter (1999). "Correctional Officer Stress: A Cause for Concern and Additional Help." *Federal Probation* **62:**65–74.

Finn, Peter, and Dale Parent (1992a). *Making the Offender Foot the Bill: A Texas Program.* Washington, DC: National Institute of Justice.

Finn, Peter, and Dale Parent (1992b). "Texas Collects Substantial Revenues from Probation Fees." *Federal Probation* **57:**17–22.

Firestone, Philip, et al. (2000). "Prediction of Recidivism in Extrafamilial Child Molesters Based on Court-Related Assessments." *Sexual Abuse: A Journal of Research and Treatment* **12:**203–221.

Fisher, Dawn, Anthony Beech, and Kevin Browne (2000). "The Effectiveness of Relapse Prevention Training in a Group of Incarcerated Child Molesters." *Psychology, Crime, and Law* **6:**181–195.

Fitzharris, Timothy L. (1971). *Work Release in Perspective—An Exploratory Analysis of Extramural Correctional Employment.* Berkeley: University of California Press.

Flanagan, Lamont W. (1997). "Prison Is a Luxury We Can No Longer Afford." *Corrections Management Quarterly* **1:**60–63.

Flanagan, Timothy J. (1996). "Community Corrections in the Public Mind." *Federal Probation* **60:**18–23.

Florida Department of Corrections (1993). *Status Report on Elderly Inmates.* Tallahassee: Florida Department of Corrections Youth and Special Needs Program Office.

Florida Department of Corrections (1999). *Time Served by Criminals Sentenced to Florida's Prisons: The Impact of Punishment Policies from 1979–1999.* Tallahassee: Florida Department of Corrections Bureau of Research and Data Analysis.

Florida Department of Corrections (2001). *Florida's Community Supervision Population Monthly Status Report.* Tallahassee: Florida Department of Corrections, Bureau of Research and Data Analysis, Community Supervision Section.

Florida House of Representatives (1994). *Alternative Sanctions in the Juvenile Justice System: Community Service Worksites, Plans, and Judicial Outcomes.* Tallahassee: Florida House of Representative Committee on Criminal Justice.

Fogel, David (1979). *We Are the Living Proof.* Cincinnati, OH: Anderson.

Fogel, David, and Joe Hudson (1981). *Justice as Fairness: Perspectives on the Justice Model.* Cincinnati, OH: Anderson.

Fogg, Vern (1992). "A Probation Model of Drug Offender Intervention in Colorado: Implementation of a Cognitive Skills Development Program." *APPA Perspectives* **16:**24–26.

Fong, Robert S., Ronald E. Vogel, and Salvador Buentello (1996). "Prison Gang Dynamics: A Research Update." In *Gangs: A Criminal Justice Approach,* J. Mitchell Miller and Jeffrey P. Rush (eds.). Cincinnati, OH: Anderson.

Fruchtman, David A., and Robert T. Sigler (1999). "Private Pre-Sentence Investigation: Procedures and Issues." *Journal of Offender Rehabilitation* 29:157–170.

Fulton, Betsy, Paul Gendreau, and Mario Paparozzi (1995). "APPA's Prototypical Intensive Supervision Program: ISP As It Was Meant to Be." *APPA Perspectives* 19:25–41.

Fulton, Betsy, and Susan Stone (1993). "Achieving Public Safety through the Provision of Intense Services: The Promise of a New ISP." *APPA Perspectives* 17:43–45.

Fulton, Betsy, et al. (1997). "The State of ISP: Research and Policy Implications." *Federal Probation* 61:65–75.

Gallemore, Johnnie (2000). "Strategies for Success: Addressing the Needs of Mentally Ill Inmates." *American Jails* 14:67–71.

Garcia, Crystal Ann (1996). *Measurement in Community Corrections: Intensive Supervision Revisited.* Ann Arbor, MI: University Microfilms International.

Gardner, William, et al. (1996). "Clinical versus Actuarial Predictions of Violence in Patients with Mental Illnesses." *Journal of Counseling and Clinical Psychology* 64:602–609.

Garner, Joel H. (1991). "The Feasibility of Predictive Classification for Inmates Held Pretrial in Federal BOP Facilities." Unpublished paper presented at the annual meeting of the American Society of Criminology, San Francisco, November.

Gatz, Nick, and Chris Murray (1981). "An Administrative Overview of Halfway Houses." *Corrections Today* 43:52–54.

Gaudin, J. M., Jr. (1993). "Effective Intervention with Neglectful Families." *Criminal Justice and Behavior* 20:66–89.

Georgia Parole Review (1990). "Georgia Rehabilitation Program Helps Disabled Parolees." *Corrections Today* 52:174–176.

Gianas, Greg (1996). "Washington's McNeil Island Work Ethic Camp: An Evolution in Corrections?" *Corrections Compendium* 21:1–9.

Gibbons, Don C. (1968). *Society, Crime, and Criminal Careers.* Englewood Cliffs, NJ: Prentice Hall.

Gido, Rosemary L. (ed.) (1998). "Evolution of the Concepts Correctional Organization and Organizational Change." *Criminal Justice Policy Review* 9:5–139.

Gilbert, James N. (2000). "Crime in the National Parks: An Analysis of Actual and Perceived Crime within Gettysburg National Military Park." *Justice Professional* 12:471–485.

Gillis, Christa A., Larry L. Motiuk, and Ray Belcourt (1998). *Prison Work Program (CORCAN) Participation: Post-Release Employment and Recidivism.* Ottawa: Research Branch, Correctional Service Canada.

Gitau, Joseph K., et al. (1997). *Improvement of the Treatment of Offenders through the Strengthening of Non-Custodial Measures.* Tokyo: Asia and Far East Institute for Prevention of Crime and Treatment of Offenders.

Glaeser, Edward L., and Bruce Sacerdote (2000). *The Determinants of Punishment: Deterrence, Incapacitation, and Vengeance.* Cambridge, MA: National Bureau of Economic Research.

Glaser, Daniel (1987). "Classification for Risk." In *Prediction and Classification: Criminal Justice Decision Making,* Don M. Gottfredson and Michael Tonry (eds.). Chicago: University of Chicago Press.

Glaser, Daniel F. (1995). *Preparing Convicts for Law-Abiding Lives: The Pioneering Penology of Richard A. McGee.* Albany: State University of New York Press.

Glasser, William (1976). *The Identity Society.* New York: Harper and Row.

Godwin, Tracy M., David J. Steinhart, and Betsy A. Fulton (1996). *Peer Justice and Youth Empowerment: An Implementation Guide for Teen Court Programs.* Washington, DC: U.S. Department of Transportation.

Goethals, Ron, and Jim Mills (1996). "Continuous Auditing: A Way to Gauge the Performance of Community Corrections Officers." *Federal Probation* 60:24–26.

Goffman, Erving (1961). *Asylums.* Garden City, NY: Anchor Press.

Goldkamp, John S. (2000). "The Drug Court Response: Issues and Implications for Justice Change." *Albany Law Review* 63:923–961.

Goldsmith, Herbert R., and DeAnna Libonate (1990). "Pilot Study of Extraneous Paperwork in a Parole/Probation Field Office." *Journal of Offender Counseling* 10:26–32.

Goldstone, Jack A., and Bert Useem (1999). "Prison Riots as Microrevolutions: An Extension of State-Centered Theories of Revolution." *American Journal of Sociology* 104:985–1029.

Goodman, Harriet, George S. Getzel, and William Ford (1996). "Group Work with High Risk Urban Youths on Probation." *Social Work* 41:375–381.

Goodman, Rebecca (1992). *Pretrial Release Study.* Minneapolis, MN: Hennepin County Bureau of Community Corrections, Planning, and Evaluation.

Goodstein, Lynne, John Kramer, and Laura Nuss (1984). "Defining Determinacy: Components of the Sentencing Process Ensuring Equity and Release Certainty." *Justice Quarterly* 1:47–73.

Gordon, Robert M. (2000). "Criminal Business Organizations: Street Gangs and 'Wanna-Be' Groups: A Vancouver Perspective." *Canadian Journal of Criminology* 42:39–60.

Gostas, Tom, and Beth Harris (1997). *Alternatives to Incarceration: Opportunities and Costs.* Boise: Office of Performance Evaluations, Idaho State Legislature.

Gottfredson, Don M., and Michael Tonry (1987). *Prediction and Classification: Criminal Justice Decision Making.* Chicago: University of Chicago Press.

Gottfredson, Don M., Leslie T. Wilkins, and Peter B. Hoffman (1978). *Guidelines for Parole and Sentencing.* Lexington, MA: Heath.

Gottfredson, Michael R., and Don M. Gottfredson (1988). *Decision Making in Criminal Justice: Toward the Rational Exercise of Discretion,* 2d ed. New York: Plenum Press.

Gottfredson, Stephen D., and Don M. Gottfredson (1990). *Classification, Prediction, and Criminal Justice Policy: Final Report to the National Institute of Justice.* Washington, DC: U.S. National Institute of Justice.

Gover, Angela R., Doris Layton MacKenzie, and Gaylene J. Styve (2000). "Boot Camps and Traditional Correctional Facilities for Juveniles: A Comparison of the Participants, Daily Activities, and Environments." *Journal of Criminal Justice* 28:53–68.

Gowdy, Voncile B., et al. (1998). *Women in Criminal Justice: A Twenty-Year Update.* Rockville, MD: U.S. National Criminal Justice Reference Service.

Gowen, Darren (1995). "Electronic Monitoring in the Southern District of Mississippi." *Federal Probation* 59:10–13.

Gowen, Darren, and Jerri B. Speyerer (1995). "Compulsive Gambling and the Criminal Offender: A Treatment and Supervision Approach." *Federal Probation* 59:36–39.

Grandberry, Gina (1998). *Moral Reconation Therapy Evaluation: Final Report.* Olympia: Planning and Research Section, Washington State Department of Corrections.

Grann, Martin, Henrik Belfrage, and Anders Tengstrom (2000). "Actuarial Assessment of Risk for Violence: Predictive Validity of the VRAG and the Historical Part of the HCR-20." *Criminal Justice and Behavior* **27:**97–114.

Gransky, Laura, and Ernest L. Cowles (1999). *An Evaluation of the Illinois Department of Corrections' Gang-Free Environment Program.* Chicago: Illinois Criminal Justice Information Authority.

Grant, Brian A., and Chris A. Beal (1998). *Work Release Program: How It Is Used and for What Purposes.* Ottawa: Research Branch, Correctional Service of Canada.

Grant, Brian A., and Marlo Gal (1998). *Case Management Preparation for Release and Day Parole Outcome.* Ottawa: Research Branch, Correctional Service of Canada.

Grant, Brian A., and Sara L. Johnson (1998). *Personal Development Temporary Absences.* Ottawa: Research Branch, Correctional Service of Canada.

Grant, Brian A., and William A. Millson (1998). *The Temporary Absence Program: A Descriptive Analysis.* Ottawa: Correctional Service of Canada.

Greenfeld, Lawrence A. (1985). *Examining Recidivism.* Washington, DC: U.S. Department of Justice.

Greenwood, Peter W. (1982). *Selective Incapacitation.* Santa Monica, CA: Rand Corporation.

Greenwood, Peter W. (1986). *Intervention Strategies for Chronic Juvenile Offenders: Some New Perspectives.* Westport, CT: Greenwood Press.

Greenwood, Peter W., and Susan Turner (1987). *The VisionQuest Program: An Evaluation.* Santa Monica, CA: Rand.

Greenwood, Peter W., and Susan Turner (1993). "Private Presentence Reports for Serious Juvenile Offenders: Implementation Issues and Impacts." *Justice Quarterly* **10:**229–243.

Grier, Leslie K. (1999). "Identity Diffusion and Development among African Americans: Implications for Crime and Corrections." *Journal of Offender Rehabilitation* **30:**81–94.

Griffiths, Curt Taylor (ed.) (1996). "World Criminal Justice." *International Journal of Comparative and Applied Criminal Justice* **20:**195–355.

Griffiths, Curt Taylor, and Gordon Bazemore (eds.) (1999). "Restorative Justice." *International Review of Victimology* **6:**261–405.

Grimes, Paul W., and Kevin E. Rogers (1999). "Truth-in-Sentencing, Law Enforcement, and Inmate Population Growth." *Journal of Socio-Economics* **28:**745–757.

Griset, Pamala L. (1996). "Determinate Sentencing and Administrative Discretion over Time Served in Prison: A Case Study of Florida." *Crime and Delinquency* **42:**127–143.

Grisso, Thomas, and Robert G. Schwartz (2000). *Youth on Trial: A Developmental Perspective on Juvenile Justice.* Chicago: University of Chicago Press.

Grisso, Thomas, Alan Tomkins, and Pamela Casey (1988). "Psychosocial Concepts in Juvenile Law." *Law and Human Behavior* **12:**403–438.

Grisso, Thomas, et al. (2000). "Violent Thoughts and Violent Behavior Following Hospitalization for Mental Disorder." *Journal of Counseling and Clinical Psychology* **68:**388–398.

Haghighi, Bahram, and Alma Lopez (1993). "Success/Failure of Group Home Treatment Programs for Juveniles." *Federal Probation* **57:**53–58.

Hahn, Paul H. (1998). *Emerging Criminal Justice: Three Pillars for a Proactive Justice System.* Thousand Oaks, CA: Sage.

Hanlon, Thomas E., et al. (1998). "The Response of Drug Abuser Parolees to a Combination of Treatment and Intensive Supervision." *Prison Journal* **78:**31–44.

Hanson, R. Karl, and David Thornton (1999). *Static 99: Improving Actuarial Risk Assessments for Sex Offenders.* Ottawa: Canada Public Works and Government Services.

Harding, Richard W. (1997). *Private Prisons and Public Accountability.* New Brunswick, NJ: Transaction.

Harding, Richard W. (1999). "Prison Privatization: The Debate Starts to Mature." *Current Issues in Criminal Justice* **11:**109–118.

Harer, Miles D. (1994). *Recidivism among Federal Prison Releasees in 1987.* Washington, DC: U.S. Federal Bureau of Prisons, Office of Research and Evaluation.

Harer, Miles D., and Christopher Eichenlaub (1992). "Prison Furloughs and Recidivism." Unpublished paper presented at the annual meeting of the American Society of Criminology, Pittsburgh, PA, November.

Harland, Alan T., Salvador Buentello, and George W. Knox (1993). "Prison Gangs." *Prison Journal* **71:**1–66.

Harlow, Caroline Wolf (1998). *Profile of Jail Inmates.* Washington, DC: U.S. Department of Justice.

Harrell, Adele, and John Roman (1999). *Process Evaluation of the Brooklyn Treatment Court and Network of Services: The First Three Years.* Washington, DC: The Urban Institute.

Harris, John C., and Paul Jesilow (2000). "It's Not the Old Ball Game: Three Strikes and the Courtroom Workgroup." *Justice Quarterly* **17:**185–203.

Harris, M. Kay (1995). *Trends and Issues in Community Corrections Acts: Final Report and Executive Summary.* Philadelphia: Crime and Justice Research Institute.

Harris, Patricia M. (ed.) (1999). *Research to Results: Effective Community Corrections.* Lanham, MD: American Correctional Association.

Harrison, Lana D., et al. (1998). "Integrating HIV-Prevention Strategies in a Therapeutic Community Work-Release Program for Criminal Offenders." *Prison Journal* **78:**232–243.

Hassine, Victor (1996). *Life without Parole: Living in Prison Today.* Los Angeles: Roxbury Press.

Hawk, Kathleen, et al. (1993). "Volunteers: Corrections' Unsung Heroes." *Corrections Today* **55:**63–139.

Heiner, Robert (ed.) (1996). *Criminology: A Cross-Cultural Perspective.* St. Paul, MN: West.

Heisel, Christine (1992). "APPA Training Seminar Brings Victim Issues to the Forefront in Nebraska State Probation System." *APPA Perspectives* **16:**38–39.

Hemmens, Craig (1999). "Legal Issues in Probation and Parole." *APPA Perspectives* **23:**16–17.

Hemmons, Craig, and Mary K. Stohr (eds.) (2000). "Ethics in Corrections." *Prison Journal* **80:**123–222.

Hendricks, James E., and Jerome B. McKean (1995). *Crisis Intervention: Contemporary Issues for On-Site Interveners.* Springfield, IL: Charles C Thomas.

Hepburn, John R., and Celesta A. Albonetti (1994). "Recidivism among Drug Offenders: A Survival Analysis of the Effects of Offender Characteristics, Type of Offense, and Two Types of Intervention." *Journal of Quantitative Criminology* **10:**159–179.

Hess, Allen K., et al. (1990). "Decision Making in the Criminal Justice System." *Criminal Justice and Behavior* **17:**300–333.

Hill, Cece (1998). "Inmate Fee for Service Programs." *Corrections Compendium* **23:**7–16.

Hill, Dina, Robert Thoma, and Christopher Birkbeck (1996). *Prison and Parole Treatment Options for Substance Abusers.* Santa Fe: New Mexico Criminal and Juvenile Coordinating Council.

Hill, Elizabeth G. (1994). *The State of California's Probation System.* Washington, DC: California Legislative Analyst's Office.

Hill, Gary (1997). "Correctional Officer Traits and Skills." *Corrections Compendium* **22:**1–12.

Hiller, Matthew L., Kevin Knight, and D. Dwayne Simpson (1999). "Prison-Based Substance Abuse Treatment, Residential Aftercare, and Recidivism." *Addiction* **94:**833–842.

Hippchen, Leonard (1981). "Some Possible Biochemical Aspects of Criminal Behavior." *Journal of Behavioral Ecology* **2:**1–6.

Hirschi, Travis (1969). *Causes of Delinquency*. Berkeley: University of California Press.

Hodgins, Sheilagh, and Rudiger Muller-Isberner (eds.) (2000). *Violence, Crime, and Mentally Disordered Offenders: Concepts and Methods for Effective Treatment and Prevention*. Chichester, U.K.: Wiley.

Hofer, Paul J., et al. (1999). "The Effect of the Federal Sentencing Guidelines on Inter-Judge Disparity." *Journal of Criminal Law and Criminology* **90:**239–321.

Hoffman, Peter B. (1983). "Screening for Risk: A Revised Salient Factor Score (SFS 81)." *Journal of Criminal Justice* **11:**539–547.

Hoffman, Peter B. (1994). "Twenty Years of Operational Use of a Risk Prediction Instrument: The United States Parole Commission's Salient Factor Score." *Journal of Criminal Justice* **22:**477–494.

Hoffman, Peter B., and Sheldon Adelberg (1980). "The Salient Factor Score: A Nontechnical Overview." *Federal Probation* **44:**44–52.

Hokanson, Shirley (1986). *The Woman Offender in Minnesota: Profile, Needs and Future Directions*. St. Paul: Minnesota Department of Corrections.

Holgate, Alina M., and Ian J. Clegg (1991). "The Path to Probation Officer Burnout: New Dogs, Old Tricks." *Journal of Criminal Justice* **19:**325–337.

Holt, Norman (1996). *Inmate Classification: A Validation Study of the California System*. Sacramento: California Department of Corrections.

Hooton, Ernest (1939). *Crime and the Man*. Westport, CT: Greenwood.

Horn, Jim (1992). "Kentucky Officers Get Involved: Political Arena." *APPA Perspectives* **16:**27–28.

Houk, Julie M. (1984). "Electronic Monitoring of Probationers: A Step toward Big Brother?" *Golden Gate University Law Review* **14:**431–436.

Houston, James, and Johan Prinsloo (1998). "Prison Gangs in South Africa: A Comparative Analysis." *Journal of Gang Research* **5:**41–52.

Howell, James C. (2000). *Youth Gang Programs and Strategies*. Washington, DC: U.S. Department of Justice.

Howell, James C., and James P. Lynch (2000). *Youth Gangs in Schools*. Washington, DC: U.S. Department of Justice.

Huddleston, C. West (1998). "Drug Courts as Jail-Based Treatment." *Corrections Today* **60:**98–101.

Hughes, Herbert (1987). *The Fatal Shore*. New York: Alfred Knopf.

Humphries, Drew (1999). *Crack Mothers: Pregnancy, Drugs, and the Media*. Columbus: Ohio State University Press.

Hunt, Geoffrey, et al. (1993). "Changes in Prison Culture: Prison Gangs and the Case of the 'Pepsi Generation.'" *Social Problems* **40:**398–409.

Huskey, Bobbie L. (1984). "Community Corrections Acts Help Promote Community-Based Programming." *Corrections Today* **46:**45.

Hutchinson, Virginia (1993). "NIC Update." *Corrections Today* **55:**132–133.

Illinois Sentencing Commission (1998). *Final Report*. Springfield: Illinois Sentencing Commission.

Indiana Department of Corrections (2001). *An Assessment of Furlough Programs: Preliminary Report*. Indianapolis: Indiana Department of Corrections.

Iowa Department of Correctional Services (1992). *Iowa Classification System: Assessment and Reassessment of Client Risk Instructions and Scoring Guide*. Davenport: Iowa Department of Correctional Services.

Irwin, John (1985). *The Jail: Managing the Underclass in American Society*. Berkeley: University of California Press.

Irwin, John, and James Austin (1994). *It's about Time: America's Imprisonment Binge*. Belmont, CA: Wadsworth.

Irwin, John, Vincent Schiraldi, and Jason Ziedenberg (1999). *America's One Million Nonviolent Prisoners*. Washington, DC: Justice Policy Institute.

Jankowski, Louis (1991). *Probation and Parole 1990*. Washington, DC: U.S. Department of Justice, Bureau of Justice Statistics.

Jayjohn, Jennifer (1995). *Analysis of 1994 Parole Decisions and Outcomes of Parole Hearings*. Columbus: Office of Management Systems, Bureau of Research, Ohio Department of Rehabilitation and Correction.

Jeffrey, C. Ray (1978). "Criminology as an Interdisciplinary Behavioral Science." *Criminology* **15:**161–162.

Jenson, Jeffrey M., and Matthew O. Howard (1998). "Correlates of Gang Involvement among Juvenile Probationers." *Journal of Gang Research* **5:**7–15.

Jesness, Carl F. (1987). "Early Identification of Delinquent-Prone Children: An Overview." In *The Prevention of Delinquent Behavior*, John D. Burchard and Sara N. Burchard (eds.). Newbury Park, CA: Sage.

Johnson, Cindy (2000). "For Better of Worse: Alternatives to Jail Time for Enviromental Crimes." *New England Journal on Criminal and Civil Confinement* **26:**265–297.

Johnson, Elmer H., and Kenneth E. Kotch (1973). "Two Factors in Development of Work Release: Size and Location of Prisons." *Journal of Criminal Justice* **1:**44–45.

Johnson, Grant M., and Raymond A. Knight (2000). "Developmental Antecedents of Sexual Coercion in Juvenile Sexual Offenders." *Sexual Abuse: A Journal of Research and Treatment* **12:**165–178.

Johnson, Knowlton W., Linda Burgess, and Sherry Hutcherson (1985). *Strengthening Kentucky's Capacity to Produce Criminal Justice Statistical Information: A Needs-Use Assessment*. Louisville: Kentucky Criminal Justice Statistical Analysis.

Johnson, Sara L., and Brian A. Grant (1999). *Review of Issues Associated with Serious Spouse Abuse among Federally Sentenced Male Offenders*. Ottawa: Research Branch, Correction Service of Canada.

Johnson, Sherri, Trina Bogle Wilson, and Sandra Wright (1999). Richmond: Virginia Department of Criminal Justice Services.

Johnson, W. Wesley, and Mark Jones (1994). "The Increased Felonization of Probation and Its Impact on the Function of Probation: A Descriptive Look at County Level Data from the 1980s and 1990s." *APPA Perspectives* **18:**42–46.

Johnson, Wesley W., et al. (1994). "Goals of Community Corrections: An Analysis of State Legal Codes." *American Journal of Criminal Justice* **18:**79–83.

Johnston, Norman (1973). *The Human Cage: A Brief History of Prison Architecture*. New York: Walker.

Jones, Mark, and Rolando V. del Carmen (1992). "When Do Probation and Parole Officers Enjoy the Same Immunity as Judges?" *Federal Probation* **56:**36–41.

Jones, Mark, and Darrell L. Ross (1997). "Electronic House Arrest and Boot Camp in North Carolina: Comparing Recidivism." *Criminal Justice Policy Review* **8:**383–403.

Jones, Marylouise E., and Arthur J. Lurigio (1997). "Ethical Considerations in Probation Practice." *APPA Perspectives* **20:**26–32.

Jones, Peter R. (1990). "Expanding the Use of Non-Custodial Sentencing Options: An Evaluation of the Kansas Community Corrections Act." *Howard Journal of Criminal Justice* **29:**114–129.

Jones, Ralph K., and John H. Lacey (1999). *Evaluation of a Day Reporting Center for Repeat DWI Offenders.* Winchester, MA: Mid-America Research Institute.

Jones, Ralph K., and John H. Lacey (2000). *State of Knowledge of Alcohol-Impaired Driving: Research on Repeat Offenders.* Winchester, MA: Mid-America Research Institute.

Jones, Ralph K., Connie H. Wiliszowski, and John H. Lacey (1999). *Examination of DWI Conviction Rate Procedures.* Winchester, MA: Mid-America Research Institute, Inc.

Jones, Richard (2000). "Digatal Rule: Punishment, Control, and Technology." *Punishment and Society* **2:**5–22.

Jones, Richard S. (1997). "Conditions of Confinement." *Journal of Contemporary Criminal Justice* **13:**3–72.

Joo, Hee Jong (1993). *Parole Release and Recidivism: Comparative Three-Year Survival Analysis of Four Successive Release Cohorts of Property Offenders in Texas.* Ann Arbor, MI: University Microfilms International.

Joo, Hee Jong, Sheldon Ekland-Olson, and William R. Kelly (1995). "Recidivism among Parole Property Offenders during a Period of Prison Reform." *Criminology* **33:**389–410.

Josi, Don A., and Dale K. Sechrest (1999). "A Pragmatic Approach to Parole Aftercare: Evaluation of a Community Reintegration Program for High-Risk Youthful Offenders." *Justice Quarterly* **16:**51–80.

Kaden, Jonathan (1998). "Therapy for Convicted Sex Offenders: Pursuing Rehabilitation without Incrimination." *Journal of Criminal Law and Criminology* **89:**347–391.

Kansas Legislative Division of Post Audit (1994). *Performance Audit Report: Reviewing the Questions of the Kansas Parole Board.* Topeka: Kansas Legislative Division of Post Audit.

Kassebaum, Gene, Janet Davidson-Coronado, and Mel Silverio (1999). *Survival on Parole: A Study of Post-Prison Adjustment and the Risk of Returning to Prison in the State of Hawaii.* Honolulu: Hawaii Department of the Attorney General.

Katz, Charles M. (1997). *Police and Gangs: A Study of a Police Gang Unit.* Ann Arbor, MI: University Microfilms International.

Kelly, Robert J. (2000). *Encyclopedia of Organized Crime in the United States: From Capone's Chicago to the New Urban Underworld.* Westport, CT: Greenwood.

Kelly, William R., and Sheldon Ekland-Olson (1991). "The Response of the Criminal Justice System to Prison Overcrowding: Recidivism Patterns among Four Successive Parolee Cohorts." *Law and Society Review* **25:**601–620.

Kennedy, David M., and Anthony A. Braga (1998). "Homicide in Minneapolis: Research for Problem Solving." *Homicide Studies* **2:**263–290.

Kerle, Kenneth E. (1998). *American Jails: Looking to the Future.* Boston: Butterworth-Heinemann.

Kingsnorth, Rodney, et al. (1999). "Criminal Sentencing and the Court Probation Officer: The Myth of Individualized Justice Revisited." *Justice System Journal* **20:**255–273.

Kirkish, Patricia, et al. (2000). "The Future of Criminal Violence: Juveniles Tried as Adults." *Journal of the American Academy of Psychiatry and the Law* **28:**38–46.

Kitsuse, J. I. (1962). "Societal Reaction to Deviant Behavior: Problems of Theory and Method." *Social Problems* **9:**247–256.

Klein, Malcolm M., Cheryl L. Maxson, and Margaret A. Gordon (1987). *Police Response to Gang Violence: Improving the Investigative Process.* Los Angeles: University of Southern California, Center for Research on Crime and Social Control.

Klingemann, Harald, and Geoffrey Hunt (1998). *Drug Treatment Systems in an International Perspective.* Thousand Oaks, CA: Sage.

Knight, Barbara B. (1992). "Women in Prison as Litigants: Prospects for Post-Prison Futures." *Women and Criminal Justice* **4:**91–116.

Knopp, Fay H., Robert Freeman-Longo, and William Ferree Stevenson (1992). *Nationwide Survey of Juvenile and Adult Sex-Offender Treatment Programs and Models.* Orwell, VT: Safer Society Program.

Knox, George W. (2000). "A National Assessment of Gangs and Security Threat Groups (STGs) in Adult Correctional Institutions." *Journal of Gang Research* **7:**1–45.

Knupfer, Anne Meis (1999). "Professionalizing Probation Work in Chicago, 1990–1935." *Social Service Review* **73:**478–495.

Kohlberg, L. (1963). "The Development of Children's Orientations toward a Moral Order: Sequence in the Development of Human Thought." *Vita Humana* **6:**11–33.

Konopka, Al (2001). *Nevada ISP Program.* Las Vegas, NV: Division of Parole and Probation.

Kowalski-Jones, Lori (2000). "Staying Out of Trouble: Community Resources and Problem Behavior among High-Risk Adolescents." *Journal of Marriage and the Family* **62:**449–464.

Kraus, Melvyn B., and Edward P. Lazear (eds.) (1991). *Searching for Alternatives: Drug-Control Policy in the United States.* Stanford, CA: Hoover Institution Press.

Krauss, Daniel A., et al. (2000). "Beyond Prediction to Explanation in Risk Assessment Research: A Comparison of Two Explanatory Theories of Criminality and Recidivism." *International Journal of Law and Psychiatry* **23:**91–112.

Krauth, Barbara (1991). "The Jail Center's Objective Jail Classification." *American Jails* **4:**131.

Kronick, Robert F., Dorothy E. Lambert, and E. Warren Lambert (1998). "Recidivism among Adult Parolees: What Makes the Difference?" *Journal of Offender Rehabilitation* **28:**61–69.

Kruttschnitt, Candace, Christopher Uggen, and Kelly Shelton (2000). "Predictors of Desistance Among Sex Offenders: The Interaction of Formal and Informal Social Controls." *Justice Quarterly* **17:**61–87.

Kulis, Chester J. (1983). "Profit in the Private Presentence Report." *Federal Probation* **47:**11–16.

Kushner, Andrea, et al. (1995). *The Organization, Caseloads, and Costs of Probation and Parole in Illinois and the United States.* Chicago: Illinois Criminal Justice Authority.

Kuznestov, Andrei, Timothy A. Pierson, and Bruce Harry (1992). "Victim Age Basis for Profiling Sex Offenders." *Federal Probation* **56:**34–38.

Landreville, P. (1997). "Electronic Surveillance of Delinquents: A Growing Trend." *Deviance et Societe* **23:**105–121.

Langan, Patrick A., and Mark A. Cunniff (1992). *Recidivism of Felons on Probation, 1986–1989.* Washington, DC: Department of Justice, Bureau of Justice Statistics.

Latessa, Edward J., and Harry E. Allen (1999). *Corrections in the Community,* 2d ed. Cincinnati, OH: Anderson.

Latessa, Edward J., Lawrence F. Travis, and Alexander Holsinger (1997). *Evaluation of Ohio's Community Corrections Act Programs and Community-Based Correctional Facilities.* Cincinnati, OH: Division of Criminal Justice, University of Cincinnati.

Latessa, Edward J., et al. (1998). *Evaluating the Prototypical ISP: Final Report.* Washington, DC: U.S. National Institute of Justice.

Latimer, H. D., J. C. Curran, and B. D. Tepper (1992). *Home Detention Electronic Monitoring Program.* Nevada City: Nevada County Probation Department Second Floor Courthouse.

Lauen, Roger J. (1997). *Positive Approaches to Corrections: Research, Policy, and Practice.* Lanham, MD: American Correctional Association.

LaVigne, Nancy (1994). *Rational Choice and Inmate Disputes over Phone Use On Rikers Island.* Monsey, NY: Criminal Justice Press.

Lavin, G. K., et al. (1984). "Group Therapy with Aggressive and Delinquent Adolescents." In *The Aggressive Adolescent: Clinical Perspectives,* C. R. Keith (ed.). New York: Free Press.

Lawrence, Richard A. (1984). "Professionals or Judicial Civil Servants? An Examination of the Probation Officer's Role." *Federal Probation* **48:**14–21.

Leadership Conference on Civil Rights (2000). *Justice on Trial: Racial Disparities in the American Criminal Justice System.* Washington, DC: Leadership Conference on Civil Rights.

Lee, Susan, Tim Auburn, and Karen Kibblewhite (1999). "Working with Sex Offenders: The Perceptions and Experiences of Professionals and Paraprofessionals." *International Journal of Offender Therapy and Comparative Criminology* **43:**103–119.

Lehman, Joseph D. (1993). "A Commissioner's Appreciation: Pennsylvania Volunteers Build Bridges between Our Prisons and the Community." *Corrections Today* **55:**84–86.

Lemert, Edwin M. (1951). *Social Pathology.* New York: McGraw-Hill.

Lemov, Penelope (1992). "The Next Best Thing to Prison." *Corrections Today* **54:**134–136.

Leonardi, Thomas J., and David R. Frew (1991). "Applying Job Characteristics Theory to Adult Probation." *Criminal Justice Policy Review* **5:**17–28.

Leonardson, Gary (1997). *Results of Early Release: Study Prompted by Passage of HB 685.* Helena: Montana Board of Crime Control.

Levin, David J., Patrick A. Langan, and Jodi M. Brown (2000). *State Court Sentencing of Convicted Felons, 1996.* Washington, DC: U.S. Bureau of Justice Statistics.

Levine, Gene N., and Ferando Parra (2000). "The Gangbangers of East Los Angeles: Sociopsycho-Analytic Considerations." *Journal of Gang Research* **7:**9–12.

Lewis, Alan Dana, and Timothy J. Howard (2000). "Parole Officers' Perceptions of Juvenile Offenders Within a Balanced and Restorative Model of Justice." *Federal Probation* **64:**40–45.

Lewis, Derek (1997). *Hidden Agendas: Politics, Law, and Disorder.* London: Hamish Hamilton.

Liberton, Michael, Mitchell Silverman, and William R. Blount (1992). "Predicting Probation Success for the First-Time Offender." *International Journal of Offender Therapy and Comparative Criminology* **36:**335–347.

Lillis, Jamie (1994). "Sentencing Guidelines Determine Penalties in 19 Systems." *Corrections Compendium* **19:**7–14.

Linden, Rick, and Don Clairmont (1998). *Making It Work: Planning and Evaluating Community Corrections and Healing Projects in Aboriginal Communities.* Ottawa: Aboriginal Corrections Policy Unit, Solicitor General Canada.

Lindner, Charles (1992a). "The Probation Field Visit and Office Report in New York State: Yesterday, Today, and Tomorrow." *Criminal Justice Review* **17:**44–60.

Lindner, Charles (1992b). "Probation Officer Victimization: An Emerging Concern." *Journal of Criminal Justice* **20:**53–62.

Lindner, Charles (1992c). "The Refocused Probation Home Visit: A Subtle But Revolutionary Change." *Federal Probation* **56:**16–21.

Lindner, Charles, and Robert L. Bonn (1996). "Probation Officer Victimization and Fieldwork Practices: Results of a National Study." *Federal Probation* **60:**16–23.

Lindner, Charles, and Margaret R. Savarese (1984). "The Evolution of Probation: University Settlement and the Beginning of Statutory Probation in New York City." *Federal Probation* **48:**3–12.

Lin-Ruey, Lin (1997). *Community Corrections: Study Prompted By Passage of HB685.* Helena: Montana Board of Crime Control.

Listug, David (1996). "Wisconsin Sheriff's Office Saves Money and Resources." *American Jails* **10:**85–86.

Litton, Gilbert, and Linda Marye (1983). *An Evaluation of the Juvenile Diversion Program in the Orleans Parish District Attorney's Office: A Preliminary Impact Evaluation.* New Orleans, LA: Mayor's Criminal Justice Coordinating Council, City of New Orleans.

Livingston, Jay (1974). *Compulsive Gamblers: Observation on Action and Abstinence.* New York: Harper Torchbooks.

Locke, Thomas P., et al. (1986). "An Evaluation of a Juvenile Education Program in a State Penitentiary." *Evaluation Review* **10:**281–298.

Logan, Gloria (1992). "In Topeka: Family Ties Take Top Priority in Women's Visiting Program." *Corrections Today* **54:** 160–161.

Lombardi, John H. (1981). "Florida's Objective Parole Guidelines: Analysis of the First Year's Implementation." Ph.D. dissertation, Florida State University, Tallahassee.

Lombardi, John H., and Donna M. Lombardi (1986). "Objective Parole Criteria: More Harm Than Good?" *Corrections Today* **48:**86–87.

Lombroso, Cesare (1918). *Crime: Its Causes and Remedies.* Boston: Little, Brown.

Londer, Randi (1987). "Can Bad Air Make Bad Things Happen?" *Parade Magazine,* August 9, 1987:6.

Love, Bill (1993). "Volunteers Make a Big Difference Inside a Maximum Security Prison." *Corrections Today* **55:**76–78.

Lovell, David, and Lorna A. Rhodes (1997). "Mobile Consultation: Crossing Correctional Boundaries to Cope with Disturbed Offenders." *Federal Probation* **61:**40–45.

Lucken, Karol (1997a). "The Dynamics of Penal Reform." *Crime, Law, and Social Change* **26:**367–384.

Lucken, Karol (1997b). "Privatizating Discretion: 'Rehabilitating' Treatment in Community Corrections." *Crime and Delinquency* **43:**243–259.

Lucker, G. William, et al. (1997). "Interventions with DWI, DUI, and Drug Offenders." *Journal of Offender Rehabilitation* **24:**1–100.

Luginbuhl, James, and Michael Burkhead (1995). "Victim Impact Evidence in a Capital Trial: Encouraging Votes for Death." *American Journal of Criminal Justice* **20:**1–16.

Lurigio, Arthur J. (ed.) (1996). *Community Corrections in America: New Directions and Sounder Investments for Persons with Mental Illness and Codisorders.* Seattle, WA: National Coalition for Mental and Substance Abuse Health Care in the Justice System.

Lurigio, Arthur J., Gad J. Bensinger, and Anna T. Laszlo (eds.) (1990). *AIDS and Community Corrections: The Development of Effective Policies.* Chicago: Loyola University Chicago.

Lurigio, Arthur J., and James A. Swartz (1999). "The Nexus between Drugs and Crime: Theory, Research, and Practice." *Federal Probation* **63:**67–71.

Lutze, Faith E., and David W. Murphy (1999). "Ultramasculine Prison Environments and Inmates' Adjustment: It's Time to Move Beyond the 'Boys Will Be Boys' Paradigm." *Justice Quarterly* **16:**709–733.

Lynch, Mona (2000). "Rehabilitation as Rhetoric: The Ideal of Reformation in Contemporary Parole Discourse and Practices." *Punishment and Society* **2:**40–65.

Lynskey, Dana Peterson, and L. Thomas Winfree Jr. (2000). "Linking Gender, Minority Group Status, and Family Matters to Self-Control Theory: A Multivariate Analysis of Key Self-Control Concepts in Youth-Gang Context." *Juvenile and Family Court Journal* **51:**1–19.

MacDonald, S. Scott, and Cynthia Baroody-Hart (1999). "Communications between Probation Officers and Judges: An Innovative Model." *Federal Probation* **63:**42–50.

MacGrady, J., W. Bemister, and B. Fontaine (1991). *Project R.E.I.D.I.D. (Recidivism and Alcohol-Related Crimes of Aggression).* Rockville, MD: National Institute of Justice, National Criminal Justice Reference Service Microfiche Program.

Mack, Dennis E. (1992). "High Impact Incarceration Program: Rikers Boot Camp." *American Jails* **6:**63–65.

MacKenzie, Doris Layton (1993). "NIJ Sponsored Studies Ask: Does Shock Incarceration Work?" *Corrections Compendium* **18:**5–12.

Maggio, Mark, and Elaine Terenzi (1993). "The Impact of Critical Incident Stress: Is Your Office Prepared to Respond?" *Federal Probation* **57:**10–16.

Mahan, Sue, and Richard Lawrence (1996). "Media and Mayhem in Corrections: The Role of the Media in Prison Riots." *Prison Journal* **76:**420–441.

Mainprize, Stephen (1992). "Electronic Monitoring in Corrections: Assessing Cost Effectiveness and the Potential for Widening the Net of Social Control." *Canadian Journal of Criminology* **34:**161–180.

Majer, Richard D. (1994). "Community Service: A Good Idea That Works." *Federal Probation* **58:**20–23.

Makkai, Toni (1999). *Drug Use Monitoring in Australia (DUMA): A Brief Description.* Canberra: Australian Institute of Criminology.

Maltz, Michael D. (1984). *Recidivism.* Orlando, FL: Academic Press.

Maltz, Michael D., and R. McCleary (1977). "The Mathematics of Behavioral Change: Recidivism and Construct Validity." *Evaluation Quarterly* **1:**421–438.

Mann, Simon (1998). *Probation Perspectives on the Curfew Order with Electronic Monitoring.* Norwich, U.K.: School of Social Work, University of East Anglia.

Manning, Peter K. (1977). *Police Work.* Cambridge, MA: MIT Press.

Marciniak, Liz Marie (1999). "The Use of Day Reporting as an Intermediate Sanction: A Study of Offender Targeting and Program Termination." *Prison Journal* **79:**205–225.

Marciniak, Liz Marie (2000). "The Addition of Day Reporting to Intensive Supervision Probation: A Comparison of Recidivism Rates." *Federal Probation* **64:**34–39.

Marcus, David K., Theodore M. Amen, and Roger Bibace (1992). "A Developmental Analysis of Prisoners' Conceptions of AIDS." *Criminal Justice and Behavior* **19:**174–188.

Markley, Greg (1994). "The Role of Mission Statements in Community Corrections." *APPA Perspectives* **18:**47–50.

Marley, C. W. (1973). "Furlough Programs and Conjugal Visiting in Adult Correctional Institutions." *Federal Probation* **37:**19–25.

Marquart, James W., et al. (1999). "The Implications of Crime Control Policy on HIV/AIDS-Related Risk among Women Prisoners." *Crime and Delinquency* **45:**82–98.

Marshall, Franklin H. (1989). "Diversion and Probation." In *The U.S. Sentencing Guidelines: Implications for Criminal Justice,* Dean J. Champion (ed.). New York: Praeger.

Marshall, William L., and Geris A. Serran (2000). "Improving the Effectiveness of Sexual Offender Treatment." *Trauma and Violence and Abuse: A Review Journal* **1:**203–222.

Martin, Nancy L., and Arthur J. Lurigio (1994). "Special Probation Programs for Drug Offenders." *APPA Perspectives* **18:**24–27.

Martinson, Robert (1974). "What Works? Questions and Answers about Prison Reform." *The Public Interest* **35:**22–54.

Marvell, Thomas B. (1995). "Sentencing Guidelines and Prison Population Growth." *Journal of Criminal Law and Criminology* **85:**696–709.

Marvell, Thomas B., and Carlisle E. Moody (1996). "Determinate Sentencing and Abolishing Parole: The Long-Term Impacts Prisons and Crime." *Criminology* **34:**107–128.

Maslach, Christina (1982a). *Burnout: The Cost of Caring.* Englewood Cliffs, NJ: Prentice Hall.

Maslach, Christina (1982b). "Understanding Burnout: Definitional Issues in Analyzing a Complex Phenomenon." In *Job Stress and Burnout,* W. S. Paine (ed.). Beverly Hills, CA: Sage.

Mason, Tom, and Dave Mercer (1999). *A Sociology of the Mentally Disordered Offender.* London: Longman.

Massachusetts Legislative Research Council (1987). *Report Relative to Alternative Sentencing.* Boston: Massachusetts Legislative Research Council.

Mastrofski, Stephen D., et al. (2000). "The Helping Hand of the Law: Police Control of Citizens on Request." *Criminology* **38:**307–342.

Matthews, Tim (1993). "Pros and Cons of Increasing Officer Authority to Impose or Remove Conditions of Supervision." *APPA Perspectives* **17:**31.

Matthewson, Terry L. (1991). "I.D. Entity." *American Jails* **5:**64–68.

Maxfield, Michael G., and Michael D. Maltz (eds.) (1999). "Special Issue on the National Incident-Based Reporting System." *Journal of Quantitative Criminology* **15:**115–248.

Maxwell, Jane Carlisle, and Lynn S. Wallisch (1998). *Substance Abuse and Crime among Probationers in Three Texas Counties: 1994–1995.* Austin: Texas Commission on Alcohol and Drug Abuse.

Maxwell, Sheila Royo (2000). "Sanction Threats in Court-Ordered Programs: Examining Their Effects on Offenders Mandated into Drug Treatment." *Crime and Delinquency* **46:**542–563.

Maxwell, Sheila Royo, and Kevin M. Gray (2000). "Deterrence: Testing the Effects of Perceived Sanction Certainty on Probation Violation." *Sociological Inquiry* **70:**117–136.

May, Tim, and Antony A. Vass (eds.) (1996). *Working with Offenders: Issues, Contexts, and Outcomes.* London: Sage.

Mays, G. Larry, and Tara Gray (eds.) (1996). *Privatization and the Provision of Correctional Services: Context and Consequences.* Cincinnati, OH: Anderson.

McClearn, Gerald E. (1969). "Biological Bases of Social Behavior with Specific Reference to Violent Behavior." In *Crimes of Violence,* D. J. Mulvhill et al. (eds.). Washington, DC: U.S. Government Printing Office.

McDevitt, Jack, Marla Domino, and Katrina Baum (1997). *Metropolitan Day Reporting Center: An Evaluation.* Boston: Center for Criminal Justice Policy Research, Northeastern University.

McDonald, Douglas C. (1993). "Private Penal Institutions." In *Crime and Justice: A Review of Research,* Vol. 16, Michael Tonry (ed.). Chicago and London: University of Chicago Press.

McDonald, Douglas C., and Elizabeth Fournier (1998). *Private Prisons in the United States: An Assessment of Current Practice.* Cambridge, MA: Abt Associates.

McDonald, Douglas C., Judith Greene, and Charles Worzella (1992). *Day Fines in American Courts: The Staten Island and Milwaukee Experiments.* Washington, DC: U.S. Department of Justice, Office of Justice Programs.

McGillis, Daniel (1998). *Resolving Community Conflict: The Dispute Settlement Center of Durham, North Carolina.* Washington, DC: U.S. Department of Justice.

McMahon, Maeve (1990). "'Net-Widening': Vagaries in the Use of a Concept." *British Journal of Criminology* **30:**121–149.

McReynolds, Veon (1987). *Variables Related to Predicting Absconding Probationers.* Ann Arbor, MI: University Microfilms International.

Meachum, Larry R. (1986). "House Arrest: The Oklahoma Experience." *Corrections Today* **48:**102–110.

Mears, Daniel P. (1998). "The Sociology of Sentencing: Reconceptualizing Decision Making Processes and Outcomes." *Law and Society Review* **32:**667–724.

Mednick, S. A., and J. Volavka (1980). "Biology and Crime." In *Crime and Justice: An Annual Review of Research,* N. Morris and M. Tonry (eds.). Chicago: University of Chicago Press.

Meeker, James W., Paul Jesilow, and Joseph Aranda (1992). "Bias in Sentencing: A Preliminary Analysis of Community Service Sentences." *Behavioral Sciences and the Law,* **10:**197–206.

Megargee, Edwin I., and Joyce Carbonell (1985). "Predicting Prison Adjustment with MMPI Correctional Scales." *Journal of Consulting and Clinical Psychology* **53:**874–883.

Memory, John M., et al. (1999). "Comparing Disciplinary Infraction Rates of North Carolina Fair Sentencing and Structured Sentencing Inmates: A Natural Experiment." *Prison Journal* **79:**45–71.

Mercer, Ron, Murray Brooks, and Paula Tully Bryant (2000). "Global Positioning Satellite System: Tracking Offenders in Real Time." *Corrections Today* **62:**76–80.

Merton, Robert King (1938). "Social Structure and Anomie." *American Sociological Review* **3:**672–682.

Merton, Robert King (1957). *Social Theory and Social Structure.* New York: Free Press.

Messina, Nena P., Eric P. Wish, and Susanna Nemes (1999). "Therapeutic Community Treatment for Substance Abusers with Antisocial Personality Disorder." *Journal of Substance Abuse Treatment* **17:**121–128.

Messinger, Sheldon L., et al. (1985). "The Foundations of Parole in California." *Law and Society Review* **19:**69–106.

MetaMetrics, Inc. (1984). *Evaluation of the Breakthrough Foundation Youth-at-Risk Program: The 10-Day Course and Followup Program.* Washington, DC: MetaMetrics, Inc.

Metchik, Eric (1992a). "Judicial Views of Parole Decision Processes: A Social Science Perspective." *Journal of Offender Rehabilitation* **18:**135–157.

Metchik, Eric (1992b). "Legal Views of Parole Decision Making: A Social Science Perspective." Unpublished paper presented at the annual meeting of the American Society of Criminology, New Orleans, LA, November.

Michigan Department of Corrections (1999). *Objective Parole Criteria: Working Paper.* Lansing: Michigan Department of Corrections.

Miclityinen, Ida (1999). *Crime and Mediation: Selection of Cases, The Significance and Meaning of Mediation to the Participants, and Reoffending.* Helsinki, Finland: National Research Institute of Legal Policy.

Middleton, Kath (1995). "Community Alternatives Reconsidered." *Howard Journal of Criminal Justice* **34:**1–9.

Midkiff, Bill (2000). "Collaborative Jail Mental Health Services." *American Jails* **14:**49–53.

Miethe, Terance D., Hong Lu, and Erin Reese (2000). "Reintegrative Shaming and Recidivism Risks in Drug Court: Explanations for Some Unexpected Findings." *Crime and Delinquency* **46:**522–541.

Miethe, Terance D., and Richard C. McCorkle (1997). "Evaluating Nevada's Anti-Gang Legislation and Gang Prosecution." Unpublished paper.

Miller, Dallas H. (1984). *A Description of Work Release Job Placements from Massachusetts State Correctional Facilities during 1982.* Boston: Massachusetts Department of Corrections.

Miller, J. Mitchell, and Jeffrey P. Rush (1996). *Gangs: A Criminal Justice Approach.* Cincinnati, OH: Anderson.

Miller, Jerome G. (1996). *Search and Destroy: African-American Males in the Criminal Justice System.* New York: Cambridge University Press.

Miller, Jody, and Rod K. Brunson (2000). "Gender Dynamics in Youth Gangs: A Comparison of Males' and Females' Accounts." *Justice Quarterly* **17:**419–448.

Mills, Darrell K. (1990). "Career Issues for Probation Officers." *Federal Probation* **54:**3–7.

Mills, Jim (1992). "Supervision Fees: APPA Issues Committee Report." *APPA Perspectives* **16:**10–12.

Minor, Kevin I., and David J. Hartmann (1992). "An Evaluation of the Kalamazoo Probation Enhancement Program." *Federal Probation* **56:**30–41.

Miranne, Alfred C., and Michael R. Geerken (1991). "The New Orleans Inmate Survey: A Test of Greenwood's Predictive Scale." *Criminology* **29:**497–518.

Mitchell, Bill, and Gene Shiller (1988). "Colorado's Shape-Up Program Gives Youth a Taste of the Inside." *Corrections Today* **50:**76–87.

Mitchell, George A. (1999). *Privatizing Parole and Probation in Wisconsin: The Path to Fewer Prisons.* Thiensville: Wisconsin Policy Research Institute.

Mitchell, George A., and David Dodenhoff (1998). *The Truth about Sentencing in Wisconsin: Plea Bargaining, Punishment, and the Public Interest.* Thiensville: Wisconsin Policy Research Institute.

Mitchell, John J., and Sharon A. Williams (1986). "SOS: Reducing Juvenile Recidivism." *Corrections Today* **48:**70–71.

Mitchell, Ojmarrh, et al. (1999). "The Environment and Working Conditions in Juvenile Boot Camps and Traditional Facilities." *Justice Research and Policy* **1:**1–22.

Montagu, A. (1968). "Chromosomes and Crime." *Psychology Today* **2:**43–49.

Montgomery, Reid H., Jr., and Gordon A. Crews (1998). *A History of Correctional Violence: An Examination of Reported Causes of Riots and Disturbances.* Lanham, MD: American Correctional Association.

Moore, John P., and Ivan L. Cook (1999). *Highlights of the 1998 National Youth Gang Survey.* Washington, DC: U.S. Department of Justice.

More, Harry W. (1998). *Special Topics in Policing,* 2d ed. Cincinnati, OH: Anderson.

Morgan, Kathryn D. (1994). "Factors Associated with Probation Outcome." *Journal of Criminal Justice* **22:**341–353.

Morgan, Kathryn D., Barbara A. Belbot, and John Clark (1997). "Liability Issues Affecting Probation and Parole Supervision." *Journal of Criminal Justice* **25:**211–222.

Morris, Norval, and Marc Miller (1985). "Predictions of Dangerousness." In *Crime and Justice: An Annual Review of Research,* Vol. 6, Michael Tonry and Norval Morris (eds.). Chicago: University of Chicago Press.

Morrisson, Richard D. (1992). "Spotting and Handling the Manipulators in Your Parole and Probation Caseload." *Corrections Today* **54:**22–24.

Mortimer, Ed, and Chris May (1997). *Electronic Monitoring in Practice: The Second Year of the Trials of Curfew Orders.* London: U.K. Home Office.

Moser, Aldine N., Jr. (1994). *Jail Privatization and Regionalization of Jails: Research in Brief.* Alexandria, VA: National Sheriff's Association.

Moses, Marilyn C. (1993). "Girl Scouts Behind Bars: New Program at Women's Prisons Benefits Mothers and Children." *Corrections Today* **55:**132–134.

Motiuk, Laurence L., and Raymond L. Belcourt (1996). *Temporary Absence Program Participation and the Release of Federal Offenders.* Ottawa: Research Division, Correctional Service Canada.

Motiuk, Laurence L., Raymond L. Belcourt, and James Bonta (1995). *Managing High-Risk Offenders: A Post-Detention Follow-Up.* Ottawa: Correctional Service Canada, Communications and Corporate Development Branch.

Motiuk, Laurence L., et al. (1994). "Special Needs Offenders." *Forum on Corrections Research* **6:**6–43.

Mumola, Christopher J., and Thomas P. Bonczar (1998). *Substance Abuse and Treatment of Adults on Probation, 1995.* Washington, DC: U.S. Office of Justice Programs.

Munden, David P., Richard Tewksbury, and Elizabeth L. Grossi (1999). "Intermediate Sanctions and the Halfway Back Program in Kentucky." *Criminal Justice Policy Review* **9:**431–449.

Munson, Michelle, and Regina E. Ygnacio (2000). *The State Jail System Today: An Update.* Austin: Texas Criminal Justice Policy Council.

Murphy, Edward M. (1985). "Handling Violent Juveniles." *Corrections Today* **47:**26–30.

Murphy, Patrick (1994). "The Invisible Minority: Irish Offenders and Criminal Justice." *Probation Journal* **4:**2–7.

Nagoshi, Jack T. (1986). *Juvenile Recidivism: Third Circuit Court.* Honolulu: Youth Development and Research Center, University of Hawaii–Manoa.

Narcotics Anonymous (1999). *The NA Way.* Van Nuys, CA: Narcotics Anonymous World Service Office.

Nasheri, Hedich (1998). *Betrayal of Due Process: A Comparative Assessment of Plea Bargaining in the United States and Canada.* Lanham, MD: University Press of America.

National Association of Pretrial Services Agencies (1995). *Performance Standards and Goals for Pretrial Release and Diversion.* Frankfort, KY: National Association of Pretrial Services Agencies.

National Commission on Law Observance and Enforcement (1931). *Wickersham Commission Reports.* Washington, DC: U.S. Government Printing Office.

National Council on Crime and Delinquency (1990a). *Development of Risk Prediction Scales for the California Youthful Offender Parole Board Based on Assessment of 1981–1982 Releases.* San Francisco: National Council on Crime and Delinquency.

National Council on Crime and Delinquency (1990b). *Tennessee Board of Paroles Risk Assessment Report.* San Francisco: National Council on Crime and Delinquency.

National Drug Court Institute (1999a). *DUI/Drug Courts: Defining a National Strategy.* Washington, DC: National Drug Court Institute.

National Drug Court Institute (1999b). *Reentry Drug Courts.* Alexandria, VA: National Drug Court Institute.

National Law Enforcement and Corrections Technology Center (1999). *Keeping Track of Electronic Monitoring.* Washington, DC: National Law Enforcement and Corrections Technology Center.

Nemes, Susanna, Eric D. Wish, and Nena Messina (1999). "Comparing the Impact of Standard and Abbreviated Treatment in a Therapeutic Community." *Journal of Substance Abuse Treatment* **17:**339–347.

Nesbitt, Charlotte A. (1992). "The Female Offender: Overview of Facility Planning and Design Issues and Considerations." *Corrections Compendium* **17:**1–7.

Nettler, Gwyn (1974). "Embezzlement without Problems." *British Journal of Criminology* **14:**70–77.

New Mexico Governor's Organized Crime Prevention Commission (1990). *New Mexico Prison Gangs.* Santa Fe: New Mexico Governor's Organized Crime Prevention Commission.

New York State Department of Correctional Services (1993). *Absconders and Parolees from Work Release: 1988–1992.* Albany: New York State Department of Correctional Services.

New York State Department of Correctional Services (1994). *Shock Incarceration and Shock Parole Supervision: The Sixth Annual Report to the Legislature.* Albany: New York State Department of Correctional Services.

New York State Division of Parole (1998). *The Ninth Annual Shock Legislative Report.* Albany: New York State Division of Parole.

Niemeyer, Mike, and David Shichor (1996). "A Preliminary Study of a Large Victim/Offender Reconciliation Program." *Federal Probation* **60:**30–34.

Nieto, Marcus (1998). *Probation for Adult and Juvenile Offenders: Options for Improved Accountability.* Sacramento: California Research Bureau.

Nieves, Kim, Jeffrey Draine, and Phyllis Solomon (2000). "The Validity of Self-Reported Criminal Arrest History among Clients of a Psychiatric Probation and Parole Service." *Journal of Offender Rehabilitation* **30:**133–151.

NIJ Reports (1991). *Electronic Monitoring.* Washington, DC: U.S. Department of Justice, no. 222.

Norman, Michael D., and Robert C. Wadman (2000). "Utah Presentence Investigation Reports: User Group Perceptions of Quality and Effectiveness." *Federal Probation* **64:**7–12.

North Carolina Administrative Office of the Courts (1988). *Presentence Reports to Judges.* Raleigh: North Carolina Administrative Office of the Courts.

Nurco, David, Thomas E. Hanlon, and Richard W. Bateman (1992). "Correlates of Parole Outcome among Drug Abusers." Unpublished paper presented at the annual meeting of the American Society of Criminology. New Orleans, LA, November.

O'Callaghan, Jerome, Alan D. Gagnon, and Serve Brochu (1990). "Alcohol and Legal Issues." *Alcoholism Treatment Quarterly* **7:**87–146.

O'Connell, Paul, and Jacquelyn M. Power (1992). "The Power of Partnerships: Establishing Literacy Programs in Community Corrections." *APPA Perspectives* **16:**6–8.

Office of Justice Programs (2001). *Rates of HIV Infection and AIDS-Related Deaths.* Washington, DC: Office of Justice Programs.

Ogburn, Kevin R. (1993). "Volunteer Program Guide." *Corrections Today* **55:**66–70.

Ogle, Robbin S. (1999). "Prison Privatization: An Environmental Catch-22." *Justice Quarterly* **16:**579–600.

Ohio Department of Correction and Rehabilitation (2001). *Guidelines for Paroling Offenders: Working Draft.* Columbus: Ohio Department of Correction and Rehabilitation.

Ohio Parole Board (1992). *The Parole Board Guidelines.* Columbus: Ohio Parole Board.

Okun, Peter (1997). *Crime and the Nation: Prison Reform and Popular Fiction in Philadelphia: 1786–1800.* Ann Arbor, MI: University Microfilms International.

Olbrich, Jeffrey Lee (1997). *Violence, Parole, and Prison Crowding: An Empirical Analysis of the Recidivism of Paroled Violent Offenders.* Ann Arbor, MI: University Microfilms International.

Olson, David E., and Arthur J. Lurigio (2000). "Predicting Probation Outcomes: Factors Associated with Probation Rearrest, Revocations, and Technical Violations During Supervision." *Justice Research and Policy* **2:**73–86.

Onek, David (1994). *Pairing College Students with Delinquents: The Missouri Intensive Case Monitoring Program.* San Francisco: National Council on Crime and Delinquency.

Orchowsky, Stan, Nancy Merritt, and Katherine Browning (1994). *Evaluation of the Virginia Department of Corrections' Intensive Supervision Program: Executive Summary.* Richmond: Virginia Department of Criminal Justice Services.

Osgood, D. Wayne, and Jeff M. Chambers (2000). "Social Disorganization Outside the Metropolis: An Analysis of Rural Youth Violence." *Criminology* **38:**81–115.

Owens, Charles E., Jeffrey A. Will, and Henry J. Camp (1997). *Inmate Risk and Needs: Developing an Objective Means for Classifying Florida's Inmate Population.* Jacksonville: University of North Florida.

Pace, Chaplain Arthur C. (1993). "Religious Volunteers Form Partnership with the Military's Chaplaincy Program." *Corrections Today* **55:**114–116.

Page, Brian (1995). *Assessment Center Handbook.* Longwood, FL: Gould Publications.

Pallone, Nathaniel J., and James J. Hennessy (1999). "Blacks and Whites as Victims and Offenders in Aggressive Crime in the U.S.: Myths and Realities." *Journal of Offender Rehabilitation* **30:**1–33.

Palmer, Carleton A., and Mark Hazelrigg (2000). "The Guilty but Mentally Ill Verdict: A Review and Conceptual Analysis of Intent and Impact." *Journal of the American Academy of Psychiatry and the Law* **28:**47–54.

Palumbo, Dennis J., and Rebecca D. Petersen (1994). "Evaluating Criminal Justice Programs." *Evaluation and Program Planning* **17:**159–164.

Palumbo, Dennis J., and Zoann Snyder-Joy (1990). "From Net-Widening to Intermediate Sanctions: The Transformation of Alternatives to Incarceration from Malevolence to Benevolence." Unpublished paper presented at the annual meeting of the American Society of Criminology, Baltimore, MD, November.

Paradis, Cheryl, et al. (2000). "Mentally Ill Elderly Jail Detainees: Psychiatric, Psychosocial, and Legal Factors." *Journal of Offender Rehabilitation* **31:**77–86.

Parent, Dale G. (1989a). "Probation Supervision Fee Collection in Texas." *APPA Perspectives* **13:**9–12.

Parent, Dale G. (1989b). *Shock Incarceration: An Overview of Existing Programs.* Washington, DC: U.S. Department of Justice, Office of Justice Programs.

Parent, Dale G., et al. (1994). *Responding to Probation and Parole Violators.* Washington, DC: U.S. National Institute of Justice.

Parker-Jimenez, Joy (1997). "An Offender's Experience with the Criminal Justice System." *Federal Probation* **11:**47–52.

Parton, Nigel, and Corinne Wattam (eds.) (1999). *Child Sexual Abuse: Responding to the Experiences of Children.* West Sussex, U.K.: Wiley.

Pastore, Ann L., and Kathleen Maguire (eds.) (2001). *Sourcebook of Criminal Justice Statistics, 1999.* Albany, NY: Hindelang Criminal Justice Research Center.

Patel, Jody, and Curt Soderlund (1994). "Getting a Piece of the Pie: Revenue Sharing with Crime Victims Compensation Programs." *APPA Perspectives* **18:**22–27.

Patterson, Bernie L. (1992). "Job Experience and Perceived Stress among Police, Correctional, and Probation/Parole Officers." *Criminal Justice and Behavior* **19:**260–285.

Payne, Brian K., and Randy R. Gainey (1998). "A Qualitative Assessment of the Pains Experienced on Electronic Monitoring." *International Journal of Offender Therapy and Comparative Criminology* **42:**149–163.

Payne, Brian K., and Randy R. Gainey (1999). "Attitudes toward Electronic Monitoring among Monitored Offenders and Criminal Justice Students." *Journal of Offender Rehabilitation* **29:**195–208.

Peach, F. J. (1999). *Corrections in the Balance: A Review of Corrective Services in Queensland.* Brisbane, Australia: Queensland Government.

Peak, Ken (1986). "Crime Victim Reparation: Legislative Revival of the Offended Ones." *Federal Probation* **50:**36–41.

Pearl, Natalie R. (1998). "Use of Community-Based Social Services to Reduce Recidivism in Female Parolees." *Women and Criminal Justice* **10:**27–52.

Pelletier, Daniel, Sylvain Coutu, and Annie Lamonde (1996). "Work and Gender Issues in Secure Juvenile Facilities." *International Journal of Offender Therapy and Comparative Criminology* **40:**32–43.

Peters, Roger H., and Mary R. Murrin (2000). "Effectiveness of Treatment-Based Drug Courts in Reducing Criminal Recidivism." *Criminal Justice and Behavior* **27:**72–96.

Peters, Roger H., et al. (1993). "Alcohol and Drug Rehabilitation." *Journal of Offender Rehabilitation* **19:**1–79.

Petersilia, Joan (1987a). *Expanding Options for Criminal Sentencing.* Santa Monica, CA: Rand Corporation.

Petersilia, Joan (1987b). "Los Angeles Experiments with House Arrest." *Corrections Today* **49:**132–134.

Petersilia, Joan (1987c). "Prisoners without Prisons." *State Legislatures,* August:22–25.

Petersilia, Joan (ed.) (1998). *Community Corrections: Probation, Parole, and Intermediate Sanctions.* New York: Oxford University Press.

Petersilia, Joan (1999a). "A Decade of Experimenting with Intermediate Sanctions: What Have We Learned?" *Justice Research and Policy* **1:**9–23.

Petersilia, Joan (1999b). "Parole and Prisoner Reentry in the United States." In *Prisons,* Michael Tonry and Joan Petersilia (eds.). Chicago: University of Chicago Press.

Petersilia, Joan M., and Susan Turner (1993). *Evaluating Intensive Supervision Probation/Parole: Results of a Nationwide Experiment.* Washington, DC: U.S. Department of Justice, Office of Justice Programs.

Petersilia, Joan M., Susan Turner, and Joyce Peterson (1986). *Prison versus Probation in California: Implications for Crime and Offender Recidivism.* Santa Monica, CA: Rand Corporation.

Petersilia, Joan M., et al. (1985). *Granting Felons Probation in California: Implications for Crime and Offender Recidivism.* Santa Monica, CA: Rand Corporation.

Philadelphia Police Department (1998). *Philadelphia Police Department Grievance Guide.* Philadelphia: Morrison Press.

Philadelphia Prison System (1990). *Philadelphia Prisons Pre-Release Program—Policy and Operations Manual.* Philadelphia: Philadelphia Prison System.

Phillips, Amy K. (1997). "Thou Shalt Not Kill Any Nice People: The Problem of Victim Impact Statements in Capital Sentencing." *American Criminal Law Review* **35:**93–118.

Piaget, J. (1948). *The Moral Judgment of the Child.* New York: Free Press.

Pizzi, William T. (1999). *Trials without Truth: Why Our System of Criminal Trials Has Become an Expensive Failure and What We Need to Do to Rebuild It.* New York: New York University Press.

Pratt, John (1996). "Reflections on Recent Trends towards the Punishment of Persistence." *Crime, Law, and Social Change* **25:**243–264.

Pratt, John (2000). "The Return of the Wheelbarrow Man: The Arrival of Postmodern Penalty?" *British Journal of Criminology* **40:**127–145.

Pratt, John, and Marny Dickson (1997). "Dangerous, Inadequate, Invisible, Out: Episodes in the Criminological Career of Habitual Criminals." *Theoretical Criminology* **1:**363–384.

Pratt, Travis C., Jeffrey Maahs, and Steven D. Stehr (1998). "The Symbolic Ownership of the Corrections 'Problem': A Framework for Understanding the Development of Corrections Policy in the United States." *Prison Journal* **78:**451–464.

Pratt, Travis C., and Melissa R. Winston (1999). "The Search for the Frugal Grail: An Empirical Assessment of the Cost-Effectiveness of Public vs. Private Correctional Facilities." *Criminal Justice Policy Review* **10:**447–471.

Prins, Herschel (1999). *Will They Do It Again? Risk Management In Criminal Justice and Psychiatry.* New York: Routledge.

Probation and Parole Employee's Association (2001). *Minutes of January 2001.* Portland, OR: Probation and Parole Employee's Association.

Probation Association (1939). *John Augustus: The First Probation Officer.* New York: Probation Association.

Proctor, Jon L., and Michael Pease (2000). "Parole as Institutional Control: A Test of Specific Deterrence and Offender Misconduct." *Prison Journal* **80:**39–55.

Project New Pride (1985). *Project New Pride.* Washington, DC: U.S. Government Printing Office.

Pullen, Suzanne (1996). *Evaluation of the Reasoning and Rehabilitation Cognitive Skills Development Program as Implemented in Juvenile ISP in Colorado.* Denver: Colorado Division of Criminal Justice.

Quay, Herbert C. (1984). *Managing Adult Inmates.* College Park, MD: American Correctional Association.

Quay, Herbert C., and L. B. Parsons (1971). *The Differential Behavioral Classification of the Adult Male Offender.* Philadelphia: Temple University. (Technical report prepared for the U.S. Department of Justice Bureau of Prisons, Contract J-1C-22, 253.)

Radli, Eric R. (1997). "Boot Camps: A 'Highly Intensive Supervision, Training, and Education Program.'" *American Jails* **11:**85–90.

Rafter, Nicole Hahn (1997). *Creating Born Criminals.* Urbana: University of Illinois Press.

Ralph, H. Paige (1992). *Texas Prison Gangs.* Ann Arbor, MI: University Microfilms International.

Rans, Laurel L. (1984). "The Validity of Models to Predict Violence in Community and Prison Settings." *Corrections Today* **46:**50–63.

Rasmussen, David W., and Bruce L. Benson (1994). *Intermediate Sanctions: A Policy Analysis Based on Program Evaluations.* Tallahassee, FL: Collins Center for Public Policy.

Rath, Quentin C. (1991). "Minnesota Corrections: Perspectives from Probation and Parole Officers." *Corrections Today* **53:**228–230.

Ratliff, Bascom W. (1988). "The Army Model: Boot Camp for Youthful Offenders." *Corrections Today* **50:**90–102.

Raynor, Peter, and Terry Honess (1998). *Drugs and Alcohol Related Offenders Project: An Evaluation of the West Glamorgan Partnership.* London: Drugs Prevention Initiative, UK Home Office.

Read, Edward M. (1990). "Twelve Steps to Sobriety: Probation Officers 'Working the Program.'" *Federal Probation* **54:**34–42.

Read, Edward M. (1992). "Euphoria on the Rocks: Understanding Crack Addiction." *Federal Probation* **56:**3–11.

Read, Edward M. (1995). "Posttreatment Supervision Challenges: Introducing Al-Anon, Nar-Anon, and Oxford House, Inc." *Federal Probation* **59:**18–36.

Read, Edward M., et al. (1997). "Variety of On-the-Job Special Skills, Special Duties in Federal Probation." *Federal Probation* **61:**25–37.

Reckless, Walter C. (1961). *The Crime Problem.* New York: Appleton-Century-Crofts.

Reckless, Walter C. (1967). *The Crime Problem,* 2d ed. New York: Appleton-Century-Crofts.

Reed, Tom (1996). *Sanctioning First-Time Convicted Felony Offenders in the Community: The Changing Profile of Offenders.* Austin, TX: Criminal Justice Policy Council.

Rees, Thomas A., Jr. (1996). "Joining the Gang: A Look at Youth Gang Recruitment." *Journal of Gang Research* **4:**19–25.

Rhine, Edward E., William R. Smith, and Ronald W. Jackson (1991). *Paroling Authorities: Recent History and Current Practice.* Laurel, MD: American Correctional Association.

Richardson, Francoise (1999). "Electronic Tagging of Offenders: Trials in England." *Howard Journal of Criminal Justice* **38:**158–172.

Richmond Times-Dispatch (1990). "Virginia County Tries Home Incarceration Program." *Corrections Today* **52:**100.

Roberts, Dorothy E., et al. (1999). "Supreme Court Review." *Journal of Criminal Law and Criminology* **89:**775–1140.

Roberts, John W. (1997). "The Federal Bureau of Prisons: Its Mission, Its History, and Its Partnership with Probation and Pretrial Services." *Federal Probation* **11:**53–57.

Robinson, Laurie (1998). "Managing Sex Offenders in the Community: Challenges and Progress." *APPA Perspectives* **22:**18.

Roche, Declan (1999). "Mandatory Sentencing." *Trends and Issues Australian Institute of Criminology* **138:**1–6.

Rogers, Joseph W. (1990). "The Predisposition Report: Maintaining the Promise of Individualized Juvenile Justice." *Federal Probation* **54:**43–57.

Rogers, Joseph W., and James D. Williams (1995). "The Predispositional Report, Decision Making, and Juvenile Court Policy." *Juvenile and Family Court Journal* **45:**47–57.

Rogers, Richard, et al. (2000). "Prototypical Analysis of Antisocial Personality Disorder: A Study of Inmate Samples." *Criminal Justice and Behavior* **27:**234–255.

Rolf, Peter Lars, and Zelma E. Greeson (1992). *Gangs USA.* Olympia, WA: FYI Limited.

Romig, Dennis A. (1978). *Justice for Our Children.* Lexington, MA: Lexington Books.

Ross, Jeffrey Ian (ed.) (2000). *Varieties of State Crime and Its Control.* Monsey, NY: Criminal Justice Press.

Rothman, David J. (1983). "Sentencing Reforms in Historical Perspective." *Crime and Delinquency* **29:**631–647.

Rottman, David, and Pamela Casey (1999). "Therapeutic Jurisprudence and the Emergence of Problem-Solving Courts." *National Institute of Justice Journal,* July:12–19.

Roulet, Sister Elaine (1993). "New York's Prison Nursery/Children's Center." *Corrections Compendium* **18**:4–6.

Roy, Sudipto (1993). "Two Types of Juvenile Restitution Programs in Two Midwestern Counties: A Comparative Study." *Federal Probation* **57**:48–53.

Roy, Sudipto (1995a). "Juvenile Restitution and Recidivism in a Midwestern County." *Federal Probation* **59**:55–62.

Roy, Sudipto (1995b). "Juvenile Offenders in an Electronic Home Detention Program." *Journal of Offender Monitoring* **8**:9–17.

Roy, Sudipto (1997). "Five Years of Electronic Monitoring of Adults and Juveniles in Lake County, Indiana: A Comparative Study on Factors Related to Failure." *Journal of Crime and Justice* **20**:141–160.

Roy, Sudipto, and Michael Brown (1992). "Victim-Offender Reconciliation Project for Adults and Juveniles: A Comparative Study in Elkhart County, Indiana." Unpublished paper presented at the annual meeting of the American Society of Criminology, San Francisco, November.

Ruddell, Rick, G. Larry Mays, and Dennis M. Giever (1998). "Transferring Juveniles to Adult Courts: Recent Trends and Issues in Canada and the United States." *Juvenile and Family Court Journal* **49**:1–15.

Runda, John C., Edward E. Rhine, and Robert E. Wetter (1994). *The Practice of Parole Boards.* Lexington, KY: Council of State Governments.

Rush, Jeffrey P. (1992). "Juvenile Probation Officer Cynicism." *American Journal of Criminal Justice* **16**:1–16.

Ryan, James E. (1997). "Who Gets Revoked? A Comparison of Intensive Supervision Successes and Failures in Vermont." *Crime and Delinquency* **43**:104–118.

Sarbin, Theodore R., and Jeffrey E. Miller (1970). "Demonism Revisited: The XYY Chromosomal Anomaly." *Issues in Criminology* **5**:195–207.

Savolainen, Jukka (2000). "Relative Cohort Size and Age-Specific Arrest Rates: A Conditional Interpretation of the Easterlin Effect." *Criminology* **38**:117–136.

Sawyer, Becki (2000). *An Evaluation of the SACRO (Fife) Young Offenders Mediation Project.* Edinburgh: Scottish Executive Central Research Unit.

Saylor, W. G., and G. G. Gaes (1992). "Post-Release Employment Project: Prison Work Has Measurable Effects on Post-Release Success." *Federal Prison Journal* **2**:32–36.

Schiff, Martha F. (1990). "Shifting Paradigms from a Presumption of Incarceration to Community Based Supervision and Sanctioning." Unpublished paper presented at the annual meeting of the American Society of Criminology, Baltimore, MD, November.

Schlatter, Gary (1989). "Electronic Monitoring: Hidden Costs of Home Arrest Programs." *Corrections Today* **51**:94–95.

Schlossman, Steven, and Joseph Spillane (1992). *Bright Hopes, Dim Realities: Vocational Innovation in American Correctional Education.* Santa Monica, CA: Rand Corporation.

Schmidt, Annesley K. (1998). "Electronic Monitoring: What Does the Literature Tell Us?" *Federal Probation* **62**:10–19.

Schmitz, Richard J., Pinky S. Wassenberg, and Marisa E. Patterson (2000). *Evaluations of the Christian County Extended Day Program, Peoria County Anti-Gang and Drug Abuse Unit, and Winnebago Day Reporting and Assessment Centers.* Chicago: Illinois Criminal Justice Information Authority.

Schneider, Thomas P., and Robert C. Davis (1995). "Speedy Trial Homicide Courts." *Criminal Justice* **9**:24–29.

Schrag, Clarence (1971). *Crime and Justice: American Style.* Washington, DC: U.S. Government Printing Office.

Schwaner, Shawn L. (1997). "They Can Run but They Can't Hide: A Profile of Parole Violators at Large." *Journal of Crime and Justice* **20**:19–32.

Schwaner, Shawn L. (1998). "Patterns of Violent Specialization: Predictors of Recidivism for a Cohort of Parolees." *American Journal of Criminal Justice* **23**:1–17.

Schwartz, Ira M. (ed.) (1999). "Will the Juvenile Court System Survive?" *Annals of the American Academy of Political and Social Science* **56**:8–184.

Sechrest, Dale K., et al. (1998). *The Riverside County Drug Court: Final Research Report.* San Bernardino: Criminal Justice Department, California State University–San Bernardino.

Seiter, Richard P. (ed.) (2000). "Restorative Justice: A Concept Whose Time Has Come." *Corrections Management Quarterly* **4**:74–85.

Senese, Jeffrey D., et al. (1992). "Evaluating Jail Reform: Inmate Infractions and Disciplinary Response in a Traditional and a Podular/Direct Supervision Jail." *American Jails* **6**:14–23.

Shah, Saleem A., and Loren H. Roth (1974). "Biological and Psychophysiological Factors in Criminality." In *Handbook of Criminology,* Daniel Glaser (ed.). Chicago: Rand-McNally.

Shane-DuBow, Sandra, Alice P. Brown, and Eric Olsen (1985). *Sentencing Reform in the United States: History, Content, and Effect.* Washington, DC: U.S. Department of Justice.

Shane-DuBow, Sandra, et al. (1998). "Structured Sentencing in the U.S.: An Experiment in Modeling Judicial Discretion." *Law and Policy* **20**:231–382.

Shapiro, Emily F. (1997). *Mandatory Sentencing Laws.* St. Paul: Research Department, Minnesota House of Representatives.

Shapiro, Walter (1990). "A Life in His Hands." *Time,* May 28, 1990:23–24.

Shaw, Clifford R., and Henry D. McKay (1929). *Juvenile Delinquency and Urban Areas.* Chicago: University of Chicago Press.

Shearer, Robert A. (2000). "Coerced Substance Abuse Counseling Revisited." *Journal of Offender Rehabilitation* **30**:153–171.

Shearer, Robert A., and Chris R. Carter (1999). "Screening and Assessing Substance-Abusing Offenders: Quantity and Quality." *Federal Probation* **63**:30–33.

Sheldon, William H. (1949). *Varieties of Delinquent Youth.* New York: Harper and Row.

Shepperd, Robert A., Jeffrey R. Geiger, and George Welborn (1996). "In Search of Security: Closed Maximum Security: The Illinois SuperMax." *Corrections Today* **58**:84–105.

Shewan, David, and John B. Davies (eds.) (2000). *Drug Use and Prisons: An International Perspective.* Amsterdam: Harwood.

Shichor, David (1992). "Following the Penological Pendulum: The Survival of Rehabilitation." *Federal Probation* **56**:19–25.

Shichor, David, and Dale K. Sechrest (1998). "A Comparison of Mediated and Non-Mediated Juvenile Offender Cases in California." *Juvenile and Family Court Journal* **49**:27–39.

Shockley, Carol (1988). "The Federal Presentence Investigation Report: Postsentence Disclosure under the Freedom of Information Act." *Administrative Law Review* **40**:79–119.

Siegel, Gayle R. (1994). "Making a Difference: The Effect of Literacy and General Education Development Programs on Adult Offenders on Probation." *APPA Perspectives* **18**:38–43.

Siegel, Michael Eric (1996). "Reinventing Management in the Public Sector." *Federal Probation* **60**:30–35.

Sieh, Edward W. (1990). "Role Perception among Probation Officers." Unpublished paper presented at the annual meeting of the Academy of Criminal Justice Sciences, Denver, CO, April.

Sieh, Edward W. (1992). "Probation Work: Mendacity and the Favorite Client." Unpublished paper presented at the annual meeting of the American Society of Criminology, New Orleans, LA, November.

Sigler, Robert T., and David Lamb (1995). "Community-Based Alternatives to Prison: How the Public and Court Personnel View Them." *Federal Probation* 59:3–9.

Sigler, Robert T., and David Lamb (1996). "Community Based Alternative Sanctions: How the Public and Court Personnel View Them." *Journal of Offender Monitoring* 9:1–8.

Silver, Eric (2000). "Race, Neighborhood Disadvantage, and Violence among Persons with Mental Disorders: The Importance of Contextual Measurement." *Law and Human Behavior* 24:449–456.

Simmons, Calvin, John K. Cochran, and William R. Blount (1997). "The Effects of Job-Related Stress and Job Satisfaction on Probation Officers' Inclinations to Quit." *American Journal of Criminal Justice* 21:213–229.

Simourd, David J., and Robert D. Hoge (2000). "Criminal Psychopathy: A Risk-and-Need Perspective." *Criminal Justice and Behavior* 27:256–272.

Sluder, Richard D., and Rolando V. del Carmen (1990). "Are Probation and Parole Officers Liable for Injuries Caused by Probationers and Parolees?" *Federal Probation* 54:3–12.

Sluder, Richard D., Anne Garner, and Kevin Cannon (1995). "The Fusion of Ideology and Technology: New Directions for Probation in the 21st Century." *Journal of Offender Monitoring* 8:1–7.

Sluder, Richard D., and Robert A. Shearer (1992). "Personality Types of Probation Officers." *Federal Probation* 56:29–35.

Sluder, Richard D., Robert A. Shearer, and Dennis W. Potts (1991). "Probation Officers' Role Perceptions and Attitudes toward Firearms." *Federal Probation* 55:3–12.

Smith, Albert G. (1992). "Proper Planning: Organizational Skills for Managing Your Probation and Parole Workload." *Corrections Today* 54:136–142.

Smith, Albert G. (1993a). "Practical Advice on Designing Probation and Parole Offices." *Corrections Today* 55:80–87.

Smith, Albert G. (1993b). "A Training Program in Probation and Parole Whose Time Has Come and Gone: Role Reversals." *APPA Perspectives* 17:24–27.

Smith, Linda G., and Ronald L. Akers (1993). "A Comparison of Recidivism of Florida's Community Control and Prison: A Five-Year Survival Analysis." *Journal of Research in Crime and Delinquency* 30:267–292.

Smith, Michael E., and Walter J. Dickey (1999). *Reforming Sentencing and Corrections for Just Punishment and Public Safety*. Washington, DC: U.S. National Institute of Justice.

Smith, Robert R., and D. A. Sabatino (1990). "American Prisoner Home Furloughs." *Journal of Offender Counseling* 10:18–25.

Snyder, Howard N., Melissa Sickmund, and Eileen Poe-Yamagata (2000). *Juvenile Transfers to Criminal Court in the 1990s: Lessons Learned from Four Studies*. Washington, DC: U.S. Office of Juvenile Justice and Delinquency Prevention.

Soma, Jerry (1994). "Group Reporting: A Sensible Way to Manage High Caseloads." *Federal Probation* 58:26–28.

Song, Lin, and Roxanne Lieb (1995). *Washington State Sex Offenders: Overview of Recidivism Studies*. Olympia: Washington State Institute for Public Policy.

Sontheimer, Henry, and Traci Duncan (1997). *Assessment of County Intermediate Punishment Programs*. Harrisburg: Pennsylvania Commission on Crime and Delinquency.

South Carolina Department of Probation, Parole, and Pardon Services (1993). *Violations Guidelines and Administrative Hearings*. Columbia: South Carolina Department of Probation, Parole, and Pardon Services.

South Carolina State Reorganization Commission (1991). *Prison Crowding in South Carolina: Is There a Solution?* Columbia: South Carolina State Reorganization Commission.

South Carolina State Reorganization Commission (1992). *An Evaluation of the Implementation of the South Carolina Department of Corrections*. Columbia: South Carolina State Reorganization Commission, A Jail and Prison Overcrowding Project Report.

Spaans, E. C., and C. Verwers (1997). *Electronic Monitoring in the Netherlands: Results of the Experiment*. The Hague: Netherlands Ministry of Justice.

Spangenberg, Robert L., et al. (1987). *Assessment of the Massachusetts Probation System*. West Newton, MA: Spangenberg Group.

Spens, Iona (ed.) (1994). *Architecture of Incarceration*. London: Academy Editions.

Spergel, Irving A. (1993). *Gang Suppression and Intervention: An Assessment*. Washington, DC: U.S. Office of Juvenile Justice and Delinquency.

Spergel, Irving A., and Susan F. Grossman (1997). "The Little Village Project: A Community Approach to the Gang Problem." *Social Work* 42:456–470.

Spergel, Irving, et al. (1994). *Gang Suppression and Intervention: Community Models*. Washington, DC: U.S. Office of Juvenile Justice and Delinquency Prevention.

Spica, Arthur R., Jr. (1993). "The Resource Referral Process: What Is between Human Services and Offender Adjustment?" *APPA Perspectives* 17:24–26.

Spiegel, Allen D., and Marc B. Spiegel (1998). "The Insanity Plea in Early Nineteenth Century America." *Journal of Community Health* 23:227–247.

Spruit, J. E., et al. (1998). "Special Issue: Forensic History." *International Journal of Law and Psychiatry* 21:315–446.

Sreenivasan, Shoba, et al. (2000). "Neuropsychological and Diagnostic Differences between Recidivistically Violent Not Criminally Responsible and Mentally Ill Prisoners." *International Journal of Law and Psychiatry* 23:161–172.

Stanz, Robert, and Richard Tewksbury (2000). "Predictors of Success and Recidivism in a Home Incarceration Program." *Prison Journal* 80:326–344.

Stastny, Charles, and Gabrielle Tyrnauer (1982). *Who Rules the Joint? The Changing Political Culture of Maximum-Security Prisons in America*. Lexington, MA: Lexington Books.

Steffensmeier, Darrell J., John Kramer, and Cathy Streifel (1993). "Gender and Imprisonment Decisions." *Criminology* 31:411–446.

Steiner, Hans, Elizabeth Cauffman, and Elaine Duxbury (1999). "Personality Traits in Juvenile Delinquents: Relation to Criminal Behavior and Recidivism." *Journal of the American Academy of Child and Adolescent Psychiatry* 38:256–262.

Stephen, Jackie (1993). *The Misrepresentation of Women Offenders: Gender Differences in Explanations of Crime in Probation Officers' Reports*. Norwich, U.K.: University of East Anglia, Social Work.

Stephens, Regina (2001). Personal letter. Sacramento, CA, Department of Corrections.

Steury, Ellen Hochstedler (1989). "Prosecutorial and Judicial Discretion." In *The U.S. Sentencing Guidelines: Implications for Criminal Justice*, Dean J. Champion (ed.). New York: Praeger.

Stevens, Dennis J. (1997). "Violence Begets Violence." *Corrections Compendium* 22:1–3.

Stewart, Sharon D. (1994). "Community-Based Drug Treatment in the Federal Bureau of Prisons." *Federal Probation* 58:24–28.

Stiles, Don R. (1994). "A Partnership for Safe Communities: Courts, Education and Literacy." *APPA Perspectives* **18:**8–9.

Stinchcomb, Jeanne B. (1999). "Recovering from the Shocking Reality of Shock Incarceration: What Correctional Administrators Can Learn from Boot Camp Failures." *Corrections Management Quarterly* **3:**43–52.

Stojkovic, Stan, and Rick Lovell (1997). *Corrections: An Introduction,* 2d ed. Cincinnati, OH: Anderson.

Stolzenberg, Lisa Ann (1993). *Unwarranted Disparity and Determinate Sentencing: A Longitudinal Study of Presumptive Sentencing Guidelines in Minnesota.* Ann Arbor, MI: University Microfilms International.

Storm, John P. (1997). "What United States Probation Officers Do." *Federal Probation* **61:**13–18.

Straub, Frank (1997). *Controlling Corruption in a Prison System: The New York State Department of Correctional Services, 1970–1990.* Ann Arbor, MI: University Microfilms International.

Strong, Ann (1981). *Case Classification Manual, Module One: Technical Aspects of Interviewing.* Austin: Texas Adult Probation Commission.

Sullivan, C., M. Q. Grant, and J. D. Grant (1957). "The Development of Interpersonal Maturity: Applications to Delinquency." *Psychiatry* **23:**373–385.

Sundt, Jody, et al. (1998). "What Will the Public Tolerate?" *APPA Perspectives* **22:**20–26.

Sweet, Joseph (1985). "Probation as Therapy." *Corrections Today* **47:**89–90.

Sykes, Gresham (1974). "The Rise of Critical Criminology." *Journal of Criminal Law and Criminology* **65:**39–45.

Sykes, Gresham M., and David Matza (1957). "Techniques of Neutralization: A Theory of Delinquency?" *American Sociological Review* **22:**664–670.

Talarico, Susette M., and Martha A. Myers (1987). "Split Sentencing in Georgia: A Test of Two Empirical Assumptions." *Justice Quarterly* **4:**611–629.

Tarr, Thomas K. (1997). "Federal and State Probation Systems in New Hampshire: A Comparison." *Federal Probation* **11:**71–75.

Taxman, Faye S. (1994). "Correctional Options and Implementation Issues: Results from a Survey of Corrections Professionals." *APPA Perspectives* **18:**32–37.

Taxman, Faye S. (1999). "Unraveling 'What Works' for Offenders in Substance Abuse Treatment Services." *National Drug Court Institute Review* **2:**93–134.

Taxman, Faye S., and James M. Byrne (1994). "Locating Absconders: Results from a Randomized Field Experiment." *Federal Probation* **58:**13–23.

Taylor, Jon Marc (1996). "Violence in Prison: A Personal Perspective." *Corrections Compendium* **21:**1–27.

Taylor, William J. (1992). "Tailoring Boot Camps to Juveniles." *Corrections Today* **54:**122–124.

Tennessee Department of Corrections (1994). *Tennessee Project CERCE (Comprehensive Education and Rehabilitation in a Correctional Environment) Resident Manual.* Nashville: Tennessee Department of Corrections.

Texas Criminal Justice Policy Council (1996). *Recidivism as a Performance Measure: The Record So Far.* Austin: Texas Criminal Justice Policy Council.

Texas Criminal Justice Policy Council (2000). *Overview of Special Needs Parole Policy and Recommendations.* Austin: Texas Criminal Justice Policy Council.

Texas Office of the Comptroller (1992). *Texas Crime, Texas Justice.* Austin: Texas Office of the Comptroller.

Texas Office of the State Auditor (1996). *A Survey of Criminal Justice Information System Users.* Austin: Texas Office of the State Auditor.

Thio, Alex (1975). "A Critical Look at Merton's Anomie Theory." *Pacific Sociological Review* **18:**83–97.

Thompson, Joel A., and G. Larry Mays (1991). *American Jails: Public Policy Issues.* Chicago: Nelson-Hall.

Thornton, William E., Jr., Jennifer James, and William G. Doerner (1982). *Delinquency and Justice.* Glenview, IL: Scott, Foresman.

Timasheff, Nicholas S. (1941). *One Hundred Years of Probation, 1841–1941.* New York: Fordham University Press.

Timonen, M., et al. (2000). "Psychiatric Admissions at Different Levels of the National Health Care Services and Male Criminality: The Northern Finland 1966 Birth Cohort Study." *Social Psychiatry and Psychiatry Epidemiology* **35:**198–201.

Toch, Hans (1995). "Inmate Involvement in Prison Governance." *Federal Probation* **59:**34–39.

Tolman, Richard M. (1996). "Expanding Sanctions for Batterers: What Can We Do Besides Jailing and Counseling Them?" In *Future Interventions with Battered Women and Their Families,* Jeffrey L. Edleson and Zvi Eisikovits (eds.). Thousand Oaks, CA: Sage.

Tonry, Michael (1997). *Intermediate Sanctions in Sentencing Guidelines.* Washington, DC: U.S. National Institute of Justice.

Tonry, Michael (ed.) (1998). *The Handbook of Crime and Punishment.* New York: Oxford University Press.

Tonry, Michael (1999a). *Fragmentation of Sentencing and Corrections in America.* Washington, DC: U.S. National Institute of Justice.

Tonry, Michael (1999b). *Reconsidering Indeterminate and Structured Sentencing.* Washington, DC: U.S. National Institute of Justice.

Toombs, Nancy J., Brent B. Benda, and Randy D. Tilmon (1999). "A Developmentally Anchored Conceptual Model of Drug Use Tested among Adult Boot Camp Inmates." *Journal of Offender Rehabilitation* **29:**49–64.

Toombs, Thomas G. (1995). "Monitoring and Controlling Criminal Offenders Using the Satellite Global Positioning System Coupled to Surgically Implanted Transponders." *Criminal Justice Policy Review* **7:**341–346.

Torbet, Patricia, and Linda Szymanski (1998). *State Legislative Responses to Violent Juvenile Crime: 1996–1997 Update.* Washington, DC: U.S. Department of Justice.

Torbet, Patricia, et al. (2000). *Juveniles Facing Criminal Sanctions: Three States That Changed the Rules.* Washington, DC: U.S. Office of Juvenile Justice and Delinquency Prevention.

Torres, Sam (1996). "The Use of a Credible Drug Testing Program for Accountability and Intervention." *Federal Probation* **60:**18–23.

Torres, Sam (1997a). "An Effective Supervision Strategy for Substance-Abusing Offenders." *Federal Probation* **61:**38–44.

Torres, Sam (1997b). "The Substance-Abusing Offender and the Initial Interview." *Federal Probation* **61:**11–17.

Torres, Sam (1998). "A Continuum of Sanctions for Substance-Abusing Offenders." *Federal Probation* **62:**36–45.

Torres, Sam, et al. (1999). *Drug-Involved Adult Offenders: Community Supervision Strategies and Considerations.* Lexington, KY: American Probation and Parole Association.

Torrey, E. Fuller (1999). "How Did So Many Mentally Ill Persons Get into America's Jails and Prisons?" *American Jails* **13:**9–13.

Travis, Lawrence F., III (1985). *Probation, Parole, and Community Corrections.* Prospect Heights, IL: Waveland Press.

Traynelis-Yurek, E., and F. G. Yurek (1990). "Increased Literacy through Unison Reading." *Journal of Correctional Education* **41:**110–114.

Tremblay, Pierre, et al. (1996). "From Childhood Physical Aggression to Adolescent Maladjustment: The Montreal Prevention Experiment." In *Preventing Childhood Disorders, Substance Abuse, and Delinquency,* R. D. Peters and R. J. McMahon (eds.). Thousand Oaks, CA: Sage.

Trester, Harold B. (1981). *Supervision of the Offender.* Englewood Cliffs, NJ: Prentice Hall.

Triplet, Rush, and Toby Ross (1998). "Developing Partnership for Gang Intervention: The Role of Community Corrections." *APPA Perspectives* **22:**29–35.

Trotter, Christopher (1996). "The Impact of Different Supervision Practices in Community Corrections: Cause for Optimism." *Australian and New Zealand Journal of Criminology* **29:**29–46.

Turpin-Petrosino, Carolyn (1999). "Are Limiting Enactments Effective? An Experimental Test of Decision Making in a Presumptive Parole State." *Journal of Criminal Justice* **27:**321–332.

Turturici, Jack, and Gregory Sheehy (1993). "How Direct Supervision Jail Design Affects Inmate Behavior Management." *Corrections Today* **55:**102–106.

Twill, Sarah E., et al. (1998). "Changes in Measured Loneliness, Control, and Social Support Among Parolees in a Halfway House." *Journal of Offender Rehabilitation* **27:**77–92.

Umbreit, Mark S. (1994). "Victim Empowerment through Mediation." *APPA Perspectives* **18:**25–28.

Umbreit, Mark S., and Robert B. Coates (1993). "Cross-Site Analysis of Victim-Offender Mediation in Four States." *Crime and Delinquency* **39:**565–585.

U.S. Bureau of Justice Assistance (1998). *1996 National Survey of State Sentencing Structures.* Washington, DC: U.S. Bureau of Justice Assistance.

U.S. Center for Mental Health Services (1995). *Double Jeopardy: Persons with Mental Illnesses in the Criminal Justice System.* Rockville, MD: U.S. Center for Mental Health Services.

U.S. Code Annotated (2001). *United States Code Annotated.* St. Paul, MN: West.

U.S. Department of Justice (1991). *Post-Release Employment Project: Summary of Preliminary Findings.* Washington, DC: U.S. Department of Justice Federal Bureau of Prisons Office of Research.

U.S. Department of Justice (1996). *Probation and Parole Population Reaches Almost 3.8 Million.* Washington, DC: U.S. Department of Justice.

U.S. Department of Justice (1997). *State and Federal PSI Report Preparation: Criteria and Regulations.* Washington, DC: U.S. Department of Justice.

U.S. Department of Justice (2000). *Probation and Parole, 1999.* Washington, DC: U.S. Department of Justice.

Useem, Bert, Camille Graham Camp, and George M. Camp (1996). *Resolution of Prison Riots: Strategies and Policies.* New York, NY: Oxford University Press.

U.S. General Accounting Office (1994). *Sentencing: Intermediate Sanctions in the Federal Criminal Justice System.* Washington, DC: U.S. General Accounting Office.

U.S. General Accounting Office (1997). *Federal Offenders: Trends in Community Corrections.* Washington, DC: U.S. General Accounting Office.

U.S. General Accounting Office (1998). *Fines and Restitution: Improvement Needed in How Offender's Payment Schedules Are Determined.* Washington, DC: U.S. General Accounting Office.

U.S. National Institute of Corrections (1996). *Community Justice: Striving for Safe, Secure and Just Communities.* Washington, DC: U.S. National Institute of Corrections.

U.S. Office of Justice Programs (1998). *Rethinking Probation: Community Supervision, Community Safety.* Washington, DC: U.S. Office of Justice Programs.

U.S. Office of National Drug Control Policy (1998). *Consensus Meeting on Drug Treatment in the Criminal Justice System: Breaking the Cycle with Science-Based Policy.* Washington, DC: U.S. Office of National Drug Control Policy.

U.S. Parole Commission (1994). *An Overview of the United States Parole Commission.* Chevy Chase, MD: U.S. Parole Commission.

U.S. Sentencing Commission (1987). *United States Sentencing Commission Guidelines Manual.* Washington, DC: U.S. Sentencing Commission.

U.S. Sentencing Commission (1994). *Report to Congress on the Maximum Utilization of Prisons Resources.* Washington, DC: U.S. Federal Bureau of Prisons.

U.S. Sentencing Commission (1996). *Reprint Series, Volume II.* Washington, DC: U.S. Government Printing Office.

Valdez, Al (1997). *Gangs: A Guide to Understanding Street Gangs,* 2d ed. San Clemente, CA: Law/Tech Publishing.

Valentine, Bill (1995). *Gang Intelligence Manual: Identifying and Understanding Modern-Day Violent Gangs in the United States.* Boulder, CO: Paladin Press.

VanderZanden, James W. (1984). *Social Psychology.* New York: Random House.

Van Voorhis, Patricia, Francis T. Cullen, and Brandon Applegate (1995). "Evaluating Interventions with Violent Offenders: A Guide for Practitioners and Policymakers." *Federal Probation* **59:**17–27.

Vaughn, Michael S. (1993). "Listening to the Experts: A National Study of Correctional Administrator's Responses to Prison Overcrowding." *Criminal Justice Review* **18:**12–25.

Vaughn, Michael S., and Linda G. Smith (1999). "Practicing Penal Harm Medicine in the United States: Prisoners' Voices from Jail." *Justice Quarterly* **16:**175–231.

Ventura County Sheriff's Department (2001). *Tattoo Removal Program.* Ventura, CA: Ventura County Sheriff's Department.

Victoria Department of Justice (1998). *Review of Suicides and Self-Harm in Victorian Prisons.* Melbourne, Australia: Victoria Department of Justice Correctional Services Task Force.

Vigdal, Gerald L., and Donald W. Stadler (1994). "Alternative to Revocation Program Offers Offenders a Second Chance." *Corrections Today* **56:**44–47.

Virginia Commission on Sentencing and Parole Reform (1995). *Report.* Richmond: Commonwealth of Virginia.

Virginia Department of Criminal Justice Services (1998). *Justice Services Pilot Program.* Richmond: Virginia Department of Criminal Justice Services.

Virginia Joint Legislative Audit and Review Commission (1996). *Review of Jail Oversight and Reporting Activities.* Richmond: Commonwealth of Virginia.

Virginia State Crime Commission (1998). *Staffing Needs and Levels within the Department of Corrections and a Reevaluation of Retirement Benefits of Probation and Parole Officers.* Richmond: Virginia State Crime Commission.

Visher, Christy A., Pamela K. Lattimore, and Richard L. Linster (1991). "Predicting the Recidivism of Serious Youthful Offenders Using Survival Models." *Criminology* **29:**329–366.

Vitiello, Michael (1997). "Three Strikes: Can We Return to Rationality?" *Journal of Criminal Law and Criminology* **87:**395–481.

Vito, Gennaro F., Ronald M. Holmes, and Deborah G. Wilson (1985). "The Effect of Shock and Regular Probation upon Recidivism: A Comparative Analysis." *American Journal of Criminal Justice* **9:**152–162.

Vito, Gennaro F., and Richard Tewksbury (1998). "The Impact of Treatment: The Jefferson County (Kentucky) Drug Court Program." *Federal Probation* **62:**46–51.

Vito, Gennaro F., and Richard Tewksbury (1999). "Improving the Educational Skills of Inmates—The Results of an Impact Evaluation." *Corrections Compendium* **24:**1–9.

Vogel, Mary E. (1999). "The Social Origins of Plea Bargaining: Conflict and the Law in the Process of State Formation, 1830–1860." *Law and Society Review* **33:**161–246.

Vohryzek-Bolden, Miki, Tim Croisdale, and Carole Barnes (1999). *Overview of Selected States' Academy and In-Service Training for Adult and Juvenile Correctional Employees.* Sacramento: California Commission on Correctional Peace Officer Standards and Training.

von Hirsch, Andrew (1992). "Proportionality in the Philosophy of Punishment." In *Crime and Justice: A Review of Research,* Vol. 16, Michael Tonry (ed.). Chicago and London: University of Chicago Press.

Vorenberg, James (1981). *Criminal Law and Procedure: Cases and Materials.* St. Paul, MN: West.

Waits, Robert (1993). *Study of Alternative Punishment Programs for Offenders.* Richmond: Virginia Department of Planning and Budget.

Waldo, Gordon P., and D. Griswold (1979). "Issues in the Measurement of Recidivism." In *The Rehabilitation of Criminal Offenders: Problems and Prospects,* Lee Sechrest, S. O. White, and E. D. Brown (eds.). Washington, DC: National Academy of Sciences.

Waldron, Thomas W. (1990). "Boot Camp Offers Second Chance to Young Felons." *Corrections Today* **52:**144–169.

Walker, Samuel (1989). *Sense and Nonsense about Crime: A Policy Guide,* 2d ed. Monterey, CA: Brooks/Cole.

Walmsley, Roy (1996). *Prison Systems in Central and Eastern Europe: Progress, Problems, and the International Standards.* Helsinki, Finland: European Institute for Crime Prevention and Control.

Walsh, Anthony (1997). *Correctional Assessment: Casework and Counseling.* Lanham, MD: American Correctional Association.

Walsh, Thomas C., et al. (1997). "Current Research and Clinical Practices." *Journal of Offender Rehabilitation* **26:**125–203.

Walters, Glenn D. et al. (1992). "The Choice Program: A Comprehensive Residential Treatment Program for Drug Involved Offenders." *International Journal of Offender Therapy and Comparative Criminology* **36:**21–29.

Warren, Roger K. (1998). "Reengineering the Court Process." Presentation to Great Lakes Court Summit, Madison, WI, September 24–25.

Washington Department of Corrections (1993). *An Integrated Approach to Education, Work, and Offender Reintegration.* Olympia: Washington Department of Corrections.

Washington State Department of Social and Mental Health Services (1991). *SSOSA Blue Ribbon Panel Final Report to the Legislature.* Olympia: Washington State Department of Social and Mental Health Services.

Watkins, John C., Jr. (1989). "Probation and Parole Malpractice in a Noninstitutional Setting: A Contemporary Analysis." *Federal Probation* **53:**29–34.

Watterson, Kathryn (1996). *Women in Prison: Inside the Concrete Tomb.* Boston: Northeastern University Press.

Welch, Michael (1999). *Punishment in America: Social Control and the Ironies of Imprisonment.* Thousand Oaks, CA: Sage.

Wellford, Charles (1975). "Labeling Theory and Criminology: An Assessment." *Social Problems* **22:**332–345.

Welsh, Wayne N. (1995). *Counties in Court: Jail Overcrowding and Court-Ordered Reform.* Philadelphia: Temple University Press.

West-Smith, Mary, Mark R. Pogrebin, and Eric D. Poole (2000). "Denial of Parole: An Inmate Perspective." *Federal Probation* **64:**3–10.

Wheeler, Gerald R., and Amy S. Rudolph (1990). "New Strategies to Improve Probation Officer's Fee Collection Rates: A Field Study in Performance Feedback." *Justice System Journal* **14:**78–94.

Wheeler-Cox, Trilby, Nancy Arrigona, and Lisa Reichers (1998). *An Overview of the Texas Youth Commission's Specialized Treatment Programs.* Austin: Texas Criminal Justice Policy Council.

Whitehead, John T. (1989). *Burnout in Probation and Parole.* New York: Praeger.

Whitehead, John T., and Charles A. Lindquist (1992). "Determinants of Probation and Parole Officer Professional Orientation." *Journal of Criminal Justice* **20:**13–24.

Whitesell, Russ, and Gordon A. Anderson (1990). *Educational Programs in Adult Correctional Institutions.* Madison: Wisconsin Legislative Council.

Whitfield, Dick (1997). *Tackling the Tag: The Electronic Monitoring of Offenders.* Winchester, U.K.: Waterside Press.

Wicharaya, Tamasak (1995). *Simple Theory, Hard Reality: The Impact of Sentencing Reforms on Courts, Prisons, and Crime.* Albany: State University of New York Press.

Wicklund, Carl (1996). "Training and Technical Assistance for Developing Correctional Options." *APPA Perspectives* **20:**44–47.

Wiebush, Richard G. (1990). "The Ohio Experience: Programmatic Variations in Intensive Supervision for Juveniles." *Perspectives* **14:**26–35.

Wiederanders, Mark R. (1983). *Success on Parole: The Influence of Self-Reported Attitudes, Experiences, and Background Characteristics on the Parole Behaviors of Youthful Offenders.* Sacramento, CA: Department of the Youth Authority.

Wiggins, Robert R. (1996). "Ten Ideas for Effective Managers." *Federal Probation* **60:**43–49.

Wilkinson, Alec (1993). *A Violent Act.* New York: Knopf.

Wilkinson, Reginald A. (1998). *Best Practices: Excellence in Conditions.* Lanham, MD: American Correctional Association.

Wilkinson, Reginald A., and Tessa Unwin (1999). "In Prison: A Recipe for Disaster." *Corrections Today* **60:**98–102.

Williams, Frank P., III, Marilyn D. McShane, and H. Michael Dolny (2000). "Predicting Parole Absconders." *Prison Journal* **80:**24–38.

Wilson, Deborah G. (1985). *Persistent Felony Offenders in Kentucky: A Profile of the Institutional Population.* Louisville: Kentucky Criminal Justice Statistical Analysis Center.

Wilson, Deborah G., and Gennaro F. Vito (1990). "Persistent Felony Offenders in Kentucky: A Comparison of Incarcerated Felons." *Journal of Contemporary Criminal Justice* **6:**237–253.

Wilson, Edward O. (1975). *Sociobiology: The New Synthesis.* Cambridge, MA: Harvard University Press.

Wilson, George P. (1985). "Halfway House Programs for Offenders." In *Probation, Parole, and Community Corrections,* Lawrence Travis III (ed.). Prospect Heights, IL: Waveland Press.

Wilson, James Q. (1997). *Moral Judgment: Does the Abuse Excuse Threaten Our Legal System?* New York: HarperCollins.

Wilson, James Q., and Richard J. Hernstein (1985). *Crime and Human Nature.* New York: Simon and Schuster.

Wilson, John J. (2000). *1998 National Youth Gang Survey.* Washington, DC: National Youth Gang Center.

Wilson, Robin J., et al. (2000). "Community-Based Sexual Offender Management: Combining Parole Supervision and Treatment to Reduce Recidivism." *Canadian Journal of Criminology* **42**:177–188.

Winfree, L. Thomas, Jr., and Dennis M. Giever (2000). "On Classifying Driving-While-Intoxicated Offenders: The Experiences of A Citywide DWI Drug Court." *Journal of Criminal Justice* **28**:13–21.

Winter, Bill (1993). "Does Corrections Need Volunteers?" *Corrections Today* **55**:20–22.

Winterfield, Laura A., and Sally T. Hillsman (1993). *The Staten Island Day-Fine Project.* Washington, DC: U.S. Department of Justice.

Wittenberg, Peter M. (1996). "Language and Communication in Prison." *Federal Probation* **60**:45–50.

Wolf, Thomas J. (1997). "What United States Pretrial Services Officers Do." *Federal Probation* **61**:19–24.

Wolfgang, Marvin E., and Franco Ferracuti (1967). *The Subculture of Violence.* London: Tavistock.

Wolfgang, Marvin E., Robert M. Figlio, and Thorsten Sellin (1972). *Delinquency in a Birth Cohort.* Chicago: University of Chicago Press.

Wood, Peter B., and Harold G. Grasmick (1995). "Inmates Rank the Severity of Ten Alternative Sanctions Compared to Prison." *Journal of the Oklahoma Criminal Justice Research Consortium* **2**:30–42.

Wood, Peter B., and Harold G. Grasmick (1999). "Toward the Development of Punishment Equivalencies: Male and Female Inmates Rate the Severity of Alternative Sanctions Compared to Prison." *Justice Quarterly* **16**:19–50.

Wooldredge, John D. (1991). "Identifying Possible Sources of Inmate Crowding in U.S. Jails." *Journal of Quantitative Criminology* **7**:373–386.

Wooldredge, John D., and Jill Gordon (1997). "Predicting the Estimated use of Alternatives to Incarceration." *Journal of Quantitative Criminology* **13**:121–142.

Wright, Kevin N. (ed.) (1997). "Managing a Changing Offender." *Corrections Management Quarterly* **1**:1–87.

Wright, Kevin N., Todd R. Clear, and Paul Dickson (1984). "Universal Applicability of Probation Risk-Assessment Instruments: A Critique." *Criminology* **22**:113–134.

Yaryura-Tobias, J. A., and F. Neziroglu (1975). "Violent Behavior Brain Dyshythmia and Glucose Dysfunction: A New Syndrome." *Journal of Orthpsychiatry* **4**:182–188.

Yeboah, David (2000). "The Evaluation of New Zealand's Habilitation Centre's Pilot Program." *Journal of Criminal Justice* **28**:227–235.

Yochelson, Samuel, and Stanton E. Samenow (1976). *The Criminal Personality.* New York: Jason Aronson.

Young, Douglas, and Rachel Porter (1999). *A Collaborative Evaluation of Pennsylvania's Program for Drug-Involved Parole Violators.* New York: Vera Institute of Justice.

Yuslum, Theresa M. (1990). "Community Service Centers in Pennsylvania: An Assessment of Post-Release Outcomes for Female Offenders." Unpublished paper presented at the annual meeting of the American Society of Criminology, Baltimore, MD, November.

Zhang, Lening, and Steven F. Messner (2000). "The Effects of Alternative Measures of Delinquent Peers on Self-Reported Delinquency." *Journal of Research in Crime and Delinquency* **37**:323–337.

Zhao, Jihong, and Nicholas Lovrich (1997). "Collective Bargaining and the Police: The Consequences for Supplemental Compensation Policies in Large Societies." *Policing* **20**:508–518.

Ziedenberg, Jason, and Vincent Schiraldi (1997). *The Risks Juveniles Face When They Are Incarcerated as Adults.* Washington, DC: The Justice Policy Institute.

Zupan, Linda L. (1993). "Direct Inmate Supervision." *American Jails* **7**:21–22.

Zurawski, James J., and Edward C. Brooks (1975). "Planning: The Dynamics of Police Administration." *FBI Law Enforcement Bulletin* **44**:2–6.

Name Index

Abt Associates, Inc., 405, 562
Adair, David N., Jr., 241
Adams, Robert, 243
Adams, Stuart, 405
Adelberg, Sheldon, 445
Adler, Jeffrey S., 217
Administrative Office of U.S. Courts, 87,
    93–94, 96, 178, 378
Aguirre, Adalberto, Jr., 79, 480
Albonetti, Celesta A., 87, 201, 241, 267,
    272
Albright, Kathleen, 190, 194
Alcoholics Anonymous World Services,
    Inc., 477
Alexander, Jack, 230, 252
Allen, G. Frederick, 315
Allen, Harry E., 33, 135
Altschuler, David M., 271, 275, 290, 534,
    538
Ambrosio, Tara Jen, 46
Amen, Theodore M., 460
American Correctional Association, 36,
    43–44, 61, 63, 67, 94, 135, 141, 145,
    195–196, 216–217, 225–231, 234, 242,
    262, 264, 268, 279, 319–320, 324, 346,
    354–355, 359–361, 363, 369, 376, 387,
    395, 413, 454, 517, 534
American Probation and Parole Associa-
    tion, 377–378, 411
Ammar, Nawal H., 289
Anderson, David C., 60, 402
Anderson, Dennis B., 289, 324
Anderson, Gordon A., 247
Anderson, H.S., 455, 463
Anderson, James F., 190
Anderson, Sara L., 324

Andrus, J.K., 461
Anno, B. Jaye, 467
Ansay, Sylvia J., 51, 54
Applegate, Brandon, 243–244, 497
Aranda, Joseph, 316
Archambeault, William G., 45, 49–50
Archwamety, Teara, 338
Arizona Department of Corrections, 387
Armstrong, Troy L., 271, 275, 290,
    527–528, 534, 538
Arnold, Charlotte S., 198–199, 289,
    411–412
Arola, Terryl, 363–365, 370
Arrigona, Nancy, 50, 275, 455
Arthur, Lindsay G., 79, 135, 137, 140, 370
Ashford, Jose B., 535
Atkins, Elliot, 98
Auburn, Tim, 417
Auerbach, Barbara J., 38, 40, 51
Augustus, John, 93–94, 136–137
Austin, James, 82, 189, 230, 252, 333, 563

Bahn, Charles, 312
Baird, S. Christopher, 347, 370–371, 523,
    525–526
Baker, David, 79, 480
Bandura, Albert, 431
Barnes, Carol, 410
Baroff, George S., 100
Baroody-Hart, Cynthia, 165
Barrineau, H.E. III, 366, 417–418
Bartlett, Shanie R., 9
Basta, Joanne, 370
Bateman, Richard W., 460
Bauer, Jere M., 140
Baum, Katrina, 70

Bayens, Gerald J., 35, 39, 177, 305
Bayse, D.J., 413–414
Bazemore, Gordon, 142, 156–157, 241,
    315, 372
Beal, Chris A., 293
Beck, Allen J., 216, 221, 223–224, 235–236,
    338, 457
Becker, Howard S., 438
Beech, Anthony, 466
Behr, Edward, 136
Belbot, Barbara A., 363, 365, 367, 376
Belcourt, Raymond L., 273, 295–296,
    393
Belenko, Steven R., 472–473
Belfrage, Henrik, 395
Bemister, W., 294
Benda, Brent B., 190
Bensinger, Gad J., 460
Benson, Bruce L., 32
Benveneste, Deena, 51, 54
Benzvy-Miller, Shereen, 45–46, 79
Berg, Bruce L., 32, 51, 56–57, 370, 546
Berliner, Lucy, 5
Bernat, Frances P., 360
Bernstein, Ilene N., 438
Bibace, Roger, 460
Bigger, Phillip J., 364
Bilchik, Shay, 190, 500, 502
Binder, Arnold, 510
Birkbeck, Chris, 140, 296–297, 325
Birmingham, Luke, 463
Bishop, Bill, 353
Bjorkly, Stal, 386, 392
Black, Henry Campbell, 7, 85, 88,
    134–135, 414, 488
Blankenship, Michael, 99

Blomberg, Thomas G., 145
Blount, William R., 252, 407
Blumstein, Alfred, 338
Boehm, L., 430
Bogard, David M., 244
Bohen, Timothy, 370–372
Bohn, Martin J., 387
Boin, R. Arjen, 243
Bolyard, Melissa, 189
Bonczar, Thomas P., 477
Bonn, Robert L., 353–354
Bonta, James, 61, 393
Boone, Harry N., Jr., 465, 548–549, 553, 558
Bork, Michael V., 142
Borum, Randy, 464
Bosoni, Anthony J., 318
Bottomley, A. Keith, 137, 260, 262, 264, 270
Bouffard, Jeffrey A., 289, 308–309, 311
Bourque, Blair B., 545
Bowers, Dan M., 56
Bowker, Arthur L., 86, 96
Bowman, Gary W., 248
Boyles, Cecilia E., 189
Braga, Anthony A., 402
Brandau, Timothy J., 47
Brandon, Ann, 248
Braswell, Michael C., 242
Breckenridge, James F., 472, 556
Brewer, Victoria E., 467
Brewster, Mary, 266
Bridges, George S., 86–87, 96
Britt, Chester L., III, 459
Brochu, Steve, 478
Brody, Arthur L., 398
Brooks, Edward C., 405
Brooks, Murray, 400
Brown, Alice P., 264
Brown, Jodi M., 141, 525
Brown, Michael, 159
Brown, Paul W., 354, 361, 364, 369
Brown, Sammie, 230
Brown, Valerie, 181
Browne, Kevin, 466
Browning, Katherine, 173, 352, 555
Bruce, A.A., 273
Brumbaugh, Susan, 140, 279
Brunson, Rod K., 480
Bryant, Paula Tully, 400
Buddress, Loren A.N., 54, 87
Buentello, Salvador, 243, 249, 251, 280
Burgess, Linda, 405
Burke, Peggy B., 241, 333, 409
Burkhead, Michael, 97
Burns, Jerald C., 185
Burns, Ronald, 245, 271–272, 332
Burpo, John, 379
Burrell, William D., 92
Burt, Grant N., 79, 140
Busher, Walter, 290
Butts, Jeffrey A., 499
Bynum, Tim, 404
Byrne, James M., 179–180, 185, 266, 317, 401

Cahalan, Margaret Werner, 218–219, 490
California Assembly, 12, 280
California Board of Corrections, 456–457
California Department of Corrections, 228, 279
California Department of Justice, 251
California Department of the Youth Authority, 557
California San Diego Association of Governments, 253
Call, Jack E., 85, 241
Camp, Camille Graham, 48, 51, 54, 57, 60, 69, 81, 190, 224, 243, 290, 293, 295, 308, 311, 317, 348, 354–355, 357, 359–360, 368–370, 399, 401, 465
Camp, George M., 48, 51, 54, 57, 60, 69, 81, 190, 224, 243, 290, 293, 295, 308, 311, 317, 348, 354–355, 357, 359–360, 368–370, 399, 401, 465
Camp, Henry J., 230
Campbell, Jacquelyn C., 388
Campbell, Ralph, Jr., 353
Campling, Jo, 243
Canada Solicitor General, 454
Cannon, Kevin, 353, 370
Capodanno, Daniel J., 459
Capretta-Wallace, Suzanne, 61
Carbonell, Joyce L., 230, 387
Carlson, Eric W., 371
Carp, Scarlett V., 196
Carpenter, Patricia, 447
Carroll, Marnie E., 51, 61, 64, 280, 324
Carter, Chris R., 467, 470–471
Casey, Pamela, 165–166, 498
Casilias, Victor A., 251
Castellano, Thomas C., 38, 40, 51, 191, 270, 290, 292
Cauffman, Elizabeth, 555
Cavanaugh, Michael J., 183
Cavender, Gray, 336, 538
Chadwick, Susan M., 43
Chaiken, Jan M., 559
Chaiken, Marcia R., 559
Chambers, Jeff M., 8
Champion, Dean J., 85, 116, 267, 273, 317, 322, 379, 387, 398, 409
Chapman, Jack, 244
Chard-Wierschem, Deborah, 248, 296, 312, 402
Charles, Michael T., 531–532
Chavaria, Frederick R., 459
Ching, James, 81
Christophersen, Kristin, 247
Church Council on Justice and Corrections, 67
Chute, C.L., 369
Ciancia, James J., 299–300, 316
Cimini, Joseph F., 157
Clagett, Arthur P., 514
Clairmont, Don, 38
Clark, John, 363, 365, 367, 376
Clark, Patricia M., 32
Clear, Todd R., 36–38, 92, 327, 408, 459
Clear, Val B., 92

Cleary, Jim, 398
Clegg, Ian J., 406, 408
Coates, Robert B., 159
Cochran, Donald, 166
Cochran, John K., 407
Cohen, Albert K., 424, 436
Cohen, Stanley, 145
Cole, Richard, 85, 241
Colling, Susan, 189
Colling-Chadwick, Susan, 305, 477
Collins, William C., 244
Colorado Legislative Council, 318
Conaboy, Richard P., 84
Conly, Catherine, 462, 464
Connecticut Board of Parole, 322
Connelly, Michael, 413
Conrad, John P., 94, 136
Cook, Ivan L., 249
Cook, Stephen S., 201, 241
Cooper, Caroline S., 9
Corbett, Ronald P., Jr., 467
Cornelius, Gary F., 222, 224, 241, 355, 361, 406–408, 410, 456
Corrado, Raymond R., 398, 457
Correctional Association of New York, 460
Corrections Compendium, 57, 67, 69, 267–268, 289–290, 364–365
Cosgrove, Edward J., 145, 354, 399
Costa, Jeralita, 411
Costanzo, Samuel A., 529–530
Courtright, Kevin E., 32, 51, 56–57, 358, 370, 546
Coutu, Sylvain, 406
Cowles, Ernest L., 191, 249
Craddock, Amy, 70
Craissati, Jackie, 143
Crank, John P., 357–358, 361, 409–410
Crew, Robert E., Jr., 201, 316
Crews, Gordon A., 243
Croisdale, Tim, 410
Cronin, Mary, 244
Crosland, Paul, 354, 369
Cullen, Francis T., 49, 243–244
Culliver, Concetta C., 197–198
Cunniff, Mark A., 553
Cunningham, John A., 477
Curran, J.C., 68
Curry, Theodore R., 79
Cushman, Robert C., 410
Cuvelier, Steven Jay, 396

D'Allessio, Stewart J., 272
Dammer, Harry R., 36–38
Davidson, William S., 446
Davidson-Coronado, Janet, 279, 324, 549
Davies, John B., 460, 466
Davis, James R., 312, 515–516
Davis, Robert C., 22, 97
Davis, Su Perk, 200, 268, 399
Dawson, Roger E., 460
Day, Michael, 247
Decker, Scott H., 404, 462
DeComo, Robert, 371
Deis, Donald R., Jr., 45, 49–50

Deitch, David A., 476
del Carmen, Rolando V., 365–368, 376
DeLeon, William Granados, 145
DelGrosso, Ernest J., 353, 361, 363
DeLisi, Matt, 8
DeLord, Ron, 379
Deschenes, Elizabeth Piper, 142, 459
Dhaliwal, Gurmeet K., 9
Dickey, Walter J., 25, 184, 266
Dickson, Marny, 12
Dickson, Paul, 327
Dieterich, William, 189
Diggs, David W., 69
DiIulio, John J., 135, 333
Dillingham, David D., 34, 40, 50, 395
Ditton, Paula M., 220, 452
DiVito, Robert J., 247
Dodenhoff, David, 21, 267
Doeren, Stephen E., 161
Doerner, William G., 424
Dolan, Richard, 458
Dolinko, David, 46
Dolny, H. Michael, 280, 402
Domino, Marla, 70
Donnelly, S.M., 316
Doyle, Patricia A., 438
Draine, Jeffrey, 275
Driggs, John, 465–466
Dubler, Nancy Neveloff, 224
Duncan, Randall W., 141, 273
Duncan, Traci, 32
Dunlap, Karen L., 34
Dutton, Donnie W., 455
Duxbury, Elaine, 555
Dyson, Laronistine, 190

Edwards, Todd, 25, 318, 454
Eichenlaub, Christopher, 297
Eisenberg, Michael, 50, 402, 455
Ekland-Olson, Sheldon, 280, 553
Elder, Alice P. Franklin, 479
Ellem, Barry, 50
Ellsworth, Thomas, 414, 459
Ely, John Frederick, 292, 310–311
Empey, Lamar T., 436
English, Kim, 43, 305, 328, 372, 477
Enos, Richard, 51, 61, 64, 280, 324, 414
Erez, Edna, 79, 97, 195, 289
Erickson, Lori, 244
Erwin, Billie S., 178, 180
Esbensen, Finn-Aage, 481
Escoto, Henry A., 398
Eskridge, Chris W., 243
Evans, Donald G., 164–165

Fagan, Jeffrey A., 396
Falkin, Gregory P., 370–372
Fannin, Leon F., 433
Farrell, Amy, 292, 476
Faulkner, David, 65
Faulkner, Rick, 33
Feeley, Malcolm M., 248
Feld, Barry C., 495–496
Ferracuti, Franco, 437–438
Ferns, Ray, 372

Fields, Charles B., 402
Figlio, Robert M., 437
Finn, Peter, 247, 404, 406, 408
Firestone, Philip, 458, 466
Fisher, Dawn, 466
Fitzharris, Timothy L., 292
Flanagan, Lamont W., 36–37, 40, 46–47
Flanagan, Timothy J., 46
Fleming, D.W., 461
Florida Advisory Council, 54
Florida Department of Corrections, 25, 81, 176–177, 272, 413
Florida House of Representatives, 315
Fogel, David, 266–267
Fogg, Vern, 471
Fong, Robert S., 249, 280
Fontaine, B., 294
Ford, William, 39
Fournier, Elizabeth, 248
Freeman-Longo, Robert, 466
Frew, David R., 354
Friedman, Sharon, 247
Fruchtman, David A., 98
Fulton, Betsy, 178, 184, 351, 358–359, 414

Gaes, G.G., 292
Gagnon, Alan D., 478
Gainey, Randy R., 60, 65, 68
Gal, Marlo, 273
Gallemore, Johnnie, 222
Garcia, Crystal Ann, 40, 305
Gardner, William, 395
Garner, Anne, 353
Garner, Joel H., 252, 370
Gatz, Nick, 309
Gaudin, J.M., Jr., 416
Geerken, Michael R., 559
Geiger, Jeffrey R., 234
Gendreau, Paul, 351
Georgia Parole Review, 462
Getzel, George S., 39
Gianas, Gregg, 245
Gibbons, Don C., 435
Gibbs, Anita, 65
Gido, Rosemary L., 235, 240
Giever, Dennis M., 497, 499
Gilbert, James N., 7
Gillis, Christina A., 273
Gitau, Joseph K., 34, 45
Glaeser, Edward L., 80
Glaser, Daniel F., 146, 296–297, 330
Glasser, William, 441–442
Godwin, Tracy M., 414
Goethals, Ron, 47
Goffman, Erving, 224
Goldkamp, John S., 459, 471–472
Goldsmith, Herbert R., 409
Goldstone, Jack A., 243
Goodman, Harriet, 39
Goodman, Rebecca, 294
Goodstein, Lynne, 268
Gordon, Jill, 9
Gordon, Margaret A., 402
Gordon, Robert M., 404
Gostas, Tom, 40, 64, 67

Gottfredson, Don M., 230, 324–326, 329–330, 369–370, 396
Gottfredson, Michael R., 230, 324–325, 369–370, 459
Gottfredson, Stephen D., 396
Gover, Angela R., 189
Gowdy, Voncile B., 454
Gowen, Darren, 64–65, 478
Graham, Laura A., 70
Grandberry, Gina, 40
Grann, Martin, 395
Gransky, Laura A., 191, 249
Grant, Brian A., 273, 293, 295, 409
Grant, J.D., 387
Grant, M.Q., 387
Grasmick, Harold G., 140, 190, 192
Gray, Kevin M., 150, 178, 305
Gray, Tara, 45, 48, 145, 248
Green, Richard, 398
Greene, Judith, 313–314
Greenfeld, Lawrence A., 558
Greenwood, Peter W., 447, 518, 559
Greeson, Zelma E., 251
Grier, Leslie K., 38
Griffiths, Curt Taylor, 47, 157
Grimes, Paul W., 82, 84, 280
Griset, Pamela L., 269
Grisso, Thomas, 463, 489, 498
Griswold, D., 553
Grossi, Elizabeth L., 280, 310–311
Grossman, Susan F., 405
Guggenheim, Martin, 396

Hageman, Mary J., 161
Haghighi, Bahram, 514–515
Hahn, Paul H., 46
Hakim, Simon, 248
Hanlon, Thomas E., 279, 460
Hanson, R. Karl, 398
Harding, Richard W., 248
Harer, Miles D., 297, 338
Harkness, Marti, 458
Harland, Alan T., 251
Harlow, Caroline Wolf, 219
Harrell, Adele, 475
Harris, Beth, 40, 64, 67
Harris, John C., 79
Harris, M. Kay, 46, 467
Harris, Patricia M., 31, 33
Harrison, Lana D., 467
Harry, Bruce, 465
Hartmann, David J., 411
Hassine, Victor, 249
Havik, Odd E., 386, 392
Hawk, Kathleen, 552
Hazelrigg, Mark, 463
Heiner, Robert, 46
Heisel, Christine, 184
Hemmens, Craig, 163–165, 190, 252
Hendricks, James E., 406
Hennessy, James J., 8
Hepburn, John R., 201, 241
Hernstein, Richard J., 424
Hess, Allen K., 332
Hickman, Laura J., 289, 308–309, 311

Hill, Cece, 293
Hill, Dina, 325
Hill, Elizabeth G., 351
Hill, Gary, 357
Hiller, Matthew L., 476
Hillsman, Sally T., 312–314
Hippchen, Leonard, 427
Hirschi, Travis, 440–441
Hodgins, Sheilagh, 463
Hofer, Paul J., 140, 272
Hoffman, Peter B., 230, 326, 330, 391, 445
Hoge, Robert D., 464
Hokanson, Shirley, 196
Holgate, Alina M., 406, 408
Holman, John E., 51, 61, 64, 280, 324
Holmes, Ronald M., 188, 308
Holsinger, Alexander, 35, 40
Holt, Norman, 230
Honess, Terry, 96
Hooten, Ernest, 424
Horn, Jim, 409
Houk, Julie M., 61
Houston, James, 249
Howard, Matthew O., 404
Howard, Timothy J., 534
Howell, James C., 461, 480
Huddleston, C. West, 471–473
Hudson, Joe, 266
Hughes, Herbert, 225, 260
Humphries, Drew, 455
Hunt, Geoffrey, 251, 477
Huskey, Bobbie L., 35–36
Hussong, Michelle, 296–297
Hutcherson, Sherry, 405

Illinois Sentencing Commission, 25
Indiana Department of Corrections, 296
Iowa Department of Correctional
    Services, 388, 397
Irwin, John, 84–85, 220, 333

Jackson, Ronald W., 270
James, Jennifer, 424
Jankowski, Louis, 269
Jayjohn, Jennifer, 319
Jeffrey, C. Ray, 424
Jenson, Jeffrey M., 404
Jesilow, Paul, 79, 316
Jesness, Carl F., 447
Johnson, Cindy, 79, 140, 142
Johnson, Elmer H., 290
Johnson, Grant M., 455
Johnson, Knowlton W., 405
Johnson, Sara L., 295, 409
Johnson, Sherri, 404
Johnson, W. Wesley, 38, 346, 399, 410
Johnston, Norman, 226
Jones, Mark, 59–60, 346, 365, 368, 399, 410
Jones, Marylouise E., 375–379
Jones, Michael, 189
Jones, Peter R., 44, 48
Jones, Ralph K., 22, 69, 178, 312, 556
Jones, Richard S., 65, 312
Joo, Hee Jong, 280, 557
Josi, Don A., 271, 538

Kaden, Jonathan, 201
Kane, Robert J., 78
Kansas Legislative Division of Post
    Audit, 322
Kassebaum, Gene, 279, 324, 549
Katsiyannis, Antonis, 338
Katz, Charles M., 402
Kelly, Robert J., 462
Kelly, William R., 280, 438, 553
Kennedy, David M., 402
Kennedy, Thomas D., 242
Kerle, Kenneth E., 217, 219–220
Kibblewhite, Karen, 417
Kingsnorth, Rodney, 86, 165
Kirkish, Patricia, 495
Kitsuse, John I., 438
Klein, Malcolm M., 402
Klingemann, Harald, 477
Knepper, Paul, 336, 538
Knight, Barbara B., 196
Knight, Kevin, 476
Knight, Raymond A., 455
Knopp, Fay H., 465
Knox, C., 461
Knox, George W., 242, 248–249, 251, 461
Knupfer, Anne Meis, 355
Kofowit, Dee, 50, 455
Kohlberg, L., 430
Konopka, Al, 307
Kotch, Kenneth E., 290
Kowalski-Jones, Lori, 489
Kramer, John, 195, 267–268
Kraus, Melvyn B., 459
Krauss, Daniel A., 388
Krauth, Barbara, 252
Kronick, Robert F., 279, 554
Kruttschnitt, Candace, 457
Kulis, Chester J., 97
Kushner, Andrea, 178, 347, 370
Kuznestov, Andrei, 465

Lacey, John H., 22, 69, 178, 312, 556
Lamb, David, 32, 38
Lambert, Dorothy E., 279, 554
Lambert, E. Warren, 279, 554
Lamonde, Annie, 406
Landreville, P., 54
Langan, Patrick A., 141, 525, 553
Laster, Kathy, 79
Laszlo, Anna T., 460
Latessa, Edward J., 33, 35, 40, 135, 305, 408
Latimer, H.D., 68
Lattimore, Pamela K., 538
Lauen, Roger J., 36–37
LaVigne, Nancy, 242
Lavin, G.K., 447
Lawrence, Richard, 243, 358, 363–365, 370
Lazear, Edward P., 459
Leadership Conference on Civil Rights,
    82
LeCroy, Craig Winston, 535
Lee, Susan, 417
Lehman, Joseph D., 411
Lemert, Edwin M., 438–439
Lemov, Penelope, 184

Leonardi, Thomas J., 354
Leonardson, Gary, 294
Levin, David J., 141, 525
Levine, Gene N., 480
Lewis, Alan Dana, 534
Lewis, Derek, 243
Liberton, Michael, 252
Libonate, DeAnna, 409
Lieb, Roxanne, 6
Lilleback, T., 455, 463
Lillis, Jamie, 273
Linden, Rick, 38
Lindner, Charles, 138, 353–354
Lindquist, Charles A., 354, 375, 406
Lin-Ruey, Lin, 33
Linster, Richard L., 538
Listug, David, 56
Litton, Gilbert, 510
Livingston, Jay, 478
Loberg, Tor, 386, 392
Locke, Thomas P., 447
Logan, Gloria, 199
Lombardi, Donna M., 326
Lombardi, John H., 326
Lombroso, Cesare, 426
Londer, Randi, 443
Lopez, Alma, 514–515
Love, Bill, 411
Lovell, David, 456
Lovell, Rick, 47
Lovrich, Nicholas, 379
Lu, Hong, 472
Lucken, Karol, 32, 35, 39, 43, 50
Lucker, G. William, 65, 555
Luginbuhl, James, 97
Lurigio, Arthur J., 40, 50, 154, 317,
    375–379, 460, 467–468, 470
Lutze, Faith E., 189
Lynch, James P., 461
Lynch, Mona, 275
Lynskey, Dana Peterson, 480

Maahs, Jeffrey, 273
MacDonald, S. Scott, 165
MacGrady, Jay, 294
MacKenzie, Doris Layton, 189, 194, 271,
    275, 289, 308–309, 311, 534, 538
Maggio, Mark, 355, 369, 407–408
Maguire, Kathleen, 24, 35, 45, 87, 195, 224,
    281, 299, 456, 465, 508, 517, 523
Mahan, Sue, 243
Mainprize, Stephen, 68
Majer, Richard D., 149, 316
Makkai, Toni, 398
Maloney, Dennis, 241, 315
Maltz, Michael D., 8, 553, 555
Mann, Simon, 65
Manning, Peter K., 441
Manske, Michael W., 35, 39, 177, 305
Marciniak, Liz Marie, 60, 68–71, 305, 555
Marcus, David K., 460
Markley, Greg, 359
Marley, C.W., 295
Marquart, James W., 466–467
Marshall, Franklin H., 116

Marshall, William L., 457, 466
Martin, Nancy L., 468
Martinson, Robert, 281, 352
Marvell, Thomas B., 82, 267, 398
Marye, Linda, 510
Maryland Commission on Criminal
    Sentencing Policy, 190
Maslach, Christina, 407, 410
Mason, Tom, 143
Massachusetts Legislative Research
    Council, 188
Mastrofski, Stephen D., 456
Matthews, Tim, 366
Matthewson, Terry L., 409
Matza, David, 434
Maxfield, Michael G., 8
Maxson, Cheryl L., 402
Maxwell, Jane Carlisle, 467
Maxwell, Sheila Royo, 79, 150, 178, 305,
    476
May, Chris, 61, 67
May, Tim, 359
Mays, G. Larry, 45, 48, 145, 248, 497, 499
McClearn, Gerald E., 427
McCleary, R., 553
McCorkle, Richard C., 402
McDevitt, Jack, 70
McDevitt, John F., 166
McDonald, Douglas C., 248, 313–314
McGillis, Daniel, 157–158
McGuire, Kathy, 458
McKay, Henry, 433, 436
McKean, Jerome B., 406
McMahon, Maeve, 48
McReynolds, Veon, 402
McShane, Marilyn D., 280, 402
Meachum, Larry R., 51
Mears, Daniel P., 86
Mednick, S.A., 424, 427
Meeker, James W., 316
Megargee, Edwin I., 230, 387
Memory, John M., 242
Mercer, Dave, 143
Mercer, Ron, 400
Meredith, Tammy, 141, 273
Merritt, Nancy, 173, 352, 555
Merton, Robert K., 434–435, 437
Messina, Nena P., 476
Messinger, Sheldon L., 270
Messner, Steven F., 489
MetaMetrics, Inc., 446, 511
Metchik, Eric, 268
Michigan Department of Corrections, 329
Miclityinen, Ida, 157
Middleton, Kath, 351
Midkiff, Bill, 224
Miethe, Terance D., 402, 472
Miller, Dallas H., 290
Miller, J. Mitchell, 249, 251
Miller, Jeffrey E., 427
Miller, Jerome G., 143–144
Miller, Jody, 480
Miller, Larry S., 242
Miller, Marc, 393, 395
Mills, Darrell K., 408

Mills, Jim, 47, 184
Millson, William A., 295
Minor, Kevin I., 411
Miranne, Alfred C., 559
Mitchell, George A., 21, 267, 333
Mitchell, John J., 511
Mitchell, Ojmarrh, 34–35, 48, 50, 190
Montagu, A., 424
Montgomery, Reid H., Jr., 243
Moody, Carlisle E., 267, 398
Moore, John P., 249
More, Harry W., 379
Morgan, Kathryn D., 201, 363, 365, 367,
    376
Morris, Norval, 393, 395
Morrison, Richard D., 410
Mortimer, Ed, 61, 67
Moser, Aldine N., Jr., 248
Moses, Marilyn C., 411
Motiuk, Laurence L., 51, 273, 295–296,
    393
Muller-Isberner, Rudiger, 463
Mullings, Janet L., 467
Mumola, Christopher J., 477
Munden, David P., 280, 310–311
Munson, Michelle, 142, 252
Murphy, David W., 189
Murphy, Edward M., 530–531
Murphy, Patrick, 359
Murray, Chris, 309
Mutchnick, Robert J., 32, 51, 56–57, 370,
    546
Myers, Martha A., 188

Nagoshi, Jack T., 446
Narcotics Anonymous, 477
Nasheri, Hedich, 20–21
National Association of Pretrial Services
    Agencies, 160, 162–163
National Law Enforcement and
    Corrections Technology Center,
    60–61, 63
National Commission on Law
    Observance and Enforcement, 265
National Council on Crime and
    Delinquency, 329
National Drug Court Institute, 472
Nemes, Susanna, 476
Nesbitt, Charlotte A., 195–196
Nettler, Gwyn, 424, 440–441
New Mexico Governor's Organized
    Crime Prevention Commission, 251
New York State Department of
    Correctional Services, 307–308,
    401–402
New York State Division of Parole, 185,
    188, 273
Newbold, Greg, 243
Neziroglu, F., 427
Niemeyer, Mike, 159
Nieto, Marcus, 59, 252, 293
Nieves, Kim, 275
Norman, Michael D., 87, 93, 95, 534–535
North Carolina Administrative Office of
    the Courts, 92

Nurco, David, 460
Nuss, Laura, 268

O'Callaghan, Jerome, 478
O'Connell, Paul, 43
Office of Justice Programs, 460
Ogburn, Kevin R., 414
Ogle, Robbin S., 248
Ohio Department of Correction and
    Rehabilitation, 327–328
Ohio Parole Board, 273, 397
Okun, Peter, 218
Olbrich, Jeffrey Lee, 326
Olsen, Eric, 264
Olson, David E., 154
Onek, David, 413
Orchowsky, Stan, 173, 352, 555
Osgood, D. Wayne, 8
Owens, Charles E., 230

Pace, Chaplain Arthur C., 411
Page, Brian, 361–362
Pallone, Nathaniel J., 8
Palmer, Carleton A., 463
Palumbo, Dennis J., 34, 184
Paparozzi, Mario, 351
Paradis, Cheryl, 456, 463
Parent, Dale G., 189, 401–402, 408
Parker-Jimenez, Joy, 370
Parks, Evalyn, 371
Parra, Ferando, 480
Parsons, L.B., 387
Parsons, Lee Anne, 218–219, 490
Parton, Nigel, 157
Pastore, Ann L., 24, 35, 45, 87, 195, 224,
    281, 299, 456, 465, 508, 517, 523
Patel, Jody, 317
Patterson, Bernie L., 407–408, 410
Patterson, Marisa E., 69–70
Payne, Brian K., 60, 65, 68
Peach, F.J., 39, 50
Peak, Ken, 293
Pearl, Natalie R., 325
Pease, Michael, 271
Pelletier, Daniel, 406
Peters, Roger H., 478
Petersen, Rebecca D., 34
Petersilia, Joan M., 33, 39, 46, 57, 142,
    144–146, 150, 172, 177–178, 184, 267,
    271, 275, 305, 317–318, 551–552, 554,
    556, 561–562
Peterson, Joyce, 561–562
Philadelphia Police Department, 379
Philadelphia Prison System, 292–293
Phillips, Amy K., 97
Piaget, Jean, 430
Pieper, Stephen L., 69
Pierson, Timothy A., 465
Pilant, James Alan, 365
Pizzi, William T., 20
Poe-Yamagata, Eileen, 496, 515
Pogrebin, Mark R., 259, 271
Poole, Eric D., 259, 271
Porporino, Frank, 9
Porter, Rachel, 280

Potts, Dennis W., 364, 396
Powell, Michelle, 398
Power, Jacquelyn M., 43
Pratt, John, 12, 556
Pratt, Travis C., 273, 308, 311
Prins, Herschel, 395
Prinsloo, Johan, 249
Probation and Parole Employees' Association, 380
Probation Association, 138
Proctor, Joe L., 271
Pullen, Suzanne K., 43, 305, 477, 527

Quay, Herbert C., 387

Rabow, Jerome, 436
Radli, Eric R., 190, 192
Rafter, Nicole Hahn, 227
Ralph, H. Paige, 251
Randolph, Amy S., 313
Rans, Laurel L., 330, 396
Rasmussen, David W., 32
Rath, Quentin C., 410
Ratliff, Bascom W., 533
Raynor, Peter, 96
Read, Edward M., 351, 354, 357–358, 363, 370, 374, 376, 399, 409, 478
Reckless, Walter C., 12, 437
Reed, Tom, 43
Rees, Thomas A., Jr., 251
Reese, Erin, 472
Regoli, Bob, 8
Reichers, Lisa, 275
Rhine, Edward E., 270, 322
Rhodes, Lorna A., 456
Richardson, Francoise, 61, 65
Richmond Times-Dispatch, 64
Roach, Kent, 79
Roberts, Dorothy E., 333
Roberts, John W., 143
Robinson, Laurie, 457, 459
Roche, Declan, 82
Rogers, Joseph W., 518, 522–523
Rogers, Kevin E., 82, 84, 280
Rolf, Peter Lars, 251
Roman, John, 475
Romig, Dennis A., 510
Rooney, Jennifer, 61
Ross, Darrell L., 59–60
Ross, Jeffrey Ian, 146
Ross, Robert R., 9
Ross, Toby, 480–481
Roth, Loren H., 427
Rothman, David J., 265
Rottman, David, 165–166
Roulet, Sister Elaine, 200
Rouse, Amelia A., 279
Roy, Sudipto, 66, 159, 316, 547
Ruddell, Rick, 497, 499
Runda, John C., 322
Rush, Jeffrey P., 249, 251, 358
Ryan, James E., 296–297

Sabatino, D.A., 295
Sacerdote, Bruce, 80

Samenow, Stanton E., 424, 430
Sandberg, Salek, 447
Sarbin, Theodore R., 427
Savarese, Margaret R., 138
Savolainen, Jukka, 8
Sawyer, Becki, 159
Saylor, W.G., 292
Schade, Linda S., 196
Schiff, Martha F., 45
Schiraldi, Vincent, 46, 84–85, 498
Schlatter, Gary, 532
Schlossman, Steven, 245
Schmidt, Annesley K., 60–61, 63, 65–67
Schmitz, Richard J., 69–70
Schneider, Thomas P., 22
Schrag, Clarence, 438–439
Schumacker, Randall E., 324
Schwaner, Shawn L., 324, 402, 544
Schwartz, Ira M., 144
Schwartz, Robert G., 489
Sechrest, Dale K., 159–160, 271, 410, 476, 538
Seidenstat, Paul, 248
Seiter, Richard P., 280, 323, 548
Sellin, Thorsten, 437
Serran, Geris A., 457, 466
Sestoft, D., 455, 463
Seymour, Anne, 411
Shah, Saleem A., 427
Shane-DuBow, Sandra, 12, 84, 264
Shannon, Michael, 379
Shapiro, Emily F., 84, 323
Shaw, Clifford, 433, 436
Shearer, Robert A., 150, 273, 361, 364, 418, 467, 470–471
Sheldon, William H., 426
Shelton, Kelly, 457
Sheppard, Robert A., 234
Shewan, David, 460, 466
Shichor, David, 159–160, 245
Shockley, Carol, 92
Sickmund, Melissa, 496, 515
Siegel, Gayle R., 293, 546
Siegel, Michael Eric, 362
Sieh, Edward W., 351, 353
Sigler, Robert T., 32, 38, 98
Silver, Eric, 392, 455
Silverio, Mel, 279, 324, 549
Silverman, Mitchell, 252
Simmons, Calvin, 407
Simourd, David J., 464
Simpson, D. Dwayne, 476
Sluder, Richard D., 353, 361, 364, 368, 370
Smith, Albert G., 361, 409
Smith, Barbara E., 97
Smith, Linda G., 466
Smith, Michael E., 25
Smith, Robert R., 295
Smith, William R., 270
Smykla, John Ortiz, 35, 39, 177, 305
Snyder, Howard N., 496, 499, 515
Snyder-Joy, Zoann, 184
Soderlund, Curt, 317

Soderstrom, Irina R., 292
Solomon, Phyllis, 275
Soma, Jerry, 370, 407
Song, Lin, 6
Sontheimer, Henry, 32
South Carolina Department of Probation, Parole, and Pardon Services, 336
South Carolina State Reorganization Commission, 188
Southern, Stephen, 414
Spaans, E.C., 61
Spangenberg, Robert L., 173
Speir, John C., 141, 273
Spens, Iona, 245
Spergel, Irving A., 280, 405
Speyerer, Jerri B., 478
Spica, Arthur R., Jr., 358
Spiegel, Allen D., 226
Spiegel, Marc B., 226
Spillane, Joseph, 245
Spruit, J.E., 217
Sreenivasan, Shoba, 463
Stadler, Donald W., 336
Stanz, Robert, 555, 557
Stastny, Charles, 136
Steen, Sara, 86–87, 96
Steffensmeier, Darrell J., 195, 267
Stehr, Steven D., 273
Steiner, Hans, 555
Steinhart, David J., 414
Steury, Ellen Hochstedler, 115–116
Stephen, Jackie, 375
Stephens, Regina, 297, 315
Stevens, Dennis J., 243
Stevenson, William Ferree, 466
Stewart, Sharon D., 359
Stiles, Don R., 294
Stinchcomb, Jeanne B., 189–190
Stohr, Mary K., 190, 252
Stojkovic, Stan, 47
Stolzenberg, Lisa, 272–273
Stone, Susan, 184
Storm, John P., 351, 354, 357–359, 369, 374, 399
Straub, Frank, 459
Strauss, Shiela, 370–372
Streifel, Cathy, 195, 267
Strong, Ann, 375
Styve, Gaylene J., 189
Sugrue, Dennis P., 447
Sullivan, C., 387
Sundt, Jody, 32, 178
Sykes, Gresham, 434, 441
Swartz, James A., 467, 470
Sweet, Joseph, 516
Szymanski, Linda, 498–499, 503

Talarico, Susette M., 188
Talty, Richard B., 299–300, 316
Tarr, Thomas K., 354
Taxman, Faye S., 44, 401, 472
Taylor, Jon Marc, 243
Taylor, William J., 189
Tengstrom, Anders, 395

Tennessee Department of Corrections, 294
Tepper, B.D., 68
Terenzi, Elaine, 355, 369, 407–408
Tewksbury, Richard, 245, 280, 310–311, 473–476, 555, 557
Texas Criminal Justice Policy Council, 36, 39, 47, 50, 454
Texas Office of the Comptroller, 280
Texas Office of the State Auditor, 358, 370
Thio, Alex, 435
Thoma, Robert, 325
Thompson, Joel A., 248
Thornton, David, 398
Thornton, William E., Jr., 424
Tilmon, Randy D., 190
Timasheff, Nicholas S., 138–139
Timonen, M., 463
Toch, Hans, 244
Tolman, Richard M., 60, 70, 145
Tomkins, Alan, 498
Tonry, Michael, 59, 70, 80–82, 150, 253, 267, 279–280, 326, 405
Tontodonato, Pamela, 97
Toombs, Nancy J., 190
Toombs, Thomas G., 65–66
Torbet, Patricia, 489, 498–499, 503
Torres, Sam, 33, 39, 372, 467–470
Torrey, E. Fuller, 222–223
Tracy, Alice, 411
Travis, Lawrence F., III, 35, 40, 309
Traynelis-Yurek, E., 415
Treger, H., 315
Tremblay, Pierre, 480
Trester, Harold B., 518
Triplet, Rush, 480–481
Trotter, Christopher, 47
Turner, Susan, 142, 459, 518, 551, 561–562
Turpin-Petrosino, Carolyn, 21
Twill, Sara E., 310
Tyrnauer, Gabrielle, 136

Uggen, Christopher, 457
Umbreit, Mark S., 159
U.S. Bureau of Justice Assistance, 82
U.S. Center for Mental Health Services, 9
U.S. Department of Justice, 150, 173, 272–273, 275, 277, 279, 294, 368, 459
U.S. General Accounting Office, 54, 93, 96, 144, 186, 188, 312
U.S. National Institute of Corrections, 146
U.S. Office of Justice Programs, 34, 40, 45, 50
U.S. Office of National Drug Control Policy, 34, 40, 51

U.S. Parole Commission, 333
U.S. Sentencing Commission, 230, 272, 300
Unwin, Tessa, 241
Useem, Bert, 243

Valdez, Al, 251
Valentine, Bill, 251
VanderZanden, James W., 430, 438–439
Van Duin, Menno J., 243
Van Voorhis, Patricia, 243–244
Vass, Antony A., 359
Vaughn, Michael S., 185, 188, 466
Ventura County Sheriff's Department, 482
Verwers, C., 61
Victoria Department of Justice, 454
Vigdal, Gerald L., 336
Virginia Commission on Sentencing and Parole Reform, 387
Virginia Department of Criminal Justice Services, 67
Virginia Joint Legislative Audit and Review Commission, 85, 240
Virginia State Crime Commission, 361
Visher, Christy A., 538
Vitiello, Michael, 64, 85
Vito, Gennaro F., 185, 188, 245, 308, 473–476, 549
Vogel, Mary E., 21
Vogel, Ronald E., 249, 280
Vohryzek-Bolden, Miki, 410
Volavka, J., 424, 427
von Hirsch, Andrew, 144
Vorenberg, James, 426

Wadman, Robert C., 87, 93, 95, 534–535
Wagner, Dennis, 184, 371
Waits, Robert, 241, 294
Waldo, Gordon P., 553
Walgrave, Lode, 156–157, 372
Walker, Samuel, 352–353
Wallisch, Lynn S., 467
Walmsley, Roy, 243
Walsh, Thomas C., 95, 162
Walters, Glenn D., 245
Warren, Roger K., 166
Washington Department of Corrections, 294
Washington State Department of Social and Mental Health Services, 466
Wassenberg, Pinky S., 69–70
Watkins, Craig, 367
Wattam, Corinne, 157
Watterson, Kathryn, 147
Weisel, Deborah, 404
Welborn, George, 234
Welch, Michael, 216, 240

Wellford, Charles, 438
Welsh, Wayne N., 85, 241
West-Smith, Mary, 259, 271
Wetter, Robert E., 322
Wheeler, Gerald R., 313
Wheeler-Cox, Trilby, 275
Whitehead, John T., 354, 375, 406
Whitesell, Russ, 247
Whitfield, Dick, 61, 64
Wicharaya, Tamasak, 386
Wicklund, Carl, 376
Wiebush, Richard G., 527–528
Wiederanders, Mark R., 280
Wiggins, Robert R., 357, 359, 361
Wiliszowski, Connie H., 22
Wilkins, Leslie T., 329–330
Wilkinson, Alec, 360
Wilkinson, Reginald A., 45, 241
Will, Jeffrey A., 230
Williams, Frank P., III, 280, 402
Williams, James D., 518
Williams, Sharon A., 511
Wilson, Deborah G., 188, 308, 549, 563
Wilson, Edward O., 424
Wilson, George P., 308–309
Wilson, James Q., 100, 424, 562–563
Wilson, John J., 402, 461, 479
Wilson, Nora Campbell, 296–297
Wilson, Robin J., 391, 404, 466
Wilson, Trina Bogle, 404
Winfree, L. Thomas, Jr., 480
Winston, Melissa R., 308, 311
Winter, Bill, 413
Winterfield, Laura A., 312–314
Wish, Eric P., 476
Wittenberg, Peter M., 404
Wolf, Thomas J., 16
Wolfgang, Marvin E., 436–438
Wood, Peter B., 140, 190, 192
Wooldredge, John D., 9, 219
Worzella, Charles, 313–314
Wright, Kevin N., 273, 327
Wright, Sandra, 404

Yaryura-Tobias, J.A., 427
Yeboah, David, 271
Ygnacio, Regina E., 142, 252
Yochelson, Samuel, 424, 430
Young, Douglas, 280
Yurek, F.G., 415
Yuslum, Theresa M., 241, 316

Zhang, Lening, 489
Zhao, Jihong, 379
Ziedenberg, Jason, 84–85, 498
Zoet, Thomas H., 465–466
Zurawski, James J., 405

Subject Index

Abnormal physical structure, 425–426
About Face, 533
Absconders, 401–402
Absolute immunity of POs, 365
Acceptance of responsibility, 89, 96, 156
   defendant's sentencing memorandum, 96
   restorative justice, 156
Accountability, 39
Act to Regulate the Treatment and Control of
   Dependent, Neglected, and Delinquent
   Children, 492
Actuarial prediction, 393–395
Adjudications, 494
Adjudicatory hearings, 507
Administrative Office of U.S. Courts, 93–94
Admin Max prisons, 233–234
Adult Internal Management System (AIMS),
   387
Agency, theory of, 49, 414
Aggravating circumstances, 99, 508
AIDS/HIV clients, 452, 456, 460–461, 466–467
Akers, Ronald, 438
Alaska Department of Corrections, 231
Alaska Long-Term Prisoner Classification Form,
   232–233
Alcatraz, 231–233
Alcohol-dependent offenders, 459–460
Alcoholics Anonymous, 43, 63, 160, 177, 222,
   247, 298, 301, 312, 333, 371, 459, 474,
   477–478
Allegheny Academy, 529–530
Alternative care cases, 526
Alternative dispute resolution (ADR), 154–155,
   157–159
   defined, 157
Alternative sentencing, 25

American Correctional Association, 227, 516
   professionalism among probation officers, 516
American Federation of State, County, and
   Municipal Employees (AFSCME), 379
American Prison Association, 227
American Probation and Parole Association,
   377–378, 516, 547
   professionalism among probation officers, 516
Americans with Disabilities Act (ADA), 43–44,
   336
   parolees and parole revocations, 336
Anamnestic prediction, 393
Anomie, 434
Anomie theory, 434–435, 437
   defined, 434
Apprehension units, 400–402
Army Model, 533
Arraignment, 21
Arrest, 4, 13
   defined, 13
Arrests of juveniles, 495–496
Assessment centers, 361–363
Auburn State Penitentiary, 226
Augustus, John, 93–94, 136–138, 140–141, 523
   PSI report preparation, 93–94
Automatic waivers, 502
Avertable recidivists, 558
Ayran Nations, 249–250

Bail, 13–16
   defined, 13
Balanced approach, 372
Ballesteros, Belinda A., personality highlight,
   90–91
Banishment, 225
Beck Depression Inventory, 63

Beyond a reasonable doubt, 22
BI Incorporated, 60
Biochemical disturbances and crime, 427
Biological theories, 425–427
Birth cohorts, 437
Body types, 426–427
Bonding theory, 440
Booking, 13
    defined, 13
Boot camps, 188–195, 532–533
    clientele profile, 190
    defined, 188–189
    effectiveness, 192–195
    examples, 191
    goals, 189–190
    juveniles, 532–533
Boston Children's Aid Society, 138
Boston House of Corrections, 136, 138
Boston Offender Project (BOP), 530–531
Bridewell Workhouse, 217
Brockway, Zebulon, 143, 227, 262
Brokers, 369, 374
Brooklyn, New York, Treatment Court, 475
Bureau of Justice Statistics, 235–236
Burnout, 405–411
    defined, 407
Burgess, Ernest W., 329
Burgess, Robert, 438
Butler (New York) Shock Incarceration Correctional Facility, 533

California Conservation Corps, 447
California scheme, 185–186
Camps, 514
Capone, Al, 233
Capote, Truman, 426
Career criminals, 9, 12
    defined, 12
Caseloads, 178, 347, 369–372
    defined, 369
    models, 371–372
    probation officer, 178
Case processing, 22
Caseworkers, 369
Castillo, Yolanda G., 493
Cellular telephone devices, 63
Certifications, 497–505
    defined, 497
    rationale, 498
Charge reduction bargaining, 21
Chicago Reform School, 491
Children in need of supervision (CHINS), 512
Children's tribunals, 491
Child savers, 491
Child-saving movement, 491
Child sexual abusers, 457–459
Choice Program, 245
Chronic offenders, 12
Citizen value system, 325
Civil procedure,   156
Civil Rights Act, 367
Clark, Benjamin C., 138
Classification of offenders, 9–12, 228–235
Classification systems, 387–398
Client-specific planning, 371

Clinical prediction, 395–396
Cocaine Anonymous, 177
Code of ethics for POs, 376–379
Cognitive development, 430
    theory, 430–431
Collective bargaining among POs, 379–381
Combination sentence, 185
Common law, 488, 490
    defined, 490
Community-based corrections, 4, 31–71
    defined, 31–33
    goals and functions, 37–45
    philosophy and history, 35–37
Community-based supervision, 40
Community control, 33, 51–54
    Florida use of, 51–54
Community control house arrest, 54
Community corrections act, 34–35
    defined, 34
Community model, 145
Community programs, 25, 476–478
    special needs offenders, 476–478
Community reintegration, 146, 292
    parole, 292
Community residential centers, 36–37, 308
Community service, 25, 177
    standard probation, 177
Community service orders, 315–316
    defined, 316
Community work, 290
Commutation, 319
Compulsary School Act, 491
Concurrent jurisdiction, 501
Conditional diversion, 160
    program, 161
Conditional release, 319
Conditional sanctions, 509–512
    defined, 510
Conflict/Marxist theory, 441
Conflict theory, 441
Congregate system, 226
Containment theory, 437–438
Continuous signalling devices, 62
Continuous signalling transmitters, 62
Contract prisoners, 216, 221, 223–224
Controlec, Inc., 60
Controller value system, 325
Conventional model, 371
    with geographic considerations,
        371–372
Cook, Rufus R., 138
Cooley, Charles Horton, 438
Correctional Adjustment Checklist, 387
Correctional Adjustment Life History, 387
Corrections, 4, 6, 23–25
    defined, 6, 23
    jails, 23
    prisons, 23–24
Corrections officers, 5–6
Corrections volunteer, 411
Counseling, individual or group, 43
Court dockets, 22
Courts, 3–4, 22
    judges, 22
Creaming, 48, 549

Creative sentencing, 25, 186
CREST (Circumstances, Motivation, Readiness, and Suitability), 292, 476
Crime, 4
Crime classification index, 7
Crime control, 146
Crimes against property, 7
Crimes against the person, 7
Crimes of violence, 7
Crime Victims Reparations Act, 317
Criminal information, 21
Criminal justice system, 4–6, 13–25
    components, 13–25
    defined, 4
    illustrated, 5
    overview, 4–6
Criminal trial, 21
Criminogenic contamination, 309
Criminogenic environment, 6, 142, 162
    diversion, 162
Criminological Diagnostic Consultants, Inc., 97–98
Critical criminology, 441
Crofton, Sir Walter, 227, 262
Cultural transmission theory, 433
Curfews, 34
Custodial sanctions, 509, 512–515

Dangerousness, 85
Dangerous-tendency test, 85
Darwin, Charles, 425, 443
Day fines, 313–315
    defined, 313
Day parole, 290
Day pass, 290
Day reporting centers, 68–71, 312
    client characteristics, 69–70
    defined, 68–69
    examples, 70–71
    guidelines for, 69–70
Defendants, 4
Defendant's sentencing memorandum, 96–98
Defense counsel, 16
Deinstitutionalization movement, 456
DeLaGarza, Nelda, personality highlight, 513
Delaware Life Skills Program, 247
Deliberate indifference, 368
Delinquency, 199
Delinquency theories, 444–445
Delinquents, 9
Delinquent subcultures, 436–437
Demand waivers, 502
Dependent and neglected children, 491–492
    defined, 492
Depo-Provera, 455
Deserts model, 144–145
Detainer warrants, 221
Detectors, 374–375
Detention, 515
    hearings, 496
Determinate sentencing, 81–82, 267–268
Deterrence, 25, 149–150
Developmentally disabled offenders, 462
Development of Correctional Staff Trainers Program, 360

Differential association theory, 433–434
    defined, 433
Differential reinforcement theory, 437–438
Direct file, 501
Discretionary waivers, 500–501
Dispute Settlement Center of Durham (DSCD) (North Carolina), 157–159
Diversion, 154–155, 160, 510
Diversion programs, 160–163
    history and philosophy, 160–161
    juveniles, 510
Divertees, 160
Double jeopardy, 3
Drug/alcohol dependent offenders, 459–460
Drug court model, 472–476
Drug court movement, 471–472
Drug courts, 471–476
Drug screening, 470–471
Due process model, 144
Durkheim, Emile, 434
DWI offenders, 56–57, 459

Early release, 4
Earned good time, 82
EARN-IT, 159
Ectomorphs, 426
Educational training, 43–44
Educator, enabler, and mediator, 375
Ego, 429
Electronic monitoring, 60–68, 531–532
    compared with home confinement, 63–64
    criticisms, 65
    defined, 60
    early uses, 60–61
    juveniles, 531–532
    profile of clients, 65–66
    types, 62–63
Elmira Reformatory, 143, 227, 262–264
Employment assistance, 40–43
Endomorphs, 426
Enforcer, 375
Ethical code for POs, 376–379
Evening Narcotics Court, 468
Exculpatory evidence, 326
Experience programs, 514
Expungement, 161
    order, 337

False negatives, 35
False positives, 35
Family Environment Scale, 63
Federal Bureau of Investigation (FBI), 7
Federal Bureau of Prisons, 143, 224, 330
Federal Juvenile Delinquency Act, 139
Federal PO ethical code, 378
Federal Rules of Criminal Procedure, 98
Federal scheme, 186
Felony, 6
    defined, 6
    probation, 85
Female probationers and parolees, 195–200
Fiering, Henry, 379
Financial/Community Service Model, 316–317
Fines, 6, 312–313
    defined, 6

Firearms in PO work, 363–365
First-offenders, 9–12, 153–154, 162
    diversion, 162
First-time offenders, 9–12
Fishman, Joseph, 219
Flat time, 82
Florida Assessment Center, 362–363
Florida community control, 53–54
Foster homes, 512
Fourth Amendment, 59, 65
Fraley, Whitney E., personality highlight, 41–42
Freedom of Information Act (FOIA), 92
Freud, Sigmund, 429–430
Front-end sentences, 25–26
Front-end solutions, 142
Furlough programs, 295–297
    defined, 295
    functions, 296–297
    goals, 295–296
    weaknesses and strengths, 297

Gamblers Anonymous, 298, 312, 477–478
Gang-Free Environment Program, 249
Gangs, 248–251, 279–280, 461–462, 478–482
    numbers in U.S., 461
Gang units, 402–405
Gaols, 216
Gender parity, 195
Georgia Intensive Supervision Probation
    Program (GISPP), 180–181
    criticisms, 184–185
Getting It Together, 447
Get-tough movement, 137
Global positioning satellite systems (GPS), 63,
    399–400
Good marks, 262–263
    illustrated, 263
Good time, 262–264
Good time credits, 81–82
    defined, 81
    earned, 81
    determinate sentencing, 81
    functions, 81
    meritorious, 81
    statutory, 81
Good time system, 262
GOSSlink, 60
Gottfredson, Don M., 329
Grand jury, 21
Gray Panthers, 411
GREAT (Gang Resistance Education and
    Training), 480
Group homes, 513–514
Guidelines-based sentencing, 82–83
Guthrie, Montie, personality highlight, 373–374

Habeas corpus, 203
Habitual offenders, 12
Habitual offender statutes, 82
Hale, Oscar Jesus, Jr., personality highlight,
    19–20
Halfway Back Program, 280
Halfway houses, 308–312
    defined, 308
    philosophy and functions, 310–311

strengths and weaknesses, 311–312
    variations, 309–310
Halfway-in houses, 309–310
Halfway-out houses, 309–310
Headstart, 447
Heightening offender accountability, 39
Heredity and criminal behavior, 427
Highly Intensive Supervision, Training, and Edu-
    cation Program (HISTEP), 192
High School Personality Questionnaire, 447
High Street Jail, 217
Home confinement, 51–60, 532
    client agreement, 52–53
    clientele profile, 57
    defined, 51
    early uses of, 51–54
    examples, 54–57
    goals, 57
    issues and criticisms, 58–60
    juveniles, 532
Home Confinement Unit, 468
Home incarceration, 51–60
Homeward Bound, 514–515
Hope Center Wilderness Camp, 514
Hope Houses, 308
House arrest, 51–60
House of Reformation, 490
Howard, John, 225
Howe, Samuel G., 262
Hubbell, Gaylord, 262
Huber Law, 290

Id, 429
Idaho Intensive Supervised Probation Program,
    181
    criticisms, 184–185
I-Level Classification, 387
Illegal searches and seizures, 59
Illinois Drug Offender Specialized Supervision
    Program, 468
Illinois Juvenile Court Act, 488
Immunity, 365–366
Implicit plea bargaining, 21
Incident reports, 81
Incidents, 8
In Cold Blood, 426
Indeterminate sentencing, 81, 264–267
    criticisms, 265–266
Index offenses, 7
Indictment, 21
Infants, 490
Information, 21
Initial appearance, 13
Inmate classification systems, 228–235
Inmate councils, 244
Inmate discipline, 242–244
Inmate violence, 242–244
Intake, 496–497
    defined, 496
    screening, 496–497
Intensive probation supervision (IPS), 177–185
Intensive supervised parole (ISP), 299–307
    defined, 299
Intensive supervised probation (ISP), 177–185,
    526–528

Intensive supervised probation *(cont.)*
  conceptual models, 178–180
  defined, 177
  juveniles, 526–528
Intermediate punishments, 32–34, 177–185
  compared with community corrections, 32–34
  defined, 32
Intermittent confinement, 186
International Halfway House Association
    (IHHA), 309
Interpersonal Maturity Level Classification System, 387
Interstate compact agreements, 279
Inwald Personality Inventory, 360
Iowa Department of Corrections Reassessment
    of Client Risk, 388–391
  illustrated, 389–391
Iowa's Classification Risk Assessment Scale,
    397
Iowa's Risk/Needs Classification System, 388
Isaac T. Hopper Home, 308
Italian school, 426

Jail
  as a condition of probation, 185–186
  boot camps, 190–192, 221–222
  design and control, 244–245
  inmates, 223–224
  overcrowding, 24–25, 45, 84, 137
  removal initiative, 220–221
Jails, 216–224
  admissions and releases, 216
  compared with prisons, 240
  defined, 216
  functions, 223
  history, 216–219
  numbers, 219
  overcrowding, 240–242
  role in parole/probation decision making,
    251–253
Jefferson County (Kentucky) Drug Court
    Program, 473–476
Job dissatisfaction, 406, 408
Judges, 22
Judicial discretion, 25, 163–166
  probation, 163–166
Judicial dispositions in juvenile courts, 509–510
Judicial plea bargaining, 21
Judicial reprieves, 135–136
Judicial waivers, 500–501
Judicial workloads, 22
Juries, 22
Jurisdiction, 6
Jurist value system, 324–325
Jury trials, 22
Just-deserts model, 144–145
Justice/due process model, 144
Justice model, 178
Juvenile Court Act, 488
Juvenile courts, 490–497
  compared with criminal courts, 492–494
  history, 490–492
Juvenile delinquency, 312
Juvenile delinquents, 488–489
  defined, 489

Juvenile Diversion/Noncustody Intake Program,
    510
Juvenile Diversion Program (JDP), 510–511
Juvenile intensive supervision programs (JISPs),
    527–528
  defined, 527
Juvenile justice system, 489–500
Juvenile offenders, 488–539
Juvenile parole, 533–539
  decision making, 534–535
  numbers, 534
Juvenile probation, 523–528, 533–539
  defined, 523
Juvenile probation officers, 515–517
  functions, 517
Juvenile rights, 505–508

Kalamazoo (Michigan) Probation Enhancement
    Program, 410–411
Kansas Department of Corrections Parolee Risk
    and Needs Assessment Coding Form, 394
Kitsuse, John, 438
Kohlberg, L., 430

Labeling theory, 438–439
  assumptions, 438
Labor turnover among POs, 368–369
Latent functions of parole, 270
Law enforcement, 3–4, 13–16
  officers, 3–4
Law Enforcement Assistance Administration
    (LEAA), 36–37, 352
Law enforcement officers, 3–4
L.E.A.R.N. (Literacy, Education, and Reading
    Network labs), 43
Legal liabilities of POs, 366–368
Legislative waivers, 502
Lemert, Edwin, 438
Level of custody, 9
Libido, 429
Lifestyle Redirection Program, 249
Limited risk control model, 178–179
Literacy services, 43–44
Little Village Gang Violence Reduction Project
    (Chicago), 404
Lockdown, 234
Lockup, 219
Lombroso, Cesare, 425, 443
Looking-glass self, 438
Lopez, Rick V., personality highlight, 403–404
Los Angeles County Officers Union,
    379–380
Louisiana Intensive Motivational Program of
    Alternative Correctional Treatment, 194
Love, Judge Jack, 61

MacArthur Violence Risk Assessment Study,
    463
Maconochie, Alexander, 227, 260–264, 290
Management by objectives (MBO), 410–411
Mandatory release, 269
Mandatory sentencing, 82–84
  defined, 82
Mandatory waivers, 500–501
Manifest functions of parole, 270

Marks of commendation, 260–264
Mark system, 227
Martinez, Sonia, personality highlight, 356–357
Martinson, Robert, 352
Marxist theory, 441
Maryland Community Criminal Justice
    Treatment Program (MCCJTP), 464
Massachusetts Parole Board Release Risk
    Classification Instrument, 392
MATCH (Mothers and Their Children), 199
Maxi-maxi prisons, 233–234
Maximum-security classification, 231–233
Maximum-security prisons, 231–233
McGill, Kay, 462
McKay, Henry, 433
Mediation, 157
Medical model, 143
Medium-security classification, 231
Medium-security prisons, 231
Megargee Inmate Typology, 230, 387
Mens rea, 488
Mentally ill offenders, 456–457, 462–465
Meritorious good time, 81
Mesomorphs, 426
Methadone treatment, 470–471
Metropolitan Day Reporting Center (MDRC),
    70
Mexican Mafia, 250
Michigan's Community Corrections Act, 32
Minimum due process rights, 333–334
Minimum-security classification, 231
Minnesota Multiphasic Personality Inventory
    (MMPI), 230, 360, 387
Minnesota sentencing grid, 82–83
    illustrated, 83
Misdemeanant, 6–7
    defined, 7
Misdemeanor(s), 6–7
    defined, 6–7
Missouri Sexual Offender Program (MOSOP),
    465
Mitigating circumstances, 99–100, 377, 508–509
Mixed sentence, 186
Model Classification Project, 523
Modes of adaptation, 434–435
Montreal Preventive Treatment Program, 480
Moral recognition therapy (MRT), 40
Mothers Against Drunk Driving (MADD), 459

Narcotics Anonymous, 177, 222, 298, 312, 333,
    474, 477–478
Narratives in PSI reports, 87–88
National Advisory Commission on Criminal Jus-
    tice Standards and Goals, 36
National Council on Crime and Delinquency,
    329–330
National Crime Victimization Survey (NCVS),
    3, 8
    compared with the *Uniform Crime Reports*, 8
    criticisms, 8
    defined, 8
National Correctional Policy on Female
    Offender Services, 195–196
National Incident-Based Reporting System
    (NIBRS), 8–12

National Prison Association, 227
National Youth Gang Survey, 478–480
Negligence in PO work, 365–368, 376, 417–418
Negligent assignment, 417
Negligent direction, 417
Negligent entrustment, 417
Negligent hiring, 417
Negligent retention, 368, 417
Negligent supervision, 417
Negligent training, 368, 417
Net-widening, 34, 47–48, 162, 184
    diversion, 162
Neutralization theory, 433–434
Nevada Intensive Supervision Program,
    305–307
New Jersey Intensive Supervision Program
    (NJISP), 299–305
New York House of Refuge, 490
New York's Prison Nursery/Children's Center,
    199–200
New York State Probation Officers Association
    (NYSPOA), 380
NIMBY syndrome, 45–46
No bill, 21
Nominal dispositions, 509–510
    defined, 509
Nominal sanctions, 509
Nonavertable recidivists, 558–559
Nonreporting, 8
Nonsecure facilities, 512–515
Norfolk Island, 260
North Carolina Day Reporting Center program,
    71
North Carolina Structured Sentencing Act,
    70–71
No true bill, 21
Numbers game model, 371

Objective parole criteria, 325–329
Offender control, 68
Offender rehabilitation, 4
    and corrections, 4
Offenders, 4
Offense seriousness score, 115–116
Offense severity, 330
Officer/client interactions, 372–376
Ohio Experience, 528–529
Ohio scheme, 186
Once an adult, always an adult, 502–503
180 Degrees, Inc., 465–466
Operating capacity, 25
Operation Night Light, 481
Operation Tracker, 481
Opportunity theory, 435
Outcome measures, 547–550
Overcharging, 21
Overcrowding, 24

PACT (Prisoner and Community Together), 159
Paraprofessionals, 414–418
    defined, 414
    legal liabilities, 416–418
Pardons, 264, 336–338
Parens patriae, 494–495
    defined, 494

Parole, 4, 25–26, 259–282
  defined, 26, 259–260
  functions, 270–275
  historical context, 260–264
  indeterminate sentencing, 265–267
  philosophy, 270
Parole agency organization, 346–355
Parole and Probation Employees' Association
  (PPEA), 380
Parole boards, 26, 317–329
  cases that do not have to be reviewed, 322–323
  cases that must be reviewed, 322
  composition and diversity, 318–319
  functions, 319–321
  orientations, 324–325
  standards, 321–322
Parole Decision-Making Project, 329–330
Parolees, 4, 275–279, 338–341
  profile, 275–279
  rights, 338–341
Parole officers (POs), 4, 355–379
  characteristics, 355–357
  duties, 357–359
  legal liabilities, 366–368
  recruitment and training, 359–368
Parole revocation, 4, 333–336, 535–539
  juveniles, 535–539
Parole revocation hearing, 336
Participative management, 410–411
Passive officers, 378
PATCH (Parents and Their Children), 199
Penitentiary, 225–226
Penitentiary Act of 1779, 225
Penn, William, 143
Pennsylvania System, 226
Persistent felony offenders, 12
Persistent offenders, 12
Personal tracking devices (PTD), 400
Petitions, 496–497
Philadelphia House of Industry, 308
Philadelphia House of Refuge, 490
Philadelphia Society for Alleviating the Miseries
  of Public Prisons, 218, 490
Piaget, Jean, 430
Pine Hills, 436
PINS (persons in need of supervision), 488,
  512
Plea bargaining, 20–21, 377
  charge reduction, 21
  defined, 20
  implicit, 21
  judicial, 21
  POs, 377
  sentence recommendation, 21
  types of, 21
Positive school, 426
Post-Release Employment Project, 292
Predictions of risk, 393–396
  actuarial, 393–395
  anamnestic, 393
  clinical, 395–396
Predispositional reports, 518–523
  defined, 518
  example, 519–520
Preliminary examination, 13

Preliminary hearing, 13
Preparole, 33
Pre-Parole Conditional Supervision Program
  (PPCSP), 289–290
Preparole programs, 289–299
Preponderance of evidence, 205
Prerelease programs, 289–299
  defined, 289
Presentence investigation reports (PSIs),
  86–98
  confidentiality, 89–92
  contents, 88–89
  criticisms, 95–96
  defined, 87
  federal PSI report, 119–129
  functions and uses, 93–94
  illustrated, 100–114, 119–129
  North Dakota PSI report, 100–105
  privatizing, 97–98
  time taken to prepare, 93
  Wisconsin PSI report, 106–114
Presentence investigations, 87, 248
Presentment, 21
President's Commission on Law Enforcement
  and Administration of Justice, 36–37,
  351, 369
PreStart Program, 290
Presumptive sentencing, 82–83
Presumptive waivers, 500–501
Pretrial detainees, 217, 220
Pretrial detention, 220
Pretrial diversion, 160–163
  criteria influencing, 162
  criticisms, 162–163
  defined, 160
  functions, 161
  history and philosophy, 160–161
  types, 160–161
Pretrial release, 33
Pretrial services, 13–16
Preventive detention, 220, 507–508
Primary deviation, 438–439
Prison design and control, 244–245
Prisoner Rehabilitation Act, 309
Prisoners, 235–239
Prison gangs, 248–251
Prison industry, 225–226
Prison overcrowding, 24–25, 45, 84, 137
Prisons, 224–240
  compared with jails, 240
  defined, 224
  functions, 227–228
  history, 224–227
  overcrowding, 240–242
  role in parole decision making, 251–253
Privatization, 48–50, 248
  community-based corrections, 48–50
  criticisms, 49–50
  defined, 48
  jails and prisons, 248
Probable cause, 13
Probatio, 134
Probation, 4, 22, 25–26, 134–154
  chronology of events, 139
  defined, 22, 134

functions, 146–150
history, 135–140
models, 142–145
philosophy, 140–142
profile of probationers, 150–154
Probation agency organization, 346–355
Probation and parole services, 346–355
administration, 347–351
functions and goals, 347
Probation conditions, 4
Probationers, 4
Probation officer caseloads, 61
Probation officers (POs), 4, 355–379
characteristics, 355–357
duties, 357–359
legal liabilities, 366–368
recruitment, 359–361
role in sentencing, 86
Probation Officers Association of Ontario (Canada) (POAO), 381
Probation revocation, 4, 200–209, 535–539
conditions for, 201–209
defined, 201
juvenile, 535–539
landmark cases, 203–209
Probation Subsidy Program, 36
Professionalism among probation officers, 516–517
Professionalization, 353, 360
Professionals, 33
Program evaluation, 544–550
defined, 544
Program for Female Offenders, Inc. (PFO), 198–199, 289, 411
Programmed contact devices, 62–63
Progressive era, 143–144
Property crimes, 7, 9–12
defined, 7
Prosecutions, 4, 16–18
Prosecutors, 4
Provo Experiment, 436
Psychoanalytic theory, 429–430
Psychological theories, 427–432
Psychopathic Personality Inventory, 470
Public defenders, 220
Public policy and recidivism, 559–560
Public risk, 316
Public safety, 40, 46–47, 59–60
electronic monitoring, 67–68
home confinement, 59–60
Pulls, 437
Punishment, 149
Punitive officers, 378
Pushes, 437

Qualified immunity of POs, 365
Quasi-judicial immunity of POs, 365

Ramirez, Linda, personality highlight, 23
Ranches, 514
Rand Corporation, 556
Rangel, Efran R., Jr., personality highlight, 229–230
Reality therapy, 441–442
defined, 441

Rearrests, 555–556
Recidivism, 6, 70, 159, 552–558
day reporting centers, 70
victim-offender reconciliation projects, 159
Recidivism rates, 6, 150
informal standards, 150
Recidivists, 6, 12, 153–154, 558–559
characteristics, 558
defined, 12
Reconstruction, 491
Reconvictions, 556
Recovery Opportunity Center, 475
Recruitment and training of POs, 359–366
Reform schools, 491
Regimented Inmate Discipline Program, 533
Regulator value system, 325
Rehabilitation, 38–39, 84–85, 140–141
model, 143–144, 225
Rehabilitative ideal, 46
Reincarcerations, 557
Reinforcement, 431
Reintegration, 38–39, 147
Reintegration model, 145
Release on own recognizance (ROR), 13, 136, 252
Reparations, 317
Repeat offenders, 12
Research units, 405
Respondeat superior, 416–417
Restitution, 25, 157, 316–317
defined, 316
parole programs, 316–317
variations, 316–317
victim-offender reconciliation, 157
Restorative case management, 372
Restorative justice, 156
Reverse waiver hearings, 502–503
Reverse waivers, 502
Revocation actions, 333
Revocation of juvenile probation and parole, 533–539
Revocations of parole or probation as recidivism, 556–557
Reynolds, James Bronson, 138
Risk assessment, 35–36, 95, 273, 386–398
applications, 397–398
defined, 386–387
effectiveness, 396
functions, 388–393
instruments, 35, 179
PSI reports, 95
types, 393–396
Risk/needs measures, 397–398
Rodriguez, Miguel Angel, Jr., personality highlight, 17–18
Role ambiguity, 409
Role conflict among POs, 374–376, 408–409
Rush, Dr. Benjamin, 225

SAFE-T, 39
Salient Factor Score 81 (SFS 81), 330–333
Salient Factor Scores, 329–333
Salvation Army, 308
Sanctioner value system, 325
Scared Straight, 511, 532–533

Screening cases, 16–18
Secondary deviation, 438–439
Secure confinement, 515
See Our Side (SOS) Program, 511–512
Selective incapacitation, 398
Self-esteem among POs, 409
Self-reported information, 7–8
Sentence recommendation plea bargaining, 21
Sentencing, 22, 25, 78–85
   defined, 78
   functions and goals, 78–80
   guidelines-based, 82–83
   determinate, 81–82
   indeterminate, 81
   issues and criticisms, 84–85
   mandatory, 82–84
   presumptive, 82–83
   types, 80–83
Sentencing hearing, 98
   defined, 98
Sentencing memorandum, 96–97
Sentencing Reform Act of 1984, 78, 202
Services delivery, 50–51
Sex offenders, 5–6, 457–459, 465–466
Sexual Predatory Act, 398
SFS 76, 330
SFS 81, 330–333
Shaw, Clifford, 433
Shire-reeves, 216–217
Shock incarceration, 188–195
Shock parole, 299, 307–308
Shock probation, 185–188, 307, 532
   defined, 185
   distinguished from split sentencing, 185
   effectiveness, 188
   juveniles, 532
   philosophy and objectives, 186–188
   programs, 185
Shock probationers, 185, 223
Sing Sing Prison, 262
Situational offenders, 9
Smart sentencing, 178
Social casework, 442–443
Social control theory, 440
Socialization, 433
Social learning theory, 431–432
   defined, 432
Social process theories, 432–441
   defined, 432
Society for the Prevention of Pauperism, 490
Sociobiology, 424–425
   defined, 424
Sociological theories, 432–441
   defined, 432
Solitary confinement, 226
South Carolina ISP Program, 181–183
   criticisms, 184–185
SpeakerID, 56
Specialized caseloads model, 372
Special needs offenders, 453–482
   coping, 454–456
   defined, 453
Special Needs Parole Program, 454
Special Sex Offender Sentencing Alternative
   (SSOSA), 5–6, 466

Speck, Richard, 427
Speedy trials, 22
Split sentences, 153
Split sentencing, 185–186
Standard parolees, 299–300
Standard parole with conditions, 297–299
   conditions, 298–299
   defined, 297
Standard probation, 172–177, 523–524
   federal probation orders, 174–175
   juveniles, 523–524
   recidivism rates, 172
   requirements, 172–173
Staten Island Day-Fine Experiment, 313–315
Status offenders, 489
Statutory exclusion, 501–502
Statutory good time, 81
Stigmatization, 157
Strain theory, 437
Stress, 354, 405–411
   defined, 406
   mitigating, 410–411
   sources, 408–410
Stroud, Robert "Birdman," 233
Study release, 293
Study release programs, 293–294
   advantages and disadvantages, 294
   defined, 293
   eligibility requirements, 294
Subculture of delinquency, 436–438
   defined, 436
Subculture of violence, 437
Subcultures, 436
Substance-abusing offenders, 467–470
Summary offense, 6
Superego, 429
Supermax prisons, 233–234
Supervised release, 116, 300
   provisions, 300
Sutherland, Edwin, 369, 433, 435, 438, 440
Synthetic officers, 379

Tattoo removal programs, 481–482
Tattoos and prison gangs, 249–250, 481–482
   illustrations, 250
Technical program violations as recidivism,
   557–558
Temporary absence programs, 295–297
Temporary Asylum for Disadvantaged Female
   Prisoners, 308
Texas Mafia, 250
Texas Special Needs Program, 454–455
Texas Syndicate, 250
Thatcher, Judge Oxenbridge, 136
Theories of criminal behavior, 423–447
Theory, 423–424, 443–444
   defined, 423
   evaluating, 443–444
Therapeutic communities, 476–478
   defined, 476
Therapeutic jurisprudence, 165–166
Tickets-of-leave, 227
Tiers, 226
Tier system, 226
Torts, 156

Total institution, 224–225
Totality of circumstances, 160
    determining pretrial diversion, 160
Traditional, treatment-oriented model,
    179–180
Transfer hearings, 504
    time considerations, 504
Transfers, 497–505
    defined, 497
    minimum ages, 499
    rationale, 498–499
Transportation, 260
Treater value system, 325
Treatment alternatives to street crime (TASC),
    460
Treatment model, 143
Treatment programs, 445–447
True bill, 21
Trujillo, Sara L., personality highlight,
    524–525
Truth-in-sentencing provisions, 82
Tuberculosis, 460–461

Unconditional diversion, 163
    program, 160
Unconditional release, 208
Uniform Crime Reports (UCR), 3, 7–8
    compared with the *National Crime
        Victimization Survey*, 8
    criticisms, 7–8
    defined, 7
Unionization of POs, 379–381
U.S. Army Correctional Activity, 533
U.S. Code Annotated, 417
U.S. Department of Justice, 219
U.S. Parole Board, 264
U.S. Parole Commission, 94, 326, 330
U.S. Sentencing Commission, 267
U.S. sentencing guidelines, 84, 89, 202
University Settlement, 138
User fees, 160

Van Dieman's Land, 260
Victim and Witness Protection Act of 1982,
    315
Victim compensation, 157
Victim impact statements (VIS), 97
    PSI reports, 97
Victimization, 8
Victimization data, 8
Victim/Offender Mediation Model, 317
Victim-offender reconciliation, 157, 159
    defined, 159

Victim-offender reconciliation projects
    (VORPs), 159
    history, 159
Victim/Reparations Model, 317
Victim restitution programs, 293
Victims of Crime Act of 1984, 293
Victim Witness Protection Act, 204
Villarreal, Victor M., personality highlight, 14–16
Violence, inmate, 242–244
Violent Crime and Law Enforcement Act
    (VCCA), 202–203
Violent crimes, 7
    defined, 7
Vocational/technical programs in jails and
    prisons, 245–248
Volunteers, 138–139, 411–414
    criticisms, 412–414
    defined, 411
    early uses in probation work, 138–139
    work performed, 411–412

Waiver hearings, 503
Waiver motion, 503
Waivers, 497–505
    defined, 497
    rationale, 498–499
Walnut Street Jail, 217–218, 225–226, 228, 490
    juveniles and, 490
Wechsler Adult Intelligence Scale, 414–415
Welfare officers, 378
Western County program, 56–57
White-collar criminals, 435
White-collar crime, 8, 435
Wickersham, George, 265
Wickersham Commission, 265
Wilderness projects, 514
Wilkins, Leslie, 329
Women in Community Service Program
    (WICS), 247
Women's Activities and Learning Center
    (WALC), 199
Work Ethic Camp (WEC), 245–247
Work furlough, 290
Workhouses, 217
Work release programs, 290–293
    defined, 290
    goals, 291–292
Write-ups, 81

XYY syndrome, 427

Youth at Risk Program, 446, 511
Youth Service Bureaus (YSBs), 510

Cases Cited

Acevedo v. Pima County Adult Probation Department, 690 P.2d 38 (1984), 367

Anderson v. State, 624 So. 2d 362 (1993), 209

Avery v. State, 844 S.W.2d 364 (1993), 537

Baker v. State, 616 So. 2d 571 (1993), 205

Bearden v. Georgia, 461 U.S. 660 (1983), 204, 207

Black v. Romano, 471 U.S. 606 (1985), 205

Bollinger v. Bd. of Parole & Post-Prison Supervision, 992 P.2d 445 (Or. Sup. December) (1999), 258

Booth v. Maryland, 107 S. Ct. 2529 (1987), 97

Breed v. Jones, 421 U.S. 519 (1975), 507, 537

Cannon v. State, 624 So. 2d 238 (1993), 208

Carroll v. Board of Parole, 859 P.2d 1203 (1993), 338–339

C.D.R. v. State, 827 S.W.2d 589 (1992), 538

Childs v. United States Board of Parole, 371 F. Supp. 1246 (1973), 330

Cobham v. State, 736 So. 2d 67 (Fla. Dist. App. June) (1999), 30

Commonwealth v. MacDonald, 736 N.E.2d 444 (Mass. App. October) (2000), 208

Crooker v. Metallo, 5 F.3d 583 (1993), 206

Davis v. State, 422 S.E.2d 546 (1992), 206

D.L.J. v. State, 765 So. 2d 740 (Fla. Dist. App. May) (2000). 486–287

Division of Corrections v. Neakok, 721 P.2d 1121 (1986), 376

Doe v. State, 595 So. 2d 212 (1992), 337

Ex parte Crouse 4 Whart. 9 (1839), 490–491, 494

Ford v. State, 758 So. 2d 1124 (Ala. Crim. App. October) (1999), 59

Gagnon v. Scarpelli, 411 U.S. 778 (1973), 85

Gibbs v. State, 760 A.2d 541 (Del. Sup. August) (2000), 204, 488

Government of Virgin Islands v. Lake, 362 F.2d 770 (1966), 205

Griffin v. Wisconsin, 483 U.S. 868 (1987), 196–197

Hamm v. Ray, 531 S.E.2d 91 (Ga. Sup. July) (2000), 30

Hammond v. District of Columbia Board of Parole, 756 A.2d 896 (D.C. App. July) (2000), 340

Heckman v. Pa. Bd. of Probation and Parole, 744 A.2d 371 (Pa. Commw. January) (2000), 287

Hill v. State, 624 So. 2d 417 (1993), 209

Hyland v. Wonder, 972 F.2d 1129 (1992), 416

Inman v. State, 684 So.2d 899 (Fla.Dist.App.Dec.) (1996), 148

In re B.K., 522 S.E.2d 255 (Ga. App. September) (1999), 486

In re Bounmy V., 17 Cal. Rptr. 2d 557 (1993), 526

In re Allen N., 100 Cal. Rptr. 2d 902 (Cal. App. October) (2000), 486

In re F.N., 624 N.E.2d 853 (1993), 536–537

In re Gault, 387 U.S. 1 (1967), 506

In re Haynes, 996 P.2d 637 (Wash. App. April) (2000), 2–3

In re Kazuo G., 27 Cal. Rptr. 2d 155 (1994), 536

In re Michael T., 17 Cal. Rptr. 2d 923 (1993), 526

In re Pedro M., 96 Cal. Rptr. 2d 839 (Cal. App. June) (2000), 486

In re Sheree M., 4 P.3d 1067 (Ariz. App. April) (2000), 31

In re Winship, 397 U.S. 358 (1970), 506–507

J.G. v. State, 604 So. 2d 1255 (1992), 537

Kelly v. State, 729 So. 2d 1007 (Fla. Dist. App. April) (1999), 30

Kent v. United States, 383 U.S. 541 (1966), 505–506

Lemon v. State, 861 S.W.d 249 (1993), 209

Matter of Jessie GG, 593 N.Y.S.2d 375 (1993), 526

Matter of J.K.A., 855 S.W.2d 58 (1993), 537–538

Matter of Tammy JJ, 47 CrL 1891 (NY. Sup. Ct.), (1993), 537

Matter of Zachary "I", 604 N.Y.S.2d 628 (1993), 512

McKeiver v. Pennsylvania, 403 U.S. 528 (1971), 502, 507

McKnight v. State, 616 So. 2d 31 (1993), 207

Mempa v. Rhay, 389 U.S. 128 (1967), 203–204, 488

Menifee v. State, 601 N.E.2d 359 (1992), 340

Minnesota v. Murphy, 465 U.S. 420 (1984), 205

Moore v. New York State Bd. of Parole, 712 N.Y.S.2d 179 (N.Y. Sup. App. Div. July) (2000), 257

Moore v. State, 623 So. 2d 842 (1993), 207

Morrissey v. Brewer, 408 U.S. 471 (1972), 204, 333–334, 488, 538, 556

Nobles v. State, 605 S02d 996 (1992), 209

Noble v. United States Parole Commission, 194 F.3d 152 (U.S.D.C. Cir. November) (1999), 286

Pareton v. Armontrout, 983 F.2d 881 (1993), 341

Patterson v. State, 612 So. 2d 692 (1992), 340

Patuxent Institution Board of Review v. Hancock, 620 A.2d 917 (1993), 538

Pennsylvania Board of Probation and Parole v. Scott, 118 S. Ct. 2014 (1998), 336

Pennsylvania Department of Corrections v. Yeskey, 118 S. Ct. 1952 (1998), 336

People ex rel. Korn v. N.Y. State Division of Parole, 710 N.Y.S.2d 124 (N.Y. Sup. App. Div.) (2000), 1–2

People v. Fleming, 3 P.3d 449 (Colo. App. June) (2000), 2

People v. Hipp, 861 S.W.2d 377 (1993), 207

People v. Matthews, 23 Cal. Rptr. 2d 434 (Cal. App. September) (1993), 338

People v. Ramos, 48 CrL 1057 (Ill. S. Ct.) (1990), 58

People v. Shafer, 491 N.W.2d 266 (1992), 340

People v. Thornton, 676 N.E.2d 1024 (Ill.App.Feb.) (1997), 148

Reynard v. State, 622 So. 2d 1026 (Fla. Dist. App.) (1993), 366

Richardson v. New York State Executive Department, 602 N.Y.S.2d 443 (1993), 339

Rodriguez v. State, 684 S0.2d 864 (Fla.Dist.App.Dec.) (1996), 149

Roller v. Cavanaugh, 984 F.2d 120 (1993), 341

Schall v. Martin, 104 S. Ct. 2403 (1984), 507–508

Shivers v. Pa. Bd. of Probation & Parole, 758 A.2d 282 (Pa. Commw. August) (2000), 339–240

Speth v. State, 6 S.W.2d 530 (Tex. Crim. App. December) (1999), 59

S.R.A. v. State, 766 So. 2d 277 (Fla. Dist. App. February) (2000), 486

S.S. v. State, 765 So. 2d 949 (Fla. Dist. App. August) (2000), 486

State v. Alves, 851 P.2d 129 (1992), 341

State v. Beauchamp, 621 A.2d 516 (1993), 341

State v. Bergman, 147 CrL 1475 (Ind. Ct. App., 2d District) (1990), 337

State v. Bradbury, 136 Me. 347 (1939)

State v. Chatagnier, 3 P.3d 586 (Kan. App. June) (2000), 2

State v. Christianson, 983 P.2d 909 (Mont. Sup. July) (1999), 287

State v. Combs, 10 P.3d 1101 (Wash. App. October) (2000), 208

State v. Fair, 736 N.E.2d 82 (Ohio App. January) (2000), 339

State v. Foshee, 756 So. 2d 693 (La. App. April) (2000), 287

State v. Gervais, 6087 A.2d 881 (R.I. Sup. May) (1992), 337–338

State v. Green, 547 So. 2d 925 (1989), 340

State v. H.B., 614 A.2d 1081 (1992), 537

State v. Hayes, 437 S.E.2d 717 (N.C. App. December) (1993), 205

State v. Johnson, 988 P.2d 460 (Wash. App. November) (1999), 30

State v. Lavoy, 614 A.2d 1077 (1992), 340

State v. Lubus, 48 CrL 1173 (Conn. SupCt.) (1990), 58

State v. Oquendo, 612 A.2d 24 (1993), 341

State v. Perez, 11 P.3d 52 (Kan. Sup. June) (2000), 339

Tarlton v. Clark, 441 F.2d 384 (1971), 323

Trantino v. N.J. State Parole Bd., 752 A.2d 761 (N.J. Sup. June) (2000), 258–259

United States v. Arch John Drummond, 967 F.2d 593 (1992), 58

United States v. Bachsian, 4 F.3d 288 (1993), 204–205

United States v. Edwards, 960 F.2d 278 (1992), 58

United States v. G.C.A., 83 F. Supp. 2d 253 (U.S.D.P.R. February) (2000), 486

United States v. Insley, 927 F.2d 185 (1991), 58

United States v. Levi, 2 F.2d 842 (1993), 209

United States v. Lombardi, 5 F.3rd 568 (1993), 207

United States v. Noonan, 47 CrL 1287 (3d Cir.) (1990), 337

United States v. Salerno, 107 S. Ct. 2095 (1987), 508

United States v. Wickman, 955 F.2d 828 (1992), 58

United States v. Zackular, 945 F.2d 23 (1991), 58

Walrath v. United States, 830 F. Supp. 444 (1993), 340

Whiteley v. Warden, 401 U.S. 560 (1971), 418

Williams v. Puckett, 624 So. 2d 496 (1993), 338

Wilson v. Ellis, 859 P.2d 744 (1993), 209

Wilson v. United States Parole Commission, 193 F.3d 195 (U.S. 3d Cir. September) (1999), 258